AF862043

PART 1 Common-Law Employment Issues

LEGISLATION	DATE
Model Uniform Employment Termination Act	1991
Sarbanes-Oxley Act	2003

PART 2 Equal Employment Opportunity

LEGISLATION	DATE
Title VII of the Civil Rights Act of 1964	1964
Amended by:	
The Equal Opportunity Act of 1972	1972
The Pregnancy Discrimination Act of 1978	1978
The Civil Rights Act of 1991	1991
The Equal Pay Act	1963
The Family and Medical Leave Act	1993
The Immigration Reform and Control Act of 1986	1986
The Age Discrimination in Employment Act	1967
The Americans with Disabilities Act of 1990	1990
The Mental Health Parity Act	1996
The Rehabilitation Act of 1973	1973
42 U.S.C. § 1981 (The Civil Rights Acts of 1866 and 1870)	1866
42 U.S.C. § 1983 (The Civil Rights Act of 1871)	1871
Executive Order No. 11246	1965
The Uniformed Services Employment and Reemployment Rights Act	1994

PART 3 Employment Law Issues

LEGISLATION	DATE
Occupational Safety and Health Act	1970
Employee Retirement Income Security Act	1974
Fair Labor Standards Act	1938
Social Security Act	1935
Welfare Reform Act	1996
Older Workers Benefits Protection Act	1990
Immigration Act of 1990	1990
Whistleblower Protection Act	1989
Immigration Reform and Control Act	1986
Multiemployer Pension Plan Amendments	1980
Equal Pay Act	1963
Jones Act (Merchant Marine Act)	1936
Walsh-Healy Act	1936
Davis-Bacon Act	1931
Longshore and Harbor Workers' Compensation Act	1927
Railway Labor Act	1926
Federal Employees' Compensation Act	1916
Federal Employers Liability Act	1908

PART 4 Labor Relations Law

LEGISLATION	DATE
The National Labor Relations Act (Wagner Act)	1935
Amended by:	
The Labor Management Relations Act (Taft-Hartley Act)	1947
The Labor-Management Reporting and Disclosure Act (Landrum Griffin Act)	1959
The Worker Adjustment and Retraining Act	1988

Employment and Labor Law

Cihon and Castagnera

THOMSON
SOUTH-WESTERN

Australia · Canada · Mexico · Singapore · Spain · United Kingdom · United States

THOMSON
SOUTH-WESTERN

Employment and Labor Law
Cihon and Castagnera

Executive Editors:
Michele Baird, Maureen Staudt &
Michael Stranz

Project Development Manager:
Linda deStefano

Sr. Marketing Coordinators:
Lindsay Annett and Sara Mercurio

Production/Manufacturing Manager:
Donna M. Brown

Production Editorial Manager:
Dan Plofchan

Pre-Media Services Supervisor:
Becki Walker

Rights and Permissions Specialist:
Kalina Ingham Hintz

Cover Image
Getty Images*

Printed in the
United States of America

For more information, please contact Thomson Custom Solutions, 5191 Natorp Boulevard, Mason, OH 45040. Or you can visit our Internet site at http://www.thomsoncustom.com

For permission to use material from this text or product, contact us by:
Tel (800) 730-2214
Fax (800) 730 2215
www.thomsonrights.com

The Adaptable Courseware Program consists of products and additions to existing Thomson products that are produced from camera-ready copy. Peer review, class testing, and accuracy are primarily the responsibility of the author(s).

Employment and Labor Law /
Cihon and Castagnera

ISBN-13: 978-0-324-69070-5
ISBN-10: 0-324-69070-3

International Divisions List

Asia (Including India):
Thomson Learning
(a division of Thomson Asia Pte Ltd)
5 Shenton Way #01-01
UIC Building
Singapore 068808
Tel: (65) 6410-1200
Fax: (65) 6410-1208

Australia/New Zealand:
Thomson Learning Australia
102 Dodds Street
Southbank, Victoria 3006
Australia

Latin America:
Thomson Learning
Seneca 53
Colonia Polano
11560 Mexico, D.F., Mexico
Tel (525) 281-2906
Fax (525) 281-2656

Canada:
Thomson Nelson
1120 Birchmount Road
Toronto, Ontario
Canada M1K 5G4
Tel (416) 752-9100
Fax (416) 752-8102

UK/Europe/Middle East/Africa:
Thomson Learning
High Holborn House
50-51 Bedford Row
London, WC1R 4LS
United Kingdom
Tel 44 (020) 7067-2500
Fax 44 (020) 7067-2600

Spain (Includes Portugal):
Thomson Paraninfo
Calle Magallanes 25
28015 Madrid
España
Tel 34 (0)91 446-3350
Fax 34 (0)91 445-6218

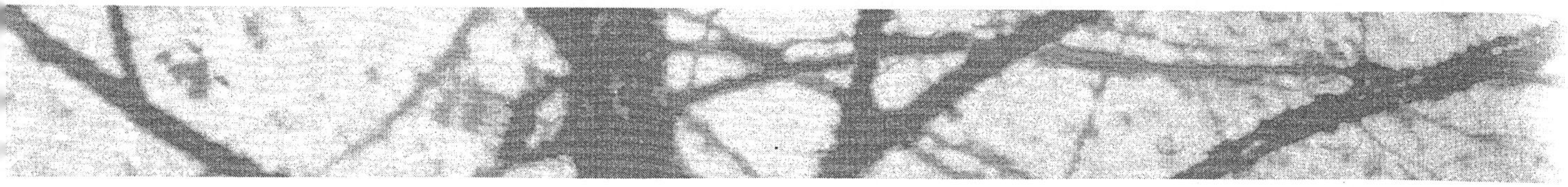

BRIEF CONTENTS

CONTENTS

PREFACE

The first four years of the 21st century define the challenges facing business, government, and organized labor in the decades ahead. As the North American Free Trade Agreement marked its tenth anniversary, millions of manufacturing jobs fled the U.S. for Mexico. Ironically, these same manufacturing jobs—at least the ones which thus far have avoided redundancy in the face of ever-increasing technological efficiency—have steadily moved from Mexico to China, Southeast Asia, and India.

While a large section of this Fifth Edition remains devoted to the National Labor Relations Act, organized labor continues to suffer diminution in the private sector. However, labor unions are as strong as ever, or even stronger, among public employees. And recent NLRB decisions have extended organizing rights to teaching assistants and other graduate and even undergraduate students on private-university campuses, while also expanding NLRA section 7 protection for concerted activity to non-union workers.

Occupational safety and health concerns have assumed a high profile following the 9/11 terrorist attacks on the World Trade Center and the Pentagon. Violence in the workplace is a fact of business life that all employers must consider and confront. The SARS epidemic is another event of these early years of the new millennium, which sets the stage for increased employer vigilance with regard to traveling employees.

The Enron and Worldcom scandals affected employees of these corporations, especially their retirement funds, which were heavily invested in their employers' own stocks. As early 2004 saw Enron's CFO sent to prison and its CEO indicted on 40 criminal counts, some questioned just how effective ERISA is in protecting employees and retirees, at a time when the graying of the Baby-Boom generation puts unprecedented pressure on the Social Security system. Similarly, the so-called "jobless recovery" of 2003–04 placed pressure on states' unemployment compensation systems just when many states were facing huge deficits and budget crunches.

All in all, the new decade poses daunting challenges in the areas of employment and labor law, which we believe we have identified and presented here.

PURPOSE AND ORGANIZATION

While *Employment and Labor Law,* 5th edition, is about law, it is a "law book" designed for use by non-lawyers. The primary audience for this book is students in business schools, human resources programs, and industrial relations programs; but the book also can be used by anyone seeking to learn about labor and employment law in the United States.

A distinguishing aspect of this book is our treatment of cases. In the crisp editing of the court opinions, it is clearly a business book with accompanying presentation of substantial case material. The case extracts, including occasional dissents and/or concurring opinions, allow the reader to experience the fact that law develops from the resolution—or at least the accommodation—of differing views. The "Working Law" and "Ethical Dilemma" features stimulate critical responses from students to this material.

We believe this exposure to differing opinions and positions, as well as the immersion in the legal reasoning process, will prove valuable to those who may become involved in arbitration, Equal Employment Opportunity Commission conciliation, collective bargaining, and other quasi-legal aspects of employee relations. In no other area of the law are nonlawyer professionals exposed to such legal regulation, and in no other area do they experience the need for "lawyer-like" skills to the extent that human resources directors and industrial relations specialists do. The human relations professional is often required to represent the employer in arbitration, in the negotiation and drafting of employment contracts, in drafting employee handbooks and policies, and in representing the employer before unemployment claims referees. While the focus of this book is not on substantive skills of negotiating, drafting, or advocacy that such situations may demand, it will develop the skills of legal reasoning and analysis which are vital for successful performance in such situations.

SUPPLEMENTARY MATERIALS

An Instructor's Manual is available to instructors only and provides solutions to end-of-chapter case problems, as well as additional information, supplemental "Working Law" and "Ethical Dilemma" articles, and extra case problems. The Instructor's Manual can be downloaded from the text Web site.

In addition, a Test Bank at the end of the Instructor's Manual contains multiple choice and true/false questions to facilitate test preparation.

- ***InfoTrac® Keywords*** at the end of each chapter direct students to articles relevant to chapter topics through the InfoTrac® library at **http://www.infotrac-college.com.** An access card with passcode is provided free with every new textbook.
- The text Web site at **http://cihon.westbuslaw.com** includes a wealth of teaching and learning resources including: Internet Applications, Court Case Updates, downloadable supplements for instructors, and more.
- Because the law impacts every aspect of our society, students of almost any discipline—including business law, political science, criminal justice and economics—can benefit from Westlaw Campus. Access to Westlaw Campus is now available with this text at a very reasonable cost. This academic version of Westlaw includes cases, statutes, administrative law, legal encyclopedias and law reviews and journals. Please ask your West Legal Studies in Business Sales Representative about obtaining access.

The availability of additional West Legal Studies in Business products may vary significantly between products and adoptions. Please contact your local Thomson Learning sales representative for more information.

A NOTE TO THE STUDENT

This book is designed for use by management or industrial relations students, but it is unique in its treatment and presentation of cases. Such cases—whether National Labor Relations Board or court decisions—and the various statutes form the framework within which all labor relations and human resource management activity takes place. You need to become familiar with the provisions of relevant statutes; for that reason we have included a number of important labor and employment law statutes in the appendix section of the text.

READING CASES

You will be required to read and understand cases in order to understand and analyze the legal decisions forming the basis of the law. A case is a bit like a parable or a fable. It presents a set of facts and events that led two opposing parties into a conflict requiring resolution by a court or agency. The judge or adjudicator is guided by legal principles developed from statutes or prior cases in the resolution of the dispute. There may be competing legal principles that must be reconciled or accommodated. The case is a self-contained record of the resolution of the dispute between the parties, but it is also an incremental step in the process of developing legal principles for resolution of future disputes.

It is the legal principles—their reconciliation and development—and the reasoning process involved that justify the inclusion of the cases we have selected. The critical task of the reader, therefore, is to sift through the facts of a case and to identify the legal principles underlying that case. In analyzing a case you may find it helpful to ask, after reading the case, "Why was this particular case included at this point in the chapter? What does this case add to the textual material immediately preceding it?"

In some instances, the answer will be that the case helps illustrate and explain a significant or difficult concept, such as the duty to bargain in good faith. Or perhaps the case demonstrates the limits of, or some important exception to, a general principle or rule of law.

In analyzing the cases, especially the longer ones, you may find it helpful to "brief" them. This simply means to make an outline. This outline can take any form that you find, with experience and experimentation, is most useful. A commonly used outline in law schools is the following:

- Case Name and Citation
  - Include the court or agency deciding the case.
  - Include the citation, which tells where to find the reported decision.
- Key Facts (in brief)
  - Indicate *why* the parties are before the court or agency.
  - Indicate *what* the parties are seeking.
  - Indicate the stage in the legal process (i.e., Trial Court, NLRB, Appeals Court, etc.).
  - Relate *what happened at the prior stages* (if any) in the legal process.

- Legal Issue(s)
  - Include the *legal problem(s)* raised by the facts of the dispute.
- Holding(s)
  - Record *how* the court or agency resolves the issue(s) in the dispute.
- Reasoning of the Decision-Maker
  - Indicate *why* the dispute was resolved the way it is.
  - Indicate how the decision-maker *applied* or *reconciled* the legal principles involved.

THE CASE PROBLEMS

One of the features that we feel distinguish this book is the set of case problems at the end of each chapter. These are real problems drawn from real cases. Sometimes our presentation of the facts is simplified to focus on a key issue or to stimulate discussion and analysis in a certain direction. Try analyzing the problems yourself; review the text if you can't identify the underlying principles and issues. Then, if the actual cases are available on campus, look them up, observe how they differ from our simplified presentation, and consider how the court, commission, or board actually ruled. This exercise, although demanding, will reinforce your understanding and round out your mastery of each chapter's subject matter.

A NOTE ON CITATIONS

The numbers and initials appearing after the names of cases mentioned or included within the text are called citations. The citations refer to the volume number and report series in which the decision in the case is printed. The citations tell where to find the case decision in the law library. We have attempted to provide citations for the cases included, or referred to, in the text. For the edited cases, the citation is given under the title of the case; citations that are indicated as "U.S." are U.S. Supreme Court cases. For cases referred to in the text, the citation is given in brackets following the case name. If you are interested in researching those cases cited in the court opinions, use the citation for the edited court opinion to find the unedited version in a law library; from the unedited version the citations for the cases referred to in the opinion can be found.

ACKNOWLEDGMENTS

The authors wish to thank the many people who contributed to the completion of this book, and our wives, Joanne Cain Castagnera and Nancy Cihon, for their support and assistance.

We also would like to thank all those who have contributed to the preparation and production of this fifth edition. In particular, we wish to acknowledge the contribution and assistance of our editors at West Legal Studies in Business/Thomson Learning: Rob Dewey for his faith in our text, Steve Silverstein for his skill in marketing the book, Lora Arduser for her attention to the details of producing the final text, and Susanna Smart for her guidance and insights during the revision of this edition.

We wish to thank the following reviewers whose helpful comments and suggestions were used during the preparation of each edition of this book:

Robert E. Allen
University of Wyoming

Thomas Apke
California State University, Fullerton

Curtiss K. Behrens
Northern Illinois University

Teresa Brady
Holy Family College

Gerald E. Calvasina
University of North Carolina

Frank J. Cavaliere
Lamar University

Melissa Dallas
Florida Atlantic University

Kiren Dosanjh
California State University, Northridge

Anne Draznin
University of Illinois at Springfield

Jan Duffy
California Polytechnic University

Bruce Elder
University of Nebraska at Kearney

Michael Garrison
North Dakota State University

Thomas L. Gossman
Western Michigan University

John A. Gray
Loyola College

Marsha E. Hass
College of Charleston

Charles Hollon
Shippensburg University of Pennsylvania

Jon Memmott
Brigham Young University

Marvin E. Newman
Rollins College

Richard O. Parry
California State University—Fullerton

Lorraine A. Schmall
Northern Illinois University

Marcia Simmering
Louisiana State University

Charles Stevens
North Dakota State University

Star Swift
Grand Valley State University

Bill Wines
Miami University (Ohio)

Lastly, the authors wish to rededicate the book to the memory of their fathers, John E. Cihon and James Ottavio Castagnera, Sr.

Patrick J. Cihon
Law and Public Policy Department
Syracuse University

James Ottavio Castagnera
President, Pinnacle Employment Law Institute
Rider University

PART 1

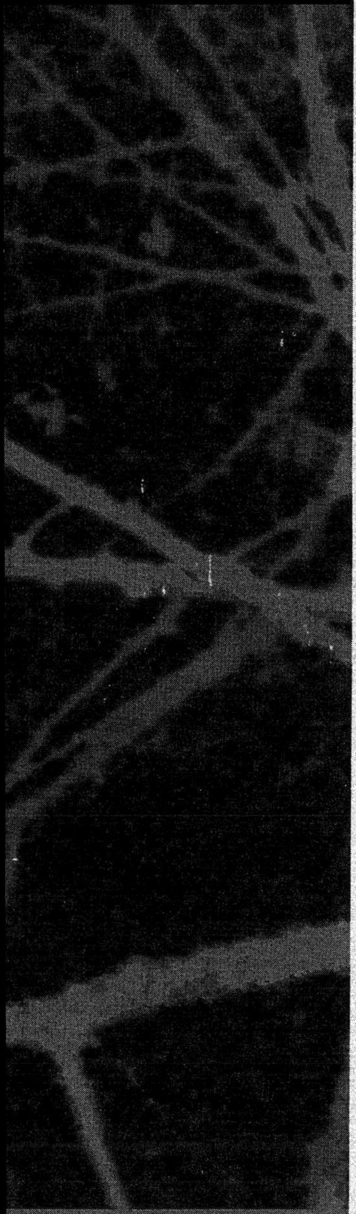

COMMON-LAW EMPLOYMENT ISSUES

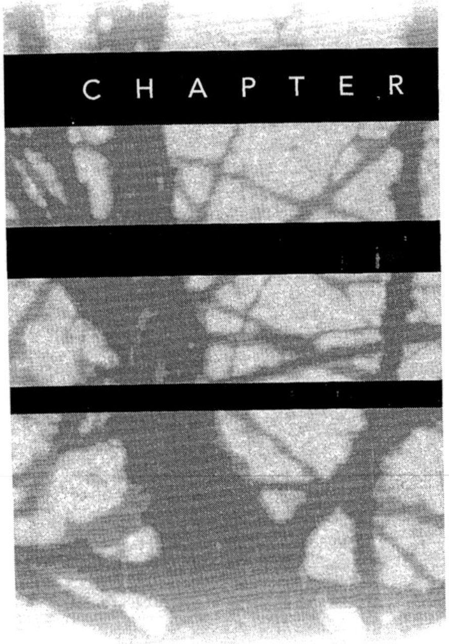

CHAPTER 1

EMPLOYMENT CONTRACTS AND WRONGFUL DISCHARGE

Common Law
Judge-made law as opposed to statutes and ordinances enacted by legislative bodies.

In this opening chapter and the one that follows, your introduction to the **common law** of employment is a survey of several major areas of the law where the court is still, by and large, sovereign. These include employment-at-will and wrongful discharge, defamation, and invasion of privacy.

EMPLOYMENT-AT-WILL

Employment-at-will
Both the employee and the employer are free to unilaterally terminate the relationship at any time and for any legally permissible reason, or for no reason at all.

To appreciate how far the courts have come, we need to look back to where they were just decades ago. In the nineteenth century, virtually every state court subscribed to the doctrine of **employment-at-will.** That doctrine in its raw form holds that an employee who has not been hired for an express period of time (say a year) can be fired at any time for any reason—or for no reason at all.

State and federal laws have narrowed this sweeping doctrine in many ways. The NLRA forbids firing employees for engaging in protected concerted activities. Title VII forbids discharge on the basis of race, color, gender, creed, or national origin. The Age Discrimination in Employment Act (ADEA) protects older workers from discriminatory discharge. The Occupational Safety and Health Act (OSHA) makes it illegal to fire an employee in retaliation for filing a safety complaint.

Although employers may complain that employment regulation is pervasive, the fact is that these laws leave broad areas of discretion for private sector employers to discharge at-will employees.[1] Except in a minority of states and cities that have adopted ordinances to the contrary, the law allows an employer to discharge homosexuals and transvestites if the company does not approve of such sexual preferences. Whistleblowers—employees who bring intraorganizational wrongdoing to the attention of the authorities—have often been fired for their trouble (frequently despite ostensible legal protection, although, as we shall see later in this chapter, much tougher protections have been put into place by the U.S. Congress very recently). Sometimes employees get fired simply because the boss does not like them. In such situations, none of these employees is covered by any of the federal and state labor laws previously discussed. Should they be protected? If so, how?

For an extensive Web resource of employment law on a state-by-state basis, see **http://www.ahipubs.com** *(Web site of the Alexander Hamilton Institute).*

Advocates of the employment-at-will doctrine defend it by pointing out that (1) the employee is likewise free to sever the working relationship at any time, and (2) in a free market, the worker with sufficient bargaining power can demand an employment contract for a set period of time if so desired. The trouble with the second point, in the view of most workers, is that as individuals they lack the bargaining power to command such a deal. This is one reason that, even in this postindustrial era, one American worker in six belongs to a union.[2]

The first of these arguments is not so easily dismissed. If the employee is free to quit at any time with or without notice, why should the employer be denied the same discretion in discharging employees? One answer to this troublesome question—an answer given by a majority of the state courts at this time—is, "The firing of an at-will employee may not be permitted if the discharge undermines an important public policy."

WRONGFUL DISCHARGE BASED ON PUBLIC POLICY

The most commonly adopted exception to the pure employment-at-will rule (the employee can be fired at any time for any reason) is the public policy exception. If a statute creates a right or a duty for the employee, he or she may not be fired for exercising that legal right or fulfilling that legal duty. A widely adopted example is jury duty: The courts of most states agree that an employer cannot fire an employee who misses work to serve on a jury (provided, of course, that the employee gives the employer proper notice).

Many courts accepting this exception, however, have kept it narrow by holding that the right or duty must be clearly spelled out by statute. For instance, in *Geary v. United States Steel Corporation* (1974), the Pennsylvania Supreme Court upheld the dismissal of a lawsuit brought by a salesman who was fired for refusing to sell what he insisted to management was an unsafe product. The court noted, "There is no suggestion that he possessed any expert qualifications or that

[1]Bear in mind that public employees enjoy constitutional rights, such as due process of law, which the Bill of Rights and the various state constitutions generally do not extend to private sector employees.

[2]Albeit, union representation in private, as opposed to public (government), employment had slipped to less than 10 percent of the eligible work force in 2003.

his duties extended to making judgments in matters of product safety." Most courts applying *Geary* have required the plaintiff-employee to point to some precise statutory right or duty before ruling the discharge wrongful.

Additionally, if the statute itself provides the employee with a cause of action, the courts are reluctant to recognize an alternative remedy in the form of a lawsuit for wrongful discharge. Thus, several Pennsylvania courts agree that an employee fired on the basis of gender or race discrimination in Pennsylvania has as his or her exclusive state law remedy the Pennsylvania Human Relations Act (PHRA), which requires that the employee initially seek redress with the commission created by that act. If the employee fails to file with the commission, thus losing the right of action under the PHRA, that person cannot come into court with the same grievance claiming wrongful discharge. Many other states' courts have reached similar conclusions regarding their states' antidiscrimination, workers' compensation, and work safety laws.

Dicta
Opinions of a judge or appellate panel of judges which are tangential to the rule, holding, and decision which are at the core of the judicial pronouncement.

Tort
A private or civil wrong or injury, caused by one party to another, either intentionally or negligently.

Staying with Pennsylvania as our example, that state has demonstrated a strong reluctance to depart from the ancient and time-tested rule of employment-at-will. In the 1970s, the Pennsylvania Supreme Court published **dicta** in one or two of its decisions that seemed to suggest that the **tort** of wrongful discharge was about to blossom in that commonwealth's common law. Taking their lead from this dicta, the federal district courts and the U.S. Court of Appeals for the Third Circuit, sitting in Pennsylvania, developed and shaped this cause of action. Then, perhaps to these federal judges' dismay, in the 1990s the high court of Pennsylvania issued opinions that virtually took these legal developments back to square one. Following is the Court's most recent ruling, which continued its tendency to keep the public policy exception to wrongful discharge narrow.

McLaughlin v. Gastrointestinal Specialists, Inc.

750 A.2d 283 (PA 2000)

Opinion: Newman, Justice

[1] In this case, we question whether the Superior Court properly upheld the decision of the trial court to sustain preliminary objections and to dismiss a cause of action for common law wrongful discharge. We affirm the Superior Court because Mary McLaughlin (Appellant) can not state a claim for wrongful discharge solely based upon an alleged retaliatory termination of her employment in violation of the Occupational Safety and Health Act of 1970.

Procedural History

Appellant avers that her former employer, Gastrointestinal Specialists, Inc. ("Employer"), fired her from her position as an office manager because she made safety complaints related to Employer's use of a chemical called gluteraldehyde. Appellant alleges that OSHA has designated gluteraldehyde as a toxic, highly noxious solution to be used only in an open, well-ventilated area and that in Employer's office, the gluteraldehyde was stored in a small closet totally lacking in ventilation. As a result, a strong, noxious odor was emitted and toxic vapors were released whenever the closet door was opened, causing Appellant to suffer from migraine headaches, nausea, fatigue, shortness of breath and dizziness.

In September of 1995, Appellant notified Employer's practice manager (manager) of her concerns regarding the use of gluteraldehyde, but she claims that no action was taken. At the end of September, Appellant learned of the dangers of gluteraldehyde and, apparently without Employer's knowledge, she obtained a sample of the air in the room in which Employer stored the chemical and sent it to a testing laboratory. The laboratory concluded in a document sent to Appellant that the gluteraldehyde was well more than OSHA's maximum exposure limit. After receiving this report, Appellant again complained to the manager, who Appellant alleges told her to keep quiet because Employer feared that other employees would file workers' compensation claims, and that a "makeshift construct" would be built to remedy the problem. Appellant informed the manager that a makeshift construct would not suffice.

On October 27, 1995, soon after this last interaction between Appellant and her manager, Employer fired Appellant. . . .

This appeal raises two issues: Whether the Superior Court erred in finding that OSHA's anti-retaliation provision was not a basis for Appellant's wrongful discharge claim and whether the state court had jurisdiction to decide this matter. For the reasons that follow, we affirm the Superior Court. . . .

Analysis

This Commonwealth has reiterated since the turn of the last century that an employer may terminate an employee for any reason, unless restrained by contract. E.g., *Henry v. Pittsburgh & Lake Erie Railroad Co.,* 139 Pa. 289, 21 A. 157 (1891). This remained the untouched law of the employment relation until our decision in *Geary v. United States Steel Corporation,* 456 Pa. 171, 319 A.2d 174 (1974) stated that an employee may bring a non-statutory cause of action against an employer for that employee's termination, under very limited exception. Although we ultimately found that *Geary* did not set forth a cause of action, in dicta we left open the possibility of a wrongful discharge claim in circumstances where a termination of an employee would violate a "clear mandate of public policy." . . .

[Since then] this Court reaffirmed the position that the employment relationship is at-will. We [have] stated that there is no common law cause of action against an employer for termination of an at-will employment relationship. Exceptions to this rule have been recognized in only the most limited of circumstances, where discharges of at-will employees would threaten clear mandates of public policy. . . .

Appellant contends that the Superior Court erred because OSHA's anti-retaliation provisions are implicated regardless of whether she complained to the agency or her Employer because the agency has promulgated administrative regulations that prohibit Employer from firing her. She then concludes that OSHA's regulations indicate that an Employee's complaints to an employer are protected activity pursuant to the anti-retaliation provisions of OSHA, therefore, she has stated a claim for a wrongful discharge pursuant to the law of this Commonwealth. We reject Appellant's arguments. Further, we do not believe that in her Complaint, or in her arguments to our courts, she has articulated that her termination threatens a clear and substantial public policy in this Commonwealth. Therefore, as a matter of law, she could not overcome the presumption that Employer was free to fire her at will.

[4] Our previous cases in this arena have not directly addressed the issue of what constitutes "public policy," but we have stated in cases outside of the wrongful termination context that "public policy is to be ascertained by reference to the laws and legal precedents and not from supposed public interest." Implicit in the previous determinations of this Court is that we declare the public policy of this Commonwealth by examining the precedent within Pennsylvania, looking to our own Constitution, court decisions and statutes promulgated by our legislature. . . .

[5] Appellant has not shown how her discharge undermines any particular public interest of this Commonwealth. At most, she made an internal complaint to her employer, and not to any public agency within the Commonwealth. She points to no Pennsylvania statutory scheme that her discharge would undermine. We believe that it is of no moment that federal regulations may provide administrative protection to employees who make safety violations known to their employers unless of course the employee is able to articulate a particular policy within the Commonwealth that is threatened.

This is not a case in which the employee avers that she made a complaint to a Commonwealth agency, . . . and was fired in retaliation. Such a case implicates the policy of the Commonwealth because it thwarts the administration of a Commonwealth agency and undermines the statutory obligations of the employer and the employee, which a Pennsylvania statute governs. Here, however, Appellant has not shown any policy of this Commonwealth that is violated, and has not established how a private report to an employer would undermine the workings of any Commonwealth agency or any statutory mechanism within the Commonwealth. Indeed, in *Geary,* supra, this Court refused to accept the premise that an employer, who might have terminated an employee in retaliation for making internal reports regarding the safety of a product, threatened the public policy of this Commonwealth to such an extent that it outweighed the presumption of at-will employment.

[6] Accordingly, we hold that in order to set forth a claim for wrongful discharge a Plaintiff must do more than show a possible violation of a federal statute that implicates only her own personal interest. . . . This is not the case here. . . .

[7] While, of course, this Commonwealth can not enact laws that contravene federal law, we are not required to override our longstanding policy regarding common law at-will employment and thus provide a common law remedy for wrongful discharge simply because Congress provides a federal statutory remedy to be brought in a federal forum. Rather, we hold that a bald reference to a violation of a federal regulation, without any more articulation of how the public policy of this Commonwealth is implicated, is insufficient to overcome the strong presumption in favor of the at-will employment relation.

Case Questions

1. If the plaintiff had filed a formal complaint with the federal Occupational Safety and Health Administration, do you think the court would have ruled differently on her wrongful discharge claim?
2. The Commonwealth of Pennsylvania has its own occupational safety and health agency. Suppose the plaintiff had filed a complaint with that agency . . . do you think this would have influenced the court's decision on her wrongful discharge action?
3. What public policies does the court say it seeks to strengthen or protect by this decision?
4. Are there any public policies that you think are undermined by the court's decision in this case?
5. Did the plaintiff have any alternative remedies besides a wrongful discharge action that she might have pursued in the alternative?

EXPRESS AND IMPLIED CONTRACTS OF EMPLOYMENT

Express Contract
A bargain the terms of which are stated explicitly in writing (or sometimes verbally), as opposed to an implied contract, terms of which must be inferred by the court from the circumstances of the parties' relationship.

Implied Contract
A contractual relationship the terms and conditions of which must be inferred from the contracting parties' behavior toward one another.

Just Cause
Sometimes called good cause, as distinct from arbitrary behavior and wrongful or illegal motivation for an act.

Some employees have express contracts of employment, usually for a definite duration. Others fall within the coverage of a collective-bargaining agreement negotiated for them by their union. Most workers, however, have no express agreement as to the term of their employment, and some were given an oral promise of a fixed term in a state in which the statute of frauds requires that contracts for performance extending for a year or more be written. Such employees have sometimes tried to convince the courts that they have been given implied promises that take them outside the ranks of their at-will co-workers. An **express contract** has terms spelled out by the parties, usually in writing. **Implied contracts** are contracts that the courts infer from company policies (such as those published in employee handbooks) and the behavior of the parties or that are implied from the law.

If a company provides its employees with a personnel handbook, and that handbook says that employees will be fired only for certain enumerated infractions of work rules or that the firm will follow certain procedures in disciplining them, a worker may later argue that the manual formed part of his or her employment contract with the firm. An increasing number of state and federal courts agree.

A few courts go further and find in the common law the basis for an implied covenant of good faith and fair dealing. According to these courts, an at-will employee can no longer be fired if the firing is unfair or in bad faith. This comes very close to saying that an involuntary termination must be for **just cause.** What constitutes "just cause" usually is defined case by case. The following case involves a determination of if and when an employer can withdraw a unilaterally promulgated policy and replace it with another, thus unilaterally altering the employment relationship.

ASMUS V. PACIFIC BELL

23 Cal. 4th 1 (2000)

Chin, Justice

We granted the request of the Ninth Circuit Court of Appeals for an answer to the following certified question of law under rule 29.5 of the California Rules of Court: "Once an employer's unilaterally adopted policy—which requires employees to be retained so long as a specified condition does not occur—has become a part of the employment contract, may the employer thereafter unilaterally [terminate] the policy, even though the specified condition has not occurred?" We conclude the answer to the certified question is yes. An employer may unilaterally terminate a policy that contains a specified condition, if the condition is one of indefinite duration, and the employer effects the change after a reasonable time, on reasonable notice, and without interfering with the employees' vested benefits.

I. Background

• • •

B. Facts

In 1986, Pacific Bell issued the following "Management Employment Security Policy" (MESP): "It will be Pacific Bell's policy to offer all management employees who continue to meet our changing business expectations employment security through reassignment to and retraining for other management positions, even if their present jobs are eliminated. This policy will be maintained so long as there is no change that will materially affect Pacific Bell's business plan achievement."

In January 1990, Pacific Bell notified its managers that industry conditions could force it to discontinue its MESP. In a letter to managers, the company's chief executive officer wrote: "[W]e intend to do everything possible to preserve our Management Employment Security Policy. However, given the reality of the marketplace, changing demographics of the workforce and the continued need for cost reduction, the prospects for continuing this policy are diminishing—perhaps, even unlikely. We will monitor the situation continuously; if we determine that business conditions no longer allow us to keep this commitment, we will inform you immediately."

Nearly two years later, in October 1991, Pacific Bell announced it would terminate its MESP on April 1, 1992, so that it could achieve more flexibility in conducting its business and compete more successfully in the marketplace. That same day, Pacific Bell announced it was adopting a new layoff policy (the Management Force Adjustment Program) that replaced the MESP but provided a generous severance program designed to decrease management through job reassignments and voluntary and involuntary terminations. Employees who chose to continue working for Pacific Bell would receive enhanced pension benefits. Those employees who opted to retire in December 1991 would receive additional enhanced pension benefits, including increases in monthly pension and annuity options. Employees who chose to resign in November 1991 would receive these additional enhanced pension benefits as well as outplacement services, medical and life insurance for one year, and severance pay equaling the employee's salary and bonus multiplied by a percentage of the employee's years of service.

Plaintiffs are 60 former Pacific Bell management employees who were affected by the MESP cancellation. They chose to remain with the company for several years after the policy termination and received increased pension benefits for their continued employment while working under the new Management Force Adjustment Program. All but eight of them signed releases waiving their right to assert claims arising from their employment under the MESP or its termination.

Plaintiffs filed an action in federal district court against Pacific Bell and its parent company, Pacific Telesis Group, seeking declaratory and injunctive relief, as well as damages for breach of contract, breach of fiduciary duty, fraud, and violations of the Employee Retirement Income Security Act (ERISA). The parties filed countermotions for partial summary judgment before conducting discovery. The district court granted summary judgment in Pacific Bell's favor against the 52 plaintiffs who signed releases. In an unpublished opinion, the Ninth Circuit affirmed the district court's judgment in this respect.

The district court granted summary judgment on the breach of contract claim in favor of the eight plaintiffs who did not sign releases. It held that even if an employer had the right unilaterally to terminate a personnel policy creating a contractual obligation, that right would not apply in cases where the original employment policy incorporated a term for duration or conditions for rescission, absent stronger evidence of the employees' assent to the policy modification than their continued employment. The court concluded that Pacific Bell could not terminate its MESP unless it first demonstrated (paraphrasing the words of the MESP) "a change that will materially alter Pacific Bell's business plan achievement." . . .

II. Discussion

A. California Employment Law

• • •

The parties agree that California law permits employers to implement policies that may become unilateral implied-in-fact contracts when employees accept them by continuing their employment. We do not further explore the issue in the context here, although we noted that whether employment policies create unilateral contracts will be a factual question in each case. The parties here disagree on how employers may terminate or modify a unilateral contract that has been accepted by the employees' performance. Plaintiffs assert that Pacific Bell was not entitled to terminate its MESP until it could demonstrate a change materially affecting its business plan, i.e., until the time referred to in a clause in the contract. Pacific Bell asserts that because it formed the contract unilaterally, it could terminate or modify that contract as long as it did so after a reasonable time, gave affected employees reasonable notice, and did not interfere with the employees' vested benefits (e.g., pension and other retirement benefits). Even if we were to require additional consideration, Pacific Bell contends it gave that consideration by offering enhanced pension benefits to those employees who chose to remain with the company after the modification took effect. Both parties rely on cases from other jurisdictions to support their respective positions.

• • •

C. Application of Legal Principles

1. Consideration

Plaintiffs contend that Pacific Bell gave no valid consideration to bind the proposed MESP termination and subsequent modification. According to plaintiffs, when Pacific Bell unilaterally terminated the contract to create a new contract with different terms, it left its employees with no opportunity to bargain for additional benefits or other consideration. The parties' obligations were unequal, and hence, there was no mutuality of obligation for the change.

We disagree. The general rule governing the proper termination of unilateral contracts is that once the promisor determines after a reasonable time that it will terminate or modify the contract, and provides employees with reasonable notice of the change, additional consideration is not required. The mutuality of obligation principle requiring new consideration for contract termination applies to bilateral contracts only. In the unilateral contract context, there is no mutuality of obligation. For an effective modification, there is consideration in the form of continued employee services. The majority rule correctly recognizes and applies this principle. Here, Pacific Bell replaced its MESP with a subsequent layoff policy. Plaintiffs' continued employment constituted acceptance of the offer of the modified unilateral contract. As we have observed, a rule requiring separate consideration in addition to continued employment as a limitation on the ability to terminate or modify an employee security agreement would contradict the general principle that the law will not concern itself with the adequacy of consideration.

The corollary is also true. Just as employers must accept the employees' continued employment as consideration for the original contract terms, employees must be bound by amendments to those terms, with the availability of continuing employment serving as adequate consideration from the employer. When Pacific Bell terminated its original MESP and then offered continuing employment to employees who received notice and signed an acknowledgement to that effect, the employees accepted the new terms, and the subsequent modified contract, by continuing to work. Continuing to work after the policy termination and subsequent modification constituted acceptance of the new employment terms.

2. Illusoriness

Plaintiffs alternatively claim that Pacific Bell's MESP would be an illusory contract if Pacific Bell could unilaterally modify it. Plaintiffs rely on the rule that when a party to a contract retains the unfettered right to terminate or modify the agreement, the contract is deemed to be illusory.

Plaintiffs are only partly correct. Scholars define illusory contracts by what they are not. As Corbin observes, "if a promise is expressly made conditional on something that the parties know cannot occur, no real promise has been made. Similarly, one who states 'I promise to render a future performance, if I want to when the time arrives,' has made no promise at all. It has been thought, also, that promissory words are illusory if they are conditional on some fact or event that is wholly under the promisor's control and bringing it about is left wholly to the promisor's own will and discretion. This is not true, however, if the words used do not leave an unlimited option to the one using them. It is true only if the words used do not in fact purport to limit future action in any way." Thus, an unqualified right to modify or terminate the contract is not enforceable. But the fact that one party reserves the implied power to terminate or modify a unilateral contract is not fatal to its enforcement, if the exercise of the power is subject to limitations, such as fairness and reasonable notice.

As Pacific Bell observes, the MESP was not illusory because plaintiffs obtained the benefits of the policy while it was operable. In other words, Pacific Bell was obligated to follow it as long as the MESP remained in effect. Although a permanent no-layoff policy would be highly prized in the modern workforce, it does not follow that anything less is without significant value to the employee or is an illusory promise. As long as the MESP remained in force, Pacific Bell could not treat the contract as illusory by refusing to adhere to its terms; the promise was not optional with the employer and was fully enforceable until terminated or modified.

3. Vested Benefits

Plaintiffs next allege that the MESP conferred a vested benefit on employees, like an accrued bonus or a pension. But as Pacific Bell observes, no court has treated an employment security policy as a vested interest for private sector employees. In addition, plaintiffs do not allege that Pacific Bell terminated its MESP in bad faith. Although we agree with plaintiffs that an employer may not generally interfere with an employee's vested benefits, we do not find that the MESP gave rise to, or created any, vested benefits in plaintiffs' favor.

4. Condition as Definite Duration Clause

Plaintiffs alternatively contend that a contract specifying termination on the occurrence (or nonoccurrence) of a future happening, in lieu of a specific date, is one of definite duration that cannot be terminated or modified until the event occurs. Because Pacific Bell declared that it would maintain its MESP "so long as" its business conditions did not substantially change, plaintiffs, like the dissent, assert that the specified condition is automatically one for a definite duration that Pacific Bell is obliged to honor until the condition occurs.

Contrary to plaintiffs and the dissent, a "specified condition" may be one for either definite or indefinite duration. Indeed, both plaintiffs and the dissent fail to recognize that courts have interpreted a contract that conditions termination on the happening of a future event as one for a definite duration or time period only when "there is an ascertainable event which necessarily implies termination." As Pacific Bell observes, even though its MESP contained language specifying that the company would continue the policy "so long as" it did not undergo changes materially affecting its business plan achievement, the condition did not state an ascertainable event that could be measured in any reasonable manner. As Pacific Bell explains, when it created its MESP, the document referred to changes that would have a significant negative effect on the company's rate of return, earnings and, "ultimately the viability of [its] business." The company noted that if the change were to occur, it would result from forces beyond Pacific Bell's control, and would include "major changes in the economy or the public policy arena." These changes would have nothing to do with a fixed or ascertainable event that would govern plaintiffs' or Pacific Bell's obligations to each other under the policy. Therefore, the condition in the MESP did not restrict Pacific Bell's ability to terminate or modify it, as long as the company made the change after a reasonable time, on reasonable notice, and in a manner that did not interfere with employees' vested benefits.

The facts show that those conditions were met here. Pacific Bell implemented the MESP in 1986, and it remained in effect until 1992, when the company determined that maintaining the policy was incompatible with its need for flexibility in the marketplace. The company then implemented a new Management Force Adjustment Program in which employees whose positions were eliminated would be given 60 days to either find another job within the company, leave the company with severance benefits after signing a release of any claims, or leave the company without severance benefits. The employees were provided with a booklet entitled Voluntary Force Management Programs detailing the new benefits the company provided following the MESP cancellation.

Thus, the MESP was in place for a reasonable time and was effectively terminated after Pacific Bell determined that it was no longer a sound policy for the company. In sum, Pacific Bell maintained the MESP for a reasonable time, it provided more than reasonable notice to the affected employees that it was terminating the policy, and it did not interfere with employees' vested benefits. The law requires nothing more.

Case Questions

1. How were the plaintiffs harmed by the company's substitution of policies?
2. Why did the company make the substitution?
3. Should it matter to the court whether the policy change occurred at a time of economic prosperity, when it might be easy for disappointed employees to change jobs, or should the rule apply regardless of conditions in the job market?
4. Explain what is meant by an illusory contract and why the court does not accept the plaintiffs' argument on this point.
5. What is meant by vesting, and why didn't the benefits promised under the old employment policy vest for the plaintiffs?

Good Faith
An honest belief, absent malice, in the statement made or the action undertaken. By comparison, *bad faith* implies malice, evil intent, fraudulent and dishonest speech or behavior.

As suggested above, the most far-ranging theory of wrongful discharge is the common law notion—adopted by only a small minority of the 50 states with regard to employment relationships—of **good faith** and fair dealing. Under this theory, the law imposes a duty to deal fairly and in good faith with every employee, even when the employment relationship is at-will. Thus, in one Delaware Supreme Court case that adopted the concept, an employee who was hired only for as long as it would take the company to find a more competent replacement, and who was shipped off to a New York City facility from his Delaware home to keep the company from losing a service contract in the "Big Apple," was deemed to have a cause of action against his Machiavellian employer. In other cases decided in some states' courts across the country, salespeople fired so as to prevent them from being on board when major sales commissions accrued have been allowed to sue for wrongful discharge, even though they admittedly were employees at-will.

MODEL EMPLOYMENT TERMINATION ACT

The National Conference of Commissioners on Uniform State Laws was organized in the 1890s as part of a movement in the American Bar Association for the reform and unification of American law. Currently, ninety-nine uniform acts and twenty-four model acts comprise the conference's list, which the states are encouraged to adopt. In 1987, the conference established a drafting committee to create a Uniform Employment Termination Act to provide employees with statutory protection against wrongful discharge. By 1991, the conference had approved a "model" act; however, division among the commissioners has prevented the act from achieving the status of "uniform." Consequently, states are encouraged to modify the model to suit each jurisdiction's particular social, economic, and legal needs. So far, only a handful of states have done so (see, e.g., Montana Wrongful Discharge from Employment Act, Mont. Code Ann. Secs. 39-2-901 through 39-2-915).

The heart and soul of the Model Employment Termination Act (META) in its present form is Section 3(a), which states that "an employer may not terminate the employment of an employee without good cause."

Section 3(b) limits application of the "good cause" limitation on employment-at-will to workers who have been with the particular employer for at least one year. Section 4(c) adds another possible exception, stating that employer and employee may substitute a severance pay agreement for the good cause standard, and the good cause standard is inapplicable to situations where termination comes at the expiration of an express oral or written contract containing a fixed duration for the employment relationship.

The META suggests that claims under it be subject to binding arbitration with arbitral awards being issued within thirty days of hearings. Section 10 forbids retaliation against employees who make claims or who testify under the procedural provisions of the META.

NEW PROTECTION FOR CORPORATE WHISTLEBLOWERS

On July 30, 2002, Congress passed and the president signed the Sarbanes-Oxley Act (SOA). The act is thus far the single most significant piece of legislation to come out of the Enron/Worldcom/Arthur Andersen accounting scandals, which helped deepen the post-9/11 stock market decline and related economic recession. SOA amends the creaky Securities and Exchange Acts of 1933 and 1934, as well as the more recent-vintage ERISA, plus the Investment Advisers Act of 1940 and the U.S. Criminal Code. The SOA includes two provisions, one criminal and the other civil, for the protection of employees who report improper conduct by corporate officials concerning securities fraud and corruption.

Dozens of federal laws, such as OSHA and Title VII, protect employees who blow the whistle on illegal practices or who cooperate in investigations and testify at hearings from employer retaliation, such as employment termination. Dozens of states have jumped on the whistleblower bandwagon, adding a dizzying variety of whistleblower laws to the panoply of rules and regs that human resource managers and employment lawyers must consider before initiating "industrial capital punishment" (i.e., firing a miscreant worker). In those increasingly rare jurisdictions or circumstances in which no federal or state anti-retaliation rule is implicated, the courts often have shown themselves willing to carve out a public policy exception to employment-at-will, where the plaintiff provides proof that he or she was fired for reporting or restricting illegal supervisory activity. But the proliferation of such laws and court rulings often fell short of protecting whistleblowers, either because of poor enforcement procedures or ineffectual remedies. The SOA is unique in making whistleblower retaliation a federal crime that can result in officer/director defendants actually going to prison.

Perhaps the scariest aspect of the SOA's criminal provision is that it can be used to punish retaliation against persons who provide information to law enforcement officials relating to the possible commission of any federal offense, not just securities fraud, albeit securities fraud was the catalyst for the legislation. The provision makes it a crime to "knowingly, with the intent to retaliate, take . . . any action harmful to any person, including interference with lawful employment or livelihood of any person, for providing a law enforcement officer any truthful information relating to the commission or possible commission of any Federal offense." Individuals found guilty under this proviso may be fined up to a quarter-million dollars and imprisoned up to ten years. Corporate defendants can face up to a half-million dollar fine if convicted.

Civil Liability under the SOA

A child of corporate greed and accounting scandals, the SOA's legislative history indicates that its whistleblower provisions are intended primarily to protect employees of publicly traded companies acting in the public interest to try to prevent officer/director wrongdoing and "to encourage and protect those who report fraudulent activity that can damage innocent investors in publicly traded companies." To the extent that Congress evinced its intent to uniformly regulate whistleblowing from within large national and multinational firms, SOA can be expected to preempt the myriad state statutes referred to earlier.

The civil-liability whistleblower language reads as follows:

> No [publicly traded] company . . . or officer, employee, contractor, subcontractor or agent of such company, may discharge, demote, suspend, threaten, harass, or in any other manner discriminate against an employee in the terms and conditions of employment because of any lawful act done by the employee—
>
> (2) to provide information, cause information to be provided, or otherwise assist in an investigation regarding conduct that the employee reasonably believes constitutes a violation of: (a) any rule or regulation of the SEC; (b) any provision of federal law relating to fraud against shareholders; or (c) federal criminal law provisions prohibiting mail fraud, bank fraud, or fraud by wire, radio, or television, when the information or assistance is provided to or the investigation is conducted by—
>
> a federal regulatory or law enforcement agency;
>
> any member of Congress or any committee of Congress; or
>
> a person with supervisory authority over the employee; [or]
>
> [a] person working for the employer who has the authority to investigate, discover, or terminate misconduct; or (2) to file, cause to be filed, testify, participate in, or otherwise assist in a proceeding filed or about to be filed . . . relating to [any of the rules, regs and statutes referenced in (1) above].
>
> This provision applies to the following employers:
>
> * All U.S. domestic publicly-traded corporations
> * All non-public companies whose debt instruments are publicly traded
> * All foreign companies registered to do business in the U.S.

SUMMARY

- In nineteenth century American common law, the employment-at-will doctrine became the norm. The at-will doctrine holds that, unless the parties expressly agree on a specific duration, the employment relationship may be severed by either the employee or the employer at any time and for any reason.
- During the second half of the twentieth century, American courts narrowed the at-will doctrine by carving out several common-law exceptions. The most common of these is the public policy exception, which holds that an employer cannot fire an employee if that termination would undermine a clear mandate of public policy. For example, many states have punished employers for firing workers who were absent from work because they had been called to jury duty.

- Another exception to the at-will rule is the legal doctrine of an implied contract. While the parties may not have agreed expressly to a duration of the employment relationship, an employee handbook or other employer policy may state that employees will not be fired except for good cause. Or such a company document may accord employees certain procedural rights, such as arbitration, before a job termination becomes final.
- Under the doctrine of good faith and fair dealing, which only a minority of American courts have adopted as a limitation on at-will employment, a terminated worker may bring a wrongful discharge action whenever the employer has failed to deal in good faith. For instance, an employer who fires a salesperson simply to escape paying commissions might run afoul of this common-law rule.
- The Model Employment Termination Act seeks to make "good cause" the basis for all employment terminations and to provide the parties with arbitration as their remedy when the propriety of a firing is in dispute. So far, only a handful of states have adopted all or some of the Model Act.
- Whistleblowers, who are ostensibly protected from retaliation under many federal and state laws, nevertheless have often been victimized by their employers, discovering too late that the laws on which they relied lacked the teeth to properly protect them. The federal Sarbanes-Oxley Act of 2002 makes such retaliation against those reporting a federal crime itself a crime that can result in the imprisonment of corporate officers. In the wake of 9/11 and Enron, whistleblower protection has come of age.

QUESTIONS

1. What were some of the socioeconomic conditions in nineteenth century America that led the majority of state courts to adopt the legal principle of employment-at-will?
2. What changes occurred in American society during the twentieth century which may have encouraged the majority of state courts to carve out exceptions to the pristine employment-at-will doctrine?
3. Of the three most widely adopted exceptions to the employment-at-will doctrine—public policy, implied contract, good faith and fair dealing—which would you accept, and which would you reject, if you were a supreme court justice in your state? Why?
4. Is it preferable to change the law by enacting a statute, such as the Model Employment Termination Act, or for a state's supreme court to make the change by judicial fiat in a court decision?
5. Given that under the Sarbanes-Oxley Act corporate official who retaliate against a whistleblower may be put in prison, what penalties should be imposed upon a so-called "whistleblower" who turns out to be a liar?

CASE PROBLEMS

1. The company's employee handbook stated clearly that employment at the firm was strictly on an at-will basis. However, at other spots, the same handbook laid out policies for progressive disciplinary action when employees violated company rules, procedures that the company said it would follow whenever a reduction in force was required by financial

circumstances, a letter from the company president saying that the company's general practice was to terminate employees only when there existed "good cause," and a policy of reassigning laid off employees who were performing satisfactorily.

Pursuant to a reduction in force, the chief financial officer terminated the financial reports supervisor after twenty-two years of good performance. Does the supervisor have a cause of action for breach of his employment contract under the employee handbook as it is described to you above? See *Guz v. Bechtel National, Inc.* [24 Cal.4th 317, 8 P.3d 1089 (2000)].

2. An at-will employee was fired for taking unpaid medical leave while his physician was trying to determine whether or not he had contracted tuberculosis. The employee claimed that the company's human resources director had told him that he "needed to take time off from work" pending the outcome of the tests. The company retorted that, while it did not dispute that the statement was made by the human resources director, the employee handbook stated that medical leaves and other unpaid leaves could only be granted in writing by enumerated company officials, specifically "by one of the principals, vice president of finance, or vice president of personnel."

The employee contended that because the human resources director told him to stay home until he had the test results, the company was estopped from asserting the handbook provision in support of its subsequent decision to terminate his employment for failing to get written leave authorization. Is the employee right? See *Honorable v. American Wyott Corporation* [11 P.3d 928 (Wyoming Supreme 2000)].

3. The corporation's vice president complained to the board of directors about what she perceived to be potential violations of state and federal antitrust laws by the corporation. The CEO, on learning of this, fired the vice president, who sued claiming that termination of her at-will employment amounted to violation of a clear mandate of public policy. While conceding that state and federal antitrust laws are significant expressions of public policy, the company contended that for the vice president to win her wrongful discharge lawsuit, she must be able to prove that the firm actually was guilty of antitrust violations.

Is the company correct in taking this position? Or should it be enough that the vice president can prove she held a good faith belief in the existence of such violations at the time that she circumvented the "chain of command" and complained to the board about the perceived violations? See *Murcott v. Best Western International, Inc.* [9 P.3d 1088 (Arizona App. 2000)].

4. The in-house legal counsel for a corporation, like all top members of management, signed an employment contract when he came to work for the company. The contract stated, among other things, that any disputes arising under the contract would be submitted to binding arbitration. Some time later, when the attorney's employment was terminated, he sought to institute a breach of contract claim in state court. The company moved to have the case dismissed on the basis of the provision in the contract that all disputes would be submitted to a private arbitrator.

The attorney countered that since his cause of action was for a material breach of the contract, and that a material breach of the contract rendered it null and void, he had no obligation to abide by the arbitration clause and subject himself to binding arbitration. Is he right? What public policy considerations should the court take into account in deciding this issue? See *Burkhart v. Semitool, Inc.* [5 P.3d 1031 (Montana Supreme 2000)].

5. A Wisconsin statute prohibits corporate employees from falsifying business records. A company's CEO requested that the company's payroll clerk cut her a bonus check without making any payroll deductions. The payroll clerk countered that in his opinion the IRS

Code required that payroll deductions be taken out of the bonus check. The CEO countered that she would be personally responsible for any tax liability that resulted from the clerk's issuing a lump sum payment. The clerk refused and was fired.

Does the payroll clerk, who was an at-will employee, have a cause of action for wrongful discharge under Wisconsin law? On what legal theory? See *Strozinsky v. School District of Brown Deer* [237 Wis.2d 19, 614 N.W.2d 443 (2000)].

6. The Iowa Civil Rights Act prohibits firing an employee in retaliation for opposing a discriminatory practice. The plaintiff in this case was fired not for opposing any such prohibited, discriminatory employment practice by the defendant company. Rather, he was terminated for voicing his opposition to the termination of a second employee, who had been previously fired for testifying against the employer's position in a discrimination case.

While the plaintiff concedes that he does not have a direct cause of action for retaliatory discharge under the Iowa antidiscrimination statute, he contends that he should have a wrongful discharge claim for violation of a clear mandate of public policy based upon the intent of the legislature as implied by the antiretaliatory provision of that statute. What do you think? See *Fitzgerald v. Salsbury Chemical, Inc.* [No. 52/98-1492 (Iowa Supreme 2000)].

7. The Oklahoma State Insurance Fund (SIF) hired the consulting firm of Alexander & Alexander to review the SIF's operations and recommend a reorganization plan. Ultimately, the consultants recommended a reduction in force of 145 employees and the outsourcing of some of the SIF's functions. Some seven state employees who lost their jobs in the SIF filed suit against the state, alleging that the real reason they were selected for termination was their report that an SIF employee working on the reorganization had taken kickbacks from vendors who hoped to participate in the outsourcing part of the plan. The state of Oklahoma had a whistleblower statute that protected public employees who reported "mismanagement" to the state's civil service agency. The seven plaintiffs in this case admitted that they had not availed themselves of this statute, but had limited their alleged whistleblowing activities to reporting their suspicions internally to other SIF employees. Consequently, it was undisputed that they could not avail themselves of the protections of the state statute. Furthermore, the statute did not define what was encompassed by the term *mismanagement*.

Based on these facts, should the courts accord the plaintiffs a common-law cause of action for wrongful discharge? If so, under which of the three major theories of common-law wrongful dismissal should they be permitted to proceed? See *Barker v. State Insurance Fund,* 2001 WL 1383604 (Okla. Supreme).

8. A secretary employed by a local branch of the United Food and Commercial Workers Union was a vocal supporter of California Proposition 226, a statewide ballot initiative which, if enacted, would prohibit unions from expending dues contributions for political purposes. When she was fired by her union, she sued, claiming that terminating her because of her political position violated a clear mandate of public policy. The union moved to dismiss her state law action on the ground that union misconduct is regulated in great detail by the federal Labor Management Reporting and Disclosure Act (LMRDA—see Chapter 19).

The relevant common-law rule is: "A state action is preempted when it is an obstacle to the accomplishment and execution of the purposes and objectives of the Congress." Applying this rule to the facts above, and assuming that the LMRDA does in fact prohibit such actions as the firing of a union employee for espousing a political position, should the state court dismiss the plaintiff's suit against the union? See *Thunderburk v. United Food and Commercial Workers Local 324,* 168 LRRM (BNA) 2623 (Cal. Ct. App. 2001).

9. The plaintiff alleged that she had been fired for refusing to have sex with her supervisor. Unfortunately for her, because the firm she worked for was tiny, it did not fall under the jurisdiction of Title VII of the federal 1964 Civil Rights Act (see Chapter 3), which covers employers with at least fifteen workers. Her alternative, the Utah Anti-discrimination Act (UADA), also exempted small businesses, having adopted the federal law's fifteen-employee threshold. She therefore contended that she should be entitled to sue under the state's common-law tort of wrongful discharge on the basis of a public policy against sexual harassment reflected in the decisions interpreting both Title VII and the UADA.

How should the court rule on her claim? Are there competing public policies at issue here? See *Gottling v. P.R., Inc.*, 2002 WL 31055952, 2002 UT 95 (Utah Supreme).

10. Assume that the defendant in the foregoing case is a law firm and the alleged harasser is an attorney practicing before the Utah bar. Assume further that the state supreme court has enacted a code of conduct covering attorneys licensed to practice in the state's courts and that this code contains a canon to the effect that all licensed Utah attorneys are required to live up to "commonly-recognized community standards of moral conduct" and to avoid acts of "moral turpitude."

Should the Utah bar association act upon a complaint of misconduct and consider disbarring the attorney if the plaintiff files a complaint with its ethics panel? Should the court's ruling on the existence or nonexistence of a cause of action in the preceding case problem have any impact upon the ethics panel's decision to initiate disciplinary proceedings?

INTERNET EXERCISES

1. The purpose of this first exercise is to acquaint you with some of the best free legal research sites on the Internet.

   Begin by going to **http://www.findlaw.com** and clicking US Laws: Cases & Codes.

   Under US State Laws, select your home state and see if you can search the site and locate any wrongful discharge cases.
2. Go to **http://www.lawguru.com** and from the Tools menu on the left choose Find Attorneys.

   Next click Browse Attorneys by State and again choose your home state. Browse the attorneys and see if you can find an attorney or firm that claims to deal with either wrongful discharge or with employment law generally.

   Click that firm's link and see what the attorneys there have posted. If there is an e-mail address or link, try writing to the attorney or firm and querying them about the status of wrongful discharge law in that jurisdiction.
3. Go to **http://www.findlaw.com**. Under Student Resources, click Law Reviews, and search the site for recent articles about wrongful discharge. Are any of the law reviews you found published by a law school in your home state?
4. Now find the Web site for the Utah branch of the Society for Human Resource Management (SHRM) and research the site for a case named *Hansen v. AmericaOnline*. What were the main facts of the case? What was SHRM's position as an *amicus curiae* (friend of the court)? Can you identify the attorney who represented SHRM by filing a friend-of-the-court brief? Can you locate his firm's Web site?

INFOTRAC KEYWORDS

http://www.infotrac-college.com

employment at will, wrongful discharge, employment contracts

2 CHAPTER

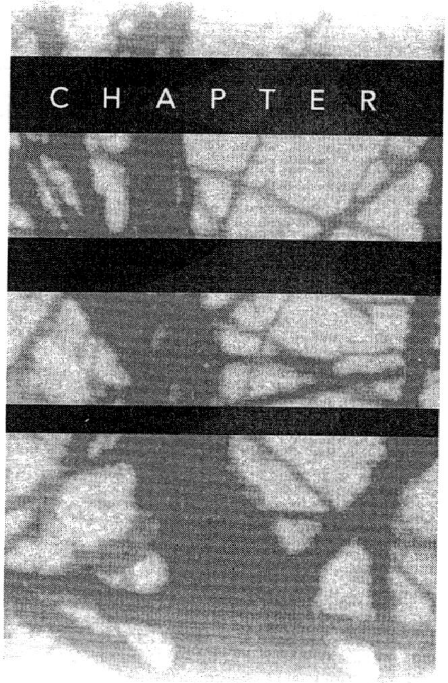

COMMONLY COMMITTED WORKPLACE TORTS

With increased frequency in the 1980s and 1990s, legal actions for wrongful termination were embellished by accompanying counts accusing employers of (and seeking additional damages for) defamation, invasion of privacy, infliction of emotional distress, and other forms of alleged improper conduct. Less frequently, employers and their defense counsels encountered such claims standing on their own.

The word *tort* derives from the French influence upon the English language and the English common law. It means a civil wrong not based upon a preexisting contractual relationship. By and large, tort law is the law of personal injury. Its application to employer/employee relationships is affected by workers' compensation insurance (see Chapter 11), which immunizes the employer from some tort liabilities; the extent of this immunity varies widely from state to state. In an effort to circumvent such employer immunity and defeat that affirmative defense, plaintiffs sometimes contend that they were not employees at all, but rather independent contractors not covered by state worker compensation statutes.

Additionally, where the work force is unionized (see Chapters 12–19) or where the employer is a public entity (see Chapter 20), the employee/plaintiff's right to bring a common-law tort action against the employer may be subject to significant restrictions. These may include National Labor Relations Act preemption, a requirement to submit the claim to binding arbitration (even nonunionized companies may add arbitration clauses to their employment contracts to ward off these proliferating claims), and sovereign immunity.

Furthermore, in this Information Age, employers are turning the tables and using the tort of trade secret theft as a means of guarding their valuable intellectual property from misappropriation by disgruntled, departing employees.

DEFAMATION AND INVASION OF PRIVACY

That defamation and invasion of privacy enjoy considerable popularity in the employer/employee context today is in part a function of our increasingly complex and heavily regulated business environment. Also, no technological innovation leaves many of us more nervous than the computer. Computers allow firms, institutions, and agencies to amass, store, and retrieve almost unlimited amounts of data on all of us. Investigative and surveillance techniques have also become highly sophisticated. In the wake of these advances, numerous commentators have predicted the death of privacy. Particularly noteworthy is the following comment by the Privacy Protection Study Commission created by the federal Privacy Act:

The text of the Privacy Act can be found at **http://www4.law.cornell.edu/uscode/5/552.html**

> One need only glance at the dramatic changes in our country during the last hundred years to understand why the relationship between organizational record keeping and personal privacy has become an issue in almost all modern societies. The records of a hundred years ago tell us little about the average American, except when he died, perhaps when and where he was born, and if he owned land, how he got his title to it. Three quarters of the adult population worked for themselves on farms or in small towns.
>
> . . . Record keeping about individuals was correspondingly limited and local in nature.
>
> . . . The past hundred years, and particularly the last three decades, have changed all that. Three out of four Americans now live in cities or their surrounding suburbs, only one in ten of the individuals in the work force today is self-employed, and education is compulsory for every child. The yeoman farmer and small-town merchant have given way to the skilled workers and white-collar employees who manage and staff organizations, both public and private, that keep society functioning.
>
> A significant consequence of this marked change in the variety and concentration of institutional relationships is that record keeping about individuals now covers almost everyone and influences everyone's life. . . .

In other words, with the great advantages that electronic technology brings to the business firm comes the necessary evil of increased likelihood and seriousness of torts of defamation and invasion of privacy, along with depersonalization and employee anxiety.

INVASION OF PRIVACY

An early U.S. Supreme Court case defined the right of privacy as

> [t]he right to be let alone; the right of a person to be free from unwarranted publicity. . . . The right of an individual (or corporation) to withhold himself and his property from public scrutiny, if he so chooses. It is said to exist only so far as its assertion is consistent with law or public policy, and in a proper case equity will interfere, if there is no remedy at law, to prevent an injury threatened by the invasion of, or infringement upon, this right from motives of curiosity, gain, or malice.

THE WORKING LAW

AOL ON THE FIRING LINE

When America Online fired three Utah-based employees for possessing guns in a company parking lot, the three turned to Utah's concealed-weapons law, one of the broadest and most tolerant pro-firearms acts in America, as the basis of a public-policy wrongful-discharge action. AOL defended with its strict "No Tolerance for Weapons at Work" policy. The Internet provider was joined by the Society for Human Resource Management and numerous other business groups in defending the action. According to a SHRM article authored on-line by Karyn-Siobhan Robinson, "The case involves the right of an employer to regulate conduct, including carrying of weapons, on its premises. The plaintiffs assert in the case, *Hansen v. America Online, Inc.*, that their termination was illegal because Utah law precludes employers from terminating an employee for lawfully possessing firearms." A SHRM attorney, Michael P. O'Brien of Salt Lake City, says, "This case addresses the fundamental question of whether or not an employer can control what occurs on the premises."

O'Brien might have added that the case has a distinctly post-Nine/Eleven flavor in that it adds to traditional notions of employee privacy rights an implicit right to look out for their own individual well-being, specifically by being well armed, a policy possibly shared by the State of Utah. SHRM and the other *amici* supporting defendant AOL strongly disagree. To the contrary, O'Brien's brief contends that "At all relevant times, it was the policy of the Governor and State of Utah, and other prominent Utah organizations, to ban guns at work." An interesting, and perhaps important, collateral question is, if the official attitude has changed in Utah since the September 11th terrorist attacks, which public policy should pertain . . . the one pervading Utah officialdom when the concealed-weapons statute was enacted or a post-Nine/Eleven attitude that may be different now? And, related to this question, the evidentiary issue of how do you demonstrate the change, given that the usual method of propounding a public policy is by citation of legal precedents, which in this case predictably predate September 11, 2001?

Four distinct species of the tort of invasion of privacy have emerged over the years since Brandeis and Warren set the stage for the tort's appearance:

1. intrusion upon plaintiff's seclusion or solitude or into his or her private affairs;
2. public disclosure of embarrassing private facts about the plaintiff;
3. publicity, the effect of which is to place the plaintiff in a "false light" in public;
4. appropriation of the plaintiff's name or likeness, without his or her permission, to the pecuniary advantage of the defendant.

It is important to note that in a privacy action the publication need not be defamatory for liability to attach; one can readily imagine (especially in situations involving the appropriation of plaintiff's name for defendant's pecuniary gain) circumstances in which a laudatory statement is tortious.

Increasingly, however, in this Information Age, the evolving common law of employee privacy rights revolves around where the employee's rights begin and the employer's rights end with regard to that ubiquitous and essential tool, the personal computer. In the decision that follows, the court wrestles with the issue of whether the trial judge erred in denying the plaintiff's former employer, defending itself against the employee's wrongful discharge action, to examine the contents of the plaintiff's home computer.

TBG Insurance Services Corporation v. The Superior Court of Los Angeles

96 Cal. App. 4th 443, 117 Cal. Rptr. 2d 155 (2002)

Vogel, Justice

An employer provided two computers for an employee's use, one for the office, the other to permit the employee to work at home. The employee, who had signed his employer's "electronic and telephone equipment policy statement" and agreed in writing that his computers could be monitored by his employer, was terminated for misuses of his office computer. After the employee sued the employer for wrongful termination, the employer demanded production of the home computer. The employee refused to produce the computer and the trial court refused to compel production. On the employer's petition, we conclude that, given the employee's consent to the employer's monitoring of both computers, the employee had no reasonable expectation of privacy when he used the home computer for personal matters. We issue the writ as prayed.

For about 12 years, Robert Zieminski worked as a senior executive for TBG Insurance Services Corporation. In the course of his employment, Zieminski used two computers owned by TBG, one at the office, the other at his residence. Zieminski signed TBG's "electronic and telephone equipment policy statement" in which he agreed, among other things, that he would use the computers "for business purposes only and not for personal benefit or non-Company purposes, unless such use was expressly approved. Under no circumstances could the equipment or systems be used for improper, derogatory, defamatory, obscene or other inappropriate purposes." Zieminski consented to have his computer "use monitored by authorized company personnel" on an "as needed" basis, and agreed that communications transmitted by computer were not private. He acknowledged his understanding that improper use of the computers could result in disciplinary action, including discharge. . . .

On November 28, 2000 . . . Zieminski's employment was terminated. According to TBG, Zieminski was terminated when TGB discovered that he "had violated TBG's electronic policies by repeatedly accessing pornographic sites on the Internet while he was at work." According to Zieminski, the pornographic Web sites were not accessed intentionally but simply "popped up" on his computer. Zieminski sued TBG, alleging that his employment had been wrongfully terminated "as a pretext to prevent his substantial stock holdings in TBG from fully vesting and to allow . . . TBG to repurchase his non-vested stock" at $.01 per share. . . .

TBG moved to compel production of the home computer, contending it has the right to discover whether information on the hard drive proves that, as claimed by TBG, Zieminski violated his employer's policy statement. . . . "[A] significant piece of evidence in this action is the home computer, as its hard drive may confirm that Zieminski has, in fact, accessed the same or similar sexually-explicit web sites at home, thereby undermining Zieminski's . . . story that, at work, such sites 'popped up' involuntarily.". . .

According to Zieminski, the home computer was provided as a "perk" given to all senior executives. He said that, "although the home computer was provided so that business related work could be done at home, it was universally accepted and understood by all that the home computer would also be used for personal purposes as well." He said his home computer was used by his wife and children, and that it "was primarily used for personal purposes and contains significant personal information and data" subject to his constitutional right of privacy. . . .

A "party may obtain discovery regarding any matter, not privileged, that is relevant to the subject matter involved in the pending action. . . ." Here, the home computer is indisputably relevant (Zieminski does not seriously contend otherwise). . . .

Zieminski's privacy claim is based on article 1, section 1, of the California Constitution, which provides: "All people are by nature free and independent and have inalienable rights. Among these are enjoying and defending life and liberty, acquiring, possessing, and protecting property, and pursuing and obtaining safety, happiness, and privacy." When affirmative relief is sought to prevent a constitutionally prohibited invasion of privacy, the plaintiff must establish "(1) a legally protected privacy interest; (2) a reasonable expectation of privacy in the circumstances; and (3) conduct by defendant constituting a serious invasion of privacy." . . . Here, we assume an abstract privacy interest in Zieminski's financial and other personal information but conclude . . . that the evidence is insufficient to support the trial court's implied finding that Zieminski had a reasonable expectation of privacy in the circumstances. . . .

Case Questions

1. In this case, the defendant-employer, defending against the former employee's wrongful discharge action, sought to discover what the plaintiff's home computer contained. The appeals court overruled the trial judge and ordered the plaintiff to grant the defendant access to his home PC. The company claimed Zieminski was fired for accessing sexually explicit Web sites; it hoped to demonstrate that the plaintiff accessed similar porno sites at home as well. Suppose the defendant's investigators also discover from records on the home PC that the plaintiff suffered from a serious disease, such as AIDS, and publicized this revelation to undermine the plaintiff's credibility. Do you think Zieminski would be allowed by the trial judge to add a count of invasion of privacy to his lawsuit against the company? If so, what would be the elements of the tort of invasion of privacy that the plaintiff would have to prove according to the appellate court's opinion? How do you think this new count of invasion of privacy would fare in light of the test enunciated by the appellate court?
2. Suppose, as suggested in question 1, that the defendant's agents, when examining the plaintiff's home computer in accordance with the appellate court's order, discovered evidence of financial wrongdoing related to the company's assets. Do you think the company should be entitled to amend its answer to the plaintiff's complaint to include this new information, as a separate and sufficient reason for firing the plaintiff, had it only known about the financial malfeasance when it fired him? If so, what effect should this new information have on the merits of the plaintiff's wrongful discharge suit? On the damages he will be awarded if he should prevail?
3. Concerning the plaintiff's "reasonable expectation of privacy" regarding the home PC, which do you feel should be given the most weight by the courts, the company policy read and signed by the employee or the practices that develop over time among the company's employees, such as the alleged use of Zieminski's computer by his wife and children? What actions or inactions by company officials might affect the balance to be set by the courts?
4. Given the issues raised by this appellate opinion, what policies on employee access and use of computers, e-mail, instant messaging, and the like would you recommend that a company institute and enforce?
5. Do you think it is sound company policy, whenever an employee is being terminated or the company is defending against a wrongful discharge action, for the company to examine the contents of the employee's desktop PC for independent grounds upon which to fire that employee?

DEFAMATION: LIBEL AND SLANDER

The tort of defamation has been defined as follows:

> A communication is defamatory if it tends so to harm the reputation of another as to lower him in the estimation of the community or to deter third persons from associating or dealing with him.

Expanding on this bare-bones definition, it is said that language is defamatory

> . . . if it tends to expose another to hatred, shame, obloquy, contempt, ridicule, aversion, ostracism, degradation, or disgrace, or to induce an evil opinion of one in the minds of right-thinking persons and to deprive him of their confidence and friendly intercourse in society.

Defamation
An intentional, false, and harmful communication. Written defamation is called *libel*. Spoken defamation is called *slander*.

Defamation is subdivided into the torts of libel and slander, the former being defamation by writing and the latter defamation through speech. These two torts may be further divided into the libel or slander that is per se and the libel or slander that is not per se. What makes this distinction critical in some cases is that libel/slander per se requires no showing of specific damages for the plaintiff to recover a judgment, whereas libel/slander that is not per se demands such a showing from the injured party. The term *per se* connotes that the third person to whom the defamation is communicated (and indeed the court) can recognize the damaging nature of the communication without being apprised of the contextual setting (innuendo) in which the communication was made. Professor Prosser has identified the commonly recognized forms of per se defamation as

> . . . the imputation of crime, of a loathsome disease, and those affecting the plaintiff in his business, trade, profession, office or calling. . . .

Business defamation thus may be defined as defamation per se having the following characteristics:

> False spoken or written words that tend to prejudice another in his business, trade, or profession are actionable without proof of special damage if they affect him in a manner that may, as a necessary consequence, or do, as a natural consequence, prevent him from deriving therefrom that pecuniary reward which probably otherwise he might have obtained.

This definition leaves the door to the courtroom wide open to the defamed employee, whose job is his or her "business, trade, or profession." Indeed, since business defamation is a per se tort, it can amount to strict liability once the plaintiff has proved that the damaging statement was published. This use of the words "strict liability" is not to say that no defenses are available. On the contrary, it is possible to identify several. First, as has already been suggested, one can dispute the contention that one published the statement or that it is defamatory. Or one can try to prove that the statement is true. Failing these, the defendant may be able to argue successfully that the statement was made from behind the shield of a privilege.

See **http://www.law.cornell.edu/topics/employment.html** *for an excellent summary of this tort as it developed and was applied to employment situations in one state's (Michigan's) common law.*

The law recognizes "qualified privileges." When a person is protected by qualified privilege, the remarks made will be immune from a defamation suit if the person made them in good faith. If the remarks were made with malice, or in bad faith, they will not be privileged. The law generally recognizes a qualified privilege where one person communicates with another who has a legitimate need to know the information. For example, comments concerning an employee's performance made to a supervisor, and communicated through the organizational structure, are privileged if made in good faith. In addition, assessments of an employee, communicated by a former employer to a prospective employer, made in good faith, are privileged. But comments or remarks, if not made in good faith and/or communicated to persons who have no legitimate need to know, are subject to a defamation action.

The following case is a good example of a dilemma that has become all too common in the American workplace at the start of the new millennium: An employer attempting to avoid liability by prompt investigation of a sexual harassment claim finds itself the target of a defamation suit by the accused supervisor.

Paulson v. Ford Motor Co.

612 N.W.2d 450 (Minn. App. 2000)

Opinion. Shumaker, Judge

Appellant Raymond Paulson challenges the district court's grant of summary judgment to respondent Ford Motor Company, contending genuine issues of material fact existed as to whether alleged defamatory statements were privileged and made with malice. . . . We affirm as to summary judgment on the defamation claim. . . .

Facts

Respondent Ford Motor Company is a Delaware corporation with its principal place of business in Dearborn, Michigan. Ford operates a St. Paul plant at which Sandra Rudebeck and Raymond Paulson worked. In 1994, Paulson became the plant's final area manager, one of the top-salaried positions. Rudebeck became a salaried supervisor in 1995.

In February 1996, another Ford supervisor asserted various claims against Ford including allegations of sexual harassment by Paulson. Gail Shirey, a personnel relations associate from Ford headquarters, conducted an investigation into the allegations against Paulson. She interviewed primarily female salaried employees, including Rudebeck. Shirey issued a report determining that Paulson's behavior constituted sexual harassment. She recommended that he be demoted and transferred to another Ford facility. Ford acted on her recommendation.

In 1997, Rudebeck sued Paulson, Ford, and another supervisor, alleging sexual harassment and related claims and defamation. Ford began discussing settlement with Rudebeck and informed Paulson. Paulson then brought claims against Ford and Rudebeck for defamation and related claims and sought indemnification from Ford.

Rudebeck settled with Ford and the other supervisor, and the district court granted summary judgment in favor of Ford on Paulson's defamation claim. . . .

Analysis

• • •

I.

[3][4][5][6][7] For a statement to meet the legal standards for defamation,

> it must be communicated to someone other than the plaintiff, it must be false, and it must tend to harm the plaintiff's reputation and to lower him in the estimation of the community.

Even publishing a defamatory statement will not lead to liability if the statement is conditionally privileged and the privilege is not abused. For a communication to be privileged, "it must be made upon a proper occasion, from a proper motive, and must be based upon reasonable or probable cause." Statements made "in the course of investigating or punishing employee misconduct" are generally privileged, based on the employer's interest in protecting against harmful employees. Once it has been shown that a conditional privilege applies, the plaintiff must prove actual malice to recover.

[8] The district court determined as a matter of law that the alleged defamatory statements about Paulson made by Ford employees were privileged and that there was no evidence of malice. Paulson contends there was

a factual question for the jury as to whether the Ford employees had reasonable or probable cause to make the statements and whether the statements were made with malice.

[9][10] "Reasonable grounds can exist if a person has valid reasons for believing a statement, even though the statement later proves to be false." In determining whether the statements were supported by reasonable or probable cause, courts will examine whether the employer took investigative steps. We do not interpret this to mean that a mere assertion that the employer conducted an investigation will suffice; instead, the court will examine the precise nature and extent of the investigation to assess the facts supporting the defamatory allegations and the efforts the employer made to ascertain their accuracy.

[11] Paulson contends the statements and reports about him were so biased and unsubstantiated that they do not show Ford had reasonable or probable cause for making the statements. We disagree. . . . Ford here conducted a thorough investigation, prompted by a complaint by another employee. Ford interviewed and took statements from a number of witnesses, reviewed Paulson's history of similar complaints, and talked to Paulson himself. The investigation provided reasonable or probable grounds to support the statements concerning Paulson, which are therefore protected by a qualified privilege.

[12][13] Once a qualified privilege applies, the plaintiff must prove actual malice to recover. Malice is "actual ill will, or a design causelessly and wantonly to injure plaintiff." While the issue of whether actual malice is present is usually a jury question, in some circumstances, it may be subject to summary judgment.

Paulson contends there was sufficient evidence of malice on the part of those making the statements to allow the issue to go to the jury. He asserts that several of the individuals who made statements had a clear vendetta against him, and that the reports used exaggerated language and false representations. But Paulson himself admitted at his deposition that Shirey and Ford were just doing their job during the investigations and no personal grudges or vendettas were involved. He acknowledged there was no evidence that Shirey handled the investigation in such a way as to intentionally harm him. We agree with the district court that Paulson did not provide evidence showing there was a factual issue as to whether actual malice was present.

Case Questions

1. What are the social and economic policies that underlie the creation by the courts of a qualified privilege in the business environment?
2. Are there any. additional policy considerations that courts need to consider when a sexual harassment investigation is the "business transaction" at issue?
3. Should the same qualified privilege apply to the woman making the sexual harassment claim if the alleged harasser decides to countersue for defamation?
4. How is "malice" defined in the preceding court opinion? How is that different from the everyday definition of malice?
5. Should a similar qualified privilege apply when a corporation is accused of invading an employee's privacy during the course of investigating alleged wrongdoing?

TORTIOUS INFLICTION OF EMOTIONAL DISTRESS

The following case involves claims of both intentional and negligent infliction of emotional distress, which arose in the context of a sexually hostile work environment. This variety of the tort is even more difficult to establish than intentional infliction, albeit mere negligence is usually a lower level of culpability than intentional conduct; as you read the opinion, see if you can discern why this is so.

Simpson v. Ohio Reformatory for Women

2003 WL 758486 (Ohio Court of Appeals 2003)

McCormac, J.

Plaintiff-appellant, Susan Simpson, appeals from a judgment of the Ohio Court of Claims ruling in favor of defendant-appellee, the Ohio Reformatory for Women ("ORW"), on her claims for negligent infliction of emotional distress, negligent supervision, and constructive discharge.

This action arises out of plaintiff's employment with ORW. From August 1996 until November 1999, plaintiff was employed at ORW in the medical records department as an "office assistant 3." According to plaintiff's trial testimony, from December 1996, until she resigned from her position at ORW in November 1999, plaintiff was subjected to almost continuous harassment by one or more unidentified co-workers. As a result of the continual workplace harassment, plaintiff claimed that she suffered severe emotional distress and was forced to quit her job with ORW.

Plaintiff's testimony reveals that the bulk of the incidents of harassment directed at her involved tampering with her work area, office equipment, or work product. For example, plaintiff testified that on various occasions when she arrived at work in the morning she found documents which she had left on her desk the night before soiled or crumpled up, all of her office equipment and supplies distributed around the office or on the floor next to her desk, her desk chair adjusted to the lowest possible level, or her desk covered in debris, including one time in which it appeared that someone had emptied the "dots" from all the office hole punches onto her desk. . . .

Plaintiff also described several incidents in which offensive or inappropriate comments were made about her. For example, plaintiff described an incident in which a "Far Side" cartoon, that had been altered such that the names of the characters in the cartoon were changed to the names of several ORW employees, including plaintiff, was placed on her chair. As altered, the cartoon suggested plaintiff was receiving favorable treatment from ORW's deputy warden. On another occasion, while plaintiff was away from her desk, someone wrote "nasty bitch" across the bottom of a document that was on plaintiff's desk.

Plaintiff testified that she reported almost every incident of harassment to Mary Miller, ORW's healthcare administrator . . . [and] to ORW's chief institutional investigator, James Hoffman, and on several occasions made her complaints known to ORW's deputy warden. Despite plaintiff's complaints, ORW did nothing to stop the harassment. In fact, plaintiff testified, after she started to complain about the harassment, the situation actually got worse.

According to plaintiff, the stress caused by the constant harassment at work eventually caused her to suffer from panic attacks, constant headaches, stomach problems, heart palpitations, anxiety, and depression. As a result of these symptoms and the fact that ORW refused to take any action to stop the workplace harassment directed at her, she resigned her position with ORW in November 1999. . . .

In pursuing her claim for intentional infliction of emotional distress against ORW, plaintiff did not seek to establish that ORW's conduct was itself "extreme and outrageous." Rather, plaintiff sought to hold ORW vicariously liable for the extreme and outrageous harassment allegedly perpetrated against her by one or more unidentified ORW employees. Ordinarily, an employer is not liable for the intentional torts of its employees unless it can be shown that the intentional tort was in the furtherance of the employer's business. . . . [T]he Ohio Supreme court held that, where an employer knows or has reason to know that an employee is sexually harassing another employee, but fails to take corrective action against the harassing employee, the employer can be held liable for the sexual harassment, even if the harassment was not in furtherance of the employer's business. In seeking to hold ORW liable on her claim for intentional infliction of emotional distress, plaintiff sought to extend the [Supreme Court's] holding to allegations of non-sexual harassment. The trial court allowed plaintiff to proceed on this theory. . . .

The record contains evidence that both plaintiff's immediate superior, Miller, and ORW's lead investigator, Hoffman, looked into plaintiff's complaints. . . .

ORW took steps to alleviate plaintiff's discomfort by allowing her to lock her office supplies up in the evening and asking other office employees to refrain from using her desk or equipment. In the sole incident in which the perpetrator was identified, the case of the altered "Far Side" cartoon, the perpetrator was required to apologize to plaintiff.

Finally, Miller testified that it was possible that one of the inmate clerks who worked in the medical records office was responsible for some of the incidents . . . , as plaintiff had angered several inmate clerks by treating them poorly. . . .

While ORW did not conduct a full-blown investigation, . . . the actions taken by ORW in response to plaintiff's complaint satisfy the requirements of [our Supreme Court]. . . .

Case Questions

1. As the court analyzes the facts of the case, are negligent infliction of emotional distress and vicarious employer liability treated as the same thing?
2. If plaintiff's immediate supervisor were responsible for the harassing activities, how would the court's analysis of the employer's liability have been different?
3. Was the harassing conduct alleged by the plaintiff so extreme and outrageous as to support a claim of either intentional or negligent infliction of emotional distress?
4. If the harassing conduct had more blatant sexual overtones, would the court's decision on the negligent infliction/vicarious liability issue have been different?
5. If you were the prison warden, would you have required a greater effort on the part of plaintiff's supervisor and the chief investigator to find and punish the people harassing the plaintiff?

TORTIOUS INTERFERENCE WITH CONTRACT

Another tort worth noting, based upon its common occurrence in the context of employment law, is tortious interference with contract.

WILLIAMS V. DOMINION TECHNOLOGY PARTNERS, L.L.C.

265 Va. 280, 576 S.E.2d 752 (Virginia Supreme Court, 2003)

Koontz, J.

This appeal arises from a judgment in favor of an employer against a former at-will employee on a motion for judgment seeking damages for an alleged breach of a fiduciary duty [and] tortious interference with a business relationship. . . .

Dominion Technology Partners, L.L.C. (Dominion) . . . is an employment firm specializing in recruiting qualified computer consultants and placing them . . . on a temporary basis with various companies. Sometime in late 1998 or early 1999, Dominion learned that Stihl, Inc. (Stihl), a power tool manufacturing firm, was seeking a computer consultant to oversee the installation of a new software package on computer systems at Stihl's facilities in Virginia Beach.

Dominion recruited Donald Williams as a possible candidate to fill the position at Stihl. . . . Williams was referred to Stihl for a placement interview. Stihl found that Williams was qualified. . . . On January 22, 1999, Stihl entered into a contract with ACSYS Information Technology, Inc. (ACSYS), an employment brokerage company with its principal offices in the State of Georgia, to employ Williams for an initial period of three months. . . .

On January 28, 1999, ACSYS entered into a contract with Dominion for Williams' services. . . .

Subsequently, Williams performed computer consulting services for Stihl under a work order from

ACSYS to Dominion beginning in January 1999. Shortly after he began work at Stihl, ACSYS required Williams to sign a "project assignment" letter that included provisions, similar to those in the contract between ACSYS and Dominion, that Williams could not directly solicit Stihl or any other ACSYS client for additional work during the term of his assignment or for one year afterwards. . . .

In a letter dated March 4, 2000, Williams formally tendered his resignation as an at-will employee of Dominion to be effective April 14, 2000. Williams stated in the letter that Dominion should advise ACSYS of his decision. . . .

In May 2000, Dominion learned that Williams had continued to work at Stihl as an ACSYS employee after April 14, 2000. Ultimately, Williams remained at Stihl as an ACSYS employee until June 1, 2001. . . .

On July 11, 2000, Dominion filed a motion for judgment against Williams alleging breach of contract, tortious interference with business relationships and prospective business relationships [and] breach of fiduciary duty. . . .

Although the judgment awarded Dominion against Williams in the trial court was founded on three different theories of liability . . . , the essential facts asserted to support each theory are intricately interrelated in this particular case. . . .

Dominion concedes that because he was an at-will employee, Williams could have terminated his employment with Dominion at any time and without any requirement, in terms of a fiduciary duty, to show good cause for doing so. . . . Thus, the essence of Dominion's assertions against Williams for damages under each theory of liability . . . is that Williams, after having learned his services as a computer consultant were likely to be needed at Stihl for an extended period of time, and while still an employee of Dominion, arranged with ACSYS to become its employee effective upon his resignation from Dominion. . . .

Dominion does not contend that the information that Stihl was considering a further upgrade to its software was a "trade secret" or "confidential information" that was exclusive and proprietary to Dominion. To the contrary, . . . Dominion subsequently obtained the same information from an independent source. . . . In this context, Williams simply knew that there was a possibility, perhaps even a probability, that within four to six months Stihl would make a business decision that would require it to continue his services. . . .

Williams tendered his resignation to Dominion in such a manner as to permit Dominion to comply with its contractual obligation to ACSYS. Williams and ACSYS both took care to assure that there was no contractual bar to their contemplated actions. . . . Dominion had not sought a non-compete agreement from Williams or ACSYS, which would have prohibited their subsequent contractual arrangement. In such circumstances, it cannot be said that Williams' conduct to safeguard his own interests was either disloyal or unfair to Dominion. Rather, we are of the opinion that Dominion's contracts provided it with nothing more than "a subjective belief or hope that the business relationships would continue and a mere possibility that future economic benefit would accrue to it."

Case Questions

1. How does Williams's at-will employment status, which typically works to the benefit of the employer against the misbehaving employee, work against Dominion's claims against Williams in this case?
2. In what ways, does the court suggest, could Dominion have strengthened its contractual right to keep Williams from "jumping ship" and helping ACSYS to claim the Stihl's IT work all for itself?
3. Why do you think Dominion didn't also name ACSYS as a defendant in its lawsuit against Williams?
4. Was Stihl guilty of any wrongdoing in this case?
5. If Williams had learned something about Stihl's future IT plans while working there, which Dominion could not learn independently, would the court have reached a different decision?

RETALIATORY DEMOTION

Students also should alert themselves to the emerging cause of action called *retaliatory demotion,* a tort that echoes the wrongful discharge cause of action considered in Chapter 1.

FREEMAN V. UNITED AIRLINES

2002 WL 31656667 (U.S. Court of Appeals, 10th Cir., 2002)

Henry, Circuit J.

In this diversity action, George Freeman appeals the district court's grant of summary judgment against him and in favor of United Airlines on his wrongful discharge claims under Colorado law. Mr. Freeman alleges that United terminated his employment in retaliation for his complaints about unlawful activity and his filing of a workers' compensation claim. In rejecting Mr. Freeman's claims on summary judgment, the district court reasoned that under Colorado law, Mr. Freeman was required to prove that he had been actually or constructively discharged and that no such discharge had occurred: United had merely placed Mr. Freeman on medical leave. The court also concluded that Mr. Freeman's remaining on medical leave resulted from "his own intransigence."...

Under Colorado law, the determination of whether an employer's action constitutes a constructive discharge depends upon whether a reasonable person under the same or similar circumstances would view the working conditions as intolerable. . . . Here, Mr. Freeman has not offered any evidence from which a reasonable factfinder could conclude that he was constructively discharged. The record indicates that Mr. Freeman had the right to come back to work if he completed a course of psychotherapy and an alcohol treatment program and that he retained seniority and other benefits. . . .

Mr. Freeman also invokes federal decisions holding that an employee may pursue a retaliation claim on an adverse employment action less severe than termination. . . .

[Such] cases applying federal statutes are not controlling in this diversity case, which is governed by Colorado law. Because Colorado courts have not extended wrongful discharge actions based on violations of public policy to actions less severe than termination, we may not apply the broader "adverse employment action" standard here. Moreover, as United noted, the issue of whether wrongful discharge actions should be available outside the termination context involves important policy questions that, in a case governed by Colorado law, would be inappropriate for this court to address in the first instance.

Case Questions

1. Why is this case governed by Colorado, rather than federal, law?
2. What are some of the "important policy questions" that underlie a decision to extend the wrongful discharge action to cases involving an adverse employment action short of job termination?
3. If the federal appeals court is uncomfortable deciding these policy issues under Colorado law, who should decide them?
4. Why might a state government reach a different conclusion with regard to these "important policy questions" than was reached by the federal government?
5. How do you feel about extending the tort of wrongful discharge to include a potential cause of action for wrongful demotion?

THEFT OF TRADE SECRETS

In all of the foregoing cases, the plaintiffs were employees and former employees, while the defendants were companies that were accused by these plaintiffs of tortious behavior that allegedly injured these workers. Less frequently, employers sue their own employees. One area of tort law in which such suits are becoming increasingly more common is trade secret protection. In this Information Age, a knowledgeable and unscrupulous employee can walk off the employer's premises with immensely valuable trade secrets encapsulated on a single compact disc.

In many states, theft of trade secrets is prosecuted under the criminal code, either with reference to the jurisdiction's general theft statute or a special "theft of trade secrets" law. Such criminal prosecutions, as well as civil actions, can become entangled in complicated legal struggles among employers, their former employees, and third parties wishing to acquire these information workers. Following is a recent example of how complex such trade secret litigation can become.

EarthWeb, Inc. v. Schlack

2000 WL 1093320 (2nd Cir., 2000)

Summary Order

On September 27, 1999, EarthWeb, Inc. ("EarthWeb") filed a complaint against Mark Schlack ("Schlack"), a former EarthWeb vice president responsible for "content" on the company's websites, alleging causes of action for misappropriation of trade secrets and breach of contract based on a confidentiality clause and restrictive covenant in Schlack's Employment Agreement. On September 28, 1999, EarthWeb filed a motion for a temporary restraining order and a preliminary injunction based on its breach of contract and misappropriation of trade secrets claims to enjoin Schlack from commencing employment with [competitor] IDG or disclosing or revealing EarthWeb's trade secrets to IDG or any third parties. The District Court entered a temporary restraining order granting the requested temporary relief, which subsequently was extended pending a determination of EarthWeb's preliminary injunction motion. Following limited discovery and oral argument, the District Court denied EarthWeb's motion for preliminary injunctive relief and lifted the temporary restraining order.

On appeal, we concluded that "the District Court did not commit any error of law or clear error of fact so as to warrant a finding of abuse of discretion with respect to EarthWeb's breach of contract claim based on the enforceability of the non-compete provision in the Employment Agreement." However, we remanded the case to the District Court for further explanation of its reasons for denying EarthWeb's motion for injunctive relief based on the confidentiality provision and EarthWeb's misappropriation of trade secrets claim while retaining jurisdiction.

On remand, the District Court reaffirmed its denial of EarthWeb's motion for a preliminary injunction and explained that it reached its decision on both issues—the confidentiality provision and the misappropriation of trade secrets—on the ground that EarthWeb had failed to show irreparable harm. . . .

> To the limited extent that EarthWeb has shown that Schlack is aware of information that could be afforded trade secret protection, EarthWeb has not established an imminent and inevitable risk of disclosure warranting preliminary relief. ITWorld.com's ability to generate the bulk of its content in-house sets it apart from EarthWeb in important ways, even though both companies will target the IT market. For example, Schlack would compromise his independence as an editor at ITWorld.com if he involved himself in the advertising aspects of the entity. Moreover, ITWorld.com has indicated that Schlack's position will simply not involve matters involving licensing, subscription pricing, or acquisitions.
>
> Based on these facts, the court finds no imminent risk that Schlack will disclose or use EarthWeb's trade secrets in connection with his employment at ITWorld.com. Consequently, EarthWeb has failed to demonstrate a likelihood of irreparable injury. . . .
>
> To be entitled to a preliminary injunction, a litigant must show "(1) that it will be irreparably harmed in the absence of an injunction, and (2) either (a) a likelihood of success on

the merits or (b) sufficiently serious questions going to the merits of the case to make them a fair ground for litigation, and a balance of hardships tipping decidedly in its favor." EarthWeb has given us no basis upon which to conclude that the District Court committed any error of law or clear error of fact with respect to its irreparable harm finding so as to warrant a finding of abuse of discretion. Indeed, we have reiterated that the irreparable harm requirement is "the single most important prerequisite for the issuance of a preliminary injunction." Thus, unless a movant can show "an injury that is neither remote nor speculative, but actual and imminent and that cannot be remedied by an award of monetary damages," a motion for a preliminary injunction should be denied.

We conclude that EarthWeb has not made a sufficient showing of likely injury to justify the issuance of a preliminary injunction. For example, EarthWeb has failed to demonstrate that Schlack has removed any of EarthWeb's proprietary documents or information or is about to violate the duties imposed by his Employment Agreement. In the absence of any evidence of this nature, the likelihood that EarthWeb will suffer irreparable injury due to Schlack's employment at *ITWorld.com* is merely speculative. . . .

For the reasons set forth above, the judgment of the District Court is hereby AFFIRMED.

Case Questions

1. What is the relationship between the plaintiff's noncompete claim and its trade secrets claim? How do they differ from one another?
2. What is the standard by which the appeals court reviewed the trial court's decision? If the appeals court conducted a *de novo* review of the facts in the trial record, do you think the outcome would have been different?
3. What does the law mean by "irreparable harm"? Why did the plaintiff in this case claim that it needed a court order, and not just money damages, to protect its interests?
4. What additional wrongdoing on the defendant's part might have changed the outcome of the case in the plaintiff's favor?

ALTERNATIVE DISPUTE RESOLUTION

Both employers and employees are increasingly coming to the realization that in long, expensive lawsuits only the lawyers win. One way around such brutal confrontations is alternative dispute resolution (ADR). Among the most common forms of ADR is binding arbitration, under which the parties mutually agree on an arbitrator and abide by that individual's decision, usually following a relatively short and informal hearing.

Stokes v. Metropolitan Life Insurance Company

351 S.C. 606, 571 S.E.2d 711 (S. C. Ct. App. 2002)

Stilwell, J.

After being terminated from his position at Metropolitan Life Insurance Company (Met Life), William B. Stokes filed suit against Met Life and Met Life employee James Drake, asserting breach of contract, trespass, and conversion. The defendants moved to compel arbitration and stay all proceedings. The circuit court granted the motion to compel as to the breach of contract but denied it as to the trespass and conversion actions. . . .

Stokes worked for Met Life as an account representative for approximately thirteen years. During his employment, Stokes applied to be registered with the National Association of Securities Dealers (NASD) as an "Investment Company and Variable Contracts Products Representative" by filing an industry application commonly know as a Form U-4. The fourth page contains a series of statements the applicant must agree to. . . . Stokes signified his agreement thereto by signing immediately under the list. The fifth paragraph of the list reads as follows:

> agree to arbitrate any dispute, claim or controversy that may arise between me and my firm, or a customer, or any other person, that is required to be arbitrated under the rules, constitutions, or by-laws of the organizations indicated in Item 10 as may be amended from time to time and that any arbitration award rendered against me may be entered as a judgment in any court of competent jurisdiction. . . .

In his suit, Stokes asserted his termination by Met Life constituted a breach of his employment contract. Regarding his trespass and conversion claims, Stokes alleged that on the approximate date of his termination, Drake, acting as Met Life's agent, broke into Stokes' rented business office without his permission and converted files and other personal property, depriving Stokes of their use. . . .

In lieu of answering Stokes' complaint, the defendants filed a motion to compel arbitration and stay proceedings. . . .

In the circuit court, Stokes conceded his breach of contract action was subject to arbitration. However, he argued that he was entitled to a jury trial on the trespass and conversion actions. . . .

As the alleged trespass and conversion appear inextricably linked to Stokes' employment and termination, we conclude they fall within the scope of the arbitration clause in Stokes' Form U-4. . . .

Having determined that Stokes' trespass and conversion actions are subject to arbitration, . . . all related state court proceedings are stayed pending resolution of the arbitration.

Case Questions

1. Why did Stokes want to pursue his claims in court instead of in front of an arbitrator? Conversely, why did Met Life want to take the case to arbitration?
2. Can you think of any reasons Stokes might be better off in front of an arbitrator? Conversely, are there any reasons Met Life might have been better off in court?
3. Form U-4 is described as a standard form that all employees in certain financial services industries must complete. Should the fact that there apparently exists little or no opportunity for the employee to engage in "arm's length" negotiation of the form's terms affect the court's decision to enforce or not to enforce the form's arbitration clause?
4. Do you agree with the court that Drake's alleged torts against the plaintiff should be subsumed in the arbitration proceedings? Why or why not?

SUMMARY

- In our post-9/11, post-Enron age, corporations are under extreme internal and external pressure to protect the safety and security of the shareholders' investment and of their employees. Because the World Trade Center and the Pentagon were successfully attacked on September 11, 2001, by terrorists who had entered this country under false pretenses, the employer's obligation to ensure that alien job applicants possess the requisite documentation to obtain U.S. employment has taken on even greater urgency than it was given by new immigration legislation in the 1990s. With the proliferation of desktop and laptop computers, as well as handheld devices of astonishing power and complexity, employers likewise are under tremendous pressure to monitor and control the uses to which their employees are putting these electronic devices. The possibility that a knowledgeable, determined employee can carry the company's most vital trade secrets out of the building on a CD or handheld computer or transmit them to a competitor as an e-mail attachment, ensures that the crime/

tort of trade secret theft will collide with employees' privacy rights with increasing frequency. E-mail and instant messaging place opportunities for defamation, infliction of emotional distress, and sexual harassment at every employee's fingertips. For all of these reasons, we can comfortably predict that the proliferation of workplace tort actions will only increase in this new century.

- Defamation can be verbal (slander) or written (libel). Many states recognize a qualified business privilege—that commercial efficiency demands that employers be able to share information about employees and applicants without undue fear of litigation. The qualified privilege requires the plaintiff/employee, who claims employer defamation, to prove the employer spoke falsely out of malice—that is, knew or should have known what was communicated was false.
- Infliction of emotional distress is a tort which usually requires proof by the plaintiff/employee that the employer's actions, which caused severe emotional distress, were outrageous. The normal stress involved in being fired from one's job, without something more, normally will not support this tort claim.
- In this Information Age, not only are employees suing their employers for a variety of alleged torts, but increasingly, employers are suing their former employees, accusing them of theft of the company's trade secrets. Some states treat misappropriation as garden-variety theft, whereas others have criminal statutes expressly directed to this particular offense. Either way, such theft is also a subset of the tort of conversion of another's property. Because the employer usually alleges irreparable harm, injunctions are a typical part of the court's remedy when the plaintiff/employer prevails.
- So ubiquitous has employment litigation become that many firms are requiring, or at least requesting, employees to agree at time of hire that they will submit any future employment disputes to an alternative dispute resolution mechanism in lieu of taking their troubles into the state and federal courthouses. The most common forms of ADR are binding arbitration, mediation, and negotiation. Many courts, too, in an effort to reduce the heavy caseloads on their dockets, now require many such claims to be submitted to nonbinding arbitration, mandatory mediation efforts, or a minitrial, before proceeding—if unresolved—to a trial by jury.

QUESTIONS

1. What are some modern technological developments that make an increase in invasion of privacy actions likely?
2. If you were a state supreme court judge, would you be willing to make it easier for employees to bring, and prevail in, invasion of privacy actions?
3. Are employers also more likely to fall prey to invasions of privacy perpetrated by their employees?
4. Define defamation. When is language defamatory? Into what two torts is defamation divided?
5. Give some examples of absolute and qualified privilege with regard to invasion of privacy and defamation as they may occur in the workplace.
6. Explain the differences between intentional and negligent infliction of emotional distress. How are they handled differently by the courts and why?
7. How is tortious interference with a contract different from breach of contract? Do the two concepts come together in a case of wrongful discharge?
8. Are there circumstances in which a demotion could constitute a breach of contract, whether or not the demotion is retaliatory?

CASE PROBLEMS

1. A regional vice president directly supervised thirty-four employees and had indirect supervision of more than 400 others. She also managed an annual budget of $20 million and made company policy in her regional facility. When offered a vice presidency at a higher salary with her employer's competitor, the vice president not only jumped ship, but she also induced seventeen key employees, who reported to her, to go along with her. Because she was well aware of all their compensation packages, she was able to help the competitor carefully tailor its counteroffers for maximum efficiency of results in luring them away.

   Do you believe the vice president owed a fiduciary duty or other duty of loyalty to her employer, such that she should be enjoined from stealing away those seventeen key employees? If so, should the injunction extend to the competitor, or is the competitor merely an innocent bystander? Is the salary information available to the departing vice president a trade secret of her current employer? If so, how should the court prevent her from taking unfair advantage of this knowledge when seeking to hire away other employees to the competitor? See *GAB Business Services, Inc. v. Lindsey & Newsom Claim Services, Inc.* [83 Cal. App. 4th 409 (2000)].

2. A popular disc jockey signed a three-year contract with a radio station under which she agreed that if she quit her job at the station, she would not go on the air with any competing station for at least six months. A year into the relationship, she left for a higher paying position with a competing station. However, for the first six months, she did not broadcast any shows for her new employer. Instead, she engaged in promotional activities and winning over advertisers from her former station, which sued her and her new affiliation.

   Do you think the disc jockey should be forbidden by court order from working in promotional and sales activities for the new station? Should the court find that her knowledge of her former employer's relationships with its advertisers are trade secrets? See *Saga Communications of New England v. Voornas* [No. 2000 ME 156 (Maine Supr. 2000)].

3. Assume that in problem 2, the disc jockey's contract with her former employer contained a provision that all disputes will be subject to arbitration. Should this provision prevent the radio station from going to court and seeking an injunction to enforce its noncompetition and trade secret rights?

   Should the court in deciding this question distinguish between the noncompetition promise, which is an express part of the disc jockey's employment contract, and the trade secret issue, which is really a tort claim under the common law? If the court decides to order an arbitration, should it dismiss the case or merely stay proceedings pending the arbitration? Do you think an arbitrator has the right to issue an "injunction" enforcing the noncompete agreement and protecting the radio station's trade secrets? Or should the arbitrator be limited to awarding money damages?

4. A firefighter was accused of fraudulently claiming an injury while fighting a fire, the alleged motive being to enhance his retirement benefits. He was suspended without pay pending the outcome of the criminal investigation. He filed a grievance through his union, and when the issue of his suspension was not resolved to his satisfaction during the steps of the grievance procedure under the collective-bargaining agreement, the union demanded binding arbitration. The city went to court, asking that the

arbitration be stayed pending the outcome of the criminal investigation. The city solicitor argued that the arbitration process would unduly interfere with the criminal investigation.

Should the court stay the arbitration? If the employee is eventually found innocent of criminal fraud, should this be dispositive of his grievance? Or should he still be forced to arbitrate his claim? See *City of New York v. Uniformed Fire Officers Association* [2000 WL 1529821 (N.Y. Ct. App.)].

5. Two former employees filed a lawsuit, alleging wrongful discharge and other workplace tort claims, against their former supervisor and the company that had employed them. The defendants sought dismissal of the suit, pointing to a standard agreement to the effect that all employees agreed to arbitrate all such disputes. The employees testified that they had never seen the arbitration policy and had never signed any agreement to abide by it. A copy of the agreement signed by a third former employee proved to have been executed by her eighteen months after she was hired.

Should the court compel the two plaintiffs to submit their claims to arbitration on these facts? See *Ryan's Family Steakhouse, Inc. v. Brooks-Shades* [2000 WL 1451563 (Alabama Supr.)].

6. The Municipality of Anchorage adopted a policy that subjects police and firefighters in safety-sensitive positions to suspicionless drug testing. The police and firefighter unions challenged the policy on the basis of privacy and search-and-seizure provisions of the Alaska constitution. The Alaskan search-and-seizure provisions are broader than the protections available under the Fourth and Fourteenth Amendments of the U.S. Constitution, which contains no express privacy guarantees at all.

Should the police and firefighters be accorded the broader protections of the Alaska constitution as opposed to those they enjoy as public employees under the U.S. Constitution, or should the U.S. Constitution preempt the broader Alaskan safeguards? Do the police and firefighters have any reasonable expectation of privacy with regard to drug testing if indeed they serve in "safety-sensitive" positions, especially in light of post-9/11 homeland security considerations? See *Anchorage Police Department Employees Association v. Municipality of Anchorage* [24 P.3d 547 (Alaska Supreme Ct. 2001)].

7. A physician at the University of California was removed from the chairmanship of the university hospital's radiology department in the wake of accusations of financial improprieties. A quarter million dollars, obtained chiefly in the form of rebates from medical equipment vendors allegedly had been inappropriately placed in the department's operating accounts. No allegations were ever made that the plaintiff had made any personal use of the funds, only that he had inappropriately deposited them in the department's accounts rather than in the medical center's general fund. The university, after learning of this, took action to reallocate the funds and also dismissed the plaintiff as chair. But he retained his tenured teaching position and his status as a staff physician.

If the plaintiff believes that he was guilty of no wrongdoing on these facts, does he have a cause of action for defamation against the university? Does he have a cause of action for retaliatory demotion? If the loss of the chairmanship occurred without a hearing, does he have a constitutional tort claim under the due process clause of the Fourteenth Amendment of the U.S. Constitution? If the plaintiff is in the right, what remedy or remedies should the court award him? Money damages? Reinstatement? Both? See *Katzberg v. Regents of University of California* [29 Cal.4th 300, 58 P.3d 339 (Cal. Supreme Ct. 2002)].

8. A supervisor was accused of sexual harassment by one of his subordinates. After an investigation, the company fired him. Contending that he was innocent, the supervisor sued his former employer, contending among other things that, since his efforts to find a new job required him to "self-publicize" the company's stated reason for his termination and that reason (sexual harassment) was false, his former employer was guilty of the tort of defamation.

Can the tort of defamation lie against an employer when it is the plaintiff/employee who is communicating the defamatory information to third parties? Assuming that as a technical matter the elements of the tort of defamation are all present in such a case, are there any public policy reasons you can think of that argue against a state supreme court recognizing a cause of action for defamation based upon admitted "self-publication" by the plaintiff/employee? See *Gonsalves v. Nissan Motor Corp.* [2002 WL 31670451 (Hawaii Supreme Ct. 2002)].

9. Randy Curtis worked for St. Onge Livestock Company as a field man, soliciting customers to sell livestock through St. Onge. In time, he worked his way up to manager of the company. Twice he discussed incentive pay plans with the company's owner. The idea behind the incentive pay plans was to enable Curtis to eventually buy the business. An agreement was worked out, including a noncompete provision, under which Curtis received some $20,000 in incentive pay over the next four years. Then, along came the owner of a rival sale-barn, who approached Curtis about managing the competing operation. Curtis advised the rival of his noncompete agreement, and the rival's attorney opined that the noncompete was valid and enforceable. All the same, Curtis and the rival decided that Curtis would "jump ship" and manage the rival firm. Once Curtis switched employers, twenty-three customers did likewise. St. Onge not only sued Curtis for breach of contract but also sued the rival for tortious interference with Curtis's St. Onge contract.

Is the rival company guilty of tortious interference with contract? If so, is there any excuse for its tortious conduct? If not, what remedy or remedies should the court accord St. Onge against the rival firm?

See *St. Onge Livestock Co., Ltd. v. Curtis* [2002 WL 1870449 (S.D. Supreme Ct. 2002)].

10. The employer was in the business of transporting developmentally disabled adults and children from their homes and care providers to various day-care centers and schools. Over a three-year period, no fewer than three male drivers filed reports of misbehavior by a male adult customer named Ernest Rocha. In one report, Rocha was alleged to have refused to remain seated and to have brandished a knife. Additionally, three female drivers had filed reports during the same general time frame, all of which alleged that Rocha had exposed himself while on the buses. The plaintiff/ driver was hired in the wake of these half-dozen reports and was required to deal with Rocha, who allegedly touched her, grabbed her purse, demanded money, refused to remain in his seat, and exposed himself to her. These repeated incidents, reported by plaintiff to her dispatcher, culminated in an incident in which Rocha allegedly touched the plaintiff "all over" and shoved his hands under her shirt. She in turn scratched his face and kicked and pushed him.

Based on these facts, should the employer be vicariously liable for Rocha's sexual harassment and tortious battering of the plaintiff? If the employer should be held vicariously liable, should that liability include intentional infliction of emotional distress upon the plaintiff?

See *Salazar v. Diversified Paratransit, Inc.* [126 Cal. Rptr.2d 475, (Cal. App. Ct. 2002)].

INTERNET EXERCISES

1. Go to **http://www.lawyertool.com**. Locate the State Legal Databases. Choose your home state.
2. Locate the link to your state's constitution and ascertain whether the constitution contains (a) an express right of privacy and (b) protection against unreasonable searches and seizures.
3. Next search the related court opinions and rules link for any cases interpreting the constitutional provision(s) you identified.
4. Finally, return to you Internet provider and, using Google or another search engine, search for sites relating to "(your home state) and invasion of privacy."

INFOTRAC KEYWORDS

http://www.infotrac-college.com

workplace torts, invasion of privacy in the workplace, retaliatory demotion, theft of trade secrets, alternative dispute resolution in the workplace

PART 2

EQUAL EMPLOYMENT OPPORTUNITY

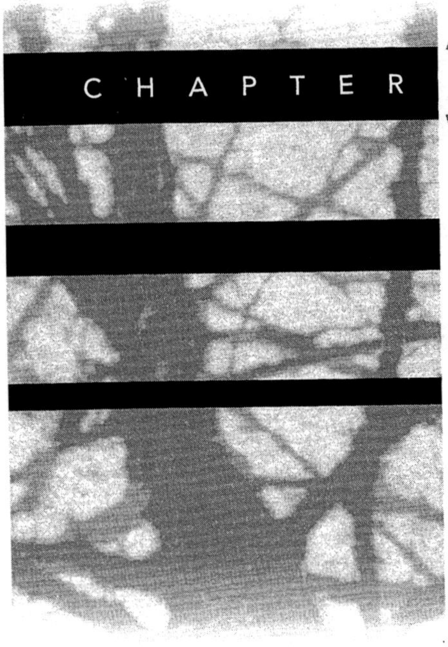

CHAPTER 3

TITLE VII OF THE CIVIL RIGHTS ACT AND RACE DISCRIMINATION

Ideally, employers should hire those employees best qualified for the particular job being filled; an employee should be selected because of his or her ability to perform the job. Determining the qualifications required for the job, however, may be difficult. In fact, required qualifications that have no relationship to job performance may disqualify prospective employees who are capable of performing satisfactorily. In addition, some employers may be influenced in their selection of employees by their biases—conscious or unconscious—regarding certain groups of people. All of these factors are part of the problem of discrimination in employment.

Discrimination in employment, whether intentional or unintentional, has been a major concern of many people who believe that our society has not lived up to its ideals of equality of opportunity for all people. The glaring inequities in our society sparked violent protests during the civil rights movement of the 1960s. African Americans, Hispanic Americans, and Native Americans constituted a disproportionate share of those living in poverty. Women of all races and colors found their access to challenging and well-paying jobs limited; they were frequently channeled into lower paying occupations traditionally viewed as "women's work."

TITLE VII OF THE CIVIL RIGHTS ACT OF 1964

To help remedy these problems of discrimination, Congress passed the Civil Rights Act of 1964, which was signed into law by President Johnson on July 2, 1964. The Civil Rights Act was aimed at discrimination in a number of areas of our society:

housing, public accommodation, education, and employment. Title VII of the Civil Rights Act deals with discrimination in employment. It became the foundation of modern federal equal employment opportunity (EEO) law.

Title VII was amended in 1968, 1972, and 1991. The most recent amendments, made by the Civil Rights Act of 1991, were substantial and were intended to reverse several Supreme Court decisions that were perceived as making it more difficult for plaintiffs to bring suit under Title VII.

This part of the book focuses on the statutory provisions requiring equal opportunity in employment. This chapter deals with the provisions of Title VII, as amended, prohibiting employment discrimination based on race. Chapter 4 will discuss the Title VII provisions regarding employment discrimination based on gender, as well as other gender-related EEO legislation. Chapter 5 will discuss discrimination based on religion and national origin, the enforcement of Title VII, and the remedies available under it. Chapter 6 will discuss the Age Discrimination in Employment Act and EEO laws dealing with discrimination based on disability. Finally, Chapter 7 will focus on other federal and state EEO legislation.

COVERAGE OF TITLE VII

Title VII of the Civil Rights Act of 1964 took effect on July 2, 1965. It prohibits the refusal or failure to hire any individual, the discharge of any individual, or the discrimination against any individual with respect to compensation, terms, conditions, or privileges of employment because of that individual's race, color, religion, sex, or national origin.

Title VII, as amended, applies to employers, labor unions, and employment agencies. An employer under Title VII is defined as a person, partnership, corporation, or other entity engaged in an industry affecting commerce that has fifteen or more employees. In *Walters v. Metropolitan Educational Enterprises, Inc.* [519 U.S. 202 (1997)], the Supreme Court held that the "payroll method" is used to determine the number of employees for coverage of Title VII. The criterion requires that the employer have at least fifteen employees on its payroll, whether they actually worked or not, for each working day of twenty or more calendar weeks in the current or preceding calendar year. According to the Supreme Court decision in *Clackamas Gastroenterology Associates, P.C. v. Wells* [123 S.Ct. 1673 (2003)], common-law principles should be applied in determining whether managing directors or physician-shareholders of professional corporations are employees for the purpose of determining coverage under Title VII. Such common-law principles include: (1) whether the organization can hire or fire the individual or set the rules and regulations of the individual's work; (2) whether, and to what extent, the organization supervises the individual's work; (3) whether the individual reports to someone higher in the organization; (4) whether, and to what extent, the individual is able to influence the organization; (5) whether the parties intended that the individual be an employee, as expressed in written agreements or contracts; and (6) whether the individual shares in the profits, losses, and liabilities of the organization.

State and local governments are also covered by Title VII; the federal government and wholly owned U.S. government corporations are covered under separate provisions of Title VII. Subsequent legislation extended the coverage of Title VII to other federal employees: (1) The Congressional Accountability Act of 1995 [2 U.S.C. § 1301] extended the coverage of Title VII of the Civil Rights Act of 1964, as amended, to the employees of the House of Representatives, the Senate, the Capitol Guide Service, the Capitol Police, the Congressional Budget Office, the Office of the Architect of the Capitol, the Office of the Attending Physician, and the Office of Technology Assessment; and (2) The Presidential and Executive Office Accountability Act [3 U.S.C. §§ 402, 411] extended the coverage of Title VII to the Executive Office of the President, the Executive Residence at the White House, and the official residence of the Vice President. Title VII does not apply to tax-exempt bona fide private membership clubs.

The 1991 amendments to Title VII extended the coverage of the act to American employers that employ U.S. citizens abroad; foreign corporations that are controlled by American employers are also covered with regard to the employment of U.S. citizens. For such employers, compliance with Title VII is not required if this compliance would force the employer to violate the law of the country where the workplace is located. The effect of this amendment was to overturn the Supreme Court decision in *EEOC v. Arabian American Oil Co.* [499 U.S. 244 (1991)].

Labor unions with at least fifteen members or that operate a hiring hall are subject to Title VII. Unions are prohibited from discriminating in employment opportunities or status against their members or applicants on the basis of race, color, religion, gender, or national origin. Employment agencies violate Title VII by discriminating on prohibited bases in announcing openings, interviewing applicants, or referring applicants to employers.

ADMINISTRATION OF TITLE VII

Title VII is administered by the Equal Employment Opportunity Commission (EEOC), a five-member commission appointed by the president that works with the commission's Office of General Counsel. The EEOC is empowered to issue binding regulations and nonbinding guidelines in its responsibility for administering and enforcing the act. Although the EEOC generally responds to complaints of discrimination filed by individuals, it can also initiate an action on its own if it finds a "pattern or practice" of discrimination in employment.

The EEOC home page address is **http://www.eeoc.gov**

The regulations and guidelines under Title VII require that employers, unions, and employment agencies post EEOC notices summarizing the act's requirements. Failure to display such notices is punishable by a fine of not more than $100 per violation. The act further requires that those covered keep records relevant to the determination of whether unlawful employment practices have been, or are being, committed. Covered employers must maintain payroll records and other records relating to applicants and to employee promotion, demotion, transfer, and discharge.

CLASS-ACTION SUIT ALLEGES RACIAL DISCRIMINATION AT REUTERS NEWS GROUP AFFILIATE

THE WORKING LAW

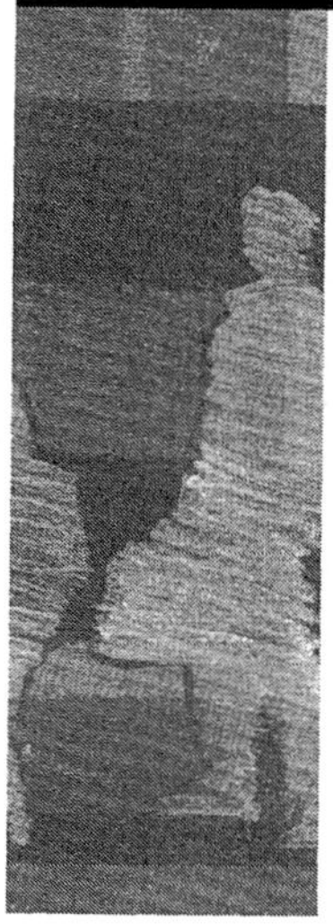

A group of African American workers at Radianz, a Manhattan-based company co-owned by Reuters, the international news service group, and Equant, a data-networking firm, recently filed a class action suit charging the employer with race discrimination in violation of Title VII. The employees had filed complaints with the Equal Employment Opportunity Commission alleging that the company had condoned "a racist, hostile" work environment and had discriminated in pay against African American employees. The alleged harassment included offensive e-mails with racist and demeaning images sent to one of the workers by his supervisor. One employee was allegedly terminated for complaining about the pay discrimination. The employees are being assisted in their class-action suit by celebrity attorney Johnnie Cochrane.

Sources: "Trio Alleges Workplace Discrimination," *Newsday* (New York), August 1, 2003, p. A51; "Reuters Accused of Widespread Racism in US Class-Action Lawsuit," *The Independent,* August 1, 2003, p.19; "Employees of New York City-Based Reuters Affiliate Complain of Racial Bias," *Knight Ridder/Tribune Business News,* August 1, 2003; "ThompsonWigdor & Gilly LLP Announces Reuters, Equant and Radianz Accused of Systemic Racism Against African-American Employees," *PR Newswire,* July 31, 2003.

DISCRIMINATION UNDER TITLE VII

It should be clear from the provisions of Section 703 that Title VII prohibits intentional discrimination in employment on the basis of race, color, religion, sex, or national origin. An employer who refuses to hire African Americans, or who will only hire women for particular positions rather than all production jobs, is in violation of Title VII. Likewise, a union that will not accept Hispanic Americans as members, or that maintains separate seniority lists for male and female members, violates the act. Such intentional discrimination is called **disparate treatment;** that is, the particular employee is subject to different treatment because of that employee's race, gender, or national origin.

Disparate Treatment
When an employee is treated differently from others due to race, color, religion, gender, or national origin.

In the years immediately following the passage of Title VII, some people believed that the act was intended to protect only minority or female employees. This issue came before the Supreme Court in the 1976 case of *McDonald v. Santa Fe Trail Transportation Co.* [427 U.S. 273]. Three employees of a trucking company were caught stealing cargo from the company. Two of the employees, who were white, were discharged; the third, an African American, was given a suspension but was not discharged. The employer justified the difference in disciplinary penalties on the ground that Title VII protected the African American employee. The white employees filed suit under Title VII. The Supreme Court emphasized that Title VII protects all employees; every individual employee is protected from any discrimination in employment because of race, color, sex, religion, and national origin. The employer had treated the white employees differently because of their race, and the employer was therefore in violation of Title VII.

BONA FIDE OCCUPATIONAL QUALIFICATIONS (BFOQS)

Bona Fide Occupational Qualification
An exception to the Civil Rights Law that allows an employer to hire employees of a specific gender, religion, or national origin when business necessity—the safe and efficient performance of the particular job—requires it.

Although Title VII prohibits intentional discrimination in employment, it does contain a limited exception that allows employers to select employees on the basis of gender, religion, or national origin when the employer can establish that being of a particular gender, religion, or national origin is a **bona fide occupational qualification** (BFOQ). To establish that a particular characteristic is a BFOQ, the employer must demonstrate that business necessity—the safe and efficient operation of the business—requires that employees be of a particular gender, religion, or national origin. Employer convenience, customer preference, or co-worker preference will not support the establishment of a BFOQ. Title VII recognizes BFOQs only on the basis of gender, religion, and national origin; the Act provides that race and color can never be used as BFOQs. (BFOQs will be discussed in more detail in the next chapter.)

UNINTENTIONAL DISCRIMINATION: DISPARATE IMPACT

Disparate Impact
The discriminatory effect of apparently neutral employment criteria.

It should be clear that intentional discrimination in employment on the basis of race, religion, gender, color, or national origin (the "prohibited grounds"), apart from a BFOQ, is prohibited, but what about unintentional discrimination? An employer may specify certain requirements for a job that operate to disqualify otherwise capable prospective employees. Although the employer is allowed to hire those employees best able to do the job, what happens if the specified requirements do not actually relate to the employee's ability to perform the job but do have the effect of disqualifying a large proportion of minority applicants? This discriminatory effect of apparently neutral requirements is known as a **disparate impact.** Should the disparate impact of such neutral job requirements be prohibited under Title VII?

Frequently, the neutral requirement at issue may be a test used by the employer to screen applicants for a job. Title VII does allow the use of employment testing. Section 703(h) provides, in part,

http://www.access.gpo.gov/nara/cfr/waisidx_00/29cfr1607_00.html
Select 1607.11 at this site for the text on disparate treatment from the Uniform Guidelines on Employee Selection Procedures (1978).

> . . . [i]t shall not be an unlawful employment practice for an employer to give and act upon the results of any professionally developed ability test provided that such test, its administration or action upon the results is not designed, intended or is used to discriminate because of race, color, religion, sex, or national origin.

The effect of that provision and the legality of using job requirements that have a disparate impact were considered by the Supreme Court in the following case.

GRIGGS V. DUKE POWER COMPANY

401 U.S. 424 (U.S. Supreme Court 1971)

Background

Duke Power Company is an electrical utility company operating in North Carolina. Prior to July 2, 1965, the effective date of Title VII of the Civil Rights Act of 1964, the Company discriminated on the basis of race in the hiring and assigning of employees at its Dan River plant. The plant was organized into five operating departments: (1) Labor, (2) Coal Handling, (3) Operations, (4) Maintenance, and (5) Laboratory and Test. African Americans were only employed in the Labor Department where the highest paying jobs paid less than the lowest paying jobs in the other four operating departments in which only whites were employed. Promotions were normally made within each department on the basis of job seniority. Transferees into a department usually began in the lowest position. In 1955 the Company instituted a policy of requiring a high school education for initial assignment to any department except Labor, and for transfer from the Coal Handling to any "inside" department (Operations, Maintenance, or Laboratory). When the Company abandoned its policy of restricting African Americans to the Labor Department in 1965, it instituted a requirement of having a high school diploma in order to transfer from the Labor Department to any other department. However, the white employees hired before the adoption of the high school diploma requirement continued to perform satisfactorily and achieve promotions in the various operating departments. The U.S. Census Bureau data from the 1960 census indicated that approximately 34 percent of white males in North Carolina had a high school diploma, compared to about 12 percent of African-American males in North Carolina who had completed high school. The Company added a further requirement for new employees on July 2, 1965, the date on which Title VII became effective. To qualify for placement in any but the Labor Department it became necessary to register satisfactory scores on two professionally prepared aptitude tests, as well as to have a high school education. However, employees with a high school diploma who had been hired prior to the adoption of the aptitude test requirements were still eligible for transfer to the four desirable departments from which African Americans had been excluded. In September 1965 the Company began to permit incumbent employees who lacked a high school education to qualify for transfer from Labor or Coal Handling to an "inside" job by passing two tests—the Wonderlic Personnel Test, which purports to measure general intelligence, and the Bennett Mechanical Comprehension Test. Neither was directed or intended to measure the ability to learn to perform a particular job or category of jobs. The requisite scores used for both initial hiring and transfer approximated the national median for high school graduates. For the employees who took the tests, the pass rate for white employees was 58 percent, while the pass rate for African American employees was 6 percent.

Griggs and a group of other African American employees brought suit against Duke Power, alleging that the high school diploma requirement and the aptitude test requirements violated Title VII because they made it more difficult for African American employees to be promoted from the Labor Department, and had the effect of continuing the previous job segregation. The District Court had found that while the Company previously followed a policy of overt racial discrimination prior to the passage of Title VII, such conduct had ceased. The District Court also concluded that Title VII was intended to be prospective only and not retroactive, and therefore, the impact of prior discrimination was beyond the reach of the Act. On appeal, the U.S. Court of Appeals for the Fourth Circuit concluded that the intent of the employer should govern, and that in this case there was no showing of intentional discrimination in the company's adoption of the diploma and test requirements. The Court of Appeals concluded there was no violation of the Act. Griggs then appealed to the U.S. Supreme Court.

Burger, Chief Justice

We granted the [appeal] in this case to resolve the question whether an employer is prohibited by . . . Title VII from requiring a high school education or passing of a standardized general intelligence test as a condition of employment in or transfer to jobs when (a) neither standard is shown to be significantly related to successful job performance, (b) both requirements operate to disqualify Negroes at a substantially higher rate than white applicants, and (c) the jobs in question formerly had been filled only by white employees as part of a longstanding practice of giving preference to whites. . . .

The objective of Congress in the enactment of Title VII . . . was to achieve equality of employment opportunities and remove barriers that have operated in the past to favor an identifiable group of white employees over other employees. Under the Act, practices, procedures, or tests neutral on their face, and even neutral in terms of intent, cannot be maintained if they operate to "freeze" the status quo of prior discriminatory employment practices.

The Court of Appeals' opinion . . . agreed that, on the record in the present case, "whites register far better on the Company's alternative requirements" than Negroes. This consequence would appear to be directly traceable to race. Basic intelligence must have the means of articulation to manifest itself fairly in a testing process. Because they are Negroes, petitioners have long received inferior education in segregated schools and this Court expressly recognized these differences . . . Congress did not intend by Title VII, however, to guarantee a job to every person regardless of qualifications. In short, the Act does not command that any person be hired simply because he was formerly the subject of discrimination, or because he is a member of a minority group. . . . What is required by Congress is the removal of artificial, arbitrary, and unnecessary barriers to employment when the barriers operate invidiously to discriminate on the basis of racial or other impermissible classification.

Congress has now provided that tests or criteria for employment or promotion may not provide equality of opportunity merely in the sense of the fabled offer of milk to the stork and the fox. On the contrary, Congress has now required that the posture and condition of the job-seeker be taken into account. It has—to resort again to the fable—provided that the vessel in which the milk is proffered be one all seekers can use. The Act proscribes not only overt discrimination but also practices that are fair in form, but discriminatory in operation. The touchstone is business necessity. If an employment practice which operates to exclude Negroes cannot be shown to be related to job performance, the practice is prohibited.

On the record before us, neither the high school completion requirement nor the general intelligence test is shown to bear a demonstrable relationship to successful performance of the jobs for which it was used. Both were adopted, as the Court of Appeals noted, without meaningful study of their relationship to job-performance ability. Rather, a vice president of the Company testified, the requirements were instituted on the Company's judgment that they generally would improve the overall quality of the work force.

The evidence, however, shows that employees who have not completed high school or taken the tests have continued to perform satisfactorily and make progress in departments for which the high school and test criteria are now used. The promotion record of present employees who would not be able to meet the new criteria thus suggests the possibility that the requirements may not be needed even for the limited purpose of preserving the avowed policy of advancement within the Company. . . .

The Court of Appeals held that the Company had adopted the diploma and test requirements without any "intention to discriminate against Negro employees." We do not suggest that either the District Court or the Court of Appeals erred in examining the employer's intent; but good intent or absence of discriminatory intent does not redeem employment procedures or testing mechanisms that operate as "built-in headwinds" for minority groups and are unrelated to measuring job capability.

. . . Congress directed the thrust of the Act to the consequences of employment practices, not simply the motivation. More than that, Congress has placed on the employer the burden of showing that any given requirement must have a manifest relationship to the employment in question. . . .

The Company contends that its general intelligence tests are specifically permitted by s 703(h) of the Act. That section authorizes the use of "any professionally developed ability test" that is not "designed, intended or used to discriminate because of race. . . ."

The Equal Employment Opportunity Commission, having enforcement responsibility, has issued guidelines interpreting s 703(h) to permit only the use of job-related tests. The administrative interpretation of the Act by the enforcing agency is entitled to great deference. . . . Since the Act and its legislative history support the Commission's construction, this affords good reason to treat the guidelines as expressing the will of Congress.

. . . Nothing in the Act precludes the use of testing or measuring procedures; obviously they are useful. What Congress has forbidden is giving these devices and mechanisms controlling force unless they are demonstrably a reasonable measure of job performance.... Far from disparaging job qualifications as such, Congress has made such qualifications the controlling factor, so that race, religion, nationality, and sex become irrelevant. What Congress has commanded is that any tests used must measure the person for the job and not the person in the abstract.

The judgment of the Court of Appeals ... is reversed.

Case Questions

1. What is the significance of the fact that Duke Power had intentionally discriminated against African Americans in hiring prior to the passage of Title VII?
2. Why did the high school diploma requirement and the aptitude tests requirement operate to disqualify African Americans from eligibility for transfer at a greater rate than whites? Explain your answer.
3. Why does the court say that the high school diploma requirement and the aptitude test requirements were "unrelated to measuring job capability"?
4. Does Title VII allow an employer to use applicants' scores on professionally developed aptitude tests as criteria for hiring? Explain your answer.
5. What is the fable of the stork and the fox that Chief Justice Burger refers to? How does it relate to this case?

The *Griggs* case dealt with objective employment selection requirements—a high school diploma and passing two aptitude tests—but in *Watson v. Fort Worth Bank & Trust* [487 U.S. 977 (1988)], the Supreme Court held that a claim of disparate impact discrimination may be brought against an employer using a subjective employment practice, such as an interview rating. The plaintiff alleging a disparate impact claim must identify the specific employment practice being challenged, and the plaintiff must offer statistical evidence sufficient to show that the challenged practice has a disparate impact on applicants for hiring or promotion because of their membership in a protected group.

SECTION 703(K) AND DISPARATE IMPACT CLAIMS

The 1991 amendments to Title VII added Section 703(k), which deals with disparate impact claims. Section 703(k) requires that the plaintiff demonstrate that the employer uses a particular employment practice that causes a disparate impact on one of the bases prohibited by Title VII. If such a showing is made, the employer must then demonstrate that the practice is job related for the position in question and is consistent with business necessity. Even if the employer makes such a showing, if the plaintiff can demonstrate that an alternative employment practice—one without a disparate impact—is available, and the employer refuses to adopt it, the employer is still in violation of the act. Section 703(k) states that a plaintiff shall demonstrate that each particular employment practice that is challenged causes a disparate impact unless the plaintiff can demonstrate that the elements of the decision-making process are not capable of separation for analysis. If the employer demonstrates that the challenged practice does not have a disparate impact, then there is no need to show that the practice is required by business necessity. Work rules that bar the employment of individuals using or possessing illegal drugs are exempt from disparate impact analysis; such rules violate Title VII only when they are adopted or applied with an intention to discriminate on grounds prohibited by Title VII.

If the employment practice at issue is shown to be sufficiently job related, and the plaintiff has not shown that alternative practices without a disparate impact are available, then the employer may continue to use the challenged employment practice because it is necessary to perform the job. Nothing in Title VII prohibits an employer from hiring only those persons who are capable of doing the job. The 1991 amendments to Title VII added a provision [Section 703(k)(2)] stating that a demonstration that an employment practice is required by business necessity may not be used as a defense to a claim of intentional discrimination under Title VII. Most of the cases dealing with disparate impact discrimination involve either race, gender, or national origin discrimination, although the language of Section 703(k) is not limited to only those bases of discrimination.

The Uniform Guidelines on Employee Selection

Uniform Guidelines on Employee Selection Procedures
A series of regulations adopted by the EEOC and other federal agencies for claims of disparate impact and unfair treatment on the job.

How can a plaintiff demonstrate a claim of disparate impact? How can an employer demonstrate that a requirement is job-related? The **Uniform Guidelines on Employee Selection Procedures** [29 C.F.R. Part 1607 (1978)], a series of regulations adopted by the EEOC and other federal agencies, provide some answers to those questions.

Showing a Disparate Impact

The Supreme Court held in *Watson v. Fort Worth Bank & Trust* that a plaintiff must "offer statistical evidence of a kind and degree sufficient to show that the practice in question has caused the exclusion of applicants for jobs or promotions because of their membership in a protected group." In *Wards Cove Packing Co. v. Atonio* [490 U.S. 642 (1989)], the Supreme Court described one way to demonstrate that hiring practices had a disparate impact on nonwhites by comparing the employer's work force with the labor market from which applicants are drawn:

> The "proper comparison [is] between the racial composition of [the at-issue jobs] and the racial composition of the qualified . . . population in the relevant labor market." It is such a comparison—between the racial composition of the qualified persons in the labor market and the persons holding at-issue jobs—that generally forms the proper basis for the initial inquiry in a disparate impact case. Alternatively, in cases where such labor market statistics will be difficult if not impossible to ascertain, we have recognized that certain other statistics—such as measures indicating the racial composition of "otherwise-qualified applicants" for at-issue jobs—are equally probative for this purpose.

Four-Fifths Rule
A mathematical formula developed by the EEOC to demonstrate *disparate impact* of a facially neutral employment practice on selection criterion.

The Uniform Guidelines, adopted before the *Watson* and *Wards Cove* decisions, set out another way to demonstrate the disparate impact of a job requirement. This procedure, known as the **Four-Fifths Rule,** compares the selection rates (the rates at which applicants meet the requirements or pass the test) for the various protected groups under Title VII. The Four-Fifths Rule states that a disparate impact will be demonstrated when the proportion of applicants from the protected group with the lowest selection rate (or pass rate) is less than 80 percent of the selection rate (pass rate) of the group with the highest selection rate.

For example, a municipal fire department requires that applicants for firefighter positions be at least five feet, six inches tall and weigh at least 130 pounds. Of the applicants for the positions, five of twenty (25 percent) of the Hispanic applicants meet the requirements, while thirty of forty (75 percent) of the white applicants meet the requirements. To determine whether the height and weight requirements have a disparate impact on Hispanics, the pass rate for Hispanics is divided by the pass rate for whites. Since .25 / .75 = .33, or 33 percent, a disparate impact according to the Four-Fifths Rule exists. Stating the rule in equation form, disparate impact exists when:

$$\frac{\text{Pass rate for group with lowest pass rate}}{\text{Pass rate for group with highest pass rate}} < .80$$

Using the numbers from our example:

$$\frac{.25\ \text{(Hispanic pass rate)}}{.75\ \text{(White pass rate)}} = .33;\ .33 < .80$$

Therefore, a disparate impact exists, establishing a prima facie case of employment discrimination. To continue using such a test, the employer must satisfy the court that the test is sufficiently job related.

VALIDATING JOB REQUIREMENTS

The fire department must demonstrate that the height and weight requirements are job related in order to continue using them in selecting employees. The Uniform Guidelines provide several methods to show that the height and weight requirements are job related. The Uniform Guidelines also require a showing of a statistical correlation demonstrating that the requirements are necessary for successful job performance. In our example, the fire department would have to show that the minimum height and weight requirements screen out those applicants who would be unable to perform safely and efficiently the tasks or duties of a firefighter.

When the job requirements involve passing an examination, it must be shown that a passing score on the exam has a high statistical correlation with successful job performance. The Uniform Guidelines set out standards for demonstrating such a correlation (known as test validity) developed by the American Psychological Association. The standards may be classified into three types: content validity, construct validity, and criterion-related validity.

Content Validity
A method of demonstrating that an employment selection device reflects the content of the job for which employees are being selected.

Content Validity

Content validity is a means of measuring whether the requirement or test actually evaluates abilities required on the job. The fire department using the height and weight requirements would have to show that the requirements determine abilities needed to do the job—that anyone shorter than five feet, six inches or weighing less than 130 pounds would be unable to do the job. That would be difficult to do, but to validate the requirements as job related, such a showing is required by the Uniform Guidelines. If the job of firefighter requires physical strength, then using a strength test as a selection device would be valid. (Height and weight requirements are sometimes used instead of a physical strength test, but they are much more difficult to validate than strength tests.) For the job of a typist, a spelling and typing test would likely have a high content validity because these tests measure abilities actually needed on the job. A strength test for typists, on the other hand, would have a low content validity rating because physical strength has little relationship to typing performance. The Uniform Guidelines set out statistical methods to demonstrate the relationship (if any) of the requirements to job performance. An employer seeking to validate such requirements must follow the procedures and conditions in the Uniform Guidelines.

Construct Validity

Construct Validity
A method of demonstrating that an employment selection device selects employees based on the traits and characteristics that are required for the job in question.

Construct validity is a means of isolating and testing for specific traits or characteristics that are deemed essential for job performance. Such traits, or constructs, may be based on observations but cannot be measured directly. For example, a teacher may be required to possess the construct "patience," or an executive may be required to possess "judgment." Such traits, or constructs, cannot be measured directly, but they may be observed based on simulations of actual job situations. The Uniform Guidelines set out procedures and methods for demonstrating that certain constructs are really necessary to the job and that means used to test for or identify these constructs actually do measure them.

Criterion-Related Validity

Criterion-Related Validity
A method of demonstrating that an employment selection device correlates with the skills and knowledge required for successful job performance.

Criterion-related validity is concerned with the statistical correlation between scores received on tests ("paper-and-pencil" tests) and job performance. An employer who administers an IQ test to prospective employees must establish that there is a high statistical correlation between successful performance on the test and successful performance on the job. That correlation may be established by giving the test to current employees and comparing their test scores with their job performance; the correlation coefficient so produced is then used to predict the job performance of other current or prospective employees taking the same test. The Uniform Guidelines provide specific procedures and requirements for demonstrating the criterion-related validity of tests used for employment selection. Failure to comply with the requirements of the Uniform Guidelines will prevent an employer from establishing that a test is job related. If the test has not been validated, its use for employment purposes will violate Title VII if such a test has a disparate impact. Furthermore, a test validated for one group, such as Hispanic Americans, may have to be separately validated for one or more other groups, such as African Americans or Asian Americans.

The following case deals with an employer's efforts to demonstrate that a physical fitness requirement is related to the job of transit police officer.

Lanning v. Southeastern Pennsylvania Transportation Authority (SEPTA)

181 F.3d 478 (3rd Cir. 1999), cert. denied, 528 U.S.1131 (Mem.) (2000)

Background

SEPTA is a regional mass transit authority in the Philadelphia, Pennsylvania area. In 1989 SEPTA initiated an extensive program to improve the quality and upgrade the physical fitness level of its transit police force. As a screening device to measure the physical fitness of applicants, SEPTA adopted a requirement that applicants for the transit police must be able to run 1.5 miles in 12 minutes or less. For the years 1991, 1993, and 1996, an average of only 12% of women applicants passed SEPTA's 1.5 mile run, while almost 60% of male applicants passed. For the years 1993 and 1996, the time period in question in this litigation, the pass rate for women was 6.7% compared to a 55.6% pass rate for men. In January 1997, five women who failed SEPTA's 1.5 mile run brought a Title VII class action against SEPTA on behalf of all 1993 female applicants . . . and future female applicants for employment as SEPTA police officers who have been or will be denied employment by reason of their inability to meet the physical entrance requirement of running 1.5 miles in 12 minutes or less. SEPTA conceded that its 1.5 mile run requirement has a disparate impact on women.

Mansmann, Circuit Judge

. . . Because SEPTA concedes that its 1.5 mile run has a disparate impact on women, . . . this appeal focuses our attention on the proper standard for evaluating whether SEPTA's 1.5 mile run is "job related for the position in question and consistent with business necessity" under the Civil Rights Act of 1991.

. . . In 1991, SEPTA hired Dr. Paul Davis to develop an appropriate physical fitness test for its police officers. Dr. Davis initially met with SEPTA officials in order to ascertain SEPTA's objectives. Dr. Davis determined that SEPTA was interested in enhancing the level of fitness, physical vigor and general productivity of its police force. Once Dr. Davis had determined SEPTA's objectives, he went on a ride-along with SEPTA transit police and, over the course of two days and approximately twenty hours, rode the SEPTA trains in order to obtain a perspective on the expectations of SEPTA transit officers.

Dr. Davis next conducted a study with twenty experienced SEPTA officers, designated "subject matter experts" (SMEs), in an effort to determine what physical abilities are required to perform the job of SEPTA transit officer. From the responses Dr. Davis received in this study, he determined that running, jogging, and walking were important SEPTA transit officer tasks and that SEPTA officers were expected to jog almost on a daily basis.

Dr. Davis then asked the SMEs to determine what level of physical exertion was necessary to perform these tasks. The SMEs estimated that it was reasonable to expect them to run one mile in full gear in 11.78 minutes. Dr. Davis rejected this estimate as too low based upon his determination that any individual could meet this requirement. Ultimately, Dr. Davis recommended a 1.5 mile run within 12 minutes. Dr. Davis explained that completion of this run would require that an officer possess an aerobic capacity of 42.5 mL/kg/min, the aerobic capacity that Dr. Davis determined would be necessary to perform the job of SEPTA transit officer.[1]

Dr. Davis recommended that SEPTA use the 1.5 mile run as an applicant screening test. Dr. Davis understood that SEPTA officers would not be required to run 1.5 miles within 12 minutes in the course of their duties, but he nevertheless recommended this test as an accurate measure of the aerobic capacity necessary to perform the job of SEPTA transit police officer. Based upon Dr. Davis' recommendation, SEPTA adopted a physical fitness screening test for its applicants which included a 1.5 mile run within 12 minutes. Beginning in 1991, the 1.5 mile run was administered as the first component of the physical fitness test; if an applicant failed to run 1.5

[1]Dr. Davis initially decided that an aerobic capacity of 50 mL/kg/min was necessary to perform the job of SEPTA transit police officer. After determining that institution of such a high standard would have a draconian effect on women applicants, however, Dr. Davis decided that the goals of SEPTA could be satisfied by using a 42.5 mL/kg/min standard.

miles in 12 minutes, the applicant would be disqualified from employment as a SEPTA transit officer.

After litigation commenced, SEPTA hired expert statisticians to submit reports examining the statistical relationship between the aerobic capacity of SEPTA's officers and their number of arrests, "arrest rates" and number of commendations. In these reports, the statisticians concluded that there was a statistically significant correlation between high aerobic capacity and arrests, arrest rates and commendations. In addition, one expert prepared a report that estimated that 51.9% of the persons arrested for serious crimes between 1991 and 1996 had an aerobic capacity of 48 mL/kg/min and 27% of those arrested had an aerobic capacity of less than 42 mL/kg/min. Based upon these reports, the District Court held that SEPTA established that its aerobic capacity requirement is job related and consistent with business necessity. . . . The District Court entered judgment in favor of SEPTA on all claims . . . [and] the individual plaintiffs have taken appeals from the District Court's final judgment. . . .

In this appeal, we must determine the appropriate legal standard to apply when evaluating an employer's business justification in an action challenging an employer's cutoff score on an employment screening exam as discriminatory under a disparate impact theory of liability. We hold today that under the Civil Rights Act of 1991, a discriminatory cutoff score on an entry level employment examination must be shown to measure the minimum qualifications necessary for successful performance of the job in question in order to survive a disparate impact challenge. . . .

. . . In conjunction with the implementation of its physical fitness screening test, SEPTA also began testing incumbent officers for aerobic capacity in 1991. SEPTA policy requires any officer who fails any portion of the incumbent fitness test to retest on the failed element within three months. For each portion of the physical fitness test that an incumbent officer fails, an interim goal is set for that officer.

SEPTA initially disciplined those incumbent officers who failed the fitness test. Due to protests by the incumbent officers' union, however, SEPTA discontinued its discipline policy and instead implemented an incentive program that rewarded incumbent officers for passing their interim fitness goals.

According to SEPTA's internal documents, significant percentages of incumbent officers of all ranks have failed SEPTA's physical fitness test. By 1996, however, 86% of incumbent officers reached SEPTA's physical fitness standards. SEPTA has never taken any steps to determine whether incumbent officers who have failed the physical fitness test have adversely affected SEPTA's ability to carry out its mission.

SEPTA has promoted incumbent officers who have failed some or all of the components of the physical fitness test. SEPTA has also given special recognition, commendations, and satisfactory performance evaluations to incumbent officers who have failed the physical fitness test. SEPTA has never disciplined, terminated, removed, reassigned, suspended or demoted any transit officer for failing to perform the physical requirements of the job.

In addition, due to a clerical error, SEPTA hired a female officer in 1991 who failed the 1.5 mile run. This officer has subsequently been "decorated" by SEPTA and has been nominated repeatedly for awards such as Officer of the Year and Officer of the Quarter. SEPTA has commended her for her outstanding performance as a police officer and has chosen her to serve as one of SEPTA's two defensive tactics instructors.

SEPTA employs an extremely low number of women in its transit police force. The District Court found that, as of July 1997, SEPTA employed only 16 women in its 234 member police force. Only two of these women hold ranks higher than that of patrol officer.

. . . The Supreme Court has yet to interpret the "job related for the position in question and consistent with business necessity" standard adopted by the [1991 amendments to the Civil Rights] Act. . . . We turn now to articulate the standard for business necessity. . . . In the context of a hiring exam with a cutoff score shown to have a discriminatory effect, the standard that best effectuates this mission is implicit in the Court's application of the business necessity doctrine to the employer in *Griggs,* i.e., that a discriminatory cutoff score is impermissible unless shown to measure the minimum qualifications necessary for successful performance of the job in question. . . .

. . . *Griggs* [and related cases] teach that in order to show the business necessity of a discriminatory cutoff score an employer must demonstrate that its cutoff measures the minimum qualifications necessary for successful performance of the job in question. . . . Furthermore we . . . conclude that the Act's business necessity language incorporates this standard.

. . . With respect to a discriminatory cutoff score, the business necessity prong must be read to demand an inquiry into whether the score reflects the minimum qualifications necessary to perform successfully the job in question. . . .

Although the District Court purported to apply the Act's "job related to the position in question and consistent with business necessity" standard to SEPTA's cutoff score on its 1.5 mile run, it is clear the District Court . . . did not apply the standard we have found to be implicit in *Griggs* and incorporated by the Act. . . . As an initial matter, the District Court seemed to conclude that Dr. Davis' expertise alone is sufficient to justify the 42.5 mL/kg/min aerobic capacity cutoff measured by the 1.5 mile run. This conclusion disregards the teachings of *Griggs* . . . in which the Court made clear that judgment alone is insufficient to validate an employer's discriminatory practices. More fundamentally, however, nowhere in its extensive opinion did the District Court consider whether Dr. Davis' 42.5 mL/kg/min cutoff reflects the minimum aerobic capacity necessary to perform successfully the job of SEPTA transit police officer.

Instead, the District Court upheld this cutoff because it was "readily justifiable." The validation studies of SEPTA's experts upon which the District Court relied to support this conclusion demonstrate the extent to which this standard is insufficient under the Act. The general import of these studies is that the higher an officer's aerobic capacity, the better the officer is able to perform the job. Setting aside the validity of these studies, this conclusion alone does not validate Dr. Davis' 42.5 mL/kg/min cutoff under the Act's business necessity standard. At best, these studies show that aerobic capacity is related to the job of SEPTA transit officer. A study showing that "more is better," however, has no bearing on the appropriate cutoff to reflect the minimal qualifications necessary to perform successfully the job in question.

. . . For the foregoing reasons, it is clear to us that the District Court did not employ the business necessity standard implicit in *Griggs* and incorporated by the Act which requires that a discriminatory cutoff score be shown to measure the minimum qualifications necessary for successful performance of the job in question in order to survive a disparate impact challenge. We will therefore vacate the judgment of the District Court and remand this appeal for the District Court to determine whether SEPTA has carried its burden of establishing that its 1.5 mile run measures the minimum aerobic capacity necessary to perform successfully the job of SEPTA transit police officer.[2] Because this is the first occasion we have had to clarify the Act's business necessity standard, on remand the District Court may wish to exercise its discretion to allow the parties to develop further the record in keeping with the standard announced here.

Case Questions

1. How did Dr. Davis determine the minimum level of aerobic capacity necessary to perform the job of SEPTA transit police officer?
2. Were police officers who could not meet the aerobic capacity standard able to perform the requirements of the SEPTA transit officer job? What evidence did the plaintiffs offer on this question?
3. Does this decision mean that SEPTA cannot establish any physical fitness requirements for its transit police? Explain your answer.

[2]The District Court rejected as irrelevant the plaintiffs' evidence that incumbent officers had failed the physical fitness test yet successfully performed the job and that other police forces function well without an aerobic capacity admission test. Under the standard implicit in Griggs and incorporated into the Act, this evidence tends to show that SEPTA's cutoff score for aerobic capacity does not correlate with the minimum qualifications necessary to perform successfully the job of SEPTA transit officer. Accordingly, this evidence is relevant and should be considered by the District Court on remand.

THE "BOTTOM LINE" AND DISCRIMINATION

Does the fact that an employer's work force contains a higher percentage of minority employees than does the general population of the surrounding area serve to insulate the employer from claims of discrimination in employment? The following case involves a similar issue: Should the fact that an employer has promoted a greater percentage of minority employees than nonminorities constitute a defense to the claim of discrimination by minority employees? The employer argues that the "bottom line"—the number of minority employees promoted—disproves any claim of discrimination. The claimants argue that the employer used a discriminatory exam (one with a disparate impact on minorities) to select those eligible for promotion. Was Title VII violated?

Connecticut v. Teal

457 U.S. 440 (1982)

Brennan, J.

We consider here whether an employer sued for violation of Title VII of the Civil Rights Act of 1964 may assert a "bottom line" theory of defense. Under that theory, as asserted in this case, an employer's acts of racial discrimination in promotions—effected by an examination having disparate impact—would not render the employer liable for the racial discrimination suffered by employees barred from promotion if the "bottom line" result of the promotional process was an appropriate racial balance. . . .

Four of the respondents, Winnie Teal, Rose Walker, Edith Latney, and Grace Clark, are black employees of the Department of Income Maintenance of the State of Connecticut. Each was promoted provisionally to the position of Welfare Eligibility Supervisor and served in that capacity for almost two years. To attain permanent status as supervisors, however, respondents had to participate in a selection process that required, as the first step, a passing score on a written examination. This written test was administered on December 2, 1978, to 329 candidates. Of these candidates, 48 identified themselves as black and 259 identified themselves as white. The results of the examination were announced in March 1979. With the passing score set at 65, 54.17 percent of the identified black candidates passed. This was approximately 68 percent of the passing rate for the identified white candidates. The four respondents were among the blacks who failed the examination, and they were thus excluded from further consideration for permanent supervisory positions. In April 1979, respondents instituted this action in the . . . District Court . . . against petitioners, the State of Connecticut, two state agencies, and two state officials. Respondents alleged, *inter alia,* that petitioners violated Title VII by imposing, as an absolute condition for consideration for promotion, that applicants pass a written test that excluded blacks in disproportionate numbers and that was not job related.

[Approximately one month before the trial, Connecticut promoted 11 of the 48 black employees and 35 of the 259 white employees who took the test. The promotions were based on test performance, past work performance, recommendations of supervisors, and seniority.] The overall result of the selection process was that, of the 48 identified black candidates who participated in the selection process, 22.9 percent were promoted and of the 259 identified white candidates, 13.5 percent were promoted. It is this "bottom-line" result, more favorable to blacks than to whites, that petitioners urge should be adjudged to be a complete defense to respondents' suit.

After trial, the District Court entered judgment for petitioners. . . . Holding that these "bottom-line" percentages precluded the finding of a Title VII violation, the court held that the employer was not required to demonstrate that the promotional examination was job related. The United States Court of Appeals for the Second Circuit reversed, holding that the District Court erred in ruling that the results of the written examination alone were insufficient to support a prima facie case of disparate impact in violation of Title VII. The Court of Appeals stated that where "an identifiable pass-fail barrier denies an employment opportunity to a disproportionately large number of minorities and prevents them from proceeding to the next step in the selection process," that barrier must be shown to be job related. We granted certiorari. . . .

Respondents base their claim on our construction of this provision in *Griggs v. Duke Power Co.* . . .

Petitioners' examination, which barred promotion and had a discriminatory impact on black employees, clearly falls within the literal language of Section 703(a)(2), as interpreted by *Griggs*. The statute speaks, not in terms of jobs and promotions, but in terms of *limitations* and *classifications* that would deprive any individual of employment *opportunities*. . . . When an employer uses a nonjob-related barrier in order to deny a minority or woman applicant employment or promotion, and that barrier has a significant adverse effect on minorities or women, then the applicant has been deprived of an employment *opportunity* "because of . . . race, color, religion, sex, or national origin." In other words, Section 703(a)(2) prohibits discriminatory "artificial, arbitrary, and unnecessary barriers to employment," that "limit . . . or classify . . . applicants for employment . . . in any way which would deprive or tend to deprive any individual of employment *opportunities*." . . .

The decisions of this Court following *Griggs* also support respondents' claim. In considering claims of disparate impact under Section 703(a)(2) this Court has consistently focused on employment and promotion requirements that create a discriminatory bar to *opportunities*. This Court has never read Section 703(a)(2) as requiring the focus to be placed instead on the overall number of minority or female applicants actually hired or promoted. . . .

The suggestion that disparate impact should be measured only at the bottom line ignores the fact that Title VII guarantees these individual respondents the *opportunity* to compete equally with white workers on the basis of job-related criteria. Title VII strives to achieve equality of opportunity by rooting out "artificial, arbitrary and unnecessary" employer-created barriers to professional development that have a discriminatory impact upon individuals. Therefore, respondents' rights under Section 703(a)(2) have been violated, unless petitioners can demonstrate that the examination given was not an artificial, arbitrary, or unnecessary barrier, because it measured skills related to effective performance in the role of Welfare Eligibility Supervisor. . . .

In sum, respondents' claim of disparate impact from the examination, a pass-fail barrier to employment opportunity, states a prima facie case of employment discrimination under Section 703(a)(2), despite their employer's nondiscriminatory "bottom line," and that "bottom line" is no defense to this prima facie case under Section 703(h). . . .

In suggesting that the "bottom line" may be a defense to a claim of discrimination against an individual employee, petitioners and *amici* appear to confuse unlawful discrimination with discriminatory intent. The Court has stated that a nondiscriminatory "bottom line" and an employer's good faith efforts to achieve a nondiscriminatory work force, might in some cases assist an employer in rebutting the inference that particular action had been intentionally discriminatory: "Proof that [a] work force was racially balanced or that it contained a disproportionately high percentage of minority employees is not wholly irrelevant on the issue of intent when that issue is yet to be decided." *Furnco Construction Corp. v. Waters* (1978). But resolution of the factual question of intent is not what is at issue in this case. Rather, petitioners seek simply to justify discrimination against respondents, on the basis of their favorable treatment of other members of respondents' racial group. Under Title VII, "A racially balanced work force cannot immunize an employer from liability for specific acts of discrimination." *Furnco Construction Corp.*

It is clear that Congress never intended to give an employer license to discriminate against some employees on the basis of race or sex merely because he favorably treats other members of the employees' group. . . .

Every *individual* employee is protected against both discriminatory treatment and against "practices that are fair in form, but discriminatory in operation." Requirements and tests that have a discriminatory impact are merely some of the more subtle, but also the more pervasive, of the "practices and devices which have fostered racially stratified job environments to the disadvantage of minority citizens."

In sum, petitioners' nondiscriminatory "bottom line" is no answer, under the terms of Title VII, to respondents' prima facie claim of employment discrimination. Accordingly, the judgment of the Court of Appeals for the Second Circuit is affirmed, and this case is remanded to the District Court for further proceedings consistent with this opinion.

It is so ordered.

Case Questions

1. What is the "bottom line" defense? How does it apply to the facts in this case?
2. Are the plaintiffs complaining of disparate impact or disparate treatment discrimination? What evidence was used to support their claim?
3. What is the relevance of the promotion rates for employees of different races to plaintiffs' claim?

SENIORITY AND TITLE VII

Seniority, or length of service on the job, is frequently used to determine entitlement to employment benefits, promotions, or transfers, and even job security itself. Seniority systems usually provide that layoffs of workers be conducted on the basis of inverse seniority; those with the least length of service, or seniority, are laid off before those with greater seniority. Seniority within a department may also be used to determine eligibility to transfer to a different department.

Seniority may have a discriminatory effect when an employer, prior to the adoption of Title VII, refused to hire women or minority workers. If, after Title VII's adoption, the employer does hire them, those workers will have the least seniority. In the event of a layoff, the workers who lose their jobs will be women and minorities, whereas white males will retain their jobs. The layoffs by inverse seniority have a disparate impact on women and minorities. Does this mean the seniority system is in violation of Title VII, as in *Griggs*?

Section 703(h) of Title VII contains an exemption for bona fide seniority systems. That section states, in part,

> Notwithstanding any other provision of this title, it shall not be an unlawful employment practice for an employer to apply different standards of compensation or different terms, conditions, or privileges of employment pursuant to a bona fide seniority or merit system provided that such differences are not the result of an intention to discriminate because of race, color, religion, sex or national origin.

What is the effect of Section 703(h) on a seniority system that has a disparate impact or that operates to perpetuate the effects of prior discrimination? In several cases decided shortly after the adoption of Title VII, courts held that departmental seniority systems that operated to deter minority employees from transferring out of low-paying and inferior jobs were in violation of Title VII because they perpetuated prior discrimination. The issue reached the Supreme Court in the case of *International Brotherhood of Teamsters v. United States.* The Court had to address the question of whether a seniority system that perpetuated the effects of prior discrimination was bona fide under Section 703(h).

International Brotherhood of Teamsters v. United States
CSC431 U.S. 324 (1977)

Stewart, J.

This litigation brings here several important questions under Title VII of the Civil Rights Act of 1964. . . . The issues grow out of alleged unlawful employment practices engaged in by an employer and a union. The employer is a common carrier of motor freight with nationwide operations, and the union represents a large group of its employees. The district court and the court of appeals held that the employer had violated Title VII by engaging in a pattern and practice of employment discrimination against Negroes and Spanish-surnamed Americans, and that the union had violated the Act by agreeing with the employer to create and maintain a seniority system that perpetuated the effects of past racial and ethnic discrimination. . . .

. . . The central claim . . . was that the company had engaged in a pattern or practice of discriminating against minorities in hiring so-called line drivers. Those Negroes and Spanish-surnamed persons who had been hired, the Government alleged, were given lower paying, less desirable jobs as servicemen or local city drivers, and were thereafter discriminated against with respect to promotions and transfers. In this connection the complaint also challenged the seniority system established by the collective-bargaining agreements between the employer and the union. The Government sought a general injunctive remedy and specific "make whole" relief for all individual discriminatees, which would allow them an opportunity to transfer to line-driver jobs with full company seniority for all purposes.

The cases went to trial and the district court found that the Government had shown "by a preponderance of the evidence that T.I.M.E.-D.C. and its predecessor companies were engaged in a plan and practice of discrimination in violation of Title VII. . . ." The court further found that the seniority system contained in the collective-bargaining contracts between the company and the union violated Title VII because it "operate[d] to impede the free transfer of minority groups into and within the company." Both the company and the union were enjoined from committing further violations of Title VII. . . .

. . . The union further contends that the seniority system contained in the collective-bargaining agreements in no way violated Title VII. If these contentions are correct, it is unnecessary, of course, to reach any of the issues concerning remedies that so occupied the attention of the court of appeals.

. . . The district court and the court of appeals, on the basis of substantial evidence, held that the Government had proved a prima facie case of systematic and purposeful employment discrimination, continuing well beyond the effective date of Title VII. The company's attempts to rebut that conclusion were held to be inadequate. For the reasons we have summarized, there is no warrant for this Court to disturb the findings of the district court and the court of appeals on this basic issue. . . .

The district court and the court of appeals also found that the seniority system contained in the collective-bargaining agreements between the company and the union operated to violate Title VII of the Act.

For purposes of calculating benefits, such as vacations, pensions, and other fringe benefits, an employee's seniority under this system runs from the date he joins the company, and takes into account his total service in all jobs and bargaining units. For competitive purposes, however, such as determining the order in which employees may bid for particular jobs, are laid off, or are recalled from layoff, it is bargaining-unit seniority that controls. Thus, a line driver's seniority, for purposes of bidding for particular runs and protection against layoff, takes into account only the length of time he has been a line driver at a particular terminal. The practical effect is that a city driver or serviceman who transfers to a line-driver job must forfeit all the competitive seniority he has accumulated in his previous bargaining unit and start at the bottom of the line drivers' "board."

The vice of this arrangement, as found by the district court and the court of appeals, was that it "locked" minority workers into inferior jobs and perpetuated prior discrimination by discouraging transfers to jobs as line drivers. While the disincentive applied to all workers, including whites, it was Negroes and Spanish-surnamed persons who, those courts found, suffered the most because many of them had been denied the equal opportunity to become line drivers when they were initially hired, whereas whites either had not sought or were refused line-driver positions for reasons unrelated to their race or national origin.

The linchpin of the theory embraced by the district court and the court of appeals was that a discriminatee who must forfeit his competitive seniority in order finally to obtain a line-driver job will never be able to "catch up" to the seniority level of his contemporary who was not subject to discrimination. Accordingly, this continued, built-in disadvantage to the prior discriminatee who transfers to a line-driver job was held to constitute a continuing violation of Title VII, for which both the employer and the union who jointly created and maintained the seniority system were liable.

The union, while acknowledging that the seniority system may in some sense perpetuate the effects of prior discrimination, asserts that the system is immunized from a finding of illegality by reason of Section 703(h) of Title VII. . . .

It argues that the seniority system in this case is "bona fide" within the meaning of Section 703(h) when judged in light of its history, intent, application, and all of the circumstances under which it was created and is maintained. More specifically, the union claims that the central purpose of Section 703(h) is to ensure that mere perpetuation of *pre-Act* discrimination is not unlawful under Title VII. And, whether or not Section 703(h) immunizes the perpetuation of *post-Act* discrimination, the union claims that the seniority system in this case has no such effect. Its position in this Court, as has been its position throughout this litigation, is that the seniority system presents no hurdles to post-Act discriminatees who seek retroactive seniority to the date they would have become line drivers but for the company's discrimination. Indeed, the union asserts that under its collective-bargaining agreements the union will itself take up the cause of the post-Act victim and attempt, through grievance procedures, to gain for him full "make whole" relief, including appropriate seniority.

The Government responds that a seniority system that perpetuates the effects of prior discrimination—pre- or post-Act—can never be "bona fide" under Section 703(h); at a minimum Title VII prohibits those applications of a seniority system that perpetuate the effects on incumbent employees of prior discriminatory job assignments.

The issues thus joined are open ones in this Court. . . .

Because the company discriminated both before and after the enactment of Title VII, the seniority system is said to have operated to perpetuate the effects of both pre- and post-Act discrimination. Post-Act discriminatees, however, may obtain full "make whole" relief, including retroactive seniority under *Franks* v. *Bowman,* without attacking the legality of the seniority system as applied to them. *Franks* made clear and the union acknowledges that retroactive seniority may be awarded as relief from an employer's discriminatory hiring and assignment policies even if the seniority system agreement itself makes no provision for such relief. Here the Government has proved that the company engaged in a post-Act pattern of discriminatory hiring, assignment, transfer, and promotion policies. Any Negro or Spanish-surnamed American injured by those policies may receive all appropriate relief as a direct remedy for this discrimination.

What remains for review is the judgment that the seniority system unlawfully perpetuated the effects of pre-Act discrimination. We must decide, in short, whether Section 703(h) validates otherwise bona fide seniority systems that afford no constructive seniority to victims discriminated against prior to the effective date of Title VII, and it is to that issue that we now turn.

. . . Were it not for Section 703(h), the seniority system in this case would seem to fall under the *Griggs* rationale. The heart of the system is its allocation of the choicest jobs, the greatest protection against layoffs, and other advantages to those employees who have been line drivers for the longest time. Where, because of the employer's prior intentional discrimination, the line drivers with the longest tenure are without exception white, the advantages of the seniority system flow disproportionately to them and away from Negro and Spanish-surnamed employees who might by now have enjoyed those advantages had not the employer discriminated before the passage of the Act. This disproportionate distribution of advantages does in a very real sense "operate to 'freeze' the status quo of prior discriminatory employment practices." But both the literal terms of Section 703(h) and the legislative history of Title VII demonstrate that Congress considered this very effect of many seniority systems and extended a measure of immunity to them. . . .

In sum, the unmistakable purpose of Section 703(h) was to make clear that the routine application of a bona fide seniority system would not be unlawful under Title VII. This was the intended result even where the employer's pre-Act discrimination resulted in whites having greater existing seniority rights than Negroes. Although a seniority system inevitably tends to perpetuate the effects of pre-Act discrimination in such cases, the congressional judgment was that Title VII should not outlaw the use of existing seniority lists and thereby destroy or water down the vested seniority rights of employees simply because their employer had engaged in discrimination prior to the passage of the Act.

To be sure, Section 703(h) does not immunize all seniority systems. It refers only to "bona fide" systems, and a proviso requires that any differences in treatment not be "the result of an intention to discriminate because of race . . . or national origin. . . ." But our reading of the legislative history compels us to reject the Government's broad argument that no seniority system that tends to perpetuate pre-Act discrimination can be "bona fide." . . . Accordingly, we hold that an otherwise neutral, legitimate seniority system does not become unlawful under Title VII simply because it may perpetuate pre-Act discrimination. Congress did not intend to make it illegal for employees with vested seniority rights to continue to exercise those rights, even at the expense of pre-Act discriminatees. . . .

The seniority system in this case is entirely bona fide. It applies equally to all races and ethnic groups. To the extent that it "locks" employees into nonline-driver jobs, it does so for all. The city drivers and servicemen who are discouraged from transferring to line-driver jobs are not all Negroes or Spanish-surnamed Americans; to the contrary, the overwhelming majority are white. The placing of line drivers in a separate bargaining unit from other employees is rational, in accord with the industry practice, and consistent with NLRB precedents. It is conceded that the seniority system did not have its genesis in racial discrimination, and that it was negotiated and has been maintained free from any illegal purpose. In these circumstances, the single fact that the system extends no retroactive seniority to pre-Act discriminatees does not make it unlawful.

Because the seniority system was protected by Section 703(h), the union's conduct in agreeing to and maintaining the system did not violate Title VII. On remand, the district court's injunction against the union must be vacated.

. . . **So ordered.**

Case Questions

1. How does the seniority system in this case operate to deter minority employees from transferring? Does it affect white employees the same way?
2. Was the Teamsters Union guilty of intentional discrimination in this case? Was the Union guilty of disparate impact discrimination? What is the relevance of § 703(h) to this case? Explain your answer.
3. When is a seniority system "bona fide" under § 703(h)?

In *American Tobacco Co. v. Patterson* [456 U.S. 63 (1982)], the Supreme Court ruled that Section 703(h) applies to seniority systems that were adopted after the passage of Title VII as well as to those in operation at the time Title VII was adopted. The protection of Section 703(h) extends to rules that determine entry into seniority classifications, according to the 1980 Supreme Court decision in *California Brewers Association v. Bryan* [444 U.S. 598]. That case involved the rule that an employee had to have worked at least forty-five weeks in a calendar year to be classified a "permanent employee." Permanent employees were given preference in layoffs and transfers over temporary employees (those not meeting the forty-five-week rule). An African American employee claimed that the forty-five-week rule had a disparate impact on minority workers. The Court, rejecting the claim, held that the forty-five-week rule was within the Section 703(h) exemption for bona fide seniority systems.

According to *Teamsters,* a seniority system is bona fide within the meaning of Section 703(h) when it is neutral on its face (it applies equally to all employees) and it is not intentionally used to discriminate. Furthermore, the court will consider whether the system had its origin in discrimination, whether it has been negotiated and maintained free from discriminatory intent, and whether the basis of the seniority system is reasonable in light of industry practice.

Section 706(e)(2), added to Title VII by the 1991 amendments, addresses the time limits for a challenge to a seniority system that allegedly is used intentionally to discriminate in violation of Title VII. According to that section, a claim may be filed after the allegedly discriminatory seniority system is adopted, after the plaintiff becomes subject to the seniority system, or after the plaintiff is injured by the application of the seniority system. Section 706(e)(2) was intended to reverse the Supreme Court decision in *Lorance v. AT&T Technologies, Inc.* [490 U.S. 900 (1989)], which held that the time limit for challenging a seniority system ran from the date on which the system was adopted, even if the plaintiff was not subjected to the system until five years later.

MIXED MOTIVE CASES UNDER TITLE VII

In *Price Waterhouse v. Hopkins* [490 U.S. 228 (1989)], the Supreme Court held that when a plaintiff shows that the employer has considered an illegal factor under Title VII (race, sex, color, religion, or national origin) in making an employment decision, the employer must demonstrate that it would have reached the same decision if it had not considered the illegal factor. According to the Supreme Court, if the employer can show this, the employer can escape liability under Title VII; that is, it will not have violated the statute.

The 1991 amendments to Title VII addressed this "mixed motive" situation and partially overruled the *Price Waterhouse* decision. Section 703(m) now states that "an unlawful employment practice is established when the complaining party demonstrates that race, color, religion, sex, or national origin was a motivating factor for any employment practice, even though other factors also motivated the practice." That is, the employer violates Title VII when an illegal factor is considered, even though there may have been other factors motivating the decision or practice. If the employer is able to show that it would have reached the same decision in the absence of the illegal factor, then the employer's liability for remedy under Title VII is reduced under Section 706(g)(2)(B). Section 706(g)(2)(B), also added by the 1991 amendments, states that the employer is subject to a court order to cease violating Title VII and is liable for the plaintiff's legal fees but is not required to pay damages or to reinstate or hire the plaintiff. In *Desert Palace, Inc. v. Costa* [123 S.Ct. 2148 (2003)], the Supreme Court held that a plaintiff need only "demonstrate" that the defendant used a prohibited factor (race, color, gender, religion, or natural origin) as one of the motives for an employment action. That demonstration can be made either by circumstantial evidence or direct evidence; the act does not require direct evidence to raise the mixed motive analysis under Section 703(m).

RETALIATION UNDER TITLE VII

Section 704 (a) of Title VII prohibits retaliation by an employer, union, or employment agency against an employee or applicant because that person has opposed any practice that is prohibited by Title VII (known as the "opposition clause") or because that person has taken part in or assisted any investigation, hearing, or proceeding under Title VII (known as the "participation clause"). To demonstrate a case of retaliation under § 704(a), plaintiffs must demonstrate that (1) they were engaged in an activity or activities protected under Title VII; (2) they suffered an adverse employment decision; and (3) there was a causal link between the protected activity and the adverse employment decision. The "protected activity" must be related to either the participation clause or the opposition clause of § 704. In *Robinson v. Shell Oil Company* [519 U.S. 337 (1997)], the Supreme Court held that § 704(a) also protects former employees from retaliation; an employer who gave a former employee a negative reference because the employee had filed a Title VII charge against the employer violated § 704(a).

AFFIRMATIVE ACTION AND TITLE VII

Affirmative action has been an extremely controversial and divisive legal and political issue since Title VII was enacted in 1964. Critics of affirmative action argue that it benefited individuals who were not, themselves, victims of illegal discrimination, and operated to discriminate against persons (usually white males) who were not personally guilty of illegal discrimination. Supporters argue that affirmative action is necessary to overcome the legacy of prior discrimination and that our society is still not free from racism and sexism.

Affirmative action programs in employment involve giving some kind of preference in hiring or promotion to qualified female or minority employees. Employees who are not members of the group being accorded the preference (usually white males) may therefore be at a disadvantage for hiring or promotion. Recall that *McDonald v. Santa Fe Trail* held that Title VII protected every individual employee from discrimination because of race, sex, color, religion, or national origin. Is the denial of preferential treatment to employees not within the preferred group (defined by race or sex) a violation of Title VII? Affirmative action programs by public sector employers raise legal issues under the U.S. Constitution as well as under Title VII: Does the affirmative action program violate the constitutional prohibitions against intentional discrimination contained in the Equal Protection Clause? The discussion of affirmative action in this chapter focuses mainly on affirmative action under Title VII. Chapter 7 will also discuss affirmative action under the Constitution.

Title VII does not require employers to enact affirmative action plans; however, the courts have often ordered affirmative action when the employer has been found in violation of Title VII. The courts have consistently held that remedial affirmative action plans—plans set up to remedy prior illegal discrimination—are permissible under Title VII because such plans may be necessary to overcome the effects of the employer's prior illegal discrimination. But if the plan is a voluntary one and the employer has not been found guilty of prior discrimination, does it violate Title VII by discriminating on the basis of race or gender?

This question was addressed by the U.S. Supreme Court in the case of *United Steelworkers of America v. Weber* [443 U.S. 193 (1979)]. Weber, a white employee, was excluded from a training program, run by the employer and union, designed to create more skilled craftworkers. Under a voluntary affirmative action program, 50 percent of the spaces in the training program were reserved for minority employees, whereas admission to the other 50 percent of the spaces was based on seniority. The affirmative action plan was temporary and would cease when the percentage of skilled craftworkers who were minorities was similar to the percentage of minority workers in the local labor market. Weber was not senior enough to qualify for the seats not reserved for minority employees, but he did have more seniority than the minority employees who were admitted under the affirmative action program. He sued, arguing that excluding him from the training program while admitting less senior minority employees was race discrimination prohibited by Title VII.

The Supreme Court upheld the legality of the voluntary affirmative action program. The majority opinion stated:

> We therefore hold that Title VII's prohibition in Sections 703(a) and (d) against racial discrimination does not condemn all private, voluntary, race-conscious affirmative action plans. . . .
>
> We need not today define in detail the line of demarcation between permissible and impermissible affirmative action plans. It suffices to hold that the challenged Kaiser-USWA affirmative action plan falls on the permissible side of the line. The purposes of the plan mirror those of the statute. Both were designed to break down old patterns of racial segregation and hierarchy. Both were structured to "open employment opportunities for Negroes in occupations that have been traditionally closed to them."
>
> At the same time, the plan does not unnecessarily trammel the interests of the white employees. The plan does not require the discharge of white workers and their replacement with new black hirees. Nor does the plan create an absolute bar to the advancement of white employees; half of those trained in the program will be white. Moreover, the plan is a temporary measure; it is not intended to maintain racial balance, but simply to eliminate a manifest racial imbalance. Preferential selection of craft trainees at the Gramercy plant will end as soon as the percentage of black skilled craftworkers in the Gramercy plant approximates the percentage of blacks in the local labor force.
>
> We conclude, therefore, that the adoption of the Kaiser-USWA plan for the Gramercy plant falls within the area of discretion left by Title VII to the private sector voluntarily to adopt affirmative action plans designed to eliminate conspicuous racial imbalance in traditionally segregated job categories.

The Court in *Weber* upheld the legality of a voluntarily adopted affirmative action program by an employer who had not been found guilty of prior discrimination. When is an employer justified in initiating a voluntary affirmative action program? What kind of evidence must the employer demonstrate to support the adoption of the affirmative action plan? What evidence must an individual who alleges discriminatory treatment by an employer acting pursuant to an affirmative action program demonstrate to establish a claim under Title VII?

In *Johnson v. Transportation Agency, Santa Clara County, California* [480 U.S. 616 (1987)], the U.S. Supreme Court held that an employer can justify the adoption of an affirmative action plan by showing that "a conspicuous . . . imbalance in traditionally segregated job categories" exists in its work force. A plaintiff challenging an employment decision based on an affirmative action plan has the burden of showing that the affirmative action plan is not valid. In *Johnson,* the Court upheld the legality of an affirmative action plan that granted a relative preference to women and minorities in hiring for positions in traditionally male-dominated jobs. The fact that the employer's plan had no definite termination date was not a problem, according to the court, because it did not set aside a specific number of positions. The plan used a flexible, case-by-case approach and was designed to attain a more balanced work force. The affirmative action plan, therefore, met the criteria set out in *Weber:* It furthered the purposes of Title VII by overcoming a manifest imbalance in traditionally segregated job categories, and it did not "unnecessarily trammel" the interests of the nonpreferred employees.

Both *Weber* and *Johnson* involved suits under Title VII. When considering the legality of affirmative action programs under the U.S. Constitution, the approach used by the courts is slightly different from the approach used in Title VII cases. In *Wygant v. Jackson Board of Education* [476 U.S. 267 (1986)] and in *Adarand Constructors, Inc. v. Pena* [515 U.S. 200 (1995)], the U.S. Supreme Court held that affirmative action plans by public sector employers must pass the strict scrutiny test under the U.S. Constitution. The strict scrutiny test, a two-part test, requires that (1) the affirmative action plan must serve a "compelling governmental interest," and (2) it must be "narrowly tailored" to further that compelling interest. Although the language of the test for the legality of affirmative action under Title VII and the test under the Constitution is similar, the Supreme Court has emphasized that the tests are distinct and different. In two cases that dealt with the constitutionality of using affirmative action criteria for admissions to the University of Michigan, and not with employment, *Grutter v. Bollinger* [123 S.Ct. 2325 (2003)] and *Gratz v. Bollinger* [123 S.Ct. 2411 (2003)], a majority of the Supreme Court held that achieving the educational benefits of a diverse student body was a compelling governmental interest. Those cases indicate that achieving the benefits of a diverse work force may be a sufficiently compelling governmental interest to justify the use of affirmative action programs for hiring or promotion decisions by public sector employers.

But in addition to being justified by a compelling governmental interest, the affirmative action program must also be narrowly tailored to achieve that purpose. The courts have held that affirmative action programs that give a relative preference rather than an absolute one—race or gender is used as a "plus factor" rather than as the determinative factor—are narrowly tailored. Programs that are temporary and that will cease when the employer achieves a more diverse work force have also been held to be narrowly tailored. However, an affirmative action program that required laying off or firing nonminority employees was held to be unconstitutional in *Wygant v. Jackson Board of Education*. The following case discusses the legality of an affirmative action plan under both Title VII and the Constitution.

University and Community College System of Nevada v. Farmer

113 Nev. 90, 930 P.2d 730 (Nev. Sup. Ct. 1997), cert. denied, 523 U.S. 1004 (March 9, 1998)

Background

Between 1989 and 1991, only one percent of the University of Nevada's full-time faculty were black, while eighty-seven to eighty-nine percent of the full-time faculty were white; twenty-five to twenty-seven percent of the full-time faculty were women. In order to remedy this racial imbalance, the University instituted the "minority bonus policy," an unwritten amendment to its affirmative action policy which allowed a department to hire an additional faculty member following the initial placement of a minority candidate.

In 1990, the University advertised for an impending vacancy in the sociology department. The announcement of the position vacancy emphasized a need for proficiency in social psychology and mentioned a salary range between $28,000.00 and $34,000.00, dependent upon experience and qualifications. The University's hiring guidelines require departments to conduct more than one interview; however, this procedure may be waived in certain cases. Yvette Farmer was one of the three finalists chosen by the search committee for the position but the University obtained a waiver to interview only one candidate, Johnson Makoba, a black African male emigrant. The department chair recalled that the search committee ranked Makoba first among the three finalists. Because of a perceived shortage of black Ph.D. candidates, coupled with Makoba's strong academic achievements, the search committee sought approval to make a job offer to Makoba at a salary of $35,000.00, with an increase to $40,000.00 upon completing his Ph.D. This initial offer exceeded the advertised salary range for the position; even though Makoba had not accepted any competing offers, the University justified its offer as a method of preempting any other institutions from hiring Makoba. Makoba accepted the job offer. Farmer was subsequently hired by the University the following year; the position for which she was hired was created under the "minority bonus policy." Her salary was set at $31,000.00 and a $2,000.00 raise after completion of her dissertation.

Farmer sued the University and Community College System of Nevada ("the University") claiming violations of Title VII of the Civil Rights Act, the Equal Pay Act and for breach of an employment contract. Farmer alleged that despite the fact that she was more qualified, the University hired a black male (Makoba) as an assistant professor of sociology instead of her because of the University's affirmative action plan. After a trial on her claims, the trial court jury awarded her $40,000 in damages, and the University appealed to the Supreme Court of Nevada. The issue on appeal was the legality of the University's affirmative action plan under both Title VII and the U.S. Constitution.

Steffen, Chief Justice

. . . Farmer claims that she was more qualified for the position initially offered to Makoba. However, the curriculum vitae for both candidates revealed comparable strengths with respect to their educational backgrounds, publishing, areas of specialization, and teaching experience. The search committee concluded that despite some inequalities, their strengths and weaknesses complemented each other; hence, as a result of the additional position created by the minority bonus policy, the department hired Farmer one year later. . . .

The University contends that the district court made a substantial error of law by failing to enter a proposed jury instruction which would have apprised the jury that Title VII does not proscribe race-based affirmative action programs designed to remedy the effects of past discrimination against traditionally disadvantaged classes. The University asserts that the district court's rejection of the proposed instruction left the jury with the impression that all race-based affirmative action programs are proscribed. . . .

Farmer . . . asserts that the University's unwritten minority bonus policy contravenes its published affirmative action plan. Finally, Farmer alleges that all race-based affirmative action plans are proscribed under Title VII of the Civil Rights Act as amended in 1991; therefore, the University discriminated against her as a female, a protected class under Title VII.

Tension exists between the goals of affirmative action and Title VII's proscription against employment practices which are motivated by considerations of race, religion, sex, or national origin, because Congress failed to provide a statutory exception for affirmative action under Title VII. Until recently, the Supreme Court's failure to achieve a majority opinion in affirmative action cases has produced schizophrenic results. . . .

United Steelworkers of America v. Weber is the seminal case defining permissible voluntary affirmative action plans [under Title VII]. . . . Under *Weber,* a permissible voluntary affirmative action plan must: (1) further Title VII's statutory purpose by "break[ing] down old patterns of racial segregation and hierarchy" in "occupations which have been traditionally closed to them"; (2) not "unnecessarily trammel the interests of white employees"; (3) be "a temporary measure; it is not intended to maintain racial balance, but simply to eliminate a manifest racial imbalance." . . .

Most recently, in *Adarand Constructors, Inc. v. Pena,* the Supreme Court revisited [the issue of the constitutionality of] affirmative action in the context of a minority set-aside program in federal highway construction. In the 5–4 opinion, the Court held that a reviewing court must apply strict scrutiny analysis for all race-based affirmative action programs, whether enacted by a federal, state, or local entity. . . . [T]he Court explicitly stated "that federal racial classifications, like those of a State, must serve a compelling governmental interest, and must be narrowly tailored to further that interest." . . .

Here, in addition to considerations of race, the University based its employment decision on such criteria as educational background, publishing, teaching experience, and areas of specialization. This satisfies [the previous cases'] commands that race must be only one of several factors used in evaluating applicants. We also view the desirability of a racially diverse faculty as sufficiently analogous to the constitutionally permissible attainment of a racially diverse student body. . . .

The University's affirmative action plan conforms to the *Weber* factors [under Title VII]. The University's attempts to diversify its faculty by opening up positions traditionally closed to minorities satisfies the first factor under *Weber*. Second, the plan does not "unnecessarily trammel the interests of white employees." The University's 1992 Affirmative Action Report revealed that whites held eighty-seven to eighty-nine percent of the full-time faculty positions. Finally, with blacks occupying only one percent of the faculty positions, it is clear that through its minority bonus policy, the University attempted to attain, as opposed to maintain, a racial balance.

The University's affirmative action plan . . . [also] passes constitutional muster. The University demonstrated that it has a compelling interest in fostering a culturally and ethnically diverse faculty. A failure to attract minority faculty perpetuates the University's white enclave and further limits student exposure to multicultural diversity. Moreover, the minority bonus policy is narrowly tailored to accelerate racial and gender diversity. Through its affirmative action policies, the University achieved greater racial and gender diversity by hiring Makoba and Farmer. Of note is the fact that Farmer's position is a direct result of the minority bonus policy.

Although Farmer contends that she was more qualified for Makoba's position, the search committee determined that Makoba's qualifications slightly exceeded Farmer's. The record, however, reveals that both candidates were equal in most respects. Therefore, given the aspect of subjectivity involved in choosing between candidates, the University must be given the latitude to make its own employment decisions provided that they are not discriminatory.

[The court then rejected Farmer's claim that the 1991 amendments to Title VII prohibit affirmative action.]

. . . we conclude that the jury was not equipped to understand the necessary legal basis upon which it could reach its factual conclusions concerning the legality of the University's affirmative action plan. Moreover, the undisputed facts of this case warranted judgment in favor of the University as a matter of law. Therefore, even if the jury had been properly instructed, the district court should have granted the University's motion for judgment notwithstanding the [jury's] verdict. Reversal of the jury's verdict on the Title VII claim is therefore in order.

The University . . . has adopted a lawful race-conscious affirmative action policy in order to remedy the effects of a manifest racial imbalance in a traditionally segregated job category. . . .

The University has aggressively sought to achieve more than employment neutrality by encouraging its departments to hire qualified minorities, women, veterans, and handicapped individuals. The minority bonus policy, albeit an unwritten one, is merely a tool for achieving cultural diversity and furthering the substantive goals of affirmative action.

For the reasons discussed above, the University's affirmative action policies pass constitutional muster. Farmer has failed to raise any material facts or law which would render the University's affirmative action policy constitutionally infirm. . . .

YOUNG and ROSE, JJ., concur.

SPRINGER, J., dissenting [omitted]

Case Questions

1. Why did the University adopt its affirmative action plan and the "minority bonus policy"?
2. How was Farmer injured or disadvantaged under the University's affirmative action plan?
3. How does the court here apply the *Weber* test for legality of affirmative action under Title VII to the facts of this case? Explain your answer.
4. According to the court here, how does the constitutional "strict scrutiny" test apply to the facts of the case here? Explain your answer.

The affirmative action plan in the previous case was a voluntary plan; that is, it was not imposed upon the employer by a court to remedy a finding of illegal discrimination. The affirmative action plans in the *Weber, Johnson,* and *Wygant* cases were also voluntary plans. Title VII specifically mentions affirmative action as a

ETHICAL DILEMMA

You are the human resource manager for Wydget Corporation, a small manufacturing company. Wydget's assembly plant is located in an inner-city neighborhood, and most of its production employees are African Americans and Hispanics, as well as some Vietnamese and Laotians who live nearby. Wydget's managers are white males who sometimes have difficulty relating to the production workers. The board of directors of Wydget is considering whether to establish a training program to groom production workers for management positions, targeting women and minorities in particular. The CEO has asked you to prepare a memo to guide the board of directors in its decision about the training program. Should you establish such a program? How can you encourage minority employees to enter the program without discouraging the white employees? What criteria should be used for determining admission into the training program? Please address these issues in a short memo, explaining and supporting your position.

possible remedy available under § 706(g)(1). In *Local 28, Sheet Metal Workers Int. Ass'n. v. EEOC* [478 U.S. 421 (1986)], the Supreme Court held that Title VII permits a court to require the adoption of an affirmative action program to remedy "persistent or egregious discrimination." The Court in *U.S. v. Paradise* [480 U.S. 149 (1987)] upheld the constitutionality of a judicially imposed affirmative action program to remedy race discrimination in promotion decisions by the Alabama State Police.

OTHER PROVISIONS OF TITLE VII

The 1991 amendments to Title VII added two other provisions to the act. One addresses the ability to challenge affirmative action programs and other employment practices that implement judicial decisions or result from consent decrees. Section 703(n) now provides that such practice may not be challenged by any person who had notice of such decision or decree and had an opportunity to present objections or by any person whose interests were adequately represented by another person who had previously challenged the judgment or decree on the same legal ground and with a similar factual situation. Challenges based on claims that the order or decree was obtained through fraud or collusion, is "transparently invalid," or was entered by a court lacking jurisdiction are not prevented by Section 703(n).

Find **http://bostonreview.net/ndf.html** *and scroll down the contents to find the forum on "The Future of Affirmative Action"; note that this discussion predates the recent Supreme Court decisions dealing with the University of Michigan—Gratz v. Bollinger and Gutter v. Bollinger*

The other added provision deals with the practice known as "race norming." Race norming refers to the use of different cutoff scores for different racial, gender, or ethnic groups of applicants or adjusting test scores or otherwise altering test results of employment-related tests on the basis of race, color, religion, sex, or national origin. Section 703(l) makes race norming an unlawful employment practice under Title VII.

SUMMARY

- Equal employment opportunity (EEO) legislation represents a statutory limitation on the employment-at-will doctrine: The EEO laws prohibit termination and other forms of employment discrimination because of an employee's race, color, gender, religion, or national origin. Title VII of the Civil Rights Act of 1964, as amended, protects all individuals from intentional discrimination (known as disparate treatment) as well as the unintentionally discriminatory effect of apparently neutral criteria that are not job related (known as disparate impact).
- Employers are free to hire employees who can effectively perform the job. The Uniform Guidelines on Employee Selection define methods for employers to demonstrate that employment selection criteria are job related; employers can use content-related, criterion-related, or construct-related validity studies to meet the requirements of § 703(k). Employers are also free to use seniority for employment decisions, as long as the seniority system is bona fide under § 703(h) of Title VII.
- Affirmative action, giving some employees preferential treatment because of their race, color, or gender, has become more controversial in recent years. Remedial affirmative action, designed to remedy the lingering effects of prior illegal discrimination, has been endorsed by the courts; the *Weber* and *Johnson* decisions allow voluntary affirmative action under Title VII when it is consistent with the purposes of the act and does not unduly harm those persons who are not of the preferred group. More recent decisions of the U.S. Supreme Court indicate that the Court will look very closely at an employer's justification for adopting an affirmative action program.

QUESTIONS

1. What are the main provisions of Title VII of the Civil Rights Act? Which employers are subject to Title VII?
2. What is meant by a bona fide occupational qualification (BFOQ)? What must be shown to establish that job-selection requirements are a BFOQ?
3. What is meant by disparate treatment? What is meant by disparate impact? How can a claim of disparate impact be demonstrated?
4. Can an employer use employment testing to select employees? Explain your answer. What must an employer show to continue to use job requirements held to have a disparate impact on a protected group of employees or applicants?
5. What is meant by the bottom line defense? Is it a sufficient answer to a claim of employment discrimination? Explain your answer.
6. When is a seniority system protected against challenge under Title VII? When is a seniority system bona fide under Title VII?
7. When are affirmative action programs legal under Title VII? Explain your answer.
8. What is the scope of protection against retaliation under § 704(a)?

CASE PROBLEMS

1. More than forty years ago, the Philadelphia Electric Company recognized the Independent Group Association (IGA) as the representative of its employee members for the presentation of grievances to management. Several employees formed the Black Grievance Committee (BGC) in response to their perception that the IGA was unresponsive to the employer's alleged discriminatory practices. The employer refused to recognize or deal with the BGC, insisting that the IGA was to have exclusive recognition for grievance purposes.

   Is the Philadelphia Electric Company guilty of race discrimination in refusing to recognize the BGC? See *Black Grievance Committee v. NLRB* [749 F.2d 1072 (3d Cir. 1984), *cert. denied*, 472 U.S. 1008 (1985)].

2. The city of Montgomery, Alabama, had a policy for its fire department that any firefighter convicted of a felony would be discharged. In August 1998, two white firefighters were fired after being convicted of felonies. However, on appealing their discharges to the Montgomery City-County Personnel Board, they were reinstated. In November 1999, Tate Williams, an African American man, was discharged, and on appeal, the board refused reinstatement.

   Was this refusal race discrimination? Does your answer depend on whether the white firefighters had committed less serious felonies than Williams? Should the board have considered each man's overall record in rendering its decisions? Are there any other factors the board should have taken into account? See *Williams v. City of Montgomery* [742 F.2d 586, 37 F.E.P. Cases 52 (11th Cir. 1984)].

3. In November 1997, a supervisor saw white employee Bill Peterson accept from an employee of another company on the same construction site what appeared to be a marijuana cigarette. Peterson subsequently confessed to taking a few puffs from the "joint," and he was fired. A day later, the company put out a general hiring call; Peterson applied and was rehired. In August 1998, the company promulgated a new rule that anyone fired could not be rehired for at least thirty days. In October 1998, Albert Leonard, an African American man, was hired as a laborer. During a routine lunchbox check by a security guard at the gate that very day, Leonard was found to be in possession of marijuana. He was fired the next day, and his termination notice contained a notation "not for rehire." Leonard was never rehired, either within or after thirty days from his discharge.

   Is he a victim of race discrimination? Explain your answer. See *Leonard v. Walsh Construction Co.* [37 F.E.P. Cases 60 (U.S. Dist. Ct. S.D. Ga. 1985)].

4. Sue Bedean, an engineer, was hired by the Tennessee Valley Authority under a voluntarily adopted affirmative action plan designed to bring females into traditionally male technical jobs. After a few months on the job, Bedean was laid off because of economic conditions; the other two engineers in her department, who were both male, were not laid off. The employer asserted that the two male engineers were more qualified than Bedean. Bedean filed suit under Title VII, arguing that the employer's failure to give her preference on layoff was a violation of the affirmative action program and of Title VII.

   Is the employer required by Title VII to continue to give preference to Bedean, after hiring her under an affirmative action program? Is a violation of the affirmative action program a violation of Title VII? Explain your answer. See *Liao v. TVA* [867 F.2d 1366 (11th Cir. 1989)].

5. Chaline, a white male, was employed as a production manager at an African-American-oriented radio station in Houston. Chaline had previously worked as a disc jockey at other radio stations. The radio station manager, for

financial reasons, decided to combine the production manager position with that of a part-time disc jockey. Chaline desired to remain as production manager and to assume the disc jockey duties. However, the station manager told him that he lacked the proper "voice" to serve as disc jockey on the station and that he was not sensitive to the listening tastes of the African American audience. The radio station had never had a white disc jockey. The station manager asked Chaline to transfer to a position in the sales department; Chaline refused and was discharged. Chaline filed a complaint with the EEOC challenging his discharge on grounds of race discrimination.

If the complaint results in a suit in federal court, will Chaline be successful? Explain your answer. See *Chaline v. KCOH, Inc.* [693 F.2d 477 (5th Cir. 1982)].

6. The city of South Bend, Indiana, adopted an affirmative action plan to give preference to minorities in hiring and promotion for police and firefighter positions. The affirmative action plan was adopted voluntarily by the city in response to the marked disparity between the percentage of African American employees in the police and fire departments with the percentage of African Americans in the general population of the city. Janowiak, a white, filed suit challenging the affirmative action plan; he argued that the city should have compared the percentage of African American employees in the police and fire departments with the percentage of African Americans in the qualified area labor pool to determine whether the affirmative action plan was necessary.

How will the court rule on his challenge? What is the proper comparison to determine whether the affirmative action plan is justified? See *Janowiak v. Corporate City of South Bend* [836 F.2d 1034 (7th Cir. 1987), *cert. denied*, 489 U.S. 1051 (1989)].

7. Crystal Chambers, a twenty-two-year-old unmarried African American woman, was employed by the Girls Club of Omaha, Nebraska. The club, whose membership was more than half African American, had as its stated goal to "provide a safe alternative from the streets and to help girls take care of themselves." Because of two incidents of unwed motherhood among staff members, the club's directors passed a Negative Role Model Policy, which stated that any unwed employee who became pregnant would be terminated. Pursuant to this policy, Chambers was fired when she became pregnant.

Can you suggest a theory under which Chambers could challenge her discharge based on race discrimination? Can the girls club articulate a bona fide business reason sufficient to overcome a finding of race discrimination? See *Chambers v. Omaha Girls Club* [834 F.2d 697 (8th Cir. 1987)].

8. King was hired by the University of Minnesota as a full, tenured professor in 1990. He was appointed to the Afro-American Studies Department and later became chairman. Four years later, he was asked to step down as chairman. The university alleged it had received many complaints from King's students and colleagues concerning poor teaching, absence from class, low enrollment, and undocumented research. Consequently, the university repeatedly denied King salary increases and ultimately approved a 9-2 vote in his department to fire him, pursuant to the complex procedures in the school's tenure code.

Assuming that King was guilty as charged, what arguments, if any, remain available to him if he tries to challenge his dismissal on the basis of race discrimination? See *King v. University of Minnesota* [774 F.2d. 224 (8th Cir. 1985), *cert. denied*, 475 U.S. 1095 (1986)].

9. Since his childhood, Dennis Walters, a white man, had dreamed of becoming director of the Atlanta Cyclorama, a gigantic display depicting a famous Civil War battle. Before ever applying for this position, Walters gained experience in historical preservation with the Georgia Historical Commission and the North Carolina Museum of History. Despite this experience, every time he applied for the post (which became available in 1996), he was rejected. First, an African American female who had been a campaign aide to Atlanta's mayor was selected. When she left the job a year later, Walters reapplied. He was judged qualified, but when an African American applicant was ruled unqualified, the position was reannounced rather than being offered to Walters or any other white candidate. Next, an African American male was hired. When he was fired a short time later, Walters again applied. This time a white female was hired. Walters filed a reverse race discrimination charge with the EEOC.

Was Walters a victim of race discrimination? Does it matter whether the white female who ultimately got the job was better qualified than Walters? If Walters wins, what remedy should he receive? See *Walters v. City of Atlanta* [803 F.2d 1135 (11th Cir. 1986)].

10. A group of African American steelworkers employed by the Lukens Steel Company alleged that they were victims of racial discrimination in their treatment by the company. At the same time, they charged their union with illegal discrimination in violation of Title VII, asserting that the union failed to vigorously pursue their grievances against the company.

Should the courts entertain this claim against the union? Is there a possible preemption problem? If allowed to sue their union, what remedy should the African American employees seek against the labor organization? See *United Steelworkers v. Goodman* [479 U.S. 982 (1986)].

INTERNET EXERCISES

1. Your boss, the vice president for human resources, informs you that the firm is considering the creation of a "diversity program" that would seek to hire qualified minority candidates into managerial and technical jobs. At present, almost all managers and technical personnel are white males. You need to determine whether the diversity program would be acceptable under the EEOC regulations on affirmative action plans. Go to the EEOC Web site at **http://www.eeoc.gov** and click the link to Laws, Regulations and Policy Guidelines. Then click the link to EEOC Regulations. Now click the link to "Affirmative action appropriate under Title VII of the Civil Rights Act of 1964, as amended."

2. What do the EEOC regulations state regarding the establishment of voluntary affirmative action plans?

What other guidance does the EEOC Web site provide for employers concerning affirmative action plans?

INFOTRAC KEYWORDS

http://www.infotrac-college.com

Title VII, disparate treatment, disparate impact, affirmative action, race norming

4 CHAPTER

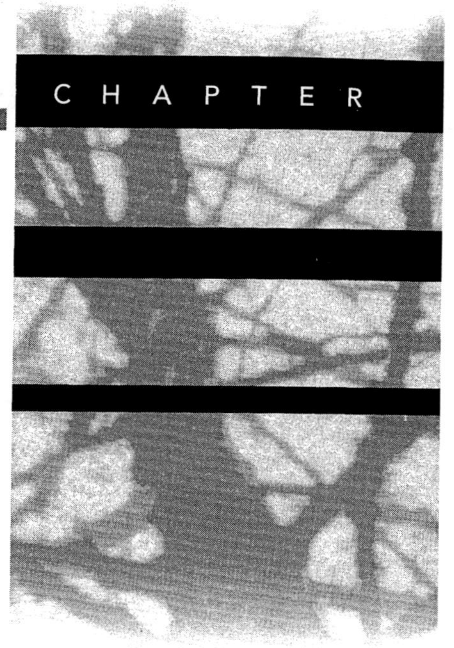

GENDER AND FAMILY ISSUES LEGISLATION: TITLE VII AND OTHER LEGISLATION

The preceding chapter introduced Title VII of the Civil Rights Act of 1964 and discussed its prohibitions on employment discrimination based on race. This chapter focuses on discrimination based on gender, family-related issues, and the relevant provisions of Title VII and other legislation.

GENDER DISCRIMINATION

Title VII prohibits any discrimination in terms or conditions of employment because of an employee's sex; it also prohibits limiting, segregating, or classifying employees or applicants in any way that would deprive individuals of employment opportunities or otherwise adversely affect their status as employees because of their sex. (While some people may argue that sex is a biological or physical construct and gender is a psychological and sociological construct, the courts have generally treated the terms *sex* and *gender* as interchangeable.) Title VII protects all individuals from employment discrimination based on sex or gender; this means both men and women are covered. Employers who refuse to hire an individual for a particular job because of that individual's gender violate Title VII, unless the employer can demonstrate that being of a particular gender is a bona fide occupational qualification (BFOQ) for that job. The act also prohibits advertising for male or female employees in

http://www.access.gpo.gov/nara/cfr/waisidx_00/29cfr1604_00.html

help-wanted notices (unless it is a BFOQ) or maintaining separate seniority lists for male and female employees. Unions that negotiate such separate seniority lists or refuse to admit female members also violate Title VII.

DRESS CODES AND GROOMING REQUIREMENTS

The act prohibits imposing different working conditions or requirements on similarly situated male and female employees because of the employee's gender. Some cases have involved employer dress codes and grooming standards. Employers need not have identical dress code or grooming requirements for men and women. For example, men may be required to wear a necktie while women are not, *Fountain v. Safeway Stores, Inc.* [555 F.2d 753 (9th Cir. 1977)]; men may be required to wear suits while women must wear "appropriate business attire," *Baker v. California Land Title Co.* [507 F.2d 895 (9th Cir. 1974), *cert. denied,* 422 U.S. 1046 (1975)]; or women may be permitted to wear long hair while males are not permitted to have hair below the collar, *Willingham v. Macon Tel. Publishing Co.* [507 F.2d 1084 (5th Cir. 1975)]. The key is that the standards are related to commonly accepted social norms and are reasonably related to legitimate business needs; however, an employer who requires women to wear a uniform but has no such requirement for men violates Title VII, *Carroll v. Talman Federal Savings & Loan Assoc.* [604 F.2d 1028 (7th Cir. 1979), *cert. denied,* 445 U.S. 929 (1980)].

GENDER AS A BFOQ

As mentioned in Chapter 3, the act does allow employers to hire only employees of one sex, or of a particular religion or national origin, if that trait is a BFOQ; most BFOQ cases involve BFOQs based on gender. Section 703(e)(1), which defines the BFOQ exemption, states that

> . . . it shall not be an unlawful employment practice for an employer to hire and employ employees, for an employment agency to classify, or refer for employment any individual, for a labor organization to classify its membership or to classify or refer for employment any individual . . . on the basis of his religion, sex, or national origin in those certain instances where religion, sex, or national origin is a bona fide occupational qualification reasonably necessary to the normal operation of that particular business or enterprise. . . .

The statute requires that an employer justify a BFOQ on the basis of business necessity; that is, the safe and efficient performance of the job in question requires that the employee be of a particular gender, religion, or national origin. Employer convenience, customer preference, or co-worker preference is not sufficient to support a BFOQ. The additional costs required by providing bathroom facilities for female workers was also not a sufficient basis to establish a BFOQ. What must an employer demonstrate to establish a claim of business necessity? The following cases illustrate the approach taken by the courts when an employer claims a BFOQ based on gender.

Diaz v. Pan American World Airways

442 F.2d 385 (U.S. Court of Appeals for the Fifth Circuit, 1971)

Tuttle, J.

. . . Celio Diaz applied for a job as flight cabin attendant with Pan American Airlines in 1967. He was rejected because Pan Am had a policy of restricting its hiring for that position to females. He then filed charges with the Equal Employment Opportunity Commission (EEOC) alleging that Pan Am had unlawfully discriminated against him on the grounds of sex. The Commission found probable cause to believe his charge, but was unable to resolve the matter through conciliation with Pan Am. Diaz next filed a class action in the United States District Court for the Southern District of Florida on behalf of himself and others similarly situated, alleging that Pan Am had violated Section 703 of the 1964 Civil Rights Act by refusing to employ him on the basis of his sex . . .

Pan Am admitted that it had a policy of restricting its hiring for the cabin attendant position to females. Thus . . . the primary issue for the District Court was whether, for the job of flight cabin attendant, being a female is a "bona fide occupational qualification (hereafter BFOQ) reasonably necessary to the normal operation" of Pan American's business. . . .

We note, at the outset, that there is little legislative history to guide our interpretation. The amendment adding the word "sex" to "race, color, religion and national origin" was adopted one day before House passage of the Civil Rights Act. . . . [H]owever, it is reasonable to assume, from a reading of the statute itself, that one of Congress' main goals was to provide equal access to the job market for both men and women. . . .

[W]e adopt the EEOC guidelines which state that "the Commission believes that the bona fide occupational qualification as to sex should be interpreted narrowly." Indeed, close scrutiny of the language of the exception compels this result. . . .

Thus, it is with this orientation that we now examine the trial court's decision. Its conclusion was based upon (1) its view of Pan Am's history of the use of flight attendants; (2) passenger preference; (3) basic psychological reasons for the preference; and (4) the actualities of the hiring process.

Having reviewed the evidence submitted by Pan American regarding its own experience with both female and male cabin attendants it had hired over the years, the trial court found that Pan Am's current hiring policy was the result of a pragmatic process, "representing a judgment made upon adequate evidence acquired through Pan Am's considerable experience, and designed to yield under Pan Am's current operating conditions better *average* performance for its passengers than would a policy of mixed male and female hiring." [emphasis added] The performance of female attendants was *better* in the sense that they were *superior* in such non-mechanical aspects of the job as "providing reassurance to anxious passengers, giving courteous personalized service and, in general, making flights as pleasurable as possible within the limitations imposed by aircraft operations."

The trial court also found that Pan Am's passengers overwhelmingly preferred to be served by female stewardesses. Moreover, on the basis of the expert testimony of a psychiatrist, the court found that an airplane cabin represents a unique environment in which an air carrier is required to take account of the special psychological needs of its passengers. These psychological needs are better attended to by females. This is not to say that there are no males who would not [sic] have the necessary qualities to perform these non-mechanical functions, but the trial court found that the actualities of the hiring process would make it more difficult to find these few males. Indeed, "the admission of men to the hiring process, in the present state of the art of employment selection, would have increased the number of unsatisfactory employees hired, and reduced the average levels of performance of Pan Am's complement of flight attendants. . . ." In what appears to be a summation of the difficulties which the trial court found would follow from admitting males to this job the court said "that to eliminate the female sex qualification would simply eliminate the best available tool for screening out applicants *likely* to be unsatisfactory and thus reduce the *average* level of performance." [emphasis added]

Because of the narrow reading we give to Section 703(e), we do not feel that these findings justify the discrimination practiced by Pan Am.

We begin with the proposition that the use of the word "necessary" in Section 703(e) requires that we apply a business *necessity* test, not a business *convenience* test. That is to say, discrimination based on sex is valid only when the *essence* of the business operation would be undermined by not hiring members of one sex exclusively.

The primary function of an airline is to transport passengers safely from one point to another. While a pleasant environment, enhanced by the obvious cosmetic effect that female stewardesses provide as well as, according to the finding of the trial court, their apparent ability to perform the non-mechanical functions of the job in a more effective manner than most men, may all be important, they are tangential to the essence of the business involved. No one has suggested that having male stewards will so seriously affect the operation of an airline as to jeopardize or even minimize its ability to provide safe transportation from one place to another. Indeed the record discloses that many airlines including Pan Am have utilized both men and women flight cabin attendants in the past and Pan Am, even at the time of this suit, has 283 male stewards employed on some of its foreign flights.

We do not mean to imply, of course, that Pan Am cannot take into consideration the ability of *individuals* to perform the non-mechanical functions of the job. What we hold is that because the non-mechanical aspects of the job of flight cabin attendant are not "reasonably necessary to the normal operation" of Pan Am's business, Pan Am cannot exclude all males simply because most males may not perform adequately. . . .

We do not agree that in this case "all or substantially all men" have been shown to be inadequate. . . .

Appellees also argue, and the trial court found, that because of the actualities of the hiring process, "the best available initial test for determining whether a particular applicant for employment is likely to have the personality characteristics conducive to high-level performance of the flight attendant's job as currently defined is consequently that applicant's biological sex." Indeed, the trial court found that it was simply not practicable to find the few males that would perform properly.

We do not feel that this alone justifies discriminating against all males. Since, as stated above, the basis of exclusion is the ability to perform non-mechanical functions which we find to be tangential to what is "reasonably *necessary*" for the business involved, the exclusion of *all* males because this is the *best* way to select the kind of personnel Pan Am desires simply cannot be justified. Before sex discrimination can be practiced, it must not only be shown that it is impracticable to find the men that possess the abilities that most women possess, but that the abilities are *necessary* to the business, not merely tangential.

Similarly, we do not feel that the fact that Pan Am's passengers prefer female stewardesses should alter our judgment. On this subject, EEOC guidelines state that a BFOQ ought not to be based on "the refusal to hire an individual because of the preferences of co-workers, the employer, clients or customers. . . ."

. . . Thus, we feel that customer preference may be taken into account only when it is based on the company's inability to perform the primary function or service it offers.

Of course, Pan Am argues that the customers' preferences are not based on "stereotyped thinking," but the ability of women stewardesses to better provide the non-mechanical aspects of the job. Again, as stated above, since these aspects are tangential to the business, the fact that customers prefer them cannot justify sex discrimination.

The judgment is reversed and the case remanded for proceedings not inconsistent with this opinion.

So ordered.

Case Questions

1. Why did Pan Am prefer female flight attendants? According to Pan Am, how were they superior to male flight attendants?
2. What was the essence of the flight attendant's job? Was being female necessary for the safe and efficient performance of that job?
3. When can an employer refuse to hire male employees for a particular job? What must be shown to support that decision? Explain your answers.

In *Dothard v. Rawlinson* [433 U.S. 321 (1977)], the U.S. Supreme Court held that the dangers presented by the conditions in Alabama maximum security prisons, characterized as "rampant violence" and "a jungle atmosphere," would reduce the ability of female guards to maintain order and would pose dangers to the female guards and to other prisoners. The Court therefore upheld as a BFOQ an Alabama state regulation restricting guard positions in maximum security prisons to persons of the same gender as the prisoners being guarded.

The courts will also allow claims of a BFOQ based on gender when community standards of morality or propriety require that employees be of a particular gender. Examples include hiring females only to work as attendants in the fitting rooms of a women's dress shop and hiring males as locker-room attendants for the men's locker rooms in an athletic club.

GENDER STEREOTYPING

If an employer refuses to promote a female employee because, despite her excellent performance, she is perceived as being too aggressive and unfeminine, has the employer engaged in sex discrimination in violation of Title VII? This question was addressed by the Supreme Court in the following case.

PRICE WATERHOUSE V. ANN B. HOPKINS

490 U.S. 228 (1989)

Background

Ann Hopkins, a senior manager in an office of Price Waterhouse, was proposed for partnership in 1982. She was neither offered nor denied admission to the partnership; instead, her candidacy was held for reconsideration the following year. When the partners in her office later refused to repropose her for partnership, she sued under Title VII of the Civil Rights Act of 1964, charging that the firm had discriminated against her on the basis of sex in its decisions regarding partnership. Judge Gesell in the District Court for the District of Columbia ruled in her favor on the question of liability and the Court of Appeals for the District of Columbia Circuit affirmed. The Supreme Court granted certiorari.

Brennan, J.

At Price Waterhouse, a nationwide professional accounting partnership, a senior manager becomes a candidate for partnership when the partners in her local office submit her name as a candidate. All the other partners in the firm are then invited to submit written comments on each candidate—either on a "long" or a "short" form, depending on the partner's degree of exposure to the candidate. Not every partner in the firm submits comments on every candidate. After reviewing the comments and interviewing the partners who submitted them, the firm's Admissions Committee makes a recommendation to the Policy Board. This recommendation will be either that the firm accept the candidate for partnership, put her application on "hold," or deny her the promotion outright. The Policy Board then decides whether to submit the candidate's name to the entire partnership for a vote, to "hold" her candidacy, or to reject her. The recommendation of the Admissions Committee, and the decision of the Policy Board, are not controlled by fixed guidelines: a certain number of positive comments from partners will not guarantee a candidate's admission to the partnership, nor will a specific quantity of negative comments necessarily defeat her application. . . .

Ann Hopkins had worked at Price Waterhouse's Office of Government Services in Washington, D.C. for five years when the partners in that office proposed her as a candidate for partnership. Of the 662 partners at the firm at that time, 7 were women. Of the 88 persons proposed for partnership that year, only 1—Hopkins—was a woman. Forty-seven of these candidates were admitted to the partnership, 21 were rejected, and 20—including Hopkins—were "held" for reconsideration the following year. Thirteen of the 32 partners who had submitted comments on Hopkins supported her bid for partnership. Three partners recommended that her candidacy be placed on hold, eight stated that they did not have an informed opinion about her, and eight recommended that she be denied partnership.

In a jointly prepared statement supporting her candidacy, the partners in Hopkins' office showcased her successful 2-year effort to secure a $25 million contract with the Department of State, labeling it "an outstanding performance" and one that Hopkins carried out "virtually at the partner level." . . . Judge Gesell specifically found that Hopkins had "played a key role in Price Waterhouse's successful effort to win a multi-million dollar contract with the Department of State." Indeed, he went on, "[n]one of the other partnership candidates at Price Waterhouse that year had a comparable record in terms of successfully securing major contracts for the partnership." The partners in Hopkins' office praised her character as well as her accomplishments, describing her in their joint statement as "an outstanding professional" who had a "deft touch," a "strong character, independence and integrity." Clients appear to have agreed with these assessments. . . . Evaluations such as these led Judge Gesell to conclude that Hopkins "had no difficulty dealing with clients and her clients appear to have been very pleased with her work" and that she "was generally viewed as a highly competent project leader who worked long hours, pushed vigorously to meet deadlines and demanded much from the multidisciplinary staffs with which she worked."

On too many occasions, however, Hopkins' aggressiveness apparently spilled over into abrasiveness. Staff members seem to have borne the brunt of Hopkins' brusqueness. Long before her bid for partnership, partners evaluating her work had counseled her to improve her relations with staff members. Although later evaluations indicate an improvement, Hopkins' perceived shortcomings in this important area eventually doomed her bid for partnership. Virtually all of the partners' negative remarks about Hopkins—even those of partners supporting her—had to do with her "interpersonal skills." Both "[s]upporters and opponents of her candidacy," stressed Judge Gesell, "indicated that she was sometimes overly aggressive, unduly harsh, difficult to work with and impatient with staff."

There were clear signs, though, that some of the partners reacted negatively to Hopkins' personality because she was a woman. One partner described her as "macho"; another suggested that she "overcompensated for being a woman"; a third advised her to take "a course at charm school." Several partners criticized her use of profanity; in response, one partner suggested that those partners objected to her swearing only "because it['] s a lady using foul language." Another supporter explained that Hopkins "ha[d] matured from a tough-talking somewhat masculine hard-nosed mgr to an authoritative, formidable, but much more appealing lady ptr candidate." But it was the man who, as Judge Gesell found, bore responsibility for explaining to Hopkins the reasons for the Policy Board's decision to place her candidacy on hold who delivered the *coup de grace:* in order to improve her chances for partnership, Thomas Beyer advised, Hopkins should "walk more femininely, talk more femininely, dress more femininely, wear make-up, have her hair styled, and wear jewelry."

Dr. Susan Fiske, a social psychologist and Associate Professor of Psychology at Carnegie-Mellon University, testified at trial that the partnership selection process at Price Waterhouse was likely influenced by sex stereotyping. Her testimony focused not only on the overtly sex-based comments of partners but also on gender-neutral remarks, made by partners who knew Hopkins only slightly, that were intensely critical of her. One partner, for example, baldly stated that Hopkins was "universally disliked" by staff, and another described her as "consistently annoying and irritating"; yet these were people who had had very little contact with Hopkins. According to Fiske, Hopkins' uniqueness (as the only woman in the pool of candidates) and the subjectivity of the evaluations made it likely that sharply critical remarks such as these were the product of sex stereotyping. . . .

In previous years, other female candidates for partnership also had been evaluated in sex-based terms. As a general matter, Judge Gesell concluded "[c]andidates were viewed favorably if partners believed they maintained their femin[in]ity while becoming effective professional managers"; in this environment, "[t]o be identified as a 'women's lib[b]er' was regarded as [a] negative comment." In fact, the judge found that in previous years "[o]ne partner repeatedly commented that he could not consider any woman seriously as a partnership candidate and believed that women were not even capable of functioning as senior managers—yet the firm took no action to discourage his comments and recorded his vote in the overall summary of the evaluations."

Judge Gesell found that Price Waterhouse legitimately emphasized interpersonal skills in its partnership decisions, and also found that the firm had not fabricated its complaints about Hopkins' interpersonal skills as a pretext for discrimination. Moreover, he concluded, the firm did not give decisive emphasis to such traits only because Hopkins was a woman; although there were male candidates who lacked these skills but who were admitted to partnership, the judge found that these candidates possessed other, positive traits that Hopkins lacked.

The judge went on to decide, however, that some of the partners' remarks about Hopkins stemmed from an impermissibly cabined view of the proper behavior of women, and that Price Waterhouse had done nothing to disavow reliance on such comments. He held that Price Waterhouse had unlawfully discriminated against Hopkins on the basis of sex by consciously giving credence and effect to partners' comments that resulted from sex stereotyping. Noting that Price Waterhouse could avoid equitable relief by proving by clear and convincing evidence that it would have placed Hopkins' candidacy on hold even absent this discrimination, the judge decided that the firm had not carried this heavy burden. . . .

Congress' intent to forbid employers to take gender into account in making employment decisions appears on the face of the statute. . . . We take these words [of Title VII] to mean that gender must be irrelevant to employment decisions. . . . The critical inquiry, the one commanded by the words of Section 703(a)(1), is whether gender was a factor in the employment decision *at the moment it was made*. Moreover, since we know that the words "because of" do not mean "*solely* because of," we also know that Title VII meant to condemn even those decisions based on a mixture of legitimate and illegitimate considerations. When, therefore, an employer considers both gender and legitimate factors at the time of making a decision, that decision was "because of" sex and the other, legitimate considerations—even if we may say later, in the context of litigation, that the decision would have been the same if gender had not been taken into account. . . .

. . . The central point is this: while an employer may not take gender into account in making an employment decision (except in those very narrow circumstances in which gender is a BFOQ), it is free to decide against a woman for other reasons. . . . the employer's burden is most appropriately deemed an affirmative defense: the plaintiff must persuade the factfinder on one point, and then the employer, if it wishes to prevail, must persuade it on another.

. . . our assumption always has been that if an employer allows gender to affect its decisionmaking process, then it must carry the burden of justifying its ultimate decision. . . .

In saying that gender played a motivating part in an employment decision, we mean that, if we asked the employer at the moment of the decision what its reasons were and if we received a truthful response, one of those reasons would be that the applicant or employee was a woman. In the specific context of sex stereotyping, an employer who acts on the basis of a belief that a woman cannot be aggressive, or that she must not be, has acted on the basis of gender. . . .

As to the existence of sex stereotyping in this case, we are not inclined to quarrel with the District Court's conclusion that a number of the partners' comments showed sex stereotyping at work. As for the legal relevance of sex stereotyping, we are beyond the day when an employer could evaluate employees by assuming or insisting that they matched the stereotype associated with their group, for "[i]n forbidding employers to discriminate against individuals because of their sex, Congress intended to strike at the entire spectrum of disparate treatment of men and women resulting from sex stereotypes." An employer who objects to aggressiveness in women but whose positions require this trait places women in an intolerable and impermissible Catch-22: out of a job if they behave aggressively and out of a job if they don't. Title VII lifts women out of this bind.

Remarks at work that are based on sex stereotypes do not inevitably prove that gender played a part in a particular employment decision. The plaintiff must show that the employer actually relied on her gender in making its decision. In making this showing, stereotyped remarks can certainly be evidence that gender played a part. In any event, the stereotyping in this case did not simply consist of stray remarks. On the contrary, Hopkins proved that Price Waterhouse invited partners to submit comments; that some of the comments stemmed from sex stereotyping; that an important part of the Policy Board's decision on Hopkins was an assessment of the submitted comments; and that Price Waterhouse in no way disclaimed reliance on the sex-linked evaluations. This is not, as Price Waterhouse suggests, "discrimination in the air"; rather, it is, as Hopkins puts it, "discrimination brought to ground and visited upon" an employee. . . .

In finding that some of the partners' comments reflected sex stereotyping, the District Court relied in part on Dr. Fiske's expert testimony. . . .

Indeed, we are tempted to say that Dr. Fiske's expert testimony was merely icing on Hopkins' cake. It takes no special training to discern sex stereotyping in a description of an aggressive female employee as requiring "a course at charm school." Nor, turning to Thomas Beyer's memorable advice to Hopkins, does it require expertise in psychology to know that, if an employee's flawed "interpersonal skills" can be corrected by a soft-hued suit or a new shade of lipstick, perhaps it is the employee's sex and not her interpersonal skills that has drawn the criticism.

. . . Hopkins showed that the partnership solicited evaluations from all of the firm's partners; that it generally relied very heavily on such evaluations in making its decision; that some of the partners' comments were the product of stereotyping; and that the firm in no way disclaimed reliance on those particular comments, either in Hopkins' case or in the past. Certainly a plausible—and, one might say, inevitable—conclusion to draw from this set of circumstances is that the Policy Board in making its decision did in fact take into account all of the partners' comments, including the comments that were motivated by stereotypical notions about women's proper deportment. . . .

Nor is the finding that sex stereotyping played a part in the Policy Board's decision undermined by the fact that many of the suspect comments were made by supporters rather than detractors of Hopkins. A negative comment, even when made in the context of a generally favorable review, nevertheless may influence the decisionmaker to think less highly of the candidate; the Policy Board, in fact, did not simply tally the "yes's" and "no's" regarding a candidate, but carefully reviewed the content of the submitted comments. The additional suggestion that the comments were made by "persons outside the decisionmaking chain"—and therefore could not have harmed Hopkins—simply ignores the critical role that partners' comments played in the Policy Board's partnership decisions.

. . . The District Judge acknowledged that Hopkins' conduct justified complaints about her behavior as a senior manager. But he also concluded that the reactions of at least some of the partners were reactions to her as a woman manager. Where an evaluation is based on a subjective assessment of a person's strengths and weaknesses, it is simply not true that each evaluator will focus on, or even mention, the same weaknesses. Thus, even if we knew that Hopkins had "personality problems," this would not tell us that the partners who cast their evaluations of Hopkins in sex-based terms would have criticized her as sharply (or criticized her at all) if she had been a man. It is not our job to review the evidence and decide that the negative reactions to Hopkins were based on reality; our perception of Hopkins' character is irrelevant. We sit not to determine whether Ms. Hopkins is nice, but to decide whether the partners reacted negatively to her personality because she is a woman.

. . . we remand the case to that court for further proceedings.

It is so ordered.

Case Questions

1. Was Hopkins qualified for promotion to partner? Explain your answer. What reasons did Price Waterhouse offer for its refusal to promote Hopkins to partner?
2. How did the partners' comments about Hopkins reflect gender stereotyping? What was the relevance of those comments? Does it matter that Price Waterhouse also had legitimate reasons for its reluctance to promote Hopkins?
3. Does an employer action based upon mixed motives, some of which include sex or race discrimination, violate Title VII? What defenses can an employer offer under such circumstances?

On remand from the Supreme Court, the District Court in *Hopkins* found that Ann Hopkins had been a victim of sex discrimination and ordered that Price Waterhouse make her a partner. See *Hopkins v. Price Waterhouse* [737 F. Supp. 1202, (D.D.C. 1990); aff'd., 970 F.2d 967 (D.C. Cir. 1990)]. In a case relying upon *Price Waterhouse v. Hopkins,* the U.S. Court of Appeals for the Ninth Circuit held that abuse and ridicule by co-workers and managers directed at a male employee because he appeared effeminate and did not conform to a male stereotype was "because of sex" for the purposes of establishing a claim under Title VII. See *Nichols v. Azteca Restaurant Enterprises, Inc.* [256 F.3d 864 (9th Cir. 2001)].

"GENDER-PLUS" DISCRIMINATION

An employer who places additional requirements on employees of a certain gender but not on employees of the opposite gender violates Title VII. For example, an employer who refuses to hire females having preschool-aged children but who does hire males with preschool-aged children is guilty of an unlawful employment practice under Title VII. Such discrimination is known as gender-plus discrimination; the additional requirement (no preschool-aged children) becomes an issue only for employees of a certain gender (female). Because similarly situated employees (men and women both with preschool-aged children) are treated differently because of their gender, the employer is guilty of gender discrimination. The Supreme Court held that an employer hiring men with preschool-aged children who refused to hire women with preschool-aged children violates Title VII in the case of *Phillips v. Martin Marietta Corp.* [400 U.S. 542 (1971)].

GENDER DISCRIMINATION IN PAY

Both Title VII and the Equal Pay Act apply to gender discrimination in pay. There is some overlap between Title VII and the Equal Pay Act, which was passed in 1963, a year before the passage of Title VII; there are also some differences in coverage, procedures, and remedies. This section discusses both the Equal Pay Act and the Title VII provisions relating to gender-based pay differentials.

THE EQUAL PAY ACT

The Equal Pay Act of 1963 requires that men and women performing substantially equal work be paid equally. The act does not reach other forms of gender discrimination or discrimination on grounds other than gender.

Coverage

The Equal Pay Act was enacted as an amendment to the Fair Labor Standards Act, which regulates minimum wages and maximum hours of employment. The Equal Pay Act's coverage is therefore similar to that of the Fair Labor Standards Act. The act applies to all employers "engaged in commerce (interstate commerce)," and it applies to all employees of an "enterprise engaged in commerce." Virtually all substantial business operations are covered. The Equal Pay Act coverage does not depend on a minimum number of employees; hence, the act may apply to firms having fewer than the fifteen employees required for Title VII coverage.

For the text of the Equal Pay Act of 1963, go to **http://www.eeoc.gov/policy/epa.html**

There are some exceptions to the coverage of the Equal Pay Act. These exceptions deal with operations that are exempted from the Fair Labor Standards Act. For example, certain small retail operations and small agricultural operations are excluded. Seasonal amusement operations and the fishing industry are also exempted from the act. The act does cover state and local government employees; the Congressional Accountability Act of 1995 [2 U.S.C. § 1301] extended the coverage of Fair Labor Standards Act, including the Equal Pay Act, to certain federal employees—the employees of the House of Representatives, the Senate, the Capitol Guide Service, the Capitol Police, the Congressional Budget Office, the Office of the Architect of the Capitol, the Office of the Attending Physician, and the Office of Technology Assessment.

Provisions

The Equal Pay Act prohibits discrimination by an employer

> between employees on the basis of sex by paying wages to employees in such establishment at a rate less than the rate at which he pays wages to employees of the opposite sex . . . for equal work on jobs the performance of which requires equal skill, effort, and responsibility, and which are performed under similar working conditions.

A plaintiff claiming violation of the Equal Pay Act must demonstrate that the employer is paying lower wages to employees of the opposite sex who are performing equal work in the same establishment. Note that the act does not require paying equal wages for work of equal value, known as comparable worth. The act requires only "equal pay for equal work." Work that is equal, or substantially equivalent, involves equal skills, effort, and responsibilities and is performed under similar working conditions.

Equal Work. When considering whether jobs involve substantially equivalent work under the Equal Pay Act, the courts do not consider job titles, job descriptions, or job classifications to be controlling. Rather, they evaluate each job on a case-by-case basis, making a detailed inquiry into the substantial duties and facts of each position.

Effort. Equal effort involves substantially equivalent physical or mental exertion needed for performance of the job. If an employer pays male employees more than female employees because of additional duties performed by the males, the employer must establish that the extra duties are a regular and recurring requirement and that they consume a substantial amount of time. Occasional or infrequent assignments of extra duties do not warrant additional pay for periods when no extra duties are performed. The employer must also show that the extra duties are commensurate with the extra pay. The employer who assigns extra duties only to male employees may face problems under Title VII unless the employer can demonstrate that being male is a bona fide occupational qualification (BFOQ) for performing the extra duties. Unless the employer can make the requisite showing of business necessity to justify a BFOQ, the extra duties must be available to both male and female employees.

Skill. Equal skill includes substantially equivalent experience, training, education, and ability. The skill, however, must relate to the performance of actual job duties. The employer cannot pay males more for possessing additional skills that are not used on the job. The act requires equal or substantially equivalent skills, not identical skills. Differences in the kinds of skills involved will not justify differentials in pay when the degree of skills required is substantially equal. For example, male hospital orderlies and female practical nurses may perform different duties requiring different skills, but if the general nature of their jobs is equivalent, the degree of skills required by each is substantially equal according to *Hodgson v. Brookhaven General Hospital* [436 F.2d 719 5th Cir. (1972)].

Responsibility. Equal responsibility includes a substantially equivalent degree of accountability required in the performance of a job, with emphasis on the importance of the job's obligations. When work of males and females is subject to similar supervisory review, the responsibility of males and females is equal. But when females work without supervision, whereas males are subject to supervision, the responsibility involved is not equal.

When considering the responsibility involved in jobs, the courts focus on the economic or social consequences of the employee's actions or decisions. Minor responsibility such as making coffee or answering telephones may not be an indication of different responsibility. The act does not require identical responsibility, only substantially equivalent responsibility. For instance, if a male employee is required to compile payroll lists and a female employee must make and deliver the payroll, the responsibilities may be substantially equivalent.

Working Conditions. The act requires that the substantially equivalent work be performed under similar working conditions. According to the 1974 Supreme Court decision in *Corning Glass Works v. Brennan* [417 U.S. 188], working conditions include the physical surroundings and hazards involved in a job. Exposure to heat, cold, noise, fumes, dust, risk of injury, or poor ventilation are examples of working conditions. Work performed outdoors involves different working conditions from work performed indoors. Work performed during the night shift, however, is not under different working conditions from the performance of the same work during the day.

The Equal Pay Act does not reach pay differentials for work that is not substantially equal in skill, effort, responsibility, and working conditions.

DEFENSES UNDER THE EQUAL PAY ACT

Although a plaintiff may establish that an employer is paying different wages for men and women performing work involving equivalent effort, skills, responsibility, and working conditions, the employer may not be in violation of the Equal Pay Act because the act provides several defenses to claims of unequal pay for equal work. When the pay differentials between the male and female employees are due to a seniority system, a merit pay system, a productivity-based pay system, or "a factor other than sex," the pay differentials do not violate the act.

Employers justifying pay differentials on seniority systems, merit pay systems, or production-based pay systems must demonstrate that the system is bona fide and applies equally to all employees. A merit pay system must be more than an ad hoc subjective determination of employees' merit, especially if there is no listing of criteria considered in establishing an employee's merit. Any such systems should be formal and objective to justify pay differentials.

The "factor other than sex" defense covers a wide variety of situations. A "shift differential," for example, involves paying a premium to employees who work during the afternoon or night shift. If the differential is uniformly available to all employees who work a particular shift, it qualifies as a "factor other than sex." But if females are precluded from working the night shift, a night-shift pay differential is not defensible under the act. A training program may be the basis of a pay differential if the program is bona fide; employees who perform similar work but are in training for higher positions may be paid more than those not in the training program. The training program should be open to both male and female employees, unless the employer can establish that gender is a BFOQ for admission to the program. In *Kouba v. Allstate Insurance Co.* [691 F.2d 873 (1982)], the U.S. Court of Appeals for the Ninth Circuit held that using an employee's prior salary to determine pay for employees in a training program was not precluded by the Equal Pay Act.

The following case is a good illustration of the court's inquiry into the alleged equality of jobs involved in an Equal Pay Act complaint.

Laffey v. Northwest Airlines

567 F.2d 429 (U.S. Court of Appeals, District of Columbia Circuit, 1976)

Robinson, J.

Northwest Airlines (NWA) appeals from a judgment of the District Court declaring certain of its personnel policies violative of the Equal Pay Act of 1963 and Title VII of the Civil Rights Act of 1964, and granting injunctive and monetary relief. The principal practice in issue here is the payment to women employed as stewardesses of salaries lower than those paid to men serving as pursers for work found by the court to be substantially equal. Others are the provision to stewardesses of less desirable layover accommodations and allowances for maintenance of uniforms. . . . NWA challenges findings of fact and conclusions of law on these matters. . . .

Between 1927 and 1947, all cabin attendants employed on NWA's aircraft were women, whom NWA classified as "stewardesses." In 1947, when the company initiated international service, it established a new cabin-attendant position of "purser," and for two decades thereafter adhered to an undeviating practice of restricting purser jobs to men alone. In implementation of this policy, NWA created another strictly all-male cabin-attendant classification—"flight service attendant"—to serve as a training and probationary position for future pursers. NWA has maintained a combined seniority list for pursers and flight service attendants, on which seniority as pursers accrued to flight service attendants immediately upon assumption of their duties as such, and a separate seniority list for stewardesses. From 1951 until 1967, flight service attendants had a contractual right to automatic promotion to purser vacancies in the order of their seniority.

It was not until 1967, when a new collective bargaining agreement was negotiated, that stewardesses first became contractually eligible to apply for purser positions. During negotiations on the issue, NWA, for both the 1967 agreement and another in 1970, rejected an additional union proposal that stewardesses, like flight service attendants, be allowed to progress to purser slots according to seniority, stating that the company "prefers males and intends to have them." The company . . . has imposed other restrictions on stewardesses seeking purser vacancies which had not previously been laid on flight service attendants.

Company policy had been to fill purser openings by hiring "men off the street" and training them for a short time, after which notices of purser vacancies would be posted. Following the 1967 collective bargaining agreement affording stewardesses access to these jobs, however, NWA hired five male purser-applicants without ever posting notices of the vacancies. In 1970, after three years of ostensibly open admission to purser status, NWA had 137 male cabin attendants—all as pursers—and 1,747 female cabin attendants—all but one as stewardesses.

The sole female purser at that time was Mary P. Laffey, who bid for a purser vacancy in 1967, after nine years' service as a stewardess. Although that purser position was scheduled to be filled in November, 1967, processing of her application was delayed assertedly for the reason that NWA needed to administer new tests to purser applicants. These tests had never previously been used in selecting pursers, and during the interim between Ms. Laffey's application and her appointment NWA hired two male pursers without benefit of any tests. Finally, in June, 1968, Ms. Laffey became a purser, but was placed on the bottom rung of the purser-salary schedule and received less than her income as a senior stewardess.

On this appeal, NWA does not challenge holdings by the District Court that Title VII was violated by NWA's refusal to hire female pursers. Rather, the appeal focuses primarily on whether the payment of unequal salaries to stewardesses and pursers, while occupying positions as such, implicates . . . the Equal Pay Act. The purser wage scale ranges from 20 to 55 percent higher than salaries paid to stewardesses of equivalent seniority. The Equal Pay Act forbids this pay differential unless greater skill, effort or responsibility is required to perform purser duties . . . the District Court analyzed in great detail NWA's flight operations . . .

Probing beneath the different titles, bidding schedules and salaries, the District Court made extensive factual findings comparing the work actually done by pursers and stewardesses, and held it to be essentially equal when considered as a whole.

Duties performed do not differ significantly in nature as between pursers and stewardesses. All must check cabins before departure, greet and seat passengers, prepare for take-off, and provide in-flight food, beverage and general services. All must complete required documentation, maintain cabin cleanliness, see that passengers comply with regulations and deplane passengers. The premier responsibility of any cabin attendant is to insure the safety of passengers during an emergency, and cabin attendants all must possess a thorough knowledge of emergency equipment and procedures on all aircraft. All attendants also must be knowledgeable in first aid techniques and must be able to handle the myriad of medical problems that arise in flight. Food service varies greatly between flights, but pursers engage in no duties that are not also performed on the same or another flight by the stewardesses. Another important duty—building goodwill between NWA and its passengers—depends on the poise, tact, friendliness, good judgment and adaptability of every cabin attendant, male or female. . . .

With respect to documentation responsibilities, the District Court found that pursers and stewardesses have different, but comparable, duties. . . .

The District Court found that "the documentary duties described which are . . . assigned only to pursers involved no greater skill, effort or responsibility than the stewardess job."

The District Court also examined another general, more intangible, duty advanced by NWA as a factor rendering the purser job different in kind from the stewardess position. The company's cabin service manual states that the senior purser on a flight will always be considered the senior cabin attendant and as such must coordinate the activities of the other attendants, and is to be held "responsible and accountable" for the proper rendering of service on that flight. But the manual further provides that if no purser is scheduled, the most senior stewardess will serve as senior flight attendant and will similarly be charged with coordination of cabin service, although she is accountable only for the conduct of service in the section of the aircraft in which she works, responsibility for the remainder being placed on the senior attendant in the other section of the aircraft.

Senior cabin attendants, be they purser or stewardess, have a number of supervisory duties. These include monitoring and, where necessary, correcting the work of other cabin attendants; determining the times of meals and movie showings; shifting cabin attendants from section to section to balance workloads; and giving pre-departure briefings on emergency equipment and procedures. On large planes, even if a purser in the first-class section is designated the senior cabin attendant, the senior in tourist shoulders these same burdens in her section of the aircraft—overseeing the great majority of passengers and cabin attendants. Stewardesses and pursers alike are subject to disciplinary action if they fail to carry out their "supervisory responsibilities."

There is, however, no merit system maintained to reward those who "supervise" better than others; all pursers and all stewardesses are on uniform, separate wage scales, regardless of whether—or how well—an individual performs. . . .

Careful evaluation of the facts comprehensively found led the District Court to conclude that NWA had discriminated against women cabin attendants on the basis of sex, in violation of Title VII and the Equal Pay Act, by compensating stewardesses and pursers unequally for equal work on "jobs the performance of which requires equal skill, effort and responsibility and which are performed under similar working conditions." More specifically the court found that NWA had discriminated in "willful violation" of the Equal Pay Act (a) by paying female stewardesses lower salaries and pensions than male pursers; (b) by providing female cabin attendants less expensive and less desirable layover accommodations than male cabin attendants; (c) by providing to male but not to female cabin attendants a uniform-cleaning allowance; and (d) "by paying Mary P. Laffey a lower salary as a purser than it pays to male pursers with equivalent length of cabin attendant service. . . ."

The claimant bears the onus of demonstrating that the work unequally recompensed was "equal" within the meaning of the Act. Once this has been done, the claimant will prevail unless the employer asserts an affirmative defense that the wage differential is justified under one of the four exceptions enumerated in the Act—"(i) a seniority system; (ii) a merit system; (iii) a system which measures earnings by quantity or quality of production; or (iv) a differential based on any other factor other than sex." If one or more of these defenses is invoked, the employer bears the burden of proving that his policies fall within an exempted area. . . .

Courts have consistently held that differences in the duties respectively assigned male and female employees must be "evaluated as part of the entire job." Thus, if in the aggregate the jobs require substantially similar skills, efforts and responsibilities, the work will be adjudged equal despite minor variations.

When there is a disparity between salaries paid men and women for similar positions bearing different titles—such as pursers and stewardesses—the courts have scrutinized the evidence to discern whether the salary differential is justified by heterogeneous duties. . . .

An employer must show a consistent pattern of performance of additional duties in order to demonstrate that added duties are genuinely the motivating factor for the substantially higher pay. It is not sufficient that an increased workload might hypothetically have commanded a higher salary if it was not in fact the basis for a significantly greater wage. The employer may not fabricate an after-the-fact rationalization for a sex-based pay difference. "[T]he semblance of [a] valid job classification system may not be allowed to mask the existence of wage discrimination based on sex." . . .

Applying these principles to the instant case, we perceive no error in the District Court's conclusion that the alleged differences in occupational duties proffered by NWA to justify the higher wage paid to pursers do not demonstrate that the stewardess and purser jobs are disparate. The court found that there is a uniform pay-scale for pursers which exceeds the pay-scale for stewardesses; and that these contrasting schemes are uncorrelated with pursers' and stewardesses' respective employment burdens. Pursers flying exclusively on domestic routes with no international documentation obligations are compensated evenly with pursers on international flights, despite the company's insistence that the onus of international flying is one of the explanations of the greater purser salary. To be sure, stewardesses who staff international flights do receive a foreign-flying supplement, but pursers' pay remains 20 to 35 percent larger than that of stewardesses of comparable seniority engaging solely in international travel.

Pursers consistently assigned to flights on which they do not function as the senior cabin attendant receive the same salary as those flying constantly in that capacity, while stewardesses rendering like service derive no supplemental income. A greater mantle of supervisory responsibility supposedly inherent in the position of senior cabin attendant thus does not exonerate the extra compensation awarded pursers. In fact, stewardesses' supervisory labors may exceed those of pursers. . . .

In sum, stewardesses are confined to the same lower salaries whether or not flying as the senior cabin attendant, regardless of how taxing the service on their flights may be, and irrespective of the performance of documentation work. Pursers, at all times and under all conditions, received substantially superior salaries. This evidence leads convincingly to the conclusion that the contrast in pay is a consequence of the historical willingness of women to accept inferior financial rewards for equivalent work—precisely the outmoded practice which the Equal Pay Act sought to eradicate. . . .

We affirm the District Court's findings that NWA purser and stewardess positions are substantially equal within the intent of the Equal Pay Act and demand financial response at the purser-level of recompense. . . .

So ordered.

Case Questions

1. What were the differences between the duties of the pursers and the duties of the stewardesses? Were those differences significant for the purposes of the Equal Pay Act? Explain your answers.
2. How did the airline treat pursers differently from stewardesses?
3. Based on the facts of this case, would NWA's differential treatment of pursers and stewardesses violate Title VII? Explain your answer.

PROCEDURES UNDER THE EQUAL PAY ACT

The Equal Pay Act is administered by the Equal Employment Opportunity Commission (EEOC). Prior to 1979, it was under the Department of Labor. In July 1979, the EEOC became the enforcement agency. The act provides for enforcement actions by individual employees (Section 16), or by the U.S. Secretary of Labor (Section 17), who has transferred that power to the EEOC.

There is no requirement that an individual filing a suit must file first with the EEOC. If the EEOC has filed a suit, it precludes individual suits on the same complaint. An individual suit must be filed within two years of the alleged violation. A violation will be held to be continuing for each payday in which unequal pay is received for equal work.

REMEDIES

An individual plaintiff's suit under Section 16 may recover the unpaid back wages due and may also receive an amount equal to the back wages as liquidated damages under the act. The trial court has discretion to deny recovery of the liquidated damages if it finds that the employer acted in good faith. An employer claiming to act in good faith must show some objective reason for its belief that it was acting legally.

The back pay recovered by a private plaintiff can be awarded for the period from two years prior to the suit; however, if the court finds the violation was "willful," it may allow recovery of back pay for three years prior to filing suit. According to *Laffey,* a violation is willful when the employer was aware of the appreciable possibility that its actions might violate the act. A successful private plaintiff also is awarded legal fees and court costs.

The remedies available under a government suit include injunctions and back pay with interest. The act does not provide for the recovery of liquidated damages in a government suit.

Unlike Title VII, the Equal Pay Act does not allow recovery of punitive damages. However, the potential recovery of liquidated damages for up to three years (in the case of willful violations) may offer recovery beyond that available under Title VII because of its limitations on punitive damages. Therefore, in certain cases, the remedies available under the Equal Pay Act may exceed those recoverable under Title VII.

TITLE VII AND THE EQUAL PAY ACT

As in *Laffey,* plaintiffs often file suit under both Title VII and the Equal Pay Act. Generally, conduct that violates the Equal Pay Act also violates Title VII; however, Title VII's coverage extends beyond that of the Equal Pay Act.

An employer paying different wages to men and women doing the same job is violating the law unless the pay differentials are due to a bona fide seniority system, a merit pay system, a productivity-based pay system, or a "factor other than sex." The Equal Pay Act prohibits paying men and women different rates if they are performing substantially equivalent work, unless the difference in pay is due to one of the factors just listed. Section 703(h) of Title VII also allows pay differentials between employees of different sexes when the differential is due to seniority, merit or productivity-based pay systems, or a factor other than sex. That provision of Section 703(h) is known as the Bennett Amendment.

The Equal Pay Act applies only when male and female employees are performing substantially equivalent work. Can Title VII be used to challenge pay differentials between men and women when they are not performing equal work? What is the effect of the Bennett Amendment?

In *County of Washington v. Gunther* [452 U.S. 161 (1981)], the Supreme Court held that the Bennett Amendment incorporates the defenses of the Equal Pay Act into Title VII; that is, pay differentials due to a seniority system, merit-pay system, productivity-based pay system, or a factor other than sex do not violate Title VII.

The *Gunther* case also held that Title VII prohibits intentional gender discrimination in pay even when the male and female employees are not performing equivalent work. In *Gunther,* the plaintiffs were able to establish a prima facie case of intentional discrimination by the employer in setting pay scales for female employees. In *Spalding v. University of Washington* [740 F.2d 686 (1984)] and *A.F.S.C.M.E. v. State of Washington* [770 F.2d 1401 (1985)], the U.S. Court of Appeals for the Ninth Circuit held that a plaintiff bringing a *Gunther*-type claim under Title VII must establish evidence of intentional discrimination (known as disparate treatment); the court held that statistical evidence purporting to show gender-based disparate salary levels for female professors, standing alone, was not sufficient to establish intentional discrimination as required by *Gunther.*

Comparable Worth

Comparable Worth
A standard of equal pay for jobs of equal value; not the same as equal-pay-for-equal-work.

Some commentators felt that the *Gunther* decision was, in effect, an endorsement of the idea of **comparable worth**—that is, that employees should receive equal pay for jobs of equal value. Notice that comparable worth is different from the equal-pay-for-equal-work requirements of the Equal Pay Act. The Supreme Court in *Gunther* emphasized that it was not endorsing comparable worth; it held simply that Title VII prohibited intentional discrimination on the basis of gender for setting pay scales. The courts of appeals have consistently maintained that Title VII does not require comparable worth standards; an employer need not pay equal wages for work of equal value as long as the pay differential is not due to intentional gender discrimination by the employer. In *Lemons v. Denver* [620 F.2d 228 (1980)], the U.S. Court of Appeals for the Tenth Circuit held that Title VII did not prohibit a public employer from paying public health nurses salaries based on the private sector wage rates for nurses, even though the public health nurses were paid less than the predominantly male jobs of garbage collector or tree trimmer. The employer was not guilty of gender discrimination simply by following the "market," even if the "market" wages for nurses reflected the effects of historical discrimination against women. Several states, however, have adopted laws requiring comparable worth pay for public sector employees.

GENDER-BASED PENSION BENEFITS

Women, on the average, live longer than men. Such differences in life expectancy are used by actuaries in determining the premium and benefit levels for annuities purchased by individuals. Gender-based actuarial tables used to determine premiums and benefits for pensions may require that women pay higher premiums to receive the same levels of benefits as men of the same age. Does an employer who uses gender-based actuarial tables to determine entitlement to pensions offered as an employment benefit violate Title VII? This question was addressed by the Supreme Court in the following case.

City of Los Angeles v. Manhart

435 U.S. 702 (1978)

Stevens, J.

As a class, women live longer than men. For this reason, the Los Angeles Department of Water and Power required its female employees to make larger contributions to its pension fund than its male employees. We granted certiorari to decide whether this practice discriminated against individual female employees because of their sex in violation of Section 703(a)(1) of the Civil Rights Act of 1964, as amended.

For many years the Department has administered retirement, disability, and death benefit programs for its employees. [Retired men and women of the same age, seniority and salary received the same monthly pension benefits, but female employees were required to pay contributions to the pension fund that were 14.84 percent higher than those paid by males. This differential was based on actuarial mortality tables and the experience of the Department, which indicates that women on average live longer than men and thus would receive more benefit payments.]

The Department . . . [contends] that . . . the differential in take-home pay between men and women was not discrimination within the meaning of Section 703(a)(1) because it was offset by a difference in the value of the pension benefits provided to the two classes of employees . . . [and] in any event, the retroactive monetary recovery is unjustified. We consider these contentions in turn. . . .

Before the Civil Rights Act of 1964 was enacted, an employer could fashion his personnel policies on the basis of assumptions about the differences between men and women, whether or not the assumptions were valid.

It is now well recognized that employment decisions cannot be predicated on mere "stereotyped" impressions about the characteristics of males or females. . . . This case does not, however, involve a fictional difference between men and women. It involves a generalization that the parties accept as unquestionably true: women, as a class, do live longer than men. The Department treated its women employees differently from its men employees because the two classes are in fact different. It is equally true, however, that all individuals in the respective classes do not share the characteristic that differentiates the average class representatives. Many women do not live as long as the average man and many men outlive the average woman. The question, therefore, is whether the existence or nonexistence of "discrimination" is to be determined by comparison of class characteristics or individual characteristics. A "stereotyped" answer to that question may not be the same as the answer which the language and purpose of the statute command.

The statute makes it unlawful "to discriminate against any *individual* with respect to his compensation, terms, conditions, or privileges of employment, because of such *individual's* race, color, religion, sex, or national origin." [emphasis added] The statute's focus on the individual is unambiguous. It precludes treatment of individuals as simply components of [a] racial, religious, sexual, or national class. If height is required for a job, a tall woman may not be refused employment merely because, on the average, women are too short. Even a true generalization about the class is an insufficient reason for disqualifying an individual to whom the generalization does not apply.

That proposition is of critical importance in this case because there is no assurance that any individual woman working for the Department will actually fit the generalization on which the Department's policy is based. Many of those individuals will not live as long as the average man. While they were working, those individuals received smaller paychecks because of their sex, but they will receive no compensating advantage when they retire.

It is true, of course, that while contributions are being collected from the employees, the Department cannot know which individuals will predecease the average woman. Therefore, unless women as a class are assessed an extra charge, they will be subsidized, to some extent, by the class of male employees. It follows, according to the Department, that fairness to its class of male employees justifies the extra assessment against all of its female employees.

But the question of fairness to various classes affected by the statute is essentially a matter of policy for the legislature to address. Congress has decided that classifications based on sex, like those based on national origin or race, are unlawful. Actuarial studies could unquestionably identify differences in life expectancy based on race or national origin, as well as sex. But a statute that was designed to make race irrelevant in the employment market, . . . could not reasonably be construed to permit a take-home pay differential based on a racial classification.

Even if the statutory language were less clear, the basic policy of the statute requires that we focus on fairness to individuals rather than fairness to classes. Practices which classify employees in terms of religion, race, or sex tend to preserve traditional assumptions about groups rather than thoughtful scrutiny of individuals. The generalization involved in this case illustrates the point. Separate mortality tables are easily interpreted as reflecting innate differences between the sexes; but a significant part of the longevity differential may be explained by the social fact that men are heavier smokers than women.

Finally, there is no reason to believe that Congress intended a special definition of discrimination in the context of employee group insurance coverage. It is true that insurance is concerned with events that are individually unpredictable, but that is characteristic of many employment decisions. Individual risks, like individual performance, may not be predicted by resort to classifications proscribed by Title VII. Indeed, the fact that this case involves a group insurance program highlights a basic flaw in the Department's fairness argument. For when insurance risks are grouped, the better risks always subsidize the poorer risks. Healthy persons subsidize medical benefits for the less healthy; unmarried workers subsidize the pensions of married workers; persons who eat, drink, or smoke to excess may subsidize pension benefits for persons whose habits are more temperate. Treating different classes of risks as though they were the same for purposes of group insurance is a common practice that has never been considered inherently unfair. To insure the flabby and the fit as though they were equivalent risks may be more common than treating men and women alike; but nothing more than habit makes one "subsidy" seem less fair than the other.

An employment practice which requires 2,000 individuals to contribute more money into a fund than 10,000 other employees simply because each of them is a woman, rather than a man, is in direct conflict with both the language and the policy of the Act. Such a practice does not pass the simple test of whether the evidence shows "treatment of a person in a manner which but for the person's sex would be different." It constitutes discrimination and is unlawful unless exempted by the Equal Pay Act or some other affirmative justification. . . .The Department argues that the different contributions exacted from men and women were based on the factor of longevity rather than sex. It is plain, however, that any individual's life expectancy is based on a number of factors, of which sex is only one. The record contains no evidence that any factor other than the employee's sex was taken into account in calculating the 14.84 percent differential between the respective contributions by men and women. We agree with Judge Duniway's observation that one cannot "say that an actuarial distinction based entirely on sex is 'based on any other factor other than sex.' Sex is exactly what it is based on."

• • •

[W]e recognize that in a case of this kind it may be necessary to take special care in fashioning appropriate relief. . . .

There can be no doubt that the prohibition against sex-differentiated employee contributions represents a marked departure from past practice. Although Title VII was enacted in 1964, this is apparently the first litigation challenging contribution differences based on valid actuarial tables. Retroactive liability could be devastating for a pension fund. The harm would fall in large part on innocent third parties. If, as the courts below apparently contemplated, the plaintiffs' contributions are recovered from the pension fund, the administrators of the fund will be forced to meet unchanged obligations with diminished assets. If the reserve proves inadequate, either the expectations of all retired employees will be disappointed or current employees will be forced to pay not only for their own future security but also for the unanticipated reduction in the contributions of past employees. . . .

So ordered.

Case Questions

1. What factors determine a person's longevity? What factors did the department's pension plan take into consideration in determining premiums employees had to pay?
2. Does Title VII allow a "reasonable cost differential" defense to a charge of gender discrimination?
3. How can an employer comply with *Manhart's* requirement of equal treatment between male and female employees for pensions? If women live longer than men, won't men be paid less under a unisex pension? Would that violate Title VII?

The Supreme Court noted in *Manhart* that it did not want to revolutionize the insurance industry. In the subsequent case of *Arizona Governing Committee v. Norris* [463 U.S. 1073 (1983)], the Supreme Court held that a deferred compensation plan for state employees, administered by a private insurance company, that used gender-based actuarial tables to determine monthly benefit payments violated Title VII. The Court held that its ruling would apply prospectively only, not retroactively.

PREGNANCY DISCRIMINATION

In the 1976 case of *General Electric v. Gilbert* [429 U.S. 125], the Supreme Court held that General Electric's refusal to cover pregnancy or related conditions under its sick-pay plan, even though male-specific disabilities such as vasectomies were covered, did not violate Title VII. In response to the *General Electric v. Gilbert* decision, Congress passed the Pregnancy Discrimination Act of 1978, which amended Title VII by adding Section 701(k) to Title VII. Section 701(k) provides

> The terms "because of sex" or "on the basis of sex" include, but are not limited to, because of or on the basis of pregnancy, childbirth, or related medical conditions; and women affected by pregnancy, childbirth, or related medical conditions shall be treated the same for all employment-related purposes, including receipt of benefits under fringe benefit programs, as other persons not so affected but similar to their ability or inability to work. . . .

Simply stated, the amendment to Title VII requires that an employer treat a pregnant employee the same as any employee suffering a nonpregnancy-related, temporary disability (unless in a relatively rare instance, the employer can establish a BFOQ for pregnancy-related discrimination). If the employer's sick-leave pay benefits cover temporary disabilities, it must also provide coverage for pregnancy-related leaves. In *Newport News Shipbuilding and Dry Dock Co. v. EEOC* [462 U.S. 669 (1983)], the Supreme Court held that an employer's medical insurance plan covering 80 percent of the cost of hospital treatment for employees' spouses or dependents, but which limited coverage of spouses' pregnancy-related costs to $500, was in violation of the pregnancy discrimination provisions of Title VII. Title VII required the employer to provide coverage for spouses' pregnancy-related conditions equal to the coverage of spouses' or dependents' other medical conditions.

Employers who fire pregnant employees are clearly in violation of Title VII, as are employers who fire pregnant employees because of the assumption that the employees will likely be absent from work for lengthy periods, *Maldonado v. U.S. Bank* [186 F.3d 759 (7th Cir. 1999)]. Discriminating against an employee who has had an abortion, or who is contemplating having an abortion, is also prohibited by Title VII, *Turic v. Holland Hospitality* [85 F.3d 1211 (6th Cir. 1996)]. The act also prohibits discharging an employee because of her efforts to become pregnant by in-vitro fertilization, *Pacourek v. Inland Steel Co.* [858 F.Supp. 1393 (N.D. Ill. 1994)]. An employer that transferred a successful sales representative to an undesirable sales territory because of her desire to start a family despite having several miscarriages was held to have violated Title VII in *Goss v. Exxon Office Systems Co.* [33 B.N.A. FEP Cas. 21 (E.D. Pa. 1983)]. The exclusion of prescription contraceptives from an employer's otherwise comprehensive prescription drug plan has also been held to violate Title VII, *Erickson v. The Bartell Drug Co.* [141 F.Supp.2d 1266 (W.D. Wash. 2001)] and *EEOC v. United Parcel Service, Inc.* [141 F.Supp.2d 1216 (D. Minn. 2001)].

Pregnancy and Hazardous Working Conditions

On-the-job exposure to harsh substances or potentially toxic chemicals may pose a hazard to the health of employees. The risk of such hazards may be greatly increased when pregnant employees are exposed to them; the hazards may also affect the health of the fetus carried by the pregnant employee. An employer wishing to avoid potential health problems for female employees and their offspring may prohibit women of childbearing age from working in jobs that involve exposure to hazardous substances. Do such restrictions violate Title VII, or may they be justified as BFOQs?

The U.S. Supreme Court in *U.A.W. v. Johnson Controls, Inc.* [499 U.S. 187 (1991)] held that the employer's restrictions were gender discrimination in violation of Title VII. For an employer to establish a BFOQ would require showing that the employee's pregnancy interfered with the employee's ability to perform the job. The Court noted

> . . . women as capable of doing their jobs as their male counterparts may not be forced to choose between having a child and having a job. . . . Johnson Controls' professed moral and ethical concerns about the welfare of the next generation do not suffice to establish a BFOQ of female sterility. Decisions about the welfare of future children must be left to the parents who conceive, bear, support, and raise them rather than to the employers who hire those parents. . . . Johnson Controls has attempted to exclude women because of their reproductive capacity. Title VII (and the pregnancy discrimination amendments) simply do not allow a woman's dismissal because of her failure to submit to sterilization.

THE FAMILY AND MEDICAL LEAVE ACT

The Family and Medical Leave Act [29 U.S.C. § 2611 *et seq.*], signed into law by President Clinton in 1993, allows eligible employees to take up to twelve weeks unpaid leave in any twelve months because of the birth, adoption, or foster care of a child; because of the need to care for a child, spouse, or parent with a serious health condition; or because the employee's own serious health condition makes the employee unable to perform functions of his or her job.

SERIOUS HEALTH CONDITION

The regulations under the FMLA [29 C.F.R. § 825.100 *et seq.*] define "serious health condition" as an illness, injury, or condition that requires inpatient hospital care, or that lasts more than three days and requires continuing treatment by a health-care provider, or that involves pregnancy, or a long-term or permanently disabling health condition. An employee's food poisoning that required one visit to a doctor but did not require hospitalization was not a serious health condition under the FLMA, nor was a child's ear infection that lasted only one day and required only a single visit to the doctor. However, a child's throat and upper respiratory infection that incapacitated the child for more than three days did qualify as a serious health condition under the FLMA.

LEAVE PROVISIONS

The leave may be taken all at once, or in certain cases, intermittently, or the employee may work at a part-time schedule. If both parents are employed by the same employer, the leave because of childbirth or to care for a sick child may be limited to a total of twelve weeks between both parents. The employee's health benefits may be maintained during leave. The employee has the right to return to the same or equivalent position, and the leave can't result in the loss of any benefit by the employee. The employer is entitled to thirty-days notice of the leave, where practicable, and may require a doctor's certification of the employee's health condition. The employer may also require certification for the employee's return to work.

COVERAGE

The Family and Medical Leave Act applies to private sector employers with fifty or more employees; public sector employers are covered without regard to the number of employees. In *Nevada Dept. of Human Resources v. Hibbs* [538 U.S. 721 (2003)], the Supreme Court held that the Eleventh Amendment of the Constitution does not grant the states immunity from suits for damages by employees under the FMLA. For employees to be eligible for leave under the act, they must have been employed by the employer for at least twelve months and must have worked at least 1,250 hours of the twelve-month period immediately preceding commencement of the leave. The employer may designate "key employees" who may be denied leave under the act; key employees are those whom it would be necessary for the employer to replace in order to prevent substantial and grievous economic injury to the operation of business. The employer must give written notice to key employees at the time such employees give notice of leave and may deny reinstatement to key employees who take leave. Key employees must be salaried employees and must be among the highest paid 10 percent of the employees at the work site. No more than 10 percent of employees at a work site can be designated key employees.

The following case discusses the requirements of the Family and Medical Leave Act for employees seeking protection for absences from work.

Price v. Marathon Cheese Corp.

119 F.3d 330 (5th Cir. 1997)

Wiener, Circuit Judge

. . . Price appeals the district court's grant of Marathon Cheese Corporation's motion for judgment as a matter of law, concluding that she failed to establish a claim under the Family and Medical Leave Act (FMLA. . . .

Price was employed by Marathon for twenty-three years. She was fired on November 7, 1994, by Marathon's plant manager, Tim Trace . . .

In August 1994, Dr. Dwight Johnson diagnosed Price with carpal tunnel syndrome and prescribed conservative treatment. Price contends that shortly thereafter she told Trace about her condition and that he inquired as to when she planned to have surgery. Trace maintains that he was never specifically informed that she had carpal tunnel syndrome and that he never stated that she would need surgery. In mid-September, Dr. Johnson restricted Price's work to light duty with limited arm movement, not to exceed eight hours per day. Price gave supervisor Carolyn Walker a note from Dr. Johnson relaying this restriction. Marathon accommodated the restricted work recommendation, placing Price on a salvage line that entailed nonrepetitive motion. Price testified that while she worked on the salvage line she was required to perform duties that were never before required of salvage line workers. She stated specifically that she first had to remove mold from the cheese by cutting through its paper wrapping, then had to place the cheese in a barrel, and finally had to remove all of the paper from the barrel. According to Price, the usual method is to remove the paper first and then remove the mold. Marathon countered that she was required to cut through the paper first, as removing the paper initially would have contaminated the entire batch of cheese.

Price requested a transfer to her old job on the two-pound line, but Trace denied this request. Her subsequent request to be placed on the random weight line was also denied.

Price obtained a release to full duties from Dr. Johnson at the end of September. In October, Price requested overtime and worked fifty-two hours in the last week of the month, which was the week before she was fired. She continued to see Dr. Johnson in October. Price claims that the October visits involved her carpal tunnel syndrome and stomach problems associated with her treatment. According to Dr. Johnson's deposition testimony, however, these visits dealt solely with her blood pressure.

On Friday, November 4, Price asked to speak with Walker and Ronnie Johnson, another plant supervisor. According to Marathon's witnesses, Price left work without permission after expressing her unwillingness to train or supervise new employees on the five-pound line, as she was not a supervisor. Rather, she stated that she would not work as a supervisor and that they could get one "back there." Price testified that she became so ill that day that she was unable to perform her duties. She contends that she informed her supervisors that she was too sick to work and was given permission to leave. Marathon's witnesses denied that Price complained of any pain; they testified that when asked whether she sought permission to leave work to see the doctor, she responded that she did not have a doctor's appointment. In fact, she did not see a doctor that day.

On the ensuing Monday, November 7, Price reported for work with a doctor's excuse that she obtained during an office visit that morning. The excuse addressed only that day; however, according to Price, she told Trace that Dr. Johnson could confirm that her condition existed prior to November 4.

Trace fired Price that morning. He testified that he did so because she had left work early without permission on the preceding workday (Friday, November 4), in violation of company policy. Marathon has a posted policy that prohibits leaving work early. Marathon rebutted Price's testimony with evidence that other employees had been discharged for leaving work without authorization. . . .

Price filed suit against Marathon in May 1995. . . . Marathon moved for judgment as a matter of law at the conclusion of all of the evidence. The trial court granted this motion, dismissing Price's claims with prejudice. [Price appealed.]

. . . The FMLA entitles an eligible employee to as much as twelve weeks leave from work when he has a serious health condition that makes him unable to perform the essential functions of his position. Such leave may be taken intermittently or on a reduced leave schedule when medically necessary. The FMLA further provides that, upon return from leave, an employee shall be restored to the position of employment he held when the leave commenced or to an equivalent position.

The FMLA defines "serious health condition" as "an illness, injury, impairment, or physical or mental condition that involves: (A) inpatient care in a hospital, hospice, or residential medical care facility; or (B) continuing treatment by a health care provider." The . . . regulations applicable to this claim clarify what is meant by a serious health condition. A "serious health condition" involves:

> (1) Any period of incapacity or treatment in connection with or consequent to inpatient care . . . in a hospital, hospice, or residential medical care facility;
> (2) Any period of incapacity requiring absence from work, school, or other regular daily activities, of more than three calendar days, that also involves continuing treatment by (or under the supervision of) a health care provider; or
> (3) Continuing treatment by (or under the supervision of) a health care provider for a chronic or long-term health condition that is incurable or so serious that, if not treated, would likely result in a period of incapacity of more than three calendar days. . . .

"Continuing treatment" means one or more of the following:

> (1) The employee or family member in question is treated two or more times for the injury or illness by a health care provider. Normally this would require visits to the health care provider. . . .
> (2) The employee or family member is treated for the injury or illness two or more times by a provider of health care services . . . under the orders of, or on referral by, a health care provider, or is treated for the injury or illness by a health care provider on at least one occasion which results in a regimen of continuing treatment under the supervision of the health care provider—for example, a course of medication or therapy—to resolve the health condition.
> (3) The employee or family member is under the continuing supervision of, but not necessarily being actively treated by, a health care provider due to a serious long-term or chronic condition or disability which cannot be cured. . . .

A "chronic serious health condition" is one that requires periodic visits for treatment, continues over an extended period of time, and may cause episodic rather than a "continuing" period of incapacity.

Price contends that on November 4, 1994, she was suffering from a serious medical condition, carpal tunnel syndrome, which kept her from performing her job. Marathon maintains that as a matter of law Price did not suffer from a serious medical condition and thus is not entitled to recover under the FMLA. Marathon asserts that she merely suffered from a short-term condition requiring brief treatment and recovery. To support this position, Marathon's evidence demonstrates that Price performed all of her job functions, and even asked for and received overtime during the week preceding her firing.

As Price did not receive inpatient care for her condition, she must meet the FMLA's requirements of receiving continuing treatment by a health care provider to qualify as having a serious health condition. Given the fact that she worked on the Friday that she left and reported for work on the following Monday, she does not satisfy the FMLA's "period of incapacity . . . of more than three consecutive calendar days" requirement. Price also contends that she suffered from a "chronic serious health condition," which eliminates the need for an absence of more than three days as well as for treatment during the absence.

. . . we conclude that Price failed to adduce sufficient evidence to allow a reasonable jury to find that she suffered from a serious health condition. The following facts are not in serious dispute. Price first visited Dr. Johnson in July 1994 with complaints of pain in her right arm and elbow. Subsequently, she obtained a nerve conduction study and visited Dr. Johnson approximately six to eight times prior to her November firing. Two of these visits had nothing to do with carpal tunnel syndrome. Dr. Johnson placed Price on modified work duties for a two-week period, but returned her to a full work schedule at her request. In his deposition, Dr. Johnson stated that she had a "mild to moderate impairment," for which he prescribed conservative treatment. He acknowledged that "[i]n more severe cases, I would consider splinting the wrist so as to prohibit movement of the wrist. I might consider taking her off work altogether." Dr. Johnson did not, however, prescribe either of these treatments for Price. We acknowledge that carpal tunnel syndrome, if sufficiently severe, can be a serious health condition; but Price's manifestation of this condition, as described by her treating physician, did not rise to the level of "serious health condition" for purposes of the FMLA. Finally, there is a dearth of evidence that she was actually incapacitated during her absence on Friday afternoon and the weekend.

Both Price and Marathon rely on *Brannon v. OshKosh B'Gosh, Inc.* to support their respective legal positions. In *Brannon,* the court held that an employee's gastroenteritis and upper respiratory infection did not constitute a serious health condition. The court stated that the regulations have developed a bright line test for determining which illnesses qualify as serious health conditions. If an employee is "(1) incapacitated for more than three days, (2) seen once by a doctor, and (3) prescribed a course of medication, such as an antibiotic, she has a 'serious health condition' worthy of FMLA protection." . . . When we follow the reasoning in *Brannon,* we find inescapable the conclusion that Price did not suffer from a serious health condition and that she failed to prove incapacity.

. . . We conclude that Price did not adduce sufficient evidence to preclude judgment as a matter of law under the FMLA. . . . Marathon was entitled to a judgment as a matter of law dismissing all of Price's claims. For the foregoing reasons, the judgment of the district court is, in all respects,

AFFIRMED.

Case Questions

1. What condition did Price claim required her absence from work and entitled her to FMLA protection?
2. Does Price's claimed condition meet the definition of a "chronic serious health condition" under the FMLA and relevant regulations? Explain your answer.
3. Does Price's claimed condition meet the definition of receiving "continuing treatment" as required under the FMLA and regulations? Explain your answer.
4. When does an employee's illness entitle the employee to protection under the FMLA?

EFFECT OF OTHER LAWS ON THE FMLA

The FMLA does not preempt or supersede any state or local law that provides for greater family or medical leave rights than those granted under the FMLA. In addition, employers are required to comply with any collective-bargaining agreement or employee benefit program that provides for greater rights than those given under the FMLA.

STATE LEGISLATION

The California Fair Employment and Housing Act Law requires employers to provide pregnant employees up to four months of unpaid pregnancy leave and to reinstate female employees returning from pregnancy leave to the job they held prior to the leave. However, if the job is unavailable due to business necessity, the employer is required to make a good-faith effort to provide a substantially similar job. The California law does not require the employer to offer such treatment to employees returning from other temporary disability leaves. California Federal Savings and Loan, a California bank, alleged that the California law violated the Pregnancy Discrimination Act because it required the employer to treat pregnant employees differently from other temporarily disabled employees. In *California Federal Savings and Loan v. Guerra* [479 U.S. 272 (1987)], the Supreme Court upheld the California law. The majority reasoned that the Pregnancy Discrimination Act amendments to Title VII were intended merely to create a minimum level of protection for pregnant employees that could be supplemented by state legislation as long as the state laws did not conflict with the terms or policies of Title

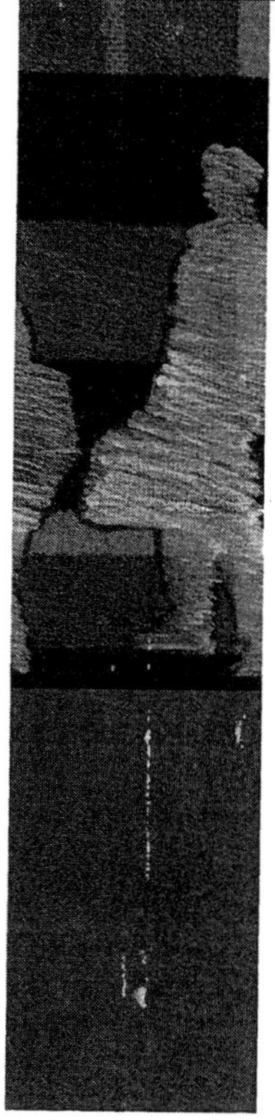

MATERNITY LEAVE PROVISIONS AROUND THE WORLD

THE WORKING LAW

As has been discussed, the FMLA allows covered employees to take up to twelve weeks of unpaid maternity or parental leave. Other countries are much more generous in their provisions for maternity or parental leave, as the following chart indicates:

Country	*Maternity Leave*	*Pay for Leave (as % of Wages)*	*Parental Leave*
Norway	18 weeks	100%	26 weeks paid leave for either parent
Denmark	18 weeks	100%	10 weeks paid leave for either parent
France	16–26 weeks	100%	
United Kingdom	14–18 weeks	90% for 6 weeks, flat rate after that	
Spain	16 weeks	100%	
Israel	12 weeks	75%	
Japan	14 weeks	60%	
India	12 weeks	100%	
Canada	17–18 weeks	55% for 15 weeks	
Mexico	12 weeks	100%	
South Africa	12 weeks	45%	
Australia	1 year	0	

Source: APESMA Professional Women's Network, Summary of **Maternity Protection ILO Convention No. 183,** June 2001, International Confederation of Free Trade Unions, the Public Services International and Education International **http://www.apesma.asn.au/women/maternity_leave_around_the_world .htm**.

VII. The Court also noted that the California law did not prevent employers from extending the right of reinstatement to employees on other temporary disability leaves; hence, the law did not require that pregnant employees be treated more generously than nonpregnant employees on temporary disability leave.

SEXUAL HARASSMENT

Sexual harassment is one of the most significant employment problems facing our society. It imposes significant costs on both employers and employees. Victims of sexual harassment may experience severe emotional anguish, physical and mental stress, frustration, humiliation, guilt, withdrawal and dysfunction in family and social relationships, medical expenses, loss of sick leave and vacation, and litigation costs. Employers suffer from absenteeism, higher turnover of employees, replacement and retraining costs, morale problems, losses in productivity, and of course, litigation expenses and damages.

http://www.eeoc.gov/facts/fs-sex.html *provides brief guidelines describing sexual harassment.*

The language of Title VII does not specifically mention sexual harassment, and in some early cases, the courts had difficulty determining whether sexual harassment was within the Title VII prohibition on gender discrimination. Now, however, the courts are clear on the position that sexual harassment is gender discrimination prohibited by Title VII. The EEOC has issued guidelines defining sexual harassment and declaring that sexual harassment constitutes gender discrimination in violation of Title VII. Sexual harassment is defined as unwelcome sexual advances, requests for sexual favors, or other verbal or physical conduct of a sexual nature, where the employee is required to accept such conduct as a condition of employment, the employee's response to such conduct is used as a basis for employment decisions such as promotion, bonuses or retention, or such conduct unreasonably interferes with the employee's work performance or creates a hostile working environment. The Title VII protections against sexual harassment apply to all individuals—both men and women—covered by Title VII. (Note that Title VII also prohibits harassment based on race, color, religion, or national origin.)

Quid Pro Quo Harassment
Harassment where the employee's response to the harassment is considered in granting employment benefits.

Hostile Environment Harassment
Harassment which may not result in economic detriment to the victim, but which subjects the victim to unwelcome conduct or comments and may interfere with the employee's work performance.

The EEOC Guidelines and the courts have recognized two general categories of sexual harassment: quid pro quo harassment and hostile environment harassment. In **quid pro quo harassment,** the employee's response to the request for sexual favors is considered in granting employment benefits, such as a male supervisor promising a female employee that she will be promoted or receive a favorable performance rating if she sleeps with him. Such harassment was held to violate Title VII in *Barnes v. Costle* [561 F.2d 983 (D.C. Cir. 1977)]. In **hostile environment harassment,** an employee may not suffer any economic detriment but is subjected to unwelcome sexual comments, propositions, jokes, or conduct that have the effect of interfering with the employee's work performance or creating a hostile work environment. The Supreme Court held hostile environment sexual harassment was prohibited by Title VII in *Meritor Savings Bank, FSB v. Vinson* [477 U.S. 57 (1986)].

EQUAL EMPLOYMENT OPPORTUNITY COMMISSION GUIDELINES ON DISCRIMINATION BECAUSE OF SEX 29 C.F.R. § 1604.11

THE WORKING LAW

Section 1604.11 Sexual Harassment

(a) Harassment on the basis of sex is a violation of § 703 of Title VII.[1] Unwelcome sexual advances, requests for sexual favors, and other verbal or physical conduct of a sexual nature constitute sexual harassment when (1) submission to such conduct is made either explicitly or implicitly a term or condition of an individual's employment, (2) submission to or rejection of such conduct by an individual is used as the basis for employment decisions affecting such individual, or (3) such conduct has the purpose or effect of unreasonably interfering with an individual's work performance or creating an intimidating, hostile, or offensive working environment.

(b) In determining whether alleged conduct constitutes sexual harassment, the Commission will look at the record as a whole and at the totality of the circumstances, such as the nature of the sexual advances and the context in which the alleged incidents occurred. The determination of the legality of a particular action will be made from the facts, on a case by case basis.

(c) Applying general Title VII principles, an employer, employment agency, joint apprenticeship committee or labor organization (hereinafter collectively referred to as "employer") is responsible for its acts and those of its agents and supervisory employees with respect to sexual harassment regardless of whether the specific acts complained of were authorized or even forbidden by the employer and regardless of whether the employer knew or should have known of their occurrence. The Commission will examine the circumstances of the particular employment relationship and the job functions performed by the individual in determining whether an individual acts in either a supervisory or agency capacity.

(d) With respect to conduct between fellow employees, an employer is responsible for acts of sexual harassment in the workplace where the employer (or its agents or supervisory employees) knows or should have known of the conduct, unless it can show that it took immediate and appropriate corrective action.

(e) An employer may also be responsible for the acts of non-employees with respect to sexual harassment of employees in the workplace, where the employer (or its agents or supervisory employees) knows or should have known of the conduct and fails to take immediate and appropriate corrective action. In reviewing these cases the Commission will consider the extent of the employer's control and any other legal responsibility which the employer may have with respect to the conduct of such non-employees.

(f) Prevention is the best tool for the elimination of sexual harassment. An employer should take all steps necessary to prevent sexual harassment from occurring, such as affirmatively raising the subject, expressing strong disapproval, developing appropriate sanctions, informing employees of their rights and procedures for raising the issue of harassment under Title VII, and developing methods to sensitize all concerned.

(g) Other related practices: Where employment opportunities or benefits are granted because of an individual's submission to the employer's sexual advances or requests for sexual favors, the employer may be held liable for unlawful sex discrimination against other persons who were qualified for but denied that employment opportunity or benefit.

---

[1]The principles involved here continue to apply to race, color, religion, or national origin.

QUID PRO QUO HARASSMENT

To establish a case of quid pro quo harassment, a plaintiff must show five things: (1) that she or he belongs to a protected group, (2) that she or he was subject to unwelcome sexual harassment, (3) that the harassment was based on sex, (4) that job benefits were conditioned on the acceptance of the harassment, and if appropriate, (5) that there is some basis to hold the employer liable. The essence of quid pro quo harassment is that the employee's submission to such conduct is made either explicitly or implicitly a term or condition of an individual's employment or that submission to or rejection of such conduct by the employee is used as the basis for employment decisions affecting the employee.

The case of *Tomkins v. Public Service Electric & Gas Co.* [568 F.2d 1044 (3rd Cir. 1977)] is a classic example of quid pro quo sexual harassment: Tomkins was told by her male supervisor that she should have sex with him if she wanted him to give her a satisfactory evaluation and recommend her for promotion. When she refused, she was subjected to a demotion, negative evaluations, disciplinary suspensions, and was ultimately fired. The U.S. Court of Appeals held that Title VII is violated when a supervisor makes sexual advances or demands toward a subordinate employee and conditions the employee's continued employment or possible promotion on a favorable response to those advances or demands.

The EEOC Guidelines on Sexual Harassment also provide that when an employer rewards one employee for entering a sexual relationship, other employees denied the same reward or benefit may have a valid harassment complaint. In *King v. Palmer* [778 F.2d 878 (D.C. Cir. 1985)], a supervisor promoted a nurse with whom he was having an affair rather than one of several more qualified nurses. The court held that the employer was guilty of gender discrimination against the superior nurses who were denied the promotion.

HOSTILE ENVIRONMENT HARASSMENT

Unlike quid pro quo harassment, hostile environment harassment does not involve the conditioning of any job status or benefit on the employee's response to the harassment; rather, the unwelcome harassment has the effect of interfering with the employee's work performance or creating a hostile work environment for the employee. Because no employment consequences are conditioned on the employee's response to the harassing conduct, some courts refused to hold that hostile environment harassment violated Title VII. The Supreme Court rejected that approach and upheld the EEOC Guidelines that declare hostile environment harassment to be sex discrimination in violation of Title VII in the case of *Meritor Savings Bank, FSB v. Vinson* [477 U.S. 57 (1986)]. After that decision, the lower courts addressed the question of just how severe the harassing conduct has to be, and how hostile the work environment must become, before such harassment is found to violate Title VII. That issue was finally settled by the Supreme Court in the following decision.

For additional discussion of sexual harassment, see **http://www.de.psu.edu/harassment**

Harris v. Forklift Systems, Inc.

510 U.S. 17 (1993)

O'Connor, J.

In this case we consider the definition of a discriminatorily "abusive work environment" (also known as a "hostile work environment") under Title VII of the Civil Rights Act of 1964.

. . . Teresa Harris worked as a manager at Forklift Systems, Inc., an equipment rental company, from April 1985 until October 1987. Charles Hardy was Forklift's president.

. . . throughout Harris' time at Forklift, Hardy often insulted her because of her gender and often made her the target of unwanted sexual innuendos. Hardy told Harris on several occasions, in the presence of other employees, "You're a woman, what do you know" and "We need a man as the rental manager"; at least once, he told her she was "a dumbass woman." Again in front of others, he suggested that the two of them "go to the Holiday Inn to negotiate [Harris'] raise." Hardy occasionally asked Harris and other female employees to get coins from his front pants pocket. He threw objects on the ground in front of Harris and other women, and asked them to pick the objects up. He made sexual innuendos about Harris' and other women's clothing.

In mid-August 1987, Harris complained to Hardy about his conduct. Hardy said he was surprised that Harris was offended, claimed he was only joking, and apologized. He also promised he would stop, and based on this assurance Harris stayed on the job. But in early September, Hardy began anew: While Harris was arranging a deal with one of Forklift's customers, he asked her, again in front of other employees, "What did you do, promise the guy . . . some [sex] Saturday night?" On October 1, Harris collected her paycheck and quit.

Harris then sued Forklift, claiming that Hardy's conduct had created an abusive work environment for her because of her gender. The . . . District Court . . . found this to be "a close case," but held that Hardy's conduct did not create an abusive environment. The court found that some of Hardy's comments "offended [Harris], and would offend the reasonable woman," but that they were not "so severe as to be expected to seriously affect [Harris'] psychological well-being."

. . . We granted certiorari, to resolve a conflict among the Circuits on whether conduct, to be actionable as "abusive work environment" harassment (no quid pro quo harassment issue is present here), must "seriously affect [an employee's] psychological well-being" or lead the plaintiff to "suffer injury." . . .

Title VII of the Civil Rights Act of 1964 makes it "an unlawful employment practice for an employer . . . to discriminate against any individual with respect to his compensation, terms, conditions, or privileges of employment, because of such individual's race, color, religion, sex, or national origin." As we made clear in *Meritor Savings Bank v. Vinson* . . . this language "is not limited to 'economic' or 'tangible' discrimination. The phrase 'terms, conditions, or privileges of employment' evinces a congressional intent 'to strike at the entire spectrum of disparate treatment of men and women' in employment," which includes requiring people to work in a discriminatorily hostile or abusive environment. When the workplace is permeated with "discriminatory intimidation, ridicule, and insult," that is "sufficiently severe or pervasive to alter the conditions of the victim's employment and create an abusive working environment," Title VII is violated. . . .

But Title VII comes into play before the harassing conduct leads to a nervous breakdown. A discriminatorily abusive work environment, even one that does not seriously affect employees' psychological well-being, can and often will detract from employees' job performance, discourage employees from remaining on the job, or keep them from advancing in their careers. Moreover, even without regard to these tangible effects, the very fact that the discriminatory conduct was so severe or pervasive that it created a work environment abusive to employees because of their race, gender, religion, or national origin offends Title VII's broad rule of workplace equality.

. . . We therefore believe the District Court erred in relying on whether the conduct "seriously affected plaintiff's psychological well-being" or led her to "suffer injury." Such an inquiry may needlessly focus the factfinder's attention on concrete psychological harm, an element Title VII does not require. Certainly Title VII bars conduct that would seriously affect a reasonable person's psychological well-being, but the statute is not limited to such conduct. So long as the environment would reasonably be perceived, and is perceived, as hostile or abusive, there is no need for it also to be psychologically injurious.

This is not, and by its nature cannot be, a mathematically precise test. We need not answer today all the potential questions it raises, nor specifically address the EEOC's new regulations on this subject. . . . But we can say that whether an environment is "hostile" or "abusive" can be determined only by looking at all the circumstances. These may include the frequency of the discriminatory conduct; its severity; whether it is physically threatening or humiliating, or a mere offensive utterance; and whether it unreasonably interferes with an employee's work performance. The effect on the employee's psychological well-being is, of course, relevant to determining whether the plaintiff actually found the environment abusive. But while psychological harm, like any other relevant factor, may be taken into account, no single factor is required.

Forklift, while conceding that a requirement that the conduct seriously affect psychological well-being is unfounded, argues that the District Court nonetheless correctly applied the *Meritor* standard. We disagree. Though the District Court did conclude that the work environment was not "intimidating or abusive to [Harris]," it did so only after finding that the conduct was not "so severe as to be expected to seriously affect plaintiff's psychological well- being" and that Harris was not "subjectively so offended that she suffered injury." The District Court's application of these incorrect standards may well have influenced its ultimate conclusion, especially given that the court found this to be a "close case."

We therefore reverse the judgment of the Court of Appeals, and remand the case for further proceedings consistent with this opinion.

So ordered.

Case Questions

1. How did the harassment directed against Harris affect her economically? How did the harassment directed against Harris affect her emotionally? Did it interfere with her work performance? Explain your answers.
2. How severe must "hostile environment" sexual harassment be before it violates Title VII?
3. Is the standard used to determine when sexual harassment becomes severe enough to create a "hostile environment" a subjective or an objective standard? Explain your answer.

Reasonable Person or Reasonable Victim?

In cases involving claims of hostile environment harassment, the courts have dealt with the question of which standard should be used to determine whether the challenged conduct was sufficiently severe and hostile. Most courts have used the "reasonable person" standard; that is, would a reasonable person find the conduct to be offensive and severe enough to create a hostile environment or to interfere with the person's work performance? The EEOC issued a policy statement declaring that courts should also consider the perspective of the victim to avoid perpetuating stereotypical notions of what behavior was acceptable to persons of a specific gender.

In response to that, some courts adopted the "reasonable victim" or "reasonable woman" standard, recognizing that men and women were likely to perceive and react differently to certain behaviors. In *Ellison v. Brady* [924 F.2d 872 (9th Cir. 1991)], the court held that the reasonable woman standard should be used to determine whether a series of unsolicited love letters sent to a female employee by a male coworker had the effect of creating a hostile work environment. Even when courts did adopt the reasonable woman standard, they emphasized that the standard was not totally subjective, but was to be based on whether an objective reasonable woman would find the conduct offensive or would have been detrimentally affected.

The Supreme Court, although not specifically addressing the issue of whether to use the reasonable person or reasonable woman standard, used the reasonable person standard in *Harris v. Forklift Systems, Inc.*

EMPLOYER LIABILITY FOR SEXUAL HARASSMENT

The EEOC Guidelines state that employers are liable for sexual harassment by supervisory or managerial employees and may also be liable for harassment by co-workers or even nonemployees under certain circumstances. The Supreme Court in *Meritor Savings Bank, FSB v. Vinson* rejected the EEOC Guidelines' position on employer liability for supervisors or managerial employees and instead held that employer liability should be determined according to traditional common-law agency principles; that is, was the harasser acting as an agent of the employer?

Agency Relationships

Whether an agency relationship is created is a question of fact to be determined on the specifics of a particular situation. Supervisors or managerial employees, acting in the course of their employment, are generally held to be agents of the employer; that is, they act with the actual, or apparent, authorization of the employer. An agency relationship can also be created by an employer's acceptance of, tolerance of, acquiescence to, or after-the-fact ratification of an employee's conduct, such as when the employer becomes aware of harassment and fails to take action to stop it.

Employer Liability for Supervisors

When is an employer liable under Title VII for sexual harassment by a supervisor or managerial employee? The courts have consistently held an employer liable for quid pro quo sexual harassment by a manager or supervisor because such conduct is related to the supervisor's or manager's job status. But courts have differed over holding an employer liable for hostile environment harassment by a supervisor or manager: Some courts held an employer liable only when the harassment was somehow aided by the supervisor's job status, while other courts held that the employer was liable when it knew or should have known of the harassment. The U.S. Supreme Court settled the issue of employer liability for hostile environment harassment by a supervisor or manager in the following case.

FARAGHER V. CITY OF BOCA RATON

524 U.S. 775 (1998)

Beth Ann Faragher worked as an ocean lifeguard for the Marine Safety Section of the Parks and Recreation Department of the City of Boca Raton, Florida (City) from 1985 to 1990. Her immediate supervisors were Bill Terry, David Silverman, and Robert Gordon. During her employment, Terry repeatedly touched the bodies of female employees without invitation, made contact with another female lifeguard in a motion of sexual simulation, and made crudely demeaning remarks about women generally. During a job interview with a woman he hired as a lifeguard, Terry said that the female lifeguards had sex with their male counterparts and asked whether she would do the same. Silverman behaved in similar ways: he made frequent, vulgar references to women and sexual matters, commented on the bodies of female lifeguards and beachgoers, and at least twice told female lifeguards that he would like to engage in sex with them.

Faragher and other female lifeguards did not complain to higher management about Terry or Silverman, although they did have informal talks with Gordon. Gordon did not feel that it was his place to report these complaints to Terry, his own supervisor, or to any other city official. In April 1990, a former lifeguard formally complained to the City's Personnel Director about Terry's and Silverman's harassment of her and other female lifeguards. The City investigated the complaint and found that Terry and Silverman had behaved improperly; the City reprimanded them, and required them to choose between a suspension without pay or the forfeiture of annual leave.

Faragher resigned in June 1990, and in 1992 filed a suit against Terry, Silverman, and the City, alleging violations of Title VII, 42 U.S.C. § 1983, and Florida law. She claimed that the harassment by Terry and Silverman created a "sexually hostile atmosphere." Because Terry and Silverman were agents of the City, and that their conduct amounted to discrimination in the terms, conditions, and privileges of her employment, Faragher sought to hold the City liable for damages, court costs, and attorney's fees. The federal trial court ruled that the conduct of Terry and Silverman was discriminatory harassment sufficiently serious to alter the conditions of Faragher's employment and constitute an abusive working environment, and held the City liable for the harassment of its supervisory employees. The trial court awarded Faragher one dollar in nominal damages on her Title VII claim. The City appealed, and the Court of Appeals for the Eleventh Circuit reversed the judgment against the City, ruling that Terry and Silverman were not acting within the scope of their employment when they engaged in the harassment, that they were not aided in their actions by the agency relationship, and that the City had no constructive knowledge of the harassment by virtue of its pervasiveness or Gordon's actual knowledge. Faragher appealed to the U.S. Supreme Court.

Justice Souter delivered the opinion of the Court.

. . . Since our decision in *Meritor,* Courts of Appeals have struggled to derive manageable standards to govern employer liability for hostile environment harassment perpetrated by supervisory employees. . . .

In the case before us, a justification for holding the offensive behavior within the scope of Terry's and Silverman's employment was well put in Judge Barkett's dissent [in the Court of Appeals]: "[A] pervasively hostile work environment of sexual harassment is never (one would hope) authorized, but the supervisor is clearly charged with maintaining a productive, safe work environment. The supervisor directs and controls the conduct of the employees, and the manner of doing so may inure to the employer's benefit or detriment, including subjecting the employer to Title VII liability." It is by now well recognized that hostile environment sexual harassment by supervisors (and, for that matter, co-employees) is a persistent problem in the workplace. An employer can, in a general sense, reasonably anticipate the possibility of such conduct occurring in its workplace, and one might justify the assignment of the burden of the untoward behavior to the employer as one of the costs of doing business, to be charged to the enterprise rather than the victim. . . .

We . . . agree with Faragher that in implementing Title VII it makes sense to hold an employer vicariously liable for some tortious conduct of a supervisor made possible by abuse of his supervisory authority. . . . Several courts, indeed, have noted what Faragher has argued, that there is a sense in which a harassing supervisor is always assisted in his misconduct by the supervisory relationship. . . . The agency relationship affords contact with an employee subjected to a supervisor's sexual harassment, and the victim may well be reluctant to accept the risks of blowing the whistle on a superior. When a person with supervisory authority discriminates in the terms and conditions of subordinates' employment, his actions necessarily draw upon his superior position over the people who report to him, or those under them, whereas an employee generally cannot check a supervisor's abusive conduct the same way that she might deal with abuse from a co-worker. When a fellow employee harasses, the victim can walk away or tell the offender where to go, but it may be difficult to offer such responses to a supervisor, whose "power to supervise—[which may be] to hire and fire, and to set work schedules and pay rates—does not disappear . . . when he chooses to harass through insults and offensive gestures rather than directly with threats of firing or promises of promotion." Recognition of employer liability when discriminatory misuse of supervisory authority alters the terms and conditions of a victim's employment is underscored by the fact that the employer has a greater opportunity to guard against misconduct by supervisors than by common workers; employers have greater opportunity and incentive to screen them, train them, and monitor their performance.

In sum, there are good reasons for vicarious liability for misuse of supervisory authority. That rationale must, however, satisfy one more condition. We are not entitled to recognize this theory under Title VII unless we can square it with *Meritor's* holding that an employer is not "automatically" liable for harassment by a supervisor who creates the requisite degree of discrimination, and there is obviously some tension between that holding and the position that a supervisor's misconduct aided by supervisory authority subjects the employer to liability vicariously; if the "aid" may be the unspoken suggestion of retaliation by misuse of supervisory authority, the risk of automatic liability is high. . . .

The . . . basic alternative to automatic liability would . . . allow an employer to show as an affirmative defense to liability that the employer had exercised reasonable care to avoid harassment and to eliminate it when it might occur, and that the complaining employee had failed to act with like reasonable care to take advantage of the employer's safeguards and otherwise to prevent harm that could have been avoided. . . .

In order to accommodate the principle of vicarious liability for harm caused by misuse of supervisory authority, as well as Title VII's equally basic policies of encouraging forethought by employers and saving action by objecting employees, we adopt the following holding in this case and in *Burlington Industries Inc. v. Ellerth* [524 U.S. 742 (1998)]. . . . An employer is subject to vicarious liability to a victimized employee for an actionable hostile environment created by a supervisor with immediate (or successively higher) authority over the employee. When no tangible employment action is taken, a defending employer may raise an affirmative defense to liability or damages, subject to proof by a preponderance of the evidence. The defense comprises two necessary elements: (a) that the employer exercised reasonable care to prevent and correct promptly any sexually harassing behavior, and (b) that the plaintiff employee unreasonably failed to take advantage of any preventive or corrective opportunities provided by the employer or to avoid harm otherwise. While proof that an employer had promulgated an antiharassment policy with complaint procedure is not necessary in every instance as a matter of law, the need for a stated policy suitable to the employment circumstances may appropriately be addressed in any case when litigating the first element of the defense. And while proof that an employee failed to fulfill the corresponding obligation of reasonable care to avoid harm is not limited to showing an unreasonable failure to use any complaint procedure provided by the employer, a demonstration of such failure will normally suffice to satisfy the employer's burden under the second element of the defense. No affirmative defense is available, however, when the supervisor's harassment culminates in a tangible employment action, such as discharge, demotion, or undesirable reassignment. . . .

Applying these rules here, we believe that the judgment of the Court of Appeals must be reversed. The District Court found that the degree of hostility in the work environment rose to the actionable level and was attributable to Silverman and Terry. It is undisputed that these supervisors "were granted virtually unchecked authority" over their subordinates, "directly controll[ing] and supervis[ing] all aspects of [Faragher's] day-to-day activities." It is also clear that Faragher and her colleagues were "completely isolated from the City's higher management." The City did not seek review of these findings.

. . . The judgment of the Court of Appeals for the Eleventh Circuit is reversed, and the case is remanded for reinstatement of the judgment of the District Court.

It is so ordered.

Case Questions

1. Why should an employer be liable for the actions of a supervisor? Does the same reasoning apply in the case of sexual harassment by a supervisor?
2. What actions can an employer take to avoid being held liable for sexual harassment by a supervisor?
3. What are the requirements of the defense for employers set out by the Supreme Court in this case? Could the City of Boca Raton use that defense here? Explain your answers.

Employer Liability for Co-Workers and Nonemployees

For both quid pro quo harassment and for hostile environment harassment by nonsupervisory or nonmanagerial employees, an employer will be liable if it knew of, or should have known of, the harassing conduct and failed to take reasonable steps to stop it. An employer may even be liable for harassment by nonemployees if the employer had some control over the harasser and failed to take reasonable steps to stop it once the employer became aware of, or should have been aware of, the harassment.

Individual Liability

The courts have held that individual employees are not liable for damages under Title VII; this means that the employee doing the harassing will not be held personally liable for damages under Title VII. They are subject to court injunctions to cease and desist from such conduct. But harassers or potential harassers should be aware that they may be held personally liable under the various state EEO laws or under common-law tort claims. The damages under state EEO laws and tort claims may include compensatory and punitive damages in addition to employment-related damages and legal fees.

Public employees who engage in sexual harassment may, in addition to the foregoing remedies, be subject to suits for damages under 42 U.S.C. § 1983 and criminal prosecution under 18 U.S.C. § 242.

EMPLOYER RESPONSES TO SEXUAL HARASSMENT CLAIMS

Employers have several defenses to raise against claims of sexual harassment. Prevention is probably the best defense: to stop sexual harassment before any legal problems develop.

Prevention

As the Supreme Court decision in *Faragher* stated, the best way for an employer to avoid liability for sexual harassment is to take active steps to prevent it. Both the EEOC Guidelines and the Supreme Court emphasize the importance of having a policy against sexual harassment and of following that policy whenever a complaint arises. The sexual harassment policy should define sexual harassment—according to the EEOC Guidelines and court decisions—and should give practical, concrete examples of such conduct. The policy must also make it very clear that such conduct by anyone in the organization will not be tolerated, and it should specify the penalties, up to and including termination, for violations of the policy. The policy should spell out the procedures for filing complaints of sexual harassment, designate specific (preferably managerial) employees who are responsible for receiving and investigating complaints, and should include reassurances that employees who file complaints will be protected from retaliation or reprisals.

The policy must be communicated to all employees, who should be educated about the policy through training and workshops; all employees must understand the policy and be aware of the employer's commitment to the policy. Above all, the employer must take steps to enforce the policy immediately upon receipt of a complaint of sexual harassment because the policy is effective only if it is followed. If the employer acts promptly to enforce the policy whenever a complaint of sexual harassment is received, it will generally avoid liability for such conduct according to *Faragher*.

Defenses

Quid Pro Quo
Something for something; giving one valuable thing for another.

In addition to the preventive approach and the defense set out in *Faragher,* employers have a few other defenses to raise when faced with charges of sexual harassment. The definition of sexual harassment indicates that the conduct complained of must be unwelcome and of a sexual nature, and it must either be **quid pro quo** or serious enough to create a hostile working environment. Generally, the courts will not consider isolated incidents or trivial comments to constitute sexual harassment; as the Supreme Court indicated in *Harris v. Forklift Systems,* factors to consider in determining whether the challenged conduct amounts to sexual harassment include its frequency, severity, whether it is physically threatening or humiliating or a mere offensive utterance, and whether it unreasonably interferes with an employee's work performance. In *Scott v. Sears, Roebuck & Co.* [798 F.2d 210 (7th Cir. 1986)], the court held that one pat on the buttocks, winks, one dinner invitation, and an offer by one employee to give a female employee a "rubdown" did not create a hostile environment. In *Rabidue v. Osceola Refining Co.* [805 F.2d 611 (6th Cir. 1986)], the court held that the display of pin-up photos and posters of nude or scantily clad women did not seriously affect female employees; but in *Barbetta v. Chemlawn Services Corp.* [669 F.Supp. 569 (W.D. N.Y. 1987)], the court held that a proliferation of pornographic material featuring nude women did create a hostile working environment for female employees.

The fact that the harassed employee failed to file a complaint through the employer's sexual harassment complaint procedure does not automatically protect the employer from liability; the employer may still be held liable if it knew of, or had reason to know of, the harassment, *Burlington Industries, Inc. v. Ellerth* [542 U.S. 742 (1998)].

Unwelcome

Conduct of a sexual nature must be unwelcome to be sexual harassment; the target of the harassment must indicate that it is unwelcome. In *Meritor,* the Supreme Court held that as long as the victim indicates that the conduct is unwelcome, it is still sexual harassment, even if the victim voluntarily complies with the harassment. A consensual sexual relationship, instigated by a female employee in an attempt to advance in her job, was held not to be sexual harassment in *Perkins v. General Motors Corporation* [709 F.Supp. 1487 (W.D. Mo. 1989)].

Provocation

Meritor also indicated that the employer can raise the defense of provocation by the victim: Did the victim instigate the allegedly harassing conduct through her or his own style of dress, comments, or conduct? The issue of provocation goes to whether the conduct was unwelcome: If the victim has encouraged the allegedly harassing conduct, is it really unwelcome? Where a female employee regularly offered to engage in sexual acts with other employees, and often lifted her skirt to show her supervisor that she wasn't wearing undergarments, a single attempt by her supervisor to hug and kiss her was held not to be sexual harassment in *McLean v. Satellite Technology Services, Inc.* [673 F.Supp. 1458 (E.D. Mo. 1987)]. However, the fact that an employee had posed nude for a national magazine did not automatically mean that she would find her boss's sexual advances welcome, *Burnes v. McGregor Electronic Industries, Inc.* [989 F.2d 959 (8th Cir. 1993)], nor did the fact that a female employee swore "like a drunken sailor" mean that she welcomed harassing conduct, *Steiner v. Showboat Operating Co.* [25 F.3d 1459 (9th Cir. 1994)].

Conduct of a Sexual Nature

In order to be sexual harassment, the conduct complained of must be based on the employee's sex. Tasteless comments or jokes or annoying behavior, while offensive, may not be sexual harassment. (Harassment based on race, color, religion, or national origin also violates Title VII.) A supervisor who is obnoxious and verbally abusive to all employees is not guilty of sexual harassment as long as the abuse is not based on sex. In *Holman v. State of Indiana* [211 F.3d 399 (7th Cir. 2000)], the U.S. Court of Appeals for the Seventh Circuit held that a supervisor's harassment and solicitation of sexual favors of both male and female employees was not conduct "because of sex."

Same-Sex Harassment

The Supreme Court decision in *Oncale v. Sundowner Offshore Services, Inc.* [523 U.S. 75 (1998)] resolved a split among the Courts of Appeals regarding whether same-sex harassment was prohibited by the sexual harassment prohibition of Title VII. The Supreme Court held that Title VII prohibits discrimination because of sex in terms or conditions of employment, including sexual harassment by employees of the same sex as the victim of the harassment. Oncale, a worker on an offshore oil platform, alleged that his male co-workers had subjected him to sexual assault and sex-related humiliating actions and had threatened him with rape. His supervisors failed to take any remedial action when he complained. The Supreme Court decision emphasized that Title VII does not reach conduct tinged with offensive sexual overtones but does forbid conduct of a sexual nature that creates a hostile work environment, conduct so severe as to alter the conditions of the victim's employment. The Court stated

> We see no justification in the statutory language or our precedents for a categorical rule excluding same-sex harassment claims from the coverage of Title VII. As some courts have observed, male-on-male sexual harassment in the workplace was assuredly not the principal evil Congress was concerned with when it enacted Title VII. But statutory prohibitions often go beyond the principal evil to cover reasonably comparable evils, and it is ultimately the provisions of our laws rather than the principal concerns of our legislators by which we are governed. Title VII prohibits

"discriminat[ion] . . . because of . . . sex" in the "terms" or "conditions" of employment. Our holding that this includes sexual harassment must extend to sexual harassment of any kind that meets the statutory requirements.

We have emphasized, moreover, that the objective severity of harassment should be judged from the perspective of a reasonable person in the plaintiff's position, considering "all the circumstances." [citing *Harris*] In same-sex (as in all) harassment cases, that inquiry requires careful consideration of the social context in which particular behavior occurs and is experienced by its target. A professional football player's working environment is not severely or pervasively abusive, for example, if the coach smacks him on the buttocks as he heads onto the field—even if the same behavior would reasonably be experienced as abusive by the coach's secretary (male or female) back at the office. The real social impact of workplace behavior often depends on a constellation of surrounding circumstances, expectations, and relationships which are not fully captured by a simple recitation of the words used or the physical acts performed. Common sense, and an appropriate sensitivity to social context, will enable courts and juries to distinguish between simple teasing or roughhousing among members of the same sex, and conduct which a reasonable person in the plaintiff's position would find severely hostile or abusive.

http://www.nolo.com/category/emp_home.html *answers frequently asked questions about sexual harassment.*

Title VII's prohibition on sexual harassment does not include harassment based on sexual orientation or sexual preference according to *Hamner v. St. Vincent Hospital and Health Care Center, Inc.* [224 F.3d 701 (7th Cir. 2000)]. However, a male employee who was harassed by managers and co-workers because he was perceived as being effeminate and did not conform to a male stereotype established a case of hostile environment sexual harassment, *Nichols v. Azteca Restaurant Enterprises, Inc.* [256 F.3d 864 (9th Cir. 2001)].

REMEDIES FOR SEXUAL HARASSMENT

Remedies for sexual harassment available under Title VII include injunctions to stop the harassment and to refrain from such conduct in the future, lost wages and benefits, compensatory and punitive damages for intentional conduct, and legal fees and reinstatement (if appropriate). Employment-related damages, such as back pay, benefits, seniority, and so on, are recoverable in their entirety. Compensatory damages (such as damages for emotional trauma and/or medical expenses) and punitive damages are available in cases of intentional violations of Title VII. Sexual harassment is generally held to be intentional conduct, so such damages are generally available to successful plaintiffs; however, there are statutory limits on the amount of compensatory and punitive damages under Title VII based on the size of the employer. In addition to Title VII, sexual harassment may also be challenged under state EEO laws and common-law torts such as intentional infliction of emotional distress, invasion of privacy, battery, and assault. Compensatory and punitive damages may be available under the various state EEO laws and are usually available under tort law; there are generally no statutory limitations on such damages available under state EEO laws and tort claims.

In addition to Title VII, state EEO laws, and tort claims, federal and state constitutional provisions may also apply to public sector employers guilty of sexual harassment. Public employees who engage in sexual harassment may be subject to suits for damages under 42 U.S.C. § 1983, which allows civil suits for damages against persons who act, under the color of law, to deprive others of legally protected rights. In *United States v. Lanier* [520 U.S. 259 (1997)], the Supreme Court upheld the criminal prosecution, under 18 U.S.C. § 242, of a public employee guilty of sexual harassment; 18 U.S.C. § 242 provides for criminal penalties of fines and prison terms of up to ten years for persons who, under the color of law, willfully subject another person to the deprivation of legally protected rights.

SEXUAL ORIENTATION OR SEXUAL PREFERENCE DISCRIMINATION

Title VII and EEO Legislation

Title VII's prohibition of discrimination based on gender does not extend to discrimination against homosexuals or lesbians; the courts have consistently held that Title VII does not protect gays or lesbians, *DeSantis v. Pacific Telephone and Telegraph Co.* [608 F.2d 327 (9th Cir. 1979)] and *Williamson v. A.G. Edwards & Sons, Inc.* [876 F.2d 69 (8th Cir. 1989)]. Nor does Title VII protect transvestites and transsexuals from employment discrimination, *Holloway v. Arthur Andersen & Co.* [566 F.2d 659 (9th Cir. 1977)], *Sommers v. Budget Marketing Inc.* [667 F.2d 748 (8th Cir. 1982)], and *Ulane v. Eastern Airlines, Inc.* [742 F.2d 1081 (7th Cir. 1984)]. The Rehabilitation Act and the Americans with Disabilities Act specifically exclude homosexuality, bisexuality, transvestism, transsexualism, and other sexual behavior conditions from their protection against discrimination based on disability or handicap. However, a number of state EEO laws, including those of California, Connecticut, Hawaii, Massachusetts, Minnesota, Nevada, New Jersey, Rhode Island, Vermont, Wisconsin, Maryland, New York, and the District of Columbia, specifically prohibit discrimination based on sexual preference or sexual orientation. Other states, including Louisiana, Michigan, New Mexico, Ohio, Pennsylvania, and Washington, prohibit sexual orientation or sexual preference discrimination by public sector employers under executive orders issued by the governor. In addition, some large cities such as New York City and San Francisco have human rights ordinances that prohibit discrimination based on sexual orientation or sexual preference. The state EEO laws of Minnesota, Rhode Island, and California also prohibit employment discrimination based on gender identity or gender expression, which means that transsexuals and persons who have undergone sex change operations are protected from discrimination on those grounds.

There are some limits to the coverage of the state laws against discrimination based on sexual orientation or sexual preference. In *Boy Scouts of America v. Dale* [530 U.S. 640 (2000)], the U.S. Supreme Court held that applying the New Jersey Law Against Discrimination's prohibition of discrimination based on sexual orientation to the Boy Scouts violated their constitutional right of expressive association under the First Amendment. The Court stated that prohibiting the Boy Scouts from dismissing a gay assistant scoutmaster would undermine the Boy Scouts' mission of instilling values in young people.

Constitutional Protection

Public employers who discriminate on the basis of homosexuality are subject to the equal protection provisions of the U.S. Constitution, which prohibit arbitrary or "invidious" discrimination. However, that has not stopped public employers from discriminating against homosexuals; the courts have generally allowed public employers to refuse to hire homosexuals when the employer can show that the ban on homosexuals has some legitimate relationship to valid employment-related concerns. In *Doe v. Gates* [981 F.2d 1316 (D.C. Cir. 1993)], the court upheld the CIA's dismissal of a gay clerk typist because he "posed a threat to national security" based on the fact that he hid information about his homosexuality. The FBI's refusal to hire a lesbian as a special agent was upheld because homosexual conduct was illegal, and the agent would be subject to blackmail to protect herself or her partner, *Padula v. Webster* [822 F.2d 97 (D.C. Cir. 1987)]. The Georgia State Attorney General's refusal to hire a lesbian as a staff attorney was affirmed on similar grounds in *Shahar v. Bowers* [114 F.3d 1097 (11th Cir. 1997)].

A number of cases dealing with discrimination against homosexuals have involved the armed services' refusal to admit homosexuals. In several decisions, the courts have upheld this general policy, but have required the military to demonstrate that an individual has engaged in homosexual conduct in order to bar that person from military service, *Watkins v. U.S. Army* [875 F.2d 699 (9th Cir. 1989)] and *Meinhold v. United States Dept. of Defense* [34 F.3d 1469 (9th Cir. 1994)]. Under President Clinton, the military adopted a "don't ask, don't tell" policy, under which persons will be barred from service if they engage in homosexual conduct or demonstrate a propensity to engage in such conduct. The policy focuses on conduct rather than a person's status; a person's declaration about his or her sexual orientation alone is not sufficient to bar that person from the military. The "don't ask, don't tell" policy has been upheld in several decisions, such as *Phillips v. Perry* [106 F.3d 1420 (9th Cir. 1997)] and *Thomasson v. Perry* [80 F.3d 915 (4th Cir. 1996)].

It must be noted that all of these cases dealing with discrimination against homosexuals were decided prior to the recent Supreme Court decision in *Lawrence v. Texas* [123 S.Ct. 2472 (June 26, 2003)]. In *Lawrence,* which was a criminal law case and not an employment case, the Court, by a 6-3 vote, declared unconstitutional state laws making it a crime for adults of the same sex to engage in consensual sexual activity in the privacy of their home. The majority held that such laws infringed upon the constitutionally protected liberty interests of homosexuals. Some commentators argue that the *Lawrence* case may signal the end of government discrimination against homosexuals; others claim that the case is more limited and deals only with laws that criminalized private, consensual sexual conduct between adults. It remains to be seen what the real impact of *Lawrence* case will be.

OTHER GENDER-DISCRIMINATION ISSUES

Section 712 of Title VII states that

> [n]othing contained in this title shall be construed to repeal or modify any Federal, State, territorial, or local law creating special rights or preference for veterans.

Because most veterans are male, any preference in employment according to veteran status will have a disparate impact on women. The effect of Section 712 is to allow such preference regardless of its disparate impact. In *Personnel Administrator of Massachusetts v. Feeney* [442 U.S. 256 (1979)], the Supreme Court held that Section 712 was permissible under the Constitution because it was not specifically aimed at discriminating against women and did not involve intentional gender discrimination. Feeney had challenged a Massachusetts law that gave combat-era veterans an absolute preference over nonveterans for state civil service jobs. Feeney alleged that the preference and Section 712, which allowed it, violated the equal protection clause of the Constitution.

SUMMARY

- Title VII allows employers to select employees based on their gender, religion, or national origin when these criteria are bona fide occupational qualifications (BFOQs) that are necessary for the safe and efficient operation of the business. As the *Diaz* and *Dothard* cases demonstrate, the courts will look closely at the particular job in question and the employer's justification for the BFOQ. Title VII does not allow the use of race or color as a BFOQ.
- Employers need to ensure that all aspects of the employment process are free from gender discrimination. Promotions and work assignments must not be based on stereotypical assumptions about men's and women's roles or capabilities. Pay and benefits must comply with the Equal Pay Act and with Title VII, and employers must not restrict the job opportunities of females because of concerns about potential hazards to pregnant women or their children. The Family and Medical Leave Act requires larger employers to allow employees unpaid leave for childbirth, adoption, and medical conditions.
- Sexual harassment in the workplace can pose serious legal and morale problems; employers should take positive steps to inform employees that sexual harassment will not be tolerated and that the employer has a policy in place to resolve sexual complaints fairly and effectively. Title VII does not prohibit discrimination based on sexual orientation or sexual preference, but some states do outlaw such discrimination. The equal protection clause of the U.S. Constitution may restrict sexual orientation or sexual preference discrimination by public sector employers.

QUESTIONS

1. Explain what is meant by gender-plus discrimination.
2. Can customer preference be used to support a restaurant's decision to hire only male waiters? What must an employer demonstrate to justify using gender as a BFOQ for hiring?
3. Must an employer offer paid pregnancy leave for employees under Title VII? How do the Pregnancy Discrimination Act provisions of Title VII affect employment benefits?
4. Under what circumstances can an employer be held liable for a supervisor's sexual harassment of another employee? For sexual harassment by a co-worker? For sexual harassment by a nonemployee?

5. When can Title VII be used to challenge gender-based pay differentials for jobs that are not equivalent? Is there a difference between coverage of the Equal Pay Act and that of the pay discrimination prohibitions of Title VII? Explain your answers.
6. Can any employer legally refuse to hire homosexuals? Explain your answer.
7. Are all employees entitled to take leave under the Family and Medical Leave Act? Explain.
8. What arguments can you make to support the position that same-sex harassment should be subject to Title VII? What arguments can you make to oppose that position? Which arguments do you find more convincing? Why?

CASE PROBLEMS

1. Anderson, a female attorney, was hired as an associate in a large law firm in 1978. She had accepted the position based on the firm's representations that associates would advance to partnership after five or six years and that being promoted to partner "was a matter of course" for associates who received satisfactory evaluations. The firm also maintained that promotions were made on a "fair and equal basis." Anderson consistently received satisfactory evaluations, yet her promotion to partnership was rejected in 1984. She again was considered and rejected in 1985. The firm's rules state that an associate passed over for promotion must seek employment elsewhere. Anderson was therefore terminated by the firm on December 31, 1985. The firm, with more than fifty partners, has never had a female partner. Anderson filed a complaint alleging gender discrimination against the firm. The firm replied that the selection of partners is not subject to Title VII because it entails a change in status "from employee to employer."

   Does Title VII apply to such partnership selection decisions? Does Anderson's complaint state a claim under Title VII? See *Hishon v. King & Spaulding* [467 U.S. 69 (U.S. Sup. Ct. 1984)].
2. John Plebani had worked as a waiter at the Cabaret Restaurant in Binghamton, New York. He was discharged when the restaurant manager decided that business would improve if the image of the restaurant was changed to that of a "gentlemen's club" featuring female staff in skimpy uniforms. Cabaret hired females for all positions involving customer contact; males were limited to kitchen positions. For a few weeks after the change, there was a slight improvement in the restaurant's business, but there was no significant long-term change. Plebani filed charges under Title VII and the New York State Human Rights Law, alleging his discharge was due to gender discrimination.

   How should the court rule on Plebani's complaint? Why? What defenses can the restaurant claim? See *Guardian Capital Corp. v. N.Y.S. Human Rights Division* [46 A.D.2d 832, 360 N.Y.S.2d 937 (N.Y. App. Div. 1974)].
3. A group of nurses employed by the State of Illinois filed a complaint charging the state with gender discrimination in classification and compensation of employees. The nurses alleged that the state had refused to implement the changes in job classifications and wage rates recommended by an evaluation study conducted by the state. The study suggested that changes in pay and classification for some female-dominated job classes should be more equitable.

   Does the nurses' complaint state a claim under Title VII? Explain your answer. See *American Nurses Association v. Illinois* [783 F.2d 716 (7th Cir. 1986)].

4. Baker, a female, was employed as a history teacher by More Science High School for three years. Although she received good evaluation reviews for her first two years, her third-year review gave her a poor evaluation. Her contract of employment was not renewed after the end of her third year. During Baker's third year, the coach of the boys' basketball team had given notice of his resignation, which was effective at the end of that school year. Baker was replaced as a history teacher by Dan Roundball, who was also hired as coach of the boys' basketball team. Baker filed a complaint with the EEOC alleging that her contract was not renewed because the school wanted to replace her with a man who would also coach the basketball team.

   Is More Science High School guilty of violating Title VII's prohibition on gender discrimination? Explain your answer. See *Carlile v. South Routt School Dist.* [739 F.2d 1496 (10th Cir. 1984)].

5. Margaret Hasselman worked as a lobby attendant at an office building located in New York City; the building was managed by Sage Realty. Lobby attendants were responsible for the security, safety, and maintenance of the building and for providing information to people entering the building. Sage furnished uniforms for lobby attendants; the style of uniforms was changed every few months. For the summer months, Sage distributed new uniforms based on a "United States Bicentennial" theme—a red, white, and blue, loosely fitted poncho, with slits down the front and sides secured by single snaps. The attendants were not permitted to wear shirts or blouses under the outfit. The uniforms were all provided in the same size, despite the fact that the sizes of the attendants varied. Hasselman found that the uniform did not fit her well; it was too short and was very revealing. She was concerned about wearing the uniform in public but was informed by Sage that her job required wearing the uniform. While wearing the uniform, Hasselman was subjected to repeated lewd, sexual comments and gestures and to sexual propositions; she found the experience humiliating and was unable to perform her job properly. Hasselman complained to her supervisor, but he ignored her complaints. Hasselman then decided to wear her prior, less revealing uniform. She also sent a letter to Sage management complaining about the revealing nature of the uniform and the harassment that she experienced. In response, she received a letter stating that lobby attendants must wear the uniform supplied, and no exceptions to that requirement would be allowed. When Hasselman reported for work the next day wearing the prior uniform, she was informed that she was being laid off and was sent home. Hasselman then contacted the EEOC to complain about her discharge.

   Was Hasselman the victim of illegal gender discrimination? Did Sage's actions toward her violate Title VII? Explain your answers. See *EEOC v. Sage Realty Corp.* [507 F.Supp. 599 (S.D.N.Y. 1981)].

6. In October 1981, Rebecca Thomas was hired as a personnel assistant by Cooper Industries, a plant that manufactures hammers and axes. In February 1982, Thomas was promoted to personnel supervisor. Her boss, the plant's employee relations manager, was fired in March 1983, whereupon she filled his job in an acting capacity. The plant manager gave her the highest possible rating on her performance evaluation, but corporate officials repeatedly refused to interview her for permanent award of the position. According to testimony, the plant manager was told by the company vice president that there was "no way" a woman could stand up to the union in the capacity of employee relations manager. A male was ultimately hired to fill the job on a permanent basis.

   Is this an example of gender discrimination? Explain your answer. See *Thomas v. Cooper Industries, Inc.* [627 F. Supp. 655 (W.D. N.C. 1986)].

7. Alvie Thompkins was employed as a full-time instructor of mathematics at Morris Brown College. Her classes were scheduled in academic year 1979–1980 in such a way that she was able to hold down a second full-time post as a math instructor at Douglas High School. Only one other faculty member, Thompkins's predecessor at Morris Brown College, ever held down two concurrent full-time jobs, and the college's vice president for academic affairs testified that he had never been aware of this earlier situation. Some male "part-time" faculty of the college were employed full-time elsewhere. Although labeled "part-timers," some of these faculty sometimes taught nine to twelve credit hours per semester, which was about the same as many "full-time" faculty. Thompkins was told to choose between her two full-time jobs; when she refused to make a choice, she was fired.

Is this a case of gender discrimination? Explain your answer. See *Thompkins v. Morris Brown College* [752 F.2d 558 37 F.E.P. Cases 24 (11th Cir. 1985)].

8. Diane L. Matthews served in the U.S. Army for four years as a field communication equipment mechanic. She received numerous awards and high performance ratings and ultimately was promoted to sergeant. She was honorably discharged in 1980. She enrolled in the University of Maine and joined the Reserve Officers Training Corps program on campus. Her ROTC instructor learned that she had attended a student senate meeting, which had been called to discuss the budget for the Wilde-Stein Club. Upon inquiring as to the nature of the club, he was told by Matthews that it was the campus homosexual organization. On further inquiry, she told the officer she was a lesbian. Although her commander did not attempt to interfere with Matthews's continued membership in the club, he reported Matthews's disclosure to his supervisor. An investigation was conducted and she was disenrolled from the ROTC program.

Was Matthews a victim of gender discrimination? Explain your answer. See *Matthews v. Marsh* [755 F.2d 182, 37 F.E.P. Cases 126 (1st Cir. 1985)].

9. Wilson, a male, applied for a job as a flight attendant with Southwest Airlines. Southwest refused to hire him because the airline hires only females for those positions. Southwest, a small commuter airline in the southwestern United States, must compete against larger, more established airlines for passengers. Southwest, which has its headquarters at Love Field in Dallas, decided that the best way to compete with those larger airlines was to establish a distinctive image. Southwest decided to base its marketing image as the "Love Airline"; its slogan is, "We're spreading love all over Texas." Southwest requires its flight attendants and ticket clerks, all female, to wear a uniform consisting of a brief halter top, hot pants, and high boots. Its quick ticketing and check-in flight counters are called "quickie machines," and the in-flight snacks and drinks are referred to as "love bites" and "love potions." Southwest claims that it is identified with the public through its "youthful, feminine" image; it cites surveys of its passengers to support its claim that business necessity requires it to hire only females for all public contact positions. The surveys asked passengers the reasons that they chose to fly with Southwest; the reason labeled "courteous and attentive hostesses" was ranked fifth in importance, after reasons relating to lower fares, frequency of flights, on-time departures, and helpful reservations personnel.

Has Southwest established that its policy of hiring only females in flight attendant and ticket clerk positions is a bona fide occupational qualification? See *Wilson v. Southwest Airlines Co.* [517 F. Supp. 292 (N.D. Texas 1981)].

10. George Vorman was being recruited by the National Aeronautics and Space Administration (NASA) as a defense intelligence coordinator; that position involved access to classified intelligence and national security information. After the preliminary round of interviews, NASA required him to undergo extensive psychological testing and expanded security clearance investigation far beyond those normally required of recruits. Vorman was informed that the expanded investigation and testing were required because he was suspected of being homosexual. Vorman refused to either affirm or deny that he was homosexual because he felt that it was irrelevant to his qualifications for the job. NASA ultimately refused to hire Vorman; he filed suit claiming he was discriminated against because of NASA's perception of his sexual orientation.

On what legal provisions can Vorman base his suit? Is he likely to win? Would the outcome be different if Vorman applied for a flight engineer position that did not involve classified national security information? Explain your answers. See *Norton v. Macy [417 F.2d 1161* (D.C. Cir. 1969)] and *High Tech Gays v. Defense Industry Security Clearance Office* [895 F.2d 563 (9th Cir. 1990)].

INTERNET EXERCISES

1. You are a human resource specialist at an international consulting firm headquartered near Palo Alto, California. You have been directed to revise your firm's policy on family and medical leave: Should the policy be extended to allow unmarried employees leave to care for their "domestic partners"? Should the definition of "domestic partners" include same-sex partners? Do the regulations under the Family and Medical Leave Act (FMLA) provide any guidance? Check the U.S. Department of Labor Web site **http://www.dol.gov** and search the FMLA regulations.
2. Can you find other resources at the U.S. Department of Labor site? You might want to consult other Web sites that may provide resource information such as **http://www.9to5.org**, and you should search the online archives of *HR Magazine* at **http://www.shrm.org**.
3. Because your firm is international, you might want to look at the European Union family leave provisions at **http://europa.eu.int/geninfo/query_en.htm**. This is a site that lets you search for specific policies and information about family and maternity leave.
4. Can you find other sites that provide assistance?

INFOTRAC KEYWORDS

http://www.infotrac-college.com

gender stereotyping, gender discrimination, equal pay act, equal work, comparable worth, pregnancy discrimination, FMLA, sexual harassment, quid pro quo harassment

5

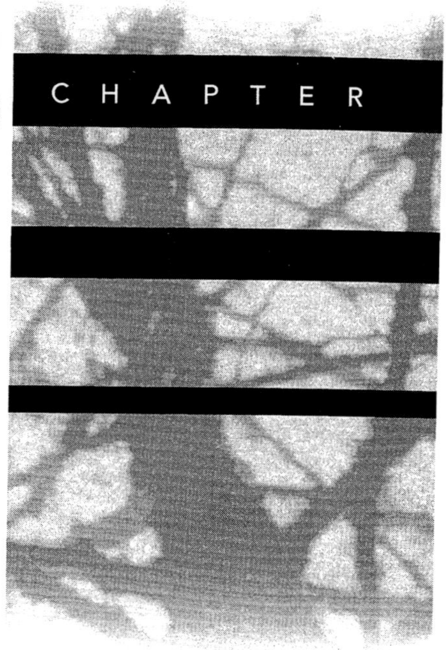

DISCRIMINATION BASED ON RELIGION AND NATIONAL ORIGIN; PROCEDURES UNDER TITLE VII

The preceding chapters dealt with Title VII of the Civil Rights Act of 1964 and its prohibitions on employment discrimination based on race and sex. This chapter deals with the Title VII provisions and procedures regarding discrimination based on religion and national origin.

DISCRIMINATION ON THE BASIS OF RELIGION

Title VII prohibits employment discrimination because of religion. The definition of religion under Title VII is fairly broad; it includes ". . . all aspects of religious observance and practice, as well as belief. . . ." Harassment because of an individual's religious beliefs (or lack thereof) that creates a hostile work environment is also prohibited under Title VII. Title VII protection extends to the beliefs and practices connected with organized religions but also includes what the EEOC Guidelines [29 C.F.R. § 1605.1] define as a person's "moral or ethical beliefs as to what is right and wrong which are sincerely held with the strength of traditional religious views." Such personal moral or ethical beliefs are protected even if the beliefs are not connected with any formal or organized religion. Atheism is included under the Title VII definition of religion according to *Young v. Southwestern Savings & Loan Association* [509 F.2d 140 (5th Cir. 1975)], but personal political or social ideologies are not protected; the racist and anti-Semitic beliefs of the Ku Klux Klan do not fall under the definition of religion. *Bellamy v. Mason's Stores, Inc.* [368 F.Supp. 1025 (W.D. Va. 1973)], *aff'd* on other grounds [508 F.2d

(4th Cir. 1974)]. Harassment of an individual because of that person's self-identification as a member of the Ku Klux Klan was not harassment because of religion and did not give rise to a claim under Title VII, *Swartzentruber v. Gunite Corp.* [99 F.Supp.2d 976 (N.D. Ind. 2000)].

For facts about religious discrimination, see **http://www.eeoc.gov/facts/fs-relig.html**

STATUTORY EXCEPTIONS FOR RELIGIOUS PREFERENCE

Title VII provides for several exceptions to the prohibition on religious discrimination.

Religion as a BFOQ

Section 703(e)(1) of Title VII includes religion within the BFOQ exception. Religion, as with gender or national origin, may be used as a BFOQ when the employer establishes that business necessity (the safe and efficient performance of the job) requires hiring individuals of a particular religion. Only rarely will a private sector business be able to establish a BFOQ based on religion; for example, an employer who is providing helicopter pilots under contract to the Saudi Arabian government to fly Muslim pilgrims to Mecca may require that all pilots be of the Muslim religion because Islamic law prohibits non-Muslims from entering the holy areas of the city of Mecca. The penalty for violating the prohibition is beheading; the employer could therefore refuse to hire non-Muslims or require all pilots to convert to Islam. See the case of *Kern v. Dynalectron Corp.* [577 F. Supp. 1196 (N.D. Texas 1983)].

Educational Institutions under Section 703(e)(2)

Religiously affiliated schools, colleges, universities, or other educational institutions are permitted to give preference to members of their particular religion in hiring. This exception is broader than that available under the BFOQ provisions; under Section 703(e)(2), the educational institution does not have to demonstrate business necessity to give preference to members of its religion when hiring employees. Therefore, a Hebrew day school can require that all of its teachers be Jewish, and a Catholic university such as Notre Dame can require that the university president be Catholic.

Section 702(a)

In addition to the exception granted to religious schools or colleges under Section 703(e)(2), Section 702(a) provides an exception under Title VII to all religious societies, religious corporations, religious educational institutions, or religious associations. This exception covers all religious entities and is wider than that under Section 703(e)(2), which is limited to religious educational institutions. Section 702(a) states

> This Title shall not apply to . . . a religious corporation, association, educational institution, or society with respect to the employment of individuals of a particular religion to perform work connected with the carrying on by such corporation, association, educational institution or society of its activities.

But how broad is the scope of the exemption under Section 702(a): Does it extend to all activities of a religious corporation, even those that are not really religious in character? The Supreme Court considered that question in the next case.

Corporation of the Presiding Bishop of The Church of Jesus Christ of Latter-day Saints v. Amos

483 U.S. 327 (1987)

[Note that this case was decided prior to the 1991 amendments to Title VII, when Section 702(a) was simply Section 702.]

White, J.

Section 702 of the Civil Rights Act of 1964, as amended, exempts religious organizations from Title VII's prohibition against discrimination in employment on the basis of religion. The question presented is whether applying the Section 702 exemption to the secular nonprofit activities of religious organizations violates the Establishment Clause of the First Amendment. The District Court held that it does, and the case is here on direct appeal.

The Deseret Gymnasium (Gymnasium) in Salt Lake City, Utah, is a nonprofit facility, open to the public, run by the Corporation of the Presiding Bishop of The Church of Jesus Christ of Latter-day Saints (CPB), and the Corporation of the President of The Church of Jesus Christ of Latter-day Saints (COP). The CPB and the COP are religious entities associated with The Church of Jesus Christ of Latter-day Saints (Church), an unincorporated religious association sometimes called the Mormon or LDS Church.

Mayson worked at the Gymnasium for some 16 years as an assistant building engineer and then building engineer. He was discharged in 1981 because he failed to qualify for a temple recommend; that is, a certificate that he is a member of the Church and eligible to attend its temples.

Mayson and others purporting to represent a class of plaintiffs brought an action against the CPB and the COP alleging, among other things, discrimination on the basis of religion in violation . . . of the Civil Rights Act of 1964. . . . The defendants moved to dismiss this claim on the ground that Section 702 shields them from liability. The plaintiffs contended that if construed to allow religious employers to discriminate on religious grounds in hiring for nonreligious jobs, Section 702 violates the Establishment Clause [of the First Amendment].

The District Court first considered whether the facts of this case require a decision on the plaintiffs' constitutional argument. Starting from the premise that the religious activities of religious employers can permissibly be exempted under Section 702, the court developed a three-part test to determine whether an activity is religious. Applying this test to Mayson's situation, the court found: first, that the Gymnasium is intimately connected to the Church financially and in matters of management; second, that there is no clear connection between the primary function which the Gymnasium performs and the religious beliefs and tenets of the Mormon Church or church administration; and third, that none of Mayson's duties at the Gymnasium are "even tangentially related to any conceivable religious belief or ritual of the Mormon Church or church administration," . . . The court concluded that Mayson's case involves nonreligious activity.

The court next considered the plaintiffs' constitutional challenge to Section 702. Applying the three-part test set out in *Lemon v. Kurtzman*. . . , the court first held that Section 702 has the permissible secular purpose of "assuring that the government remains neutral and does not meddle in religious affairs by interfering with the decision-making process in religions. . . ." The court concluded, however, that Section 702 fails the second part of the *Lemon* test because the provision has the primary effect of advancing religion. Among the considerations mentioned by the court were: that Section 702 singles out religious entities for a benefit, rather than benefiting a broad grouping of which religious organizations are only a part; that Section 702 is not supported by long historical tradition; and that Section 702 burdens the free exercise rights of employees of religious institutions who work in nonreligious jobs.

Finding that Section 702 impermissibly sponsors religious organizations by granting them "an exclusive authorization to engage in conduct which can directly and immediately advance religious tenets and practices," the court declared the statute unconstitutional as applied to secular activity. The court entered summary judgment in favor of Mayson and ordered him reinstated with backpay. Subsequently, the court vacated its judgment so that the United States could intervene to defend the constitutionality of Section 702. After further briefing and argument the court affirmed its prior determination and reentered a final judgment for Mayson. . . .

We find unpersuasive the District Court's reliance on the fact that Section 702 singles out religious entities for a benefit. Although the Court has given weight to this consideration in its past decisions, it has never indicated that statutes that give special consideration to religious groups are *per se* invalid. That would run contrary to the teaching of our cases that there is ample room for accommodation of religion under the Establishment Clause.

Where, as here, government acts with the proper purpose of lifting a regulation that burdens the exercise of religion, we see no reason to require that the exemption come packaged with benefits to secular entities. We are also unpersuaded by the District Court's reliance on the argument that Section 702 is unsupported by long historical tradition. There was simply no need to consider the scope of the Section 702 exemption until the 1964 Civil Rights Act was passed, and the fact that Congress concluded after eight years that the original exemption was unnecessarily narrow is a decision entitled to deference, not suspicion.

Appellees argue that Section 702 offends equal protection principles by giving less protection to the employees of religious employers than to the employees of secular employers.

. . . In a case such as this, where a statute is neutral on its face and motivated by a permissible purpose of limiting governmental interference with the exercise of religion, we see no justification for applying strict scrutiny to a statute that passes the *Lemon* test. The proper inquiry is whether Congress has chosen a rational classification to further a legitimate end. We have already indicated that Congress acted with a legitimate purpose in expanding the Section 702 exemption to cover all activities of religious employers. . . . it suffices to hold—as we now do—that as applied to the nonprofit activities of religious employers, Section 702 is rationally related to the legitimate purpose of alleviating significant governmental interference with the ability of religious organizations to define and carry out their religious missions.

It cannot be seriously contended that Section 702 impermissibly entangles church and state; the statute effectuates a more complete separation of the two and avoids the kind of intrusive inquiry into religious belief that the District Court engaged in this case. The statute easily passes muster under the third part of the *Lemon* test.

The judgment of the District Court is reversed, and the case is remanded for further proceedings consistent with this opinion.

It is so ordered.

Brennan, J., with whom Marshall, J. joins (concurring)

. . . my concurrence in the judgment rests on the fact that this case involves a challenge to the application of Section 702's categorical exemption to the activities of a nonprofit organization. I believe that the particular character of nonprofit activity makes inappropriate a case-by-case determination whether its nature is religious or secular. . . .

. . . I concur in the Court's judgment that the nonprofit Deseret Gymnasium may avail itself of an automatic exemption from Title VII's proscription on religious discrimination.

O'Connor, J. (concurring)

. . . I emphasize that under the holding of the Court, and under my view of the appropriate Establishment Clause analysis, the question of the constitutionality of the Section 702 exemption as applied to for-profit activities of religious organizations remains open.

Case Questions

1. What is the relevance of the three-part test set out in *Lemon v. Kurtzman* to a claim under Title VII?
2. What, according to the Supreme Court, was the rationale for the enactment of the Section 702(a) exemption for religious organizations? How does that purpose relate to the three-part test from *Lemon v. Kurtzman*?
3. Does the Section 702(a) exemption apply to all activities of religious organizations, even to commercial activities? Does the exemption allow religious organizations to discriminate on the basis of race or gender? Explain your answers.

Reasonable Accommodation

Even when religion is not a BFOQ and the employer is not within the Section 702 exemption, the prohibition against discrimination on the basis of religion is not absolute. Section 701(j) defines religion as

> includ[ing] all aspects of religious observance and practice, as well as belief, unless an employer demonstrates that he is unable to reasonably accommodate to an employee's religious observance or practice without undue hardship on the conduct of the employer's business.

An employer must make reasonable attempts to accommodate an employee's religious beliefs or practices, but if such attempts are not successful or involve undue hardship, the employer may discharge the employee. The following case explores the extent to which an employer is required to accommodate an employee's beliefs.

Trans World Airlines v. Hardison

432 U.S. 63 (1977)

White, J.

Petitioner Trans World Airlines (TWA) operates a large maintenance and overhaul base in Kansas City, Mo. On June 5, 1967, respondent Larry G. Hardison was hired by TWA to work as a clerk in the Stores Department at its Kansas City base. Because of its essential role in the Kansas City operation, the Stores Department must operate 24 hours per day, 365 days per year, and whenever an employee's job in that department is not filled, an employee must be shifted from another department, or a supervisor must cover the job, even if the work in other areas may suffer.

Hardison, like other employees at the Kansas City base, was subject to a seniority system contained in a collective-bargaining agreement which TWA maintains with petitioner International Association of Machinists and Aerospace Workers (IAM). The seniority system is implemented by the union steward through a system of bidding by employees for particular shift assignments as they become available. The most senior employees have first choice for job and shift assignments, and the most junior employees are required to work when the union steward is unable to find enough people willing to work at a particular time or in a particular job to fill TWA's needs.

In the spring of 1968 Hardison began to study the religion known as the Worldwide Church of God. One of the tenets of that religion is that one must observe the Sabbath by refraining from performing any work from sunset on Friday until sunset on Saturday. The religion also proscribes work on certain specified religious holidays.

When Hardison informed Everett Kussman, the manager of the Stores Department, of his religious conviction regarding observance of the Sabbath, Kussman agreed that the union steward should seek a job swap for Hardison or a change of days off; that Hardison would have his religious holidays off whenever possible if Hardison agreed to work the traditional holidays when asked; and that Kussman would try to find Hardison another job that would be more compatible with his religious beliefs. The problem was temporarily solved when Hardison transferred to the 11 P.M.–7 A.M. shift. Working this shift permitted Hardison to observe his Sabbath.

The problem soon reappeared when Hardison bid for and received a transfer from Building 1, where he had been employed, to Building 2, where he would work the day shift. The two buildings had entirely separate seniority lists; and while in Building 1 Hardison had sufficient seniority to observe the Sabbath regularly, he was second from the bottom on the Building 2 seniority list.

In Building 2 Hardison was asked to work Saturdays when a fellow employee went on vacation. TWA agreed to permit the union to seek a change of work assignments for Hardison, but the union was not willing to violate the seniority provisions set out in the collective-bargaining contract, and Hardison had insufficient seniority to bid for a shift having Saturdays off.

A proposal that Hardison work only four days a week was rejected by the company. Hardison's job was essential, and on weekends he was the only available person on his shift to perform it. To leave the position empty would have impaired Supply Shop functions, which were critical to airline operations; to fill Hardison's position with a supervisor or an employee from another area would simply have undermanned another operation; and to employ someone not regularly assigned to work Saturdays would have required TWA to pay premium wages.

When an accommodation was not reached, Hardison refused to report for work on Saturdays. . . . [Hardison was fired by TWA.]

The Court of Appeals found that TWA had committed an unlawful employment practice under Section 703(a)(1) of the Act. . . .

In 1967 the EEOC amended its guidelines to require employers "to make reasonable accommodations to the religious needs of employees and prospective employees where such accommodations can be made without undue hardship on the conduct of the employer's business." The Commission did not suggest what sort of accommodations are "reasonable" or when hardship to an employer becomes "undue."

This question—the extent of the required accommodation—remained unsettled . . . Congress [then] included the following definition of religion in its 1972 amendments to Title VII:

> The term "religion" includes all aspects of religious observance and practice, as well as belief, unless an employer demonstrates that he is unable to reasonably accommodate to an employee's or prospective employee's religious observance or practice without undue hardship on the conduct of the employer's business. [Section 701(j)] . . .

The Court of Appeals held that TWA had not made reasonable efforts to accommodate Hardison's religious needs. . . .

We disagree. . . .

. . . As the record shows, Hardison himself testified that Kussman was willing, but the union was not, to work out a shift or job trade with another employee.

. . . it appears to us that the [seniority] system itself represented a significant accommodation to the needs, both religious and secular, of all of TWA's employees. As will become apparent, the seniority system represents a neutral way of minimizing the number of occasions when an employee must work on a day that he would prefer to have off. . . .

We are also convinced, contrary to the Court of Appeals, that TWA cannot be faulted for having failed itself to work out a shift or job swap for Hardison. Both the union and TWA had agreed to the seniority system; the union was unwilling to entertain a variance over the objections of men senior to Hardison. . . .

Had TWA nevertheless circumvented the seniority system by relieving Hardison of Saturday work and ordering a senior employee to replace him, it would have denied the latter his shift preference so that Hardison could be given his. The senior employee would also have been deprived of his contractual rights under the collective-bargaining agreement.

Title VII does not contemplate such unequal treatment. . . . we conclude that Title VII does not require an employer to go that far.

. . . [T]he Court of Appeals suggested that TWA could have replaced Hardison on his Saturday shift with other available employees through the payment of premium wages. Both of these alternatives would involve costs to TWA, either in the form of lost efficiency in other jobs or as higher wages.

To require TWA to bear more than a *de minimis* cost in order to give Hardison Saturdays off is an undue hardship. . . .

As we have seen, the paramount concern of Congress in enacting Title VII was the elimination of discrimination in employment. In the absence of clear statutory language or legislative history to the contrary, we will not readily construe the statute to require an employer to discriminate against some employees in order to enable others to observe their Sabbath.

Reversed.

Case Questions

1. Did Hardison's religious beliefs present a scheduling problem when he was hired? Is the employer required to accommodate religious beliefs if a conflict

arises only after the employee has been hired? Explain your answers.

2. Did the union's refusal to grant Hardison a variance from the seniority requirements of the collective-bargaining agreement violate the union's duty to accommodate Hardison's beliefs under Title VII? Explain.

3. Why is TWA unwilling to pay some other employee overtime to work for Hardison on Saturdays? Is TWA required to do so under Title VII? Explain.

The Duty of Reasonable Accommodation

As the *Hardison* case illustrates, the prohibition of religious discrimination under Title VII is not absolute; an employee may not be protected under Title VII if the employer is unable to make reasonable accommodation to the employee's religious beliefs or practices without undue hardship to the employer's business. The determination of what accommodation is reasonable, and whether it would impose an undue hardship on the employer, is to be based on each individual case and the facts of each situation. The EEOC Guidelines indicate that the following factors will be considered in determining what is a reasonable accommodation and whether it results in undue hardship: the size of the employer's work force and the number of employees requiring accommodation, the nature of the job or jobs that present a conflict, the cost of the accommodation, the administrative requirements of the accommodation, whether the employees affected are under a collective bargaining agreement, and what alternatives are available and have been considered by the employer. The employee seeking accommodation must first inform the employer of the conflict with his or her religious beliefs or practices and must request accommodation; the employee is also required to act reasonably in considering the alternative means of accommodation available, *Jordan v. North Carolina National Bank* [565 F.2d 72 (4th Cir. 1977)].

Some employees may find a co-worker's exercise of his or her religious beliefs offensive. How should the employer accommodate the employee's right to express her or his religious beliefs with the concerns of the co-workers? Must the employer allow an employee continually to ask co-workers if they "have been born again" or to invite them to attend religious services, when the co-workers have made it clear that they find such conduct offensive? In *Wilson v. U.S. West Communications* [58 F.3d 1337 (8th Cir. 1995)], an employee insisted on wearing an antiabortion button featuring a color photo of a fetus as an expression of her religious beliefs; she also occasionally wore a T-shirt with a color image of a fetus. Other employees found the button and the T-shirt offensive or disturbing. Their reactions to the button and T-shirt caused disruptions at work, and the employer documented a 40 percent decline in productivity of the unit after the employee began wearing the button. The employer offered the employee three choices: (1) she could wear the button while she was in her cubicle, but must take it off when she moved around the office; (2) she could cover the button while at work; or (3) she could wear a different antiabortion button without the photograph. The employee refused, insisting that she had to wear the button to be a "living witness" to her religious beliefs. The employer ultimately fired the employee, and the former employee filed suit under Title VII, alleging religious discrimination. She argued that the disruption in the workplace was caused by the reaction of the co-workers, not by her wearing the button. The court of appeals held that the employer did not violate Title VII by firing the employee; Title VII requires that an employer reasonably accommodate an employee's religious beliefs but does not require that the employer allow that employee to impose her or his religious views on others.

If there are several ways to accommodate the employee's religious beliefs, is the employer required to provide the accommodation that is preferred by the employee? In *Ansonia Board of Education v. Philbrook* [479 U.S. 60 (1986)], the Supreme Court held the following:

> . . . We find no basis in either the statute or its legislative history for requiring an employer to choose any particular reasonable accommodation. By its very terms the statute directs that any reasonable accommodation by the employer is sufficient to meet its accommodation obligation. The employer violates the statute unless it "demonstrates that [it] is unable to reasonably accommodate . . . an employee's . . . religious observance or practice without undue hardship on the conduct of the employer's business." Thus, where the employer has already reasonably accommodated the employee's religious needs, the statutory inquiry is at an end. The employer need not further show that each of the employee's alternative accommodations would result in undue hardship. As *Hardison* illustrates, the extent of undue hardship on the employer's business is at issue only where the employer claims that it is unable to offer any reasonable accommodation without such hardship. Once the Court of Appeals assumed that the school board had offered to Philbrook a reasonable alternative, it erred by requiring the board to nonetheless demonstrate the hardship of Philbrook's alternatives. . . . We accordingly hold that an employer has met its obligation under Section 701(j) when it demonstrates that it has offered a reasonable accommodation to the employee.

Public Employers

In addition to the obligations to attempt to accommodate employees' religious beliefs or practices under Title VII, public sector employers are also subject to the constitutional protections for freedom of religion under the First Amendment of the U.S. Constitution. The First Amendment prohibits the establishment of religion by government (generally interpreted as government conduct favoring or promoting religion) and also prohibits undue government interference with the free exercise of religion. The Supreme Court has broadly interpreted religion in determining the scope of protection under the First Amendment, requiring only that the plaintiff demonstrate that her belief is "religious" in her own scheme of things and that it is sincerely held with the strength of traditional religious beliefs, *Welsh v. United States* [398 U.S. 333 (1970)], *United States v. Seeger* [380 U.S. 163 (1965)], and *Frazee v. Illinois Dept. of Employment Security* [489 U.S. 829 (1989)]. The case of *Lemon v. Kurtzman* [403 U.S. 602 (1971)] (discussed in the *Amos* case) set out a three-part test to determine if government action affecting religion violates the First Amendment: (1) Does the government action have a secular purpose? (2) Does the action neither advance nor inhibit religion? (3) Does the government action involve "entanglement" of church and state? In *Estate of Thornton v. Caldor, Inc.* [472 U.S. 703 (1985)], the Supreme Court held that a Connecticut statute requiring employers to allow employees to take off work on their religious Sabbath was unconstitutional. That statute violated the First Amendment because it advanced a religious purpose: It gave Sabbath observers an unqualified right not to work, and it ignored the interests and convenience of the employer and other employees who did not observe a Sabbath.

DISCRIMINATION BASED ON NATIONAL ORIGIN

Title VII prohibits employment discrimination against any applicant or employee because of national origin, although it does recognize that national origin may be a BFOQ, where the employer demonstrates that hiring employees of a particular ethnic or national origin is a business necessity for the safe and efficient performance of the job in question. The government's response to the terrorist attacks on the World Trade Center and the Pentagon on September 11, 2001, and the public's heightened awareness regarding security and fear of potential threats led to increased scrutiny of individuals who appeared to be Muslims or of Middle Eastern origin. Incidents of "ethnic profiling" were common; persons (primarily males) perceived to be from Middle Eastern countries were subjected to security checks, searches, interrogation by authorities, and general public suspicion. Is such ethnic profiling permissible under Title VII? In general, no. Any employment discrimination against an individual because of that individual's (actual or perceived) national origin, ethnicity, or religion is a violation of Title VII unless it is justified by a BFOQ.

http://www.eeoc.gov/facts/fs-nator.html *discusses issues in national origin discrimination.*

Following the events of September 11, 2001, the EEOC reported an increase in complaints alleging discrimination against individuals because they were perceived as being Muslim, Arabic, Middle Eastern, South Asian, or Sikh. More than 800 complaints of "backlash" discrimination were filed by individuals who alleged that they were discriminated against because of their religion or national origin; most of the complaints involved discharge or harassment. EEOC enforcement efforts have resulted in nearly 100 individuals receiving over $1.45 million in benefits as resolution of employment discrimination complaints related to the September 11 attacks. The EEOC has also conducted numerous outreach and education efforts for employers to promote voluntary compliance with Title VII. [1]

DEFINITION

National origin discrimination includes any discrimination based upon the place of origin of an applicant or employee or his or her ancestor(s) and any discrimination

[1]EEOC Press Release, 7/17/2003, "Muslim Pilot Fired Due to Religion and Appearance, EEOC Says in post-9/11 Backlash Discrimination Suit," **http://www.EEOC.gov/press/7-17-03a.html**.

based upon the physical, cultural, or linguistic characteristics of an ethnic group. Title VII's prohibition on national origin discrimination includes harassment of employees because of their national origin and extends to discrimination based upon reasons related to national origin or ethnic considerations, such as: (1) a person's marriage to a person of, or association with persons of, an ethnic or national origin group; (2) a person's membership in, or association with, an organization identified with or seeking to promote the interests of any ethnic or national origin group; (3) a person's attendance or participation in schools, churches, temples, or mosques generally used by persons of an ethnic or national origin group; or (4) a person's name, or the name of the person's spouse, which is associated with an ethnic or national origin group. An employer may violate the statute by discriminating against an applicant or employee whose education or training is foreign or, conversely, by requiring that training or education be done abroad.

Title VII does allow employers to hire employees based on legitimate business, safety, or security concerns; employers may impose heightened background screening for employees or applicants, as long as such requirements are related to legitimate job concerns and are applied uniformly to the employees in similar situations or job classes. Section 703(g) states that it is not a violation of Title VII for an employer to refuse to hire or to discharge an employee who is unable to meet the requirements for a national security clearance where federal law or regulations require such a clearance for the job in question.

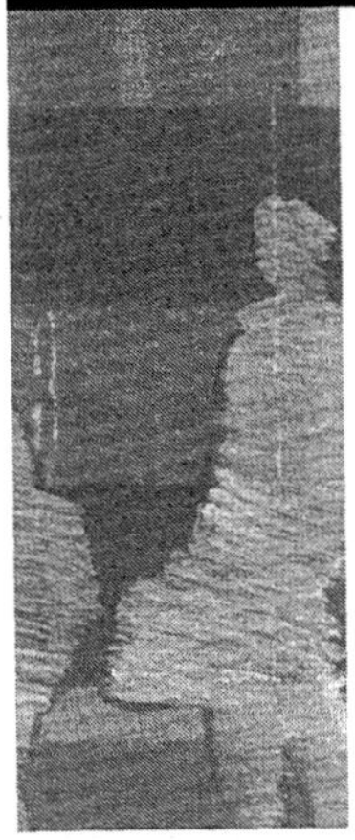

THE WORKING LAW

EEOC SETTLES HARASSMENT SUIT ON BEHALF OF PAKISTANI AMERICAN EMPLOYEES

The Equal Employment Opportunity Commission announced the settlement of a Title VII suit filed against Stockton Steel, a subsidiary of the Herrick Corporation. The suit alleged that the company had discriminated against Pakistani American employees; the employees alleged that they were given undesirable work assignments, were subjected to harassment based on their national origin, and were ridiculed while performing their daily Islamic prayer obligations. The workers claimed that they were repeatedly called derogatory names, such as "camel jockeys" and "ragheads." Under the terms of the settlement agreement, Stockton Steel agreed to pay damages of $1.1 million to four former employees, to conduct training to prevent future discrimination, and to implement a policy to guarantee employees' rights to request accommodations for religious beliefs.

Sources: "Pakistani-American Workers to Share $1.11 Million in Harassment Settlement with Stockton Steel," *States News Service*, March 19, 2003; "Pakistani-American Workers to Share $1.11 Million in Harassment Settlement with Stockton Steel," EEOC Press Release, March 19, 2003.

DISPARATE IMPACT

Employers should avoid arbitrary employment criteria, such as height or weight requirements, for applicants or employees because such requirements may have a disparate impact on national origin; they have the effect of excluding large numbers of certain ethnic groups. For example, height requirements may exclude most persons of Asian or Hispanic origin; the refusal to recognize educational qualifications from foreign institutions may exclude foreign-born applicants. If such requirements or practices have a disparate impact, they constitute discrimination in violation of Title VII, unless they can be shown to be required for the effective performance of the job in question.

ENGLISH-ONLY RULES

An employer may violate Title VII by denying employment opportunities because of an applicant's or employee's foreign accent or inability to communicate well in English, unless the job in question involves public contact (such as sales clerks or receptionists). One issue of specific concern to the EEOC is the use by employers of ***English-only rules,*** which prohibit employees from speaking any language but English at work. Absolute or "blanket" English-only rules, requiring employees to speak English exclusively during all their time in the workplace, are generally more difficult to justify than more limited English-only rules, which require employees to speak English only at certain times—such as when they are with customers—or in certain places—such as the sales floor or other "public contact" areas. The employer must clearly notify the employees of when and where the restriction applies.

The EEOC Guidelines on Discrimination Because of National Origin [29 C.F.R. § 1606] take the position that blanket English-only rules violate Title VII unless they are required by business necessity. The EEOC believes that such rules may create an "atmosphere of inferiority, isolation and intimidation" based on an employee's ethnicity which could result in a discriminatory working environment and tend to be "a burdensome term and condition of employment." However, not all courts have agreed with the EEOC position on blanket English-only rules, as the following case illustrates.

GARCIA V. SPUN STEAK COMPANY

998 F.2d 1480 (9th Cir. 1993), rehearing denied, 13 F.3d 296, cert. denied, 512 U.S. 1228 (1994)

O'Scannlain, C. J.

... Spun Steak Company ... produces poultry and meat products in south San Francisco for wholesale distribution. Spun Steak employs 33 workers, 24 of whom are Spanish-speaking. Virtually all of the Spanish-speaking employees are Hispanic. While two employees speak no English, the others have varying degrees of proficiency in English. Spun Steak has never required job applicants to speak or to understand English as a condition of employment.

Approximately two-thirds of Spun Steak's employees are . . . involved in the production process. Appellees Garcia and Buitrago are production line workers; they stand before a conveyor belt, remove poultry or other meat products from the belt and place the product into cases or trays for resale. Their work is done individually. Both Garcia and Buitrago are fully bilingual, speaking both English and Spanish. . . .

Prior to September 1990, these Spun Steak employees spoke Spanish freely to their co-workers during work hours. . . . Spun Steak began to investigate the possibility of requiring its employees to speak only English in the workplace [after it] . . . received complaints that Garcia and Buitrago made derogatory, racist comments in Spanish about two co-workers, one of whom is African-American and the other Chinese-American.

The company's president, Kenneth Bertelson, concluded that an English-only rule would promote racial harmony in the workplace. In addition, he concluded that the English-only rule would enhance worker safety because some employees who did not understand Spanish claimed that the use of Spanish distracted them while they were operating machinery, and would enhance product quality because the U.S.D.A. inspector in the plant spoke only English and thus could not understand if a product-related concern was raised in Spanish. Accordingly, the following rule was adopted:

> [I]t is hereafter the policy of this Company that only English will be spoken in connection with work. During lunch, breaks, and employees' own time, they are obviously free to speak Spanish if they wish. However, we urge all of you not to use your fluency in Spanish in a fashion which may lead other employees to suffer humiliation.

In addition to the English-only policy, Spun Steak adopted a rule forbidding offensive racial, sexual, or personal remarks of any kind.

It is unclear from the record whether Spun Steak strictly enforced the English-only rule. According to the plaintiffs-appellees, some workers continued to speak Spanish without incident. Spun Steak issued written exceptions to the policy allowing its clean-up crew to speak Spanish, allowing its foreman to speak Spanish, and authorizing certain workers to speak Spanish to the foreman at the foreman's discretion. One of the two employees who speak only Spanish is a member of the clean-up crew and thus is unaffected by the policy.

In November 1990, Garcia and Buitrago received warning letters for speaking Spanish during working hours. For approximately two months thereafter, they were not permitted to work next to each other. Local 115 (the union representing the Spun Steak employees) protested the English-only policy and requested that it be rescinded but to no avail.

On May 6, 1991, Garcia, Buitrago, and Local 115 filed charges of discrimination against Spun Steak with the U.S. Equal Employment Opportunity Commission. The EEOC conducted an investigation and determined that there was reasonable cause to believe that Spun Steak violated Title VII. . . . Garcia, Buitrago, and Local 115, on behalf of all Spanish-speaking employees of Spun Steak, filed suit, alleging that the English-only policy violated Title VII. . . . The district court . . . granted the Spanish-speaking employees' motion for summary judgment, concluding that the English-only policy disparately impacted Hispanic workers without sufficient business justification, and thus violated Title VII. [Spun Steak appealed.]

The Spanish-speaking employees do not contend that Spun Steak intentionally discriminated against them in enacting the English-only policy. Rather, they contend that the policy had a discriminatory impact on them because it imposes a burdensome term or condition of employment exclusively upon Hispanic workers and denies them a privilege of employment that non-Spanish-speaking workers enjoy. . . . We are satisfied that a disparate impact claim may be based upon a challenge to a practice or policy that has a significant adverse impact on the "terms, conditions, or privileges" of the employment of a protected group under Section 703(a)(1).

. . . It is beyond dispute that, in this case, if the English-only policy causes any adverse effects, those effects will be suffered disproportionately by those of Hispanic origin. The vast majority of those workers at Spun Steak who speak a language other than English—and virtually all those employees for whom English is not a first language—are Hispanic. It is of no consequence that not all Hispanic employees of Spun Steak speak Spanish; nor is it relevant that some non-Hispanic workers may speak Spanish. If the adverse effects are proved, it is enough under Title VII that Hispanics are disproportionately impacted.

. . . The Spanish-speaking employees argue that the policy adversely affects them in the following ways:

(1) it denies them the ability to express their cultural heritage on the job; (2) it denies them a privilege of employment that is enjoyed by monolingual speakers of English; and (3) it creates an atmosphere of inferiority, isolation, and intimidation. We discuss each of these contentions in turn.

The employees argue that denying them the ability to speak Spanish on the job denies them the right to cultural expression. . . . Title VII, however, does not protect the ability of workers to express their cultural heritage at the workplace. Title VII is concerned only with disparities in the treatment of workers; it does not confer substantive privileges. . . . Just as a private employer is not required to allow other types of self-expression, there is nothing in Title VII which requires an employer to allow employees to express their cultural identity.

Next, the Spanish-speaking employees argue that the English-only policy has a disparate impact on them because it deprives them of a privilege given by the employer to native-English speakers: the ability to converse on the job in the language with which they feel most comfortable. It is undisputed that Spun Steak allows its employees to converse on the job. The ability to converse—especially to make small talk—is a privilege of employment, and may in fact be a significant privilege of employment in an assembly-line job. It is inaccurate, however, to describe the privilege as broadly as the Spanish-speaking employees urge us to do.

The employees have attempted to define the privilege as the ability to speak in the language of their choice. A privilege, however, is by definition given at the employer's discretion; an employer has the right to define its contours. Thus, an employer may allow employees to converse on the job, but only during certain times of the day or during the performance of certain tasks. The employer may proscribe certain topics as inappropriate during working hours or may even forbid the use of certain words, such as profanity.

Here, as is its prerogative, the employer has defined the privilege narrowly. When the privilege is defined at its narrowest (as merely the ability to speak on the job), we cannot conclude that those employees fluent in both English and Spanish are adversely impacted by the policy. Because they are able to speak English, bilingual employees can engage in conversation on the job. It is axiomatic that "the language a person who is multi-lingual elects to speak at a particular time is . . . a matter of choice." The bilingual employee can readily comply with the English-only rule and still enjoy the privilege of speaking on the job. "There is no disparate impact . . ." with respect to a privilege of employment "if the rule is one that the affected employee can readily observe and nonobservance is a matter of individual preference." . . .

Title VII is not meant to protect against rules that merely inconvenience some employees, even if the inconvenience falls regularly on a protected class. Rather, Title VII protects against only those policies that have a significant impact. The fact that an employee may have to catch himself or herself from occasionally slipping into Spanish does not impose a burden significant enough to amount to the denial of equal opportunity. . . .

Finally, the Spanish-speaking employees argue that the policy creates an atmosphere of inferiority, isolation, and intimidation. Under this theory, the employees do not assert that the policy directly affects a term, condition, or privilege of employment. Instead, the argument must be that the policy causes the work environment to become infused with ethnic tensions. The tense environment, the argument goes, itself amounts to a condition of employment. . . .

Here, the employees urge us to adopt a per se rule that English-only policies always infect the working environment to such a degree as to amount to a hostile or abusive work environment. This we cannot do. Whether a working environment is infused with discrimination is a factual question, one for which a per se rule is particularly inappropriate. The dynamics of an individual workplace are enormously complex; we cannot conclude, as a matter of law, that the introduction of an English-only policy, in every workplace, will always have the same effect.

The Spanish-speaking employees in this case have presented no evidence other than conclusory statements that the policy has contributed to an atmosphere of "isolation, inferiority or intimidation." The bilingual employees are able to comply with the rule, and there is no evidence to show that the atmosphere at Spun Steak in general is infused with hostility toward Hispanic workers. Indeed, there is substantial evidence in the record demonstrating that the policy was enacted to prevent the employees from intentionally using their fluency in Spanish to isolate and to intimidate members of other ethnic groups. In light of the specific factual context of this case, we conclude that the bilingual employees have not raised a genuine issue of material fact that the effect is so pronounced as to amount to a hostile environment.

We do not foreclose the prospect that in some circumstances English-only rules can exacerbate existing tensions, or, when combined with other discriminatory behavior, contribute to an overall environment of discrimination. Likewise, we can envision a case in which such rules are enforced in such a draconian manner that the enforcement itself amounts to harassment. In evaluating such a claim, however, a court must look to the totality of the circumstances in the particular factual context in which the claim arises.

In holding that the enactment of an English-only while working policy does not inexorably lead to an abusive environment for those whose primary language is not English, we reach a conclusion opposite to the EEOC's long-standing position. The EEOC Guidelines provide that an employee meets the prima facie case in a disparate impact cause of action merely by proving the existence of the English-only policy. Under the EEOC's scheme, an employer must always provide a business justification for such a rule. . . .

. . . we are not bound by the Guidelines. . . . Nothing in the plain language of Section 703(a)(1) supports the EEOC's English-only rule Guideline. . . . We are not aware of, nor has counsel shown us, anything in the legislative history to Title VII that indicates that English-only policies are to be presumed discriminatory. Indeed, nowhere in the legislative history is there a discussion of English-only policies at all.

Because the bilingual employees have failed to make out a prima facie case, we need not consider the business justifications offered for the policy as applied to them. On remand, if Local 115 is able to make out a prima facie case with regard to employees with limited proficiency in English, the district court could then consider any business justification offered by Spun Steak.

. . . we conclude that the bilingual employees have not made out a prima facie case and that Spun Steak has not violated Title VII in adopting an English-only rule as to them. Thus, we reverse the grant of summary judgment in favor of Garcia, Buitrago, and Local 115 to the extent it represents the bilingual employees, and remand with instructions to grant summary judgment in favor of Spun Steak on their claims. A genuine issue of material fact exists as to whether there are one or more employees represented by Local 115 with limited proficiency in English who were adversely impacted by the policy. As to such employee or employees, we reverse the grant of summary judgment in favor of Local 115, and remand for further proceedings.

Reversed and Remanded.

Case Questions

1. Why did Spun Steak adopt the English-only rule? Did Spun Steak establish that the rule was required by business necessity?
2. Did the bilingual employees allege a claim of disparate treatment or disparate impact discrimination? What was the basis of their claim; that is, how did the rule affect them? Did the Court of Appeals agree?
3. Does the Court of Appeals' decision mean that all employers are free to impose English-only rules? Is Spun Steak's rule legal in all circumstances? Explain your answers.

CITIZENSHIP

Title VII protects all individuals, both citizens and noncitizens, who reside in or are employed in the United States from employment discrimination based on race, color, religion, sex, or national origin. However, the Supreme Court in *Espinoza v. Farah Mfg. Co.* [414 U.S. 86 (1973)] held that Title VII's prohibition on national origin discrimination does not include discrimination on the basis of citizenship. Section 703(g) of Title VII also allows employers to refuse to hire applicants who are denied national security clearances for positions subject to federal security requirements.

THE IMMIGRATION REFORM AND CONTROL ACT OF 1986 AND DISCRIMINATION BASED ON NATIONAL ORIGIN OR CITIZENSHIP

The Immigration Reform and Control Act of 1986 (IRCA) prohibits employment discrimination because of national origin or citizenship against applicants or employees, other than illegal aliens, with respect to hiring, recruitment, discharge, or referral for a fee. Employers may, however, discriminate based upon citizenship when it is necessary to comply with other laws or federal, state, or local government contracts or when determined by the attorney general to be essential for an employer to do business with a government agency. Employers are permitted under the IRCA to give a U.S. citizen preference over an alien when both the citizen and the alien are "equally qualified" for the job for which they are being considered.

The Immigration Act of 1990 expanded the protection of the IRCA to cover seasonal agricultural workers. It is unlawful to intimidate, threaten, coerce, or retaliate against any person for the purpose of interfering with the rights secured under the IRCA's antidiscrimination provisions. Employers are also prohibited from requesting more or different employment-eligibility documents than are required under the IRCA and from refusing to honor documents that reasonably appear to be genuine.

The IRCA is enforced by the Department of Justice through the Special Counsel for Immigration-Related Unfair Employment Practices, a position created by the act. The nondiscrimination provisions of the IRCA apply to employers with more than three employees, but they do not extend to national origin discrimination that is prohibited by Title VII. Consequently, employers who are subject to Title VII (those with fifteen or more employees) are not subject to the IRCA's provisions on national origin discrimination. However, because Title VII does not expressly prohibit discrimination based upon citizenship, all employers with more than three employees are covered by the IRCA's provisions against discrimination based upon citizenship.

ETHICAL DILEMMA: ALLAH IN THE WORKPLACE?

A small group of employees at Wydget are Muslims; some wear turbans and burques (robes covering their body). They have asked you, the human resource manager, to allow them to conduct religious prayer services in the plant cafeteria during their morning and afternoon coffee breaks and their lunch break. In general, those employees are good workers, and you don't want to do anything that would undermine their morale. However, a number of other Wydget employees have complained to you that they are suspicious of such meetings, which they fear may be a cover for terrorist or subversive activities. You are concerned that if you allow the lunchtime prayer services, other employees who are Buddhists, Hindus, or Christians may also seek to conduct religious or prayer services.

Should you allow the Muslim employees to hold the prayer services? What arguments can you make in favor of allowing the services? What arguments can you make against allowing them? How should you respond to the fears and perceptions of the other employees? Can Wydget allow the prayer services for the Muslims while refusing other employees the right to hold their own prayer services? Prepare a memo for the CEO on this question. The memo should list the arguments in favor of, and against, allowing the prayer services and should recommend a decision, with appropriate explanation and justification, for the CEO.

ENFORCEMENT OF TITLE VII

This section focuses on the procedures for filing and resolving complaints of employment discrimination that arise under Title VII.

THE EQUAL EMPLOYMENT OPPORTUNITY COMMISSION

Title VII is administered and enforced by the Equal Employment Opportunity Commission (EEOC). The EEOC is headed by a five-member commission; the commissioners are appointed by the president with Senate confirmation. The general counsel of the EEOC is also appointed by the president, also with Senate confirmation.

Unlike the National Labor Relations Board (NLRB), the EEOC does not adjudicate, or decide, complaints alleging violations of Title VII, nor is it the exclusive enforcement agency for discrimination complaints. The EEOC staff investigates complaints filed with it and attempts to settle such complaints voluntarily. If a settlement is not reached voluntarily, the EEOC may file suit against the alleged discriminator in the federal courts.

The EEOC also differs from the NLRB in that the EEOC may initiate complaints on its own when it believes a party is involved in a "pattern or practice" of discrimination. In these cases, the EEOC need not wait for an individual to file a complaint with it. When a complaint alleges discrimination by a state or local government, Title VII requires that the Department of Justice initiate any court action against the public sector employer.

PROCEDURES UNDER TITLE VII

Filing a Complaint

Title VII, unlike the National Labor Relations Act, does not give the federal government exclusive authority over employment discrimination issues. Section 706(c) of Title VII requires that an individual filing a complaint of illegal employment discrimination must first file with a state or local agency authorized to deal with the issue, if such an agency exists. The EEOC may consider the complaint only after the state or local agency has had the complaint for sixty days or ceased processing the complaint, whichever occurs first.

State Agency Role

A number of states and municipalities have created equal employment opportunity agencies, also known as "fair employment" or "human rights" commissions. Some state agencies have powers and jurisdiction beyond those given to the EEOC. The New York State Human Rights Division enforces the New York State Human Rights Law; in addition to prohibiting discrimination in employment on the basis of race, color, religion, gender, and national origin, the New York legislation also prohibits employment discrimination on the basis of age, marital status, disability, and criminal record. The Pennsylvania Human Relations Act established the Human Rights Commission, which is empowered to hold hearings before administrative law judges to determine whether the act has been violated. The Pennsylvania legislation goes beyond Title VII's prohibitions by forbidding employment discrimination on the basis of disability.

Filing with the EEOC

When the complaint must first be filed with a state or local agency, Section 706(e) requires that it be filed with the EEOC within 300 days of the act of alleged discrimination. If there is no state or local agency, the complaint must be filed with the EEOC within 180 days of the alleged violation. By contrast, the limitation for filing a complaint under the New York State Human Rights Law is one year; the limitations period under the Pennsylvania Human Relations Act is ninety days.

For a description of filing procedures in cases of employment discrimination, see **http://www.eeoc.gov/facts/howtofil.html**

As noted earlier, an individual alleging employment discrimination must first file a complaint with the appropriate state or local agency, if such an agency exists. Once the complaint is filed with the state or local agency, the complainant must wait sixty days before filing the complaint with the EEOC; if the state or local agency terminates proceedings on the complaint prior to the passage of sixty days, the complaint may then be filed with the EEOC. This means that the individual filing the complaint with the state or local agency must wait for that agency to terminate proceedings or for sixty days, whichever comes first. *Mohasco Corp. v. Silver* [447 U.S. 807 (1980)] involved a situation in which an individual filed a complaint alleging that he was discharged because of religious discrimination with the New York Division of Human Rights 291 days after the discharge. The state agency began to process and investigate the complaint; the EEOC began to process the complaint some 357 days after the discharge. The Supreme Court held that the complaint had not been properly filed with the EEOC within the 300-day limit; the Court held that the EEOC has a duty, under the statute, to begin processing a complaint within 300 days of the alleged violation. In order to allow the state agency the required sixty days for processing, the complaint must have been filed with the state agency within 240 days so that, when the EEOC began to process the complaint, it would be within the 300-day limit. However, as noted, when the state or local agency terminates proceedings on the complaint before sixty days have passed, the EEOC may begin to process the complaint upon the other agency's termination.

EEOC PROCEDURE AND ITS RELATION TO STATE PROCEEDINGS

The EEOC has entered into "work-sharing" agreements with most state equal employment opportunity agencies to deal with the situation that arose in the *Mohasco* decision. Under such agreements, the agency that initially receives the complaint processes it. When the EEOC receives the complaint first, it refers the complaint to the appropriate state agency. The state agency then waives its right to process the complaint and refers it back to the EEOC; the state agency does retain jurisdiction to proceed on the complaint in the future, after the EEOC has completed its processing of the complaint. The EEOC treats the referral of the complaint to the state agency as the filing of the complaint with the state agency, and the state's waiver of the right to process the complaint is treated as termination of state proceedings, allowing the filing of the complaint with the EEOC under Section 706(c) of Title VII.

In *EEOC v. Commercial Office Products Co.* [486 U.S. 107 (1988)], the complainant filed a sex discrimination complaint with the EEOC on the 289th day after her discharge. The EEOC, under a work-sharing agreement, sent the complaint to the state agency, which returned the complaint to the EEOC after indicating that it waived its right to proceed on the complaint. The EEOC then began its investigation into the complaint and ultimately brought suit against the employer. The trial court and the court of appeals held that Section 706(c) required that either sixty days must elapse from the filing of the complaint with the state agency, or the state agency must both commence and terminate its proceedings, before the complaint could be deemed to have been filed with the EEOC. The Supreme Court, on appeal, reversed the court of appeals; the Supreme Court held that the state agency's waiver of its right to proceed on the complaint constituted a termination of the state proceedings under Section 706(c), allowing the EEOC to proceed with the complaint. As a result of this decision, in states where the EEOC and the state agency have work-sharing agreements, a complaint filed with the EEOC anytime within the 300-day time limit will be considered properly filed, and the EEOC can proceed with its processing of the complaint.

When Does the Violation Occur?

Because the time for filing a complaint under Title VII is limited, it is important to determine when the alleged violation occurred. In most situations, it is not difficult to determine the date of the violation from which the time limit begins to run, but in some instances, it may present a problem. The Supreme Court, in *Delaware State College v. Ricks* [449 U.S. 250 (1982)], held that the time limit for a Title VII violation begins to run on the date that the individual is aware, or should be aware, of the alleged violation, not on the date that the alleged violation has an effect on the individual.

In *Lorance v. AT&T Technologies, Inc.* [490 U.S. 900 (1989)] (see Chapter 3), the Supreme Court ruled that the time limit for filing a complaint against an allegedly discriminatory change to a seniority system begins to run at the time the actual change is made. However, the effect of the decision in *Lorance* was reversed by the 1991 amendments to Title VII. Section 706(e)(2) now provides that for claims involving the adoption of a seniority system for allegedly discriminatory reasons, the violation can occur when the seniority system is adopted, when the complainant becomes subject to the seniority system, or when the complainant is injured by the application of the seniority system.

Continuing Violation

In *Bazemore v. Friday* [478 U.S. 385 (1986)], the plaintiffs challenged a pay policy that allegedly discriminated against African American employees. The pay policy had its origins prior to the date that Title VII applied to the employer, but the

Supreme Court held that the violation was a continuing one—a new violation occurred every time the employees received a paycheck based on the racially discriminatory policy. Where the plaintiff alleges a continuing violation of Title VII, the plaintiff need only file within 180 or 300 days (depending on whether there is an appropriate local or state agency involved) of the latest incident of the alleged continuing violation.

Hostile Environment Harassment

Employees alleging harassment creating a hostile environment in violation of Title VII must file their complaint with the EEOC within 180 days (if there is no state or local agency involved) or 300 days (it there is an appropriate state and local agency) of the most recent discrete incident of harassment according to *National Railroad Passenger Corp. v. Morgan* [536 U.S. 101 (2002)].

EEOC PROCEDURE FOR HANDLING COMPLAINTS

Upon receipt of a properly filed complaint, the EEOC has ten days to serve a notice of the complaint with the employer, union, or agency alleged to have discriminated (the respondent). Following service upon the respondent, the EEOC staff conducts an investigation into the complaint to determine whether reasonable cause exists to believe it is true. If no reasonable cause is found, the charge is dismissed. If reasonable cause to believe the complaint is found, the commission will attempt to settle the complaint through voluntary conciliation, persuasion, and negotiation. If the voluntary procedures are unsuccessful in resolving the complaint after thirty days from its filing, the EEOC may file suit in a federal district court.

If the EEOC dismisses the complaint or decides not to file suit, it notifies the complainant that he or she may file suit on his or her own. The complainant must file suit within ninety days of receiving the right-to-sue notice.

When the EEOC has not dismissed the complaint but has also not filed suit or acted upon the complaint within 180 days of its filing, the complainant may request a right-to-sue letter. Again, the complainant has ninety days from the notification to file suit. The suit may be filed in the district court in the district where the alleged unlawful employment practice occurred, where the relevant employment records are kept, or where the complainant would have been employed.

In *Yellow Freight System, Inc. v. Donnelly* [494 U.S. 820 (1990)], the Supreme Court held that the federal courts do not have exclusive jurisdiction over Title VII claims; state courts are competent to adjudicate claims based on federal law such as Title VII. This means that the individual may file suit in either the federal or appropriate state court.

Because the complainant may be required to file first with a state or local agency and may file his or her own suit if the EEOC has not acted within 180 days, several legal proceedings involving the complaint may occur at the same time. What is the effect of a state court decision dismissing the complaint on a subsequent suit filed in federal court? In *Kremer v. Chemical Construction Co.* [456 U.S. 461 (1982)], the U.S. Supreme Court held that a plaintiff who loses a discrimination suit in a state court is precluded from filing a Title VII suit based on the same facts in federal court. According to *Kremer,* the complainant who is unsuccessful in the state courts does not get a second chance to file a suit based on the same facts in federal court because of the full-faith-and-credit doctrine. However, the holding in *Kremer* was limited only to the effect of a state court decision.

What is the effect of a negative determination by a state administrative agency on the complainant's right to sue in federal court? In *University of Tennessee v. Elliot* [478 U.S. 788 (1986)], the Supreme Court held that the full-faith-and-credit doctrine did not apply to state administrative agency decisions; hence, a negative determination by the state agency would not preclude the complainant from suing in federal court under Title VII. (The Court in *Elliot* did hold that the findings of fact made by the state agency should be given preclusive effect by the federal courts in suits filed under 42 U.S. 1981 and 1983.)

The Relationship between Title VII and Other Statutory Remedies

The U.S. Court of Appeals for the Sixth Circuit held that the NLRB's rejection of an unfair labor practice charge alleging racial discrimination does not preclude the filing of a Title VII suit growing out of the same situation [*Tipler v. E. I. du Pont de Nemours,* 433 F.2d 125 (1971)]. However, if an employee had voluntarily accepted reinstatement with back pay in settlement of his or her grievance against the employer, the U.S. Court of Appeals for the Fifth Circuit held that the employee had waived his or her right to sue under Title VII on the same facts. See *Strozier v. General Motors* [635 F.2d 424 (1981)].

In the case of *Johnson v. Railway Express Agency* [421 U.S. 454 (1975)], the Supreme Court held that an action under Title VII is separate and distinct from an action alleging race discrimination under the Civil Rights Act of 1866, 42 U.S.C., Section 1981. (That legislation will be discussed in Chapter 7.)

BURDENS OF PROOF: ESTABLISHING A CASE

Once the complaint of an unlawful employment practice under Title VII has become the subject of a suit in a federal district court, the question of the burden of proof arises. What must the plaintiff show to establish a valid claim of discrimination? What must the defendant show to defeat a claim of discrimination?

Prima Facie Case
A case "on the face of it" or "at first sight"; often used to establish that if a certain set of facts are proven, then it is apparent that another fact is established.

The plaintiff in a suit under Title VII always carries the burden of proof; that is, the plaintiff must persuade the trier of fact (the jury or the judge if there is no jury) that there has been a violation of Title VII. To do this, the plaintiff must establish a **prima facie** case of discrimination—enough evidence to raise a presumption of discrimination. If the plaintiff is unable to establish a prima facie case of discrimination, the case will be dismissed. The specific elements of a prima facie case, or the means to establish it, will vary depending on whether the complaint involves disparate treatment (intentional discrimination) or disparate impact (the discriminatory effects of apparently neutral criteria).

The plaintiff may use either anecdotal evidence or statistical evidence to establish the prima facie case. In *Bazemore v. Friday* [478 U.S. 385 (1986)], the plaintiffs offered a statistical multiple-regression analysis to demonstrate that pay policies discriminated against African American employees. The employer argued that the multiple-regression analysis did not consider several variables that were important in determining employees' pay. The trial court and the court of appeals refused to admit the multiple-regression analysis as evidence because it did not include all relevant variables. On appeal, however, the Supreme Court held that the multiple-regression-analysis evidence should have been admitted; the failure of the analysis to include all relevant variables affects its probative value (the weight given to it by the trier of fact), not its admissibility.

DISPARATE TREATMENT CLAIMS

Claims of disparate treatment involve allegations of intentional discrimination in employment. An individual is treated differently by the employer because of that individual's race, color, religion, gender, or national origin. A plaintiff alleging disparate treatment must establish that he or she was subjected to less favorable treatment because of his or her race, color, religion, gender, or national origin. The specific elements of a prima facie case of disparate treatment under Title VII are discussed in the following case.

McDonnell Douglas Corp. v. Green

411 U.S. 792 (1973)

Powell, J.

The case before us raises significant questions as to the proper order and nature of proof in actions under Title VII of the Civil Rights Act of 1964.

Petitioner, McDonnell Douglas Corporation, is an aerospace and aircraft manufacturer headquartered in St. Louis, Missouri, where it employs over 30,000 people. Respondent, a black citizen of St. Louis, worked for petitioner as a mechanic and laboratory technician from 1956 until August 28, 1964 when he was laid off in the course of a general reduction in petitioner's work force. Respondent, a long-time activist in the civil rights movement, protested vigorously that his discharge and the general hiring practices of petitioner were racially motivated. As part of this protest, respondent and other members of the Congress on Racial Equality illegally stalled their cars on the main roads leading to petitioner's plant for the purpose of blocking access to it at the time of the morning shift change. The District Judge described the plan for, and respondent's participation in, the "stall-in" as follows:

> ... five teams, each consisting of four cars, would "tie-up" five main access roads into McDonnell at the time of the morning rush hour. The drivers of the cars were instructed to line up next to each other completely blocking the intersections or roads. The drivers were also instructed to stop their cars, turn off the engines, pull the emergency brake, raise all windows, lock the doors, and remain in their cars until the police arrived. The plan was to have the cars remain in position for one hour....

... On July 2, 1965, a "lock-in" took place wherein a chain and padlock were placed on the front door of a building to prevent the occupants, certain of petitioner's employees, from leaving. Though respondent apparently knew beforehand of the "lock-in," the full extent of his involvement remains uncertain.

Some three weeks following the "lock-in," on July 25, 1965, petitioner publicly advertised for qualified mechanics, respondent's trade, and respondent promptly applied for reemployment. Petitioner turned down respondent, basing its rejection on respondent's participation in the "stall-in" and "lock-in." Shortly thereafter, respondent filed a formal complaint with the Equal Employment Opportunity Commission, claiming that petitioner had refused to rehire him because of his race and persistent involvement in the civil rights movement in violation of Sections 703(a)(1) and 704(a). . . . The former section generally prohibits racial discrimination in any employment decision while the latter forbids discrimination against applicants or employees for attempting to protest or correct allegedly discriminatory conditions of employment.

The Commission made no finding on respondent's allegation of racial bias under Section 703(a)(1), but it did find reasonable cause to believe petitioner had violated Section 704(a) by refusing to rehire respondent because of his civil rights activity. After the Commission unsuccessfully attempted to conciliate the dispute, it advised respondent in March 1968, of his right to institute a civil action in federal court within 30 days.

On April 15, 1968, respondent brought the present action, claiming initially a violation of Section 704(a) and, in an amended complaint, a violation of Section 703(a)(1) as well. The District Court dismissed the latter claim of racial discrimination in petitioner's hiring procedures. . . . The District Court also found that petitioner's refusal to rehire respondent was based solely on his participation in the illegal demonstrations and not on his legitimate civil rights activities. The court concluded that nothing in Title VII or Section 704 protected "such activity as employed by the plaintiff in the 'stall-in' and 'lock-in' demonstrations."

. . . On appeal, the Eighth Circuit affirmed that unlawful protests were not protected activities under Section 704(a), but reversed the dismissal of respondent's Section 703(a)(1) claim relating to racially discriminatory hiring practices . . . The court ordered the case remanded for trial of respondent's claim under Section 703(a)(1).

. . . The critical issue before us concerns the order and allocation of proof in a private, single-plaintiff action challenging employment discrimination. The language of Title VII makes plain the purpose of Congress to assure equality of employment opportunities and to eliminate those discriminatory practices and devices which have fostered racially stratified job environments to the disadvantage of minority citizens.

As noted in [*Griggs v. Duke Power Co.*]:

> Congress did not intend Title VII, however, to guarantee a job to every person regardless of qualifications. In short, the Act does not command that any person be hired simply because he was formerly the subject of discrimination, or because he is a member of a minority group. Discriminatory preference for any group, minority or majority, is precisely and only what Congress has proscribed. What is required by Congress is the removal of artificial, arbitrary, and unnecessary barriers to employment when the barriers operate invidiously to discriminate on the basis of racial or other impermissible classification. . . .

There are societal as well as personal interests on both sides of this equation. The broad, overriding interest shared by employer, employee, and consumer, is efficient and trustworthy workmanship assured through fair and racially neutral employment and personnel decisions. In the implementation of such decisions, it is abundantly clear that Title VII tolerates no racial discrimination, subtle or otherwise.

In this case respondent, the complainant below, charges that he was denied employment "because of his involvement in civil rights activities" and "because of his race and color." Petitioner denied discrimination of any kind, asserting that its failure to re-employ respondent was based upon and justified by his participation in the unlawful conduct against it. Thus, the issue at the trial on remand is framed by those opposing factual contentions. . . .

The complainant in a Title VII trial must carry the initial burden under the statute of establishing a prima facie case of racial discrimination. This may be done by showing (i) that he belongs to a racial minority; (ii) that he had applied and was qualified for a job for which the employer was seeking applicants; (iii) that, despite his qualifications, he was rejected; and (iv) that, after his rejection, the position remained open and the employer continued to seek applicants from persons of complainant's qualifications. In the instant case, we agree with the Court of Appeals that respondent proved a prima facie case. . . . Petitioner sought mechanics, respondent's trade, and continued to do so after respondent's rejection. Petitioner, moreover, does not dispute respondent's qualifications and acknowledges that his past work performance in petitioner's employ was "satisfactory."

The burden then must shift to the employer to articulate some legitimate, nondiscriminatory reason for respondent's rejection. We need not attempt in the instant case to detail every matter which fairly could be recognized as a reasonable basis for a refusal to hire. Here petitioner has assigned respondent's participation in unlawful conduct against it as the cause for his rejection. We think that this suffices to discharge petitioner's burden of proof at this stage and to meet respondent's prima facie case of discrimination.

The Court of Appeals intimated, however, that petitioner's stated reason for refusing to rehire respondent was a "subjective" rather than objective criterion which "carries little weight in rebutting charges of discrimination." Regardless of whether this was the intended import of the opinion, we think the court below seriously underestimated the rebuttal weight to which petitioner's reasons were entitled. Respondent admittedly had taken part in a carefully planned "stall-in," designed to tie up access and egress to petitioner's plant at a peak traffic hour. Nothing in Title VII compels an employer to absolve and rehire one who has engaged in such deliberate, unlawful activity against it. . . .

. . . Petitioner's reason for rejection thus suffices to meet the prima facie case, but the inquiry must not end here. While Title VII does not, without more, compel rehiring of respondent, neither does it permit petitioner to use respondent's conduct as a pretext for the sort of discrimination prohibited by Section 703(a)(1). On remand, respondent must, as the Court of Appeals recognized, be afforded a fair opportunity to show that petitioner's stated reason for respondent's rejection was in fact pretextual. Especially relevant to such a showing would be evidence that white employees involved in acts against petitioner of comparable seriousness to the "stall-in" were nevertheless retained or rehired. Petitioner may justifiably refuse to rehire one who was engaged in unlawful, disruptive acts against it, but only if this criterion is applied alike to members of all races. Other evidence that may be relevant to any showing of pretextuality includes facts as to the petitioner's treatment of respondent during his prior term of employment, petitioner's reaction, if any, to respondent's legitimate civil rights activities, and petitioner's general policy and practice with respect to minority employment. On the latter point, statistics as to petitioner's employment policy and practice may be helpful to a determination of whether petitioner's refusal to rehire respondent in this case conformed to a general pattern of discrimination against blacks. In short, on the retrial respondent must be given a full and fair opportunity to demonstrate by competent evidence that the presumptively valid reasons for his rejection were in fact a coverup for a racially discriminatory decision. . . .

Case Questions

1. How can a plaintiff establish a prima facie case of disparate treatment discrimination?
2. What was McDonnell Douglas's reason for refusing to rehire Green? Why did Green argue that the reason was a pretext for illegal discrimination?
3. How could Green convince the court that McDonnell Douglas's reason was a pretext? What evidence would be relevant to such a showing? What would be the effect of such a showing?

Defendant's Burden

If the plaintiff is successful in establishing a prima facie case of disparate treatment, the defendant must then try to overcome the plaintiff's claims. Is the defendant required to disprove those claims, prove that there was no discrimination, or merely explain the apparent discrimination? What is the nature of the defendant's burden in a disparate treatment case? In *Texas Department of Community Affairs v. Burdine* [450 U.S. 248 (1979)], the U.S. Supreme Court stated:

> The nature of the burden that shifts to the defendant should be understood in light of the plaintiff's ultimate and intermediate burdens. The ultimate burden of

> persuading the trier of fact that the defendant intentionally discriminated against the plaintiff remains at all time with the plaintiff. . . . The burden that shifts to the defendant, therefore, is to rebut the presumption of discrimination by producing evidence that the plaintiff was rejected, or someone else was preferred, for a legitimate, nondiscriminatory reason. The defendant need not persuade the court that it was actually motivated by the proffered reasons. It is sufficient if the defendant's evidence raises a genuine issue of fact as to whether it discriminated against the plaintiff. To accomplish this, the defendant must clearly set forth, through the introduction of admissible evidence, the reasons for the plaintiff's rejection. The explanation provided must be legally sufficient to justify a judgment for the defendant. If the defendant carries this burden of production, the presumption raised by the prima facie case is rebutted. . . .

According to *Burdine,* the defendant need only "articulate" some legitimate justification for its actions; the burden of proof—of persuading the trier of fact—remains with the plaintiff. Although the defendant need not *prove* that there was no discrimination, the nondiscriminatory justification or explanation offered by the defendant must be believable. Obviously, if the defendant's justification is not credible, then the plaintiff's prima facie case will not be rebutted, and the plaintiff will prevail.

Plaintiff's Burden of Showing Pretext

After the defendant has advanced a legitimate justification to counter, or rebut, the plaintiff's prima facie case, the focus of the proceeding shifts back to the plaintiff. The plaintiff, as was discussed in the *McDonnell Douglas* case, must be afforded an opportunity to show that the employer's justification is a mere pretext, or cover-up. This can be shown either directly, by persuading the court that a discriminatory reason likely motivated the defendant, or indirectly, by showing that the offered justification is not worthy of credence. The burden of showing that the defendant's offered justification is a pretext for discrimination is a very difficult one. According to the Supreme Court decision in *St. Mary's Honor Center v. Hicks* [509 U.S. 502 (1993)], the plaintiff, in addition to demonstrating that the defendant's justification is false, still has to convince the trier of fact that the defendant was motivated by illegal discrimination. When the plaintiff has established a prima facie case of discrimination, and in doing so has provided enough evidence for the trier of fact (jury or judge) to reject the employer's offered excuse as false, there was sufficient evidence to support a finding that the employer had intentionally discriminated against the plaintiff, *Reeves v. Sanderson Plumbing Products, Inc.* [530 U.S. 133 (2000)]. (Note that the *Reeves* case involved a claim under the Age Discrimination in Employment Act, which is discussed in the next chapter, but the burden of proof analysis is also applicable under Title VII.)

DISPARATE IMPACT CLAIMS

Unlike a disparate treatment claim, a claim of disparate impact does not involve an allegation of intentional discrimination. Rather, as in *Griggs v. Duke Power Co.,* it involves a claim that neutral job requirements have a discriminatory effect. The plaintiff, in order to establish a prima facie case, must show that the apparently neutral employment requirements or practices have a disproportionate impact upon a class protected by Title VII. (A protected class under Title VII is a group of individuals defined on the basis of race, color, religion, sex, or national origin.) The Supreme Court in the *Wards Cove Packing Co. v. Atonio* and *Watson v. Fort Worth Bank & Trust* decisions (see Chapter 3) held that a plaintiff alleging a disparate impact claim must "offer statistical evidence of a kind and degree sufficient to show that the practice in question has caused the exclusion of applicants for jobs or promotions because of their membership in a protected group."

Four-Fifths Rule

As discussed in Chapter 3, one way to establish proof of a disproportionate impact is by using the Four-Fifths Rule from the EEOC Guidelines. The rule states that a disparate impact will be presumed to exist when the selection or pass rate for the protected class with the lowest selection rate is less than 80 percent of the selection or pass rate of the protected class with the highest rate. The Four-Fifths Rule is used primarily when challenging employment tests or requirements such as a high school diploma or minimum height and weight requirements.

Using Statistics

Another method of establishing a disparate impact may be by making a statistical comparison of the minority representation in the employers' work force and the minority representation in the population as a whole (or in the relevant area or labor market). When a job requires specific skills and training, the population used for comparison with the work force may be limited to available qualified individuals within the relevant area or labor market. The court may require specific demographic and geographic comparisons when using statistical evidence, as demonstrated in *Hazelwood School Dist. v. U.S.* [433 U.S. 299 (1977)].

Defendant's Burden

When the plaintiff has established a prima facie case of disparate impact, the defendant has two methods of responding. The defendant may challenge the statistical analysis, the methods of data collection, or the significance of the plaintiff's evidence. The defendant may also submit alternative statistical proof that leads to conclusions that contradict those of the plaintiff's evidence.

Rather than attacking the plaintiff's statistical evidence, the defendant alternatively may show that the employment practice, test, or requirement having the disparate impact is job related.

Although the Supreme Court decisions in *Watson v. Fort Worth Bank & Trust* and *Wards Cove Packing Co. v. Atonio* both held that the employer need only show some business justification for the challenged practice, and the plaintiff has the burden of persuasion for showing that the challenged practice is not job related, the 1991 amendments to Title VII overruled those cases. Section 703(k) requires that, once the plaintiff has demonstrated that the challenged practice has a disparate impact, the employer has the burden of persuasion for convincing the court that the practice is job related.

A defense of job-relatedness can be established by using the methods of demonstrating validity set out in the Uniform Guidelines for Employee Selection. (The methods of demonstrating that a test or requirement is content valid, construct valid, or criterion valid are described in Chapter 3.)

If the defendant establishes that the practice, requirement, or test is job related, the plaintiff may still prevail by showing that other tests, practices, or requirements that do not have disparate impacts on protected classes are available and would satisfy the defendant's legitimate business concerns. The plaintiff may also try to show that the job-related justification is really just a pretext for intentional discrimination.

After-Acquired Evidence

What happens when the employer, after an employee who was allegedly fired for discriminatory reasons has filed a Title VII claim, discovers that the employee had falsified credentials on the application for employment? Does the evidence of the plaintiff employee's misconduct (known as *after-acquired evidence*) preclude the right of the plaintiff to sue? In *McKennon v. Nashville Banner Publishing Co.* [513 U.S. 352 (1995)], the Supreme Court held that the after-acquired evidence does not preclude the plaintiff's suit, but rather goes to the issue of the remedies available. If the employer can demonstrate that the employee's wrongdoing is severe enough to result in termination had the employer known of the misconduct at the time the alleged discrimination occurred, the court must then consider the effect of the wrongdoing on the remedies available to the plaintiff. In such a case, the Supreme Court held that reinstatement would not be appropriate, and back pay may be awarded from the date of the alleged discrimination by the employer to the date upon which the plaintiff's misconduct was discovered. *McKennon* involved a suit under the Age Discrimination in Employment Act, but the after-acquired evidence rule has also been applied in Title VII suits, *Wallace v. Dunn Construction Co.* [62 F.3d 374 (11th Cir. 1995)]. Evidence of the plaintiff's misconduct that occurs after the plaintiff was terminated was not relevant to the plaintiff's claim of discrimination and was excluded by the court in *Carr v. Woodbury County Juvenile Detention Center* [905 F. Supp. 619 (N.D. Iowa 1995), *aff'd* by 97 F.3d 1456 (8th Cir. 1996)].

ARBITRATION OF STATUTORY EEO CLAIMS

Unions and employers generally agree that any disputes arising under their collective agreements will be settled through arbitration. More recently, an increasing number of employers whose employees are not unionized are requiring their employees to agree to settle any employment disputes through arbitration rather than litigation in the courts. Employers tend to favor arbitration because it is generally quicker than litigation, is confidential while court decisions are public, and the remedies available under arbitration may be less generous than those available through the courts. What is the effect of such arbitration agreements on the employee's ability to bring a suit under Title VII or other EEO legislation?

In *Alexander v. Gardner Denver Co.* [415 U.S. 147 (1974)], the Supreme Court held that an arbitration proceeding under a collective agreement did not prevent an employee from filing suit alleging a violation of Title VII; the employee had lost in an arbitration challenging his discharge under the collective agreement but was still permitted to bring a Title VII suit in court. The Supreme Court held that the arbitration dealt with the employee's rights under the collective agreement, which were distinct from the employee's statutory rights under Title VII.

Seventeen years later, in *Gilmer v. Interstate/Johnson Lane Corp.* [500 U.S. 20 (1991)], the Supreme Court held that a securities broker was required to arbitrate, rather than litigate, his age discrimination claim because he had signed an agreement to arbitrate all disputes arising from his employment. The arbitration agreement was included in Gilmer's registration with the New York Securities Exchange, which was required for him to work as a broker. The Supreme Court in *Gilmer* held that the individual agreement to arbitrate, voluntarily agreed to by Gilmer, was enforceable under the Federal Arbitration Act and required Gilmer to submit all employment disputes, including those under EEO legislation, to arbitration. The agreement to arbitrate did not waive Gilmer's rights under the statutes but simply required that those rights be determined by the arbitrator rather than the courts. The Court in *Gilmer* emphasized that it involved a different situation from *Alexander v. Gardner Denver,* which continued to apply when arbitration under a collective agreement was involved.

The distinctions between the *Alexander* case and the *Gilmer* case need to be emphasized. In *Gilmer,* the individual employee had agreed, as part of an agreement connected with his employment, to arbitrate all disputes growing out of that employment. In *Alexander,* the union and the employer had agreed, as part of a collective agreement, to arbitrate employment disputes arising under that collective agreement; the individual employee, while subject to the collective agreement, had not personally agreed to arbitrate any disputes.

Arbitration Clauses in Collective Agreements

Most courts continue to recognize the distinction between *Gilmer* and *Alexander:* Individual agreements to arbitrate will generally be enforced, but a collective agreement's arbitration clause will generally not be held to require individual employees to arbitrate claims of employment discrimination, as in *Pryner v. Tractor Supply Co.* [109 F.3d 354 (7th Cir. 1997)]. In *Wright v. Universal Marine Supply* [525 U.S. 70 (1998)], the U.S. Supreme Court held that, to waive individual employee's rights to sue over employment discrimination claims, the arbitration clause of a collective agreement must contain a "clear and unmistakable waiver" of the individual employee's rights to sue. Applying the *Wright* decision, the U.S. Court for the Sixth Circuit in *Kennedy v. Superior Printing Co.* [215 F.3d 650 (2000)] held that an employee who had arbitrated a claim of employment discrimination was not prevented from bringing a court suit over the same discrimination claim; the Sixth Circuit stated that the collective agreement's general nondiscrimination clause did not constitute the required "clear and unmistakable waiver."

Individual Agreements to Arbitrate Employment Discrimination Disputes

The *Gilmer* case involved a claim of age discrimination under the Age Discrimination in Employment Act, but courts soon applied its reasoning to discrimination claims under Title VII and other federal and state employment discrimination legislation.

The Federal Arbitration Act [FAA] requires federal courts to enforce agreements to arbitrate if they are voluntary and knowing. However, Section 1 of the FAA states that it does not apply to "contracts of employment of seamen, railroad employees, or any other class of workers engaged in foreign or interstate commerce." How broadly should the courts read the exception for "contracts of employment" in Section 1 of the FAA? Does it encompass all employment contracts or is it limited to the specific kinds of contracts mentioned ("seamen, railroad employees, or any other class of workers engaged in foreign or interstate commerce")? This issue, which was not directly addressed by the *Gilmer* case, was decided by the U.S. Supreme Court in the case of *Circuit City Stores, Inc. v. Adams* [532 U.S. 105 (2001)]. The Supreme Court held that Section 1 of the FAA excludes only contracts of employment of the specific classes of workers listed in the statute. In *Circuit City,* the employer's application for employment contained a Dispute Resolution Agreement requiring employees to submit all employment disputes to binding arbitration; applicants who refused to sign the Dispute Resolution Agreement were not hired. The Supreme Court held that such an agreement is enforceable under the FAA and that employees signing the agreement are precluded from suing the employer over employment disputes. While individual employees may be bound by arbitration agreements in their contracts of employment, the individual arbitration agreements do not prevent the EEOC from bringing suit against an employer to enforce EEO laws according to *EEOC v. Waffle House, Inc.* [534 U.S. 279 (2003)]. The EEOC can bring legal action to enforce the EEO statutes, and may also seek individual remedies (such as back pay and reinstatement) for the employee who had signed the arbitration agreement.

Challenges to the Enforceability of Agreements to Arbitrate

The *Circuit City* decision means that employers may insist upon employees agreeing to arbitrate employment disputes as a condition of employment; applicants or employees who refuse to agree to such provisions will not be hired or will be fired. Because employers can force such arbitration agreements upon employees, a court asked to enforce an agreement to arbitrate must be satisfied that the agreement is knowing and reasonable. In *Brisentine v. Stone & Webster Engineering Corp.* [117 F.3d 519 (11th Cir. 1997)], the U.S. Court of Appeals for the Eleventh Circuit stated that, for an arbitration agreement to be enforced, it must meet three requirements: (1) the employee must have individually agreed to the arbitration provision, (2) the arbitration must authorize the arbitrator to resolve the statutory EEO claims, and (3) the agreement must give the employee the right to insist on arbitration if the statutory EEO claim is not resolved to his or her satisfaction in any grievance procedure or dispute resolution process of the employer.

Most courts now take the position that an agreement to arbitrate, knowingly and voluntarily agreed to by an employee, is binding and requires the employee to arbitrate EEO claims instead of taking them to court. Arbitration agreements that were not knowingly agreed to will not be enforced, *Prudential Insurance Co. v. Lai* [42 F.3d 1299 (9th Cir. 1994)], nor will the courts enforce agreements that are not binding upon the employer or that are unfair to the employee, *Hooters of America, Inc. v. Phillips* [9173 F.3d 933 (4th Cir. 1999)] and *Floss v. Ryan's Family Steak Houses* [211 F.3d 306 (6th Cir. 2000)]. The courts will also refuse to enforce arbitration agreements that restrict remedies available to employees less than those remedies available under the appropriate EEO statute, *Circuit City Stores, Inc. v. Adams* [279 F.3d 889 (9th Cir. 2002), *cert. denied,* 535 U.S. 1112 (2002)].

The California Supreme Court, in the case of *Armendariz v. Foundation Health Psychcare Services, Inc.* [99 Cal. Rptr.2d 745, 24 Cal.4th 83 (2000)], set out requirements for enforcing agreements requiring arbitration of claims under California state employment discrimination legislation: (1) the arbitration must be by a neutral arbitrator; (2) the arbitration procedures must allow the parties access to witnesses and essential documents; (3) the arbitrator must provide a written decision; (4) the remedies available under the arbitration must be similar to those available in court; and (5) the employee may not be required to pay any arbitrators' fees or expenses or any unreasonable costs as a condition of going to arbitration. While *Armendariz* deals with state law, some federal courts have adopted its analysis with regard to enforcing mandatory agreements to arbitrate.

Costs of Arbitration

Some challenges to the enforceability of arbitration agreements involve the question of cost: Does the arbitration agreement require the employee to bear unreasonable costs? As mentioned in *Armendariz,* arbitration agreements that impose excessive costs on employees could operate to deter those employees from bringing complaints of employment discrimination. Because the employees may be required to arbitrate rather than litigate their claims, they are effectively denied the protection of the EEO laws. As a result, the courts have refused to enforce arbitration agreements that require the employee to bear unreasonable expenses associated with the arbitration. In *Green Tree Financial Corp. v. Randolph* [531 U.S. 79 (2000)], which was not an employment case, the Supreme Court held that the party seeking to invalidate an arbitration agreement because it would be prohibitively expensive has the burden of demonstrating the likelihood of incurring such costs.

After *Green Tree,* the federal courts have struggled with the question of when the cost requirements of arbitration become prohibitively or unreasonably expensive. Plaintiffs who file EEO suits in the federal courts are required to pay a filing fee (currently less than $300) and must also bear the cost of legal representation; attorneys for plaintiffs are likely to take such cases on a contingency basis (they will only charge legal fees if the plaintiff wins the suit). Title VII also provides that successful plaintiffs may recover legal fees as part of the statutory remedies available. In contrast, the employee filing for arbitration will be required to pay a filing fee and will also generally be held to pay at least half of the arbitrator's fees and expenses. There may be additional fees for administrative costs, for discovery proceedings, and for subpoenas of witnesses. One study estimated that the costs of filing for arbitration (based on holding three days of hearings) ranged between $3,950 and $10,925.[2] Requiring an employee to pay such expenses to pursue an employment discrimination claim may have the effect of deterring the employee from doing so; some employers may have an incentive to impose arbitration requirements with high costs to prevent employees from filing employment discrimination claims. As a result, the courts have been sensitive to claims that the arbitration agreement imposes unreasonable costs on the employee.

In *Armendariz v. Foundation Health Psychcare Services, Inc.* [99 Cal. Rptr.2d 745, 24 Cal.4th 83 (2000)], the California Supreme Court held that an arbitration agreement that required the employee to pay any expenses beyond that which would be required to file a suit in court would be unreasonable and not enforceable. In *Morrison v. Circuit City Stores, Inc.* [317 F.3d 646 (6th Cir. 2003)(*en banc*)], the court held that a "fee-splitting" clause (which required the employee and the employer to split the costs of the arbitration and the arbitrator's fees) would be unreasonable and unenforceable when it would deter a substantial number of potential claimants from exerting their statutory rights.

The court, in making such a determination, should consider the employee's income and resources available, the potential costs of arbitration, and the costs of litigation as an alternative to arbitration. Such an approach may yield different results for different employees: For highly paid executive employees, fee-splitting requirements would be affordable and therefore enforceable, but for lower level employees, such cost requirements would not be enforceable. In the *Morrison* case, the court required the employee to arbitrate her claim but held that the employer had to pay the costs of the arbitration. Other courts have held fee-splitting clauses unreasonable per se; such requirements are unenforceable because, by requiring the employee to pay at least some of the costs of arbitration, they automatically limit the remedies that would be available to the employee under Title VII, *Perez v. Globe Airport Security Services* [253 F.3d 1280 (11th Cir. 2001)], *Circuit City Stores, Inc. v. Adams* [279 F.3d 889 (9th Cir. 20020, *cert. denied,* 535 U.S. 1112 (2002)], and *Ingle v. Circuit City Stores, Inc.*, 328 F.3d 1165 (9th Cir. 2003)].

REMEDIES UNDER TITLE VII

Plaintiffs under Title VII are entitled to a jury trial on their claims. The remedies available to a successful plaintiff under Title VII are spelled out in Section 706(g). These remedies include judicial orders requiring hiring or reinstatement of employees, awarding of back pay and seniority, injunctions against unlawful employment practices, and "such affirmative action as may be appropriate." Section 706(k) provides that the court, in its discretion, may award legal fees to a prevailing party other than the EEOC or the United States. The Civil Rights Act of 1991 added the right to recover compensatory and punitive damages for intentional violations of Title VII. Individual employ-

http://www.eeoc.gov/policy/cra91.html *contains the text of the Civil Rights Act of 1991 regarding damages.*

[2]"The Costs of Arbitration," *Public Citizen,* April 2002.

ees, even those in supervisory or managerial positions, are not personally liable under Title VII, *Tomka v. The Seiler Corp.* [66 F.3d 1295 (2d Cir. 1995)].

Back Pay

Section 706(g) states that the court may award back pay to a successful plaintiff. Back-pay orders spelled out by that section have some limitations, however. Section 706(g) provides that no back-pay order shall extend to a period prior to two years before the date of the filing of a complaint with the EEOC. It also provides that "Interim earnings or amounts earnable with reasonable diligence by the person or persons discriminated against shall operate to reduce the back pay otherwise allowable." That section imposes a duty to mitigate damages upon the plaintiff.

Although Section 706(g) states that a court may award back pay, it does not require that such an award always be made. What principles should guide the court on the issue of whether to award back pay?

According to the Supreme Court in *Albemarle Paper Co. v. Moody* [422 U.S. 405 (1975)], Title VII is remedial in nature and is intended to "make whole" victims of discrimination. Therefore, a successful plaintiff should be awarded back pay as a matter of course; back pay should be denied only in exceptional circumstances, such as when it would frustrate the purpose of Title VII.

In *Ford Motor Co. v. EEOC* [456 U.S. 923 (1982)], the Supreme Court held that an employer's back-pay liability may be limited to the period prior to the date of an unconditional offer of a job to the plaintiff, even though the offer did not include seniority retroactive to the date of the alleged discrimination. The plaintiff's rejection of the offer, in the absence of special circumstances, would end the accrual of back-pay liability of the employer.

In addition, Section 706(g)(2)(B), added by the 1991 amendments to Title VII, limits an employer's liability in mixed motive cases, provided that the employer can demonstrate that it would have reached the same decision even without consideration of the illegal factor. In these situations, the employer is subject to the court's injunctive or declaratory remedies and is liable for legal fees but is not liable for back pay or other damages, nor is the employer required to hire or reinstate the complainant.

Front Pay

Front Pay
Monetary damages awarded a plaintiff instead of reinstatement or hiring.

In some cases, if a hiring or reinstatement order may not be appropriate or if there is excessive animosity between the parties, the court may award the plaintiff **front pay**—monetary damages in lieu of reinstatement or hiring. The question of whether front pay is appropriate is a question for the judge, as is the determination of the amount of front pay. The amount of front pay depends upon the circumstances of each case; the court will consider factors such as the employability of the plaintiff and the likely duration of the employment. Any front pay awarded to the plaintiff by the court is separate from any compensatory and punitive damages awarded; the front-pay award is not subject to the statutory limits (discussed below) placed on the compensatory and punitive damages awards according to the Supreme Court decision in *Pollard v. E. I. du Pont de Nemours & Co.* [532 U.S. 843 (2001)].

COMPENSATORY AND PUNITIVE DAMAGES

The right to recover compensatory and punitive damages for intentional violations of Title VII was created by the Civil Rights Act of 1991, which amended Title VII. The 1991 act allows claims for compensatory and punitive damages, in addition to any remedies recoverable under Section 706(g) of Title VII, to be brought under 42 U.S.C. Section 1981, as amended by the 1991 act. Section 1981 (discussed in detail in Chapter 7) allows recovery of damages for intentional race discrimination. The Civil Rights Act of 1991 added a section to 42 U.S.C. Section 1981 that allows damages suits for intentional discrimination in violation of Title VII, for which the plaintiff could not recover under Section 1981 (that is, discrimination because of gender, religion, or national origin).

If the plaintiff can demonstrate that a private sector defendant (not a governmental unit, agency, or other public sector entity) has engaged "in a discriminatory practice or discriminatory practices with malice or with reckless indifference to the federally protected rights of an aggrieved individual," the plaintiff can recover compensatory and punitive damages. Punitive damages are not recoverable against public sector defendants. The compensatory and punitive damages are separate from, and in addition to, any back pay, interest, front pay, legal fees, or other remedies recovered under Section 706(g) of Title VII.

The compensatory and punitive damages recoverable under the amended Section 1981 are subject to statutory limits, depending on the number of employees of the defendant/employer. For employers with more than 14 but fewer than 101 employees, the damages recoverable are limited to $50,000; for defendants with more than 100 but fewer than 201 employees, the limit is $100,000; for more than 200 but fewer than 501 employees, it is $200,000; and for employers with more than 500 employees, the limit is $300,000. The number of people employed by a defendant/employer is determined by considering the number employed in each week of twenty or more calendar weeks in the current or preceding year.

Plaintiffs bringing a claim for damages under the amended Section 1981 have the right to a jury trial. As noted, punitive and compensatory damages are not recoverable against a public sector employer; punitive and compensatory damages are only recoverable for intentional discrimination and not for claims of disparate impact discrimination. Punitive and compensatory damages under the amended Section 1981 are also recoverable for intentional violations of the Americans with Disabilities Act of 1990 (discussed in Chapter 6).

When an employee has convinced the court that there was hostile environment harassment (based on race, sex, religion, or national origin) in violation of Title VII, the employer may be held liable for damages for all the acts that contributed to the hostile environment, even though some of those acts may have occurred more than 300 days (or 180 days, if appropriate) prior to the date on which the employee filed the complaint according to *National Railroad Passenger Corp. v. Morgan* [536 U.S. 101 (2002)].

Limitations on Remedies for Mixed Motive Discrimination

In cases involving mixed motive discrimination claims under Section 703(m) of Title VII [see the discussion of the *Hopkins* case and Section 703(m) in Chapter 3],

Section 706(g)(2)(B) provides that an employer will not be liable for damages when the employer can demonstrate that it would have reached the same decision even without consideration of the illegal factor. Where the employer has met the "same decision" test, the court will only issue a declaration or injunction and award the plaintiff legal fees; the plaintiff is not entitled to be hired, reinstated, or receive back pay, front pay, or compensatory and punitive damages.

Employer Liability for Punitive Damages under Title VII

Prior to being amended in 1991, Title VII did not provide for the recovery of punitive or compensatory damages; successful plaintiffs were limited to recovering wages, benefits, and legal fees. The Civil Rights Act of 1991 amended Title VII to allow recovery of punitive damages in cases in which the employer has engaged in intentional discrimination and has done so "with malice or with reckless indifference to the federally protected rights of an aggrieved individual." Under what circumstances should employers be held liable for punitive damages under Title VII? Are there any defenses that employers may raise to avoid liability for punitive damages? In *Kolstad v. American Dental Association* [527 U.S. 526 (1999)], the Supreme Court answered those questions:

> The employer must act with "malice or with reckless indifference to [the plaintiff's] federally protected rights." The terms "malice" or "reckless indifference" pertain to the employer's knowledge that it may be acting in violation of federal law, not its awareness that it is engaging in discrimination. . . . an employer must at least discriminate in the face of a perceived risk that its actions will violate federal law to be liable in punitive damages. There will be circumstances where intentional discrimination does not give rise to punitive damages liability under this standard. In some instances, the employer may simply be unaware of the relevant federal prohibition. There will be cases, moreover, in which the employer discriminates with the distinct belief that its discrimination is lawful. The underlying theory of discrimination may be novel or otherwise poorly recognized, or an employer may reasonably believe that its discrimination satisfies a bona fide occupational qualification defense or other statutory exception to liability. . . . Holding employers liable for punitive damages when they engage in good faith efforts to comply with Title VII, however, is in some tension with the very principles underlying common law limitations on vicarious liability for punitive damages—that it is "improper ordinarily to award punitive damages against one who himself is personally innocent and therefore liable only vicariously." Where an employer has undertaken such good faith efforts at Title VII compliance, it "demonstrat[es] that it never acted in reckless disregard of federally protected rights."
>
> . . . we agree that, in the punitive damages context, an employer may not be vicariously liable for the discriminatory employment decisions of managerial agents where these decisions are contrary to the employer's "good-faith efforts to comply with Title VII."

REMEDIAL SENIORITY

The *Teamsters* case, discussed in Chapter 3, held that a bona fide seniority system is protected by Section 703(h), even when it perpetuates the effects of prior discrimination. If the court is prevented from restructuring the bona fide seniority system, how can the court remedy the prior discrimination suffered by the plaintiffs? In *Franks v. Bowman Transportation Co.* [424 U.S. 747 (1976)], the Supreme Court held that remedial seniority may be awarded to the victims of prior discrimination to overcome the effects of discrimination perpetuated by the bona fide seniority system. The Court stated that "the denial of seniority relief to victims of illegal . . . discrimination in hiring is permissible 'only for reasons which, if applied generally, would not frustrate the central statutory purposes of eradicating discrimination . . . and making persons whole for injuries suffered through past discrimination.' . . ."

The granting of remedial seniority may be necessary to place the victims of discrimination in the position they would have been in had no illegal discrimination occurred.

LEGAL FEES

Section 706(k) provides that the court, in its discretion, may award "reasonable attorney's fees" under Title VII. The section also states that the United States or the EEOC may not recover legal fees if they prevail, but shall be liable for costs "the same as a private person" if they do not prevail.

In *New York Gaslight Club v. Carey* [447 U.S. 54 (1980)], the Supreme Court held that an award of attorney's fees under Section 706(k) can include fees for the legal proceedings before the state or local agency when the complainant is required to file with that agency by Section 706(c).

Section 706(k) does not require that attorney's fees be awarded to a prevailing party; the award is at the court's discretion. In *Christianburg Garment Co. v. EEOC* [434 U.S. 412 (1978)], the Supreme Court held that a successful plaintiff should generally be awarded legal fees except in special circumstances; a prevailing defendant should be awarded legal fees only when the court determines that the plaintiff's case was frivolous, unreasonable, vexatious, or meritless. A case is meritless, according to the Court, not simply because the plaintiff lost, but where the plaintiff's case was "groundless or without foundation." Why should prevailing defendants be treated differently than prevailing plaintiffs under Title VII?

CLASS ACTIONS

The rules of procedure for the federal courts allow an individual plaintiff to sue on behalf of a whole class of individuals allegedly suffering the same harm. Rule 23 of the Federal Rules of Civil Procedure allows such suits, known as *class actions,* when several conditions are met. First, the number of members of the class is so numerous that it would be "impracticable" to have them join the suit individually. Second, there must be issues of fact or law common to the claims of all members. Third, the claims of the individual seeking to represent the entire class must be typical of the claims of the members of the class. Finally, the individual representative must fairly and adequately protect the interests of the class.

When these conditions are met, the court may certify the suit as a class-action suit on behalf of all members of the class. Individuals challenging employment discrimination under Title VII may sue on behalf of all individuals affected by the alleged discrimination by complying with the requirements of Rule 23. In *General Telephone Co. of the Southwest v. Falcon* [457 U.S. 147 (1982)], the Supreme Court held that an employee alleging that he was denied promotion due to national origin discrimination is not a proper representative of the class of individuals denied hiring by the employer due to discrimination. The plaintiff had not suffered the same injuries allegedly suffered by the class members.

The EEOC need not seek certification as a class representative under Rule 23 to seek classwide remedies under Title VII according to the Supreme Court decision in *General Telephone v. EEOC* [446 U.S. 318 (1980)]. The EEOC, said the Court, acts to vindicate public policy and not just to protect personal interests.

Remedies in Class Actions

Classwide remedies are appropriate under Title VII according to the Supreme Court's holding in *Franks v. Bowman Transportation Co.* [424 U.S. 747 (1976)], which authorized such classwide "make whole" orders. In *Local 28, Sheet Metal Workers v. EEOC* (see Chapter 3), the Supreme Court upheld court-ordered affirmative action to remedy prior employment discrimination. The Court specifically said affirmative relief may be available to minority group members who were not personally victimized by the employer's prior discrimination. Additionally, in *Local 93, Int'l Ass'n. of Firefighters v. Cleveland* (see Chapter 3), the Supreme Court approved a consent decree that imposed affirmative action to remedy prior discrimination, again upholding the right of nonvictims to benefit from the affirmative remedy.

PUBLIC EMPLOYEES UNDER TITLE VII

Title VII was amended in 1972 to cover the employees of state and local employers; these employees are subject to the same procedural requirements as private employees. However, Section 706(f)(1) authorizes the U.S. Attorney General, rather than the EEOC, to file suit under Title VII against a state or local public employer.

http://www.eeoc.gov/facts/fs-fed.html *covers the facts about federal sector compliant processing regulations.*

Most federal employees are covered by Title VII but are subject to different procedural requirements. Section 701(b) excludes the United States, wholly owned federal government corporations, and any department or agency of the District of Columbia subject to civil service regulations from the definition of "employer" under Title VII. Section 717 of the act does provide, however, that "All personnel actions affecting employees or applicants for employment . . . in positions under the federal civil service, the D.C. Civil Service and the U.S. Postal Service . . . shall be made free from any discrimination based on race, color, religion, sex or national origin."

Section 717 also designated the federal Civil Service Commission as the agency having jurisdiction over complaints of discrimination by federal employees. However, in 1978, that authority was transferred to the EEOC under Reorganization Plan

No. 1 of 1978. The EEOC adopted procedural regulations regarding Title VII complaints by federal employees. A federal employee alleging employment discrimination must first consult with an Equal Employment Opportunity (EEO) counselor within the employee's own agency. If the employee is not satisfied with the counselor's resolution of the complaint, the employee can file a formal complaint with the agency's designated EEO official. The EEO official, after investigating and holding a hearing, renders a decision; that decision can be appealed to the head of the agency. If the employee is not satisfied with that decision, he or she can either seek judicial review of it or file an appeal with the EEOC. If the employee chooses to file with the EEOC, the complaint is subject to the general EEOC procedures. The employee has ninety days from receiving notice of the EEOC taking final action on the complaint to file suit. The employee may file suit, as well, when the EEOC has not made a decision on the complaint after 180 days from its filing with the EEOC.

Employees of Congress and the White House

The Civil Rights Act of 1991 extended the coverage of Title VII to employees of Congress. Employees of the House of Representatives, the Senate, the Capitol Guide Service, the Capitol Police, the Congressional Budget Office, the Office of the Architect of the Capitol, the Office of the Attending Physician, and the Office of Technology Assessment are subject to Title VII through the Congressional Accountability Act of 1995 as well. Those employees can file complaints of illegal discrimination with the Office of Compliance, created by the act, within 180 days of the alleged violation. The Office of Compliance initially attempts to resolve the complaint through counseling and mediation; if the complaint is still unresolved after the counseling and mediation period, the employee may either seek administrative resolution of the complaint through the Office of Compliance or file suit in federal court. Employees of the Executive Office of the President, the Executive Residence at the White House, and the official residence of the Vice President are subject to Title VII through the Presidential and Executive Office Accountability Act. Complaints by those employees of violations of Title VII are subject to an initial counseling and mediation period; the employee may then choose to pursue the complaint with the EEOC or file suit in federal court.

SUMMARY

- The protection that Title VII provides for employees from religious discrimination is not absolute. Religion may be a BFOQ, and the employer is not required to accommodate an employee's religious beliefs or practices if doing so would impose undue hardship on the employer, as defined in the *Hardison* case. Religious corporations and religiously affiliated educational institutions may give preference in employment to members of their particular religion according to Section 702(a) of Title VII and the *Amos* decision. Public sector employers are also subject to the First Amendment of the U.S. Constitution, which may further restrict their dealings with employees' religious beliefs and practices.

- Title VII prohibits employment discrimination based on national origin, although national origin may be used as a BFOQ when necessary for safe and efficient performance of the particular job. Employer English-only rules may also present problems under Title VII, unless supported by specific business justification. Title VII does not prohibit discrimination based on citizenship, but the Immigration Reform and Control Act of 1986 prohibits employment discrimination based on citizenship or national origin.
- The enforcement procedures under Title VII require that individuals claiming illegal discrimination go first to the appropriate state or local agency and then file their complaint with the Equal Employment Opportunity Commission (EEOC) after sixty days or the termination of proceedings at the state or local level, whichever comes first. The EEOC may decide to file suit on the complaint, and if it chooses not to sue, the individual may do so. Title VII suits can be brought in either federal or state courts. The plaintiff in a suit under Title VII must establish a prima facie case of discrimination; the defendant must then offer some legitimate explanation for the apparently discriminatory action to rebut the plaintiff's claims. If the defendant does offer a legitimate explanation for the challenged conduct, the plaintiff still has the opportunity to demonstrate that the employer's explanation was a pretext for illegal discrimination. Successful plaintiffs under Title VII may get an order of reinstatement, may recover back pay and benefits, legal fees, and in cases of intentional discrimination, can recover compensatory and punitive damages up to the appropriate statutory limit. Prevailing defendants may recover legal fees if the plaintiff's case was frivolous, groundless, or brought in bad faith. Plaintiffs claiming discrimination may be required to take their cases to arbitration rather than sue in court if they have knowingly and voluntarily agreed to arbitrate such complaints.

QUESTIONS

1. How does Title VII's prohibition of religious discrimination differ from the prohibition of discrimination based on race or color? Explain your answer.
2. What is meant by national origin under Title VII? Does Title VII prohibit discrimination based on ancestry? Explain.
3. Under what circumstances is an employer permitted to discriminate based on citizenship under Title VII? Under the IRCA?
4. What is necessary for an employer to require employees to arbitrate, rather than litigate, employment discrimination claims? Would employers or employees be more likely to favor arbitration over litigation? Explain your answers.
5. Explain the differences between the exemption for religious organizations under Section 702(a) and the exemption under Section 703(e)(2). Does one exemption supersede the other? Explain. How do those exemptions differ from a BFOQ based on religion?
6. What is the effect of a state court's dismissal of a discrimination complaint on the complainant's right to file suit in federal court? What is the effect of a state EEO agency dismissal of a discrimination complaint on the right of the complainant to file suit in federal court?
7. What remedies are available to a successful plaintiff under Title VII? When are punitive damages recoverable?
8. Must a complainant always file a complaint of illegal discrimination with the relevant state or local agency before filing a complaint with the EEOC? Explain.

CASE PROBLEMS

1. Morgan was an untenured faculty member at Ivy University. In February 1995, he was informed that the Faculty Tenure Committee recommended that he not be offered a tenured position with the university. Failure to achieve tenure requires that the faculty member seek employment elsewhere; the university offers such faculty members a one-year contract following denial of tenure. At the expiration of the one-year contract, the faculty member's employment is terminated.

   Morgan appealed to the tenure committee for a reconsideration. The committee granted him a one-year extension for a reconsideration. In February 1996, the committee again denied Morgan tenure at Ivy University. The university board of trustees affirmed the committee's decision. Morgan was informed of the trustees' decision and offered a one-year contract on June 26, 1996.

   Morgan accepted the one-year contract, which would expire on June 30, 1997. On June 1, 1997, Morgan filed charges with the EEOC alleging race and sex discrimination by Ivy University in denying him tenure. The one-year contract expired on June 30, 1997, and Morgan's employment was terminated.

   Assuming no state or local EEOC agency is involved, is Morgan's complaint validly filed with the EEOC? What employment practice is he challenging? When did it occur? See *Delaware State College v. Ricks* [449 U.S. 250 (1980)].

2. Cohen, a college graduate with a degree in journalism, applied for a position with *The Christian Science Monitor,* a daily newspaper published by the Christian Science Publishing Society, a branch of the Christian Science Church. The church board of directors elects the editors and managers of the *Monitor* and is responsible for the editorial content of the *Monitor.* The church subsidizes the *Monitor,* which otherwise would run at a significant loss. The application for employment at the *Monitor* is the same one used for general positions with the church. It contains many questions relating to membership in the Christian Science Church and to its religious affiliation.

   Cohen, who is not a member of the Christian Science Church, was rejected for employment with the *Monitor.* He filed a complaint with the EEOC alleging that his application was not given full consideration by the *Monitor* because he is not a member of the Christian Science Church. The *Monitor* claimed that it can apply a test of religious qualifications to its employment practices.

   Is the *Monitor* in violation of Title VII? Explain your answer. See *Feldstein v. Christian Science Monitor* [555 F.Supp. 974 (D.C. Mass. 1983)].

3. Dewhurst was a female flight attendant with Sub-Central airlines. Sub-Central's employment policies prohibited female attendants from being married, but married male employees were employed by Sub-Central. Dewhurst was married on June 15, 1980; she was discharged by Sub-Central the next day. Sub-Central, under pressure from the EEOC, eliminated the "no-married females" rule in March 1982.

   Dewhurst was rehired by Sub-Central on February 1, 1983. Sub-Central refused to recognize her seniority for her past employment with Sub-Central; the company's policy is to refuse to recognize prior service for all former employees who are rehired. Dewhurst filed a complaint with the EEOC on March 1, 1983, alleging that Sub-Central's refusal to credit her with prior seniority violated Title VII.

   Is her complaint validly filed with EEOC? See *United Airlines v. Evans* [431 U.S. 553 (1977)].

4. Smith, Washington, and Bailey are African American bricklayers. They had applied for work with Constructo Co., a brick and masonry

contractor. Constructo refused their applications for the reason that company policy is to hire only bricklayers referred by Constructo employees. The three filed charges with the EEOC, which decided not to file suit against Constructo. The bricklayers then filed suit in federal court against Constructo, alleging race discrimination in hiring.

At the trial, the three presented evidence of their rejection by Constructo. Constructo denied any racial discrimination in hiring and introduced evidence showing that African Americans make up 13 percent of its work force. Only 5.7 percent of all certified bricklayers in the greater metropolitan area are African American.

Has Constructo met its burden under Title VII? Have the three African Americans met their burden under Title VII? See *Furnco Construction Co. v. Waters* [438 U.S. 567 (1978)].

5. Walker is a clerk with the U.S. Postal Service. The Postal Service distributes the materials for the draft registration required of young men. Walker, although not a formal member of the Society of Friends (known as Quakers), had a long history of involvement with the Quakers. She therefore refused to distribute draft registration materials when she was working. The Postal Service fired her.

Is Walker's refusal to distribute the draft registration materials protected by Title VII? Explain your answer. See *McGinnis v. U.S. Postal Service* [512 F.Supp. 517 (U.S. Dist. Ct., N.D. Cal. 1980)].

6. Denora Sarin, a Cambodian immigrant and a practicing Buddhist, was employed as a systems engineer with Raytheon Company. Shortly after Sarin was assigned to work on a particular project, Goldberg, one of the workers he supervised, approached and taunted Sarin saying, "What's Buddhism? What kind of Buddha do you worship? The skinny Buddha or the fat one? I want to fight you. You don't fight me back." Sarin also claimed to be physically harassed by another employee, but after Sarin reported the conduct to his supervisor, it was not repeated. Goldberg continued to mock Sarin's religion on several occasions, and when Sarin later asked him to perform certain work, Goldberg shouted at him, "You're not my boss. You have no right to tell me what to do. You don't know me very well—I can do a lot of things that you cannot imagine." Goldberg also told Sarin that he (Sarin) came to the United States to "destroy and ruin the system of this country." Sarin again reported the conduct to Goldberg's supervisor. Sarin was extremely disturbed by the incident and took the rest of the day off. When he returned to work the next day, Goldberg had been transferred to a different work area. Goldberg was subjected to a discipline hearing because of Sarin's complaints. Goldberg denied Sarin's allegations, and there were no other witnesses to the incidents. No discipline was imposed on Goldberg, but he was warned that he would be severely disciplined if he harassed Sarin in the future. Sarin continued to experience anxiety attacks and suffered chest pains; he denied the company's offer to change shifts because the new shift would still overlap with that of Goldberg. On the recommendation of his doctor, Sarin resigned from his job. He then filed a complaint against Raytheon with the state EEO agency and with the EEOC and later filed suit against Raytheon under Title VII.

Should Raytheon be held in violation of Title VII? Could Sarin sue Goldberg? Explain your answers. See *Sarin v. Raytheon Company* [905 F.Supp. 49 (D.Mass. 1995)].

7. Elizabeth Westman was employed by Valley Technologies as an engineering technician. On June 15, 1997, she was terminated after being informed by her supervisor that the company was experiencing financial difficulties and could no longer afford to employ her. Westman subsequently learned, on May 15, 1998, that she was terminated so that her supervisor could hire a less qualified male technician in her place. Upon learning of the real reason for her discharge, Westman immediately filed a complaint with the EEOC; the employer argued that her complaint should be dismissed because it was not filed within the time limit required under Title VII.

Will her complaint be dismissed or was it properly filed? Explain your answer. See *Reeb v. Economic Opportunity Atlanta, Inc.* [516 F.2d 924 (5th Cir. 1975)].

8. S. A. Bouzoukis was employed as a member of the faculty of Enormous State University; she was denied tenure and offered a one-year terminal contract. Bouzoukis alleged that she was denied tenure because of gender discrimination, and she retained an attorney to pursue her claim against the university. Her attorney met with university officials to discuss the complaint, and the university requested that Bouzoukis allow the university time to conduct an investigation into her complaint. The university officials stated that if Bouzoukis agreed to delay filing her complaint with the EEOC, they would not raise the issue of time limits as a defense if the complaint could not be settled through negotiations. The university's investigation and subsequent negotiations dragged on for ten months; no settlement was reached. Bouzoukis then filed the complaint with the EEOC; she later filed suit in federal court. The university argued in court that the suit should be dismissed because the complaint was not filed with the EEOC within 300 days of the alleged violation.

How should the court rule on the time limit issue? Explain your answer. See *Leake v. University of Cincinnati* [605 F.2d 255 (6th Cir. 1979)].

9. Bernardo Huerta, an employee of the Adams Corp., was transferred to a position that prevented him from being eligible for overtime work. Huerta filed a complaint with the EEOC alleging that he had been discriminated against because of his national origin. After negotiations subsequent to the filing of the complaint, Huerta and the Adams Corp. reached a settlement agreement on his complaint. A year later, Huerta claimed that Adams had broken the settlement agreement, and he filed suit in federal court. The court granted judgment for Huerta, and he asked the court to award him legal fees. Adams Corp. argued that the action to enforce the settlement agreement was not the same as an action under Title VII; therefore, Huerta should not be awarded legal fees as a prevailing party under Title VII. Should the court award Huerta legal fees? Explain your answer. See *Robles v. United States* [54 Emp. Prac. Dec. (CCH) P 40, 193 (D.D.C. 1990)].

10. Marjorie Reiley Maguire was a professor in the theology department at Marquette University, a Roman Catholic institution. Approximately half of the twenty-seven members of the department were Jesuits, and only one other member was female at the time Maguire came up for tenure. The school denied her tenure because of her pro-choice view on the abortion issue—that is, because she favored personal choice rather than the Church's strict ban on abortions.

Was she a victim of gender discrimination? See *Maguire v. Marquette University* [814 F. 2d 1213 (7th Cir. 1987)].

INTERNET EXERCISES

1. You are an employee at a new Internet start-up company in Silicon Valley, but you suspect that you are being denied a promotion because of your race. Use the Web site of the California Department of Fair Employment and Housing at **http://www.dfeh.ca.gov** to find the nearest office of the California Fair Employment and Housing Commission.

2. Use the EEOC's home page at **http://www.eeoc.gov** to find the location of the nearest office of the EEOC.
3. Go to the Web site of the New York State Division of Human Rights at **http://www.nysdhr.com** and click on the link "How to File a Complaint" to find the location of offices and procedures for filing a complaint under the New York Human Rights Law.

   Go to the website **http://www.findlaw.com** and click the "US State Resources", then click on the links for a particular state, and try to find the Web sites of that state's EEO enforcement agency. What are the similarities between that state's EEO enforcement procedures and those under Title VII with the EEOC? What are the differences?

INFOTRAC KEYWORDS

http://www.infotrac-college.com

religious discrimination, national origin discrimination, English-only rules, disparate impact

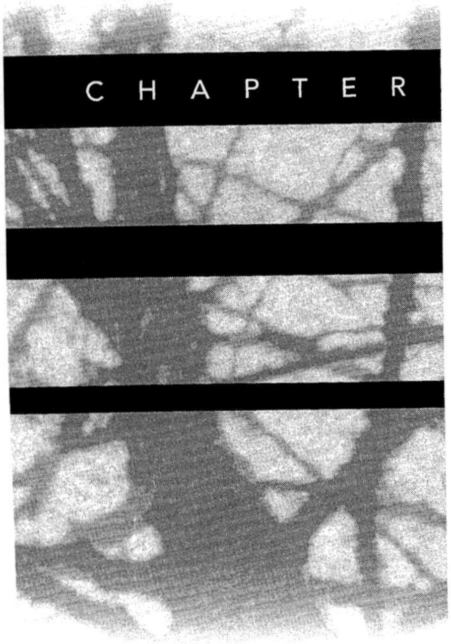

CHAPTER 6

DISCRIMINATION BASED ON AGE AND DISABILITY

Title VII of the Civil Rights Act, which was discussed in the preceding chapters, prohibits employment discrimination based on race, color, religion, gender, or national origin. In addition to Title VII, other federal legislation deals with employment discrimination because of other factors. This chapter covers the Age Discrimination in Employment Act, which prohibits employment discrimination based on age, and the Americans with Disabilities Act and the Rehabilitation Act, which prohibit discrimination based on disability.

THE AGE DISCRIMINATION IN EMPLOYMENT ACT

Discrimination in terms or conditions of employment because of age is prohibited by the Age Discrimination in Employment Act of 1967 (ADEA). The act's prohibitions, however, are limited to age discrimination against employees aged forty and older. It was intended to protect older workers who were more likely to be subjected to age discrimination in employment. (Although the ADEA's protection is limited to older workers, state equal employment opportunity laws may provide greater protection against age discrimination; the New York Human Rights Law, for example, prohibits age discrimination in employment against persons eighteen and older.)

http://www.eeoc.gov/policy/adea.html *contains the text of the ADEA.*

COVERAGE

The ADEA applies to employers, labor unions, and employment agencies. Employers involved in an industry affecting commerce, with twenty or more employees, are covered by the act. U.S. firms that employ American workers in a foreign country are subject to the ADEA. Labor unions are covered if they operate a hiring hall or if they have twenty-five or more members and represent the employees of an employer covered by the act.

The definition of employer under the ADEA includes state and local governments; the U.S. Supreme Court upheld the inclusion of state and local governments under the ADEA in *EEOC v. Wyoming* [460 U.S. 226 (1983)]. However, in January 2000, the Supreme Court held that the Eleventh Amendment of the U.S. Constitution provides state governments with immunity from suits by private individuals under the ADEA, *Kimel v. Florida Board of Regents* [528 U.S. 62 (2000)].

PROVISIONS

The ADEA prohibits the refusal or failure to hire, the discharge, or any discrimination in compensation, terms, conditions, or privileges of employment because of an individual's age (forty and older). The act applies to employers, labor unions, and employment agencies. The main effect of the act is to prohibit the mandatory retirement of employees. The act does not affect voluntary retirement by employees. It does provide for some limited exceptions and recognizes that age may be a BFOQ.

A plaintiff alleging a violation of the ADEA must establish a prima facie case that the employer has discriminated against the employee because of age. The employee must demonstrate that age was "a determining factor" in the employer's decision; it need not be the only determining factor.

The courts have adopted the Title VII procedures for establishing a claim under the ADEA; that is, the plaintiff must establish a prima facie case of age discrimination. The employer defendant must then offer a legitimate justification for the challenged action. If the defendant offers such a justification, the plaintiff can still show that the offered justification is a pretext for age discrimination.

Examples of violations of the ADEA include the mandatory retirement of workers over age fifty-five while allowing workers under fifty-five to transfer to another plant location or the denial of a promotion to a qualified worker because the employee is over fifty.

Must the plaintiff alleging that he was fired because of his age show that the employer replaced him with a person under forty to establish a prima facie case of age discrimination? That was the issue addressed by the Supreme Court in the following case.

O'Connor v. Consolidated Coin Caterers Corp.

517 U.S. 308 (1996)

Justice Scalia

. . . Petitioner James O'Connor was employed by respondent Consolidated Coin Caterers Corporation from 1978 until August 10, 1990, when, at age 56, he was fired. Claiming that he had been dismissed because of his age in violation of the ADEA, petitioner brought suit in the United States District Court . . . [which] granted respondent's motion for summary judgment, and petitioner appealed. The Court of Appeals for the Fourth Circuit stated that petitioner could establish a prima facie case . . . only if he could prove that (1) he was in the age group protected by the ADEA (40 or older); (2) he was discharged or demoted; (3) at the time of his discharge or demotion, he was performing his job at a level that met his employer's legitimate expectations; and (4) following his discharge or demotion, he was replaced by someone, of comparable qualifications outside the protected class (under 40). Since petitioner's replacement was 40 years old, the Court of Appeals concluded that the last element of the prima facie case had not been made out. Finding that petitioner's claim could not survive a motion for summary judgment . . . the Court of Appeals affirmed the judgment of dismissal. We granted O'Connor's petition for certiorari.

In *McDonnell Douglas,* we established an allocation of the burden of production and an order for the presentation of proof in . . . discriminatory-treatment cases. . . . Once the plaintiff has met this initial burden, the burden of production shifts to the employer

> to articulate some legitimate, nondiscriminatory reason for the employee's rejection. If the trier of fact finds that the elements of the prima facie case are supported by a preponderance of the evidence and the employer remains silent, the court must enter judgment for the plaintiff.
>
> In assessing claims of age discrimination brought under the ADEA, the Fourth Circuit . . . has applied some variant of the basic evidentiary framework set forth in *McDonnell Douglas*. . . .
>
> As the very name prima facie case suggests, there must be at least a logical connection between each element of the prima facie case and the illegal discrimination for which it establishes a legally mandatory, rebuttable presumption.

The element of replacement by someone under 40 fails this requirement. The discrimination prohibited by the ADEA is discrimination because of [an] individual's age, though the prohibition is limited to individuals who are at least 40 years of age. This language does not ban discrimination against employees because they are aged 40 or older; it bans discrimination against employees because of their age, but limits the protected class to those who are 40 or older. The fact that one person in the protected class has lost out to another person in the protected class is thus irrelevant, so long as he has lost out *because of his age*. Or to put the point more concretely, there can be no greater inference of age discrimination (as opposed to 40 or over discrimination) when a 40 year-old is replaced by a 39 year-old than when a 56 year-old is replaced by a 40 year-old. Because it lacks probative value, the fact that an ADEA plaintiff was replaced by someone outside the protected class is not a proper element of the . . . prima facie case.

Perhaps some courts have been induced to adopt the principle urged by respondent in order to avoid creating a prima facie case on the basis of very thin evidence—for example, the replacement of a 68 year-old by a 65 year-old. While the respondent's principle theoretically permits such thin evidence (consider the example above of a 40 year-old replaced by a 39 year-old), as a practical matter it will rarely do so, since the vast majority of age-discrimination claims come from older employees. In our view, however, the proper solution to the problem lies not in making an utterly irrelevant factor an element of the prima facie case, but rather in recognizing that the prima facie case requires *evidence adequate to create an inference that an employment decision was based on a[n] [illegal] discriminatory criterion*. . . . In the age-discrimination context, such an inference cannot be drawn from the replacement of one worker with another worker insignificantly younger. Because the ADEA prohibits discrimination on the basis of age and not class membership, the fact that a replacement is substantially younger than the plaintiff is a far more reliable indicator of age discrimination than is the fact that the plaintiff was replaced by someone outside the protected class.

The judgment of the Fourth Circuit is reversed, and the case is remanded for proceedings consistent with this opinion.

It is so ordered.

Case Questions

1. What is the function of a prima facie case? What is the significance of the Court of Appeals for the Fourth Circuit requirement that the plaintiff must show that he was replaced by someone under forty in order to establish a prima facie case?
2. Why does the Supreme Court reject the Court of Appeals requirement that the plaintiff must show that he was replaced by someone under forty to establish a claim under the ADEA? Explain your answer.
3. Can a sixty-eight-year-old employee who is replaced by a sixty-five-year-old employee establish a prima facie case of age discrimination? Explain your answer.

Defenses

When the plaintiff has established a prima facie case of age discrimination, the defendant must articulate some legitimate justification for the challenged action. The ADEA provides some specific exemptions and defenses on which the defendant may rely. The act recognizes that age may be a BFOQ and exempts executive employees from the prohibition on mandatory retirement. The act also provides that actions pursuant to a bona fide seniority system, retirement, pension or benefit system, for good cause, or for a "reasonable factor other than age" are not violations.

The ADEA was amended in 1990 to provide an additional defense for employers: Where the employer employs American workers in a foreign country and compliance with the ADEA would cause the employer to violate foreign law, the employer is excused from complying with the ADEA.

In *Mahoney v. RFE/RL Inc.* [47 F.3d 447 (D.C. Cir. 1995)], the employer's compliance with German law requiring employees to enforce a labor contract setting retirement age at sixty-five was held to be a defense under the foreign law exception of the ADEA.

Bona Fide Seniority or Benefit Plan

The ADEA allows an employer to observe the terms of a bona fide seniority system or employee benefit plan such as a retirement or pension plan as long as the plan or system is not "subterfuge to evade the purpose of this Act." The ADEA provides, however, that no seniority system or benefit plan "shall require or permit the involuntary retirement of any individual."

In *Public Employees' Retirement System of Ohio v. Betts* [492 U.S. 158 (1989)], the Supreme Court held that the ADEA exception protected any age-based decisions taken pursuant to a bona fide benefit plan as long as the plan did not require mandatory retirement. In response to that decision, Congress passed the Older Workers Benefit Protection Act, which became law in October 1990. The law amended the ADEA to require that any differential treatment of older employees under benefit plans must be "cost-justified"; that is, the employer must demonstrate that the reduction in benefits is only to the extent required to achieve approximate cost equivalence in providing benefits to older and younger employees. General claims that the cost of insuring individuals increases with age are not sufficient; the employer must show that the specific level of reductions for older workers in a particular benefit program is no greater than necessary to compensate for the higher cost of providing such benefits for older workers.

Factor Other Than Age

The ADEA allows employers to differentiate between employees when the differentiation is based on a reasonable factor other than age. For example, an employer may use a productivity-based pay system, even if older employees earn less than younger employees because they do not produce as much as younger employees. The basis for determining pay would be the employees' production, not their age. Similarly, when a work force reduction is carried out pursuant to an objective evaluation of all employees, it does not violate the act simply because a greater number of older workers than younger workers were laid off according to *Mastie v. Great Lakes Steel Co.* [424 F. Supp. 1299 (E.D. Mich. 1976)].

As well, the employer is permitted to discipline or discharge employees over forty for good cause. In *Hazen Paper Co. v. Biggins* [507 U.S. 604 (1993)], the Supreme Court held that discrimination directed against an employee because of his years of service is not the same as discrimination because of age; hence, the employer's conduct in allegedly firing an employee to prevent him from becoming eligible for vesting under the pension plan was based on a factor other than age.

The Supreme Court's decision in *Hazen Paper* was based on the fact that the ADEA has a specific exemption for employer actions based on a factor other than age. The Court did not decide the question of whether a disparate impact claim may be brought under the ADEA. (Disparate impact claims, you recall, involve challenges to apparently neutral employment criteria that have a disproportionate impact on a protected group of employees—in the case of the ADEA, employees forty and older.) After the *Hazen Paper* decision, the federal courts of appeals have differed on the question of whether an age discrimination claim based on the disparate impact theory is possible. The U.S. Courts of Appeals for the Second Circuit and the Eighth Circuit have held that disparate impact claims may be brought under the ADEA [see the cases of *Maresco v. Evans Chemetics, Div. of W.R. Grace & Co.,* 964 F.2d 106 (2d Cir. 1992); *District Council 37, A.F.S.C.M.E. v. New York City Dept. of Parks & Recreation,* 113 F.3d 347 (2d Cir. 1997); *Smith v. City of Des Moines,* 99 F.3d 1466 (8th Cir. 1996); and *Houghton v. SIPCO,* 38 F.3d 953 (8th Cir. 1994)]. But that is opposite the position taken by several other U.S. Courts of Appeals, which have read *Hazen Paper* as precluding disparate impact claims under the ADEA [see *EEOC v. Francis W. Parker School,* 41 F.3d 1073 (7th Cir. 1994), *cert. denied,* 515 U.S. 1142 (1995); *Banas v. Public Service Co. of Colorado,* 103 F.3d 144 (10th Cir. 1996); and *DiBiase v. Smithkline Beecham Corp.,* 48 F.3d 719 (3d Cir. 1995)].

Executive Exemption

Section 631(c) of the ADEA allows the mandatory retirement of executive employees who are over the age of sixty-five. To qualify under this exemption, the employee must have been in a bona fide executive or high policymaking position for at least two years and, upon retirement, must be entitled to nonforfeitable retirement benefits of at least $44,000 annually. An employee who is within the executive exemption can be required to retire upon reaching age sixty-five; mandatory retirement prior to sixty-five is still prohibited.

State or Local Government Firefighters or Law Enforcement Officers

Section 623(j) of the ADEA allows state and local governments to set, by law, retirement ages for firefighters and law enforcement officers. Where the state or local retirement age law was in effect as of March 3, 1983, the retirement age set by that law may be enforced. Where the state or local legislation setting the retirement age was enacted after September 30, 1996, the retirement age must be at least fifty-five.

This original version of this exception was inserted into the ADEA in response to the Supreme Court decision in *Johnson v. Mayor and City Council of Baltimore* [472 U.S. 353 (1985)], but that provision expired at the end of 1993; the current version of this exception was added to the ADEA in 1996.

Bona Fide Occupational Qualification

The ADEA does recognize that age may be a BFOQ for some jobs. The act states that a BFOQ must be reasonably necessary to the normal operation of the employer's business. In *Hodgson v. Greyhound Lines, Inc.* [499 F.2d 859 (7th Cir. 1974)], the court held that Greyhound could refuse to hire applicants for bus driver positions if the candidates were over thirty-five years old because of passenger safety considerations; a test pilot could not be mandatorily retired at age fifty-two according to *Houghton v. McDonnell Douglas Corp.* [553 F.2d 561 (8th Cir. 1977)]. The Supreme Court considered the question of what is required to qualify as a BFOQ under the ADEA in the following case.

Western Air Lines v. Criswell

472 U.S. 400 (1985)

Stevens, J.

The petitioner, Western Air Lines, Inc., requires that its flight engineers retire at age 60. Although the Age Discrimination in Employment Act of 1967 (ADEA) generally prohibits mandatory retirement . . . the Act provides an exception "where age is a bona fide occupational qualification [BFOQ] reasonably necessary to the normal operation of the particular business." A jury concluded that Western's mandatory retirement rule did not qualify as a BFOQ even though it purportedly was adopted for safety reasons. The question here is whether the jury was properly instructed on the elements of the BFOQ defense.

In its commercial airline operations, Western operates a variety of aircraft . . . [that] require three crew members in the cockpit: a captain, a first officer, and a flight engineer. "The 'captain' is the pilot and controls the aircraft. He is responsible for all phases of its operation. The 'first officer' is the copilot and assists the captain. The 'flight engineer' usually monitors a side-facing instrument panel. He does not operate the flight controls unless the captain and the first officer become incapacitated."

A regulation of the Federal Aviation Administration prohibits any person from serving as a pilot or first officer on a commercial flight "if that person has reached his 60th birthday." The FAA has justified the retention of mandatory retirement for the pilots on the theory that "incapacitating medical events" and "adverse psychological, emotional and physical changes" occur as a consequence of aging. "The inability to detect or predict with precision an individual's risk of sudden or subtle incapacitation, in the face of known age-related risks, counsels against relaxation of the rule."

At the same time, the FAA has refused to establish a mandatory retirement age for flight engineers. "While a flight engineer has important duties which contribute to the safe operation of the airplane, he or she may not assume the responsibilities of the pilot in command." Moreover, available statistics establish that flight engineers have rarely been a contributing cause or factor in commercial aircraft "accidents" or "incidents."

In 1978, respondents Criswell and Starley were captains operating DC-10s for Western. Both men celebrated their 60th birthdays in July 1978. Under the collective-bargaining agreement in effect between Western and the union, cockpit crew members could obtain open positions by bidding in order of seniority. In order to avoid mandatory retirement under the FAA's under-age-60 rule for pilots, Criswell and Starley applied for reassignment as flight engineers. Western denied both requests, ostensibly on the ground that both employees were members of the company's retirement plan which required all crew members to retire at age 60. . . .

Criswell [and] Starley . . . brought this action against Western contending that the under-age-60 qualification for the position of flight engineer violated the ADEA. In the District Court, Western defended, in part, on the theory that the age-60 rule is a BFOQ reasonably necessary to the safe operation of the airline. All parties submitted evidence concerning the nature of the flight engineer's tasks, the physiological and psychological traits required to perform them, and the availability of those traits among persons over age 60.

As the District Court summarized, the evidence at trial established that the flight engineer's "normal duties are less critical to the safety of flight than those of a pilot." The flight engineer, however, does have critical functions in emergency situations and, of course, might cause considerable disruption in the event of his own medical emergency.

The actual capabilities of persons over age 60, and the ability to detect disease or a precipitous decline in their faculties, were the subject of conflicting medical testimony. Western's expert witness, a former FAA Deputy Federal Air Surgeon, was especially concerned about the possibility of a "cardiovascular event" such as a heart attack. He testified that "with advancing age the likelihood of onset of disease increases and that in persons over age 60 it could not be predicted whether and when such diseases would occur."

The plaintiff's experts, on the other hand, testified that physiological deterioration is caused by disease, not aging, and that "it was feasible to determine on the basis of individual medical examinations whether flight deck crew members, including those over age 60, were physically qualified to continue to fly." These conclusions were corroborated by the nonmedical evidence. . . . Moreover, several large commercial airlines have flight engineers over age 60 "flying the line" without any reduction in their safety record.

The jury was instructed that the "BFOQ defense is available only if it is reasonably necessary to the normal operation or essence of defendant's business." The jury was informed that the "essence of Western's business is the safe transportation of their passengers." The jury was also instructed:

> One method by which defendant Western may establish a BFOQ in this case is to prove:
>
> (1) That in 1978, when these plaintiffs were retired, it was highly impractical for Western to deal with each second officer over age 60 on an individualized basis to determine his particular ability to perform his job safely; and
>
> (2) That some second officers over age 60 possess traits of a physiological, psychological or other nature which preclude safe and efficient job performance that cannot be ascertained by means other than knowing their age.
>
> In evaluating the practicability to defendant Western of dealing with second officers over age 60 on an individualized basis, with respect to the medical testimony, you should consider the state of the medical art as it existed in July 1978.

The jury rendered a verdict for the plaintiffs and awarded damages. After trial, the District Court [judge] granted equitable relief . . . [and] found no merit in Western's BFOQ defense to the mandatory retirement rule.

On appeal, Western made various arguments attacking the verdict and judgment below, but the Court of Appeals affirmed in all respects. In particular, the Court of Appeals rejected Western's contention that the instruction on the BFOQ defense was insufficiently deferential to the airline's legitimate concern for the safety of its passengers. We granted certiorari to consider the merits of this question.

Throughout the legislative history of the ADEA, one empirical fact is repeatedly emphasized: the process of psychological and physiological degeneration caused by aging varies with each individual. "The basic research in the field of aging has established that there is a wide range of individual physical ability regardless of age." As a result, many older American workers perform at levels equal or superior to their younger colleagues. . . .

. . . Congress responded with the enactment of the ADEA. The preamble declares that the purpose of the ADEA is "to promote employment of older persons based on their ability rather than age [and] to prohibit arbitrary age discrimination in employment." Section 4(a)(1) makes it "unlawful for an employer . . . to fail or refuse to hire or to discharge any individual or otherwise discriminate against any individual with respect to his compensation, terms, conditions, or privileges of employment, because of such individual's age." . . .

. . . Congress recognized that classifications based on age, like classifications based on religion, sex, or national origin, may sometimes serve as a necessary proxy for neutral employment qualifications essential to the employer's business. The diverse employment situations in various industries, however, forced Congress to adopt a "case-by-case basis . . . as the underlying rule in the administration of the legislation." Congress offered only general guidance on when an age classification might be permissible . . . "where age is a bona fide occupational qualification reasonably necessary to the normal operation of the particular business."

In *Usery v. Tamiami Trail Tours, Inc.,* the Court of Appeals for the Fifth Circuit was called upon to evaluate the merits of a BFOQ defense to a claim of age discrimination. Tamiami Trail Tours, Inc., had a policy of refusing to hire persons over age 40 as intercity bus drivers. At trial, the bus company introduced testimony supporting its theory that the hiring policy was a BFOQ based upon safety considerations—the need to employ persons who have a low risk of accidents. In evaluating this contention, the Court of Appeals drew on its Title VII precedents, and concluded that two inquiries were relevant.

First, the court recognized that some job qualifications may be so peripheral to the central mission of the employer's business that *no* age discrimination can be "reasonably *necessary* to the normal operation of the particular business." The bus company justified the age qualification for hiring its drivers on safety considerations, but the court concluded that this claim was to be evaluated under an objective standard:

> [T]he job qualifications which the employer invokes to justify his discrimination must be reasonably necessary to the essence of his business—here the safe transportation of bus passengers from one point to another. The greater the safety factor, measured by the likelihood of harm and the probable severity of that harm in case of an accident, the more stringent may be the job qualifications designed to insure safe driving.

This inquiry "adjusts to the safety factor" by ensuring that the employer's restrictive job qualifications are "reasonably necessary" to further the overriding interest in public safety. In *Tamiami,* the court noted that no one had seriously challenged the bus company's safety justification for hiring drivers with a low risk of having accidents.

Second, the court recognized that the ADEA requires that age qualifications be something more than "convenient" or "reasonable"; they must be "reasonably necessary . . . to the particular business," and this is only so when the employer is compelled to rely on age as a proxy for the safety-related job qualifications validated in the first inquiry. This showing could be made in two ways. The employer could establish that it "had reasonable cause to believe, that is, a factual basis for believing, that all or substantially all [persons over the age qualifications] would be unable to perform safely and efficiently the duties of the job involved." . . .

Alternatively, the employer could establish that age was a legitimate proxy for the safety-related job qualifications by proving that it is "impossible or highly impractical" to deal with the older employees on an individualized basis. "One method by which the employer can carry this burden is to establish that some members of the discriminated-against class possess a trait precluding safe and efficient job performance that cannot be ascertained by means other than knowledge of the applicant's membership in the class." In *Tamiami,* the medical evidence on this point was conflicting, but the District Court had found that individual examinations could not determine which individuals over the age of 40 would be unable to operate the buses safely. The Court of Appeals found that this finding of fact was not "clearly erroneous," and affirmed the District Court's judgment for the bus company on the BFOQ defense. . . .

Considering the narrow language of the BFOQ exception . . . we conclude that this two-part inquiry properly identifies the relevant considerations for resolving a BFOQ defense to an age-based qualification purportedly justified by considerations of safety. . . .

Western relied on two different kinds of job qualifications to justify its mandatory retirement policy. First, it argued that flight engineers should have a low risk of incapacitation or psychological and physiological deterioration. . . .

On a more specific level, Western argues that flight engineers must meet the same stringent qualifications as pilots, and that it was therefore quite logical to extend to flight engineers the FAA's age-60 retirement rule for pilots. Although the FAA's rule for pilots, adopted for safety reasons, is relevant evidence in the airline's BFOQ defense, it is not to be accorded conclusive weight. The extent to which the rule is probative varies with the weight of the evidence supporting its safety rationale and "the congruity between the . . . occupations at issue." In this case, the evidence clearly established that the FAA,

Western, and other airlines all recognized that the qualifications for a flight engineer were less rigorous than those required for a pilot.

In the absence of persuasive evidence supporting its position, Western nevertheless argues that the jury should have been instructed to defer to "Western's selection of job qualifications for the position of [flight engineer] that are reasonable in light of the safety risks." This proposal is plainly at odds with Congress' decision, in adopting the ADEA, to subject such management decisions to a test of objective justification in a court of law. The BFOQ standard adopted in the statute is one of "reasonable necessity," not reasonableness. . . .

. . . Under the Act, employers are to evaluate employees . . . on their merits and not their age. In the BFOQ defense, Congress provided a limited exception to this general principle, but required that employers validate any discrimination as "reasonably necessary to the normal operation of the particular business." . . .

When an employee covered by the Act is able to point to reputable businesses in the same industry that choose to eschew reliance on mandatory retirement . . . when the employer itself relies on individualized testing in similar circumstances, and when the administrative agency with primary responsibility for maintaining airline safety has determined that individualized testing is not impractical for the relevant position, the employer's attempt to justify its decision on the basis of the contrary opinion of experts—solicited for the purposes of litigation—is hardly convincing on any objective standard short of complete deference. Even in cases involving public safety, the ADEA plainly does not permit the trier of fact to give complete deference to the employer's decision.

The judgment of the Court of Appeals is

Affirmed.

Case Questions

1. Why does the FAA require that airline pilots retire at age sixty? Does the FAA requirement apply to flight engineers? Why?
2. Why does Western seek to retire flight engineers at sixty? What is the practice at other airlines?
3. Should the court defer to the judgment of Western's expert witnesses that retirement of flight engineers at age sixty is reasonable? Does the court do so in this case? Explain your answers.

Early Retirement and Work Force Reductions

The ADEA does not prohibit voluntary retirement as long as it is truly voluntary. The Older Workers Benefit Protection Act of 1990, which amended the ADEA, contained several provisions concerning work force reductions. Employers seeking to reduce their work force may offer employees early retirement incentives, such as subsidized benefits for early retirees or paying higher benefits until retirees are eligible for social security, as long as the practice is a permanent feature of a plan that is continually available to all who meet eligibility requirements and participation in the early retirement program is voluntary. Severance pay made available because of an event unrelated to age (such as a plant closing or work force reduction) may be reduced by the amount of health benefits or additional benefits received by individuals eligible for an immediate pension.

Waivers

Employers may require employees receiving special benefits upon early retirement to execute a waiver of claims under the ADEA if the waiver is knowing and voluntary and the employees receive additional compensation for the waiver, over and above that to which they are already entitled. The waivers must be in writing and must specifically refer to rights under the ADEA; the waivers do not operate to waive any rights of the employee that arise after the waiver was executed. The employees required to execute a waiver must be advised, in writing, to consult an attorney about the waiver and must be given at least twenty-one days to consider the matter before deciding whether to execute the waiver. The employees must also be allowed to revoke the waivers up to seven days after signing. If the waivers are part of a termination incentive program offered to a group or class of employees, the employer must give the employees forty-five days to consider the waiver. If the early retirement and waiver are offered to a class of employees, the employer must provide employees with the following information: a list of the class eligible for early retirement, the factors to determine eligibility for early retirement, the time limits for deciding upon early retirement, and any possible adverse action if the employee declines to accept early retirement and the date of such possible action.

For any waiver involving a claim that is already before the EEOC or a court, employees must be given "reasonable time" to consider the waiver. No waiver affects an employee's right to contact the EEOC or the EEOC's right to pursue any claim under the ADEA. In any suit involving a waiver of ADEA rights, the burden of proving that the waiver complies with ADEA requirements is on the person asserting that the waiver is valid (usually the employer).

When an employee accepts an employer's offer of severance benefits in return for signing a waiver that does not comply with the waiver requirements set out in the ADEA, does the employee's retention of those benefits operate to "ratify" the waiver and make it effective? The U.S. Supreme Court addressed that question in the following case.

Oubre v. Entergy Operations, Inc.

522 U.S. 422 (1998)

Justice Kennedy

Petitioner Dolores Oubre worked as a scheduler at a power plant in Killona, Louisiana, run by her employer, respondent Entergy Operations, Inc. In 1994, she received a poor performance rating. Oubre's supervisor met with her on January 17, 1995, and gave her the option of either improving her performance during the coming year or accepting a voluntary arrangement for her severance. She received a packet of information about the severance agreement and had 14 days to consider her options, during which she consulted with attorneys. On January 31, Oubre decided to accept. She signed a release, in which she "agree[d] to waive, settle, release, and discharge any and all claims, demands, damages, actions, or causes of action . . . that I may have against Entergy. . . ." In exchange, she received six installment payments over the next four months, totaling $6,258.

The Older Workers Benefit Protection Act (OWBPA) imposes specific requirements for releases covering ADEA claims. In procuring the release, Entergy did not comply with the OWBPA in at least three respects: (1) Entergy did not give Oubre enough time to consider her options, (2) Entergy did not give Oubre seven days after she signed the release to change her mind, and

(3) the release made no specific reference to claims under the ADEA.

Oubre filed a charge of age discrimination with the Equal Employment Opportunity Commission, which dismissed her charge on the merits but issued a right-to-sue letter. She filed this suit against Entergy in the United States District Court for the Eastern District of Louisiana, alleging constructive discharge on the basis of her age in violation of the ADEA and state law. Oubre has not offered or tried to return the $6,258 to Entergy, nor is it clear she has the means to do so. Entergy moved for summary judgment, claiming Oubre had ratified the defective release by failing to return or offer to return the monies she had received. The District Court agreed and entered summary judgment for Entergy. The Court of Appeals affirmed. . . .

The employer rests its case upon general principles of state contract jurisprudence. As the employer recites the rule, contracts tainted by mistake, duress, or even fraud are voidable at the option of the innocent party. The employer maintains, however, that before the innocent party can elect avoidance, she must first tender back any benefits received under the contract. If she fails to do so within a reasonable time after learning of her rights, the employer contends, she ratifies the contract and so makes it binding. The employer also invokes the doctrine of equitable estoppel. As a rule, equitable estoppel bars a party from shirking the burdens of a voidable transaction for as long as she retains the benefits received under it. Applying these principles, the employer claims the employee ratified the ineffective release (or faces estoppel) by retaining all the sums paid in consideration of it. The employer, then, relies not upon the execution of the release but upon a later, distinct ratification of its terms. . . .

In 1990, Congress amended the ADEA by passing the OWBPA. The OWBPA provides: "An individual may not waive any right or claim under [the ADEA] unless the waiver is knowing and voluntary. . . . [A] waiver may not be considered knowing and voluntary unless at a minimum" it satisfies certain enumerated requirements . . .

The statutory command is clear: An employee "may not waive" an ADEA claim unless the waiver or release satisfies the OWBPA's requirements. The policy of the Older Workers Benefit Protection Act is likewise clear from its title: It is designed to protect the rights and benefits of older workers. The OWBPA implements Congress' policy via a strict, unqualified statutory stricture on waivers, and we are bound to take Congress at its word. Congress imposed specific duties on employers who seek releases of certain claims created by statute. Congress delineated these duties with precision and without qualification: An employee "may not waive" an ADEA claim unless the employer complies with the statute. Courts cannot with ease presume ratification of that which Congress forbids.

The OWBPA sets up its own regime for assessing the effect of ADEA waivers, separate and apart from contract law. The statute creates a series of prerequisites for knowing and voluntary waivers and imposes affirmative duties of disclosure and waiting periods. The OWBPA governs the effect under federal law of waivers or releases on ADEA claims and incorporates no exceptions or qualifications. The text of the OWBPA forecloses the employer's defense, notwithstanding how general contract principles would apply to non-ADEA claims.

The rule proposed by the employer would frustrate the statute's practical operation as well as its formal command. In many instances a discharged employee likely will have spent the monies received and will lack the means to tender their return. These realities might tempt employers to risk noncompliance with the OWBPA's waiver provisions, knowing it will be difficult to repay the monies and relying on ratification. We ought not to open the door to an evasion of the statute by this device.

Oubre's cause of action arises under the ADEA, and the release can have no effect on her ADEA claim unless it complies with the OWBPA. In this case, both sides concede the release the employee signed did not comply with the requirements of the OWBPA. Since Oubre's release did not comply with the OWBPA's stringent safeguards, it is unenforceable against her insofar as it purports to waive or release her ADEA claim. As a statutory matter, the release cannot bar her ADEA suit, irrespective of the validity of the contract as to other claims. . . .

It suffices to hold that the release cannot bar the ADEA claim because it does not conform to the statute. Nor did the employee's mere retention of monies amount to a ratification equivalent to a valid release of her ADEA claims, since the retention did not comply with the OWBPA any more than the original release did. The statute governs the effect of the release on ADEA claims, and the employer cannot invoke the employee's failure to tender back as a way of excusing its own failure to comply.

We reverse the judgment of the Court of Appeals and remand for further proceedings consistent with this opinion.

It is so ordered.

Appendix to Opinion of the Court

Older Workers Benefit Protection Act, § 201, 104 Stat. 983, 29 U.S.C. § 626(f)

(f) Waiver

(1) An individual may not waive any right or claim under this chapter unless the waiver is knowing and voluntary. Except as provided in paragraph (2), a waiver may not be considered knowing and voluntary unless at a minimum—

(A) the waiver is part of an agreement between the individual and the employer that is written in a manner calculated to be understood by such individual, or by the average individual eligible to participate;

(B) the waiver specifically refers to rights or claims arising under this Act;

(C) the individual does not waive rights or claims that may arise after the date the waiver is executed;

(D) the individual waives rights or claims only in exchange for consideration in addition to anything of value to which the individual already is entitled;

(E) the individual is advised in writing to consult with an attorney prior to executing the agreement;

(F)(i) the individual is given a period of at least 21 days within which to consider the agreement; or

(ii) if a waiver is requested in connection with an exit incentive or other employment termination program offered to a group or class of employees, the individual is given a period of at least 45 days within which to consider the agreement;

(G) the agreement provides that for a period of at least 7 days following the execution of such agreement, the individual may revoke the agreement, and the agreement shall not become effective or enforceable until the revocation period has expired;

(H) if a waiver is requested in connection with an exit incentive or other employment termination program offered to a group or class of employees, the employer (at the commencement of the period specified in subparagraph (F)) informs the individual in writing in a manner calculated to be understood by the average individual eligible to participate, as to—

(i) any class, unit, or group of individuals covered by such program, any eligibility factors for such program, and any time limits applicable to such program; and

(ii) the job titles and ages of all individuals eligible or selected for the program, and the ages of all individuals in the same job classification or organizational unit who are not eligible or selected for the program.

(2) A waiver in settlement of a charge filed with the Equal Employment Opportunity Commission, or an action filed in court by the individual or the individual's representative, alleging age discrimination of a kind prohibited under section 4 or 15 may not be considered knowing and voluntary unless at a minimum—

(A) subparagraphs (A) through (E) of paragraph (1) have been met; and

(B) the individual is given a reasonable period of time within which to consider the settlement agreement.

(3) In any dispute that may arise over whether any of the requirements, conditions, and circumstances set forth in subparagraph (A), (B), (C), (D), (E), (F), (G), or (H) of paragraph (1), or subparagraph (A) or (B) of paragraph (2), have been met, the party asserting the validity of a waiver shall have the burden of proving in a court of competent jurisdiction that a waiver was knowing and voluntary pursuant to paragraph (1) or (2).

(4) No waiver agreement may affect the Commission's rights and responsibilities to enforce this Act. No waiver may be used to justify interfering with the protected right of an employee to file a charge or participate in an investigation or proceeding conducted by the Commission.

Case Questions

1. Why was the waiver signed by Oubre not valid under the ADEA?
2. Does Entergy argue that the waiver did comply with the ADEA? Why does Entergy argue that the waiver should be binding on Oubre?
3. Must Oubre return the money Entergy gave her for signing the waiver before she can sue Entergy under the ADEA? Explain your answer.

NEW REGULATION ADDRESSES SUPREME COURT RULING ON WAIVERS UNDER AGE BIAS LAW

THE WORKING LAW

In December 2000, the EEOC published the final regulation prohibiting the return, or "tender back," of consideration in connection with challenges to waivers under the ADEA. The new rule addresses the Supreme Court's 1998 decision *in Oubre v. Entergy Operations, Inc.* [522 U.S. 422] and related issues regarding waivers. The full text of the rule, as well as a supplementary question-and-answer document, is on the EEOC's Web site at http://www.eeoc.gov.

"The issuance of this regulation supports the vigorous enforcement of the ADEA's provisions regarding the use of waivers in layoffs and reductions in force, in accordance with the Supreme Court's decision in *Oubre,*" said EEOC Chairwoman Ida L. Castro. "By providing detailed guidance on the tender back question, the rule will enhance the ability of both employers and employees to understand and comply with the law."

An ADEA waiver is an agreement between an employer and employee in which the employee gives up the right to pursue an age discrimination claim against the employer in exchange for severance or early retirement benefits or something else of value. Employees are often asked to sign waivers in connection with layoffs or reductions in force. Consistent with the Supreme Court's ruling in *Oubre,* the regulation provides that an employer may not require an employee to return, or "tender back," severance pay or other benefits in order to challenge a waiver as inconsistent with the ADEA.

In addition, the rule prohibits the imposition of other financial penalties against an employee simply for challenging a waiver in court. It does, however, protect an employer's ability to recover attorney's fees if a challenge is filed in bad faith. The rule also sets out standards regarding when an employer may obtain restitution of funds it has paid an employee and what an employer's duties are when a waiver is challenged.

Employers paid $38.6 million dollars to settle age discrimination complaints filed with the EEOC during the years 1991–1999.

Source: EEOC, December 11, 2000.

PROCEDURES UNDER THE ADEA

The ADEA is enforced and administered by the EEOC. The EEOC acquired the enforcement responsibility from the Department of Labor pursuant to a reorganization in 1978. The ADEA allows suits by private individuals as well as by the EEOC.

An individual alleging a violation of the ADEA must file a written complaint with the EEOC and with the state or local equal employment opportunity (EEO) agency if one exists. Unlike Title VII, however, the individual may file simultaneously with both the EEOC and the state or local agency; there is no need to go to the state or local agency prior to filing with the EEOC. The complaint must be filed with the EEOC within 180 days of the alleged violation if no state or local agency exists. If such an agency does exist, the complaint must be filed with the EEOC within thirty days of the termination of proceedings by the state or local agency, and it must be filed not later than 300 days from the alleged violation.

After filing with the EEOC and the state or local EEO agency, the individual must wait sixty days before filing suit in federal court. Although there is no requirement that the individual wait for a right-to-sue notice from the EEOC, the sixty-day period is to allow time for a voluntary settlement of the complaint. If the EEOC dismisses the complaint or otherwise terminates proceedings on the complaint, it is required to notify the individual filing the complaint. The individual then has ninety days from receipt of the notice to file suit. Even though the individual must wait at least sixty days from filing with the agencies before bringing suit in court, the court suit must be filed no later than ninety days from receiving the right-to-sue notice from the EEOC. An individual can file an age discrimination suit in federal court even if the state or local EEO agency has ruled that the employee was not the victim of age discrimination according to the Supreme Court decision in *Astoria Federal Savings & Loan v. Solimino* [501 U.S. 104 (1991)]. If the EEOC files suit under the ADEA, the EEOC suit supersedes any ADEA suit filed by the individual or any state agency. As with Title VII, the ADEA allows for a jury trial.

After-Acquired Evidence

In *McKennon v. Nashville Banner Publishing Co.* [513 U.S. 352 (1995)], the employer discovered that an employee allegedly fired because of her age had copied confidential documents prior to her discharge. The employer argued that the evidence of the plaintiff/employee's misconduct (known as *after-acquired evidence*) precluded the right of the plaintiff to sue under the ADEA. The Supreme Court held that the after-acquired evidence does not preclude the plaintiff's suit but rather goes to the issue of what remedies are available. If the employer can demonstrate that the employee's wrongdoing was severe enough to result in termination had the employer known of the misconduct at the time the alleged discrimination occurred, the court must then consider the effect of the wrongdoing on the remedies available to the plaintiff. In such a case, reinstatement might not be appropriate, and back pay could be awarded only from the date of the alleged discrimination by the employer to the date upon which the plaintiff's misconduct was discovered.

Arbitration of ADEA Claims

In *Gilmer v. Interstate/Johnson Lane Corp.* [500 U.S. 20 (1991)], the Supreme Court held that a securities broker was required to arbitrate, rather than litigate, his age discrimination claim because he had signed an agreement to arbitrate all disputes arising from his employment. The individual agreement to arbitrate, voluntarily agreed to by Gilmer, was enforceable under the Federal Arbitration Act and required Gilmer to submit all employment disputes, including those under EEO legislation, to arbitration. The agreement to arbitrate did not waive Gilmer's rights under the statutes but simply required that those rights be determined by the arbitrator rather than the courts. In general, agreements to arbitrate ADEA claims will be enforced when they were voluntarily and knowingly agreed to by the employees, but such arbitration agreements do not prevent the EEOC from bringing a suit on behalf of the individual employees subject to the arbitration agreements. (See the discussion of this topic in Chapter 5.)

Suits by Federal Employees

Despite the fact that the federal government is not included in the ADEA's definition of employer, Section 15 of the act provides that personnel actions in most federal government positions shall be made free from discrimination based on age. The ADEA protects federal workers "who are at least 40 years of age."

Complaints of age discrimination involving federal employees are now handled by the EEOC. A federal employee agency must file the complaint with the EEOC within 180 days of the alleged violation; the employee may file suit in federal court after thirty days from filing with the EEOC. The ADEA provides only for private suits in cases involving complaints by federal employees. No provision is made for suits by the EEOC.

Government Suits

In addition to private suits, the ADEA provides for suits by the responsible government agency (now the EEOC, formerly the secretary of labor) against nonfederal employers. The EEOC must attempt to settle the complaint voluntarily before filing suit; there is no specific time limitation for this required conciliation effort. Once conciliation has been attempted, the EEOC may file suit.

The 1991 amendments to the ADEA eliminated the previous time limits spelled out for suits by the EEOC; as a result, at present, the courts are split on the question of when the EEOC suit must be filed. Some courts have held that there is no specific statute of limitations on ADEA suits filed by the EEOC, *EEOC v. Tire Kingdom* [80 F.3d 449 (11th Cir. 1996)]; other courts have held that the EEOC is also subject to the ninety-day limitation, *McConnell v. Thomson Newspapers, Inc.* [802 F.Supp. 1484 (E.D.Tex. 1992)].

REMEDIES UNDER THE ADEA

The remedies available under the ADEA are similar to those available under the Equal Pay Act. Successful private plaintiffs can recover any back wages owing and legal fees; they may also recover an equal amount as liquidated damages if the employer acted "willfully." The Supreme Court, in the 1985 case of *Trans World Airlines, Inc. v. Thurston* [469 U.S. 111], held that an employer acts willfully when "the employer either knew or showed reckless disregard for the matter of whether its conduct was prohibited by the ADEA." Injunctive relief is also available, and legal fees and costs are recoverable by the successful private plaintiff. Back pay and liquidated damages recovered under the ADEA are subject to income taxation according to *Commissioner of IRS v. Schleier* [515 U.S. 323 (1995)].

Remedies in suits by the EEOC may include injunctions and back pay. Liquidated damages, however, are not available in such suits.

http://www.eeoc.gov/abouteeoc/plan/nep.html *is the site for the text of the U.S. EEOC National Enforcement Plan.*

DISCRIMINATION BECAUSE OF DISABILITY

The legislation prohibiting employment discrimination because of disability is more recent than the other equal employment opportunity legislation. The Rehabilitation Act of 1973 prohibits discrimination because of disability by the federal government, by government contractors, and by recipients of federal financial assistance. The Americans with Disabilities Act of 1990 (ADA) also prohibits discrimination in employment because of disability; the ADA is patterned after the Civil Rights Act of 1964. The coverage of the ADA is much broader than the Rehabilitation Act; the ADA covers all employers with fifteen or more employees. This section discusses both the ADA and the Rehabilitation Act.

THE AMERICANS WITH DISABILITIES ACT

http://www.dol.gov/esa/regs/statutes/ofccp/ada.htm *provides the full text of the Americans with Disabilities Act.*

The ADA is a comprehensive piece of civil rights legislation for individuals with disabilities; Title I of the act, which applies to employment, prohibits discrimination against individuals who are otherwise qualified for employment. The act became law on July 26, 1990, effective two years after that date for employers with twenty-five or more employees and three years from that date for employers with fifteen or more employees.

Coverage

The ADA applies to both private and public sector employers with fifteen or more employees but does not apply to most federal government employers, American Indian tribes, or bona fide private membership clubs. The Congressional Accountability Act of 1995 [Pub. L. 104-1, 109 Stat. 3] extended the coverage of the ADA and the Rehabilitation Act to the employees of the House of Representatives, the Senate, the Capitol Guide Service, the Capitol Police, the Congressional Budget Office, the Office of the Architect of the Capitol, the Office of the Attending Physician, and the Office of Technology Assessment. The Presidential and Executive Office Accountability Act [Pub. L. 104-331, 110 Stat. 4053] extended coverage of the ADA and the Rehabilitation Act to the Executive Office of the President, the Executive Residence at the White House, and the official residence of the Vice President. United States employers operating abroad or controlling foreign corporations are covered with regard to the employment of U.S. citizens, unless compliance with the ADA would cause the employer to violate the law of the foreign country in which the workplace is located.

The U.S. Supreme Court, in a 5-4 decision, ruled that the Eleventh Amendment of the U.S. Constitution gave the states immunity from individual suits for damages under the ADA, *Board of Trustees of the University of Alabama v. Garrett* [531 U.S. 356 (2001)]. The Court's reasoning in *Garrett* was consistent with its earlier decision in *Kimel v. Florida Board of Regents* [528 U.S. 62 (2000)].

Provisions

The ADA prohibits covered employers from discriminating in any aspect of employment because of disability against an otherwise qualified individual with a disability. Illegal discrimination under the ADA includes

> . . . limiting, segregating, or classifying employees or applicants in a way that adversely affects employment opportunities because of disability, using standards or criteria that have the effect of discriminating on the basis of disability or perpetuating discrimination against others, excluding or denying jobs or benefits to qualified individuals because of the disability of an individual with whom a qualified individual is known to associate, failing to make reasonable accommodation to the known limitations of an otherwise qualified individual unless such accommodation would impose an undue hardship, failing to hire an individual who would require reasonable accommodation, and failing to select or administer employment tests in the most effective manner to ensure that the results reflect the skills of applicants or employees with disabilities.

The ADA also prohibits retaliation against any individual because the individual has opposed any act or practice unlawful under the ADA or because the individual has filed a charge or participated in any manner in a proceeding under the ADA. The act also prohibits coercion or intimidation of, threats against, or interference with an individual's exercise of or enjoyment of any rights granted under the act.

QUALIFIED INDIVIDUAL WITH A DISABILITY

The ADA and the Rehabilitation Act impose obligations not to discriminate against otherwise qualified individuals with disabilities. According to the Supreme Court decision in *Southeastern Community College v. Davis* [442 U.S. 397 (1979)], a person is a qualified individual with a disability if the person "is able to meet all . . . requirements in spite of his disability." The individual claiming to be qualified has the burden of demonstrating his or her ability to meet all physical requirements legitimately necessary for the performance of duties. An employer is not required to hire a person with a disability who is not capable of performing the duties of the job; however, the regulations under the act require the employer to make "reasonable accommodation" to the disabilities of individuals.

The ADA defines "qualified individual with a disability" as "an individual with a disability who, with or without reasonable accommodation, can perform the essential functions of the employment position that such individual holds or desires." When determining the essential functions of a job, the court or the EEOC, which administers and enforces the ADA, is to consider the employer's judgment as to what is essential; if a written job description is used for advertising the position or interviewing job applicants, that description is to be considered evidence of the essential functions of the job.

In *Cleveland v. Policy Management Systems* [526 U.S. 795 (1999)], the Supreme Court held that an individual who applies for Social Security disability benefits may still be a "qualified individual with a disability" within the meaning of the ADA. In *Albertsons, Inc. v. Kirkingburg* [527 U.S. 555 (1999)], the Supreme Court held that a truck driver who was not able to meet federal safety standards for commercial motor vehicle operators was not "a qualified individual with a disability" under the ADA; the employer was not required to participate in an experimental program that would have waived the safety standards.

DEFINITION OF DISABILITY

The ADA defines "individual with a disability" very broadly: Disability means, with respect to an individual,

(a) a physical or mental impairment that substantially limits one or more of the major life activities of such individual;
(b) a record of such an impairment; or
(c) being regarded as having such an impairment.

Employees who use illegal drugs are not protected by the ADA, nor are alcoholics who use alcohol at the workplace or who are under the influence of alcohol at the workplace. Individuals who are former drug users or recovering drug users, including persons participating in a supervised rehabilitation program and individuals "erroneously regarded" as using drugs but who do not use drugs, are under the ADA's protection.

The definition of disability under the ADA includes infectious or contagious diseases, unless the disease presents a direct threat to the health or safety of others and that threat cannot be eliminated by reasonable accommodation. Temporary or short-term nonchronic conditions, with little or no long-term or permanent impact, are usually not considered disabilities. The act's protection does not apply to an individual who is a transvestite, nor are homosexuality, bisexuality, or sexual behavior disorders such as exhibitionism or transsexualism considered disabilities. Compulsive gambling, kleptomania, pyromania, and psychoactive substance use disorders resulting from current illegal use of drugs are also not within the definition of disability.

In *Sutton v. United Air Lines, Inc.* [527 U.S. 471 (1999)], the Supreme Court held that when determining whether an individual has a disability that substantially limits one or more major life activities, a court must also consider the existence of corrective, mitigating, or remedial measures that may reduce the effect of the disability. Sutton sought a job as a commercial airline pilot but suffered from severe myopia, which rendered her vision at 20/200 or worse in each eye. With corrective lenses (either glasses or contact lenses), however, her vision was functionally equivalent to normal vision. Although her vision problems disqualified her from serving as an airline pilot, the Court held that she was not disabled within the meaning of the ADA definition. Her corrected vision did not substantially limit her in any major life activity, and her myopia was therefore not a disability within the meaning of the ADA. Sutton also claimed that her condition prevented her from being a commercial pilot and thus substantially limited her ability to work, which is a major life activity. The Court rejected that argument, holding that a disability must preclude an individual from a class or range of jobs, rather than simply disqualifying her from a particular or specialized job, to substantially limit her ability to work.

A person claiming protection of the ADA must have a disability, but the mere existence of such a disability is not, in itself, sufficient to establish ADA coverage. The individual's disability must "substantially limit one or more major life activities" for the individual to be disabled within the meaning of the ADA. In the following case, the U.S. Supreme Court considered what an individual must demonstrate in order to establish that the disabling condition substantially limits one or more major life activities.

Toyota Motor Manufacturing, Kentucky, Inc. v. Williams

534 U.S. 184 (2002)

Background

[Williams was hired at Toyota's Georgetown, Kentucky, manufacturing plant in August 1990. She was placed on an engine fabrication assembly line, where she worked with pneumatic tools, which eventually caused pain in her hands, wrists, and arms. She sought medical treatment and was diagnosed with bilateral carpal tunnel syndrome and bilateral tendinitis. Her physician placed her on permanent work restrictions, preventing her from lifting more than twenty pounds or from frequently lifting or carrying objects weighing up to ten pounds, engaging in constant repetitive flexion or extension of her wrists or elbows, performing overhead work, or using vibrating or pneumatic tools.

Because of these restrictions, she was assigned to various modified duty jobs for the next two years. She eventually filed a workers' compensation claim, which was settled with Toyota, and she returned to work. Toyota then placed her on a team in Quality Control Inspection Operations (QCIO). QCIO performs four jobs: (1) assembly paint; (2) paint second inspection; (3) shell body audit; and (4) ED surface repair. Williams initially performed only the first two of these jobs, and for a few years, she rotated between them. Her jobs were modified to include only visual inspection with few or no manual tasks. Toyota agreed that Williams was physically capable of performing both of these jobs and that her performance was satisfactory.

In the fall of 1996, Toyota announced that it wanted QCIO employees to be able to rotate through all four of the QCIO jobs. Williams received training for the shell body audit job, which required the worker to apply a highlight oil to the body of passing cars at a rate of approximately one car per minute. That job required Williams to hold her hands and arms up around shoulder height for several hours at a time. Shortly after Williams began to perform the shell body audit job, she began to experience pain in her neck and shoulders. She sought medical care and was diagnosed with an inflammation of the muscles and tendons around both of her shoulder blades, myotendinitis and myositis bilateral forearms with nerve compression causing median nerve irritation, and a condition that causes pain in the nerves that lead to the upper extremities. She requested that Toyota accommodate her medical conditions by allowing her to perform only her original two jobs in QCIO, which she could still perform without difficulty. Williams claimed that Toyota refused her request and forced her to continue working in the shell body audit job, causing her even greater physical injury. Toyota claimed that she began missing work regularly.

On December 6, 1996, her doctors placed her under a no-work-of-any-kind restriction, and she did not report for work after that. On January 27, 1997, Toyota informed her by letter that her employment was terminated because of her poor attendance record. Williams filed suit against Toyota under the ADA.]

Justice O'Connor

. . . Under the ADA, a physical impairment that "substantially limits one or more . . . major life activities" is a "disability." Respondent [Williams], claiming to be disabled because of her carpal tunnel syndrome and other related impairments, sued petitioner [Toyota] . . . for failing to provide her with a reasonable accommodation as required by the ADA. . . .

Respondent based her claim that she was "disabled" under the ADA on the ground that her physical impairments substantially limited her in (1) manual tasks; (2) housework; (3) gardening; (4) playing with her children; (5) lifting; and (6) working, all of which, she argued, constituted major life activities under the Act. Respondent also argued, in the alternative, that she was disabled under the ADA because she had a record of a substantially limiting impairment and because she was regarded as having such an impairment.

. . . the District Court granted summary judgment to petitioner. The court found that respondent had not been disabled, as defined by the ADA, at the time of petitioner's alleged refusal to accommodate her, and that she had therefore not been covered by the [ADA]. . . . The District Court held that respondent had suffered from a physical impairment, but that the impairment did not qualify as a disability because it had not "substantially limit[ed]" any "major life activit[y]." The court rejected respondent's arguments that gardening, doing housework, and playing with children are major life activities. Although the court agreed that performing manual tasks, lifting, and working are major life activities, it found the evidence insufficient to demonstrate that respondent had been substantially limited in lifting or working. The court found respondent's claim that she was substantially limited in performing manual tasks to be "irretrievably contradicted by [respondent's] continual insistence that she could perform the tasks in assembly [paint] and paint [second] inspection without difficulty." The court also found no evidence that respondent had had a record of a substantially limiting impairment, or that petitioner had regarded her as having such an impairment. . . .

Respondent appealed. . . . The Court of Appeals for the Sixth Circuit reversed the District Court's ruling on whether respondent was disabled at the time she sought an accommodation. . . . The Court of Appeals held that in order for respondent to demonstrate that she was disabled due to a substantial limitation in the ability to perform manual tasks at the time of her accommodation request, she had to "show that her manual disability involve[d] a 'class' of manual activities affecting the ability to perform tasks at work." Respondent satisfied this test, according to the Court of Appeals, because her ailments "prevent[ed] her from doing the tasks associated with certain types of manual assembly line jobs, manual product handling jobs and manual building trade jobs (painting, plumbing, roofing, etc.) that require the gripping of tools and repetitive work with hands and arms extended at or above shoulder levels for extended periods of time." In reaching this conclusion, the court disregarded evidence that respondent could "ten[d] to her personal hygiene [and] carr[y] out personal or household chores," finding that such evidence "does not affect a determination that her impairment substantially limit[ed] her ability to perform the range of manual tasks associated with an assembly line job." . . .

We granted [Toyota's appeal] . . . to consider the proper standard for assessing whether an individual is substantially limited in performing manual tasks. . . .

The ADA requires covered entities, including private employers, to provide "reasonable accommodations to the known physical or mental limitations of an otherwise qualified individual with a disability who is an applicant or employee, unless such covered entity can demonstrate that the accommodation would impose an undue hardship." . . . The Act defines a "qualified individual with a disability" as "an individual with a disability who, with or without reasonable accommodation, can perform the essential functions of the employment position that such individual holds or desires." In turn, a "disability" is:

> (A) a physical or mental impairment that substantially limits one or more of the major life activities of such individual;
>
> (B) a record of such an impairment; or
>
> (C) being regarded as having such an impairment. . . .

To qualify as disabled under subsection (A) of the ADA's definition of disability, a claimant must initially prove that he or she has a physical or mental impairment. The . . . regulations [under the ADA] . . . define "physical impairment," the type of impairment relevant to this case, to mean "any physiological disorder or condition, cosmetic disfigurement, or anatomical loss affecting one or more of the following body systems. . . ."

Merely having an impairment does not make one disabled for purposes of the ADA. Claimants also need to demonstrate that the impairment limits a major life activity. The . . . regulations provide a list of examples of "major life activities" that includes "walking, seeing, hearing," and, as relevant here, "performing manual tasks."

To qualify as disabled, a claimant must further show that the limitation on the major life activity is "substantia[l]." Unlike "physical impairment" and "major life activities," the . . . regulations do not define the term "substantially limits." . . . The EEOC, therefore, has created its own definition for purposes of the ADA. According to the EEOC regulations, "substantially limit[ed]" means "[u]nable to perform a major life activity that the average person in the general population can perform"; or "[s]ignificantly restricted as to the condition, manner or duration under which an individual can perform a particular major life activity as compared to the condition, manner or duration under which the average person in the general population can perform that same major life activity." In determining whether an individual is substantially limited in a major life activity, the . . . following factors should be considered: "[t]he nature and severity of the impairment; [t]he duration or expected duration of the impairment; and [t]he permanent or long-term impact, or the expected permanent or long-term impact of or resulting from the impairment." . . .

. . . The parties do not dispute that respondent's medical conditions . . . amount to physical impairments. The relevant question, therefore, is whether the Sixth Circuit correctly analyzed whether these impairments substantially limited respondent in the major life activity of performing manual tasks. Answering this requires us to address . . . what a plaintiff must demonstrate to establish a substantial limitation in the specific major life activity of performing manual tasks.

Our consideration of this issue is guided first and foremost by the words of the disability definition itself. "[S]ubstantially" in the phrase "substantially limits" suggests "considerable" or "to a large degree." . . . The word "substantial" thus clearly precludes impairments that interfere in only a minor way with the performance of manual tasks from qualifying as disabilities. . . .

"Major" in the phrase "major life activities" means important. . . . "Major life activities" thus refers to those activities that are of central importance to daily life. . . .

We therefore hold that to be substantially limited in performing manual tasks, an individual must have an impairment that prevents or severely restricts the individual from doing activities that are of central importance to most people's daily lives. The impairment's impact must also be permanent or long term.

. . . [Rather than merely submitting evidence of a medical diagnosis of an impairment] the ADA requires [plaintiffs] . . . to prove a disability by offering evidence that the extent of the limitation [caused by their impairment] in terms of their own experience . . . is substantial. That the Act defines "disability" "with respect to an individual," makes clear that Congress intended the existence of a disability to be determined in such a case-by-case manner. . . .

An individualized assessment of the effect of an impairment is particularly necessary when the impairment is one whose symptoms vary widely from person to person. . . . an individual's carpal tunnel syndrome diagnosis, on its own, does not indicate whether the individual has a disability within the meaning of the ADA.

The Court of Appeals . . . suggested that in order to prove a substantial limitation in the major life activity of performing manual tasks, a "plaintiff must show that her manual disability involves a 'class' of manual activities," and that those activities "affec[t] the ability to perform tasks at work." Both of these ideas lack support.

. . . While the Court of Appeals in this case addressed the different major life activity of performing manual tasks . . . [it focused] on respondent's inability to perform manual tasks associated only with her job. This was [an] error. When addressing the major life activity of performing manual tasks, the central inquiry must be whether the claimant is unable to perform the variety of tasks central to most people's daily lives, not whether the claimant is unable to perform the tasks associated with her specific job. . . .

There is also no support . . . for the Court of Appeals' idea that the question of whether an impairment constitutes a disability is to be answered only by analyzing the effect of the impairment in the workplace. . . . the manual tasks unique to any particular job are not necessarily important parts of most people's lives. . . . The court, therefore, should not have considered respondent's inability to do such manual work in her specialized assembly line job as sufficient proof that she was substantially limited in performing manual tasks.

At the same time, the Court of Appeals . . . treated as irrelevant "[t]he fact that [Williams] can . . . ten[d] to her personal hygiene [and] carr[y] out personal or household chores." Yet household chores, bathing, and brushing one's teeth are among the types of manual tasks of central importance to people's daily lives, and should have been part of the assessment of whether respondent was substantially limited in performing manual tasks.

The District Court noted that [Williams] . . . admitted that she was able to do the manual tasks required by her original two jobs in QCIO. In addition . . . even after her condition worsened, she could still brush her teeth, wash her face, bathe, tend her flower garden, fix breakfast, do laundry, and pick up around the house. The record also indicates that her medical conditions caused her to avoid sweeping, to quit dancing, to occasionally seek help dressing, and to reduce how often she plays with her children, gardens, and drives long distances. But these changes in her life did not amount to such severe restrictions in the activities that are of central importance to most people's daily lives that they establish a manual task disability as a matter of law. . . . [I]t was therefore inappropriate for the Court of Appeals to grant . . . judgment to [Williams] on the issue of whether she was substantially limited in performing manual tasks, and its decision to do so must be reversed. . . .

Accordingly, we reverse the Court of Appeals' judgment . . . and remand the case for further proceedings consistent with this opinion.

So ordered.

Case Questions

1. What was Williams's medical condition? How did it affect her ability to perform life activities? How did it affect her ability to perform her job? Explain your answers.
2. What kind of activities should the court consider in determining whether the plaintiff's condition substantially limits major life activities? What activities should the court consider if the plaintiff claims that her condition substantially limits her ability to work?
3. Did the Court hold that Williams was disabled within the meaning of the ADA? Why? Explain.

MEDICAL EXAMS AND TESTS

The ADA limits the ability of an employer to test for or inquire into the disabilities of job applicants and employees. Employers are prohibited from asking about the existence, nature, or severity of a disability; however, an employer may ask about the individual's ability to perform the functions and requirements of the job. Employers are likewise not permitted to require preemployment medical examinations of applicants. However, once an offer of a job has been extended to an applicant, employers can require a medical exam, provided that such an exam is required of all entering employees. Current employees are similarly protected from inquiries or exams, unless those requirements can be shown to be "job-related and consistent with business necessity." The act does not consider a drug test to be a medical examination, and it does not prohibit an employer from administering drug tests to its employees or from making employment decisions based on the results of such tests.

REASONABLE ACCOMMODATION

The definition of a "qualified individual with a disability" includes the individual who is capable of performing the essential functions of a job with reasonable accommodation on the part of the employer. The ADA and the Rehabilitation Act impose on employers the obligation to make reasonable accommodations for such individuals or employees, unless the accommodation would impose "undue hardship" on the employer. Examples of accommodations listed in the ADA include making facilities accessible to disabled individuals; restructuring jobs; providing part-time or modified work schedules; acquiring or modifying equipment; adjusting or modifying examinations, training materials, or policies; and providing qualified readers or interpreters. Failure to make such reasonable accommodation (which would not impose an undue hardship), or failure to hire an individual because of the need to make accommodation for that individual, is included in the definition of illegal discrimination under the act. Employers are not required to create a new position for the disabled applicant or employee, nor are they required to offer the individual the most expensive means of accommodation.

When an employee requests an accommodation that conflicts with the seniority provisions of a collective-bargaining agreement, the employer ordinarily need only demonstrate the conflict to establish that the accommodation is unreasonable; however, according to the Supreme Court decision in *U.S. Airways, Inc. v. Barnett* [535 U.S. 391 (2002)], the employee may present evidence of special circumstances that would make an exception to the seniority rules reasonable under the particular facts.

UPS SETTLES DISCRIMINATION SUIT BY DEAF EMPLOYEES

THE WORKING LAW

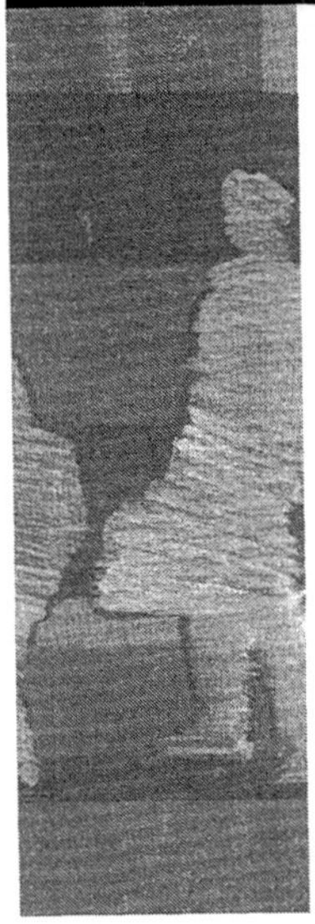

United Parcel Service agreed to pay $5.8 million in damages to settle a class-action suit filed on behalf of more than 1,000 workers with hearing impairments. The employees had alleged that UPS did not provide interpreters for them during training and safety sessions, denied them opportunities for promotion, patronized them, and treated them as having "second class" status. UPS denied that it had discriminated against the hearing impaired employees. Under the terms of the settlement agreement, UPS will provide interpreters for interviews, orientation, training, disciplinary meetings, and annual performance reviews. UPS will also evaluate the workers' communication needs, designate human resource contact persons, install text telephones, and distribute vibrating pagers to the employees. UPS will also set aside $100,000 for a monitoring program and will pay $4.1 million in legal fees for the employees. The suit was filed under the Americans with Disabilities Act by five employees, who were assisted by Disability Rights Advocates, a non-profit organization in Oakland, California. The settlement agreement must still be approved by the U.S. District Court for Northern California.

Sources: "Deaf UPS Workers Settle Case for $10M," Washingtonpost.com, July 22, 2003; "Hearing Impaired Collect Damages in Suit Against UPS," *San Francisco Chronicle,* July 22, 2003; "UPS Settles Class-Action Lawsuit, Agrees to Pay Millions to Deaf Workers," *San Jose Mercury News,* July 22, 2003.

Reasonable accommodations may include the minimal realignment or assignment of job duties or the provision of certain assistance devices. For example, an employer could reassign certain filing or reception duties from the requirements of a typist position to accommodate an individual confined to a wheelchair. An employer could also be required to equip telephones with amplifiers to accommodate an employee's hearing disability. Although the extent of accommodation required must be determined case by case, drastic realignment of work assignments or the undertaking of severe financial costs by an employer would be considered "unreasonable" and would not be required. In *PGA Tour, Inc. v. Martin* [532 U.S. 661 (2001)] (which involved the public accommodation provisions of

Title III of the ADA and not the ADA's employment-related provisions under Title I), the Court held that allowing a disabled golfer to ride in a golf cart, rather than walk during a golf tournament, was a reasonable accommodation that did not fundamentally alter the nature of the event.

How should an employer respond to an employee's request for reasonable accommodation? This is discussed in the following case.

Humphrey v. Memorial Hospitals Association

239 F.3d 1128 (9th Cir. 2001)

Background

[Carolyn Humphrey worked for Memorial Hospitals Association (MHA) as a medical transcriptionist from 1986 until her termination in 1995. Throughout her employment at MHA, Humphrey's transcription performance was excellent and consistently exceeded MHA's standards for speed, accuracy, and productivity. In 1989, she began to experience problems getting to work on time or at all. She engaged in a series of obsessive rituals that hindered her ability to arrive at work on time. She felt compelled to rinse her hair for up to an hour, and if, after brushing her hair, it didn't "feel right," she would return to the shower and wash it again. This process of washing and preparing her hair could take up to three hours. She would also feel compelled to dress very slowly, to repeatedly check for papers she needed, and to pull out strands of her hair and examine them closely because she felt as though something was crawling on her scalp. These obsessive thoughts and rituals made it very difficult for her to get to work on time. Because of Humphrey's tardiness and absenteeism, MHA gave her a disciplinary warning in June 1994. Humphrey's mental obsessions and peculiar rituals only grew worse after the warning, and her attendance record did not improve; in December 1994, she received a "Level III" warning, which documented four tardy days and one unreported absence over a two-week period. Humphrey began to suspect that her debilitating symptoms and inability to get to work on time might be related to a medical condition. In May 1995, after a diagnostic evaluation and psychological testing, Dr. John Jacisin diagnosed her with obsessive-compulsive disorder (OCD). He sent a letter explaining that diagnosis to her supervisor on May 18, 1995, telling her that Humphrey's OCD "is directly contributing to her problems with lateness." The letter also stated that Jacisin would like to see Humphrey continue to work, but it may be necessary for her to take some time off until her symptoms are under better control.

On June 7, 1995, Humphrey met with her supervisor to review Dr. Jacisin's letter. What happened at this meeting is disputed. MHA contends that Humphrey rejected the leave of absence alluded to in the doctor's letter. Humphrey claims that she was never offered a leave of absence and never rejected one. Instead, she testified that "they asked if I would like to keep working. And I said yes." Humphrey wanted to try to keep working, if possible, and her supervisor told her that she could have an "accommodation" that would allow her to do so. The supervisor suggested a flexible start time arrangement in which Humphrey could begin work anytime within a twenty-four-hour period on days on which she was scheduled to work. Humphrey accepted the flexible start-time arrangement. However, she continued to miss work; no one from MHA broached the subject of modifying the accommodation. On September 18, 1995, Humphrey, upset about her continuing problems, sent her supervisor an e-mail message requesting that she be allowed to work from her home as a new accommodation, because the flexible start time was not working. MHA did allow some medical transcriptionists to work out of their homes; no one at MHA asked Dr. Jacisin for his opinion on the work-at-home request. MHA denied the request to work from her home because of Humphrey's disciplinary warnings for tardiness and absenteeism. The supervisor did not suggest an alternative accommodation or indicate that MHA would reassess its arrangements to accommodate Humphrey in light of the failure of the flexible work schedule arrangement.

Humphrey continued to perform well when she was at work; her evaluation indicates that were it not for her ailment, she would have been a model employee. While meeting with her supervisor, Humphrey again raised the issue of working at home but was told that she would have to be free of attendance problems for a year before she could be considered for an at-home transcriptionist position. Neither Humphrey nor her supervisor suggested a medical leave of absence at this meeting. Humphrey was absent two more times, and on October 10, 1995, she was fired. MHA's stated reason for the termination was Humphrey's history of tardiness and absenteeism. Humphrey testified that after learning of her termination, she went across the hall to her supervisor's office and asked if she might take a leave of absence instead, but her request was refused. MHA concedes that it would have granted the request if Humphrey had asked for a leave of absence prior to her termination, as MHA had a policy of permitting medical leaves of absence to employees with disabilities.

Humphrey filed suit against MHA alleging a violation of the ADA. The district court granted MHA's motion for summary judgment, and Humphrey appealed to the U.S. Court of Appeals for the Ninth Circuit.]

Reinhardt, Circuit Judge

Humphrey contends that MHA violated the ADA and the FEHA by failing to reasonably accommodate her disability and by terminating her because of that disability. . . . To prevail on a claim of unlawful discharge under the ADA, the plaintiff must establish that he is a qualified individual with a disability and that the employer terminated him because of his disability. . . . It is undisputed that Humphrey had the skills, training, and experience to transcribe medical records. . . . Humphrey is a "qualified individual" under the ADA so long as she is able to perform the essential functions of her job "with or without reasonable accommodation." Either of two potential reasonable accommodations might have made it possible for Humphrey to perform the essential functions of her job: granting her a leave of absence or allowing her to become a "home-based transcriptionist." . . .

Working at home is a reasonable accommodation when the essential functions of the position can be performed at home and a work-at-home arrangement would not cause undue hardship for the employer. [EEOC Enforcement Guidance: Reasonable Accommodation and Undue Hardship Under the Americans with Disabilities Act, FEP (BNA) 405:7601, at 7626 (March 1, 1999).] Humphrey does not dispute that regular and predictable performance of the job is an essential part of the transcriptionist position because many of the medical records must be transcribed within twenty-four hours, and frequent and unscheduled absences would prevent the department from meeting its deadlines. However, physical attendance at the MHA offices is not an essential job duty; in fact . . . MHA permits some of its medical transcriptionists to work at home.

MHA denied Humphrey's application for a work-at-home position because of her disciplinary record, which consisted of . . . warnings for tardiness and absenteeism prior to her diagnosis of OCD. It would be inconsistent with the purposes of the ADA to permit an employer to deny an otherwise reasonable accommodation because of past disciplinary action taken due to the disability sought to be accommodated. Thus, Humphrey's disciplinary record does not constitute an appropriate basis for denying her a work-at-home accommodation. . . .

. . . We conclude, as a matter of law, that . . . MHA had an affirmative duty under the ADA to explore further methods of accommodation before terminating Humphrey.

Once an employer becomes aware of the need for accommodation, that employer has a mandatory obligation under the ADA to engage in an interactive process with the employee to identify and implement appropriate reasonable accommodations. "An appropriate reasonable accommodation must be effective, in enabling the employee to perform the duties of the position." The interactive process requires communication and good-faith exploration of possible accommodations between employers and individual employees, and neither side can delay or obstruct the process. Employers, who fail to engage in the interactive process in good faith, face liability for the remedies imposed by the statute if a reasonable accommodation would have been possible.

Moreover, we have held that the duty to accommodate "is a 'continuing' duty that is 'not exhausted by one effort.'" . . . the employer's obligation to engage in the interactive process extends beyond the first attempt at accommodation and continues when the employee asks for a different accommodation or where the employer is aware that the initial accommodation is failing and further accommodation is needed. This rule fosters the framework of cooperative problem-solving contemplated by the ADA, by encouraging employers to seek to find accommodations that really work, and by avoiding the creation of a perverse incentive for employees to request the most drastic and burdensome accommodation possible out of fear that a lesser accommodation might be ineffective.

. . . Even if we assume that Humphrey turned down the leave of absence in June in favor of a flexible start-time arrangement, her attempt to perform her job functions by means of a less drastic accommodation does not forfeit her right to a more substantial one upon the failure of the initial effort.

By the time of her annual performance review in September, it was abundantly clear to MHA that the flexible start time accommodation was not succeeding; Humphrey had accumulated six unreported absences in each of the months of August and September, and her evaluation stated that her attendance record was "unacceptable." At this point, MHA had a duty to explore further arrangements to reasonably accommodate Humphrey's disability.

Humphrey also realized that the accommodation was not working, and requested a work at home position. When it received that request, MHA could have either granted it or initiated discussions with Humphrey regarding other alternatives. Instead, MHA denied her request without suggesting any alternative solutions, or exploring with her the possibility of other accommodations. Rather than fulfill its obligation to engage in a cooperative dialogue with Humphrey, Pierson's e-mail suggested that the matter was closed: "During our 6/7/95 meeting, you requested to be accommodated for your disability by having a flexible start time, stating that you would have no problems staying for a full shift once you arrived. You were given this flexible start time accommodation which continues to remain in effect." . . . [A]n employer fails to engage in the interactive process as a matter of law where it rejects the employee's proposed accommodations by letter and offers no practical alternatives. Similarly, MHA's rejection of Humphrey's work-at-home request and its failure to explore with Humphrey the possibility of other accommodations, once it was aware that the initial arrangement was not effective, constitutes a violation of its duty regarding the mandatory interactive process.

Given MHA's failure to engage in the interactive process, liability is appropriate if a reasonable accommodation without undue hardship to the employer would otherwise have been possible. As we have already discussed, a leave of absence was a reasonable accommodation for Humphrey's disability. Ordinarily, whether an accommodation would pose an undue hardship on the employer is a factual question. Here, however, MHA has conceded that granting a leave of absence would not have posed an undue hardship. MHA had a policy of granting leaves to disabled employees, and admits that it would have given Humphrey a leave had she asked for one at any time before her termination. MHA's ultimate position, therefore, is simply that Humphrey is not entitled to a leave of absence because she failed to ask for one before she was fired. As we have explained, however, MHA was under a continuing duty to offer a reasonable accommodation. Accordingly, we hold as a matter of law . . . that MHA violated the ADA's reasonable accommodation requirement.

Unlike a simple failure to accommodate claim, an unlawful discharge claim requires a showing that the employer terminated the employee because of his disability. . . . In this case, MHA's stated reason for Humphrey's termination was absenteeism and tardiness. For purposes of the ADA, with a few exceptions, conduct resulting from a disability is considered to be part of the disability, rather than a separate basis for termination. The link between the disability and termination is particularly strong where it is the employer's failure to reasonably accommodate a known disability that leads to discharge for performance inadequacies resulting from that disability. . . . Humphrey has presented sufficient evidence to create a triable issue of fact as to whether her attendance problems were caused by OCD. In sum, a jury could reasonably find the requisite causal link between a disability of OCD and Humphrey's absenteeism and conclude that MHA fired Humphrey because of her disability.

For the foregoing reasons, the district court's grant of summary judgment to MHA on Humphrey's ADA and FEHA claims is hereby REVERSED and the case is REMANDED for proceedings consistent with this opinion.

It is so ordered.

Case Questions

1. How did Humphrey's condition affect her ability to perform her job? Was Humphrey "an otherwise qualified individual with a disability" under the ADA? Explain your answers.
2. What accommodation did the employer initially offer to Humphrey? Was the accommodation effective? Explain.
3. What accommodation did Humphrey then request from her employer? How did the employer respond to her request? Why?
4. Was the employer's decision to terminate Humphrey a violation of the ADA? Explain your answer.

A court's consideration of what would be a reasonable accommodation to the individual's disability is to be done on a case-by-case basis. What may be a reasonable accommodation in one situation may not be reasonable under differing circumstances. In *Vande Zande v. State of Wisconsin Dept. of Administration* [44 F.3d 538 (7th Cir. 1995)], the court held that an employer's refusal to allow a disabled employee to work at home was not a violation of the ADA. The court there stated

> Most jobs in organizations public or private involve teamwork under supervision rather than solitary unsupervised work, and teamwork under supervision generally cannot be performed at home without a substantial reduction in the quality of the employee's performance. This will no doubt change as communications technology advances, but is the situation today. Generally, therefore, an employer is not required to accommodate a disability by allowing the disabled worker to work, by himself, without supervision, at home. . . . An employer is not required to allow disabled workers to work at home, where their productivity inevitably would be greatly reduced.

Undue Hardship

An employer is not required to make accommodation for an individual if that accommodation would impose "undue hardship on the operation of the business of the covered entity." The ADA provides a complex definition of what constitutes an "undue hardship," including a list of factors to be considered in determining the impact of the accommodation on the employer. An accommodation imposes an undue hardship if it requires significant difficulty or expense when considered in light of the following factors:

(i) the nature and cost of the accommodation needed under this act;

(ii) the overall financial resources of the facility or facilities involved in the provision of the reasonable accommodation; the number of persons employed at such facility; the effect on expenses and resources, or the impact otherwise of such accommodation upon the operation of the facility;

(iii) the overall financial resources of the covered entity; the overall size of the business of a covered entity with respect to the number of its employees; the number, type, and location of its facilities; and

(iv) the type of operation or operations of the covered entity, including the composition, structure, and functions of the work force of such entity; the geographic separateness, administrative, or fiscal relationship of the facility or facilities in question to the covered entity.

It should be obvious that the definition of undue hardship is intended to be flexible. What would be a reasonable accommodation for General Motors or Microsoft could be a significant expense or difficulty for a much smaller employer.

DEFENSES UNDER THE ADA

In addition to the defense of undue hardship, the ADA sets out four other possible defenses for employers.

Direct Threat to Safety or Health of Others

Employers may refuse to hire or accommodate an individual if that individual's condition poses a "direct threat" to the health or safety of others in the workplace. Direct threat is defined as a "significant risk to the health or safety of others that cannot be eliminated by reasonable accommodation." The definition of disability under the act includes infectious or contagious diseases; in determining if such a disease presents a direct threat to others, the employer's considerations must be based on objective and accepted public health guidelines, not on stereotypes or public attitudes or fears, according to *School Board of Nassau County, Florida v. Arline* [480 U.S. 273 (1987)]. An employer would probably not be required to hire an individual with an active case of hepatitis or tuberculosis, but could not discriminate against an individual who has been treated for cancer, exposed to the HIV virus (associated with AIDS), or has had a history of mental illness. An employer may refuse to hire an individual when performance of the job would endanger the individual's own health due to an existing disability, *Chevron, U.S.A. v. Echazabal* [536 U.S. 73 (2002)].

Job-Related Criteria

Employers may hire, select, or promote individuals based on tests, standards, or criteria that are job related or are consistent with business necessity. Employers could refuse to hire or promote individuals with a disability who are unable to meet such standards, tests, or criteria or when performance of the job cannot be accomplished by reasonable accommodation. For example, an employer would be justified in refusing to hire a blind person for a bus driver position.

ETHICAL DILEMMA: INSURANCE COVERAGE FOR MENTAL DISABILITIES?

You are the employee benefits manager at Immense Multinational Business Corporation (IMB), responsible for administering the company's medical insurance plan. At present, IMB provides employees with medical and hospitalization insurance. Because the IMB insurance plan does not include coverage for mental conditions, employees who have sought counseling because of personal and/or family problems, or who have undergone rehabilitation and counseling for drug and alcohol abuse problems, have not been reimbursed for such treatment. The employees' association requests that IMB expand their medical insurance plan to include mental health conditions and rehabilitation counseling.

The vice president for human resources directs you to make a presentation to the CEO and the board of directors on whether IMB should expand its insurance plan to include mental health conditions and counseling. What are the benefits of offering expanded coverage? What are the costs and other problems associated with offering expanded coverage? What, if any, legal requirements are applicable to the decision? Should IMB offer the expanded coverage? Explain and support your answer.

Food Handler Defense

An employer in the food service industry may refuse to assign or transfer to a job involving food handling any individual who has an infectious or communicable disease that can be transmitted to others through the handling of food, when the risk of infection cannot be eliminated by reasonable accommodation. The ADA requires the secretary of health and human services to develop a list of diseases that can be transmitted through food handling; only the diseases on that list (which is to be updated annually) may be used as a basis for refusal under this defense. The Secretary of Health and Human Services has stated that HIV infection (associated with AIDS) cannot be transmitted through food handling.

Religious Entities

Title I of the ADA does not prohibit a religious corporation, association, educational institution, or society from giving preference in employment to individuals of a particular religion to perform work connected with the carrying on by such corporation, association, educational institution, or society of its activities. Thus, as in the *Amos* case (see Chapter 5), a gymnasium operated by The Church of Jesus Christ of Latter-day Saints may refuse to hire an individual with a disability who is not a member of that church.

ENFORCEMENT OF THE ADA

The ADA is enforced by the EEOC. The act specifically provides that the procedures and remedies under Title VII of the Civil Rights Act of 1964 shall be those used or available under the ADA. This means that an individual must first file a complaint with a state or local agency, where appropriate, and then with the EEOC; the EEOC, or the individual if the EEOC declines, may file suit against an employer. Remedies available include injunctions, hiring or reinstatement order (with or without back pay), and attorney fees. The Civil Rights Act of 1991 amended 42 U.S.C. Section 1981A to allow suits for compensatory and punitive damages against parties accused of intentional discrimination in violation of the Americans with Disabilities Act. Such damages are not available where the alleged discrimination involves provision of a reasonable accommodation of an individual's disability and the employer demonstrates that it made a good-faith effort to accommodate the individual's disability. Punitive damages are not available against public sector employers. The ADA also directs the EEOC to develop and issue regulations to enforce the act.

See **http://www.eeoc.gov/litigation/index.html** *for a listing of active and resolved cases.*

THE REHABILITATION ACT

The Rehabilitation Act of 1973 protects the employment rights of individuals with a disability; the act's provisions prohibit discrimination against otherwise qualified individuals with a disability. The definition of "individual with a disability" under the Rehabilitation Act is similar to that under the ADA:

> any person who (a) has a physical or mental impairment, which substantially limits one or more of such person's major life activities, (b) has a record of such an impairment, or (c) is regarded as having such an impairment.

The Supreme Court decision in *School Board of Nassau County, Fla. v. Arline* [480 U.S. 273 (1987)] held that the definition of disability under the Rehabilitation Act included contagious diseases; the employee with an infectious disease is "otherwise qualified" within the meaning of the act if the threat posed to others by the disease can be eliminated or avoided through reasonable accommodation by the employer.

The Civil Rights Restoration Act of 1988, passed by Congress over President Reagan's veto, amended the definition of "individual with a disability" under the Rehabilitation Act to exclude a person with

> a currently contagious disease or infection and who, by reason of such disease or infection, would constitute a direct threat to the health or safety of other individuals or who, by reason of the currently contagious disease or infection, is unable to perform the duties of the job.

PROVISIONS

The Rehabilitation Act imposes obligations not to discriminate against otherwise qualified individuals with a disability. According to *Southeastern Community College v. Davis* [442 U.S. 397 (1979)], a person is "an otherwise qualified individual with a disability" under the Rehabilitation Act (as with the ADA) if the person is able to meet the requirements of the position in spite of the disability or with reasonable accommodation of the disability. The individual claiming to be qualified has the burden of demonstrating her or his ability to meet all physical requirements legitimately necessary for the performance of the duties of the position. An employer is not required to hire a person with a disability who is not capable of performing the duties of the position; however, the employer is required to make reasonable accommodation to the disability of the individual if such accommodation will not impose undue hardship on the employer.

Three main provisions of the Rehabilitation Act deal with discrimination against otherwise qualified individuals with a disability: Section 501 prohibits such discrimination by federal government employers, Section 503 prohibits such discrimination by employers with federal contracts, and Section 504 prohibits the denial of participation in, or the benefits of, any federally funded activity to an otherwise qualified individual with a disability.

Section 501: Federal Government Employers

Section 501 of the Rehabilitation Act prohibits discrimination on the basis of disability by federal executive agencies, departments, and instrumentalities; it also requires them to develop affirmative action plans for the hiring, placement, and advancement of individuals with disabilities. The plans are to be updated annually and reviewed and approved by the Equal Employment Opportunity Commission (EEOC).

Enforcement of Section 501

Section 505(a) of the act provides that Section 501 is enforced through the provisions under Title VII of the Civil Rights Act of 1964, as amended. While federal executive employees with complaints of alleged violations may bring a private suit, they must first seek review of the alleged violation with their agency's Equal Employment Opportunity counselor, whose decision is subject to a formal review through the agency's EEO complaint procedures. The employee can then either seek judicial review of the final decision of the agency or appeal the action to the EEOC. If the employee elects to seek judicial review, a civil action may be filed in federal court within ninety days of receipt of notice of the agency's final decision or within 180 days of filing with the agency if there has been no decision. Employees choosing to refer the complaint to the EEOC may file a civil action within ninety days of receipt of the EEOC's notice of final action or within 180 days of filing with the EEOC if there has been no EEOC decision within that time.

Remedies available include injunctions, orders directing hiring or reinstatement, with or without back pay and interest, attorney fees, and expert witness fees. In addition to the remedies under the Civil Rights Act, plaintiffs alleging intentional discrimination in violation of Section 501 can bring an action seeking compensatory damages under 42 U.S.C. Section 1981A. Such damages are not available when the alleged discriminatory practice involves reasonable accommodation and the respondent showed good-faith efforts. Punitive damages under 42 U.S.C. Section 1981A are not available against public sector employers.

Section 503: Federal Contractors

Section 503 of the Rehabilitation Act prohibits discrimination on the basis of disability by federal contractors with annual contracts in excess of $10,000. Federal contractors with contracts of $50,000 or more are also required to develop affirmative action plans as to the hiring of otherwise qualified individuals with a disability. Enforcement of Section 503 is through the administrative procedures of the Office of Federal Contract Compliance Programs (OFCCP) under the Department of Labor. Aggrieved individuals must file a complaint with the OFCCP; there is no individual right to file suit under Section 503. Employers found in violation of Section 503 may be subject to injunctions, withholding of progress payments under the contract, termination of the contract, or debarment from future contracts. Remedies available under the administrative procedures for individuals who are victims of discrimination in violation of Section 503 include hiring or reinstatement, back pay, and benefits.

Section 504: Federally Assisted Programs

Section 504 of the Rehabilitation Act prohibits discrimination on the basis of disability against otherwise qualified individuals with a disability by persons or entities operating or administering any federally funded programs. To be covered by Section 504, the entities must be the direct recipient of federal financial assistance; according to *U.S. Department of Transportation v. Paralyzed Veterans of America* [477 U.S. 597 (1986)], indirect beneficiaries are not recipients within the meaning of the section. The statutory language provides that "No otherwise qualified individual with a disability . . . shall . . . (solely by reason of the disability) be excluded from participation in, be denied the benefits of, or be subjected to discrimination under . . ." any program receiving federal financial assistance. If any part of the entity receives any federal funding, the nondiscrimination requirement applies to the entire entity; there is no minimum funding amount required for coverage under Section 504. While the language of Section 504 does not specifically refer to employment, its prohibition against discrimination extends to employment discrimination, even though the primary purpose of the federal financial assistance is not providing employment, according to the Supreme Court decision in *Consolidated Rail Corp. v. Darrone* [465 U.S. 624 (1984)].

http://www.dol.gov/dol/compliance/comp-rehab.htm *is the site for the Rehabilitation Act of 1973.*

Employers are required to make reasonable accommodation to the otherwise qualified employee's or applicant's condition; any employment requirements that adversely affect disabled persons must be directly and substantially related to business necessity and safe job performance. In *Southeastern Community College v. Davis* [442 U.S. 397 (1979)], the Supreme Court upheld the college's refusal to admit a woman with a severe hearing disability to the registered nurses training program. The woman's disability was not correctable with a hearing aid and would create problems in carrying out her duties during the clinical portions of her training. The college was not required to redesign the program to accommodate her disability because the components of the nursing program were required by state law.

Enforcement of Section 504

The regulations under Section 504 make the agencies administering the funding the primary enforcement authority for complaints against the recipients of such funding. Most agencies have developed their own administrative procedures for investigating and adjudicating claims of discrimination; the federal Department of Education coordinates and oversees enforcement of Section 504 by the other federal agencies. Unlike Section 503, there is an individual right to sue under Section 504. Persons claiming a violation of Section 504 may seek equitable relief and recover back pay, monetary damages, and legal fees; they are not required to pursue the agency's administrative procedures before filing suit. Punitive damages are not recoverable in private suits brought under Section 504, *Barnes v. Gorman* [536 U.S. 181 (2002)].

AIDS AND THE DISABILITY DISCRIMINATION LEGISLATION

Recall that the definition of disability under both the ADA and the Rehabilitation Act includes contagious diseases, such as AIDS. Although AIDS is contagious, medical authorities agree that it is not transmitted through the casual contact likely to occur in the workplace. The courts have consistently held that persons who are

Choose a site about AIDS in the workplace at the CDC site, **http://www.brta-lrta.org/**

HIV-positive suffering from AIDS or AIDS-related conditions are individuals with a disability under the Rehabilitation Act and the ADA. Therefore, employers are required to make reasonable accommodation for employees with AIDS or related conditions, as long as the employees are capable of performing the essential functions of the job and do not present a direct threat to the health or safety of others.

The nature of the risk posed by the employee's HIV-positive status, or AIDS infection, depends on the nature of the job in question. In *Chalk v. U.S. District Court* [840 F.2d 701 (9th Cir. 1988)], a teacher who was diagnosed with AIDS was granted an injunction against transfer to an administrative position because the risk of AIDS transmission in the classroom was minimal. However, an HIV-positive neurosurgeon was not entitled to continue his residence because he posed a significant risk to his patients, *Doe v. University of Md. Medical Systems Corp.* [50 F.3d 1261 (4th Cir. 1995)], and in *Doe v. Washington University* [780 F.Supp. 628 (E.D. Mo. 1991)], an HIV-positive dental student was not permitted to continue his dental education. *Severino v. North Fort Meyers Fire Control Dist.* [935 F.2d 1179 (11th Cir. 1991)] held that a firefighter who was HIV-positive was reasonably accommodated under the Rehabilitation Act by being reassigned to light duties because the medical evidence indicated a risk of transmission of his disease to others during rescue operations. In *Leckelt v. Board of Comm. of Hosp. District No. 1* [909 F.2d 820 (5th Cir. 1990)], a licensed practical nurse who refused to report the results of an HIV test was legally discharged for violating a hospital policy requiring employees to report any infectious disease to protect patients, co-workers, and the infected employees themselves.

Because the definition of individual with disability under both the ADA and the Rehabilitation Act includes an individual regarded as having a physical or mental condition that impairs a major life activity, an employee who is discharged because of a false and unfounded rumor that he or she was infected with HIV is protected as an individual with a disability. Do individuals who are HIV positive, but who do not present any evidence of impairment and who suffer from no ailments that affect the manner in which they live, fall under the definition of "individual with a disability" under the ADA or the Rehabilitation Act? The U.S. Supreme Court, in *Bragdon v. Abbott* [524 U.S. 624 (1998)], held that asymptomatic HIV was a disability within the meaning of the ADA because it was a medical condition that impaired the major life activity of reproduction.

More on AIDS can be found on the American Red Cross site at **http://www.redcross.org/services/hss/hivaids** *or at* **http://www.brta-lrta.org/main/ta.htm**

STATE DISABILITY DISCRIMINATION LEGISLATION

All fifty states have laws that prohibit discrimination against individuals with disabilities. The coverage of such laws varies; some cover both private and public sector employers, while others apply only to the public sector. The provisions of such laws generally parallel those of the ADA but in some instances go beyond the ADA protections; the California Fair Employment and Housing Act requires only that physical and mental disabilities place a "limitation" on a major life activity, rather than the "substantial limitation" required under the ADA (as discussed in the *Toyota Motor Manufacturing* case earlier in this chapter). Some states have specific legislation prohibiting discrimination against individuals with specific conditions, such as the sickle cell trait, Tay-Sachs disease, HIV, or AIDS. Kentucky, for example, prohibits employers from requiring that applicants or employees take an HIV test, unless the employer can establish that the absence of HIV infection is a bona fide occupational qualification for the job in question. New York, New Jersey, and North Carolina prohibit discrimination against applicants or employees because of genetic traits or conditions and prohibit requiring individuals to undergo genetic testing as a condition of employment.

DRUG ABUSE AND DRUG TESTING

Neither the ADA nor the Rehabilitation Act prohibits drug testing by employers; the ADA specifically states that drug tests are not considered medical exams under its provisions. Section 104 of the ADA specifically excludes from the definition of "qualified individual with a disability" any persons who are currently engaged in the illegal use of drugs and allows employers to prohibit the use of alcohol and illegal drugs at the workplace. The Rehabilitation Act also excludes from its protection individuals who are alcoholics or drug abusers whose current use of alcohol or drugs prevents them from performing the duties of the job or whose employment constitutes a direct threat to the property or safety of others. Note that the ADA and the Rehabilitation Act refer to the current use of drugs or alcohol; both laws specifically protect former drug users who have successfully been rehabilitated, persons who are participating in or have completed a supervised drug rehabilitation program and who no longer use drugs, and persons who are "erroneously regarded" as using illegal drugs but who do not actually use such drugs.

http://www.eeoc.gov/facts/fs-ada.html
briefly lists facts on ADA regarding drug testing.

The following case deals with the question of whether an employee who was addicted to cocaine and who voluntarily entered a drug rehabilitation program is protected under the ADA.

ZENOR V. EL PASO HEALTHCARE SYSTEM, LIMITED

176 F.3d 847 (5th Cir. 1999)

Garwood, Circuit Judge

Plaintiff-appellant Tom Zenor (Zenor) appeals the district court's grant of judgment as a matter of law in favor of his former employer, Vista Hills Medical Center, now defendant-appellee El Paso Healthcare Ltd. . . .

In 1991, Columbia hired Zenor to work as a pharmacist in the pharmacy at its Columbia Medical Center-East hospital. When Zenor began his employment, he received an employment manual expressing the at-will nature of his employment and disclaiming any contractual obligations between the employer and employee. Zenor also received a copy of Vista Hills' then-existing drug and alcohol policy. In 1993, Zenor received a copy of Columbia's Drug-Free/Alcohol-Free Workplace Policy (the Policy), which was in effect at all times relevant to this case.

In 1993, Zenor became addicted to cocaine. Between 1993 and 1995, Zenor injected himself with cocaine as many as four to five times a week. He also smoked marijuana on three or four occasions and more frequently used tranquilizers to offset the cocaine's effects. Despite his drug use, Zenor remained a generally adequate employee and usually received favorable employment evaluations. . . . Zenor testified he never used drugs at work, nor came to work under the influence of drugs. Columbia was unaware of Zenor's addiction until August 15, 1995.

Zenor had been working the night shift at the pharmacy. When Zenor left work on August 15, 1995, at approximately 8:30 A.M., he injected himself with cocaine. As Zenor prepared to return to work that night, he became dizzy and had difficulty walking. Suspecting that he was still impaired from the morning's cocaine injection, Zenor called the pharmacy director, Joe Quintana (Quintana), and stated that he could not report to work because he was under the influence of cocaine. During the conversation, Quintana asked whether Zenor would take advantage of Columbia's Employee Assistance Program, "ACCESS." Zenor replied that he would. Quintana then stated that he was on vacation, and instructed Zenor to contact Quintana's supervisor, Paschall Ike (Ike).

Zenor spoke to Ike, who was also on vacation and told Zenor to call his (Zenor's) own doctor. Zenor then called his personal physician, who arranged for Zenor to receive emergency treatment that evening. . . . The next morning, Zenor was transferred to the El Paso Alcohol and Drug Abuse Service Detox Center, where he remained hospitalized for nine days.

On August 23, while still at the Detox Center, Zenor became concerned about losing his job. Zenor and one of his Detox Center counselors, Pete McMillian (McMillian), contacted Yolanda Mendoza (Mendoza), Columbia's Human Resources Director. This was the first time Zenor had contacted Columbia since his conversation with Ike eight days earlier. Nobody at Columbia knew where Zenor had been since the night of August 15.

Zenor told Mendoza that he wished to enter a rehabilitation program and asked her whether his job would be secure until he returned. Although the evidence is disputed, there is evidence that Mendoza assured Zenor that his job would be secure until he completed the program. Mendoza then told McMillian that Zenor was eligible for a twelve-week leave of absence under the Family Medical Leave Act (FMLA). Later that afternoon, McMillian retrieved from Mendoza the paperwork necessary for Zenor to take FMLA leave. Zenor completed the paperwork. The next day, August 24, Zenor checked into an independent residential rehabilitation facility, Landmark Adult Intensive Residential Services Center (Landmark).

After consulting with Columbia's lawyers, Mendoza and Quintana decided to terminate Zenor's employment. On September 20, 1995, Mendoza, Quintana, and ACCESS director Joe Provencio had a meeting with Zenor, his Landmark counselor, and Landmark's Director of Adult Treatment Services Dorrance Guy (Guy). Zenor was told that he would remain an employee of Columbia until his medical leave expired, and then he would be terminated.

Zenor protested that Columbia could not fire him because the Policy stated that employees who completed rehabilitation would be returned to work. Zenor also argued that he had been told if he "self-reported" his addiction he would not be fired. Mendoza explained that Columbia was concerned because pharmaceutical cocaine would be readily available to Zenor in the pharmacy, and therefore Columbia would not allow Zenor to return to work. . . .

Zenor completed the residential portion of his treatment program and was released from Landmark on October 9, 1995. On October 18, Zenor met with Mendoza and again asked to keep his job. Mendoza told Zenor that his termination stood. Zenor then requested that Mendoza write an official letter regarding his termination, in order to assist Zenor in continuing his medical benefits.

Zenor later sued Columbia, alleging that he was fired in violation of the Americans with Disabilities Act (ADA) and the Texas Commission on Human Rights Act (TCHRA). The case proceeded to trial. . . . At the conclusion of Zenor's case-in-chief, Columbia moved for judgment as a matter of law. The district court granted Columbia judgment as a matter of law. . . . Zenor appeals and in this Court challenges . . . the dismissal of his ADA claim. . . .

On appeal, the parties raise three separate questions with respect to the ADA claim: (1) whether Zenor was disqualified from the ADA's protection because he was a "current user" of illegal drugs at the relevant time, (2) whether Zenor was an otherwise qualified individual, and (3) whether Zenor established that he suffered from a disability.

. . . The district court correctly granted judgment in favor of Columbia. First, Zenor is excluded from the definition of "qualified individual" under the ADA because he was a current user of illegal drugs. Similarly, due to Zenor's cocaine use, he was not otherwise qualified for the job of a pharmacist. Alternatively, regardless of whether Zenor was a current user of illegal drugs, Zenor failed to prove that he was disabled within the meaning of the statute.

The first issue is whether Zenor was "currently engaging in the illegal use of drugs" at the time the adverse employment action was taken. 42 U.S.C. § 12114 specifically exempts current illegal drug users from the definition of qualified individuals. . . . In other words, federal law does not proscribe an employer's firing someone who currently uses illegal drugs, regardless of whether or not that drug use could otherwise be considered a disability. The issue in this case, therefore, is whether Zenor was a "current" drug user within the meaning of the statute.

As a threshold matter, this Court must determine the proper time at which to evaluate whether Zenor was "currently engaging in the illegal use of drugs." . . .

. . . Columbia decided to terminate Zenor on or before September 20, 1995, and that decision was adequately conveyed to Zenor on September 20, 1995. The relevant employment action for Zenor's ADA case thus occurred on September 20, 1995. Therefore, the question is whether Zenor, who had used cocaine on August 15, 1995, was currently engaging in the illegal use of drugs when Columbia informed him on September 20, 1995, of its decision to terminate him. We conclude, as a matter of law, that he was.

Under the ADA, "currently" means that the drug use was sufficiently recent to justify the employer's reasonable belief that the drug abuse remained an ongoing problem. Thus, the characterization of "currently engaging in the illegal use of drugs" is properly applied to persons who have used illegal drugs in the weeks and months preceding a negative employment action. . . .

The EEOC Compliance Manual on Title I of the ADA also supports this interpretation.

"'Current' drug use means that the illegal use of drugs occurred recently enough to justify an employer's reasonable belief that involvement with drugs is an ongoing problem. It is not limited to the day of use, or recent weeks or days, in terms of an employment action. It is determined on a case-by-case basis." [EEOC-M-1A Title VIII § 8.3 Illegal Use of Drugs.]

Additionally, [other courts have] suggested several factors which courts should examine to determine whether a person is a current substance abuser, including "the level of responsibility entrusted to the employee; the employer's applicable job and performance requirements; the level of competence ordinarily required to adequately perform the task in question; and the employee's past performance record." Rather than focusing solely on the timing of the employee's drug use, courts should consider whether an employer could reasonably conclude that the employee's substance abuse prohibited the employee from performing the essential job duties.

Zenor admits to having used cocaine as much as five times a week for approximately two years and to having been addicted. On September 20, 1995, Zenor had refrained from using cocaine for only five weeks, all while having been hospitalized or in a residential program. Such a short period of abstinence, particularly following such a severe drug problem, does not remove from the employer's mind a reasonable belief that the drug use remains a problem. Zenor's position as a pharmacist required a great deal of care and skill, and Zenor admits that any mistakes could gravely injure Columbia's patients. Moreover, Columbia presented substantial testimony about the extremely high relapse rate of cocaine addiction. Zenor's own counselors, while supportive and speaking highly of Zenor's progress, could not say with any real assurance that Zenor wouldn't relapse. Finally, Columbia presented substantial evidence regarding the on-going nature of cocaine-addiction recovery. The fact that Zenor completed the residential portion of his treatment was only the first step in a long-term recovery program. Based on these factors, Columbia was justified in believing that the risk of harm from a potential relapse was significant, and that Zenor's drug abuse remained an on-going threat.

Nonetheless, Zenor argues that because he voluntarily enrolled in a rehabilitation program, he is entitled to protection under the ADA's "safe harbor" provision for drug users. The safe harbor provides an exception to the current user exclusion of 42 U.S.C. §12114(a) for individuals who are rehabilitated and no longer using drugs. See 42 U.S.C. § 12114(b):

> "(b) Rules of construction. Nothing in subsection (a) shall be construed to exclude as a qualified individual with a disability an individual who—
> (1) has successfully completed a supervised drug rehabilitation program and is no longer engaging in the illegal use of drugs, or has otherwise been rehabilitated successfully and is no longer engaging in such use; [or]
> (2) is participating in a supervised rehabilitation program and is no longer engaging in such use. . . ."

However, the mere fact that an employee has entered a rehabilitation program does not automatically bring that employee within the safe harbor's protection. . . . the safe harbor provision applies only to individuals who have been drug-free for a significant period of time. . . .

Zenor argues that he should be protected by the safe harbor provision because he "self-reported" his addiction and voluntarily entered the rehabilitation program . . . [but] it does not propel Zenor into the safe harbor's protection simply because he had entered a rehabilitation program before the adverse employment action was taken.

For similar reasons, Columbia was free to find that Zenor was not a "qualified individual" even in the absence of the statutory exclusion for illegal drug users. A qualified individual under the ADA must be able to perform essential job requirements. The ADA directs courts to consider employers' definitions of essential job requirements. Columbia reasonably may have felt that having a pharmacist who had recently been treated for cocaine addiction undermined the integrity of its hospital pharmacy operation. . . . Such conclusions do not violate the ADA.

Columbia was also entitled to consider the relapse rate for cocaine addiction in determining that Zenor was not qualified to work as a pharmacist. . . . As noted, cocaine addiction has a very high relapse rate, and the risk of harm from a potential relapse was great. . . .

Finally, this evidence should be viewed in light of what was known to Columbia on the date it fired Zenor. . . . As an alternate basis for our holding, we determine that Zenor was not disabled within the meaning of the ADA. . . . Zenor argues that he was perceived as being a drug addict and therefore established a disability under the ADA.

. . . Zenor argues that he was not a current drug user, but was regarded by Columbia as a drug addict. Zenor thus attempts to establish a disability by citing testimony that Columbia officials regarded him as an addict.

However, Zenor's burden under the ADA is not satisfied merely by showing that Columbia regarded him as a drug addict: the fact that a person is perceived to be a drug addict does not necessarily mean that person is perceived to be disabled under the ADA. Zenor must also show that Columbia regarded Zenor's addiction as substantially limiting one of Zenor's major life activities. . . .

. . . Zenor argues that Columbia perceived him as substantially limited in the major life activity of working. In this context, "[t]he term substantially limits means significantly restricted in the ability to perform either a class of jobs or a broad range of jobs in various classes as compared to the average person having comparable training, skills and abilities." . . . Zenor presented no evidence that Columbia regarded him as limited in his ability to work in a broad range of jobs. Zenor does not argue that he was qualified for, or sought, alternative employment positions at Columbia other than as pharmacist. . . . Here . . . Columbia felt that a recent cocaine addict was unqualified for one specific job: that of a pharmacist. Columbia was entitled to conclude that if a person is a pharmacist, cocaine addiction is not acceptable.

. . . Zenor failed to establish that he was regarded as suffering from a disability within the meaning of the ADA. Nor, for the reasons discussed above, could a reasonable jury find that Zenor was an "otherwise qualified individual" for the position of a pharmacist. Therefore, the district court correctly granted judgment as a matter of law for Columbia on Zenor's ADA claim. . . .

The district court's judgment dismissing Zenor's suit is accordingly in all things

AFFIRMED.

Case Questions

1. When did Zenor inform Columbia that he was addicted to cocaine? When did he enter the drug treatment program? When did Columbia decide to terminate Zenor? When did Zenor complete the drug treatment program?
2. Why did Columbia refuse to rehire Zenor after he completed the drug treatment program?
3. Was Zenor's drug addiction a disability within the meaning of the ADA? Was Zenor covered by the ADA protection for persons who have completed a supervised drug treatment program? Explain your answers.

An employer's policy against rehiring former employees discharged for workplace misconduct was a legitimate, non-discriminatory reason for refusing to rehire a former employee who was discharged after testing positive for cocaine use, and was not a violation of the ADA, according to *Raytheon Co. v. Hernandez* [124 S.Ct. 513 (U.S. 2003)].

Federal Drug Testing Legislation

Drug testing by employers is not generally prohibited by any federal legislation; indeed, federal laws or regulations may require that certain employees, such as those in the airline or transportation industry, undergo periodic or random drug testing. The Drug-Free Workplace Act, passed by Congress in 1988, requires that government contractors doing more than $25,000 of business annually and recipients of federal grants of more than $25,000 establish written drug-free workplace policies and establish drug-free awareness programs.

State Drug Testing Legislation

A number of states have passed legislation regarding drug testing of employees. Most such laws set mandatory procedural requirements for employers who subject employees or applicants to drug testing. In general, these laws require that employers (1) provide employees with a written statement of their drug testing policy, (2) require confirmatory tests in the case of an initial positive test result, (3) allow employees or applicants who have tested positive to have the sample retested at their own expense, (4) offer employees who test positive the opportunity to enroll in a drug rehabilitation program, and (5) allow termination of employees testing positive only when they refuse to participate in such a program, fail to complete such a program, or violate the terms of the rehabilitation program. Several states, including Connecticut and West Virginia, require employers to have reasonable grounds to suspect that employees are using drugs before subjecting employees (other than employees in safety-sensitive positions or subject to federal drug testing requirements) to drug tests.

Drug Testing by Private Sector Employers

As noted, neither the ADA nor the Rehabilitation Act prohibits drug testing by employers. Private sector employers may be subject to federal laws or regulations that require drug testing of certain employees and may be required by the Drug-Free Workplace Act to establish a drug-free workplace policy. In general, federal and state laws do not prohibit drug testing by private sector employers; such testing may be subject to the procedural requirements of any relevant state laws. Employers whose work forces are unionized are required to bargain in good faith with the union representing their employees before instituting a drug testing program for those employees.

Drug Testing by Public Sector Employers

In addition to the legal issues that may arise under specific drug testing laws, drug testing of employees or applicants by a public sector employer could raise questions of its legality under the Constitution. In a case that arose prior to the passage of the ADA, *New York City Transit Authority v. Beazer* [438 U.S. 904 (1978); 440 U.S. 568 (1979)], the Supreme Court upheld the constitutionality of a New York City Transit Authority rule prohibiting the employment of persons using methadone; the rule was held to serve the purposes of safety and efficiency and was a policy choice that the public sector employer was empowered to make.

The constitutional challenges to public sector drug testing are based on the Fourth Amendment, which forbids unreasonable searches or seizures by the government. Drug testing is considered a search; the general requirement under the Fourth Amendment is that the government must show some reasonable cause to justify the drug testing. In *Skinner v. Railway Labor Executives Association* [489 U.S. 602 (1989)], the Supreme Court upheld the constitutionality of Federal Railroad Administration regulations that required drug tests of all railroad employees involved in accidents, regardless of whether there was any reason to suspect individual employees of drug use. The Supreme Court held that the testing program served a compelling government interest by regulating conduct of railroad employees to ensure public safety, and that interest outweighed the privacy concerns of the employees; the fact that the employees had been involved in an accident was sufficient reason to subject them to drug testing.

http://said.dol.gov/stateLawList.asp *is the Web site for information on State laws concerning drug testing in the workplace.*

In *National Treasury Employees Union v. Von Raab* [489 U.S. 656 (1989)], the Supreme Court upheld rules of the U.S. Customs Service that required drug tests of all employees in, or applicants for, positions that involved the interdiction of drug smuggling, carrying a firearm, or access to classified materials. The government interest in public safety and in preventing law enforcement officials from being subjected to bribery or blackmail because of their own drug use justified the drug testing program under the Fourth Amendment. The unique mission of the Customs Service and the important government interests served by the testing justified the testing of all employees in the particular positions even without any showing of individualized suspicion that they were using drugs.

Subsequent to its decisions in *Skinner* and *Von Raab,* the Supreme Court held in *Chandler v. Miller* [520 U.S. 305 (1997)] that a Georgia law that required all candidates for state political offices to pass a drug test was unconstitutional because there was no evidence of a drug problem among elected officials, and the political offices did not involve high risk or safety-sensitive positions or drug-interdiction efforts.

A number of lower federal court decisions have also dealt with drug testing by public sector employers. In *American Fed. of Govt. Employees v. Thornburgh (INS)* [713 F. Supp. 359 (N.D.Cal. 1989)], the court confined drug testing by the Immigration and Naturalization Service to the job classes specified in *Von Raab:* those employees involved directly in drug interdiction, carrying firearms, and with access to classified information. In *AFGE v. Thornburgh (Bureau of Prisons)* [720 F. Supp. 154 (N.D.Cal. 1989)], the court enjoined the Bureau of Prisons' program of mandatory random testing of all employees, regardless of their job function, because the employer had failed to demonstrate a special need for the testing, as required by the Supreme Court decisions. *NTEU v. Watkins* [722 F. Supp. 766 (D.D.C. 1989)] upheld the Department of Energy's drug testing of employees in "sensitive" positions: those with access to sensitive information; presidential appointees; law enforcement officers; those whose duties pertain to law enforcement or national security or to protection of lives or property; those occupied with public health or safety; and those positions involved with a high degree of trust.

The court in *Watkins* also held that testing employees carrying firearms was not justified unless they also had law enforcement duties, and merely holding a security clearance does not decrease one's privacy expectation to justify testing with no other justification present.

In *Harmon v. Thornburgh* [878 F.2d 484 (D.C. Cir. 1989)], the court held that the *Von Raab* and *Skinner* public safety rationale to justify testing focuses on the immediacy of the threat posed. Therefore, the Department of Justice program of random drug testing of prosecutors, those with access to grand jury proceedings, and those with top-secret security clearances was not justified here; the court did allow the testing of employees with access to top-secret national security information. In *AFGE v. Skinner* [885 F.2d 884 (D.C. Cir. 1989)], the Department of Transportation's drug testing of employees in jobs with a direct impact on public health, safety, or national security, such as air traffic controllers, safety inspectors, aircraft mechanics, and motor vehicle operators, was upheld by the court of appeals.

In the case of *Georgia Association of Educators v. Harris* [749 F. Supp. 1110 (N.D.Ga., 1990)], a federal court in Georgia issued an injunction against the enforcement of Georgia legislation requiring drug tests of all applicants for state employment. The court held that the testing requirement could not stand under the standards set out in *Von Raab.*

Drug Testing and the NLRB

A number of National Labor Relations Board (NLRB) decisions have dealt with drug testing. An employer's mandatory drug testing program for all employees who suffered work-related injuries was held to be a mandatory bargaining subject in *Johnson–Bateman Co.* [295 NLRB No. 26, 131 L.R.R.M. 1393 (1989)], requiring that employers must bargain in good faith with the union(s) representing their employees before instituting drug testing requirements. In *Oil, Chemical and Atomic Workers Int. Union, Local 2-286 v. Amoco Oil Co.* [885 F.2d 697 (10th Cir. 1989)], the court of appeals issued an injunction to prevent an employer from unilaterally implementing a drug testing program, pending the outcome of arbitration over whether the collective agreement gave the employer the right to institute such a program. However, drug testing of job applicants is not a mandatory bargaining subject according to *Star Tribune* [295 NLRB No. 63, 131 L.R.R.M. 1404 (1989)], which means that employers may unilaterally adopt drug testing for applicants for employment.

SUMMARY

- The Age Discrimination in Employment Act (ADEA) prohibits discrimination in employment based on age; the ADEA protects only employees aged forty and older from such discrimination, but some state laws protect employees aged eighteen and older. Mandatory retirement is prohibited, except where age is a BFOQ necessary for the safe and efficient performance of the job in question; the *Western Airlines* case interprets the BFOQ provisions of the ADEA. Exceptions under the ADEA allow certain executives to be retired at age sixty-five and allow public sector employers to establish retirement ages for law enforcement officers and firefighters. Employers may differentiate among employees because of age in the provision of employment benefits, as long as the differentiation is cost justified and pursuant to a bona fide benefits plan. Voluntary early retirement is not prohibited, and employers may offer supplemental benefits as an inducement for early retirement. The ADEA imposes certain requirements on employers who require employees to sign a waiver as a condition of receiving early retirement incentives.

- Both the Americans with Disabilities Act (ADA) and the Rehabilitation Act prohibit employment discrimination against otherwise qualified individuals with a disability. Both acts have the same broad definition of disability. Persons otherwise qualified, but who are perceived by others as having a disability, are protected under both acts. Persons with AIDS or who are HIV-positive have generally been held to be protected from employment discrimination under both acts. The Rehabilitation Act covers only employers who are government contractors or who operate or administer federally funded activities; the ADA covers both public and private employers with fifteen or more employees. Both acts require employers to make reasonable accommodation to the conditions of otherwise qualified individuals with a disability, as discussed in the *Humphrey* case.
- Neither the ADA nor the Rehabilitation Act requires or forbids drug testing of employees, although the ADA does protect employees who have successfully completed a drug rehabilitation program or who are "erroneously regarded as using drugs." Public employers who require employees to be tested for drugs may face problems under the Fourth Amendment of the U.S. Constitution; private sector employers who impose drug testing programs may be subject to appropriate state laws.

QUESTIONS

1. How does the coverage of the Americans with Disabilities Act differ from that of the Rehabilitation Act? Is there any overlap between the coverage of the acts? Explain your answers.
2. What must a plaintiff establish to support a claim of age discrimination under the ADEA? Must the plaintiff demonstrate that he or she was replaced by someone under forty? Explain.
3. What constitutes a disability under the ADA? Are all individuals with disabilities protected under the ADA?
4. Under what circumstances can public sector employers require their employees to take drug tests? How do the circumstances under which private sector employers may require employees to take drug tests differ from those of public sector employers?
5. What is necessary to establish a BFOQ under the ADEA? What other defenses are available to an employer under the ADEA?
6. What are the differences in the procedures for filing complaints under Section 503 and Section 504 of the Rehabilitation Act?
7. How far must an employer go to accommodate an otherwise qualified individual's disability? What constitutes undue hardship?
8. When can an employer institute a mandatory retirement age for employees?
9. What, if any, incentives can an employer offer employees to retire voluntarily? Can an employer require employees to waive their rights under the ADEA as a condition of receiving such incentives? Explain your answers.
10. Must employers hire persons who are HIV positive? Explain.

CASE PROBLEMS

1. Annie Miners worked as promotions director for REV 105, a radio station owned by Cargill Communications, Inc. Miners used a company van in her work, which required her to organize promotional events in bars and nightclubs. Cargill issued a memorandum to all employees prohibiting consumption of alcoholic beverages while working at company events; violation of the policy was grounds for discharge.

   In May 1994, Mark Lang became Miners's supervisor. One month prior to that date, Miners missed work one day, explaining that she had been out late drinking the night before. The incident was noted in her file. Lang was aware of the entry in her file; he was particularly sensitive to issues of drug and alcohol abuse because he had received treatment himself for chemical dependence. About a year later, management became suspicious that Miners had driven the company van after drinking. Management hired a private investigator, Seman, to follow her. On June 6, 1995, Seman observed Miners drinking at several bars and then driving away in the van. He also observed her drinking with some of the station's advertising clients two days later. Miners, who weighed about 250 pounds, admitted that she had about five drinks over the course of six hours, during which time she also consumed food. Seman called Lang, and when Miners left the bar, Lang was waiting for her at the van. Lang demanded the keys, which Miners surrendered to him. The next day, Miners was informed that her actions the previous night were reason for termination; she was offered the opportunity to enroll in a chemical dependence treatment program "due to the possibility that [she] might be an alcoholic."

   Miners was informed that she could complete the program with no loss in pay, or she would be fired. She rejected the treatment and was fired. She sued Cargill under the ADA and under the state Human Rights Act, alleging that Cargill fired her because it regarded her as an alcoholic.

   How should the court rule on her case? Explain your answer. See *Miners v. Cargill Communications, Inc.* [113 F.3d 820 (8th Cir. 1997)].

2. Ann Lindsey and Linda York, both over forty years old, were employed as head waitresses shortly after the opening of the Cabaret Royale, an upscale gentlemen's club in Dallas. Its facilities include a gourmet restaurant, conference room with office services, a boutique, wide-screen viewing of sports events, and topless dancing. Lindsey was hired in January 1989. Two months later, she sought promotion to dancer. She spoke with one of the managers, and that same evening, she was summoned into the office of the general manager, Brian Paul, and told that she was "too old" to be a dancer. York was present at the time. In ensuing weeks, several younger waitresses were promoted to dancer. Finally, on May 8, 1989, Lindsey resigned and immediately became employed as a dancer at the Million Dollar Saloon. Cabaret Royale contends that Lindsey was not qualified to be one of its dancers because she failed to meet its attractiveness standard; specifically, she was not "beautiful, gorgeous, and sophisticated." York also began working as a waitress in January 1989. On May 8, 1989, she left work around 1:30 a.m. claiming to be ill. As she left, she saw a regular customer, Kevin Hale, waiting for a cab and she gave him a ride home. When she returned to work two days later, she was informed that she was fired. She maintains that no reasons were assigned for her dismissal. Cabaret Royale responds that she was terminated because she violated the club's prohibition against leaving with customers. York counters that younger waitresses were not disciplined for the identical behavior. The Cabaret employed only one other

nonmanagement female over age forty, Joy Tarver, a dancer who also was terminated at the same time. York and Lindsey filed suit under the ADEA.

Can they establish a prima facie case of age discrimination? Are they likely to be successful in their claim? Explain your answers. See *Lindsey v. Prive Corp.* [987 F.2d 324 (5th Cir. 1993)].

3. The El Paso Natural Gas Company had a rule that pilots of the company's private planes must either accept ground jobs or retire at age sixty. Pilots' duties included night flying, visual flying, and instrument flying. Transfer to a ground job at age sixty was permitted if one was available. Otherwise, the pilot was forced to retire. El Paso argued that it was impractical for the company to try to monitor the health of a pilot after age sixty and that the FAA regulation requiring retirement of commercial pilots after age sixty was prima facie proof of the legality of the company's rule under the ADEA BFOQ provisions.

   Do you agree? Explain your answer. See *EEOC v. El Paso Natural Gas Co.* [626 F. Supp. 182 (W.D. Tex. 1985)].

4. Alan Labonte was hired as executive director of the Hutchins & Wheeler law firm in June 1992. In his first year in the position, he created a timekeeping system that saved the firm $13,000 per month, negotiated leases to lower rental payments by $43,000, lowered client disbursement costs by $200,000, and reduced overtime costs by $40,000. The firm's partners gave him a performance evaluation stating that they were "very satisfied" with his performance; he received a raise of $4,600. After about a year, Labonte developed a limp; when he consulted a doctor about the problem, he was informed that he had multiple sclerosis. After his diagnosis, he informed the firm and requested that the partners meet with his doctors to determine what measures could be taken to accommodate his condition. One partner had a brief lunch meeting with one doctor, who suggested that the firm limit the amount of walking that Labonte would be required to do. The firm made no effort to limit Labonte's walking, to move his office, or to rearrange his job; instead, the firm assigned additional duties to him and pressured him to cancel a personal trip to Florida that he had planned. On one occasion, a partner told him to go home if he was tired, so he wouldn't wear himself out and become ineffective. In January 1994, the firm terminated Labonte because his condition affected his performance; the firm claimed that his thinking was "not as crisp as it needed to be." After he was terminated, Labonte applied for, and was granted, disability benefits under the firm's insurance policy, stating that he was "unable to work long hours in a stressful job" and "needed a flexible work schedule." He then worked as a consultant and enrolled in a graduate program at a local university. Labonte brought a claim of disability discrimination against the firm under both state and federal law; after following the administrative procedures, he filed suit in federal court. The firm argued that Labonte was precluded from bringing suit because he accepted disability benefits.

   How should the court rule on his claim? Can he pursue the suit despite accepting disability benefits? Why should that matter for his claim? Explain your answers. See *Labonte v. Hutchins & Wheeler* [424 Mass. 813, 678 N.E.2d 853 (Mass. Sup. Ct., 1997)].

5. Giles Parkinson had been Chief General Counsel for Cordmaker, Inc. for a number of years; he was nearly sixty years old. After experiencing financial difficulties and a severe downturn in business, Cordmaker eliminated Parkinson's position and informed him that he was being terminated. Most of his duties were reassigned to other employees, including a thirty-seven-year-old attorney. Parkinson informed the board of directors of Cordmaker that he believed their decision to fire him was illegal and that he would file suit. Parkinson was then placed on a leave of absence and

paid full salary for six months and 70 percent of his salary for three months thereafter. He requested that he be able to use his former office, and the company's phones and computers, to conduct a job search but was barred from using any company facilities. Parkinson filed suit under the ADEA and the New York Human Rights Law, alleging that Cordmaker had discriminated against him because of his age and had retaliated against him for complaining of age discrimination by denying him use of company facilities.

How should the court rule on his suit? Explain your answer. See *Wanamaker v. Columbian Rope Co.* [108 F.3d 462 (2d Cir. 1997)].

6. Gerald Woythal was Chief Engineer for Tex-Tenn Corp.; he was one of the company's original employees and sixty-two years old. His boss was Operating Manager James Carico. Carico found it difficult to communicate with Woythal, whom he characterized as having a negative attitude, being apathetic about the company's future, and sometimes unavailable when Carico needed to talk to him. The company was experiencing rapid growth, and Carico was concerned about the Engineering Department's ability to meet the increased demands placed upon it. He decided to hire an additional engineer to serve as Woythal's assistant. Woythal showed no interest in the hiring decision or in recruiting the new engineer. When Carico asked Woythal about his plans for the future and what he wanted to do for Tex-Tenn, Woythal simply replied that he would work until he was seventy. When Carico pressed Woythal about his plans for the Engineering Department, Woythal was uninterested and evasive. Carico then called Woythal into his office for a discussion and told him that "the company needed his participation, and if he chose not to participate, he would not be needed." Carico then asked Woythal if he intended to be an active participant in the company and told him to make his mind up by the end of the month. Woythal interpreted Carico's remarks to mean that he was fired, and he left the company at the end of the month. Tex-Tenn hired a younger engineer to replace Woythal. Woythal then filed suit under the ADEA, alleging age discrimination.

Can Woythal establish a legitimate claim of age discrimination? What defenses can Tex-Tenn raise? How should the court rule on the suit? Explain your answers. See *Woythal v. Tex-Tenn Corp.* [112 F.3d 243 (6th Cir. 1997)].

7. Bonnie Cook applied for employment as an attendant at a Rhode Island hospital for the developmentally disabled. She had previously worked at the hospital and had a good work record but left voluntarily. She was not rehired because she was extremely obese; She was five feet two inches tall and weighed more than 320 pounds. The hospital's human resources director stated that she felt Cook's obesity would limit her ability to evacuate patients in case of an emergency and make her more susceptible to developing serious health problems. Cook sued the hospital under the ADA.

Is Cook's obesity a disability under the ADA? Does her obesity prevent her from being an "otherwise qualified individual with a disability" under the ADA? Does it matter that Cook's weight may change? How should the court decide this case? Explain your answers. See *Cook v. State of Rhode Island Dept. of Mental Health, Retardation and Hospitals* [10 F.3d 17 (1st Cir. 1993)].

8. Rotert had been working as a mortgage processing officer when the company told her that her duties were being changed to those of a loan consultant and that she would be transferred to another branch. The company told the fifty-nine-year-old Rotert her salary would be the same. Rotert protested the new work assignment and resigned. She filed a claim for unemployment benefits, which was denied because she was not "constructively discharged" due to the new assignment. Rather, the state agency held, she had voluntarily quit.

When Rotert filed an ADEA complaint, again stating that she was constructively discharged in favor of a younger employee who took her former job as mortgage processing officer, the company argued for dismissal because the issue of "constructive discharge" had already been decided against her by the state agency.

How should the court rule? See *Rotert v. Jefferson Federal Savings & Loan Ass'n.* [623 F. Supp. 1114 (D. Conn. 1985)].

9. Ralph Sheehan was an assistant editor at Racing Form, Inc., a publisher that prints horse racing newsletters, programs, and tout sheets. Racing Form decided to computerize its operations, which would eliminate several jobs. The company human resources manager prepared a list of the jobs to be eliminated and the employees occupying those jobs, the jobs to be retained and the employees filling those jobs, and the birth dates of those employees. Sheehan, age fifty, was informed that his job would be eliminated; he noticed from the listing that most of the employees losing their jobs were older, while those being retained were younger. Sheehan filed an age discrimination complaint and argued that including the employees' birth dates was evidence of age discrimination.

Is the court likely to agree with Sheehan? Are there other legitimate reasons for including the employees' birth dates on the listing? Explain. See *Sheehan v. Daily Racing Form* [104 F.3d 940 (7th Cir. 1997)].

10. The administrators at Wayzatta Central High School, in Wayzatta, Mississippi, were concerned about rumors of illegal drug use by the high school students. The school administrators decided to require all high school varsity athletes to undergo drug tests. Although there was no specific evidence that the athletes were using drugs, the administration reasoned that athletes tend to be role models and opinion leaders for the student body; hence, requiring them to take drug tests would also send a strong antidrug message to the rest of the students. When some students complained that the faculty were not subject to the drug testing, the administration adopted a policy that also required all faculty and staff at the school to take drug tests, despite the fact that there was no evidence of drug use by the faculty, and anyone testing positive would be discharged. The teachers protested the drug testing policy and decided to file suit to challenge it.

On what grounds can the teachers challenge the drug testing policy? Is their legal challenge likely to be successful? Is the drug testing of the student athletes legal? Explain. See *Board of Education of Indpt. School Dist. No. 92 of Pottawatomie County v. Earls* [536 U.S. 822 (2002)], *Georgia Assoc. of Educators v. Harris* [749 F. Supp. 1110 (N.D. Ga. 1990)], and *Vernonia School Dist. v. Acton* [515 U.S. 646 (1995)].

INTERNET EXERCISES

1. Your employer, Immense Multinational Business (IMB), is approached by a local social service agency that works with persons with disabilities. The social service agency asks IMB to undertake a program to hire individuals with disabilities. Your boss, the human resources director, asks you to investigate methods of accommodating the disabilities of potential employees referred by the social service agency. Consult the U.S. Department of Justice's ADA site at **http://www.usdoj.gov/crt/ada/adahom1.htm** and click the Technical Assistance Program link to determine what information may be available.

2. Consult IBM's Accessibility Center Web site at **http://www-3.ibm.com/able/guidelines/web/accessweb.html** for information on how technology may make it easier to accommodate a potential employee's disability. What other resources can you find on the Web?

INFOTRAC KEYWORDS

http://www.infotrac-college.com

age discrimination, Age Discrimination In Employment Act, Older Workers Benefit Protection Act, Americans with Disability Act, Rehabilitation Act, Federal drug testing legislation, drug testing

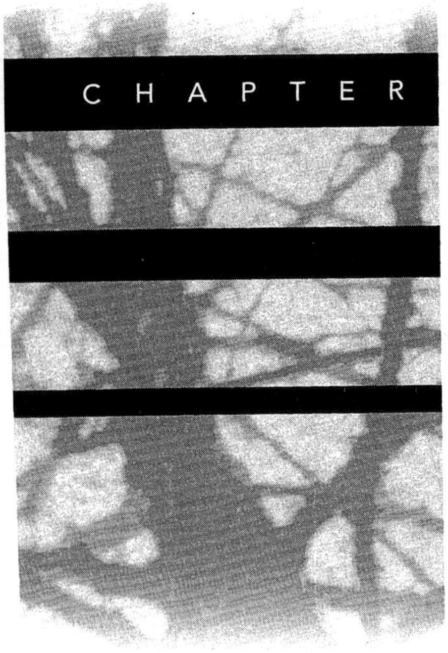

CHAPTER 7

OTHER EEO LEGISLATION

In addition to the legislation discussed in the preceding chapters, there are other legal provisions that can be used to attack discrimination in employment. Those other provisions include the Civil Rights Acts of 1866 and 1870, Executive Order 11246, the Uniformed Services Employment and Reemployment Act, the National Labor Relations Act, the Constitution, and the various state EEO laws. This chapter discusses these provisions in some detail.

THE CIVIL RIGHTS ACTS OF 1866 AND 1870

The Civil Rights Acts of 1866 and 1870 were passed during the Reconstruction era immediately following the Civil War. They were intended to ensure that the newly freed slaves were granted the full legal rights of U.S. citizens. The acts are presently codified in Sections 1981, 1983, and 1985 of Chapter 42 of the U.S. Code (referred to as 42 U.S.C. Sections 1981, 1983, 1985).

SECTION 1981

Section 1981 provides, in part, that

> All persons within the jurisdiction of the United States shall have the same right in every State and Territory to make and enforce contracts . . . as is enjoyed by white citizens. . . .

The Supreme Court held in *Jones v. Alfred H. Mayer Co.* [392 U.S. 409 (1968)] that the acts could be used to attack discrimination in private employment. Following *Jones,* Section 1981 was increasingly used, in addition to Title VII, to challenge employment discrimination. In *Johnson v. Railway Express Agency* [421 U.S. 454 (1975)], the Supreme Court held that Section 1981 provided for an independent cause of action (right to sue) against employment discrimination. A suit under Section 1981 was separate and distinct from a suit under Title VII.

In the 1989 decision of *Patterson v. McLean Credit Union* [491 U.S. 164], the Supreme Court held that Section 1981 covered only those aspects of racial discrimination in employment that related to the formation and enforcement of contracts and did not cover harassment based on race. The Civil Rights Act of 1991 amended Section 1981 and effectively overturned the *Patterson* decision by adding Section 1981(b), which states

> For the purposes of this section, the term "make and enforce contracts" includes the making, performance, modification, and termination of contracts, and the enjoyment of all benefits, privileges, terms and conditions of the contractual relationship.

The 1991 act also added Section 1981A, which gives the right to sue for compensatory and punitive damages to victims of intentional discrimination in violation of Title VII, the Americans with Disabilities Act of 1990, and the Rehabilitation Act.

The wording of Section 1981 (". . . as is enjoyed by white citizens . . .") seems to indicate a concern with racial discrimination. In *Saint Francis College v. Al-Khazraji* [481 U.S. 604 (1987)], a college professor alleged that he was denied tenure because he was an Arab. The college argued that Arabs are members of the Caucasian (white) race and that the professor was therefore not a victim of race discrimination subject to Section 1981. In determining whether Section 1981 applied to the professor's claim, the Supreme Court held that

> Based on the history of Section 1981, we have little trouble in concluding that Congress intended to protect from discrimination identifiable classes of persons who are subjected to intentional discrimination solely because of their ancestry or ethnic characteristics. Such discrimination is racial discrimination that Congress intended Section 1981 to forbid, whether or not it would be classified as racial in terms of modern scientific theory. The Court of Appeals was thus quite right in holding that Section 1981, "at a minimum," reaches discrimination against an individual "because he or she is genetically part of an ethnically and physiognomically distinctive subgrouping of *homo sapiens*." It is clear from our holding, however, that a distinctive physiognomy is not essential to qualify for Section 1981 protection. If respondent on remand can prove that he was subjected to intentional discrimination based on the fact that he was born an Arab, rather than solely on the place or nation of his origin, or his religion, he will have made out a case under Section 1981.

Based on *Saint Francis College v. Al-Khazraji,* the courts now interpret "race" under Section 1981 broadly to include claims of ethnic discrimination that are racial in character, such as claiming that an individual was treated differently because he was Hispanic rather than "Anglo," *Lopez v. S. B. Thomas, Inc.* [831 F.2d 1184 (2d Cir. 1987)]. Plaintiffs may bring suits under Section 1981 to challenge racial or ethnic harassment or retaliation, *Manatt v. Bank of America, N.A.* [339 F.3d 792 (9th Cir. 2003)].

SECTION 1983

Section 1983 of 42 U.S.C. provides that

> Every person who, under the color of any statute, ordinance, regulation, custom or usage, of any State or Territory, subjects, or causes to be subjected, any citizen of the United States or other person within the jurisdiction thereof to the deprivation of any rights, privileges, or immunities secured by the Constitution and laws, shall be liable to the party injured in an action at law equity, or other proper proceeding for redress.

As with Section 1981, Section 1983 is restricted to claims of intentional discrimination. But unlike Section 1981, the prohibitions of Section 1983 extend to the deprivation of any rights guaranteed by the Constitution or by law. In *Maine v. Thiboutot* [448 U.S. 1 (1980)], the Supreme Court held that Section 1983 encompasses claims based on deprivation of rights granted under federal statutory law. This means that claims alleging discrimination on grounds prohibited by federal law, such as gender, age, religion, national origin, and so forth, can be brought under Section 1983. But because of the wording of Section 1983 (". . . under the color of any statute, . . . of any state"), claims under Section 1983 are restricted to cases in which the alleged discrimination is by someone acting (or claiming to act) under government authority. That means employment discrimination by public employers is subject to challenge because such employers act under specific legal authority. In general, claims against private sector employers can rarely be filed under Section 1983. Any claims against private employers under Section 1983 must establish that the employer acted pursuant to some specific government authority; this is the "state action" requirement. In addition, in *Brown v. GSA* [425 U.S. 820 (1976)], the Supreme Court held that the only remedy available to federal government employees complaining of race discrimination in employment is provided by Section 717 of Title VII.

SECTION 1985(C)

Section 1985(c) of 42 U.S.C. prohibits two or more persons from conspiring to deprive a person or class of persons "of the equal protection of the laws, or of equal privileges and immunities under the law." The provision was enacted in 1871 to protect blacks from the violent activities of the Ku Klux Klan.

In *Griffin v. Breckenridge* [403 U.S. 88 (1971)], the Supreme Court held that a group of African Americans alleging that they were attacked and beaten by a group of whites could bring suit under Section 1985(c). It appeared that the provision could be used to attack intentional discrimination in private employment when two or more persons were involved in the discrimination. But in 1979, the Supreme Court held in *Great American Federal Savings & Loan Ass'n. v. Novotny* [442 U.S. 366] that Section 1985(c) could not be used to sue for violation of a right created by Title VII. Relying on *Novotny,* lower courts have held that Section

1985(c) cannot be used to challenge violations of the Equal Pay Act or the Age Discrimination in Employment Act.

PROCEDURE UNDER SECTIONS 1981 AND 1983

A suit under Section 1981 is not subject to the same procedural requirements as a suit under Title VII. There is no requirement to file a claim with any administrative agency, such as the Equal Employment Opportunity Commission, before filing suit under Section 1981 or Section 1983. The plaintiff may file suit in federal district court and is entitled to a jury trial; a successful plaintiff may recover punitive damages in addition to compensatory damages such as back pay, benefits, and legal fees.

The right to sue under Section 1981A for compensatory and punitive damages for intentional violations of Title VII and the Americans with Disabilities Act of 1990 was added by the Civil Rights Act of 1991. The act also set upper limits on the amount of damages recoverable based on the size of the employer (as specified in Chapter 5). Punitive damages are not recoverable against public sector employers.

EXECUTIVE ORDER NO. 11246

Executive Order No. 11246, originally signed by President Johnson in 1965 and amended by President Nixon in 1969, provides the basis for the federal government contract compliance program. Under that executive order, as amended, firms doing business with the federal government must agree not to discriminate in employment on the basis of race, color, religion, national origin, or gender.

EQUAL EMPLOYMENT REQUIREMENTS

Contract Compliance Program
Regulations which provide that all firms having contracts or subcontracts exceeding $10,000 with the federal government must agree to include a no-discrimination clause in the contract.

The **contract compliance program** is administered by the U.S. Secretary of Labor through the Office of Federal Contract Compliance Programs (OFCCP). The OFCCP has issued extensive regulations spelling out the requirements and procedures under the contract compliance program. The regulations provide that all firms having contracts or subcontracts exceeding $10,000 with the federal government must agree to include a no-discrimination clause in the contract. The clause, which is binding on the firm for the duration of the contract, requires the contractor to agree not to discriminate in employment on the basis of race, color, religion, gender, or national origin. The contractor also agrees to state in all employment advertisements that all qualified applicants will be considered without regard to race, color, religion, gender, or national origin and to inform each labor union representing its employees of its obligations under the program. The contracting firm is also required to include the same type of no-discrimination clause in every subcontract or purchase order pursuant to the federal contract.

Look up the OFCCP at **http://www.dol.gov/esa/ofccp/index.htm**

The Secretary of Labor, through the OFCCP, may investigate any allegations of violations by contracting firms. Penalties for violation include the suspension or cancellation of the firm's government contract and the disbarment of the firm from future government contracts.

AFFIRMATIVE ACTION REQUIREMENTS

Affirmative Action Plans
Programs which involve giving preference in hiring or promotion to qualified female or minority employees.

In addition to requiring the no-discrimination clause, the OFCCP regulations may require that a contracting firm develop a written plan regarding its employees. Firms with contracts of services or supply for over $50,000 and having fifty or more employees are required to maintain formal written programs, called **affirmative action plans,** for the utilization of women and minorities in their work force. Affirmative action plans, which must be updated annually, must contain an analysis of the employer's use of women and minorities for each job category in the work force. When job categories reveal an underutilization of women and minorities—that is, fewer women or minorities employed than would reasonably be expected based on their availability in the relevant labor market—the plan must set out specific hiring goals and timetables for improving the employment of women and minorities. The firm is expected to make a good-faith effort to reach those goals; the goals set are more in the nature of targets than hard-and-fast "quotas." The firms must submit annual reports of the results of their efforts to meet the goals set out in the affirmative action plan.

See **http://www.dol.gov/esa/regs/statutes/ofccp/eo11246.htm** *for information on affirmative action.*

Firms holding federal or federally assisted construction contracts or subcontracts over $10,000 are also subject to affirmative action requirements. The contracting firm must comply with the goals and timetables for employment of women and minorities set periodically by the OFCCP. Those construction industry goals are set for "covered geographic areas" of the country based on census data for the areas. The "goals and timetables" approach to affirmative action for construction industry employees was held to be constitutional and legal under Title VII in *Contractors Ass'n. of Eastern Pennsylvania v. Shultz* [442 F.2d 159 (3rd Cir. 1971)].

PROCEDURE UNDER EXECUTIVE ORDER NO. 11246

Individuals alleging a violation of a firm's obligations under Executive Order No. 11246 may file complaints with the OFCCP within 180 days of the alleged violation. The OFCCP may refer the complaint to the EEOC for investigation, or it may make its own investigation. If it makes its own investigation, it must report to the director of the OFCCP within sixty days.

If there is reason to believe that a violation has occurred, the firm is issued a show-cause notice, directing it to show why enforcement proceedings should not be instituted; the firm has thirty days to provide such evidence. During this thirty-day period, the OFCCP is also required to make efforts to resolve the violation through mediation and conciliation.

If the firm fails to show cause or if the conciliation is unsuccessful, the director of the OFCCP may refer the complaint to the Secretary of Labor for administrative enforcement proceedings or to the Department of Justice for judicial enforcement proceedings. The individual filing the complaint may not file suit privately against the firm alleged to be in violation, but the individual may bring suit to force the OFCCP to enforce the regulations and requirements under the Executive Order, *Legal Aid Society v. Brennan* [608 F.2d 1319 (9th Cir. 1979)].

Administrative enforcement proceedings involve a hearing before an administrative law judge (ALJ). The ALJ's decision is subject to review by the secretary of labor; the secretary's decision may be subjected to judicial review in the federal courts, *Firestone Co. v. Marshall* [507 F. Supp. 1330 (E.D. Texas 1981)].

Firms found to be in violation of the obligations under the Executive Order, either through the courts or the administrative proceedings, may be subject to injunctions and required to provide back pay and grant retroactive seniority to affected employees. The firm may also have its government contract suspended or canceled and may be declared ineligible for future government contracts. Firms declared ineligible must demonstrate compliance with the Executive Order's requirements to be reinstated by the director of the OFCCP.

EMPLOYMENT DISCRIMINATION BECAUSE OF MILITARY SERVICE: THE UNIFORMED SERVICES EMPLOYMENT AND REEMPLOYMENT RIGHTS ACT

During the recent U.S. military actions in Afghanistan and Iraq, many persons who were members of the National Guard or military reserves were called to active duty; in some instances, the tour of active duty lasted more than one year. What are the legal rights of employees who are called to active duty? Do they have the right to return to their job after their active duty service is over? Federal legislation protects the reemployment rights of employees who serve in the military services or who are members of the reserves and are called into active duty.

THE UNIFORMED SERVICES EMPLOYMENT AND REEMPLOYMENT RIGHTS ACT

The Uniformed Services Employment and Reemployment Rights Act (USERRA), enacted in 1994, replaced the Veterans' Reemployment Rights Act. USERRA covers both private and public sector employers, including the federal government; it prohibits employers from discriminating against employees because of their service in the military. USERRA applies only to noncareer military service—that is, to employees who are called to active duty from their civilian jobs. It does not apply to career military service, *Woodman v. Office of Personnel Management* [258 F.3d 1372 (Fed. Cir. 2001)].

Employees who are absent from employment because they were ordered to active military service are entitled to reinstatement and employment benefits if they meet the following requirements: (1) they gave the employer notice of the period of military service; (2) they are absent for a cumulative total of less than five years; and (3) they submitted an application for reemployment within the designated time period. The time period for submitting the notice of reemployment to the employer depends on the length of the military service. For military service less than thirty-one days, the employee need only report to work on the first full workday after completion of the service and transportation to the employee's residence. For service longer than 30 days but less than 181 days, the notice must be submitted not later than fourteen days after completing the period of military service. For service longer than 180 days, the notice must be submitted not later than ninety days after completion of the period of military service.

Employers are not required to reinstate employees after their military service if: (1) the employer's circumstances have changed so that reemployment would be unreasonable or impossible; (2) the reemployment would cause undue hardship in accommodation, training, or effort; or (3) the initial employment was for a brief, nonrecurring period. In any such case, the employer has the burden of proving that the denial of reemployment was permissible under the act.

Employees reemployed after military service are entitled to the seniority, rights, and benefits they had as of the date the military service began, plus any seniority, rights, and benefits that they would have received had they remained continuously employed. Persons who are reemployed under the act after military service of more than 180 days may not be discharged without cause within one year of reemployment; persons reemployed after military service of more than 30 days but less than 180 days may not be discharged without cause within 180 days of reemployment. Persons who are affected by alleged violations of the USERRA must file written complaints with the federal Secretary of Labor; the Secretary will investigate any complaint and make reasonable attempts to settle it. If such attempts are unsuccessful, affected persons may request that the secretary refer a complaint to the U.S. Attorney General to take court action to enforce the act or may file legal action themselves in the appropriate federal district court.

Remedies available under such a suit include ordering the employer to comply with the act and compensation for lost wages, benefits, and legal fees. Liquidated damages are available where the employer's violation was willful. According to *Gummo v. Village of Depew, N.Y.* [75 F.3d 98 (2d. Cir. 1996)], the employee only needs to show that the military service was a substantial or motivating factor in the employer's decision to discharge the employee; it need not be the sole reason. An employer can escape liability by showing that the employee would have been discharged even without military service.

The following case involves a claim of termination and refusal to reemploy an individual in violation of USERRA.

Leisek v. Brightwood Corporation

278 F.3d 895 (9th Cir. 2002)

Tashima, Circuit Judge

John C. Leisek was a full-time employee of Brightwood from December 10, 1991, until the effective date of the termination of his employment, July 3, 1996. . . . He was also a member of the Oregon National Guard (the "Guard") at all times during his employment with Brightwood. Leisek owned and operated a hot-air balloon that had the National Guard insignia on it. Starting in 1995, he attended various events around the country, using the balloon as a recruiting and promotional tool for the National Guard. He designated his balloon program "H.A.B.I.T." (Hot Air Balloon Interaction Team).

Throughout the spring and summer of 1996, Leisek received several written orders to perform temporary active duty by attending and participating in ballooning events for the National Guard. Leisek provided Brightwood with a list of several events that he expected to attend from May 1996 to September 1996, although he did not have orders for all the events at the time. Because of the large number of events taking place during the summer months, Leisek requested a leave of absence for the summer months of 1996. Unlike in the previous year, however, when he had been granted leave, Brightwood denied Leisek's request and instructed him to stop soliciting ballooning events because his absences would be a hardship for Brightwood due to his specialized position.

The H.A.B.I.T. schedule that Leisek submitted to Brightwood included temporary duty dates for events in Boise, Idaho, from June 23 to June 30; Montrose, Colorado, from July 3 to 7; Monroe, Wisconsin, from July 8 to 14; and several other events from July through September. Leisek eventually received written orders for his participation in the events to take place in Idaho and Wisconsin, but he at no time received any Guard orders, either oral or written, for the event in Colorado.

In telephone conversations that took place during and shortly after Leisek's temporary duty in Boise, Idaho, David Duncan, the plant personnel manager at Brightwood, informed him that he was expected to report back to work upon completion of his Guard duties in Boise, because his request for leave to attend the event in Colorado had been denied; Brightwood had not received any written or oral Guard orders, which it required in order to authorize the leave. Duncan also told Leisek that Brightwood would not honor any future orders involving the balloon project, other than those for which it had already received orders, and that, if he chose to proceed on to the Colorado event rather than return to work, he would be considered to have quit voluntarily by abandoning his employment without authorization on July 1, 2, and 3. Leisek told Duncan that he would at that time "pursue his other options," which Duncan assumed meant he would be pursuing a full-time career in the Guard. Despite Duncan's warning, Leisek continued on to Colorado, where he remained until July 7. He remained in Colorado, even though he had Guard orders to attend the Wisconsin event between July 8 and 14. Leisek understood that his employment with Brightwood had been terminated.

Leisek fulfilled his remaining Guard assignments in July, August, and September 1996. He had no further contact with anyone at Brightwood until September 25, when he sought reemployment at the company. Leisek was invited to resubmit an employment application, but he refused to do so and was not reemployed.

Leisek then commenced this action, alleging unlawful employment practices in violation of USERRA on the basis of his termination and Brightwood's failure to reemploy him. . . . the district court granted summary judgment in favor of Brightwood . . . Leisek timely appeals.

USERRA "prohibit[s] discrimination against persons because of their service in the uniformed services." . . . A violation of USERRA occurs when a person's

> membership, application for membership, service, application for service, or obligation for service in the uniformed services is a *motivating factor* in the employer's action, unless the employer can prove that the action would have been taken in the absence of such membership, application for membership, service, application for service, or obligation for service. [38 U.S.C. § 4311(c)(1)]

. . . USERRA . . . requires only that the employee's military status was "a motivating factor" in the employer's action. . . . the employee first has the burden of showing, by a preponderance of the evidence, that his or her protected status was "a substantial or motivating factor in the adverse [employment] action;" the employer may then avoid liability only by showing, as an affirmative defense, that the employer would have taken the same action without regard to the employee's protected status.

We must determine: (1) whether there is sufficient evidence from which a jury could find that Leisek's Guard status or conduct was a substantial or "motivating factor" in Brightwood's decision to terminate his employment; and (2) if there is such evidence, whether Brightwood has established as an uncontroverted fact that it would have terminated his employment even if he had not been a member of the Guard.

USERRA defines "service in the uniformed services" as

> the performance of duty on a voluntary or involuntary basis in a uniformed service *under competent authority* and includes active duty, active duty for training, initial active duty

> for training, inactive duty training, full-time National Guard duty, a period for which a person is absent from a position of employment for the purpose of an examination to determine the fitness of the person to perform any such duty. [38 U.S.C. § 4303(13)] [emphasis added]

Thus, in order to be considered "service in the uniformed services," the performance of duty must be "under competent authority."

Leisek was not acting under Guard orders, or under any other "competent authority," when he traveled to the Colorado event, rather than returning to work, and Brightwood was aware of this fact. The record contains evidence that Brightwood's corporate policy made unexcused absences a ground for termination of employment. Even though Leisek's unexcused absences would be a legitimate basis for Brightwood's decision to terminate his employment for the resulting absences from work on July 1 through 3, we nonetheless must examine whether the record supports the inference that Brightwood was also motivated by some other factor, namely, Leisek's Guard status, in terminating his employment. As noted, USERRA requires only that military status be a "motivating factor" in Brightwood's adverse employment action.

. . . Under USERRA, discriminatory motivation of the employer "may be reasonably inferred from a variety of factors, including proximity in time between the employee's military activity and the adverse employment action, inconsistencies between proffered reason and other actions of the employer, an employer's expressed hostility towards members protected by the statute together with knowledge of the employee's military activity, and disparate treatment of certain employees compared to other employees with similar work records or offenses." [citation omitted] The court may consider "all record evidence," including the employer's "explanation for the actions taken."

Here, the evidence supports an inference that Leisek's military status was a "motivating factor" in Brightwood's decision to terminate his employment due to its concern regarding the significant number of absences from work that Leisek's participation in the H.A.B.I.T. program required. The record includes testimony supporting an inference that Leisek's Guard-duty absences since his promotion to the position of quality assurance inspector had created an increased burden for Brightwood and that it had proposed a plan that would restrict Leisek's future Guard-related absences to a period of three weeks and would deduct those absences from his vacation time. In addition, Duncan had informed Leisek that Brightwood had decided not to honor any future Guard orders, except for those that it already had in hand, and had instructed him to discontinue his solicitation of ballooning events. This evidence is sufficient to support an inference that Leisek's military status or conduct was a substantial or motivating factor in Brightwood's decision to terminate his employment.

Brightwood further contends that summary judgment was proper because it presented evidence that established the affirmative defense that it would have terminated Leisek's employment for his unauthorized absences, regardless of his Guard status or conduct. The burden of proof with respect to this affirmative defense is on the employer. As we have noted, the record contains evidence that Brightwood's corporate policy made unexcused absences a reason for termination of employment. However, even though Leisek's unexcused absences would be a legitimate reason for terminating his employment, Brightwood has not established as an uncontroverted fact that it would have terminated Leisek even if he had not been active in the Guard's H.A.B.I.T. program.

There are thus genuine issues of material fact both as to whether Leisek's Guard status and duty was a "motivating factor" in Brightwood's decision to terminate Leisek's employment and, if so, whether Brightwood would have made the same decision to terminate Leisek without regard to his protected status.

With respect to reemployment rights, USERRA provides that, subject to certain conditions, "any person whose absence from a position of employment is necessitated by reason of service in the uniformed services shall be entitled to the reemployment rights" under USERRA. Leisek attended the Colorado ballooning event without any Guard orders that he do so. His absence from employment while attending the Colorado event was thus not "necessitated by reason of service in the uniformed services." He is, therefore, not entitled to the reemployment benefits provided by USERRA. Summary judgment was properly granted to Brightwood on Leisek's reemployment claim.

In sum, because there are material issues of fact about whether Leisek's termination was motivated by his Guard status and whether Brightwood has established that it would have terminated his employment even if he had not been a Guard member, the district court erred in granting summary judgment in favor of Brightwood on Leisek's termination claim. The district court, however, properly granted summary judgment to

Brightwood on Leisek's reemployment claim. Accordingly, the decision of the district court is affirmed in part and reversed in part, and Leisek's termination claim under USERRA is remanded for further proceedings. . . .

AFFIRMED in part, REVERSED in part, and REMANDED.

Case Questions

1. What temporary duty military service was Leisek ordered to perform? Was his service at the Colorado event pursuant to written orders from the National Guard?
2. Why did Brightwood terminate Leisek's employment? When was Leisek terminated?
3. Was Brightwood's termination of Leisek in violation of USERRA? Was Brightwood's refusal to rehire Leisek in violation of USERRA? Explain your answers.

THE NATIONAL LABOR RELATIONS ACT

The unfair labor practice prohibitions of the National Labor Relations Act (NLRA) may be used to attack discrimination in employment in some instances. In *United Packinghouse Workers Union v. NLRB* [416 F.2d 1126 (D.C. Cir. 1969)], the court held that race discrimination by an employer was an unfair labor practice in violation of Section 8(a)(1) of the NLRA. Retaliation against employees who filed charges with the EEOC, by refusing to recall them from layoff, was held to violate Section 8(a)(1) in *Frank Briscoe Inc. v. NLRB* [637 F.2d 946 (3rd Cir. 1981)].

Unions that discriminate against African Americans in membership or in conditions of employment are in violation of Section 8(b)(1)(A) and their duty of fair representation of all employees in the bargaining unit according to the Supreme Court decision of *Syres v. Oil Workers* [350 U.S. 892 (1955)]. (See the *Steele v. Louisville & Nashville R.R.* case in Chapter 19.) In *Hughes Tool Co.* [56 L.R.R.M. 1289 (1964)], the NLRB held that a union's refusal to represent African American workers violated Section 8(b)(1)(A) and was grounds to rescind the union's certification as bargaining agent. Discrimination against female employees by a union also violates Section 8(b)(1)(A) as held in *NLRB v. Glass Bottle Blowers Local 106* [520 F.2d 693 (6th Cir. 1975)]. (See Chapter 19 for a discussion of the duty of fair representation.)

Employers and unions that negotiate, or attempt to negotiate, discriminatory provisions in seniority systems, pay scales, or promotion policies may commit unfair labor practices in violation of Section 8(a)(5) or Section 8(b)(3) by refusing to bargain in good faith.

CONSTITUTIONAL PROHIBITIONS AGAINST DISCRIMINATION

Certain provisions of the U.S. Constitution may be used by public sector employees to challenge discrimination in their employment. The Constitution regulates the relationship between the government and individuals; therefore, the Constitution's prohibitions against discrimination apply only to government employers and to private employers acting under government support or compulsion (state action).

DUE PROCESS AND EQUAL PROTECTION

The primary constitutional provisions used to attack discrimination are the guarantees of due process of law and equal protection found in the Fifth and Fourteenth Amendments. The Fifth Amendment applies to the federal government, and the Fourteenth Amendment applies to state and local governments. In addition, specific enactments such as the First Amendment guarantee of freedom of religion may be used to challenge discrimination. In *Brown v. GSA* [425 U.S. 820 (1976)], the Supreme Court held that the only remedy available to persons complaining of race discrimination in federal government employment is provided by Section 717 of Title VII. However, not all federal employees are covered by Title VII. For example, members of the armed forces or the personal staff members of elected officials, who are not covered by Title VII, could file constitutional challenges to alleged discrimination.

At **http://www.law.cornell.edu/constitution/constitution.table.html** *select the 5th and 14th Amendments to read their text.*

In the case of ***Davis v. Passman*** [442 U.S. 228 (1979)], the Supreme Court held that a member of a congressman's staff, who was not covered by Title VII, could bring a suit under the Fifth Amendment against her employer for discharging her because of intentional gender discrimination.

Challenges to employment discrimination under the due process and equal protection guarantees involve claims that the discriminatory practices deny the victims of the discrimination rights equal, or treatment equal, to those who are not targets of the discrimination. Blanket prohibitions on employment of females, or of members of a minority group, deny those employees due process of law by presuming that all women, or members of the minority group, are unable to perform the requirements of a particular job.

In *Washington v. Davis* [426 U.S. 229 (1976)], the Supreme Court held that the constitutional prohibitions applied only to invidious, or intentional, discrimination; claims alleging disparate impact could not be brought under the constitutional provisions.

Not all intentional discrimination on the basis of race, gender, and so on is unconstitutional, however. In considering claims of discrimination under the Constitution, the court will first consider the basis of discrimination. Some bases of discrimination, or "classifications" by government action, will be considered "suspect classes"; that is, there is little justification for treating persons differently because they fall within a particular class. For example, racial discrimination involves classifying, and treating differently, employees by race. Such conduct can rarely be justified. The court will strictly scrutinize any offered justification for such conduct. The government must show that such classification, or treatment, is required because of a compelling government interest, and no less discriminatory alternatives exist. For example, classifying employees by race, while discriminatory, may be justified if the reason is to compensate employees who had been victims of prior racial discrimination.

AFFIRMATIVE ACTION AND THE CONSTITUTION

Affirmative action has become an extremely controversial issue in recent years (see the discussion in Chapter 3). The courts have been growing more skeptical about the legality of affirmative action requirements imposed by government entities.

The U.S. Supreme Court, in the 1995 decision *Adarand Constructors, Inc. v. Pena* [515 U.S. 200], held that federal government affirmative action programs giving preferential treatment based on race or color must be justified under the "strict scrutiny" test. This test requires the government to demonstrate that the affirmative action program was necessary to achieve a compelling government purpose and that the program was "narrowly tailored" to achieve the compelling purpose. It must also show that it did not unduly harm those who were not given the preferential treatment.

A majority of the Supreme Court upheld the use of affirmative action in admissions by a public university, the University of Michigan, in two cases, *Grutter v. Bollinger* [123 S.Ct. 2325 (2003)] and *Gratz v. Bollinger* [123 S.Ct. 2411 (2003)]. In these cases, which did not deal with employment, the Supreme Court held that achieving the educational benefits of a diverse student body was a compelling governmental interest. Extending the rationale of these cases to employment would indicate that achieving the benefits of a diverse work force may be a sufficiently compelling governmental interest to justify the use of affirmative action programs for hiring or promotion decisions by public sector employers. However, an affirmative action program must also be narrowly tailored to achieve the compelling governmental purpose. The courts have held that affirmative action programs that give a relative preference rather than an absolute one—race or gender is used as a "plus factor" rather than as the determinative factor—are narrowly tailored. Programs that are temporary and that will cease when the employer achieves a more diverse work force have also been held to be narrowly tailored.

Wygant v. Jackson Board of Education [476 U.S. 267 (1986)] involved an affirmative action program that was not narrowly tailored. In this case, the collective-bargaining agreement between a public school board and the teachers' union contained an affirmative action program in the event that layoffs of teachers were necessary. Layoffs would be based on seniority ("last hired, first fired") unless the effect of the seniority-based layoffs would reduce the percentage of minority teachers at a given school below the percentage of minority students in that school. If that were the case, the affirmative action program would require the layoff of senior nonminority teachers ahead of minority teachers with less seniority. The purpose of the plan was to ensure the presence of minority teachers in the schools so that the minority teachers could serve as role models for minority students and encourage them to get an education. Wygant, a white teacher who lost her job under the affirmative action plan, brought suit, arguing that the plan calling for race-based layoffs was in violation of the Equal Protection Clause of the Fourteenth Amendment. The Supreme Court held that although providing role models for minority students might be a compelling governmental purpose, a plan requiring the layoff of teachers because of their race was "not sufficiently narrowly tailored" to the achievement of that purpose. The Court stated "the . . . selection of layoffs as the means to accomplish even a valid purpose cannot satisfy the demands of the Equal Protection Clause."

Remedial affirmative action programs—that is, programs adopted to remedy illegal discrimination—have generally been held to be constitutional. In *Local 28, Sheet Metal Workers Int. Ass'n. v. EEOC* [478 U.S. 421 (1986)], the U.S. Supreme Court held that courts may impose affirmative action programs to remedy "persistent or egregious discrimination," even if the affirmative action plan had the effect of benefiting individuals who were not themselves victims of discrimination. The Court emphasized that affirmative action programs should be imposed by a court only as a last resort and that such programs should be "tailor[ed] . . . to fit the nature of the violation" the court seeks to remedy. In *Local 93, Int. Ass'n. of Firefighters v. Cleveland* [478 U.S. 501 (1986)], the Supreme Court held that the parties in an employment discrimination suit may enter into a settlement agreement (known as a consent decree) requiring an affirmative action program where the employer has been found guilty of discrimination. The consent decree's affirmative action program may benefit minority employees who were not personally victims of illegal employment discrimination.

In *U.S. v. Paradise* [480 U.S. 149 (1987)], the Supreme Court upheld a court-ordered affirmative action plan that required the Alabama Public Safety Department to promote to corporal one African American state trooper for every white trooper promoted, until either African Americans occupied 25 percent of the corporal positions or until the department instituted a promotion policy that did not have an adverse impact on African American troopers. The majority held that the order was necessary to remedy past "pervasive, systematic and obstinate" discrimination by the department.

DIFFERING VIEWS OF AFFIRMATIVE ACTION

THE WORKING LAW

These extracts from the Supreme Court opinion in *Grutter v. Bollinger* [123 S.Ct. 2325 (2003)] reflect the differing views on the legality of government racial preferences.

Justice O'Connor for the court:

. . . It is true that some language in [prior Supreme Court] opinions might be read to suggest that remedying past discrimination is the only permissible justification for race-based governmental action. [citations omitted] But we have never held that the only governmental use of race that can survive strict scrutiny is remedying past discrimination. . . . Today, we hold that the Law School has a compelling interest in attaining a diverse student body.

The Law School's educational judgment that such diversity is essential to its educational mission is one to which we defer. The Law School's assessment that diversity will, in fact, yield educational benefits is substantiated by respondents and their *amici*. Our scrutiny of the interest asserted by the Law School is no less strict for taking into account complex educational judgments in an area that lies primarily within the expertise of the university. . . .

We have long recognized that, given the important purpose of public education and the expansive freedoms of speech and thought associated with the university environment, universities occupy a special niche in our constitutional tradition. . . . Our conclusion that the Law School has a compelling interest in a diverse student body is informed by our view that attaining a diverse student body is at the heart of the Law School's proper institutional mission, and that "good faith" on the part of a university is "presumed" absent "a showing to the contrary." . . .

Even in the limited circumstance when drawing racial distinctions is permissible to further a compelling state interest, government is still "constrained in how it may pursue that end: [T]he means chosen to accomplish the [government's] asserted purpose must be specifically and narrowly framed to accomplish that purpose." The purpose of the narrow tailoring requirement is to ensure that "the means chosen 'fit' . . . th[e] compelling goal so closely that there is little or no possibility that the motive for the classification was illegitimate racial prejudice or stereotype." . . . That inquiry must be calibrated to fit the distinct issues raised by the use of race to achieve student body diversity in public higher education. . . .

To be narrowly tailored, a race-conscious admissions program cannot use a quota system—it cannot "insulat[e] each category of applicants with certain desired qualifications from competition with all other applicants." Instead, a university may consider race or ethnicity only as a "'plus' in a particular applicant's file," without "insulat[ing] the individual from comparison with all other candidates for the available seats." In other words, an admissions program must be "flexible enough to consider all pertinent elements of diversity in light of the particular qualifications of each applicant, and to place them on the same footing for consideration, although not necessarily according them the same weight."

We find that the Law School's admissions program bears the hallmarks of a narrowly tailored plan. . . .

Justice Thomas, in dissent:

A close reading of the Court's opinion reveals that all of its legal work is done through one conclusory statement: The Law School has a "compelling interest in securing the educational benefits of a diverse student body." No serious effort is made to explain how these benefits fit with the state interests the Court has recognized (or rejected) as compelling, or to place any theoretical constraints on an enterprising court's desire to discover still more justifications for racial discrimination. . . .

Justice Powell's opinion in *Bakke* and the Court's decision today rest on the fundamentally flawed proposition that racial discrimination can be contextualized so that a goal, such as classroom aesthetics, can be compelling in one context but not in another. This "we know it when we see it" approach to evaluating state interests is not capable of judicial application. Today, the Court insists on radically expanding the range of permissible uses of race to something as trivial (by comparison) as the assembling of a law school class. I can only presume that the majority's failure to justify its decision by reference to any principle arises from the absence of any such principle.

Under the proper standard, there is no pressing public necessity in maintaining a public law school at all and, it follows, certainly not an elite law school. Likewise, marginal improvements in legal education do not qualify as a compelling state interest. . . .

OTHER CONSTITUTIONAL ISSUES

Some forms of discrimination involve classifications that may be more neutral than racial classifications. The courts refer to such classifications as "nonsuspect" classes. When discrimination is based on nonsuspect classes, the court will consider whether the discriminatory classification bears a reasonable relationship to a valid state interest. For example, in *Personnel Administrator of Massachusetts v. Feeney* [442 U.S. 256 (1979)], the Supreme Court upheld a Massachusetts law that required all veterans to be given preference for state civil service positions over nonveterans, even though the law had the effect of discriminating against women because veterans were overwhelmingly male. The classification of applicants on the basis of veteran status was reasonably necessary for the valid government objective of rewarding veterans for the sacrifices of military service.

In *Cleveland Board of Education v. LaFleur* [414 U.S. 632 (1974)], the Supreme Court struck down a rule imposing a mandatory maternity leave on teachers reaching the fifth month of pregnancy on grounds that it violated the due process rights of the teachers. The rule denied the teachers the freedom of personal choice over matters of family life, and it was not shown to be sufficiently related to the school-board interests of administrative scheduling and protecting the health of teachers. The rule had the effect of classifying every teacher reaching the fifth month of pregnancy as being physically incapable of performing the duties of the job, when such teacher's ability or inability to perform during pregnancy is an individual matter.

Personal grooming requirements and restrictions on hair length and facial hair for police officers were upheld by the Supreme Court in *Kelley v. Johnson* [425 U.S. 238 (1976)] because they were reasonably related to the maintenance of discipline among members of the police force. In *Goldman v. Weinberger* [475 U.S. 503 (1976)], the Supreme Court dismissed a challenge under the First Amendment to an Air Force uniform regulation that prevented an Orthodox Jew from wearing his yarmulke while on duty. Despite the fact that the yarmulke was unobtrusive, the regulations were justified by the Air Force interest in maintaining morale and discipline, which were held to be legitimate military ends.

STATE EEO AND EMPLOYMENT LAWS

The discussion of EEO law in this and preceding chapters has focused mainly on federal legislation. In addition to the various federal laws, most states also have their own equal employment opportunity legislation or regulations. State laws figure into the enforcement of federal laws. Recall that under Title VII, persons complaining of employment discrimination must file with the appropriate state or local EEO agency before taking their complaint to the federal Equal Employment Opportunity Commission. Such state or local EEO laws may provide greater protection than the federal legislation does. For example, the Michigan Civil Rights Act specifically prohibits discrimination based on height or weight, and the District of Columbia Human Rights Law prohibits discrimination based on personal appearance or political affiliation. The New York State Human Rights Law prohibits age discrimination in employment against employees aged eighteen or older (unless age is a bona fide occupational qualification [BFOQ]).

Choose a state from the lists at **http://www.law.cornell.edu:80/topics/state_statutes.html#labor,** *or* **http://www.law.cornell.edu/states/index.html**

Gender Discrimination

All state EEO laws prohibit gender discrimination in terms or conditions of employment, except in those instances where sex may be a BFOQ. Some state laws, such as Minnesota's Human Rights Act, specifically prohibit sexual harassment in addition to the general prohibition on gender discrimination. Maine law requires employers to post a notice in the workplace informing employees that sexual harassment is illegal and describing how to file a complaint of sexual harassment with the Maine Human Rights Commission.

Sexual Orientation Discrimination

Although federal law does not prohibit discrimination because of sexual orientation or sexual preference, a number of states have legislation prohibiting such discrimination. California, Connecticut, Hawaii, Massachusetts, Minnesota, Nevada, New Jersey, Rhode Island, Vermont, Wisconsin, Maryland, New York, and the District of Columbia prohibit employment discrimination based on sexual orientation or sexual preference by public and private sector employers. Several other states, including Louisiana, Michigan, New Mexico, Ohio, Pennsylvania, and Washington, prohibit public sector employers from discriminating because of sexual orientation or sexual preference through executive orders issued by the governor. In some large cities, including New York City and San Francisco, local ordinances prohibit employment discrimination because of sexual orientation or sexual preference.

Family Friendly Legislation

A number of states have legislation similar to the federal Family and Medical Leave Act, which allows employees to take unpaid leave for childbirth, adoption, or serious illness of a child, parent, or spouse. California's Fair Employment and Housing Act requires that an employer reinstate an employee returning from pregnancy leave to her previous job, unless that job was unavailable because of business necessity. In that case, an employer is required to make a reasonable, good-faith effort to provide a similar position for the employee. New York law protects the right of a mother to breast-feed her child in any public or private place where she is authorized to be. Several states require that employers allow employees time off (without pay) to attend their children's school meetings or conferences if held during normal working hours. The number of hours allowed per year varies by state, and Nevada simply prohibits an employer from discharging an employee for absences due to school conferences or meetings. In each case, the employee is required to give appropriate advance notice to the employer.

OTHER EMPLOYMENT LEGISLATION

Whistleblower Laws

A number of federal and state laws provide some protection for whistleblowers—employees who report employer wrongdoing or actions threatening public health or safety. The federal Civil Service Reform Act [5 U.S.C. § 2303] provides general protection for civil service workers from any discipline or retaliation because they have disclosed a violation of laws or regulations, gross mismanagement or a gross waste of funds, or a substantial and specific danger to the public health or safety. The federal Office of Special Counsel is responsible for investigating and pursuing claims of whistleblowers. A number of specific federal laws provide protection from retaliation for employees who report violations of those laws. Examples include the Safe Drinking Water Act, which protects employees who report illegal pollution of water, and the Federal Mine Health and Safety Act, which protects employees reporting mine safety violations.

The Sarbanes-Oxley Act of 2002, which was passed in response to the corporate scandals involving Enron and Worldcom, imposes both civil and criminal penalties for employers who take adverse employment actions against whistleblowers. The criminal provisions make it a federal crime to retaliate knowingly against persons who provide information to law enforcement officials relating to the possible commission of any federal offense. Penalties include fines of up to \$250,000 and imprisonment of up to ten years for individual violators and fines of up to \$500,000 for corporations. The civil provisions are administered by the Department of Labor; remedies available under the civil provisions include reinstatement, back pay, legal fees and costs, and compensatory damages.

All fifty states and the District of Columbia have some form of whistleblower laws. Some state laws, such as those of Connecticut, Florida, Hawaii, and Maine, cover both private and public sector employees; most such laws, however, cover only public sector workers. In California, Louisiana, and New Jersey, both public and private sector employees who reasonably believe that an employer is acting illegally are protected if they report such actions to the authorities. New York has separate legislation for public and private employers. In New York, public sector employees who reasonably believe that their employer has violated the law, and that the violation poses a "substantial and specific danger" to public health or safety, are protected.

The following case raises the question of whether that same "reasonable belief" standard should apply to employees who report alleged wrongdoing under New York's private sector whistleblower law [N.Y.S. Labor Law § 740].

Green v. Saratoga A.R.C.

233 A.D.2d 821, 650 N.Y.S.2d 441 (N.Y. App. Div. 1996)

Carpinello, Justice

. . . Plaintiff [Green] was formerly employed as a residence counselor at defendant's Washington Street Intermediate Care Facility (hereinafter the facility) in the City of Saratoga Springs, Saratoga County. In her capacity as residence counselor, plaintiff was responsible for taking care of the needs of the developmentally disabled clients who lived in the facility. In late 1988 and early 1989, she reported to her immediate supervisor that she had observed two other employees using illegal drugs during the late-night shift. Plaintiff's supervisor instructed plaintiff to call her at home if she observed any other suspicious behavior and came into the facility one evening after receiving a telephone call from plaintiff about potential trouble there. However, unsatisfied with the supervisor's response, plaintiff arranged a meeting with a higher-level supervisor, who did undertake an investigation of the allegations.

Plaintiff also contacted the Saratoga County Sheriff's Department, who referred the matter to the Office of Mental Retardation and Developmental Disabilities [OMRDD], the State agency with regulatory oversight over defendant. OMRDD undertook its own investigation of plaintiff's allegations. Defendant, OMRDD and the Sheriff's Department all found plaintiff's allegations to be unsubstantiated.

. . . [The] plaintiff claims that as the result of her reports to public authorities of suspected drug use at the facility, she was subjected to a campaign of harassment, intimidation and retaliation in violation of [the New York whistleblower law]. . . . Specifically, she alleges that defendant placed written reprimands in her file, tried to force her to resign, placed her on two-week suspension and ultimately sought to transfer her to another facility. [Green filed suit against her former employer, alleging a violation of the New York State whistleblower law and claims for defamation and intentional infliction of emotional distress. The trial court granted the employer's motion for summary judgment, dismissing Green's suit. Green appealed.] The . . . [trial court] stated that it was constrained by . . . *Bordell v. General Elec. Co.*, which held that Labor Law § 740 requires proof of an actual violation of a law, rule or regulation and that an employee's good-faith reasonable belief that a violation may have occurred is not enough. . . .

Plaintiff argues that we should reconsider our decision in *Bordell v. General Elec. Co.*, and hold that Labor Law § 740 requires only that an employee have a "reasonable belief" that a law, rule or regulation has been violated in order to qualify for the statute's protections. Since plaintiff's main brief was filed, however, the [New York] Court of Appeals affirmed our decision in *Bordell v. General Elec. Co.*, and held that a plaintiff must demonstrate an actual violation of law to sustain a cause of action under the statute. Plaintiff's argument that a different standard should be applied is, therefore, without merit.

In the alternative, plaintiff contends that defendant retaliated against her for reporting to the Sheriff's Department that defendant had failed to comply with its own personnel policy. However, Labor Law § 740 is triggered only by a violation of a law, rule or regulation that creates and presents a substantial and specific danger to the public health and safety. . . . Even assuming for the sake of argument that defendant violated its own personnel policy or the [New York State] regulation requiring the implementation of that policy, plaintiff has failed to demonstrate that the alleged violation threatened the health or safety of the public-at-large. . . . While the alleged misconduct may have posed a danger to certain individual residents of the facility, plaintiff has completely failed to show that it posed a danger to the public. . . .

Ordered that the order is affirmed, without costs.

Case Questions

1. What alleged violations of law did Green report? Did the investigations resulting from Green's complaints establish that there were legal violations by her employer?
2. According to Green, how did her employer respond to her reports of wrongdoing? Did the employer's actions against Green violate the New York whistleblower law? Explain your answers.
3. Did Green have a reasonable belief that the conduct she reported involved violations of the law? Why should that matter for her whistleblower law claim? Would the result of this case have been different if Green actually established that the employer was involved in illegal conduct? Explain.

Criminal Record

Federal EEO laws do not specifically prohibit employment discrimination based on criminal record; however, refusing to hire applicants because of their arrest records (as opposed to convictions) may violate Title VII. Some states have specific prohibitions on discrimination because of criminal records. The New York State Human Rights Law prohibits employment discrimination because of prior criminal convictions, unless such convictions have a direct and specific relationship to the job being sought or when granting employment to the individual would involve an unreasonable risk to the property or safety of others or the general public. The New York Human Rights Law also specifically prohibits employers from seeking information about arrests that did not result in a conviction, although this restriction does not apply to applicants for employment as law enforcement officers or to governmental bodies that grant licenses for guns or firearms.

Some states require that employers conduct criminal record background checks on applicants for certain positions: Tennessee law requires applicants for jobs with public schools to disclose any prior convictions; Texas law allows institutions of higher education to obtain background checks on applicants for security-sensitive positions; Vermont requires persons employed as private security officers, armed guards or couriers, guard dog handlers, and applicants for private detective licenses to undergo background checks for prior convictions; Missouri requires criminal background checks for persons working as home care providers, youth service workers, school bus drivers, and nursing home workers; North Carolina requires a background check for applicants and employees in nuclear power plants; and Indiana law requires criminal background checks for employees of the state Lottery Commission. A growing number of states, including Delaware, Florida, Hawaii, Indiana, Missouri, Nebraska, New York, and Virginia, require criminal background checks for employees involved in child care or day care.

Polygraph Testing

The federal Employee Polygraph Protection Act of 1988 (EPPA) severely restricts the right of private employers to require employees to take polygraph, or "lie detector," tests; many states have similar laws. The EPPA does not apply to public sector employers; it prohibits private sector employers, unless they fall under one of four exceptions, from requiring employees or applicants to submit to polygraph tests as a condition of employment. Employers are also prohibited from disciplining or discharging any employees because they refused to submit to a polygraph test. The exceptions under the EPPA allow polygraph testing under the following circumstances: (1) private employees who are working as consultants to, or employees of, firms that are contractors to federal national security intelligence operations; (2) employers engaged in the provision of private security services, armored car services, or the installation and maintenance of security alarm systems may require polygraph testing of certain prospective employees; (3) employers whose business involves the manufacture, sale, or distribution of controlled substances (drugs) are authorized to test employees who have direct access to the controlled substances; and (4) employers who have a reasonable basis to suspect that employees may have been involved in an incident that resulted in economic loss to the employer may request that those employees take polygraph tests.

The EPPA requires that any polygraph test must be administered by a validly licensed examiner. An employer that requests employees to submit to a polygraph test under the fourth exception (ongoing investigation into an economic loss) must meet specific procedural requirements: (1) the employer must provide the employees with a written statement describing the incident being investigated, specifically identifying the economic loss and the reason for testing the particular employees; (2) the employees must be given a written notice of the date, time, and location of the test; (3) the employees must read, and sign, a written notice that they cannot be required to submit to the test as a condition of employment; and (4) the employees have the right to review all questions that will be asked during the test and are informed that they have the right to terminate the test at any time. The EPPA specifically forbids the polygraph operator from asking any questions relating to religious beliefs, beliefs or opinions on racial matters, political beliefs or affiliations, any questions relating to sexual behavior, and any questions relating to beliefs, affiliations, or lawful activities of labor unions.

After the test has been administered, the employer must furnish the employees with a written copy of the examiner's conclusions regarding their test, a copy of questions asked, and their charted responses. The polygraph examiner may only disclose information acquired through the test to the employer requesting the test and to the employees subjected to the test; the employer may only disclose information to the employees involved.

Even when an employer may legally administer a polygraph test under the EPPA, and the employer has complied with the procedural requirements, the employer may not discharge, discipline, or otherwise deny employment to an individual solely on the basis of the polygraph test results. The employer must have additional evidence to support any employment action taken against the tested employees. The EPPA is enforced by the federal Secretary of Labor, who may assess civil penalties of up to $10,000 against violators. In addition, individual employees or applicants who allege violations of the EPPA may bring a civil suit for damages, reinstatement, back pay, benefits, and legal fees; the time limit for bringing such suits is three years from the alleged violation. *Rubin v. Tourneau, Inc.* [797 F.Supp. 247 (S.D.N.Y. 1992)] held that the company performing the polygraph test may be sued, along with the employer, by an employee alleging violations of the EPPA. Failure to comply with the EPPA's procedural requirements is a violation subject to civil suit according to *Mennen v. Easter Stores* [951 F.Supp. 838 (N.D. Iowa 1997)] and *Long v. Mango's Tropical Cafe, Inc.* [958 F.Supp. 612 (S.D. Fla. 1997)].

Honesty Testing

Because federal and state legislation generally prohibits employers from requiring employees to take polygraph tests, some employers have turned to other "honesty" tests in an attempt to evaluate employees or applicants. These are usually "paper-and-pencil" tests and may include psychological profile testing. (Most psychological profile tests are generally not intended to be used as an employment screening device, but employers may choose to use them as part of the hiring process.) The honesty tests seek to measure various workplace behaviors such as truthfulness, perceptions about the pervasiveness of employee theft, illegal drug use, and admissions of theft. There is some controversy over the validity of honesty tests: A 1990 study by the federal Office of Technology and Assessment found research on the effectiveness of such tests inconclusive, but a 1991 study by the American Psychological Association was much more positive and favorable.

The federal EPPA does not prohibit honesty testing, and neither does most state legislation. However, Massachusetts specifically prohibits employers from using honesty tests; Rhode Island bars using honesty tests as the primary basis of employment decisions, and Wisconsin also limits the use of honesty tests by employers. The use of psychological profile tests as an employee selection device could possibly raise issues under the Americans with Disabilities Act or state antidiscrimination legislation (see Chapter 6). Employers desiring to use psychological profile tests should have a legitimate, work-related rationale for the testing.

Off-Duty Conduct

A number of states protect employees from employment discrimination because of their lawful, off-the-job conduct. This legislation is mainly designed to protect smokers or tobacco users from employment discrimination as long as their tobacco use is off duty. Tennessee law protects the off-duty use of "agricultural products not regulated by the alcoholic beverage commission." New York and Minnesota protect the "legal use of consumable products" off duty, covering alcohol as well as tobacco. States such as Illinois, Minnesota, Montana, New York, North Carolina, South Dakota, West Virginia, Wisconsin, and Wyoming protect off-duty smokers from employment discrimination but do allow employers to differentiate between smokers and nonsmokers in the costs of insurance and medical benefits, as long as the cost differential reflects the actual difference in the cost of coverage.

The New York State Labor Law [§ 201-d] probably goes the farthest in protecting off-the-job activities; it prohibits employers from discriminating against employees because of their legal off-duty recreational or political activities. On the question of whether an employee's affair with a co-worker was protected "recreational activity" under the legislation, there is a split among the courts: A state appellate court, *NYS v. Wal-Mart Stores* [207 A.D.2d 150, 621 N.Y.S.2d 158 (N.Y.A.D. 1995)], and the U.S. Court of Appeals for the Second Circuit, *McCavitt v. Swiss Reinsurance America Corp.* [237 F.3d 166 (2001)], have held that such conduct is

ETHICAL DILEMMA: AN ADDITIONAL CHARGE FOR SMOKERS?

As the Employee Benefits Manager at Immense Multinational Business (IMB), you are responsible for trying to hold down the cost of employee medical insurance while still providing comprehensive quality medical care to IMB employees. Lately, you have noticed that some employees, usually those who smoke, have significantly higher medical claims than nonsmokers. Studies indicate that employees who smoke a pack of cigarettes a day have claims that are 18 percent higher than those of nonsmokers; smokers are 29 percent more likely than nonsmokers to have annual medical claims over $5,000. Estimates by the American Lung Association indicate that the medical benefits for smokers cost at least $1,000 more per year than for nonsmokers.

Based on such information, you are considering whether IMB should impose an additional annual charge of $500 for medical benefits and insurance coverage on employees who are smokers. Would such an additional charge for smokers be legal? What arguments can you make for imposing the additional charge on smokers? What arguments can you make for not imposing the additional charge? Should IMB impose the additional charge? Explain your answers.

not protected, but a federal district court has held that an employee's cohabitation with a former employee was protected, *Pasch v. Katz Media Corp.* [101 I.E.R. Cas. 1574, 1995 WL 469719 (S.D.N.Y. 1995)].

SUMMARY

- In addition to the primary EEO laws at the federal level, other legislation protects employees from some other forms of discrimination in employment. The Civil Rights Acts of 1866 and 1870 allow persons who are victims of intentional discrimination to sue for damages: 42 U.S.C. Section 1981 can be used against intentional race or national origin discrimination, and 42 U.S.C. Section 1983 can be used for intentional discrimination by public sector employers.
- Government contractors are subject to the affirmative action requirements of Executive Order 11246, and employees who serve in the military are protected from employment discrimination by the Uniformed Services Employment and Reemployment Rights Act. The National Labor Relations Act may provide employees with legal remedies against employment discrimination.
- Public sector employers are subject to the constitutional equal protection and due process provisions that prohibit intentional discrimination. The federal courts are becoming increasingly skeptical about governmental affirmative action programs, which entail preferential discrimination based on race or gender. State employment discrimination and employment laws supplement federal legislation and provide additional protection for employees.

QUESTIONS

1. Against which kinds of discrimination can 42 U.S.C. Section 1981 be used? What remedies are available to plaintiffs under 42 U.S.C. Section 1981?
2. When are employees protected from discrimination because of their service in the U.S. military forces? What must the employees do to receive such protection? What remedies are available under the USERRA?
3. Against which kinds of discrimination can 42 U.S.C. Section 1983 be used? What remedies are available under 42 U.S.C. Section 1983?
4. When are employers subject to the obligations of E.O. 11246? What does E.O. 11246 require of employers?
5. Can a public sector employer use affirmative action to give hiring preference to female applicants? Can that public sector employer give females preference when deciding which employees to lay off? Explain your answers.
6. Must employers grant their employees time off to attend meetings with their children's teachers? Explain.
7. Can federal government employees bring an employment discrimination suit under 42 U.S.C. Section 1981? Under 42 U.S.C. Section 1983? Explain. What other remedies can they pursue?
8. Does the U.S. Constitution prohibit all employment discrimination based on race? Explain your answer.

CASE PROBLEMS

1. Keller worked for the Maryland Department of Social Services. She sued both the department and the state after she was denied promotion to case worker associate III. She argued that the state had violated Title VII and Section 1983 by refusing to promote her because she was African American. The state moved for dismissal of Keller's Section 1983 count, arguing that Title VII provides a concurrent and more comprehensive remedy and, therefore, preempts Keller from coming under Section 1983.

   How should the court rule? See *Keller v. Prince George's County Department of Social Services* [616 F. Supp. 540 (D. Md. 1985)].

2. Marta Davis sued her employer under Section 1981 of the 1866 Civil Rights Act, claiming she was discriminated against because of her Hispanic ancestry. The company contended that Section 1981 was passed in 1866 in response to the enactment of "black codes" in several states, which prevented African Americans from exercising fundamental rights to which they were entitled as part of their newly acquired citizenship. The company asserts that because this was the clear congressional purpose for passing Section 1981, it cannot be stretched to cover national origin discrimination.

   Do you agree? See *Davis v. Boyle-Midway, Inc.* [615 F. Supp. 560 (N.D. Ga. 1985)].

3. Alice Bobo, an African American woman, was employed by Continental Baking Company in a production position. She was fired because she refused to wear a hat as part of her uniform; she claimed that her male co-workers were not required to wear such hats. She filed suit against Continental Baking under 42 U.S.C. Section 1981, alleging that her discharge was due to gender and race discrimination.

   Can she pursue her claims under 42 U.S.C. Section 1981? Explain your answer. See *Bobo v. Continental Baking Co.* [662 F.2d 340 (5th Cir. 1981)].

4. Rita Novak was employed by Dakota Industries as General Manager: she was also a member of the U.S. Army Reserves. Her reserve unit was called up to active duty in Bosnia for six months in December 1996, and she gave the employer appropriate notice of her need to be absent from her job for that period. Upon completion of her duty in Bosnia, she returned to the job at Dakota Industries on July 7, 1997. She was reemployed at the same rate of pay as she received prior to leaving for Bosnia, but the employer did not give her the general pay increase granted by Dakota to all employees in May 1997. Novak informed the employer that she was entitled to receive the May 1997 pay increase, but the employer refused and told her she was lucky to have a job at all. Three weeks later, Novak informed her employer that she was required to attend a two-day training program for the Reserves and that she would be absent from work on August 14 and 15, 1997. The employer complained about the disruption caused by her absence during her service in Bosnia and informed her that her Reserve duty was "too much trouble" and that she was needed on the job. Novak then presented a copy of her reserve orders to report for the training session, along with a written request for a two-day leave; the employer told her that if she went, she "shouldn't come back." When Novak did not appear for work on August 14, the employer prepared a check for her, with the notation "final pay owing as of termination date, August 14, 1997." The employer presented the check to Novak when she reported for work August 18, told her she was fired, and asked for her keys.

   What legal remedies can Novak pursue against Dakota Industries? What steps should she take to pursue a claim, and what is her likelihood of success? What remedies can she recover? Explain your answers. See *Novak v. Mackintosh* [937 F.Supp. 873 (D.S.D. 1996)].

5. Porter, an African American male, was rejected as an applicant for the Washington, D.C., Police Department because he failed to pass Test 21, a verbal facility and reading comprehension test. Porter discovers that African Americans fail Test 21 at a rate four times higher than that of Caucasian applicants. Porter files suit against the D.C. Police Department, alleging that the use of Test 21 constitutes race discrimination in violation of the Constitution's Equal Protection clause.

How should the court rule on his claim? Can he bring any other legal challenges to the use of Test 21? Explain. See *Washington v. Davis* [426 U.S. 229 (1976)].

6. Joseph K. Bonacorsa had been involved in the harness racing industry for a number of years; he was licensed by the New York State Racing and Wagering Board as both a harness owner and a driver. He had been convicted of perjury for lying under oath that he and his wife owned several horses. These horses were in fact owned by Gerald Forrest, who had previously been found guilty of conspiring to fix races at harness tracks and was therefore legally barred from owning licensed race horses. When Bonacorsa was convicted of perjury, the New York State Racing and Wagering Board revoked his harness owner and driver license. Bonacorsa served two years in prison and was on probation for a number of years. When his probation period ended, he was issued a certificate of good conduct by the N.Y. Board of Parole. Upon receiving the certificate, Bonacorsa applied to the State Racing and Wagering Board to reinstate his harness owner and driver license; the Racing and Wagering Board refused to reinstate his license because his prior conviction was conduct that "impugned the integrity of racing within the state." Bonacorsa decided to pursue a legal challenge to the board's refusal to grant him a license.

Under what legal provisions can he sue to challenge the refusal to grant him a license? What is his likelihood of success? Explain. See *Bonacorsa v. Lindt* [129 A.D.2d 518, 514 N.Y.S.2d 370 (N.Y.A.D. 1987)].

7. Christine Noland was employed as an administrative assistant in the County Assessor's Office in Comanche County, Oklahoma. Her immediate supervisor was Robert McAdoo; McAdoo was initially the county Deputy Assessor and was later promoted to the Assessor position. Throughout the period of her employment, Noland claims that McAdoo subjected her to unwelcome sexual advances, remarks, and physical contact. McAdoo would put his arm around her waist or neck despite the fact that she continually told him to stop. McAdoo would also stand in a doorway so that Noland had to rub against him to pass through. When Noland refused McAdoo's request that he and she attend an out-of-town conference, she was fired. Noland filed suit under 42 U.S.C. Section 1983 against both the county and McAdoo personally, alleging sexual harassment.

Can Noland bring a sexual harassment claim under 42 U.S.C. Section 1983? Can McAdoo personally be held liable under 42 U.S.C. Section 1983? Does Noland have any other statutory remedies available? Explain your answers. See *Noland v. McAdoo* [39 F.3d 269 (10th Cir. 1994)].

8. Neves sued the U.S. Department of Housing and Urban Development (HUD), alleging employment discrimination in violation of Title VII and also, in the alternative, violation of her rights under the Constitution. HUD argues that Neves's exclusive remedy is under Title VII, and therefore, the constitutional count should be dismissed.

Is HUD correct? Explain your answer. See *Neves v. Kolaski* [602 F. Supp. 645 (D. Rhode Is. 1985)].

9. Green, an African American male, applied for a clerical position with the Missouri-Pacific Railroad but was not hired because he had a criminal record. Green had been convicted of refusing to report for induction into the armed forces in 1971 and had served four years in federal prison. Green's refusal to report for induction was based on his religious beliefs. After serving his sentence, he had been employed by a public service agency for eighteen years; his work record was excellent. Green had no other arrests or convictions on his record. Missouri-Pacific had a policy of refusing to hire any person convicted of a criminal offense.

What, if any, legal remedies can Green pursue against Missouri-Pacific? Would he have any additional remedies if the office where he applied was located in Alabama? In New York? Explain your answers. See *Green v. Missouri-Pacific Railroad* [549 F.2d 1158 (8th Cir. 1977)].

10. A New York State constitutional provision and a civil service statute required that military veterans with wartime service be granted extra points on competitive exams for state civil service jobs. Wartime vets received a five-point bonus on the exam, and disabled vets received an extra ten points. However, this bonus was limited to veterans who were New York residents at the time they entered military service.

Is this affirmative action program permissible under the Constitution and federal statutory law? See *Attorney General of the State of New York v. Soto-Lopez* [476 U.S. 898 (1986)].

INTERNET EXERCISE

You are about to start a small business in your home state. In addition to the various federal laws outlined in this book, does your state have any specific protective legislative provisions that might affect your hiring or employment practices? Use the FindLaw site at **http://www.findlaw.com/index.html**. Under Legal Professionals, click the US State Resources link. Then click your state and follow the appropriate links to find any applicable protective employment or labor legislation. You might also want to visit the Web site of the Legal Information Institute of Cornell Law School at **http://www.law.cornell.edu** and click the appropriate links.

INFOTRAC KEYWORDS

http://www.infotrac-college.com

EEOC, OFCCP, Uniformed Services Employment and Reemployment Act, NLRA, affirmative action programs, whistleblowing, polygraph testing

PART 3

EMPLOYMENT LAW ISSUES

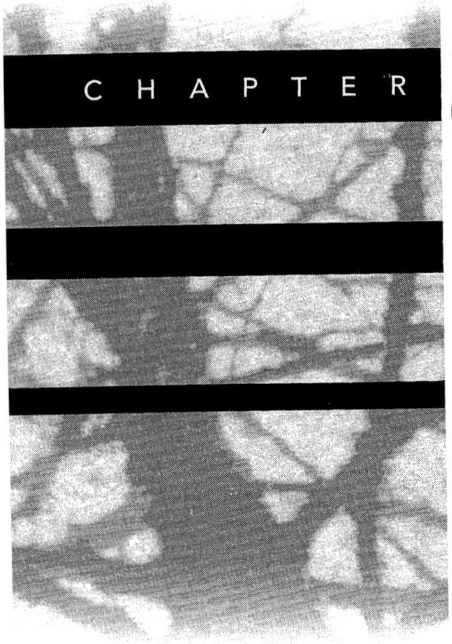

CHAPTER 8

OCCUPATIONAL SAFETY AND HEALTH

The AFL-CIO Web site has a safety section that advises visitors, "When you go to work, you shouldn't have to worry about whether you will return home at the end of the day; and you shouldn't have to return home sick, injured or maimed because your job is unsafe or unhealthy" (visit **http://www.aflcio.org/safety**). The site then offers the following facts:

- 5.7 million Americans were injured or sickened on the job in 2000.
- That year, 50,000 died from occupational illnesses.
- 5,915 were fatally injured on the job.

On September 25, 2002, the Bureau of Labor Statistics released 2001's workplace fatality data:

- Total fatalities stayed about the same at around 5,900, or 4.3 per 100,000 workers.
  - Work-related highway crashes, as usual, led the pack, accounting for 1,404 deaths.
  - Mining—including oil and gas production—remained the most dangerous occupation, killing 170, or 30 per 100,000 in the industry.
  - Agriculture, forestry, and fishing logged 740 fatalities—that is, 22.8 per 100,000.
- The "prize" for largest number of injuries in an industry went to the construction trades, which posted 1,225 fatal accidents.

For a discussion of state job safety and health programs, see **http://www.osha.gov/fso/osp/index.html**

- Not coincidentally, deaths among Hispanic workers were up 9 percent; these deaths were concentrated in construction and agricultural occupations.
- Among types of accidents, falls and electrocutions stood out as disproportionately on the increase.
- States posting spikes of +25 or more in their death rates were Alabama, Florida, Georgia, Illinois, Oklahoma, Pennsylvania, and Washington.
- In contrast to these states, Massachusetts took a bow for halving the national death rate during the decade of the nineties.[1]

As America marked the first anniversary of 9/11, the federal Centers for Disease Control reported that some 700 firefighters and paramedics who participated in the rescue and cleanup at the World Trade Center remained on medical leaves or light duty assignments. Rescue workers, lacking appropriate eye and respiratory protection in the first hours after the attack, were exposed to substantial amounts of airborne particulates. Common complaints include (1) eye, nose, and throat irritation and (2) nausea and shortness of breath.

Additionally, nearly a third of these rescue workers reported symptoms consistent with major depression according to the CDC survey. This result correlates with the fact that nearly half actually witnessed the collapse or at least the immediate aftermath. Another, probably inevitable, aspect of the aftermath is litigation. A much-publicized class action seeks to recover on behalf of the victims from a motley crew of defendants, including Osama Bin Laden, his terrorist network, and several suspected terrorist states, but less noticed is a lawsuit brought in 2002 against New York City and the Port Authority of New York and New Jersey. Styled *Graybill v. New York City,* the case accuses the defendants of negligent conduct during the cleanup. The plaintiff was injured when an unsecured, half-ton girder dropped from an unattended hydraulic-claw machine and landed in his work area. He cites sections 240 and 241 of the New York Labor Law in pleading a failure to comply with established safety standards. Commenced in state court, the case was removed to the U.S. District Court for the Southern District of New York in Manhattan by the Port Authority, which assumed the post-September 11 Air Safety Act accorded exclusive jurisdiction to the federal courts for terrorist-related aircraft crashes. However, holding that Graybill's injuries were too far removed from the initial Trade Center attack, the federal judge remanded the case to state court for adjudication. The action remained pending as this new edition was being prepared.[2]

Meanwhile, corporations across the country added disaster planning to their ever-lengthening lists of health and safety policies, procedures, and training protocols. The Occupational Health and Safety Administration for its part continued its efforts to emphasize cooperation over coercion, while—somewhat inappositely—keeping the pressure on employers to voluntarily pay attention to ergonomics, despite the demise of the agency's proposed rule in the early days of the Bush administration.

---

[1] *BNA Occupational Safety & Health Daily,* Sept. 25 & 26, 2002.

[2] *BNA Occupational Safety & Health Daily,* September 10 & 16, 2002.

PURPOSE OF THE OCCUPATIONAL SAFETY AND HEALTH ACT

The Occupational Safety and Health Act (OSHA) was enacted by Congress in 1970. The statute has two broad goals: (1) to assure safe and healthful working conditions for working men and women; and (2) to provide a framework for research, education, training, and information in the field of occupational safety and health. The act requires employers to furnish their employees a workplace that is free from recognized hazards that cause, or are likely to cause, serious injury or death. A recognized hazard is one that is known to be hazardous, taking into account the standard of knowledge of the industry.

http://www.dol.gov/dol/compliance/comp-osha.htm
describes provisions of the Occupational Safety and Health Act of 1970.

In addition to the general duty of employers to furnish a workplace free from hazards, the act requires that employers meet the various health and safety standards set under the act and keep records of injuries, deaths, accidents, illnesses, and particular hazards.

The Occupational Safety and Health Act applies to all employees who work for an employer that is engaged in a business affecting interstate commerce. This broad coverage reaches almost all employers and employees in the United States and its territories, with some exceptions. The act does not apply to the federal and state governments in their capacity as employers, nor does it apply to domestic servants or self-employed persons.

The act contains no specific industry-wide exemptions. However, if other federal agencies exercise statutory authority to prescribe or enforce standards or regulations affecting occupational safety or health, the Occupational Safety and Health Act does not apply. For this exemption to operate, it must be shown that the working conditions of the affected employees are covered by another federal statute that has the protection of employees as one of its purposes. The other agency must also have exercised its jurisdiction to make regulations or standards applying to specific working conditions that would otherwise be covered by the act. An example of such a situation involves the workers on offshore oil platforms. Their working conditions were governed by health and safety regulations enacted and enforced by both the U.S. Coast Guard and the U.S. Geological Survey. In *Marshall v. Nichols* [486 F. Supp. 615 (E.D. Texas 1980)], the court held that the Occupational Safety and Health Administration was precluded from exerting its jurisdiction over offshore oil platforms because of the coverage by the Coast Guard and the Geological Survey.

ADMINISTRATION AND ENFORCEMENT

The Occupational Safety and Health Act created three federal agencies for administration and enforcement. The Occupational Safety and Health Administration (OSHA) is the primary agency created for enforcement of the act. An independent agency within the Department of Labor, it has the authority to promulgate standards, conduct inspections of workplaces, issue citations for violations, and recommend penalties. OSHA acts on behalf of the secretary of labor.

Industry Division	All Establishments	Establishment Employment Size (workers)				
		1 to 10	11 to 49	50 to 249	250 to 999	1,000 or more
Private industry (2)	5.3	2.0	4.6	6.7	6.2	6.0
Agriculture, forestry, and fishing (2)	6.4	3.5	6.4	8.6	6.0	4.3
Mining (3)	4.0	2.1	4.0	5.3	3.9	1.3
Construction	7.1	4.0	8.0	8.6	6.2	5.5
Manufacturing	7.2	3.1	7.3	8.2	7.1	6.7
Durable goods	7.9	4.2	8.4	9.0	7.8	7.0
Nondurable goods	6.2	1.4	5.3	7.1	6.2	6.1
Transportation and public utilities (4)	6.1	2.6	5.2	7.2	6.4	6.7
Wholesale and retail trade	5.3	2.0	4.6	7.0	7.3	4.3
Wholesale trade	5.2	2.0	4.9	6.8	6.8	3.1
Retail trade	5.3	2.1	4.5	7.0	7.5	4.7
Finance, insurance, and real estate	1.7	1.2	1.6	2.3	2.0	1.3
Services	4.6	1.3	3.0	5.9	5.8	6.8

1 The incidence rates represent the number of injuries and illnesses per 100 full-time workers and were calculated as: (N/EH) x 200,000, where
N = number of injuries and illnesses
EH = total hours worked by all employees during the calendar year
200,000 = base for 100 equivalent full-time workers (working 40 hours per week, 50 weeks per year)

2 Excludes farms with fewer than 11 employees.

3 Data for mining (Division B in the Standard Industrial Classification Manual, 1987 Edition) include establishments not governed by the Mine Safety and Health Administration (MSHA) rules and reporting, such as those in oil and gas extraction. Data for mining operators in coal, metal, and nonmetal mining are provided to BLS by the Mine Safety and Health Administration, U.S. Department of Labor. Independent mining contractors are excluded from the coal, metal, and nonmetal mining industries. These data do not reflect the changes OSHA made to its recordkeeping requirements effective January 1, 2002; therefore, estimates for these industries are not comparable with estimates for other industries.

4 Data for employers in railroad transportation are provided to BLS by the Federal Railroad Administration, U.S. Department of Transportation. These data do not reflect the changes OSHA made to its recordkeeping requirements effective January 1, 2002; Therefore, estimates for these industries are not comparable with estimates for other industries.

FIGURE 8.1 Incidence rates (1) of nonfatal occupational injuries and illnesses by industry division and employment size, 2002.
Source: Bureau of Labor Statistics, U.S. Department of Labor.

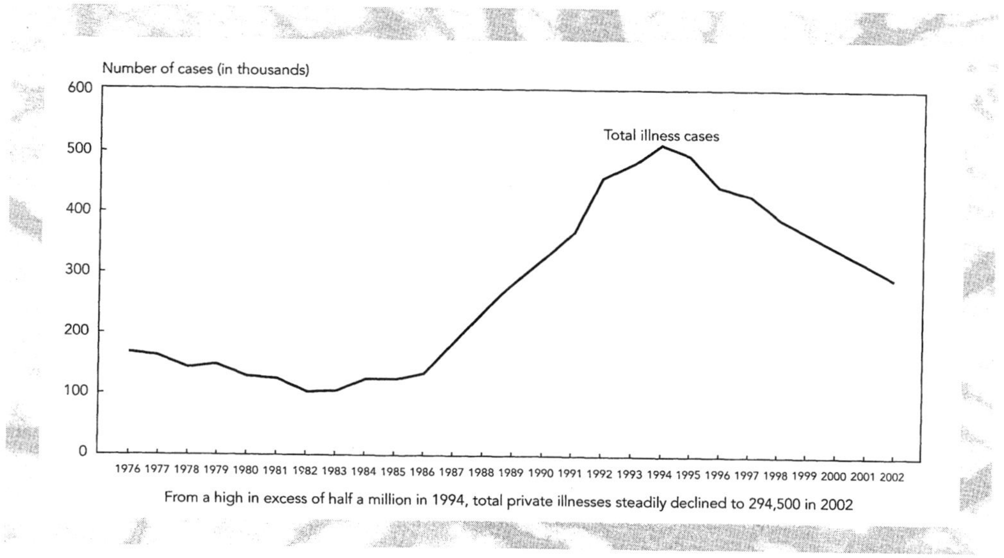

FIGURE 8.2 Occupational illness cases, private industry, 1976–2002.
Source: Bureau of Labor Statistics, U.S. Department of Labor, December 18, 2003.

http://www.osha.gov *is the main index for standards and related documents, and for OSHA programs.* **http://www.cdc.gov/niosh/homepage.html** *is the NIOSH home page.*

The National Institute of Occupational Safety and Health (NIOSH) is an agency created to conduct research and promote the application of the research results to ensure that no worker will suffer diminished health, reduced functional capacity, or decreased life expectancy as a result of his or her work experience.

The Occupational Safety and Health Review Commission (OSHRC) is a quasi-judicial agency created to adjudicate contested enforcement actions of OSHA. Whereas OSHA may issue citations and recommend penalties for violations of the act, only OSHRC can actually assess and enforce the penalties. The decisions of OSHRC can be appealed to the U.S. courts of appeals. OSHRC has three members appointed by the president for overlapping six-year terms and a number of administrative law judges who have career tenure.

Standards, Feasibility, and Variances

To reach the goal of providing hazard-free workplaces for all employees, the act provides for the setting of standards regulating the health and safety of working conditions. The secretary of labor is granted authority under the act to promulgate occupational safety and health standards through OSHA. The act provides for the issuance of three kinds of standards: interim standards, permanent standards, and emergency standards.

http://www.osha.gov/comp-links.html *is the site for OSHA standards and related documents.*

Interim Standards. Interim standards are those that the secretary of labor had power to issue for the first two years following the effective date of the act. These standards were generally modeled on various preexisting industry consensus standards. The secretary, in adopting previously accepted national consensus standards, was not required to hold public hearings or any other formal proceedings.

Permanent Standards. Permanent standards are both newly created standards and revised interim standards. These standards are developed by OSHA and NIOSH and are frequently based on suggestions made by interested parties, such as employers, employees, states and other political subdivisions, and labor unions. The secretary of labor is also empowered to appoint an advisory committee to assist in the promulgation of permanent standards. This committee has ninety days from its date of appointment, unless a longer or shorter period is prescribed by the secretary, to make its recommendations regarding a proposed rule.

After OSHA has developed a proposed rule that promulgates, modifies, or revokes an occupational safety or health standard, the secretary must publish a notice in the *Federal Register*. Included in this notice must be a statement of the reasons for either adopting a new, changing an existing, or revoking a prior standard. Interested parties are then allowed thirty days after publication to submit written data, objections, or comments relating to the proposed standards. If the interested party files written objections and requests a public hearing concerning these objections, the secretary must publish a notice in the *Federal Register* specifying the time and place of the hearing and the standard to which the objection has been filed.

Within sixty days after the expiration of the period for comment or after the completion of any hearing, the secretary must issue a rule promulgating, modifying, or revoking the standard or make a determination that the rule should not be issued. If adopted, the rule must state its effective date. This date must ensure a sufficient period for affected employers and employees to be informed of the existence of the standard and of its terms.

Emergency Standards. The secretary of labor may, under special circumstances, avoid the procedures just described by issuing temporary emergency standards. These standards are issued when the secretary believes that employees are exposed to grave dangers from substances or agents determined to be toxic or physically harmful. Actual injury does not have to occur before a temporary emergency standard can be promulgated, although there must be a genuinely serious emergency.

Emergency standards take effect immediately upon publication in the *Federal Register*. After publication, the secretary must then follow the procedure for formally adopting a permanent standard to make the emergency standard into a permanent standard. That new permanent standard must be issued within six months after its publication as an emergency standard.

Appeals of Standards. After a standard has been promulgated by the secretary, any person adversely affected by it can file a challenge to the validity of the standard. Such challenges must be filed with the appropriate federal court of appeals before the sixtieth day after the issuance of the standard.

Upon reviewing the standard, the court of appeals will uphold the standard if it is supported by substantial evidence. The secretary must demonstrate that the standard was in response to a significant risk of material health impairment.

Feasibility. The act grants the secretary authority to issue standards dealing with toxic materials or harmful physical agents. A standard must be one that most adequately assures, to the extent feasible and on the basis of the best available evidence, that no employee will suffer material impairment of health or functional capacity, even if the employee has regular exposure to the hazard. The feasibility of a standard must be examined from two perspectives: technological feasibility and economic feasibility. Further, OSHA can force an industry to develop and diffuse new technology to satisfy precise permissible exposure limits to toxic materials or harmful physical agents that have never before been attained, if OSHA can present substantial evidence showing that companies acting vigorously and in good faith can develop the technology. The standard also must satisfy the requirement of economic feasibility.

Burden of Proof. The secretary must carry the burden of proving both technological and economic feasibility when promulgating and enforcing standards governing toxic materials and harmful physical agents. However, the secretary does not have to establish that the cost of a standard bears a reasonable relationship to its benefits, as demonstrated in the case of *American Textile Mfr.'s Inst. v. Donovan* [101 S.Ct. 2478 (1981)].

In general, the secretary bears the burden of proving by "substantial evidence on the record considered as a whole" that the cited employer violated the act. The prima facie case which the secretary must prove to make an OSHA citation "stick" is well illustrated in the following case.

Trinity Industries, Inc. v. Occupational Safety and Health Review Commission

206 F.3d 539 (5th Cir., 2000)

Reynaldo G. Garza, Circuit Judge

Background

Trinity Industries operates plants that manufacture and repair railcars. Trinity also "lines" new "hopper" railcars by spraying their insides with a chemical coating designed to seal and protect the interior of a railcar. Absent proper ventilation, this lining process has the potential to create a hazardous atmosphere inside the railcar. A hazardous atmosphere is defined as one that is oxygen deficient or which contains toxic levels of a hazardous gas or dust of flammable vapors in excess of ten percent of the lower flammable limit (LFL) or lower explosive limit (LEL). At issue in this case are citations issued against Trinity based on an OSHA inspector's finding that the atmosphere inside at least one of Trinity's railcars exceeded ten percent of the LEL during the lining process.

Trinity designed a ventilation system to prevent the build up of a hazardous atmosphere, consisting of a ventilation duct on top of the railcar which pulls air out of the railcar, thus forcing fresh air to be drawn into the railcar through its bottom opening. The entire process exchanges all of the air in the railcar with air from outside the railcar every minute.

Railcars are "confined spaces" per OSHA regulations. OSHA's standard for employee entry into confined spaces governs work activities in confined spaces. A confined space is "permit required" if it contains, or has the potential to contain, a hazardous atmosphere. . . . [The applicable regulation], however, allows alternative methods of compliance if the confined space only contains a "potentially hazardous atmosphere," and if continuous ventilation alone is sufficient to maintain safe conditions. According to Trinity, . . . the employer need not comply with the costly and time consuming requirements set forth in [the remainder of the regulation].

Over a ten-year period ending with his departure from the company, Trinity's former corporate and environmental director, Jerry Riddles, tested the inside of more than a thousand railcars during the actual lining operation while the cars were ventilated. The levels of combustible and toxic vapors inside the railcars were tested with direct reading instruments placed inside the railcars. During this testing, Riddles never received a reading above ten percent of the LEL no matter which lining material was used. Based on this testing, Trinity concluded that its railcar lining operation was governed by subpart (c) rather than by subpart (d), and that its ventilation system maintained safe conditions inside the railcars during the lining operations.

The alleged violation in this case occurred at a plant in Bessemer, Alabama. Riddles tested about sixty cars at this plant as part of his ten-year program. The Bessemer plant safety directors also tested the cars periodically and found no hazardous atmosphere inside the cars during the lining process. However, during a subsequent OSHA inspection, an inspector detected levels of flammable vapor at 24–26 percent of the LEL. Notably, all of his measurements were taken from outside the railcar. Apparently, the reading instruments were placed at the opening at the bottom of the railcar where outside air is pulled in, presumably measuring the air being pulled into the car rather than directly measuring the air in the car. The inspector conceded that these readings did not tell him "the actual concentrations inside the hopper car." Trinity suggested that open paint cans in the area may have been the source for the high readings outside of the railcar, but denied that the readings were evidence of concentrations inside the railcar.

Based on these readings from outside the railcar, the Secretary of Labor found that there was a hazardous atmosphere inside the railcars despite Trinity's ventilation system. . . . Trinity was cited for, *inter alia,* failure to comply with [the regulation].

Trinity appealed the citation to an Administrative Law Judge (ALJ) who noted that there was "no evidence to dispute Trinity's claim that, under usual conditions, the ventilation system maintained flammable vapors below ten percent of the LEL," but concluded that the OSHA test established the existence of a hazardous atmosphere at the time of the inspection and therefore that the lining operation did not qualify for the . . . exception.

Trinity then petitioned the Commission for review on the grounds that the ALJ's decision was inconsistent and illogical, and that the ALJ had affirmed the confined space citation without requiring the Secretary to prove that Trinity knew or should have known of the violations. On review, the Commission held that the inspector's tests showed at least a "potential" for the atmosphere inside the cars to be hazardous when ventilated. The Commission also held that Trinity was not eligible for the . . . exception and affirmed the citations as violations. . . . Notably, the Commission declined to consider the knowledge issue, finding that it need not be addressed since it was not raised in the petition for review. On appeal, Trinity argues that even if there was a hazardous atmosphere inside the railcar (or the potential for one), there is no basis for finding that Trinity knew or should have known of this condition and thus the citations must be dismissed.

Discussion

• • •

[5][6] Since the Commission declined to address the issue of knowledge, we will conduct *de novo* review of whether the evidence of knowledge is sufficient to sustain the violation. To prove the knowledge element of its burden, the Secretary must show that the employer knew of, or with exercise of reasonable diligence could have known of the non-complying condition. When the Secretary alleges that a contaminant is present in impermissible levels, but the employer shows that it had made measurements and determined that the concentration was not excessive, the burden is on the Secretary to show that the employer's failure to discover the excessive concentration resulted from a failure to exercise reasonable diligence. Thus, in this case, the Secretary must show that Trinity knew or should have known that its ventilation was not maintaining an atmosphere below ten percent of the LEL during the lining operation.

[7] Trinity argues that the uncontroverted evidence consists of sworn testimony describing more than a thousand tests which demonstrated that its ventilation system was maintaining an atmosphere below ten percent of LEL during the lining operation. These tests were explicitly credited by the ALJ. The Secretary responds that the OSHA inspection demonstrates that Trinity was out of compliance on the day in question. Additionally, we note that the Secretary alleges that there are issues over the documentation of the tests on which Trinity relied, worker imperfection in maintaining the ventilation system, and general sloppiness, all of which are alleged to demonstrate a lack of reasonable diligence on Trinity's part. However, the most thorough evidence of the vapor levels remains the extensive testing conducted by Trinity as described by sworn testimony of the railroad safety experts who conducted the tests. On the basis of this evidence, we find that the Secretary failed in its burden of proving that Trinity knew or should have known that the levels in the railcars were improper. Therefore, we VACATE the citations issued against Trinity.

Conclusion

The citations issued against Trinity by the Secretary of Labor are hereby **VACATED.**

Case Questions

1. Why should the secretary of labor be required to prove that the employer had knowledge of a non-complying condition? Wouldn't a safer workplace result from holding employers strictly liable for conditions that don't comply with OSHA regulations?
2. How might the secretary of labor have proven that the employer had knowledge of the non-complying condition in this case?
3. How did the OSHA investigator's testing technique differ from that of the employer's own safety manager? Which technique do you feel was more appropriate?
4. Should courts second-guess the OSHA's experts when it comes to determining whether unsafe conditions exist in a workplace? Or in determining the appropriate burden of proof to place on the secretary of labor, should judges defer to the agency's judgment in these matters?

Variances If an employer, or a class of employers, believes that the OSHA standard is inappropriate to its particular situation, an exemption, or variance, may be sought. This variance may be temporary or permanent.

A temporary variance may be granted when the employer is unable to comply with a standard by its effective date because of the unavailability of professional or technological personnel or of materials or equipment necessary to come into compliance with the standard. The employer must show that all possible actions have been taken to protect employees and that all actions necessary for compliance are being undertaken. A temporary variance can be granted only after the affected employees have been given notice of the request and an opportunity for a hearing. Temporary variances can be granted for a one-year period and may then be renewed for two six-month periods.

Permanent variances are granted when the employer establishes by a preponderance of the evidence that its particular procedures provide as safe and healthful a workplace as the OSHA standard would provide. The affected employees must be informed of the request for the permanent variance and may request a hearing. If the variance is granted, either the employees or OSHA may petition to modify or revoke the variance.

The secretary of labor also has authority to issue experimental variances involving new or improved techniques to safeguard worker safety or health.

EMPLOYEE RIGHTS

In addition to being granted the right to a workplace free from recognized hazards, employees under the Occupational Safety and Health Act are protected from retaliation or discrimination by their employer because they have exercised any rights granted by the act. Section 11(c)(1) of the act provides that

See **http://www.dol.gov** *on whistleblower protection.*

> No person shall discharge or in any manner discriminate against any employee because such employee has filed any complaint or instituted or caused to be instituted any proceeding under or related to this Act or has testified or is about to testify in any such proceeding or because of the exercise by such employee on behalf of himself or others of any right afforded by this Act.

Pursuant to Section 11(c)(1), the secretary of labor has adopted a regulation that protects employees from discrimination because they refuse to work in the face of a dangerous condition. The right to refuse can be exercised when employees are exposed to a dangerous condition posing the risk of serious injury or death and when there is insufficient time, due to the nature of the hazard, to resort to the regular statutory procedures for enforcement. When possible, the employees should attempt to have the employer correct the hazardous condition before exercising their right to refuse. The dangerous condition triggering the employees' refusal must be of such a nature that a reasonable person, under the circumstances facing the employees, would conclude that there is a real danger of death or serious injury. However, as the following case amply illustrates, a worker refuses to perform his duties at his own peril, should OSHA find he behaved unreasonably.

Wood v. Herman

104 F.Supp.2d 43 (D.D.C. 2000)

Memorandum Opinion

Huvelle, District Judge

Before the Court are defendants' motion to dismiss, or in the alternative, for summary judgment, and plaintiff Wood's cross motion for summary judgment. Having considered the motions, the oppositions, the replies and the entire record herein, the Court grants defendants' motion and dismisses plaintiff's complaint with prejudice on the grounds that the Secretary of Labor's decision not to bring an enforcement action under § 11(c) of the Occupational Safety and Health Act is not reviewable by the court but is committed to the agency's discretion.

Background

Plaintiff Roger Wood appeals the decision of the Department of Labor (DoL) declining to file a complaint on his behalf for retaliatory discharge under § 11(c) of the Occupational Safety and Health Act. Wood was formerly employed as an electrician by a subsidiary of Raytheon at Johnston Atoll Chemical Agent System ("JACADS"), a chemical weapons incinerator which was located on Johnston Atoll in the Pacific Ocean and was being used to destroy a lethal chemical weapons stockpile.

Plaintiff began working at the incinerator on June 18, 1990, and he frequently complained about safety conditions at JACADS. On February 4, 1991, after repeated reprimands, plaintiff refused an assignment to work in a toxic area because Raytheon did not provide him with new corrective lenses for the facepiece of his protective mask. As a result, plaintiff was discharged. Plaintiff claims that the difference between the old prescription and the new prescription for the corrective lenses was significant, while Raytheon and the Secretary claim that it was minor. Plaintiff asserts that the discharge was in retaliation for his reporting safety violations and refusing to work under unsafe conditions. On February 15, 1991, plaintiff filed a § 11(c) complaint with the Occupational Safety and Health Administration (OSHA).

OSHA 11(c) Investigator John Braeutigam investigated plaintiff's complaint, and OSHA's San Francisco Area Office made a preliminary determination that plaintiff's complaint had merit. In compliance with standard OSHA procedure, the Area Office attempted to settle the case informally, but when this proved unsuccessful, the case was forwarded to the Regional Solicitor of Labor for legal review and possible litigation. After further research, the Secretary determined that the case was inappropriate for litigation and referred the case to the Department of Defense. In February 1996, the case was returned to OSHA, and in April 1996 National OSHA and the Solicitor's Office reviewed the case again. In a letter dated May 3, 1996, the Assistant Secretary for OSHA notified Wood that OSHA would take no further action because the right to refuse to work is very limited and plaintiff's refusal did not meet the applicable legal test. Furthermore, the Secretary explained that OSHA may not have authority in this area since the hazardous workplace in question was under the control of the Department of the Army, and Raytheon could therefore have a legal defense that would "further complicate the litigation of this matter."

Wood seeks a declaratory judgment that DoL's decision declining to bring suit pursuant to § 11(c) on his behalf was arbitrary and capricious. In response, the DoL and the Secretary of Labor have filed a motion to dismiss or, in the alternative, for summary judgment, arguing that the Secretary's decision to decline to file a § 11(c) OSHA suit is not judicially reviewable. Alternatively, the government argues that the Secretary's decision not to bring suit was reasonable under the facts and the law. Given the Court's conclusion that the Secretary's declination to bring an enforcement action is not reviewable, it need not address defendant's alternative argument.

Legal Analysis

A. The Reviewability of the Secretary's Nonenforcement Decision

[1] The Administrative Procedure Act ("APA") provides that there is a presumption of reviewability of administrative decisions unless the decision falls within one of two exceptions. The first exception is where Congress has expressly precluded judicial review by

statute. The second exception, the focus of this case, occurs when the agency action is "committed to agency discretion by law." In the seminal case relating to judicial review of enforcement actions, the Supreme Court ruled that "an agency's decision not to prosecute or enforce, whether through civil or criminal process, is a decision generally committed to an agency's absolute discretion." In [that case] prison inmates who had been sentenced to death petitioned the Food and Drug Administration, alleging that the use of certain drugs for lethal injection violated the Food, Drug and Cosmetic Act (FDCA). The prison inmates further requested that the FDA take enforcement action in light of these violations, but the FDA refused. In finding this nonenforcement decision by the FDA to be unreviewable, the Supreme Court explained:

> [A]n agency decision not to enforce often involves a complicated balancing of a number of factors which are peculiarly within its expertise. Thus, the agency must not only assess whether a violation has occurred, but whether agency resources are best spent on this violation or another, whether the agency is likely to succeed if it acts, whether the particular enforcement action requested best fits the agency's overall policies, and indeed, whether the agency has enough resources to undertake the action at all. An agency generally cannot act against each technical violation of the statute it is charged with enforcing. The agency is far better equipped than the courts to deal with the many variables involved in the proper ordering of its priorities.

Based on these policy concerns, the Court found that an agency's decision to refuse to bring an enforcement action is unsuitable for review, and therefore, it "should be presumed immune from judicial review under § 701(a)(2)," unless the statute "has provided guidelines for the agency to follow in exercising its enforcement powers." Applying this test to the FDCA, the Court found no "law to apply," for there were no "meaningful standards for defining the limits of . . . [agency enforcement] discretion." It thus concluded that the FDA's decision not to institute enforcement proceedings was "committed to agency discretion by law" within the meaning of the APA, and it left "to Congress, and not to the courts, the decision as to whether an agency's refusal to institute proceedings should be judicially reviewable."

• • •

[2] In the instant case, Section 11(c) of OSHA states: the Secretary shall cause such investigation to be made as he deems appropriate. If upon such investigation, the Secretary determines that the provisions of this subsection have been violated, he shall bring an action.

Applying the reasoning set forth in *Chaney* and its progeny, this Court is unable to discern any meaningful guidelines for the Secretary to follow in deciding whether to bring an enforcement action. The Court therefore has no standards to apply to determine if the Secretary has abused her discretion. In the absence of such standards, the *Chaney* presumption of nonreviewability must govern, and as discussed below, plaintiff cannot overcome this presumption.

• • •

Plaintiff . . . argues that the use of the word "shall" in § 11(c) demonstrates Congress' intent to limit the Secretary of Labor's discretion. While it is a recognized tenet of statutory construction that the word "shall" is usually a command, this principle has not been applied in cases involving administrative enforcement decisions. For instance, in [one recent case], the Fifth Circuit acknowledged that "shall" is typically mandatory, but "when duties within the traditional realm of prosecutorial discretion are involved, the courts have not found this maxim controlling."

• • •

Plaintiff attempts to distinguish [such] cases by arguing that they did not involve the protection of individual rights, as opposed to the public interest, and . . . the statute at issue provided for a private right of action which is not permitted under § 11(c). However, [the leading case] did not base its holding regarding reviewability on whether the statute's purpose was to protect public rights versus individual rights or whether the statute provided for a private right of action. Rather, the sole issue is whether a court has meaningful standards to apply to the agency's exercise of discretion.

Finally, plaintiff's reliance on the statutory purpose and the agency's regulations provide little support for his efforts to overcome the presumption against reviewability. While there can be no doubt that the OSH Act was intended to be a strong remedial statute and that employee reporting of violations was an important provision in achieving the goal of worker safety, it is not possible to extrapolate from this purpose a Congressional intent to provide for judicial review of the Secretary's enforcement decisions. On the contrary, § 13 of the OSH Act explicitly provides employees a right to bring an action in United States District Court against the Secretary "[i]f the Secretary arbitrarily and capriciously fails to seek relief under this section . . ." . This section demonstrates that Congress, if it so desires, knows how to place an express provision in the Act allowing for judicial review. The lack of such a clause in § 11 of the same Act argues against finding such Congressional intent. Nor do the DoL regulations pertaining to § 11(c) provide the requisite standards for judicial review of the agency's action. While these regulations address the question of what constitutes protected activity, they do not establish any guidance for determining whether the Secretary should institute enforcement proceedings.

In sum, the case law makes clear that the holding in *Dunlop* constitutes a narrow, if not unique, exception to the presumption established in *Chaney* that an agency decision to decline enforcement is not reviewable, but is committed to the Secretary's discretion. Plaintiff has failed to overcome this presumption, since Congress has not evidenced a clear intent to subject § 11(c) decisions to judicial review. While the facts presented by the plaintiff may well raise a forceful argument in favor of the institution of a civil action by the agency, authority to review the decision whether to bring such an action has not been granted to the courts.

Conclusion

Based on the foregoing, the Court concludes that the Secretary's decision not to institute enforcement proceedings on plaintiff's behalf is not reviewable, and thus, defendants' motion to dismiss is

GRANTED.

Case Questions

1. Explain the legal test for whether an employee's refusal to work is protected activity under the applicable OSHA regulations.
2. Do you think this test is too hard on employees who have to make judgments on the spot and who risk job loss if their judgments are wrong?
3. Why did the court defer to the secretary of labor's discretion in this case?
4. Is this a case in which the Department of Labor's expertise deserves greater weight than the court's own expertise in what is fair treatment and due process of law?

INSPECTIONS, INVESTIGATIONS, AND RECORDKEEPING

OSHA's occupational safety and health standards are enforced through physical inspections of workplaces. Practical realities in enforcing the act have forced OSHA to prioritize the inspection process. Thus, inspections are targeted first to the investigation of complaints of imminent danger and then to investigation of fatal and catastrophic accidents, investigation of complaints filed by employees alleging hazardous working conditions, investigation of high-hazard industries, and finally, random general investigations.

Recordkeeping Requirements

OSHA relies on several sources of information to determine when and where inspections will occur. First, employers with eight or more employees are required under the act to keep records of and to make periodic reports to OSHA on occupational injuries and illnesses. Occupational injuries must be recorded if they involve or result in death, loss of consciousness, medical treatment other than minor first aid, one or more lost workdays, the restriction of work or motion, or transfer to another job. Second, the employer is required to maintain accurate records of employee exposures to potentially toxic materials or harmful physical agents required to be monitored under the act. Third, any employee or representative of an employee who believes that a violation of a safety or health standard exists that threatens physical harm, or believes that an imminent danger exists, may request an inspection.

The site for Section 8 on Inspections, Investigations, and Recordkeeping is **http://www.osha.gov/recordkeeping/index.html**

Inspections

The compliance officer conducting the inspection may enter without delay and at reasonable times any factory, business establishment, construction site, or workplace covered by the act. This inspection may include all pertinent conditions, structures, machines, apparatus, devices, equipment, and materials on the inspection site. The office is also given authority to question privately any employer, owner, operator, agent, or employee.

The act allows the employer and a representative authorized by the employees to accompany the inspector during the physical inspection of the work site.

In *Marshall v. Barlow's Inc.* (436 U.S. 307, 1973) the Supreme Court held that an employer subject to an OSHA inspection may insist upon a search warrant.

As a result of *Marshall v. Barlow's,* the compliance officer now must request permission to enter the workplace or other area that is to be the subject of the search. If the employer refuses entry or forbids the continuation of an inspection, the compliance officer must terminate the inspection or confine it to those areas where no objection has been raised. Following such a refusal, an ex parte application for an inspection warrant can be obtained from either a U.S. district judge or a U.S. magistrate.

Sometimes the legitimacy of the inspection becomes entwined with the even knottier question of overlapping jurisdiction. For example, the U.S. Coast Guard—now a part of the new cabinet-level Department of Homeland Security created by the Homeland Security Act in 2003—enjoys jurisdiction over the navigable waterways and vessels sailing those waters. In the following case, fatal injuries aboard an oil exploration barge led to a Coast Guard investigation of the accident. Neither the Coast Guard nor OSHA had ever before inspected the vessel, and in fact, under USCG regulations, no regular inspections were required. On the basis of the investigation results, OSHA cited the vessel's owners for violations of the Occupational Safety and Health Act. Ultimately, it fell to the U.S. Supreme Court to ascertain whether OSHA has jurisdiction to piggyback onto a Coast Guard inspection/investigation and sanction the offending employer under the OSH Act and its implementing regulations.

Chao v. Mallard Bay Drilling, Inc.

534 U.S. 235 (U.S. Supreme Court 2002)

Stevens, J

Respondent operates a fleet of barges used for oil and gas exploration. On April 9, 1997, one of those barges, "Rig 52," was towed to a location in the territorial waters of Louisiana, where it drilled a well over two miles deep. On June 16, 1997, when the crew had nearly completed drilling, an explosion occurred, killing four members of the crew and injuring two others. Under United States Coast Guard regulations, the incident qualified as a "marine casualty" because it involved a commercial vessel operating "upon the navigable waters of the United States."

Pursuant to its statutory authority, the Coast Guard conducted an investigation of the casualty. The resulting report was limited in scope to what the Guard described as "purely vessel issues," and noted that the Guard "does not regulate mineral drilling operations in state waters, and does not have the expertise to adequately analyze all issues relating to the failure of an oil/natural gas well." The Coast Guard determined that natural gas had leaked from the well, spread throughout the barge, and was likely ignited by sparks in the pump room. The report made factual findings concerning the crew's actions, but did not accuse respondent of violating any Coast Guard regulations. Indeed, the report noted the limits of the Coast Guard's regulation of vessels such as Rig 52: The report explained that, although Rig 52 held a Coast Guard Certificate of Documentation, it had "never been inspected by the Coast Guard." In Coast Guard terminology, Rig 52 was an "uninspected vessel," as opposed to one of the 14 varieties of "inspected vessels" subject to comprehensive Coast Guard regulation.

Based largely on information obtained from the Coast Guard concerning this incident, the Occupational Safety and Health Administration (OSHA) cited respondent for three violations of the Occupational Safety and Health Act of 1970 (OSH Act or Act), implementing regulations. The citations alleged that the respondent failed promptly to evacuate employees on board the drilling rig; failed to develop and implement an emergency response plan to handle anticipated emergencies; and failed to train employees in emergency response. Respondent did not deny the charges, but challenged OSHA's jurisdiction to issue the citations on two grounds: that Rig 52 was not a "workplace" within the meaning of sec. 4(a) of the Act; and that sec. 4(b)(1) of the Act pre-empted OSHA occupational safety and health on vessels in navigable waters. . . .

Congress has assigned a broad and important mission to the Coast Guard. Its governing statute provides, in part:

> "The Coast Guard . . . shall administer laws and promulgate and enforce regulations for the promotion of safety of life and property on and under the high seas and waters subject to the jurisdiction of the United States covering all matters not specifically delegated by law to some other executive department . . ." 14 U. S. C. 2 (2000 ed.).

Under this provision, the Guard possesses authority to promulgate and enforce regulations promoting the safety of vessels anchored in state navigable waters, such as Rig 52. As mentioned above, however, in defining the Coast Guard's regulatory authority, Congress has divided the universe of vessels into two classes: "inspected vessels" and "uninspected vessels." . . . Congress has listed 14 types of vessels that are "subject to inspection" by the Guard pursuant to a substantial body of rules mandated by Congress. . . .

The parties do not dispute that OSHA's regulations have been pre-empted with respect to *inspected* vessels, because the Coast Guard has broad statutory authority to regulate the occupational health and safety of workers aboard inspected vessels, and it has exercised that authority. Indeed, the Coast Guard and OSHA signed a "Memorandum of Understanding" (MOU) on March 17, 1983, evidencing their agreement that, as a result of the Guard's exercise of comprehensive authority over inspected vessels, OSHA "may not enforce the OSH Act with respect to the working conditions of seamen aboard inspected vessels." The MOU recognizes that the exercise of the Coast Guard's authority—and hence the displacement of OSHA jurisdiction—extends not only to those working conditions on inspected vessels specifically discussed by Coast Guard regulations, but to all working conditions on inspected vessels, including those "not addressed by the specific regulations." . . .

Uninspected vessels such as Rig 52, however, present an entirely different regulatory situation. Nearly all of the Coast Guard regulations responsible for displacing OSHA's jurisdiction over inspected vessels, as described in the MOU, do not apply to uninspected vessels like Rig 52. Rather, in the context of uninspected vessels, the Coast Guard's regulatory authority—and exercise thereof—is more limited. With respect to uninspected vessels, the Coast Guard regulates matters related to marine safety, such as fire extinguishers, life preservers, engine flame arrestors, engine ventilation, and emergency locating equipment. Because these general marine safety regulations do not address the occupational safety and health concerns faced by inland drilling operations on uninspected vessels, they do not pre-empt OSHA's authority under sec. 4(b)(1) in this case. . . .

We think it equally clear that Rig 52 was a "workplace" as that term is defined in sec. 4(a) of the Act. The vessel was located within the geographic area described in the definition: "a State," namely Louisiana. Nothing in the text of sec. 4(a) attaches any significance to the fact that the barge was anchored in navigable waters. . . .

Accordingly, the judgment of the Court of Appeals is reversed.

Case Questions

1. Why didn't the Coast Guard conduct inspections of vessels such as Rig 52?
2. Since the Coast Guard has chosen not to inspect such vessels, should OSHA inspect them? Does it have the legal right to inspect them under this Supreme Court decision?
3. Since neither the USCG nor OSHA chose to inspect Rig 52 in the past, is it fair to fine the owners of the vessel for OSH Act violations?
4. Since OSHA piggybacked its citations and penalties upon another agency's investigation/inspection, should the cited owners/employers have objected that OSHA's decision was based on inadmissible or unreliable information?

NEW HEALTH AND SAFETY CHALLENGES IN THE POST-9/11 WORKPLACE

THE WORKING LAW

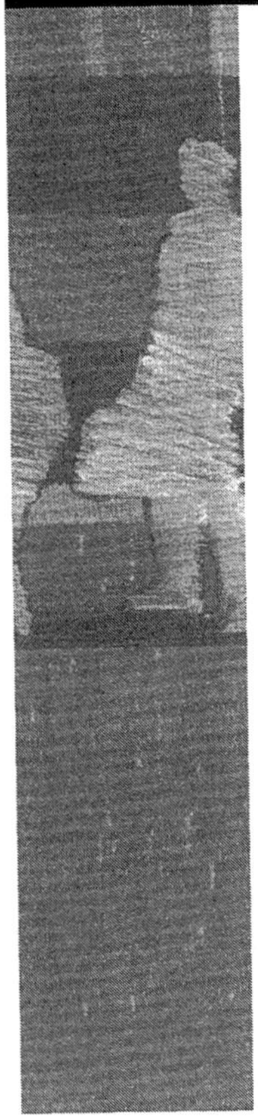

As noted in the introduction to this chapter, environmental health and safety concerns have taken on new urgency in our post-9/11 world of terrorist threats. Shortly after the attacks on the World Trade Center and the Pentagon, anthrax spores were discovered in U.S. post offices from Connecticut to Washington, D.C. Even the U.S. congressional postal facility was contaminated, and a number of people died from exposure to anthrax. One frequently articulated reason the Bush administration decided to extend its "War on Terrorism" to Sadaam Hussein's regime in Iraq was alleged intelligence information that the Middle Eastern dictator was developing chemical and biological weapons of mass destruction. When, simultaneous with the U.S. invasion of Iraq, an epidemic involving a hitherto unheard-of virus began in southern China, Hong Kong, and Singapore, memories of the fall 2001 anthrax incidents led to renewed fears of biological attacks on the United States. Employers in so-called "clean" industries, such as international finance, found themselves faced with quarantining employees returning from business in the Far East during the late winter and into the spring and summer of 2003. "SARS," which stands for severe acute respiratory syndrome, became the newest acronym in the news media, as thousands were stricken, hundreds died, and cases popped up in Toronto and elsewhere in North America.

Needless to say, OSHA was drawn into the new crisis. In the spring of 2003, the agency issued "Information Regarding Severe Acute Respiratory Syndrome (SARS)" on its Web site at **http.www.osha.gov/dep/sars/index.html**. What follows is a brief excerpt from this set of broad guidelines, which is heavily cross-linked to Web sites and online documents of the World Health Organization and the Centers for Disease Control.

Background on SARS

Severe acute respiratory syndrome (SARS) is an emerging, sometimes fatal, respiratory illness. The first identified cases occurred in China in late 2002, and the disease has now spread throughout the world. Although SARS is believed to be caused by a virus, the specific agent has not been identified, and there is not yet any laboratory or other test that can definitively identify cases. Suspected SARS cases in the United States have involved individuals returning from travel to Asia and health care workers and other contacts of those patients. SARS does not appear to be caused by casual contact; transmission appears to be primarily through close contact with a symptomatic patient.

The Centers for Disease Control and Prevention (CDC) has defined a suspect case of SARS as an illness of unknown cause that began in February 2003 or later and meets the following criteria:

- Fever of at least 100.5 degrees F.
- One or more clinical findings of respiratory illness, such as cough, shortness of breath, difficulty breathing, hypoxia, or x-ray evidence of either pneumonia or acute respiratory distress syndrome; and
- The onset of symptoms occurs within 10 days of either (1) travel to an area with documented or suspected community transmission of SARS; or (2) close contact with either a person with a respiratory illness who traveled to a SARS area or a known suspect SARS case. Close contact means having cared for, lived with, or had direct contact with respiratory secretions and/or body fluids. A list of areas with documented or suspected community transmission of SARS can be found on the Updated Interim U.S. Case Definition of Severe Acute Respiratory Syndrome (SARS) website. Suspect cases with radiographic evidence of pneumonia, respiratory distress syndrome, or evidence of unexplained respiratory distress syndrome by autopsy are designated "probable causes" by the World Health Organization (WHO) case definition.

In addition to fever, reports indicated that the majority of SARS patients experienced chills, and about half had muscle aches and dry cough. Fewer than half have also shown other symptoms such as dizziness. The incubation period is typically 2 to 7 days, although some reports suggest an incubation period as long as 10 to 12 days. Signs of the illness include a decreased white blood cell count in most patients as well as below normal blood platelet counts, liver enzyme increase, and electrolyte disturbance in a number of patients.

Most people with SARS are adults. Those age 40 and older and those with certain medical conditions appear to be at increased risk of more severe disease and of death. Treatment consists of antibiotics and steroids, with other options being explored. Between 10 and 20 percent of SARS patients have required ventilator support for a period of time. To date, about 4 percent of identified SARS cases have been fatal.

Employee Training

All employees with potential occupational exposure to SARS, as described in this document, should be trained on the hazards associated with that exposure and on the protocols in place in their facilities to isolate and report cases and to reduce exposures.

Employers and employees may obtain further information on OSHA training regulations and policies including the revised bloodborne pathogen standard 29 CFR 1910.1030 and needlestick prevention information located on the *Bloodborne Pathogen: Technical Links page*. Additional information can also be obtained from the *CDC's SARS web site*.

CITATIONS, PENALTIES, ABATEMENT, AND APPEAL

When an inspection leads to the discovery of a violation of a standard under the act, the employer is issued either a written citation describing the particular nature of the violation or a notice of *de minimis* violations. A *de minimis* violation is one that has no direct or immediate relationship to the health or safety of the workers or the workplace affected, and no citations or proposed penalties are issued.

Visit the OSHA site at **http://www.osha.gov** *and do a search for citations or noncompliance.*

If a citation is issued, the employer must be notified by certified mail within a reasonable time, but in no event longer than six months after the identification of the violation, of any proposed penalty to be assessed. The employer then has fifteen working days within which to notify OSHA that it intends to contest the citation or the proposed penalty. If the employer does not contest, the citation becomes final and is not subject to appeal or review.

The citation must set a reasonable time for the abatement of the violation, usually not to exceed thirty days. The employer is required to post the citation, or a copy, prominently at or near each place the violation occurred. The employees or representatives of the employees may file a notice challenging the period of time set in the citation for the abatement.

If the employer challenges the citation, the penalty assessed, or the period for abatement, a hearing is held before an administrative law judge, who makes findings of fact and conclusions of law that either affirm, modify, or vacate the citation. This order becomes final thirty days after it is filed with OSHA unless, within that time, a member of OSHRC exercises the statutory right to direct review by the full commission. Any party to the proceeding may file a petition requesting this discretionary review. A final order of the commission may be appealed to the appropriate U.S. court of appeals.

The penalty and citation may be separately challenged by the employer. However, if only the penalty is contested, the violation is not subject to review.

When the citation and proposed penalty are contested, the employer has an absolute defense to the citation if it can prove that compliance to the standard is impossible. A showing that the standards are merely impractical or difficult to meet will not excuse performance.

In the event the violation is not corrected within the allowed time, the employer is notified by certified mail of the failure to abate and of the proposed penalty. This notice and proposed penalty are final unless, here again, the employer files a notice of contest within fifteen working days. If the order is not contested, it is deemed a final order and is not subject to judicial review.

If the employer has made a good-faith effort to comply with the abatement requirements of the initial citation but the abatement has not occurred because of factors beyond the reasonable control of the employer, a petition for modification of abatement can be filed. If OSHA or an employee objects to the requested extension or modification, a hearing is held before OSHRC.

If the employer files a petition for modification, the petition must state in detail the steps taken by the employer to abate the hazard, the additional time necessary to abate, the reasons additional time is necessary, including unavailability of technical or professional personnel or equipment, and interim steps being taken to protect employees.

If the employer fails to correct a cited violation after it has become final, a fine may be imposed of not more than $1,000 per day. If the violation is found to be willful, a repeat violation, or results in the death of an employee, OSHA can impose fines of up to $70,000. In the past, OSHA had a practice of imposing a large fine and then allowing the offender to negotiate a reduction in the fine. In 1990, Congress amended the act to prohibit OSHA from reducing a fine for a willful violation below $7,000. The act also provides for criminal penalties of up to six months imprisonment, with the maximum increased to twelve months for a repeat violation.

STATE PLANS

The Occupational Safety and Health Act requires that OSHA encourage the states to develop and operate their own workplace safety and health programs, which must be "at least as effective as" the federal programs. When a state plan has been accepted by OSHA, it is monitored immediately after its approval to determine its compliance, and OSHA retains discretionary enforcement authority for three years. The state agency must file quarterly and semiannual reports with OSHA. Once the effectiveness of the state program is determined, OSHA decides whether federal enforcement will be reinstituted or fully delegated to the state. If the state plan is fully certified, it is still required to change its standards to conform to any changes made in the federal standards, unless it can show a compelling local reason against making the change.

Some states, such as California, have detailed and well-developed enforcement programs that are fully certified by OSHA. At present, nearly half of the states have plans at some level of the implementation process.

Some states have also adopted right-to-know laws, which grant employees the right to know if hazardous or toxic substances are used in their workplace. Employers may be required to label containers of toxic substances, to inform employees of toxic substances in the workplace, to train employees in the proper handling of such substances, and to inform employees' physicians of the chemical composition of substances in the workplace in connection with a physician's diagnosis or treatment of an employee.

http://www.epa.gov/iedweb00/pubs/hpguide.html
is an EPA site on indoor air pollution with links to sites on specific topics, including environmental tobacco smoke.
http://www.osha.gov/SLTC/indoorairquality/index.html
contains the abstract of the OSHA proposal on Indoor Air Quality.

PRIVATE ENFORCEMENT ACTIONS: THE TOBACCO CASES

The Occupational Safety and Health Administration's role in workplace safety is something of a shared role; its duties and enforcement initiatives often overlap those of state agencies, as just discussed, and other federal agencies, such as the Environmental Protection Agency, as well as private rights of action by individuals. One example of this overlap is the regulation of smoking in the workplace.

In addition to OSHA, the Environmental Protection Agency and the Federal Aviation Agency, as well as numerous state and local agencies, have taken a hand in regulating tobacco smoking in transportation, office, restaurant, educational, and many other public and private facilities. Litigation against the major tobacco manufacturers by a consortium of states' attorneys general led to the multibillion-dollar "tobacco settlement," under which the treasuries of participating states stand to collect billions of dollars in revenues from the participating defendants.

Yet, despite this massive monetary settlement, which the U.S. Department of Justice played a key role in brokering, Big Tobacco was not successful in obtaining either congressionally mandated immunity from further lawsuits or some statutory limit on the size of judgments that juries might award in future lawsuits. Consequently, during the past half-dozen years, the legal battle has shifted to the alleged victims of secondary smoke. Such suits have tended to focus on the plight of flight attendants for the major airlines, who contend that their health has been permanently damaged by being forced to contend with passengers' smoking habits in the confined spaces of commercial aircraft on a workaday basis.

In early 2003, two such cases reached crucial phases in Florida courtrooms.

- On January 8, 2003, Miami-Dade Circuit Court Judge Leslie B. Rothenberg ordered a new trial, overturning a defense verdict, in the case of *Janoff v. Philip Morris*. Former American Airlines flight attendant Suzette Janoff had sued Philip Morris, Lorillard Tobacco, R. J. Reynolds, and Brown & Williamson on the theory that secondhand smoke that she inhaled during her years of working aboard airliners had caused her chronic sinusitis. In ordering a new trial, her honor cited tobacco industry attorneys for misleading her on the applicable evidentiary law. Her order was a "warning to lawyers who argue positions to the court that they [know] or should [know are] contrary to the law. . . ." During the trial, the judge had candidly admitted her limited knowledge of key evidentiary issues and solicited the lawyers' guidance. She subsequently discovered, posttrial, that the defense attorneys had prevailed on an argument that had been rejected in a similar secondhand-smoke, flight-attendant case that was a controlling precedent in *Janoff*.
- Less than a month after Judge Rothenberg's ruling in *Janoff*, the same defendants won a second jury verdict in the case of James Seal, who had claimed that thirty years as a flight attendant for United Airlines had aggravated his asthmatic condition. The defendants here again succeeded in persuading the jurors that the plaintiff's breathing problems were not the result of secondhand smoke on the job.

But the most interesting development in this evolving health and safety hassle occurred in a case in which the involved flight attendants were not the plaintiffs/alleged victims, but rather were the purported culprits, bringing down liability upon their employer's head. The following case is of interest not only because it involved affirmation of a $1.4 million verdict in a single-plaintiff claim but also because it illustrates how the legal fight over tobacco liability is shifting in the new century from the national arena, where it was played out during the 1990s (climaxing in the national tobacco settlement mentioned earlier), onto the global stage. In seeking to escape the huge verdict awarded by a federal district court judge, the defendant tried to rely on an international treaty to limit its liability in this wrongful death case.

Husain v. Olympic Airways

316 F.3d 829 (U.S. Ct. of Appeals, 9th Cir. 2002)

Molloy, D. J. (sitting by designation)

After a non-jury trial, the district court determined that Dr. Abid M. Hanson's death on Olympic Airways ("Olympic") Flight 417 was caused by an accident as defined in Article 17 of the Warsaw Convention. The trial judge also found the accident resulted from willful misconduct by Olympic's employees. The district court awarded $1,400,000 in damages. Olympic appeals the determination of the district court and the award of damages. We hold that the district court's findings are not clearly erroneous and we AFFIRM.

On January 4, 1998, 52-year-old Dr. Abid M. Hanson died while passenger on Olympic Flight 417 between Athens, Greece and New York City. His death occurred after he suffered complications when he was exposed to ambient second-hand smoke while seated in the airplane's non-smoking section three rows in front of the smoking section.... Dr. Hanson's wife, Rubina Husain, had asked Olympic's employees on multiple occasions with increasing urgency to move Dr. Hanson to another seat away from the smoking section. She explained the critical reasons Dr. Hanson had to move and made her concerns known about the consequences of leaving him exposed to the offensive smoke. Ms. Husain's requests were ignored, primarily by flight attendant Maria Leptougou. Dr. Hanson died from a severe asthma attack caused by the smoke exposure....

Plaintiffs in essence contend that a flight attendant who does nothing to deal with a known risk to a passenger's health-related travel problems is negligent. Because Ms. Leptougou's conduct was negligent, it fits the definition of accident under Article 17. Plaintiffs argue that crew negligence is external to the passenger and is not a reasonably expected part of international travel....

The district court found, after examining evidence establishing industry standards and Olympic's policies regarding passengers with medical needs, that this failure to act was a "blatant disregard of industry standards and airline policies." ... Ms. Leptougou's failure to act was more egregious in light of the simple nature of Ms. Husain's request, which could easily have been satisfied without interference with the airplane's normal operation. Combined, these factors bring Ms. Leptougou's failure to assist Dr. Hanson within the meaning of an "accident" for Article 17 purposes....

Carrier liability for injuries caused by an accident is usually limited to $75,000 per passenger. However, Article 25 [of the Warsaw Convention] provides that injuries that result from the carrier's willful misconduct or the willful misconduct of an employee acting within the scope of her employment are excluded from the liability limits....

Ms. Leptougou's failure to take action, either by moving Dr. Hanson or by notifying the chief cabin attendant of Ms. Husain's request to have her husband moved, was willful misconduct. The district court concluded "Ms. Leptougou *must have known* that the cabin was not full, that Dr. Hanson had a medical problem and a special susceptibility to smoke, and that her failure to move him would aggravate his condition and cause his probable injury." ...

We decide that the district court's findings and conclusions are well-grounded in the record. Olympic's argument asks this Court to substitute its judgment and second guess the district court. This we cannot do....

Therefore, we affirm the judgment of the district court.

Case Questions

1. In affirming the district judge's judgment in favor of the plaintiff, the appeals panel notes that the flight attendant, Ms. Leptougou, failed to testify. Do you think the defendant had a reason for not calling its employee as a witness at the trial? Would you have called her if you were Olympic's trial attorney?
2. Do you agree that the flight attendant, Ms. Leptougou, was acting within the scope of her employment in refusing to assist Dr. Hanson? Are there any arguments to be made to the contrary?
3. Olympic's own policies seem to have been used against it in this case. Shouldn't employer policies aimed at ensuring the health and safety of its customers,

if communicated to the employees, serve to shield the employer from customer liability when an employee chooses to ignore such policies on her own?

4. Can you think of any policy reasons for arguing that a case such as this would be better handled by an international equivalent of OSHA or the EPA instead of being fought out between the parties in a lawsuit?

5. Should flight attendant Leptougou be subject to employee discipline? If you had been Olympic's HR director, what discipline would you recommend to management? If the flight attendants had a union and Ms. Leptougou was discharged by Olympic, would you as union president have filed a grievance challenging her termination of employment?

6. If Dr. Hanson knew, before he boarded the plane, or shortly after taking his seat, that he was only three rows away from the smoking section, should this knowledge change the outcome of the case? And if so, could the *Hanson* case then be used as a favorable precedent by the tobacco companies in defending against the pending secondhand-smoke cases brought by flight attendants?

WORKPLACE VIOLENCE

Workplace violence has emerged as an important safety concern in the twenty-first century. Its most extreme form—homicide—is the second leading cause of fatal occupational injury in the United States. Every year, almost 1,000 workers are murdered and about 1.5 million are assaulted in their places of employment. Concern about workplace violence has intensified exponentially in the wake of the terrorist attacks and anthrax events of autumn 2001. Businesses based primarily in office buildings, which once thought themselves above and beyond the workplace safety concerns of heavy industry and hermetically sealed from the violent intrusions endemic to convenience food stores and other retail establishments, now find themselves in need of policies and procedures to deal with all manner of threats from inside and outside their organizations. Most large businesses have felt compelled to go so far as to develop evacuation plans in anticipation of the day when it is their high-rise office building or corporate office park that is the target of a terrorist attack or a biological or chemical incursion. Following is a brief set of guidelines, prepared by this text's authors for a West newsletter which they write on a monthly basis.[3]

Workplace Violence and Those Who Commit It

Workplace violence can be classified as follows:

1. Violence by emotionally enraged persons
2. Violence by an angry spouse or relative of an employee
3. Random acts of violence
4. Violence against law enforcement or security
5. Terrorism and hate crimes

[3]Based on Castagnera, Cihon & Morris, *West's Termination of Employment Bulletin,* April 2003.

Persons who commit workplace violence often share one or more of the following characteristics:

- A history of violence
- Psychosis
- Romantic obsession
- Chemical dependence
- Depression
- Paranoia or pathological blaming
- Impaired neurological functioning
- Elevated frustration with the work environment
- Interest in or obsession with weapons
- Personality disorder

Other documented indicators of a potential for workplace violence are:

- Alcohol abuse
- Drug abuse
- Impaired judgment
- Emotional difficulties
- Financial problems
- Legal problems
- Strained family relations
- Occupational failure
- Threats
- Absenteeism
- Deterioration of personal appearance, attitude, and behavior
- Deterioration of interpersonal relations
- Inefficiency

Documenting Behavior

Incidents of workplace violence or possible violent behavior should be documented as follows:

1. Record incidents promptly.
2. Indicate date, time, and location.
3. Detail the behavior.
4. List all persons and work products involved.
5. Identify the performance standards and disciplinary rules violated.
6. Record the consequences of the action.
7. Record management's response.
8. Record the employee's reaction to management's response.

A Supervisor's Response

Supervisors should respond as follows to indicators of potential workplace violence:

1. Don't try to diagnose the behavior personally.
2. Don't discuss drinking unless it occurs on the job.
3. Don't moralize.
4. Don't be misled by sympathy-evoking tactics.
5. Don't cover up for a friend.
6. Don't put the individual into an isolated work area.
7. Don't ignore the problem or the signs of trouble.
8. Do remember that chemical dependence is progressive and likely will only get worse over time.
9. Do bring to the attention of suspected employees the company's employee assistance program.
10. Do make it clear that your organization is concerned with job performance and that, if performance does not improve, the job is in jeopardy.
11. Do explain that the employee must make the personal decision to seek help.
12. Do emphasize that the employee assistance program is confidential.

Prevention

To prevent workplace violence:

1. Develop a written policy.
2. Form a crisis management team.
3. Develop policies on counseling, suspension, and termination.
4. Immediately investigate all incidents, such as threats.
5. Contact specialists for assistance.
6. Be flexible: Revise plans, policies, and procedures as information develops.

Evacuation Plans

In the words of labor lawyer Louis Lessig of the Pinnacle Employment Law Institute, "Employers of all sizes are now drafting and revising emergency evacuation procedures. But, in order to adequately prepare, it is necessary to know in advance which employees, if any, will need assistance." In line with Lessig's observation, the EEOC recently released guidelines concerning the creation of emergency plans that comply with the Americans with Disabilities Act. The guide lists three ways in which employers can obtain the information Mr. Lessig says they need:

1. The employer can ask about a new hire's needs in this regard after making an offer of employment and prior to the commencement of work.
2. The employer is allowed to send out periodic surveys to all employees to ascertain such special needs; however, self-identification must be strictly

voluntary and be used only in conjunction with construction of the emergency plan.

3. The employer may ask all employees with declared disabilities if they will require such special assistance in the event of an evacuation of the work site.

Also worth noting is the ADA provision that while, in general, medical information must be maintained in confidentiality, relevant information can be provided by the employer to:

- Health-care workers
- Emergency coordinators
- Floor captains
- A colleague designated to provide the special assistance required

Particularly regarding small businesses, OSHA has posted an "eTool" on the Internet. This resource is intended to help small employers wrestle with relevant OSH Act standards such as:

- Means of egress (29 CFR 1910.37)
- Emergency action and fire prevention plans (29 CFR 1910.38)
- Portable fire extinguishers (29 CFR 1910.157)
- Fixed extinguishing systems (29 CFR 1910.160)
- Fire detection systems (29 CFR 1910.164)
- Employee alarm systems (29 CFR 1910.165)

The Web site covers

- Evacuation procedures
- Emergency escape route assignments
- Procedures for employees who remain behind to handle critical systems
- Procedures to account for all employees
- Rescue and medical duties of designated employees
- Means of reporting fires and other emergencies
- Names and titles of persons to be contacted for explanation of procedures and duties
- Tips on evaluating your workplace

See the National Safety Council's Emergencies and Disasters Web site at **http://www.nsc.org/issues/prepare.htm**.

Packages and Mail

Although the East Coast anthrax scare is behind us and there have been no publicized repetitions, employees should still be alert. The OSHA offers the following guidelines.

General Mail Handling

- Be observant for suspicious envelopes and packages.
- Open all mail with a letter opener or by the method least likely to disturb the contents.
- Do not blow into envelopes.
- Do not shake or pour out the contents.
- Keep hands away from nose and mouth.
- Wash hands after handling the mail.

Things That Should Trigger Suspicion

- Discoloration, crystallization, strange odor, or oil stains
- Powder or residue
- Protruding wires or aluminum foil
- Excessive tape or string
- Unusual size or unusual weight for its size
- Lopsided or oddly shaped envelope
- Postmark that does not match return address
- Restrictive endorsement such as Personal or Confidential

The Centers for Disease Control has issued guidelines for clean-up workers exposed to anthrax. These are based in part upon OSH Act regulations for hazardous waste clean-up operations (29 CFR 1910.120). These CDC guidelines are available at **http://www.bt.cdc.gov/agent/anthrax/index.asp**.

Yet another resource for employers concerned about developing disaster preparedness plans post-9/11 is a federal report entitled "Learning from Disasters: Weapons of Mass Destruction Preparedness through Worker Training." The report is the result of a Worker Education and Training Program Conference held in Raleigh, North Carolina, on April 25–26, 2002. It was funded out of EPA's superfund coffers and is available from the Government Printing Office.

Studying Violence

NIOSH is funding a two-year, $200,000 study at the University of Maryland. The main purpose of the study is a better understanding of the scope of the problem of violence. Preliminary data indicate that workers most often victimized by workplace violence are:

- Special education teachers
- Mental health professionals
- Home health-care workers
- All-night convenience store clerks
- Cab drivers

SUMMARY

- The Occupational Safety and Health Act was enacted by Congress in response to the large number of workplace deaths, diseases, and injuries occurring in the United States every year. Scholars and critics disagree about how effective the OSH Act has been in reducing or preventing such occurrences.
- The OSH Act empowers the Occupational Safety and Health Administration to promulgate rules and set standards for workplace safety. These rules are subject to challenge in our federal courts.
- The Occupational Safety and Health Administration is also empowered to enforce the law and the regulations by means of workplace inspections and citations. Its agents are not required to meet the same strict search warrant requirements imposed upon police officers by the Fourth Amendment to the U.S. Constitution. Furthermore, while OSHA's jurisdiction can sometimes become entangled with that of other agencies, such as the Environmental Protection Agency and the U.S. Coast Guard, recent case law suggests that in this post-9/11 world of heightened health and safety concerns, the U.S. Supreme Court is prepared to allow OSHA a substantial amount of leverage in conducting inspections and enforcing the OSH Act and its implementing regulations.
- Not only is OSHA's jurisdiction over workplace safety not exclusive, but in some major areas—workplace smoking being a very significant one—private litigation has played a significant role in securing employee rights and recompensing employee injuries. Most recently, Big Tobacco has been the target of "secondhand smoke" lawsuits by employees, such as airline attendants, who claim to have been harmed by the necessity of working in closely confined workspaces where secondhand smoke has been present daily. The U.S. Supreme Court in May 2003 agreed to review the $1.4 million judgment in one the most significant of these lawsuits.
- Another emerging area of OSHA concern is workplace violence, a complicated issue that implicates multiple government agencies, professions, and causes. Here, too, the September 11, 2001, terrorist attacks and the anthrax crisis that followed have led many corporations to develop policies and procedures for dealing with a wide range of health and safety threats that might come from within as well as from outside their workplaces, including in the case of many larger corporations and organizations detailed work site evacuation plans.

QUESTIONS

1. What are the goals of the Occupational Safety and Health Act? How does the act attempt to meet those goals?
2. What agencies are created by the Occupational Safety and Health Act, and what are the roles of those agencies?
3. Describe the procedures used to create permanent standards under OSHA.
4. When can employees exercise the right to refuse to work under OSHA without fear of reprisal?

5. What is the purpose of workplace inspections under OSHA? What is the effect of the *Barlow's* case on that purpose?
6. What procedures must be followed in issuing a citation under OSHA? What penalties may be imposed for violations of OSHA?
7. What is the effect of state right-to-know laws?

CASE PROBLEMS

1. An employee filed a complaint with the Occupational Safety and Health Administration, accusing her employer—a printing plant—of assorted safety violations. A few days after filing the complaint, she held a lunchtime meeting with her co-workers in an effort to get them to protest their work conditions. Later that same afternoon, she was called to her supervisor's office where she was fired.

   The Department of Labor brought this action, claiming that the employee's termination was retaliatory. The company contended that during the meeting with her supervisor, the employee became loud, abusive, and even threatened him.

   If the threatening and abusive language can be proven, should this constitute an independent reason for the discharge, such that the DOL's claim of retaliatory firing should be defeated? Does the lunchtime meeting with her coworkers implicate any other federal labor statute in your consideration of this case? Does this consideration change the outcome? See *Herman v. Crescent Publishing Group, Inc.* [2000 WL 1371311 (S.D.N.Y.)].

2. The U.S. Department of Labor's Wage and Hour Division audited an employer and determined that the company had committed violations of the minimum wage and overtime provisions of the federal Fair Labor Standards Act (see Chapter 10). The company wished to appeal this determination.

   The firm's human resources director called the main number of the Department of Labor's offices in the corporation's home city. She was put through to an official in the OSHA office in the local federal building. This OSHA official, responding to the human resources director's inquiry, advised her that she need not count weekends and holidays when calculating the deadline date for filing her company's appeal. It turned out that this information was incorrect, and as a result, the appeal was dismissed by the Wage and Hour Division's appellate office as untimely.

   Should a court order the Department of Labor to honor the appeal, since one of its agencies gave the human resources manager the incorrect information upon which her company relied to its detriment? What are the policy considerations pro and con regarding such a ruling? Is there a constitutional issue involved in this case? See *Atlantic Adjustment Co. v. U.S. Dept. of Labor* [90 F.Supp.2d 627 (E.D. Pa. 2000)].

3. Following an explosion and fire at an employer's petrochemical facility, OSHA investigators interviewed numerous employees of the company. While OSHA's investigation was still pending, the company sent the agency a Freedom of Information Act (FOIA) request, asking for transcriptions of all witness statements taken by the investigators. When OSHA declined to provide these statements, the company sued, seeking a writ of mandamus that would require the agency to comply with the FOIA request.

   What policy considerations favor requiring OSHA to provide the company with copies of these statements? What policy considerations are against requiring disclosure? Do these policy considerations change in any way as the underlying case progresses from the investigative to later stages in OSHA's procedures? Are there constitutional considerations involved? See *Cooper Cameron Corp. v. U.S. Dept. of Labor* [118 F.Supp.25 757 (S.D. Texas 2000)]; see also *Freedom of Information Act* [5 U.S.C. 552 (West 2000)].

4. Because the availability of new plots was becoming very limited, a cemetery company in a major metropolitan area began selling single plots wherein a husband and wife ultimately would be interred one on top of the other. When the first spouse died, a grave was excavated to a depth sufficient to leave room for the future interment of the surviving spouse. To "square off" the corners of the grave, a member of the cemetery's grounds crew would enter the newly dug grave with a spade or trowel to perform the task.

One of the groundskeepers filed a complaint with OSHA claiming that it was unsafe to work in the graves without shoring. An inspector from OSHA decided that the double graves were deep enough to require proper shoring before a gravedigger enters them to square them off. The cemetery's general manager replied that no other cemetery's procedure included shoring and that if required to do so, his company would become uncompetitive.

What recourse does the general manager have? (This case problem is drawn from the experience of one of the authors in legal practice.)

5. Employees of the state's Department of Environmental Management (DEM) complained to the state's attorney general that their agency was not properly implementing the requirements of the federal Solid Waste Disposal Act. DEM fired them after it learned of their complaint.

The Solid Waste Disposal Act contains a whistleblower protection clause. See 42 U.S.C. 6971 (West 2000). The employees sued in federal court to collect damages from the state under this provision. The state moved to dismiss the action on the basis of its sovereign immunity.

What is sovereign immunity and when do you think a state should be able to rely upon this legal principle to avoid liability? Should the fact that this case creates a potential clash between state and federal government influence the court's decision on whether or not to dismiss the action? See *Rhode Island v. United States* [16 BNA IER Cases 1258 (D. R.I. 2000)].

6. Sami Al-Arian was a tenured professor of computer engineering at the University of South Florida. Early in 2002, the university terminated his employment, citing his public statements, reported by the media and broadcast on TV, in support of Islamic *jihad*. The university claimed in terminating Al-Arian that he posed a threat to the safety of other university employees.

Do you think the university was justified in firing the Palestinian professor? What arguments could you make in favor of his reinstatement if you were his attorney? Did OSHA have any jurisdiction in this case? Would OSHA have had grounds to issue a citation for a safety violation if the university had failed to fire the professor and his presence on campus had in fact resulted in a violent third-party action that killed or injured university employees?

7. About one year later, Al-Arian was charged by federal law enforcement officials with raising money to support a terrorist organization, Palestinian Islamic Jihad, allegedly responsible for more than 100 murders in Israel and the Israeli-occupied territories.

Does this indictment strengthen the university's case for firing Al-Arian? Is your answer the same whether or not the university knew of these indictable activities prior to the indictment? See *West's Termination of Employment Bulletin,* May 2003, at 11.

8. We have seen in this chapter that OSHA shares responsibility for workplace health and safety with a variety of other federal agencies (such as the U.S. Coast Guard), as well as state and local governmental bodies and even private rights of action (as in the secondhand smoke cases). In this case, the Teamsters Union was endeavoring to unionize the Overnite Transportation Company's Bedford, Illinois, facility. In furtherance of those organizing efforts, Teamster-paid pickets appeared at the work site armed with ax handles disguised as picket signs. In the ensuing confrontation, some of the company's employees, mainly security guards, were injured.

Which governmental body should have jurisdiction over this case: OSHA, the National Labor Relations Board, the U.S. District Court, or an appropriate state court?

See *Overnite Transportation Co. v. International Brotherhood of Teamsters, Chauffeurs, Warehousemen and Helpers of America* [773 N.E.2d 26 (Ill. App. 2002)].

9. Plaintiff drove a bus for defendant Diversified Paratransit, Inc., which was in the business of transporting developmentally disabled adults and children from their homes and care providers to various day-care centers and schools. One such adult client harassed the plaintiff regularly, including exposing himself to her and ultimately grabbing her and trying to kiss her. Her complaints to her employer were largely ignored. Following the incident involving physical contact, she quit her job.

Does the plaintiff have the right to file an OSHA complaint in this case? Does she have a private right of action to sue her employer? If so, what is her legal theory? Does the lawsuit have any OSHA preemption problems? See *Salazar v. Diversified Paratransit, Inc.* [126 Cal. Rptr.2d 475 (Cal. App. 2002)].

10. The plaintiff in this case was employed by United Engineers and Constructors at its chemical weapons incinerator on the Johnston Atoll in the South Pacific. Due to the types of weapons handled at the facility, the court observed, "the working conditions . . . are probably as dangerous as any undertaken in the world." Plaintiff had previously been employed at the Pine Bluff Arsenal in Arkansas, where he had made more than 1,000 "toxic entries"—that is, entries into a contaminated area of a plant, requiring protective clothing and other precautions. Upon his arrival at the atoll, he concluded that the company's managers and his co-workers failed to appreciate the risks they were running. In particular, he concluded that the basic training and the safety equipment were both inadequate. Consequently, he began complaining. His complaints were vindicated by the subsequent issuance of two "serious" citations by OSHA following the agency's inspection of the facility in reaction to plaintiff's complaints. The citations related to unapproved respirators and the standby-team's use of improper equipment. (A "serious" violation means that the hazard poses a "substantial probability of death or serious physical harm.")

Disputes between plaintiff and his superiors continued. The situation came to a climax when plaintiff refused to work in a toxic area because the company had failed to provide him with a new set of corrective lenses for his face mask. Plaintiff was discharged for insubordination. He again filed an OSH Act complaint, and the agency's regional investigator made an initial finding that the complaint had merit. However, after several local attempts to amicably resolve the dispute, the case was forwarded to the OSHA regional solicitor in San Francisco with a recommendation that the case be adjudicated. However, the regional solicitor decided to dismiss the case due to a possible jurisdictional dispute with the U.S. Army, which conducted its own inspection/ investigation but failed to act. Instead, the army turned the file over to the Department of Labor, where OSHA gave the case one final review but still refused to take adjudicative action.

Based on these facts, what are the policy considerations in favor and against allowing the plaintiff to pursue a lawsuit against OSHA, seeking a writ of mandamus from a federal judge, and requiring OSHA to adjudicate plaintiff's retaliation claim against the employer? See *Wood v. Department of Labor* [275 F.3d 107 (D.C. Cir. 2001)].

INTERNET EXERCISES

The purpose of these Internet Exercises is to give you some hands-on experience working with two "hot" health and safety issues that are highlighted in The Working Law features of this chapter: workplace violence and SARS.

1. Go to **http://www.osha.gov** and locate the "evacuation_eTool" that OSHA has made available for small businesses seeking to develop worksite evacuation plans that comply with OSH Act regulations.
2. Assume that you or your student group is a health clinic and work on developing an evacuation plan for your facility using this eTool to help you.
3. Now go to **http://www.osha.gov/dep/sars** and ascertain whether the information published by OSHA there provides any guidelines or suggestions that should be incorporated into your draft plan.
4. And finally, click the link you find on OSHA's SARS site for the CDC's Updated Interim Infection Control Guidance and determine whether this set of guidelines suggests or requires any amendments to your draft plan.

INFOTRAC KEYWORDS

http://www.infotrac-college.com

OSHA, OSHA citations, NIOSH, workplace safety, employee rights, OSHA penalties, workplace violence

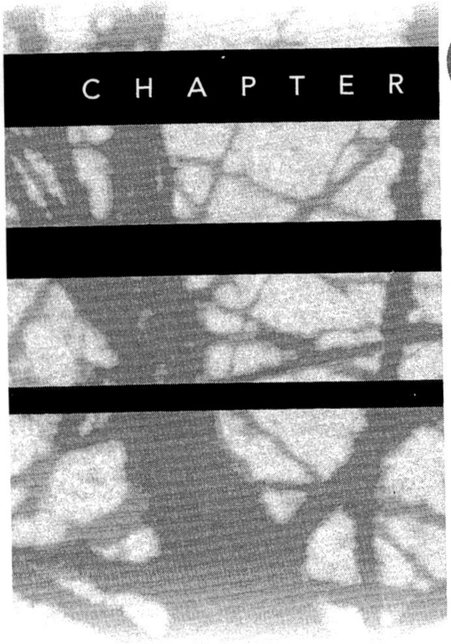

CHAPTER 9

EMPLOYEE RETIREMENT INCOME SECURITY ACT (ERISA)

During the summer of 2003, President Bush proposed a significant change in how corporations calculate their pension fund liabilities. In early July 2003, the Bush administration announced its desire to end the present practice of using long-term Treasury bond rates as the benchmark for calculating corporate pension liabilities. These Treasury rates had fallen to historic lows due to repeated lowering of the prime interest rate by the Federal Reserve in an effort to jump-start a lagging U.S. economy. Such low rates required companies to place substantial additional funds into their pension plans to meet federal funding requirements. Bipartisan legislation was also under consideration, which if enacted would facilitate a switch from the long-term Treasury rate to a composite corporate bond rate. Meanwhile, union officials and some labor economists complained that adoption of either the Bush or the congressional plan would hurt older, more mature industrial companies with troubled pensions plans, encouraging these corporations to cut back or terminate their defined-benefit pension plans or even begin shifting their payrolls toward a younger work force.[1]

This latest controversy, following hot on the heels of the Enron-WorldCom scandals (see below), serves to emphasize that even after more than a quarter century of close federal regulation of employee pension plans, the pension fund abuses that led to the enactment of sweeping federal employee-benefit legislation in the mid-1970s have not yet been eradicated by our national government.

---

[1]"Concerns Raised Over Bush Pension Proposal," *Benefits Next,* July 9, 2003 at **http://www2.benefitsnext.com/Article.cfm/Nav/5.0.0.2.27818**.

ERISA: BACKGROUND AND PURPOSE

For a brief description of ERISA with hyperlinks to other relevant sites, go to **http://www.dol.gov/dol/topic/retirement/erisa.htm**

In 1974, Congress enacted the Employee Retirement Income Security Act, known as ERISA. The act was passed in response to numerous instances of pension fund mismanagement and abuse. Retired employees had their pension benefits reduced or terminated because their pension plan had been inadequately funded or depleted through mismanagement. In other instances, employees retiring after as many as twenty years or more of service with an employer were ineligible for pensions because of complex and strict eligibility requirements.

ERISA is intended to prevent such abuses and to protect the interests of employees and their beneficiaries in employee benefit plans. The act imposes standards of conduct and responsibility upon pension fund fiduciaries (persons having authority or control over the management of pension fund assets). The act also requires that pension plan administrators disclose relevant financial information to employees and the government. The act sets certain minimum standards that pension plans must meet to qualify for preferential tax treatment, and it provides legal remedies to employees and their beneficiaries in the event of violations.

The provisions of ERISA apply to employee benefit plans established by employers. The act recognizes two types of benefit plans: welfare plans and pension plans. Welfare plans usually provide participating employees and their beneficiaries with medical coverage, disability benefits, death benefits, vacation pay, and/or unemployment benefits. Welfare plans may also include apprenticeship programs, prepaid legal services, day-care centers, and scholarship funds. Pension plans are defined as including any plan intended to provide retirement income to employees and resulting in deferral of income for such employees.

ERISA's main focus is on pension plans. It seeks to ensure that all employees covered by pension plans receive the benefits due them under the plans. ERISA does not require an employer to provide a pension plan for its employees. However, if a pension plan is offered, ERISA sets the minimum standards and requirements that the pension plan must meet.

COVERAGE

The provisions of ERISA do not apply to employee benefit plans that are established by federal, state, or local government employers. Nor does the act apply to plans covering employees of tax-exempt churches or to plans maintained solely for the purpose of complying with state workers' compensation, unemployment compensation, or disability insurance laws. Neither does ERISA apply to plans maintained outside the United States primarily for the benefit of nonresident aliens. But these exemptions are relatively narrow; ERISA's reach is very broad.

The two main features of ERISA—the imposition of standards for fiduciary conduct and responsibility and the setting of minimum standards for pension plan requirements—have different bases for their coverage. The fiduciary duties and conduct standards apply to any employee benefit plan established or maintained by an employer engaged in interstate commerce or in an industry or activity affecting interstate commerce. They also apply to plans established and maintained by unions representing employees engaged in an industry or activity affecting interstate commerce.

The minimum standards for pension plans must be met for the employee pension plans to qualify for preferential tax treatment. Because such tax treatment enables an employer to deduct contributions to qualified benefit plans immediately but does not consider the payments as income to participating employees until they receive the payments after retirement, most employers seek to "qualify" their plans by complying with ERISA's minimum standards. Such compliance, however, is not required. Some employers who view the ERISA requirements as too stringent have chosen not to qualify their pension and other benefit plans for preferential tax treatment. Those employers are still subject to the fiduciary duties of ERISA if they are engaged in, or affect, interstate commerce (which today includes the vast majority of enterprises).

Preemption

Despite the broad preemptive power that the federal courts have given to ERISA, as defined in *Shaw v. Delta Airlines, Inc.* [463 U.S. 85 (1983)], several courts have allowed plaintiffs raising claims of discrimination in employee benefit plans to pursue them under state anti-discrimination laws.

The following case involves a state law claim by an employee who alleged that he was fired two days after informing his employer that his daughter required an expensive liver transplant operation.

Le v. Applied Biosystems

886 F.Supp. 717 (N.D. Cal. 1995)

Order of Remand

Jensen, District Judge

On April 26, 1995, the Court heard arguments on plaintiff's motion for remand. Having considered the arguments of counsel, the applicable law, and the papers submitted, the Court hereby GRANTS plaintiff's motion.

I. Background

A. Procedural History

Plaintiff Joe Le's Second Amended Complaint was filed on January 24, 1995. Defendants timely answered the complaint in San Mateo County Superior Court on February 24, 1995. Also on February 24, 1995, defendants removed the action to this Court, contending that the Employee Retirement Income Security Act (ERISA), 29 U.S.C. § 1001 et seq. preempted plaintiff's fourth cause of action.

B. Factual Background

After approximately seven years of employment with defendant Applied Biosystems, plaintiff Joe Le's employment was terminated. Plaintiff says that defendants, including plaintiff's supervisor, defendant Bruce Alleman, claimed that plaintiff had played a computer game during work hours, in contravention of purported company policy. Despite plaintiff's denial of this allegation, he was fired. He was terminated just two days after he informed his employer that his daughter required a liver transplant operation and that, if no donor were found, plaintiff would be the donor. Plaintiff added that the procedure was an expensive one, and that, if he were the donor, he would require a two- or three-month leave of absence.

Plaintiff's complaint states causes of action for breach of implied-in-fact contract, breach of the covenant of good faith and fair dealing, race and national origin discrimination in violation of California law, disability discrimination in violation of California law, and wrongful termination in violation of California Government Code § 12945.2. Defendants removed the case on the grounds that plaintiff's fourth cause of action for state law disability discrimination is preempted by ERISA.

C. Applicable Law

28 U.S.C. § 1447(c) requires the remand of a case [to the state court where the plaintiff initiated it] if subject matter jurisdiction is lacking [in the federal court to which the defendant removed it.]

II. Discussion

A. Parties' Arguments

Defendants assert that plaintiff's fourth cause of action for disability discrimination is, in reality, a claim arising under ERISA. ERISA prohibits discharge of employees to avoid payment of medical benefits. As part of his fourth cause of action, plaintiff claims that he was discharged so that his employer would not have to pay for his daughter's liver transplant. As such, defendant argues that ERISA preempts the fourth cause of action, and removal was proper.

Plaintiff concedes that, if no exception to preemption exists, his fourth cause of action would be preempted by ERISA. He argues, however, that the claim falls within a narrow exception to ERISA preemption. In *Shaw v. Delta Air Lines, Inc.*, the Supreme Court held that a state anti-discrimination law is not preempted by ERISA where the state law prohibits practices which are also unlawful under federal law. Plaintiff claims that the conduct alleged as part of his fourth cause of action—that he was terminated because defendants wished to avoid paying medical benefits to him, an individual perceived to have a disability, or to his daughter, a family member with a disability—is unlawful under the Americans with Disabilities Act (ADA), 42 U.S.C. § 12101 et seq. and therefore not preempted by ERISA. . . .

B. Analysis

Plaintiff claims that he was terminated because his employer wished to avoid paying for his daughter's medical treatment. He claims that this is unlawful discrimination which is prohibited by both the California Fair Employment and Housing Act (FEHA), Gov't Code § 12940, and the ADA, 42 U.S.C. § 12101.

ERISA preempts state laws "insofar as they may now or hereafter relate to any employee benefit plan" covered by ERISA. If no exception to ERISA preemption exists, a claim of termination to avoid payment of benefits would be preempted. *Ingersoll-Rand Company v. McClendon*. An exception to preemption will be found, however, whenever preemption of the law would serve "to alter, amend, modify, invalidate, impair, or supersede any law of the United States . . . or any rule or regulation issued under any such law." 29 U.S.C. § 1144(d).

In *Shaw v. Delta Air Lines, Inc.*, the Supreme Court held that a state anti-discrimination statute is preempted under ERISA only insofar as it prohibits practices otherwise lawful under federal law. If the state law prohibits conduct which is unlawful under federal law, then the state law is not preempted.

In *Shaw*, a New York state statute forbade discrimination in employee benefit plans on the basis of pregnancy and required employers to pay sick leave to employees unable to work because of pregnancy. The Supreme Court determined that the state statute did "relate to" an employee benefit plan within the meaning of 29 U.S.C. § 1144(a), but that an exception to preemption under 29 U.S.C. § 1144(d) saved the law from preemption. The Court reasoned that state anti-discrimination laws play a significant role in the enforcement of Title VII. In fact, state fair employment laws play such a pivotal role in the federal enforcement scheme by providing a means of enforcing Title VII's commands that, were such laws to be preempted by ERISA, Title VII itself would be impaired and its goals frustrated. Therefore, the Court found that it was not Congress's intent to preempt the application of federal statutes or their state counterparts.

Although *Shaw* dealt with a state statute that was parallel to Title VII, the same reasoning applies to a state statute that is parallel to the ADA. In *Bennett v. Hallmark Cards,* the Court applied *Shaw* and held that because the ADA utilizes the same administrative procedures as Title VII and has similar goals and objectives, state laws which themselves prohibit practices unlawful under the ADA are not subject to preemption, as preemption would impair the enforcement of the ADA.

Parties agree that if plaintiff's fourth cause of action prohibits practices which are unlawful under the ADA, then the claim is not preempted by ERISA. The pivotal question, then, is whether or not plaintiff's allegation that he was fired to avoid payment of medical benefits for his daughter's liver transplant violates the ADA.

It appears that such conduct does violate the ADA. 42 U.S.C. § 12112(a) declares that

> no covered entity shall discriminate against a qualified individual with a disability because of the disability of such individual in regard to job application procedures, the hiring, advancement, or discharge of employees, employee compensation, job training, and other terms, conditions, and privileges of employment.

2 U.S.C. § 12112(b)(4) explains that the term "discriminate" includes

> excluding or otherwise denying equal jobs or benefits to a qualified individual because of the known disability of an individual with whom the qualified individual is known to have a relationship or association.

The EEOC has amplified this prohibition in Section 7.9 of its *Technical Assistance Manual.* Section 7.9 notifies employers that the prohibitions of the ADA apply to the provision and administration of health insurance, as well as other benefit plans.
This means that:

> . . . An employer cannot fire or refuse to hire an individual with a disability because the employer's current health insurance plan does not cover the individual's disability, or because the individual may increase the employer's future health care costs.
>
> An employer cannot fire or refuse to hire an individual (whether or not that individual has a disability) because the individual has a family member or dependent with a disability that is not covered by the employer's current health insurance plan, or that may increase the employer's future health care costs.

The language of the ADA, coupled with the explanatory provisions of the EEOC *Technical Assistance Manual,* clearly prohibit terminating an individual with a disability (or an individual with a family member with a disability) so as to avoid paying the increased costs of the individual's medical benefits. Plaintiff alleges that this was the reason he was terminated. Taking plaintiff's allegation as true, it states a claim under the ADA. As such, plaintiff's fourth cause of action is not preempted by ERISA, and the Court must remand the case to state court.

III. Conclusion

Plaintiff's state law discrimination claim that he was fired to avoid paying benefits for his daughter's liver transplant is within the scope of ERISA. However, because the alleged conduct also violates another federal law—the ADA—an exception to preemption exists. As such, the claim is not preempted; no federal question is presented; this Court does not have subject-matter jurisdiction; and the case must be remanded to state court. . . .
It is so ordered.

Case Questions

1. Explain what the terms "removal" and "remand" mean in the context of this case.
2. Are there any reasons the defendant/employer might have preferred to have this case heard in federal, rather than state, court?
3. Suppose the federal court had decided not to remand the case to state court for trial of the plaintiff's state law claims. Would the plaintiff have had a federal law cause of action to pursue?
4. Assuming that the plaintiff had federal law claims available, can you suggest any reasons he apparently preferred instead to pursue state law causes of action?
5. Can you think of any circumstances in which provisions of the two federal laws discussed here—ERISA and ADA—might be in conflict?

FIDUCIARY RESPONSIBILITY

As noted, ERISA imposes standards of conduct and responsibility on fiduciaries of benefit plans established or maintained by employers and unions engaged in or affecting interstate commerce. The act requires that all such plans must be in writing and must designate at least one named fiduciary that has the authority to manage and control the plan's operation and management. The plan must also provide a written procedure for establishing and carrying out a funding policy that is consistent with the plan's objectives and with ERISA's requirements. The written provisions must also specify the basis on which contributions to the fund and payments from the fund will be made. Finally, the written plan must describe the procedure for allocation of responsibility for administering and operating the benefit plan.

ERISA requires that all assets of the benefit plan must be held in trust for the benefit of participating employees and their beneficiaries. The plan must establish a procedure for handling claims on the fund by participants and their beneficiaries. Any individual with a claim against the fund must exhaust these internal procedures before seeking legal remedies from the courts.

Fiduciary
ERISA defines fiduciary as including any person exercising discretionary authority or control respecting the management of the benefit plan, or disposition of plan assets; or who renders, or has authority or responsibility to render, investment advice with respect to any money or property of the plan; or, last, who has *any* discretionary authority or responsibility in the administration of the plan.

Fiduciary

ERISA defines a **fiduciary** as including any person exercising discretionary authority or control respecting the management of the benefit plan, or disposition of plan assets; or who renders, or has authority or responsibility to render, investment advice (for which he or she is compensated) with respect to any money or property of the plan; or who has *any* discretionary authority or responsibility in the administration of the plan. Persons not normally considered fiduciaries, such as consultants or advisers, *may* be found to be fiduciaries when their expertise is used in a managerial, administrative, or advisory capacity by the plan.

In June 2000, the U.S. Supreme Court answered the question of whether treatment decisions by health maintenance organizations (HMOs)—a source of great controversy at the start of this new century—made HMOs and their physicians into fiduciaries.

PEGRAM V. HERDRICH

120 S.Ct. 2143 (2000)

Justice Souter delivered the opinion of the Court.

The question in this case is whether treatment decisions made by a health maintenance organization, acting through its physician employees, are fiduciary acts within the meaning of the Employee Retirement Income Security Act of 1974 (ERISA). We hold that they are not.

I

Petitioners, Carle Clinic Association, P.C., Health Alliance Medical Plans, Inc., and Carle Health Insurance Management Co., Inc. (collectively Carle) function as a health maintenance organization (HMO) organized for profit. Its owners are physicians providing prepaid medical services to participants whose employers contract with Carle to provide such coverage. Respondent, Cynthia Herdrich, was covered by Carle through her husband's employer, State Farm Insurance Company.

The events in question began when a Carle physician, petitioner Lori Pegram, examined Herdrich, who was experiencing pain in the midline area of her groin. Six days later, Dr. Pegram discovered a six by eight centimeter inflamed mass in Herdrich's abdomen. Despite the noticeable inflammation, Dr. Pegram did not order an ultrasound diagnostic procedure at a local hospital, but decided that Herdrich would have to wait eight more days for an ultrasound, to be performed at a facility staffed by Carle more than 50 miles away. Before the eight days were over, Herdrich's appendix ruptured, causing peritonitis.

Herdrich sued Pegram and Carle in state court for medical malpractice, and she later added two counts charging state-law fraud. Carle and Pegram responded that ERISA preempted the new counts, and removed the case to federal court, where they then sought summary judgment on the state-law fraud counts. The District Court granted their motion as to the second fraud count but granted Herdrich leave to amend the one remaining. This she did by alleging that provision of medical services under the terms of the Carle HMO organization, rewarding its physician owners for limiting medical care, entailed an inherent or anticipatory breach of an ERISA fiduciary duty, since these terms created an incentive to make decisions in the physicians' self-interest, rather than the exclusive interests of plan participants.

Herdrich sought relief under 29 U.S.C. § 1109(a), which provides that

> "[a]ny person who is a fiduciary with respect to a plan who breaches any of the responsibilities, obligations, or duties imposed upon fiduciaries by this subchapter shall be personally liable to make good to such plan any losses to the plan resulting from each such breach, and to restore to such plan any profits of such fiduciary which have been made through use of assets of the plan by the fiduciary, and shall be subject to such other equitable or remedial relief as the court may deem appropriate, including removal of such fiduciary."

When Carle moved to dismiss the ERISA count for failure to state a claim upon which relief could be granted, the District Court granted the motion, accepting the Magistrate Judge's determination that Carle was not "involved [in these events] as" an ERISA fiduciary. The original malpractice counts were then tried to a jury, and Herdrich prevailed on both, receiving $35,000 in compensation for her injury. She then appealed the dismissal of the ERISA claim to the Court of Appeals for the Seventh Circuit, which reversed. The court held that Carle was acting as a fiduciary when its physicians made the challenged decisions and that Herdrich's allegations were sufficient to state a claim:

> "Our decision does not stand for the proposition that the existence of incentives automatically gives rise to a breach of fiduciary duty. Rather, we hold that incentives can rise to the level of a breach where, as pleaded here, the fiduciary trust between plan participants and plan fiduciaries no longer exists (i.e., where physicians delay providing necessary treatment to, or withhold administering proper care to, plan beneficiaries for the sole purpose of increasing their bonuses)."

We granted certiorari, and now reverse the Court of Appeals.

II

Whether Carle is a fiduciary when it acts through its physician owners as pleaded in the ERISA count depends on some background of fact and law about HMO organizations, medical benefit plans, fiduciary obligation, and the meaning of Herdrich's allegations.

A

Traditionally, medical care in the United States has been provided on a "fee-for-service" basis. A physician charges so much for a general physical exam, a vaccination, a tonsillectomy, and so on. The physician bills the patient for services provided or, if there is insurance and the doctor is willing, submits the bill for the patient's care to the insurer, for payment subject to the terms of the insurance agreement. In a fee-for-service system, a physician's financial incentive is to provide more care, not less, so long as payment is forthcoming. The check on this incentive is a physician's obligation to exercise reasonable medical skill and judgment in the patient's interest.

Beginning in the late 1960's, insurers and others developed new models for health-care delivery, including HMOs. The defining feature of an HMO is receipt of a fixed fee for each patient enrolled under the terms of a contract to provide specified health care if needed. The HMO thus assumes the financial risk of providing the benefits promised: if a participant never gets sick, the HMO keeps the money regardless, and if a participant becomes expensively ill, the HMO is responsible for the treatment agreed upon even if its cost exceeds the participant's premiums.

Like other risk-bearing organizations, HMOs take steps to control costs. At the least, HMOs, like traditional insurers, will in some fashion make coverage determinations, scrutinizing requested services against the contractual provisions to make sure that a request for care falls within the scope of covered circumstances (pregnancy, for example), or that a given treatment falls within the scope of the care promised (surgery, for instance). They customarily issue general guidelines for their physicians about appropriate levels of care. And they commonly require utilization review (in which specific treatment decisions are reviewed by a decisionmaker other than the treating physician) and approval in advance (precertification) for many types of care, keyed to standards of medical necessity or the reasonableness of the proposed treatment. These cost-controlling measures are commonly complemented by specific financial incentives to physicians, rewarding them for decreasing utilization of health-care services, and penalizing them for what may be found to be excessive treatment. Hence, in an HMO system, a physician's financial interest lies in providing less care, not more. The check on this influence (like that on the converse, fee-for-service incentive) is the professional obligation to provide covered services with a reasonable degree of skill and judgment in the patient's interest.

• • •

B

Herdrich focuses on the Carle scheme's provision for a "year-end distribution," to the HMO's physician owners. She argues that this particular incentive device of annually paying physician owners the profit resulting from their own decisions rationing care can distinguish Carle's organization from HMOs generally, so that reviewing Carle's decisions under a fiduciary standard as pleaded in Herdrich's complaint would not open the door to like claims about other HMO structures. While the Court of Appeals agreed, we think otherwise, under the law as now written.

Although it is true that the relationship between sparing medical treatment and physician reward is not a subtle one under the Carle scheme, no HMO organization could survive without some incentive connecting physician reward with treatment rationing. The essence of an HMO is that salaries and profits are limited by the HMO's fixed membership fees. This is not to suggest that the Carle provisions are as socially desirable as some other HMO organizational schemes; they may not be.

• • •

We think, then, that courts are not in a position to derive a sound legal principle to differentiate an HMO like Carle from other HMOs. For that reason, we proceed on the assumption that the decisions listed in Herdrich's complaint cannot be subject to a claim that they violate fiduciary standards unless all such decisions by all HMOs acting through their owner or employee physicians are to be judged by the same standards and subject to the same claims.

C

[1][2] We turn now from the structure of HMOs to the requirements of ERISA. A fiduciary within the meaning of ERISA must be someone acting in the capacity of manager, administrator, or financial adviser to a "plan," and Herdrich's ERISA count accordingly charged Carle with a breach of fiduciary duty in discharging its obligations under State Farm's medical plan. ERISA's definition of an employee welfare benefit plan is ultimately circular: "any plan, fund, or program . . . to the extent that such plan, fund, or program was established . . . for the purpose of providing . . . through the purchase of insurance or otherwise . . . medical, surgical, or hospital care or benefits." One is thus left to the common understanding of the word "plan" as referring to a scheme decided upon in advance. Here the scheme comprises a set of rules that define the rights of a beneficiary and provide for their enforcement. Rules governing collection of premiums, definition of benefits, submission of claims, and resolution of disagreements over entitlement to services are the sorts of provisions that constitute a plan. Thus, when employers contract with an HMO to provide benefits to employees subject to ERISA, the provisions of documents that set up the HMO are not, as such, an ERISA plan, but the agreement between an HMO and an employer who pays the premiums may, as here, provide elements of a plan by setting out rules under which beneficiaries will be entitled to care.

• • •

D

The allegations of Herdrich's ERISA count that identify the claimed fiduciary breach are difficult to understand. In this count, Herdrich does not point to a particular act by any Carle physician owner as a breach. She does not complain about Pegram's actions, and at oral argument her counsel confirmed that the ERISA count could have been brought, and would have been no different, if Herdrich had never had a sick day in her life.

What she does claim is that Carle, acting through its physician owners, breached its duty to act solely in the interest of beneficiaries by making decisions affecting medical treatment while influenced by the terms of the Carle HMO scheme, under which the physician owners ultimately profit from their own choices to minimize the medical services provided. She emphasizes the threat to fiduciary responsibility in the Carle scheme's feature of a year-end distribution to the physicians of profit derived from the spread between subscription income and expenses of care and administration.

• • •

[6][7] The pleadings must also be parsed very carefully to understand what acts by physician owners acting on Carle's behalf are alleged to be fiduciary in nature. It will help to keep two sorts of arguably administrative acts in mind. What we will call pure "eligibility decisions" turn on the plan's coverage of a particular condition or medical procedure for its treatment. "Treatment decisions," by contrast, are choices about how to go about diagnosing and treating a patient's condition: given a patient's constellation of symptoms, what is the appropriate medical response?

These decisions are often practically inextricable from one another, as amici on both sides agree. This is so not merely because, under a scheme like Carle's, treatment and eligibility decisions are made by the same person, the treating physician. It is so because a great many and possibly most coverage questions are not simple yes-or-no questions, like whether appendicitis is a covered condition (when there is no dispute that a patient has appendicitis), or whether acupuncture is a covered procedure for pain relief (when the claim of pain is unchallenged). The more common coverage question is a when-and-how question. Although coverage for many conditions will be clear and various treatment options will be indisputably compensable, physicians still must decide what to do in particular cases. The issue may be, say, whether one treatment option is so superior to another under the circumstances, and needed so promptly, that a decision to proceed with it would meet the medical necessity requirement that conditions the HMO's obligation to provide or pay for that particular procedure at that time in that case. The Government in its brief alludes to a similar example when it discusses an HMO's refusal to pay for emergency care on the ground that the situation giving rise to the need for care was not an emergency. In practical terms, these eligibility decisions cannot be untangled from physicians' judgments about reasonable medical treatment, and in the case before us, Dr. Pegram's decision was one of that sort. She decided (wrongly, as it turned out) that Herdrich's condition did not warrant immediate action; the consequence of that medical determination was that Carle would not cover immediate care, whereas it would have done so if Dr. Pegram had made the proper diagnosis and judgment to treat. The eligibility decision and the treatment decision were inextricably mixed, as they are in countless medical administrative decisions every day.

• • •

[8] Based on our understanding of the matters just discussed, we think Congress did not intend Carle or any other HMO to be treated as a fiduciary to the extent that it makes mixed eligibility decisions acting through its physicians.

Case Questions

1. Discuss whether HMOs on balance have improved or damaged the delivery of medical services in the United States.
2. What do you think are the policy considerations behind the Supreme Court's decision in this case?
3. Without benefit of ERISA protection, are future litigants left with sufficient legal remedies against HMOs that make similar mistakes in diagnosis and treatment?
4. Does what happened to the plaintiff in this case suggest that the federal government should nationalize HMOs?

CORPORATE CORRUPTION CONTINUES DESPITE ERISA: THE ENRON EXAMPLE

THE WORKING LAW

On June 27, 2003, the U.S. Department of Labor filed suit against current and former officers of Enron Corporation and its pension plan. The DOL contended in its complaint that the defendants had breached their fiduciary duty of protecting Enron employees from the

huge losses these workers endured when Enron's stock price collapsed in 2001. The retirement accounts of many Enron employees were heavily invested in Enron's own stock, which in the late 1990s had been one of the hottest equity investments on Wall Street. Enron, a Fortune 500 company that dealt in energy contracts, was considered a rock-solid investment until an accounting scandal, instigated by a whistleblower inside the company, revealed that most of Enron's substantial profits existed only on paper.

The pension fund lawsuit followed hard on the heels of a decision by federal energy regulators to bar Enron from engaging in competitive electricity and natural gas sales. According to the DOL complaint, more than 20,700 employee/participants in Enron's 401(k) plan had nearly two-thirds of their pension fund assets tied up in the company's common stock. The accounting scandal caused the publicly traded securities' value to collapse, driving the firm into bankruptcy by December 2001.The lawsuit named former Enron Chairman Kenneth Lay, who succeeded in cashing out before his company's stock value collapsed, as well as former directors of the corporation, including the wife of former Senator Phil Gramm of Texas, Enron's home state.

Critics on the political left complained that the Enron debacle demonstrates the weak condition of other company pension plans grounded upon investment in their own securities and a gap in the federal pension plan regulatory "safety net" intended to protect employees from such financial catastrophes.

Sources: "Enron Sued on Pensions," *International Herald Tribune Online,* June 27, 2003, **http://www.iht.com/articles/100950.htm**; Leigh Strope, "Labor Dept. to Sue Enron over Pensions," *Washington Post,* June 26, 2003, p. E12; Robin Blackburn, "The Enron Debacle and the Pension Crisis," *New Left Review,* March–April 2002.

Fiduciary Duties

ERISA generally codifies and expands the common-law concepts defining the role of a fiduciary. Under ERISA, fiduciaries must discharge their duties solely in the interest of the participants and their beneficiaries for the exclusive purpose of providing them with plan benefits.

Fiduciaries under ERISA are held to the common-law "prudent person rule"; that is, the fiduciary must act "with the care, skill, prudence and diligence that a prudent person acting in a like capacity and familiar with such matters would use in the conduct of an enterprise of like character and with like aims." For instance, the fiduciary must diversify the investments of the plan to minimize the risk of large losses, unless under the particular circumstances it would be prudent not to diversify. (See the discussion of Enron in The Working Law above).

Prohibited Transactions

The act prohibits self-serving transactions by fiduciaries or persons "with an interest" in the benefit plan. The act defines a person "with an interest" as including a fiduciary, a person providing services to the plan, an employer whose employees are covered by the plan, or an owner having a 50 percent or greater interest in such an enterprise/employer. The transactions prohibited between the plan and the person with an interest include the sale or lease of property, the extension of credit, and the furnishing of goods, services, or facilities. Also prohibited is the transfer of plan assets to, or for the use of, a person with an interest.

Fiduciaries are forbidden to engage in self-dealing with the plan—that is, dealing with the assets of the plan for their own interests. Fiduciaries are also prohibited from receiving any consideration or benefit personally from persons dealing with the plan in connection with a transaction involving the assets of the plan. The act prohibits the plan from investing more than 10 percent of its assets in the securities or property of an employer of employees participating in the plan. (Investments in such employer securities or property involving less than 10 percent of the plan's assets must still meet the prudent person test.

Liability for Breach of Fiduciary Duty

Fiduciaries are liable to the plan for any losses resulting from the breach of any of their duties, responsibilities, or obligations. Such a fiduciary must also refund any personal profits made through personal use of the plan's assets. The miscreant fiduciary may also be subject to any other equitable or remedial measures that the court may deem appropriate, including his or her removal.

Fiduciaries may also be liable for the breach of duty by a cofiduciary under the following circumstances:

1. knowingly participating in, or undertaking to conceal, an act or omission of a cofiduciary;
2. enabling a cofiduciary to commit a breach by failing to comply with their own fiduciary responsibilities;
3. failing to make reasonable efforts to remedy a breach by a cofiduciary of which they have knowledge.

Exculpatory provisions, which seek to protect fiduciaries from liability for the breach of their duties, are generally held to be void as against public policy. The fiduciary may insure against liability for breach of duty; however, if the benefit plan provides such insurance for the fiduciary, the insurance company must be allowed to recover from the fiduciary any amounts paid out under the policy.

Fiduciaries are not liable for any breaches that occur either before they become fiduciaries or after they cease to be fiduciaries of the plan.

Bonding

The act requires every fiduciary of an employee pension plan and every person who handles funds or property of a plan to be bonded in an amount equal to at least 10 percent of the funds handled, but not less than $1,000 and not more than $500,000. The form of the bond must be approved by the secretary of labor and must provide protection to the plan against any loss caused by fraud or dishonesty of the plan official.

No bonding is required for the administrator, officers, or employees of a plan under which only the general assets of a union are used to pay benefits. In addition, no bond is required of a fiduciary that is a U.S. corporation exercising trust powers or conducting an insurance business if it is subject to supervision or examination by federal or state authorities and, at all times, has combined capital and surplus in excess of a minimum amount set by regulation, at not less than $1 million.

ERISA also authorizes a plan administrator to apply to the secretary of labor for exemption from the bonding requirements on the ground that the overall financial condition of the plan is sound enough to provide protection for participants and their beneficiaries.

Enforcement of Fiduciary Duties

The fiduciary duty and responsibility provisions of ERISA are enforced by the Department of Labor and by plan participants and their beneficiaries. The Department of Labor is authorized by the act to bring suit against a fiduciary who breaches any duties, obligations, or responsibilities under the act. Such suits may also be brought by plan participants or the beneficiaries, who may, if successful, also recover their legal fees and costs.

If an employee benefit plan has engaged in certain prohibited transactions, the secretary of labor may assess a civil penalty to be paid by the plan. If the plan engaging in the prohibited transactions is qualified for preferential tax treatment, the Internal Revenue Service may impose and collect an excise tax against the plan, rather than having the secretary of labor levy a civil penalty.

CORPORATE CORRUPTION CONTINUES DESPITE ERISA: THE WORLDCOM EXAMPLE

THE WORKING LAW

In 2002, WorldCom—little more than a year earlier one of the hottest communications stocks in a booming bull market fueled by upstart dot-com companies—became the target of multiple lawsuits brought in federal and state courts by major retirement funds that had invested heavily in the corporation's stock. When WorldCom reported in mid-2002 that $3.8 billion dollars was wrongly reflected on its corporate books as capital expenses during the preceding two fiscal years—meaning that the red-hot communications company had actually suffered net losses when it was reporting record profits to its investors—its stock value (like that of Enron) plummeted. New York State's pension fund for its public employees reported a loss of $300 million due to WorldCom's debacle. It was the largest loss from a single security in the fund's whole history. Michigan reported a $116 million decline, and Florida reported $90 million.

In March 2003, the U.S. District Court for the Southern District of New York, which sits in Manhattan, ruled that an action brought by the New York City Employees' Retirement System in a New York State court, and which named WorldCom directors, executives, and accountants as defendants, was so closely entangled with WorldCom's bankruptcy proceedings that it must be pursued in the federal court arena. Two of these defendants, former WorldCom CFO Scott Sullivan and Controller David Myers, had already been arrested and charged by federal prosecutors with securities fraud and filing false statements with the Securities and Exchange Commission. At the time of these arrests in late July 2002, the Department of Justice was also looking into a $400 million loan borrowed from WorldCom by its cofounder and CEO Bernard Ebbers shortly before the company's stock value crashed. Additionally, some twenty class actions, including two by WorldCom employees under ERISA, were pending when WorldCom filed for Chapter 11 bankruptcy court protection in June 2002. And still other pension funds had filed lawsuits in various state courts. The U.S. Bankruptcy Court in Manhattan heard WorldCom's case in September 2003 and the court's decision was pending as this fifth edition went to press.

Sources: "Pensions' Lawsuits against WorldCom to Proceed in New York Federal Court," *Bankruptcy Law Daily,* March 10, 2003, **http://subscript.bna.com/SAMPLES/bky.nsf/0/a357bbf1c26704e885256ce0007ba50f?OpenDocument**; Marc Humbert, "Pensions Reel under WorldCom's Loss," *San Francisco Examiner,* March 28, 2002, **http://www.examiner.com/business/default.jsp?story=b.worldcom.0628w**; "WorldCom Executives Arrested," *BBC News,* August 1, 2002, **http://news.bbc.co.uk/1/hi/business/2166426.stm**

MINIMUM REQUIREMENTS FOR QUALIFIED PENSION PLANS

In addition to imposing standards of conduct for benefit plan fiduciaries, ERISA sets certain minimum requirements that plans must meet to qualify for preferential tax treatment. The act also requires plan administrators to disclose certain relevant financial information, and it provides an insurance fund for benefits payable under certain pensions.

Types of Pension Plans

The act recognizes two types of pension plans: defined-benefit plans and defined-contribution plans.

http://www.pbgc.gov *will take you to the home page of the PBGC.*

Defined-Benefit Plan
A pension plan that ensures eligible employees and their beneficiaries a specified monthly income for life.

Defined-Constribution Plan
Plan under which employer makes a fixed-share contribution into a retirement account each year.

Defined-Benefit Plans. A **defined-benefit plan** is a pension plan that ensures eligible employees and their beneficiaries a specified monthly income for life. ERISA provides an insurance scheme to guarantee the benefits under defined-benefit plans. The insurance scheme is administered by the Pension Benefit Guaranty Corporation (PBGC) set up under the act. The PBGC collects a premium from employers offering such pensions to provide an insurance fund. If an employer is unable to meet the payment requirements of a defined-benefit plan, the PBGC will pay monthly benefits to the participating employees up to a maximum monthly amount. Despite the substantial sums raised by the PBGC through employer premiums, the insurance fund is inadequate to cover all potential liability under defined-benefit pension plans. And employers, by and large, have shied away from defined-benefit plans in recent years. It's easy to understand why: The graying of the work force, the retirement of the huge population of baby boomers, and fluctuations in financial markets conspire to make defined-benefit plans pricey and unpredictable.

Defined-Contribution Plans. Under **defined-contribution plans,** an employer makes a fixed-share contribution into a retirement account each year. These funds are invested on behalf of the participating employee, who receives the proceeds upon retirement. The pension benefits under a defined-contribution plan are not insured against failure of the company and are not covered by the PBGC. In contrast to defined-benefit plans, defined-contribution plans shift the risk from the employer to the employee. The employer knows exactly how much it must contribute annually per employee. The employee runs the risk that these contributions will fall short of his or her retirement requirements. During the 2002 stock market decline, which included the dot-com meltdown and the Enron/WorldCom scandals, many would-be retirees postponed their departures from the work force as their pension plan gains of the 1990s eroded and, in some instances, even evaporated.

Plans Qualifying for Preferential Tax Treatment

ERISA sets certain minimum requirements that pension plans must meet to qualify for preferential tax treatment. Such requirements involve participation of employees and vesting—that is, entitlement to non-forfeitable benefits under the plan. The requirements specified under ERISA are minimum requirements; the employer may offer more generous provisions in a pension plan. However, if the plan's requirements are more stringent than ERISA's minimum provisions, the pension plan will not qualify for preferential tax treatment.

Participation and Coverage Requirements. Although a company's tax-qualified retirement plan need not cover all its employees, certain minimal coverage and participation requirements must be met. In reviewing these requirements, keep in mind that they constitute the "floor" below which coverage and participation cannot be permitted to drop; a company can be more liberal with the participation rules in its particular plan if it wishes.

The Internal Revenue Code permits a qualified retirement plan to require an employee to reach the age of twenty-one and to complete a year of service before being eligible to participate. If a plan provides for full and immediate vesting of company contributions into it, then participation can be conditioned upon up to two years of service. [This exception does not apply to 401(k) plans, for which the maximum period before participation remains one year of service regardless of the vesting schedule.] A plan is no longer permitted to set a maximum age for an employee's participation. Although the law once stated that new hires who were less than five years away from the plan's specified normal retirement age could be excluded, this is no longer the case.

Plans that are permitted to require two years of service prior to plan participation cannot demand that the two years be consecutive. But employees who incur a one-year break in service can be required to start the qualification process over again when they resume employment with the sponsoring company.

A plan can exclude specified classes of employees from participation based on factors other than failure to meet minimum age and length of service requirements. The most common exclusion is of unionized employees subject to a collective-bargaining agreement, which may include a provision for participation in a multi-employer pension plan sponsored by the union. Sometimes, too, unions succeed in negotiating superior terms with the employer. For example, at Rider University in New Jersey, the faculty, represented for collective bargaining by the American

Association of University Professors, receives a 0.25 percent higher pension contribution than the university's nonunion employees.

The length of service requirement (that is, the eligibility computation period) is defined as any consecutive twelve months, whether specified in the plan as a calendar year or plan year, during which the employee works at least 1,000 hours. If the employee falls short of the 1,000-hour requirement during the initial computation period, the next computation period commences on the anniversary of employment or the first day of the plan year in which that anniversary falls, if the plan so specifies. For purposes of computing the 1,000 hours, the law calls for including all hours for which the employee is paid or is entitled to be paid. Hours of service thus include paid vacation, sick days, holidays, days missed because of disability, and the like. Back pay, awarded under one of the federal labor or employment laws, is also included.

A one-year break in service similarly means a calendar year, plan year, or any other consecutive twelve months designated by the plan, during which for whatever reason the employee fails to complete more than 500 hours of service. (One significant exception is parenting leave, which does not constitute such a break in service.)

In addition to participation requirements, the law also imposes coverage requirements as a condition of tax qualification. A pension plan must satisfy one of two coverage tests: the ratio percentage test or the average benefit test. (A plan having no "non-highly compensated" employees will automatically meet the Internal Revenue Code's coverage requirements.)

Using the ratio percentage test, the number of nonhighly compensated active employees participating must equal at least 70 percent of the highly compensated ($75,000-plus per year or owners, officers, and best-paid employees even if earning as little as $45,000 to $50,000) active employees.

If the average benefit test is used, the plan must not discriminate in favor of the company's highly compensated employees. The nonhighly compensated workers once again must receive at least 70 percent of the highly compensated participants' average benefits.

Vesting Requirements. Vesting means that a plan participant has gained a nonforfeitable right to some plan benefit. In the case of a defined-contribution plan, the right is to the employee's accrued account balance, which may fluctuate with the financial markets if the account is invested in securities. (Thus, for example, Enron employees may have been vested in their pension plan, but since the plan was invested in Enron's own stock, when the stock value collapsed, these hapless employees enjoyed a nonforfeitable right to little or nothing.) If the plan is of the defined-benefit variety, the non-forfeitable right is to the accrued benefit. (But if the plan is under-funded and the employer is in financial trouble, reaping that benefit on retirement may be problematic.) Vesting turns upon length of service. Until a participant's length of service compels vesting, that participant can accrue benefits but will not have a non-forfeitable right to those benefits. In other words, if an employee quits or is fired before vesting begins, his or her accrued benefits will be lost (unless the employee moves to a related company in the same corporation or is rehired by the same company before a one-year break in service has occurred).[2]

Not long ago, it was not unusual for plans to require ten years of service for full vesting. Changes to federal law liberalized that requirement, and plans must now choose between two minimum vesting schedules. Under a five-year vesting schedule, no vesting occurs until the participant completes five years of service, when 100 percent occurs. Under seven-year graded vesting, the minimum acceptable schedule is as follows:

Years of Service	Vested Percentage
Less than 3	0
3	20
4	40
5	60
6	80
7 or more	100

Two important points should be kept in mind. First, as with participation and coverage requirements, the above schedules are minimums; a particular employer's plan(s) can permit faster vesting if the employer desires. Second, these schedules count years of service, not years of participation. Thus, in the five-year vesting option, for example, a plan that called for a year of service to participate plus five years of participation would not meet the minimum vesting schedule.

Interruptions in Service. All vesting schedules require some period of continuous employment, and breaks in service become important in computing the time at which benefits become vested. In computing an employee's years of service, any years of service completed prior to any one-year break in service are not required to be taken into account until the employee has completed a year of service after returning to employment. Thereafter, if the number of consecutive one-year breaks totals five or more or exceeds the employee's pre-break years of service (regardless of number) and no vesting has occurred before the break in service, then the pre-break service can be ignored for vesting purposes. Additionally, years of service before the employee turned eighteen, years of service before the plan was put into effect, and if the plan is contributory, years in which the participant declined to contribute can be disregarded.

Integration of Benefits. Although an employee has a vested right to participate in pension plan benefits after the requisite time period, in some circumstances the amounts the employer must pay out to the employee under the plan may be reduced by the amount of payments the employee receives from some other program. For example, some pension plans may take into account the social security

---

[2]However, remember that under ERISA it is illegal to fire an employee for the express purpose of preventing him or her from reaping the benefits of the plan. See *Le v. Applied Biosystems* [886 F. Supp. 717 (N.D. Cal. 1995)] at page 258 in this chapter.

payments received by employees in calculating the monthly pension benefits paid to such employees. ERISA provides that a qualified plan may be offset by $83\frac{1}{3}$ percent of the social security payments received by an employee; that is, the monthly pension benefits paid to the employee under the plan may be reduced by the amount equal to $83\frac{1}{3}$ percent of the monthly social security benefits received by the employee. But after benefits to a participant have commenced, they cannot later be reduced by an increase in social security.

Integration
The right to offset benefits against those paid by other sources.

This right of offsetting benefits against those paid by other sources is known as **integration.** Integration is an extraordinarily complex area, even by ERISA's intricate standards, beyond the scope of this book.

POTENTIAL PLUSES OF DEFINED-BENEFIT PLANS FOR OWNER-EMPLOYEES

THE WORKING LAW

A defined-benefit plan can pose problems for a corporation, especially if that company is in a declining sector of the economy or when, as now, interest rates are extremely low—thus leading the Bush administration and the Congress to propose replacing the long-term Treasury bond rate with a melded rate derived from a basket of corporate debt securities (see the introduction to this chapter). However, a defined-benefit plan can create a windfall in the form of tax savings for an owner-employee of a closely held corporation.

After years of hard work, good management, and outstanding customer service, a business owner had a profitable company and an excellent income. But he believed that too much of his income was being turned over to the IRS, so he approached his financial adviser, who suggested a defined-benefit pension plan as the solution.

While the IRS in 2003 allowed a maximum annual contribution of $40,000 for a defined-contribution plan (and even less for a 401[k] plan), the agency allowed the business owner to contribute up to $160,000 per year into a defined-benefit plan. This regulatory difference exists in recognition of the historical problem of underfunding such plans, which (as you now know) specify the vested benefit that each plan participant must receive upon retirement, the state of the corporation and the state of the economy notwithstanding.

Furthermore, new government regulations allow for creation of a much-simplified defined-benefit plan tailored to the needs of small businesses. This so-called 412(i) plan actually contains a sliding scale of contributions so that "Johnny-come-latelies" can use catch-up provisions to contribute nearly a quarter-million dollars per year on a tax-deductible basis.

Secondary benefits of establishing such a plan can include creditor protection and a disability supplement. This latter supplement can eventually replace a business owner's traditional self-employment disability insurance, a second area of savings.

Source: William Gevers, "Defined Benefit Plan Secures Pension for Business Owners," *Puget Sound Business Journal,* April 28, 2003, **http://seattle.bizjournals.com/seattle/stories/2003/04/28/focus11.html**.

Minimum Funding Requirements

Employers with pension plans are required by ERISA to set aside a sufficient amount of funds each year to cover the benefit liabilities that accrued under the plan during that year. These funds are maintained in a funding standard account. The act also requires that past-service costs (costs for earned benefits that had been unfunded prior to the passage of ERISA) must be paid each year. The plan must pay the normal cost of plan administration for that year, plus the amount necessary to amortize (in equal installments until fully amortized) those earned benefits that had been unfunded prior to ERISA's passage. The rate at which these past-service costs are **amortized** depends on the time at which the pension plan came into existence.

Amortize
To liquidate a debt by means of installment payments.

Liability due to experience gains and deficiencies of the plan must be amortized in equal installments over a maximum fifteen-year period. The determination of experience gains or losses and a valuation of the plan's liabilities must be made at least every three years. Net amounts lost due to changes in actuarial assumptions used under the plan must be amortized over a thirty-year period.

http://www.pbgc.gov *provides guidance and FAQs for business and participants on pension fund topics.*

Waivers The funding requirements of a plan for any given year may be waived by the IRS upon the plan's showing of hardship. It must be shown that the waiver will not be adverse to the plan's participants as a group. Any amounts waived must be amortized over a maximum fifteen-year period. A plan may not be granted more than five waivers during a fifteen-year period.

Funding Penalties If the required funding standards are not met by the employer, a 5 percent excise tax may be imposed by the IRS against the accumulated funding deficiency. If the deficiency is not corrected within a specified time, a penalty of up to 100 percent of the deficiency may be levied by the IRS.

In the following case, the plaintiffs rely on the terms of their summary plan description in contending that their pension plan was illegally underfunded, notwithstanding the plan documents, which arguably legitimized the lower retirement benefits they received.

Burnstein v. Retirement Account Plan for Employees of Allegheny Health Education Research Foundation

2003 WL 21509028 (3rd Cir.)

Garth, Circuit Judge

The plaintiff-appellants in this ERISA case appeal from the district court's dismissal of their First Amended Complaint for failure to state a claim and also challenge the denial of their motion to file a Second Amended Complaint as futile.

The plaintiffs are five former employees of the now-bankrupt Allegheny Health Education and Research Foundation ("AHERF"). These plaintiffs sought to recover benefits that they believed they had accrued through AHERF's Retirement Account Plan. . . .

In 1988, AHERF, which operated hospitals and other health-care facilities in western Pennsylvania, began acquiring hospitals and associated physician practices and medical schools in the Philadelphia area.

AHERF had begun to experience significant financial losses by the late 1990s. In July 1998, AHERF filed for bankruptcy. The complaint alleges that AHERF, a non-profit corporation, was profligate in its expenditures and generous (to a fault) in furnishing its executives with compensation, stock options, travel opportunities and the like. . . .

AHERF's Retirement Account Plan was a defined benefit pension plan under ERISA. The AHERF Plan was a "cash balance plan," a form of a defined benefit plan under ERISA in which "the employer's contribution is made into hypothetical individual employee accounts." The complaint alleged that because the Plan "speaks in terms of a participant's 'account,' many participants are fooled into thinking that the cash balance plan works like a defined contribution plan." Under a cash balance plan, however, if the plan terminates, "it is possible that the plan will be underfunded as to some or all of the participants." . . .

Burnstein alleges that he was surprised to learn that AHERF had not funded the Plan for the benefits he believed had accrued. . . .

The complaint alleged that the Summary Plan Description "reinforces the impression created by the Plan Brochure that each participant had a fully funded account in which retirement benefits were accrued and grew each year." . . .

Today, we join the other Courts of Appeals that have considered this issue, and hold that, where a summary plan description conflicts with the plan language, it is the summary plan description that will control. . . .

Case Questions

1. Do you agree with the court's holding, or should the pension plan, as the official legal contract, be the controlling document in the case? What are the arguments for and against the respective positions?
2. If, as is suggested by the plaintiffs in their complaint in this case, the corporation's top executives generously rewarded themselves while failing to insure that the rank-and-file employee pension plan was fully funded, should that be viewed as a prima facie breach of a fiduciary duty?
3. How should the fact that Allegheny started out as a not-for-profit corporation affect the court's view of this case?
4. How is a cash-balance pension plan different from a traditional defined-benefit plan?

Discrimination

To qualify for preferential tax treatment under ERISA, pension plans must not, either by design or operation, discriminate in favor of officers, shareholders, or highly compensated employees. The act prohibits discrimination in benefits, contributions, and coverage of employee classifications under a plan. A plan may be limited to only salaried workers; employees earning only wages may be excluded from the plan. The key factor is that contributions and benefits of employees bear a uniform relationship to total compensation. Any variation in treatment under the plan must be applied consistently and may not discriminate in favor of the "prohibited class" of employees (officers, shareholders, and those who are defined as highly compensated).

Reporting and Disclosure Requirements

ERISA imposes a series of reporting and disclosure requirements on the administrators of pension plans. These requirements are designed to provide the government and plan participants with the information necessary to enforce and protect participants' rights, to assure nondiscriminatory operation of the plan, to disclose prohibited transactions, and to give advance warnings of possible plan failures.

The plan must furnish plan participants and beneficiaries with a summary plan description (SPD), which must provide the name and address of the plan, its administrator and trustees, the requirements for participation, vesting and disqualification under the plan, procedures for presenting claims, and procedures for appealing denials of claims. The plan must also provide participants and beneficiaries with a summary of material modifications to the plan and with a summary annual report of the plan.

The plan must file a summary description of the plan (similar to that given to participants) and summaries of all material modifications to the plan with the Department of Labor. The plan must file a detailed annual premium filing form and a notice of any "reportable event," such as changes reducing benefits payable, inability to pay benefits due, failure to meet minimum funding standards, or transactions with the Pension Benefit Guaranty Corporation (PBGC). In addition, the plan must file a notice of intention to terminate with the PBGC at least ten days prior to the plan's termination. Finally, the plan must file extremely detailed financial disclosure forms with the IRS annually.

TERMINATION OF A PLAN

ERISA allows the termination of any existing pension plan, subject to provisions intended to protect those persons receiving benefits and to guarantee the preservation of the benefits vested before the plan is terminated. As just mentioned, a notice of the intention to terminate the plan must be filed with the PBGC at least ten days prior to the termination. ERISA created the PBGC, financed by a premium levied against employers, to insure employees against the loss of their benefits when a defined-benefit plan is terminated. If the plan is unable to meet its obligations, PBGC will pay minimum monthly benefits to those entitled to payments under the plan.

Upon termination of a plan, the plan's assets are allocated pursuant to the following priorities: voluntary employee contributions, required employee contributions, benefits to participants receiving benefits for at least three years based on plan provisions in effect for five years, all other insured benefits, all other non-forfeitable benefits, and all other benefits. If the assets are insufficient to cover all claims within one of the described classes, then the assets will be allocated pro rata within the last class to receive benefits under the allocation.

When the assets of a plan are insufficient to satisfy benefit claims, the employer is liable to the PBGC for 100 percent of the under-funding, subject to a limit of 30 percent of the net worth of the employer. This liability is a government lien against the property of the employer and is treated as a federal tax lien.

If there are surplus funds in the pension fund upon its termination, the employer may recover those surplus funds under certain circumstances. Section 4044(d)(1) of ERISA provides that the employer may recover any surplus assets remaining in the pension fund if (1) all liabilities to participating employees and beneficiaries for benefits under the pension plan have been satisfied, (2) the recovery of surplus assets by the employer does not violate any section of ERISA, and (3) the pension plan itself provides that the employer may recover any surplus funds in these circumstances. The employer is subject to an excise tax on the amount of the surplus funds; nevertheless, over the years since ERISA's enactment, numerous corporations have terminated pension plans to recapture excess contributions, and occasionally, corporate raiders have captured control of publicly traded companies to cash in on overfunded pension plans.

Multiemployer Plan Terminations or Withdrawals. When ERISA was enacted, the PBGC insurance provisions applied only to pension plans operated by single employers. PBGC coverage was not extended to multiemployer pension plans until 1980. The Multiemployer Pension Plan Amendments Act of 1980 extended PBGC coverage to employers withdrawing from a multiemployer pension plan. Employers must pay a fixed amount into the fund. The amount, to be paid upon withdrawal, is the withdrawing employer's proportionate share of the plan's unfunded vested benefits. Unfunded vested benefits are defined as the difference between the present value of the plan's vested benefits and the current value of the plan's assets.

http://www.pbgc.gov/legal_info.htm *lists parts of the Code of Federal Regulations dealing with PBGC regulations.*

The following case considers whether an employer-member of a multiemployer plan can escape liability because it misunderstood the terms of the relevant collective bargaining agreement.

Laborers' Pension Fund v. A&C Environmental, Inc.

301 F.3d 768 (7th Cir. 2002)

Ripple, Circuit Judge

The Laborers' Pension Fund and the Laborers' Welfare Fund of the Health and Welfare Department of the Construction and General Laborers' District Council of Chicago and Vicinity . . . brought this action under ERISA section 515 and section 301 of the Labor-Management Relations Act to recover delinquent contributions and union dues allegedly owed to them by A&C Environmental, Inc. ("A&C"). . . .

A&C is a corporation specializing in the transportation and disposal of hazardous and nonhazardous waste. In April 1999 . . . [the collective-bargaining agreement] that [A&C] signed states that A&C . . . "agrees to pay the amounts that it is bound to pay under the said Collective Bargaining Agreements to the Health and Welfare Department of the Construction and General Laborers' District Council of Chicago and Vicinity and the Laborers' Pension Fund." . . .

A&C failed to contribute to the Funds or to remit all of the dues that the Union claimed were due.

The Funds brought suit against A&C . . . to recover the delinquent contributions and hired an auditing firm to determine how much A&C owed. . . .

At trial A&C presented its defense of fraud in the execution, seeking to prove that [its representative] had not known that the contract he signed with the Union obligated A&C to make contributions to the Funds and that his ignorance was excusable. . . .

[The jury found in A&C's favor, and the plaintiffs appealed.]

Although fraud in the execution is a viable defense under ERISA section 515, A&C has not made out the defense. In order to establish the defense of fraud in the execution, A&C had to prove that it did not know that it was signing a collective bargaining agreement that obligated it to make contributions to the Funds and that its ignorance was excusable because it had reasonably relied upon the representations of the union representative. . . . The Funds do not contest that the Union representative, Mr. Frattini, misrepresented the nature of the contract to [A&C's representative]. They submit, however, that [A&C's] ignorance of the nature of the contract was inexcusable because [A&C's representative] had a reasonable opportunity to review the document. . . .

Here, [A&C's representative] signed a one-page document written in English and entitled "Collective Bargaining Agreement." . . . A&C insists that [its representative] did not understand that the contract would require the company to contribute to the pension funds; if he had reviewed the single page he would have learned that it did. In short, [his] ignorance of the nature of the contract was not excusable. Thus, as a matter of law, A&C did not prove fraud in the execution; it simply failed to show that there was any reasonable basis for [its] reliance on the earlier representations of the union representative. . . .

REVERSED AND REMANDED

Case Questions

1. Define "fraud in the execution" of a contract.
2. What facts would have satisfied the court that A&C was a victim of fraud?
3. Shouldn't the court punish the plaintiffs for the admitted fraud committed by the union business agent when dealing with A&C's representative?
4. What lesson does this case teach with regard to dealing with labor unions?

Administration and Enforcement

http://www.pbgc.gov *is the PBGC's home page.*

ERISA's provisions and requirements are enforced by the Department of Labor, the Internal Revenue Service, and individual participants and beneficiaries. The fiduciary duties and the reporting and disclosure provisions are enforced by the Department of Labor. The IRS enforces the minimum vesting and participation requirements and levies tax penalties for funding violations and prohibited transactions. Individual participants and beneficiaries may bring suit to enforce their rights under the act.

The act provides criminal penalties for willful violations of the reporting and disclosure requirements. Persons willfully violating those requirements are subject to a fine of not more than $5,000, a prison term of up to one year, or both. Violations by corporate or union fiduciaries may be subject to a fine of up to $100,000.

Civil actions may be brought by a participant or beneficiary if the plan administrator fails to furnish requested materials about the plan. Civil suits may also be brought to recover benefits due under the plan. Participants may also collect penalties of up to $100 per day from an administrator who fails to provide, upon request, information to which a participant is entitled. Participants and beneficiaries, and the secretary of labor, may bring actions to clarify rights to future benefits, to enjoin any violation of the act or terms of the plan, and to obtain relief from a breach of fiduciary responsibilities.

Where private rights of action and the secretary of labor's power overlap remained in Y2K a gray area requiring Supreme Court oversight and clarification.

Harris Trust and Savings Bank v. Salomon Smith Barney Inc.

120 S.Ct. 2180 (2000)

Justice Thomas delivered the opinion of the Court.

Section 406(a) of the Employee Retirement Income Security Act of 1974 (ERISA) bars a fiduciary of an employee benefit plan from causing the plan to engage in certain transactions with a "party in interest." Section 502(a)(3) authorizes a "participant, beneficiary, or fiduciary" of a plan to bring a civil action to obtain "appropriate equitable relief" to redress violations of ERISA Title I. The question is whether that authorization extends to a suit against a nonfiduciary "party in interest" to a transaction barred by § 406(a). We hold that it does.

I

• • •

Ameritech Pension Trust (APT) provides pension benefits to employees and retirees of Ameritech Corporation and its subsidiaries and affiliates. Salomon [Salomon Smith Barney], during the late 1980's, provided broker-dealer services to APT, executing nondiscretionary equity trades at the direction of APT's fiduciaries, thus qualifying itself (we assume) as a "party in interest." . . . Salomon sold interests in several motel properties to APT for nearly $21 million. APT's purchase of the motel interests was directed by National Investment Services of America (NISA), an investment manager to which Ameritech had delegated investment discretion over a portion of the plan's assets, and hence a fiduciary of APT.

This litigation arose when APT's fiduciaries—its trustee, petitioner Harris Trust and Savings Bank, and its administrator, petitioner Ameritech Corporation—discovered that the motel interests were nearly worthless. Petitioners maintain that the interests had been worthless all along; Salomon asserts, to the contrary, that the interests declined in value due to a downturn in the motel industry. Whatever the true cause, petitioners sued Salomon in 1992. . . .

Salomon moved for summary judgment, arguing that § 502(a)(3), when used to remedy a transaction prohibited by § 406(a), authorizes a suit only against the party expressly constrained by § 406(a)—the fiduciary who caused the plan to enter the transaction—and not against the counterparty to the transaction.

The District Court denied the motion, holding that ERISA does provide a private cause of action against nonfiduciaries who participate in a prohibited transaction, but granted Salomon's subsequent motion for certification of the issue for interlocutory appeal under 28 U.S.C. § 1292(b).

The Court of Appeals for the Seventh Circuit reversed.

• • •

II

[5] We agree with the Seventh Circuit's and Salomon's interpretation of § 406(a). They rightly note that § 406(a) imposes a duty only on the fiduciary that causes the plan to engage in the transaction. We reject, however, the Seventh Circuit's and Salomon's conclusion that, absent a substantive provision of ERISA expressly imposing a duty upon a nonfiduciary party in interest, the nonfiduciary party may not be held liable under § 502(a)(3), one of ERISA's remedial provisions. Petitioners contend, and we agree, that § 502(a)(3) itself imposes certain duties, and therefore that liability under that provision does not depend on whether ERISA's substantive provisions impose a specific duty on the party being sued.

[6] Section 502 [a] provides:

". . . A civil action may be brought—

"(3) by a participant, beneficiary, or fiduciary (A) to enjoin any act or practice which violates any provision of [ERISA Title I] or the terms of the plan, or (B) to obtain other appropriate equitable relief (i) to redress such violations or (ii) to enforce any provisions of this title or the terms of the plan."

• • •

Section 502(1) provides in relevant part:

> "(1) In the case of—
> "(A) any breach of fiduciary responsibility under (or other violation of) part 4 of this subtitle by a fiduciary, or
> "(B) any knowing participation in such a breach or violation by any other person,
> "the Secretary shall assess a civil penalty against such fiduciary or other person in an

amount equal to 20 percent of the applicable recovery amount.

"(2) For purposes of paragraph (1), the term 'applicable recovery amount' means any amount which is recovered from a fiduciary or other person with respect to a breach or violation described in paragraph (1)—

"(A) pursuant to any settlement agreement with the Secretary, or

"(B) ordered by a court to be paid by such fiduciary or other person to a plan or its participants and beneficiaries in a judicial proceeding instituted by the Secretary under subsection (a)(2) or (a)(5) of this section." 29 U.S.C. §§ 1132(l)(1)–(2).

Section 502(l) contemplates civil penalty actions by the Secretary against two classes of defendants, fiduciaries and "other person[s]." The latter class concerns us here. Paraphrasing, the Secretary shall assess a civil penalty against an "other person" who "knowing[ly] participat[es] in" "any . . . violation of . . . part 4 . . . by a fiduciary." And the amount of such penalty is defined by reference to the amount "ordered by a court to be paid by such . . . other person to a plan or its participants and beneficiaries in a judicial proceeding instituted by the Secretary under subsection (a)(2) or (a)(5)." Ibid.

[8] The plain implication is that the Secretary may bring a civil action under § 502(a)(5) against an "other person" who "knowing[ly] participat[es]" in a fiduciary's violation; otherwise, there could be no "applicable recovery amount" from which to determine the amount of the civil penalty to be imposed on the "other person." This § 502(a)(5) action is available notwithstanding the absence of any ERISA provision explicitly imposing a duty upon an "other person" not to engage in such "knowing participation." And if the Secretary may bring suit against an "other person" under subsection (a)(5), it follows that a participant, beneficiary, or fiduciary may bring suit against an "other person" under the similarly worded subsection (a)(3).

• • •

III

Notwithstanding the text of § 502(a)(3) (as informed by § 502(l)), Salomon protests that it would contravene common sense for Congress to have imposed civil liability on a party, such as a nonfiduciary party in interest to a § 406(a) transaction, that is not a "wrongdoer" in the sense of violating a duty expressly imposed by the substantive provisions of ERISA Title I. Salomon raises the specter of § 502(a)(3) suits being brought against innocent parties—even those having no connection to the allegedly unlawful "act or practice"—rather than against the true wrongdoer, i.e., the fiduciary that caused the plan to engage in the transaction.

[9][10][11] But this *reductio ad absurdum* ignores the limiting principle explicit in § 502(a)(3): that the retrospective relief sought be "appropriate equitable relief." The common law of trusts, which offers a "starting point for analysis [of ERISA] . . . [unless] it is inconsistent with the language of the statute, its structure, or its purposes," plainly countenances the sort of relief sought by petitioners against Salomon here. As petitioners and amicus curiae the United States observe, it has long been settled that when a trustee in breach of his fiduciary duty to the beneficiaries transfers trust property to a third person, the third person takes the property subject to the trust, unless he has purchased the property for value and without notice of the fiduciary's breach of duty. The trustee or beneficiaries may then maintain an action for restitution of the property (if not already disposed of) or disgorgement of proceeds (if already disposed of), and disgorgement of the third person's profits derived therefrom. As we long ago explained in the analogous situation of property obtained by fraud:

> "Whenever the legal title to property is obtained through means or under circumstances 'which render it unconscientious for the holder of the legal title to retain and enjoy the beneficial interest, equity impresses a constructive trust on the property thus acquired in favor of the one who is truly and equitably entitled to the same, although he may never, perhaps, have had any legal estate therein; and a court of equity has jurisdiction to reach the property either in the hands of the original wrongdoer, or in the hands of any subsequent holder, until a purchaser of it in good faith and without notice acquires a higher right and takes the property relieved from the trust.'" *Moore v. Crawford,* 130 U.S. 122, 128, 9 S.Ct. 447, 32 L.Ed. 878 (1889) (quoting 2 J. Pomeroy, Equity Jurisprudence § 1053, pp. 628–629 (1886)).

[12][13][14] Importantly, that a transferee was not "the original wrongdoer" does not insulate him from liability for restitution.

• • •

Accordingly, we reverse the Seventh Circuit's judgment and remand the case for further proceedings consistent with this opinion.

It is so ordered.

Case Questions

1. What is the gist of Salomon's argument that it should not be the target of a private party's lawsuit under ERISA?
2. Is Salomon really an innocent bystander to a breach of a fiduciary duty?
3. Is Salomon right in cautioning that the decision against it could open a flood of third-party litigation under ERISA?
4. How can third parties protect themselves against suits such as this one?

SUMMARY

- The Employee Retirement Income Security Act (ERISA) was enacted to protect older employees from what Congress perceived as rampant abuses by employers with regard to pension funds. The act also regulated other employee welfare benefits.
- ERISA preempts most state laws on the same subject matter. However, state banking and insurance laws may coexist with ERISA.
- Under ERISA, those who help manage pension funds, such as employers that establish them, are considered fiduciaries and are held to a high standard of accountability for how they manage these funds.
- One of the main ways ERISA seeks to prevent employee pension funds from being abused by employers is in vesting. Vesting rules require that after reasonable lengths of employment, employees gain legal title to some or all of the benefits earmarked for them in employer pension funds. Thus, even if their employment is terminated, these benefits will not be forfeited.
- Other employee benefits, such as vacations and health insurance, do not vest. Nevertheless, ERISA imposes fiduciary duties on those who administer such benefits and forbids arbitrary and capricious denials of them.
- Multiemployer pension plans, often administrated in trust by labor unions, pose particularly difficult issues, such as who will be responsible for vested employee benefits when one of the participating employers withdraws from the plan or goes bankrupt.
- The Pension Benefit Guarantee Corporation is the government agency created by Congress to supervise employer handling of employee pension plans and to take over for bankrupt and otherwise defunct employers.

QUESTIONS

1. What problems led to the passage of ERISA? How does the act attempt to correct those problems?
2. What are the bases of coverage for the dual obligations ERISA places upon pension and benefit plans?

3. What is a fiduciary? What obligations does ERISA impose upon fiduciaries?
4. What is a defined-contribution pension plan? What is a defined-benefit pension plan? Why are defined-benefit plans subject to more requirements and regulations than defined-contribution plans?
5. What is vesting? What alternative minimum requirements for vesting are imposed by ERISA?
6. What are the minimum funding requirements ERISA imposes on qualified pension plans? When may a waiver from such requirements be granted?
7. What is the role of the Pension Benefit Guaranty Corporation under ERISA? What obligations apply in the event of an employer's withdrawal from a multiemployer defined-benefit pension plan?
8. What are the enforcement procedures for ERISA's fiduciary obligations? For the minimum standards required of qualified plans under ERISA?

CASE PROBLEMS

1. The union pension fund sued an employer under ERISA, seeking the right to audit the company's books and to recover delinquent pension payments. The defendant company filed a motion, asking the court to permit it to bring the labor union into the case by means of a procedure called "impleading."

   The company's claims against the union are that the collective-bargaining agreement should be voided because it was not entered into voluntarily and the union lacks majority support among the company's workers. However, the union has no obligation to indemnify the company should it be found liable for delinquent pension contributions. Furthermore, the pension plan is a separate contractual arrangement in which the employer is indisputably a participant, albeit the company would not be involved with the pension plan had it not first become a party to the collective agreement.

   Should the court permit the union to be dragged into the lawsuit? Or is justice for the employees better served by leaving the union on the sidelines while the contribution delinquency issue is resolved by the court? See *Laborers' Pension Fund v. McKinney Construction Corp.* [2000 WL 1727779 (N.D. Ill.)].

2. A medical center sued a major insurance company in state court, contending that the insurance carrier had breached its contract with the center's hospital by failing to reimburse it for the full contractual amounts when the hospital rendered services to the carrier's insured patients.

   The insurance company removed the case to federal district court, claiming that the controversy was essentially federal in nature, involving a welfare benefit plan regulated by ERISA. The medical center moved to have the case remanded to state court, pointing out that ERISA exempts from its coverage, among other things, insurance contracts.

   Who is right? See *Lakeview Medical Center v. Aetna Health Management, Inc.* [2000 WL 1727553 (E.D. La.)].

3. The administrator of a major corporation's employee benefit plans filed suit, seeking to preempt claims by obtaining a declaratory judgment that certain sales personnel were not actually employees and therefore were not entitled to benefits under the plans. The personnel in question performed sales services for the marketing subsidiary of the parent corporation. The evidence showed that these personnel were paid neither wages nor salaries.

Instead they earned fees by selling magazine subscriptions. These salespeople claimed they were subject to substantial supervision such as:

- review of sales presentations;
- review of correspondence;
- occasional accompaniment by managers to meetings with clients; and
- management direction on the handling of clients.

They were required to file periodic reports. However, they were not required to work any particular hours or any particular number of hours in a week. Nor did they have to obtain advance approval to take a vacation.

The company claims they are independent contractors and therefore not entitled to employee benefits. What do you say? See *Administrative Committee of Time Warner, Inc. v. Biscardi* [2000 WL 1721168 (S.D.N.Y.)].

4. Cypress Mountain Coals Corporation entered into a collective-bargaining agreement with the United Mine Workers of America under which the company agreed, among other things, to add disability pensions to its existing obligations under the union's multiemployer pension plan. The plan documents were silent as to whether or not an injured employee could qualify if his disability was not exclusively caused by a mining accident. A year after the collective agreement was consummated, Cypress employee Donald Miller was injured in a mine accident. But when he applied for a disability pension, the company denied his application, contending that his disability was partly caused by preexisting conditions. The union sued Cypress for breach of the collective agreement and the pension plan.

   How should the courts rule? See *United Mine Workers of America v. Cypress Mountain Coals Corp.* [171 BNA LRRM 2512 (6th Cir. 2002)].

5. Summit Bancorp maintained a defined-benefit pension plan for salaried employees only. John Bauer, employed as a sales representative by Summit for some eighteen years on an hourly basis, sued at time of retirement, contending he was entitled to be included in the pension plan.

   Reviewing the rules laid out in this chapter, do you think Bauer was right? See *Bauer v. Summit Bancorp* [325 F.3d 155 (3d Cir. 2002)].

INTERNET EXERCISES

One of The Working Law pieces in this chapter concerns the collapse of WorldCom, a major communications corporation that saw its stock value collapse when it admitted to misaccounting for billions in operating costs that would have vastly diminished net profits. The collapse led to loss of pension funds, heavily invested in WorldCom stock, by numerous public and private pension funds around the nation. This exercise is intended to help you to explore this debacle more deeply and see what you can learn from it.

1. Go to **http://www.dol.gov** and search the index for the Employee Benefits Security Administration page.
2. On this page, find the link for 10 Warning Signs that Pension Contributions are being Misused. Print these ten signs out or else keep this page open.
3. Then go back to Google and search WorldCom.
4. Read some posted news stories and commentaries about the WorldCom debacle and see how many of the ten warning signs you can identify in the facts that have been reported about WorldCom.
5. Now, armed with this list, go to **http://www.findlaw.com** and go to Search Findlaw.

6. Choosing U.S. Federal Case Law, use the drop down menu to search All Circuit Courts for WorldCom.
7. Find a case entitled *Kerkof v. MCI WorldCom, Inc.* (1st Cir. 2002).
8. Read and brief the case. What were Kerkof's claims against the defendant? How did the jury decide in her case? How did the appeals court rule on defendant's objections to the jury's verdict? Do Kerkof's claims reflect any of the warning signs you associated with WorldCom?
9. How does MCI fit into this picture? Hint: Visit **http://www.financialdirector.co.uk/News/1133600**.
10. Summarize what you've learned about WorldCom's activities that might help you someday in safeguarding your own pension rights against your employer's possible wrongdoing.

INFOTRAC KEYWORDS

http://www.infotrac-college.com

ERISA, qualified pension plans, defined-benefit plans, defined contribution plans, cash-balance pension plans, ERISA discrimination

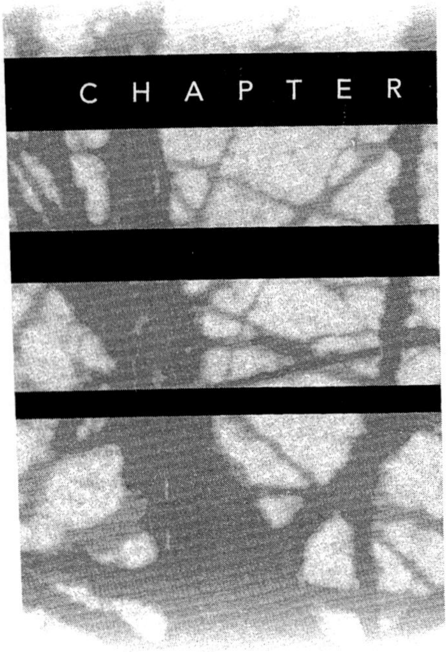

CHAPTER 10

THE FAIR LABOR STANDARDS ACT

Since the Fair Labor Standards Act (FLSA) was first enacted in 1938, the temptation may be to view FLSA issues such as minimum wages, overtime entitlements, and even child labor as long-settled and of little immediate import in twenty-first century America.

http://www.dol.gov/dol/compliance/comp-flsa.htm *will take you to a reference guide to the Fair Labor Standards Act.*

But to the contrary, globalization has put new pressure on American free enterprise, which all too often has succumbed to the lure of faraway places where sweatshops can be established to replace high-wage, frequently unionized factories in the United States or to the temptation to hire illegal aliens to staff sweatshops here in our own cities. "Globalization" has been described by one noted labor historian as follows:

> Globalization has been used to describe a variety of developments including the spread of popular music, movies and fashion, the increasing ease of global communication and transportation, the rapid international diffusion of new technologies and the increasingly international scope of large corporations. . . . Many of the Western nations ha[ve] reached the late stage of development and huge private corporations in partnership with governments range[ ] across the globe seeking industrial markets, investment areas, trading partners and . . . sources of cheap labor and raw materials. . . . Finally, in the midst of this . . . globalization . . . a third wave is looming, a global information economy, the emergence and dominance of the information sector—the sector that produces, manipulates, processes, distributes and markets information products—a sector now controlled by the wealthy nations.[1]

[1]Dr. Joseph Gowaskie, Rider University, Lawrenceville, N.J., unpublished paper quoted with permission.

Even more fundamentally, while slavery was abolished by the United States by a bloody Civil War and the subsequent Thirteenth Amendment to the Constitution, slavery and trafficking of human beings throughout the world exacerbate the worst symptoms of globalization. The U.S. Department of State has recently estimated that at least 700,000 beings are annually trafficked across international borders to be enslaved in sweatshops, on vast construction projects, on plantations, and in brothels.[2] According to one Internet source,

> Modern-day slaves can be found laboring as servants or concubines in Sudan, as child "carpet slaves" in India, or as cane-cutters in Haiti and southern Pakistan. . . . According to Anti-Slavery International . . . there are currently over 200 million people in bondage.[3]

Faced with such facts and figures, Americans can no longer take for granted the sanctity of the minimum wage, their entitlement to premium pay or compensatory time off for hours worked in excess of forty per week, or that child and/or "sweated" labor is a historical artifact to be experienced only in the display cases of the Smithsonian Institution's museum of American history. To the contrary, a thorough understanding and appreciation of the FLSA have assumed new urgency in the new millennium.

BACKGROUND OF THE FLSA

- In 1931, Congress passed the Davis-Bacon Act, which provides that contractors working on government construction projects must pay the prevailing wage rates in the geographic area, as determined by the secretary of labor. The Davis-Bacon Act is still in force.
- The federal government attempted the general regulation of wages and hours through the National Industrial Recovery Act (NIRA). The NIRA, passed in 1933, was an attempt to improve general conditions during the Great Depression. The NIRA provided for the development of "codes of fair competition" for various industries. The codes, to be developed by trade associations within each industry, would specify the minimum wages to be paid, the maximum hours to be worked, and limitations on child labor. When approved by the president, the codes would have the force of law. The Supreme Court held that the NIRA was an unconstitutional delegation of congressional power in the 1935 case of *Schecter Poultry Corp. v. U.S.*
- In 1936, the Walsh-Healy Act was passed. Like the Davis-Bacon Act, it regulates working conditions for government contractors. The Walsh-Healy Act sets minimum standards for wages for contractors providing at least $10,000

[2] "Trafficking in Persons Report," U.S. State Department, July 2001, **http://www.state.gov**.
[3] Ricco Villanueva Siasoco, "Modern Slavery," Infoplease.com, September 29, 2002, **http://www.infoplease.com/spot/slavery1.html**.

worth of goods to the federal government. It also requires that hours worked in excess of forty per week be paid at time-and-a half the regular rate of pay. The Walsh-Healy Act, like Davis-Bacon, is also still in force.

In 1937, the Supreme Court was presented with a case that challenged the legality of a Washington state law that set a minimum wage for women. In several prior cases, the court had held minimum wage laws to be unconstitutional, as it had done with the NIRA. Though the case is now sixty-five years old, the principles it enunciates are as pertinent to the body of employment law as they ever were.

West Coast Hotel Co. v. Parrish

300 U.S. 379 (1937)

Hughes, C.J.

This case presents the question of the constitutional validity of the minimum wage law of the State of Washington.

The Act, entitled "Minimum Wages for Women," authorizes the fixing of minimum wages for women and minors. It provides:

> SECTION 1. The welfare of the State of Washington demands that women and minors be protected from conditions of labor which have a pernicious effect on their health and morals. The State of Washington, therefore, exercising herein its police and sovereign power declares that inadequate wages and unsanitary conditions of labor exert such pernicious effect.
>
> SEC. 2. It shall be unlawful to employ women or minors in any industry or occupation within the State of Washington under conditions of labor detrimental to their health or morals; and it shall be unlawful to employ women workers in any industry within the State of Washington at wages which are not adequate for their maintenance.
>
> SEC. 3. There is hereby created a commission to be known as the "Industrial Welfare Commission" for the State of Washington, to establish such standards of wages and conditions of labor for women and minors employed within the State of Washington, as shall be held hereunder to be reasonable and not detrimental to health and morals, and which shall be sufficient for the decent maintenance of women.

The appellant conducts a hotel business. The appellee Elsie Parrish was employed as a chambermaid and (with her husband) brought this suit to recover the difference between the wages paid her and the minimum wage fixed pursuant to the state law. The minimum wage was $14.50 per week of 48 hours. The appellant challenged the act as repugnant to the due process clause of the Fourteenth Amendment of the Constitution of the United States. The Supreme Court of the State, reversing the trial court, sustained the statute and directed judgment for the plaintiffs. The case is here on appeal.

We think that the question [regarding the validity of the New York Minimum Wage Act] which was not deemed to be open in the *Morehead* [*v. New York ex rel. Tipaldo*] case is open and is necessarily presented here. The Supreme Court of Washington has upheld the minimum wage statute of that State. It has decided that the statute is a reasonable exercise of the police power of the State. In reaching that conclusion the state court has invoked principles long established by the Court in the application of the Fourteenth Amendment. The state court has refused to regard the decision in the *Adkins v. Children's Hospital* case, where the District of Columbia Minimum Wage Act was held invalid, as determinative and has pointed to our decisions both before and since that case as justifying its position. We are of the opinion that this ruling of the state court demands on our part a reexamination of the *Adkins* case. The importance of the question, in which many States having similar laws are concerned, the close division by which the decision in the *Adkins* case was reached, and the economic conditions which have supervened, and in the light of which the reasonableness of the exercise of the protective power of the State must be considered, make it not only appropriate, but we think imperative, that in deciding the present case the subject should receive fresh consideration. . . .

The principle which must control our decision is not in doubt. The constitutional provision invoked is the due process clause of the Fourteenth Amendment governing the States, as the due process clause invoked in the *Adkins* case governed Congress. In each case the violation alleged by those attacking minimum wage regulation for women is deprivation of freedom of contract. What is this freedom? The Constitution does not speak of freedom of contract. It speaks of liberty and prohibits the deprivation of liberty without due process of law. In prohibiting that deprivation the Constitution does not recognize an absolute and uncontrollable liberty. Liberty in each of its phases has its history and connotation. But the liberty safeguarded is liberty in a social organization which requires the protection of law against the evils which menace the health, safety, morals, and welfare of the people. Liberty under the Constitution is thus necessarily subject to the restraints of due process, and regulation which is reasonable in relation to its subject and is adopted in the interests of the community is due process.

This essential limitation of liberty in general governs freedom of contract in particular. More than twenty-five years ago we set forth the applicable principle in these words, after referring to the cases where the liberty guaranteed by the Fourteenth Amendment had been broadly described:

> But it was recognized in the cases cited, as in many others, that freedom of contract is a qualified and not an absolute right. There is no absolute freedom to do as one wills or to contract as one chooses. The guaranty of liberty does not withdraw from legislative supervision that wide department of activity which consists of the making of contracts, or deny to government the power to provide restrictive safeguards. Liberty implies the absence of arbitrary restraint, not immunity from reasonable regulations and prohibitions imposed in the interests of the community.

This power under the Constitution to restrict freedom of contract has had many illustrations. That it may be exercised in the public interest with respect to contracts between employer and employee is undeniable. . . . In dealing with the relation of employer and employed, the legislature has necessarily a wide field of discretion in order that there may be suitable protection of health and safety, and that peace and good order may be promoted through regulations designed to insure wholesome conditions of work and freedom from oppression.

The point that has been strongly stressed that adult employees should be deemed competent to make their own contracts was decisively met nearly forty years ago in *Holden v. Hardy,* where we pointed out the inequality in the footing of the parties. We said:

> The legislature has also recognized the fact, which the experience of legislators in many States has corroborated, that the proprietors of these establishments and their operatives do not stand upon an equality, and that their interests are, to a certain extent, conflicting. The former naturally desire to obtain as much labor as possible from their employees, while the latter are often induced by the fear of discharge to conform to regulations which their judgment, fairly exercised, would pronounce to be detrimental to their health or strength. In other words, the proprietors lay down the rules and the laborers are practically constrained to obey them. In such cases self-interest is often an unsafe guide, and the legislature may properly interpose its authority.

And we added that the fact "that both parties are of full age and competent to contract does not necessarily deprive the State of the powers to interfere where the parties do not stand upon an equality, or where the public health demands that one party to the contract shall be protected against himself. The State still retains an interest in his welfare, however reckless he may be. The whole is no greater than the sum of all the parts, and when the individual health, safety and welfare are sacrificed or neglected, the State must suffer."

It is manifest that this established principle is peculiarly applicable in relation to the employment of women in whose protection the State has a special interest. That phase of the subject received elaborate consideration in *Muller v. Oregon,* where the constitutional authority of the State to limit the working hours of women was sustained. We emphasized the consideration that "woman's physical structure and the performance of maternal functions place her at a disadvantage in the struggle for subsistence" and that her physical well-being "becomes an object of public interest and care in order to preserve the strength and vigor of the race." We emphasized the need of protecting woman against oppression despite her possession of contractual rights. We said that "though limitations upon personal and contractual rights may be removed by legislation, there is that in her disposition and habits of life which will operate against a full assertion of those rights. She will still be where some legislation to protect her seems necessary to secure a real equality of right." Hence she was "properly placed in a class by herself, and legislation designed for her protection may be sustained even when like legislation is not necessary for men and could not be sustained." We concluded that the limitations which the statute there in question "placed upon her contractual powers, upon her right to agree with her employer as to the time she shall labor" were "not imposed solely for her benefit, but also largely for the benefit of all." . . .

This array of precedents and the principles they applied were thought by the dissenting Justices in the *Adkins* case to demand that the minimum wage statute be sustained. The validity of the distinction made by the Court between a minimum wage and a maximum of hours in limiting liberty of contract was especially challenged. . . .

One of the points which was pressed by the Court in supporting its ruling in the *Adkins* case was that the standard set up by the District of Columbia Act did not take appropriate account of the value of the services rendered. In the *Morehead* case, the minority thought that the New York statute had met that point in its definition of a "fair wage" and that it accordingly presented a distinguishable feature which the Court could recognize within the limits which the *Morehead* petition for certiorari was deemed to present. The Court, however, did not take that view and the New York Act was held to be essentially the same as that for the District of Columbia. The statute now before us is like the latter, but we are unable to conclude that in its minimum wage requirement the State has passed beyond the boundary of its broad protective power.

The minimum wage to be paid under the Washington statute is fixed after full consideration by representatives of employers, employees and the public. It may be assumed that the minimum wage is fixed in consideration of the services that are performed in the particular occupations under normal conditions. Provision is made for special licenses at less wages in the case of women who are incapable of full service. The statement of Mr. Justice Holmes in the *Adkins* case is pertinent: "This statute does not compel anybody to pay anything. It simply forbids employment at rates below those fixed as the minimum requirement of health and right living. It is safe to assume that women will not be employed at even the lowest wages allowed unless they earn them, or unless the employer's business can sustain the burden. In short the law in its character and operation is like hundreds of so-called police laws that have been upheld." And Chief Justice Taft forcibly pointed out the consideration which is basic in a statute of this character:

> Legislatures which adopt a requirement of maximum hours or minimum wages may be presumed to believe that when sweating employers are prevented from paying unduly low wages by positive law they will continue their business, abating that part of their profits, which were wrung from the necessities of their employees, and will concede the better terms required by the law; and that while in individual cases hardship may result, the restriction will inure to the benefit of the general class of employees in whose interest the law is passed and so to that of the community at large.

We think that the views thus expressed are sound and that the decision in the *Adkins* case was a departure from the true application of the principles governing the regulation by the State of the relation of employer and employed. . . .

With full recognition of the earnestness and vigor which characterize the prevailing opinion in the *Adkins* case we find it impossible to reconcile that ruling with these well-considered declarations. What can be closer to the public interest than the health of women and their protection from unscrupulous and overreaching employers? And if the protection of women is a legitimate end of the exercise of state power, how can it be said that the requirement of the payment of a minimum wage fairly fixed in order to meet the very necessities of existence is not an admissible means to that end? The legislature of the State was clearly entitled to consider the situation of women in employment, the fact that they are in the class receiving the least pay, that their bargaining power is relatively weak, and that they are the ready victims of those who would take advantage of their necessitous circumstances. The legislature was entitled to adopt measures to reduce the evils of the "sweating system," the exploiting of workers at wages so low as to be insufficient to meet the bare cost of living, thus making their very helplessness the occasion of a most injurious competition. The legislature had the right to consider that its minimum wage requirements would be an important aid in carrying out its policy of protection. The adoption of similar requirements by many States evidences a deep seated conviction both as to the presence of the evil and as to the means adopted to check it. Legislative response to that conviction cannot be regarded as arbitrary or capricious, and that is all we have to decide. Even if the wisdom of the policy be regarded as debatable and its effects uncertain, still the legislature is entitled to its judgment.

There is an additional and compelling consideration which recent economic experience has brought into a strong light. The exploitation of a class of workers who are in an unequal position with respect to bargaining power and are thus relatively defenseless against the denial of a living wage is not only detrimental to their health and well-being but casts a direct burden for their support upon the community. What these workers lose in wages the taxpayers are called upon to pay. The bare cost of living must be met. We may take judicial notice of the unparalleled demands for relief which arose during the recent period of depression and still continue to an alarming extent despite the degree of economic recovery which has been achieved. It is unnecessary to cite official statistics to establish what is of common knowledge through the length and breadth of the land. While in the instant case no factual brief has been presented, there is no reason to doubt that the State of Washington has encountered the same social problem that is present elsewhere. The community is not bound to provide what is in effect a subsidy for unconscionable employers. The community may direct its law-making power to correct the abuse which springs from their selfish disregard of the public interest. The argument that the legislation in question constitutes an arbitrary discrimination, because it does not extend to men, is unavailing. This Court has frequently held that the legislative authority, acting within its proper field, is not bound to extend its regulation to all cases which it might possibly reach. The legislature "is free to recognize degrees of harm and it may confine its restrictions to those classes of cases where the need is deemed to be clearest." If "the law presumably hits the evil where it is most felt, it is not to be overthrown because there are other instances to which it might have been applied." There is no "doctrinaire requirement" that the legislation should be couched in all embracing terms. This familiar principle has repeatedly been applied to legislation which singles out women, and particular classes of women, in the exercise of the State's protective power. Their relative need in the presence of the evil, no less than the existence of the evil itself, is a matter for the legislative judgment.

Our conclusion is that the case of *Adkins v. Children's Hospital,* should be, and it is, overruled. The judgment of the Supreme Court of the State of Washington is

Affirmed.

Case Questions

1. What does the "due process" clause of the Fourteenth Amendment of the U.S. Constitution say? What interest protected by that language did the West Coast Hotel claim was threatened by the minimum wage law?
2. What competing interests does the Court claim the state of Washington had in regulating wages?
3. Why does the Court agree with the Washington legislature that women should be accorded special protection? Do you agree or disagree with this reasoning? Do you think such special protection for women is legal today?
4. Of what significance to the case's outcome is the minimum wage law's requirement that hearings be held?
5. Why did the Court overrule *Adkins v. Children's Hospital?* Why did the Court wait until this case to do so?
6. Does West Coast Hotel prefigure how the Court is likely to rule regarding the constitutionality of the Fair Labor Standards Act? Or is the ruling limited to wage laws which protect only women and children?

ORIGIN AND PURPOSE OF THE FAIR LABOR STANDARDS ACT

The *Schecter Poultry* decision and the *West Coast Hotel* case were the main factors behind the FLSA. The *Schecter* case, which struck down the National Industrial Recovery Act, forced the federal government to attempt direct regulation of hours and wages in general. The *West Coast Hotel* case demonstrated that some regulation of working conditions was viewed by the Supreme Court as a valid exercise of government power.

http://www4.law.cornell.edu/uscode/29/ch8.html *will take you to a list of sections of the FLSA.*

After the *West Coast Hotel* decision, President Roosevelt told Congress

> All but the hopelessly reactionary will agree that to conserve our primary resources of manpower, Government must have some control over maximum hours, minimum wages, the evil of child labor, and the exploitation of unorganized labor.

The FLSA was passed by Congress and signed into law on June 25, 1938. The Supreme Court held the FLSA to be constitutional in the 1941 case of *U.S. v. Darby Lumber Co.* (312 U.S. 100). The FLSA, as amended over the years, continues in force today. It is the essential, although unglamorous, foundation for more recent federal regulation of working conditions through OSHA, ERISA, and even ADEA. The FLSA deals with four areas: minimum wages, overtime pay provisions, child labor, and equal pay for equal work. (The Equal Pay Act is an amendment to the FLSA. See Chapter 4 for a discussion of the provisions of the Equal Pay Act.)

COVERAGE

The FLSA, as amended, provides for three bases of coverage. Employees who are engaged in interstate commerce, including both import and export, are covered. In addition, employees who are engaged in the production of goods for interstate commerce are subject to the FLSA. The "production" of goods includes "any closely related process or occupation directly essential" to the production of goods for interstate commerce. Finally, all employees employed in an "enterprise engaged in" interstate commerce are subject to the FLSA, regardless of the relationship of their duties to commerce or the production of goods for commerce. This basis, the "enterprise" test, is subject to minimum dollar-volume limits for certain types of businesses. Employees of small employers would have to qualify for FLSA coverage under one of the other two bases of coverage. Employers and employees not covered by FLSA are generally subject to state laws, similar to the FLSA, which regulate minimum wages and maximum hours of work.

In 1966, the FLSA was extended to cover some federal employees and to include state and local hospitals and educational institutions. In 1974, FLSA coverage was extended to most federal employees, to state and local government employees, and to private household domestic workers.

The Congressional Accountability Act of 1995 [Pub. L. 104-1, 109 Stat. 3 (January 23, 1995)] extended the coverage of Fair Labor Standards Act to the employees of the House of Representatives, the Senate, the Capitol Guide Service, the Capitol Police, the Congressional Budget Office, the Office of the Architect of the Capitol, the Office of the Attending Physician, and the Office of Technology Assessment.

The extension of FLSA coverage to state and local government employees spawned a controversy under provisions of the U.S. Constitution. In the 1976 decision of *National League of Cities v. Usery* (426 U.S. 833), the Supreme Court held that federal regulation of the working conditions of state and local government employees infringed upon state sovereignty. The question was addressed again, in 1985, by the Supreme Court in *Garcia v. San Antonio Metropolitan Transit Authority* (469 U.S. 528), which overruled *National League of Cities,* stating, "we perceive nothing in the overtime and minimum-wage requirements of the FLSA . . . that is destructive of state sovereignty or violative of any constitutional provision." One event that helped persuade the court to overrule *National League of Cities* a mere nine years after it was decided was an intervening congressional amendment of the FLSA permitting states and municipalities to provide their nonexempt employees with compensatory time off in lieu of overtime pay.

This FLSA amendment generated even more litigation. As recently as May 2000, the Supreme Court felt compelled to speak yet again on this contentious problem of federal regulation of public employers' wage and hour obligations.

CHRISTENSEN V. HARRIS COUNTY

120 S. Ct. 1655 (2000)

Justice Thomas

Under the Fair Labor Standards Act of 1938 (FLSA), States and their political subdivisions may compensate their employees for overtime by granting them compensatory time or "comp time," which entitles them to take time off work with full pay. If the employees do not use their accumulated compensatory time, the employer is obligated to pay cash compensation under certain circumstances. Fearing the fiscal consequences of having to pay for accrued compensatory time, Harris County adopted a policy requiring its employees to schedule time off in order to reduce the amount of accrued compensatory time. Employees of the Harris County Sheriff's Department sued, claiming that the FLSA prohibits such a policy. The Court of Appeals rejected their claim. Finding that nothing in the FLSA or its implementing regulations prohibits an employer from compelling the use of compensatory time, we affirm.

I

A

The FLSA generally provides that hourly employees who work in excess of 40 hours per week must be compensated for the excess hours at a rate not less than $1\frac{1}{2}$ times their regular hourly wage. Although this requirement did not initially apply to public-sector employers, Congress amended the FLSA to subject States and their political subdivisions to its constraints, at first on a limited basis, and then more broadly. States and their political subdivisions, however, did not feel the full force of this latter extension until our decision in *Garcia v. San Antonio Metropolitan Transit Authority,* 469 U.S. 528, which overruled our holding in *National League of Cities v. Usery,* 426 U.S. 833, that the FLSA could not constitutionally restrain traditional governmental functions.

In the months following *Garcia,* Congress acted to mitigate the effects of applying the FLSA to States and their political subdivisions, passing the Fair Labor Standards Amendments of 1985. Those amendments permit States and their political subdivisions to compensate employees for overtime by granting them compensatory time at a rate of $1\frac{1}{2}$ hours for every hour worked. To provide this form of compensation, the employer must arrive at an agreement or understanding with employees that compensatory time will be granted instead of cash compensation.

The FLSA expressly regulates some aspects of accrual and preservation of compensatory time. For example, the FLSA provides that an employer must honor an employee's request to use compensatory time within a "reasonable period" of time following the request, so long as the use of the compensatory time would not "unduly disrupt" the employer's operations. The FLSA also caps the number of compensatory time hours that an employee may accrue. After an employee reaches that maximum, the employer must pay cash compensation for additional overtime hours worked. In addition, the FLSA permits the employer at any time to cancel or "cash out" accrued compensatory time hours by paying the employee cash compensation for unused compensatory time. And the FLSA entitles the employee to cash payment for any accrued compensatory time remaining upon the termination of employment.

B

Petitioners are 127 deputy sheriffs employed by respondents Harris County, Texas, and its sheriff, Tommy B. Thomas (collectively, Harris County). It is undisputed that each of the petitioners individually agreed to accept compensatory time, in lieu of cash, as compensation for overtime.

As petitioners accumulated compensatory time, Harris County became concerned that it lacked the resources to pay monetary compensation to employees who worked overtime after reaching the statutory cap on compensatory time accrual and to employees who left their jobs with sizable reserves of accrued time. As a result, the county began looking for a way to reduce accumulated compensatory time. It wrote to the United States Department of Labor's Wage and Hour Division, asking "whether the Sheriff may schedule non-exempt employees to use or take compensatory time."

The Acting Administrator of the Division replied:

> "[I]t is our position that a public employer may schedule its nonexempt employees to use their accrued FLSA compensatory time as directed if the prior agreement specifically provides such a provision. . . .
>
> "Absent such an agreement, it is our position that neither the statute nor the regulations permit an employer to require an employee to use accrued compensatory time." Opinion Letter from Dept. of Labor, Wage and Hour Div. (Sept. 14, 1992), 1992 WL 845100 (Opinion Letter).

After receiving the letter, Harris County implemented a policy under which the employees' supervisor sets a maximum number of compensatory hours that may be accumulated. When an employee's stock of hours approaches that maximum, the employee is advised of the maximum and is asked to take steps to reduce accumulated compensatory time. If the employee does not do so voluntarily, a supervisor may order the employee to use his compensatory time at specified times.

Petitioners sued, claiming that the county's policy violates the FLSA because § 207(o)(5)—which requires that an employer reasonably accommodate employee requests to use compensatory time—provides the exclusive means of utilizing accrued time in the absence of an agreement or understanding permitting some other method. The District Court agreed, granting summary judgment for petitioners and entering a declaratory judgment that the county's policy violated the FLSA. The Court of Appeals for the Fifth Circuit reversed, holding that the FLSA did not speak to the issue and thus did not prohibit the county from implementing its compensatory time policy.

II

Both parties, and the United States as *amicus curiae,* concede that nothing in the FLSA expressly prohibits a State or subdivision thereof from compelling employees to utilize accrued compensatory time. Petitioners and the United States, however, contend that the FLSA implicitly prohibits such a practice in the absence of an agreement or understanding authorizing compelled use.

Title 29 U.S.C. § 207(o)(5) provides:

> "An employee . . .
>
> "(A) who has accrued compensatory time off . . . , and
>
> "(B) who has requested the use of such compensatory time,
>
> "shall be permitted by the employee's employer to use such time within a reasonable period after making the request if the use of the compensatory time does not unduly disrupt the operations of the public agency."

Petitioners and the United States rely upon the canon *expressio unius est exclusio alterius,* contending that the express grant of control to employees to use compensatory time, subject to the limitation regarding undue disruptions of workplace operations, implies that all other methods of spending compensatory time are precluded.

[1][2] We find this reading unpersuasive. We accept the proposition that "[w]hen a statute limits a thing to be done in a particular mode, it includes a negative of

any other mode." But that canon does not resolve this case in petitioners' favor. The "thing to be done" as defined by § 207(o)(5) is not the expenditure of compensatory time, as petitioners would have it. Instead, § 207(o)(5) is more properly read as a minimal guarantee that an employee will be able to make some use of compensatory time when he requests to use it. As such, the proper *expressio unius* inference is that an employer may not, at least in the absence of an agreement, deny an employee's request to use compensatory time for a reason other than that provided in § 207(o)(5). The canon's application simply does not prohibit an employer from telling an employee to take the benefits of compensatory time by scheduling time off work with full pay.

In other words, viewed in the context of the overall statutory scheme, § 207(o)(5) is better read not as setting forth the exclusive method by which compensatory time can be used, but as setting up a safeguard to ensure that an employee will receive timely compensation for working overtime. Section 207(o)(5) guarantees that, at the very minimum, an employee will get to use his compensatory time (i.e., take time off work with full pay) unless doing so would disrupt the employer's operations. And it is precisely this concern over ensuring that employees can timely "liquidate" compensatory time that the Secretary of Labor identified in her own regulations governing § 207(o)(5):

> "Compensatory time cannot be used as a means to avoid statutory overtime compensation. An employee has the right to use compensatory time earned and must not be coerced to accept more compensatory time than an employer can realistically and in good faith expect to be able to grant within a reasonable period of his or her making a request for use of such time."

[3] At bottom, we think the better reading of § 207(o)(5) is that it imposes a restriction upon an employer's efforts to prohibit the use of compensatory time when employees request to do so; that provision says nothing about restricting an employer's efforts to require employees to use compensatory time. Because the statute is silent on this issue and because Harris County's policy is entirely compatible with § 207(o)(5), petitioners cannot prove that Harris County has violated § 207.

[4] Our interpretation of § 207(o)(5)—one that does not prohibit employers from forcing employees to use compensatory time—finds support in two other features of the FLSA. First, employers remain free under the FLSA to decrease the number of hours that employees work. An employer may tell the employee to take off an afternoon, a day, or even an entire week. Thus, under the FLSA an employer is free to require an employee to take time off work, and an employer is also free to use the money it would have paid in wages to cash out accrued compensatory time. The compelled use of compensatory time challenged in this case merely involves doing both of these steps at once. It would make little sense to interpret § 207(o)(5) to make the combination of the two steps unlawful when each independently is lawful.

III

In an attempt to avoid the conclusion that the FLSA does not prohibit compelled use of compensatory time, petitioners and the United States contend that we should defer to the Department of Labor's opinion letter, which takes the position that an employer may compel the use of compensatory time only if the employee has agreed in advance to such a practice. [A] court must give effect to an agency's regulation containing a reasonable interpretation of an ambiguous statute.

[5][6] Here, however, we confront an interpretation contained in an opinion letter, not one arrived at after, for example, a formal adjudication or notice-and-comment rulemaking. Interpretations such as those in opinion letters—like interpretations contained in policy statements, agency manuals, and enforcement guidelines, all of which lack the force of law—do not warrant . . . deference. Instead, interpretations contained in formats such as opinion letters are "entitled to respect" . . . but only to the extent that those interpretations have the "power to persuade." As explained above, we find unpersuasive the agency's interpretation of the statute at issue in this case.

[7] Of course, the framework of deference . . . does apply to an agency interpretation contained in a regulation. But in this case the Department of Labor's regulation does not address the issue of compelled compensatory time. The regulation provides only that "[t]he agreement or understanding [between the employer and employee] may include other provisions governing the preservation, use, or cashing out of compensatory time so long as these provisions are consistent with [§ 207(o)]." Nothing in the regulation even arguably requires that an employer's compelled use policy must be included in an agreement. The text of the regulation itself indicates that its command is permissive, not mandatory.

• • •

As we have noted, no relevant statutory provision expressly or implicitly prohibits Harris County from pursuing its policy of forcing employees to utilize their compensatory time. In its opinion letter siding with the petitioners, the Department of Labor opined that "it is our position that neither the statute nor the regulations permit an employer to require an employee to use accrued compensatory time." Opinion Letter. But this view is exactly backwards. Unless the FLSA prohibits respondents from adopting its policy, petitioners cannot show that Harris County has violated the FLSA. And the FLSA contains no such prohibition. The judgment of the Court of Appeals is affirmed.

It is so ordered

Case Questions

1. Why do you suppose the FLSA amendment, permitting states and municipalities to give their employees compensatory time off in lieu of paying overtime pay, helped persuade the Supreme Court that the FLSA unconstitutionally infringed upon state sovereignty? How does this amendment relate to the age-old constitutional principle that "the power to tax is the power to destroy"?
2. Explain the reasoning as to why the FLSA does not forbid public employers from forcing their employees to take compensatory time off, even when those employees would prefer not to do so.
3. Why should a public employee mind being ordered to take some time off?
4. Suppose that Harris County had lost this case. Could the county, in order to prevent its employees from accumulating more compensatory time, lay them off? If so, would this in effect force such employees to fall back on their accumulated comp time anyway?
5. If such employees were represented by a labor union, what should the union's position appropriately be with respect to this controversy? In light of the court's ruling, what provisions might that union try to negotiate into the relevant collective-bargaining agreement to provide its members with as much discretion in their use of comp time as legally possible?

MINIMUM WAGES

Minimum Wage
The wage limit, set by the government, under which an employer is not allowed to pay an employee.

The government regulation of the **minimum wage** is an attempt to reduce poverty and bring the earnings of workers closer to the cost of living. The setting of the minimum wage was also an attempt to maintain the purchasing power of the public to lift the country out of the economic depths of the Great Depression.

The concept of a minimum wage may seem simple: The employer may not pay employees less than the minimum wage per hour. In 1938, the minimum wage was set at $0.25 per hour, and it was raised to $0.40 per hour through the next seven years.

http://www.dol.gov/esa *is the site of the ESA Code of Federal Regulation entries.*

The federal minimum wage was raised from $4.25 to $4.75 on October 1, 1996, and to $5.15 on September 1, 1997, Public Law 104-188 (August 20, 1996). The legislation raising the minimum wage also allows employers to pay employees under twenty years of age $4.25 per hour for the first ninety days after they are hired.

Although the concept of the minimum wage seems simple, administering it may present some problems because of the wide variation in methods of compensating employees. For example, many employees are paid on an hourly basis, whereas others receive a weekly or monthly salary. Waiters and waitresses often rely on tips from customers for a large percentage of their earnings. Machinists and sewing machine operators are usually paid on a "piece-rate" basis; that is, they earn a certain amount of money for each piece completed. Salespeople usu-

http://www4.law.cornell.edu/uscode/29/206.html *contains the text of the section on the minimum wage from the FLSA.*

ally earn a commission, which may or may not be supplemented by a base salary. Musicians may be paid a flat rate per engagement, and umpires or referees may be paid by the game.

Such atypical compensation methods are subject to regulations developed by the administrator of the Wage and Hour Division of the Department of Labor. The regulations are designed to ensure that all workers receive at least the minimum wage. If a worker is a "tipped worker"—that is, one who receives tips from customers—the employer is allowed to reduce the minimum wage paid to that worker by up to 40 percent, with the difference to be made up by tips received. The earnings of workers who are paid on a piece-rate basis must average out to at least the minimum wage; the time period over which the earnings are averaged cannot be longer than a single workweek. This means that the earnings of such an employee may be less than the minimum wage for any single hour, as long as the total earnings for the week average out to the minimum wage. Some persons being paid for the work may not even be viewed as employees at all for purposes of Fair Labor Standards Act coverage.

Barnett v. Young Men's Christian Association, Inc.

175 F.3d 1023 (8th Cir. 1999)

PER CURIAM

Missouri inmate Matthew W. Barnett appeals from the district court's dismissal under 28 U.S.C. § 1915 of his action under the Fair Labor Standards Act (FLSA), 29 U.S.C. §§ 201-219, and state law. We reverse.

Barnett filed this action against Young Men's Christian Association, Inc. (YMCA), and George Hartsfield, a general manager employed by YMCA, seeking punitive and compensatory damages, and to proceed *in forma pauperis* (IFP). In relevant part, Barnett alleged that he worked at a YMCA as part of a work-release furlough program. YMCA employees would pick up Barnett at the prison and take him to the YMCA where he worked forty hours a week, essentially as a maintenance worker. Prison officials did not supervise or make "spot checks" of Barnett at the YMCA, and Hartsfield, who maintained employment records, had the power to hire and fire Barnett, and to control his schedule, conditions of employment, and rate of pay. Barnett "freely contracted with the YMCA" to sell his labor for which YMCA directly paid him $1.00 an hour. Barnett claimed that he was thus an "employee" under the FLSA, and was entitled to be paid at the minimum wage. Barnett also asserted state law claims arising from YMCA's failure to pay him the minimum wage, and from his discharge after he voiced his opinions about the inadequacy of his wage.

Under 28 U.S.C. § 1915(e)(2), district courts "shall dismiss" cases filed IFP "at any time if the court determines" that the action "is frivolous or malicious" or "fails to state a claim on which relief may be granted." We conclude Barnett's complaint neither is frivolous nor fails to state a claim.

The FLSA provides that "[e]very employer shall pay to each of his employees" not less than the minimum wage. An "employee" is defined as "any individual employed by an employer," and "employer" is defined as "any person acting directly or indirectly in the interest of an employer in relation to an employee." The Supreme Court has suggested that "employee" is expansively defined under the FLSA, and has stated that courts should determine whether an individual is an "employee" in light of the "economic reality" of the situation under the totality of the circumstances, rather than rely on technical labels.

Two circuit courts have held that a prisoner may be an employee for purposes of the FLSA when the prisoner voluntarily works outside the prison for a private company that supervises and directly pays the prisoner. {One case found that prisoners working for a construction company were employees since they were not sentenced to hard labor and were not guarded by corrections officers. The other stated that, where a college proposed to hire qualified inmates as tutors for an in-prison program and the college had the discretion concerning who to hire and who it rejected, the chosen tutors would be college employees.}

• • •

In deciding that Barnett was not covered by the FLSA, the district court relied on *McMaster v. Minnesota,* 30 F.3d 976 (8th Cir. 1994), *cert. denied,* 513 U.S. 1157 (1995). In *McMaster,* we held that inmates "who are required to work as part of their sentences and perform labor within a correctional facility as part of a state-run prison industries program are not 'employees'" under the FLSA. We noted that the primary purpose of the FLSA—providing minimum standards of living for workers—had no application in the prison context, and that the second purpose of the FLSA—protecting competition—was addressed by the Ashurst-Sumners Act, 18 U.S.C. §§ 1761, 1762 (criminalizing transport in interstate commerce of any goods produced by prisoner). *McMaster* does not control here for two reasons.

First, we note that the FLSA's goal of protecting competition is not served by denying coverage to Barnett because the Ashurst-Sumners Act would not apply to preserve competition here: Barnett did not make goods to be sold in interstate commerce—he provided maintenance services. Second, this suit presents materially different facts than those before us in *McMaster.* This case is factually much closer to *Watson* or *Carter,* both of which we distinguished in *McMaster.* See id. at 979–80 (finding *Watson* distinguishable because inmates did not work in jail, were picked up at jail by private contractor, were left unguarded, were not assigned to work as part of their sentences but volunteered, and were paid directly; finding *Carter* distinguishable because inmates there sought relief against private company rather than prison, and because inmates were not required to work as part of their sentences). This suit was brought against a private entity, as was the case in both *Watson* and *Carter,* and not against a branch or representative of the county, state, or federal government, or against the prison or prison industries—where courts have denied FLSA coverage to prisoners.

Although the district court suggested YMCA's status as a nonprofit organization formed for a public purpose—rather than a private company—distinguished the present case . . . we see no reason why this status should immunize YMCA from the requirements of the FLSA in the present case.

Thus, treating Barnett's allegations as true, we conclude he has stated a claim under the FLSA. Accordingly, we reverse and remand for further proceedings consistent with this opinion.

Case Questions

1. How did the plaintiff's status as a convict and prisoner affect the court's decision?
2. How did the impact, or lack of impact, on the larger economy affect the court's decision?
3. Did the appellee's status as a nonprofit organization have any effect upon the court's reasoning?
4. Might prisoner rehabilitation be improved by requiring prisons to pay FLSA minimum wages in all cases?
5. What objections might a state's taxpayers legitimately have to a state being forced to pay prisoners the minimum wage?
6. Should a prisoner's receipt of free room and board be considered by courts in such cases?

Another tricky issue with which the DOL and courts have wrestled is the time required for an employee to prepare to perform the job and the time required to end the day's performance. This issue has arisen, for instance:

- Where the shifts of incoming and outgoing retail clerks must effectuate a transfer of the store's cash register between their shifts;

- Where miners and factory workers must don uniforms or equipment in a locker room at the start of their shifts and perhaps shower and change at the end of their workdays.

A closely related and equally thorny issue is when time spent by an employee waiting to work or "on call" is compensable and when it is not. Both of these issues arose in the recent case reported next.

Hiner v. Penn-Harris-Madison School Corporation

256 F. Supp. 2d 854 (N.D. Indiana 2003)

Nuechterlein, U.S. Magistrate Judge

Plaintiffs, twenty bus operators employed by Defendant . . . , filed a claim for unpaid overtime compensation pursuant to the Fair Labor Standards Act ("the FLSA") and the Indiana Wage Statute on October 15, 2001. Plaintiffs move for Partial Summary Judgment under the FLSA. On October 17, 2002, Defendant moved for Partial Summary Judgment, alleging that certain compensated time was not working time under the FLSA. For the following reasons, Plaintiffs' motion is granted in part and Defendant's motion is granted in part. . . .

While fact issues remain regarding each individual driver's schedule, Plaintiffs' typical daily schedule is as follows. Most Plaintiffs drive two daily routes, the first, or secondary school route, delivers secondary students to and from school, while the second, or elementary school route, delivers elementary students. Both routes occur in the morning and afternoon with some drivers driving additional mid-day routes in between their other responsibilities.

Prior to embarking on their secondary student routes, Plaintiffs are required to conduct pre-trip bus inspection. After dropping off the secondary students, Plaintiffs have a period of "down-time" until beginning their elementary school routes. The period of down-time varies for each driver, ranging anywhere from twelve minutes to one hour. Under [their Collective Bargaining] Agreement, Plaintiffs are paid for their down-time in addition to a paid morning break which is included as part of their morning route. Following their morning breaks/down-time, the drivers begin picking up elementary school students. The time at which the drivers begin their elementary routes varies depending on individual elementary schools' start times. Following their elementary routes, the drivers have another period of down-time until some drivers begin their mid-day routes. . . .

As in the morning, Plaintiffs pick up secondary students first, conduct their routes, and return to the elementary schools for their elementary routes. As previously stated, Plaintiffs' pay begins ten minutes prior to student dismissal for the first student pick-up and ends with the last students drop-off. . . .

Plaintiffs' employment agreement only pays them from their first morning pick-up until their final afternoon-drop-off. Hence, Plaintiffs are not compensated for the time it takes them to drive to their first morning pick-up and from their final afternoon drop-off. . . .

Plaintiffs moved for partial summary judgment on October 15, 2002, arguing that their daily bus inspections and all pre and post route drive time should be included as hours worked for purposes of overtime compensation under the FLSA.

The Portal-to-Portal Act eliminates certain preliminary and postliminary activities that do not include any principal work activities from "hours worked" under the FLSA. . . .

Two examples of what is meant by an integral part of the principal activity are . . .

> (1) In connection with the operation of a lathe, an employee will frequently, at the commencement of his workday, oil, grease, or clean his machine, or install a new cutting tool. Such activities are an integral part of the principal activity, and are included within such term.
> (2) In the case of a garment worker in a textile mill, who is required to report 30 minutes before other employees report to commence

> their principal activities, and who during such 30 minutes distributes clothing or parts of clothing at the workbenches of other employees and gets machines in readiness for operation by other employees, such activities are among the principal activities of such employees. . . .

[B]ecause Defendant concedes that the mandatory inspections as well as Plaintiffs' pre and post route driving time constitute hours worked under the FLSA, Plaintiffs' motion for partial summary judgment is granted in part. Because the Court has insufficient evidence to determine the length of each individual plaintiff's pre and post route drive time, as well as the duration of individual plaintiff's inspections, this Court is unable to grant or deny Plaintiffs' motion for partial summary judgment as to each individual plaintiff. . . .

Defendant filed a motion for partial summary judgment on October 17, 2002, arguing that the down-time taken by Plaintiffs between their morning bus routes; their outgoing and return trips for extra-curricular events; and their compensated time after completion of their mid-day routes exceeding twenty minutes does not constitute hours worked . . . for purposes of overtime compensation. . . .

In determining whether on-call time is compensable, the key question is whether time is spent predominantly for the employer's benefit or for the benefit of the employee. . . .

This Court . . . finds that individual plaintiff's compensated down-time is not considered working time under the FLSA in cases where an individual employee's down-time exceeds twenty minutes and the employee is not required to perform services for Defendant, but is instead free to use his or her down-time for personal pursuits.

Due to the multiple number of plaintiffs in this case, however, it cannot be said that all the plaintiff bus operators are actually using their down-time for personal purposes. . . . Therefore, Defendant's motion for partial summary judgment is granted in part. . . .

Case Questions

1. With regard to the time spent in driving buses to and from their first pick-ups, should it make a difference to the outcome of the case if the drivers are allowed to take their buses home at night and drive from home in the morning?
2. With regard to the hypothetical facts in question 1, does your answer change once again if, before driving from home to their first pick-up, the drivers conduct a safety inspection of their buses? How about if, when they get the buses home, they clean them before they quit for the day?
3. Why do you think twenty minutes has been chosen by the drafters of DOL wage and hour regulations as the dividing line between compensable and non-compensable waiting time? Does this number make sense to you? How about if it involves a lunch break?
4. How is waiting time different from on-call time? Which is more likely to be compensable?

OVERTIME PAY

Overtime Pay
Employees covered by FLSA are entitled to overtime pay, at one-and-a-half times their regular pay rate, for hours worked in excess of forty hours per workweek.

Workweek
A term the FLSA uses to signify seven consecutive days, but the law does not require that the workweek start or end on any particular day of the calendar week.

In addition to being entitled to earn the minimum wage, employees covered by the FLSA are entitled to **overtime pay,** at one-and-a-half times their regular pay rate, for hours worked in excess of forty hours per workweek.

The term **workweek** has special significance under the FLSA. It is a "term of art" with a fairly precise meaning. A workweek consists of seven consecutive days, but the law does not require that the workweek start or end on any particular day of the calendar week. For instance, a workweek may run from Tuesday to Monday or from Friday to Thursday. The starting day of the workweek may be changed from time to time, provided that the purpose of the change is not to avoid the requirements of the law (such as avoiding the payment of overtime to a group of workers).

As with the minimum wage, regulations have been developed to compute the hourly wages of workers paid by commission, piece-rate, and so forth for the purpose of calculating overtime pay. A more difficult question is deciding whether

ETHICAL DILEMMA: CONVENIENCE STORE CLERK'S CONUNDRUM

College sophomore Suzy Smart works part-time in the Handi Mart convenience store near campus. The manager at Handi Mart requires that each clerk arrive fifteen minutes prior to the start of the shift so that the clerk going off duty can review the sales figures and cash status with the replacement before leaving. The clerk going off duty punches her timecard after this review, but the oncoming clerk is not allowed to clock in until the review is completed and she has agreed that the sales and cash figures are accurate. Sometimes this exercise takes more than fifteen minutes; no matter how long it takes, the clerk coming on duty may not punch her timecard and start earning wages until the process is completed.

This semester, Suzy is taking a course on labor and employment law. After reading the text chapter concerning minimum wage and overtime rules under the Fair Labor Standards Act, she realizes that the store manager is violating the law by not allowing the oncoming clerk to punch the time clock as soon as she arrives. She brings this up with the store manager.

The store manager tells Suzy that he is not allowed by the parent corporation of Handi Mart to compensate two clerks for the same period of time, no matter how brief, because this is classified by the corporation as a "single coverage" store. Furthermore, he adds ominously, if Suzy complains to the Wage and Hour Division of the U.S. Department of Labor, he probably will be forced by the company to lay off Suzy and the other part-timers and cover the evening shifts himself. "You may get everyone a few dollars in back pay," he adds, "but you'll also cost everybody their jobs. Remember, some of your co-workers are single parents who need this extra income to make ends meet."

Should Suzy file a minimum wage complaint with the U.S. Department of Labor?

http://www.dol.gov *is the Department of Labor home page. Once there, initiate a search for overtime pay, then select a topic from the list of regulations.*

certain hours, not strictly part of working hours, should be included in working time for the calculation of wages and overtime. The Portal to Portal Act of 1947, which amended the FLSA, provides that preliminary or post-work activities are to be included in compensable time only if they are called for under contract or industry custom or practice.

EXEMPTIONS FROM OVERTIME AND MINIMUM WAGE PROVISIONS

Exempt Employees
Employees whose hours of work and compensation are not stipulated by the FLSA.

Not all employees under the FLSA are entitled to overtime pay or subject to the minimum wage. The FLSA sets out four general categories of **exempt employees:** executives, administrators, professionals, and outside salespeople.

Executive Employees

The regulations under the FLSA spell out two different tests for determining whether employees are executives and therefore exempt. The first test, known as the *short test,* applies to employees earning more than $250 per week. Those employees must meet two requirements: (1) their primary duty must be management, and (2) they must regularly direct the work of at least two other employees. For workers earning more than $155 but less than $250 per week to be exempted as executives, they must meet the requirements of the *long test*.[4] The long test includes the two requirements of the short test, and in addition, the employees must (1) have the authority to hire or fire employees or to make recommendations, which are given "particular weight," as to hiring, firing, or disciplining other workers; (2) customarily and regularly exercise discretionary powers in their work; and (3) not spend more than 20 percent (40 percent for employees of retail establishments) of their time in any week on activities that are not directly and closely related to their management duties.

http://www.dol.gov/dol/topic/wages/minimumwage.htm *is the site for the minimum wage and overtime regulations and exemptions.*

Administrative Employees

The regulations under the FLSA set out a short test and a long test for determining whether employees in administrative positions are exempt from the overtime and minimum wage provisions of the FLSA. Employees earning more than $250 per week are exempt under the short test if their primary duty consists of either (1) the performance of office or nonmanual work directly related to management policies or general business operations of their employer or their employer's customers or (2) the performance of administrative functions of a school system or educational institution in work directly related to the instruction or training carried on in them. Employees earning more than $155 but less than $250 per week are exempted if they meet the requirements of the long test. The long test includes the requirements of the short test plus the following other requirements: (1) the employee must customarily and regularly exercise discretion and independent judgment; (2) the employee must regularly perform, under general supervision only, specialized or technical work requiring special training or experience, perform special assignments, or regularly assist a proprietor or person in an executive or administrative capacity; and (3) the employee must not devote more than 20 percent (40 percent for employees of retail establishments) of time in a workweek to activities not directly and closely related to the performance of administrative duties.

Professional Employees

Employees in bona fide professional positions are exempted from the FLSA's overtime and minimum wage provisions if they meet one of several tests set out in the regulations. Persons engaged in the practice of law or medicine and persons employed as teachers in a school system or educational institution are exempt regardless of salary level. Persons employed in professional positions and earning more than $250 per week must meet the short test requirements. Their primary

[4]If these salaries seem extremely low, it is because Congress has not seen fit to revise them upward for decades. As this fifth edition went to press, Congress was taking up this question for the first time in many, many years.

duty must consist of (1) work requiring advanced knowledge in a field of science or acquired customarily through a prolonged course of specialized instruction; (2) work original and creative in character in a recognized field of artistic endeavor; or (3) teaching, tutoring, or lecturing as a certified or recognized teacher in a school system or educational institution. Persons in professional positions who earn between $170 and $250 per week must meet the long test requirements to be exempted. The long test requirements include the requirements of the short test plus these other requirements: (1) the person's work must require the consistent exercise of discretion and judgment in its performance; (2) the work must be predominantly intellectual and varied in character, and its output cannot be standardized in relation to a given period of time; and (3) the person must not devote more than 20 percent of time in a workweek to activities not an essential part of, or incident to, his or her professional duties.

Outside Salespeople

The regulations under the FLSA exempt outside salespeople from both the overtime and minimum wage provisions. To be exempt, the following requirements must be met: (1) the person must be employed in, and regularly engage in, making sales or obtaining orders or contracts, away from his or her employer's place of business; and (2) the person must not spend more than 20 percent of the hours in a workweek in duties other than sales duties.

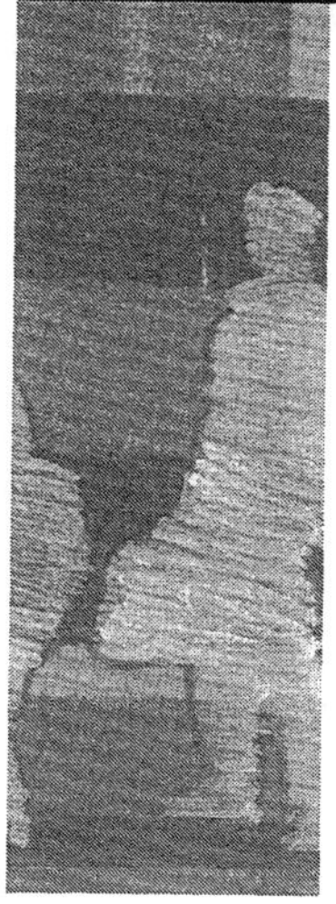

CALIFORNIA LAW NOW EXEMPTS HIGHLY PAID TECH PROFESSIONALS FROM STATE'S OVERTIME RULES

THE WORKING LAW

Under the Fair Labor Standards Act, states are permitted to enact their own wage and hours laws as long as such state statutes and their implementing regulations do not diminish or deny any rights accorded employees by the FLSA. California has improved upon the FLSA by requiring the payment of overtime for all hours in excess of eight in any single workday. However, in September 2000, the California legislature amended the wage and hour law to the effect that "highly paid" tech professionals in Silicon Valley and elsewhere throughout the state would no longer receive overtime pay on this basis.

California's overtime law requires time and a half for more than eight hours a day, unlike most states, which only require overtime after forty hours in a week. The daily overtime law exempts employees who work flexible schedules, such as four ten-hour days, and requires anyone exempt from overtime to be salaried rather than hourly. Under federal law, temporary computer programmers and some other computer professionals are exempt from overtime if they earn at least $27.63 an hour. But California's more stringent law allows workers earning between $27.63 and $41 an hour to be eligible for overtime.

Source: *San Jose Mercury News,* September 19, 2000. Byline: Hallye Jordan and Margaret Stern.

LIMITATIONS ON CHILD LABOR

The problems of child labor are graphically demonstrated by photographs from the late nineteenth and early twentieth centuries showing children who had spent their youth toiling in coal mines or factories. The children, often immigrants, were subjected to the same hazardous conditions and occupational diseases as were their parents. The children received little or no formal education. Their wages were usually meager and had the effect of depressing the wages paid to adult workers in the same jobs.

http://www.dol.gov/dol/topic/youthlabor/nonagricultural employment.htm
is the site of the regulation on nonagricultural child labor.

The social and economic problems of child labor were recognized by government; many states passed legislation attempting to limit child labor. Those early laws were restricted in their effectiveness, though, and the number of children employed continued to rise until about 1910. Congress made several attempts to enact federal limitations on child labor. In 1916, a law prohibiting the shipment in interstate commerce of goods produced by factories or mines employing child labor was passed. The Supreme Court, however, in the 1918 case of *Hammer v. Dagenhart* (247 U.S. 1), held that the law was unconstitutional because it exceeded the limited power granted to the federal government under the commerce clause of the Constitution.

THE STRAIGHT STORY ABOUT THOSE AWFUL OVERSEAS SWEATSHOPS

THE WORKING LAW

In Bangkok a girl of 15 works in a factory making clothing for export to America. She is paid $2 a day for a nine-hour shift, six days a week. Her father says, "It's good pay. I hope she can keep that job." Sweatshops that seem brutal from an American perspective can appear tantalizing to a Thai laborer getting by on beetles. Workers regard it as a plus that the factory allows them to work long hours, and in fact seek out those companies that offer them the chance to earn more. For an impoverished Indonesian or Bangladeshi woman—with a handful of kids who would otherwise drop out of school and risk dying of mundane diseases like diarrhea—$1 or $2 a day can be a life-transforming wage. For all their misery, sweatshops offer a precarious escape from the poverty that is the developing world's greatest problem.

Nothing captures the difference in mind-set between East and West more than attitudes towards sweatshops. American companies have been hammered in the press over the last decade for producing shoes, toys and other products in grim factories with dismal conditions. Protests against sweatshops have become common at meetings of the World Bank and the World Trade Organization.

Agitation for improved safety conditions can be helpful, just as it was in 19th-century Europe. But Asian workers would be appalled if American consumers boycotted certain toys or clothing in protest. The simplest way to help the poorest Asians would be to buy more from sweatshops, not less, because the truth is that those grim factories have contributed to a remarkable explosion of wealth in Asia. In fact, the most vibrant parts of Asia are nearly all in what might be called the Sweatshop Belt—from China and South Korea to Malaysia, Indonesia and even Bangladesh and India. Today these sweatshop countries control about one-quarter of the global economy, and have helped lay the groundwork for a historic economic realignment that is putting Asia back on its feet.

Over the past 50 years, countries such as India resisted foreign exploitation, while countries that started at a similar economic level—like Taiwan and South Korea—accepted sweatshops as the price of development. Today there can be no doubt about which approach worked better. Taiwan and South Korea are modern countries with low rates of infant mortality and high levels of education, while every year 3.1 million Indian children die before the age of 5, mostly from diseases of poverty like diarrhea.

Source: Nicholas D. Kristof and Sheryl WuDunn. *The Portland Oregonian,* October 1, 2000.

The National Industrial Recovery Act (NIRA) provided that the codes of fair competition for each industry could limit child labor, but in 1935, the NIRA was held unconstitutional by the Supreme Court in *Schecter Poultry v. U.S.* In 1936, the Walsh-Healy Act prohibited contractors under government contracts from using child labor to produce, manufacture, or furnish materials for the contract. The Fair Labor Standards Act of 1938 at last provided for general federal regulation of child labor. In 1941, it was upheld by the Supreme Court in *U.S. v. Darby Lumber Co.*

The FLSA and Child Labor

The FLSA does not prohibit all child labor; rather it proscribes only "oppressive" child labor. The act prohibits the interstate shipment of goods from establishments employing oppressive child labor. It also prohibits oppressive child labor in any enterprise with two or more employees engaged in the production of goods for interstate commerce. The definition of "oppressive child labor" is crucial to the administration of the act. The act defines oppressive child labor by using age restrictions and identifying hazardous occupations.

Employing minors under age eighteen in any occupation identified as hazardous by the secretary of labor is prohibited. Minors aged sixteen to eighteen may work in certain non-hazardous occupations, and minors aged fourteen to sixteen may be employed in non-manufacturing or non-mining occupations for limited hours outside school hours. Minors under age fourteen can be employed only in agriculture under specific limitations and with parental consent.

The regulations limiting work by minors aged fourteen to sixteen further specify that the minors' hours between 7 A.M. and 7 P.M. may not exceed eighteen hours per week when school is in session or forty hours per week when school is not in session; nor may they exceed three hours per day when school is in session or eight hours per day when school is not in session.

Specific exemptions from the category of oppressive child labor include the employment of newspaper carriers who are engaged in delivering papers to consumers; minors who are hired as actors or performers in movies, radio, television, or theatrical productions; and minors who are employed by their parents, or persons standing in the place of parents, in occupations other than manufacturing, mining, or others identified as hazardous by the secretary of labor.

At present, a number of occupations have been identified as hazardous by the secretary of labor, including the following:

- coal mining or mining other than coal;
- occupations in or about plants manufacturing explosives or articles containing explosive components;
- occupations involving operation of motor-driven hoisting apparatus;
- logging or saw milling occupations;
- occupations involving exposure to radioactive substances;
- occupations of motor-vehicle operator or helper;
- occupations involving operation of power-driven woodworking machines;
- occupations involving operation of power-driven metalworking, forming, punching, or shearing machines;
- occupations in or about slaughtering or meatpacking plants or rendering plants;
- occupations involving the manufacture of brick, tile, or related products;
- occupations involving the operation of circular saws, handsaws, and guillotine shears;
- occupations involving wrecking, demolition, and shipbreaking.

Although child labor cases have become relatively rare in recent years, the Department of Labor strictly enforces the FLSA provision.

Chao v. Vidtape, Inc

196 F. Supp. 2d 281 (E.D.N.Y. 2002)

Boyle, U.S. Magistrate Judge

The Secretary of Labor . . . commenced this action on May 1, 1998 . . . after an investigation of the labor practices of the defendants. This court held a bench trial on April 23, 2001 to May 1, 2001, and the parties gave summations on October 18, 2001. At the conclusion of the trial, . . . [t]his court granted judgment in favor of the Secretary on March 29, 2002. . . . .

Wilber Amaya testified that he was fourteen years old when Vidtape hired him to pack videos and boxes using a "hand truck." At his interview, he presented his INS work permit . . . which indicated that Amaya was born on September 2, 1982. Amaya worked ten hour days, six days a week, during the months when school was in session. Vidtape terminated Amaya after the Department of Labor began its investigation. The court credits this testimony. . . .

In employing Wilbur Amaya, defendants violated the Act's child labor provision. Section 212(c) of the Act provides that "no employer shall employ any oppressive child labor in commerce or in the production of goods for commerce or in any enterprise engaged in commerce or the production of goods for commerce." "Oppressive child labor" is defined as a "condition of employment under which . . . any employee under the age of sixteen is employed by an employer . . . in any occupation." Children between the age of 14 and 16 cannot be employed for more than three hours a day, 18 hours per week when school is in session, and 8 hours a day, 40 hours a week when school is not in session. . . . The regulations also state that minors are not permitted to work in occupations that involve manufacturing of goods. . . .

Although . . . defendants asserted as an affirmative defense that the minor child was hired at the request of a relative and that defendants were not aware they violated child labor law, intent or willfulness is not an element of this offense.

The defendants violated the "hot goods" provision by manufacturing products in violation of the Act. The "hot goods" provision in sec. 215(a)(1) provides that it is unlawful for any person to "transport, . . . ship, . . . deliver or sell in commerce . . . any goods in the production of which any employee was employed" in violation of minimum wage, overtime or child labor restrictions. The remedy for violation of this provision is an injunction. Vidtape violated the "hot goods" provision by manufacturing videotapes in violation of the Act and then shipping them in interstate commerce. An injunction is warranted. . . .

Case Questions

1. The defendants claim that Wilbur Amaya was employed by them as a favor to his relatives. The court rejects this defense. Do you think the outcome would or should be any different if Wilbur's relatives were the owners of Vidtape?
2. Suppose that Wilbur were being home-schooled, as is permitted in many states. Should that excuse his full-time employment while school is in session?
3. Aside from the fact that he was missing school, do Wilbur's work conditions seem to have been "oppressive" for a fourteen year old?
4. Why is an injunction appropriate in this case? Why aren't money damage and/or a fine sufficient?

ENFORCEMENT AND REMEDIES UNDER FLSA

The FLSA is enforced by the Department of Labor. The Wage and Hour Division of the Department of Labor performs inspections and investigations and issues rules and regulations. The secretary of labor is authorized to file suit on behalf of employees seeking to collect wages and overtime and may also recover liquidated damages in an amount equal to the amount of wages owed. The secretary may also seek injunctions against violations of the act. Criminal proceedings for willful violations may be instituted by the Department of Justice.

Employees may file suit to recover back wages and overtime plus liquidated damages in an equal amount. They may also seek reinstatement and may recover legal fees. The statute of limitations for violations is two years; for willful violations it is extended to three years. The Supreme Court discussed the definition of "willful" in *McLaughlin v. Richland Shoe Co.* [486 U.S. 128 (1988)]; the court defined "willful" as "that the employer either knew or showed reckless disregard as to whether its conduct was prohibited by the FLSA." Employees generally may not release employers for less than the full amount owing, nor may employees waive their rights to compensation under the act.

The child labor prohibitions are enforced by the prohibition of interstate shipment of goods produced by child labor and by fines. Fines may also be levied against employers who keep inadequate wage and hour records.

The following case involves a discussion of the standard used by the court in determining whether to award liquidated damages in addition to back pay.

Mogilevsky v. Bally Total Fitness Corporation

2003 WL 21098646 (U.S. District Court, D. Mass. 2003)

Young, Chief Judge

The plaintiff . . . has brought claims regarding unpaid wages against his former employer . . . pursuant to the Fair Labor Standards Act and the common law. The Court held a bench trial on [his] claims in September 2002. . . .

The Court begins by noting that the hours in question accrued between January 1998 and December 1999. Mogilevsky filed the instant action on May 18, 2001. The Fair Labor Standards Act sets forth a two-year statute of limitations, unless the employer's violation was willful, in which case the statute of limitations is extended to three years. . . .

The Supreme Court has stated that an employer's violation is willful within the meaning of the Fair Labor Standards Act when it can be shown that the employer knew, or recklessly disregarded, that it was acting in violation of the Act. . . . Here the Court rules that although Bally's failure to pay Mogilevsky his proper wages may well have been negligent, that failure does not rise to the level of reckless disregard, given the lack of clarity in Mogilevsky's own records and his unorthodox approach to scheduling training sessions. Accordingly, the appropriate statute of limitations period for Mogilevsky's claims under . . . the Fair Labor Standards Act . . . is two years.

The question remains, however, whether Mogilevsky can recover for the hours accrued prior to May 18, 1999. With respect to these hours . . . Bally can potentially be held liable [under] Mogilevsky's common law breach of contract claim, which carries a six-year statute of limitations. . . .

The Court rules that a common law breach of contract claim is inapplicable here. The documents that Mogilevsky cites as giving rise to this "contract"—the Employee Information and Acknowledgment Form and the Employee Handbook—simply contain what are essentially promises to adhere to federal and state law regarding payment of overtime wages. . . .

[W]ith respect to [the] payment of $1482.50 that Bally owes Mogilevsky under the Fair Labor Standards Act, the Court rules that Mogilevsky is entitled to liquidated damages—that is, an additional equal amount. Although Bally's failure to comply with the Fair Labor Standards Act was not willful or reckless, the Court rules, on the basis of the evidence presented at the bench trial, that Bally cannot meet its burden of proving good faith and reasonableness as it must do to avoid liquidated damages. First, the Court found at the conclusion of the bench trial that Bally issued mandates of "no overtime" when it should have known that professional trainers had already booked overtime and that—more specifically—Mogilevsky's own supervisors knew that Mogilevsky would have to work overtime in some such instances. Moreover the Court also found that, at the Bally gym where Mogilevsky worked, there was a practice—albeit not one condoned by the company—by trainers of passing their sales to each other in order to meet certain targets. Based on these findings, the Court concludes that liquidated damages are warranted and that Mogilevsky is entitled to an additional equal amount. . . .

Case Questions

1. What is meant by the term "liquidated damages" under the FLSA? How are such damages different from punitive damages as allowed by the American common law and the 1991 Civil Rights Act?
2. What is meant by "good faith" required to avoid liquidated damages, and whose burden is it to establish the presence of good-faith behavior?
3. How is employer negligence distinguished from recklessness in this decision? Is the distinction drawn by the judge persuasive?
4. Attorney fees are also allowed to be assessed by the judge against the defendant to be paid to the plaintiff's lawyer. Do you think Mogilevsky should be entitled to an award of attorney fees in this case? Do you think that possibility was a significant factor in his attorney's initial decision to take this case? If so, what does that suggest to you about the public policy underlying this "fee-shifting" aspect of the FLSA?

SUMMARY

- The Fair Labor Standards Act (FLSA) is the primary federal law governing minimum wages, overtime compensation, and child labor in the United States. It does not preempt similar state laws that provide employees with greater protections in these key categories. The FLSA has been declared by the Supreme Court not to be an unconstitutional taking of employers' property or an unconstitutional interference with the right to make contracts.
- Minimum hourly wages need not be paid to bona fide executives, administrators, professionals, and outside salespeople, who typically receives salaries and commissions. Hourly workers, who are entitled to at least the federal minimum wage, cannot be penalized by deductions for tools, uniforms, or cash register losses.
- Executives, administrators, professionals, and outside salespeople also are not entitled to overtime pay. Hourly employees are entitled to at least one-and-a-half times their regular hourly pay rates for all hours over forty in any workweek.
- FLSA child labor provisions limit the use of children and teens in dangerous workplaces. Since the law does not extend to American corporations' activities outside the United States and its territories, critics of corporate practices in Third-World countries recently have accused a number of major corporations of exploiting child labor, as well as workers generally, in offshore operations.

QUESTIONS

1. What are the main provisions of the FLSA? What are the bases of coverage for the FLSA?
2. What deductions may be made from an employee's wages under the FLSA? Explain your answer.
3. Does the FLSA require the payment of overtime? Under what circumstances?
4. What are the major exceptions from the overtime and minimum wage requirements of the FLSA? What are the tests used to determine whether an employee falls under one of those exemptions?
5. What is meant by "oppressive child labor"? What is the significance of oppressive child labor under the FLSA?
6. What remedies are available for violations of the minimum wage and overtime provisions of the FLSA? What penalties may be imposed for violations of the child labor prohibitions?

CASE PROBLEMS

1. The employer is a not-for-profit corporation that provides services to mentally retarded and developmentally disabled individuals. It operates residential group homes for its clientele. Each such geographically separate house is under the sole charge of a house manager. The house manager's job includes (1) managing the house's budget; (2) hiring and managing other employees at the house; and (3) maintaining employment records. However,

these house managers also perform nonmanagerial tasks such as transporting clients, assisting them with bathing and dressing, and numerous other chores normally performed by their subordinates.

Should these house managers be classified as exempt executive employees for purposes of minimum wage and overtime pay under the FLSA? See *Department of Labor, Wage and Hour Division, Opinion Letter of July 14, 2000* [2000 WL 1537209].

2. Company A sells airtime and infomercials on television. It employs telephone callers at $9 per hour. Company B, which is owned by the same parent company, does telephone collection calling of its clients' debtors, paying the same hourly rate of $9.

Employee C works forty hours per week for Company A. He also is employed evenings for a total of ten hours per week for Company B.

Should Company B be required to pay Employee C time-and-one-half for overtime compensation? See *Department of Labor, Wage and Hour Division, Opinion Letter of July 14, 2000, Attachment 1* [2000 WL 1537209].

3. A volunteer ambulance company contracts with a for-profit corporation to provide drivers and emergency medical technicians (EMTs). The for-profit company then bills the volunteer ambulance company for the services of these employees. Sometimes, however, these very same drivers and EMTs provide their services to the volunteer ambulance company as volunteers in their off-duty hours. Should the volunteer ambulance company be required to pay these drivers and EMTs either minimum wages and/or overtime compensation for their "volunteer" hours? See *Department of Labor, Wage and Hour Division, Opinion Letter of May 22, 2000* [2000 WL 1537253].

4. The employer established a performance-based bonus plan under which workers who were not exempt from the minimum wage and overtime provisions of the FLSA were evaluated on various productivity criteria. At year's end, some of the company's top performers were given lump-sum, one-time bonuses. Who received the bonuses and in what amounts were determinations made by the CEO in her sole discretion. The company was under no advance contractual obligation to give any bonuses or to give any particular employees a bonus.

Should the employer be permitted to exclude these lump-sum bonuses when calculating a recipient's hourly rate of pay for purposes of determining whether she or he has been receiving the proper amount when entitled to overtime compensation? See *Department of Labor, Wage and Hour Division, Opinion Letter of May 19, 2000* [2000 WL 1537273].

5. A company allowed its employees to take a half-hour lunch break. However, the break was uncompensated, and the employees were not permitted to leave the employer's premises during the break. Nevertheless, these employees did leave their positions on the production line and eat in an employee lunchroom. They also went outdoors at their discretion.

Should the employer be required under the FLSA to compensate these hourly production workers for their thirty-minute lunch breaks? What about maintenance workers who might be recalled early from their lunch breaks if an equipment breakdown required it? See *Brown v. Howard Industries, Inc.* [116 F.Supp.2d 764 (S.D. Miss. 2000)].

6. Pursuant to the FLSA exception, which allows public employers to give their hourly workers compensatory time in lieu of overtime pay, a town provided its police officers with compensatory time credits in place of overtime premiums. However, when police officers tried to "cash in" their compensatory entitlements, the chief of police—following the instructions of the town council—approved such requests only when a police officer's absence on "comp time" did not require the town to pay a replacement officer overtime/comp time.

Should the town be permitted to restrict the police officers' enjoyment of their comp time entitlements in this fashion? See *Canney v. Town of Brookline* [2000 WL 1612703 (D. Mass.)].

7. The employee, an immigrant, filed a claim with state's labor commission, claiming unpaid overtime entitlements. The employer then reported her immigration status to the Immigration and Naturalization Service (now the Bureau of Citizenship and Immigration Services in the Department of Homeland Security), which upon investigation found that the employee in fact was in violation of INS regulations.

Should the employee be permitted to pursue a lawsuit against the employer, alleging retaliation in violation of Section 215(a)(3) of the FLSA, which makes it illegal to punish an employee for exercising her rights under the FLSA? Does your answer change if the INS fails to find that the employee is working in violation of INS regulations? What if the reporting employer honestly believed in good faith that the violation existed?

What are the competing public policy considerations for and against permitting such a lawsuit under these two different sets of facts? See *Contreras v. Corinthian Vigor Insurance Brokerage, Inc.* [2000 WL 1521369 (N.D. Cal.)].

8. The employee was employed as a "floating" pharmacist by a small chain of drug stores. As the floater, he was shifted from store to store to fill in for ill and vacationing regular pharmacists. He was paid an hourly wage of $27 but no overtime, even though he sometimes worked more than forty hours in a single week.

When he sued for his unpaid overtime compensation, the company contended that he is a professional employee and therefore not entitled to overtime compensation under the FLSA. Is the company correct? What different or additional facts, if any, might cause you to change your answer? See *Iheanacho v. Safeway, Inc.* [2000 WL 1364239 (D. Oregon)].

9. A university provided free housing for its male security guards but not for its female guards. The university claimed that its purpose was to ensure round-the-clock availability of public safety officers on the campus in case of emergencies, and therefore, the housing was for its benefit and convenience and not an added form of compensation to the male officers. University officials also claimed that it would be unduly expensive to try to make the facilities coed to accommodate the female guards.

The female guards brought suit under the Equal Pay Act provisions of the FLSA (see Chapter 4). Who should win? See *Stewart v. S.U.N.Y. Maritime College* [2000 WL 1218379 (S.D.N.Y.)].

10. A local bus company makes its money by transporting passengers to and from the local train station and to bus depots, where they catch interstate buses. The company runs no buses outside state lines but is strictly local. Nevertheless, the company is regulated by the U.S. Department of Transportation. The FLSA exempts interstate transportation activities.

The local bus company admits it never pays its drivers overtime compensation when they exceed forty hours of work in a week. But it argues that it is exempt because it is engaged in interstate transportation.

Do you agree? See *United Transportation Local Union 759 v. Orange Newark Elizabeth Bus, Inc.* [111 F.Supp.2d 514 (D.N.J. 2000)].

INTERNET EXERCISES

1. Go to **http://www.dol.gov**.
2. Locate the Department of Labor's Wage and Hour Division home page.
3. Find the link to Farm Labor and locate the fact sheet relating to child labor.
4. What are the relevant rules involving child labor in agriculture and to whom do they apply?
5. Now go to Google and search Child Labor.
6. Find the Web site for the Children's World Congress on Child Labor.
7. Locate the link to Child Labor in the U.S.
8. What does this link offer with regard to child labor in U.S. agriculture? What are the hot topics? Does the information suggest that the U.S. Department of Labor is doing a good job or a poor job of enforcing its child labor regulations in the area of agriculture?

INFOTRAC KEYWORDS

http://www.infotrac-college.com

FLSA, wage regulation, minimum wage, overtime pay, child labor laws

11 CHAPTER

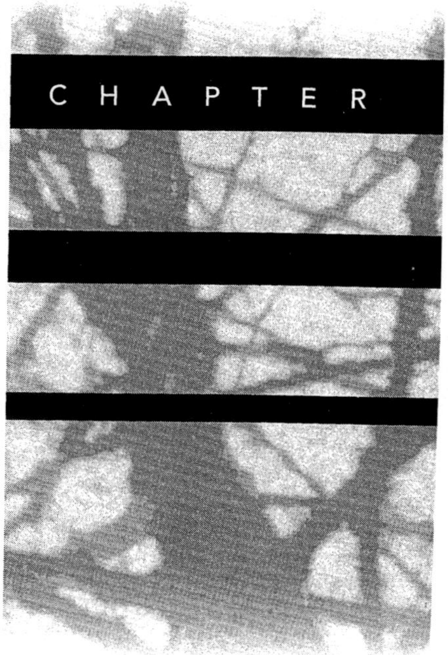

EMPLOYEE WELFARE PROGRAMS: SOCIAL SECURITY, WORKERS' COMPENSATION, AND UNEMPLOYMENT COMPENSATION

Not until the 1900s, and for a substantial number of Americans not even until the 1930s, did the government provide any assistance to workers affected by unemployment, on-the-job injury, work-related disability, or old age. Until that time, Americans (like workers around the world then and even today) relied on their families, ethnic communities, churches, and social clubs for aid when their incomes were temporarily or permanently disrupted. For instance, Irish coal miners in Pennsylvania in the 1870s might belong to the Ancient Order of Hibernians, a benevolent society with a fund dedicated to assisting the widows and orphans of miners killed in the "pits." Increasingly, too, workers organized and looked to their unions for help in times of trouble. But before Congress passed the National Labor Relations Act (NLRA) in 1935, most unions were mere shadows of what they would later become.

> **http://www4.law.cornell.edu/uscode/45/ch8.html** *is the site for the index of sections of the Railway Labor Act.*

Congress did occasionally become involved in the welfare of employees in private industry, even before the groundbreaking legislation of the 1930s. The Railway Labor Act (governing labor relations), which was passed in 1926, and the Federal Employment Liability Act (FELA), which was passed in 1908, predate the NLRA and workers' compensation laws, respectively. The FELA was enacted in recognition of the incredible number of casualties in the railroad industry (about 25,000 deaths annually around the turn of the last century) and of the realities of workers trying to sue their employers in those days. In the early days of the railroad industry, a shocking number of railway workers suffered accidents or were killed at work. Those injured, or the families of those killed, often found attempts at getting recourse from the railway companies an exercise in frustration or futility. The legal realities of going up against the railroad were daunting.

The text of Section 51 of FELA regarding employer responsibility can be found at **http://www4.law.cornell.edu/uscode/45/51.html**

Suppose a railroad worker in 1900 was hit by a railcar that rolled in deadly silence down the track because of a faultily set brake. The injured, perhaps permanently disabled, worker might hold the railroad responsible and seek to sue it for money damages. To do so, he would first have to find a lawyer willing to take the case. Having little or no savings, he might find it difficult to obtain an attorney prepared to take on one of the great financial juggernauts of the era. If he did, he faced a daunting set of defenses that the railroad company could raise. The railroad's lawyers most likely would first argue that the hapless employee, by taking the job, had assumed the risk of injury. They would then seek to establish that he somehow had been contributorily negligent, such as by not being alert while in the rail yard. Finally, they would invoke the fellow-servant doctrine; that is, they would say that he was not injured by their client, "the railroad," but by a co-worker who had negligently failed to set the brake properly.

As you can see, any worker who recovered what his injuries deserved from the railroad had to have been both very persistent and very lucky. For most workers, or their widows and orphans, the alternative was one of the forms of charity previously mentioned, perhaps in combination with some modest form of public dole. But being employed in the key industry of industrialized America, railroad workers were the first able to exert unified pressure to better their circumstances. Theirs was the first major industry to be organized by several railway brotherhoods, such as the Brotherhood of Railway Clerks. Once organized, they successfully lobbied for passage of the FELA.

Although the FELA still requires an injured railroad worker to file suit in a federal or state court, it substantially reduces the burden of proof placed upon the employee/plaintiff, while depriving the railroad/defendant of some of its most potent defenses. Thus, injured employees generally win their cases under the FELA, which is still in force today.

Not until the New Deal era of the 1930s did such legislation become widespread in the United States. The Pennsylvania Superior Court summarized the development of such U.S. laws in a 1946 unemployment compensation decision, *Bliley Electric Company v. Unemployment Compensation Board of Review* [45 A.2d 898, 901 (1946)]:

> The statute, almost ten years old, introduced into our law a new concept of social obligation, extended the police power of the State into a virgin field, and created a body of rights and duties unknown to the common law. England was the first common law country to operate a similar system, and its experience began as an experiment in 1911. Its law, revised as trial exposed error, became the basis for the American unemployment compensation system, although in detail there are vast variances between the American and British systems. Wisconsin passed an act in 1932, but it required the enactment of the Social Security Act by Congress on August 14, 1935 to induce other states to adopt the system. All of the states have enacted conforming legislation, and their statutes include the basic requirements laid down by the Act of Congress, but they differ widely and sharply in respect to the details, which Congress left open to state legislation.

The pattern of the genesis of unemployment benefits identified by the Pennsylvania Superior Court also matches the historical pattern for social security and workers' compensation. Although the roots of these laws can be traced to the second decade of the twentieth century (just a bit behind England and Germany), the widespread availability of these important benefits is indebted to President Franklin Roosevelt's New Deal.

All three social welfare programs—social security pensions, workers' compensation, and unemployment compensation—descend from a common history and came into being about the same time. A major distinction between unemployment and workers' compensation versus social security is that the states have primary responsibility for the first two (with some notable exceptions), whereas social security is a federally supervised program applied uniformly across the country. But despite this difference, plus many distinctions between the various states' systems of unemployment or workers' compensation, the common threads, like the common ancestry, make it possible to discuss each of these forms of worker welfare in general terms. Wherever you wind up working in the United States, you will find that state's systems readily recognizable.

This chapter begins with the federal social security program and then examines workers' compensation and unemployment compensation.

THE SOCIAL SECURITY AND SUPPLEMENTAL SECURITY ACTS

Nearly one in every seven Americans are recipients of social security benefits. The social security system was originally entitled "old age and survivor's insurance" (OASI), and the notion that it really was insurance was a significant component of Franklin Roosevelt's success in selling the program to Congress and the country. Yet in reality, for its first three decades of existence, the OASI was financed from current payroll taxes charged to employers and their employees. Those who looked forward to drawing benefits when they got old paid for the benefits being received by current pensioners. This was pay as you go, not a real vested pension fund or paid-up retirement insurance. But it worked as long as retirees were a modest percentage of the active work force and benefits were low.

As post–World War II baby boomers entered the work force, and especially as employment peaked during the Vietnam War, a surplus actually piled up in the OASI. But during this same time, another trend was set in motion that by the mid-1970s placed the OASI's solvency in jeopardy. For years, the Social Security Administration career staff aimed toward converting social security from a minimal safety net into an adequate pension. This goal was shared by many congressional liberals and by organized labor. Gradually, these players won their way, not only increasing the typical retiree's benefit and insulating it against inflation, but also expanding the program to cover other needy Americans, such as the permanently disabled.

Meanwhile, the baby boom became a baby bust, while life spans lengthened. Public information from the Census Bureau and the Department of Labor reveals that during the 1970s, 24.1 million young workers entered the labor pool. Only 9 million joined the labor force in the 1980s. The 1990s produced only 15.6 million new workers. Persons fifty-five and older constituted 20 percent of our population at the turn of this century and will constitute 32.3 percent by 2030. The average American woman produced 3.4 to 3.6 offspring between 1946 and 1964. Today, she gives birth to an average of 1.8 children. In 1900, people over seventy-four years old made up only 1.2 percent of the population. By 1982, they were 5 percent of the populace. By 2030, their ranks will represent a hefty 10 percent of the country. These figures eloquently illustrate the pressures on the social security system.

These pressures were first felt during Gerald Ford's presidency (1973–1976), hard on the heels of some of the most generous (and shortsighted) social security legislation in the system's history. By 1977, talk of a social security bankruptcy was common not only in Washington but around the country. Jimmy Carter came into office with the problem on his agenda, and by the time Ronald Reagan took office in 1981, the problem had become critical.

To better understand the system as it is administered and maintained today, we must look at three legislative phases: the original passage of the act, the early 1970s amendments that built in automatic cost-of-living increases and other costly expansions, and the bailout legislation of the early 1980s.

TITLES II AND VIII OF THE SOCIAL SECURITY ACT OF 1935

Old-age pensions were near and dear to Franklin Roosevelt well before he was elected president in 1932. Although he was from wealthy and famous New York society stock, his interest in the issue came at least in part from personal experience. In a campaign speech delivered on October 2, 1932, in Detroit, he recounted one such personal perspective on the plight of old people:

> I had been away during the winter time and when I came back I found that a tragedy had occurred. I had had an old farm neighbor, who had been a splendid old fellow—supervisor of his town, highway commissioner of his town, one of the best of our citizens. Before I left, around Christmastime, I had seen the old man, who was eighty-nine, his old brother, who was eighty-seven, his other brother, who was eighty-five, and his kid sister, who was eighty-three.
>
> When I came back in the spring, I found that in the severe winter that followed there had been a heavy fall of snow and one of the old brothers had fallen down on his way out to the barn to milk the cow and had perished in the snow drift.
>
> The town authorities had come along and had taken the two old men and had put them in the county poorhouse, and they had taken the old lady and had sent her down for want of a better place, to the insane asylum although she was not insane but just old.

As governor of New York, Roosevelt had not gotten very far pushing the notion of old-age pensions. Few other states had done any better. When he took over the Oval Office in 1933, fifteen of forty-eight states had no provisions whatever for aged Americans. The rest paid an average pension of about $16 a month, not enough even in those hard times to pay for one square meal a day. In June 1934, the new president set up the Cabinet Committee on Economic Security with Labor Secretary Frances Perkins, herself a former New York social worker and member of that state's industrial commission, as chairperson.

The committee was pushed along by the efforts of Californian Everett Townsend to lobby through Congress his own Townsend Plan for the elderly. The committee also addressed other issues covered in this chapter, such as unemployment compensation, which they decided should be administered by the states. As for social security, they favored federal centralization because workers might be employed in many places during a career and then ultimately retire somewhere they had never worked. Roosevelt's major contribution to the final plan, a contribution that proved prophetic, was to insist it be called old-age insurance.

Each contributor was to have her or his own account, even though the fund operated pay as you go and there was no vesting of actual individual contributions. Roosevelt told one colleague that the purpose of that approach was ". . . so those sons of bitches up on the Hill can't ever abandon this system when I'm gone." His idea worked brilliantly. As stated by Harvard's Neustadt and May in *Thinking in Time: The Uses of History for Decision-Makers,* ". . . by 1939 it turned out that the symbols of the thing sufficed—the term, the trappings, the account numbers—never mind the vesting."

THE 1970S: SOCIAL SECURITY CRISIS

The social security crisis began in 1972. The Social Security Act was amended twice that year. In July 1972, social security benefits were increased by Congress 20 percent, effective September 1 of that year. That amendment also introduced automatic cost-of-living increases, tied to the Consumer Price Index, starting in 1975. Then, in October 1972, more amendments, effective the following January, were enacted into law; some 3.4 million widows of deceased retirees received enhanced benefits, and all retirees were permitted to earn more income without diminution in their pensions.

http://www.ssa.gov/OP_Home/ssact/comp-toc.htm *provides an index to provisions of the Social Security Act.*

A number of factors had combined to cause Congress and President Nixon to permit these very expensive amendments to the thirty-year-old system. OASI funds had piled up into a tidy surplus during the Vietnam War. Nixon wanted to be reelected; signing the social security amendments was only a minor excess of his reelection efforts (as compared to the Watergate scandal that was soon to materialize and eclipse all other issues on the political scene). Presidential politics led lobby opposition, such as from the National Association of Manufacturers, to be muted as well. And so, for perhaps the first time in three decades, social security became an adequate pension, not merely a minimal safety net. But at what price?

Three unexpected trends converged to threaten the fattened fund with fiscal disaster. First, as mentioned earlier, the birthrate dropped while life spans of Americans lengthened. Second, inflation began galloping, spurred in part by the first of several successive oil crises. Third came a recession. The term *stagflation,* which means persistent inflation together with stagnant consumer demand and relatively high unemployment, entered the economists' lexicon, and by 1977, talk of a social security bankruptcy was common.

Meanwhile, President Carter resisted attempts to reduce pensioners' benefits. When the new president, Ronald Reagan, appeared to endorse some delays in increases in 1981, public opinion lashed back at him with a vengeance.

THE 1980S: RECOVERY?

Reagan's response was to set up a bipartisan commission in the autumn of 1981 to study the problems facing social security. He appointed five members, and the speaker of the House and Senate majority leader each got to appoint five more. Most key players and key interests received some representation on the commission. After six weeks of discussions and negotiations, there was a commission report. The result was a combination of benefit reductions and delays, and tax increases that have kept the program solvent into the foreseeable future. One key to the continued viability of the program in the twenty-first century may be the continued reformation of entitlement programs generally, exemplified by the Welfare Reform Act of 1996.

SOCIAL SECURITY BENEFIT PROGRAMS TODAY

Retirement Insurance Benefits

The original and still the main purpose of social security is to provide partial replacement of earnings when a worker decides it is time to retire. Although benefits have increased substantially in the last two decades, both in relative and absolute terms, this retirement benefit is still not, and never was, intended to totally replace what that worker was earning prior to retirement. And yet, for many Americans over sixty-five, social security is the main, or even the only, source of income. This is true in part because the other major piece of federal legislation dealing with pensions, the Employee Retirement Income Security Act (ERISA), goes a long way toward protecting an employee's accrued pension benefits. But remember from Chapter 9 that it does not require an employer to establish a pension plan for its employees in the first place. And many workers still do not have significant pension plans where they work. Social security is often the only safety net when it is no longer possible to continue working.

Monthly benefits are payable to a retired insured worker from age sixty-two onward. Under some circumstances, a spouse and children may also be eligible. For a person to be "fully insured" by social security, he or she must accrue a minimum of forty quarters (that is, ten years) of contributions. These contributions are shared by the employer and the employee, who has no choice but to have the tax taken directly out of each paycheck, until a maximum amount of taxable income (for social security purposes only) has been earned in a calendar year. Once that income level has been reached (approximately $75,000 in 2003), no more social security tax is deducted until the start of the next calendar year.

Being fully insured does not guarantee any particular benefit amount; it only means that some benefit is guaranteed. The average monthly benefit for an individual in the 1990s was approximately $600. The average for a married couple, both of whom were fully insured upon retirement, is a little over $1,000. These averages take into account aged retirees who started receiving benefits years ago, as well as new pensioners, who could receive as much as $975 per month. The average also includes those who retired before sixty-five, which is the age when the maximum available benefit is granted. Those choosing to retire at sixty-two got only 80 percent of the maximum benefit, whereas applicants aged sixty-three and sixty-four were awarded 87 percent and 93 percent of the maximum, respectively.

Benefits can wind up being reduced in yet another way. A retiree applying for social security may be fully insured and age sixty-five, and thus will receive the maximum monthly benefit. But if this retiree continues earning income in excess of $25,000 per year, both this income and the social security benefits themselves will be subject to taxation.

WILL SOCIAL SECURITY BE THERE FOR YOU?

THE WORKING LAW

The Center on Budget and Policy Priorities predicts that, if no substantial changes are made in the near future mandating a major tax cut, the "projected cost of the tax cut over 75 years amounts to 1.68 percent of GDP, or $8.7 trillion in present value." Thus, the center's report continues, "the cost of the tax cut over the next 75 years is more than twice as large as the long-term deficit in Social Security. . . ."[1] On March 17, 2003, the Social Security Board of Trustees stated that the program, as currently constituted, cannot be sustained over this long term. In its 2003 Annual Report to Congress, the board indicated that:

- The likely point at which federal tax revenues will fall short of program costs is 2018.
- The likely point at which the trust fund will be entirely exhausted is 2042.
- The trust fund will require a transfusion of 3.5 trillion of today's dollars, earning interest at today's Treasury rates, to pay all the anticipated entitlements of the next 75 years.[2]

Other observers are far more sanguine. One points out that, "With over $1 trillion in assets, the U.S. Social Security Trust Fund is the largest pension reserve in the world, and potentially a model for other developed countries facing future financing problems."[3] Another adds, "The United States government has never defaulted on its bonds throughout its entire history. . . . SS tax revenues currently exceed benefit payments, and will continue to do so for some time."[4] Yet another commentator argued, "[T]he Social Security trust fund will not be exhausted, at the current rate, until 2042; after this, payroll taxes would not quite cover the outlay to retirees and disabled. Horrors! But wait. The projected Social Security deficit is less than three quarters of one percent of national income. And by 2042, real wages will be some 40 percent higher than today because of higher productivity, yielding a proportionately higher available payroll tax."[5]

Many students using this textbook in 2004 will be almost 60 years old by 2042. Do you think social security will be waiting there for you four decades from now?

---

[1]Center on Budget and Policy Priorities, "Social Security and the Tax Cut," **http://www.cbpp.org**, April 9, 2002.

[2]U.S. Government Info/Resources, "Social Security Trust Fund Gone by 2042," **http://www.usgovinfo.about.com/cs/socialsecurity/a/aassgone_p.htm**, July 31, 2003.

[3]Kent Smetters, "Is the Social Security Trust Fund Worth Anything?" National Bureau of Economic Research, **http://papers.nber.org/papers/W9845**, July 2003.

[4]Center for Economic and Policy Research, "Defaulting on the Social Security Trust Fund: Winners and Losers," **http://www.cepr.net/Social_Security/defaulting_ss.htm**, July 23, 2001.

[5]Nick O'Dell, "Gloomy Deficit Predictions Are Unfounded," *The Philadelphia Inquirer*, July 27, 2003, at D2.

Medicare

In addition to basic benefits, retired Americans receive a form of health insurance under the social security system. Medicare benefits cover a portion of the costs of hospitalization and the medical expenses of insured workers and their spouses age sixty-five and older, as well as younger disabled workers in some circumstances. This insurance is divided into two parts designated by the federal bureaucracy as A and B.

http://www.ssa.gov/pubs/10043.html *is the site for information on Medicare.*

Part A is hospital insurance for inpatient hospital care, inpatient skilled nursing care, and hospice care. Part B is supplementary medical insurance, which helps defray the costs of doctors' services and other medical expenses not covered by part A.

A worker who applies for social security benefits and is receiving them at age sixty-five is automatically covered under part A. The same is true for someone who has been receiving social security disability benefits (discussed briefly below) for at least twenty-four months. Part B is not entirely free. One-fourth of the premium is paid by the beneficiary, whereas the other three-fourths are covered by the federal government's general revenues. In the 1990s, the basic monthly premium of around $30 was deducted directly from the insured's social security check.

In December 2003, Congress enacted and the President signed on what may be the first major overhaul of Medicare in many, many years. This major revision includes a prescription drug benefit for retirees.

Disability

Under the social security system, a worker is considered disabled when a severe physical or mental impairment prevents that person from working for a year or more or is expected to result in the victim's death. The disability does not have to be work related (as is the case for workers' compensation disability, discussed later in this chapter), but it must be total. In other words, if the injured or ailing worker can do some sort of work, though not necessarily the same work as before the disability, then this program probably will not apply. Under some circumstances, a disabled worker's spouse, children, or surviving family members are also eligible for benefits.

Just as older workers must accrue forty quarters of credit to be fully insured, so too, younger people must earn some social security credits to qualify for disability benefits. For instance, before reaching age twenty-four, a member of the work force would need six credits (six quarters of work subject to social security tax) during the preceding three years. A worker who becomes disabled between ages thirty-one and forty-two must be credited with twenty quarters on his or her account.

After twenty-four months of disability, Medicare is made available, just as in the case of retired Americans. Additionally, the social security system provides services intended to get disabled people back into the work force and off the benefit rolls. Usually, vocational rehabilitation services are provided by state rehabilitation agencies in cooperation with the federal Social Security Administration. The law provides that disability benefits can continue during a nine-month return-to-work trial period. Generally, if the trial is successful, benefits will be continued during a three-month "adjustment period" and then stopped.

Related to this aspect of the social security system is supplemental security income, a program financed by general funds from the U.S. Treasury (not social security taxes) and aimed at aiding legally blind, elderly, or partially disabled workers. The law also allows blind workers to earn as much as $780 per month without being considered as holding substantial gainful employment rendering them ineligible for one or both of these federal subsidies.

As noted earlier, although the principal purpose of social security is to provide retirement benefits, the disability coverage is also extremely significant in this country's welfare system because most states and many employers fail to provide disability insurance for non-job-related illnesses and injuries. A minority of states (New Jersey, for example) do tax payrolls and paychecks to provide disability coverage. And many companies offer short- and/or long-term disability insurance. But many more do not. Nor does social security comprehensively fill this gap: It applies only after a year of total disability. Thus, it is less than a complete solution, but it is a safety net that can help keep some individuals off state welfare.

OTHER FEDERAL AND STATE BENEFIT PROGRAMS

Social security programs focus upon working Americans who for one of several reasons—old age, disability, black lung disease—can no longer do their jobs but who have paid into the fund and therefore are entitled to draw benefits from it. But what about people who have never earned such eligibility? As noted earlier, a worker's dependents and survivors can sometimes collect benefits based on that worker's social security account. For others, a variety of other federal and state programs are available.

http://www.ssa.gov/OP_Home/ssact/comp-toc.htm
lists social security programs, including grants to states. State Web sites will also provide specific information.

Food Stamps

The Department of Agriculture provides food stamps to low-income households to supplement their purchasing ability. Not only the unemployed but also lower paid workers may qualify for those "coupons," which can be used in most grocery stores and supermarkets, provided they are "spent" on necessities and not on items such as cigarettes and alcoholic beverages. The program is administered by state public assistance (welfare) offices. A major overhaul of the federal welfare system during the second Clinton administration, plus abysmal budgetary deficits in many states during the first three years of the twenty-first century, combined to dramatically limit the amount and duration of benefits that welfare recipients could anticipate in the new American century.

Railroad Retirement

This program was set up under its own act and with its own board. It is coordinated with the social security system. Payments by employees and covered railroads are at a higher level than social security. The quid pro quo is that retirement can be taken as early as age sixty, and disability benefits are more readily available as well.

Medicaid

Medicaid is a health service vendor payment program that makes direct payments to providers on behalf of eligible individuals. The program is run by the states with federal financial participation. People who qualify for two other benefit programs, supplemental security income and aid for dependent children, also automatically qualify for Medicaid. In addition to these so-called categorically needy, states are also allowed to elect to cover aged, blind, and disabled individuals, and many states do.

Can Medicaid funds be used to pay for services at a religiously affiliated institution to provide for patients who, for religious reasons, refuse to accept medical care from health-care providers?

CHILDREN'S HEALTHCARE IS A LEGAL DUTY, INCORPORATED V. MIN DE PARLE
212 F.3d 1084 (8th Cir. 2000)

Wollman, Chief Judge

Section 4454 of the Balanced Budget Act of 1997 creates exceptions to the Medicare and Medicaid Acts for persons who have religious objections to the receipt of medical care. These exceptions enable such individuals to receive government assistance for nonmedical care that they receive in facilities that, for religious reasons, administer only nonmedical services. Appellants Bruce Bostrom, Steven Peterson, and Children's Healthcare is a Legal Duty, Inc., utilizing taxpayer standing, filed suit in federal district claiming that section 4454 impermissibly establishes religion in violation of the First Amendment of the United States Constitution. The district court found that section 4454 is a permissible accommodation of religion and thus does not transgress the Establishment Clause. We affirm.

I. Factual Background

In 1965, Congress enacted the Medicare Act, 42 U.S.C. §§ 1395 et seq., and the Medicaid Act, 42 U.S.C. §§ 1396 et seq., in an attempt to make health care more readily available to certain segments of the public. The Medicare Act creates a system of comprehensive health insurance for the disabled and the elderly. Funded by federal employment taxes, Medicare reimburses hospitals and skilled nursing facilities for the costs of providing hospital and post-hospital care to program beneficiaries. The Medicaid Act, in contrast, provides medical assistance to low-income families with dependent children and to impoverished individuals who are aged, blind, or disabled. Medicaid is jointly financed by the federal and state governments and is administered by the states, which must submit plans that meet broad statutory requirements in order to receive federal funding.

From their enactment until 1996, both the Medicare and Medicaid Acts contained express exceptions for members of the First Church of Christ, Scientist (Christian Scientists), a religious group that objects to medical care and embraces prayer as the sole means of healing. The exceptions sought to extend to Christian Scientists the nonmedical elements of Medicare- and Medicaid-funded services, and also to except Christian Science sanitoria, the facilities providing such care, from the Acts' medical oversight requirements. The exceptions remained in effect until August 7, 1996, when the United States District Court for the District of Minnesota declared them unconstitutional as facially discriminating among religious sects in violation of the Establishment Clause.

In response to [that decision] Congress enacted section 4454 of the Balanced Budget Act of 1997. With section 4454, Congress sought to replace the sect-specific portions of the Medicare and Medicaid Acts "with a sect-neutral accommodation available to any person who is relying on a religious method of healing and for whom the acceptance of the medical health services would be inconsistent with his or her religious beliefs." To achieve this end, Congress struck all references to "Christian Science sanitoria" contained within the Medicare and Medicaid Acts and replaced them with the phrase "religious nonmedical health care institutions" (RNHCIs). Congress then defined an RNHCI as an institution that, among other things, "provides only nonmedical nursing items and services exclusively to patients who choose to rely solely upon a religious method of healing or for whom the acceptance of medical health services would be inconsistent with their religious beliefs," and that "on the basis of its religious beliefs, does not provide . . . medical items and services . . . for its patients."

Section 4454's incorporation of RNHCI terminology into the Medicare and Medicaid Acts enables individuals who hold religious objections to medical care to receive government assistance for care that they receive at RNHCIs, and it also frees RNHCIs from all medically based supervision. Section 4454 achieves these results under the Medicare Act through three primary provisions. First, section 4454 expressly includes RNHCIs within Medicare's definition of "hospital" and "skilled nursing facility," designations required for Medicare coverage, even though RNHCIs do not meet the technical criteria necessary to qualify as either of these facilities. Second, section 4454 provides that Medicare will pay for services rendered in an RNHCI if the recipient of the services has a condition such that the recipient would have been entitled to Medicare benefits if the recipient had received the same services in a medical facility. Third, section 4454 exempts RNHCIs from the medical oversight requirements of 42 U.S.C. § 1320c, which establishes "peer review organizations" that oversee the services provided in facilities that qualify for Medicare funding.

• • •

[1] In response to the enactment of section 4454, appellants brought the present action against the United States, contending that section 4454 violates the Establishment Clause both on its face and as applied to Christian Science sanitoria. The district court rejected appellants' claim, granting summary judgment in favor of the government and intervenor Christian Scientists. The court found that section 4454 does not facially discriminate among religious sects and therefore is not subject to strict scrutiny review . . . and concluded that section 4454 is a permissible accommodation of religion under the Establishment Clause. This appeal followed.

• • •

II. Facial Challenge to Section 4454

Section 4454 is by its terms sect-neutral. It does not include or disqualify any particular sect by name, but instead uses religiously neutral terms to define RNHCIs, and those persons who may receive Medicare and Medicaid coverage for care received in RNHCIs. Indeed, an individual may elect to receive Medicare- and Medicaid-funded services in an RNHCI simply by stating that he or she is "conscientiously opposed" to medical treatment and that such treatment is "inconsistent with his or her sincere religious beliefs."

Section 4454's legislative history suggests that it is facially neutral among religions. Although Congress enacted section 4454 in response to [a court decision], appellants' characterization of section 4454 as nothing more than an attempt to "reinstate" to Christian Scientists the benefits invalidated in [that court decision] is supported only by a selective and strained reading of the legislative history. A more accurate reading, in our view, reveals that the legislative impetus behind section 4454 was to accommodate all persons who object to medical care for religious reasons, not only Christian Scientists. Congress was explicit that section 4454 was intended to provide "a sect-neutral accommodation available to any person . . . for whom the acceptance of medical health services would be inconsistent with his or her religious beliefs." Whether the religious objector is of the Christian Science faith or some other sect is immaterial; section 4454's benefits were intended for all persons who embrace spiritual healing over medical treatment.

• • •

[6][7] Finally, the practical effect of section 4454 does not render it facially discriminatory. Appellants contend that section 4454 effectively discriminates among sects because the "criteria for a RNHCI were carefully gerrymandered to include only the Christian Science sanitoria, and to exclude as many other institutions as possible that could render the same care." However, even if appellants are correct that few facilities other than Christian Science sanitoria qualify as RNHCIs, this alone is insufficient to make section 4454 impermissibly discriminatory. In addition to disparate impact, a "claimant

alleging 'gerrymander' must be able to show the absence of a neutral, secular basis for the lines government has drawn." Because we believe that the detailed eligibility requirements set forth by Congress for RNHCI status reflect valid secular justifications, we conclude that section 4454 does not, in effect, constitute a religious gerrymander subject to strict scrutiny.

Case Questions

1. Should the court look through the non-specific language of the amended statute and acknowledge the alleged Congressional intent to extend benefits to Christian Science facilities?
2. If we assume that the court should, and would, look through the form to the underlying substance of the amendment (per question 1, above), do you think it necessarily follows that the provision is unconstitutional? Can you make an argument that the provision would still pass constitutional muster?
3. Suppose that a patient wants to reject established medical practices, such as medication or surgery, in favor of an experimental cure. Should that person be covered by Medicare and Medicaid or not?
4. Should benefits be extended to organizations which use non-Western medical techniques, such as Chinese acupuncture or Indian hermetic practices? Does the court's opinion support or undermine your position?

WHO MUST PARTICIPATE IN SOCIAL SECURITY?

Most American workers and their employers must pay into the social security system. This has led some religious groups, such as the Amish in Pennsylvania, to object on the basis of their unique religious and social organization. Some members of such religious sects have gone so far as to refuse even to provide prospective employers with their social security numbers. And when denied employment, they have sued under a wide variety of legal theories.

SUTTON V. PROVIDENCE ST. JOSEPH MEDICAL CENTER

192 F.2d 826 (9th Cir. 1999)

Graber, Circuit Judge

Defendant, the Providence St. Joseph Medical Center, refused to hire plaintiff Kenneth E. Sutton, Jr., after he failed to provide a social security number as required by federal law. Plaintiff brought this action alleging that Defendant thereby violated Title VII of the 1964 Civil Rights Act, as amended (Title VII), 42 U.S.C. § 2000e et seq.; the Religious Freedom Restoration Act (RFRA), 42 U.S.C. § 2000bb et seq.; the free speech guarantee of the First Amendment; the Privacy Act, 5 U.S.C. § 552a; and the Paperwork Reduction Act, 44 U.S.C. § 3512. Plaintiff also brought various state claims. The district court dismissed the federal claims pursuant to Federal Rule of Civil Procedure 12(b)(6) and, thereafter, refused to exercise supplemental jurisdiction over the state claims. For the reasons that follow, we affirm.

Factual and Procedural Background

• • •

On June 25, 1997, Defendant offered Plaintiff a position as a Senior Network Analyst. Plaintiff accepted. Before he could begin working for Defendant, however, Plaintiff was required to fill out employment forms that required, among other information, his social security number. Plaintiff believes that a social security number is the "Mark of the Beast" prophesied in the Book of Revelations, Chapters 13 and 14. Plaintiff therefore told Defendant that his religion prevented him from providing such a number. Because Plaintiff would not provide his social security number, Defendant refused to hire Plaintiff.

On February 24, 1998, Plaintiff brought this action, alleging that Defendant had violated Title VII, RFRA, the First Amendment, the Privacy Act, and various state constitutional provisions and laws. On June 1, 1998, Plaintiff amended his complaint to allege, in addition, that Defendant had violated the Paperwork Reduction Act. Thereafter, Defendant moved to dismiss the action pursuant to Federal Rule of Civil Procedure 12(b)(6). The district court granted the motion, dismissing Plaintiff's federal claims with prejudice. The district court then declined to exercise supplemental jurisdiction over Plaintiff's state claims and, accordingly, the court dismissed those claims without prejudice. This timely appeal ensued.

• • •

Title VII

Title VII provides in part:

> It shall be an unlawful employment practice for an employer—
>
> (1) to fail or refuse to hire . . . any individual . . . because of such individual's . . . religion . . . [.]
>
> 42 U.S.C. § 2000e-2(a)(1). "Religion" includes all aspects of religious observance and practice, as well as belief, unless an employer demonstrates that he is unable to reasonably accommodate to an employee's or prospective employee's religious observance or practice without undue hardship on the conduct of the employer's business.
>
> 42 U.S.C. § 2000e(j).

[1][2] This court has adopted [the following] test for analyzing religious discrimination claims under Title VII. First, "the employee must establish a prima facie case [of discrimination] by proving that (1) she had a bona fide religious belief, the practice of which conflicted with an employment duty; (2) she informed her employer of the belief and conflict; and (3) the employer threatened her or subjected her to discriminatory treatment, including discharge, because of her inability to fulfill the job requirements." "[I]f the employee proves a prima facie case of discrimination, the burden shifts to the employer to show either that it initiated good faith efforts to accommodate reasonably the employee's religious practices or that it could not reasonably accommodate the employee without undue hardship."

[3] It is uncontested that (1) Plaintiff sincerely believes that his religion prevents him from providing a social security number, (2) Plaintiff informed Defendant of his belief, and (3) Defendant refused to hire Plaintiff because he did not provide Defendant with a social security number. Nevertheless, Defendant argues, and the district court held, that Plaintiff cannot establish a prima facie case, because Defendant is required by law to obtain Plaintiff's social security number. Specifically, the Immigration and Naturalization Service (INS), Immigration Form I-9, and the Internal Revenue Code (IRC), require employers to provide the social security numbers of their employees.

Although they have disagreed on the rationale, courts agree that an employer is not liable under Title VII when accommodating an employee's religious beliefs would require the employer to violate federal or state law.

• • •

RFRA

Plaintiff next alleges that Defendant violated RFRA. The district court dismissed Plaintiff's claim, holding that . . . Defendant was not acting under "color of law" as required by RFRA. We . . . agree that Plaintiff cannot state a RFRA claim against Defendant, a private employer, in the circumstances presented.

• • •

As an initial matter, we note that RFRA does not expressly include private employers within its reach. When Congress has intended to regulate private employers, in statutes such as Title VII and the Americans with Disabilities Act (ADA), it has done so explicitly. Congress chose not to include similar wording in RFRA. Ordinarily, this court must give effect to such a difference in wording.

[6] We also note another guide to the interpretation of statutes. When a statute contains a list of specific items and a general item, we usually deem the general item to be of the same category or class as the more specifically enumerated items. Here, the enumerated list includes parts of government and agents acting on behalf of government, not purely private entities. Ordinarily, we would interpret the phrase "acting under color of law" accordingly.

• • •

First Amendment

[15][16] Plaintiff next brought a *Bivens v. Six Unknown Named Agents of the Federal Bureau of Narcotics,* 403 U.S. 388, 91 S.Ct. 1999, 29 L.Ed.2d 619 (1971), claim, alleging that Defendant violated his First Amendment right to freedom of speech. A *Bivens* claim, like a RFRA claim, can be brought only "against one who is engaged in governmental (or 'state') action." "Whatever the proper standard for finding governmental action may be, it can be no more inclusive than the standard used to find state action for the purposes of section 1983." As noted in the previous section, Plaintiff cannot satisfy the requirements of § 1983 (as incorporated in RFRA). We therefore affirm the district court's dismissal of Plaintiff's First Amendment claim.

Privacy Act

[17][18] The district court dismissed Plaintiff's Privacy Act claim, in part because Defendant is not a federal agency. Section 7(a)(1) of the Privacy Act provides that "[I]t shall be unlawful for any Federal . . . agency to deny to any individual any right, benefit, or privilege provided by law because of such individual's refusal to disclose his social security account number." "The private right of civil action created by the Act is specifically limited to actions against agencies of the United States Government. The civil remedy provisions of the statute do not apply against private individuals . . . [or] private entities." Defendant is not a federal agency but, instead, is a private entity. The district court properly dismissed Plaintiff's Privacy Act claim.

Paperwork Reduction Act

[19] Finally, Plaintiff brought a claim under the Paperwork Reduction Act. The district court dismissed that claim, holding that the Paperwork Reduction Act does not create a private right of action. The Paperwork Reduction Act provides:

> (a) Notwithstanding any other provision of law, no person shall be subject to any penalty for failing to comply with a collection of information that is subject to this chapter if [listing certain conditions].
>
> (b) The protection provided by this section may be raised in the form of a complete defense, bar, or otherwise at any time during the agency administrative process or judicial action applicable thereto.

As is apparent from subsection (b), the Act authorizes its protections to be used as a defense. The Act does not authorize a private right of action. That being so, the district court properly dismissed Plaintiff's Paperwork Reduction Act claim.

AFFIRMED.

Case Questions

1. The plaintiff's claims fail him in large part because the defendant is a private employer. Would the plaintiff have had a better reception in court if he had chosen to sue the federal government?
2. Should an American worker who holds a sincere religious conviction that he or she should not have a social security number be permitted to decline the assignment of such a number?
3. If your answer to question 2 is yes, should the declining worker also be disqualified from receiving any social security benefits?
4. Should such a worker, even if allowed to decline a number and/or if disqualified from receiving benefits, still be required to make contributions to the social security fund from his or her wages?

WORKERS' COMPENSATION: LIMITED LIABILITY AND EASY RECOVERY

Workers' Compensation Benefits awarded an employee when injuries are work related.

Workers' compensation, as it has been instituted in virtually every state, is a statutory trade-off. As noted earlier in this chapter, the employer loses several highly successful defenses to the injured employee's claim: assumption of risk, contributory negligence, and the fellow-servant doctrine. In return, employers get immunity from suits by injured employees, with some limited exceptions. (Typically, the exceptions are failure to carry the requisite compensation insurance; intentional, as opposed to accidental, injuries to employees; and those rare circumstances in which the employer—a hospital, for example—deals with, and harms, the employee in its capacity as a third-party provider of a service and not as employer.)

http://www.dol.gov/dol/topic/workcomp/index.htm
is a site on workers' compensation programs, with links to information on compliance, eligibility, and procedures.

For the worker, typical compensation schemes permit easy access to benefits, relatively simple adjudication of disputed claims, plus the possibility of an additional, perhaps more substantial, recovery in a related third-party tort action against, say, the manufacturer of the machine that caused the work-related injury. Employers and insurance carriers often complain about fraudulent claims, usually involving hard-to-disprove back injuries. Perhaps the only possible response to claims of fraud is that any system conceived and run by human beings will be subject to some abuses. The concept of workers' compensation is eminently fair, and in practice, it has spared millions of injured workers and their families untold hardship.

A FETUS IS NOT AN EMPLOYEE, SAY CALIFORNIA SUPREMES

THE WORKING LAW

In a unanimous decision, the California Supreme Court has upheld an appellate court holding that a child injured in utero could sue the mother's employer for civil (tort) damages. The child, Mikayla Snyder, was born with cerebral palsy and other disabling conditions.

Her mother, Naomi, was two months pregnant when her retail store employer "negligently allowed a janitorial contractor to operate a propane-powered floor-buffing machine in the store without adequate ventilation. . . . Several customers and employees fainted from the fumes. Some, including Naomi, were taken to the hospital with symptoms including nausea, headaches and respiratory distress." The Snyders alleged that both Naomi and her unborn child were exposed to toxic levels of carbon monoxide, "which impairs the ability of red blood cells to transport oxygen." It was that deprivation that disabled Mikayla, the Snyders alleged.

The trial court dismissed the suit, saying it was barred by workers' compensation law and an earlier appeal court decision which stated that because the fetus was harmed at work, the baby's injury "was a collateral consequence of the treatment of [the mother]." The Court of Appeals' decision in the Snyder case reversed that earlier decision, saying a worker's fetus is no more constrained by workers' compensation law than a customer's would be.

The employer "contends that permitting children to pursue civil actions for prenatal injuries suffered in their parents' workplaces exposes employers to 'liability for injuries allegedly arising out of commonplace industrial accidents and thus defeats the compensation bargain'." The California Supreme Court observed that the concern is "more properly addressed to the Legislature than this court," and the judgment of the Court of Appeals was affirmed.

Source: *Cal-OSHA Reporter,* News, Vol. 24, No. 46 (November 17, 1997).

ELIGIBILITY FOR BENEFITS

To be eligible for workers' compensation benefits, an employee's injury must be work related. This does not mean that an employee who is hurt in an off-the-job accident (such as an automobile accident while driving to a sports event on a Sunday afternoon) is necessarily without any benefits. If the company provides health insurance, this coverage will probably pay the hospital and doctor bills. Many firms have disability insurance, short term and/or long term, in their fringe benefit packages, ensuring some income flow while the injured worker recuperates. Workers' compensation is not a matter of employer choice, but of state law; it is often more generous in amount and/or duration than the employer's disability program (if the company carries one at all).

The issue of work-relatedness has given rise to some interesting litigation. For instance, if the auto accident just described occurred while the employee was commuting to or from the job, it would not be work related and therefore would not be covered by workers' compensation insurance. But if the employee were traveling directly from home to a business meeting at which he was delivering a project proposal, if she were making some deliveries for her employer on the way home, or if the accident occurred in the company parking lot, the employee may be covered by workers' compensation. Some states have held that accidents such as these are work related.

Other cases have involved sports injuries sustained on the company's premises during lunch hour, injuries sustained going to or from the premises for lunch, and many other borderline circumstances. The next case briefly examines a slightly different set of circumstances in which the employee's underlying physical condition clearly was not caused by any workplace activity, but in which the employee allegedly was seeking medical attention in furtherance of his "workplace comfort" when he was killed in a traffic accident.

ESTATE OF FRY V. LABOR AND INDUSTRY REVIEW COMMISSION

2000 WL 1618417 (Wis. App.)

Background

This case was submitted to the administrative law judge and LIRC on stipulated facts. Fry died on April 14, 1994, in a traffic accident. Fry, a stockbroker paid solely on commission, had arrived at his Piper Jaffray office at the usual time that morning, but left the office midday after informing office personnel that he had a scheduled appointment to have radiological testing for kidney stones at St. Mary's Hospital. Fry had a history of kidney stone problems and earlier that day was experiencing kidney pain symptoms. Fry told the receptionist that he had an appointment later that afternoon and expected to return to the office after medical testing was completed. Although not explicitly stated in the stipulation of facts, it appears undisputed that Fry scheduled the appointment sometime that morning.

The parties agree that the most direct route from Fry's office to the hospital required Fry, who was driving his own vehicle, to cross Highway 172, proceed

North on Highway 41, and exit at the Shawano Avenue exit. At approximately 12:50 P.M., Fry was spotted by several motorists on the side of Highway 41, apparently trying to flag down traffic. He had parked his van, leaving the engine running. The Brown County Sheriff's Department concluded that Fry had been overcome by kidney stone pain, was unable to drive further, and removed himself from his vehicle in order to obtain assistance. Fry was killed when he stepped onto the road and was struck by a truck.

• • •

The Personal Comfort Doctrine

Generally, an employee's exclusive remedy for a work-related injury lies under the WCA. An employer may only be held liable under the WCA for injuries that occur while an employee is "performing service growing out of and incidental to his or her employment." In limited circumstances, an employee may be performing services growing out of and incidental to employment even when the employee is engaged in activities related to the employee's own personal comfort pursuant to the personal comfort doctrine. The personal comfort doctrine was developed

> to cover the situation where an employee is injured while taking a brief pause from his labors to minister to the various necessities of life. Although technically the employee is performing no services for his employer in the sense that his actions do not contribute directly to the employer's profits, compensation is justified on the rationale that the employer does receive indirect benefits in the form of better work from a happy and rested workman, and on the theory that such a minor deviation does not take the employee out of his employment.

Under the liberal construction given to Wis. Stat. ch. 102, an employee acts within the course of employment when he or she is otherwise within the time and space limits of employment, and briefly turns away from his or her other work to tend to matters necessary or convenient to his or her own personal health and comfort.

Once an employee has entered into the course of his employment,

> the test to be applied in determining whether he has removed himself therefrom is that of deviation. In other words, has the employee engaged in some activity of his own which has no relation to his employer's business? An act which ministers to the employee's comfort while on the job is not such deviation because it is incidental to, and not wholly apart from, the employment.

The personal comfort doctrine does not apply, and an employee is not within the course of employment, if the "extent of the departure is so great that an intent to abandon the job temporarily may be inferred, or . . . the method chosen is so unusual and unreasonable that the conduct cannot be considered an incident of the employment."

• • •

Discussion

The estate argues that Fry's trip to the hospital falls within the personal comfort doctrine because like the claimant in *Van Roy,* Fry left his work site to satisfy a basic personal need, during working hours, and with his employer's consent. LIRC in its decision concedes that Fry had permission to leave his workplace to seek medical attention, but disputes whether Fry, whose salary was based on commission, was being paid at the time of the accident. In other words, the parties dispute the legal significance of the fact that Fry was paid on commission. We need not address this disputed issue, because even if Fry had consent to leave and was being paid at the time of the accident, LIRC's legal conclusion that the extent of Fry's departure from the workplace goes beyond the personal comfort doctrine is a reasonable one.

• • •

LIRC concluded as a matter of law that the extent of Fry's departure was so great that an intent to abandon the job temporarily can be inferred. It is undisputed that Fry intended to drive to the hospital and undergo medical testing. Even though Fry planned to return to work after medical testing was completed, Fry's intended activities suggest a greater break from the work day than the activities of employees who briefly pause from work to get a drink, use the restroom or eat a snack.

Our supreme court has refused to establish a line of demarcation and declare that all personal comfort trips by an employee off the premises of the employer that fall within a certain area of space or time arise out of the employee's employment. We are nevertheless satisfied that the stipulated facts in this case support

LIRC's legal conclusion that Fry's trip constituted such a sufficient departure from work that LIRC could reasonably conclude that Fry intended to abandon his job temporarily, so that he was no longer performing services incidental to employment pursuant to WIS. STAT. § 102.03(1)(c)1. Each worker's compensation case is governed by its own facts and circumstances, and in this case LIRC's conclusion of law, based on its application of § 102.03(1)(c)1 and the personal comfort doctrine to the unique facts of this case, was not unreasonable. Accordingly, we uphold the circuit court's order and LIRC's decision denying benefits.

Judgment affirmed.

Case Questions

1. Explain the court's reasoning in the *Fry* case.
2. Suppose that Fry appeared to his supervisor to be in obvious pain and that the supervisor ordered Fry to go to see his doctor. Would the outcome of the case have been different?
3. Suppose that Fry collapsed in pain at his workstation and an ambulance was called by the company. Suppose further that Fry died while being treated by the emergency medical technicians who arrived with the ambulance. Would the outcome of the case have been different?

WORKERS' COMPENSATION PROCEDURES

If the fifty states were surveyed, not surprisingly at least minor differences would be discovered among all fifty with respect to the procedural aspects of workers' compensation claims (just as states will differ on exactly what constitutes a work-related injury). There are even fairly dramatic procedural differences between some states. Notably, the majority of jurisdictions use a system of compensation referees or administrative law judges (ALJs) to adjudicate claims at the lowest level. But others (the minority) place disputed claims directly into the regular state court system. The discussion that follows gives a rough outline of the "typical" procedures most states follow.

A claim is usually initiated by the injured employee, who reports an accident to the employer (more specifically, to the employee's immediate supervisor, the human resources manager, or someone else designated to process such claims). The employer in turn submits a report of the alleged accident to its insurance carrier. After receiving the report, the carrier will usually require subsequent submission of amplifying information, such as doctor and hospital reports. If the carrier is satisfied with what it sees, it may grant the injured employee benefits. Benefits consist of medical bill payments plus payments in lieu of paychecks, usually at something like one-half to two-thirds of the worker's regular pay.

The carrier may decide that the injury was not work related or for some other reason should not be accepted as a valid claim. If so, it will notify the employee accordingly. This notice starts the clock running on a statute of limitations, often two or three years, during which time the employee must contest the denial within the context of the state workers' compensation system. This will probably involve retaining an attorney, since the procedures are simple compared to what occurs in a typical courtroom but are not so simple that claimants can effectively represent themselves. Attorney fees are limited by statute, usually to a maximum of about 20 percent of the claimant's nonmedical (that is, salary substitution) benefits.

Hearings are held in front of a compensation referee or an ALJ. But these proceedings may be supplemented (and thereby abbreviated) with deposition testimony, particularly from medical experts, such as physicians, who are difficult and expensive to schedule for hearings. A deposition is a formal procedure, usually held in the doctor's office, during which the physician is placed under oath and questioned in turn by the two attorneys representing the claimant and the insurance carrier. If the doctor is the claimant's expert, the claimant's lawyer will conduct a direct examination, after which the carrier's legal counsel will cross-examine. If the physician represents the carrier, then its counsel will go first. Objections, such as to hearsay testimony, will be made on the record, which is transcribed by a court reporter, for later rulings by the referee. Sometimes these depositions are taken on videotape. Whether on tape or in transcript form, such depositions are later submitted to the referee for review and consideration along with the hearing testimony of the claimant, possibly the employer, other witnesses to the accident, and the like.

WORKERS' COMPENSATION PREEMPTION BY FEDERAL LAW

Although workers' compensation has been left primarily to the states to administer, the system does brush up against various federal acts for compensating workers for whom Congress now or at some time in the past considered requiring special protection. Railroad workers have long had recourse to the Federal Employers Liability Act (FELA); sailors come under the Jones Act (46 U.S.C. Section 688); and many other maritime workers are covered by the Longshoremen's and Harbor Workers' Compensation Act (33 U.S.C. Section 901, et seq.). U.S. government workers have their own Federal Employees Compensation Act (5 U.S.C. Section 1801). In all cases, these acts supersede state workers' compensation laws.

The FELA has given rise to some difficult litigation. Suppose a railroad subsidiary is a trucking company that picks up and delivers goods to the railroad's freight yard, where the subsidiary's drivers are supervised by the railroad yardmaster. Does this make the railroad a joint employer of the driver? If so, can a driver injured at the yard claim workers' compensation benefits against the trucking subsidiary and then turn around and sue the railroad for even more money, such as for pain and suffering, under the FELA? The answer to this question typically turns on the railroad's right to control the driver's activities, as well as the legal relationship between the two companies.

A similar problem can arise when a worker contends that although the employer's liability under state law is limited to paying workers' compensation, separate employer liability exists under a preemptive federal law. In the 1990 case of *Adams Fruit Co., Inc. v. Barrett* (494 U.S. 638, 58 U.S.L.W. 4367), the Supreme Court held that workers could bring suit for violations of specific federal legislation despite the fact that they had received benefits under the state workers' compensation law. The court held that the specific federal legislation superseded the exclusivity provisions of the state workers' compensation law.

On the other hand, although ERISA (Chapter 9) has sweeping preemptive impact on most state laws, it specifically exempts state workers' compensation laws from its preemptive powers. In the following case, the U.S. Court of Appeals for the Fifth Circuit (New Orleans) was called upon to determine whether the workers' compensation exemption to the ERISA preemption protected a private employer's occupational injury plan, permitted by Texas law as an alternative to participation in the state's workers' compensation system, against ERISA's intrusive effects.

HERNANDEZ V. JOBE CONCRETE PRODUCTS, INC.

282 F.3d 360 (5th Cir. 2002)

Garza, C.J.

Plaintiff-Appellant Jose Hernandez ("Hernandez") brought this suit in state court against his former employer Jobe Concrete Products, Inc. ("Jobe") after he suffered an on-the-job injury. After Jobe successfully removed the case to federal court, the district court issued a judgment dismissing Hernandez's complaint and compelling arbitration between the parties. On appeal, Hernandez challenges the subject matter jurisdiction of the district court. We must decide whether ERISA's preemption provisions confer federal jurisdiction, or whether the district court should have granted Hernandez's motion to remand the case to state court.

Hernandez injured his back in the course of his employment for Jobe. Hernandez contends that after his return to work following his injury, he was required to perform "arduous manual work" in contravention of his doctor's instructions. As a result, Hernandez quit his job with Jobe, and his medical benefits under Jobe's occupational injury plan ceased. Hernandez subsequently brought suit against Jobe, asserting claims for unlawful retaliation, negligence, breach of contract, breach of the covenant of good faith and fair dealing, and intentional infliction of emotional distress. . . .

ERISA, a comprehensive federal scheme designed to protect the participants and beneficiaries of employee benefit plans, supercedes "any and all State laws in so far as they may now or hereafter relate to any employee benefit plan." . . . The parties agree that Jobe's plan is a benefit plan that would normally fall within the scope of ERISA. However, they disagree as to whether the plan falls within one of the statute's exceptions to preemption. Section 1003(b)(3) exempts from ERISA coverage any employee benefit plan if "such plan is maintained solely for the purpose of complying with applicable workmen's compensation laws or unemployment compensation or disability insurance laws." . . .

The Texas Workers' Compensation Act ("TWCA") governs the distribution of benefits to workers who are injured on the job. The Texas statute is different from most other states in that it gives employers the option not to carry insurance coverage under the TWCA. If an employer chooses not to carry such coverage, then the non-subscriber's employees retain the right to sue their employer in state court, and the employer is deprived of traditional common law defenses. Jobe is a "non-subscriber" under the TWCA, because it elected to adopt its own occupational injury plan to cover on-site injuries. This plan, titled the "Jobe Concrete Products, Inc. Occupational Benefit Program" (the "Jobe Plan"), provides benefits resulting from a work-related injury for (1) short term disability; (2) death, dismemberment, and permanent total disability; and (3) medical care. The plan also includes a waiver that provides all claims for damages or harm resulting from an on-the-job injury will be subject to binding arbitration.

Jobe argues that because Texas does not require employers to provide workers' compensation insurance, either by subscribing to the state plan or by offering an equivalent alternative, the Jobe Plan is not maintained solely for the purpose of complying with Texas workers' compensation law, as required by section 1003(b). We agree. No Texas law requires Jobe to provide or maintain its plan. Instead, Jobe has undoubtedly created and maintained its plan in order to avoid the high cost of insurance under the TWCA, and in an effort to limit its liability in the absence of such insurance. . . .

If Jobe had opted to maintain workers' compensation insurance in compliance with the TWCA, ERISA would not have preempted Hernandez's state law claims. . . .

For the foregoing reasons, we hold that remand of Hernandez's claims to the state court is inappropriate in this action. Thus we affirm the judgment of the district court compelling arbitration and dismissing Hernandez's complaint.

Case Questions

1. Can you come up with any reasons why the Texas legislature may have chosen to diverge from the pattern set by the overwhelming majority of other states and passed a law that allows employers to opt out of the state's workers' compensation law? Do you think this opt-out provision generally favors employers or employees?
2. Employers who opt out of the TWCA lose their traditional common-law defenses in any subsequent suit by an injured employee. What defenses are the TWCA referring to here?
3. Consider Hernandez's common-law claims against Jobe in light of Chapters 1 and 2 of this textbook. Had the appeals court ruled in Hernandez's favor, what would have happened to Hernandez's lawsuit? Based on the few facts of his case, what do you think his chances of success might have been on these various common-law causes of action?
4. Now that the appeals court has ruled as it has, what happens to Hernandez's case? (You may want to review Chapter 9 in answering this question.) What remedies might he hope for if he ultimately prevails?
5. On balance, do you think Jobe made a good or a bad business decision in adopting its plan?

UNEMPLOYMENT COMPENSATION

http://www.doleta.gov/ *will link you to various sites on unemployment compensation. You can also check sites for specific states, such as* **http://www.labor.state.ny.us/index.html** *for New York.*

Just as social security requires attaining a certain age and contributing over the years to an "account" and workers' compensation requires that the injury occur under working conditions, so eligibility for **unemployment compensation** requires that the "idleness" occur in a specific set of circumstances: The employee must be out of work through no fault of his or her own and be available for suitable work if and when it becomes available.

The concept of fault is an attenuated one; that is, only a high level of fault, termed **willful misconduct,** will serve to disqualify the out-of-work worker from these benefits. Incompetence is considered to be an unfortunate condition, not a basis for affixing guilt, under this branch of employment law. So although an at-will employee, or even one protected by a "good cause" provision in a labor contract, may properly be dismissed for poor performance, that alone will not disqualify him or her from receiving unemployment benefits.

Unemployment Compensation
Benefits paid to employees out of work through no fault of their own and who are available for suitable work if and when it becomes available.

Willful Misconduct
The high level of fault that disqualifies an out-of-work worker from unemployment benefits.

As the concept of "work related" is the focus of much litigation in the workers' compensation arena, so too is "willful misconduct" an issue of constant debate and redefinition in the unemployment compensation systems of our fifty states. For example, is absenteeism "misconduct"? If it is, when is it "willful"? The employee who is "excessively" (itself a tough term to define) absent or tardy may be lazy, or he or she may have children to get to day care and a bus to catch that is unreliable. In the latter instance, the employee can probably still be discharged but most likely will not be denied benefits until she or he can find another job.

Even if the conduct is clearly willful and wrong, this still may not be enough to disqualify the applicant for unemployment benefits. If, for instance, the misconduct is not readily discernible to the average worker and the employer failed to promulgate a rule or give a warning for prior infractions, an unemployment referee may be most reluctant to deny benefits.

As with workers' compensation, unemployment compensation litigation usually starts with a terminated worker's application for benefits. Instead of an insurance carrier evaluating the claim, the unemployment claim is usually evaluated in the first instance by an unemployment office or agency in the area where the worker resides. Regardless of whether the decision is favorable or unfavorable, an appeal is possible. The worker's motive for appealing an unfavorable decision is obvious. But why would an employer challenge the grant of benefits to someone it had let go? The answer is that unemployment benefits are paid for by a tax on the wages of the workers and an equal levy on the employer's total payroll. In most jurisdictions, this tax is variable, rising and falling with the particular company's experience in drawing upon the state fund. Consequently, if undeserving discharges are permitted to receive benefits, the employer will experience a gradual increase in these payroll taxes.

The unemployment system is similar to workers' compensation in that challenged decisions go to a referee and from there can usually be appealed into the state court system. A case can potentially go all the way to a state's supreme court, which typically reviews a few selected cases of special significance each year. Following is a case decided by the Supreme Court of Pennsylvania, reviewing a case that had already been passed upon by the state's Unemployment Compensation Board of Review and the state's Commonwealth Court, a midlevel appellate forum.

McCann v. Unemployment Compensation Board of Review

756 A.2d 1 (Pa. Supr. 2000)

Opinion

Saylor, Justice

This case concerns the propriety of an assessment of counsel fees against Appellant, the Unemployment Compensation Board of Review (the "Board"), under Pennsylvania Rule of Appellate Procedure 2744.

Appellee, Virginia McCann ("McCann"), was employed by CR's Friendly Market ("Employer") until April 30, 1996, when she was discharged for allegedly looking through a co-employee's purse. McCann subsequently applied for unemployment compensation benefits, which were initially denied by the Job Center upon a finding of willful misconduct. At the ensuing hearing before the unemployment compensation referee, Employer's manager, Gregory Golden, testified that McCann had searched the purse of another employee, Katina Fisher, looking for a two-dollar bill that had previously been in the drawer of the cash register. Mr. Golden explained that, although he did not personally observe the incident, the circumstances of its occurrence were conveyed to him by Ms. Fisher and another employee, John Watts. Mr. Golden specifically stated that McCann was discharged for "looking through another employee's personal property without their permission." Employer also offered an unsworn statement signed by Mr. Watts explaining the incident. McCann, acting pro se, testified that she had tried to purchase the two-dollar bill from the cash register only to learn that it was missing. McCann denied having searched Ms. Fisher's purse, explaining that she had accidentally observed the two-dollar bill in the side pocket of the purse while picking it up and showed the subject bill to her co-worker, Mr. Watts.

Following the hearing, the referee awarded benefits upon concluding that Employer offered no evidence of willful misconduct by McCann. On Employer's appeal, rejecting McCann's testimony as not credible, the Board found that McCann intentionally and purposefully looked into Ms. Fisher's purse, thus invading the privacy of a co-worker, without good cause. Concluding that McCann's conduct violated the standards of behavior that Employer could rightfully expect from its employees, the Board held that McCann engaged in willful misconduct disqualifying her from receiving unemployment compensation benefits.

McCann, by counsel, sought reconsideration of the Board's decision on the basis that all of Employer's evidence of willful misconduct consisted of uncorroborated hearsay statements and, thus, was insufficient to support the Board's adjudication. The Board denied McCann's request, and an appeal to the Commonwealth Court followed. During the pendency of that appeal, counsel for McCann unsuccessfully sought agreement from the Board for a remand, again raising the hearsay nature of Employer's evidence, and arguing that such evidence could not be corroborated solely by the Board's disbelief of McCann's testimony. The Board maintained that its adjudication was sustainable on the ground that McCann engaged in willful misconduct, not only by looking into Ms. Fisher's purse, but also by showing the two-dollar bill to her co-worker.

Following submission of briefs, a three-judge panel of the Commonwealth Court held that Employer's proofs, comprised, as they were, of hearsay statements, did not provide the requisite substantial evidence necessary to support the finding that McCann had intentionally searched a co-employee's purse. Nor, the Commonwealth Court held, was Employer's evidence sufficiently corroborated by the Board's credibility determination concerning McCann's testimony. The Commonwealth Court then rejected the Board's alternative theory of affirmance, explaining that:

> The Board essentially agrees that there is no substantial evidence in the record to support a finding that Claimant intentionally searched a fellow employee's purse. Instead of agreeing with Claimant's arguments and withdrawing its opposition thereto, the Board contends that Claimant had nevertheless engaged in willful misconduct by showing the two dollar bill to her co-worker. However, Employer did not raise Claimant's showing the two dollar bill to a co-worker as a basis for her discharge, there was no work rule prohibiting such conduct on the part of Claimant, and the Board, in its decision, did not state that such conduct was the basis for its determination that Claimant had engaged in willful misconduct. As such, the Board is precluded from raising that issue as a grounds for discharge for the first time on appeal, and we refuse to consider the Board's argument on that issue.

Expressing displeasure with the Board's argument in this regard, the Commonwealth Court also stated:

> In the past, when its decision was unsupported by the record, the Board indicated as such and withdrew its opposition to the claimant's appeal rather than proceed on the merits. Here, however, the Board raises a different reason for Claimant's discharge than it did in its decision, i.e., that Claimant had shown the two dollar bill to her co-worker, in a last ditch effort to justify its otherwise insupportable action.

Relying upon the Commonwealth Court's expressed dissatisfaction, as well as the Board's denial of the request for reconsideration and its refusal to agree to a remand, McCann's counsel filed a motion for attorney's fees under Pennsylvania Rule of Appellate Procedure 2744, claiming that the Board's position was frivolous. Counsel sought $126.72 for costs in reproducing briefs and $1,635.00 in attorney's fees.

The majority of the Commonwealth Court, sitting en banc, held that counsel fees can be assessed under Rule 2744 against an administrative tribunal that subsequently defends its decision on appeal, explaining that such an award is predicated upon a showing that the Board's conduct as a party before the court was dilatory, obdurate or vexatious and does not impinge upon an administrative tribunal's adjudicatory functions. The majority proceeded to examine the Board's conduct during the appellate process, concluding that the advancement of a different but unsupported theory for affirmance, made in the Board's capacity as an advocate, constituted vexatious and obdurate conduct warranting the imposition of counsel fees under Rule 2744. In a dissenting opinion, Judge Smith, joined by Judge Doyle, explained that attorney's fees may only be awarded against a state agency if expressly authorized by statute. Judge Smith found no express statutory authority pertaining to adjudicative agencies, such as the Board, and reasoned that the majority's distinction between the Board's actions as a quasi-judicial entity and its conduct as a respondent on appeal was too subtle and would lead to applications for fees under Rule 2744 whenever a party disagreed with an agency decision or argument. In a separate dissenting opinion, Judge Leadbetter agreed that an adjudicative tribunal can be subject to fees under Rule 2744 for conduct undertaken in defense of its decision during appellate review, but would have concluded that the Board's conduct in the present case was not obdurate, dilatory or vexatious. Judge Leadbetter viewed the Board's advocacy, like that of any other party on appeal, as permissibly seeking affirmance on an alternative ground.

Presently, the Board argues that the imposition of attorney's fees under Rule 2744 encroaches upon its quasi-judicial immunity; penalizes its adjudicative functions; renders those functions subject to the threat of external pressures; and compels the Board to admit error in its decision-making process. The Board further contends that the award of attorney's fees violates the doctrine of sovereign immunity, as there exists no express statutory authorization for the assessment of fees against an administrative agency defending its adjudication on appeal. McCann, on the other hand, following the reasoning of the majority opinion of the Commonwealth Court, explains that attorney's fees were not awarded against the Board for actions occurring in the adjudicatory process, but rather, for its conduct as an appellate litigant, thus negating any claim of quasi-judicial immunity. Regarding the Board's assertion of sovereign immunity, McCann posits that the Legislature's authorization of the underlying action against the Board for unemployment compensation benefits constituted a waiver of sovereign immunity, rendered the Board a party subject to an award of benefits, and sanctioned the imposition of counsel fees under Rule 2744 as an exercise of judicial authority.

[1] Resolution of these competing arguments would necessarily implicate questions touching upon the respective roles and interests of coordinate but constitutionally separate branches of government. Quasi-judicial agencies should be afforded the ability to perform their administrative and adjudicative functions as part of the executive branch of government free from excessive interference by the judiciary. At the same time, however, courts possess an inherent authority to guard the integrity of judicial proceedings by sanctioning egregious conduct of litigants. In determining whether and under what circumstances this latter power can be invoked to impose sanctions against the Commonwealth and its agencies, courts must be particularly circumspect, as, in our systems of checks and balances, this is one area in which the judiciary by necessity must render the final pronouncement.

[2] Here, however, we need not reach this issue, since we conclude that the Board's conduct during the appellate process was not dilatory, obdurate and vexatious within the meaning of Appellate Rule 2744. The Commonwealth Court's contrary statement notwithstanding, the Board never conceded that its decision was unsupported by substantial evidence, nor were the Board's findings based entirely upon uncorroborated hearsay testimony. The undisputed facts, arising primarily from McCann's own statements, establish that McCann did look in her co-worker's purse; the only controverted issue centered upon whether she did so accidentally or intentionally. Although Employer offered no direct evidence of McCann's intent, such direct proof of an actor's state of mind, often being impossible to obtain, is frequently inferred from the circumstances surrounding the actor's conduct. The circumstantial evidence associated with the incident at issue, including McCann's frustrated desire to purchase the missing two-dollar bill, suggests a course of conduct that provides arguable support for the Board's inference that McCann deliberately looked into the purse. Furthermore, although the Board's alternative argument for affirmance, namely, that McCann knowingly conveyed private information in pursuit of a personal economic interest, was contrary to the Commonwealth Court's precedent because it was not a reason for discharge specifically raised by Employer, the Board could, quite properly, have argued that McCann's admitted showing of the contents of her co-worker's purse to another employee constituted some corroborating circumstantial evidence that McCann's actions were not inadvertent. Viewed in this light, the Board's formulation of its arguments, although ultimately unavailing, was not so egregious as to warrant the imposition of monetary sanctions.

Accordingly, the order of the Commonwealth Court assessing attorney's fees against the Board under Rule 2744 is **reversed.**

Case Questions

1. When should a court require a government agency to pay a claimant's legal fees?
2. What are the public policy pros and cons of permitting a private citizen to collect legal fees from a government agency/defendant?
3. Should your proposed legal rule apply with equal force to welfare agencies, such as unemployment compensation and workers' compensation agencies, on the one hand, and to the police and prosecutors' offices, on the other?

VOLUNTARY QUITTING

Under normal conditions, an employee cannot quit his job and then apply for unemployment benefits. In other words, when a worker is discontented, she is expected to stick with her current job until she finds another—not quit and collect benefits pending reemployment.

However, in some compelling circumstances, the law will allow an employee to leave the employment. In these cases, the quit is considered involuntary because it amounts to a constructive discharge from the job. Some such cases have involved extreme instances of sexual or racial harassment by the employee's immediate supervisor to the extent that the boards and courts held that no worker should be required to submit to such abuse or risk denial of unemployment compensation. Others have concerned an employee's extreme allergic reaction to substances in the workplace. In all such cases, the employee must remain available for alternative jobs that the state employment agency might direct him or her to apply for. (In some instances, such as when an allergy is so severe and general that the employee cannot work at all, workers' compensation might be the more appropriate remedy.)

DRUG TESTS AND WILLFUL MISCONDUCT

The next case deals with one of the most hotly debated employment topics: drug testing. The federal Drug-Free Workplace Act and the so-called war on drugs have focused nationwide attention on what is perceived as a major employment problem. Many companies have enlisted in this "war" with great enthusiasm, not necessarily taking into account the impact their drug testing programs may have on their employees. In the following case, the worker was denied benefits after being fired for alleged willful misconduct, including refusal to submit to a drug test after a pair of driving accidents.

LEE V. EMPLOYMENT APPEAL BOARD

616 N.W.2d 661 (Iowa Supr. 2000)

Lavorato, Justice

Mitchell County Secondary Roads (county) and the Employment Appeal Board (agency) appealed from a district court decision on judicial review reversing the agency's decision to deny John W. Lee unemployment benefits based on misconduct. The county and the agency contended that the district court erred because there was substantial evidence to support the agency's finding of misconduct. We transferred the case to the court of appeals, which agreed and reversed. We granted further review and now hold that there was no substantial evidence of misconduct. We therefore vacate the court of appeals decision and affirm the district court judgment.

Background Facts and Proceedings

The county hired Lee on August 30, 1982. His duties included plowing snow and using a dump truck to spread gravel and sand during and after snowstorms.

On December 5, 1991, Mitchell County Engineer James Hyde gave Lee an oral warning about his poor job performance. The written record of the warning mentioned that Lee had experienced a drop in attitude and morale and had damaged property but failed to report the damage. The written record also mentioned that the county had received several public complaints about his snowplowing. The written record concluded that Lee's "job is apparently of little importance" to him and that "[i]mprovements need to be made in attitude, morale, job performance, initiative, and desire."

On January 26, 1995, Lee received another written warning about his job performance. The warning noted that Lee had "continued to destroy county property" and avoided work assignments. The warning also noted that employees had expressed "concern for their safety working around" Lee as well as their "concern for the safety of the traveling public when [he is] operating heavy equipment on the highway." The warning concluded that Lee continued to "exhibit a poor attitude, lack of respect for county property, low morale, poor job performance, and little or no initiative or desire to perform the task at hand." The warning demanded that Lee improve in these areas or otherwise face possible termination.

Shortly after this warning, the county issued Lee a notice of termination with the understanding that he could return to work if he successfully completed an alcohol treatment program. Lee successfully completed the program.

Later in 1995, Lee hit an overhead electrical wire with a county truck, tearing away one end of the wire from a nearby house. The incident caused damage to the house, and a resulting power surge damaged several household electrical appliances. Apparently, the county issued Lee no warning following this incident. Lee received no warnings between the January 25, 1995 warning and 1998.

Hyde testified that despite the warnings that Lee received he—Hyde—saw no effort on Lee's part to improve his job performance. According to Hyde, Lee's typical response to any comment about his job performance was "get the union in here." Hyde farther testified that he saw no concern on Lee's part about his job performance nor any effort by Lee to initiate any discussion on how he could improve.

On April 14, 1998, Lee was spreading rock and gravel on a slippery road. At the time, he was driving a county dump truck. He was traveling at the recommended speed limit of twenty miles per hour when he was forced to swerve the truck off to the right side of the road to avoid hitting an oncoming car. In doing so, Lee hit and broke an overhead utility wire with the box of the truck that he had earlier raised to spread the rock and gravel.

Two days later, Lee, while driving a county dump truck, hit and broke a support wire for an overhead utility line partially hidden by overhanging trees. At the time, Lee was spreading rock at an intersection in a wooded area.

Lee immediately reported both incidents to the county.

On April 21 Hyde met with the county board of supervisors to discuss the two incidents. Shortly after this meeting, Lee was notified that the board had decided to conduct a termination hearing on April 27. Lee attended the hearing with his union representative.

In lieu of termination, Hyde recommended to the board a two-week suspension provided Lee would submit to a physical exam and agree to four drug and alcohol tests per year. The county would pay for one test and Lee would be responsible for the other three. (The union contract provided for only one annual drug test.) Several days later, Lee rejected the offer. Lee testified he rejected the offer because he did not want to pay for three drug and alcohol tests per year.

Thereafter, the county issued Lee a written notice of termination on May 4, 1998. The notice explained that the decision to terminate Lee's employment was "based on Section 4.02 of the current contract which addresses the history of similar and/or past offenses, and Section 4.03(D) gross negligence resulting in willful destruction of property."

Shortly thereafter, Lee applied for unemployment insurance benefits. On May 19, 1998, the Iowa Workforce Development Center determined that Lee was eligible for benefits. The decision determined that the "employer did not furnish sufficient evidence to show misconduct." The county, as intervenor, appealed the decision.

On June 9 an Administrative Law Judge (ALJ) held a hearing at which Lee and Hyde testified. On June 18, in a written decision, the ALJ reversed the earlier decision that had allowed benefits. The ALJ found that the county had established misconduct on the part of Lee. The decision resulted in a disqualification for benefits.

Lee appealed to the Employment Appeal Board, which affirmed the ALJ's decision. Lee petitioned for judicial review in the district court. The district court reversed, concluding that "the Employment Appeal Board erred as a matter of law in finding that Lee's conduct was misconduct for which he could be denied benefits."

• • •

Did Substantial Evidence Support the Agency's Decision That Lee's Actions Constituted Misconduct?

A. The law regarding misconduct

Iowa Code section 96.5(2) (1997) provides that a claimant is disqualified from unemployment benefits if the department of workforce development finds that the claimant has been discharged for misconduct in connection with the individual's employment. The Iowa Administrative Code defines misconduct

> as a deliberate act or omission by a worker which constitutes a material breach of the duties and obligations arising out of such worker's contract of employment. Misconduct as the term is used in the disqualification provision [is] limited to conduct evincing such willful or wanton disregard of an employer's interest as is found in deliberate violation or disregard of standards of behavior which the employer has the right to expect of employees, or in carelessness or negligence of such degree of recurrence as to manifest equal culpability, wrongful intent or evil design, or to show an intentional and substantial disregard of the employer's interests or of the employee's duties and obligations to the employer. On the other hand mere inefficiency, unsatisfactory conduct, failure in good performance as the result of inability or incapacity, inadvertencies or ordinary negligence in isolated instances, or good faith errors in judgment or discretion are not to be deemed misconduct within the meaning of the statute.

• • •

B. Analysis

[9] 1. Negligent acts. The agency first found that Lee was negligent in the performance of his job duties. In support of this finding, the agency noted that there was (1) no other explanation "for having two accidents of the same type within a three-day period" and (2) no evidence that "Lee was somehow physically or mentally incapable of performing his job duties in a safe and prudent manner." Based on this evidence, the agency jumped to the conclusion that Lee "simply did not care to give enough attention and caution to his responsibilities to perform them well and safely." This leap in reasoning—in the agency's view—satisfied the intentional requirement for misconduct.

There seems to be no dispute that the two accidents in April 1998 precipitated Lee's employment termination. However, there is no record evidence that Lee intentionally or deliberately damaged the utility lines. We conclude as a matter of law that these accidents standing alone do not constitute misconduct.

[10] Of course, the definition of misconduct recognizes that multiple negligent acts may amount to misconduct:

> Misconduct . . . is . . . limited to conduct evincing such willful or wanton disregard of an employer's interest as is found in . . . carelessness or negligence of such degree of recurrence as to manifest equal culpability, wrongful intent or evil design, or to show an intentional and substantial disregard of the employer's interests or of the employee's duties and obligations to the employer.

We hold, however, as a matter of law, that under the facts here the property damage in 1991 and three accidents involving electrical wires (two in April 1998 and the one in 1995), even when taken together, do not amount to misconduct. There is no explanation in the record as to the property damage in 1991. The agency therefore made no finding of negligence as to this incident.

The accident in 1995 happened when Lee's dump truck came into contact with an overhead electrical wire. The agency also made no finding that this accident happened because of Lee's negligence. Instead, the agency focused on the two accidents in 1998 and concluded that these accidents happened because Lee was negligent.

One of the 1998 accidents happened when Lee swerved his truck off the road to avoid hitting an oncoming car, and the other happened when Lee hit a power line partially obstructed from view by overhanging tree limbs. The only finding that the agency made to support its conclusion that Lee was negligent was that two accidents of the same nature happened within a three-day period. So, the agency concluded Lee must have been negligent. The fact that two accidents of the same nature happened within a three-day period is speculative at best on the question of negligence.

There is no evidence other than Lee's testimony as to how these accidents happened. Under his testimony, we find, as a matter of law, no negligence. There was no evidence that Lee violated any traffic laws. Additionally, the uncontroverted evidence is that the two accidents were beyond Lee's control. In fact, Lee's action in swerving to miss an oncoming car demonstrates he had his employer's best interests in mind because his evasive action avoided a potentially serious accident and monetary loss for the employer. In short, there was nothing about these two accidents that would support an inference that Lee "did not care to give enough attention and caution to his responsibilities to perform them well and safely."

We conclude the evidence falls short of establishing "carelessness or negligence of such degree of recurrence as to manifest equal culpability, wrongful intent or evil design, or to show an intentional and substantial disregard of the employer's interest or of the employee's duties and obligations to the employer."

[11] 2. Failure to improve job performance. Additionally, the agency found that Lee failed to perform his job to the best level of his ability. This failure, the agency concluded, constituted misconduct. On this point, the agency expressly found as follows:

> The claimant was certainly aware the employer expected a certain standard of performance from him as evidenced from his performance evaluations and the previous incident of possible termination in 1995. For whatever reason, the claimant refused to improve his performance by exercising more caution. . . . Failure to perform a job to the best level of one's ability is misconduct.

[T]he agency here simply accepted the employer's subjective proof that Lee's failure to live up to the employer's expectation was intentional. The undisputed testimony in this case is that Lee never improved his performance, even after receiving warnings. Therefore, there is no quantifiable or objective evidence that shows Lee was capable of performing at a level better than that at which he usually worked. The employer had the burden to provide this objective evidence. The burden was not on Lee to show he was not capable of working to his employer's satisfaction. Although Lee's conduct might have been unsatisfactory as far as the employer was concerned, such conduct does not amount to misconduct. The last part of the definition of misconduct makes clear that "mere inefficiency, unsatisfactory conduct, failure in good performance as the result of inability or incapacity . . . are not to be deemed misconduct."

In sum, contrary to the conclusion reached by the agency, the mere fact that Lee's performance did not improve is not evidence of an intent not to improve. Such a conclusion can only be drawn if there is first established objective proof that the claimant was actually capable of improved performance. Because there was no such evidence here, substantial evidence of misconduct was lacking.

[12] 3. Refusal to accept suspension and undergo drug and alcohol testing. Additionally, on the issue of Lee's failure to improve his work performance, the agency found that Lee could have shown good faith in an attempt to improve by accepting the two-week suspension and the attendant agreement for drug and alcohol testing. His decision not to make this good faith effort is further evidence of the fact he simply did not have sufficient interest in his job to do it well.

We conclude the agency should not have relied on this evidence because Lee was not discharged because he refused to accept a two-week suspension and undergo drug testing four times a year. As the record clearly shows, the employer's reason for discharging Lee was the "history of similar and/or past offenses" under section 4.02 of the union contract and "gross negligence in willful destruction of property" under section 4.03 of that contract. Lee's refusal occurred after the last incident that gave rise to the employer's decision to discharge him. Therefore, Lee's refusal had nothing to do with the reason the county discharged him. The employer cannot now rely on such refusal as additional proof of misconduct.

Case Questions

1. Do you think some individuals are genuinely "accident prone"?
2. Are there times when mere carelessness by an employee should be deemed by the state's unemployment agency to rise to the level of willful misconduct?
3. Suppose the accident is not the result of illegal substance abuse, but the purposeful misuse of a legal drug, such as a prescription cold remedy legitimately obtained by the employee from his physician. Is such misuse of the legitimate prescription "willful misconduct" in its own right? Whether or not such misuse is mentioned in the employer's drug policy? Whether or not the misuse results in an accident?

SUMMARY

- The United States social security system provides older Americans with modest pensions. The system has been extended to aid permanently disabled younger American workers as well. A significant policy issue is whether a social security pension should be enough to support a retiree or is merely a supplement to ensure that all retired Americans have at least a financial safety net. Severe fiscal problems in recent years have brought these issues to the political forefront.
- Workers' compensation is a state-by-state system that provides workers injured in the course of their employment with medical care and income supplementation while they are disabled. All states have adopted such a program, although the rules, procedures, and benefits vary markedly from one state to another.
- Unemployment compensation is also a state-by-state system that exists in every state of the union. Employees who lose their jobs for any reason, except abandonment or willful misconduct, receive weekly cash benefits and assistance in finding new employment. What constitutes unexcused abandonment of a job or willful misconduct (justifying firing by the employer) is a matter of frequent litigation before unemployment boards and state courts.

QUESTIONS

1. Explain the policy consideration that led the U.S. government to retain federal control of the social security system, while permitting the states to assume primary responsibility for their workers' compensation and unemployment compensation programs.
2. Should the government require employers to provide disability insurance for their employees, which would be available whether or not the disability is work related? If your answer is yes, should this be done at the federal or the state level? Should it be done by means of payroll taxes (like unemployment compensation) or insurance (such as workers' compensation)?
3. Should drug abusers be treated (for purposes of social security, workers' compensation, and unemployment benefits) as wrongdoers who are rendered ineligible or ill persons who should receive such benefits? Is your answer different for any of the three social welfare benefits? If so, what are the underlying policy considerations that cause you to vary your response?
4. What exactly is meant by a work-related injury?
5. What constitutes willful misconduct? How does the worker's mental status figure into the definition?

CASE PROBLEMS

1. The plaintiff, a ski instructor and member of the ski patrol in the Oregon Cascades resort region, was married to a woman who was HIV-positive. When she developed full-fledged AIDS, she applied for and was awarded social security disability benefits. After the plaintiff's employer learned of his wife's total-disability status under the social security program and the cause of her disability, it demanded that the plaintiff submit to a blood test to ascertain

whether or not he was HIV-positive. When he refused, he was fired.

What rights do you think the plaintiff has under federal employment laws based on these facts? See *John Doe v. An Oregon Resort* [2001 WL 880165 (D. Oregon)].

2. Plaintiff suffered a heart attack. He applied for Social Security Disability Insurance (SSDI). His claim was initially rejected, but he appealed and was successful on appeal. The social security administrative law judge found that plaintiff was unable to perform the work he had done in the past. During the pendency of this social security claim, the plaintiff was also a part of an unfair labor practice complaint against his employer. The National Labor Relations Board administrative law judge found that the plaintiff and his co-workers had been the victims of their employer's unfair labor practices and therefore would ordinarily be entitled to back-pay awards for any periods of unemployment related to the unfair labor practices. However, the employer contended that plaintiff should not be eligible for any back pay under the National Labor Relations Act because he had a total-disability claim concurrently pending with the Social Security Administration and would not have reported for work during the pendency of that claim anyway.

What do you think? See *Performance Friction Corporation* [335 NLRB No. 86, 2001 WL 1126575 (NLRB)].

3. A discharged U.S. Navy officer filed claims for back pay and reinstatement, claiming that he was wrongfully discharged after he refused, on religious grounds, to sign reenlistment papers that required him to use his social security number as his personal military identification number. He argued that the Navy erroneously listed his discharge as "voluntary" and that in fact he was constructively discharged.

Should the officer be reinstated with back pay? See *Carmichael v. United States* [298 F.3d 1367 (Fed. Cir. 2002)].

4. Plaintiff was injured on the job when she was attacked by a co-worker. She sued the employer on the basis of negligent hiring and negligent supervision. The employer sought dismissal of the lawsuit on the ground that the attack was a work-related accident that is covered by the exclusivity provisions of workers' compensation and that workers' compensation benefits should be the plaintiff's sole remedy in this case.

What are the arguments for and against the employer's defense? How should the court rule? See *Caple v. Bullard Restaurants, Inc.* [152 N.C. App. 421, 567 S.E.2d 828 (2002)].

5. The plaintiff was fired by his employer, along with a co-worker, as a result of a fistfight that the two of them conducted on the company's premises. The plaintiff subsequently sued the employer for wrongful discharge, claiming that he was only defending himself and that the state's public policy favoring victim compensation in cases of violent crime created a cause of action. The state also has a well-established common-law rule favoring at-will employment.

What are the arguments for and against a wrongful discharge cause of action in this case?

Are plaintiff's injuries arguably compensable under the state's workers' compensation act? How should the workers' compensation act be factored into the court's consideration of the plaintiff's public policy wrongful discharge claim? See *Quebedeaux v. Dow Chemical Company* [820 So.2d 542 (La. Supreme 2002)].

6. The plaintiff was employed in one of the defendant's stores. She suffered a back injury and made a workers' compensation claim. When she was partially recovered, she returned to the store on a light-duty assignment that allowed her to work four hours per day. Upon her return, co-workers made fun of her injury and mocked her limitations, sometimes implying by their barbs that the injury was faked. The plaintiff sued for disability discrimination under the state's antidiscrimination statute, retaliation under the state's workers' compensation act, and intentional infliction of emotional distress.

How should the court rule on each of these claims as against plaintiff's employer? Does it make a difference whether the store manager was aware of her co-workers' behavior? Whether she complained to higher company officials about it? Whether the manager took part in the behavior?

If the court finds retaliation for pursuing a workers' compensation claim, should this finding insulate the employer from liability under the state's antidiscrimination statute? Under state tort law? See *Robel v. Roundup Corporation* [148 Wash. 2d 35, 59 P.3d 611 (Wash. Supreme 2002)].

7. Plaintiff/employee suffered mental/emotional trauma but no physical injuries as the result of an armed robbery that occurred in the store while the plaintiff was on the job. Her post-traumatic stress disorder was manifest by nausea, cramps, confusion, and the side effects of her prescribed medication. She sued her employer for negligence in failing to maintain appropriate security measures in the store.

What are the arguments for and against an employer defense of workers' compensation exclusivity with regard to plaintiff's injuries? How should the court rule? See *Rivers v. Grimsley Oil Company, Inc.* [842 So.2d 975 (Fla. App. 2003)].

8. Plaintiff/truck driver was fired after he tested positive for use of marijuana on the job. Under applicable federal interstate-trucking regulations, the driver had the right to a second test at the employer's expense within seventy-two hours of the positive result. The employer failed to advise the employee of this right. But the employee paid for his own test, which came up negative. The employer then refused to consider the results of that second test but instead let the discharge stand.

When plaintiff applies for unemployment compensation, if the referee considers only the employer's evidence of a positive drug test, should the plaintiff be found guilty of willful misconduct and denied benefits? Should the referee allow the plaintiff/employee to submit evidence of his personally purchased drug test? How much weight should the referee give this test? See *Southwood Door Company v. Burton* [847 SO.2d 833 (Miss. Supreme 2003)].

9. Plaintiff/employee tested positive for marijuana use in a random drug test at work and was terminated for willful misconduct. At his unemployment compensation hearing, plaintiff presented undisputed testimony that he had inhaled secondary marijuana smoke while off duty. The employer was unable to refute this testimony.

Based on these facts, how should the court rule on plaintiff's claim for unemployment compensation? See *Baldor Electric Company v. Reasoner* [66 S.W.3d 256 (Mo. App. 2001)].

10. A terminated sales representative claimed he was fired because he was HIV-positive. The company contended that he was let go due to intentional disrespect for his supervisors and contravention of company rules. On appeal of the unemployment referee's decision, the state superior court ruled that the plaintiff's supervisor knew nothing of plaintiff's health condition. This ruling became a final judgment on the unemployment compensation claim, which therefore was denied due to plaintiff's willful misconduct.

Should this judgment collaterally estop the plaintiff from relitigating his disability claim against the former employer under the state's antidiscrimination statute? See *Shields v. Bellsouth Advertising and Publishing Co.* [273 Ga. 774, 545 S.E.2d 898 (Ga. Supreme 2001)].

INTERNET EXERCISES

Many nations have social welfare programs analogous to the ones discussed in this chapter. The U.S. Department of State has negotiated a complex web of agreements with foreign nations to ensure that Americans working abroad will have their benefits protected while not being subjected to double taxation. The purpose of this exercise is to explore this complex web of international law and bilateral tax treaties, which you undoubtedly will encounter should your career require you to work abroad.

1. Go to **http://www.ssa.gov/international/inter_intro.html** and review the site carefully.
2. Now select a nation where you think you might like to live and work someday, should the opportunity present itself. Click the link for that nation and review the tax treaty that's presented there. What obligations, if any, does the bilateral agreement place upon American corporations doing business in that country? Upon American workers there? Upon the host nation? Upon the United States?
3. Next, suppose that you like the host nation so well that you decide to remain there permanently. Can you locate the link on this site that can tell you what social security benefits you can hope to enjoy should you end up retiring in your chosen country?

INFOTRAC KEYWORDS

http://www.infotrac-college.com

Social Security Act, ERISA, medicare, social security disability, food stamps, railroad retirement, medicaid, workers compensation, unemployment compensation, willful misconduct

PART 4

LABOR RELATIONS LAW

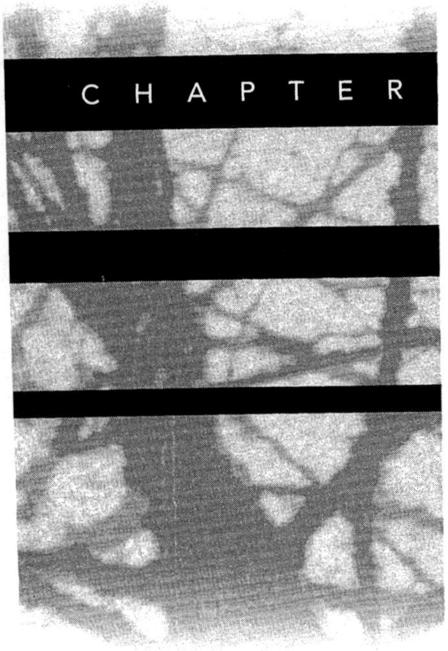

CHAPTER 12

THE DEVELOPMENT OF AMERICAN LABOR UNIONS AND THE NATIONAL LABOR RELATIONS ACT

Common Law
Law developed from court decisions rather than through statutes.

In 1721, an English court declared that a combination of journeymen-taylors [tailors], created to improve their bargaining position with the master-taylors, was a criminal conspiracy under **common law.** When that case, *King against the Journeymen-Taylors of Cambridge,* was decided, it was well-settled law that individual workers were free to make the best bargains they could with prospective employers. Individual workers were also free to withhold their services if they were dissatisfied with the bargain. Such individual freedom was known as "freedom of contract." The judges in the *Journeymen-Taylors* case found the journeymen guilty of an illegal conspiracy on the basis of the common (judge-made) law. The judges held that public policy objectives recognized by the common law as being in the best interests of society required holding the combination illegal. Although freedom of contract was a laudable principle when pursued by individuals, it took on antisocial aspects when individual workers combined to improve their bargaining power.

The *Journeymen-Taylors* case was one example of legal restrictions placed on laborers. Such restrictions, the roots of our labor laws, go back to the fourteenth century. In 1349, an ordinance was adopted that required laborers to work for the same pay as they had received in 1347. The ordinance was an attempt to prevent laborers from demanding higher pay because of the severe shortage of workers resulting from the Black Death plague that devastated the country during 1348.

That ordinance was followed in 1351 by the Statute of Laborers, which provided that able-bodied persons under age sixty with no means of subsistence must work for whoever required them. The statute also prohibited giving alms to able-bodied beggars and held that vagrant serfs could be forced to work for anyone claiming them. This statute was succeeded in 1562 by the Tudor Industrial Code, which made combinations of workers illegal.

The legal restrictions just mentioned were attempts to prevent the laborers of society from improving their lot in life at the expense of the landed class, or the employers. The Industrial Revolution brought about the rise of centralized manufacturing, with factories replacing the cottage industry in which craftsmen produced their own goods. These factories required laborers, who were subjected to harsh conditions and long hours. Despite the hardships that the new Industrial Age presented, it also carried the promise of a vast increase both in wealth and in mass-produced consumer goods. That increase would be sufficient to make possible a vastly improved standard of living for all classes, including the factory workers. It would be necessary, however, for laborers to join together to ensure that they would get their share of the increasing wealth of the nation. Although initial attempts at joining together were held illegal as combinations or conspiracies, the ruling class and public opinion gradually came to recognize the legitimacy of joint action by workers. This recognition was reflected in an easing of legal restrictions on such activities; the Conspiracy and Protection Act of 1875 and the Trades Disputes Act of 1906 legitimized the role of organized labor in England.

LABOR DEVELOPMENT IN AMERICA

The English events just chronicled contained the seeds of the American labor relations system. Although industrialization came to America much later than to England, the craftsmen and journeymen of late eighteenth and early nineteenth century America recognized the importance of organized activity to resist employer attempts to reduce wages. The American courts reacted to these activities in much the same way as had the English courts.

One of the earliest recorded American labor cases is the *Philadelphia Cordwainers* case, decided in 1806. The cordwainers, or shoemakers, had united into a club and had presented the master cordwainers, their employers, with a rate schedule for production of various types of shoes. The wage increases they demanded ranged from twenty-five to seventy-five cents per pair. The employers were attempting to compete with shoe producers in other cities for the expanding markets of the South and West; they sought to lower prices to compete more effectively. In response to the workers' wage demands, the employers took their complaint to the public prosecutor. The workers were charged with "contriving and intending unjustly and oppressively, to increase and augment the prices and rates usually paid to them" and with preventing, by "threats, menaces, and other unlawful means" other journeymen from working for lower wages. They were also accused of conspiring to refuse to work for any master who employed workers who did not abide by the club's rules.

In directing the jury to consider the case, the judge gave the following charge:

> What is the case now before us? . . . A combination of workmen to raise their wages may be considered in a two fold point of view: one is to benefit themselves . . . the

> other is to injure those who do not join their society. The rule of law condemns both. If the rule be clear, we are bound to conform to it even though we do not comprehend the principle upon which it is founded. We are not to reject it because we do not see the reason of it. It is enough, that it is the will of the majority. It is law because it is their will—if it is law, there may be good reasons for it though we cannot find them out. But the rule in this case is pregnant with sound sense and all the authorities are clear upon the subject. Hawkins, the greatest authority on the criminal law, has laid it down, that a combination to maintaining one another, carrying a particular object, whether true or false, is criminal. . . .
>
> . . . One man determines not to work under a certain price and it may be individually the opinion of all: in such a case it would be lawful in each to refuse to do so, for if each stands, alone, either may extract from his determination when he pleases. In the turnout of last fall, if each member of the body had stood alone, fettered by no promises to the rest, many of them might have changed their opinion as to the price of wages and gone to work; but it has been given to you in evidence, that they were bound down by their agreement, and pledged by mutual engagements, to persist in it, however contrary to their own judgment. The continuance in improper conduct may therefore well be attributed to the combination. The good sense of those individuals was prevented by this agreement, from having its free exercise.
>
> . . . It is now, therefore, left to you upon the law, and the evidence, to find the verdict. If you can reconcile it to your consciences, to find the defendants not guilty, you will do so; if not, the alternative that remains, is a verdict of guilty.

The jury found the defendants guilty of conspiracy to raise their wages; the judge fined each man eight dollars. The effect of the decision was to render combinations of workers for the purpose of raising wages illegal. The case produced a public outcry by the Jeffersonians and in the press.

Not all of labor's activities were held illegal; for example, in *People v. Melvin* [2 Wheeler C.C. 262, Yates Sel. Cas. 112], a New York cordwainers' case decided in 1809, the charge of an illegal combination to raise wages was dismissed. The court declared that the journeymen were free to join together, but they could not use means "of a nature too arbitrary and coercive, and which went to deprive their fellow citizens of rights as precious as any they contended for."

Criminal Conspiracy
A crime that may be committed when two or more persons agree to do something unlawful

Although that language may have sounded promising, the law remained in a most unsettled state. In 1835, the New York Supreme Court in *People v. Fisher* [14 Wend. 9] found unionized workers guilty of **criminal conspiracy** under a statute that vaguely stated, "If two or more persons shall conspire . . . to commit any act injurious to the public health, to public morals, or to trade or commerce; or for the perversion or obstruction of justice or the due administration of the laws—they shall be deemed guilty of a misdemeanor." The workers—again shoemakers and again organized into a club—had struck to force the discharge of a co-worker who had accepted wages below the minimum set by the club. The defendants were guilty of conspiring to commit an act "injurious to trade or commerce," the court reasoned. Artificially high wages meant correspondingly higher prices for boots, which prevented local manufacturers from selling as cheaply as their competitors elsewhere. Furthermore, the court observed, the community was deprived of the services of the worker whose discharge was procured by the shoemakers' union.

Such decisions provoked outrage among workers in the eastern states. In the wake of these trials, mobs of workers sometimes held their own mock trials and hanged unpopular judges in effigy. Despite such popular sentiments, the courts and the law remained major obstacles to organized labor's achieving a legitimate place in society. The first step toward that achievement was the law's recognition that a labor organization was not per se an illegal conspiracy. That legal development came in the landmark decision of the Massachusetts Supreme Court in 1842 in the case of *Commonwealth v. Hunt*.

Commonwealth v. Hunt

45 Mass. (4 Met.) 111 (Supreme Court of Massachusetts, 1842)

[Seven members of the Boston Journeymen Bootmakers' Society were convicted of criminal conspiracy for organizing a strike against an employer, Isaac B. Wait, who had hired one Jeremiah Horne, a journeyman who did not belong to the society. The indictment charged the bootmakers with having "unlawfully, perniciously, deceitfully, unjustly and corruptly" conspired to withhold their services from Master Wait until such time as he discharged Horne, and with the "wicked and unlawful intent to impoverish" Horne by keeping him from the pursuit of his trade. The trial judge had instructed the jury that if the course of conduct set forth in the indictment was found by them to be true, then it amounted to criminal conspiracy and a verdict of guilty should follow. The jury so found, and the hapless defendants appealed their conviction to the state's highest court.

Chief Justice Shaw, who wrote the court's decision, anticipated that Massachusetts workers would react violently if the high court affirmed the conviction. Some historians suggest that he also knew that the fortunes of many old Boston families were tied to the new shoe and clothing mills and that a wave of work stoppages in the wake of an adverse ruling could jeopardize these youthful business ventures. The opinion that follows should be read with these considerations in mind.]

Shaw, C.J.

The general rule of the common law is, that it is a criminal and indictable offence, for two or more to confederate and combine together, by concerted means, to do that which is unlawful or criminal, to the injury of the public, or portions or classes of the community, or even to the rights of an individual. This rule of law may be equally in force as a rule of common law, in England and in this Commonwealth; and yet it must depend upon the local laws of each country to determine, whether the purpose to be accomplished by the combination, or the concerted means of accomplishing it, be unlawful or criminal in the respective countries.

. . . But the great difficulty is, in framing any definition or description, to be drawn from the decided cases, which shall specifically identify this offence—a description broad enough to include all cases punishable under this description, without including acts which are not punishable. Without attempting to review and reconcile all the cases, we are of opinion, that as a general description, though perhaps not a precise and accurate definition, a conspiracy must be a combination of two or more persons, by some concerted action, to accomplish some criminal or unlawful purpose, or to accomplish some purpose, not in itself criminal or unlawful, by criminal or unlawful means.

. . . With these general views of the law, it becomes necessary to consider the circumstances of the present case, as they appear from the indictment itself, and from the bill of exceptions filed and allowed.

. . . The first count set forth, that the defendants, with diverse others unknown, on the day and at the place named, being workmen, and journeymen, in the art and occupation of bootmakers, unlawfully, perniciously, and deceitfully designing and intending to continue, keep up, form, and unite themselves, into an unlawful club, society and combination, and make unlawful by-laws, rules and orders among themselves, and thereby govern themselves and other workmen, in the said art, and unlawfully and unjustly to extort great sums of money by means thereof, did unlawfully assemble and meet together, and being so assembled, did unjustly and corruptly conspire, combine, confederate and agree together, that none of them should thereafter, and that none of them would, work for any master or person whatsoever, in the said art, mystery and occupation, who should employ any workman or journeyman, or other person, in the said art, who was not a member of said club, society or combination, after notice given him to discharge such workman, from the employ of such master; to the great damage and oppression. . . .

The manifest intent of the association is, to induce all those engaged in the same occupation to become members of it. Such a purpose is not unlawful. It would give them a power which might be exerted for useful and honorable purposes, or for dangerous and pernicious ones. If the latter were the real and actual object, and susceptible of proof, it should have been specially charged. Such an association might be used to afford each other assistance in times of poverty, sickness and distress; or to raise their intellectual, moral and social condition; or to make improvement in their art; or for other proper purposes. Or the association might be designed for purposes of oppression and injustice. But in order to charge all those, who become members of an association, with the guilt of a criminal conspiracy, it must be averred and proved that the actual, if not the avowed object of the association, was criminal. An association may be formed, the declared objects of which are innocent and laudable, and yet they may have secret articles, or an agreement communicated only to the members, by which they are banded together for purposes injurious to the peace of society or the rights of its members. Such would undoubtedly be a criminal conspiracy, on proof of the fact, however meritorious and praiseworthy the declared objects might be. The law is not to be hoodwinked by colorable pretences. It looks at truth and reality, through whatever disguise it may assume. . . . But when an association is formed for purposes actually innocent, and afterwards its powers are abused, by those who have the control and management of it, to purposes of oppression and injustice, it will be criminal in those who thus misuse it, or give consent thereto, but not in the other members of the association. In this case, no such secret agreement, varying the objects of the association from those avowed, is set forth in this count of the indictment.

Nor can we perceive that the objects of this association, whatever they may have been, were to be attained by criminal means. The means which they proposed to employ, as averred in this count, and which, as we are now to presume, were established by the proof, were, that they would not work for a person, who, after due notice, should employ a journeyman not a member of their society. Supposing the object of the association to be laudable and lawful, or at least not unlawful, are these means criminal? The case supposes that these persons are not bound by contract, but free to work for whom they please, or not to work, if they so prefer. In this state of things, we cannot perceive, that it is criminal for men to agree together to exercise their own acknowledged rights, in such a manner as best to subserve their own interests. One way to test this is, to consider the effect of such an agreement, where the object of the association is acknowledged on all hands to be a laudable one. Suppose a class of workmen, impressed with the manifold evils of intemperance, should agree with each other not to work in a shop in which ardent spirit was furnished, or not to work in a shop with any one who used it, or not to work for an employer, who should, after notice, employ a journeyman who habitually used it. The consequences might be the same. A workman, who should still persist in the use of ardent spirit, would find it more difficult to get employment; a master employing such a one might, at times, experience inconvenience in his work, in losing the services of a skilful but intemperate workman. Still it seems to us, that as the object would be lawful, and the means not unlawful, such an agreement could not be pronounced a criminal conspiracy. . . .

We think, therefore, that associations may be entered into, the object of which is to adopt measures that may have a tendency to impoverish another, that is, to diminish his gains and profits, and yet so far from being criminal or unlawful, the object may be highly meritorious and public spirited. The legality of such an association will therefore depend upon the means to be used for its accomplishment. If it is to be carried into effect by fair or honorable and lawful means, it is, to say the least, innocent; if by falsehood or force, it may be stamped with the character of conspiracy. It follows as a necessary consequence, that if criminal and indictable, it is so by reason of the criminal means intended to be employed for its accomplishment; and as a further legal consequence, that as the criminality will depend on the means, those means must be stated in the indictment.

... [L]ooking solely at the indictment, disregarding the qualifying epithets, recitals and immaterial allegations, and confining ourselves to facts so averred as to be capable of being traversed and put in issue, we cannot perceive that it charges a criminal conspiracy punishable by law. The exceptions must, therefore, be sustained, and the judgment arrested.

Case Questions

1. Why was the union engaging in a strike against the employer? How was the strike a "conspiracy"? Explain your answers.
2. How did Chief Justice Shaw characterize the purposes of the union's strike? What is necessary to establish a "criminal conspiracy"?
3. What test does Chief Justice Shaw use to determine the legality of the union's actions? Does the case hold that all union activity is legal? Explain.

Although *Commonwealth v. Hunt* did not abolish the doctrine of criminal conspiracy with regard to unions, it did make it extremely difficult to apply the doctrine to labor activities. After 1842, the legality of labor unions was accepted by mainstream judicial opinion. Furthermore, in the post–Civil War period, most state appellate courts accepted the legality of peaceful strikes, provided that the purpose of the work stoppage was determined by the court to be legal.

THE POST–CIVIL WAR PERIOD

After *Commonwealth v. Hunt,* the courts grudgingly accorded labor unions a measure of legitimacy, but the labor movement was forced to struggle—sometimes violently—with employers for recognition. The years following the Civil War were a turbulent period for the American labor movement. Those years saw not only a great increase in the growth and development of unions, but they were also marked by violent strikes in several industries.

The Civil War created a shortage of laborers to work in the factories producing materials for the war effort; the war years were a prosperous time for labor. After the war, however, the returning soldiers swelled the ranks of the work force, thus depressing wages. The Panic of 1873, with its widespread economic depression, also greatly weakened the labor movement because workers, desperate for employment, could easily be dissuaded from union activity by their employers. Nearly fifteen years passed before labor recovered from the effects of these events.

The last decades of the nineteenth century saw three centers of labor activity: the Knights of Labor, the Socialists, and the American Federation of Labor. Each group sought to rejuvenate organized labor after the declines suffered during the 1870s.

The Knights of Labor

The Noble Order of the Knights of Labor grew out of a garment workers' local union in Philadelphia. The local had been blacklisted during the years following the Civil War. Its leaders, including Uriah Stevens, believed that the union had

http://www.nv.cc.va.us/users/nvsageh/hist122/part1/koflaborconst.html *displays the text of the Constitution of the Knights of Labor.*

failed because its members were too well known and were confined to specific crafts. In 1869, they dissolved the old organization and formed Local Assembly 1 of the Noble Order of the Knights of Labor. Members were sworn to secrecy. (Such secrecy and rituals were later abolished in an attempt to attract immigrant labor into the order.)

By 1873, there were thirty-one local assemblies, all in the Philadelphia area. The Knights spread into Camden, New Jersey, and into Pittsburgh by 1875, but they still remained largely a regional organization. Not until the Railway Strike of 1877 did the Knights become a national movement.

That railway strike was a response to successive wage cuts by various railroads. It began among railway workers on the Baltimore and Ohio line at Camden on July 16, 1877, and quickly spread to workers on other lines as far west as Chicago and St. Louis. Government troops took over operation of the railroads, which resulted in numerous violent confrontations with the strikers. The strike ended in August 1877, but not before exacting a toll of hundreds of deaths and $10 million worth of property damage.

Following the strike, there was a rush of labor into the Knights. By the end of 1877, district assemblies had been established in New York, Massachusetts, Ohio, West Virginia, Illinois, and Indiana. A convention held at Reading, Pennsylvania, on January 1, 1878, officially transformed the Knights into a national organization.

From 1878 to 1884, the Order of the Knights of Labor conducted a large number of strikes as it sought to organize unskilled workers as well as skilled laborers. The Knights continued to favor industrywide organizations rather than craft unions. This attitude, however, posed problems because the unskilled workers of mixed locals (those containing both skilled and unskilled workers) could easily be replaced during a strike. Membership in the Knights grew but turnover was high, as members were suspended for nonpayment of dues, usually in the wake of unsuccessful strikes. In 1883, for example, 84,000 members were initiated but 54,000 were suspended. Some locals disbanded when employers, following unsuccessful strikes, forced workers to sign **yellow-dog contracts** (contracts in which they agreed not to join any union).

Yellow-Dog Contracts
Employment contracts requiring employees to agree not to join a union.

The Knights suffered a number of defeats in strikes in 1886. After these setbacks, they sought to form a political alliance with the agrarian reform movement and the socialists. This United Front sought to gain through political means what the Knights had failed to win through strikes, but it had only moderate success and gradually disintegrated. The Knights of Labor began to decline as the skilled trade unions pulled out; those unions believed they could more effectively achieve their goals through a more narrowly based organization that emphasized labor actions rather than political actions.

The Socialists

The establishment of the International Workingmen's Association (the First International) by Karl Marx in London in 1864 stirred interest in socialism in the United States. In 1865, the German Workingmen's Union was formed in New York City; it was later reorganized as the Social Party. In 1868, after poor electoral showings, it was reorganized as Section 2 of the First International.

The socialist movement grew from 1868 to 1875, but it also experienced internal dissension and fragmentation. Although the movement had initially sought to organize unions, it turned to political activities in the aftermath of the Railway Strike of 1877. The political arm of the movement became the Socialist Labor Party, which was able to elect some local officials and state legislators in 1878. In 1880, the party aligned itself with the Greenback Party.

The Haymarket Riot of 1886 greatly injured the socialist movement. The riot erupted during a rally for a general strike over the eight-hour workday; almost 3,000 people turned out to hear three anarchists speak in support of the strike at Chicago's Haymarket Square. A bomb was thrown into a group of policemen trying to disperse the crowd. Both the public outcry following the riot and the trial and conviction of the anarchist speakers and associates (who were not even present at the riot) for the bombing served to deny the socialist movement public acceptance and legitimacy.

The labor activities of the socialist movement came to be represented by the Industrial Workers of the World (the IWW, or "Wobblies") during the early decades of the twentieth century. The Wobblies were a radical union that engaged in a number of violent strikes; their counterpart in the western United States was the Western Federation of Miners, led by William "Big Bill" Haywood, a socialist labor leader.

Following the Russian Revolution in 1917, the Wobblies were eclipsed by the American Communist Party, an outgrowth of the Third International organized in Moscow in 1919. The American Communist Party, although maintaining interest in labor organizing, emphasized political activities. The influence of the Communist Party in labor activities, although important during the Depression, declined during World War II and the late 1940s; the Cold War and the McCarthy "red hunts" in the late 1940s and early 1950s effectively brought an end to organized labor's links to the American Communist Party.

The American Federation of Labor

The American Federation of Labor (AFL), which has become the dominant organization of the American labor movement, was the rival of both the Socialists and the Knights of Labor. The AFL emphasized union activities in contrast to the political activities of the Knights and the Socialists. This "pure and simple" trade union movement was started by Samuel Gompers and Adolph Strasser of the Cigarmakers' Union. They pulled together a national convention in 1879, which adopted a pattern of union organization based on the British trade union system. Local unions were to be organized under the authority of a national association; dues were to be raised to create a large financial reserve; and sick and death benefits were to be provided. The national organization's focus was on wages and practical, immediate goals rather than on the ideological and political aims of the Knights of Labor and the Socialists.

A federation of trade unions developed. Although the federation was open to unskilled workers, it was dominated by groups of workers from the skilled trades or crafts. The federation's unions faced stiff rivalry from the Knights of Labor; the Knights continually "raided" the trade unions for new members. The trade unions, for their part, believed they could be more effective organizing their own crafts rather than affiliating with the unskilled workers in the Knights of Labor. The Cigarmakers chose Gompers to rally the other trade unions in opposition to the Knights of Labor. He convened a conference of trade unions in Philadelphia in 1886. The conference demanded that the Knights not interfere with the unions' activities nor compete with the unions for members. The Knights responded by affirming that they represented all workers—both skilled and unskilled. The Knights also ordered all members affiliated with the Cigarmakers' International to quit that union or forfeit membership in the Knights.

Although the struggle between the Knights of Labor and the AFL continued for a number of years, over the next decade the Knights suffered a drastic decline in membership. Employer animosity toward the Knights ran high, and a number of employers broke their contracts with the Knights. In addition, the Knights' involvement in a great many unsuccessful strikes hurt their image among workers. Skilled tradesmen, already alienated by the Knights' policy of including all workers, deserted the Knights for the AFL. From a high of 700,000 members in 1886, the Knights' membership dwindled to 100,000 by mid-1890.

As the Knights declined, the AFL grew in size and importance. By 1900, organized labor was largely composed of the 500,000 skilled workers in AFL-affiliated unions. For the next few decades, the AFL and its affiliated craft unions dominated the organized labor movement in America. That dominance was to be challenged by the Congress of Industrial Organizations, which developed in the late 1930s in reaction to the refusal of the AFL to sponsor a drive to organize industrial workers.

The Congress of Industrial Organizations

The Congress of Industrial Organizations (CIO) was a federation of unions that sought to organize the unskilled production workers largely ignored by the AFL. It grew out of a renewed industrywide interest in organizing activity led by the autoworkers, steel workers, and the mine workers under John L. Lewis. The AFL opposed the new organization and in 1938 expelled all unions associated with the CIO.

Browse the AFL-CIO home page at **http://www.aflcio.org**

The CIO, which emphasized political activity as well as organizing activity, had spectacular success in organizing the workers of the steel, automobile, rubber, electrical, manufacturing, and machinery industries. After years of bitter rivalry, the AFL was finally forced to recognize the success and permanence of the CIO with its 4.5 million members; the result was that the 10.5 million members of the AFL at last merged with the CIO in 1955. The resulting organization, the AFL-CIO, continues to be the dominant body in the American labor movement.

RECENT TRENDS IN THE LABOR MOVEMENT

The years following World War II were boom years for the labor movement. Unions grew in strength in the manufacturing industries until approximately one-third of the American labor force was unionized. Union membership in the private sector reached a peak in the early 1950s and has been slowly declining since then; by 2000, only about 14 percent of the work force was unionized. Since the 1960s, unionized employers have faced increasing competition from domestic nonunion firms and foreign competitors. The "oil-induced" inflation of the 1970s also increased the economic pressures on manufacturers and employers, making them very sensitive to production costs—of which labor costs are a significant component. The manufacturing sector of the U.S. economy, in which the labor movement's strength was concentrated, has been hit hardest by the changing economic conditions and competition.

The late 1970s and the 1980s were marked by the "restructuring" of American industry. Mergers, takeovers, plant relocations to the mostly nonunion Sun Belt and overseas, and plant closings all became common occurrences, as did collective bargaining, where the employer asked the union for "give backs"—reductions in wages and benefits and relaxation of restrictive work rules. The mid-1980s were characterized by the decline of the manufacturing sector and the rise of the service economy, the indifference (or hostility) of the Reagan administration toward organized labor, and an aggressiveness toward unions on the part of management. Even the owners of the football teams of the National Football League were willing to take on the union representing their employees by forcing a strike, and they succeeded; the National Football League Players Association ultimately ceased to represent the professional football players.

Although unions in the private sector have been in decline, unions in the public sector have been growing strongly since the 1960s. The increase in the number of unionized government employees at the local, state, and federal levels has somewhat offset the decline of union members in the private sector. But the 1980s were difficult for public sector unions as well. Although public sector employers do not face foreign competition, the "tax revolts" by American voters and the antigovernment attitude of the Reagan and Bush administrations put limits on the ability of government employers to improve wages and benefits for public sector employees. After twelve years of Republican administrations, the Clinton administration provided unions with a friendly and sympathetic ear at the White House. Clinton appointed the Dunlop Commission to report on the future of worker-management relations and make suggestions for an overhaul of federal labor law, but the commission's report had little effect and was largely ignored. The Republican-controlled Congress blocked Clinton's ability to make legislative changes and limited the extent to which organized labor could take advantage of the Democratic president's years in office.

Now, in the first years of the twenty-first century, the percentage of the American work force in organized labor is at an all time low. Labor unions have had a few moments of triumph: The Saturn Corporation agreement between the United Automobile Workers and General Motors was hailed as the template for a new relationship between labor and management; professional athletes waged successful strikes against Major League Baseball owners and the National Hockey League; the players of the National Basketball Association defeated an attempt to decertify their union; white-collar engineering workers conducted a successful strike against Boeing; and organized labor's pressure on President Clinton was the reason for his

1996 veto of the TEAM Act, which unions claimed would have legalized company-controlled unions.

But the few triumphs for organized labor in the late 1990s did not signal the resurgence of a new labor movement. What political influence labor enjoyed during the Clinton administration vanished under Republican George W. Bush. Yet, despite labor's dwindling membership and declining political power, some workers still value the collective voice that unions can offer as a means of communicating with management to determine wages, benefits, and working conditions. Recognition of that potential power was the reason that the American Medical Association (AMA) voted at its 1999 national meeting to seek legislative changes that would allow independent medical practitioners to form unions. The AMA sees unions as a means to counter the increasing power and control that insurance companies and health maintenance organizations (HMOs) exercise over the practice of medicine and to provide doctors with bargaining power to negotiate collectively with HMOs and insurance companies over reimbursement rates and steps to ensure quality medical care for patients. While such legislative action is unlikely, the AMA's actions indicate the importance individuals attach to being able to participate in the determination of their wages, benefits, and working conditions.

MAKING LABOR RELEVANT IN THE "NEW ECONOMY": ORGANIZING IN SILICON VALLEY

THE WORKING LAW

Amy Dean has been working in Silicon Valley for several years, but she's not just another "dot-com" millionaire or wannabee; she is the head of the South Bay regional labor council and a national strategist for the AFL-CIO. She coordinates the efforts of some 110 local unions in the Silicon Valley area and was recruited by AFL-CIO President John Sweeney to direct a committee of national labor leaders considering the future directions of the organized labor movement. She also led a successful political campaign to force the San Jose, California, city council to adopt "living wage" legislation for all municipal contractors. San Jose now has the highest minimum wage in the country.

Amy Dean admits that the labor movement has to change to be relevant to workers in the "new economy." Today's workers and employers desire flexibility and innovation, and the days of a job for life are gone. Toward that end, she set up Working Partnerships USA, a nonprofit research arm of the labor council. The research institute has focused on the challenges facing working families in Silicon Valley: the shift from permanent jobs in larger companies to temporary jobs with small firms, the problems facing low-wage workers, and the effects of government policies. While dealing with issues such as building union membership, she also emphasizes that the labor movement needs to be involved with broader concerns such as building social justice. Working with local community groups, Ms. Dean started the Labor/Community Leadership Institute to train activists and to provide leaders for community organizations. She helped found the Interfaith Council, a clearinghouse for local community groups and churches, and has pressed the local governments to use money from tobacco litigation settlements to provide medical care for low-income children.

One feature of the "new economy" that makes traditional union organizing difficult is the temporary nature of jobs—the average length of a job in California is now about three years, and turnover is even faster in highly specialized positions. Firms hire workers as temporary employees, with few protections and little or no benefits. Through Working Partnerships USA, Ms. Dean has created a temporary employment agency, Together@Work, to train and place clerical workers in new jobs and to improve pay and working conditions for temporary workers; it also plans to offer medical benefits and pensions.

If organized labor is to adapt to the "new economy" of the twenty-first century, it will be due to the efforts of people like Amy Dean. She recognizes that it won't be easy: "Change takes place over a lifetime. . . . That's going to take 30 years of working very, very hard."

Sources: "Mother Jones Meets the Microchip," *The Economist,* June 12, 1999; "Silicon Valley Isn't Exactly Known as a Stronghold of Organized Labor," *Mother Jones,* Sept.–Oct. 2000.

LEGAL RESPONSES TO THE LABOR MOVEMENT

We have seen that the courts reacted with hostility to the early activities of organized labor. The common-law conspiracy doctrine was used effectively during the early and mid-nineteenth century to prohibit organized activity by workers. As judicial hostility decreased (as seen in *Commonwealth v. Hunt*), organized labor grew in size and effectiveness.

Employers facing threats of strikes or boycotts by unions sought new legal weapons to use against labor activists. The development of the labor injunction in the late 1880s provided a powerful weapon for use against the activities of organized labor.

THE INJUNCTION

Injunction
A court order to provide remedies prohibiting some action or commanding the righting of some wrongdoing.

The **injunction** is a legal device developed centuries earlier in England. As the system of law courts was established in England following the Norman Conquest, the remedies provided by such courts were limited to monetary damage awards. When legal remedies proved inadequate, plaintiffs seeking recompense petitioned the king for relief. These petitions were referred to the chancellor, the king's secretary, to be decided in the name of the king. When appropriate, the chancellor issued a writ, or order, commanding in the name of the king that a person act, or refrain from acting, in a particular way. Over time, courts of chancery developed to provide such court orders (injunctions) when legal remedies proved inadequate; these courts, also called courts of equity, developed their own rules as to the availability of special remedies such as the injunction. The dual system of courts of law and courts of equity was carried to America with the English colonists and was preserved following the Revolution.

At the present time, according to the rules of equity, an injunction is available whenever monetary damages alone are inadequate and when the plaintiff's interests are facing irreparable harm from the defendant's actions. A defendant who ignores such a court order can be jailed and fined for contempt of the court.

The reputed first use of the injunction against labor activities involved a strike by employees of a railroad that had been placed under a court-appointed receiver because of financial problems. The court-appointed receiver asked the court to prohibit the union representing the employees from interfering with the receiver's court-ordered duties. The court responded by directing the union to cease the strike and by holding its leaders guilty of contempt of court when they refused. The strike ended in a matter of hours.

The Pullman Strike of 1894 clearly demonstrated the effective power of a labor injunction in preventing organized activity by labor unions. The Pullman Palace Car Company housed its workers in a "company town"; workers had to pay rent, utility bills, and even taxes to the company. When the company cut wages by 22 percent in 1893, it refused to reduce rents and service charges. The employees turned to their union for help. The American Railway Union, led by its president, Eugene Debs, commenced a boycott of all Pullman rolling stock in June 1894. Within hours, 60,000 workers on the railways in the west ceased working; the boycott soon spread to the south and the east.

The railroad General Managers Association turned to the U.S. attorney general for help. The attorney general, Richard Olney, secured the promise of President Grover Cleveland to use federal troops, if necessary, to support the "judicial tribunes" in dealing with the strike. The attorney general then turned to the federal courts. Using the theory that railroads were, in effect, "public highways" and that any obstruction of such highways should be dealt with by the federal government as a restraint of interstate commerce, the U.S. attorney general convinced the federal district court in Chicago to issue an injunction against the strikers. The court ordered all persons "to refrain from interfering with or stopping any of the business of any of the railroads in Chicago engaged as common carriers."

Federal marshals were dispatched to enforce the writ of injunction; when they were resisted by crowds of strikers, federal troops were brought into Chicago to subdue the crowds. Eugene Debs was indicted for conspiracy in restraint of commerce and obstructing the U.S. mail. When the U.S. Supreme Court upheld the legal actions in the case of *In re Debs* [158 U.S. 564 (1895)], the effectiveness of the labor injunction was convincingly established.

Throughout the last decade of the nineteenth century and the first two decades of the twentieth century, the courts willingly granted injunctions against actual or threatened strikes or boycotts by unions. The courts did not require any showing that the strike or boycott actually harmed the employer's business. The courts were also willing to assume that legal remedies such as damage awards were inadequate. Generally, the injunctions granted were written in very broad terms and directed against unnamed persons. The injunctions were often granted in ex parte proceedings, so-called because they occurred without any representative of the union present. Once an injunction had been granted, court officers would enforce it against the union. Union members who resisted risked jail terms and/or fines for being in contempt of the court order. In the face of such threatened sanctions, union leaders generally had to comply by stopping the strike or boycott.

The labor injunction became a potent weapon for management to use against any union pressure tactics. The unions were deprived of their chief weapons to pressure employers for economic improvements. Although the AFL emphasized union activity over political activity, it soon made the passage of anti-injunction legislation a top priority in its program.

YELLOW-DOG CONTRACTS

In addition to securing labor injunctions against union activities, employers were able to use the courts to enforce yellow-dog contracts, or contracts of employment that required employees to agree not to join a union. By incorporating the antiunion promise in the contract, employers could legally make nonmembership in unions a condition of employment. Employees who joined a union could be fired for breach of their employment contract.

http://www4.law.cornell.edu/uscode/29/103.html *is the site of the text of the U.S. Code on yellow-dog contracts.*

In the 1917 case of *Hitchman Coal Co. v. Mitchell* [245 U.S. 229], the Supreme Court upheld an injunction against a strike that was intended to force the employer to abandon the yellow-dog contracts. The majority of the Court held that the union, by inducing the workers to break their contracts, was guilty of wrongly interfering with contractual relations. The Court's decision confirmed the importance of the yellow-dog contract as another weapon in the employers' legal arsenal against unions.

THE ANTITRUST LAWS

In addition to the labor injunction and the yellow-dog contract, the antitrust laws provided yet another legal weapon for employers. Congress passed the Sherman Antitrust Act in 1890 in response to public agitation against such giant business monopolies as the Standard Oil Company and the American Tobacco Company. The act outlawed restraints of trade and monopolizing of trade. Section 1 contained the following provision:

> Every contract, combination in the form of trust or otherwise, or conspiracy, in restraint of trade or commerce among the several states, or with foreign nations, is hereby declared to be illegal. Every person who shall make any such contract or engage in any such combination or conspiracy, shall be deemed guilty of a misdemeanor, and, on conviction thereof, shall be punished by fine not exceeding five thousand dollars, or by imprisonment not exceeding one year, or by both said punishments, in the discretion of the court.

Other provisions of the act allowed private parties to sue for damages if they were injured by restraints of trade and gave the federal courts power to issue injunctions against violators of the act. Most observers assumed the act was limited to business trusts and predatory corporate behavior. *Loewe v. Lawlor* [208 U.S. 274 (1908)], the *Danbury Hatters'* case, however, made it clear that organized labor activities were also subject to the Sherman Act.

The *Danbury Hatters'* case grew out of an AFL boycott of the D. E. Loewe Company of Danbury, Connecticut. To assist efforts by the United Hatters' Union to organize the Loewe workers, the AFL called for a nationwide boycott of all Loewe products. The company responded by filing a suit under the Sherman Act in 1903. The company alleged that the boycott was a conspiracy to restrain trade, and it sought damages totaling $240,000 against the individual union members. The district court, rejecting the union's argument that the boycott did not interfere with "trade or commerce among the states," found the defendants liable for damages. The union appealed to the U.S. Supreme Court.

The Supreme Court, in this 1908 decision, held that the boycott was a combination in restraint of trade within the meaning of the Sherman Act. The Court refused to read into the act an exemption for labor activities, citing the words of Section 1 that "every . . . combination or conspiracy in restraint of trade" was illegal.

After the Supreme Court's decision in the *Danbury Hatters'* case, other employers also successfully attacked union boycotts under the Sherman Act. In the face of such actions, the AFL lobbied Congress for legislative relief. The passage of the Clayton Act in 1914 appeared to provide the relief sought by labor.

The key provisions of the Clayton Act, which also amended the Sherman Act, were Sections 6 and 20. Section 6 stated that

> the labor of a human being is not a commodity or article of commerce. Nothing contained in the antitrust laws shall be construed to forbid the existence and operation of labor . . . organizations, . . . nor shall such organizations, or the members thereof, be held or construed to be illegal combinations or conspiracies in restraint of trade, under the antitrust laws.

Section 20 restricted the issuance of labor injunctions. It provided that no injunction could be issued against employees unless irreparable harm to the employer's property or property rights was threatened and the legal remedy of monetary damages would be inadequate. Samuel Gompers of the AFL declared those sections to be "labor's Magna Carta."

The effect of those sections was the subject of the 1921 Supreme Court decision of *Duplex Printing Press Company v. Deering* [254 U.S. 443]. The case grew out of a boycott of the products of the Duplex Printing Press Company, organized by the Machinists' Union. The union was attempting to get the employer to agree to a closed shop provision, to accept an eight-hour workday, and to adopt a union-proposed wage scale. When a strike proved unsuccessful, the union called for a national boycott of Duplex products. Duplex responded by filing suit for an injunction under the Clayton Act against the officers of the New York City Local of the Machinists' Union. The union argued that Sections 6 and 20 of the Clayton Act prevented the issuance of an injunction against the union and its officers.

A majority of the Supreme Court held that Section 6

> assumes the normal objects of a labor organization to be legitimate, and declares that nothing in the antitrust laws shall be construed to forbid the existence and operation of such organizations or to forbid their members from lawfully carrying out their legitimate objects. . . . But there is nothing in the section to exempt such an organization or its members from accountability where it or they depart from its normal and legitimate objects and engage in actual combination of conspiracy in restraint of trade. And by no fair or permissible construction can it be taken as authorizing any activity otherwise unlawful, or enabling a normally lawful organization to become a cloak for an illegal combination or conspiracy in restraint of trade as defined by the antitrust laws.

The Court, finding no legislative intent in Section 6 or Section 20 for a general grant of immunity for conduct otherwise violative of the antitrust laws, upheld the injunction against the union and its officers. The Court's decision effectively gutted the Clayton Act provisions hailed by Gompers.

The Supreme Court did grant labor a small concession in the 1922 case of *United Mine Workers of America v. Coronado Coal Company* [259 U.S. 344]. The mining company brought suit under the Sherman Act for damages resulting from a violent strike by the union. The Court held that whereas all strikes were not necessarily legal under the Sherman Act, the strike here had only an indirect effect on interstate commerce and was therefore not in violation of the act.

Although *Coronado Coal* provided a slight glimmer of hope for organized labor, the effects of the labor injunction and the *Danbury Hatters'* and *Duplex* cases continued to make things extremely difficult. Labor would have to wait for the effects of the Great Depression, as well as the accession of the Democratic Party to national power, before the legal and judicial impediments to its activities would be removed.

THE DEVELOPMENT OF THE NATIONAL LABOR RELATIONS ACT

Organized labor reacted to the judicial endorsement of employer antiunion tactics by engaging in coordinated political pressure for legislative controls on judicial involvement in labor disputes. This political activity yielded results in 1932 when a federal anti-injunction act, sponsored by Senator Norris and Congressman La Guardia, was enacted. The Norris–La Guardia Act was reputedly drafted by Harvard law professor (and later Supreme Court Justice) Felix Frankfurter, who was a leading critic of judicial abuses of the labor injunction.

THE NORRIS–LA GUARDIA ACT

The Norris–La Guardia Act, in effect, was a legislative reversal of the prevailing view of the judiciary that economic injury inflicted by unions pursuing their economic self-interest was unlawful both at common law and under the antitrust laws. The act created a laissez-faire environment for organized labor's self-help activities. Labor finally had its Magna Carta.

http://www4.law.cornell.edu/uscode/29/101.html *will take you to the wording of the Norris–La Guardia Act.*

Provisions

Section 1 of the Norris–La Guardia Act prohibited the federal courts from issuing injunctions in labor disputes except in strict conformity with the provisions set out in the act. Those provisions, contained in Section 7, required that the court hold an open-court hearing, with opportunity for cross-examination of all witnesses and participation by representatives of both sides to the controversy. The court could issue an injunction only if the hearing had established that unlawful acts had actually been threatened or committed and would be committed or continue to be committed unless restraints were ordered. The party seeking the injunction would have to establish that substantial and irreparable injury to its property would follow and that it had no adequate remedy at law. Finally, the court would have to be convinced that the public officials charged with the duty to protect the threatened property were unable or unwilling to provide adequate protection. Only after complying with this procedure and making such findings could the court issue an injunction in a labor dispute.

Section 4 of the act set out a list of activities that were protected from injunctions, even when the foregoing safeguards might be observed. The section states that

> [n]o court of the United States shall have jurisdiction to issue any restraining order or temporary or permanent injunction in any case involving or growing out of any labor dispute to prohibit any person or persons participating or interested in such dispute (as these terms are herein defined) from doing, whether singly or in concert, any of the following acts:
>
> (a) Ceasing or refusing to perform any work or to remain in any relation of employment;
>
> (b) Becoming or remaining a member of any labor organization or of any employer organization, regardless of any such undertaking or promise as is described in Section 3 of this act;
>
> (c) Paying or giving to, or withholding from, any person participating or interested in such labor dispute, any strike or unemployment benefits or insurance, or other moneys or things of value;
>
> (d) By all lawful means aiding any person participating or interested in any labor dispute who is being proceeded against in, or is prosecuting, any action or suit in any court of the United States or of any State;
>
> (e) Giving publicity to the existence of, or the facts involved in, any labor dispute, whether by advertising, speaking, patrolling, or by any other method not involving fraud or violence;
>
> (f) Assembling peaceably to act or to organize to act in promotion of their interests in a labor dispute;
>
> (g) Advising or notifying any person of an intention to do any of the acts heretofore specified;
>
> (h) Agreeing with other persons to do or not to do any of the acts heretofore specified; and
>
> (i) Advising, urging, or otherwise causing or inducing without fraud or violence the acts heretofore specified, regardless of any such undertaking or promise as is described in Section 3 of this act.

The term *labor dispute* was defined in Section 13(c) of the act, which states:

> The term "labor dispute" includes any controversy concerning the terms or conditions of employment, or concerning the association or representation of persons in negotiating, fixing, maintaining, changing, or seeking to arrange terms or conditions of employment, regardless of whether or not the disputants stand in the proximate relation of employer and employee.

Finally, Section 3 of the act declared that yellow-dog contracts were contrary to public policy of the United States and were not enforceable by any federal court. Nor could the courts use such contracts as the basis for granting any legal or equitable remedies (such as injunctions).

State Anti-Injunction Laws

Although the Norris–La Guardia Act applied only to the federal courts, a number of states passed similar legislation restricting their court systems in issuing labor injunctions. These acts are known as "little Norris–La Guardia Acts." The Supreme Court upheld the constitutionality of Wisconsin's little Norris–La Guardia Act in the 1937 decision of *Senn v. Tile Layers' Protective Union* [301 U.S. 468]. Although the case did not involve the federal act, it did raise the same legal issues as would an attack on the constitutionality of the federal act; the decision in *Senn* was regarded as settling the question of the federal act's constitutionality.

Validity and Scope of the Norris–La Guardia Act

The following case illustrates the Supreme Court's approach to the validity and the broad scope of the provisions of the Norris–La Guardia Act.

New Negro Alliance v. Sanitary Grocery Co., Inc.

303 U.S. 552 (1938)

Roberts, J.

The matter in controversy is whether the case made by the pleadings involves or grows out of a labor dispute within the meaning of Section 13 of the Norris–La Guardia Act.

The respondent sought an injunction restraining the petitioners and their agents from picketing its stores and engaging in other activities injurious to its business. . . .

The case, then, as it stood for judgment was this: The petitioners requested the respondent to adopt a policy of employing negro clerks in certain of its stores in the course of personnel changes; the respondent ignored the request and the petitioners caused one person to patrol in front of one of the respondent's stores on one day carrying a placard which said, "Do Your Part! Buy Where You Can Work! No Negroes Employed Here!" and caused or threatened a similar patrol of two other stores of respondent. The information borne by the placard was true. The patrolling did not coerce or intimidate respondent's customers; did not physically obstruct, interfere with, or harass persons desiring to enter the store; the picket acted in an orderly manner, and his conduct did not cause crowds to gather in front of the store.

The trial judge was of the view that the laws relating to labor disputes had no application to the case. He entered a decree enjoining the petitioners and their agents and employees from picketing or patrolling any of the respondent's stores, boycotting or urging others to boycott respondent; restraining them, whether by inducements, threats, intimidation, or actual or threatened physical force, from hindering any person entering respondent's places of business, from destroying or damaging or threatening to destroy or damage respondent's property, and from aiding or abetting others in doing any of the prohibited things. The Court of Appeals thought that the dispute was not a labor dispute within the Norris–La Guardia Act because it did not involve terms and conditions of employment such as wages, hours, unionization or betterment of working conditions, and that the trial court, therefore, had jurisdiction to issue the injunction. We think the conclusion that the dispute was not a labor dispute within the meaning of the act, because it did not involve terms and conditions of employment in the sense of wages, hours, unionization or betterment of working conditions is erroneous.

Subsection (a) of Section 13 provides: "A case shall be held to involve or to grow out of a labor dispute when the case involves persons who are engaged in the same industry, trade, craft, or occupation; or have direct or indirect interests therein; . . . or when the case involves any conflicting or competing interests in a 'labor dispute' (as hereinafter defined) of 'persons participating or interested' therein (as hereinafter defined)." Subsection (b) characterizes a person or association as participating or interested in a labor dispute "if relief is sought against him or it, and if he or it . . . has a direct or indirect interest therein." Subsection (c) defines the term "labor dispute" as including "any controversy concerning terms or conditions of employment, . . . regardless of whether or not the disputants stand in the proximate relation of employer and employee." These definitions plainly embrace the controversy which gave rise to the instant suit and classify it as one arising out of a dispute defined as a labor dispute. They leave no doubt that the New Negro Alliance and the individual petitioners are, in contemplation of the act, persons interested in the dispute.

In quoting the clauses of Section 13 we have omitted those that deal with disputes between employers and employees and disputes between associations of persons engaged in a particular trade or craft, and employers in the same industry. It is to be noted, however, that the inclusion in the definitions of such disputes, and the persons interested in them, serves to emphasize the fact that the quoted portions were intended to embrace controversies other than those between employers and employees; between labor unions seeking to represent employees and employers; and between persons seeking employment and employers.

The act does not concern itself with the background or the motives of the dispute. The desire for fair and equitable conditions of employment on the part of persons of any race, color, or persuasion, and the removal of discriminations against them by reason of their race or religious beliefs is quite as important to those concerned as fairness and equity in terms and conditions of employment can be to trade or craft unions or any form of labor organization or association. Race discrimination by an employer may reasonably be deemed more unfair and less excusable than discrimination against workers on the ground of union affiliation. There is no justification in the apparent purposes or the express terms of the act for limiting its definition of labor disputes and cases arising therefrom by excluding those which arise with respect to discrimination in terms and conditions of employment based upon differences of race or color.

The purpose and policy of the act respecting the jurisdiction of the federal courts is set forth in Sections 4 and 7. The former deprives those courts of jurisdiction to issue an injunction against, inter alia, giving publicity to the existence of, or the facts involved in, any labor dispute, whether by advertising, speaking, patrolling, or by any other method not involving fraud or violence; against assembling peaceably to act or to organize to act in promotion of their interests in a labor dispute; against advising or notifying any person of an intention to do any of the acts specified; against agreeing with other persons to do any of the acts specified. Section 7 deprives the courts of jurisdiction to issue an injunction in any case involving or growing out of a labor dispute, except after hearing sworn testimony in open court in support of the allegations of the complaint, and upon findings of fact to the effect (a) that unlawful acts have been threatened and will be committed unless restrained, or have been committed and will be continued, unless restrained, and then only against the person or persons, association or organization making the threat or permitting the unlawful act or authorizing or ratifying it; (b) that substantial and irreparable injury to complainant's property will follow; (c) that, as to each item of relief granted, greater injury will be inflicted upon the complainant by denial of the relief than will be inflicted on the defendant by granting it; (d) that complainant has no adequate remedy at law; and (e) that the public officers charged with the duty to protect complainant's property are unable or unwilling to furnish adequate protection.

The legislative history of the act demonstrates that it was the purpose of the Congress further to extend the prohibitions of the Clayton Act respecting the exercise of jurisdiction by federal courts and to obviate the results of the judicial construction of the act. It was intended that peaceful and orderly dissemination of information by those defined as persons interested in a labor dispute concerning "terms and conditions of employment" in an industry or a plant or a place of business should be lawful; that, short of fraud, breach of the peace, violence, or conduct otherwise unlawful, those having a direct or indirect interest in such terms and conditions of employment should be at liberty to advertise and disseminate facts and information with respect to terms and conditions of employment, and peacefully to persuade others to concur in their views respecting an employer's practices. The District Court erred in not complying with the provisions of the act.

The decree must be reversed, and the cause remanded to the District Court for further proceedings in conformity with this opinion.

[Dissent omitted.]

Case Questions

1. Why was the New Negro Alliance picketing the grocery store(s)?
2. Were the picketer(s) employed by the store(s)? How could this dispute be characterized as a "labor dispute" within the Norris–La Guardia Act? What is the significance of the Supreme Court's determination that the picketing here was part of a labor dispute under the Norris–La Guardia Act?
3. Under the Norris–La Guardia Act, when can a federal court issue an injunction in a labor dispute? What must be shown to support issuing such an injunction?

THE RAILWAY LABOR ACT

The Railway Labor Act, passed in 1926, allowed railroad employees to designate bargaining representatives of their own choosing, free from employer interference. This legislation introduced some of the ideas and approaches later incorporated in the National Labor Relations Act.

The railroads were one of the earliest industries in which employees were unionized. As noted earlier, the railroads were the target of several violent strikes during the late nineteenth century. The importance of the railroads for the nation's economic development and the railroads' position as essentially being public utilities made them the subject of government regulation; the Interstate Commerce Commission was created in 1887 to regulate freight rates and routes. The disruptive effects of labor disputes involving the railroads were also a subject for government concern. Congress passed several laws aimed at minimizing or avoiding labor strife in the railroad industry.

See **http://www4.law.cornell.edu/uscode/45/ch8.html** *for the text of the Railway Labor Act.*

During World War I, the federal government took over operation of the nation's railroads. Upon return of the railways to their private owners following the war, Congress enacted the Transportation Act of 1920. This act revised the Newlands Act and created a Railway Labor Board. The board had three members, one each representing the carriers, the employees, and the public. The board would investigate labor disputes and publish its decisions. However, the board lacked enforcement power and had to rely on public opinion for enforcing its decisions.

Provisions

Finally, in 1926, Congress passed the Railway Labor Act, which established a three-step procedure for settling disputes. The first step involved using a federal mediation board to attempt to facilitate negotiation of the parties' differences. If that failed, the board would then try to induce the parties to arbitrate the dispute. Although not compelled to submit the dispute to arbitration, the parties would be legally bound by the results if they agreed to arbitration. Finally, if arbitration was refused, the board could recommend to the president that an emergency board of investigation be created. If the president created the emergency board, the parties in dispute were required to maintain the status quo for thirty days while the investigation proceeded. Even if an emergency board was not appointed, the parties were still required to maintain the status quo for thirty days. This mandatory cooling-off period was designed to allow the dispute to be settled through negotiation. The union retained its right to strike, and the employer could lock out once the cooling-off period expired.

The act also provided that both labor and management had the right to designate bargaining representatives without the "interference, influence or coercion" of the other party. That provision was the subject of the Supreme Court's 1930 decision of *Texas & New Orleans Railroad v. Brotherhood of Railway Clerks* [281 U.S. 548]. The union had sought, and was granted, an injunction against employer interference with the employees' designation of a bargaining representative under the act. The railroad argued that the act did not create any legally enforceable right of free choice for employees and that the act's provisions were an unconstitutional interference with management's right to operate the railroad. The Supreme Court upheld the injunction and the constitutionality of the Railway Labor Act, rejecting the railroad's challenges.

The Railway Labor Act was amended by Congress in 1934, 1936, 1951, and 1966. The act was extended to cover airline employees, and a duty to bargain with the duly designated representative of each side was spelled out. The amendments also provided that unions representing the airline or railway employees could bargain for a union shop provision. The National Railroad Adjustment Board was created to arbitrate disputes involving the railroads and unions; its awards are final and binding upon the parties. The amendments also created sanctions for enforcement of the act by declaring violations to be misdemeanors. Such violations included the interference with the designation of representatives by either party, the use of yellow-dog contracts, and the changing of any terms or conditions of employment without complying with the provisions of a collective agreement.

The amendments creating the duty to bargain with representatives of the employees were the subject of a challenge in the 1937 Supreme Court case of *Virginia Railway Co. v. System Federation No. 40* [300 U.S. 515]. The union representing railway employees sought an injunction to force the railroad to recognize and bargain with it. The trial court ordered the railroad to "treat with" the union and to "exert every reasonable effort to make and maintain agreements" covering conditions of employment and settling of disputes. The order was affirmed by the court of appeals, over the objections of the employer that the act imposed no legally enforceable duty to bargain. The Supreme Court, affirming the order, held that the act created a mandatory requirement of recognizing and negotiating with the bargaining representatives duly designated by the parties and that this requirement could be enforced by court order.

THE NATIONAL INDUSTRIAL RECOVERY ACT

The other statutory predecessor of the National Labor Relations Act was the National Industrial Recovery Act (NIRA). This legislation was the centerpiece of President Franklin D. Roosevelt's New Deal. Roosevelt took office in 1933, the fourth year of the Great Depression; some 15 million people were unemployed, and there was a widespread belief that the nation's economic growth had come to a permanent halt. Roosevelt proposed his New Deal program to pull the nation out of the Depression. It involved government working closely and actively with business to revive the economy.

The NIRA set up a system in which major industries would operate under codes of fair competition, which would be developed by trade associations for each industry. These associations would be under the supervision and guidance of the National Recovery Administration (NRA). The NIRA, in Section 7(a), also provided that the codes of fair competition contain the following conditions:

> (1) That employees shall have the right to organize and bargain collectively through representatives of their own choosing, and shall be free from interference, restraint, or coercion of employers of labor, or their agents, in the designation of such representatives or in self-organization or in other concerted activities for the purpose of collective bargaining or other mutual aid or protection; (2) that no employee . . . shall be required as a condition of employment to join any company union or to refrain from joining, organizing, or assisting a labor organization of his own choosing; and (3) that employers shall comply with the maximum hours of labor, minimum rates of pay, and other conditions of employment, approved or prescribed by the President.

The NRA, responsible for administering the codes of fair competition under the NIRA, had to rely on voluntary cooperation from the industries being regulated. The NRA announced that codes containing provisions concerning hours, rates of pay, and other conditions of employment would be subject to NRA approval, although such conditions had not been arrived at through collective bargaining. The practical effect of this announcement was to allow industry to develop such codes unilaterally, without input from organized labor. While employees rushed to join unions, employers refused to recognize and bargain with the unions. A wave of strikes resulted, with more strikes in 1933 than in any year since 1921.

President Roosevelt issued a plea for industrial peace and created the National Labor Board to "consider, adjust and settle differences and controversies that may arise through differing interpretations" of the NIRA provisions.

THE NATIONAL LABOR BOARD

The National Labor Board (NLB) was created in August 1933. It was composed of seven members; three representatives each would be chosen by the NRA's Industrial Advisory Board and Labor Advisory Board. The seventh member was Senator Robert Wagner of New York, who was chairman. The NLB initially functioned as a mediation board, seeking to persuade the parties to settle their differences peacefully. It had considerable early success, relying on public sentiment and the prestige of its members. Despite its early success, however, the NLB had several serious flaws.

The partisan members of the NLB tended to vote in blocks, undermining the credibility and effectiveness of the board. The board was also inexperienced and understaffed. The most serious drawback, however, was the weakness of enforcement powers given to the NLB. The only sanctions available to the NLB were either to request that the NRA withdraw an offending company's "Blue Eagle"—a sign of compliance with the NIRA and of NRA approval (which was necessary to contract with the federal government)—or to ask the Department of Justice to seek a court order to enforce a board ruling. In practice, the NLB relied mainly on the power of persuasion.

The NLB's persuasive power, however, was effective only as long as an employer was not overtly antagonistic to organized labor. In major industries such as steel and automobiles, there was a strong inclination to defy NLB orders. Several major employers refused to conduct, or to abide by the results of, representation elections under Section 7(a) of the NIRA. William Green, president of the AFL, publicly lamented the destruction of the "faith that . . . workers have in . . . the National Labor Board." In March 1934, the nation's automobile manufacturers all refused to recognize the United Automobile Workers Union or to allow the board to conduct a representative election. President Roosevelt chose to have General Hugh Johnson, head of the NRA, negotiate a settlement rather than stand behind the NLB order. That decision destroyed what little effectiveness the NLB retained.

Despite its short tenure, the NLB did make several contributions to modern labor law. It evolved from a mediation service into an adjudicative body akin to the present National Labor Relations Board (NLRB). It also established the principles of majority rule and exclusive representation of the employees in a particular bargaining unit. In addition, the board developed other rules that have come to be basic principles of labor relations law, among them the following: (1) an employer was obligated to bargain with a union that had been chosen as representative by a majority of employees; (2) employers had no right to know of an employee's membership in, or vote for, a union when a secret ballot representation election was held; and (3) strikers remained employees while on strike and were entitled to displace any replacements hired if the strike was the result of employer violations of the NIRA.

THE "OLD" NATIONAL LABOR RELATIONS BOARD

In June 1934, President Roosevelt formulated Public Resolution No. 44. This resolution, which was then passed by Congress, authorized the president to establish a "board or boards" empowered to investigate disputes arising under Section 7(a) of the NIRA and to conduct secret ballot representation elections among employees. Enforcement of board decisions would remain with the NRA and the Department of Justice. Roosevelt then abolished the NLB and transferred its funds, personnel, and pending cases to the National Labor Relations Board (the "old" NLRB). The NLRB was denied all jurisdiction over disputes in the steel and auto industries. The NLRB reaffirmed the key rulings of the NLB; it also issued guidelines to assist regional offices in handling common types of cases and began organizing its decisions into a body of precedents guiding future action.

When the Supreme Court declared the NIRA to be unconstitutional in its 1935 decision *Schechter Poultry Corp. v. U.S.* [295 U.S. 495], it also destroyed the "old" NLRB.

THE NATIONAL LABOR RELATIONS ACT

Senator Wagner introduced a proposed National Labor Relations Act (NLRA) in the Senate in 1935, but the bill faced stiff opposition. The National Association of Manufacturers and the general business community opposed it. Certain union leaders within the AFL, fearing the law would give equal organizing advantages to the rival CIO unions, also opposed it. Opposition to the bill declined after the Supreme Court's *Schechter Poultry* decision; opponents were certain that the Court would also strike down the NLRA, just as it had done with the NIRA.

http://www4.law.cornell.edu/uscode/29/151.html *is the site for the NLRA.*

The NLRA was passed by Congress and enacted into law in 1935. Because of the doubts over the NLRA's constitutionality, President Roosevelt had difficulty finding qualified people willing to be appointed to the National Labor Relations Board (NLRB) established under the NLRA. The main concern over the constitutionality of the NLRA dealt with whether it was a valid exercise of the interstate commerce power given to Congress under the Constitution. In *Schechter Poultry,* the Supreme Court had held that the NIRA was not within the authority given the federal government under the commerce clause of the Constitution. In passing the NLRA, Congress had relied on the power to regulate commerce among the states given to it under the commerce clause. The findings of fact incorporated in Section 1 of the NLRA contained the following statement:

http://www.nlrb.gov/ *will take you to the home page of the NLRB.*

> The denial by employers of the right of employees to organize and the refusal by employers to accept the procedure of collective bargaining lead to strikes and other forms of industrial strife or unrest, which have the intent or the necessary effect of burdening or obstructing commerce. . . .

For more than a year after the passage of the NLRA, there was only limited activity by the NLRB. The board set out to develop economic data supporting the findings of fact in Section 1 of the NLRA. It also sought the best possible case to take to the Supreme Court to settle the constitutionality issue.

During the same period, the Supreme Court came under heavy criticism from President Roosevelt for its opposition to his New Deal initiatives. Roosevelt at one point proposed expanding the Court from nine to fifteen justices, allowing him to "pack the Court" by appointing justices sympathetic to his program. The pressure on the Court and the retirement of some of its members resulted in a dramatic shift in the Court's attitudes toward Roosevelt's New Deal. It also meant that the NLRA might get a more sympathetic reception at the Court than the NIRA had gotten.

Finally, the NLRB brought five cases to the federal courts of appeals. The cases involved an interstate bus company, the Associated Press news service, and three manufacturing firms. The board lost all three of the manufacturing company cases in the courts of appeals on the interstate commerce issue. All five of the cases were taken to the Supreme Court and were heard by the Court in February 1937. The NLRB developed its arguments in the *Jones & Laughlin Steel* case, one of the manufacturing cases, almost entirely on the interstate commerce issue. That case became the crucial litigation in the test of the NLRA's constitutionality.

The Supreme Court in its 1937 decision in *NLRB v. Jones & Laughlin Steel Corp.* [301 U.S. 1] upheld the constitutionality of the NLRA by a 5-4 vote. The majority opinion, by Chief Justice Hughes, held that the disruption of operations of Jones & Laughlin due to industrial strife would have a serious and direct effect on interstate commerce. In the words of the Court,

> When industries organize themselves on a national scale, making their relation to interstate commerce the dominant factor in their activities, how can it be maintained that their industrial labor relations constitute a forbidden field into which Congress may not enter when it is necessary to protect interstate commerce from the paralyzing consequences of industrial war?

By the slimmest of margins, the Supreme Court had upheld the validity of the National Labor Relations Act. The decision also meant that a labor relations board effectively empowered to deal with disputes between labor and management had finally been established.

OVERVIEW OF THE NATIONAL LABOR RELATIONS ACT

The passage of the National Labor Relations Act, or the Wagner Act, constituted a revolutionary change in national labor policy. Workers were now to be legally protected by the federal government in their rights to organize for mutual aid and security and to bargain collectively through representatives of their own choice.

Go to **http://www.nlrb.gov/nlrb/legal/manuals/rules** *and choose "The Act" for the text of the NLRA.*

The purpose of the act, as stated in Section 1, was to

> eliminate the causes of certain substantial obstructions to the free flow of commerce . . . by encouraging the practice and procedure of collective bargaining and by protecting the exercise by workers of full freedom of association, self-organization, and designation of representatives of their own choosing, for the purpose of negotiating the terms and conditions of their employment or other mutual aid or protection.

The basis of the act was the protection of the rights of employees, defined by Section 7:

> Employees shall have the right to self-organization, to form, join, or assist labor organizations, to bargain collectively through representatives of their own choosing, and to engage in concerted activities for the purpose of collective bargaining or other mutual aid or protection.

To protect these basic rights of employees, the act prohibited certain practices of employers that would interfere with or prevent the exercise of such rights. Those practices were designated unfair labor practices, and the act listed five of them:

1. interference with, or restraint or coercion of, employees in the exercise of their Section 7 rights;
2. domination of, or interference with, a labor organization (including financial or other contributions to it);
3. discrimination in terms or conditions of employment of employees for the purpose of encouraging or discouraging union membership;

4. discrimination against an employee for filing a charge or testifying in a proceeding under the act;
5. refusal to bargain collectively with the employees' legal bargaining representative.

The act reconstituted the National Labor Relations Board to enforce and administer the statute. The board created a nationwide organization, developed a body of legal precedents (drawing heavily upon decisions of its predecessors), and developed and refined its procedures. In its efforts to carry out the policies of the legislation, the board was frequently criticized for being too prounion. Indeed, the entire orientation of the Wagner Act was prounion in its definition of employee rights and unfair practices by employers.

Under the protection of the Wagner Act, unions were able to develop to a great extent; their powers relative to employers grew accordingly. Even during World War II, when labor and management pledged cooperation to ensure production for the war effort, some unions were accused of abusing their newly gained power under the act. A 1946 strike by the United Mine Workers, in defiance of a Supreme Court order to remain on the job, seemed to crystallize public opinion that unions had grown too powerful.

This public concern was reflected in congressional action to limit unions' abuse of their powers. Congressional critics were especially concerned over jurisdictional disputes, in which two unions claimed the right to represent the workers of an employer, leaving the employer "trapped" between them, and recognitional picketing, which was aimed at forcing an employer to recognize the union regardless of the sentiments of the employees.[1] These kinds of congressional concerns resulted in the passage of the Taft-Hartley Act in 1947. The Taft-Hartley Act outlawed the **closed shop,** a term describing an employer who agrees to hire only employees who are already union members. It also added a list of unfair labor practices by unions and emphasized that employees had the right, under Section 7, to refrain from collective activity as well as engage in it. The purpose and effect of the Taft-Hartley Act were to balance the rights and duties of both unions and employers.

Closed Shop
An employer who agrees to hire only those employees who are already union members.

After Taft-Hartley, the National Labor Relations Act was amended several times, the most significant version being the Landrum-Griffin Act of 1959. Landrum-Griffin was passed in response to concerns about union racketeering and abusive practices aimed at union members. The act set out specific rights for individual union members against the union, and it proscribed certain kinds of conduct by union officials, such as financial abuse, racketeering, and manipulation of union-election procedures.

[1]The Teamsters Union was particularly notorious for using this tactic with firms employing primarily African American workers. The Teamsters would force the firm to recognize them as a bargaining agent for the employees and collect union dues, but wages and working conditions would remain unaffected.

SUMMARY

- Organized labor developed slowly in the United States, with the post–Civil War industrialization spurring the rise of the Knights of Labor, the socialists, and the American Federation of Labor (AFL). The AFL ultimately developed into the dominant organization of the American labor movement; its merger with the CIO in 1955 marked the high point for organized labor in the United States. Since the mid-1950s, the percentage of the American work force that is unionized has steadily dwindled, from around 35 percent to the current level of approximately 15 percent. Unions still exert political influence, but there has been no resurgence of the labor movement since the mid-1950s. The U.S. legal system responded to organized labor by initially trying to suppress it through the use of the conspiracy doctrine, the labor injunction, and yellow-dog contracts. The antitrust laws, intended to attack anticompetitive business practices, were also used against union strikes and boycotts.
- It was not until the Great Depression of the 1930s that organized labor received legislative protection. The Norris–La Guardia Act, passed in 1932, greatly limited the use of labor injunctions by the federal courts. The National Industrial Recovery Act, the centerpiece of Franklin Roosevelt's New Deal, provided protection for employees organizing unions and encouraged collective bargaining. The National Labor Board (NLB) was created in 1933 to mediate labor disputes, but it had to rely on persuasion rather than legal authority. The NLB was replaced by the "old" National Labor Relations Board in 1934. When the Supreme Court declared the National Industrial Recovery Act unconstitutional in 1935, it meant the end of the old NLRB.
- Congress passed the Wagner Act shortly thereafter; the NLRA, and the NLRB it created, survived a constitutional challenge in the 1937 decision of *NLRB v. Jones & Laughlin Steel Corp.* The Wagner Act became the foundation for the development of the current National Labor Relations Act, the legal framework for labor relations in the United States.

QUESTIONS

1. How was the criminal conspiracy doctrine used against labor union activities in the United States?
2. What were the main objectives of the Knights of Labor? What factors contributed to the decline of the Knights of Labor? How did the objectives of the American Federation of Labor differ from those of the Knights of Labor? Why was the AFL more successful than the Knights of Labor?
3. Why was the labor injunction an effective weapon against union activities?
4. What are yellow-dog contracts? How could they be used to deter union organizing activity?
5. How were the antitrust laws used to deter union activities?
6. What were the main provisions of the Norris–La Guardia Act? How did the Norris–La Guardia Act affect union activities?
7. What dispute resolution procedures are available under the Railway Labor Act? Which employees are covered by the Railway Labor Act?

8. How did the National Industrial Recovery Act attempt to encourage collective bargaining? Why was the NRA unsuccessful in promoting collective bargaining?

9. What factors undermined the effectiveness of the National Labor Board?

10. What was the basis of federal jurisdiction over labor relations to support the National Labor Relations Act? What was the effect of the Supreme Court decision in the *Jones & Laughlin Steel Corp.* case?

INTERNET EXERCISES

Why do people join unions? What do unions have to offer today's employees? Using the Web site of the AFL-CIO at **http://www.aflcio.org**, how would you answer these questions? How is the labor movement tailoring its message to reach minority workers?

INFOTRAC KEYWORDS

http://www.infotrac-college.com

common law, knights of labor, american federation of labor AND AFL, labor concessions, AFL-CIO, antitrust laws, Norris-La Guardia act, railway labor act, NLRA

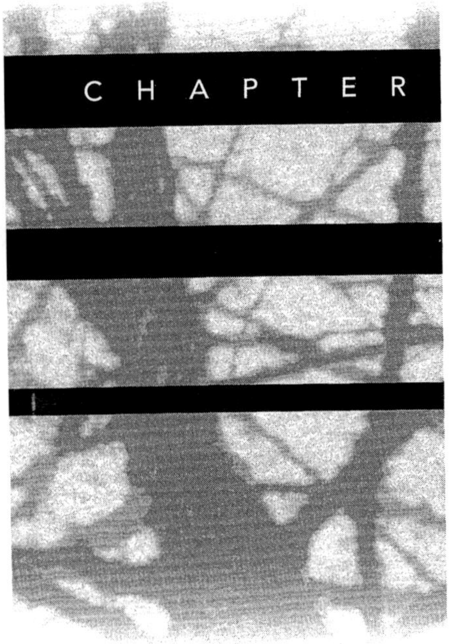

CHAPTER 13

THE NATIONAL LABOR RELATIONS BOARD: ORGANIZATION, PROCEDURES, AND JURISDICTION

This chapter discusses the National Labor Relations Board, the agency that administers and enforces the National Labor Relations Act.

THE NATIONAL LABOR RELATIONS BOARD

Unless otherwise specified, the discussion throughout this and subsequent chapters will focus on the current National Labor Relations Act[1] and the present National Labor Relations Board's organization, jurisdiction, and procedure.

ORGANIZATION

Because the Wagner Act gave little guidance concerning the administrative structure of the newly created agency, the NLRB adopted an administrative organization that made it prosecutor, judge, and jury with regard to complaints under the act. The board investigated charges of unfair labor practices, prosecuted complaints, conducted hearings, and rendered decisions. Pursuant to its statutory authority, the

[1]The Taft-Hartley Act incorporated the National Labor Relations Act. Scholars and labor lawyers differ over whether the modern act should be referred to as the NLRA or the Labor Management Relations Act, or both. For convenience, and since the enforcing agency is still called the NLRB, we will continue to refer to the act as the National Labor Relations Act.

Check **http://www.nlrb.gov/nlrb/press/facts.asp** *for facts on the organization and structure of the NLRB.*

board did appoint a general counsel to serve as legal adviser and direct litigation, but the general counsel was subordinate to the board in virtually all matters.

The combination of prosecutorial and judicial functions was one of the major criticisms leveled by commentators and attorneys against the board in the years prior to the passage of the Taft-Hartley Act. This issue, not surprisingly, was addressed by Taft-Hartley in 1947. Although retaining the concept of a single enforcement agency, Taft-Hartley made the Office of the General Counsel an independent unit to direct the administrative and enforcement efforts of the NLRB regional offices. The board itself was expanded from three to five members. It continued to exercise the judicial function of deciding complaints filed under the act.

The newly organized NLRB represented a unique type of administrative agency structure in that it was bifurcated into two independent authorities within the single agency: the five-member board and the general counsel. Figure 13.1 depicts the organization of the two authorities of the bifurcated agency.

The Board

The board itself is the judicial branch of the agency. The five members of the board are nominated by the president and must be confirmed by the Senate. They serve five-year terms. Members of the board can be removed from office by the president only for neglect of duty or malfeasance in office. One member is to be designated by the president as chairperson. Members have a staff of about twenty-five legal clerks and assistants to help in deciding the numerous cases that come before them. The executive secretary of the board is the chief administrative officer, charged with ruling on procedural questions, assigning cases to members, setting priorities in case handling, and conferring with parties to cases that come before the board. There is also a solicitor, whose function is to advise members on questions of law and policy. Finally, an information director assists the board on public relations issues.

Administrative Law Judges (ALJ) Formerly called trial examiners, these judges are independent of both the board and the general counsel.

The NLRB also has a branch called the Division of Judges. These **administrative law judges (ALJs),** formerly called trial examiners, are independent of both the board and the general counsel. Appointed for life, they are subject to the federal Civil Service Commission rules governing appointment and tenure. This organizational independence is necessary because the ALJs conduct hearings and issue initial decisions on unfair labor practice complaints issued by regional offices throughout the United States, under the authority delegated to these offices by the general counsel.

The board is prohibited by law from reviewing an ALJ's findings or recommendations before the issuance of the ALJ's formal report. The ALJ's function is that of a specialized trial court judge: to decide unfair labor practice complaints. ALJ decisions may be appealed to the board, which functions as a specialized court of appeal. After rendering their initial decisions, ALJs (like trial court judges) have nothing to do with the disposition of the case if it is appealed to the board.

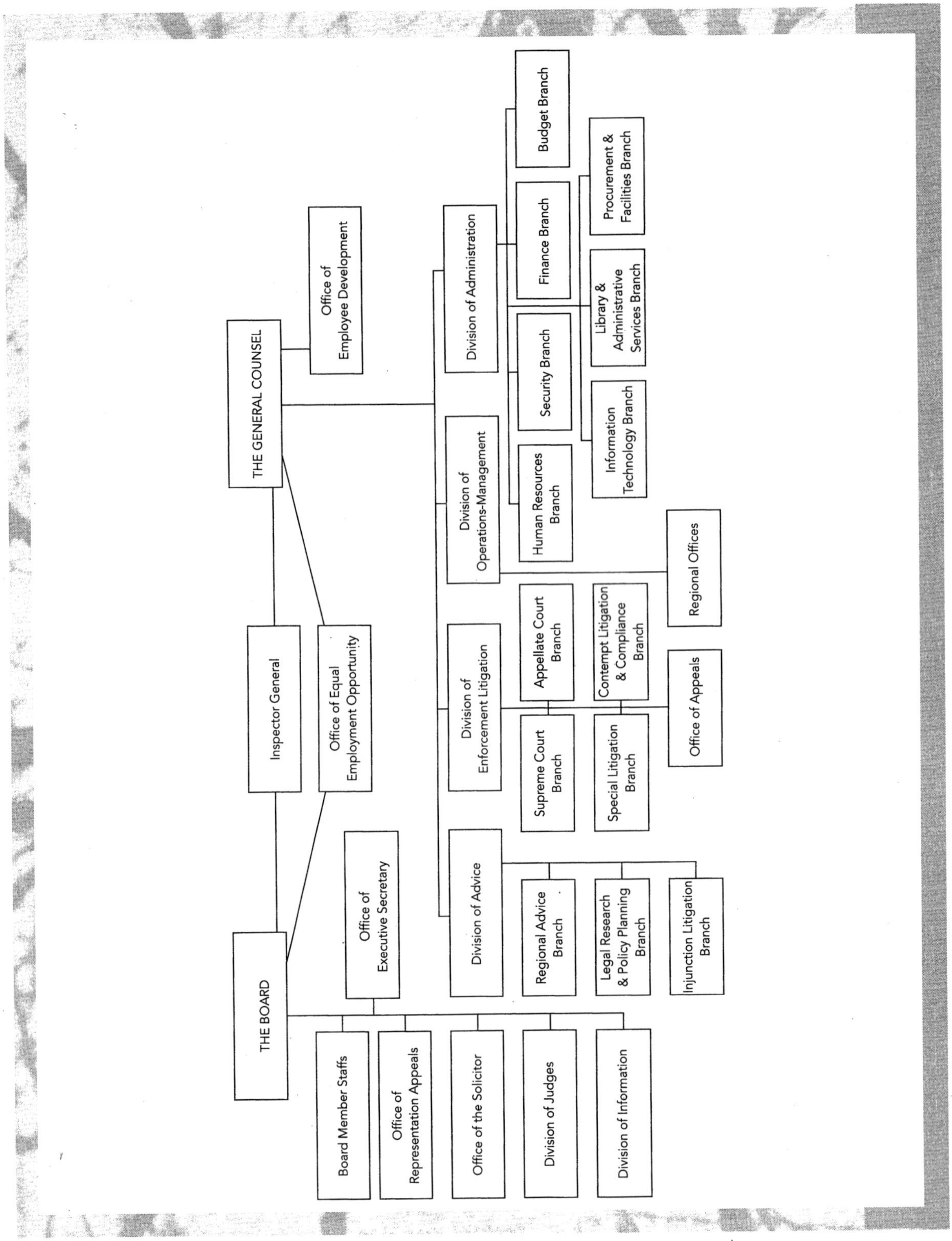

FIGURE 13.1 Organization chart of the National Labor Relations Board

Prepared by: Organization & Management Branch Division of Administration 7.74 (**http://www.nlrb.gov/nlrb/legal/manuals/rules/rrorgchart.asp**).

BATTISTA SWORN IN AS CHAIRMAN OF NLRB

THE WORKING LAW

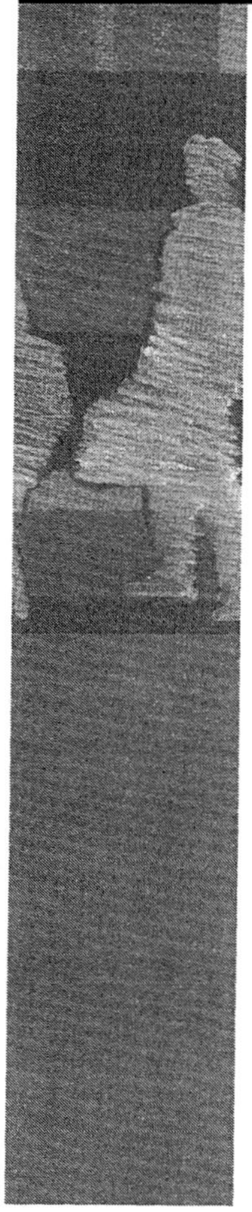

Robert J. Battista was sworn in as Chairman of the National Labor Relations Board on December 17, 2002; Battista was nominated to the post by President George W. Bush and confirmed by the U.S. Senate. His term will expire December 16, 2007. Chairman Battista had practiced labor and employment law with the Detroit, Michigan, law firm of Butzel Long since 1965. He is a graduate of the University of Notre Dame and the University of Michigan Law School.

Other current members of the National Labor Relations Board include:

Wilma B. Liebman, appointed to the NLRB initially by Bill Clinton and reappointed by George W. Bush; her term expires August 27, 2006. She had previously served as Special Assistant to the Director of the Federal Mediation and Conciliation Service and prior to that had been legal counsel to the Bricklayers and Allied Craftsmen union and the International Brotherhood of Teamsters union. Liebman is a graduate of Barnard College and the George Washington University Law Center.

Peter C. Schaumber, appointed to the NLRB by George W. Bush for a term that expires August 27, 2005. Schaumber had previously been in private practice in Washington, D.C., and also had been Associate Director of a Law Department Division in the Office of the Comptroller of the Currency, an Assistant United States Attorney for the District of Columbia, and an Assistant Corporation Counsel for the District of Columbia. Schaumber is a graduate of Georgetown University and the Georgetown University Law Center.

Dennis P. Walsh, initially appointed to the NLRB by Bill Clinton in December 2000, and reappointed by George W. Bush in December 2001. His current term expires December 16, 2004. Prior to his appointment to the NLRB, Walsh had served as Chief Counsel to NLRB member Wilma B. Liebman and to member Margaret A. Browning. He had previously been an associate at the Philadelphia law firm of Spear, Wilderman, Borish, Endy, Browing and Spear; he had also been a staff attorney at the NLRB. Walsh is a graduate of Hamilton College and Cornell Law School.

At the present time (December, 2003) one position on the N.L.R.B. is vacant.

Sources: "Robert Battista Is Sworn in as Chairman of the National Labor Relations Board," *N.L.R.B. Press Release,* December 17, 2002; NLRB Web site at **http://www.nlrb.gov** Press Release link.

The General Counsel

The Office of the General Counsel is the prosecutorial branch of the NLRB and is also in charge of the day-to-day administration of the NLRB regional offices. The general counsel is nominated by the president, with Senate confirmation for a four-year term. The structure of this branch of the NLRB is more complex than that of the board (see Figure 13.1). The Office of the General Counsel has four divisions:

1. the Division of Operations Management, which supervises operations of field offices and the management of all cases in the Washington, D.C., divisions;

2. the Division of Advice, which oversees the function of legal advice to the regional offices, the injunction work of the district court branch, and the legal research and special projects office;
3. the Division of Enforcement Litigation, which is responsible for the conduct of agency litigation enforcing or defending board orders in the federal courts of appeal or the Supreme Court;
4. the Division of Administration, which directs the management, financial, and personnel work of the Office of the General Counsel.

The NLRB has thirty-four regional offices and a number of subregional offices. The staff of each regional office consists of a regional director, regional attorney, field examiners, and field attorneys. Although Section 3(d) of the act gives the general counsel "final authority, on behalf of the Board, in respect of investigation of charges and issuance of complaints . . . and in respect of the prosecution of such complaints before the Board," the Office of General Counsel has exercised its statutory right to delegate this power to the regional directors, who make most of the day-to-day decisions affecting enforcement of the act.

PROCEDURES

The NLRB handles two kinds of legal questions: (1) those alleging that an unfair labor practice has taken place in violation of the act and (2) representation questions concerning whether, and if so how, employees will be represented for collective bargaining. In either type of case, the NLRB does not initiate the proceeding; rather, it responds to a complaint of unfair practice or a petition for an election filed by a party to the case. (The board refers to unfair practice cases as C cases and to representation cases as R cases.)

Unfair Labor Practice Charges

See **http://www.nlrb.gov/nlrb/legal/decisions** *on unfair labor practice cases.*

The filing of an unfair practice charge initiates NLRB proceedings in unfair labor practice cases. The act does not restrict who can file a charge; the most common charging parties are employees, unions, and employers. However, in *NLRB v. Indiana & Michigan Electric Co.* [318 U.S. 9 (1943)], the Supreme Court held that an individual who was a "stranger" to the dispute could file an unfair labor practice charge. The NLRB has adopted a special form for the filing of unfair practice charges (see Figure 13.2). In its fiscal year 2001, there were 28,124 unfair labor practice charges filed with the NLRB.

See **http://www.nlrb.gov/nlrb/shared_files/reports/default.asp?useShared=/nlrb/legal/reports/default.asp** *on unfair labor practice cases.*

Section 10(b) of the act requires that unfair practice charges must be filed within six months of the occurrence of the alleged unfair practice. Once a charge has been timely filed, the procedure is as follows:

- The charge is investigated by a field examiner. A charge can be resolved at this stage through mutual adjustment, voluntary withdrawal, or agency dismissal for lack of merit.
- If the charge is found to have merit and the case has not been settled by adjustment, a formal complaint is issued by the regional director.

INTERNET
FORM NLRB-501
(11-94)

UNITED STATES OF AMERICA
NATIONAL LABOR RELATIONS BOARD
CHARGE AGAINST EMPLOYER

FORM EXEMPT UNDER 44 U.S.C. 3512

DO NOT WRITE IN THIS SPACE	
Case	Date Filed

INSTRUCTIONS:
File an original and 4 copies of this charge with NLRB Regional Director for the region in which the alleged unfair labor practice occurred or is occurring.

1. EMPLOYER AGAINST WHOM CHARGE IS BROUGHT

a. Name of Employer | b. Number of Workers Employed

c. Address *(street, city, State, ZIP, Code)* | d. Employer Representative | e. Telephone No. | Fax No.

f. Type of Establishment *(factory, mine, wholesaler, etc.)* | g. Identify Principal Product or Service

h. The above-named employer has engaged in and is engaging in unfair labor practices within the meaning of Section 8(a), subsections (1) and *(list subsections)* ______________________ of the National Labor Relations Act, and these unfair labor practices are unfair practices affecting commerce within the meaning of the Act.

2. Basis of the Charge *(set forth a clear and concise statement of the facts constituting the alleged unfair labor practices.)*

By the above and other acts, the above-named employer has interfered with, restrained, and coerced employees in the exercise of the rights guaranteed in Section 7 of the Act.

3. Full name of party filing charge *(if labor organization, give full name, including local name and number)*

4a. Address *(street and number, city, State, and ZIP Code)* | 4b. Telephone No. | Fax No.

5. Full name of national or international labor organization of which it is an affiliate or constituent unit *(to be filled in when charge is filed by a labor organization)*

6. DECLARATION
I declare that I have read the above charge and that the statements are true to the best of my knowledge and belief.

By ______________________ ______________________
(Signature of representative or person making charge) *(Title, if any)*

Fax No. __________

Address ______________________ __________ __________
(Telephone No.) *Date*

WILLFUL FALSE STATEMENTS ON THIS CHARGE CAN BE PUNISHED BY FINE AND IMPRISONMENT (U.S. CODE, TITLE 18, SECTION 1001)

FIGURE 13.2 Unfair labor practice charge form. (Source: NLRB Web site at **http://www.nlrb.gov**. Click on Forms link.)

(In recent years, approximately one-third of all charges filed were voluntarily withdrawn, another one-third were dismissed as having no merit, and approximately one-third were found to have merit. Of the charges having merit, approximately 60 percent were settled with no formal complaint being issued. Thus, approximately 86 percent of all charges filed were disposed of before reaching the hearing stage in the procedure.)

- A public hearing on the complaint is held in front of an ALJ. (The Taft-Hartley amendments added the requirement that "so far as practicable" this hearing shall be conducted in accordance with the rules of evidence applicable to federal district courts.) At the conclusion of the hearing, the ALJ issues a report with findings of fact and recommendations of law.
- The ALJ's report is served on the parties and forwarded to the board in Washington, D.C. Each party then has twenty days to file exceptions to the report. These exceptions are in effect an appeal to the board. If no exceptions are taken, the ALJ's report is automatically accepted by the board as a final order.
- If exceptions have been filed to the ALJ's report by one or more parties, the board reviews the case and issues a decision and remedial order. The parties will normally have filed briefs with the board, explaining their respective positions on the exceptions. Sometimes (although rarely) a party will also request and be granted the opportunity to make oral arguments before the board. Normally, a three-member panel of the board handles any single case at this stage. (In 40 percent of all the "appeals," the board approves the ALJ's report in its entirety).

See Figure 13.3 for a summary of unfair labor practice procedures.

Orders of the board are not self-enforcing; if a party against whom an order is issued refuses to comply, the NLRB must ask the appropriate federal circuit court of appeals for a judgment enforcing the order. In addition, any party to the case may seek review of the board's decision in the appropriate federal court of appeal. The scope of this judicial review of the board's order is not the same as an appeal from the verdict of a federal trial court; the appeals court is required to accept the board's findings of fact provided that the findings are supported by substantial evidence in the case record. Any party to the case decided by the federal circuit court of appeals may petition the U.S. Supreme Court to grant certiorari to review the appellate court's decision. The Supreme Court generally restricts its review to cases in which a novel legal issue is raised or in which there is a conflict among the courts of appeal. (Only a minuscule percentage of labor cases reach this final step of the procedure.)

If the regional director refuses to issue a complaint after investigating a charge, that decision can be appealed to the Office of Appeals of the General Counsel in Washington, D.C. Approximately 30 percent of the charges dismissed by the regional offices are appealed to the Office of Appeals of the General Counsel. The Office of Appeals reverses the dismissal by the regional offices only rarely—in less than 10 percent of the cases appealed. The courts have upheld the general counsel's absolute discretion in these decisions; a conclusion that the charge lacks significant merit to issue a complaint cannot be appealed beyond the General Counsel's

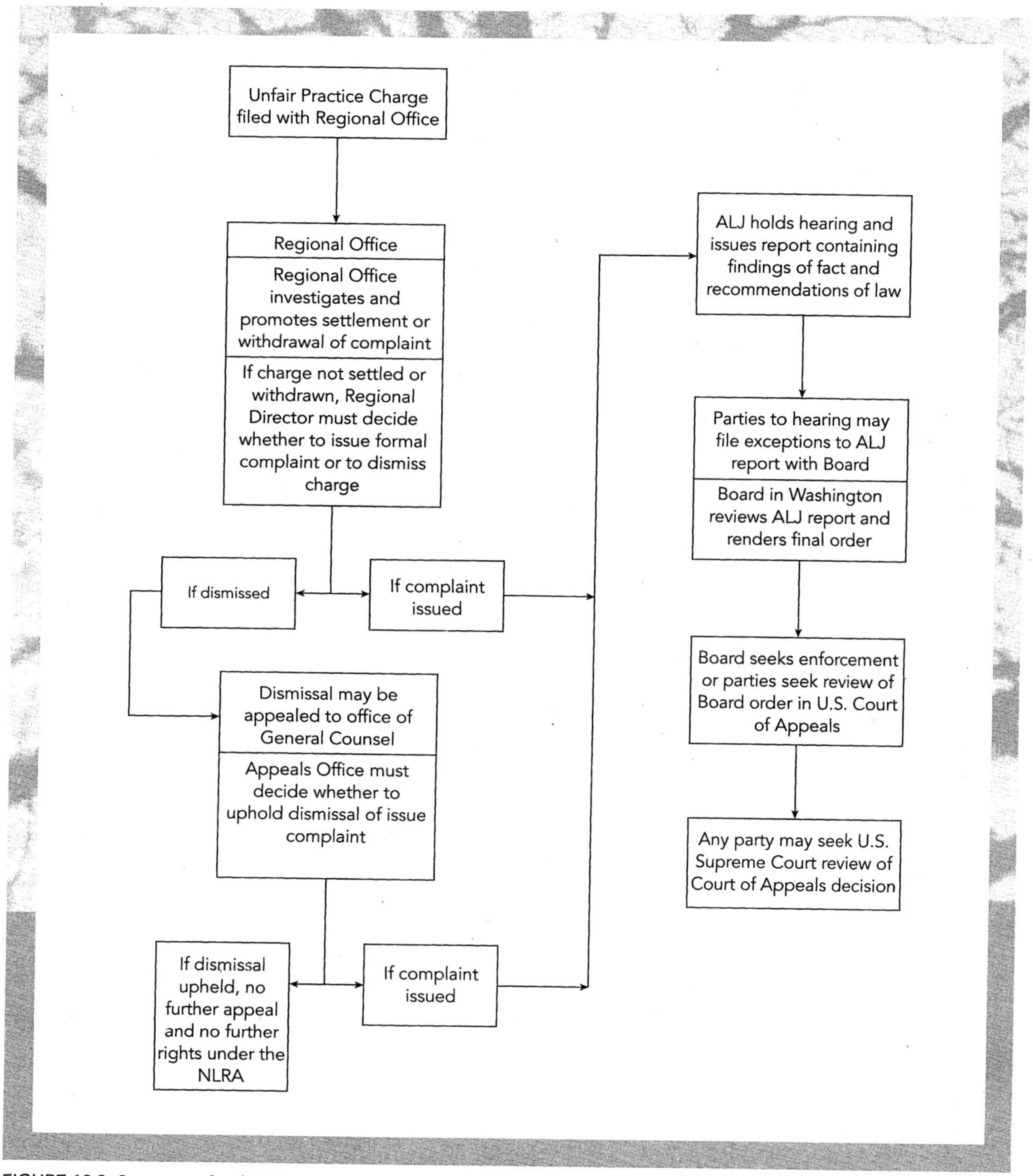

FIGURE 13.3 Summary of unfair labor practice procedures. (Based on National Labor Relations Board Basic Procedures in Cases Involving Charges of Unfair Labor Practices Exhibit on NLRB Web site at **http://www.nlrb.gov/nlrb/about/reports/gpra_03attach_b.pdf**.)

Office of Appeals. As such, the charging party's statutory rights have been procedurally exhausted and terminate without any hearing or judicial review.

Representation Elections

The other type of cases coming before the NLRB involve representation questions—employees choosing whether or not to be represented by a labor union as their exclusive bargaining agent. Although the issues and procedures involved in representation questions are discussed in detail in Chapter 14, a few points are highlighted in this discussion of NLRB procedures.

See **http://www.nlrb.gov/nlrb/shared_files/reports/default.asp?useShared=/nlrb/legal/reports/default.asp** *on representation cases.*

Representation proceedings are at the very heart of the National Labor Relations Act because the acceptance or rejection of a union as bargaining agent by a group of employees is the essence of the exercise of the rights guaranteed by Section 7 of the act—to engage in, or refrain from, concerted activity for purposes of collective bargaining or mutual aid or protection. Section 9 of the act outlines the procedures available to employees for exercising their rights under Section 7.

For nearly twenty-five years, the board had primary responsibility for the conduct of all representation elections. Then, in 1959, Congress decided that election procedures were sufficiently settled that the board could delegate its duties in this area to the regional directors. The board did so in 1961. Specifically, the regional directors are authorized by the board to

- decide whether a question concerning representation exists;
- determine the appropriate collective-bargaining unit;
- order and conduct an election;
- certify the election's results;
- resolve challenges to ballots by making findings of fact and issuing rulings.

The board has retained limited review, as the statute suggests, to ensure uniform and consistent application of its interpretation of law and policy. There are four grounds on which the board will review an election:

1. if a significant issue of *law* or policy is raised due to an absence of or departure from reported board precedent;
2. if the regional director has made a clear error regarding some *factual* issue and this error is prejudicial to the rights of one of the parties;
3. if the *procedure* involved some error that prejudiced a party;
4. if the board believes that one of its rules or policies is due for a *reconsideration*.

Ordinarily, once the regional director has decided that a representation election should be held involving a particular unit of employees, a Notice and a Direction of Election are issued by the regional office, even though one of the parties has appealed some aspect of the director's decision to the board in Washington. However, unless the parties have waived their right to request board review, the director will set the election date no earlier than twenty-five days from the notices. On the other hand, the date will usually not be set any later than thirty days after the director's decision to proceed.

JURISDICTION

Under the National Labor Relations Act, the NLRB is given authority to deal with labor disputes occurring "in commerce" or "affecting commerce" [as defined in Section 2(7) of the act]. Consistent with the federal courts' traditional view of the scope of federal commerce clause powers, the Supreme Court has held that the NLRB can regulate labor disputes in virtually any company, unless the firm's contact with interstate commerce is de minimus (minuscule and merely incidental).

Rather than exercise its jurisdiction to the full extent of the federal commerce power, the NLRB has chosen to set certain minimum jurisdictional standards. These standards specify the limits beyond which the NLRB will decline jurisdiction over any labor dispute. The Landrum-Griffin Act recognized this policy by providing that the NLRB may decline jurisdiction over any labor dispute that would have been outside the NLRB's minimum jurisdictional standards as of August 1, 1959. The NLRB may expand its jurisdictional standards, but it cannot contract them beyond their position as of August 1, 1959. The 1959 amendments to the act also provide that the states under certain circumstances may assert jurisdiction over labor disputes on which the NLRB declines to assert jurisdiction.

General Jurisdictional Standards

The NLRB jurisdictional standards are set in terms of the dollar volume of business that a firm does annually. The current NLRB jurisdictional standards are as follows:

General Nonretail Firms. Sales of goods to consumers in other states, directly or indirectly (termed outflow) or purchases of goods from suppliers in other states, directly or indirectly (termed inflow) of at least $50,000 per year.

Retail Businesses. Annual volume of business of at least $500,000, including sales and excise taxes.

Combined Manufacturing and Retail Enterprises. When an integrated enterprise manufactures a product and sells it directly to the public, either the retail or the nonretail standard can be applied.

Combined Wholesale and Retail Companies. When a company is involved in both wholesale and retail sales, the nonretail standard is applicable.

Instrumentalities, Channels, and Links of Interstate Commerce. Annual income of at least $50,000 from interstate transportation services or the performing of $50,000 or more in services for firms that meet any of the other standards, except indirect inflow and outflow established for nonretail businesses.

National Defense. Any enterprise having a substantial impact on the national defense.

U.S. Territories and the District of Columbia. Same standards are applied to the territories as to enterprises operating in the fifty states; plenary (total) jurisdiction is exercised in the District of Columbia.

Public Utilities. At least $250,000 total annual volume of business.

Newspapers. At least $200,000 total annual volume of business.

Radio, Telegraph, Telephone, and Television Companies. At least $100,000 total annual volume of business.

Hotels, Motels, and Residential Apartment Houses. At least $500,000 total annual volume of business.

Taxicab Companies. At least $500,000 total annual volume of business.

Transit Systems. At least $250,000 total annual volume of business.

Privately Operated Health-Care Institutions. Nursing homes, visiting nurses' associations, and similar facilities and services, $100,000; all others, including hospitals, $250,000 total annual volume of business.

Nonprofit, Private Educational Institutions. $1 million annual operating expenditures.

U.S. Postal Service. The board was empowered to assert jurisdiction under the Postal Reorganization Act of 1970.

Multiemployer Bargaining Associations. Regarded as a single employer for the purpose of totaling up annual business with relation to the above standards.

Multistate Establishments. Annual business of all branches is totaled with regard to the board's standards.

Unions as Employers. The appropriate nonretail standard.

Exempted Employers

Not all employers—or employees of such employers—meeting the NLRB jurisdictional standards are subject to the provisions of the National Labor Relations Act. Certain kinds of employers have been excluded from coverage of the act by specific provisions in the act; other employers have been exempted as a result of judicial decisions interpreting the act.

Section 2(2) of the act defines the term *employer* as "including any person acting as an agent of an employer, directly or indirectly," but not including:

- the federal government or any wholly owned government corporation;
- any state or political subdivision thereof (county, local, or municipal governments); railroads, airlines, or related companies that are subject to the Railway Labor Act (In 1996, Congress amended the Railway Labor Act to include Federal Express under its jurisdiction, rather than under the NLRA; United Parcel Service, however, remains under the NLRA.);
- labor organizations in their representational capacity. (Unions are covered by the act in the hiring and treatment of their own employees.)

In addition to these statutory exclusions, judicial decisions have created other exclusions. The NLRB will usually refuse to exercise jurisdiction over an employer that has a close relationship to a foreign government, even if such employers would otherwise come under its jurisdiction. The Supreme Court has held that the act does not apply to labor disputes of foreign crews on foreign flag vessels temporarily in U.S. ports, even if such ships deal primarily in American contracts. See *Incres S.S. v. Maritime Workers* [372 U.S. 24 (1963)]. However, when the dispute involves American residents working while the vessel is in port, the dispute is subject to the act. In *Int. Longshore Assoc. v. Allied International, Inc.* [456 U.S. 212 (1982)], the Supreme Court held that a politically motivated refusal by American longshoremen to service American ships carrying Russian cargo, to protest the Soviet invasion of Afghanistan, was subject to the jurisdiction of the NLRB.

The Supreme Court has also held in *NLRB v. Catholic Bishop* [440 U.S. 490 (1979)] that the NLRB lacked jurisdiction over a parochial high school. The Court stated that its holding was necessary to avoid excessive government entanglement with religion, as prohibited by the First Amendment. The NLRB has taken the position that the Court's decision exempts from NLRB jurisdiction only those organizations devoted principally to the promulgation of the faith of a religion. For example, the NLRB has refused jurisdiction over a television station owned by a church in which over 90 percent of the station's broadcasts were religious in nature. However, hospitals operated by religious organizations, or religious charity services providing aid to the elderly, have been held subject to NLRB jurisdiction because they were not principally involved with promulgating the religion's faith.

Exempted Employees

Just as with employers, not all employees employed by employers in or affecting commerce are subject to the provisions of the National Labor Relations Act. These exclusions from coverage are the result of both statutory provisions and judicial decisions.

Statutory Exemptions. Section 2(3) of the National Labor Relations Act, in its definition of *employee,* expressly excludes

- individuals employed as agricultural laborers;
- individuals employed as domestics within a person's home;
- individuals employed by a parent or spouse;
- independent contractors;
- supervisors;
- individuals employed by employers subject to the Railway Labor Act.

Several of these statutory exclusions require some discussion. For example, the NLRA does not specifically define the term "agricultural laborer"; rather, Congress has directed the NLRB to consider the definition of "agriculture" found in Section 3(f) of the Fair Labor Standards Act [29 U.S.C. § 203(f)], which is very broad. It includes cultivating, tilling, growing, dairying, producing, or harvesting any agricultural commodity, raising livestock, or any operations or practices performed by a farmer or on a farm as incident to, or in conjunction with such farming operations. The NLRB considers the facts of each case, looking to the specific duties and the time spent at the duties to determine whether persons are agricultural laborers within the meaning of the NLRA.

In *Holly Farms Corp. v. NLRB* [517 U.S. 392 (1996)], the Supreme Court (by a 5-4 decision) held that the "live haul" crews of a poultry processor, who drive from the processor's location to independent farms and there collect and cage chickens, lift the cages on a truck, and transport them back to the processor, were not agricultural laborers within the meaning of Section 2(3) and were therefore covered by the NLRA. Agricultural employees exempted from the NLRA may be covered by state legislation; several states, such as California and Arizona, have created agricultural labor relations boards to cover the labor disputes of agricultural laborers.

Independent Contractor
A person working as a separate business entity.

An **independent contractor** is a person working as a separate business entity; these individuals are not subject to the direction and control of an employer. For example, a person who owns and operates a dump truck and who contracts to provide rubbish disposal service to a firm might be an independent contractor and not an employee of the firm. If the firm used its own truck and directed a worker to haul away its rubbish, the worker would be an employee and not an independent contractor. The NLRB looks to the degree of control and direction exercised by the firm over the worker to determine whether the worker is an employee or an independent contractor.

Supervisor
Person with authority to direct, hire, fire, or discipline employees in the interests of the employer.

The term **supervisor** is defined in Section 2(11) of the NLRA as someone who, in the interests of the employer, has the authority to direct, hire, fire, discipline, transfer, or suspend other employees and who uses independent judgment in the exercise of such authority. The NLRB, applying Section 2(11) to nurses in the health-care industry, had held that nurses who directed other employees in patient care were not acting in the interests of their employer and therefore were not supervisors within the meaning of Section 2(11). The Supreme Court rejected the NLRB's decision in *NLRB v. Health Care & Retirement Corporation of America* [511 U.S. 571 (1994)]. The NLRB then held that nurses did not exercise "independent judgment" within the meaning of Section 2(11) because the nurses were exercising "ordinary professional or technical judgment" in directing other employees to deliver patient care in accordance with employer-specified standards.

The following case involves the Supreme Court's consideration of the NLRB's determination that those nurses were not supervisors under the NLRA.

National Labor Relations Board v. Kentucky River Community Care, Inc.

532 U.S. 706 (2001)

[Kentucky River Community Care, Inc. (Kentucky River) operates a residential care facility for persons suffering from mental retardation and mental illness. The facility, Caney Creek, employs approximately 110 professional and nonprofessional employees and about 12 managerial or supervisory employees. In 1997, the Carpenters Union petitioned the NLRB to represent a single unit of all 110 potentially eligible employees at Caney Creek. At the hearing on the petition, Kentucky River objected to the inclusion of Caney Creek's six registered nurses in the bargaining unit, arguing that they were supervisors under § 2(11) of the Act and therefore were excluded from the class of employees covered by the NLRA and included in the bargaining unit. The Board's Regional Director initially held that Kentucky River had the burden of proving supervisory status; the Regional Director then held that Kentucky River had not carried that burden and therefore included the nurses in the bargaining unit. The regional director directed an election to determine whether the union would represent the unit; the union won the election and was certified as the representative of the Caney Creek employees.

Kentucky River then refused to bargain with the union in order to get judicial review of the certification decision. The NLRB's General Counsel filed an unfair labor practice complaint under § § 8(a)(1) and 8(a)(5) of the Act. The Board granted summary judgment to the General Counsel, holding Kentucky River had violated the NLRA. Kentucky River then petitioned the U.S. Court of Appeals for the Sixth Circuit. The Sixth Circuit held that the Board had erred in placing the burden of proving supervisory status on respondent rather than on its General Counsel, and it also rejected the Board's determination that the registered nurses did not exercise "independent judgment." The court stated that the Board had erred by classifying the nurses' supervision of nurse's aides in administering patient care as "routine" because the nurses have the ability to direct patient care by virtue of their training and expertise, not because of their connection with management. The NLRB then appealed to the U.S. Supreme Court.]

Justice Scalia delivered the opinion of the Court.

Under the National Labor Relations Act, employees are deemed to be "supervisors" and thereby excluded from the protections of the Act if, *inter alia,* they exercise "independent judgment" in "responsibly . . . direct[ing]" other employees "in the interest of the employer." This case presents two questions: which party in an unfair-labor-practice proceeding bears the burden of proving or disproving an employee's supervisory status; and whether judgment is not "independent judgment" to the extent that it is informed by professional or technical training or experience. . . .

The Act expressly defines the term "supervisor" in § 2(11) . . . [but] does not, however, expressly allocate the burden of proving or disproving a challenged employee's supervisory status. The Board therefore has filled the statutory gap with the consistent rule that the burden is borne by the party claiming that the employee is a supervisor. . . .

The Board argues that the Court of Appeals for the Sixth Circuit erred in not deferring to its resolution of the statutory ambiguity, and we agree. The Board's rule is supported by "the general rule of statutory construction that the burden of proving justification or exemption under a special exception to the prohibitions of a statute generally rests on one who claims its benefits. The burden of proving the applicability of the supervisory exception . . . should thus fall on the party asserting it. In addition, it is easier to prove an employee's authority to exercise 1 of the 12 listed supervisory functions than to disprove an employee's authority to exercise any of those functions, and practicality therefore favors placing the burden on the party asserting supervisory status. We find that the Board's rule for allocating the burden of proof is reasonable and consistent with the Act . . .

The text of § 2(11) of the Act . . . sets forth a three-part test for determining supervisory status. Employees are statutory supervisors if (1) they hold the authority to engage in any 1 of the 12 listed supervisory functions, (2) their "exercise of such authority is not of a merely routine or clerical nature, but requires the use of independent judgment," and (3) their authority is held "in the interest of the employer." [*NLRB v. Health Care & Retirement Corp. of America*] The only basis asserted by the Board, before the Court of Appeals and here, for rejecting respondent's proof of supervisory status with respect to directing patient care was the Board's interpretation of the second part of the test— . . . that employees do not use "independent judgment" when they exercise "ordinary professional or technical judgment in directing less-skilled employees to deliver services in accordance with employer-specified standards." The Court of Appeals rejected that interpretation . . .

The Board . . . argues further that the judgment even of employees who are permitted by their employer to exercise a sufficient *degree* of discretion is not "independent judgment" if it is a particular *kind* of judgment, namely, "ordinary professional or technical judgment in directing less-skilled employees to deliver services." . . . The text, by focusing on the "clerical" or "routine" (as opposed to "independent") nature of the judgment, introduces the question of degree of judgment . . . But the Board's categorical exclusion turns on factors that have nothing to do with the degree of discretion an employee exercises. Let the judgment be significant and only loosely constrained by the employer; if it is "professional or technical" it will nonetheless not be independent. The breadth of this exclusion is made all the more startling by virtue of the Board's extension of it to judgment based on greater "experience" as well as formal training. What supervisory judgment worth exercising, one must wonder, does not rest on "professional or technical skill or experience"? If the Board applied this aspect of its test to every exercise of a supervisory function, it would virtually eliminate "supervisors" from the Act.

As it happens, though, only one class of supervisors would be eliminated in practice, because the Board limits its categorical exclusion with a qualifier: Only professional judgment that is applied "in directing less-skilled employees to deliver services" is excluded from the statutory category of "independent judgment." This second rule is no less striking than the first, and is directly contrary to the text of the statute. *Every* supervisory function listed by the Act is accompanied by the statutory requirement that its exercise "requir[e] the use of independent judgment" before supervisory status will obtain, but the Board would apply its restriction upon "independent judgment" to just 1 of the 12 listed functions: "responsibly to direct." There is no apparent textual justification for this asymmetrical limitation, and the Board has offered none. Surely no conceptual justification can be found in the proposition that supervisors exercise professional, technical, or experienced judgment only when they direct other employees. Decisions "to hire, . . . suspend, lay off, recall, promote, discharge, . . . or discipline" other employees, must often depend upon that same judgment, which enables assessment of the employee's proficiency in performing his job. . . . Yet in no opinion that we were able to discover has the Board held that a supervisor's judgment in hiring, disciplining, or promoting another employee ceased to be "independent judgment" because it depended upon the supervisor's professional or technical training or experience. When an employee exercises one of these functions with judgment that possesses a sufficient degree of independence, the Board invariably finds supervisory status.

The Board's refusal to apply its limiting interpretation of "independent judgment" to any supervisory function other than responsibly directing other employees is particularly troubling because just seven years ago we rejected the Board's interpretation of part three of the supervisory test that similarly was applied only to the same supervisory function. [*NLRB v. Health Care & Retirement Corp. of America*] In *Health Care,* the Board argued that nurses did not exercise their authority "in the interest of the employer," as § 2(11) requires, when their "independent judgment [was] exercised incidental to professional or technical judgment" instead of for "disciplinary or other matters, i.e., in addition to treatment of patients." It did not escape our notice that the target of this analysis was the supervisory function of responsible direction. "Under § 2(11)," we noted, "an employee who in the course of employment uses independent judgment to engage in 1 of the 12 listed activities, including responsible direction of other employees, is a supervisor. Under the Board's test, however, a nurse who in the course of employment uses independent judgment to engage in responsible direction of other employees is not a supervisor." We therefore rejected the Board's analysis as "inconsistent with . . . the statutory language," because it "rea[d] the responsible direction portion of § 2(11) out of the statute in nurse cases." It is impossible to avoid the conclusion that the Board's interpretation of "independent judgment," applied to nurses for the first time after our decision in *Health Care,* has precisely the same object. . . . The Labor Management Relations Act, 1947 (Taft-Hartley Act) expressly excluded "supervisors" from the definition of "employees" and thereby from the protections of the Act. § 2(3) . . . The term "supervisor" means any individual having authority . . . "to hire, transfer, suspend, lay off, recall, promote, discharge, assign, reward, or discipline other employees, *or* responsibly to direct them, or to adjust their grievances." Moreover, the Act assuredly did *not* incorporate the Board's current interpretation of the term "independent judgment" as applied to the function of responsible direction . . . because it had limited the category of supervisors more directly, by requiring functions *in addition* to responsible direction.

. . . What is at issue is the Board's contention that the policy of covering professional employees under the Act justifies the categorical exclusion of professional judgments from a term, "independent judgment," that naturally includes them. And further, that it justifies limiting this categorical exclusion to the supervisory function of responsibly directing other employees. These contentions contradict both the text and structure of the statute, and they contradict as well the rule of *Health Care* that the test for supervisory status applies no differently to professionals than to other employees. We therefore find the Board's interpretation unlawful . . .

. . . the Board's error in interpreting "independent judgment" precludes us from enforcing its order. . . . Our conclusion that the Court of Appeals was correct to find the Board's test inconsistent with the statute . . . suffices to resolve the case. The judgment of the Court of Appeals is affirmed.

It is so ordered.

Case Questions

1. What test determines whether an employee is a supervisor under the NLRA?
2. What is the basis of the NLRB position that nurses who direct other employees in delivering patient care are not exercising independent judgment within the meaning of Section 2(11)? Is the NLRB's position based upon the language of the NLRA? Explain your answers.
3. What is the significance of the determination that the staff nurses are supervisors under the NLRA? What implications does this case have for other professional employees? Explain.

Managerial Employees
Persons involved in the formulation or effectuation of management policies.

Judicial Exemptions. In addition to the statutory exclusions of employees from NLRA coverage, the U.S. Supreme Court has created other exemptions. **Managerial employees,** persons whose positions involve the formulation or effectuation of management policies, were held to be excluded from NLRA coverage in *NLRB v. Textron* [416 U.S. 267 (1974)]. In the 1980 decision in *NLRB v. Yeshiva University* [444 U.S. 672], the Supreme Court held that faculty at a private university, who play a significant role in developing and implementing university academic policies, were managerial employees and thus excluded from the protection of the NLRA. Following *Yeshiva,* the U.S. Court of Appeals for the First Circuit held that faculty at Boston University were managerial employees, *Boston Univ. Chapter, AAUP v. NLRB* [835 F.2d 399 (1987)]. However, where faculty do not have input in developing or implementing policy and exercise no supervisory duties, they have been held to be employees under the coverage of the NLRA, *Stevens Inst. v. NLRB* [620 F.2d 720 (9th Cir. 1980)] and *Bradford College* [261 NLRB 565 (1982)].

The NLRB recently reversed its position on the question of whether graduate students who teach classes, and medical residents and interns, are employees under the NLRA. In *Boston Medical Center* [330 NLRB No. 30 (Nov. 26, 1999)], the NLRB reversed its previous position and held that medical residents and interns are employees within the definition of Section 2(3) of the NLRA. Following the *Boston Medical Center* decision, the NLRB held that graduate assistants, graduate

ETHICAL DILEMMA: FACULTY CONSULTATION RIGHTS AT PRESTIGIOUS UNIVERSITY?

You are the Vice President for Faculty Relations at Prestigious University, a private university in New Jersey. The major portion of your duties involves negotiation and communication with the Prestigious University Chapter of the American Association of University Professors [AAUP]. The Prestigious Chapter of the AAUP has functioned as the representative of the faculty for discussions over salary, benefits, and working conditions for a number of years. Although there is no formal collective agreement between the university administration and the AAUP Chapter, the administration has never instituted any policies or changes to benefits or working conditions without first getting the approval of the AAUP Chapter.

Because of declining enrollment, increased building maintenance costs, and the expenses of updating computer facilities all across the campus, the university is experiencing financial difficulties. The administration decides to freeze faculty salaries and reduce its contribution to the faculty's medical insurance and pension plans. The AAUP Chapter strongly objects to such actions and will not cooperate with the university administration to implement them. The great majority of the faculty at Prestigious University supports the AAUP's position.

Should the university administration continue to work with the AAUP in its capacity as faculty representative, or should the administration impose its financial proposals over the AAUP's objections? The university president has asked you to prepare a memo that outlines the advantages and disadvantages of the two approaches and recommends a course of action. Which approach would you recommend? Why? Prepare the requested memo and explain your position.

students who teach courses, are employees within the definition of the NLRA in *New York University* [332 NLRB No. 111 (Oct. 31, 2000)]; the NLRB affirmed the decision of the Regional Director of the New York City Regional Office, directing that a representation election be held among graduate assistants at New York University.

Employees excluded from the act's coverage are not prevented from organizing and attempting to bargain collectively with their employer. There is nothing in the National Labor Relations Act to prohibit such action. Exclusion means that those employees cannot invoke the act's protection for the exercise of rights to organize and bargain. There is no requirement that their employer recognize or bargain with their union or even tolerate such activity. Because those employees are denied the act's protections, the employer is free to discipline or discharge excluded employees who attempt to organize and bargain. Therefore, the faculty members in *Boston University* may attempt to organize and bargain with their employer, but the university need not recognize and bargain with them.

Confidential Employees
Persons whose job involves access to confidential labor relations information.

Confidential employees are neither supervisors nor managerial employees, but those persons whose position involves access to confidential labor relations information. The following case discusses the scope of the confidential employee exemption.

NLRB v. Meenan Oil Co., L.P.

139 F.3d 311 (2d Cir. 1998)

Jacobs, Circuit Judge

The National Labor Relations Board (the "Board") petitions for enforcement of its order finding that Meenan Oil Co., L.P. ("Meenan" or the "Company") violated Sections 8 (a) (1) and (5) of the National Labor Relations Act (the "NLRA"), by refusing to bargain with a properly certified union and requiring Meenan to bargain with the union on demand. Meenan contends that the two collective-bargaining units at issue were improperly certified because they include employees who are outside the protection of the NLRA. Specifically, Meenan asserts that . . . its administrator for payroll and personnel matters is . . . a confidential employee; and the executive secretary to its general manager is a confidential employee. . . .

Rosemary Gould is [General Manager] Zaweski's executive secretary. She sits outside his office and spends most of her time answering telephones, typing, filing, and performing other clerical tasks. She also opens Zaweski's mail, including items marked "confidential." Gould types documents dealing with employee discipline, including disciplinary notices, termination notices, minutes of union grievance meetings, and grievance settlement documents. Ordinarily, she prepares the documents after a decision has been made, and often after their contents have been disclosed to the relevant employees or union representatives, or discussed with them; copies are generally sent to the employees and union immediately after they are produced. Gould also types some internal memoranda dealing with various personnel issues. These memoranda give her access to intra-management communications that affect union employees generally, even if they do not specifically concern labor issues or strategies. Thus Gould is responsible for typing the Company's annual profit plan, which forecasts the salary increase or decrease planned for every Meenan employee. Meenan asserts that her access to all of these materials makes Gould a confidential employee, and that it was error to include her in a collective-bargaining unit.

Angela Gabriel, the Company's payroll/personnel administrator, had worked for the Company for about twelve years at the time of the election. . . . Gabriel reports to the Company's accounting supervisor on most matters, but reports to Zaweski on issues of personnel. Her primary responsibility is to handle the paperwork for payroll and personnel matters. Specifically, she: prepares the weekly payroll figures; collects personnel forms when new employees are hired; receives and files copies of insurance claims, disciplinary notices, and other notices; maintains a complete set of personnel files; calculates and fills out the forms for employees' benefit fund contributions; helps managers keep track of employees' absences and overtime, and is expected to point out any discrepancies she observes; fills out unemployment compensation forms using information provided by the Company's managers; and occasionally copies documents from an employee's file in order to assist a manager who is testifying at an unemployment hearing.

. . . Gabriel's duties give her access to potentially sensitive information about the Company. Copies of all employees' personnel files are filed in Gabriel's office. She receives employees' drug-test results, though she plays no role in deciding what to do about the results. Gabriel is privy to some union-related information (such as impending layoffs), but she generally acquires that information only when it is in the process of being forwarded to the union. Most important for present purposes, she assists Zaweski with the preparation of the Company's annual profit plan, and in that way has access to the current salary as well as salary changes forecast by the Company for all employees and supervisors, and at least some managers. Because she has access to all of this information, Meenan contends that Gabriel, like Gould, is a confidential employee who for that reason must be excluded from any bargaining unit. . . .

The Board excludes from collective-bargaining units individuals who fit the definition of "confidential employees." *NLRB v. Hendricks County Rural Elec. Membership Corp.*, 454 U.S. 170, 189 (1981). . . .

The Supreme Court has identified two categories of confidential employees who are excluded from the NLRA's protection: (i) employees who "assist and act in a confidential capacity to persons who formulate, determine, and effectuate management policies in the field of labor relations," and (ii) employees who "regularly have access to confidential information concerning anticipated changes which may result from collective-bargaining negotiations."

There are arguably some confidential aspects to many employment relationships, but the Board (for that reason) hews strictly to a narrow definition of a confidential employee. . . . In *Hendricks County,* the Supreme Court approved the Board's use of this "labor nexus" test; so employees who have access to confidential business information are not for that reason excludible from collective-bargaining units. The Board looks to "the confidentiality of the relationship between the employee and persons who exercise managerial functions in the field of labor relations." Moreover, the confidential labor-related information available to the employee must be information that is not already known to the union or in the process of being disclosed to it.

The rationale for the exclusion of confidential employees (as so defined) is that management should not be forced to negotiate with a union that includes employees "who in the normal performance of their duties may obtain advance information of the [c]ompany's position with regard to contract negotiations, the disposition of grievances, and other labor relations matters." An individual who routinely sees data which would enable the union to predict, understand or evaluate the bargaining position of the employer is therefore excluded from union membership.

We conclude that Angela Gabriel, the payroll/personnel administrator, and Rosemary Gould, the executive secretary to the general manager, are confidential employees. Both are in a confidential employment relationship with General Manager Zaweski, who is largely responsible for conducting Meenan's labor relations. Both women fit neatly within the category of confidential employee, identified by the Supreme Court in *Hendricks County,* as those who "assist and act in a confidential capacity to persons who formulate, determine, and effectuate management policies in the field of labor relations."

Zaweski has responsibility for preparing the Company's annual profit plan. Gabriel assists him in that project by filling out forms that show the current salaries and most recent pay raises of the Company's employees, including supervisors and at least some members of management. The forms containing this information, as prepared by Gabriel, are forwarded to the Company's managers, who apply corporate salary increase guidelines to arrive at a recommendation for the timing and size of each employee's next raise, and review these recommendations with Zaweski. A copy of the revised recommendations is then sent to the Company's corporate department, and a copy is retained by Gabriel. If the corporate department revises the figures, Gabriel receives a copy of the updated document. Gabriel thus has knowledge of the proposed salary increase—or decrease—of every Meenan employee. Often she learns of these proposed changes six to seven months before they are implemented.

Zaweski's executive secretary, Rosemary Gould, types the initial draft of the annual profit plan, and in so doing she gets to see the proposed wage and salary figures before they are sent to the corporate department and to Gabriel. Gould testified that she, Gabriel and Zaweski are the only non-corporate employees who see this document.

Because Gabriel and Gould assist Zaweski with the preparation of the Company's annual profit plan, they have access to projected wage and salary data for both union and non-union employees. This information, in the hands of the Union, would give it a significant strategic advantage in negotiations. The Union could predict the size of the raises that management already planned to give both union and non-union employees, prior to any collective-bargaining session, and use that level of compensation as a floor for its demands. At the same time, information about the present and projected compensation of managers would afford leverage in bargaining for comparable raises for union members. Even if this information is never mentioned, it would enable the Union to anticipate and gauge management's resistance to its demands.

In summary, the projected wage and salary data contained in the profit plan influences and signals "the [c]ompany's position with regard to contract negotiations." Meenan is not required to bargain with a union whose members have this advantage.

The Board's finding that Gabriel and Gould are not confidential employees is unsupported by substantial evidence, and we therefore decline to enforce the Board's order insofar as Gabriel and Gould are included in the Office Clerical collective-bargaining unit. . . .

For the foregoing reasons, we modify the Board's order to remove Meenan's "payroll/personnel administrator" and its "executive secretary" from the Office Clerical collective-bargaining unit. The order as modified is enforced.

Case Questions

1. What is the rationale for the exclusion of confidential employees?
2. Does the confidential employee exclusion apply to all employees who have access to the employer's confidential information? What is the "labor nexus" test?
3. What are the key features of Gould's and Gabriel's job duties for the purposes of the "labor nexus" test? Would including Gabriel and Gould in the bargaining unit place the employer at a disadvantage when dealing with the union? Explain.

Although managerial employees are excluded from the act's coverage, it is not clear whether "confidential" employees are excluded from the act's coverage or are simply excluded from bargaining units with other employees. If confidential employees, like managers, are excluded from the act's coverage, they are denied the protections of the act. If, however, they are excluded only from bargaining units, they remain employees under the act and are entitled to its statutory protection. The Supreme Court did not specifically address this question in *Hendricks,* nor did the court in *Meenan Oil Co.*

Can persons who are on the payroll of a union as organizers also be employees under the meaning of Section 2(3)? The following case involves that question in the context of the legality of an employer's refusal to hire persons who are also on the union payroll as organizers.

NLRB v. Town & Country Electric, Inc.

516 U.S. 85 (1995)

Breyer, J.

Can a worker be a company's "employee" within the terms of the National Labor Relations Act if, at the same time, a union pays that worker to help the union organize the company? . . .

The relevant background is the following: Town & Country Electric, Inc., a nonunion electrical contractor, wanted to hire several licensed Minnesota electricians for construction work in Minnesota. Town & Country . . . advertised for job applicants, but it refused to interview 10 of 11 union applicants (including two professional union staff) who responded to the advertisement. Its employment agency hired the one union applicant whom Town & Country interviewed, but he was dismissed after only a few days on the job.

The members of the union (the International Brotherhood of Electrical Workers, Locals 292 and 343) filed a complaint with the National Labor Relations Board claiming that Town & Country and the employment agency had refused to interview (or retain) them because of their union membership. An administrative law judge ruled in favor of the union members, and the Board affirmed that ruling.

In the course of its decision, the Board determined that all 11 job applicants (including the two union officials and the one member briefly hired) were "employees" as the Act defines that word. The Board recognized that under well-established law, it made no difference that the 10 members who were simply applicants were never hired. . . . Neither, in the Board's view, did it matter (with respect to the meaning of the word "employee") that the union members intended to try to organize the company if they secured the advertised jobs, nor that the union would pay them while they set about their organizing. The Board then rejected the company's fact-based explanations for its refusals to interview or to retain these 11 "employees," and held that the company had committed "unfair labor practices" by discriminating on the basis of union membership.

The United States Court of Appeals for the Eighth Circuit reversed the Board. It held that the Board had incorrectly interpreted the statutory word "employee." In the court's view, that key word does not cover (and therefore the Act does not protect from anti-union discrimination) those who work for a company while a union simultaneously pays them to organize that company. For this . . . reason, the court refused to enforce the Board's order.

Because other Circuits have interpreted the word "employee" differently, we granted certiorari. . . .

The National Labor Relations Act seeks to improve labor relations in large part by granting specific sets of rights to employers and to employees. This case grows out of a controversy about rights that the Act grants to "employees," namely, rights

> to self-organization, to form, join, or assist labor organizations, to bargain collectively . . . and to engage in other concerted activities for the purpose of collective bargaining or other mutual aid or protection. [§ 7]

We granted certiorari to decide only that part of the controversy that focuses upon the meaning of the word "employee," a key term in the statute, since these rights belong only to those workers who qualify as "employees" as that term is defined in the Act. . . .

The relevant statutory language is the following:

> The term "employee" shall include any employee, and shall not be limited to the employees of a particular employer, unless this subchapter explicitly states otherwise, and shall include any individual whose work has ceased as a consequence of, or in connection with, any current labor dispute or because of any unfair labor practice, and who has not obtained any other regular and substantially equivalent employment, but shall not include any individual employed as an agricultural laborer, or in the domestic service of any family or person at his home, or any individual employed by his parent or spouse, or any individual having the status of an independent contractor, or any individual employed as a supervisor, or any individual employed by an employer subject to the Railway Labor Act, as amended from time to time, or by any other person who is not an employer as herein defined. [§ 2(3)]

We must specifically decide whether the Board may lawfully interpret this language to include company workers who are also paid union organizers. . . .

Several strong general arguments favor the Board's position. For one thing, the Board's decision is consistent with the broad language of the Act itself—language that is broad enough to include those company workers whom a union also pays for organizing. The ordinary dictionary definition of "employee" includes any "person who works for another in return for financial or other compensation. . . ." The phrasing of the Act seems to reiterate the breadth of the ordinary dictionary definition, for it says "[t]he term 'employee' shall include any employee." [§ 2(3)]

For another thing, the Board's broad, literal interpretation of the word "employee" is consistent with several of the Act's purposes, such as protecting "the right of employees to organize for mutual aid without employer interference," and "encouraging and protecting the collective bargaining process." And, insofar as one can infer purpose from congressional reports and floor statements, those sources too are consistent with the Board's broad interpretation of the word. . . .

Finally, at least one other provision of the 1947 Labor Management Relations Act seems specifically to contemplate the possibility that a company's employee might also work for a union. This provision forbids an employer (say, the company) from making payments to a person employed by a union, but simultaneously exempts from that ban wages paid by the company to "any . . . employee of a labor organization, who is also an employee" of the company. [§ 302(c)(1)] If Town & Country is right, there would not seem to be many (or any) human beings to which this last phrase could apply.

Town & Country believes that it can overcome these general considerations, favoring a broad, literal interpretation of the Act, through an argument that rests primarily upon the common law of agency. It first argues that our prior decisions resort to common law principles in defining the term "employee." . . . And it also points out that the Board itself, in its decision, found "no bar to applying common law agency principles to the determination whether a paid union organizer is an 'employee.' "

Town & Country goes on to argue that application of common law agency principles requires an interpretation of "employee" that excludes paid union organizers. . . . It argues that, when the paid union organizer serves the union—at least at certain times in certain ways—the organizer is acting adversely to the company. Indeed, it says, the organizer may stand ready to desert the company upon request by the union, in which case, the union, not the company, would have "the right . . . to control the conduct of the servant." Thus, it concludes, the worker must be the servant (i.e., the "employee") of the union alone. . . . In some cases, there may be a question about whether the Board's departure from the common law of agency with respect to particular questions and in a particular statutory context, renders its interpretation unreasonable. But no such question is presented here since the Board's interpretation of the term "employee" is consistent with the common law.

Town & Country's common law argument fails, quite simply, because, in our view, the Board correctly found that it lacks sufficient support in common law. . . . The Board . . . concluded that service to the union for pay does not "involve abandonment of . . . service" to the company.

And that conclusion seems correct. Common sense suggests that as a worker goes about his ordinary tasks during a working day, say, wiring sockets or laying cable, he or she is subject to the control of the company employer, whether or not the union also pays the worker. The company, the worker, the union, all would expect that to be so. And, that being so, that union and company interests or control might sometimes differ should make no difference. . . . Moreover, union organizers may limit their organizing to nonwork hours. If so, union organizing, when done for pay but during nonwork hours, would seem equivalent to simple moonlighting, a practice wholly consistent with a company's control over its workers as to their assigned duties.

Town & Country's "abandonment" argument is yet weaker insofar as the activity that constitutes an "abandonment," i.e., ordinary union organizing activity, is itself specifically protected by the Act. This is true even if a company perceives those protected activities as disloyal. After all, the employer has no legal right to require that, as part of his or her service to the company, a worker refrain from engaging in protected activity.

Neither are we convinced by the practical considerations that Town & Country adds to its agency law argument. The company refers to a union resolution permitting members to work for nonunion firms, which, the company says, reflects a union effort to "salt" nonunion companies with union members seeking to organize them. . . . It argues that "salts" might try to harm the company, perhaps quitting when the company needs them, perhaps disparaging the company to others, perhaps even sabotaging the firm or its products. Therefore, the company concludes, Congress could not have meant paid union organizers to have been included as "employees" under the Act.

This practical argument suffers from several serious problems. For one thing, nothing in this record suggests that such acts of disloyalty were present, in kind or degree, to the point where the company might lose control over the worker's normal workplace tasks. Certainly the union's resolution contains nothing that suggests, requires, encourages, or condones impermissible or unlawful activity. For another thing, the argument proves too much. If a paid union organizer might quit, leaving a company employer in the lurch, so too might an unpaid organizer, or a worker who has found a better job, or one whose family wants to move elsewhere. And if an overly zealous union organizer might hurt the company through unlawful acts, so might another unpaid zealot (who may know less about the law), or a dissatisfied worker (who may lack an outlet for his grievances). This does not mean they are not "employees."

Further, the law offers alternative remedies for Town & Country's concerns, short of excluding paid or unpaid union organizers from all protection under the Act. For example, a company disturbed by legal but undesirable activity, such as quitting without notice, can offer its employees fixed-term contracts, rather than hiring them "at will" as in the case before us; or it can negotiate with its workers for a notice period. A company faced with unlawful (or possibly unlawful) activity can discipline or dismiss the worker, file a complaint with the Board, or notify law enforcement authorities. . . .

. . . We hold only that the Board's construction of the word "employee" is lawful; that term does not exclude paid union organizers.

For these reasons, the judgment of the Court of Appeals is vacated, and the case is remanded for further proceedings consistent with this opinion.

It is so ordered.

Case Questions

1. What is the union's purpose in seeking to have its organizers employed by Town & Country?
2. What arguments does Town & Country make to support its position that the union organizers should not be considered "employees" under the NLRA?
3. How does the Court deal with Town & Country's arguments? Does the Court suggest other ways that Town & Country might address its concerns? Explain.

Jurisdiction over Labor Organizations

Section 2(5) of the National Labor Relations Act defines *labor organization* as "any organization of any kind, or any agency or employee representation committee or plan, in which employees participate and which exists for the purpose, in whole or in part, of dealing with employers concerning grievances, labor disputes, wages, rates of pay, hours of employment, or conditions of work."

NLRB and Supreme Court decisions have held that the words "dealing with" are broad enough to encompass relationships that fall short of collective bargaining. For example, in *NLRB v. Cabot Carbon* [360 U.S. 203 (1959)], the Supreme Court held that the act encompassed employee committees that functioned merely to discuss with management, but not bargain over, such matters of mutual interest as grievances, seniority, and working conditions. There is also case law to suggest that a single individual cannot be considered a labor organization "in any literal sense." See *Bonnaz v. NLRB* [230 F.2d 47 (D.C. Cir. 1956)].

PREEMPTION AND THE NRLA

Because of the broad reach of NLRB jurisdiction under the federal commerce power, it is important to consider whether the states have any authority to legislate regarding labor relations in the private sector. Although state laws that conflict with federal laws are void under the supremacy clause of Article VI of the Constitution, the Supreme Court has consistently held that states may regulate activities involving interstate commerce where such regulation is pursuant to a valid state purpose. In such situations, the states have concurrent jurisdiction with the federal government: The regulated firm or activity is subject to both the state and federal regulations. But where an activity is characterized by pervasive federal regulation, the Supreme Court has held that Congress has, under the supremacy clause powers, "occupied the field" so that the federal law preempts any state regulation. (One example of such preemption is the regulation of radio and television broadcasting by the Federal Communications Commission.) Has Congress, through the enactment of the National Labor Relations Act, preempted state regulation of private sector labor disputes?

The Supreme Court tried to answer this question in two leading decisions. In *San Diego Building Trades Council v. Garmon* [359 U.S. 236 (1959)], the Supreme Court held that state and federal district courts are deprived of jurisdiction over conduct that is "arguably subject" to Section 7 or Section 9 of the NLRA. More recently, in *Sears Roebuck v. San Diego County District Council of Carpenters* [436 U.S. 180 (1978)], the Supreme Court held that state courts may deal with matters arising out of a labor dispute when the issue presented to the state court is not the same as that which would be before the NLRB. The Court said it would consider the nature of the particular state interests being asserted and the effect on national labor policies of allowing the state court to proceed. *Sears* involved a trespassing charge filed against picketing by the carpenters; no unfair practice charges were filed with the NLRB by either party to the dispute. The Court upheld the right of the state court to order the picketers to stop trespassing on Sears's property, recognizing that Congress did not preempt all state regulation of matters growing out of a labor dispute.

In *Wisconsin Dept. of Industry, Labor & Human Relations v. Gould* [475 U.S. 282 (1986)], the Supreme Court held that the NLRA preempted a Wisconsin law that barred any firm violating the NLRA three times within five years from doing business with the state; the Court held that the law sought to supplement the sanctions for violations of the NLRA and so was in conflict with the NLRB's comprehensive regulation of industrial relations.

The Supreme Court summarized the principles of the preemption of state laws by federal labor relations law in the 1993 case of *Building & Construction Trades Council of the Met. Dist. v. Assoc. Builders and Contractors of Mass.* [507 U.S. 218], which upheld a state regulation requiring contractors working on public contracts to abide by the terms of a collective agreement. The Court noted that federal labor relations law preempts state regulation of activities that are protected by Section 7 or are defined as unfair labor practices by the NLRA (as in *San Diego Building Trades v. Garmon*), and state regulation of areas left to the control of market and economic forces (as in *Wisconsin Dept. of Industry, Labor & Human Relations v. Gould*).

President Clinton's Executive Order No. 12954 disqualified firms that hired permanent replacement workers during lawful strikes from federal contracts over

$100,000. This order, however, was held to be preempted by the NRLA, which allows employers to hire permanent replacements in economic strikes, *Chamber of Commerce v. Reich* [74 F.3d 1322 (D.C. Cir. 1996), *rehearing denied* 83 F.3d 439 (D.C. Cir. 1996)].

Federal legislation may also expressly preserve the right of the states to regulate activities. For example, Section 103 of the Labor-Management Reporting and Disclosure Act, dealing with internal union affairs, states that "Nothing contained in this title shall limit the rights and remedies of any member of a labor organization under any State . . . law or before any court or other tribunal. . . ." Because of this provision, states are free to legislate greater protection for union members vis-à-vis their unions, and state courts are free to hear suits that may arise under such laws.

SUMMARY

- The National Labor Relations Act (NRLA) regulates private sector labor relations; the NLRA is administered by the National Labor Relations Board (NLRB). The NLRA defines the basic rights of employees and prohibits actions by employers or unions that interfere with or restrict those rights—defined as unfair labor practices. The NLRB adjudicates complaints of unfair labor practices under the NLRA and conducts representation elections.
- The NLRA excludes public sector employers, railroads, and airlines subject to the Railway Labor Act from its definition of employer; and the NLRB has adopted guidelines to define the scope of its jurisdiction over private sector employers. The NRLA also excludes certain employees from the act's coverage: agricultural laborers, persons employed as domestics in the homes of others, individuals employed by parents or spouses, independent contractors, supervisors, and employees of Railway Labor Act employers. In addition to the statutory exclusions, the courts have excluded managerial employees and confidential employees.
- The NLRA preempts state laws that purport to regulate conduct protected by or prohibited by the NLRA and that seek to regulate areas left by the NLRA to the market and economic forces.

QUESTIONS

1. What were the major provisions of the Wagner Act? What were the effects of this act?
2. What factors led to the passage of the Taft-Hartley Act? What were the effects of this act?
3. Describe the structural organization of the National Labor Relations Board. What are the functions of the board's various branches?
4. Describe the NLRB procedures for handling unfair labor practice complaints.
5. What is the effect of the NLRB jurisdictional guidelines? What role do states have in regulating labor relations?
6. Which employers are exempt from NLRA coverage? Which employers are covered by the NLRA?
7. Which employees are excluded from NLRA coverage?

8. What is an independent contractor? What test does the NLRA use to determine whether employees are supervisors?
9. What is the test for managerial employees? What is the test for confidential employees?
10. What is the effect of the exclusion of supervisory employees? What is the effect of the exclusion of confidential employees?

CASE PROBLEMS

1. The legislature of West Virginia enacted a law in 1983 (effective July 1, 1984) requiring that at least 40 percent of the board of directors of all nonprofit and local government hospitals in the state be composed of an equal proportion of "consumer representatives" from "small businesses, organized labor, elderly persons, and persons whose income is less than the national median income." The American Hospital Association joined with a number of West Virginia hospitals in seeking an injunction against enforcement of the law and a declaratory judgment that, among other things, the law interfered with bargaining rights between the hospitals and their employees and was therefore preempted by federal labor law.

   If you were arguing for the plaintiff hospitals, how would you contend that this West Virginia law might interfere with the collective-bargaining relationship? If you were the federal judge hearing the case, how would you rule and why? See *American Hospital Association v. Hansbarger* [600 F. Supp. 465, 118 L.R.R.M. 2389 (N.D. W.Va. 1984)].

2. Spring Valley Farms, Inc. supplied poultry feed to farmers who raised broiler and egg-laying poultry. Sarah F. Jones had the title of feed delivery manager with the company in Cullman, Alabama, and she dispatched the drivers who delivered the feed. Drivers could earn more money on "long hauls" (more than fifty miles from the mill) than on "short hauls." Therefore, Spring Valley Farms instructed Jones to "equalize" the number of long and short hauls so that all drivers would earn approximately the same wages. The company also instructed her to work the drivers as close to forty hours per week as possible and then to "knock them off" by seniority. It was left to Jones's discretion to devise methods for accomplishing these objectives.

   Does Spring Valley Farms fall under the jurisdiction of the NLRB? Is Jones as manager excluded from the Board's jurisdiction? See *Spring Valley Farms* [272 NLRB No. 205, 118 L.R.R.M. 1015 (1984)].

3. In 1976, the citizens of New Jersey amended their state constitution to permit the legislative authorization of casino gambling in Atlantic City. Determined to prevent the infiltration of organized crime into its nascent casino industry, the New Jersey legislature enacted the Casino Control Act, which provides for the comprehensive regulation of casino gambling, including the regulation of unions representing industry employees. Sections 86 and 93 of the act specifically impose certain qualification criteria on officials of labor organizations representing casino industry employees. (Section 86, for example, contains a list of crimes, conviction of which disqualifies a union officer from representing casino employees.) A hotel employees' union challenged the state law, arguing that it was preempted by the NLRA, which gives employees the right to select collective-bargaining representatives of their own choosing. The case reached the U.S. Supreme Court.

   How should the Supreme Court have ruled? Why? See *Brown v. Hotel Employees Local 54* [468 U.S. 491, 116 L.R.R.M. 2921 (1984)].

4. The Volunteers of America (VOA) is a religious movement founded in New York City in 1896. Its purpose is "to reach and uplift all segments of the population and to bring them to a knowledge of God." The Denver Post of the VOA, founded in 1898, is an unincorporated association operated under the direction of the national society. It maintains three chapels in the Denver area, at which it conducts regular religious services and Bible study groups. The VOA also operates a number of social programs in Denver, including temporary care, shelter, and counseling centers for women and children.

   The United Nurses, Professionals and Health Care Employees Union filed a petition with the NLRB to represent the counselors at these shelters. The VOA argued it was not subject to the board's jurisdiction because (1) the First Amendment to the U.S. Constitution precludes NLRB jurisdiction over a religious organization, and (2) it received partial funding from the city and county governments under contracts specifying the services it was to perform so that the government, not the VOA, was the true employer. The case reached the Tenth Circuit Court of Appeals.

   How should the court have ruled on these two arguments? See *Denver Post of VOA v. NLRB* [732 F.2d 769 (10th Cir. 1984)] and *Aramark Corp. v. NLRB* [179 F.3d 872 (10th Cir. 1999)].

5. The *Alcoa Seaprobe* was a U.S. flagged ocean-going vessel engaged in offshore geophysical and geotechnical research. While berthed in Woods Hole, Massachusetts, its owner, Alcoa Marine Corporation (a Delaware corporation headquartered in Houston, Texas), had contracted with Brazil's national oil company to use *Alcoa Seaprobe* for offshore exploration of Brazil's continental shelf. When Alcoa sent the *Seaprobe* to Brazil, it did not intend to return the vessel to the United States.

   The Masters, Mates & Pilots Union (International Longshoremen) filed a petition to represent the crew of *Alcoa Seaprobe*. Alcoa Marine Corporation argued that since *Seaprobe* was not expected to operate in U.S. territorial waters, the NLRA did not apply.

   How should the NLRB have ruled? See *Alcoa Marine Corp.* [240 NLRB No. 18, 100 L.R.R.M. 1433 (1979)].

6. National Detective Agencies, Inc., of Washington, D.C., provided security officers to various clients in the District of Columbia. Among these clients was the Inter-American Development Bank, "an international economic organization whose purpose is to aid in the economic development and growth of its member nations, who are primarily members of the Organization of American States." The Federation of Special Police petitioned the NLRB to represent National's employees, including those who worked at the bank.

   National argued that the bank could require National to issue orders and regulations to its guards and to remove any guard the bank considered unsatisfactory. The bank had the right to interview all job applicants and to suggest wage scales. Consequently, National argued, the bank was a joint employer of the guards and, as an international organization, enjoyed "sovereign immunity" from NLRA jurisdiction. Therefore, these guards should not be included in the proposed bargaining unit.

   How do you think the NLRB ruled on this argument? Is this case conceptually distinguishable from the *Alcoa Seaprobe* case in problem 5? See *National Detective Agencies* [237 NLRB No. 72, 99 L.R.R.M. 1007 (1978)].

7. Burman was employed as a production supervisor at Vincow, Inc. until he was fired because his brother and cousin had led a union organizing campaign among the workers at Vincow. Burman filed an unfair labor practice complaint with the NLRB, alleging that his discharge was a violation of Section 8(a)(1). Subsequent to the firing of Burman, Vincow recognized the union as the exclusive bargaining agent of its employees.

How should the NLRB rule on Burman's complaint? Explain your answer. See *Kenrich Petrochemicals v. NLRB* [893 F.2d 1468 (3d Cir. 1990)].

8. The faculty at the Universidad Central de Bayamon in Puerto Rico seek to unionize in order to bargain collectively with the university over wages, working conditions, and so on. The university, which describes itself as a "Catholic-oriented civil institution," is governed by a board of trustees, of whom a majority are to be members of the Dominican religious order.

Is the Universidad subject to NLRB jurisdiction, or is it exempt under the Catholic Bishop doctrine? See *Universidad Central de Bayamon* [273 NLRB No. 138 (1984); 778 F.2d 906 (1st Cir.) *rev'd. on rehearing,* 793 F.2d 383 (1985)].

9. Callaghan, an employee of Smith Transportation, is one of the leaders of an effort to unionize the Smith employees. Biggins, the personnel manager of Smith, suspects Callaghan is involved in the organizing campaign and decides to fire him. Callaghan is given notice on January 15, 2001, that his employment will be terminated on January 31, 2001. On July 20, 2001, Callaghan files a complaint with the appropriate regional office of the NLRB, alleging that he was fired in violation of Sections 8(a)1 and 3 of the NLRA. Smith Transportation argues that the complaint was not filed within the required six-month limitations period.

Was the complaint filed in a timely fashion? Does the time limit run from when the employee is notified of the impending discharge or from when the discharge becomes effective? See *United States Postal Service* [271 NLRB No. 61, 116 L.R.R.M. 1417 (1984)].

10. Speedy Clean Service, Inc. provides janitorial services for office buildings; a number of its employees are Hispanics who have entered the United States illegally. When several employees try to organize a union to represent them, Speedy Clean fires all of its workers. The discharged employees file unfair labor practice charges with the NLRB; the employer argues that the illegal aliens are not entitled to protection under the act.

Are illegal aliens included within the definition of "employee" under Section 2(3)? Explain your answer.

INTERNET EXERCISE

Which office of the NLRB has jurisdiction over employers in your vicinity? Whom would you contact to file a charge or petition with the NLRB? Using the NLRB's Web site at **http://www.nlrb.gov**, find the address and phone number of the NLRB office nearest to you. Who is the current chairman of the NLRB? Who is the General Counsel of the NLRB? When do their terms expire?

INFOTRAC KEYWORDS

http://www.infotrac-college.com

NLRB, unfair labor practices

14 CHAPTER

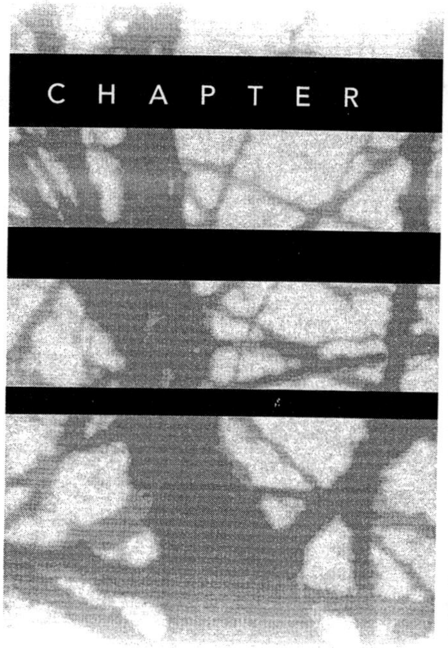

THE UNIONIZATION PROCESS

In the preceding chapter, we discussed briefly the National Labor Relations Board's (NLRB) administrative structure and procedures in representation (R) cases. In this chapter, we consider in greater detail the mechanisms created by the board for determining whether a company's employees will be represented by a union for purposes of collective bargaining. (The Railway Labor Act, which covers companies and employees in the railroad and airline industries, contains provisions that are analogous in many respects to the National Labor Relations Act [NLRA] procedures discussed in this chapter.)

EXCLUSIVE BARGAINING REPRESENTATIVE

We have seen that Section 7 of the NLRA entitles employees "to bargain collectively through representatives of their own choosing." Section 9(a) adds that

> Representatives designated or selected for the purposes of collective bargaining by the majority of the employees in a unit appropriate for such purposes, shall be the exclusive representatives of all the employees in such unit for the purposes of collective bargaining in respect to rates of pay, wages, hours of employment, or other conditions of employment.

The position of the union as exclusive bargaining agent supersedes any individual contracts of employment made between the employer and the unit employees. Any dealings with individual unit employees must be in accordance with the collective-bargaining agreement.

> *See*
> **http://www4.law.cornell.edu/uscode/29/159.html**
> *for the NLRA text on representatives and elections.*

The Taft-Hartley Act added some protection for minority factions within bargaining units by adding to Section 9(a) the stipulation that

> any individual or a group of employees shall have the right at any time to present grievances to their employer and to have such grievances adjusted, without the intervention of the bargaining representative, as long as the adjustment is not inconsistent with the terms of a collective-bargaining contract . . . then in effect.

The extent to which this provision allows the employer to deal with individual employee grievances, and its effect on the union's position as exclusive bargaining agent, will be discussed in Chapter 16.

EMPLOYEES' CHOICE OF BARGAINING AGENT

Although the most common method of determining the employees' choice of a bargaining representative is to hold a secret ballot election, the NLRA does not require such procedures. Employers confronted by a union claiming to have the support of a majority of their employees may recognize the union as the exclusive bargaining agent for those employees. Section 9(a) requires only that the union, in order to become the exclusive bargaining agent, be designated or selected by a majority of the employees. It does not require that an election be held to determine employee choice. The propriety of this method of recognition, called a voluntary recognition, is well established, provided that the employer has no reasonable doubt of the employees' preference and that recognition is not granted for the purpose of assisting one particular union at the expense of another seeking to represent the same employees.

Bargaining status achieved through a voluntary recognition imposes on the employer the duty to bargain with the union in good faith, just the same as with a union victory in a representation election conducted by the board. But the representation election method has several advantages over the voluntary recognition method. The representation election procedures involve the determination of the bargaining unit—that is, which of the employer's workers should be grouped together for purposes of representation and bargaining. Following a union victory in an election, the employer is obligated to recognize and bargain with the union for at least twelve months following the election. No petitions seeking a new representation (or decertification) election can be filed for that unit of employees during the twelve-month period. For a voluntary recognition, the employer is obligated to recognize and bargain with the union only for a "reasonable length" of time, unless a collective-bargaining agreement is agreed upon. In the absence of an agreement, the voluntary recognition does not prevent the filing of a petition seeking a representation election for that same group of employees. In addition, an employer who voluntarily recognizes a union claiming to have majority support commits an unfair labor practice if the union does not actually have the support of a majority of the employees in the bargaining unit. Thus, a representation election conducted by the board is the method of recognition preferred by the parties in most cases.

Just as filing a charge initiates the administrative process in an unfair labor practice (C) case, so too a petition from an interested party is needed to initiate a board-sponsored election under Section 9(c)(1)(A). Any employee, group of employees, or labor organization can file such a petition seeking a representation election or a decertification election on behalf of the employees as a whole (see Figure 14.1). An employer is entitled to file a petition only after one or more individuals or unions present that employer with a claim for recognition as the bargaining representative according to Section 9(c)(1)(B).

If it is a union or employees who file a petition with the appropriate regional office of the board, the NLRB will not proceed with the election until the petitioning union or employee group presents evidence that at least 30 percent of the employee group support the election request. (If an employer files the petition under the circumstances outlined above, this rule does not apply.) Usually, this showing of support is reflected in signed and dated authorization cards obtained by the union from the individual employees. These cards may simply state that the signatories desire an election to be held, or they may state that the signing employee authorizes the union to be his or her bargaining representative. Other acceptable showings of employee interest can include a letter or similar informal document bearing a list of signatures and applications for union membership.

Forty-Eight-Hour Rule
NLRB requirement that a party filing a petition for a representation election must provide evidence to support the petition within 48 hours of the filing.

Under the board's **forty-eight-hour rule,** an employer who files a petition must submit to the regional office proof of a union's recognition demand within two days of filing the petition. Likewise, a petitioning union or employee group has forty-eight hours after filing in which to proffer authorization cards or other proof of 30 percent employee support for the requested election. Upon the docketing (logging in) of a petition, a written notification of its filing is sent by the regional director to the employer and any labor organizations claiming to represent any employees in the proposed unit or known to have an interest in the case's disposition. Employers are asked to submit a payroll list covering the proposed bargaining unit, data showing the nature and volume of the company's business for jurisdictional purposes, and a statement of company position on the appropriateness of the requested bargaining unit.

The new R case is then assigned to a board agent, who investigates to determine whether the following conditions exist:

1. The employer's operations affect commerce within the act's meaning.
2. A question about representation really exists (that is, no union presently represents the employees and is shielded by the election bar rule, or some similar impediment to the election).
3. The proposed bargaining unit is appropriate.
4. The petitioning union, if any, has garnered a 30 percent showing of interest among the employees.

If the agent finds some impediment to an election, the regional director can dismiss the petition. The decision to dismiss can be appealed to the board in Washington, D.C. Conversely, the petitioning party may choose to withdraw the petition. The usual penalty for withdrawal is imposition of a six-month waiting

FORM EXEMPT UNDER 44 U.S.C. 3512

FORM NLRB-502
(3-96)

UNITED STATES GOVERNMENT
NATIONAL LABOR RELATIONS BOARD
PETITION

DO NOT WRITE IN THIS SPACE	
Case No.	Date Filed

INSTRUCTIONS: Submit an original and 4 copies of this Petition to the NLRB Regional Office in the Region in which the employer concerned is located. If more space is required for any one item, attach additional sheets, numbering item accordingly.

The Petitioner alleges that the following circumstances exist and requests that the National Labor Relations Board proceed under its proper authority pursuant to Section 9 of the National Labor Relations Act.

1. **PURPOSE OF THIS PETITION** *(If box RC, RM, or RD is checked and a charge under Section 8(b)(7) of the Act has been filed involving the Employer named herein, the statement following the description of the type of petition shall not be deemed made.)* **(Check One)**

☐ **RC-CERTIFICATION OF REPRESENTATIVE** - A substantial number of employees wish to be represented for purposes of collective bargaining by Petitioner and Petitioner desires to be certified as representative of the employees.

☐ **RM-REPRESENTATION (EMPLOYER PETITION)** - One or more individuals or labor organizations have presented a claim to Petitioner to be recognized as the representative of employees of Petitioner.

☐ **RD-DECERTIFICATION (REMOVAL OF REPRESENTATIVE)** - A substantial number of employees assert that the certified or currently recognized bargaining representative is no longer their representative.

☐ **UD-WITHDRAWAL OF UNION SHOP AUTHORITY (REMOVAL OF OBLIGATION TO PAY DUES)** - Thirty percent (30%) or more of employees in a bargaining unit covered by an agreement between their employer and a labor organization desire that such authority be rescinded.

☐ **UC-UNIT CLARIFICATION** - A labor organization is currently recognized by Employer, but Petitioner seeks clarification of placement of certain employees: *(Check one)* ☐ In unit not previously certified. ☐ In unit previously certified in Case No. ____________

☐ **AC-AMENDMENT OF CERTIFICATION** - Petitioner seeks amendment of certification issued in Case No. ____________
Attach statement describing the specific amendment sought.

2. Name of Employer	Employer Representative to contact	Telephone Number
3. Address(es) of Establishment(s) involved *(Street and number, city, State, ZIP code)*		Telecopier Number (Fax)
4a. Type of Establishment *(Factory, mine, wholesaler, etc.)*	4b. Identify principal product or service	

5. Unit involved *(In UC petition, describe present bargaining unit and attached description of proposed clarification.)*	6a. Number of Employees in Unit:
Included	Present
	Proposed *(By UC/AC)*
Excluded	6b. Is this petition supported by 30% or more of the employees in the unit?* ☐ Yes ☐ No *Not applicable in RM, UC, and AC

(If you have checked box RC in 1 above, check and complete EITHER item 7a or 7b, whichever is applicable.)

7a. ☐ Request for recognition as Bargaining Representative was made on *(Date)* ____________ and Employer declined recognition on or about *(Date)* ____________ *(If no reply received, so state.)*

7b. ☐ Petitioner is currently recognized as Bargaining Representative and desires certification under the Act.

8. Name of Recognized or Certified Bargaining Agent *(If none, so state.)*	Affiliation
Address, Telephone No. and Telecopier No. (Fax)	Date of Recognition or Certification

9. Expiration Date of Current Contract. If any *(Month, Day, Year)*	10. If you have checked box UD in 1 above, show here the date of execution of agreement granting union shop *(Month, Day, and Year)*
11a. Is there now a strike or picketing at the Employer's establishment(s) involved? Yes ______ No ______	11b. If so, approximately how many employees are participating?

11c. The Employer has been picketed by or on behalf of *(Insert Name)* ____________, a labor organization, of *(Insert Address)* ____________ Since *(Month, Day, Year)* ____________

12. Organizations or individuals other than Petitioner *(and other than those named in items 8 and 11c)*, which have claimed recognition as representatives and other organizations and individuals known to have a representative interest in any employees in unit described in item 5 above. *(If none, so state.)*

Name	Affiliation	Address	Date of Claim
			Telecopier No. (Fax)

13. Full name of party filing petition (If labor organization, give full name, including local name and number)

14a. Address *(street and number, city, state, and ZIP code)*	14b. Telephone No.
	14c. Telecopier No. (Fax)

15. Full name of national or international labor organization of which it is an affiliate or constituent unit *(to be filled in when petition is filed by a labor organization)*

I declare that I have read the above petition and that the statements are true to the best of my knowledge and belief.

Name *(Print)*	Signature	Title *(if any)*
Address *(street and number, city, state, and ZIP code)*		Telephone No.
		Telecopier No. (Fax)

WILLFUL FALSE STATEMENTS ON THIS PETITION CAN BE PUNISHED BY FINE AND IMPRISONMENT (U.S. CODE, TITLE 18, SECTION 1001)

FIGURE 14.1 Petition to initiate NLRB election. (Source: NLRB web site at **http://www.nlrb.gov**. Click on Forms link.)

period before the same party can petition again. (If the employer has submitted the petition, the named union may disclaim interest, also leading to dismissal.)

If the petition survives this initial investigation, the parties may still require the resolution of issues raised by the petition. Questions such as the definition of the bargaining unit, the eligibility of certain employees to participate in the election, and the number of polling places need to be settled prior to holding the election. The parties may agree to waive their rights to a hearing on these issues and proceed to a **consent election.** In so doing, they may either agree that all rulings of the regional director on these questions are final and binding, or they may reserve the right to appeal the regional director's decisions to the board.

Consent Election
Election conducted by the regional office giving the regional director final authority over any disputes.

If the parties fail to agree on some of these issues and have not agreed to a consent election, then a representation hearing will be held before a presiding officer, who may be a board attorney, field examiner, or ALJ. The act does not prescribe rules of evidence to be used in this proceeding (in contrast to the C case hearing); indeed, the board's rules and regulations state that federal court rules of evidence shall not be controlling.

A second union, with a 10 percent showing of interest from among the employees, is entitled to intervene and participate in the hearing. Such an intervention can also block a consent election and compel a hearing to take place.

Shortly after the hearing, the hearing officer will submit a report to the director, who will then render a decision either to hold an election or to dismiss the petition. This decision can be appealed by a party to the board in Washington only on the following grounds:

- A board legal precedent was not followed or should be reconsidered.
- A substantial factual issue is clearly erroneous in the record.
- The conduct of the hearing was prejudicial to the appealing party.

The board will act expeditiously on the appeal. Meanwhile, the regional director will proceed with plans for the election, which usually occurs twenty-five to thirty days after it has been ordered.

http://www4.law.cornell.edu/uscode/29/481.html
contains a description of the terms of office and election procedures.

RULES THAT BAR HOLDING AN ELECTION

The philosophy of the NLRB and the courts is that a board-sponsored election is a serious step, which the affected employees should not be permitted to disavow or overrule frivolously or hastily. Furthermore, the newly certified bargaining agent should be given a reasonable opportunity to fulfill its mandate by successfully negotiating a collective-bargaining agreement with the company. If the board failed to protect the successfully elected bargaining representative from worker fickleness or rival union challenges, the employer would be encouraged to avoid timely and sincere bargaining in an effort to erode the union's support before an agreement is reached. The board has, therefore, fashioned several election bar rules.

Contract Bar Rule
A written labor contract bars an election during the life of the bargaining agreement, subject to the "open season" exception.

Under the **contract bar rule,** a written labor contract—signed and binding on the parties and dealing with substantial terms and conditions of employment—bars an election among the affected bargaining unit during the life of that bargaining agreement. This rule has two exceptions. First, the board provides a window, or "open season," during which a rival union can offer its challenge by filing an election petition. This window is open between the ninetieth day and sixtieth day prior to the expiration of the current collective-bargaining agreement. The rationale here is that a rival union should not be completely prevented from filing an election petition; otherwise, the employer and incumbent union could continually bargain new contracts regardless of whether the employees wished to continue to be represented by the incumbent union.

If no new petition is filed during the open-season period, then the last sixty days of the contract provide a period during which the parties can negotiate a new agreement insulated from any outside challenges. If a petition is filed during this insulated period, it will be dismissed as untimely. In the event that the employer and the incumbent union fail to reach a new agreement and the old agreement expires, then petitions may be filed anytime after the expiration of the existing agreement.

The second exception to the contract bar rule is that a contract for longer than three years will operate only as a bar to an election for three years. In the *American Seating Co.* decision [106 NLRB 250 (1953)], the board held that an agreement of excessive duration cannot be used to preclude challenges to the incumbent union indefinitely. Therefore, any contract longer than three years duration will be treated as if it were three years long for the purposes of filing petitions; that is, the open-season period would occur between the ninetieth and the sixtieth day prior to the end of the third year of the agreement.

Section 9(C)(3) of the NLRA provides that when a valid election has been held in a bargaining unit, no new election can be held for a twelve-month period for that unit or any subdivision of the unit. When the employees of a unit have voted not to be represented by a union, no other union may file for an election for those employees for twelve months. By the same token, when a union has been certified as the winner of the election, it is free from challenge to its status for at least twelve months. This twelve-month period usually runs from the date of certification, but when an employer refuses to bargain with the certified union, the board may extend the period to twelve months from when good-faith bargaining actually commences. The twelve-month period under Section 9(C)(3) applies only when an election has been held. When an employer has voluntarily recognized a union, the board will allow a "reasonable time" for the parties to reach an agreement before it will accept election petitions from rival unions. Although a reasonable time may vary depending on the circumstances of each specific case, it may be less than twelve months.

DEFINING THE APPROPRIATE BARGAINING UNIT

Bargaining Unit
Group of employees being represented by a union.

The **bargaining unit** is a concept central to labor relations under both the Railway Labor Act and the National Labor Relations Act. The bargaining unit is the basic constituency of the labor union; it is the group of employees for which the union seeks to acquire recognition as bargaining agent and to negotiate regarding employment conditions. In order for collective bargaining to produce results fair

ETHICAL DILEMMA: EMPLOYEE UNION SUPPORT TO SURVEY OR NOT TO SURVEY?

You are the human resource manager at Southwestco, a small manufacturing company. The office clerical and technical employees at Southwestco are not unionized, but the production employees are. You have heard rumors that some clerical and technical employees are starting a campaign to become unionized, and several employees have specifically told you that they don't want to join. One morning, you receive a letter via certified mail from the union local representing the production workers. The union now claims to have the support of an overwhelming majority of the office clerical and technical employees and requests that the company recognize the union as the exclusive bargaining representative for all clerical and technical employees. How should you respond to the union demand?

You are considering whether to conduct a survey of the clerical and technical employees to determine whether a majority of them support the union. What arguments can you make in favor of conducting such a survey? What arguments can you make against it? Prepare a memo for the board of directors recommending (1) a response to the union demand for recognition and (2) whether or not to conduct a survey of the employees. Explain and support your positions.

to both sides, it is essential that the bargaining unit be defined appropriately. The bargaining unit should encompass all employees who share a community of interests regarding working conditions. It should not be so broad as to include divergent or antagonistic interests. Nor should it submerge the interests of a small yet well-defined group of employees within the larger unit.

Section 9(b) of the NLRA provides that the definition of an appropriate bargaining unit is a matter left to the board's discretion. What constitutes an appropriate bargaining unit is the most commonly disputed issue in representative case hearings. It is also one of the most complex and difficult questions for the board and the courts to resolve. The Supreme Court in *Packard Motor Car v. NLRB* [330 U.S. 485 (1947)] observed that "The issue as to what unit is appropriate is one for which no absolute rule of law is laid down by statute. . . . The decision of the Board, if not final, is rarely to be disturbed." This statement is a bit misleading because Section 9(b) of the NLRA does set out some guidelines for the board in determining the appropriate unit. Section 9(b) states that the goal in defining a bargaining unit is to "assure the employees the fullest freedom in exercising the rights guaranteed by this Act." Section 9(b) also contains the following five provisions:

1. The options open to the board in determining a bargaining unit include an employerwide unit, a craft unit, a single-plant unit, or a subdivision thereof.
2. The unit cannot contain both professional employees [as defined by Section 2(12) of the act] and nonprofessional employees, unless a majority of the professional employees have voted to be included in the unit.
3. A craft unit cannot be found to be inappropriate simply on the ground that a different unit (e.g., a plantwide unit) was established by a previous board

determination, unless a majority of the employees in the proposed craft unit vote against representation in such a separate craft unit.

4. A unit including nonguard or security employees cannot include plant guards or security personnel; conversely, a union representing plant guards cannot be certified if it also includes workers other than guards as members or if it is directly or indirectly affiliated with a union representing persons other than guards.[1]
5. The extent to which employees have already been organized at the time of the filing of the election petition is not to be controlling of the board's definition of the appropriate bargaining unit.

In addition to the statutory commands, the board has fashioned a number of other factors to be considered in determining the appropriate unit. Those factors include the following:

- the community of interest of included employees concerning wages, hours, working conditions, the nature of duties performed, and the skills, training, or qualifications required;
- geographical and physical proximity of included workers;
- any history of prior collective bargaining tending to prove that a workable relationship exists or can exist between the employer and the proposed unit;
- similarity of the unit to the employer's administrative or territorial divisions, the functional integration of the company's operations, and the frequency of employee interchange;
- the desires of the employees concerning the bargaining unit, such as might be determined through a secret ballot among workers who have the statutory prerogative of choosing between a plantwide unit or a separate craft unit. (This right to self-determination by election is referred to as the *Globe* doctrine, after the case in which the standards for such elections were set out, *Globe Machine and Stamping* [3 NLRB 294 (1937)] pursuant to Section 9(b)(2) of the act.)

The NLRB has ruled that temporary employees are to be included in the same bargaining unit with permanent employees when the temporary employees are jointly employed by the employer and the firm supplying the temporary employees, *M. B. Sturgis, Inc.* [331 NLRB No. 173 (Aug. 25, 2000)] and *Tree of Life, Inc. d/b/a Gourmet Award Foods* [336 NLRB No. 77 (2001)].

The following case illustrates the NLRB's application of the "community of interest" test, where the union seeks to include both office clerical workers and outside field workers.

---

[1]By requiring that guards and security personnel be organized in a separate bargaining unit and separate unions, Congress appears to hold the view that the normal duties of plant guards can create conflicts of interest with their union loyalties. Section 9(b) prohibits the NLRB from certifying a "mixed" bargaining unit—one containing guards and nonguards—but it does not preclude voluntary recognition of a union representing a mixed unit, *General Service Employees Union, Local No. 73 v. NLRB* [230 F.3d 909 (7th Cir. 2000)].

Syracuse University and Local 200A, Service Employees Int. Union

325 NLRB No. 15 (NLRB 1997)

Decision on Review and Order

By Chairman Gould and Members Fox and Higgins

[The employer, Syracuse University, sought, and the NLRB granted, review of the decision of the Regional Director to direct an election in a bargaining unit of the university's parking service employees, including parking lot attendants, parking enforcement officers, and parking control officers, including the Employer's Parking and Transit Service department (Parking Service) clerical employees. The decision of the Regional Director follows:]

Decision and Direction of Election

. . . The Employer is a large, private, nonprofit institution of higher learning in Syracuse, New York. The Petitioner [union] . . . seeks to represent all regularly scheduled full-time and part-time employees, including clerical employees, in the Parking Services Department, excluding all temporary employees, confidential employees, supervisors, and guards as defined in the Act, and all other employees. In this regard, the record reveals that the Parking and Transit Services department, hereinafter called Parking Services, consists of at least 26 field staff, having the job titles of parking lot attendants and parking control officers, and 7 office staff, who are classified as office coordinators and data coordinators. . . .

The Parking Services department is engaged in overseeing vehicular parking access on the Employer's facility and providing shuttle services to students, faculty, staff, and visitors for academic purposes throughout the campus, including the Carrier Dome.

Parking Services clerical employees work on the Employer's South campus in the Skytop office building, where the Parking Services' office and most of the Employer's other administrative offices are situated. Parking Services field staff mainly conduct their work duties on the Employer's North (main) campus where they report to a trailer at the Veterans Administration Hospital parking lot and where most of the Employer's 100–150 parking lots and 11,000 parking spaces are located. . . .

. . . The Employer contends that the Parking Services field employees referred to as enforcement officers are guards as defined in Section 9(b)(3) of the Act, inasmuch as their principal responsibilities involve issuing tickets and tow warnings for parking violations. Based on such work duties, the Employer argues that enforcement officers, thus, enforce rules against employees and other persons to protect the Employer's property. In this regard, the record reveals that the duties of Parking Services field employees referred to as enforcement officers include issuing parking tickets and tow warnings. However, the record discloses that other parking lot attendants and parking control officers also issue parking tickets and tow warnings, but are not claimed by the Employer to be guards. Thus, the Employer essentially concedes that such job duty, standing alone, does not render an employee a statutory guard. . . . I conclude that Parking Services field employees referred to as enforcement officers are not statutory guards. Thus, I conclude that they share a community of interest with the petitioned-for unit employees. I shall, therefore, include Parking Services field employees referred to as enforcement officers in the bargaining unit found appropriate herein and find them eligible to vote in the election to be directed.

The Petitioner [union] maintains that Parking Services clerical employees are plant (service) clericals who share a community of interest with Parking Services field employees and should, therefore, be included in the bargaining unit found appropriate herein. [T]he Employer argues that Parking Services clerical employees are office clericals who, pursuant to Board precedent, are not to be included in other bargaining units and, thereby, should be excluded from the bargaining unit found appropriate herein. In this regard, the Employer contends that Parking Services clerical employees have a community of interest with office clerical employees in the Employer's other numerous departments.

The Board has generally excluded office clericals from a production and maintenance unit. However, plant clerical employees are customarily included in a production and maintenance bargaining unit because they generally share a community of interest with the employees in the unit. The Board has noted that "the distinction drawn between office and plant clericals is not always clear." In this regard, the test is usually whether the employees' duties are related to the production or service process (plant clericals) or related to general office operations (office clericals). The distinction is rooted in community of interest concepts. . . .

I find, pursuant to the record evidence herein, that the functions and duties performed by Parking Services clerical employees are more akin to plant clericals than office clericals. In this regard, the facts reveal that Parking Services clerical employees spend a significant amount of time engaging in duties closely associated with Parking Services field employees, as well as the service process which they perform. In particular, Parking Services clerical employees: prepare and issue parking permits to faculty, staff, students, and visitors, similar to Parking Services field employees who grant access to the Employer's parking lots and sometimes issue temporary parking permits; collect money for parking permits, as well as collecting payment or appeals for parking violations, similar to Parking Services field employees who at times collect payment from customers upon entrance to the Employer's parking lots; enter data from parking ticket transactions on a computer which are then utilized by the Parking Services field employees; develop and distribute to Parking Services office and field employees, for their regular use, a calendar of the Employer's special events, a list of VIP reserved parking spaces, and a list of vehicles that must be towed due to excessive parking violations; handle "starting banks" and tickets that are used at the Employer's parking pay lots for its special events; and personally monitor, throughout the Employer's facility, shuttle bus service for proper maintenance of time schedules. Thus, Parking Services clerical employees are intimately connected with the work performed by Parking Services field employees.

Moreover, Parking Services clerical and field employees interact often with each other. In this regard, Parking Services clerical employees communicate daily with the field employees in [the course of their work.]

. . . Hence, even though Parking Services clerical employees exercise some clerical skills they are intimately connected with the work performed by Parking Services field employees and require regular and substantial work contacts with unit employees.

Furthermore, there is regular and frequent interchange of work duties between Parking Services clerical and field employees. In this regard, Parking Services field employees consistently engage in work performed by clerical employees in the Parking Services office. Likewise, Parking Services clerical employees typically perform work in the field engaged in by Parking Services field employees during the Employer's special events and on other several occasions. Consequently . . . even though Parking Services clerical employees have separate work locations in an enclosed office and exercise some inherent clerical functions, I conclude that their tasks are functionally integrated with the service process performed by Parking Services field employees and are, thus, plant clericals who share a community of interest with Parking Services field employees. Accordingly, Parking Services clerical and field employees have equivalent qualifications for their job classifications, have similar wages and benefits and are generally under the same direction by the department manager.

. . . In sum, I find that the Parking Services clerical employees are plant clericals based on the fact that they perform work duties in close association with the Parking Services field employees and the entire service process related to parking on the Employer's facility. Thus, I conclude that Parking Services clerical employees share a community of interest with the petitioned-for unit employees. I shall, therefore, include Parking Services clerical employees in the bargaining unit found appropriate herein and find them eligible to vote in the election to be directed. . . .

Appropriate Unit

The following employees of the Employer constitute a unit appropriate for the purposes of collective bargaining within the meaning of Section 9(b) of the Act:

> All regularly scheduled full-time and part-time employees, including plant (service) clerical employees and all other employees regularly scheduled to perform work in the Parking and Transit Services department, including parking lot attendants, parking enforcement officers, parking control officers, office coordinators, and data coordinators; but excluding all temporary employees, confidential employees, professional employees, supervisors, and guards as defined in the Act. . . .

[On review, the NLRB affirmed the Regional Director's finding that the unit including both clerical and field service workers was appropriate.]

Case Questions

1. Why does the NLRB reject the employer's arguments that some Parking Services employees are guards and therefore excluded from the proposed bargaining unit?
2. What arguments does the employer make against including the Parking Services clerical employees with the field workers in the proposed bargaining unit?
3. What factors does the NLRB consider in deciding whether to include the clerical workers with the field workers? How do those factors apply to the facts here according to the NLRB decision?

Craft Unit Severance

One of the most complex issues in bargaining unit determination involves the questions of craft unit severance: When is it appropriate to certify a craft bargaining unit representing employees who were previously included in a larger bargaining unit? The NLRB decision *Mallinckrodt Chemical Works* [162 NLRB 387 (1966)] is the leading pronouncement on the matter. In that case, the NLRB indicated that it will look to the following factors:

- if the proposed craft unit consists of skilled crafts workers performing functions on a non-repetitive basis, or if it is a functionally distinct department;
- the history of collective bargaining of the employees involved and other plants of the employer;
- the extent to which the employees in the proposed unit have established and maintained their separate identity during inclusion in the larger unit;
- the history and pattern of collective bargaining in the industry involved;
- the degree of integration of the employer's production processes;
- the qualifications of the union seeking to represent the separate craft unit; and
- the union's experience in representing employees like those in the proposed craft unit.

Bargaining Unit Definition in the Health-Care Industry

The 1974 amendments to the NLRA extended NLRB jurisdiction over nonprofit health-care institutions. The congressional committee reports accompanying the amending legislation stated that "Due consideration should be given by the Board to preventing proliferation of bargaining units in the health care industry." The board issued its final rule for such determinations in 1989; the final rule was printed in 54 *Federal Register* 16336 (1989). The rule states that the board will recognize the following eight bargaining units for acute-care hospitals: physicians, registered nurses, other professional employees, medical technicians, skilled maintenance workers, clerical workers, guards, and other nonprofessional employees. No unit with fewer than six employees will be certified (except for guard units).

The NLRB rules for bargaining unit determination are available as Part 103 from the NLRB Web site
http://www.nlrb.gov/nlrb/legal/manuals/rules

The U.S. Supreme Court upheld the NLRB's health-care industry bargaining unit rules and the power of the NLRB to establish bargaining units through its rule-making authority in *American Hospital Association v. NLRB* [499 U.S. 606 (1991)]. In certain circumstances, such as where other bargaining units already exist at the health-care facility, or where there are fewer than six employees in any of the specific categories, the NLRB will apply the traditional "community of interest" test bargaining units, *Kaiser Foundation Hospitals* [312 NLRB 933 (1993)].

NLRB DISMISSES EMPLOYER OBJECTIONS IN HOSPITAL ELECTIONS

THE WORKING LAW

The NRLB has dismissed objections filed by the hospital employers in two representation elections held to determine whether registered nurses wished to be represented by a union. After dismissing the employers' objections, the NLRB certified the Service Employees International Union Nurse Alliance Local 121RN as the exclusive bargaining representative of approximately 700 registered nurses at Pomona Valley Hospital Medical Center in Pomona, California and for about 600 nurses at Provident Saint Joseph Medical Center in Burbank, California. In each case, a majority of the employees voted for the union in representation elections held in September 2002; objections filed by the hospitals delayed the NLRB's certification of the election results until June 2003.

Sources: "U.S. Officials Certify Burbank, Calif., Nurses' Union Effort," *Knight Ridder/Tribune Business News, Daily News,* Los Angeles, Calif., June 4, 2003; "Federal Government Throws Out Hospital Objections, Certifies Nation's Largest Nurse Union to Represent RNs at Pomona Valley Hospital Medical Center," *PR Newswire,* June 3, 2003.

VOTER ELIGIBILITY

Along with determining the appropriate bargaining unit, the question of which employees are actually eligible to vote in the election must be resolved. Factors to be considered are whether an employee is within the bargaining unit and whether striking employees are able to vote.

In general, when the election has been directed (or agreed to, for consent elections), the board establishes an eligibility date—that is, the date by which an employee must be on the employer's payroll in order to be eligible to vote. The eligibility date is usually the end of the payroll period immediately preceding the direction of (or agreement to hold) the election. Employees must be on the payroll as of the eligibility date, and they must also continue to be on the payroll on the date the election is held. Employees hired after the eligibility date but before the election date are not eligible to vote.

Employees may be on strike when an election is held; this is most often the case in decertification elections, when the employees not striking seek to get rid of the union. Section 2(3) of the NLRA defines *employee* to include "any individual whose work has ceased as a consequence of . . . any current labor dispute . . . and who has not obtained any other regular and substantially equivalent employment." The board has adopted several rules clarifying the voting rights of striking employees.

Unfair Labor Practice Strike
A strike to protest employer unfair practices.

The board distinguishes whether the employees are on an unfair labor practice strike or an economic strike. An **unfair labor practice strike** is a strike by employees in protest of, or precipitated by, employer unfair labor practices. The board holds that unfair labor practice strikers cannot be permanently replaced by the employer. Unfair labor practice strikers are eligible to vote in any election held during the strike.

Economic Strike
A strike over economic issues such as a new contract or a grievance.

Economic strikes are strikes over economic issues, such as grievances or a new contract. Unlike unfair labor practice strikers, economic strikers may be permanently replaced by the employer. Economic strikers who have not been permanently replaced may vote in any election during the strike, but economic strikers who have been permanently replaced may vote only in elections held within twelve months after the strike begins. After twelve months, they lose their eligibility to vote. The employees hired to replace economic strikers may vote if they are permanent replacements—that is, if the employer intends to retain them after the strike is over. Replacements hired on a temporary basis, who will not be retained after the strike ends, are not eligible to vote. As a result of these rules, during the first twelve months of a strike, permanent replacements and all economic strikers may vote; after twelve months, only the permanent replacements and those economic strikers who have not been permanently replaced may vote.

Economic strikers or unfair labor practice strikers who obtain permanent employment elsewhere and who abandon their prior jobs lose their eligibility to vote. Although the board generally presumes that other employment by strikers during a strike is temporary, they will hold that a striker has lost eligibility to vote if it can be shown that he or she does not intend to return to the prior job. Also, strikers fired for wrongdoing during the strike are not eligible to vote.

When the eligibility of employees to vote is challenged, the NLRB holds that, in the case of both unfair labor practice strikes and economic strikes, the employer has the burden of proving that replacements hired during the strike are permanent employees in order for the replacements to be qualified to vote in a representation election, *O. E. Butterfield, Inc.* [319 NLRB 1004 (1995)]. Although the board prefers that challenges to voter eligibility be resolved at a hearing prior to the election, such challenges may also be raised at the time the challenged employee votes. When an employee's right to vote is challenged, the ballot at issue is placed in a sealed envelope rather than in the ballot box. After all employees have voted, the board first counts the unchallenged ballots. If the results of the election will not be changed by the challenged ballots—because there are not enough of them to change the outcome—the board will not rule on the challenges. However, if the challenged ballots could affect the election results, the board will hold a hearing to resolve the challenges, count those ballots from the eligible voters, and then certify the election results.

REPRESENTATION ELECTIONS

***Excelsior* List**
A list of the names and addresses of the employees eligible to vote in a representation election.

Within seven days after the regional director approves a consent election or directs that an election be held, the employer must file an election eligibility list with the regional office. This list, called an ***Excelsior* list** after the decision in which the board set out this requirement, *Excelsior Underwear, Inc.* [156 NLRB No. 111 (1966)], contains the names and home addresses of all employees eligible to vote so that the union can contact them outside their work environment, beyond the boss's observation and control. A board agent will then arrange a conference with all parties to settle the details of the election. The NLRB will set aside elections won by the employer where the employer has failed to provide the union with an *Excelsior* list containing the full first and last names of all employees in the bargaining unit, *North Macon Health Care Facility* [322 NLRB No. 82 (1996)].

The election is generally held on company premises; however, if the union objects, it can be held elsewhere. In *San Diego Gas & Electric* [325 NLRB No. 218 (1998)], the NLRB held that the Regional Director may authorize the use of mail-in ballots in cases where (1) the eligible employees are scattered over a wide geographic area because of their job duties; (2) the eligible employees are scattered because of their work schedules; or (3) there is a strike, lockout, or picketing in progress at the employer's location. The NLRB agent supervises the conduct of the election, and all parties are entitled to have observers present during the voting. All parties to the election will undoubtedly have engaged in an election campaign prior to the vote. The board regards such an election as an experiment to determine the employees' choice. The board therefore strives for "laboratory conditions" in the conduct of the election and requires that neither side engage in conduct that could unduly affect the employees' free choice.

Captive-Audience Speeches
Meetings or speeches held by the employer during working hours, which employees are required to attend.

The laboratory conditions can be violated by unfair practices committed by either side. Conduct that does not amount to an unfair practice may also violate the laboratory conditions if the board believes that wrongful misconduct will unduly affect the employees' choice. **Captive-audience speeches** given by representatives of the employers or mass meetings by the union within twenty-four hours of an election at which the union promises to waive initiation fees for members who join before the election are examples of such conduct. Elections have been set aside where a supervisor distributed antiunion hats to the employees, *Barton Nelson, Inc.* [318 NLRB 712 (1995)]; where the employer offered employees who were not scheduled to work two hours' pay to come in to vote, *Sunrise Rehabilitation Hospital* [320 NLRB 212 (1995)]; and where the union used a sound truck to broadcast prounion songs into the plant on the day of the election, *Bro-Tech Corp. v. NLRB* [105 F.3d 890 (3d Cir. 1997)]. A supervisor's comment that he would "kick [the employees'] asses" if they voted for the union was grounds to set aside an election, *Medic One, Inc.* [331 NLRB No. 56 (2000)]. An employer's failure to prevent employees urging decertification of the union from sending e-mail messages to the employees was not a reason to set aside the election when the union also had access to the employer's e-mail system, *Lockheed Martin Skunk Works* [331 NLRB No. 104 (2000)].

The NLRB has adopted a rule barring employers and unions from conducting any election raffles where eligibility to participate in the raffle is tied in any way to voting in the election or being at the election site on election day, or if the raffle is conducted at any time during a period beginning twenty-four hours before the scheduled opening of the polls and ending with the closing of the polls, *Atlantic Limousine, Inc.* [331 NLRB No. 134 (2000)]. Violations of the rule will result in setting aside the election upon filing an objection. The rule against raffles includes announcing a raffle, distributing raffle tickets, identifying raffle winners, and awarding raffle prizes.

Actions by third parties, other than the employer and union, may also violate the laboratory conditions. In one case, the local newspaper in a small southern town printed racially inflammatory articles about the union attempting to organize the work force of a local employer. The board held that the injection of racial propaganda into the election violated the laboratory conditions and was reason to invalidate the election, which the union lost.

A local pastor who met with employees and discussed possible plant closure if the union won the election was acting as an agent of the employer. His comments were held to be an unfair labor practice and were grounds to set aside the election, *Southern Pride Catfish* [331 NLRB No. 81 (2000)].

The board has decided that it will not monitor the truthfulness of the election propaganda of either side. Misrepresentations in campaign promises or propaganda will not, of themselves, be grounds to set aside the election results. The NLRB will intervene if either party uses a forged document that renders the voting employees unable to recognize the propaganda for what it is, *NLRB v. St. Francis Healthcare Center* [212 F.3d 945 (6th Cir. 2000)].

Twenty-Four-Hour Silent Period
The 24-hour period prior to the representation election, during which the parties must refrain from formal campaign meetings.

The board requires that the parties in an election refrain from formal campaigning for twenty-four hours prior to the election. This **twenty-four-hour silent period** is intended to give the employees time to reflect upon their choice free from electioneering pressures. Any mass union rallies or employer captive-audience speeches during the silent period will be grounds to set aside the election results, *Comet Electric* [314 NLRB 1215 (1994)] and *Bro-Tech Corp. v. NLRB* [105 F.3d 890 (3d Cir. 1997)]. Figure 14.2 shows a sample ballot for a representation election.

If either party believes the election laboratory conditions were violated, that party may file objections to the other party's conduct with the regional director within five days of the election. Postelection unfair labor practice charges could also result in the election results being set aside.

After the election is held, the parties have five days in which to file any objections with the regional director. If the director finds the objections to be valid, the election will be set aside. If the objections are held to be invalid, the results of the election will be certified. To be victorious, a party to the election must receive a majority of the votes cast; that is, either the union or the no-union choice must garner a majority of the votes cast by the eligible employees. If the election involved more than one union and no choice received a simple majority, the board will hold a run-off election between the two choices getting the highest number of votes. If a union wins, it will be certified as the bargaining agent for all the employees in the bargaining unit.

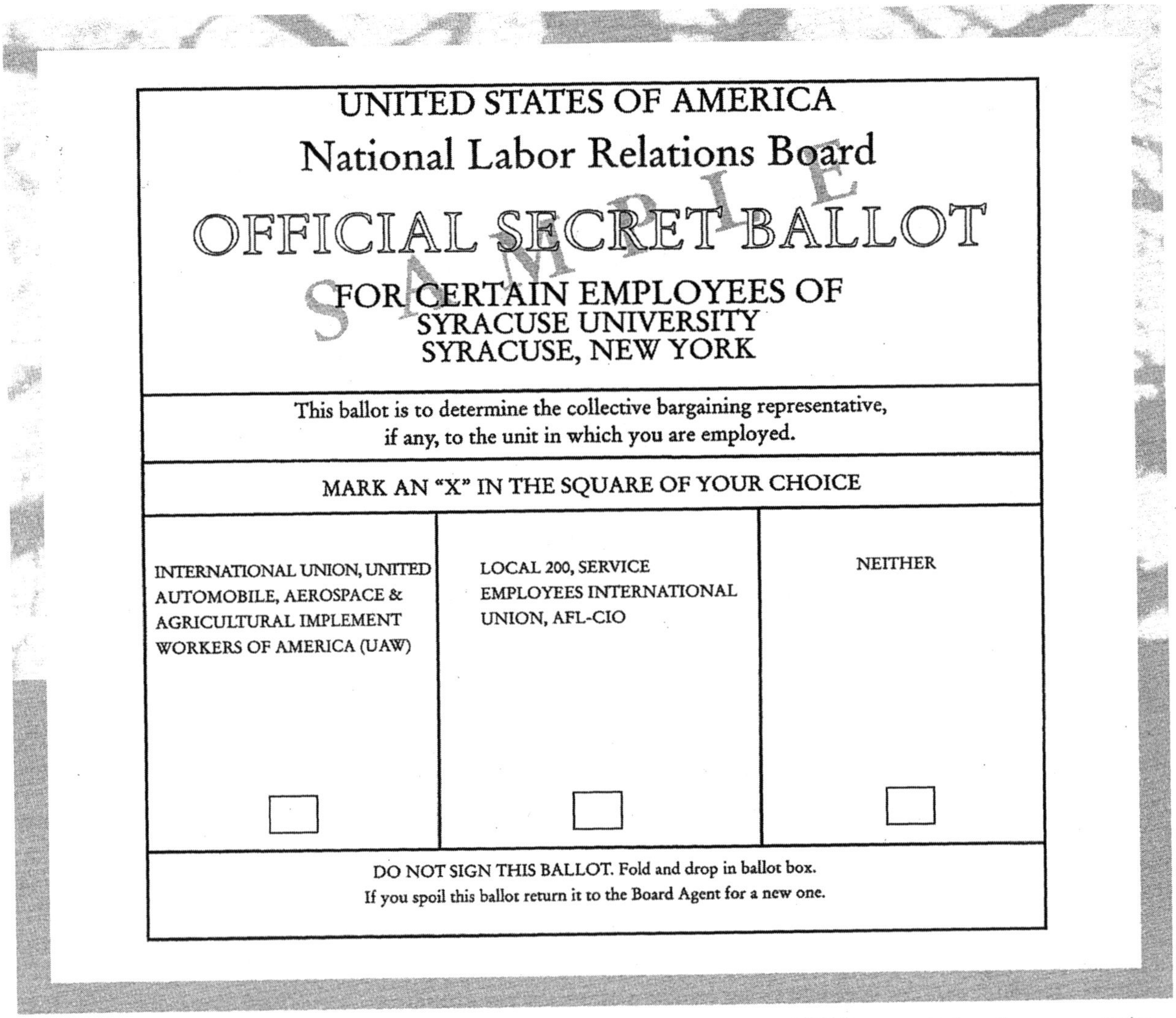

UNITED STATES OF AMERICA

National Labor Relations Board

OFFICIAL SECRET BALLOT

SAMPLE

FOR CERTAIN EMPLOYEES OF
SYRACUSE UNIVERSITY
SYRACUSE, NEW YORK

This ballot is to determine the collective bargaining representative, if any, to the unit in which you are employed.

MARK AN "X" IN THE SQUARE OF YOUR CHOICE

INTERNATIONAL UNION, UNITED AUTOMOBILE, AEROSPACE & AGRICULTURAL IMPLEMENT WORKERS OF AMERICA (UAW)	LOCAL 200, SERVICE EMPLOYEES INTERNATIONAL UNION, AFL-CIO	NEITHER
☐	☐	☐

DO NOT SIGN THIS BALLOT. Fold and drop in ballot box.
If you spoil this ballot return it to the Board Agent for a new one.

FIGURE 14.2 Sample NLRB representation election ballot. (Source: NLRB poster at 1979 Syracuse University representation election.)

Because the conduct of representation elections is a matter subject to the discretion of the regional directors and the board, only limited judicial review of certification decisions is available. However, as a practical matter, an employer can obtain review of the board's certification decision by refusing to bargain with the certified union and contesting the issue in the subsequent unfair labor practice proceeding.

Decertification Petition
Petition stating that a current bargaining representative no longer has the support of a majority of the employees in the bargaining unit.

DECERTIFICATION OF THE BARGAINING AGENT

An employee or group of employees, or a union or individual acting on their behalf, may file a **decertification petition** under Section 9(c)(1) of the act, asserting that "the individual or labor organization, which has been certified or is being currently recognized by their employer as the bargaining representative" no longer enjoys the unit's support. The board also requires the showing of 30 percent employee interest in support of a decertification petition to entertain it. This 30 percent rule has been criticized by some commentators in that the petition signifies nothing more than that fewer than half the employees are unhappy with their representative. Yet the mere filing of the petition can totally disrupt the bargaining process because the employer may refuse to bargain while the petition is pending.

An employer is not permitted to file a decertification petition; the board will dismiss a decertification petition by employees if it discovers that the employer instigated the filing. However, a company can file an election petition if it can demonstrate by objective evidence that it has reasonable grounds for believing that the incumbent union has lost its majority status. Such petitions must be filed during the open-season periods, just as with petitions seeking representation elections.

Deauthorization Elections

Union Shop Clause
Clause in an agreement requiring all present and future members of a bargaining unit to be union members.

Section 9(e)(1) of the NLRA provides for the holding of a deauthorization election to rescind the union shop clause in a collective agreement. The **union shop clause,** which may be included in a collective agreement, requires that all present and future members of the bargaining unit become, and remain, union members. They typically must join the union after thirty days from the date on which they were hired. Failure to join the union or to remain a union member is grounds for discharge. The provisions of Section 9(e)(1) state that a petition for a deauthorization election may be filed by an employee or group of employees. The petition must have the support of at least 30 percent of the bargaining unit. If a valid petition is filed, along with the requisite show of support, the board will conduct a secret ballot election to determine whether a majority of employees in the unit wish to remove the union shop clause from the agreement. As is the case with representation and decertification elections, no deauthorization election can be held for a bargaining unit (or subdivision of the unit) if a valid deauthorization election has been held in the preceding twelve-month period. Unlike representation elections and decertification elections, which are determined by a majority of the votes actually cast, deauthorization elections require that a majority of the members in the bargaining unit vote in favor of rescinding the union shop clause for it to be rescinded.

ACQUIRING REPRESENTATION RIGHTS THROUGH UNFAIR LABOR PRACTICE PROCEEDINGS

Unfair labor practice charges filed with the board while representation proceedings are pending may invoke the board's blocking charge policy. The filing of such charges usually halts the representation case, and no election will be held pending the resolution of the unfair labor practice charges. An employer may wish to forestall the election and erode the union's support by committing various unfair labor practices, thereby taking unfair advantage of this policy.

Go to **http://www4.law.cornell.edu/uscode/29/158.html** *for the text on Unfair Labor Practices.*

A union may wish to proceed with the pending election despite the unfair labor practice charges. It can do so by filing a request-to-proceed notice with the board. If the union proceeds and wins the election, then the effect of the unfair labor practice charges is not very important. However, if the union loses the election, it may be because of the effect of the employer's illegal actions. In that case, the union could file objections to the election and request that a new election be held. But how could the union overcome the lingering effects of the employer's unfair practices? Rather than seek a new election or proceed with the original election, the union may rely on the unfair practice charges and ask the board, as a remedy for the unfair labor practices, to order the employer to recognize and bargain with the union without its ever winning an election.

In the case of *NLRB v. Gissel Packing Co.* [395 U.S. 575 (1969)], the Supreme Court held that the NLRB may issue a bargaining order, requiring the employer to recognize and bargain with the union, as a remedy for the employer's unfair labor practices where those practices were pervasive, outrageous, and precluded the union from ever demonstrating majority support. The Court in *Gissel Packing* also held that a bargaining order might be an appropriate remedy where the employer's unfair labor practices, although not pervasive and outrageous, nevertheless had the effect of preventing any election from being a true demonstration of the employees' desires as to union representation; however, in such situations, a bargaining order should only be granted where the union, at some point during the organizing campaign, had majority support.

The following case illustrates the application of the *Gissel Packing* bargaining order remedy.

Kinney Drugs, Inc. v. NLRB

74 F.3d 1419 (2d Cir. 1996)

Jacobs, J.

. . . [T]he National Labor Relations Board ("Board" or "NLRB") has issued an order (1) finding that during a 1991 union organizing election petitioner crossrespondent Kinney Drugs, Inc. ("Kinney") engaged in unfair labor practices sufficiently egregious as to justify a bargaining order. . . .

In this appeal, the NLRB seeks enforcement of its bargaining orders, and Kinney asks us to reject the NLRB's findings that (1) Kinney engaged in unfair labor practices justifying the issuance of the initial bargaining order. . . .

Kinney sells pharmaceutical and other products at stores in Vermont and northern New York. This appeal arises out of a November 22, 1991 election in a stipulated unit at a Kinney warehouse and distribution center in Gouverneur, New York. The election was held to determine whether the Kinney warehouse employees wished to be represented by Local 687, affiliated with the International Brotherhood of Teamsters, Chauffeurs, Warehousemen and Helpers of America (the "union"). A total of 41 employees cast votes in the election. Kinney challenged six of these ballots and the union challenged one. Only Kinney's challenges are pursued on appeal. When the unchallenged 34 ballots were opened immediately following the election, they split 17 for the union and 17 against it. Since this tie vote defeats union certification, the challenged ballots have become potentially determinative.

Administrative Law Judge Joel A. Harmatz conducted hearings in June 1992 and issued his decision in June 1993, (1) finding that Kinney had committed numerous unfair labor practices that warranted the issuance of a bargaining order. . . . The NLRB adopted virtually all of the ALJ's report in an order dated July 12, 1994. . . . Based on Kinney's unfair labor practices, the NLRB issued a bargaining order compelling Kinney to negotiate with the union without regard to the vote (the "July 12, 1994 bargaining order").

. . . The NLRB found that a number of the actions taken by Kinney constituted unfair labor practices in violation of [the NLRA]. According to the NLRB order, Kinney violated the labor laws in the following ways, among others:

- Threatening to close the warehouse if the union won the election.
- Threatening employees Woods and Les McClure with discharge unless they supported management.
- Soliciting grievances with implicit or explicit promises to rectify them.
- Taking corrective action in response to complaints raised by employees during the course of the election.
- Threatening loss of benefits.
- Interrogating various employees regarding their position on the union and the election.

Discussion

We review . . . the findings of unfair labor practices committed by Kinney during the 1991 election campaign and the resulting bargaining order. . . .

The NLRB's July 12, 1994 bargaining order was based on the ALJ's finding that Kinney management had engaged in unfair labor practices so egregious as to foreclose irreparably the prospect of a fair second election. On appeal, Kinney argues (1) that the NLRB's findings of unfair labor practices were unsupported by substantial evidence and (2) that even if the NLRB's findings were supportable and the union's allegations were accepted as true, a bargaining order was an unwarranted and excessive remedy.

. . . A bargaining order can be an acceptable response to a series of unfair labor practices "which have made the holding of a fair election unlikely. . . ." But such an order is only an "appropriate remedy for those practices [that] . . . are of 'such a nature that their coercive effects cannot be eliminated by the application of traditional remedies, with the result that a fair and reliable election cannot be had.'"

In this circuit, "(a)n election, not a bargaining order remains the preferred remedy. . . . [A] bargaining order is a rare remedy warranted only when it is clearly established that traditional remedies cannot eliminate the effects of the employer's past unfair labor practices."

In *NLRB v. Windsor Industries, Inc.*, we analyzed the framework erected by *Gissel* and concluded that bargaining orders are proper remedies in two kinds of cases:

> The Court first identified those cases, described in *Gissel* as "exceptional," which were "marked by 'outrageous' and 'pervasive' unfair labor practices." In these cases an order to bargain might issue irrespective of whether the union had ever demonstrated majority support.
>
> *Gissel* also recognized a second tier of "less extraordinary cases marked by less pervasive practices which nonetheless still have the tendency to undermine majority strength and impede the election processes," and which might therefore call for the issuance by the Board of a bargaining order. In fashioning remedies in those cases, involving a "lesser showing of employer misconduct," the Board "can properly take into consideration the extensiveness of an employer's unfair practices in terms of their past effect on election conditions and the likelihood of their recurrence in the future." The Court then stated that if the Board finds "the possibility of erasing the effects of past practices and of ensuring a fair election (or a fair rerun) by the use of traditional remedies, though present, is slight and that employee sentiment once expressed through cards would, on balance, be better protected by a bargaining order, then such an order should issue. . . ."

. . . The *Gissel* category of "exceptional misconduct" is limited to what are termed "hallmark" violations. "Such violations include closing of a plant or threats of closure or loss of employment, granting of benefits to employees, or reassignment, demotion or discharge of union adherents." The only violations by Kinney that potentially amount to exceptional misconduct are the threat of plant closure and the threat to discharge Woods and Les McClure. The second *Gissel* category applies to a group of more pallid unfair labor practices such as "interrogation of employees, promises of benefits, expressions of antiunion resolve, or threats of decreased benefits. . . ." Such lesser misconduct . . . will not support a bargaining order absent serious and longlasting untoward effects on employees." Most of the unfair labor practices cited by the NLRB in this case . . . are of this lesser variety.

We consider in detail the two "hallmark" violations that arguably constitute exceptional misconduct under *Gissel.*

1. The NLRB found that supervisor Dave McClure, in a one-on-one conversation, told employee Donald Bush that if the union won the election, the warehouse might be shut down. . . . Kinney had decided, McClure allegedly told Woods, that it might be cheaper to replace the warehouse functions with an outside trucking firm if the warehouse employees formed a union. Such a statement is the type of "reasonable prediction" based on "economic necessities" envisioned by *Gissel.* Kinney had the right to spell out the possible economic consequences of unionization; and Kinney's employees, who could hardly rely on the union for a neutral view, had a profound interest in receiving that information. The labor laws do not suppress one side of the debate. The NLRB therefore erred in finding that the McClure-Bush conversation constituted a violation of § 8(a)(1).
2. The other arguably hallmark violation committed by Kinney involved Cognetti's threat to fire Les McClure and Otis Woods unless they gave active support to management in the election. . . . Because our inquiry is restricted to the question of whether the NLRB's findings are supported by substantial evidence, we accept the finding that Kinney engaged in the unfair labor practice of an unrepudiated threatened discharge.

At worst, Kinney committed one sustainable hallmark violation during the course of the 1991 election, plus an assortment of lesser infractions. . . .

As discussed above, *Gissel* bargaining orders may be issued either (a) if an employer has engaged in exceptional misconduct, or (b) if the employer has engaged in lesser misconduct under *Gissel,* and the union can demonstrate that "(1) the union was at some point supported by a majority of the bargaining unit employees; and (2) the employer's unfair labor practices undermined the union's majority strength and the possibility of erasing the effects of past practices and of ensuring a fair election (or a fair rerun) by the use of traditional remedies, though present, is slight." This case falls into neither of these categories.

1. Not every "hallmark" violation amounts to exceptional misconduct under *Gissel.* . . . Kinney has engaged in no exceptional, pervasive, and outrageous behavior: a threat is by nature less outrageous than actual dismissal; actual dismissal is a management message calculated to reach all the members of the unit whereas Kinney's threat was made to two employees and disseminated to others by them, not by Kinney; and Kinney acted to limit its threat. . . .
2. If the Board's bargaining order is to be enforced, it must satisfy the requirements outlined by *Gissel* for cases marked by a lesser degree of misconduct than exceptional hallmark violations. The Board must first establish that there existed majority "employee sentiment once expressed through cards" in favor of the union. . . . Twenty-five signature cards are included in the record. The unit contained 41 individuals, including the seven whose votes were contested. We conclude below that the NLRB erred in rejecting Kinney's challenges to four of the seven contested ballots. Of these four employees, two had signed cards. Retrospectively, therefore, the original unit consisted of 37 individuals, a majority of 23 of whom signed cards. . . . Nevertheless, even if the union had majority support in September 1991, the bargaining order was an excessive remedy. Absent exceptional misconduct (as defined in *Gissel*), a bargaining order is justifiable only if "the possibility of erasing the effects of past practices and of ensuring a fair election (or a fair rerun) by the use of traditional remedies . . . is slight." The test is whether or not "a fair and reliable election can be had."

The finding of a hallmark violation, such as the threats to Woods and Les McClure, does not necessarily justify a bargaining order, even in the absence of mitigating factors. . . .

In considering whether to enforce a bargaining order in the absence of exceptional misconduct, courts may also consider whether the alleged violations involved acts or mere threats to act. . . . Our preference not to enforce a bargaining order in all but the most extreme of circumstances "reflects the important policy that employees not have union representation forced upon them when, by exercise of their free will, they might choose otherwise." . . .

... Kinney's hallmark violation was far less egregious than that committed [in other cases where the court held a bargaining order was not appropriate] ... and Kinney's other alleged labor practices are trivial even in the aggregate. Moreover, the bargaining order in this case was entered without consideration of other circumstances that bear upon fairness: the turnover in the unit (as to which no inquiry was apparently made) and the thin margin of the vote. In short, the NLRB has "failed to convince us that a bargaining order is warranted. . . ."

We decline to enforce the NLRB's July 12, 1994 bargaining order insofar as it is based upon the unfair labor practices committed by Kinney in connection with the November 1991 election.

Case Questions

1. What unfair labor practices had Kinney committed according to the NLRB? Which unfair labor practices did the court of appeals find were warranted?
2. Did the court of appeals find that the unfair labor practices justified the issuance of a bargaining order? Why? Explain.
3. According to the court of appeals, when is a bargaining order justified? Why does the court of appeals favor holding a new election rather than issuing a bargaining order?

Other Bargaining Order Remedy Issues

The Supreme Court's *Gissel Packing* decision indicated that the NLRB could issue a bargaining order to remedy outrageous and pervasive unfair labor practices by the employer, even if the union never had established majority support of the employees in the appropriate bargaining unit. The U.S. Court of Appeals for the Third Circuit held that the Board had the power to issue such an order, *United Dairy Farmers Co-op. Assoc. v. NLRB* [633 F.2d 1054 (1980)]; however, the U.S. Court of Appeals for the D.C. Circuit held that it was inappropriate for the Board to issue a bargaining order where the union never established evidence of majority support, *Conair Corp. v. NLRB* [721 F.2d 1355 (1983), *cert. denied,* 467 U.S. 1241 (1984)]. The NLRB now takes the position that it will not issue a bargaining order unless the union had, at some point, shown evidence of majority support during the organizing campaign, *Gourmet Foods, Inc.* [270 NLRB 578 (1984)].

A second area of dispute over bargaining order remedies is the question of whether the NLRB should consider subsequent events and changed circumstances when determining whether a bargaining order remedy is appropriate: Has the passage of time, the turnover of employees in the unit, or other factors limited the effects of the employer's unfair labor practices? The NLRB takes the position that it will not consider subsequent events or changed circumstances because to do so would allow the employer to capitalize on its misconduct. The courts of appeals are divided on this issue: The Seventh Circuit enforced a bargaining order despite a delay of four years and turnover of most the bargaining unit employees, *America's Best Quality Coatings v. NLRB* [44 F.3d 106, *cert. denied,* 515 U.S. 1158 (1995)], while the Sixth Circuit, the Second Circuit, and the D.C. Circuit held that the Board must consider subsequent events and the effect of the passage of time when deciding to issue a bargaining order, *DTR Industries v. NLRB* [39 F.3d 106 (6th Cir. 1994)], *Kinney Drugs, Inc. v. NLRB* [74 F.3d 1419 (2d Cir. 1996)], and *Charlotte Amphitheater Corp. v. NLRB* [82 F.3d 1074 (D.C. Cir. 1996)].

Employer Response to Union Recognition Demand

The *Gissel Packing* case involved an employer who committed unfair labor practices after the union claimed majority support. But what about the situation in which an employer, after being confronted by the union claiming recognition, simply refuses to recognize the union but refrains from committing any unfair labor practices? Is the employer required to petition for an election or recognize the union? Or is it up to the union to initiate the election process? In *Linden Lumber Div., Summer & Co. v. NLRB* [419 U.S. 301 (1974)], the U.S. Supreme Court held that an employer who receives a request for voluntary recognition from a union claiming to have the majority support of the employer's employees is not required to recognize the union, provided that the employer has no knowledge of the union's support (independent of the union's claim to have majority support) and does not commit any unfair labor practices. Neither is the employer required to petition the NLRB for a representation election in response to the union's request for recognition; it is then up to the union either to file a petition for an election or to institute unfair labor practice charges. Of course, if the employer does engage in unfair labor practices after receiving the union's request for recognition, the union is free to seek a *Gissel*-type bargaining order from the NLRB as a remedy. Such bargaining orders are granted infrequently, however, as the *Kinney Drugs* case indicates.

SUMMARY

- The NLRA gives employees the right to determine for themselves whether they wish to be represented by a union. If the majority of the employees in an appropriate bargaining unit indicate that they support a union, the NLRA provides that the union then becomes the exclusive bargaining representative of that bargaining unit. Although representation elections conducted by the NLRB are the most common means through which unions acquire representation rights, an employer may also voluntarily recognize a union as bargaining representative for a group of employees when the union demonstrates majority support.
- Unions, employees, or employers may file a petition with the NLRB seeking a representation election. Unions or employees may file a petition for a decertification election. When a petition is filed, the NLRB will determine whether the contract bar rule precludes holding an election; if not, the NLRB must then determine an appropriate bargaining unit. The NLRB uses the "community of interest" test to define the bargaining unit. While the bargaining unit determination depends on the facts of each case, in the health-care industry the NLRB will apply its rules for bargaining unit determination.
- The NLRB conducts representation elections under "laboratory conditions" to ensure that the election represents the free choice of the employees. Violations of the laboratory conditions or of the twenty-four-hour silent period rule may result in the NLRB invalidating the election results. Representation and decertification elections are by secret ballot, and the winner is determined by a majority of the votes cast. If no choice captures a majority of votes, a runoff election is held between the two choices getting the most votes. For deau-

thorization elections, which seek to rescind agency shop or union shop dues requirements, the result is determined by whether any choice gets a majority of the votes of all employees in the bargaining unit. Either party may file challenges to votes or to the election itself; valid challenges will be determined after a hearing by either the Regional Director or the NLRB itself.

- Unions may also acquire representation rights through unfair labor practice proceedings. The NLRB may issue a bargaining order when the effects of unfair labor practices by employers prevent a fair election from being held. Such remedies are the exception, with the NLRB and the courts preferring elections as the means to give effect to employees' right of free choice under the NLRA.

QUESTIONS

1. What are the methods by which a union can acquire representation rights for a group of employees?
2. What steps are necessary to get the NLRB to hold a representation election? A decertification election?
3. What is the contract bar rule? What are the exceptions to it?
4. What is a bargaining unit? What factors does the NLRB consider in determining the appropriate bargaining unit?
5. Under what conditions are economic strikers ineligible to vote in representation elections? Under what conditions are unfair labor practice strikers ineligible to vote in representation elections?
6. What is the *Excelsior* list? What is the significance of the twenty-four-hour silent period?
7. Under what circumstances can a union acquire representation rights through unfair labor practice proceedings?
8. When must an employer recognize a union requesting voluntary recognition?

CASE PROBLEMS

1. In 2000, employees of the Kent Corporation elected an independent union as their collective-bargaining representative. A collective-bargaining agreement was hammered out and ultimately ratified by the employees, effective until December 31, 2003. In November 2003, the two sides again negotiated, the result being a contract to be in effect until December 31, 2006. This agreement was signed by the Association committee members but was never ratified by the rank and file. In fact, evidence showed there had been no association membership meetings, no election of officers, no dues ever collected, and no association treasury since 2000.

   In August 2004, the Steelworkers Union filed a representation petition. The NLRB regional director ruled that the association was a defunct union and that its current contract was no bar to an election. The company filed a request for review of the decision with the NLRB in Washington, D.C. The association vice president and a member of the bargaining committee attested to their willingness to continue representing the employees. There was no evidence that the association had ever failed to act on a bargaining unit member's behalf.

How should the NLRB rule on the association's representative status? See *Kent Corporation* [272 NLRB No. 115, 117 L.R.R.M. 1333 (1984)].

2. L&J Equipment Company was engaged in the surface mining of coal, with its principal site in Hatfield, Pennsylvania, and six satellite sites in other parts of western Pennsylvania. In early 2001, the United Mine Workers of America began organizing L&J's mining employees. A few days after the first organizing meeting, a company-owned truck was destroyed by fire. Authorities determined the fire had been deliberately set. Three weeks later, the United Mine Workers filed a petition for an election. The date set for the election was November 4, 2001.

During the intense election campaign, promanagement employees were threatened. A week before the election, a company-owned barn burned to the ground. The United Mine Workers won the election by a vote of 39-33.

L&J refused to bargain. The union filed a Section 8(a)(5) charge, and the board found that L&J was guilty of an unfair labor practice. L&J appealed to the U.S. Court of Appeals for the Third Circuit, claiming that the board abused its discretion in certifying the union in light of its pre-election improprieties.

How should the appellate court have ruled on this challenge? See *NLRB v. L&J Equipment Co.* [745 F.2d 224, 117 L.R.R.M. 2592 (3d Cir. 1984)].

3. Action Automotive, Inc., a retail auto parts and gasoline dealer, had stores in a number of Michigan cities. In March 2003, Local 40 of the Retail Store Employees Union filed a petition for a representation election. The union got a plurality of the unchallenged votes. But the challenged ballots could have made the difference.

The union challenged the ballots of the wife of the company's coowner/president, who worked as a general ledger clerk at the company's headquarters, and of the mother of the three owner/brothers, who worked as a cashier in one of the nine stores. The company argued that since neither received any special benefits, neither should be excluded from the employee unit or denied her vote.

The case reached the U.S. Supreme Court. What arguments could you make to the Court for the union's view? For the company's view? See *NLRB v. Action Automotive, Inc.* [469 U.S. 970 (1985)].

4. Micronesian Telecommunications Corporation (MTC) had its principal office on Saipan, a Pacific island held as a U.S. trust territory. Electrical Workers Local 1357 (IBEW) sought to represent the employees of MTC, including its employees on neighboring islands.

What jurisdictional issues should the NLRB have addressed before asserting jurisdiction of the case? What result? If the board asserted jurisdiction, what factors should it have considered with respect to whether employees on the neighboring islands belonged in the same bargaining unit with the workers on Saipan? See *Micronesian Tel. Corp.* [273 NLRB No. 56, 118 L.R.R.M. 1067 (1984)].

5. Kirksville College in Missouri was a nonprofit corporation providing health-care services, medical education, and medical research. Service Employees Local 50 filed three representation petitions seeking to represent separate units composed, respectively, of all technical, all professional, and all service/maintenance employees at the Kirksville Health Center, an unincorporated subsidiary of the college. The college also had several affiliated hospitals and rural clinics within a sixty-mile radius of the main campus.

What factors should the NLRB consider in deciding whether technical, professional, and service employees should be in separate units? What factors must be looked at to decide whether clinic employees should properly have their own bargaining unit(s) or be part of a broader unit taking in (a) the college,

(b) affiliated hospitals, and/or (c) satellite facilities? See *Kirksville College* [274 NLRB No. 121, 118 L.R.R.M. 1443 (1985)].

6. The Steelworkers Union sought to represent a unit composed of four occupational health nurses in an aluminum plant. The company argued that the nurses were managerial employees, exempt from the act, or in the alternative, professional employees who must be part of a bargaining unit of all the plant's professional employees. The nurses' primary responsibilities were treating employees' injuries and illnesses, administering routine physical examinations to applicants and employees, and maintaining logs and records.

What additional facts did the NLRB need to decide the issues raised by the company? See *Noranda Aluminum Inc. v. NLRB* [751 F.2d 268, 118 L.R.R.M. 2136 (8th Cir. 1984)].

7. Because of the mixture of ethnic groups in the plant, the NLRB conducted the election using a ballot translated from English into Spanish, Vietnamese, and Laotian. Food & Commercial Workers Local 34 won the election 119-112.

The translations were line by line. Some English-reading employees claimed this made it difficult to read. Some of the translations were later found to be somewhat inaccurate. Neither side challenged any ballots.

How should the NLRB have ruled on the company's challenge to the election outcome based on the flawed ballots? See *Kraft, Inc.* [273 NLRB 1484, 118 L.R.R.M. 1242 (1985)].

8. One employee ballot in a close election was marked with a large "X" in the "No Union" box and the word "Yes" written above the box.

Should the NLRB count this ballot? If so, how? See *NLRB v. Newly Wed Foods Inc.* [758 F.2d 4, 118 L.R.R.M. 3213 (1st Cir. 1985)].

9. The International Brotherhood of Electrical Workers, Local Unions 605 and 985, AFL-CIO ("the union") have represented a bargaining unit comprised of MP&L's service and maintenance employees since 1938. The most recent collective-bargaining agreement concerning these employees is for the term of October 15, 2003, until October 15, 2005. That agreement does not include MP&L's storeroom and warehouse employees.

In January 2004, the union petitioned the NLRB for certification as bargaining representative of these storeroom and warehouse employees. MP&L opposed the petition, urging that the board's contract bar rule barred the election required for the union to be certified. MP&L contended that the contract bar rule must be applied to employees intentionally excluded from an existing collective-bargaining agreement.

The regional director rejected MP&L's contention. The board affirmed this decision. An election was held, and a slim majority of the storeroom and warehouse employees voted to be represented by the union. The NLRB certified the results of the election.

To obtain judicial review of the board's decision to permit a representation election, MP&L refused to bargain with the union on behalf of the newly represented employees. The union filed an unfair labor practice charge with the board.

How should the board have ruled on this challenge by MP&L? See *NLRB v. Mississippi Power & Light Co.* [769 F.2d 276 (5th Cir. 1985)].

10. The source of dispute was a representation election held at Kusan's Franklin, Tennessee, plant on October 19, 2002. The union won that election by a vote of 118-107. Kusan, however, filed objections with the board over the conduct of the election. The objections charged that the union interfered with the election by conducting a poll of the employees and threatening and coercing employees during the course of the polling.

In December 2002, the regional director of the NLRB investigated Kusan's objections and issued a report recommending that the objections be overruled. The results of the election were certified by the board in April 2003.

Kusan's objections centered on a petition that Kusan employees who supported the union circulated among their fellow workers prior to the election. The petition, which bore approximately 100 names, read as follows:

> We, the undersigned, are voting YES for the IAM. We don't mind being on the firing line because we know it's something that has to be done. Please join with us. VOTE YES and help us to make Kusan, Inc. a better place to work and earn a living.

Kusan contends that the circulation and distribution of the petition constituted impermissible "polling" of the employees by the union.

How should the board have ruled on Kusan's objections? See *Kusan Mfg. Co. v. NLRB* [749 F.2d 362, 117 L.R.R.M. 3394 (6th Cir. 1984)].

INTERNET EXERCISE

You are a human resource associate at a small Web design firm. Your boss, the firm's owner and president, informs you that she has just received a request for recognition from a union that claims to represent the firm's production employees. The president asks you to gather information about the representation election process. Using the NLRB's Web site at **http://www.nlrb.gov/**, what information can you discover about the board's procedures and regulations regarding the holding of a representation election? Click the link to Rules and Regulations for the detailed description of the NLRB's procedures; click the Manuals link to see the board's manual for law and procedure in representation election cases; click the Forms link for the Petition form (#502) to seek an election; and finally, click the Other Publications link to print copies of "The NLRB and You—Representation Cases" and "Your Government Conducts an Election."

INFOTRAC KEYWORDS

http://www.infotrac-college.com

unionization, union elections, bargaining unit, labor strike, union recognition

15

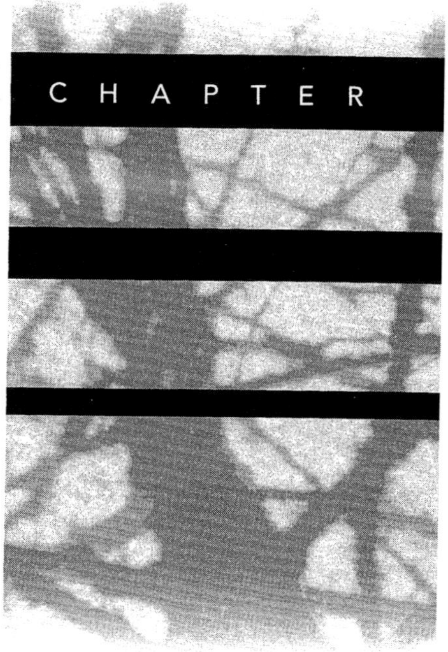

UNFAIR LABOR PRACTICES BY EMPLOYERS AND UNIONS

The National Labor Relations Act (NLRA) defines a list of unfair labor practices by both employers and unions. Such unfair labor practices are various forms of conduct or activities that adversely affect employees in the exercise of their rights under Section 7 of the act. The unfair labor practices by employers in Section 8(a) were in the Wagner Act; the union unfair labor practices in Section 8(b) were added by the Taft-Hartley Act in 1947 and amended by the Landrum-Griffin Act of 1959.

Section 8(a) makes it illegal for an employer to engage in the following conduct:

- interfere with, restrain, or coerce employees in the exercise of rights guaranteed to them by Section 7 of the act;
- dominate, interfere with, or contribute financial or other support to a labor organization;
- discriminate in the hiring or terms or conditions of employment of employees in order to encourage or discourage membership in any labor organization;
- discharge or discriminate against an employee for filing charges or giving testimony under the NLRA;
- refuse to bargain collectively with the bargaining representatives of the employees, as designated in Section 9(a).

Section 8(b) makes it illegal for unions to engage in the following conduct:

- restrain or coerce employees in the exercise of their rights under Section 7, or restrain or coerce an employer in the selection of a representative for collective bargaining purposes;

- cause or attempt to cause an employer to discriminate against an employee in terms or conditions of employment in order to encourage (or discourage) union membership;
- refuse to bargain collectively with an employer (when the union is the bargaining agent of the employees);
- engage in secondary picketing or encourage secondary boycotts of certain employers;
- require employees to pay excessive or discriminatory union dues or membership fees;
- cause an employer to pay for services that are not performed (feather-bedding);
- picket an employer in order to force the employer to recognize the union as bargaining agent when the union is not entitled to recognition under the act (recognition picketing).

Because both employer and union unfair practices involve, for the most part, the same kinds of conduct, we examine them together in this chapter. The refusal to bargain by either employer or union will be discussed in Chapter 16, which deals with the duty to bargain in good faith. The union offenses of secondary picketing and recognition picketing will be discussed in Chapter 17, along with other forms of union pressure tactics.

SECTION 7: RIGHTS OF EMPLOYEES

Because all unfair practices involve conduct that interferes with employees in the exercise of their rights under Section 7 of the NLRA, it is important to determine the exact rights granted employees by Section 7. Section 7 contains this statement:

> Employees shall have the right to self-organization, to form, join or assist labor organizations, to bargain collectively through representatives of their own choosing, and to engage in other concerted activities for the purpose of collective bargaining or other mutual aid or protection, and shall also have the right to refrain from any or all such activities. . . .

http://www4.law.cornell.edu/uscode/29/157.html *contains the text of Section 7 on Rights of Employees.*

The rights under Section 7 are given to all employees covered by the NLRA; the employees need not be organized union members to enjoy such rights. In addition, because the rights are given to the individual employee, they may not be waived by a union purporting to act on behalf of the employees.

For conduct of employees to be protected under Section 7, it must be *concerted* and it must be for the purpose of collective bargaining or other mutual aid or protection. A group of employees discussing the need for a union in order to improve working conditions is obviously under the protection of Section 7, as are employees who attempt to get their co-workers to join a union. But the protection of Section 7 also extends to activities not directly associated with formal unionization. For example, a group of nonunion employees who walked off the job to protest the extremely cold temperatures inside the shop were held to be exercising their Section 7 rights, as was an employee who circulated a petition about the management of the company's credit union. An employee collecting signatures of co-workers on a letter to management protesting the selection of a new supervisor was held to be engaged in protected activity in *Atlantic-Pacific Coast Inc. v. NLRB* [52 F.3d 260 (9th Cir. 1995)]. Section 7 protects employees in these situations from discipline or discharge for their conduct.

There are, of course, limits to the extent of Section 7 protection. Employees acting individually may not be protected; in addition, conduct not related to collective bargaining or mutual aid or protection purposes is not protected. For example, an employee seeking to have a foreman removed because of a personal "grudge" was held not protected by Section 7; nor was a group of employees striking to protest company sales to South Africa protected.

Perhaps the most difficult aspect of determining whether conduct is protected under Section 7 deals with the "concerted action" requirement: When is an individual employee, acting alone, protected? The following Supreme Court decision addresses this question.

NLRB v. City Disposal Systems

465 U.S. 822 (1984)

Brennan, J.

James Brown, a truck driver employed by respondent, was discharged when he refused to drive a truck that he honestly and reasonably believed to be unsafe because of faulty brakes. Article XXI of the collective-bargaining agreement between respondent and Local 247 of the International Brotherhood of Teamsters, Chauffeurs, Warehousemen and Helpers of America, which covered Brown, provides:

> [T]he Employer shall not require employees to take out on the street or highways any vehicle that is not in safe operating condition or equipped with safety appliances prescribed by law. It shall not be a violation of the Agreement where employees refuse to operate such equipment unless such refusal is unjustified.

The question to be decided is whether Brown's honest and reasonable assertion of his right to be free of the obligation to drive unsafe trucks constituted "concerted activit[y]" within the meaning of Section 7 of the National Labor Relations Act. The National Labor Relations Board (NLRB) held that Brown's refusal was concerted activity within Section 7, and that his discharge was, therefore, an unfair labor practice under Section 8(a)(1) of the Act. The Court of Appeals disagreed and declined enforcement.

James Brown was assigned to truck No. 245. On Saturday, May 12, 1979, Brown observed that a fellow driver had difficulty with the brakes of another truck, truck No. 244. As a result of the brake problem, truck No. 244 nearly collided with Brown's truck. After unloading their garbage at the landfill, Brown and the driver of truck No. 244 brought No. 244 to respondent's truck-repair facility, where they were told that the brakes would be repaired either over the weekend or in the morning of Monday, May 14.

Early in the morning of Monday, May 14, while transporting a load of garbage to the landfill, Brown experienced difficulty with one of the wheels of his own truck—No. 245—and brought that truck in for repair. At the repair facility, Brown was told that, because of a backlog at the facility, No. 245 could not be repaired that day. Brown reported the situation to his supervisor, Otto Jasmund, who ordered Brown to punch out and go home. Before Brown could leave, however, Jasmund changed his mind and asked Brown to drive truck No. 244 instead. Brown refused explaining that "there's something wrong with that truck. . . . [S]omething was wrong with the brakes . . . there was a grease seal or something leaking causing it to be affecting the brakes."

Brown did not, however, explicitly refer to Article XXI of the collective-bargaining agreement or to the agreement in general. In response to Brown's refusal to drive truck No. 244, Jasmund angrily told Brown to go home. At that point, an argument ensued and Robert Madary, another supervisor, intervened, repeating Jasmund's request that Brown drive truck No. 244. Again, Brown refused, explaining that No. 244 "has got problems and I don't want to drive it." Madary replied that half the trucks had problems and that if respondent tried to fix all of them it would be unable to do business. He went on to tell Brown that "[w]e've got all this garbage out here to haul and you tell me about you don't want to drive." Brown responded, "Bob, what you going to do, put the garbage ahead of the safety of the men?" Finally, Madary went to his office and Brown went home. Later that day, Brown received word that he had been discharged. He immediately returned to work in an attempt to gain reinstatement but was unsuccessful.

... Brown filed an unfair labor practice charge with the NLRB, challenging his discharge. The Administrative Law Judge (ALJ) found that Brown had been discharged for refusing to operate truck No. 244, that Brown's refusal was covered by Section 7 of the NLRA, and that respondent had therefore committed an unfair labor practice under Section 8(a)(1) of the Act. The ALJ held that an employee who acts alone in asserting a contractual right can nevertheless be engaged in concerted activity within the meaning of Section 7. . . .

The NLRB adopted the findings and conclusions of the ALJ and ordered that Brown be reinstated with back pay. On a petition for enforcement of the Board's order, the Court of Appeals disagreed with the ALJ and the Board. Finding that Brown's refusal to drive truck No. 244 was an action taken solely on his own behalf, the Court of Appeals concluded that the refusal was not a concerted activity within the meaning of Section 7.

Section 7 of the NLRA provides that "[e]mployees shall have the right to . . . join or assist labor organizations, to bargain collectively through representatives of their own choosing, and to engage in other concerted activities for the purpose of collective bargaining or other mutual aid or protection." The NLRB's decision in this case applied the Board's longstanding "*Interboro* doctrine," under which an individual's assertion of a right grounded in a collective-bargaining agreement is recognized as "concerted activit[y]" and therefore accorded the protection of Section 7. The Board has relied on two justifications for the doctrine: First, the assertion of a right contained in a collective-bargaining agreement is an extension of the concerted action that produced the agreement; and second, the assertion of such a right affects the rights of all employees covered by the collective-bargaining agreement.

Neither the Court of Appeals nor respondent appears to question that an employee's invocation of a right derived from a collective-bargaining agreement meets Section 7's requirement that an employee's action be taken "for purposes of collective bargaining or other mutual aid or protection." As the Board first explained in the *Interboro* case, a single employee's invocation of such rights affects all the employees that are covered by the collective-bargaining agreement. This type of generalized effect, as our cases have demonstrated, is sufficient to bring the actions of an individual employee within the "mutual aid or protection" standard, regardless of whether the employee has his own interests most immediately in mind.

The term "concerted activit[y]" is not defined in the Act but it clearly enough embraces the activities of employees who have joined together in order to achieve common goals. What is not self-evident from the language of the Act, however, and what we must elucidate, is the precise manner in which particular actions of an individual employee must be linked to the actions of fellow employees in order to permit it to be said that the individual is engaged in concerted activity. We now turn to consider the Board's analysis of that question as expressed in the *Interboro* doctrine.

Although one could interpret the phrase, "to engage in concerted activities," to refer to a situation in which two or more employees are working together at the same time and the same place toward a common goal, the language of Section 7 does not confine itself to such a narrow meaning. In fact, Section 7 itself defines both joining and assisting labor organizations—activities in which a single employee can engage—as concerted activities. Indeed, even the courts that have rejected the *Interboro* doctrine recognize the possibility that an individual employee may be engaged in concerted activity when he acts alone. They have limited their recognition of this type of concerted activity, however, to two situations: (1) that in which the lone employee intends to induce group activity, and (2) that in which the employee acts as a representative of at least one other employee. The disagreement over the *Interboro* doctrine, therefore, merely reflects differing views regarding the nature of the relationship that must exist between the action of the individual employee and the actions of the group in order for Section 7 to apply. We cannot say that the Board's view of that relationship, as applied in the *Interboro* doctrine, is unreasonable.

The invocation of a right rooted in a collective-bargaining agreement is unquestionably an integral part of the process that gave rise to the agreement. That process—beginning with the organization of a union, continuing into the negotiation of a collective-bargaining agreement, and extending through the enforcement of the agreement—is a single, collective activity. Obviously, an employee could not invoke a right grounded in a collective-bargaining agreement were it not for the prior negotiating activities of his fellow employees. Nor would it make sense for a union to negotiate a collective-bargaining agreement if individual employees could not invoke the rights thereby created against their employer. Moreover, when an employee invokes a right grounded in the collective-bargaining agreement, he does not stand alone. Instead, he brings to bear on his employer the power and resolve of all his fellow employees. When, for instance, James Brown refused to drive a truck he believed to be unsafe, he was in effect reminding his employer that he and his fellow employees, at the time their collective-bargaining agreement was signed, had extracted a promise from City Disposal that they would not be asked to drive unsafe trucks. He was also reminding his employer that if it persisted in ordering him to drive an unsafe truck, he could reharness the power of that group to ensure the enforcement of that promise. It was just as though James Brown was reassembling his fellow union members to reenact their decision not to drive unsafe trucks. A lone employee's invocation of a right grounded in his collective-bargaining agreement is, therefore, a concerted activity in a very real sense. . . .

. . . By applying Section 7 to the actions of individual employees invoking their rights under a collective-bargaining agreement, the *Interboro* doctrine preserves the integrity of the entire collective-bargaining process; for by invoking a right grounded in a collective-bargaining agreement, the employee makes that right a reality, and breathes life, not only into the promises contained in the collective-bargaining agreement, but also into the entire process envisioned by Congress as the means by which to achieve industrial peace.

To be sure, the principal tool by which an employee invokes the rights granted him in a collective-bargaining agreement is the processing of a grievance according to whatever procedures his collective-bargaining agreement establishes. . . . Indeed, it would make little sense for Section 7 to cover an employee's conduct while negotiating a collective-bargaining agreement, including a grievance mechanism by which to protect the rights created by the agreement, but not to cover an employee's attempt to utilize that mechanism to enforce the agreement.

. . . As long as the employee's statement or action is based on a reasonable and honest belief that he is being, or has been, asked to perform a task that he is not required to perform under his collective-bargaining agreement, and the statement or action is reasonably directed toward the enforcement of a collectively bargained right, there is no justification for overturning the Board's judgment that the employee is engaged in concerted activity, just as he would have been had he filed a formal grievance. . . .

In this case, the Board found that James Brown's refusal to drive truck No. 244 was based on an honest and reasonable belief that the brakes on the truck were faulty. Brown explained to each of his supervisors his reason for refusing to drive the truck. Although he did not refer to his collective-bargaining agreement in either of these confrontations, the agreement provided not only that "[t]he . . . .employer shall not require employees to take out on the streets or highways any vehicle that is not in safe operating condition," but also that "[i]t shall not be a violation of the Agreement where employees refuse to operate such equipment, unless such refusal is unjustified." There is no doubt, therefore, nor could there have been any doubt during Brown's confrontations with his supervisors, that by refusing to drive truck No. 244, Brown was invoking the right granted him in his collective-bargaining agreement to be free of the obligation to drive unsafe trucks. . . . Accordingly, we accept the Board's conclusion that James Brown was engaged in concerted activity when he refused to drive truck No. 244. We therefore reverse the judgment of the Court of Appeals and remand the case for further proceedings consistent with this opinion. . . .

It is so ordered.

Case Questions

1. What is the relationship of the collective-bargaining process to the right to refuse to operate unsafe equipment that was invoked by Brown? Did Brown mention the collective agreement when he refused to operate the truck?
2. How was Brown's individual refusal to operate the truck he felt was unsafe "concerted activity" within the meaning of Section 7 of the NLRA? Explain your answer.
3. Under what other circumstances, if any, can individual action be regarded as concerted within the meaning of Section 7?

In a National Labor Relations Board (NLRB) decision handed down before the Supreme Court decided *City Disposal Systems,* the board held that in order for an individual employee's action to be concerted, it would require "that the conduct be engaged in with or on the authority of other employees, and not solely by and on behalf of the employee himself." See *Meyers Industries* [268 NLRB No. 73 (1984)]. The case involved an employee who was discharged after refusing to drive his truck and reporting safety problems with his truck to state transportation authorities; the employee had acted alone and the workers were not unionized. Is this holding consistent with the Supreme Court's decision in *City Disposal Systems*?

The U.S. Court of Appeals for the District of Columbia remanded the board's decision in *Meyers Industries* to the board for reconsideration [755 F.2d 941 (1985)]. On rehearing, the board reaffirmed its decision that the employee had not been engaged in concerted activity. When the case again came before the court of appeals, the D.C. Circuit Court upheld the board's decision, holding that it was a reasonable interpretation of the act. See *Prill v. NLRB* [835 F.2d 1481 (1987)]. In *Ewing v. NLRB* [861 F.2d 353 (2d Cir. 1988)], the court of appeals upheld the board in a case similar to *Meyers Industries* on the board's third try at justifying the conclusion that the employee did not engage in concerted activity.

Even though conduct may be concerted under Section 7, it may not be protected by the act. As noted in the *City Disposal Systems* decision, the employee may not act in an abusive manner. The board has held that illegal, destructive, or unreasonable conduct is not protected, even if such conduct was concerted and for purposes of mutual aid or protection. For example, workers who engaged in on-the-job slowdowns by refusing to process orders were not protected because they could not refuse to work yet continue to get paid. Threats or physical violence by employees are not protected, nor is the public disparagement of the employer's product by employees or the referral of customers to competitors of the employer. The rights of employees under Section 7 are at the heart of the act; they are enforced and protected through unfair labor practice proceedings under Sections 8(a) and 8(b).

SECTIONS 8(A)(1) AND 8(B)(1): VIOLATION OF EMPLOYEE RIGHTS BY EMPLOYERS OR UNIONS

Interference with, coercion, or restraint of employees in the exercise of their Section 7 rights by employers or unions is prohibited by Section 8(a)(1) and Section 8(b)(1), respectively. While violations of other specific unfair labor practice provisions may also violate Sections 8(a)(1) or 8(b)(1), certain kinds of conduct involve violations of Sections 8(a)(1) or 8(b)(1) only. This section discusses conduct that violates those specific sections only.

The NLRB has held that any conduct that has the natural tendency to restrain or coerce employees in the exercise of their Section 7 rights is a violation; actual coercion or restraint of the employees need not be shown. Intention is not a requirement for a violation of Sections 8(a)(1) and 8(b)(1); the employer or union need not have intended to coerce or restrain employees. All that is necessary is

http://www4.law.cornell.edu/uscode/29/158.html
is the site of the section on unfair labor practices in the NRLA.

that they engage in conduct that the board believes has the natural tendency to restrain employees in the exercise of their Section 7 rights.

Most employer violations of Section 8(a)(1) occur in the context of union organizing campaigns. Such violations usually involve restrictions on the soliciting activities of employees or coercive or threatening remarks made by the employer. The employer's ability to make antiunion remarks is discussed first.

ANTIUNION REMARKS BY EMPLOYER

During a union organizing campaign, the employer might attempt to persuade employees not to support the union. Such attempts may involve statements of opinion regarding the prospects of unionization and may also involve implicit promises or threats of reprisal. The extent to which the employer may communicate its position has been the subject of numerous board and court decisions. Section 8(c) of the act states that

> The expressing of any views, argument or opinion . . . shall not constitute or be evidence of an unfair labor practice under any of the provisions of this Act, if such expression contains no threat of reprisal or force or promise of benefit.

It should be clear from the wording of Section 8(c) that explicit threats to fire union sympathizers are not protected by Section 8(c) and are therefore violations of Section 8(a)(1). The board believes that because employees are economically dependent on the employer for their livelihood, they will be especially sensitive to the views explicitly or implicitly expressed by the employer. The board will therefore examine closely the "totality of circumstances" of any employer's antiunion remarks to determine if they go beyond the protections of Section 8(c) and thus violate Section 8(a)(1).

In the *Gissel Packing* decision, mentioned in Chapter 14, the Supreme Court defined the limits to which an employer may predict the consequences of unionization. The employer may make a prediction based on objective facts to convey the employer's reasonable belief as to demonstrably probable effects or consequences, provided that such factors are beyond the employer's control. If the employer makes predictions about matters within the control of the employer, the board is likely to view such statements as implicit threats because the employer is in a position to make those predictions come true. Statements such as, "The union almost put us out of business last time and the new management wouldn't hesitate to close this plant," have been held to be violations of Section 8(a)(1), whereas comments such as, "If the union gets in, it will have to bargain from scratch for everything it gets," have been held to be within Section 8(c)'s protection.

In *American Spring Wire Co.* [237 NLRB No. 185 (1978)], the company's president made the following speech to employees in response to rumors that a union was trying to organize the workers:

> . . . We have beaten the Union on two occasions in this plant by overwhelming majorities and I know the majority of us are tired of such activity. The majority of us do not deserve such continuing harassment. We have set up in this Company all the means of communication possible, and to those of you who still think you can

> win more with the Union than you have with us in the past 9 years, well—you are dead wrong—leave us alone—get the hell out of our plant. . . .
>
> I want to say something to you as clearly as I possibly can. Whether or not ASW has a union is really not significant to the Corporation's future, or to myself, Dave Carruthers, or other major employees of this Company. As far as I am concerned those of us who are loyal to each other as a group can make valve spring wire, music wire, alloy wire, in Moline, Illinois; Saskatchewan, Canada; Puerto Rico; or Hawaii. We don't need Cleveland, Ohio, or all this beautiful property. Remember nine years ago we had nothing. Today our Company has developed a certain amount of wealth and goodwill at the banks, a fantastic organization of people and friends who supply us goods, and above all a long and growing list of customers. These people do business with us, not with this building or this land. We do not intend to have this statement appear as a threat because it is not. It is a statement of fact. Facts are that our real concern regarding a union is with the majority of you who have opposed it in the past, and who would be locked into it should it come to this plant.
>
> With that in mind, I want to tell you that those of us in management do not wish to become involved in another election. We need the time to do the things that will continue to promote our Company, ourselves, and hopefully, you. I am asking you as your friend not to sign union cards, as we don't have the patience to put up with it again. This next battle is yours, not ours. It is up to each one of you who is against the union to stop the card signing before it gets started. I don't care how you do it. Organize yourselves and get it done. . . .

The NLRB held that the statement directing union supporters to ". . . get the hell out of our plant" and telling those employees who opposed the union to ". . . stop the card signing before it gets started. I don't care how you do it. . . ." were threatening and coercive. The statement that "We don't need Cleveland, Ohio. . . ." was held to be a clear threat to close the plant if the employees joined a union. The remarks were held to be a violation of Section 8(a)(1). In *NLRB v. Exchange Parts* [375 U.S. 405 (1964)], the Supreme Court held that the announcement of improved vacation pay and salary benefits during a union organizing campaign violated Section 8(a)(1). The Court reasoned that

> The danger inherent in the well-timed increases in benefits is the suggestion of the fist inside the velvet glove. Employees are not likely to miss the inference that the source of benefits now conferred is also the source from which future benefits must flow and which may dry up if it is not obliged.

Why is the promise of benefits not protected under Section 8(c)? How does it interfere with the employees' exercise of Section 7 rights?

In *Heck's, Inc.* [293 NLRB No. 132, 131 L.R.R.M. 1281 (1989)], the board declared that an employer did not commit an unfair labor practice by informing its unionized employees that it was opposed to their union and to unionization in general. However, the employer did commit an unfair labor practice by including its anti-union policy in its employee handbook and unilaterally requesting that all employees sign a statement agreeing to be bound by that policy.

EMPLOYER LIMITATIONS ON SOLICITING AND ORGANIZING

For employees to exercise their right, under Section 7, to choose their bargaining representative free from coercion, the employees must have access to information that will enable them to exercise this right intelligently. Such information may come from fellow employees who are active in union organizing attempts, or it may come from nonemployee union organizers. Although the union may attempt to reach the employees individually at their homes, it is more convenient and more effective to contact the employees at the work site when they are all assembled there. But organizing activities at the workplace may disrupt production and will certainly conflict with the employer's right to control and direct the work force. The employer's property rights at the workplace also include the right to control access to the premises. Clearly, then, the right of employees to organize is in conflict with the employer's property rights over the enterprise. How is such a conflict to be reconciled?

In *NLRB v. Babcock & Wilcox* [351 U.S. 105 (1956)], the Supreme Court upheld a series of NLRB rules for employer restrictions upon nonemployee access to the premises and soliciting activity of employees. In the following case, the Supreme Court reconsidered the issues raised in *Babcock & Wilcox*.

Lechmere, Inc. v. NLRB

502 U.S. 527 (1992)

Thomas, J.

. . . This case stems from the efforts of Local 919 of the United Food and Commercial Workers Union, AFL-CIO, to organize employees at a retail store in Newington, Connecticut, owned and operated by petitioner Lechmere, Inc. The store is located in the Lechmere Shopping Plaza. . . . Lechmere's store is situated at the Plaza's south end, with the main parking lot to its north. A strip of 13 smaller "satellite stores" not owned by Lechmere runs along the west side of the Plaza, facing the parking lot. To the Plaza's east (where the main entrance is located) runs the Berlin Turnpike, a four-lane divided highway. The parking lot, however, does not abut the Turnpike; they are separated by a 46-foot-wide grassy strip, broken only by the Plaza's entrance. The parking lot is owned jointly by Lechmere and the developer of the satellite stores. The grassy strip is public property (except for a four-foot-wide band adjoining the parking lot, which belongs to Lechmere).

The union began its campaign to organize the store's 200 employees, none of whom was represented by a union, in June 1987. After a full-page advertisement in a local newspaper drew little response, nonemployee union organizers entered Lechmere's parking lot and began placing handbills on the windshields of cars parked in a corner of the lot used mostly by employees. Lechmere's manager immediately confronted the organizers, informed them that Lechmere prohibited solicitation or handbill distribution of any kind on its property,[1] and asked them to leave. They did so, and Lechmere personnel removed the handbills. The union organizers renewed this handbilling effort in the parking lot on several subsequent occasions; each time they were asked to leave and the handbills were removed. The organizers then relocated to the public grassy strip, from where they attempted to pass out handbills to cars

[1]Lechmere had established this policy several years prior to the union's organizing efforts. The store's official policy statement provided, in relevant part: "Non-associates [i.e., nonemployees] are prohibited from soliciting and distributing literature at all times anywhere on Company property, including parking lots. Non-associates have no right of access to the non-working areas and only to the public and selling areas of the store in connection with its public use." On each door to the store Lechmere had posted a six-inch by eight-inch sign reading: "TO THE PUBLIC. No Soliciting, Canvassing, Distribution of Literature or Trespassing by Non-Employees in or on Premises." Lechmere consistently enforced this policy inside the store as well as on the parking lot (against, among others, the Salvation Army and the Girl Scouts).

entering the lot during hours (before opening and after closing) when the drivers were assumed to be primarily store employees. For one month, the union organizers returned daily to the grassy strip to picket Lechmere; after that, they picketed intermittently for another six months. They also recorded the license plate numbers of cars parked in the employee parking area; with the cooperation of the Connecticut Department of Motor Vehicles, they thus secured the names and addresses of some 41 nonsupervisory employees (roughly 20 percent of the store's total). The union sent four mailings to these employees; it also made some attempts to contact them by phone or home visits. These mailings and visits resulted in one signed union authorization card.

Alleging that Lechmere had violated the National Labor Relations Act by barring the nonemployee organizers from its property, the union filed an unfair labor practice charge with respondent National Labor Relations Board (Board).... [A]n administrative law judge (ALJ) ruled in the union's favor. He recommended that Lechmere be ordered, among other things, to cease and desist from barring the union organizers from the parking lot....

The Board affirmed the ALJ's judgment and adopted the recommended order.... A divided panel of the United States Court of Appeals for the First Circuit denied Lechmere's petition for review and enforced the Board's order. This Court granted certiorari.

... By its plain terms, the NLRA confers rights only on employees, not on unions or their nonemployee organizers. In *NLRB v. Babcock & Wilcox Co.* (1956), however, we recognized that insofar as the employees' "right of self-organization depends in some measure on [their] ability ... to learn the advantages of self-organization from others," § 7 of the NLRA may, in certain limited circumstances, restrict an employer's right to exclude nonemployee union organizers from his property. It is the nature of those circumstances that we explore today....

[In *Babcock,* the Supreme Court held] ... that the Board had erred by failing to make the critical distinction between the organizing activities of employees (to whom § 7 guarantees the right of self-organization) and non-employees (to whom § 7 applies only derivatively). Thus, while "no restriction may be placed on the employees' right to discuss self-organization among themselves, unless the employer can demonstrate that a restriction is necessary to maintain production or discipline, ... no such obligation is owed nonemployee organizers...." As a rule, then, an employer cannot be compelled to allow distribution of union literature by nonemployee organizers on his property. As with many other rules, however, we recognized an exception. Where "the location of a plant and the living quarters of the employees place the employees beyond the reach of reasonable union efforts to communicate with them," employers' property rights may be "required to yield to the extent needed to permit communication of information on the right to organize...."

Although we have not had occasion to apply *Babcock's* analysis in the ensuing decades, we have described it in cases arising in related contexts.... In both cases, we quoted approvingly *Babcock's* admonition that accommodation between employees' § 7 rights and employers' property rights "must be obtained with as little destruction of the one as is consistent with the maintenance of the other." There is no hint in [either of the two cases], however, that our invocation of *Babcock's* language of "accommodation" was intended to repudiate or modify *Babcock's* holding that an employer need not accommodate nonemployee organizers unless the employees are otherwise inaccessible. Indeed, in one case we expressly noted that nonemployee organizers cannot claim even a limited right of access to a nonconsenting employer's property until "after the requisite need for access to the employer's property has been shown"....

We further noted that, in practice, nonemployee organizational trespassing had generally been prohibited except where "unique obstacles" prevented nontrespassory methods of communication with the employees....

In *Babcock,* as explained above, we held that the Act drew a distinction "of substance" between the union activities of employees and nonemployees. In cases involving employee activities, we noted with approval, the Board "balanced the conflicting interests of employees to receive information on self-organization on the company's property from fellow employees during nonworking time, with the employer's right to control the use of his property." In cases involving nonemployee activities (like those at issue in *Babcock* itself), however, the Board was not permitted to engage in that same balancing (and we reversed the Board for having done so).... *Babcock's* teaching is straightforward: § 7 simply does not protect nonemployee union organizers except in the rare case where "the inaccessibility of employees makes ineffective the reasonable attempts by nonemployees to communicate with them through the usual channels." Our reference to "reasonable" attempts was nothing more than a commonsense recognition that unions need not engage in extraordinary feats to communicate with inaccessible employees—not an endorsement of the view (which we expressly rejected) that the Act protects "reasonable" trespasses. Where reasonable alternative means of access exist, § 7's guarantees do not authorize trespasses by nonemployee organizers, even . . . "under . . . reasonable regulations" established by the Board.

. . . To say that our cases require accommodation between employees' and employers' rights is a true but incomplete statement, for the cases also go far in establishing the locus of that accommodation where nonemployee organizing is at issue. So long as nonemployee union organizers have reasonable access to employees outside an employer's property, the requisite accommodation has taken place. It is only where such access is infeasible that it becomes necessary and proper to take the accommodation inquiry to a second level, balancing the employees' and employers' rights. . . .

. . . The threshold inquiry in this case, then, is whether the facts here justify application of *Babcock's* inaccessibility exception. The ALJ below observed that "the facts herein convince me that reasonable alternative means [of communicating with Lechmere's employees] were available to the Union. . . ." Reviewing the ALJ's decision . . . however, the Board reached a different conclusion on this point, asserting that "there was no reasonable, effective alternative means available for the Union to communicate its message to [Lechmere's] employees."

We cannot accept the Board's conclusion, because it "rests on erroneous legal foundations." . . . As we have explained, the exception to *Babcock's* rule is a narrow one. It does not apply wherever nontrespassory access to employees may be cumbersome or less-than-ideally effective, but only where "the location of a plant and the living quarters of the employees place the employees beyond the reach of reasonable union efforts to communicate with them." Classic examples include logging camps . . . , mining camps . . . and mountain resort hotels. . . . *Babcock's* exception was crafted precisely to protect the § 7 rights of those employees who, by virtue of their employment, are isolated from the ordinary flow of information that characterizes our society. The union's burden of establishing such isolation is, as we have explained, "a heavy one," and one not satisfied by mere conjecture or the expression of doubts concerning the effectiveness of nontrespassory means of communication.

The Board's conclusion in this case that the union had no reasonable means short of trespass to make Lechmere's employees aware of its organizational efforts is based on a misunderstanding of the limited scope of this exception. Because the employees do not reside on Lechmere's property, they are presumptively not "beyond the reach," of the union's message. Although the employees live in a large metropolitan area (Greater Hartford), that fact does not in itself render them "inaccessible" in the sense contemplated by *Babcock*. . . . Such direct contact, of course, is not a necessary element of "reasonably effective" communication; signs or advertising also may suffice. In this case, the union tried advertising in local newspapers; the Board said that this was not reasonably effective because it was expensive and might not reach the employees. Whatever the merits of that conclusion, other alternative means of communication were readily available. Thus, signs (displayed, for example, from the public grassy strip adjoining Lechmere's parking lot) would have informed the employees about the union's organizational efforts. (Indeed, union organizers picketed the shopping center's main entrance for months as employees came and went every day.) Access to employees, not success in winning them over, is the critical issue—although success, or lack thereof, may be relevant in determining whether reasonable access exists. Because the union in this case failed to establish the existence of any "unique obstacles," that frustrated access to Lechmere's employees, the Board erred in concluding that Lechmere committed an unfair labor practice by barring the nonemployee organizers from its property.

The judgment of the First Circuit is therefore reversed, and enforcement of the Board's order denied.

It is so ordered.

Case Questions

1. What means were available to the union to contact the Lechmere employees? Which, if any, did the union use to try to reach those employees? How successful were the union's efforts?
2. When, according to *Babcock & Wilcox,* must an employer allow nonemployee organizers on the employer's property? What examples of such instances does the majority opinion give?
3. What was the basis of the NLRB's decision in this case? Why does the Court reverse the NLRB's decision? Explain.

As the Supreme Court noted in *Lechmere,* under certain circumstances the employer may be required to allow union organizers access to its property when there are no other reasonable alternative means of access available. In *Thunder Basin Coal v. Reich* [510 U.S. 200 (1994)], the Supreme Court stated that the employer's right to exclude union organizers comes from state property law, not from the NLRA; nothing in the NLRA requires that employers exclude organizers. Where the employer has no state law property right to exclude union organizers, *Lechmere* does not apply, and the employer may not prohibit access by the union, *NLRB v. Calkins* [187 F.3d (9th Cir. 1999)]. In *United Food and Commercial Workers v. NLRB* [222 F.3d 1030 (D.C. Cir. 2000)], the U.S. Court of Appeals for the D.C. Circuit held that an employer leasing the property had no right, under state law, to deny access to union organizers.

Restrictions on Employees

Although nonemployees may be barred completely, an employer may place only "reasonable restrictions" on the soliciting activities of employees. Employer rules limiting soliciting activities must have a valid workplace purpose, such as ensuring worker safety or maintaining the efficient operation of the business, and must be applied uniformly to all soliciting, not just to union activities. The employer may limit the distribution of literature where it poses a litter problem. Employee soliciting activity may be limited to nonworking areas such as cafeterias, restrooms, or parking lots. Such activities may also be restricted to "nonworking times" such as coffee breaks and lunch breaks. However, an employer may not completely prohibit such activities. In the absence of exceptional circumstances, blanket prohibitions on soliciting have been held unreasonable and in violation of Section 8(a)(1).

Employer rules requiring that employees get prior approval from the employer for solicitation are overly restrictive and violate section 8(a)(1), *Opryland Hotel* [323 NLRB 723 (1997)]. Employers have the right to restrict the use of company bulletin boards and telephones during working time, but the employer may not enforce such rules in a discriminatory manner to exclude or restrict union activities. If the employer allows employees the occasional personal use of company telephones or e-mail systems, it could not lawfully exclude union activities as a subject of discussion, *Adtranz* [331 NLRB No. 40 (2000), *enforced in part,* 253 F.3d 19 (D.C. Cir. 2001)]. Employers may not restrict "visual-only" solicitations such as hats, buttons, and so forth in the absence of exceptional circumstances.

When the workplace is a department store or hospital, "no-solicitation" rules may present particular problems. An employer will attempt to ensure that soliciting activity does not interfere with customer access or patient care, yet the board will ensure that the employees are still able to exercise their Section 7 rights. In *Beth Israel Hospital v. NLRB* [437 U.S. 483 (1978)], the U.S. Supreme Court upheld the board order allowing a hospital to prohibit soliciting by employees in patient-care areas, but prohibiting the hospital from denying employees the right to solicit in the hospital cafeteria.

OTHER SECTION 8(A)(1) VIOLATIONS

An employer filing an ultimately unsuccessful suit against unions engaged in protected activity is not automatically in violation of Section 8(a)(1) when there were reasonable grounds for the suit, *BE & K Construction Co. v. NLRB* [536 U.S. 516 (2002)].[2] Other employer practices likely to produce Section 8(a)(1) complaints may involve interrogation of employees regarding union sympathies and the denial of employee requests to have a representative present during disciplinary proceedings.

Polling and Interrogation

An employer approached by a union claiming to have the support of a majority of employees may wish to get some independent verification of the union's claim. In *Struknes Construction* [165 NLRB 1062 (1967)], the NLRB set out guidelines to reconcile the legitimate interests of an employer in polling employees regarding union support with the tendency of such a poll to restrain employees in the free exercise of their Section 7 rights. The NLRB requires that the employer have a "good faith reasonable doubt" about a union's claim of majority support in order to conduct a poll of employees regarding their support of a union. The Supreme Court upheld the Board's "good faith reasonable doubt" requirement in *Allentown Mack Sales and Service, Inc. v. NLRB* [522 U.S. 359 (1998)]. If the employer chooses to poll its employees, the poll must be conducted according to the following guidelines:

1. It must be done in response to a union claim of majority support.
2. The employees must be informed of the purpose of the poll.
3. The employees must be given assurances that no reprisals will result from their choice.
4. The poll must be by secret ballot.

In addition, the employer must not have created a coercive atmosphere through unfair labor practices or other behavior; and the poll must not be taken if a representation election is pending. Why should the board preclude such a poll when an election is pending? In light of *Linden Lumber* (in Chapter 14), what happens when the poll by the employer discloses that the union has majority support?

The employer polling pursuant to the *Struknes* rules needs to be distinguished from the interrogation of employees regarding their union sympathies. Polling is to be done by secret ballot and only in response to a union claim for voluntary recognition. Interrogation may involve confronting individual employees and questioning

---

[2]See "Case Handling Instructions for Cases Concerning *Bill Johnson's Restaurant* and *BE & K Construction Company v. NLRB*," Memorandum of the General Counsel, Memorandum 02-09, Sept. 20, 2002, available from the NLRB Website at **http://www.nlrb.gov**. Click on the link to "GC Memos" and then scroll down to the link for GC Memo 02-09.

them about their union sympathies. Such interrogation may be in response to a union organizing campaign or a request for voluntary recognition.

The NLRB has held that interrogation of individual employees, even known union adherents, is not an unfair labor practice if it is done without threats or the promise of benefits by the employer [*Rossmore House,* 269 NLRB No. 198 (1984); affirmed sub nom *Hotel & Restaurant Employees Local 11 v. NLRB,* 760 F.2d 1006 (9th Cir. 1985)]. If the interrogation is accompanied by threats against the employees or other unfair labor practices by the employer, however, it may be a violation of Section 8(a)(1).

In *Alliance Rubber* [126 L.R.R.M. 1217, 286 NLRB No. 57 (1987)], the board, in a 2-1 decision, held that two polygraph examiners, hired by the employer to help in an investigation of suspected plant sabotage and drug use, were acting as agents of the employer when they interrogated employees about union activities in the course of administering polygraph exams to the employees. The board held that the questioning was made even more stressful because of its connection with the investigation into drug use and sabotage, and it implicitly gave the employees the message that engaging in union activity might result in them being suspected of engaging in unlawful activity in the plant. The company vice president's conduct reasonably led employees to believe that the examiners asked the questions about union activities on behalf of the employer; therefore, the employer and the polygraph operators were held to have violated Section 8(a)(1).

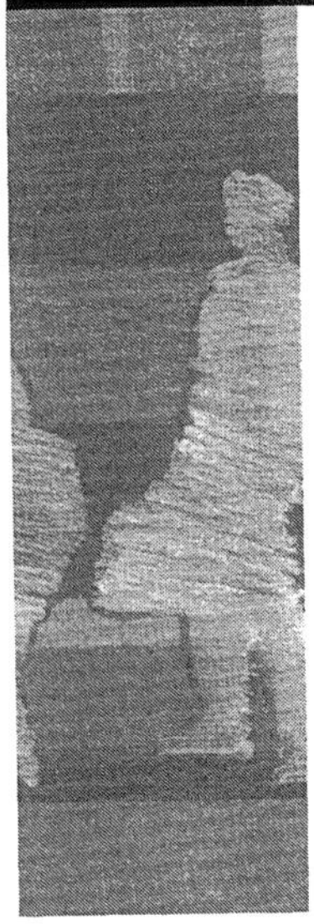

BODY ARMOR FIRM HELD GUILTY OF ULPS

THE WORKING LAW

An NLRB administrative law judge (ALJ) ordered Point Blank Body Armor, Inc., a Florida firm that makes personal body armor for the U.S. Army and various city police departments, to stop threatening employees with dismissal or loss of jobs. The NLRB unfair labor practice charges grew out of events surrounding a union organizing campaign for the firm's workers. On July 17, 2002, a group of employees sought to present two documents to their supervisors during the workers' morning break. The documents were a request for voluntary recognition and a request that the company remain neutral during any representation election. The supervisors refused to accept the documents and informed the employees that they were doing something illegal. One supervisor told them, "You made a mistake . . . It will get bad. It will get worse for you . . ." The workers began to chant in support of the union "Si, se puede"; in response to the workers' demonstration, the employer called police and ultimately closed the plant for the day at 11:00 A.M. The employees left the premises but gathered in a parking lot across the street and continued to chant and protest the early closing.

That afternoon, the firm fired the employee who had acted as spokesman for the employees, and over the next few weeks, it fired several other employees who were perceived as leading union supporters. The firm also reduced overtime and informed the employees that it was making arrangements to contract out work and to lay off employees if they engaged in any "slowdown" of work production. When another employee wearing a union button was fired on Friday, August 9, allegedly for taking an overly long bathroom break, approximately 175 other workers walked off the job in protest. Managers told the workers that they would be fired if they did not return to work within three days. On August 28, the firm sent letters to the strikers informing them that they had been permanently replaced.

The NLRB sought an injunction under Section 10(j), and on January 30, 2003, the U.S. District Court for the Southern District of Florida issued an injunction ordering the firm to stop disciplining, terminating, or otherwise adversely affecting the working conditions of the workers because of their support and activities for the union. The court also ordered the firm to reinstate the fired workers and the striking workers who made unconditional offers to return to work. The NLRB issued an unfair labor practice complaint against the firm, and on July 16, 2003, the NLRB administrative law judge found the company in violation of Sections 8(a)(1) and 8(a)(3) and ordered the firm to stop threatening the employees with loss of work, discharge, layoff, or plant closure in retaliation for their union activities or support. The ALJ also ordered that the firm pay the discharged workers back pay and pay all the employees for the loss of overtime that was taken away in retaliation for union activity. The firm vowed to appeal the ALJ's decision.

Sources: *Kentov v. Point Blank Body Armor, Inc.* [2003 WL 253063 (S.D. Fla. Jan. 30, 2003)]; "Body Armor Firm Ordered to Stop Threatening Employees," *Newsday,* July 17, 2003; "Board Finds Broward County Body Armor Maker in Violation of Labor Laws," *The Miami Herald,* July 17, 2003.

Weingarten Rights

***Weingarten* Rights**
The right of employees to have a representative of their choice present at meetings that may result in disciplinary action against the employees.

In *NLRB v. Weingarten* [420 U.S. 251 (1975)], an employer refused to allow an employee to have a union representative present during the questioning of the employee about thefts from the employer. The Supreme Court upheld the NLRB ruling that such a refusal violated Section 8(a)(1). The Court reasoned that "the action of an employee in seeking to have the assistance of his union representative at a confrontation with his employer clearly falls within the literal wording of Section 7 that '[e]mployees shall have the right . . . to engage in concerted activities for the purpose of . . . mutual aid or protection.'" Shortly after its decision in *Weingarten,* the board extended ***Weingarten* rights** to nonunion employees as well, *Materials Research Corp.* [262 NLRB 1010 (1982)]; however, in *E. I. DuPont & Co.* [2899 NLRB 627 (1988)], the NLRB decided to restrict such rights to unionized employees only. More recently, the NLRB reversed that position and again held that nonunion employees are also entitled to have a representative present during investigatory interviews, *Epilepsy Foundation of Northeast Ohio* [331 NLRB No. 92 (2000)]; that decision was enforced by the U.S. Court of Appeals for the District of Columbia, *Epilepsy Foundation of Northeast Ohio v. NLRB* [268 F.3d 1095 (2001)]. The *Weingarten* right to have a representative present applies whenever the meeting with management will have the "probable" result of the imposition of discipline or where such a result is "seriously considered." The NLRB also holds that, absent extenuating circumstances, the employee is entitled to the union representative of his or her choice, *Anheuser-Busch v. NLRB* [2003 WL 21773845 (4th Cir. Aug. 1, 2003)].

The board has set the following two requirements on the exercise of *Weingarten* rights by employees: (1) the employee must actually request the presence of a representative to have the right, *Montgomery Ward* [269 NLRB No. 156, 115 L.R.R.M. 1321 (1984)], and (2) an employer who violates an employee's *Weingarten* rights is not prevented from disciplining the employee, provided that the employer has independent evidence, not resulting from the "tainted" interview, to justify the discipline, *ITT Lighting Fixtures, Div. of ITT* [261 NLRB 229 (1982)].

Violence and Surveillance

One last area of employer violations of Section 8(a)(1) involves violence and surveillance of employees. It should be clear from the wording of Section 8(a)(1) that violence or threats of violence directed against employees by the employer (or agents of the employer) violate Section 8(a)(1) because they interfere with the free exercise of the employees' Section 7 rights. Employer surveillance of employee activities, or even creating the impression that the employees are under surveillance, also violates Section 8(a)(1) because such a practice has the natural tendency to restrict the free exercise of the employees' Section 7 rights. An employer photographing or videotaping employees who are engaging in protected activity is a violation of Section 8(a)(1), *F. W. Woolworth Co.* [310 NLRB 1197 (1993)]. An employer asking employees to agree to be filmed for use in an antiunion video was a violation of Section 8(a)(1), *Allegheny Ludlum Corp. v. NLRB* [301 F.3d 167 (3d Cir. 2002)].

UNION COERCION OF EMPLOYEES AND EMPLOYERS

Whereas Section 8(a)(1) prohibits employer interference with employees' Section 7 rights, Section 8(b)(1)(A) prohibits union restraint or coercion of the exercise of Section 7 rights by the employee. It is important to remember that Section 7 also gives employees the right to refrain from concerted activity. (There is an important qualification on the employees' right to refrain from union activities; Section 7 recognizes that a union shop or agency shop provision requiring employees to join the union or to pay union dues may be valid. We discuss these provisions later in this chapter.)

Section 8(b)(1)(A)

In *Radio Officers Union v. NLRB* [347 U.S. 17 (1954)], the Supreme Court stated that the policy behind Section 7 and Section 8(b) was "to allow employees to freely exercise their right to join unions, be good, bad or indifferent members, or to abstain from joining any union, without imperiling their livelihood."

Union threats or violence directed at employees are clear violations of Section 8(b)(1)(A); such actions tend to coerce or interfere with the employees' free choice of whether or not to support the union. But just as with employer actions under Section 8(a)(1), less blatant conduct may also be an unfair labor practice. Where the union has waived its initiation fees for employees who join prior to a representation election, the board has found a Section 8(b)(1)(A) violation. By the same reasoning, union statements such as, "Things will be tough for employees who don't join the union before the election," were also held to violate Section 8(b)(1)(A). A statement by a union business agent, in response to an internal union investigation into alleged financial improprieties initiated by other union members, that "when this is over with, someone's going to get hurt . . ." was held to be a threat of reprisal violating Section 8(b)(1)(A), *Local 466, Int. Brotherhood of Painters and Allied Trades (Skidmore College)* [332 NLRB No. 41 (2000)]. However, a union representative photographing employees distributing union literature outside the employer's facility is not per se a violation of Section 8(b)(1)(A), nor does it violate the laboratory conditions for holding a representation election, *Randall Warehouse of Arizona, Inc.* [328 NLRB 1034 (1999)].

Section 8(b)(1)(A) does recognize the need for unions to make rules regarding membership qualifications. A proviso to the section declares "[t]his paragraph shall not impair the right of a labor organization to prescribe its own rules with respect to the acquisition or retention of membership therein." The courts have tended to construe this provision liberally, provided that the union action does not affect the job tenure of an employee. The courts have allowed unions to fine members who refused to go on strike; they have also upheld the right of unions to file suit in state court to collect such fines. However, when a union has expelled a member for filing an unfair labor practice charge with the NLRB without exhausting available internal union remedies, the Supreme Court has found the union in violation of Section 8(b)(1)(A). The Court reasoned, "Any coercion used to discourage, retard or defeat that access [to the NLRB] is beyond the legitimate interests of a labor organization." See *NLRB v Industrial Union of Marine and Shipbuilding Workers* [391 U.S. 418 (1968)].

Section 8(b)(1)(B)

Section 8(b)(1)(B) protects employers from union coercion in their choice of a representative for purposes of collective bargaining or the adjustment of grievances. The legislative history of this section suggests that it was intended to prevent unions from coercing firms into multiemployer bargaining units.

In a number of industries, employers bargain with a union on a multiemployer basis. This is particularly true in industries characterized by a number of small firms and a single large union. Examples are coal mining, the trucking industry, construction, and the longshoring industry. To offset the power of the large union, the employers join together and bargain through an employers' association or multiemployer bargaining unit. This joint bargaining by employers prevents the union from engaging in **whipsaw strikes**—that is, strikes in which the union selectively strikes one firm in the industry. Because that firm's competitors are not struck, they can continue to operate and draw business from the struck firm. The struck firm is under great pressure to concede to union demands to regain lost business. When the firm capitulates, the union repeats the process against other firms. Multiemployer bargaining resists such efforts because all firms bargain together; if the union strikes one firm, the others can lock out their employees to undermine the union's pressure.

Whipsaw Strikes
Strikes by a union selectively pitting one firm in an industry against the other firms.

In addition to preventing whipsaw strikes, other reasons for engaging in multiemployer bargaining include the following:

- It eases each company's administrative burden by reducing the number of negotiating sessions and aiding information exchange.

- When one large company is the pacesetter in the industry and the union is likely to insist that other firms adopt approximately the same contract terms, smaller employers may have more input into the bargaining process by joining the leader in a multiemployer bargaining arrangement.
- Establishment of uniform wages, hours, and working conditions among the members of the bargaining group means firms will not have to engage in economic competition in the labor market.

Despite the legislative history of Section 8(b)(1)(B), the section does not mention multiemployer bargaining. The board and the courts have taken the position that multiemployer bargaining cannot be demanded by the interested employers or by the relevant union; rather, it must be consented to by both sides. The union need not agree to bargain with the employers' association, nor can it insist that any company or companies form or join such a bargaining group. However, once the parties have agreed to multiemployer bargaining and negotiations have begun, neither an employer nor the union may withdraw without the consent of the other side, except in the event of "unusual circumstances." This rule prevents one side from pulling out just because the bargaining has taken an undesirable turn. (The board has held that an impasse, or deadlock in negotiations, does not constitute "unusual circumstances.")

Unions have been found guilty of violating Section 8(b)(1)(B) when they struck to force a company to accept a multiemployer association for bargaining purposes and when they tried to force a firm to enter an individual contract in conflict with the established multiemployer unit. In addition, unions that have insisted on bargaining with company executives rather than an attorney hired by management have been held to violate Section 8(b)(1)(B).

SECTION 8(A)(2): EMPLOYER DOMINATION OF LABOR UNIONS

In-house Unions
Unions created and controlled by the employer.

In the years just prior to and shortly after the passage of the Wagner Act in 1935, employer-formed and dominated unions were common. Firms that decided they could no longer completely resist worker demands for collective action created **in-house unions,** or captive unions. Such unions or employee associations created an impression of collective bargaining while allowing management to retain complete control. This type of employer domination is outlawed by Section 8(a)(2). That section also outlaws employer interference in the formation or administration of a labor organization, as well as employer support (financial or otherwise) of the same.

As remedies for Section 8(a)(2) violations, the board may order the employer to cease recognizing the union, to cancel any agreements reached with the union, to cease giving support or assistance to the union, or to disband an in-house or captive union.

Although in-house unions are not a common problem today, the problem of employer support is of continuing interest. Support such as secretarial help, office equipment, or financial aid is prohibited. An employer is permitted by Section 8(a)(2) to allow "employees to confer with him during working hours without loss of time or pay."

An employer who agrees to recognize a union that does not have the support of a majority of employees violates Section 8(a)(2); such recognition is a violation even if the employer acted on a good-faith belief that the union had majority support. An employer is also prohibited from recognizing one union while another union has a petition for a representation election pending before the NLRB. However, the board has held that an employer may continue negotiations with an incumbent union even though a rival union has filed a petition for a representation election. See *RCA Del Caribe* [262 NLRB No. 116 (1982)]. Are these two positions consistent? How can they be reconciled?

In addition to being prohibited from recognizing a nonmajority union, the employer is forbidden from helping a union solicit membership or dues checkoff cards and from allowing a supervisor to serve as a union officer.

One area of interest under Section 8(a)(2) has developed recently as many employers initiated innovative work arrangements among employees. To improve productivity and worker morale, some employers have created autonomous work groups, quality circles, or work teams in which groups of employees are given greater responsibility for determining work schedules, methods, and so forth. When these work groups or teams discuss working conditions, pay, or worker grievances with representatives of the employer, they could be classified as labor organizations under the NLRA. Section 2(5) defines a labor organization as

> any organization of any kind, or any agency or employee representation committee or plan, in which employees participate and which exists for the purpose, in whole or in part, of dealing with employers concerning grievances, labor disputes, wages, rates of pay, hours of employment, or conditions of work.

The following case deals with the question of whether employer-created "employee action committees" were employer dominated or controlled labor organizations in violation of Section 8(a)(2).

Electromation, Inc. v. NLRB

35 F.3d 1148 (7th Cir. 1994)

[Electromation, a manufacturer of small electrical and electronic components and related products, employed approximately 200 employees, most of whom were women; the employees were not represented by a union. In response to financial losses, the company decided to cut expenses by revising its employee attendance policy and replacing the scheduled wage increases with lump-sum payments based on the length of each employee's service at the company. When Electromation informed its employees of these changes at the 1988 employee Christmas party, a number of employees signed a letter to the company expressing their dissatisfaction with the changes and asking the company to reconsider. The company president met with randomly selected employees to discuss wages, bonuses, incentive pay, tardiness, attendance programs, and bereavement and sick leave policy. Following this meeting, the president and supervisors concluded that the company would involve the employees to come up with solutions to these issues through the use of "action committees" of employees and management.

At a meeting to explain the action committees, the employees initially reacted negatively to the concept. They reluctantly agreed to the proposed committees and suggested that they be allowed to sign up for specific committees. The next day, the company informed the employees of the formation of five action committees and posted sign-up sheets for the following committees: (1) Absenteeism/Infractions; (2) No Smoking Policy; (3) Communication Network; (4) Pay Progression for Premium Positions; and (5) Attendance Bonus Program. Each committee was to consist of employees and one or two members of management, as well as the company's Employee Benefits Manager, Loretta Dickey, who was in charge of the coordination of all the committees. No employees were involved in the drafting of any aspect of the memorandum or the statement of subjects that the committees were to consider. The company then posted a memo announcing the members of each committee and dates of the initial committee meetings. The company's Employee Benefits Manager had determined which employees would participate on each committee. In late January and early February 1989, four of the action committees began to meet, but the No Smoking Policy Committee was never organized.

During the Attendance Bonus Program Committee's first meeting, management officials solicited employee ideas regarding a good attendance award program. Through the discussions, the committee developed a proposal, which was declared by management members to be too costly and was not pursued further for that reason.

Then on February 13, 1989, the International Brotherhood of Teamsters, Local Union No. 1049 (the "union") demanded recognition from the company. Until that time, the company was unaware that any organizing efforts had occurred at the plant. In late February, the president informed Employee Benefits Manager Dickey of the union's demand. Upon the advice of counsel, Dickey announced at the next meeting of each committee that, due to the union demand, the company could no longer participate in the committees, but that the employee members could continue to meet if they so desired. Finally, on March 15, 1989, the president formally announced to the employees that "due to the Union's campaign, the Company would be unable to participate in the committee meetings and could not continue to work with the committees until after the union election."

The union election took place on March 31, 1989; the employees voted 95-82 against union representation. On April 24, 1989, a regional director of the Board issued a complaint alleging that Electromation had violated the Act; the NLRB ultimately found that Electromation violated Sections 8(a)(2) and (1) of the NLRA through its establishment and administration of "action committees" consisting of employees and management. Electromation sought judicial review of the NLRB order.]

Will, J.

. . . In this appeal, we consider a petition to set aside and a cross-petition to enforce an order of the National Labor Relations Board.

. . . An allegation that Electromation has violated Section 8(a)(2) and (1) of the Act raises two distinct issues: first, whether the action committees in this case constituted "labor organizations" within the meaning of Section 2(5); and second, whether the employer dominated, influenced, or interfered with the formation or administration of the organization or contributed financial or other support to it, in violation of Section 8(a)(2) and (1) of the Act. . . .

. . . Under [the] statutory definition [of labor organization, § 2(5)] the action committees would constitute labor organizations if: (1) the Electromation employees participated in the committees; (2) the committees existed, at least in part, for the purpose of "dealing with" the employer; and (3) these dealings concerned "grievances, labor disputes, wages, rates of pay, hours of employment, or conditions of work."

In reaching its decision in this case, the Board also noted that "if the organization has as a purpose the representation of employees, it meets the statutory definition of 'employee representation committee or plan' under Section 2(5) and will constitute a labor organization if it also meets the criteria of employee participation and dealing with conditions of work or other statutory subjects." Because the Board found that the employee members of the action committees had acted in a representational capacity, it did not decide whether an employee group could ever be found to constitute a labor organization in the absence of a finding that it acted as a representative of the other employees. . . .

With respect to the first factor, there is no question that the Electromation employees participated in the action committees. Turning to the second factor, which is the most seriously contested on appeal, the Board found that the activities of the action committees constituted "dealing with" the employer. In this appeal, the company primarily argues that the Board erred in finding that Section 8(a)(2) was violated. However, as an alternative ground for setting aside part of the Board's order, the company contends that there is not substantial evidence to support the finding that at least three of the action committees—the Absenteeism/Infractions

Committee, the Communication Network Committee, and the Pay Progression for Premium Positions Committee—existed for the purpose of "dealing with" Electromation. Interestingly, the company concedes on appeal that there is enough evidence to support a finding that the fourth committee—the Attendance Bonus Program Committee—existed for the purpose of dealing with the company. The company argues that the other three action committees existed only as simple communication devices not engaged in collective bargaining of any sort, so they are not labor organizations under the statutory definition.

... Given the facts surrounding the formation and administration of all the action committees in this case, we cannot treat each committee separately. First, in their formation and administration, the individual committees were constituted as part of a single entity or program. They were initially conceived as an integrated employer response to deal with growing employee dissatisfaction. It was not until later that individual committee subject areas were identified and categorized by management. Also, a single management representative, Loretta Dickey, was assigned the responsibility for coordinating all action committee activities. The interrelatedness of these committees is further demonstrated by the company's determination that an employee could serve on only one committee at a time.

The company in fact posted only a single announcement identifying the members of each committee. Without consulting each committee individually, Dickey drafted a single statement summarizing the contemplated activities of all the committees. We agree with the Board that the action committees can be differentiated only in the specific subject matter with which each dealt. Each committee had an identical relationship to the company: the purpose, structure, and administration of each committee was essentially the same....

... even if the committees are considered individually, there exists substantial evidence that each was formed and existed for the purpose of "dealing with" the company. It is in fact the shared similarities among the committee structures which compels unitary treatment of them for the purposes of the issues raised in this appeal....

We have previously noted that the broad construction of [the definition of] labor organization applies not only with regard to the "absence of formal organization, [but also to] the type of interchange between parties which may be deemed 'dealing'" with employers. Moreover, an organization may satisfy the statutory requirement that it exist for the purpose in whole or in part of dealing with employers even if it has not engaged in actual bargaining or concluded a bargaining agreement.

... the Supreme Court [in *Cabot Carbon* (1959)] expressly rejected the contention that "dealing with" means "bargaining with," noting that Congress had declined to accept a proposal to substitute the phrase "bargaining with" for "dealing with" under Section 2 (5).... First, the Court found that nothing in the plain words of Section 2(5), its legislative history, or the decisions construing it, supported the contention that an employee committee which does not "bargain with" employers in the usual concept of collective bargaining does not engage in "dealing with" employers and, therefore, is not a labor organization.... According to the *Cabot Carbon* Court, by adopting the broader term "dealing with" and rejecting the more limited term "bargaining collectively," Congress clearly did not intend that the broad term "dealing with" should be limited to and mean only "bargaining with." ...

Relying in large part on these principles, the Board here explained that "dealing with" is a bilateral mechanism involving proposals from the employee organization concerning the subjects listed in Section 2(5), coupled with real or apparent consideration of those proposals by management....

Given the ... holding in *Cabot Carbon* that "dealing with" includes conduct much broader than collective bargaining, the Board did not err in determining that the Electromation action committees constituted labor organizations within the meaning of Sections 2(5) and 8(a)(2) of the Act. Although it is true that [the company] ... made no guarantees as to the results regarding the employee recommendations, the activities of the action committees nonetheless constituted "dealing with" the employer. Finally, with respect to the third factor, the subject matter of that dealing—for example, the treatment of employee absenteeism and employee bonuses—obviously concerned conditions of employment. We further agree with the Board that the purpose of the action committees was not limited to the improvement of company efficiency or product quality, but rather that they were designed to function and in fact functioned in an essentially representative capacity. Accordingly, given the statute's traditionally broad construction, there is substantial evidence to support the Board's finding that the action committees constituted labor organizations....

... [W]e must next consider whether, through their creation and administration of the action committees, the company acted unlawfully in violation of Section 8(a)(2) and (1) of the Act.

. . . the Board focused its analysis on the relationship between Electromation's actions in creating and administering the action committees and the resulting effect upon its employees' rights under the Act. . . . The Board correctly focused on management's participation in the action committees and its effect on the employees and found domination in that the company defined the committee structures and committee subject matters, appointed a manager to coordinate and monitor the committee meetings, structured each committee to include one or two management representatives, and permitted those managers to review and reject committee proposals before they could be presented to upper level management. The Board's interpretation of Section 8(a)(2) simply does not contravene the statutory language. . . .

Electromation . . . also argues that Section 8(a)(2) requires proof of actual domination or interference with the employees' free choice. . . .

As the Board found, substantial evidence supports the finding of company domination of the action committees. First, the company proposed and essentially imposed the action committees upon its employees as the only acceptable mechanism for resolution of their acknowledged grievances regarding the newly announced attendance bonus policies. . . .

The record also clearly shows that the employees were initially reluctant to accept the company's proposal of the action committees as a means to address their concerns; their reaction was "not positive." Nonetheless, the company continued to press the idea until the employees eventually accepted. Moreover, although the company informed the employees that they could continue to meet on their own, shortly after Electromation removed its management representatives from the committees due to the union recognition demand and announced that it would not work with the committees until after the union election, several of the committees disbanded. . . .

The company played a pivotal role in establishing both the framework and the agenda for the action committees. Electromation unilaterally selected the size, structure, and procedural functioning of the committees; it decided the number of committees and the topic(s) to be addressed by each. The company unilaterally drafted the action committees' purposes and goal statements, which identified from the start the focus of each committee's work.

. . . Electromation actually controlled which issues received attention by the committees and which did not. . . .

Although the company acceded to the employees' request that volunteers form the committees, it unilaterally determined how many could serve on each committee, decided that an employee could serve on only one committee at a time, and determined which committee certain employees would serve on, thus exercising significant control over the employees' participation and voice at the committee meetings. . . . Also, the company designated management representatives to serve on the committees. Employee Benefits Manager Dickey was assigned to coordinate and serve on all committees. In the case of the Attendance Bonus Program Committee, the management representative . . . reviewed employee proposals, determined whether they were economically feasible, and further decided whether they would be presented to higher management. This role of the management committee members effectively put the employer on both sides of the bargaining table, an avowed proscription of the Act. Finally, the company paid the employees for their time spent on committee activities, provided meeting space, and furnished all necessary supplies for the committees' activities. While such financial support is clearly not a violation of Section 8(a)(2) by itself, . . . in the totality of the circumstances in this case such support may reasonably be characterized to be in furtherance of the company's domination of the action committees. We therefore conclude that there is substantial evidence to support the Board's finding of unlawful employer domination and interference in violation of Section 8(a)(2) and (1).

. . . Accordingly, because we find that substantial evidence supports the Board's factual findings and that its legal conclusions have a reasonable basis in the law, we affirm the Board's findings and enforce the Board's order.

Enforced.

Case Questions

1. What was the purpose of the action committees created by Electromation? Did the committees constitute labor organizations within the meaning of Section 2(5) of the NLRA? Explain your answer.
2. When does a labor organization "deal with" an employer within the meaning of Section 2(5)? Did Electromation "deal with" the action committees? Explain.
3. On what basis did the NLRB and the court determine that Electromation dominated and controlled the action committees?

ETHICAL DILEMMA: "EMPLOYEE INVOLVEMENT GROUP FOR WYDGET?"

You are the human resources manager of Wydget Corporation, a small manufacturing firm. The employees of Wydget are not unionized. Because of difficult business conditions, the workers' wages have not increased in several years, and their medical insurance benefits have been reduced. As a result, morale among employees is low, and there has been high turnover in the work force. You are considering creating an employee involvement group to provide an opportunity for workers to share their concerns and ideas with management and to discuss production problems and working conditions. How can you structure the group to ensure that employees feel their role is effective, without running afoul of Section 8(a)(2)? What are the potential problems associated with the creation of such a group? Should you establish the employee involvement group? Explain the reasons for your opinion.

An employer-created group of managers and employees that discussed matters such as medical benefits, stock ownership plans, and termination policy was held to be an employer-dominated labor organization in violation of Section 8(a)(2), *Polaroid Corp.* [329 NLRB No. 47 (1999)].

SECTIONS 8(A)(3) AND 8(B)(2): DISCRIMINATION IN TERMS OR CONDITIONS OF EMPLOYMENT

Under Section 8(a)(3) of the NLRA, employers are forbidden to discriminate "in regard to hire or tenure or employment or any term or condition of employment to encourage or discourage membership in any labor organization." Unions, under Section 8(b)(2), are forbidden to

> cause or attempt to cause an employer to discriminate against an employee in violation of Subsection 8(a)(3) or to discriminate against an employee with respect to whom membership in such organization has been denied or terminated on some ground other than . . . failure to tender the periodic dues and the initiation fees uniformly required as a condition of . . . membership. . . .

The intent of these sections is to insulate an employee's employment from conditions based on his or her union sympathies or lack thereof. If an employee is to have the free choice, under Section 7, to join or refrain from joining a union, then that employee must not be made to suffer economically for his or her choice. The wording of Sections 8(a)(3) and 8(b)(2) indicates that a violation of these sections has two elements. First, there must be some discrimination in the terms or conditions of employment—either a refusal to hire, discharge, lay off, or discipline—or a union attempt to get the employer to so discriminate. Second, the discrimination or attempt to cause discrimination must be for the purpose of encouraging or discouraging union membership. For example, in *USF Red Star, Inc.* [330 NLRB No. 15 (1999)], a union's efforts to get the employer to discharge an employee because of his internal union activities violated Section 8(b)(2) [and Section

8(b)(1)(A)]; when the employer discharged the employee because of the union's demands, it violated Section 8(a)(3) [and Section 8(a)(1)].

Because the discrimination (or attempt to cause it) must be for the purpose of encouraging or discouraging union membership, intention is a necessary part of a violation of these sections. If an employer (or union) states that an employee should be fired because of participation in union activities (or lack of participation), demonstrating the requisite intention for a violation is no problem. But most complaints involving Section 8(a)(3) or Section 8(b)(2) are not as clear-cut. For example, what happens if an employee who supports the union's organizing campaign also has a poor work record? How should the board and the courts handle a case in which the employer or union has mixed motives for its actions? That is the subject of the following case.

NLRB v. Transportation Management Corp.

462 U.S. 393 (1983)

White, J.

The National Labor Relations Act makes unlawful the discharge of workers because of union activity, but employers retain the right to discharge workers for any number of other reasons unrelated to the employee's union activities. When the General Counsel of the National Labor Relations Board (Board) files a complaint alleging that an employee was discharged because of his union activities, the employer may assert legitimate motives for his decision. In *Wright Line* . . . the National Labor Relations Board reformulated the allocation of the burden of proof in such cases. It determined that the General Counsel carried the burden of persuading the Board that an anti-union animus contributed to the employer's decision to discharge an employee, a burden that does not shift, but that the employer, even if it failed to meet or neutralize the General Counsel's showing, could avoid the finding that it violated the statute by demonstrating by a preponderance of the evidence that the worker would have been fired even if he had not been involved with the Union. The question presented in this case is whether the burden placed on the employer in *Wright Line* is consistent with Sections 8(a)(1) and 8(a)(3), as well as with Section 10(c) of the NLRA, which provides that the Board must prove an unlawful labor practice by a "preponderance of the evidence."

Prior to his discharge, Sam Santillo was a bus driver for respondent Transportation Management Corporation. On March 19, 1979, Santillo talked to officials of the Teamster's Union about organizing the drivers who worked with him. Over the next four days Santillo discussed with his fellow drivers the possibility of joining the Teamsters and distributed authorization cards. On the night of March 23, George Patterson, who supervised Santillo and the other drivers, told one of the drivers that he had heard of Santillo's activities. Patterson referred to Santillo as two-faced, and promised to get even with him.

Later that evening Patterson talked to Ed West who was also a bus driver for respondent. Patterson asked, "What's with Sam and the Union?" Patterson said that he took Santillo's actions personally, recounted several favors he had done for Santillo, and added that he would remember Santillo's activities when Santillo again asked for a favor. On Monday, March 26, Santillo was discharged. Patterson told Santillo that he was being fired for leaving his keys in the bus and taking unauthorized breaks.

Santillo filed a complaint with the Board alleging that he had been discharged because of his union activities, contrary to Sections 8(a)(1) and 8(a)(3) of the NLRA. The General Counsel issued a complaint. The administrative law judge (ALJ) determined by a preponderance of the evidence that Patterson clearly had an anti-union animus and that Santillo's discharge was motivated by a desire to discourage union activities. The ALJ also found that the asserted reasons for the discharge could not withstand scrutiny. Patterson's disapproval of Santillo's practice of leaving his keys in the bus was clearly a pretext, for Patterson had not known about Santillo's practice until after he had decided to discharge Santillo; moreover, the practice of leaving keys in buses was commonplace among respondent's employees. Respondent identified two types of unauthorized breaks, coffee breaks and stops at home. With respect to both coffee breaks and stopping at home, the ALJ found that Santillo was never cautioned or admonished about such behavior, and that the employer had not followed its customary practice of issuing three written warnings before discharging a driver. The ALJ also found that the taking of coffee breaks during working hours was normal practice, and that respondent tolerated the practice unless the breaks interfered with the driver's performance of his duties. In any event, said the ALJ, respondent had never taken any adverse personnel action against an employee because of such behavior. While acknowledging that Santillo had engaged in some unsatisfactory conduct, the ALJ was not persuaded that Santillo would have been fired had it not been for his union activities.

The Board affirmed, adopting with some clarification the ALJ's findings and conclusions and expressly applying its *Wright Line* decision. It stated that respondent had failed to carry its burden of persuading the Board that the discharge would have taken place had Santillo not engaged in activity protected by the Act. The First Circuit Court of Appeals, relying on its previous decision rejecting the Board's *Wright Line* test . . . refused to enforce the Board's order and remanded for consideration of whether the General Counsel had proved by a preponderance of the evidence that Santillo would not have been fired had it not been for his union activities. . . .

As we understand the Board's decisions, they have consistently held that the unfair labor practice consists of a discharge or other adverse action that is based in whole or in part on anti-union animus—or as the Board now puts it, that the employee's protected conduct was a substantial or motivating factor in the adverse action. The General Counsel has the burden of proving these elements under Section 10(c). But the Board's construction of the statute permits an employer to avoid being adjudicated a violator by showing what his actions would have been regardless of his forbidden motivation. It extends to the employer what the Board considers to be an affirmative defense but does not change or add to the elements of the unfair labor practice that the General Counsel has the burden of proving under Section 10(c). The Board has instead chosen to recognize, as it insists it has done for many years, what it designates as an affirmative defense that the employer has the burden of sustaining. We are unprepared to hold that this is an impermissible construction of the Act. "[T]he Board's construction here, while it may not be required by the Act, is at least permissible under it . . ." and in these circumstances its position is entitled to deference.

The Board's allocation of the burden of proof is clearly reasonable in this context. . . .The employer is a wrongdoer; he has acted out of a motive that is declared illegitimate by the statute. It is fair that he bear the risk that the influence of legal and illegal motives cannot be separated, because he knowingly created the risk and because the risk was created not by innocent activity but by his own wrongdoing.

For these reasons, we conclude that the Court of Appeals erred in refusing to enforce the Board's orders, which rested on the Board's *Wright Line* decision.

The Board was justified in this case in concluding that Santillo would not have been discharged had the employer not considered his efforts to establish a union. At least two of the transgressions that purportedly would have in any event prompted Santillo's discharge were commonplace, and yet no transgressor had ever before received any kind of discipline. Moreover, the employer departed from its usual practice in dealing with rules infractions; indeed, not only did the employer not warn Santillo that his actions would result in being subjected to discipline, it never even expressed its disapproval of his conduct. In addition, Patterson, the person who made the initial decision to discharge Santillo, was obviously upset with Santillo for engaging in such protected activity. It is thus clear that the Board's finding that Santillo would not have been fired even if the employer had not had an anti-union animus was "supported by substantial evidence on the record considered as a whole". . . . Accordingly, the judgment is

Reversed.

Case Questions

1. What reasons did the employer offer to justify Santillo's discharge? What, according to Santillo, prompted his discharge?
2. What evidence did the NLRB present to challenge the employer's reasons for the discharge?
3. When does the NLRB's *Wright Line* test apply? What does it require? Does the Supreme Court uphold the *Wright Line* test?

DISCRIMINATION IN EMPLOYMENT TO ENCOURAGE UNION MEMBERSHIP

Union Security Agreements

Union Security Agreements
Contract provisions requiring employees to join the union or pay union dues.

Although Section 8(a)(3) and Section 8(b)(2) prohibit discrimination to encourage or discourage union membership, there is an important exception regarding the "encouragement" of union membership. That exception deals with **union security agreements**—when an employer and union agree that employees must either join the union or at least pay union dues in order to remain employees. This exception requires some discussion.

Prior to the Taft-Hartley Act of 1947, unions and employers could agree that an employer would hire only employees who were already union members. These agreements, called closed shop agreements, had the effect of encouraging (or requiring) workers to join unions if they wished to get a job. Such agreements clearly restrict the employee's free exercise of Section 7 rights; for that reason, they were prohibited. But the Taft-Hartley amendments did not completely prohibit all "union security" arrangements. Section 8(a)(3), as amended by Taft-Hartley, contains the following provision:

> Provided, that nothing in this Act . . . shall preclude an employer from making an agreement with a labor organization . . . to require as a condition of employment membership therein on or after the thirtieth day following the beginning of such agreement, whichever is later. . . .

Section 8(a)(3) also provides that an employer can justify discharging an employee for nonmembership in a union only if membership was denied or terminated because of the employee's failure to pay the dues and initiation fees required of all members.

Union Shop Agreement
Agreement requiring employees to join the union after a certain period of time.

Agency Shop Agreement
Agreement requiring employees to pay union dues, but not requiring them to join the union.

The effect of these provisions is to allow an employer and union to agree to a union shop or agency shop provision. A **union shop agreement** requires that all employees hired by the employer must join the union after a certain period of time, not less than thirty days. Although employees need not be union members to be hired, they must become union members if they are to remain employed past the specified time period. An **agency shop agreement** does not require that employees actually join the union, but they must at least pay the dues and fees required of union members.

Although Section 8(a)(3) states that an employer and a union can agree "to require as a condition of employment membership" in the union on or after thirty days of hiring, Section 8(b)(2) and the second proviso to Section 8(a)(3) state that an employee cannot be fired except for failure to pay dues and initiation fees. In effect, this latter language has the legal effect of reducing all union shops to the level of agency shops. Under an agency shop agreement, remember, employees need not become formal members of the union but must pay union dues. Under the language of Section 8(b)(2), formal union members cannot be fired for disobeying the union's internal rules or failing to participate in union affairs. The only difference is that they may be fined by the union for these infractions, and the fines may be enforceable in a state court. Furthermore, the law is clear that an employee who pays dues but refuses to assume full union membership cannot be held to these rules and sanctions.

Unions argue that union security provisions are needed to prevent "free riders"; since all members of the bargaining unit get the benefits of the union's agreement, whether or not they are union members, they should be required to pay the costs of negotiating and administering the agreement—union dues. Only by paying the costs of such union representation can free riders be prevented.

Although such agreements do prevent free riders, they are also coercive to the extent that they may override an employee's free choice of whether or not to join a union. For that reason, the act permits states to outlaw such union security agreements. Section 14(b) states that

> Nothing in this Act shall be construed as authorizing the execution or application of agreements requiring membership in a labor organization as a condition of employment in any state or territory in which such execution or application is prohibited by State or Territorial law.

Right-to-Work Laws
Law which prohibit union security agreements.

This section allows for the passage of **right-to-work laws,** which prohibit such union security agreements. In states that have passed such a law, the union shop and agency shop agreements are illegal. A number of states, mainly in the South and West (the Sun Belt) have passed such laws. It is also worth noting that Section 19 of the act was amended to allow employees with bona fide religious objections to joining unions or paying union dues to make arrangements to pay the required fees or dues to a charitable organization.

When a union security agreement is in effect, the employer must discharge an employee, upon the union's request, if the employee has been denied membership in or expelled from the union for failure to pay the required union dues or fees. Under Section 8(b)(2), the union cannot legally demand the discharge of an employee for refusing to pay "back dues" or "reinstatement fees" after a lapse of membership in a prior job. Other examples of union violations of Section 8(b)(2) are forcing an employer to agree to hire only applicants satisfactory to the union or causing an employee to be discharged for opposition to the manner in which internal union affairs are conducted or because the worker was disliked or considered a troublemaker by the union leadership.

Hiring Halls

Hiring Halls
A job-referral mechanism operated by unions whereby unions refer members to prospective employers.

In some industries, employers rely on unions to refer prospective employees to the various employers. Such arrangements, known as **hiring halls,** are common in industries such as trucking, construction, and longshoring. Hiring halls and other job-referral mechanisms operated by unions may have the effect of encouraging membership in the union because an employee must go through the union to get a job. The NLRB and the Supreme Court have held such hiring halls or referral mechanisms to be legal as long as they meet the following conditions:

1. The union must not discriminate on grounds of union membership for job referrals.
2. The employer may reject any applicant referred by the union.

3. A notice of the nondiscriminatory operation of the referral service must be posted in the hiring hall.

It is also legal for the union to set skill levels necessary for membership or for referral to employers through a hiring hall.

Preferential Treatment for Union Officers: Super Seniority

In some collective agreements, an employer will agree to give union officers or stewards preferential treatment in the event of layoffs or recall of employees. Such provisions, known as super seniority because layoff and recall are usually done on the basis of seniority, may have the effect of encouraging union membership. Yet they also serve to ensure that employees responsible for the enforcement and administration of the collective agreement remain on the job to ensure the protection of all employees' rights under the contract. However, preferential treatment that goes beyond layoff and recall rights is not so readily justified. For that reason, and because it clearly discriminates in employment conditions to encourage union activity, broad super seniority clauses may involve violations of Sections 8(a)(3) and 8(b)(2).

DISCRIMINATION IN EMPLOYMENT TO DISCOURAGE UNION MEMBERSHIP

Just as discrimination in terms or conditions of employment to encourage union membership violates Section 8(a)(3), so does discrimination that is intended to discourage union membership or activities. Most complaints alleging discrimination to discourage such activities occur in the context of union organizing campaigns or strikes.

Activity protected under Section 7 includes union organizing activity as well as strikes over economic issues or to protest unfair labor practices. The employer that refuses to hire, or discharges, lays off, or disciplines an employee for such activity, is in violation of Section 8(a)(3). Although the employer must have acted with the intention of discouraging union membership, the board has held that specific evidence of such an intention need not be shown if the employer's conduct is inherently destructive of the employee's Section 7 rights.

As noted earlier, several reasons may be behind an employer's action; anti-union motives may play a part, along with legitimate work-related reasons. Recall that in *NLRB v. Transportation Management,* the Supreme Court upheld the board practice of requiring the employer to show that the discipline or discharge would have occurred even without the employee's protected conduct. If the employer can meet that burden, then it is not a violation of Section 8(a)(3). However, if there are no legitimate business reasons for the employer's actions, then the conduct is a violation, *Huck Store Fixture Co. v. NLRB* [327 F.3d 528 (7th Cir. 2003)].

An employer who fires employees for engaging in a union organizing campaign is in violation of Section 8(a)(3). Firing employees for striking over economic demands is also a violation. Other examples of Section 8(a)(3) violations include:

- layoffs that violate seniority rules and that fall mainly upon union supporters;
- disproportionately severe discipline of union officers or supporters;

- discharging a union supporter without the customary warning prior to discharge;
- discharging a union supporter based on past misconduct that had previously been condoned;
- selective enforcement of rules against union supporters.

STRIKES AS PROTECTED ACTIVITY

Strikes by employees are the essence of concerted activity; workers agree to withhold their labor from the employer in order to pressure the employer to accept their demands. A strike for collective-bargaining purposes or for purposes of mutual aid and protection comes under the protection of Section 7. However, despite the purposes of the strike, if it violates the collective agreement or if workers are attempting to strike while still collecting their pay, the strike may not be protected.

When discussing the rights of strikers under the NLRA and the employer's response to the strike, the board and the courts distinguish between economic strikes and unfair labor practice strikes. As discussed in Chapter 14, an *economic strike* is called to pressure the employer to accept the union's negotiating demands. It occurs after the old collective agreement has expired and negotiations for a new agreement break down. By contrast, an *unfair labor practice strike* is called to protest an employer's illegal actions. It does not involve contract demands or negotiations. The rights of strikers thus may depend on whether the strike is an unfair labor practice or economic strike. An economic strike may be converted into an unfair labor practice strike by an employer's unfair practices that are committed during the strike, as in *Ryan Iron Works, Inc.* [332 NLRB No. 49 (2000)].

Unfair Labor Practice Strikes

The Supreme Court has held, in *Mastro Plastics v. NLRB* [350 U.S. 270 (1956)], that unfair labor practice strikes are protected activity under the act. This means that unfair labor practice strikers may not be fired for going on strike, nor may they be permanently replaced. Strikes that begin as economic strikes may become unfair labor practice strikes if the employer commits serious unfair labor practices during the strike. For example, if the employer refused to bargain with the union over a new agreement and discharged the strikers, the strike would become an unfair labor practice strike.

An employer may hire workers to replace the strikers during an unfair labor practice strike, but the strikers must be reinstated when the strike is over. Although misconduct on the picket line may normally be a sufficient reason for an employer to discharge a striker, the board has held in prior decisions that severe misconduct (such as physical assault) is needed to justify the discharge of an unfair labor practice striker. However, in *Clear Pine Mouldings, Inc.* [268 NLRB No. 173 (1984)], the board held that the existence of an unfair labor practice strike

> does not in any way privilege those employees [on strike] to engage in other than peaceful picketing and persuasion. . . . There is nothing in the statute to support the notion that striking employees are free to engage in or escalate violence or misconduct in proportion to their estimates of the degree of seriousness of an employer's unfair labor practices.

Economic Strikes

Economic strikes, as previously noted, are work stoppages by the employees designed to force the employer to meet their bargaining demands for increased wages or other benefits. As with unfair labor practice strikes, economic strikes are protected activity; however, the protections afforded economic strikers are not as great as those given unfair labor practice strikers. As mentioned earlier in the discussion of protected activity under Section 7, on-the-job slowdowns are not protected, and employees who engage in such conduct may be discharged. In addition, economic strikes in violation of the collective agreement are not protected.

When the economic strike is protected, the striking employees may not be discharged for going on strike; however, the employer may hire permanent replacements for the striking employees. The right to hire permanent replacements was affirmed by the Supreme Court in 1938 in the case of *NLRB v. MacKay Radio & Telegraph* [304 U.S. 333]. Although the striking employees may be permanently replaced, they still retain their status as "employees" under the act. [See the definition of employee in Section 2(3).] Because they retain their status as employees, the strikers are entitled to be reinstated if they make an unconditional application for reinstatement and if vacancies are available. If no positions are available at the time of their application, even if the lack of vacancies is due to the hiring of replacements, the employer need not reinstate the strikers. However, if the strikers continue to indicate an interest in reinstatement, the employer is required to rehire them as positions become available. This requirement was upheld by the Supreme Court in *NLRB v. Fleetwood Trailers Co.* [389 U.S. 375 (1967)].

In *Laidlaw Corp.* [171 NLRB No. 175 (1968)], the NLRB held that economic strikers who had made an unconditional application for reinstatement and who continued to make known their availability for employment were entitled to be recalled by the employer prior to the employer's hiring of new employees.

In *David R. Webb Co., Inc. v. NLRB* [888 F.2d 501 (7th Cir. 1990)], the Court of Appeals held that the employer's duty to reinstate strikers continues until the strikers have been reinstated to their former positions or to substantially equivalent positions; reinstating them to lower positions does not satisfy the employer's obligation. The following case discusses when, if ever, the employer may have a legitimate justification to refuse to reinstate strikers.

Diamond Walnut Growers, Inc. v. NLRB

113 F.3d 1259 (D.C. Cir. 1997) (en banc)

[Diamond Walnut Growers (Diamond) processes, packages, and distributes walnuts; it hires seasonal employees during the fall harvesting season to supplement its regular work force. Diamond's employees had been represented by the Cannery Workers Local 601 of the International Brotherhood of Teamsters (the union). In September 1991, following expiration of the most recent collective-bargaining agreement, nearly 500 of Diamond's permanent and seasonal employees went on strike. Diamond hired replacement workers to continue operations. The strike was bitter and divisive: Strikers are alleged to have engaged in acts of violence against the replacement workers, and injunctions were issued against both the strikers and replacements. The union encouraged a public boycott of Diamond's products to exert economic pressure on Diamond. The boycott included a well-publicized national bus tour during which union members publicly distributed leaflets describing Diamond's work force as "scabs" who packaged walnuts contaminated with "mold, dirt, oil, worms and debris."

One year into the strike, the NLRB held a representation election; the union lost but filed objections with the NLRB, and the NLRB ordered that a new election be held in October 1993. Two weeks prior to the new election, four striking employees approached Diamond with an unconditional offer to return to work. In a letter presented to the company, the employees stated that they were convinced that a fair election was impossible; the employees felt that it was important for the replacement workers to have an opportunity to hear from some Union sympathizers.

Neither the permanent jobs they held before the strike, nor substantially equivalent jobs were available for three of the returning strikers at the time of their return, and Diamond placed them in seasonal jobs. Willa Miller, who had been a quality control supervisor prior to the strike, was placed in a seasonal packing position even though a seasonal inspection job was available; Alfonsina Munoz had been employed as a lift truck operator and, despite the availability of a seasonal forklift job, was given a seasonal job cracking and inspecting nuts in the inspection department; and Mohammed Kussair, formerly an air separator machine operator, was also placed in a seasonal cracking and inspecting position.

The union lost the rerun election. The NLRB General Counsel then filed a complaint alleging that Diamond had violated Sections 8(a)(3) and 8(a)(1) of the National Labor Relations Act by unlawfully discriminating against Miller, Munoz, and Kussair. The General Counsel alleged that because of their protected strike activity, Diamond declined to put them in certain available seasonal positions for which they were qualified and that were preferable to the positions in which they were placed. After a hearing, the ALJ recommended that the charges be dismissed because, while he found that Diamond had discriminated against the employees by considering their protected activity when placing them in jobs, such discrimination was not unlawful because no vacancies were available in their former jobs or in substantially equivalent jobs. On review, the NLRB reversed the ALJ's decision. The Board held that, while Diamond was under no legal obligation to reinstate the strikers, once it voluntarily decided to reinstate them, it was required to act in a nondiscriminatory fashion toward them. The NLRB held that Diamond had discriminated against Miller, Munoz, and Kussair by declining to place them in seasonal positions of quality control assistant, lift truck operator, and loader, respectively, because of their union status and/or because of certain protected activity they engaged in while on strike. The Board rejected Diamond's justifications for placing the three returning strikers as it did: the employer's concern that the replacement workers might instigate violence against the three and that the placements of Miller and Munoz were justified by their participation in the boycott and the circulation of disparaging leaflets. The NLRB held that Diamond had failed to justify its discrimination and was guilty of unfair labor practices. Diamond sought judicial review of the NLRB decision.]

Silberman, J.

. . . Diamond challenges the NLRB's determination that it lacked substantial business justification for refusing to place the three employees in the specific jobs they sought—quality control assistant, lift truck operator, and loader. . . . It is undisputed that the *Fleetwood* framework governs this case. The General Counsel . . . must make out a prima facie case that the employer discriminated within the meaning of the Act, which means the employer's decision as to how to treat the three returning strikers was attributable to their protected activity.

. . . A struck employer faced with an unconditional offer to return to work is obliged to treat the returning employee like any other applicant for work (unless the employee's former job or its substantial equivalent is available, in which case the employee is preferred to any other applicant). But Miller and Munoz were not treated like any other applicant for work. Miller was qualified for a seasonal position in quality control that paid 32 cents per hour more than the packing job to which she was assigned. And Munoz was qualified to fill a forklift operating job, a position that paid between $2.75 and $5.00 per hour more than the walnut cracking and inspecting job she received. Diamond admits that it took into account Miller's and Munoz's protected activity in choosing to place them in jobs that were objectively less desirable than those for which they were qualified. [Diamond], although it contended that the discrimination was comparatively slight, does not dispute that its action discriminated against Munoz and Miller within the meaning of the Act. . . .

Under *Fleetwood* after discrimination is shown, the burden shifts to the employer to establish that its treatment of the employees has a legitimate and substantial business justification. [Diamond] declined to give Munoz the forklift driver job because of its concern that driving [it] throughout the plant would be unduly risky in two respects. First, because of the bad feeling between strikers and replacements, Munoz would be endangered if confronted by hostile replacement workers in an isolated area. Second, since Munoz had participated in the bus tour during which the union had accused the company of producing tainted walnuts, Munoz would be tempted to engage in sabotage by using the 11,000 pound vehicle to cause unspecified damage. As for Miller, who was also on the bus tour, the company declined to put her in the "sensitive position of quality control assistant" where "the final visual inspection of walnuts is made prior to leaving the plant." In that position, she would have "an easy opportunity to let defective nuts go by undetected . . . or to place a foreign object into the final product, thereby legitimizing the Union's claim of tainted walnuts."

. . . The Board rejected [Diamond's] proffered justifications for its placement of Munoz on the same grounds as did the ALJ. As to Diamond's purported fear for her safety, no evidence had been produced that Munoz was thought to be responsible for any violence, so there was no reason to believe she would have been a special target. The Board said, "[T]here is no specific evidence that any replacements harbored hostility toward these three strikers, and, if such evidence did exist as [Diamond] claims, we fail to see how placing them in the positions to which they were assigned would lessen the perceived danger of retaliatory acts being committed against them." The Board discounted Diamond's contention that Munoz would be under greater protection if closely supervised, noting that petitioner had admitted that "Munoz freely roamed the plant unsupervised during her breaks." The Board did not dismiss out of hand, however, the proposition that concern for a returning striker's safety could ever amount to a substantial business justification for a "discriminating" placement; it was careful to state "we find that [Diamond] was not justified in restricting the strikers' job placements out of fear that the replacement employees would retaliate against these three strikers." . . .

As for the possibility that Munoz would engage in forklift sabotage, the Board was more terse, stating only that "the strikers' conduct [referring to the bus tour] constituted protected . . . activity," and there was no evidence indicating that such protection was lost because of threats made by Miller and Munoz. If Munoz had uttered specific threats of sabotage, however, she would have lost her protected status . . . ; the General Counsel would not even have established a prima facie case. . . . [T]he Board necessarily . . . concluded that the possibility of Munoz engaging in future sabotage by misuse of her forklift was simply not a sufficient risk to constitute a substantial business justification for her treatment.

. . . An employer's concern for the safety of a few returning strikers, put in the midst of a majority of replacements in a strike marked by violence, may be genuine, but it is hardly unreasonable for the Board to insist, at minimum, on evidence of a concrete threat to those strikers. Otherwise, such a generalized concern could all too easily serve as a handy pretext for disfavoring returning strikers. Moreover, if there were such a threat, the employer might well be obliged to take adequate prophylactic measures that bear upon those who threatened the violence rather than those who were threatened. . . . Similarly, the Board was reasonable in its determination that the risk of Munoz engaging in sabotage while riding around on her 11,000 pound forklift—the petitioner seems to most fear her crashing the forklift into machinery—is not a substantial justification for her disadvantageous placement in another job. Strikes tend to be hard struggles, and although this one may have been more bitter than most, there is always a potential danger of returning strikers, particularly while the strike is still ongoing, engaging in some form of sabotage. There is therefore undeniably some risk in employing returning strikers during a strike. But it could not be seriously argued that an employer cannot be forced to assume any risk of sabotage, because that would be equivalent to holding that an employer need not take back strikers during an ongoing strike at all. . . .

. . . The Miller case is another matter. It will be recalled that [Diamond] declined to assign her to the post of quality control assistant, the job responsible for the final inspection of walnuts leaving the plant (she received a job paying 32 cents an hour less). The Board rejected the employer's justification, which was based on Miller's participation in the product boycott and bus tour leafletting, saying only . . . "the strikers' conduct constituted protected . . . activity and there is no evidence indicating that such protection was lost because of threats made by Miller and Munoz to damage or sabotage . . . equipment or products." . . . With respect to Miller, we think the Board's determination that petitioner's business justification is insubstantial is flat unreasonable.

All strikes . . . are a form of economic warfare, but when a union claims that a food product produced by a struck company is actually tainted . . . the unpleasant effects will long survive the battle. The company's ability to sell the product, even if the strike is subsequently settled, could well be destroyed. . . . [Once the NLRB has shown discrimination because of protected activity] . . . the burden shifts to the employer to produce a legitimate and substantial business justification.

We therefore take the Board to mean . . . that [Diamond] was obliged to show something more than it presented to support its concern that putting Miller in the quality control position would provide her "with an easy opportunity to let defective nuts go by undetected or to place a foreign object into the final product thereby legitimizing the Union's claim of tainted walnuts." Again, we emphasize that if petitioner had actual evidence that Miller had sabotaged the walnuts . . . Miller would be unprotected by the Act, and [Diamond] need not offer any justification for discriminating against her. The issue, then, is . . . whether the employer had a legitimate concern, based on the undisputed evidence and the employer's claimed factual inferences—presented to and unchallenged by the Board—that her employment as a quality control assistant would have posed an unusual and serious risk that she would engage in future misconduct of a particular kind, at great cost to petitioner . . . The Board seems to have ignored those concerns . . .

The Board does not quarrel with petitioner's contention that the potential damage if the public learned of impurities in Diamond's walnuts would be extraordinary. . . . Nor does the Board dispute that Miller in the quality control position would have had the capacity to cause such damage to the company.

The Board's counsel argues . . . that it is unfair to assume that an employee would behave in a disloyal and improper fashion. It is unnecessary, however, for us to make that assumption to decide the Board was unreasonable. The Board accepted petitioner's contention that Miller would have been placed "in the sensitive position . . . where final visual inspection of walnuts is made prior to leaving the plant," . . . In short, she would have had a special motive, a unique opportunity and little risk of detection to cause severe harm. Both the risk Diamond faced in its placement of Miller was qualitatively different than a normal risk of sabotage, and the deterrence to Miller's possible misbehavior was peculiarly inadequate.

. . . There may well be other situations in which an employer could produce compelling grounds for a relatively unfavorable assignment of a returning striker. The Board itself implied that a serious threat of violence against the striker might suffice. The legal proposition that governs this case, however, is that the Board must consider whatever special circumstances are presented by an employer asserting the defense of substantial justification, and it may not summarily reject an employer's specific and persuasive explanation.

. . . In this case, at least with respect to one part of the Board's decision, we conclude the Board exceeded the reasonableness limits.

So ordered.

[Concurring and dissenting opinions omitted.]

Case Questions

1. What was the basis of the NLRB unfair labor practice charges against Diamond? How did Diamond justify its actions that led to the unfair labor practice charges? Did the NLRB accept Diamond's justifications? Did the court of appeals? Explain your answers.
2. What are an employer's obligations when an economic striker makes an unconditional application to return to work?
3. When can an employer refuse to reinstate a returning economic striker?

The NLRB has held that a union may waive the right of strikers to be reinstated with full seniority in exchange for an end to a strike. See *Gem City Ready Mix* [279 NLRB 191, 116 L.R.R.M. 1266 (1984)] and *NLRB v. Harrison Ready Mix Concrete* [770 F.2d 78 (6th Cir. 1985)].

Other Strike-Related Issues

Recall that under Section 7, employees have the right to refrain from concerted activity, which includes the right to remain working rather than go on strike. As noted in our discussion of Section 8(b)(2), a union may impose some disciplinary sanctions upon union members who refuse to go on strike, but they may not cause an employer to discriminate against such employees in terms or conditions of employment. Nor may the employer offer incentives or benefits to the replacements or those employees not going on strike when such benefits are not available to the strikers. In the case of *NLRB v. Erie Resistor Co.* [373 U.S. 221 (1963)], the Supreme Court held that the employer's granting of twenty years' seniority to all replacements violated Section 8(a)(3). The effect of such seniority was to insulate the replacements from layoff, while exposing employees who went on strike to layoff. This effect would continue long after the strike was over; it would place the former strikers at a disadvantage simply because they went on strike. Although *Erie Resistor* involved rather severe actions by the employer, the NLRB has held that any preferential treatment in terms or conditions of employment accorded to the nonstrikers or replacements, and not to the strikers, violates Section 8(a)(3).

A 1983 Supreme Court decision involved the rights of the workers hired to replace economic strikers. In *Belknap v. Hale* [463 U.S. 491 (1983)], the Court held that replacements hired under the promise of permanent employment could sue the employer for breach of contract if they were laid off at the end of the strike. Does *Belknap v. Hale* undermine the rights of strikers to be reinstated?

Employer Response to Strike Activity

Lockout
An employer's temporary withdrawal of employment to pressure employees to agree to the employer's bargaining proposals.

Just as employees are free to go on strike to promote their economic demands, employers are free to withdraw employment from employees to pressure them to accept the employer's demands. This tactic, called a **lockout,** is the temporary withdrawal of employment to pressure employees to agree to the employer's bargaining proposals. A lockout needs to be distinguished from a permanent closure of a plant to avoid unionization.

When the employees have not gone on strike, the employer may be reluctant to "lock them out." (Why?) But when the threat of a "quickie strike" or unannounced walkout poses the prospect of damage to equipment or disruption of business, the employer may lock out to avoid such problems. The board has consistently held that such "defensive" lockouts are not unfair labor practices. Lockouts by the employers in a multiemployer bargaining unit, to avoid a whipsaw strike by the union, have been held legal by the board and the Supreme Court. What about the situation in which an employer locks out the unionized employees and hires replacements? This issue is addressed in the following Supreme Court decision.

NLRB v. Brown
380 U.S. 278 (1965)

Brennan, J.

The respondents, who are members of a multiemployer bargaining group, locked out their employees in response to a whipsaw strike against another member of the group. They and the struck employer continued operations with temporary replacements. The National Labor Relations Board found that the struck employer's use of temporary replacements was lawful, but that the respondents had violated ss. 8(a)(1) and (3) of the National Labor Relations Act by locking out their regular employees and using temporary replacements to carry on business. The Court of Appeals for the Tenth Circuit disagreed and refused to enforce the Board's order. . . .

Five operators of six retail food stores in Carlsbad, New Mexico, make up the employer group. The stores had bargained successfully on a group basis for many years with Local 462 of the Retail Clerks International Association. Negotiations for a new collective agreement to replace the expiring one began in January 1960. Agreement was reached by mid-February on all terms except the amount and effective date of a wage increase. Bargaining continued without result, and on March 2 the Local informed the employers that a strike had been authorized. The employers responded that a strike against any member of the employer group would be regarded as a strike against all. On March 16, the union struck Food Jet, Inc., one of the group. The four respondents, operating five stores, immediately locked out all employees represented by the Local, telling them and the Local that they would be recalled to work when the strike against Food Jet ended. The stores, including Food Jet, continued to carry on business by using management personnel, relatives of such personnel, and a few temporary employees; all of the temporary replacements were expressly told that the arrangement would be discontinued when the whipsaw strike ended. Bargaining continued until April 22 when an agreement was reached. The employers immediately released the temporary replacements and restored the strikers and the locked out employees to their jobs. . . .

We begin with the proposition that the Act does not constitute the Board as an "arbiter of the sort of economic weapons the parties can use in seeking to gain acceptance of their bargaining demands." In the absence of proof of unlawful motivation, there are many economic weapons which an employer may use that either interfere in some measure with concerted employee activities, or which are in some degree discriminatory and discourage union membership, and yet the use of such economic weapons does not constitute conduct that is within the prohibition of either s. 8(a)(1) or s. 8(a)(3). Even the Board concedes that an employer may legitimately blunt the effectiveness of an anticipated strike by stockpiling inventories, readjusting contract schedules, or transferring work from one plant to another, even if he thereby makes himself "virtually strike-proof." . . .

Specifically, he may in various circumstances use the lockout as a legitimate economic weapon. . . .

In the circumstances of this case, we do not see how the continued operations of respondents and their use of temporary replacements any more implies hostile motivation, nor how it is inherently more destructive of employee rights, than the lockout itself. Rather, the compelling inference is that this was all part and parcel of respondents' defensive measure to preserve the multiemployer group in the face of the whipsaw strike. Since Food Jet legitimately continued business operations, it is only reasonable to regard respondents' actions as evincing concern that the integrity of the employer group was threatened unless they also managed to stay open for business during the lockout. For with Food Jet open for business and respondents' stores closed, the prospect that the whipsaw strike would succeed in breaking up the employer association was not at all fanciful. The retail food industry is very competitive and repetitive patronage is highly important. Faced with the prospect of a loss of patronage to Food Jet, it is logical that respondents should have been concerned that one or more of their number might bolt the group and come to terms with the Local, thus destroying the common front essential to multiemployer bargaining. The Court of Appeals correctly pictured the respondents' dilemma in saying, "If . . . the struck employer does choose to operate with replacements and the other employers cannot replace after lockout, the economic advantage passes to the struck member, the nonstruck members are deterred in exercising the defensive lockout, and the whipsaw strike ... enjoys an almost inescapable prospect of success." Clearly, respondents' continued operations with the use of temporary replacements following the lockout was wholly consistent with a legitimate business purpose.

The Board's finding of a Section 8(a)(1) violation emphasized the impact of respondents' conduct upon the effectiveness of the whipsaw strike. It is no doubt true that the collective strength of the stores to resist that strike is maintained, and even increased, when all stores stay open with temporary replacements. The pressures on the employees are necessarily greater when none of the union employees is working and the stores remain open. But these pressures are no more than the result of the Local's inability to make effective use of the whipsaw tactic. Moreover, these effects are no different from those that result from the legitimate use of any economic weapon by an employer. Continued operations with the use of temporary replacements may result in the failure of the whipsaw strike, but this does not mean that the employers' conduct is demonstrably so destructive of employee rights or so devoid of significant service to any legitimate business end that it cannot be tolerated consistently with the Act. Certainly then, in the absence of evidentiary findings of hostile motive, there is no support for the conclusion that respondents violated Section 8(a)(1).

Nor does the record show any basis for concluding that respondents violated Section 8(a)(3). Under that section both discrimination and a resulting discouragement of union membership are necessary, but the added element of unlawful intent is also required. In *Buffalo Linen* itself the employers treated the locked-out employees less favorably because of their union membership, and this may have tended to discourage continued membership, but we rejected the notion that the use of the lockout violated the statute. The discriminatory act is not by itself unlawful unless intended to prejudice the employees' position because of their membership in the union; some element of antiunion animus is necessary.

We agree with the Court of Appeals that respondents' conduct here clearly fits into the latter category, where actual subjective intent is determinative, and where the Board must find from evidence independent of the mere conduct involved that the conduct was primarily motivated by an antiunion animus. While the use of temporary nonunion personnel in preference to the locked-out union members is discriminatory, we think that any resulting tendency to discourage union membership is comparatively remote, and that this use of temporary personnel constitutes a measure reasonably adapted to the effectuation of a legitimate business end. Here discontent on the part of the Local's membership in all likelihood is attributable largely to the fact that the membership was locked out as the result of the Local's whipsaw stratagem. But the lockout itself is concededly within the rule of *Buffalo Linen*. We think that the added dissatisfaction and resultant pressure on membership attributable to the fact that the nonstruck employers remain in business with temporary replacements is comparatively insubstantial. First, the replacements were expressly used for the duration of the labor dispute only; thus, the displaced employees could not have looked upon the replacements as threatening their jobs. At most the union would be forced to capitulate and return its members to work on terms which, while not as desirable as hoped for, were still better than under the contract. Second, the membership, through its control of union policy, could end the dispute and terminate the lockout at any time simply by agreeing to the employers' terms and returning to work on a regular basis. Third, in light of the union-shop provision that had been carried forward into the new contract from the old collective agreement, it would appear that a union member would have nothing to gain and much to lose by quitting the union. Under all these circumstances, we cannot say that the employers' conduct had any great tendency to discourage union membership. Not only was the prospect of discouragement of membership comparatively remote, but the respondents' attempt to remain open for business with the help of temporary replacements was a measure reasonably adapted to the achievement of legitimate end—preserving the integrity of the multi-employer bargaining unit.

When the resulting harm to employee rights is thus comparatively slight, and a substantial and legitimate business end is served, the employers' conduct is prima facie lawful. Under these circumstances the finding of an unfair labor practice under Section 8(a)(3) requires a showing of improper subjective intent. Here, there is no assertion by either the union or the Board that the respondents were motivated by antiunion animus, nor is there any evidence that this was the case.... Thus, not only is there absent in the record any independent evidence of improper motive, but the record contains positive evidence of the employers' good faith. In sum, the Court of Appeals was required to conclude that there was not sufficient evidence gathered from the record as a whole to support the Board's finding that respondents' conduct violates Section 8(a)(3). . . .

Courts must, of course, set aside Board decisions which rest on "an erroneous legal foundation." Congress has not given the Board untrammeled authority to catalogue which economic devices shall be deemed freighted with indicia of unlawful intent. In determining here that the respondents' conduct carried its own badge of improper motive, the Board's decision, for the reasons stated, supplied the criteria governing the application of Sections 8(a)(1) and (3). Since the order therefore rested on "an erroneous legal foundation," the Court of Appeals properly refused to enforce it.

Affirmed.

Case Questions

1. Why are employers usually not willing to lock out employees?
2. What reasons did the employers give for locking out their employees in this case? Is this lockout a "defensive lockout"? Explain your answer.
3. Why did the Court state that there was no antiunion intent on the part of the employers in this case? What evidence did the Court use to support that statement? Explain.

Whereas *Brown* dealt with a defensive lockout in response to a strike against one employer, the Supreme Court in *American Shipbuilding Co. v. NLRB* [380 U.S. 300 (1965)] held that an employer is free to lock out employees in anticipation of the union going on strike. That decision allows the employer to use a lockout as an offensive weapon to promote its bargaining position; the employer need not wait for the union to strike first. An employer may not engage in a lockout unless negotiations have reached an impasse, or deadlock, and exceptional circumstances are required by the board to justify lockouts prior to a bargaining impasse.

In *Ancor Concepts, Inc.* [323 NLRB No. 134 (1997)], the NLRB held that the use of permanent replacements after a lockout was a violation of Section 8(a)(3).

How does that situation differ from *NLRB v. Brown*? The NLRB upheld the use of temporary replacements after an offensive lockout in *Harter Equipment* [280 NLRB No. 71, 122 L.R.R.M. 1219 (1986)].

Plant Closing to Avoid Unionization

The preceding discussion dealt with an employer's response to the economic demands of organized workers; the employer is free to lock out to avoid union bargaining demands. But what about the situation in which the employees are just in the process of forming a union? Can the employer shut down the plant to avoid unionization? Recall that Section 8(a)(1) prohibits threats of closure or layoff to dissuade employees from joining a union. Should it make any difference whether the shutdown to avoid unionization is complete (the entire operation) or partial (only part of the operation)? The following Supreme Court decision addresses this issue.

Textile Workers Union v. Darlington Mfg. Co.

380 U.S. 263 (1965)

Harlan, J.

Darlington Manufacturing Company was a South Carolina corporation operating one textile mill. A majority of Darlington's stock was held by Deering Milliken & Co., a New York "selling house" marketing textiles produced by others. Deering Milliken in turn was controlled by Roger Milliken, president of Darlington, and by other members of the Milliken family. The National Labor Relations Board found that the Milliken family, through Deering Milliken, operated 17 textile manufacturers, including Darlington, whose products, manufactured in 27 different mills, were marketed through Deering Milliken.

In March 1956 petitioner Textile Workers Union initiated an organizational campaign at Darlington which the company resisted vigorously in various ways, including threats to close the mill if the union won a representation election. On September 6, 1956, the union won an election by a narrow margin. When Roger Milliken was advised of the union victory, he decided to call a meeting of the Darlington board of directors to consider closing the mill. . . . The board of directors met on September 12 and voted to liquidate the corporation, action which was approved by the stockholders on October 17. The plant ceased operations entirely in November, and all plant machinery and equipment was sold piecemeal at auction in December.

The union filed charges with the Labor Board claiming that Darlington had violated Sections 8(a)(1) and 8(a)(3) of the National Labor Relations Act by closing its plant, and Section 8(a)(5) by refusing to bargain with the union after the election. The Board, by a divided vote, found that Darlington had been closed because of the anti-union animus of Roger Milliken, and held that to be a violation of Section 8(a)(3). The Board also found Darlington to be part of a single integrated employer group controlled by the Milliken family through Deering Milliken; therefore Deering Milliken could be held liable for the unfair labor practices of Darlington. Alternatively, since Darlington was a part of the Deering Milliken enterprise, Deering Milliken had violated the Act by closing part of its business for a discriminatory purpose. The Board ordered back pay for all Darlington employees until they obtained substantially equivalent work or were put on preferential hiring lists at the other Deering Milliken mills. Respondent Deering Milliken was ordered to bargain with the union in regard to details of compliance with the Board order.

On review, the Court of Appeals . . . denied enforcement by a divided vote. The Court of Appeals held that even accepting arguendo the Board's determination that Deering Milliken had the status of a single employer, a company has the absolute right to close out a part or all of its business regardless of anti-union motives. The court therefore did not review the Board's finding that Deering Milliken was a single integrated employer. We hold that so far as the Labor Act is concerned, an employer has the absolute right to terminate his entire business for any reason he pleases, but disagree with the Court of Appeals that such right includes the ability to close part of a business no matter what the reason. We conclude that the case must be remanded to the Board for further proceedings.

Preliminarily it should be observed that both petitioners argue that the Darlington closing violated Section 8(a)(1) as well as Section 8(a)(3) of the Act. We think, however, that the Board was correct in treating the closing only under Section 8(a)(3). Section 8(a)(1) provides that it is unfair labor practice for an employer "to interfere with, restrain, or coerce employees in the exercise of" Section 7 rights. Naturally, certain business decisions will, to some degree, interfere with concerted activities by employees. . . .

. . . The AFL-CIO suggests in its *amicus* brief that Darlington's action was similar to a discriminatory lockout, which is prohibited "because [it is] designed to frustrate organizational efforts, to destroy or undermine bargaining representation, or to evade the duty to bargain." One of the purposes of the Labor Act is to prohibit the discriminatory use of economic weapons in an effort to obtain future benefits. The discriminatory lockout designed to destroy a union, like a "runaway shop," is a lever which has been used to discourage collective employee activities in the future. But a complete liquidation of a business yields no such future benefit for the employer, if the termination is bona fide. It may be motivated more by spite against the union than by business reasons, but it is not the type of discrimination which is prohibited by the Act. The personal satisfaction that such an employer may derive from standing on his beliefs or the mere possibility that other employers will follow his example are surely too remote to be considered dangers at which the labor statutes were aimed. Although employees may be prohibited from engaging in a strike under certain conditions, no one would consider it a violation of the Act for the same employees to quit their employment *en masse,* even if motivated by a desire to ruin the employer. The very permanence of such action would negate any future economic benefit to the employees. The employer's right to go out of business is no different.

We are not presented here with the case of a "runaway shop," whereby Darlington would transfer its work to another plant or open a new plant in another locality to replace its closed plant. Nor are we concerned with a shutdown where the employees, by renouncing the union, could cause the plant to reopen. Such cases would involve discriminatory employer action for the purpose of obtaining some benefit in the future from the new employees. We hold here only that when an employer closes his entire business, even if the liquidation is motivated by vindictiveness towards the union, such action is not an unfair labor practice.

While we thus agree with the Court of Appeals that viewing Darlington as an independent employer, the liquidation of its business was not an unfair labor practice, we cannot accept the lower court's view that the same conclusion necessarily follows if Darlington is regarded as an integral part of the Deering Milliken enterprise.

The closing of an entire business, even though discriminatory, ends the employer-employee relationship; the force of such a closing is entirely spent as to that business when termination of the enterprise takes place. On the other hand, a discriminatory partial closing may have repercussions on what remains of the business, affording employer leverage for discouraging the free exercise of Section 7 rights among remaining employees of much the same kind as that found to exist in the "runaway shop" and "temporary closing" cases. Moreover, a possible remedy open to the Board in such a case, like the remedies available in the "runaway shop" and "temporary closing" cases, is to order reinstatement of the discharged employees in the other parts of the business. No such remedy is available when an entire business has been terminated. By analogy to those cases involving a continuing enterprise we are constrained to hold, in disagreement with the Court of Appeals, that a partial closing is an unfair labor practice under Section 8(a)(3) if motivated by a purpose to chill unionism in any of the remaining plants of the single employer and if the employer may reasonably have foreseen that such closing will likely have that effect.

. . . In these circumstances, we think the proper disposition of this case is to require that it be remanded to the Board so as to afford the Board the opportunity to make further findings on the issue of purpose and effect. . . .

So ordered.

Case Questions

1. Why should it matter whether the Darlington mill was a single employer or part of a much larger integrated operation? Is the closure of an entire business to avoid a union illegal? Explain your answers.
2. What is the difference between the closure of an entire business and a "runaway shop"? Do the facts here present a total closure or a runaway shop? Explain.
3. What did the NLRB determine would be the likely effect of closing the Darlington mill on the other employees of Deering Milliken? Why is that relevant to the determination of whether the Darlington closure was illegal?

On remand, the board held that the Darlington plant was closed to deter union organizing at other plants controlled by the Millikens and therefore violated Section 8(a)(3). The decision and order were enforced by the U.S. Court of Appeals for the Fourth Circuit in *Darlington Mfg. v. NLRB* [397 F.2d 760 (1968)].

Runaway Shop
An employer who closes in one location and opens in another to avoid unionization.

The Court in *Darlington* noted that a complete shutdown to avoid unionization is different from a **runaway shop,** in which the employer closes in one location and opens in another to avoid unionization. Such runaway conduct is in violation of Section 8(a)(3). However, the motive requirement under Section 8(a)(3) may pose a problem in determining whether the relocation of the operation violates the act. If the employer raises some legitimate business reasons for the relocation, the NLRB counsel must demonstrate that the runaway would not have happened except for the employees' unionizing efforts. (See the *Transportation Management* case discussed earlier in this chapter.)

As remedy for a runaway shop, the board will order that the offending employer offer the old employees positions at the new location; the employer must also pay the employees' moving or travel expenses. If the employer has shut down part of the operation, the board may order the employer to reopen the closed portion or to reinstate the affected employees in the remaining parts of the operation. The employees will also be awarded back pay lost because of the employer's violation. Remedies are discussed more fully later in this chapter.

OTHER UNFAIR LABOR PRACTICES

In addition to the unfair labor practices already discussed, the NLRA prohibits several other kinds of conduct. Refusing to bargain in good faith, the subject of Section 8(a)(5) and Section 8(b)(3), will be discussed in Chapter 16, and union unfair practices involving picketing and secondary boycotts will be dealt with in Chapter 17. The remaining unfair labor practices are the focus of this section.

EMPLOYER REPRISALS AGAINST EMPLOYEES

Section 8(a)(4) prohibits an employer from discharging or otherwise discriminating against an employee who has filed charges or given testimony under the act. Because employees must be free to avail themselves of the act's procedures to give effect to their Section 7 rights, reprisals against employees for exercising their rights must also infringe on those rights. Violations of Section 8(a)(4) include the discharge or disciplining of an employee filing unfair practice charges and the layoff of such employees. Refusing to consider an employee for promotion because that employee filed unfair practice charges is also a violation. Section 8(a)(4) is directed only against employers; union reprisals against employees for exercising their statutory rights are dealt with under Section 8(b)(1)(A).

EXCESSIVE UNION DUES OR MEMBERSHIP FEES

Section 8(b)(5) prohibits a union from requiring excessive dues or membership fees of employees covered by a union security agreement. Because a union security agreement requires that employees join the union (or at least pay all dues and fees) to retain their jobs, some protection against union abuse or extortion must be given to the affected employees. In deciding a complaint under Section 8(b)(5), the board is directed by the act to consider "the practices and customs of labor organizations in the particular industry, and the wages currently paid to the employees affected."

FEATHERBEDDING

Section 8(b)(6) makes it unfair labor practice for a union "to cause or attempt to cause an employer to pay or deliver or agree to pay or deliver any money or other thing of value, in the nature of an extraction, for services which are not performed or not to be performed." The practice of getting paid for services not performed or not to be performed is known as **featherbedding.**

Featherbedding
The practice of getting paid for services not performed or not to be performed.

Although this statutory prohibition may seem straightforward, it may not be easy to discern featherbedding from legal activities. For instance, a union steward may be employed to run a drill press. In reality, she may be spending much of her time assisting co-workers for the union's benefit and may even draw additional compensation for this service from the union. If the collective-bargaining agreement allows for this activity, then it is legal.

In another situation, the employer may pay for work that is not really needed—because, for instance, of technological innovations in the industry—but through industrial custom and usage, the work is still performed by union members. This, too, is legal under the NLRA.

In *American Newspaper Publisher's Assoc. v. NLRB* [345 U.S. 100 (1953)], the Supreme Court held that Section 8(b)(6) is limited only to payment (or demanding of payment) for services not actually rendered. In that case, the payment by the employers for the setting of type that was not needed did not violate the act because the services, although not needed, were actually performed. Because of increasing economic competition from nonunionized firms and because of labor-saving technological developments, complaints of union featherbedding under Section 8(b)(6) are relatively rare today.

REMEDIES FOR UNFAIR LABOR PRACTICES

Under Section 10 of the NLRA, the NLRB is empowered to prevent any person from engaging in any unfair labor practice. Section 10(a) authorizes the board to investigate charges, issue complaints, and order hearings in unfair labor practice cases. If the ALJ (or the board on review) finds that an employer or union has been or is engaging in unfair labor practices, the NLRB will so state in its findings and issue a cease-and-desist order with regard to those practices. If the employer (or union) chooses not to comply with the order, the board will petition the appropriate federal court of appeals for enforcement of its order as provided in Section 10(e).

The board may also order the offending party to take affirmative action in the wake of the unfair labor practices. For instance, when an employee has been discriminatorily discharged in violation of Section 8(a)(1), (3), or (4), the board will commonly require that the employee be reinstated, usually with back pay.

Finally, under Section 10(j) of the act, the board in its discretion may seek an injunction in a federal district court to put a halt to unfair labor practices while the parties to a dispute await its final resolution by the board.[3] The purpose is to

[3]See "Utilization of Section 10(j) Proceedings," Memorandum of the General Counsel, Memorandum GC02-07, Aug. 9, 2002, available at the NLRB Website **http://www.nlrb.gov**. Click on the GC Memos link and scroll down to GC Memo 02-07.

preserve the status quo while the adjudicative process works itself out. The NLRB obtained an injunction against the Major League Baseball owners for their refusal to bargain in good faith with the Major League Baseball Players' Association in 1995, *Silverman v. Major League Baseball Players Relations Committee, Inc.* [67 F.3d 1054 (2d Cir. 1995)]. That injunction forced the owners back to the bargaining table with the players' union and was instrumental in getting the parties to settle the baseball strike in April 1995. Section 10(l) requires the board to seek a temporary restraining order from a court when a union is engaging in a secondary boycott, hot cargo agreements, recognitional picketing, or a jurisdictional dispute. (Those unfair practices will be discussed in Chapter 17.)

REINSTATEMENT

When an employee has been discharged or laid off in violation of the act, the board is empowered by Section 10(c) to order reinstatement with back pay. However, Section 10(c) also states that the board shall not order reinstatement of, or back pay for, an employee who has been discharged "for cause." Therefore, an employee guilty of misconduct may not be entitled to reinstatement. This provision is of particular interest in strike situations. Employees on an economic strike may be discharged for misconduct such as violence, destruction of property, and so on. In a 1984 decision, the board held that verbal threats alone may justify discharge when they "reasonably tend to coerce or intimidate employees in the exercise of rights protected under the Act." The board had held that in the case of unfair practice strikers, more severe misconduct is required to justify discharge. But in *Clear Pine Mouldings* [268 NLRB No. 173 (1984)], the board stated that unfair practice strikers are not given any privilege to engage in misconduct or violence just because they are on strike over employer unfair labor practices. In any situation, physical assaults or violence will not be tolerated by the board.

What should the NLRB do when an employee who was fired illegally by the employer has lied under oath in the NLRB hearing? Is the employee entitled to be reinstated, or should the misconduct of lying justify dismissal? That is the question in the following case.

ABF Freight System, Inc. v. NLRB

510 U.S. 317 (1994)

Stevens, J.

. . . Michael Manso gave his employer a false excuse for being late to work and repeated that falsehood while testifying under oath before an Administrative Law Judge (ALJ). Notwithstanding Manso's dishonesty, the National Labor Relations Board (Board) ordered Manso's former employer to reinstate him with back pay. Our interest in preserving the integrity of administrative proceedings prompted us to grant certiorari to consider whether Manso's misconduct should have precluded the Board from granting him that relief.

Manso worked as a casual dockworker at petitioner ABF Freight's (ABF's) trucking terminal in Albuquerque, New Mexico, from the summer of 1987 to August 1989. He was fired three times. The first time, Manso was one of 12 employees discharged in June 1988 in a dispute over a contractual provision relating to so-called "preferential casual" dockworkers. The grievance Manso's union filed eventually secured his reinstatement; Manso also filed an unfair labor practice charge against ABF over the incident..

Manso's return to work was short-lived. Three supervisors warned him of likely retaliation from top management—alerting him, for example, that ABF was "gunning" for him, and that "the higher echelon was after [him]". . . . Within six weeks ABF discharged Manso for a second time on pretextual grounds—ostensibly for failing to respond to a call to work made under a stringent verification procedure ABF had recently imposed upon preferential casuals. Once again, a grievance panel ordered Manso reinstated.

Manso's third discharge came less than two months later. On August 11, 1989, Manso arrived four minutes late for the 5 A.M. shift. At the time, ABF had no policy regarding lateness. After Manso was late to work, however, ABF decided to discharge preferential casuals—though not other employees—who were late twice without good cause. Six days later Manso triggered the policy's first application when he arrived at work nearly an hour late for the same shift. Manso telephoned at 5:25 A.M. to explain that he was having car trouble on the highway, and repeated that excuse when he arrived. ABF conducted a prompt investigation, ascertained that he was lying, and fired him for tardiness under its new policy on lateness.

Manso filed a second unfair labor practice charge. In the hearing before the ALJ, Manso repeated his story about the car trouble that preceded his third discharge.. The ALJ credited most of his testimony about events surrounding his dismissals, but expressly concluded that Manso lied when he told ABF that car trouble made him late to work. Accordingly, although the ALJ decided that ABF had illegally discharged Manso the second time because he was a party to the earlier union grievance, the ALJ denied Manso relief for the third discharge based on his finding that ABF had dismissed Manso for cause.

The Board affirmed the ALJ's finding that Manso's second discharge was unlawful, but reversed with respect to the third discharge. Acknowledging that Manso lied to his employer and that ABF presumably could have discharged him for that dishonesty, the Board nevertheless emphasized that ABF did not in fact discharge him for lying and that the ALJ's conclusion to the contrary was "a plainly erroneous factual statement of [ABF]'s asserted reasons." Instead, Manso's lie "established only that he did not have a legitimate excuse for the August 17 lateness." The Board focused primarily on ABF's retroactive application of its lateness policy to include Manso's first time late to work, holding that ABF had "seized upon" Manso's tardiness "as a pretext to discharge him again and for the same unlawful reasons it discharged him on June 19." In addition, though the Board deemed Manso's discharge unlawful even assuming the validity of ABF's general disciplinary treatment of preferential casuals, it observed that ABF's disciplinary approach and lack of uniform rules for all dockworkers "raise[d] more questions than they resolve[d]." The Board ordered ABF to reinstate Manso with back pay.

The Court of Appeals enforced the Board's order. Its review of the record revealed "abundant evidence of anti-union animus in ABF's conduct towards Manso," including "ample evidence" that Manso's third discharge was not for cause. . . .

. . . We assume that the Board correctly found that ABF discharged Manso unlawfully in August 1989. We also assume, more importantly, that the Board did not abuse its discretion in ordering reinstatement even though Manso gave ABF a false reason for being late to work. We are concerned only with the ramifications of Manso's false testimony under oath in a formal proceeding before the ALJ. We recognize that the Board might have decided that such misconduct disqualified Manso from profiting from the proceeding, or it might even have adopted a flat rule precluding reinstatement when a former employee so testifies . . . however, the issue is not whether the Board might adopt such a rule, but whether it must do so.

False testimony in a formal proceeding is intolerable. We must neither reward nor condone such a "flagrant affront" to the truthseeking function of adversary proceedings.

ABF submits that the false testimony of a former employee who was the victim of an unfair labor practice should always preclude him from winning reinstatement with back pay. . . . The Act expressly authorizes the Board "to take such affirmative action including reinstatement of employees with or without back pay, as will effectuate the policies of [the Act]." Only in cases of discharge for cause does the statute restrict the Board's authority to order reinstatement. This is not such a case.

When Congress expressly delegates to an administrative agency the authority to make specific policy determinations, courts must give the agency's decision controlling weight unless it is "arbitrary, capricious, or manifestly contrary to the statute." Because this case involves that kind of express delegation, the Board's views merit the greatest deference. This has been our consistent appraisal of the Board's remedial authority throughout its long history of administering the Act. . . .

Notwithstanding our concern about the seriousness of Manso's ill-advised decision to repeat under oath his false excuse for tardiness, we cannot say that the Board's remedial order in this case was an abuse of its broad discretion or that it was obligated to adopt a rigid rule that would foreclose relief in all comparable cases. Nor can we fault the Board's conclusions that Manso's reason for being late to work was ultimately irrelevant to whether anti-union animus actually motivated his discharge and that ordering effective relief in a case of this character promotes a vital public interest. Notably, the ALJ refused to credit the testimony of several ABF witnesses . . . and the Board affirmed those credibility findings. The unfairness of sanctioning Manso while indirectly rewarding those witnesses' lack of candor is obvious. Moreover, the rule ABF advocates might force the Board to divert its attention from its primary mission and devote unnecessary time and energy to resolving collateral disputes about credibility. Its decision to rely on "other civil and criminal remedies" for false testimony rather than a categorical exception to the familiar remedy of reinstatement is well within its broad discretion. The judgment of the Court of Appeals is affirmed.

It is so ordered.

Case Questions

1. What was ABF's justification for discharging Manso the third time? Did the ALJ find that discharge illegal under the NLRA? Did the ALJ order that Manso be reinstated? Why?
2. Did the NLRB agree with the ALJ's decision as to what remedy Manso is entitled? Why?
3. Why does the Supreme Court uphold the NLRB's decision? Does the Court's decision encourage or reward lying under oath? Explain.

Front Pay
Monetary award for loss of anticipated future earnings.

While the NLRB generally seeks reinstatement for employees discharged illegally, there are some instances when it may seek **front pay** rather than reinstatement. Front pay is a monetary award for loss of anticipated future earnings because of the unfair labor practice. The Board's General Counsel[4] has indicated that front pay may be appropriate where the unfair labor practice has impaired the ability of the employee to return to work, where the employer or other employees remain hostile to the discharged employee, or where the discharged employee is close to retirement. Front pay may also be used as a substitute for a "preferential hire" list.

BACK PAY

When calculating back-pay awards due employees under Section 10(c), the board requires that the affected employees mitigate their damages; the board will deduct from the back-pay wages to reflect income that the employee earned or might have earned while the case was pending. (Welfare benefits and unemployment insurance payments are not deducted from back-pay awards by the board.) The board also requires that interest (at a rate based on the Treasury bills index) be paid on back-pay awards under the act.

[4]See "Guideline Memorandum Concerning Frontpay," Office of the General Counsel, Feb. 3, 2000, available online at the NLRB Website **http://www.nlrb.gov**. Click on the GC Memos link, then scroll down to GC Memo 00-01.

The Internal Revenue Service considers back-pay awards to be taxable income for the year in which the award is received. In some instances, an employee receiving a lump-sum back-pay award representing more than one year's worth of pay may have increased income tax liability due to the award. In such cases, the NLRB has indicated that it will seek an additional monetary award to cover the additional income taxes owed by the employee because of the lump sum-award, plus interest.[5]

The NLRB is precluded by the Immigration Reform and Control Act of 1986 (discussed in Chapter 5) from awarding back pay to an undocumented alien who is not legally entitled to work in the United States, *Hoffman Plastic Compounds, Inc. v. NLRB* [122 S.Ct. 1275 (2002)].[6]

The general wording of Section 10(c) allows the board great flexibility in fashioning remedies in various unfair practice cases. Such flexibility is exemplified by the bargaining order remedy in *Gissel Packing,* considered in Chapter 14. Furthermore, the board has required the guilty party to pay the legal fees of the complainant in cases involving severe or blatant violations. In one case involving an employer's unfair practices that destroyed a union's majority support, the board ordered the employer to pay the union's organizing expenses for those employees.

DELAY PROBLEMS IN NLRB REMEDIES

Although the NLRB has rather broad remedial powers under the NLRA, the delays involved in pursuing the board's remedial procedures limit somewhat the effectiveness of its powers. The increasing caseload of the board has delayed the procedural process to the point at which a determined employer can dilute the effectiveness of any remedy in a particular case.

Because unfair practice cases take so long to resolve, the affected employees may be left financially and emotionally exhausted by the process. Furthermore, the remedy, when it comes, may be too little, too late. One study found that when reinstatement was offered more than six months after the violation of the act occurred, only 5 percent of those discriminatorily discharged accepted their old jobs back.

Indeed, the final resolution of the back-pay claims of the employees in the *Darlington* case (presented earlier) did not occur until 1980—fully twenty-four years from the closing of their plant to avoid the union!

Obviously, a firm that can afford the litigation expenses may find it advantageous to delay a representation election by committing unfair practices or refusing to bargain with a certified union in violation of Section 8(a)(5), reasoning that

---

[5]See "Reimbursement for Excess Federal and State Income Taxes which Discriminatees Owe as a Result of Receiving a Lump-sum Backpay Award," Office of the General Counsel, Sept. 22, 2000, available online at **http://www.nlrb.gov**. Click on the GC Memos link, and scroll down to GC Memo 00-07.

[6]See "Procedures and Remedies for Discriminatees Who May Be Undocumented Aliens after *Hoffman Plastic Compounds, Inc.*," Memorandum of the General Counsel, Memorandum GC02-06, July 19, 2002, available at **http://www.nlrb.gov**. Click on the GC Memos link and scroll down to GC Memo 02-06.

the lawyers' fees plus any back-pay awards will total less of a cost of doing business than will increased wages and fringes under a collective-bargaining agreement.

An attempt to remedy the delay in processing unfair practice cases was made in 1978; the Labor Law Reform Bill would have expedited board review of ALJ decisions and limited judicial review. That bill was passed by the House of Representatives but was the victim of a filibuster by opponents in the Senate. Although the NLRB has attempted to reduce the backlog of cases pending (and the attendant delay in the resolution process) by increasing the workloads of ALJs and board members, the delay problem remains. That problem, with its effects on the rights of employees under the act, poses a serious threat to the effectiveness of our national labor relations policies.

The NLRB has made reducing the time needed to resolve unfair labor practice cases a priority. In its 1998 fiscal year, the NLRB median time for handling unfair labor practice complaints was 271 days from the issuance of a complaint until the close of the hearing. In its Annual Performance Plans,[7] the NLRB sets annual goals for significantly reducing the time it takes to resolve unfair labor practice charges.

SUMMARY

- Section 7 of the NLRA provides protection for employees who engage in concerted activity for collective bargaining or for mutual aid and protection. All employees under the NLRA enjoy the right to engage in protected activity; conduct by employers or unions that undercuts or interferes with employees' Section 7 rights is an unfair labor practice.
- Section 8 of the NLRA defines a list of unfair labor practices by employers and by unions. Restrictions on employees' organizing or soliciting activity may violate Section 8(a)(1) or 8(b)(1); employer support, domination, or control of a labor organization [as defined by Section 2(5)] may be in violation of Section 8(a)(2). Employers that discriminate in terms or conditions of employment against employees either to encourage or discourage union membership violate Section 8(a)(3), and unions that attempt to get an employer to engage in such discrimination against employees violate Section 8(b)(2). The NLRA does allow employers and unions to adopt union security provisions such as an agency shop or union shop agreement; however, closed shop agreements, which require that a person be a union member to be hired, are prohibited under the NLRA.
- Economic strikes are protected activities under the NLRA, but economic strikers may be permanently replaced and are not guaranteed to get their jobs back after the strike. Unfair labor practice strikes are also protected activities, and unfair labor practice strikers may not be permanently replaced. An employer may lock out employees in a bargaining dispute but may not permanently replace the locked-out workers.
- The NLRB has broad powers to remedy unfair labor practices, but in practice, the procedures for resolving unfair labor practice complaints may take a long time. Such delays may operate to undermine the effectiveness of the remedies available and the intent of the NLRA in protecting the free choice of employees.

[7]The NLRB Annual Performance Plan for the current fiscal year is available online at the NLRB's Web site at **http://www.nlrb.gov**. Click the Public Notices link, next click the Government Performance and Results Act of 1993, and then click the link for the appropriate annual performance plan.

QUESTIONS

1. What kind of activity is protected by Section 7 of the NLRA? What is the effect of such protection?
2. To what extent may an employer limit union soliciting by employees? By nonemployees?
3. When can an individual acting alone be considered to be engaged in concerted activity under Section 7 of the NLRA? Explain your answer.
4. What is the relevance of motive under Section 8(a)(1)? What is the relevance of motive under Section 8(a)(3)? Explain.
5. What are union security provisions? Why would unions want to negotiate such provisions? Why are closed shop agreements outlawed?
6. When does an employee group constitute a labor organization under Section 2(5) of the NLRA? Can an employer organize an employee-management committee to discuss working conditions without violating Section 8(a)(2)? Explain.
7. What is featherbedding?
8. Why are lockouts by employers uncommon? When may an employer use an "offensive lockout" under the NLRA?
9. To what extent is an economic strike protected activity? To what extent is an unfair labor practice strike protected activity? What is the practical significance of the difference in the treatment of the different types of strikers under the NLRA?
10. What is the effect of delay in the NLRB disposition of unfair labor practice complaints?

CASE PROBLEMS

1. Sandra Falcone was employed as a dental hygiene assistant. During a staff meeting, Dr. Trufolo discussed some work-related problems. Falcone and a co-worker interrupted the meeting several times to disagree with Dr. Trufolo's comments. After the meeting, the office manager reprimanded Falcone and her co-worker for disrupting the meeting by questioning Dr. Trufolo and by giggling and elbowing each other. On the following Monday, Falcone presented a list of grievances to the office manager, which Falcone had discussed with co-workers. Shortly thereafter, she was fired.

   Based on these facts, did the employer commit an unfair labor practice by discharging Falcone? Upon what facts should the NLRB determine the true motive for the discharge? See *Joseph DeRario, DMD, P.A.* [283 NLRB No. 86, 125 L.R.R.M. 1024 (1987)].

2. Potter Manufacturing Co. laid off fifteen employees because of economic conditions and lack of business. The union representing the employees at Potter subsequently discovered that the employer had laid off employees that the employer believed were most likely to honor a picket line in the event of a strike. The union filed an unfair labor practice complaint with the NLRB, alleging that the layoffs violated Sections 8(a)1 and 8(a)3.

   How should the NLRB rule on the complaint? See *National Fabricators* [295 NLRB No. 126, 131 L.R.R.M. 1761 (1989)].

3. Shortly after the union won a representation election in a Philadelphia-area hospital, the hospital fired the union steward, allegedly for failing to report to work. Some eighteen months after the discharge, and while the unfair labor practice charge was still in litigation, a majority of the bargaining unit presented the president of the hospital with a petition requesting that the president withdraw recognition from the union and cease bargaining with

it. Pursuant to the petition, after confirming the authenticity of the signatures and that it contained a majority of the bargaining unit members, the president withdrew recognition. The union filed another unfair labor practice charge.

If the hospital was found guilty of discriminatorily discharging the union steward, can you make an argument that it committed a second unfair labor practice by withdrawing recognition from the union while the unfair labor practice charge was pending? Do you reach a different result if at the time the petition was presented the hospital had been found guilty of the discriminatory discharge but was in the process of appealing the board's decision? Would the result be different if the hospital had been found guilty but had immediately remedied the illegal action by reinstating the employee with back pay? See *Taylor Hospital v. NLRB* [770 F.2d 1075 (3d Cir. 1985)].

4. During a strike by the employees at Gillen, Inc., the picketers carried signs referring to the company and its president as "scabs." The president of Gillen, Inc., D. C. Gillen, filed a defamation suit against the union for its picketing and signs. Gillen sought $500,000 in damages, despite the fact that he could identify no business losses because of the picketing and signs. Gillen's suit was dismissed by the court as "groundless." The union then filed an unfair labor practice complaint against Gillen, Inc., alleging that filing the suit against the picketing and signs served to coerce the employees in the exercise of their rights under Section 7.

   How should the NLRB rule on the complaint? Explain your answer. See *H. S. Barss Co.* [296 NLRB No. 151, 132 L.R.R.M. 1339 (1989)].

5. Rubber Workers District No. 8 began an organizing campaign at Bardcor Corporation, a small manufacturing company in Guthrie, Kentucky, during the summer of 1981. Shortly after the campaign began, the president of the corporation began taking pictures of workers in the plant. Employee Maxine Dukes asked supervisor Mike Loreille why the pictures were being taken. Loreille responded that the president wanted something to remember the employees by after he fired them for union activity.

   A majority of the company's thirty-seven employees signed union authorization cards. The next day, the employer discharged eight workers, seven of whom had signed cards. After the discharge, the union filed a series of unfair labor practice charges. The company was able to justify the discharges for economic reasons and argued that the picture-taking incident and Loreille's comment were nothing but jokes.

   What provision of the NLRA did the company allegedly violate by the picture-taking incident and the supervisor's comment to Ms. Dukes? Try to formulate an argument for and against finding a violation of the act by the employer in one or both of these actions. Could the picture-taking incident alone violate the act? Did the supervisor's comment alone violate the act? See *Bardcor Corporation* [270 NLRB No. 157 (1984)].

6. Employees of New Hope Industries' Donaldsonville, Louisiana, plant went on strike to protest the company's failure to pay them on time and to force assurance that they would be paid on time in the future. Emil Thiac, the sole owner of this manufacturer of children's clothing, threatened to discharge the employees in the event of a strike and subsequently did fire them when they struck. Thiac later informed an NLRB attorney investigating the situation that he would close down the plant rather than reinstate or give back pay to the discharged strikers. He also informed the attorney that efforts to obtain back pay could be futile because the company's money was tied up in trust funds for his children. Thiac ultimately closed the plant and refused to give the NLRB his home address or provide the board with any means to communicate with him.

   Based on these facts, do you think the board has any way of preventing Thiac from dissipating or hiding the company's assets while the unfair labor practice charges are pending? See *Norton v. New Hope Industries, Inc.*, unpublished opinion (U.S. Dist. Ct., M.D. La., 1985).

7. Handicabs, Inc. provides transportation services to disabled and elderly persons in the Minneapolis–St. Paul metropolitan area. Handicabs established a policy prohibiting the discussion of company-related problems with clients. The policy, addendum no. 2 in the employee handbook, states in relevant part:

> "Discussing complaints or problems about the company with our clients will be grounds for immediate dismissal.
>
> ... All of our clients are protected by the Vulnerable Adults Act. According to this law, you must not tease them, take monies (other than ride-fare or tip) from them, curse or use profanity while in their presence, or do anything verbal or physical or of a sexual nature. Also, you must not put these people in a threatening or uncomfortable position by discussing any personal or company-related problems that may make them feel coerced or obligated to act upon or react to."

In addition, Handicabs maintained a company policy, addendum no. 1, that prohibited its employees from discussing their wages among themselves, violation of which was also grounds for immediate termination.

On September 20, 1994, Handicabs discharged one of its drivers, Ronald F. Trail, after receiving a complaint that he had been "talking about the union" with his passengers. The complaint was made by Claudia Fuglie, a Handicabs employee and paying client; Fuglie, who suffers from spina bifida, is wheelchair bound and dependent on the handicapped-accessible transit service. Fuglie complained that the talk of unionization and potential work stoppage distressed her.

In response to his termination, Trail filed an unfair labor practice charge with the NLRB. How should the NLRB rule on his complaint? Which, if any, sections of the NLRA has Handicabs violated? Explain. See *Handicabs, Inc. v. NLRB* [95 F.3d 681 (8th Cir. 1996)].

8. In response to rumors that the employees of Tristeel Fabrication, Inc. were seeking to join a union, Strodel, the plant manager, held a meeting with the employees. Strodel informed them that if they voted to join a union, "things will no longer be the same—they could get stricter. Any collective bargaining would start from scratch, with no guarantee that the company would agree to continue any of the benefits the employees presently had. Everything will be conducted by the book (meaning the collective agreement)."

Do Strodel's comments constitute an unfair labor practice? Explain. See *Jamaica Towing, Inc.* [236 NLRB No. 223 (1978)] and *Fidelity Telephone Co.* [236 NLRB No. 26 (1978)].

9. Santos Diaz, Antonio Lopez, Rafael Naraes, and Jose Rivera worked on the dock crew for Mike Yurosek & Son, Inc., a vegetable packing company. Each had been employed by Yurosek between nine and fifteen years. In early September 1990, warehouse manager Juan Garza announced to the dock crew members that he was reducing their hours to approximately thirty-six a week. Some of the employees complained that the new schedule would not provide enough time to finish their work. Garza apparently responded: "That's the way it's going to be. . . . You are going to punch [out] . . . exactly at the time that I tell you."

On September 24, pursuant to the new schedule, the crew was scheduled to work from 10:00 A.M. to 4:30 P.M. Shortly before 4:30, foreman Jaime Ortiz approached each of the four employees individually and instructed each to work an additional hour. All four employees refused to stay. They told Ortiz that they were required to follow the new schedule imposed by Garza. The employees then proceeded to punch out. Ortiz met them at the time clock and instructed them not to punch in the next morning but to meet him in the company dining hall.

The following day, the four employees were asked to wait in the company waiting room. Each employee was then individually called in turn into the personnel office and questioned by Garza, Ortiz, and three other company officers. When each employee was asked why he did not work the extra hour, each responded that he was adhering to the new schedule posted by Garza. After the interviews, the employees waited while the company officials discussed the matter. Each employee was then individually called back into the office and terminated for insubordination. The employees filed an unfair labor practice complaint with the NLRB over their termination.

Was their conduct protected under Section 7? Was it concerted? How should the NLRB rule on their complaint? Explain. See *NLRB v. Mike Yurosek & Son, Inc.* [53 F.3d 261 (9th Cir. 1995)].

10. Lawson runs 700 convenience food stores in Ohio, Indiana, Pennsylvania, and Michigan. Following the murder of an employee in a Lawson store, the United Food and Commercial Workers Union (UFCW) began to organize Lawson sales assistants in northeastern Ohio. Some employees refused to report to work for two days after the murder as a protest against lax security measures.

In response to the complaints, Lawson installed outdoor lights at its stores, adopted a policy that no one would be required to work alone at night, and began paying overtime for work done after closing hours.

Following the initiation of the UFCW campaign, Lawson placed no-solicitation signs in all its stores and told employees that anyone violating the no-solicitation rule would be subject to discharge.

When the UFCW filed a representation petition with the NLRB, seeking an election, employees were told that the stores would close if they voted in the union. One store manager told employees not to discuss the union at work because Lawson planned to install listening devices in the stores.

What, if any, unfair labor practices has Lawson committed? See *The Lawson Co. v. NLRB* [753 F.2d 471 (6th Cir. 1985)].

INTERNET EXERCISE

You have been asked to develop an Internet and e-mail use policy for your employer. One of the issues you need to address is whether the employer must make the company's e-mail system available to employees seeking to organize a union. What can you find on the NLRB's Web site on this topic? Go to the **http://www.nlrb.gov** and click the Press Releases link. Now enter the 2000 in the search term and click "Go". Then enter the document number R-2416 in the search term and click "Go" to find the item Dec. 14, 2000 year link [NLRB General Counsel Leonard Page Issues Report on Case Developments, (R-2416), issued Dec. 14, 2000]. Scroll through the report. What does it say about union use of e-mail systems? Then go back to the NLRB home page and click the Board Decisions link. Then click the link to Bound Volume 331. Then scroll down to the *Adtranz* AFF Daimler-Bentz case link decision [331 NLRB 291]. What advice does that case have to offer on the issue? What was *Adtranz's* rule regarding employee personal e-mail use? Did the *Adtranz* rule violate Section 8(a)(1)? Explain.

INFOTRAC KEYWORDS

http://www.infotrac-college.com

unfair labor practice, employee rights, weingarten rights, right-to-work laws, lockout

16

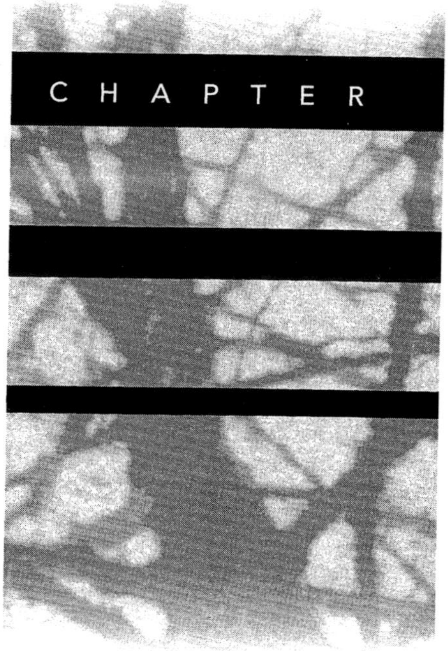

COLLECTIVE BARGAINING

Collective Bargaining
Process by which a union and employer meet and confer with respect to wages, hours, and other terms and conditions of employment.

Employees join unions to gain some influence over their working conditions and wages; that influence is achieved through the process called **collective bargaining** Section 8(d) of the National Labor Relations Act (NLRA) defines collective bargaining as

> [t]he performance of the mutual obligation of the employer and the representative of the employees to meet at reasonable times and confer in good faith with respect to wages, hours, and other terms and conditions of employment, or the negotiation of an agreement or any question arising thereunder. . . .

This process of meeting and discussing working conditions is actually a highly stylized and heavily regulated form of economic conflict. Within the limits of conduct spelled out by the National Labor Relations Board (NLRB) under the NLRA, the parties exert pressure on each other to force some concession or agreement. The union's economic pressure comes from its ability to withhold the services of its members—a strike. The employer's bargaining pressure comes from its potential to lock out the employees or to permanently replace striking workers. The NLRB and the courts, through their interpretation and administration of the NLRA, have limited the kinds of pressure either side may exert and how such pressure may be applied. This chapter examines the collective-bargaining process and the legal limits placed on that process.

THE DUTY TO BARGAIN

An employer is required to recognize a union as the exclusive bargaining representative of its employees when a majority of those employees support the union. The union may demonstrate its majority support either through signed authorization cards or by winning a representation election. Once aware of the union's majority support, the employer must recognize and bargain with the union according to the process spelled out in Section 8(d). Section 8(a)(5) makes it an unfair labor practice for an employer to refuse to bargain with the representative of its employees, and Section 8(b)(3) makes it an unfair practice for a union representing a group of employees to refuse to bargain with their employer.

See **http://www.nlrb.gov/nlrb/shared_files/brochures/basicguide.asp** *select "NLRA, a guide to basic law and procedures."*

Although the NLRA imposes an obligation to bargain collectively upon both employer and union, it does not control the results of the bargaining process. Section 8(d) makes it clear that the obligation to bargain "does not compel either party to agree to a proposal or require the making of a concession." The act thus reflects an ambivalence regarding the duty to bargain in good faith. The parties, to promote industrial relations harmony, are required to come together and negotiate, but in deference to the principle of freedom of contract, they are not required to reach an agreement. This tension between the goal of promoting industrial peace and the principle of freedom of contract underlies the various NLRB and court decisions dealing with the duty to bargain. The accommodation of these conflicting ideas makes the area a difficult and interesting aspect of labor relations law.

If the parties are required to negotiate, yet are not required to reach an agreement or even to make a concession, how can the board determine whether either side is bargaining in good faith? Section 8(d) requires that the parties meet at reasonable times to discuss wages, hours, and terms and conditions of employment; it also requires that any agreement reached must be put in writing if either party so requests. But Section 8(d) does not speak to bargaining tactics. Is either side free to insist upon its proposal as a "take-it-or-leave-it" proposition? Can either side refuse to make any proposal? These questions must be addressed in determining what constitutes bargaining in good faith.

See **http://www.nlrb.gov/nlrb/legal/manuals/rules/act.asp** *select the NLRA, and scroll to view the full text of Section 8(d).*

BARGAINING IN GOOD FAITH

Section 8(a)(5) requires that the employer bargain with a union that is the representative of its employees according to Section 9(a). Section 9(a) states that a union that has the support of a majority of employees in a bargaining unit becomes the exclusive bargaining representative of all employees in the unit. That section also states that the employer may address the grievances of individual employees as long as it is done in a manner consistent with the collective agreement and the union has been given an opportunity to be present at such adjustment. That provision raises the question of how far the employer can go in dealing with individuals rather than the union. In *J. I. Case Co. v. NLRB* [321 U.S. 332

(1944)], the Supreme Court held that contracts of employment made with individual employees were not impediments to negotiating a collective agreement with the union. J. I. Case had made it a practice to sign yearly contracts of employment with its employees. When the union, which won a representation election, requested bargaining over working conditions, the company refused. The employer argued that the individual contracts covered those issues and no bargaining could take place until those individual contracts had expired. The Supreme Court held that the individual contracts must give way to allow the negotiation of a collective agreement. Once the union is certified as the exclusive bargaining representative of the employees, the employer cannot deal with the individual employees in a manner inconsistent with the union's status as exclusive representative. To allow individual contracts of employment to prevent collective bargaining would undercut the union's position. Therefore, the individual contracts must give way to the union's collective negotiations.

What about the situation in which individual employees attempt to discuss their grievances with the employer in a manner inconsistent with the union's role as exclusive representative? How far does the Section 9(a) proviso go to allow such discussion? That question is addressed in the following Supreme Court decision.

Emporium Capwell Co. v. Western Addition Community Organization

420 U.S. 50 (1975)

[Emporium Capwell Co. operates a department store in San Francisco; the company had a collective-bargaining agreement with the Dept. Store Employees Union. The agreement, among other things, included a prohibition of employment discrimination by reason of race, color, religion, national origin, age, or sex. The agreement also set up a grievance and arbitration process to resolve any claimed violation of the agreement, including a violation of the nondiscrimination clause.]

Marshall, J.

This litigation presents the question whether, in light of the national policy against racial discrimination in employment, the National Labor Relations Act protects concerted activity by a group of minority employees to bargain with their employer over issues of employment discrimination. The National Labor Relations Board held that the employees could not circumvent their elected representative to engage in such bargaining. The Court of Appeals for the District of Columbia Circuit reversed, holding that in certain circumstances the activity would be protected. . . .

On April 3, 1968, a group of Company employees covered by the agreement met with the Secretary-Treasurer of the Union, Walter Johnson, to present a list of grievances including a claim that the Company was discriminating on the basis of race in making assignments and promotions. The Union official agreed to take certain of the grievances and to investigate the charge of racial discrimination. He appointed an investigating committee and prepared a report on the employees' grievances, which he submitted to the Retailer's Council and which the Council in turn referred to the Company. The report described "the possibility of racial discrimination" as perhaps the most important issue raised by the employees and termed the situation at the Company as potentially explosive if corrective action were not taken. It offered as an example of the problem the Company's failure to promote a Negro stock employee regarded by other employees as an outstanding candidate but a victim of racial discrimination.

Shortly after receiving the report, the Company's labor relations director met with Union representatives and agreed to "look into the matter" of discrimination and see what needed to be done. Apparently unsatisfied with these representations, the Union held a meeting in September attended by Union officials, Company employees, and representatives of the California Fair Employment Practices Committee (FEPC) and the local antipoverty agency. The Secretary-Treasurer of the Union announced that the Union had concluded that the Company was discriminating, and that it would process every such grievance through to arbitration if necessary. Testimony about the Company's practices was taken and transcribed by a court reporter, and the next day the Union notified the Company of its formal charge and demanded that the joint union-management Adjustment Board be convened "to hear the entire case."

At the September meeting some of the Company's employees had expressed their view that the contract procedures were inadequate to handle a systemic grievance of this sort; they suggested that the Union instead begin picketing the store in protest. Johnson explained that the collective agreement bound the Union to its processes and expressed his view that successful grievants would be helping not only themselves but all others who might be the victims of invidious discrimination as well. The FEPC and antipoverty agency representatives offered the same advice. Nonetheless, when the Adjustment Board meeting convened on October 16, James Joseph Hollins, Tom Hawkins, and two other employees whose testimony the Union had intended to elicit refused to participate in the grievance procedure. Instead, Hollins read a statement objecting to reliance on correction of individual inequities as an approach to the problem of discrimination at the store and demanding that the president of the Company meet with the four protestants to work out a broader agreement for dealing with the issue as they saw it. The four employees then walked out of the hearing.

Hollins attempted to discuss the question of racial discrimination with the Company president shortly after the incidents of October 16. The president refused to be drawn into such a discussion but suggested to Hollins that he see the personnel director about the matter. Hollins, who had spoken to the personnel director before, made no effort to do so again. Rather, he and Hawkins and several other dissident employees held a press conference on October 22 at which they denounced the store's employment policy as racist, reiterated their desire to deal directly with "the top management" of the Company over minority employment conditions, and announced their intention to picket and institute a boycott of the store. On Saturday, November 2, Hollins, Hawkins, and at least two other employees picketed the store throughout the day and distributed at the entrance handbills urging consumers not to patronize the store. Johnson encountered the picketing employees, again urged them to rely on the grievance process, and warned that they might be fired for their activities. The picketers, however, were not dissuaded, and they continued to press their demand to deal directly with the Company president.

On November 7, Hollins and Hawkins were given written warnings that a repetition of the picketing or public statements about the Company could lead to their discharge. When the conduct was repeated the following Saturday, the two employees were fired.

Respondent Western Addition Community Organization, a local civil rights association of which Hollins and Hawkins were members, filed a charge against the Company with the National Labor Relations Board. After a hearing the NLRB Trial Examiner found that the discharged employees had believed in good faith that the Company was discriminating against minority employees, and that they had resorted to concerted activity on the basis of that belief. He concluded, however, that their activity was not protected by Section 7 of the Act and that their discharges did not, therefore, violate Section 8(a)(1).

The Board, after oral argument, adopted the findings and conclusions of its Trial Examiner and dismissed the complaint. Among the findings adopted by the Board was that the discharged employees' course of conduct

> . . . was no mere presentation of a grievance, but nothing short of a demand that the [Company] bargain with the picketing employees for the entire group of minority employees.

Central to the policy of fostering collective bargaining, where the employees elect that course, is the principle of majority rule. If the majority of a unit chooses union representation, the NLRA permits them to bargain with their employer to make union membership a condition of employment, thereby imposing their choice upon the minority. . . . In establishing a regime of majority rule, Congress sought to secure to all members of the unit the benefits of their collective strength and bargaining power, in full awareness that the superior strength of some individuals or groups might be subordinated to the interest of the majority.

In vesting the representatives of the majority with this broad power Congress did not, of course, authorize a tyranny of the majority over minority interests. . . . we have held, by the very nature of the exclusive bargaining representative's status as representative of all unit employees, Congress implicitly imposed upon [the union] a duty fairly and in good faith to represent the interests of minorities within the unit. And the Board has taken the position that a union's refusal to process grievances against racial discrimination, in violation of that duty, is an unfair labor practice. Indeed, the Board had ordered a union implicated by a collective bargaining agreement in discrimination with an employer to propose specific contractual provisions to prohibit racial discrimination. . . .

Plainly, national labor policy embodies the principles of nondiscrimination as a matter of highest priority, and it is a common-place that we must construe the NLRA in light of the broad national labor policy of which it is a part. These general principles do not aid respondent, however, as it is far from clear that separate bargaining is necessary to help eliminate discrimination. Indeed, as the facts of this case demonstrate, the proposed remedy might have just the opposite effect. The collective bargaining agreement in this case prohibited without qualification all manner of invidious discrimination and made any claimed violation a grievable issue. The grievance procedure is directed precisely at determining whether discrimination has occurred. That orderly determination, if affirmative, could lead to an arbitral award enforceable in court. Nor is there any reason to believe that the processing of grievances is inherently limited to the correction of individual cases of discrimination. Quite apart from the essentially contractual question of whether the Union could grieve against a "pattern or practice" it deems inconsistent with the nondiscrimination clause of the contract, one would hardly expect an employer to continue in effect an employment practice that routinely results in adverse arbitral decisions.

The decision by a handful of employees to bypass the grievance procedure in favor of attempting to bargain with their employer, by contrast, may or may not be predicated upon the actual existence of discrimination. An employer confronted with bargaining demands from each of several minority groups would not necessarily, or even probably, be able to agree to remedial steps satisfactory to all at once. Competing claims on the employer's ability to accommodate each group's demands, e.g., for reassignments and promotions to a limited number of positions, could only set one group against the other even if it is not the employer's intention to divide and overcome them. Having divided themselves, the minority employees will not be in position to advance their cause unless it be by recourse seriatim to economic coercion, which can only have the effect of further dividing them along racial or other lines. Nor is the situation materially different where, as apparently happened here, self-designated representatives purport to speak for all groups that might consider themselves to be victims of discrimination. Even if in actual bargaining the various groups did not perceive their interests as divergent and further subdivide themselves, the employer would be bound to bargain with them in a field largely preempted by the current collective bargaining agreement with the elected bargaining representatives. . . .

The elimination of discrimination and its vestiges is an appropriate subject of bargaining, and an employer may have no objection to incorporating into a collective agreement the substance of his obligation not to discriminate in personnel decisions; the Company here has done as much, making any claimed dereliction a matter subject to the grievance-arbitration machinery as well as to the processes of Title VII. But that does not mean that he may not have strong and legitimate objections to bargaining on several fronts over the implementation of the right to be free of discrimination for some of the reasons set forth above. Similarly, while a union cannot lawfully bargain for the establishment or continuation of discriminatory practices, it has legitimate interest in presenting a united front on this as on other issues and in not seeing its strength dissipated and its stature denigrated by subgroups within the unit separately pursuing what they see as separate interests. . . .

. . . The policy of industrial self-determination as expressed in Section 7 does not require fragmentation of the bargaining unit along racial or other lines in order to consist with the national labor policy against discrimination. And in the face of such fragmentation, whatever its effect on discriminatory practices, the bargaining process that the principle of exclusive representation is meant to lubricate could not endure unhampered. . . .

Respondent objects that reliance on the remedies provided by Title VII is inadequate effectively to secure the rights conferred by Title VII. . . .

Whatever its factual merit, this argument is properly addressed to the Congress and not to this Court or the NLRB. In order to hold that employer conduct violates

Section 8(a)(1) of the NLRA because it violates Section 704(a) of Title VII, we would have to override a host of consciously made decisions well within the exclusive competence of the Legislature. This obviously, we cannot do.

Reversed.

Case Questions

1. What were the complaints of the minority employees against the company? How did the union respond to their complaints?
2. Why did the employees reject using the procedures under the collective-bargaining agreement? What happened to them when they insisted on picketing the store to publicize their complaints?
3. Did the NLRB hold that their conduct was protected under Section 7? Why? Did the Supreme Court protect their conduct? Why?

Although the employer in *J. I. Case* and the employees in *Emporium Capwell* were held to have acted improperly, there is some room for individual discussions of working conditions and grievances. Where the collective agreement permits individual negotiation, an employer may discuss such matters with individual employees. Examples of such agreements are the collective agreements covering professional baseball and football players; the collective agreement sets minimum levels of conditions and compensation, while allowing the athletes to negotiate salary and other compensation on an individual basis.

Procedural Requirements of the Duty to Bargain in Good Faith

A union or employer seeking to bargain with the other party must notify that other party of its desire to bargain at least sixty days prior to the expiration of the existing collective agreement or, if no agreement is in effect, sixty days prior to the date it proposes the agreement to go into effect. Section 8(d) requires that such notice must be given at the proper time; failure to do so may make any strike by the union or lockout by the employer an unfair labor practice. Section 8(d) also requires that the parties must continue in effect any existing collective agreement for sixty days from the giving of the notice to bargain or until the agreement expires, whichever occurs later. Strikes or lockouts are prohibited during this sixty-day "cooling-off" period; employees who go on an economic strike during this period lose their status as "employees" and the protections of the act. Therefore, if the parties have given the notice to bargain later than sixty days prior to the expiration of the contract, they must wait the full sixty days to go on strike or lockout, even if the old agreement has already expired.

When negotiations result in matters in dispute, the party seeking contract termination must notify the Federal Mediation and Conciliation Service (FMCS) and the appropriate state mediation agency within thirty days from giving the notice to bargain. Neither side may resort to a strike or lockout until thirty days after the FMCS and state agency have been notified.

The NLRA provides for longer notice periods when the collective bargaining involves the employees of a health-care institution. In that case, the parties must give notice to bargain at least ninety days prior to the expiration of the agreement; no strike or lockout can take place for at least ninety days from the giving of the notice or the expiration of the agreement, whichever is later. Furthermore, the FMCS and state agency must be notified sixty days prior to the termination of the agreement. Finally, Section 8(g) requires that a labor organization seeking to picket or strike against a health-care institution must give both the employer and the FMCS written notice of its intention to strike or picket at least ten days prior to taking such action. Why should a labor organization be required to give health-care institutions advance notice of any strike or picketing?

As noted, Section 8(d) prohibits any strike or lockout during the notice period. Employees who go on strike during that period are deprived of the protection of the act. In *Mastro Plastics Co. v. NLRB* [350 U.S. 270 (1956)], the Supreme Court held that the prohibition applied only to economic strikes—strikes designed to pressure the employer to "terminate or modify" the collective agreement. Unfair labor practice strikes, which are called to protest the employer's violation of the NLRA, are not covered by the Section 8(d) prohibition. Therefore, the employees in *Mastro Plastics* who went on strike during the sixty-day cooling-off period to protest the illegal firing of an employee were not in violation of Section 8(d) and were not deprived of the protection of the act.

Creation of the Duty to Bargain

As has been discussed, the duty to bargain arises when the union gets the support of a majority of the employees in a bargaining unit. When a union is certified as the winner of a representation election, the employer is required by Section 8(a)(5) to bargain with it. (An employer with knowledge of a union's majority support, independent of the union's claim of such support, must also recognize and bargain with the union without resort to an election.)

When an employer is approached by two unions, each claiming to represent a majority of the employees, how should the employer respond? One way would be to refuse to recognize either union (provided, of course, that the employer had no independent knowledge of either union's majority support) and to insist on an election. Can the employer recognize voluntarily one of the two unions claiming to represent the employees?

In *Bruckner Nursing Home* [262 NLRB 955 (1982)], the NLRB held that an employer may recognize a union that claims to have majority support of the employees in the bargaining unit even though another union is also engaged in an organizing campaign, as long as the second union has not filed a petition for a representation election. The Board reasoned that the rival union, unable to muster even the support of 30 percent of the employees necessary to file a petition, should not be permitted to prevent the recognition of the union with majority support. If, however, a valid petition for a representation election has been filed, then the employer must refrain from recognizing either union and must wait for the outcome of the election to determine if either union has majority support.

The *Bruckner Nursing Home* decision dealt with a situation in which the employees were not previously represented by a union. When an incumbent union's status has been challenged by a rival union that has petitioned for a representation election, is the employer still required to negotiate with the incumbent union? In *RCA Del Caribe* [262 NLRB 963 (1982)], the Board held that

> the mere filing of a representation petition by an outside, challenging union will no longer require or permit an employer to withdraw from bargaining or executing a contract with an incumbent union. Under this rule . . . an employer will violate Section 8(a)(5) by withdrawing from bargaining based solely on the fact that a petition has been filed by an outside union. . . .
>
> If the incumbent prevails in the election held, any contract executed with the incumbent will be valid and binding. If the challenging union prevails, however, any contract executed with the incumbent will be null and void. . . .

The *Bruckner Nursing Home* and *RCA Del Caribe* decisions were departures from prior Board decisions, which required that an employer stay neutral in the event of rival organizing campaigns or when the incumbent union faced a petition filed by a challenging union. Which approach do you think is more likely to protect the desires of the individual employees? Do *Bruckner Nursing Home* and *RCA Del Caribe* make it more difficult to unseat an incumbent union?

When craft employees who had previously been included in a larger bargaining unit vote to be represented by a craft union, and a smaller craft bargaining unit is severed from the larger one, what is the effect of the agreement covering the larger unit? In *American Seating Co.* [106 NLRB 250 (1953)], the NLRB held that the old agreement no longer applies to the newly severed bargaining unit, and the old agreement does not prevent the employer from negotiating with the craft union on behalf of the new bargaining unit. Is this decision surprising? [Recall the *J. I. Case* decision discussed earlier and reexamine the wording of Section 8(d) in its entirety.]

Duration of the Duty to Bargain

When the union is certified as bargaining representative after winning an election, the NLRB requires that the employer recognize and bargain with the union for at least a year from certification, regardless of any doubts the employer may have about the union's continued majority support. This one-year period applies only when no collective agreement has been made. When an agreement exists, the employer must bargain with the union for the term of the agreement. Unfair labor practices committed by the employer, such as refusal to bargain in good faith, may have the effect of extending the one-year period, as the Board held in *Mar-Jac Poultry* [136 NLRB 785 (1962)].

When a union acquires bargaining rights by voluntary recognition rather than certification, the employer is required to recognize and bargain with the union only for "a reasonable period of time" if no agreement is in effect. What constitutes a reasonable period of time depends on the circumstances in each case. If an agreement has been reached after the voluntary recognition, then the employer must bargain with the union for the duration of the agreement.

After the one-year period or a reasonable period of time—whichever is appropriate—has expired, and no collective agreement is in effect, the employer may refuse to bargain with the union if the employer can establish that the union has lost the support of the majority of the bargaining unit, *Levitz Furniture Co. of the*

Pacific [333 NLRB No. 105 (2001)]. The employer's evidence to support the fact that the union has lost majority support must have a reasonable basis in fact and, in the case of a certified union, must be based only on events that occur after the expiration of the one-year period from the certification of the union, *Chelsea Industries* [331 NLRB No. 184 (2000)]. In a successorship situation (see Chapter 18), the incumbent union is entitled to a rebuttable presumption of continuing majority support; that presumption will not serve as a bar to an otherwise timely petition for a representation election or a decertification election, *MV Transportation* [337 NLRB No. 129 (2002)]. The U.S. Supreme Court upheld the NLRB's requirement that the employer have a "good faith reasonable doubt" about the union's majority support in order to take a poll of employees about their support of the union, *Allentown Mack Sales and Services, Inc. v. NLRB* [522 U.S. 359 (1998)]. The Board held in *NLRB v. Flex Plastics* [726 F.2d 272 (6th Cir. 1984)] that filing a decertification petition alone does not suffice to establish a reason to doubt the union's majority support. When the employer can establish some reasonable factual basis for its claim that the union has lost majority support, it may refuse to negotiate with the union. To find a violation of Section 8(a)(5), the Board must then prove that the union in fact represented a majority of the employees on the date the employer refused to bargain.

What happens if the employer agrees with the union on a contract but then tries to raise a claim that the union has lost majority support? That is the subject of the following case.

Auciello Iron Works, Inc. v. NLRB

517 U.S. 781 (1996)

Souter, J.

The question here is whether an employer may disavow a collective bargaining agreement because of a good faith doubt about a union's majority status at the time the contract was made when the doubt arises from facts known to the employer before its contract offer had been accepted by the union. . . .

Petitioner Auciello Iron Works of Hudson, Massachusetts, had 23 production and maintenance employees during the period in question. After a union election in 1977, the NLRB certified Shopmen's Local No. 501, a/w International Association of Bridge, Structural, and Ornamental Iron Workers, AFL-CIO, as the collective bargaining representative of Auciello's employees. Over the following years, the company and the Union were able to negotiate a series of collective bargaining agreements, one of which expired on September 25, 1988. Negotiations for a new one were unsuccessful throughout September and October, 1988, however, and when Auciello and the Union had not made a new contract by October 14, 1988, the employees went on strike. Negotiations continued, nonetheless, and, on November 17, 1988, Auciello presented the Union with a complete contract proposal. On November 18, 1988, the picketing stopped, and nine days later, on a Sunday evening, the Union telegraphed its acceptance of the outstanding offer. The very next day, however, Auciello told the Union that it doubted that a majority of the bargaining unit's employees supported the Union, and for that reason disavowed the collective bargaining agreement and denied it had any duty to continue negotiating. Auciello traced its doubt to knowledge acquired before the Union accepted the contract offer, including the facts that 9 employees had crossed the picket line, that 13 employees had given it signed forms indicating their resignation from the Union, and that 16 had expressed dissatisfaction with the Union.

In January, 1989, the Board . . . issued [a] . . . complaint charging Auciello with violation of Secs. 8(a)(1) and (5) of the NLRA. An administrative law judge found that a contract existed between the parties and that Auciello's withdrawal from it violated the Act. The Board affirmed the administrative law judge's decision; it treated Auciello's claim of good faith doubt as irrelevant and ordered Auciello to reduce the collective bargaining agreement to a formal written instrument. . . . [The Court of Appeals enforced the order and Auciello appealed to the Supreme Court.]

The object of the National Labor Relations Act is industrial peace and stability, fostered by collective bargaining agreements providing for the orderly resolution of labor disputes between workers and employees. To such ends, the Board has adopted various presumptions about the existence of majority support for a union within a bargaining unit, the precondition for service as its exclusive representative. The first two are conclusive presumptions. A union "usually is entitled to a conclusive presumption of majority status for one year following" Board certification as such a representative. A union is likewise entitled under Board precedent to a conclusive presumption of majority status during the term of any collective bargaining agreement, up to three years. . . .

There is a third presumption, though not a conclusive one. At the end of the certification year or upon expiration of the collective bargaining agreement, the presumption of majority status becomes a rebuttable one. Then, an employer may overcome the presumption (when, for example, defending against an unfair labor practice charge) by showing that, at the time of [its] refusal to bargain, either (1) the union did not in fact enjoy majority support, or (2) the employer had a "good faith" doubt, founded on a sufficient objective basis, of the union's majority support. . . . Auciello asks this Court to hold that it may raise the latter defense even after a collective bargaining contract period has apparently begun to run upon a union's acceptance of an employer's outstanding offer.

The same need for repose that first prompted the Board to adopt the rule presuming the union's majority status during the term of a collective bargaining agreement also led the Board to rule out an exception for the benefit of an employer with doubts arising from facts antedating the contract. The Board said that such an exception would allow an employer to control the timing of its assertion of good faith doubt and thus to "'sit' on that doubt and . . . raise it after the offer is accepted." The Board thought that the risks associated with giving employers such "unilatera[l] control [over] a vital part of the collective bargaining process," would undermine the stability of the collective bargaining relationship, and thus outweigh any benefit that might in theory follow from vindicating a doubt that ultimately proved to be sound.

The Board's judgment in the matter is entitled to prevail. . . . It might be tempting to think that Auciello's doubt was expressed so soon after the apparent contract formation that little would be lost by vindicating that doubt and wiping the contractual slate clean, if in fact the company can make a convincing case for the doubt it claims. On this view, the loss of repose would be slight. But if doubts about the union's majority status would justify repudiating a contract one day after its ostensible formation, why should the same doubt not serve as well a year into the contract's term? . . .

The Board's approach generally allows companies an adequate chance to act on their pre-acceptance doubts before contract formation, just as Auciello could have acted effectively under the Board's rule in this case. Auciello knew that the picket line had been crossed and that a number of its employees had expressed dissatisfaction with the Union at least nine days before the contract's acceptance, and all of the resignation forms Auciello received were dated at least five days before the acceptance date. During the week preceding the apparent formation of the contract, Auciello had at least three alternatives to doing nothing. It could have withdrawn the outstanding offer and then, like its employees, petitioned for a representation election. . . .

Following withdrawal, it could also have refused to bargain further on the basis of its good faith doubt, leaving it to the Union to charge an unfair labor practice, against which it could defend on the basis of the doubt. And, of course, it could have withdrawn its offer to allow it time to investigate while it continued to fulfill its duty to bargain in good faith with the Union. The company thus had generous opportunities to avoid the presumption before the moment of acceptance.

. . . As Auciello would have it, any employer with genuine doubt about a union's hold on its employees would be invited to go right on bargaining, with the prospect of locking in a favorable contract that it could, if it wished, then challenge. Here, for example, if Auciello had acted before the Union's telegram by withdrawing its offer and declining further negotiation based on its doubt (or petitioning for decertification), flames would have been fanned, and if it ultimately had been obliged to bargain further, a favorable agreement would have been more difficult to obtain. But by saving its challenge until after a contract had apparently been formed, it could not end up with a worse agreement than the one it had. The Board could reasonably say that giving employers some flexibility in raising their scruples would not be worth skewing bargaining relationships by such one-sided leverage, and the fact that any collective bargaining agreement might be vulnerable to such a post-formation challenge would hardly serve the Act's goal of achieving industrial peace by promoting stable collective bargaining relationships. . . .

. . . We hold that the Board reasonably found an employer's pre-contractual, good faith doubt inadequate to support an exception to the conclusive presumption arising at the moment a collective bargaining contract offer has been accepted. We accordingly affirm the judgment of the Court of Appeals for the First Circuit.

It is so ordered.

Case Questions

1. When did Auciello become aware of the question about the union's majority support? When did Auciello act on that question?
2. What presumptions does the NLRB apply to the question of the existence of a union's majority support? Which of those assumptions is involved in this case?
3. What must an employer show to overcome the NLRB presumption applied in this case? Why does the court reject Auciello's attempt to establish its doubts about the union's majority support?

What happens if the union employees go on strike and are permanently replaced by the employer? Must the employer continue to recognize and bargain with the union? In *Pioneer Flour Mills* [174 NLRB 1202 (1969)], the NLRB held that economic strikers must be considered members of the bargaining unit for the purpose of determining whether the union has majority support for the first twelve months of the strike. After twelve months, if they have been permanently replaced, the strikers need not be considered part of the bargaining unit by the employer. Unfair labor practice strikers may not be permanently replaced and must be considered members of the bargaining unit.

Where an employer has hired replacements during an economic strike and now seeks to determine whether the union still has majority support, can the employer presume that the replacement workers oppose the union? The NLRB takes the position that it will not presume the replacements oppose the union, but rather will consider each case on its own facts: Has the employer presented sufficient objective evidence to indicate that the replacements do not support the union? The NLRB's approach was upheld by the Supreme Court in *NLRB v. Curtin Matheson Scientific, Inc.* [494 U.S. 775 (1990)].

THE NATURE OF THE DUTY TO BARGAIN IN GOOD FAITH

After having considered how the duty to bargain in good faith arises and how long it lasts, we now turn to exactly what it means: What is "good-faith" bargaining?

As we have seen, the wording of Section 8(d) states that making concessions or reaching agreement is not necessary to good-faith bargaining. The imposition of such requirements would infringe upon either party's freedom of contract and would destroy the voluntary nature of collective bargaining, which is essential to its success. What is required for good-faith bargaining, according to the NLRB, is that the parties enter negotiations with "an open and fair mind" and "a sincere purpose to find a basis of agreement."

As long as the parties bargain with an intention to find a basis of agreement, the breakdown or deadlock of negotiations is not a violation of the duty to bargain in good faith. When talks reach a deadlock—known as an **impasse**—as a result of sincere bargaining, either side may break off talks on the deadlocked issue. In determining whether an impasse exists, the board considers the totality of circumstances: the number of times the parties have met, the likelihood of progress on the issue, the use of mediation, and so on. The board considers that a change in the position of either party or a change in the circumstances may break an impasse; in that case, the parties would not be able to break off all talks on the issue.

Impasse
A deadlock in negotiations.

When the impasse results from a party's rigid insistence upon a particular proposal, it is not a violation of the duty to bargain if the proposal relates to wages, hours, or terms and conditions of employment. In *NLRB v. American National Insurance Co.* [343 U.S. 395 (1952)], the Supreme Court held that the employer's insistence upon contract language giving it discretionary control over promotions, discipline, work scheduling, and denying arbitration on such matters was not in violation of the duty to bargain in good faith. In *NLRB v. General Electric Co.* [418 F.2d 736 (2d Cir. 1969), *cert. denied,* 397 U.S. 965 (1970)], the Court of Appeals held that "take-it-or-leave-it" bargaining is not, by itself, in violation of the duty to bargain. But when an employer engages in other conduct indicating lack of good faith—such as refusing to sign a written agreement, attempting to deal with individual employees rather than the union, and refusing to provide the union with information regarding bargaining proposals—then the combined effect of the employer's conduct is to violate the duty to negotiate in good faith. But hard bargaining, in and of itself, is not a violation; at some point in negotiations, either side may make a "final" offer and hold to it firmly.

While negotiations are being conducted, is either side free to engage in tactics designed to pressure the other into making a concession? Is such pressure during bargaining consistent with negotiating in good faith? In *NLRB v. Insurance Agents International Union* [361 U.S. 477 (1960)], the U.S. Supreme Court held that the use of economic pressure such as "work to rule" and "on the job slow-downs" is not inconsistent with the duty of bargaining in good faith; indeed, the use of economic pressure is "part and parcel" of the collective-bargaining process.

SUBJECT MATTER OF BARGAINING

As the preceding cases indicate, the NLRB and the courts are reluctant to control the bargaining tactics available to either party. This reluctance reflects a philosophical aversion to government intrusion into the bargaining process. Yet some regulation of bargaining is necessary if the bargaining process is to be meaningful. Some control is required to prevent the parties from making a charade of the process by holding firmly to arbitrary or frivolous positions. One means of control is the distinction between mandatory and permissive subjects of bargaining.

MANDATORY BARGAINING SUBJECTS

Mandatory Bargaining Subjects
Those matters that vitally affect the terms and conditions of employment of the employees in the bargaining unit; the parties must bargain in good faith over such subjects.

Mandatory bargaining subjects, according to the Supreme Court decision in *Allied Chemical & Alkalai Workers v. PPG* [404 U.S. 157 (1971)], are those subjects that "vitally affect the terms and conditions of employment" of the employees in the bargaining unit. The Supreme Court in *PPG* held that changes in medical insurance coverage of former employees who were retired were not a mandatory subject, and the company need not bargain over such changes with the union. The fact that the company had bargained over these issues in the past did not convert a permissive subject into a mandatory one; the company was free to change the insurance policy coverage unilaterally.

The NLRB and the Court have broadly interpreted the matters subject to mandatory bargaining as being related to "wages, hours, terms and conditions of employment" specified in Sections 8(d) and 9(a). Wages have been held to include all forms of employee compensation and fringe benefits, including items such as pensions, stock options, annual bonuses, employee discounts, shift differentials, and incentive plans. Hours and terms and conditions of employment have received similar broadening. The Supreme Court, in *Ford Motor Co. v. NLRB* [441 U.S. 488 (1979)], held that the prices of food sold in vending machines in the plant cafeteria were mandatory subjects for bargaining when the employer had some control over pricing.

The aspect of mandatory bargaining subjects that has attracted the most controversy has been the duty to bargain over management decisions to subcontract work or to close down a plant. In *Fibreboard Paper Products v. NLRB* [379 U.S. 203 (1964)], the Supreme Court held that an employer must bargain with the union over a decision to subcontract out work previously done by bargaining unit employees. Later NLRB and Court decisions held that subcontracting that had never been done by bargaining unit employees was not a mandatory issue; in addition, decisions to change the corporate structure of a business or to terminate manufacturing operations were not mandatory subjects but rather were inherent management rights. Even the decision to go out of business entirely is not a mandatory subject of bargaining. But while the employer need not discuss such decisions with the union, the board has held that the effects of such decisions upon the employees are mandatory bargaining subjects. The employer must therefore discuss the effects of such decisions with the union; matters such as severance pay, transfer policies, retraining, and the procedure to be used for layoffs must be negotiated with the union.

The following case illustrates the test used to determine whether a managerial decision, such as the decision to close part of the firm's operations, is a mandatory bargaining subject.

First National Maintenance Corp. v. NLRB

452 U.S. 666 (1981)

Blackmun, J.

Must an employer, under its duty to bargain in good faith "with respect to wages, hours, and other terms and conditions of employment," Sections 8(d) and 8(a)(5) of the National Labor Relations Act, negotiate with the certified representative of its employees over its decision to close a part of its business? In this case, the National Labor Relations Board (Board) imposed such a duty on petitioner with respect to its decision to terminate a contract with a customer, and the United States Court of Appeals, although differing over the appropriate rationale, enforced its order.

Petitioner, First National Maintenance Corporation (FNM), is a New York corporation engaged in the business of providing housekeeping, cleaning maintenance, and related services for commercial customers in the New York City area. It contracts for and hires personnel separately for each customer, and it does not transfer employees between locations.

During the spring of 1977, petitioner was performing maintenance work for the Greenpark Care Center, a nursing home in Brooklyn. Petitioner employed approximately 35 workers in its Greenpark operation.

Petitioner's business relationship with Greenpark, seemingly, was not very remunerative or smooth. In March 1977, Greenpark gave petitioner the 30 days' written notice of cancellation specified by the contract, because of "lack of efficiency." This cancellation did not become effective, for FNM's work continued after the expiration of that 30-day period. Petitioner, however, became aware that it was losing money at Greenpark. On June 30, by telephone, it asked that its weekly fee be restored at the $500 figure, and, on July 6, it informed Greenpark in writing that it would discontinue its operations there on August 1 unless the increase were granted. By telegram on July 25, petitioner gave final notice of termination.

While FNM was experiencing these difficulties, District 1199, National Union of Hospital and Health Care Employees, Retail, Wholesale and Department Store Union, AFL-CIO (Union), was conducting an organization campaign among petitioner's Greenpark employees. On March 31, 1977, at a Board-conducted election, a majority of the employees selected the union as their bargaining agent. Petitioner neither responded nor sought to consult with the union.

On July 28, petitioner notified its Greenpark employees that they would be discharged three days later.

With nothing but perfunctory further discussion, petitioner on July 31 discontinued its Greenpark operation and discharged the employees.

The union filed an unfair labor practice charge against petitioner, alleging violations of the Act's Section 8(a)(1) and (5). After a hearing held upon the Regional Director's complaint, the Administrative Law Judge made findings in the union's favor. . . . [H]e ruled that petitioner had failed to satisfy its duty to bargain concerning both the decision to terminate the Greenpark contract and the effect of that change upon the unit employees.

The Administrative Law Judge recommended an order requiring petitioner to bargain in good faith with the union about its decision to terminate its Greenpark service operation and its consequent discharge of the employees, as well as the effects of the termination. He recommended, also, that petitioner be ordered to pay the discharged employees back pay from the date of discharge until the parties bargained to agreement, or the bargaining reached an impasse, or the union failed timely to request bargaining or the union failed to bargain in good faith.

The National Labor Relations Board adopted the Administrative Law Judge's findings without further analysis, and additionally required petitioner, if it agreed to resume its Greenpark operations, to offer the terminated employees reinstatement to their former jobs or substantial equivalents; conversely, if agreement was not reached, petitioner was ordered to offer the employees equivalent positions, to be made available by discharge of subsequently hired employees, if necessary, at its other operations.

The United States Court of Appeals for the Second Circuit, with one judge dissenting in part, enforced the Board's order.

The Court of Appeals' decision in this case appears to be at odds with decisions of other Courts of Appeals, some of which decline to require bargaining over any management decision involving "a major commitment of capital investment" or a "basic operational change" in the scope or direction of an enterprise, and some of which indicate that bargaining is not mandated unless a violation of Section 8(a)(3) (a partial closing motivated by antiunion animus) is involved. The Board itself has not been fully consistent in its rulings applicable to this type of management decision.

A fundamental aim of the National Labor Relations Act is the establishment and maintenance of industrial peace to preserve the flow of interstate commerce. Central to achievement of this purpose is the promotion of collective bargaining as a method of defusing and channeling conflict between labor and management.

Although parties are free to bargain about any legal subject, Congress has limited the mandate or duty to bargain to matters of "wages, hours, and other terms and conditions of employment." Congress deliberately left the words "wages, hours, and other terms and conditions of employment" without further definition, for it did not intend to deprive the Board of the power further to define those terms in light of specific industrial practices.

Nonetheless, in establishing what issues must be submitted to the process of bargaining, Congress had no expectation that the elected union representative would become an equal partner in the running of the business enterprise in which the union's members are employed.

Some management decisions, such as choice of advertising and promotion, product type and design, and financing arrangements, have only an indirect and attenuated impact on the employment relationship. Other management decisions, such as the order of succession of layoffs and recalls, production quotas, and work rules, are almost exclusively "an aspect of the relationship" between employer and employee. The present case concerns a third type of management decision, one that had a direct impact on employment, since jobs were inexorably eliminated by the termination, but had as its focus only the economic profitability of the contract with Greenpark, a concern under these facts wholly apart from the employment relationship. This decision, involving a change in the scope and direction of the enterprise, is akin to the decision whether to be in business at all, "not in [itself] primarily about conditions of employment, though the effect of the decision may be necessarily to terminate employment." At the same time this decision touches on a matter of central and pressing concern to the union and its member employees: the possibility of continued employment and the retention of the employees' very jobs.

Petitioner contends it had no duty to bargain about its decision to terminate its operations at Greenpark. This contention requires that we determine whether the decision itself should be considered part of petitioner's retained freedom to manage its affairs unrelated to employment. The aim of labeling a matter a mandatory subject of bargaining, rather than simply permitting, but not requiring, bargaining, is to "promote the fundamental purpose of the Act by bringing a problem of vital concern to labor and management within the framework established by Congress as most conducive to industrial peace." The concept of mandatory bargaining is premised on the belief that collective discussions backed by the parties' economic weapons will result in decisions that are better for both management and labor and for society as a whole. This will be true, however, only if the subject proposed for discussion is amenable to resolution through the bargaining process. Management must be free from the constraints of the bargaining process to the extent essential for the running of a profitable business. It also must have some degree of certainty beforehand as to when it may proceed to reach decisions without fear of later evaluations labeling its conduct an unfair labor practice. Congress did not explicitly state what issues of mutual concern to union and management it intended to exclude from mandatory bargaining. Nonetheless, in view of an employer's need for unencumbered decisionmaking, bargaining over management decisions that have a substantial impact on the continued availability of employment should be required only if the benefit, for labor-management relations and the collective-bargaining process, outweighs the burden placed on the conduct of the business.

Both union and management regard control of the decision to shut down an operation with the utmost seriousness. As has been noted, however, the Act is not intended to serve either party's individual interest, but to foster in a neutral manner a system in which the conflict between these interests may be resolved. It seems particularly important, therefore, to consider whether requiring bargaining over this sort of decision will advance the neutral purposes of the Act.

A union's interest in participating in the decision to close a particular facility or part of an employer's operations springs from its legitimate concern over job security. The Court has observed: "The words of [Section 8(d)] . . . plainly cover termination of employment which . . . necessarily results" from closing an operation. The union's practical purpose in participation, however, will be largely uniform: it will seek to delay or halt the closing. No doubt it will be impelled, in seeking these ends, to offer concessions, information, and alternatives that might be helpful to management or forestall or prevent the termination of jobs. It is unlikely, however, that requiring bargaining over the decision itself, as well as its effects, will augment this flow of information and suggestions. There is no dispute that the union must be given a significant opportunity to bargain about these matters of job security as part of the "effects" bargaining mandated by Section 8(a)(5). A union, pursuing such bargaining rights, may achieve valuable concessions from an employer engaged in a partial closing.

Moreover, the union's legitimate interest in fair dealing is protected by Section 8(a)(3), which prohibits partial closings motivated by antiunion animus, when done to gain an unfair advantage.

Thus, although the union has a natural concern that a partial closing decision not be hastily or unnecessarily entered into, it has some control over the effects of the decision and indirectly may ensure that the decision itself is deliberately considered. It also has direct protection against a partial closing decision that is motivated by an intent to harm a union.

Management's interest in whether it should discuss a decision of this kind is much more complex and varies with the particular circumstances. If labor costs are an important factor in a failing operation and the decision to close, management will have an incentive to confer voluntarily with the union to seek concessions that may make continuing the business profitable. At other times, management may have great need for speed, flexibility, and secrecy in meeting business opportunities and exigencies. It may face significant tax or securities consequences that hinge on confidentiality, the timing of a plant closing, or a reorganization of the corporate structure. The publicity incident to the normal process of bargaining may injure the possibility of a successful transition or increase the economic damage to the business. The employer also may have no feasible alternative to the closing, and even good-faith bargaining over it may both be futile and cause the employer additional loss.

There is an important difference, also, between permitted bargaining and mandated bargaining. Labeling this type of decision mandatory could afford a union a powerful tool for achieving delay, a power that might be used to thwart management's intentions in a manner unrelated to any feasible solution the union might propose.

We conclude that the harm likely to be done to an employer's need to operate freely in deciding whether to shut down part of its business purely for economic reasons outweighs the incremental benefit that might be gained through the union's participation in making the decision, and we hold that the decision itself is not part of Section 8(d)'s "terms and conditions," over which Congress has mandated bargaining. . . .

Case Questions

1. Why did First National Maintenance decide to close its operations at Greenpark? Could bargaining with the union affect those reasons? Explain your answer.
2. What test does the Supreme Court use to determine whether the decision to close operations is a mandatory bargaining subject? How does that test apply to the facts of this case?
3. What is the significance of labeling a decision a mandatory bargaining subject? Is the employer completely prohibited from acting alone on a mandatory subject? Explain.

Subsequent to the *First National Maintenance* decision, the NLRB has interpreted the "balancing test" set out by the court as focusing on whether the employer's decision is based on labor costs. A decision to relocate production to another plant was not a mandatory subject because the decision did not turn on labor costs, *Local 2179, United Steelworkers of America v. NLRB* [822 F.2d 559 (5th Cir. 1987)].

In short, the question whether the employer must bargain with the union over a management decision such as plant closing, work relocation, or corporate reorganization is whether or not the decision is motivated by a desire to reduce labor

ETHICAL DILEMMA: POSSIBLE PLANT CLOSING—TO MEET OR NOT TO MEET?

You are the human resource manager at Immense Multinational Business's production facility located in Utica, New York. The Utica plant is seventy-five years old. The plant is profitable but barely so; its production costs are the highest in the corporation's manufacturing division. The workers at the Utica facility are unionized, and the wages at Utica are higher than at most of the company's other manufacturing plants. But the utility costs, real estate taxes, and N.Y. Workers' Compensation and Unemployment Insurance payroll taxes at the Utica plant are very high and are the main reasons for the plant's high production costs.

The company has recently opened a manufacturing plant in Puerto Rico; corporate headquarters is considering expanding the production at that facility by transferring production from the Utica plant. The Utica workers have heard rumors that the plant will be closed. The officials of the local union at the Utica plant offer to meet with you to discuss the plant closing rumors and concessions that they are willing to make to keep the Utica plant open. Should you meet with them to discuss the plant closing and possible concessions? What arguments can you make for meeting with the union? What arguments can you make for not meeting with the union? Would refusing to meet and discuss those matters with the union be an unfair labor practice? Prepare a memo for corporate headquarters addressing these questions.

costs or to escape the collective-bargaining agreement. If the decision is based on other business considerations, apart from labor costs, then the employer's duty to bargain is limited to the effects of the decision on the employees rather than the decision itself.

What is the effect of labeling a subject as a mandatory bargaining issue upon the employer's ability to make decisions necessary to the efficient operation of the enterprise? The Supreme Court opinion in *First National Maintenance* was concerned about placing burdens on the employer that would interfere with the need to act promptly. But rather than preventing employer action over mandatory subjects, the duty to bargain requires only that the employer negotiate with the union. If the union agrees or makes concessions, then the employer is free to act. If the union fails to agree and an impasse results from good-faith bargaining, the employer is then free to implement the decision. The duty to bargain over mandatory subjects requires only that the employer bargain in good faith to the point of impasse over the issue. Once impasse has been reached, the employer is free to act unilaterally. In the case of *NLRB v. Katz* [369 U.S. 736 (1962)], the Supreme Court stated that an employer may institute unilateral changes on mandatory subjects after bargaining to impasse; however, when the impasse results from the employer's failure to bargain in good faith, any unilateral changes would be an unfair labor practice in violation of Section 8(a)(5). An employer is under no duty to bargain over changes in permissive subjects; according to thc Supreme Court opinion in *Allied Chemical & Alkalai Workers v. PPG,* cited earlier, unilateral changes on permissive subjects are not unfair practices.

The following case involves the application of the *Katz* decision.

Visiting Nurse Services of Western Massachusetts, Inc. v. NLRB

177 F.3d 52 (1st Cir. 1999), cert. denied, 528 U.S. 1074 (2000)

Lynch, Circuit Judge

. . . VNS is a corporation based in Holyoke, Massachusetts, which provides home-based nursing home services. The last collective bargaining agreement between VNS and the Union expired on October 31, 1992; between July 1995 and March 1997, the parties attempted to negotiate a successor agreement. . . .

VNS's package proposal provided for a two-percent wage increase and for a change from a weekly to a bi-weekly payroll system, to become effective on November 6, 1995. The Union did not accept the proposal but expressed a willingness to bargain about various proposed alterations to the job classifications for employee nurses. VNS presented a "substantially identical" proposal on December 6, 1995, but this proposal also granted VNS "the sole and unqualified right to designate [job] classifications as it deemed necessary based on operational needs."

On February 29, 1996, VNS again offered the Union a two-percent wage increase, effective retroactively to November 6, 1995, in return for the Union's agreement to its proposals for a bi-weekly payroll system and the job classification changes. The Union, acknowledging the broad opposition (within its membership) to the bi-weekly payroll system, rejected the proposal. Nevertheless, on March 21, 1996, VNS notified the Union that "based on operational and economic realities [VNS] intend[ed] to implement 'both' the wage increase and the bi-weekly pay proposals that, to date, [VNS and the Union had] been unable to agree on." Five days later, the Union replied: "We oppose the unilateral implementation of the bi-weekly payroll system. . . . You have decided to tie your proposed two percent increase in employee wages to the implementation of a bi-weekly payroll system and we have rejected that combined proposal." VNS implemented the wage increase on April 7, 1996, and the biweekly payroll system on May 3, 1996.

On June 18, 1996, VNS presented another "package proposal." This proposal retained the earlier proposed job classification changes and included a second two-percent wage increase (to become effective July 7, 1996). The proposal also added three new provisions: 1) the transformation of three holidays into "floating" holidays to be taken at a time requested by the employee; 2) the implementation of a "clinical ladders" program; and 3) the adoption of an enterostomal therapist classification and program. On the same day, VNS also proposed a smaller, alternative package (the "mini package") which also included a second two-percent wage increase along with the above proposals on floating holidays and the clinical ladders and enterostomal therapist and classification programs.

The parties did not reach agreement on either proposal. In a letter dated August 20, 1996, VNS advised the Union that as of September 6, 1996, it was contemplating implementing the "mini package" and that "all of the above items [were] the 'positives' that [the parties] discussed that could be implemented while bargaining for a successor agreement continued." The Union responded on September 5, 1996: "We oppose the unilateral implementation of these proposals. The Union request[s] that you not make any changes to wages, hours or working conditions. Please do not hesitate to call me to arrange a meeting as soon as possible to discuss this and other outstanding issues."

VNS then sent a memorandum, dated September 13, 1996, to the bargaining unit employees (but not to the Union) informing them that it had implemented the mini package with the wage increase to be applied retroactively to July 7, 1996. Ten days later, VNS advised the Union that the wage increase had already been implemented and that the other programs (floating holidays, clinical ladders, and enterostomal therapist and classification) were "already in process." After emphasizing its view that these were "only 'positive items'" meant to enhance the staff's economic conditions while bargaining continued, VNS declared that "it [was] the Agency's position that the mini package involved ha[d] been properly implemented."

The Union filed a charge with the NLRB. . . . Based on these charges, the General Counsel of the NLRB issued a complaint against VNS. . . .

The NLRB order found that VNS violated §§ 8(a)(1) and (5) of the Act by unilaterally implementing 1) a bi-weekly payroll system on or about May 3, 1996; 2) changes in holidays on or about September 6, 1996; 3) a clinical ladder program on or about September 6, 1996; 4) an enterostomal therapist classification and program on or about September 6, 1996; and 5) changes in job classifications at some time subsequent to May 3, 1996. VNS made these changes while it was still bargaining with the Union and had not yet reached general impasse. There is no dispute that all of these are mandatory subjects of bargaining under § 8(d) of the Act.

Before the NLRB, the parties stipulated that they had not reached impasse in their bargaining on the agreement as a whole. Thus, under controlling law, because impasse had not been reached, the employer could take unilateral action on a mandatory subject of bargaining only under a narrow range of circumstances. No economic exigencies or business emergencies existed here which would warrant unilateral action. The NLRB found that the usual rule applied and there were no exceptions. The NLRB issued a broad remedial order based on a finding that VNS has a proclivity to violate the Act. . . .

VNS argues that once it had given the Union notice of its position on a particular issue and an opportunity to respond, it was free to unilaterally declare impasse on specific issues and to take action.

In response to the employer's contention, the Board held:

> [A]s a general rule, when, as here, parties are engaged in negotiations for a collective-bargaining agreement, an employer's obligation to refrain from unilateral changes extends beyond the mere duty to provide a union with notice and an opportunity to bargain about a particular subject matter before implementing such changes. Rather, an employer's obligation under such circumstances encompasses a duty to refrain from implementing such changes at all, absent overall impasse on bargaining for the agreement as a whole. There are two limited exceptions to that general rule: (1) when a union, in response to an employer's diligent and earnest efforts to engage in bargaining, insists on continually avoiding or delaying bargaining, or (2) when economic exigencies or business emergencies compel prompt action.

The Board found that neither exception applied.

Both the Supreme Court and this court have affirmed the rule that unless the employer has bargained to impasse on the agreement as a whole, there is a violation of §§ 8(a)(1) and (5) if the employer makes unilateral changes in mandatory subjects of bargaining (subject to the very limited exceptions described above). . . . The doctrine applies where an existing contract has expired and the negotiations for a new one are not concluded.

This court has long said that an employer must bargain to impasse before making a unilateral change. The basic principles were established in 1962 by the Supreme Court's decision in *N.L.R.B. v. Katz* . . . .

The Supreme Court has applied the *Katz* rule to situations, as here, where an existing agreement has expired but negotiations on a new one had not been completed. Further, in *Litton* [*Litton Financial Printing Div. v. NLRB,* 501 U.S. 190 (1991)] the Court reaffirmed that "an employer commits an unfair labor practice if, without bargaining to impasse, it effects a unilateral change of an existing term or condition of employment."

We reject VNS's position that parties are at impasse merely because the Union rejects or does not accept the employer's position on a particular issue. Whether there is an impasse is an intensely fact-driven question, with the initial determination to be made by the Board. Our role is to review the Board's factual determinations to determine whether there is substantial evidence in the record as a whole to support the Board's finding on impasse. There may be instances where one or two issues so dominate and drive the collective bargaining negotiations that the Board would be justified in finding that impasse on those one or two issues amounts to a bargaining deadlock. But that is a far cry from this case. As this court has said, "[i]mpasse occurs when, after good faith bargaining, the parties are deadlocked so that any further bargaining would be futile."

The Supreme Court has commented on the difficulty of applying the concept of "impasse" to a given set of facts, noting: "perhaps all that can be said with confidence is that an impasse is a state of facts in which the parties, despite the best of faith, are simply deadlocked."

The NLRB has similarly interpreted the scope of the statutory duty to bargain. Congress delegated to the Board, in § 8(d) of the Act, the responsibility to make that interpretation. The Board's interpretation is rational and consistent with the Act.

Collective bargaining involves give and take on a number of issues. The effect of VNS's position would be to permit the employer to remove, one by one, issues from the table and impair the ability to reach an overall agreement through compromise on particular items. In addition, it would undercut the role of the Union as the collective bargaining representative, effectively communicating that the Union lacked the power to keep issues at the table. . . .

For the foregoing reasons we dismiss VNS's petition and we grant the cross-petition of the NLRB to enforce the Board's order.

Case Questions

1. What were the changes unilaterally imposed by VNS? Were these changes on mandatory or permissive bargaining subjects?
2. Had the negotiations for a new collective agreement broken down when VNS initiated the changes? Had the union rejected any further discussions on the proposed changes? Why is that significant?
3. What are the two exceptions to the *Katz* doctrine recognized by the courts? Do either of those exceptions apply here? Explain.

Even if an employer has bargained to impasse over a mandatory subject and is free to implement changes, the changes made must be consistent with the proposal offered to the union. To institute changes unilaterally that are more generous than the proposals the employer was willing to offer the union is a violation of Section 8(a)(5) according to the Supreme Court decision in *NLRB v. Crompton-Highland Mills* [337 U.S. 217 (1949)]. Thus, the employer is not free to offer replacements wages that are higher than those offered to the union before the union went on strike. In some very exceptional circumstances, when changes must be made out of business necessity, the employer may institute unilateral changes without reaching an impasse, but those changes must be consistent with the offers made to the union, *Raleigh Water Heating* [136 NLRB 76 (1962)].

PERMISSIVE BARGAINING SUBJECTS

Permissive Bargaining Subjects
Those subjects that are neither mandatory or illegal; the parties may, but are not required to, bargain over such subjects.

The previous discussion dealt with mandatory bargaining subjects; the Supreme Court in *NLRB v. Wooster Div. of Borg-Warner Corp.* [356 U.S. 342 (1958)] also recognized that there are permissive subjects and prohibited subjects. **Permissive bargaining subjects** are those matters not directly related to wages, hours, terms and conditions of employment, and not prohibited. Either party may raise permissive items in bargaining, but such matters cannot be insisted upon to the point of impasse. If the other party refuses the permissive-item proposal, it must be dropped. *Borg-Warner* held that insisting upon permissive items to impasse and conditioning agreement on mandatory subjects upon agreement to permissive items was a violation of the duty to bargain in good faith. An interest arbitration clause in the collective-bargaining agreement, which would require that all future contract disputes be settled by an arbitrator rather than by a strike or lockout, was held to be a permissive bargaining subject; the employer's insistence that the union agree to the interest arbitration clause as a condition of the employer signing the collective-bargaining agreement was a violation of Section 8(a)(5), *Laidlaw Transit, Inc.* [323 NLRB No. 156 (1997)]. Other examples of permissive items are proposals regarding union procedure for ratifying contracts, attempts to modify the union certification, strike settlement agreements, corporate social or charitable activities, and the proposal to require a transcript of all bargaining sessions. Matters that are "inherent management rights" or "inherent union rights" are also permissive subjects.

PROHIBITED BARGAINING SUBJECTS

Prohibited bargaining subjects are proposals that involve violations of the NLRA or other laws. Examples would be a union attempt to negotiate a closed shop provision or to require an employer to agree to a "hot cargo clause" prohibited by Section 8(e) of the act. Any attempt to bargain over a prohibited subject may violate Section 8(a)(5) or Section 8(b)(3); any agreement reached on such items is null and void. It should be clear that prohibited subjects may not be used to precipitate an impasse.

MODIFICATION OF COLLECTIVE AGREEMENTS

Section 8(d) of the act prohibits any modifications or changes in a collective agreement's provisions relating to mandatory bargaining subjects during the term of the agreement unless both parties to the agreement consent to such changes. (When the agreement has expired, either party may implement changes in the mandatory subjects covered by the agreement after having first bargained, in good faith, to impasse.)

In *Milwaukee Spring Div. of Illinois Coil Spring* [268 NLRB 601 (1984)], the question before the NLRB was whether the employer's action to transfer its assembly operations from its unionized Milwaukee Spring facility to its nonunion operations in Illinois during the term of a collective agreement was a violation of Sections 8(a)(1), 8(a)(3), and 8(a)(5). The transfer of operations was made because of the higher labor costs of the unionized operations; as a result of the transfer, the employees at Milwaukee Spring were laid off. Prior to the decision to relocate operations, the employer had advised the union that it needed reductions in wages and benefit costs because it had lost a major customer, but the union had rejected any concessions. The employer had also proposed terms upon which it would retain operations in Milwaukee, but again, the union had rejected the proposals and declined to bargain further over alternatives to transfer. The NLRB had initially held that the actions constituted a violation of Sections 8(a)(1), 8(a)(3), and 8(a)(5); but on rehearing, the board reversed the prior decision and found no violation. The majority of the board reasoned that the decision to transfer operations did not constitute a unilateral modification of the collective agreement in violation of Section 8(d) because no term of the agreement required the operations to remain at the Milwaukee Spring facility. Had there been a work-preservation clause stating that the functions the bargaining unit employees performed must remain at the Milwaukee plant, the employer would have been guilty of a unilateral modification of the collective agreement, in violation of Section 8(d). The employer's offers to discuss concessions and the terms upon which it would retain operations in Milwaukee satisfied the employer's duty to bargain under Section 8(a)(5). The majority also held that the layoff of the unionized employees after the operations were transferred did not violate Section 8(a)(3). The effect of their decision, reasoned the majority, would be to encourage "realistic and meaningful collective bargaining that the Act contemplates." The dissent argued that the employer was prohibited from transferring operations during the term of the agreement without the consent of the union. The Court of Appeals for the D.C. Circuit affirmed the majority's decision in *U.A.W. v. NLRB* [765 F.2d 175 (1985)].

Plant Closing Legislation

Because of concerns over plant closings, Congress passed the Worker Adjustment and Retraining Act (WARN) in August 1988. The law, which went into effect February 4, 1989, requires employers with 100 or more employees to give sixty days' advance notice prior to any plant closings or mass layoffs. The employer must give written notice of the closing or mass layoff to the employees or their representative, to the state economic development officials, and to the chief elected local government official. WARN defines a *plant closing* as being when fifty or more employees lose their jobs during any thirty-day period, because of a permanent plant closing, or a temporary shutdown exceeding six months. A plant closing may also occur when fifty or more employees experience more than a 50 percent reduction in the hours of work during each month of any six-month period. *Mass layoffs* are defined as layoffs creating an employment loss during any thirty-day period for 500 or more employees or for fifty or more employees who constitute at least one-third of the full-time labor force at a unit of the facility. The act also requires a sixty-day notice when a series of employment losses adds up to the requisite levels over a ninety-day period. The notice requirement has two exceptions. One exception is the so-called *failing firm exception,* when the employer can demonstrate that giving the required notice would prevent the firm from obtaining capital or business necessary to maintain the operation of the firm. The other exception is when the work loss is due to "unforeseen circumstances."

Although the legislation speaks of plant closings, and Congress had industrial plant closings as a primary concern when passing WARN, the courts have held that it applies to employers such as law firms, brokerage firms, hotels, and casinos. The act imposes a penalty for failure to give the required notice; the employer is required to pay each affected employee up to sixty days' pay and benefits if the required notice is not given. The act also provides for fines of up to $500 for each day the notice is not given, up to a maximum of $30,000; however, the fines can be imposed only in suits brought by local governments against the employer. WARN does not create any separate enforcement agency, nor does it give any enforcement authority to the Department of Labor.

The act requires only that advance notice of the plant closings or mass layoffs be given; it does not require that the employer negotiate over the decision to close or lay off. To that extent, WARN does not affect the duty to bargain under the NLRA or the results of the *First National Maintenance* decision.

The Duty to Furnish Information

In *NLRB v. Truitt Mfg.* [351 U.S. 149 (1956)], the Supreme Court held that an employer that pleads inability to pay in response to union demands must provide some financial information in an attempt to support that claim. The Court reasoned that such a duty was necessary if bargaining was to be meaningful; the employer is not allowed to "hide behind" claims that it cannot afford the union's pay demands. The rationale behind this requirement is that the union will be able to determine if the employer's claims are valid; if so, the union will moderate its demands accordingly.

The *Truitt* requirement to furnish information is not a "truth in bargaining" requirement. It relates only to claims of financial inability to meet union proposals. If the employer pleads inability to pay, the union must make a good-faith demand for financial information supporting the employer's claim. In responding to the union request, the employer need not provide all the information requested by the union, but it must provide financial information in a reasonably usable and accessible form.

While the *Truitt* duty relates to financial information when the employer has pleaded inability to pay, another duty to furnish information is far greater in scope. Information relating to the enforcement and administration of the collective agreement must be provided to the union. This information is necessary for the union to perform its role as collective representative of the employees. This duty continues beyond negotiations to cover grievance arbitration during the life of the agreement as well. Such information includes wage scales, factors entering into compensation, job rates, job classifications, statistical data on the employer's minority employment practices, and a list of the names and addresses of the employees in the bargaining unit.

The employer's refusal to provide the union with a copy of the contract for the sale of the employer's business was a violation of Section 8(a)(5) when the union sought the contract to determine whether the employees were adequately provided for after the sale and the union had agreed to keep the sales information confidential and to allow the employer to delete the sale price from the contract, *NLRB v. New England Newspapers, Inc.* [856 F.2d 409 (1st Cir. 1988)]. Employers using toxic substances have been required to furnish unions with information on the generic names of substances used, their health effects, and toxicological studies. Employers are not required to turn over medical records of identified individual employees. To safeguard the privacy of individual employees, the courts have required that individual employees must consent to the disclosure of individual health records and scores on aptitude or psychological tests. An employer is entitled, however, to protect trade secrets and confidential information such as affirmative action plans or privately developed psychological aptitude tests.

Information provided to the union does not have to be in the exact format requested by the union, but it must be in a form that is not burdensome to use or interpret. An employer may not prohibit union photocopying of the information provided, *Communications Workers Local 1051 v. NLRB* [644 F.2d 923 (1st Cir. 1981)].

BARGAINING REMEDIES

We have seen that the requirements of the duty to bargain in good faith reflect a balance between promoting industrial peace and recognizing the principle of freedom of contract. To preserve the voluntary nature of collective bargaining, the Board and the courts will not require either party to make a concession or agree to a proposal.

When the violation of Section 8(a)(5) or Section 8(b)(3) involves specific practices, such as the refusal to furnish information or the refusal to sign an already agreed-upon contract, the Board orders the offending party to comply. Likewise, when an employer has illegally made unilateral changes, the Board requires that the prior conditions be restored and any reduction in wages or benefits be paid back. However, if the violation of the duty to bargain in good faith involves either side's refusal to recognize or negotiate seriously with the other side, the board is limited in remedies available. In such cases, the Board will issue a "cease-and-desist" order directing the offending party to stop the illegal conduct and a "bargaining order" directing the party to begin to negotiate in good faith. But the Board cannot require that the parties make concessions or reach an agreement; it can only require that the parties return to the bargaining table and make an effort to explore the basis for an agreement. The following case deals with the limits on the Board's remedial powers in bargaining order situations.

H. K. Porter Co. v. NLRB

397 U.S. 99 (1970)

Black, J.

After an election, respondent United Steelworkers Union was, on October 5, 1961, certified by the National Labor Relations Board as the bargaining agent for the employees at the Danville, Virginia, plant of the H. K. Porter Co. Thereafter negotiations commenced for a collective bargaining agreement. Since that time the controversy has seesawed between the Board, the Court of Appeals for the District of Columbia Circuit, and this Court. This delay of over eight years is not because the case is exceedingly complex, but appears to have occurred chiefly because of the skill of the company's negotiators in taking advantage of every opportunity for delay in an Act more noticeable for its generality than for its precise prescriptions. The entire lengthy dispute mainly revolves around the union's desire to have the company agree to "check off" the dues owed to the union by its members, that is, to deduct those dues periodically from the company's wage payments to the employees. The record shows, as the Board found, that the company's objection to a checkoff was not due to any general principle or policy against making deductions from employees' wages. The company does deduct charges for things like insurance, taxes, and contributions to charities, and at some other plants it has a checkoff arrangement for union dues. The evidence shows, and the court below found, that the company's objection was not because of inconvenience, but solely on the ground that the company was "not going to aid and comfort the union." Based on this and other evidence the Board found, and the Court of Appeals approved the finding, that the refusal of the company to bargain about the checkoff was not made in good faith, but was done solely to frustrate the making of any collective bargaining agreement. In May 1966, the Court of Appeals upheld the Board's order requiring the company to cease and desist from refusing to bargain in good faith and directing it to engage in further collective bargaining, if requested by the union to do so, over the checkoff.

In the course of that opinion, the Court of Appeals intimated that the Board conceivably might have required petitioner to agree to a checkoff provision as a remedy for the prior bad-faith bargaining, although the order enforced at that time did not contain any such provision. In the ensuing negotiations the company offered to discuss alternative arrangements for collecting the union's dues, but the union insisted that the company was required to agree to the checkoff proposal without modification. Because of this disagreement over the proper interpretation of the court's opinion, the union, in February 1967, filed a motion for clarification of the 1966 opinion. The motion was denied by the court on March 22, 1967, in an order suggesting that contempt proceedings before the Board would be the proper avenue for testing the employer's compliance with the original order. A request for the institution of such proceedings was made by the union, and in June 1967, the

Regional Director of the Board declined to prosecute a contempt charge, finding that the employer had "satisfactorily complied with the affirmative requirements of the Order." . . . The union then filed in the Court of Appeals a motion for reconsideration of the earlier motion to clarify the 1966 opinion. The court granted that motion and issued a new opinion in which it held that in certain circumstances a "checkoff may be imposed as a remedy for bad-faith bargaining." The case was then remanded to the Board and on July 3, 1968, the Board issued a supplemental order requiring the petitioner to "[g]rant to the Union a contract clause providing for the checkoff of union dues." . . . The Board had found that the refusal was based on a desire to frustrate agreement and not on any legitimate business reason. On the basis of that finding the Court of Appeals approved the further finding that the employer had not bargained in good faith, and the validity of that finding is not now before us. Where the record thus revealed repeated refusals by the employer to bargain in good faith on this issue, the Court of Appeals concluded that ordering agreement to the checkoff clause "may be the only means of assuring the Board, and the court, that [the employer] no longer harbors an illegal intent."

In reaching this conclusion the Court of Appeals held that Section 8(d) did not forbid the Board from compelling agreement. That court felt that "Section 8(d) defines collective bargaining and relates to a determination of whether a . . . violation has occurred and not to the scope of the remedy which may be necessary to cure violations which have already occurred." We may agree with the Court of Appeals that as a matter of strict, literal interpretation of that section it refers only to deciding when a violation has occurred, but we do not agree that that observation justifies the conclusion that the remedial powers of the Board are not also limited by the same considerations that led Congress to enact Section 8(d). It is implicit in the entire structure of the Act that the Board acts to oversee and referee the process of collective bargaining, leaving the results of the contest to the bargaining strengths of the parties. It would be anomalous indeed to hold that while Section 8(d) prohibits the Board from relying on a refusal to agree as the sole evidence of bad faith bargaining, the Act permits the Board to compel agreement in that same dispute. The Board's remedial powers under Section 10 of the Act are broad, but they are limited to carry out the policies of the Act itself. One of these fundamental policies is freedom of contract. While the parties' freedom of contract is not absolute under the Act, allowing the Board to compel agreement when the parties themselves are unable to do so would violate the fundamental premise on which the Act is based—private bargaining under governmental supervision of the procedure alone, without any official compulsion over the actual terms of the contract.

In reaching its decision, the Court of Appeals relied extensively on the equally important policy of the Act that workers' rights to collective bargaining are to be secured. In this case the Court apparently felt that the employer was trying effectively to destroy the union by refusing to agree to what the union may have considered its most important demand. Perhaps the court, fearing that the parties might resort to economic combat, was also trying to maintain the industrial peace which the Act is designed to further. But the Act, as presently drawn, does not contemplate that unions will always be secure and able to achieve agreement even when their economic position is weak, nor that strikes and lockouts will never result from a bargaining to impasse. It cannot be said that the Act forbids an employer or a union to rely ultimately on its economic strength to try to secure what it cannot obtain through bargaining. It may well be true, as the Court of Appeals felt, that the present remedial powers of the Board are insufficiently broad to cope with important labor problems. But it is the job of Congress, not the Board or the courts, to decide when and if it is necessary to allow governmental review of proposals for collective bargaining agreements and compulsory submission to one side's demands. The present Act does not envision such a process.

The judgment is reversed and the case is remanded to the Court of Appeals for further action consistent with this opinion.

Reversed and remanded.

Case Questions

1. Had the employer agreed to the union dues checkoff clause? Why did the court of appeals hold that the NLRB had the power to impose a checkoff clause on the employer?
2. Does the Supreme Court agree that the NLRB has the power to impose the checkoff clause? Why?
3. In light of this Supreme Court decision, what is the extent of the NLRB's power to remedy violations of the duty to bargain in good faith?

Because of the limitations on the NLRB's remedial powers in bargaining cases, an intransigent party can effectively frustrate the policies of the NLRA. If a union or employer is willing to incur the legal expenses and possible contempt-of-court fines, it can avoid reaching an agreement with the other side. Although unions are occasionally involved in such situations, most often employers have more to gain from refusing to bargain. The legal fees and fines may amount to less money than the employer would be required to pay in wages under a collective agreement (and the legal expenses are tax deductible). Perhaps the most extreme example of such intransigence was the J. P. Stevens Company; in the late 1970s, the company was found guilty of numerous unfair practices and was subjected to a number of bargaining orders, yet in only one case did it reach a collective agreement with the union.

Extreme cases like J. P. Stevens are the exception, however. Despite the Board's remedial shortcomings, most negotiations culminate in the signing of a collective agreement. That fact is a testament to the vitality of the collective-bargaining process and a vindication of a policy emphasis on the voluntary nature of the process.

ANTITRUST ASPECTS OF COLLECTIVE BARGAINING

When a union and a group of employers agree upon specified wages and working conditions, the effect may be to reduce competition among the employers with respect to those wages or working conditions. In addition, when the parties negotiate limits on subcontracting work or the use of prefabricated materials, the effect may be to reduce or prevent competition among firms producing these materials. Although the parties may be pursuing legitimate goals of collective bargaining, those goals may conflict with the policies of the antitrust laws designed to promote competition.

http://www4.law.cornell.edu/uscode/15/17.html *is the site of the text on "Antitrust laws not applicable to labor organizations."*

In the case of *U.S. v. Hutcheson* [312 U.S. 219 (1941)], the Supreme Court held that a union acting in its self-interest, which does not combine with nonlabor groups, is exempt from the antitrust laws. *Hutcheson* involved union picketing of Anheuser-Busch and a call for a boycott of Anheuser-Busch products as a result of a dispute over work-assignment decisions. The Court ruled that such conduct was legal as long as it was not done in concert with nonlabor groups.

The scope of the labor relations exemption from the antitrust laws was further clarified by the Supreme Court in *Amalgamated Meat Cutters v. Jewel Tea Co.* [381 U.S. 676 (1965)]. In that case, the union and a group of grocery stores negotiated restrictions on the hours its members would work, since the contract required the presence of union butchers for fresh meat sales. The effect of the agreement was to restrict the hours during which the grocery stores could sell fresh (rather than prepackaged) meat. Jewel Tea argued that such a restriction of competition among the grocery stores violated the Sherman Antitrust Act. The Supreme Court held that since the union was pursuing its legitimate interests—that is, setting hours of work through a collective-bargaining relationship—and did not act in concert with one group of employers to impose restrictions on another group of employers, the contract did not violate the Sherman Act.

Despite the broad scope of the antitrust exemption for labor relations activities, several cases have held unions in violation of the antitrust laws. In *United Mine Workers v. Pennington* [381 U.S. 657 (1965)], the union agreed with one group of mine operators to impose wage and pension demands on a different group of mines. The union and the first group of mine owners were held by the Court to have been aware that the second group, composed of smaller mining operations, would be unable to meet the demands and could be forced to cease operations. The Supreme Court stated that if the union had agreed with the first group of employers in order to eliminate competition from the smaller mines, the union would be in violation of the antitrust laws. Although the union, acting alone, could attempt to force the smaller mines to agree to its demands, the union lost its exemption from the antitrust laws when it combined with one group of employers to force demands on the second group.

In *Connell Construction Co. v. Plumbers Local 100* [421 U.S. 616 (1975)], a union attempted to force a general contractor to agree to hire only plumbing subcontractors who had contracts with the union. The general contractor did not itself employ any plumbers, and the union did not represent the employees of the general contractor. The effect of the union demand would be to restrict competition among plumbing subcontractors. Nonunion firms, and even unionized firms that had contracts with other unions, would be denied access to plumbing jobs. The Supreme Court held that the union conduct was not exempt from the antitrust laws because the union did not have a collective-bargaining relationship with Connell, the general contractor. Although a union may attempt to impose restrictions on employers with whom it has a bargaining relationship, it may not attempt to impose such restrictions on employers outside that bargaining relationship.

In *Brown v. Pro Football, Inc.* [518 U.S. 231 (1996)], the U.S. Supreme Court held that the nonstatutory exemption from the antitrust laws continued past the expiration of the collective agreement and the point of impasse and lasted as long as a collective-bargaining relationship existed. The Court therefore upheld the legality of salary restrictions imposed by the members of a multiemployer bargaining unit—the teams of the National Football League—unilaterally after the expiration of their collective agreement and after bargaining in good faith to impasse.

In summary, then, the parties are generally exempt from the antitrust laws when they act alone to pursue legitimate concerns within the context of a collective-bargaining relationship. If a union agrees with one group of employers to impose demands on another group or if it attempts to impose work restrictions on employers outside a collective-bargaining relationship, it is subject to the antitrust laws.

THE WORKING LAW

STRIP CLUB AGREES TO CONTRACT WITH DANCERS' UNION

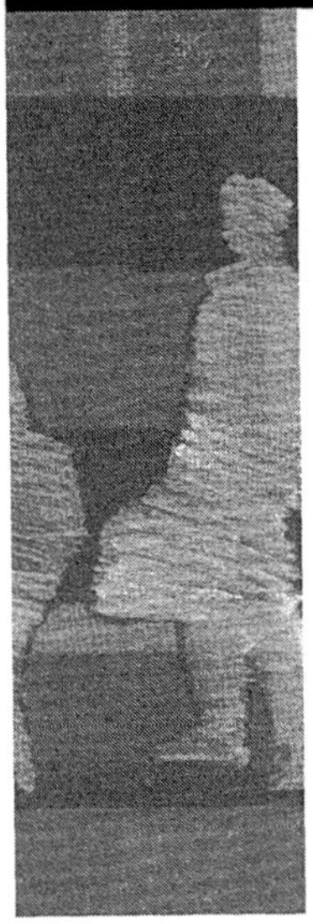

After members of the Exotic Dancers Union engaged in an informational picket line to protest wage cuts and to seek improved health benefits, the owners of the Lusty Lady Theater agreed to a contract with the union. The Lusty Lady is the nation's only unionized strip club; the dancers organized their union in 1995. The new contract is for two years and increases wages by $3 per hour over the life of the contract; it also adds a $2 per dance shift allowance (rising to $4 per shift in the second year) for prep time for the dancers to do their hair and makeup. The new contract provides the dancers with 1 and a half sick days per year and lowers a hiring cap to ensure that the dancers get sufficient dance shifts. The dancers' union members ratified the contract January 17, 2003.

In December 2002, the dancers had engaged in an informational picket to pressure the club to negotiate with the union, which is affiliated with the Service Employees International Union, Local 790. The dancers wore hot pink T-shirts bearing the slogan "Bad girls like good contracts," and they chanted, "Two, four, six, eight, pay us more to gyrate."

Sources: "Lusty Lady Dancers Ratify Union Contract," *The San Francisco Chronicle,* p. A27, January 31, 2003; "Unionized Strippers Ratify Contract with San Francisco Club," *Associated Press State & Local Wire,* January 30, 2003; "Strippers' Union Ratifies Contract," CNN.com, January 31, 2003; "Unionized Strippers Picket for More Booty," *The San Francisco Chronicle,* p. A17, December 3, 2003.

SUMMARY

- The duty to bargain in good faith arises under Section 9(a) of the NLRA because of a union's status as exclusive bargaining agent. When a union demonstrates the support of a majority of the employees in the bargaining unit, both the union and the employer are required to bargain in good faith, as defined in Section 8(d).
- The NLRB presumptions regarding the union's majority status require that the employer recognize and bargain with the union for at least one year following the union's victory in a representation election or for a reasonable period of time following a voluntary recognition of the union by the employer. If the parties have negotiated a collective-bargaining agreement, the presumption of union majority support continues for the length of the collective agreement or for the first three years of the agreement if it is for a longer term. After the expiration of the collective agreement, the employer must demonstrate a good-faith doubt as to the union's majority support, based on some objective evidence, to refuse to bargain with the union.
- Bargaining in good faith, as defined in Section 8(d), requires that the parties meet and discuss matters with an open mind to explore the basis of an agreement. The parties are not required to make concessions or to reach an agreement.
- The NLRB has classified bargaining subject matter as either mandatory, permissive, or illegal. Attempts to negotiate illegal subjects, or taking an illegal subject to impasse, are a violation of the duty to bargain in good faith. Mandatory

subjects are those that directly affect the wages, hours, and terms and conditions of employment of the employees in the bargaining unit; the parties are required to discuss such issues and, after reaching impasse, may strike or lock out over mandatory subjects. Permissive subjects are those that are neither mandatory nor illegal; while the parties are free to discuss these matters, they cannot take permissive subjects to impasse.

- The NLRB's remedies for violations of the duty to bargain in good faith are limited to cease-and-desist orders; the NLRB cannot order parties to reach an agreement, nor can it impose contractual terms on the parties.

QUESTIONS

1. Under what circumstances may an employer whose employees are unionized bargain legally with individual employees?
2. What procedural requirements for collective bargaining does Section 8(d) impose?
3. Must an employer refuse to bargain with either union when two unions are seeking to represent the employer's workers? Explain your answer.
4. When is a "take-it-or-leave-it" bargaining position legal under the NLRA? Explain your answer.
5. What are mandatory bargaining subjects? What is the significance of an item being classified as a mandatory bargaining subject?
6. Under what circumstances may an employer institute unilateral changes in matters covered by a collective agreement? Explain your answer.
7. When is an employer required to provide financial information to a union?
8. What conduct by unions is subject to the antitrust laws?

CASE PROBLEMS

1. During bargaining, the employer reached an impasse on (a) a detailed "management rights" clause, (b) a broad "zipper" clause, (c) a waiver-of-past-practices provision, and (d) a no-strike provision. The employer's final economic offer consisted of an increase of ten cents per hour for seven of the nine bargaining unit employees and a wage review for the remaining two.

   Based on these facts, the NLRB concluded that the employer had engaged in mere surface bargaining and condemned the employer's final proposals as "terms which no self respecting union could be expected to accept." The company appealed the case to the Ninth Circuit.

   If you had sat on the panel at the appellate court level, would you have agreed or disagreed with the board's conclusions? See *NLRB v. Tomco Communications, Inc.* [567 F.2d 871, 97 L.R.R.M. 2660 (9th Cir. 1978)].

2. The personnel department at an electrical utility had a policy of giving all new employees a "psychological aptitude test." The union demanded access to the test questions, answers, and individual scores for the employees in the bargaining unit. The union pointed out that among similar types of information that the NLRB had ordered disclosed in other cases were seniority lists, employees' ages, names and addresses of successful and unsuccessful job applicants, information

about benefits received by retirees under employer's pension and insurance plans, information on employee grievances, and information on possible loss of work due to a proposed leasing arrangement.

The company claimed that if it released the information the union sought, its test security program would be severely compromised. Furthermore, employee confidence in the confidentiality of the testing program would be shattered.

How do you think the NLRB would rule in this case? See *Detroit Edison Co. v. NLRB* [440 U.S. 301, 100 L.R.R.M. 2728 (1979)].

3. During negotiations for renewing the collective agreement, the union representing the employees at Mercy Hospital presented a proposal that the hospital cafeteria be open for all employees from the hours of 6:30 A.M.–8:00 P.M. and 2:00 A.M.–4:00 A.M. The cafeteria had been open for those hours for the past ten years, but the hospital had considered closing it overnight. The union argued that there were approximately 175 employees working the overnight shift, and many of them used the cafeteria for lunch and breaks. The hospital responded that the cafeteria had been losing money during the 2:00 A.M.–4:00 A.M. operations. The union proposal was made on May 15, 1992; on May 19, without any notice to and discussions with the union, the hospital closed the cafeteria overnight. The hospital installed additional vending machines and provided a toaster and microwave for use by the employees. The union filed an unfair labor practice complaint with the NLRB over the hospital's closing of the cafeteria overnight.

How should the NLRB rule on the complaint? Was the hospital required to bargain with the union over the decision to close the cafeteria overnight? Why? See *Mercy Hospital of Buffalo* [311 NLRB 869 (1993)].

4. Sonat Marine was engaged in the business of transporting petroleum and petrochemical products. The Seafarers International Union (SIU) represented two separate bargaining units of Sonat's employees. One unit consisted of licensed employees—that is, the tugboat masters, mates, and pilots. In 1984, Sonat advised the union that it intended to withdraw recognition of the SIU as the bargaining representative of these licensed personnel at the expiration of the current collective-bargaining agreement. Sonat's stated reason was that it had determined that these personnel were supervisors who were not subject to the NLRA as employees. The union demanded information on the factual basis for Sonat's position. Sonat refused to provide a response.

The union filed an unfair labor practice charge, asserting that Sonat was not bargaining in good faith. Was the union right? See *Sonat Marine, Inc.* [279 NLRB No. 16 (1986)].

5. Pratt-Farnsworth, Inc., a unionized construction contractor in New Orleans, owned a nonunion subsidiary, Halmar. During negotiations of a new collective-bargaining agreement with Pratt-Farnsworth, the Carpenters' Union demanded that the company provide information concerning Halmar's business activities; the union was suspicious that the subsidiary was being used by the parent to siphon off work that could have been done by union members.

If you represented the union, what arguments would you make to support your demand for information? If you were on the company's side, how would you respond? See *Carpenters Local 1846 v. Pratt-Farnsworth, Inc.* [690 F.2d 489, 111 L.R.R.M. 2787 (5th Cir. 1982)].

6. The company and the union commenced collective bargaining in April 1982. After four sessions, the company submitted, on June 15, a contract package for union ratification. Two days later, the union's membership rejected the package. No strike ensued.

Following rejection, the union's chief negotiator contacted the company and pointed out four stumbling blocks to ratification: union security, wages, overtime pay, and sickness and accident benefits. On July 7, the company resubmitted its original contract package unchanged. The union agreed to put it to a second ratification vote. However, before the vote took place, the company's president withdrew the package from the bargaining table. His reasoning was that the union's failure to strike indicated that the company had earlier overestimated the union's economic power. When in subsequent bargaining sessions the company proposed wages and benefits below those in the original package, the union charged it with bad-faith bargaining.

How should the NLRB have ruled on this complaint? See *Pennex Aluminum Corp.* [271 NLRB No. 197, 117 L.R.R.M. 1057 (1984)].

7. For more than thirty years without challenge by the union, the Brod & McClung-Pace Co.'s bargaining unit employees performed warranty work at customers' facilities. Then the international union altered its constitution to forbid its members to do such warranty work. Pursuant to this constitutional change, the local union, which was subject to the international's constitution, sought a midterm modification of its collective-bargaining agreement with the company to eliminate the warranty work. When the firm refused, the union sought to achieve a unilateral change by threatening its members with court-collectible fines if they continued to perform the work.

   Did the union violate the NLRA? If so, how? See *Sheet Metal Workers Int'l. Ass'n., Local 16* [271 NLRB No. 49, 117 L.R.R.M. 1085 (1984)].

8. After five sessions of multiemployer bargaining, the Carpenters' Union and the Lake Charles District of the Associated General Contractors of Louisiana reached a new agreement. However, the printed contract inadvertently omitted a "weather clause," which was to state that an employee who reported for work but was sent home because of inclement weather would get four hours' pay, and an employee sent home because of weather after having started work would get paid only for hours actually worked, but not less than two hours. When the omission was discovered, the contract was already ratified and signed. The union refused to add the clause. The company then asked to reopen bargaining over the wage and reporting clauses that were affected by the omission. The union refused. Who, if anyone, has committed an unfair labor practice? See *International Brotherhood of Carpenters Local 1476* [270 NLRB 1432, 117 L.R.R.M. 1097 (1984)].

9. The production workers at Molded Products Co., represented by the Allied Workers Union, went on strike in June 1992, after their collective agreement expired. The strike lasted two months, and during the strike, almost half of the 150 workers crossed the picket line and returned to work. When the strike ended, the company recalled sixty of the strikers and operated with a work force of 135. Some of the workers then circulated a petition stating that they no longer wished to be represented by the union, and seventy of the workers signed it. The company then notified the union that it was withdrawing recognition and refused to bargain with the union over renewing the collective agreement. The union filed a complaint with the NLRB, arguing that the company's withdrawal of recognition violated Sections 8(a)(1) and (5).

   How should the NLRB rule on the complaint? Why? Explain your answer. See *Quazite Div. of Morrison Molded Fiberglass Co. v. NLRB* [87 F.3d 493 (D.C. Cir. 1996)].

10. Plymouth Stamping, an automotive parts company located in Michigan, decided to contract out its parts assembly operations in response to deteriorating sales and financial conditions. It notified the union on February 11, 1980, of its plans to subcontract. The notice stated that the operation would be discontinued as of February 15, that the assembly operation employees would be either laid off or transferred, and that the action was necessary "due to economic and business reasons." The union requested a meeting, which was held on February 14, 1980. At this meeting, the company explained

that the action was the result of a number of factors, including declining sales, noncompetitive wage rates, burdensome state taxes, and high workers' compensation costs. The company, in response to a question concerning possible ways to retain the jobs, stated that the union would have to accept substantial wage cuts, a cost-of-living freeze, a reduction in some benefits, and a modification in work rules. The union requested that the company delay any action until at least the following week; the company, while stating that its decision was not final, requested a reply from the union by February 15 as to whether it would agree to concessions. The union failed to respond by February 15, and over the weekend (February 16 and 17), the company moved its assembly equipment to a plant in Ohio. Meanwhile, unbeknownst to the company, the union, in a letter dated February 14, had requested information regarding the specifics of the decision; the company received the union's letter on February 20. The company responded to the union's letter on March 11; it stated that the decision was not irreversible and that it was prepared to discuss the matter with the union. The company repeated that the decision to subcontract was taken because "assembly operations are labor intensive and the costs (wages/benefits) associated with supporting this labor group have made the company noncompetitive." On March 1, the company entered into a formal leasing agreement with the subcontracting company; the lease allowed the company to terminate the lease and repossess the equipment and gave the subcontractor the option to purchase the equipment. The subcontractor purchased the equipment on July 1, 1980. The union filed an unfair labor practice complaint with the NLRB, charging the company with violations of Sections 8(a)(1) and 8(a)(5) for failing to bargain over a mandatory subject of bargaining and making a unilateral change in a mandatory subject without bargaining to impasse.

How should the NLRB decide the union's complaint? What would have been the effect of the WARN law if it had applied to this case? See *NLRB v. Plymouth Stamping Division, Eltec Corp.* [870 F.2d 1112 (6th Cir. 1989)].

INTERNET EXERCISE

Why would unions and companies be willing to discuss, much less agree upon, matters that are characterized as "permissive bargaining subjects"? For example, why would the United Auto Workers Union (UAW) and Ford Motor Company be willing to negotiate the creation of a partnership to provide community support services for working families? To find out more about the Ford-UAW partnership to set up Family Service and Learning Centers (FSLC), which will offer an integrated array of family and community services—child-care programs, before- and after-school programs for preteens, programs for teens, adult and family education classes, and programs for retirees—go to the FSLC Web site at **http://www.familycenteronline.org/**Click the link to Press Room and then click the link for the Factsheet. The centers provide these services to UAW members from Ford, salaried Ford employees, and family members and retirees. How do such programs benefit Ford, the UAW, and the community?

INFOTRAC KEYWORDS

http://www.infotrac-college.com

collective bargaining, bargaining in good faith

17 CHAPTER

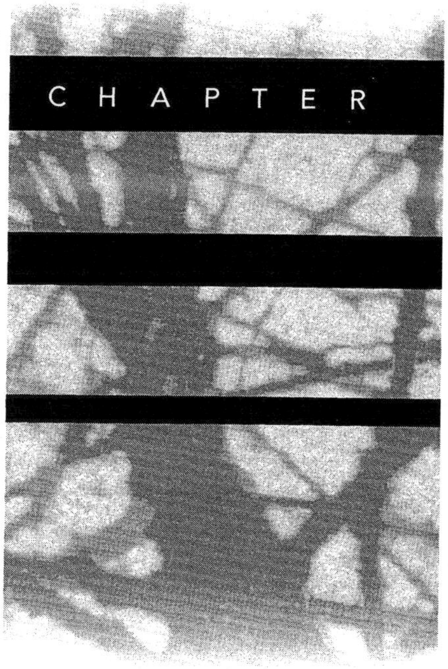

PICKETING AND STRIKES

Collective bargaining involves economic conflict: Each party to the negotiations seeks to protect its economic interests by extracting concessions from the other side. Both union and management back up their demands with the threat of pressure tactics that would inflict economic harm upon the other party. If the negotiations reach an impasse, the union may go on strike, or the employer may lock out to force concessions. This chapter discusses the limitations placed on the use of such pressure tactics.

PRESSURE TACTICS

Pressure Tactics
Union pressure tactics involve strikes and calls for boycotts, while employers may resort to lockouts.

Pressure tactics include picketing, patrolling, strikes, and boycotts by unions and lockouts by employers. *Picketing* is the placing of persons outside the premises of an employer to convey information to the public. The information may be conveyed by words, signs, or the distribution of literature. Picketing is usually accompanied by *patrolling,* which is the movement of persons back and forth around the premises of an employer. A *strike*—the organized withholding of labor by workers—is the traditional weapon by which workers attempt to pressure employers. If the strike is successful, the economic harm resulting from the cessation of production will force the employer to accede to the union's demands. Strikes are usually accompanied by picketing and patrolling as means of enforcing the strike. Unions may also instigate a boycott of the employer's product to increase the economic pressure upon the employer.

See **http://www4.law.cornell.edu/uscode/29/158.html** *for details on picketing and striking.*

Employers are free to replace employees who go on strike. If the strike is an economic strike, replacement may be permanent. Employers are also free to lock out the employees—that is, to intentionally withhold work from them—to force the union to make concessions. An employer may resort to a lockout only after bargaining in good faith to an impasse; however, the bargaining dispute must be over a mandatory bargaining subject. Limitations on the right of an employer to lock out were discussed in Chapter 15 in the cases of *NLRB v. Brown* and *American Shipbuilding v. NLRB.*

Strikes may be economic strikes or unfair labor practice strikes. (The rights of the striking workers to reinstatement and their protection under the National Labor Relations Act [NLRA] were discussed in Chapter 15.) Strikes in violation of contractual no-strike clauses may give rise to union liability for damages and to judicial "back-to-work" orders; the enforcement of no-strike clauses is discussed in Chapter 18. The focus in this chapter is on economic strikes and picketing. When the word *strike* is used, it refers to an economic strike unless otherwise specified.

THE LEGAL PROTECTION OF STRIKES

There is no constitutional right to strike. In fact, courts have traditionally held strikes to be criminal conspiracies (see Chapter 12). Constitutional restrictions, however, apply only to government activity; private sector strikes generally raise no constitutional issues. Strikes by private sector employees are regulated by the NLRA and are protected activity under Section 7 of the act. For public sector employees, there may be no right to strike (see Chapter 20).

Although there is no recognized constitutional right to strike, there is a constitutional right to picket. The courts have held that picketing involves the expression and communication of opinions and ideas and is therefore protected under the First Amendment's freedom of speech. In *Thornhill v. Alabama* [310 U.S. 88 (1940)], the Supreme Court held a state statute that prohibited all picketing, including even peaceful picketing, to be unconstitutional. Courts did, however, recognize that picketing involves conduct apart from speech so that there may be some reason for limitations upon the conduct of picketing. In *Teamsters Local 695 v. Vogt* [354 U.S. 284 (1957)], the Supreme Court held that picketing, because it involves speech plus patrolling, may be regulated by the government more readily than pure speech activity.

THE NORRIS–LA GUARDIA ACT

As you recall from Chapter 12, the Norris–La Guardia Act, passed in 1932, severely restricted the ability of federal courts to issue injunctions in labor disputes. The act did not "protect" strikes; it simply restricted the ability of federal courts to issue injunctions. The act defines "labor dispute" very broadly to cover disputes even when the parties are not in an employer-employee relationship. Furthermore, the dispute need not be the result of economic concerns, as illustrated by the following case.

Jacksonville Bulk Terminals v. ILA

457 U.S. 702 (1982)

Marshall, J.

In this case, we consider the power of a federal court to enjoin a politically motivated work stoppage in an action brought by an employer pursuant to Section 301(a) of the Labor Management Relations Act (LMRA), 29 U.S.C., Section 185(a), to enforce a union's obligations under a collective-bargaining agreement. We first address whether the broad anti-injunction provisions of the Norris–La Guardia Act apply to politically motivated work stoppages. . . .

On January 4, 1980, President Carter announced that, due to the Soviet Union's intervention in Afghanistan, certain trade with the Soviet Union would be restricted. Superphosphoric acid (SPA), used in agricultural fertilizer, was not included in the presidential embargo. On January 9, 1980, respondent International Longshoremen's Association (ILA) announced that its members would not handle any cargo bound to, or coming from, the Soviet Union or carried on Russian ships. In accordance with this resolution, respondent local union, an ILA affiliate, refused to load SPA bound for the Soviet Union aboard three ships that arrived at the shipping terminal operated by petitioner Jacksonville Bulk Terminals, Inc. (JBT) at the Port of Jacksonville, Florida during the month of January 1980.

In response to this work stoppage, petitioners JBT, Hooker Chemical Corporation, and Occidental Petroleum Company (collectively referred to as the Employer) brought this action pursuant to Section 301(a) of the LMRA, against respondents ILA, its affiliated local union, and its officers and agents (collectively referred to as the Union). The Employer alleged that the Union's work stoppage violated the collective-bargaining agreement between the Union and JBT. The Employer . . . requested a temporary restraining order. . . . The United States District Court for the Middle District of Florida . . . granted the Employer's request for a preliminary injunction . . . reasoning that the political motivation behind the work stoppage rendered the Norris–La Guardia Act's anti-injunction provisions inapplicable.

The United States Court of Appeals for the Fifth Circuit . . . disagreed with the District Court's conclusion that the provisions of the Norris–La Guardia Act are inapplicable to politically motivated work stoppages. . . .

Section 4 of the Norris–La Guardia Act provides in part:

> No court of the United States shall have jurisdiction to issue any restraining order or temporary or permanent injunction in any case involving or growing out of any labor dispute to prohibit any person or persons participating or interested in such dispute . . . from doing, whether singly or in concert, any of the following acts:
> (a) Ceasing or refusing to perform any work or to remain in any relation of employment. . . .

Congress adopted this broad prohibition to remedy the growing tendency of federal courts to enjoin strikes by narrowly construing the Clayton Act's labor exemption from the Sherman Act's prohibition against conspiracies to restrain trade. This Court has consistently given the anti-injunction provisions of the Norris–La Guardia Act a broad interpretation, recognizing exceptions only in limited situations where necessary to accommodate the Act to specific federal legislation or paramount congressional policy.

The Employer argues that the Norris–La Guardia Act does not apply in this case because the political motivation underlying the Union's work stoppage removes this controversy from that Act's definition of a "labor dispute." . . .

At the outset, we must determine whether this is a "case involving or growing out of any labor dispute" within the meaning of Section 4 of the Norris–La Guardia Act. Section 13(c) of the Act broadly defines the term labor dispute to include "any controversy concerning terms or conditions of employment." The Employer argues that the existence of political motives takes this work stoppage controversy outside the broad scope of this definition. This argument, however, has no basis in the plain statutory language of the Norris–La Guardia Act or in our prior interpretations of that Act. Furthermore, the argument is contradicted by the legislative history of not only the Norris–La Guardia Act but also the 1947 amendments to the National Labor Relations Act (NLRA).

An action brought by an employer against the union representing its employees to enforce a no-strike pledge generally involves two controversies. First, there is the "underlying dispute," which is the event or condition that triggers the work stoppage. This dispute may not be political, and it may or may not be arbitrable under the parties' collective-bargaining agreement. Second, there is the parties' dispute over whether the no-strike pledge prohibits the work stoppage at issue. This second dispute can always form the basis for federal court jurisdiction, because Section 301(a) gives federal courts jurisdiction over "[s]uits for violation of contracts between an employer and a labor organization."

It is beyond cavil that the second form of dispute—whether the collective-bargaining agreement either forbids or permits the union to refuse to perform certain work—is a "controversy concerning the terms or conditions of employment." This Section 301 action was brought to resolve just such a controversy. In its complaint, the Employer did not seek to enjoin the intervention of the Soviet Union in Afghanistan, nor did it ask the District Court to decide whether the Union was justified in expressing disapproval of the Soviet Union's actions. Instead, the Employer sought to enjoin the Union's decision not to provide labor, a decision which the Employer believed violated the terms of the collective-bargaining agreement. It is this contract dispute, and not the political dispute, that the arbitrator will resolve, and on which the courts are asked to rule.

The language of the Norris–La Guardia Act does not except labor disputes having their genesis in political protests. Nor is there any basis in the statutory language for the argument that the Act requires that *each* dispute relevant to the case be a labor dispute. The Act merely requires that the case involve "any" labor dispute. Therefore, the plain terms of Section 4(a) and Section 13 of the Norris–La Guardia Act deprive the federal courts of the power to enjoin the Union's work stoppage in this Section 301 action, without regard to whether the Union also has a nonlabor dispute with another entity.

The conclusion that this case involves a labor dispute within the meaning of the Norris–La Guardia Act comports with this Court's consistent interpretation of that Act. Our decisions have recognized that the term "labor dispute" must not be narrowly construed because the statutory definition itself is extremely broad. . . .

The critical element in determining whether the provisions of the Norris–La Guardia Act apply is whether "the employer-employee relationship [is] the matrix of the controversy." In this case, the Employer and the Union representing its employees are the disputants, and their dispute concerns the interpretation of the labor contract that defines their relationship. Thus, the employer-employee relationship is the matrix of this controversy. . . .

Even in cases where the disputants did not stand in the relationship of employer and employee, this Court had held that the existence of noneconomic motives does not make the Norris–La Guardia Act inapplicable. The Employer's argument that the Union's motivation for engaging in a work stoppage determines whether the Norris–La Guardia Act applies is also contrary to the legislative history of that Act. The Act was enacted in response to federal court intervention on behalf of employers through the use of injunctive powers against unions and other associations of employees. This intervention had caused the federal judiciary to fall into disrepute among large segments of this Nation's population. . . .

Further support for our conclusion that Congress believed that the Norris–La Guardia Act applies to work stoppages instituted for political reasons can be found in the legislative history of the 1947 amendments to the NLRA. That history reveals that Congress rejected a proposal to repeal the Norris–La Guardia Act with respect to one broad category of political strikes. . . .

This case, brought by the Employer to enforce its collective-bargaining agreement with the Union, involves a "labor dispute" within any common-sense meaning of that term. . . .

Case Questions

1. Why was the union refusing to load the cargo bound for the Soviet Union? With whom does the union have a dispute?
2. Does the Norris–La Guardia Act distinguish between politically motivated strikes and other strikes or labor disputes? Is this strike a "labor dispute" within the meaning of the Norris–La Guardia Act? Explain.
3. What was the purpose of the Norris–La Guardia Act? How does the Supreme Court's decision in this case support that purpose?

The Norris–La Guardia Act applied only to federal courts, but a number of states passed similar legislation restricting the issuance of labor injunctions by their courts.

Some exceptions to the Norris–La Guardia restrictions have been recognized. Sections 10(j) and 10(l) of the NLRA authorize the National Labor Relations Board (NLRB) to seek injunctions against unfair labor practices. Section 10(h) of the NLRA provides that Norris–La Guardia does not apply to actions brought under Sections 10(j) and (l) or to actions to enforce NLRB orders in the courts. The Supreme Court upheld this exemption in the case of *Bakery Sales Drivers, Local 33 v. Wagshal* [333 U.S. 437 (1948)]. The ability to initiate or maintain an action for an injunction under Sections 10(j) or (l) is restricted to the NLRB, *Solien v. Misc. Drivers & Helpers Union, Local 610* [440 F.2d 124 (8th Cir. 1971) cert. denied, 403 U.S. 905 (1971), 405 U.S. 996 (1972)].

Another exception to the Norris–La Guardia restrictions has been recognized when a union strikes over an issue that is subject to arbitration. That exception is discussed in Chapter 18.

GENERAL ELECTRIC WORKERS STRIKE OVER HEALTH INSURANCE COSTS

THE WORKING LAW

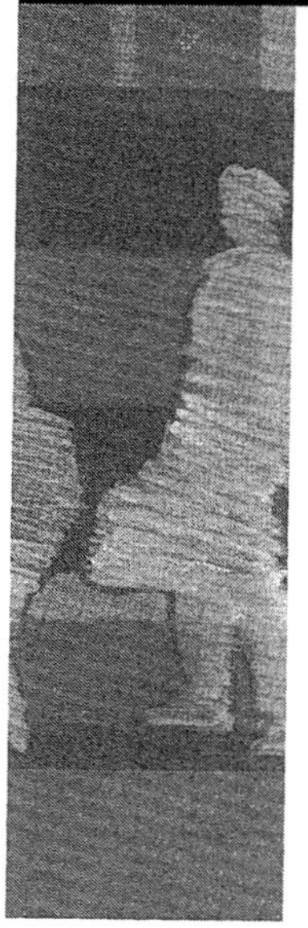

Approximately 17,000 employees of General Electric staged a two-day strike in January 2003 to protest the company's attempts to increase the share of health insurance costs paid by the employees. The striking workers, members of the International Union of Electronic Workers-Communications Workers of America (IUE-CWA) and the United Electrical Radio and Machine Workers of America (UE), went on strike at GE plants in Lynn, Massachusetts, Erie, Pennsylvania, Cleveland, Ohio, Schenectady, New York, and Louisville, Kentucky. The unions argued that GE, which was expected to report annual profits of $16 billion, should not require its workers to pay for the increased cost of health insurance.

The dispute at GE is just one example of a continuing trend where companies faced with rising health-care costs attempt to pass on a share of those costs to their employees. Hershey, the chocolate maker, suffered a forty-four-day strike in 2002 over health-care costs; the strike at Hershey was the first in more than twenty-two years. Unions are emphatic about resisting employer cutbacks in health benefits and in limiting the share of health-care costs borne by employees.

Sources: "17,000 G.E. Workers Strike over Higher Health Costs," *The New York Times*, January 15, 2003, p. 13; "This Month's Strike at General Electric Highlights Tensions between Management and Workers over Healthcare and Retirement Benefits," *Financial Times*, January 30, 2003, p. 11; "GE Unions End Two-Day National Strike," *Reuters News Service*, January 27, 2003.

THE NLRA

The National Labor Relations Act, as mentioned earlier, makes strikes protected activity. The NLRA also contains several provisions that deal with picketing. Section 8(b)(4) outlaws secondary boycotts, and Section 8(b)(7) prohibits recognitional picketing in some situations. In *NLRB v. Drivers, Chauffeurs, Helpers Local 639* [362 U.S. 274 (1960)], the Supreme Court held that the NLRB may not regulate peaceful picketing that does not run afoul of Section 8(b)(4) or Section 8(b)(7). Section 8(b)(1)(A) may be used to prohibit union violence on the picket line, but it does not extend to peaceful picketing. As a result, NLRB regulation of picketing under the NLRA is limited to specific situations such as recognition picketing or secondary picketing.

State Regulation of Picketing

Although the NLRB role in regulating picketing is limited, the states enjoy a major role in the legal regulation of picketing. *Thornhill v. Alabama,* mentioned earlier, prohibited the states from banning all picketing, including peaceful picketing. In *International Brotherhood of Teamsters, Local 695 v. Vogt, Inc.* [354 U.S. 284 (1957)], the Supreme Court held that the states may regulate picketing when it conflicts with valid state interests. The state interest in protecting the safety of its citizens and enforcing the criminal law justifies state regulation of violent picketing. State courts may issue injunctions against acts of violence by strikers, but an outright ban on all picketing because of violence can be justified only when "the fear generated by past violence would survive even though future picketing might be wholly peaceful" according to the Supreme Court in *Milk Wagon Drivers, Local 753 v. Meadowmoor Dairies, Inc.* [312 U.S. 287 (1941)].

State courts may also issue injunctions against mass picketing—picketing in which pickets march so closely together that they block access to the plant—even though it is peaceful. See *Westinghouse Electric Co. v. U.E., Local 410* [139 N.J. Eq. 97 (1946)]. Picketing intended to force an employer to join a conspiracy in violation of state antitrust laws may be enjoined by a state court, *Giboney v. Empire Storage & Ice Co.* [336 U.S. 490 (1949)]. State courts may also enjoin the use of language by pickets that constitutes fraud, misrepresentation, libel, or inciting a breach of the peace, *Linn v. United Plant Guard Workers Local 114* [383 U.S. 53 (1966)].

All of these cases involved picketing activity on public property. Can trespass laws be used to prohibit peaceful picketing on private property? That is the question addressed by the following case.

Hudgens v. NLRB

424 U.S. 507 (1976)

Stewart, J.

The petitioner, Scott Hudgens, is the owner of the North DeKalb Shopping Center, located in suburban Atlanta, Ga. The center consists of a single large building with an enclosed mall. Surrounding the building is a parking area which can accommodate 2,640 automobiles. The shopping center houses 60 retail stores leased to various business. One of the lessees is the Butler Shoe Co. Most of the stores, including Butler's, can be entered only from the interior mall.

In January 1971, warehouse employees of the Butler Shoe Co. went on strike to protest the company's failure to agree to demands made by their union in contract negotiations. The strikers decided to picket not only Butler's warehouse but its nine retail stores in the Atlanta area as well, including the store in the North DeKalb Shopping Center. On January 22, 1971, four of the striking warehouse employees entered the center's enclosed mall carrying placards which read: "Butler Shoe Warehouse on Strike, AFL-CIO, Local 315." The general manager of the shopping center informed the employees that they could not picket within the mall or on the parking lot and threatened them with arrest if they did not leave. The employees departed but returned a short time later and began picketing in an area of the mall immediately adjacent to the entrances of the Butler store. After the picketing had continued for approximately 30 minutes, the shopping center manager again informed the pickets that if they did not leave they would be arrested for trespassing. The pickets departed.

The union subsequently filed with the Board an unfair labor practice charge against Hudgens, alleging interference with rights protected by Section 7 of the Act. Relying on this Court's decision in *Food Employees v. Logan Valley Plaza,* the Board entered a cease-and-desist order against Hudgens, reasoning that because the warehouse employees enjoyed a First Amendment right to picket on the shopping center property, the owner's threat of arrest violated Section 8(a)(1) of the Act. Hudgens filed a petition for review in the Court of Appeals for the Fifth Circuit. Soon thereafter this Court decided *Lloyd Corp. v. Tanner,* and *Central Hardware Co. v. NLRB,* and the Court of Appeals remanded the case to the Board for reconsideration in light of those two decisions.

The Board, in turn, remanded to an Administrative Law Judge, who made findings of fact, recommendations, and conclusions to the effect that Hudgens had committed an unfair labor practice by excluding the pickets. This result was ostensibly reached under the statutory criteria set forth in *NLRB v. Babcock & Wilcox Co.*, a case which held that union organizers who seek to solicit for union membership may intrude on an employer's private property if no alternative means exist for communicating with the employees. But the Administrative Law Judge's opinion also relied on the Court's constitutional decision in *Logan Valley* for a "realistic view of the facts." The Board agreed with the findings and recommendations of the Administrative Law Judge, but departed somewhat from his reasoning. It concluded that the pickets were within the scope of Hudgens' invitation to members of the public to do business at the shopping center, and that it was, therefore, immaterial whether or not there existed an alternative means of communicating with the customers and employees of the Butler store.

Hudgens again petitioned for review in the Court of Appeals for the Fifth Circuit, and there the Board changed its tack and urged that the case was controlled not by *Babcock & Wilcox,* but by *Republic Aviation Corp. v. NLRB,* a case which held that an employer commits an unfair labor practice if he enforces a no-solicitation rule against employees on his premises who are also union organizers, unless he can prove that the rule is necessitated by special circumstances. The Court of Appeals enforced the Board's cease-and-desist order but on the basis of yet another theory. While acknowledging that the source of the pickets' rights was Section 7 of the Act, the Court of Appeals held that the competing constitutional and property right considerations discussed in *Lloyd Corp. v. Tanner,* "burde[n] the General Counsel with the duty to prove that other locations less intrusive upon Hudgens' property rights than picketing inside the mall were either unavailable or ineffective," and that the Board's General Counsel had met that burden in this case.

In this Court the petitioner Hudgens continues to urge that *Babcock & Wilcox Co.* is the controlling precedent, and that under the criteria of that case the judgment of the Court of Appeals should be reversed. The respondent union agrees that a statutory standard governs, but insists that, since the Section 7 activity here was not organizational as in *Babcock* but picketing in support of a lawful economic strike, an appropriate accommodation of the competing interests must lead to an affirmance of the Court of Appeals' judgment. The respondent Board now contends that the conflict between employee picketing rights and employer property rights in a case like this musts be measured in accord with the commands of the First Amendment, pursuant to the Board's asserted understanding of *Lloyd Corp. v. Tanner,* and that the judgment of the Court of Appeals should be affirmed on the basis of that standard.

As the above recital discloses, the history of this litigation has been a history of shifting positions on the part of the litigants, the Board, and the Court of Appeals. It has been a history, in short, of considerable confusion, engendered at least in part by decisions of this Court that intervened during the course of the litigation. In the present posture of the case the most basic question is whether the respective rights and liabilities of the parties are to be decided under the criteria of the National Labor Relations Act alone, under a First

Amendment standard, or under some combination of the two. It is to that question, accordingly, that we now turn.

It is, of course, a commonplace that the constitutional guarantee of free speech is a guarantee only against abridgment by government, federal or state. . . . [T]he rights and liabilities of the parties in this case are dependent exclusively upon the National Labor Relations Act. Under the Act the task of the Board, subject to review by the courts, is to resolve conflicts between Section 7 rights and private property rights, "and to seek a proper accommodation between the two." What is "a proper accommodation" in any situation may largely depend upon the content and the context of the Section 7 rights being asserted. The task of the Board and the reviewing courts under the Act, therefore, stands in conspicuous contrast to the duty of a court in applying the standards of the First Amendment, which requires "above all else" that expression must not be restricted by government "because of its message, its ideas, its subject matter, or its content."

In the *Central Hardware* case, and earlier in the case of *NLRB v. Babcock & Wilcox Co.*, the Court considered the nature of the Board's task in this area under the Act. Accommodation between employees' Section 7 rights and employers' property rights, the Court said in *Babcock & Wilcox*, "must be obtained with as little destruction of one as is consistent with the maintenance of the other."

Both *Central Hardware* and *Babcock & Wilcox* involved organizational activity carried on by nonemployees on the employers' property. The context of the Section 7 activity in the present case was different in several respects which may or may not be relevant in striking the proper balance. First, it involved lawful economic strike activity rather than organizational activity. Second, the Section 7 activity here was carried on by Butler's employees (albeit not employees of its shopping center store), not by outsiders. Third, the property interests impinged upon in this case were not those of the employer against whom the Section 7 activity was directed, but of another.

The *Babcock & Wilcox* opinion established the basic objective under the Act: accommodation of Section 7 rights and private property rights "with as little destruction of one as is consistent with the maintenance of the other." The locus of that accommodation, however, may fall at differing points along the spectrum depending on the nature and strength of the respective Section 7 rights and private property rights asserted in any given context. In each generic situation, the primary responsibility for making this accommodation must rest with the Board in the first instance. . . .

For the reasons stated in this opinion, the judgment is vacated and the case is remanded to the Court of Appeals with directions to remand to the National Labor Relations Board, so that the case may be there considered under the statutory criteria of the National Labor Relations Act alone.

It is so ordered.

Case Questions

1. With whom does the union have the dispute? Where is the union picketing? Who seeks to prevent the union from picketing there? What is the purpose of the union's picketing there?
2. According to the *Babcock & Wilcox* decision (see Chapter 15), what factors should the court consider in determining whether a union can picket on private property?
3. Are the picketers employees of Butler Shoe Co.? How does their picketing affect the employer's property rights? Explain.

PICKETING UNDER THE NLRA

As has been noted, Sections 8(b)(4) and 8(b)(7) of the NLRA prohibit certain kinds of picketing. Peaceful picketing is protected activity under the NLRA. However, violent picketing and mass picketing, as well as threatening conduct by the pickets, are not protected under Section 7. Employees who engage in such conduct may be disciplined or discharged by the employer and may also be subject to injunctions, criminal charges, and civil tort suits.

Section 8(b)(4) deals with secondary boycotts—certain union pressure tactics aimed at employers that are not involved in a labor dispute with the union. Section 8(b)(7) regulates picketing by unions for organizational or recognitional purposes.

Section 8(b)(7): Recognitional and Organizational Picketing

Section 8(b)(7) was added to the NLRA by the 1959 Landrum-Griffin Act. It prohibits recognitional picketing by an uncertified union in certain situations. Section 8(b)(7) contains the following provisions:

> [It is an unfair practice for a labor organization] (7) to picket or cause to be picketed, or threaten to picket or cause to be picketed, any employer where an object thereof is forcing or requiring an employer to recognize or bargain with a labor organization as the representative of his employees, or forcing or requiring the employees of an employer to accept or select such labor organization as their collective-bargaining representative, unless such labor organization is currently certified as the representative of such employees:
>
> (A) where the employer has lawfully recognized in accordance with this Act any other labor organization and a question concerning representation may not appropriately be raised under Section 9(c) of this Act,
>
> (B) where within the preceding twelve months a valid election under Section 9(c) of this Act has been conducted, or
>
> (C) where such picketing has been conducted without a petition under Section 9(c) being filed within a reasonable period of time not to exceed thirty days from the commencement of such picketing: Provided, That when such a petition has been filed the Board shall forthwith, without regard to the provisions of Section 9(c)(1) or the absence of a showing of a substantial interest on the part of the labor organization, direct an election in such unit as the Board finds to be appropriate and shall certify the results thereof: Provided further, That nothing in this subparagraph (C) shall be construed to prohibit any picketing or other publicity for the purpose of truthfully advising the public (including consumers) that an employer does not employ members of, or have a contract with, a labor organization, unless an effect of such picketing is to induce any individual employed by any other person in the course of his employment, not to pick up, deliver or transport any goods or not to perform any services.
>
> Nothing in this paragraph (7) shall be construed to permit any act which would otherwise be an unfair labor practice under this Section 8(b).

See **http://www4.law.cornell.edu/uscode/29/522.html** *about extortionate picketing.*

The interpretation of Section 8(b)(7) and its application to recognitional picketing are the subjects of the following case.

SMITLEY V. NLRB

327 F.2d 351 (U.S. Court of Appeals, 9th Cir. 1964)

[After the NLRB dismissed a complaint that the union had violated Section 8(b)(7)(C), the company sought judicial review of the board's decision.]

Duniway, J.

The findings of the Board as to the facts are not attacked. It found, in substance, that the unions picketed the cafeteria for more than thirty days before filing a representation petition under Section 9(c) of the act, that an object of the picketing was to secure recognition, that the purpose of the picketing was truthfully to advise the public that petitioners employed nonunion employees or had no contract with the unions, and that the picketing did not have the effect of inducing any stoppage of deliveries or services to the cafeteria by employees of any other employer. . . . We conclude that the views of the Board, as stated after its second consideration of the matter, are correct, and that the statute has not been violated. . . .

It will be noted that Subdivision (7) of Subsection (b), Section 8, starts with the general prohibition of picketing "where an object thereof is forcing or requiring an employer to recognize or bargain with a labor organization" (this is often called recognitional picketing) ". . . or forcing or requiring the employees of an employer to accept or select such labor organization. . . ." (this is often called organizational picketing), ". . . unless such labor organization is currently certified as the representative of such employees: . . ." This is followed by three subparagraphs, (A), (B), and (C). Each begins with the same word, "where." (A) deals with the situation "where" the employer has lawfully recognized another labor organization and a question of representation cannot be raised under Section 9(c). (B) refers to the situation "where," within the preceding 12 months, a valid election under Section 9(c) has been conducted. (C), with which we are concerned, refers to a situation "where" there has been no petition for an election under Section 9(c) filed within a reasonable period of time, not to exceed thirty days, from the commencement of the picketing. Thus, Section 8(b)(7) does not purport to prohibit all picketing having the named "object" of recognitional or organizational picketing. It limits the prohibition of such picketing to three specific situations.

There are no exceptions or provisos in subparagraphs (A) and (B), which describe two of those situations. There are, however, two provisos in subparagraph (C). The first sets up a special procedure for an expedited election under Section 9(c). The second is one with which we are concerned. It is an exception to the prohibition of "such picketing," i.e., recognitional or organizational picketing, being a proviso to a prohibition of such picketing "where" certain conditions exist. . . .

. . . We think that, in substance, the effect of the second proviso to subparagraph (C) is to allow recognitional or organizational picketing to continue if it meets two important restrictions: (1) it must be addressed to the public and be truthful and (2) it must not induce other unions to stop deliveries or services. The picketing here met those criteria. . . .

[The court affirmed the board's dismissal of the complaint.]

Case Questions

1. Why was the union picketing the cafeteria? How long had it been picketing?
2. What kind of picketing is allowed under the proviso to Section 8(b)(7)(C)? What two conditions must be met for picketing to fall under the proviso's protection?
3. Does the picketing in this case fall under the proviso? Explain.

If a union pickets in violation of Section 8(b)(7)(C), the employer may request that the NLRB hold an expedited election. The NLRB will determine the appropriate bargaining unit and hold an election. No showing of interest on the part of the union is necessary. The NLRB will certify the results of the election; if the union is certified, the employer must bargain with it. If the union loses, continued picketing will violate Section 8(b)(7)(B). Why? Section 10(1) requires the board to seek an injunction against the picketing when it issues a complaint for an alleged Section 8(b)(7) violation.

As *Smitley* emphasizes, not all recognitional picketing violates Section 8(b)(7). The proviso in Section 8(b)(7)(C) allows recognitional picketing directed at the public to inform them that the picketed employer does not have a contract with the union. Such picketing for publicity may continue beyond thirty days, unless it causes other employees to refuse to work.

Picketing to protest substandard wages paid by an employer, as long as the union does not have a recognitional object, is not subject to Section 8(b)(7). Such picketing may continue indefinitely and is not unlawful, even if it has the effect of disrupting deliveries to the employer, according to *Houston Building & Con-*

struction Trades Council [136 NLRB 321 (1962)]. Similarly, picketing to protest unfair practices by the employer, when there is no recognitional objective, is not prohibited according to *UAW Local 259* [133 NLRB 1468 (1961)].

Section 8(b)(4): Secondary Boycotts

Section 8(b)(4), which deals with secondary boycotts, is one of the most complex provisions of the NLRA. Section 8(b)(4) contains the following provisions:

> [It is an unfair practice for a labor organization] (4) (i) to engage in, or to induce or encourage any individual employed by any person engaged in commerce or in an industry affecting commerce to engage in, a strike or refusal in the course of his employment to use, manufacture, process, transport, or otherwise handle or work on any goods, articles, materials, or commodities or to perform any services; or (ii) to threaten, coerce, or restrain any person engaged in commerce or in an industry affecting commerce, where in either case an object thereof is:
>
> (A) forcing or requiring any employer or self-employed person to join any labor or employer organization to enter into any agreement which is prohibited by Section 8(e);
>
> (B) forcing or requiring any person to cease using, selling, handling, transporting, or otherwise dealing in the products of any other producer, processor, or manufacturer, or to cease doing business with any other person, or forcing or requiring any other employer to recognize or bargain with a labor organization as the representative of his employees unless such labor organization has been certified as the representative of such employees under the provisions of Section 9: Provided, That nothing contained in this clause (B) shall be construed to make unlawful, where not otherwise unlawful, any primary strike or primary picketing;
>
> (C) forcing or requiring any employer to recognize or bargain with a particular labor organization as the representative of his employees if another labor organization has been certified as the representative of such employees under the provisions of Section 9;
>
> (D) forcing or requiring any employer to assign particular work to employees in a particular labor organization or in a particular trade, craft, or class rather than to employees in another labor organization or in another trade, craft, or class, unless such employer is failing to conform to an order or certification of the Board determining the bargaining representative for employees performing such work:
>
> Provided, That nothing contained in this Subsection (b) shall be construed to make unlawful a refusal by any person to enter upon the premises of any employer (other than his own employer), if the employees of such employer are engaged in a strike ratified or approved by a representative of such employees whom such employer is required under this Act: Provided further, That for the purposes of this paragraph (4) only, nothing contained in such paragraph shall be construed to prohibit publicity, other than picketing, for the purpose of truthfully advising the public, including consumers and members of a labor organization, that a product or products are produced by an employer with whom the labor organization has a primary dispute and are distributed by another employer, as long as such publicity does not have an effect of inducing any individual employed by any person other than the primary employer in the course of his employment to refuse to pick up, deliver, or transport any goods, or not to perform any services, at the establishment of the employer engaged in such distributions. . . .

When considering Section 8(b)(4), the courts and the board generally consider the intention behind the provisions rather than its literal wording. The intention is to protect employers who are not involved in a dispute with a union from pressure by that union. For example, if the union representing the workers of a toy manufacturing company goes on strike, it is free to picket the manufacturer (the primary employer). But if the union pickets the premises of a wholesaler who distributes the toys of the primary employer, such picketing may be secondary and prohibited by Section 8(b)(4)(B). Whether the picketing is prohibited depends on whether the union's picketing has the objective of trying to force the wholesaler to cease doing business with the manufacturer.

Most secondary picketing situations, however, are more complicated than this simple example. For instance, if the primary employer's location of business is mobile, such as a cement-mix delivery truck, is the union allowed to picket a construction site where the cement truck is making a delivery? What if the union has a dispute with a subcontractor on a construction site? Can it picket the entire construction site?

Primary picketing by a union is against an employer with which it has a dispute. Section 8(b)(4) does not prohibit such picketing, even though it is intended to persuade customers to cease doing business with the primary employer. It is important, therefore, to identify which employer is the primary employer—the employer with whom the union has the dispute. It is helpful to consider three questions when confronting a potential secondary picketing situation. The first is: With whom does the union have the dispute? This question identifies the primary employer. Question two is: Is the union picketing at the primary employer's premises or at the site of a neutral employer? Question three is: What is the object of the union's picketing? If the union is picketing at a secondary employer to force that employer to cease doing business with the primary employer, then it is illegal. But if the picketing is intended only to inform the public that the secondary employer handles the primary product, it is legal. The objective of the picketing is the key to its legality: Does the picketing have an objective prohibited by Section 8(b)(4)?

Ambulatory Situs Picketing

Ambulatory Situs Picketing
Union picketing that follows the primary employer's mobile business.

When the primary employer's business location is mobile, picketing by a union following that mobile location is called **ambulatory situs picketing.** The following board decision sets out the conditions under which the union may engage in ambulatory situs picketing.

SAILORS' UNION OF THE PACIFIC AND MOORE DRY DOCK CO.

92 NLRB 547 (NLRB, 1950)

[Samsoc, a shipping company, contracted with Kaiser Gypsum to ship gypsum from Mexico in the ship *Phopho.* Samsoc replaced the crew of the ship with a foreign crew. The union demanded bargaining rights for the ship; Samsoc refused. The ship was in dry dock being outfitted for the voyage, and the foreign crew was on board for training. The union posted pickets at the entrances to the dry dock; the dry-dock workers refused to work on the ship but did perform other work. The dry-dock company filed an unfair practice charge with the NLRB.]

Picketing at the premises of a primary employer is traditionally recognized as primary action, even though it is "necessarily designed to induce and encourage third persons to cease doing business with the picketed employer. . . ."

Hence, if Samsoc, the owner of the *S.S. Phopho,* had had a dock of its own in California to which the *Phopho* had been tied up while undergoing conversion by Moore Dry Dock employees, picketing by the Respondent at the dock site would unquestionably have constituted *primary* action even though the Respondent might have expected that the picketing would be more effective in persuading Moore employees not to work on the ship than to persuade the seamen aboard the *Phopho* to quit that vessel. The difficulty in the present case arises therefore, not because of any difference in picketing objectives, but from the fact that the *Phopho* was not tied up at its own dock, but at that of Moore, while the picketing was going on in front of the Moore premises.

In the usual case, the *situs* of a labor dispute is the premises of the primary employer. Picketing of the premises is also picketing of the *situs,* . . . But in some cases the situs of the dispute may not be limited to a fixed location; it may be ambulatory. Thus, in the *Schultz* case, a majority of the Board held that the truck upon which a truck driver worked was the situs of a labor dispute between him and the owner of the truck. Similarly, we hold in the present case that, as the *Phopho* was the place of employment of the seamen, it was the *situs* of the dispute between Samsoc and the Respondent over working conditions aboard the vessel.

When the *situs* is ambulatory, it may come to rest temporarily at the premises of another employer. The perplexing question is: Does the right to picket follow the *situs* while it is stationed at the premises of a secondary employer, when the only way to picket that *situs* is in front of the secondary employer's premises? . . . Essentially the problem is one of balancing the right of a union to picket at the site of its dispute as against the right of a secondary employer to be free from picketing in a controversy in which it is not directly involved.

When a secondary employer is harboring the *situs* of a dispute between a union and a primary employer, the right of neither the union to picket nor of the secondary employer to be free from picketing can be absolute. The enmeshing of premises and *situs* qualifies both rights. In the kind of situation that exists in this case, we believe that picketing of the premises of a secondary employer is primary if it meets the following conditions: (a) The picketing is strictly limited to times when the *situs* of dispute is located on the secondary employer's premises; (b) at the time of the picketing the primary employer is engaged in its normal business at the *situs;* (c) the picketing is limited to places reasonably close to the location of the *situs;* (d) the picketing discloses clearly that the dispute is with the primary employer. All these conditions were met in the present case.

(a) During the entire period of the picketing the *Phopho* was tied up at a dock in the Moore shipyard.

(b) Under its contract with Samsoc, Moore agreed to permit the former to put a crew on board the *Phopho* for training purposes during the last two weeks before the vessel's delivery to Samsoc. . . . The various members of the crew commenced work as soon as they reported aboard the *Phopho.* Those in the deck compartment did painting and cleaning up, those in the steward's department, cooking and cleaning up; and those in the engine department, oiling and cleaning up. The crew were thus getting the ship ready for sea. They were on board to serve the purposes of Samsoc, the *Phopho's* owners, and not Moore. The normal business of a ship does not only begin with its departure on a scheduled voyage. The multitudinous steps of preparation, including hiring and training a crew and putting stores aboard, are as much a part of the normal business of a ship as the voyage itself. We find, therefore, that the *Phopho* was engaged in its normal business.

(c) Before placing its pickets outside the entrance to the Moore shipyard, the Respondent Union asked, but was refused, permission to place its pickets at the dock where the *Phopho* was tied up. The Respondent, therefore, posted its pickets at the yard entrance which, as the parties stipulated, was as close to the *Phopho* as they could get under the circumstances.

(d) Finally, by its picketing and other conduct the Respondent was scrupulously careful to indicate that its dispute was solely with the primary employer, the owners of the *Phopho.* Thus the signs carried by the pickets said only that the *Phopho* was unfair to the Respondent. The *Phopho* and not Moore was declared "hot." Similarly, in asking co-operation of other unions, the Respondent clearly revealed that its dispute was with the *Phopho*. Finally, Moore's own witnesses admitted that no attempt was made to interfere with other work in progress in the Moore yard. . . .

We are only holding that, if a shipyard permits the owner of a vessel to use its dock for the purpose of readying and training a crew and putting stores aboard a ship, a union representing seamen may then within the careful limitations laid down in this decision, lawfully picket the front of the shipyard premises to advertise its dispute with the shipowner. . . .

[The complaint was dismissed.]

Case Questions

1. With whom did the union have the dispute? Where did the union seek to picket? Why?
2. Why did the NLRB characterize the picketing as primary? Was the primary employer engaged in its normal operations? Explain.
3. What four conditions does the NLRB establish to ensure that ambulatory situs picketing does not disrupt the secondary employer's operations? How did those conditions apply to the facts of this case?

Reserved Gate Picketing: Secondary Employees at the Primary Site

The *Moore Dry Dock* case deals with the legality of picketing at a secondary, or neutral, location. What about the legality of picketing that affects secondary employees at a primary site? The following case, also called the *General Electric* case, deals with that situation.

Local 761, International Union of Electrical Radio & Machine Workers [General Electric] v. NLRB

366 U.S. 667 (1961)

Frankfurter, J.

General Electric Corporation operates a plant outside of Louisville, Kentucky, where it manufactures washers, dryers, and other electrical household appliances. The square-shaped, thousand-acre, unfenced plant is known as Appliance Park. A large drainage ditch makes ingress and egress impossible except over five roadways across culverts, designated as gates.

Since 1954, General Electric sought to confine the employees of independent contractors, described hereafter, who work on the premises of the Park, to the use of Gate 3-A and confine its use to them. The undisputed reason for doing so was to insulate General Electric employees from the frequent labor disputes in which the contractors were involved. Gate 3-A is 550 feet away from the nearest entrance available for General Electric employees, suppliers, and deliverymen. Although anyone can pass the gate without challenge, the roadway leads to a guardhouse where identification must be presented. Vehicle stickers of various shapes and colors enable a guard to check on sight whether a vehicle is authorized to use Gate 3-A. Since January 1958, a prominent sign has been posted at the gate which states: *"Gate 3-A for Employees of Contractors Only—G.E. Employees Use Other Gates."* On rare occasions, it appears, a General Electric employee was allowed to pass the guardhouse, but such occurrence was in violation of company instructions. There was no proof of any unauthorized attempts to pass the gate during the strike in question.

The independent contractors are utilized for a great variety of tasks on the Appliance Park premises. Some do construction work on new buildings; some install and repair ventilating and heating equipment; some engage in retooling and rearranging operations necessary to the manufacture of new models; others do "general maintenance work." . . .

The Union, . . . here, is the certified bargaining representative for the production and maintenance workers who constitute approximately 7,600 of the 10,500 employees of General Electric at Appliance Park. On July 27, 1958, the Union called a strike [against GE]. . . . Picketing occurred at all the gates, including Gate 3-A, and continued until August 9 when an injunction was issued by a Federal District Court. The signs carried by the pickets at all gates read: *"Local 761 on Strike G.E. Unfair."* Because of the picketing, almost all of the employees of independent contractors refused to enter the company premises.

Neither the legality of the strike or of the picketing at any of the gates except 3-A nor the peaceful nature of the picketing is in dispute. The sole claim is that the picketing before the gate exclusively used by employees of independent contractors was conduct proscribed by 8(b)(4)[(B)].

The Trial Examiner recommended that the Board dismiss the complaint. He concluded that the limitations on picketing which the Board had prescribed in so-called "common situs" cases were not applicable to the situation before him, in that the picketing at Gate 3-A represented traditional primary action which necessarily had a secondary effect of inconveniencing those who did business with the struck employer. . . .

The Board rejected the Trial Examiner's conclusion. It held that, since only the employees of the independent contractors were allowed to use Gate 3-A, the Union's object in picketing there was "to enmesh these employees of the neutral employers in its dispute with the Company," thereby constituting a violation of Section 8(b)(4)[(B)] because the independent employees were encouraged to engage in a concerted refusal to work "with an object of forcing the independent contractors to cease doing business with the Company."

The Court of Appeals for the District of Columbia granted enforcement of the Board's order. . . . [I]t concluded that the Board was correct in finding that the objective of the Gate 3-A picketing was to encourage the independent-contractor employees to engage in a concerted refusal to perform services for their employers in order to bring pressure on General Electric. Since the incidence of the problem involved in this case is extensive and the treatment it has received calls for clarification, we brought the case here.

Section 8(b)(4)[(B)] of the National Labor Relations Act provided that it shall be an unfair labor practice for a labor organization

> to engage in, or to induce or encourage the employees of any employer to engage in, a strike or a concerted refusal in the course of their employment to use, manufacture, process, transport, or otherwise handle or work on any goods, articles, materials, or commodities or to perform any services, where an object thereof is: [(B)] forcing or requiring . . . any employer or other person . . . to cease doing business with any other person. . . .

This provision could not be literally construed; otherwise it would ban most strikes historically considered to be lawful, so-called primary activity ". . . Congress did not seek, by Section 8(b)(4), to interfere with the ordinary strike. . . ." The impact of the section was directed toward what is known as the secondary boycott whose "sanctions bear, not upon the employer who alone is a party to the dispute, but upon some third party who has no concern in it." Thus the section "left a striking labor organization free to use persuasion, including picketing, not only on the primary employer and his employees but on numerous others. Among these were secondary employers who were customers or suppliers of the primary employer and persons dealing with them . . . and even employees of secondary employers so long as the labor organization did not . . . 'induce or encourage the employees of any employer to engage in a strike or a concerted refusal in the course of their employment'. . . ."

But not all so-called secondary boycotts were outlawed in Section 8(b)(4)[(B)]. "The section does not speak generally of secondary boycotts. It describes and condemns specific union conduct directed to specific objectives. . . . Employees must be induced; they must be induced to engage in a strike or concerted refusal; an object must be to force or require their employer or another person to cease doing business with a third person. Thus, much that might argumentatively be found to fall within the broad and somewhat vague concept of secondary boycott is not in terms prohibited."

Important as is the distinction between legitimate "primary activity" and banned "secondary activity," it does not present a glaringly bright line. The objectives of any picketing include a desire to influence others from withholding from the employer their services or trade. . . . But picketing which induces secondary employees to respect a picket line is not the equivalent of picketing which has an object of inducing those employees to engage in concerted conduct against their employer in order to force him to refuse to deal with the struck employer.

. . . the question is whether the Board may apply the *Dry Dock* criteria so as to make unlawful picketing at a gate utilized exclusively by employees of independent contractors who work on the struck employer's premises. . . . The key to the problem is found in the type of work that is being performed by those who use the separate gate. It is significant that the Board has since applied its rationale, first stated in the present case, only to situations where the independent workers were performing tasks unconnected to the normal operations of the struck employer—usually construction work on his buildings. In such situations, the indicated limitations on picketing activity respect the balance of competing interests that Congress has required the Board to enforce. On the other hand, if a separate gate were devised for regular plant deliveries, the barring of picketing at that location would make a clear invasion on traditional primary activity of appealing to neutral employees whose tasks aid the employer's everyday operations. The 1959 Amendments to the National Labor Relations Act, which removed the word "concerted" from the boycott provisions, included a proviso that "nothing contained in this clause (b) shall be construed to make unlawful, where not otherwise unlawful, any primary strike or primary picketing. . . ."

In a case similar to the one now before us, the Court of Appeals of the Second Circuit sustained the Board in its application of Section 8(b)(4)(A) to a separate-gate situation. "There must be a separate gate marked and set apart from other gates; the work done by the men who use the gate must be unrelated to the normal operations of the employer and the work must be of a kind that would not, if done when the plant were engaged in its regular operations, necessitate curtailing those operations." These seem to us controlling considerations.

The foregoing course of reasoning would require that the judgment below sustaining the Board's order be affirmed but for one consideration, even though this consideration may turn out not to affect the result . . . the Board and the Court of Appeals . . . did not take into account that if Gate 3-A was in fact used by employees of independent contractors who performed conventional maintenance work necessary to the normal operations of General Electric, the use of the gate would have been a mingled one outside the bar of Section 8(b)(4)[(B)]. In short, such mixed use of this portion of the struck employer's premises would not bar picketing rights of the striking employees. While the record shows some such mingled use, it sheds no light on its extent. It may well turn out to be that the instances of these maintenance tasks were so insubstantial as to be treated by the Board as de minimis. We cannot here guess at the quantitative aspect of this problem. It calls for Board determination. For determination of the questions thus raised, the case must be remanded by the Court of Appeals to the Board.

Reversed.

Case Questions

1. With whom does the union have a dispute here? Why is the union picketing at the GE plant?
2. Why is the union's picketing of all gates except Gate 3-A primary? Why does this case focus on the legality of the picketing at Gate 3-A?
3. What test does the Court use to determine whether the union's picketing at Gate 3-A is primary or secondary? What is "mixed" or "mingled" use of the gate? Explain how that relates to whether picketing of the gate is primary or secondary.

Common Situs Picketing

The *General Electric* case made the nature of the work performed by the secondary employees at the primary site the key to whether the union may target secondary employees with picketing. In the construction industry, subcontractors and the general contractor are all working on the same project: erecting a building. Does this mean a union that has a dispute with the general contractor may picket

Common Situs Picketing
Union picketing of an entire construction site.

the entire construction site (known as **common situs picketing**)? Should the NLRB apply the *General Electric* separate gate approach to picketing at construction sites, or does the legality of common situs picketing require a different approach? In *Building and Construction Trades Council of New Orleans, AFL-CIO and Markwell and Hartz, Inc.* [155 NLRB 319 (1965)], the NLRB held that the *Moore Dry Dock* approach applied to common situs picketing. The following case illustrates the application of the *Moore Dry Dock* doctrine to a case of common situs picketing.

International Union of Operating Engineers, Local 150, AFL-CIO v. NLRB

47 F.3d 218 (7th Cir. 1995)

Coffin, Circuit Judge

Local 150 of the International Union of Operating Engineers, AFL-CIO, seeks review of a decision by the National Labor Relations Board (Board) that the Union violated the secondary boycott provisions of the National Labor Relations Act (NLRA), Section 8(b)(4)(i), (ii)(B). The Board, which cross-petitions for enforcement of its order, found that the Union . . . picketed neutral gates at a multi-employer workplace in an effort to force the uninvolved employers to pressure the struck employer into settling the dispute more quickly. . . .

LTV Steel operates a large steel making plant in East Chicago, Indiana. Located on the grounds of the 1,150-acre facility are two companies that serve as subcontractors to LTV for the processing and disposal of slag, a by-product of the steelmaking process. The strike at issue in this case was aimed at one of those companies, Edward C. Levy Co. (Levy), whose collective bargaining agreement with Local 150 expired at the end of September 1991. Employees of the other slag processing firm, the Heckett Division of Harsco Corp. (Heckett), also are represented by Local 150. . . .

The LTV plant has three entrances, designated as the East Bridge gate, the West Bridge gate, and the Burma Road gate. The East and West Bridge gates are the entrances normally used for access to the facility by employees and vendors. The ALJ found that the Burma Road entrance is used only in strike situations, as part of a so-called "reserved gate" system. Such a system is common where employers share a site but only one is experiencing labor strife. One entrance is "reserved" for the exclusive use of traffic related to the struck firm, and all picketing must be directed there. This system is designed to keep neutral parties out of the dispute, and avoids the need for them to cross picket lines.

The strike against Levy began on October 12, 1991, and ended on October 18. On the first day of the strike, LTV posted signs at each of the three gates. All of them identified the East and West Bridge gates as "neutral" gates reserved for the use of LTV Steel and all persons having business with the company, except for anyone connected with Levy. The signs directed Levy's traffic to the Burma Road gate, "which has been reserved solely and exclusively for Levy's employees, their suppliers, their delivery men, their subcontractors and all others having business with Levy." LTV expected the Union to picket only at this gate.

It is undisputed that no one from LTV gave written notice, or any other formal notification, of the gate arrangement to the Union, which established picket lines on public property near each of the three gates. The signs posted by LTV at the East and West Bridge gates could be seen by the picketers, but the words probably were not visible. Two company officials testified, however, that they told picketers at both the East and West Bridge locations on October 12 that a Levy gate had been set up at the Burma Road entrance and that the picketing should be confined to that location. An LTV security officer also testified that he informed four picketers near the East Bridge gate entrance that they would have to picket at Burma Road.

. . . Burma Road . . . is a distinctly non-road-like path that lies between the Amoco Oil gate and the EJ & E property. A large pole placed there by Amoco usually blocks the entrance to Burma Road from Front Street, but this was removed at LTV's request during the strike. The truck traffic generated by Levy made the location of the road "obvious" as the strike progressed.

Burma Road is central to this case because the Board maintains that, once the Levy reserved gate was established, the Union was legally permitted to picket only at that location. The Union claims that it . . . received no notice of the reserved gate system. . . .

Also of significance is the role of Heckett's employees during the strike. Heckett and Levy are direct competitors and, consequently, there apparently was some concern on the part of the Union about whether LTV would look to Heckett for help during a strike by Levy. Heckett's employees, meanwhile, were concerned about what the Union expected of them if a strike were called against Levy; their contract had a no-strike provision and they feared losing their jobs if they did not report to work. . . . Several Heckett employees testified that they were told either before the strike, or at its outset, that a neutral gate would be set up. On two occasions, however, Union officials at least implicitly urged members to respect picket signs established at their worksite, thereby disdaining the reserved gate system. . . .

About 53 of the 69 Union members employed by Heckett worked during the strike. On October 14, during the strike, the Union filed internal charges against them for "refus[ing] to honor the picket line," in violation of the Union's by-laws.

. . . the Board found that various of the Union's actions constituted unfair labor practices under the NLRA: (1) picketing at neutral gates; (2) distributing pamphlets encouraging employees of neutral employers to stay out of work; (3) bringing internal charges against members employed by a neutral employer; and (4) applying to employees of a neutral employer the Union bylaw barring members from working on a job where a strike has been called.

The Union challenges only the finding that it violated the NLRA by picketing at the East and West Bridge gates. . . .

The question before us, therefore, is whether substantial evidence in the record supports the Board's finding that the Union's picketing ran afoul of the NLRA's secondary boycott provisions. Union conduct violates section 8(b)(4) of the NLRA "if any object of that activity is to exert improper influence on secondary or neutral parties. . . ." Whether the Union was motivated by a secondary objective is a question of fact, and is to be determined through examination of "the totality of [the] union's conduct in [the] given situation."

. . . Because not all union conduct that interferes with uninvolved employers is banned, the distinction between permissible "primary" activity and unlawful "secondary" activity "is often more nice than obvious." This is particularly true where the primary and secondary employers occupy a common work site. As an evidentiary tool for determining the dispositive point—the union's intent—the NLRB has adopted the so-called *Moore Dry Dock* standards. Under these standards, a union's picketing is presumed to be lawful primary activity if (1) it is "strictly limited to times when the situs of the dispute is located on the secondary employer's premises"; (2) "the primary employer is engaged in its normal business at the situs"; (3) it is "limited to places reasonably close to the location of the situs"; and (4) it "discloses clearly that the dispute is with the primary employer."

The third [*Moore Dry Dock*] standard is the one of significance in this case. When an employer implements a valid reserved gate system, and a union continues to picket a gate designated exclusively for neutrals, a violation of the third *Dry Dock* criterion is established because the picketing is not limited to the "location" of the dispute as permissibly confined. This gives rise to a presumption of illegitimate, secondary intent. The question remains, however, "a factual inquiry into the union's actual state of mind under the totality of the circumstances."

. . . Under these standards, we have little difficulty affirming the Board's determination that the Union violated section 8(b)(4) by intentionally enmeshing neutrals in its dispute with Levy. The ALJ's most crucial finding, that the Union knew about the reserved gate system, yet "consciously chose" to ignore it, is amply supported by the record. The evidence recounted by the ALJ showed that Union officials anticipated the establishment of a reserved gate system and had indicated to some Heckett employees that the Union itself was working toward setting up a safe gate. In addition, Union officials knew that Levy was using the Burma Road entrance, and it is undisputed that [the Burma Road] gate was used only during strikes as part of a reserved gate system. Thus, the fact that the Union sent pickets to Burma Road by itself reflects knowledge that a reserved gate system was in place. Moreover, while the wording on the signs posted at the East and West

Bridge gates may not have been visible to picketers and supervising Union officials, they certainly could see that signs had been posted and so must have realized that the anticipated reserved gates had been designated. Indeed, LTV officials testified that they told Union members at both the East and West Bridge gates to move to the Levy gate at Burma Road. . . .

The Union contends that, in the absence of formal notice of a reserved gate system, it may not be penalized for failing to confine its picketing to the Burma Road location. We acknowledge that it would be better if employers gave written or other formal notice of such a system, even when it appears that the Union must have gained actual knowledge through an informal method. In these circumstances, however, we cannot say that the ALJ improperly imposed responsibility on the Union based, among other factors, on its having received sufficient notice of the system. . . . Moreover, misuse of the reserved gate system was not the only evidence of the Union's intent to engage in secondary activity. As the Board found, the Union unlawfully distributed pamphlets to Heckett employees advising them that they had the right not to work "no matter how many gates the employer sets up." In addition, on the first day of the strike, a picketer who identified himself as picket captain, told LTV's labor relations manager that a Union official had directed that all three gates be picketed and that the Union's "intent was to impact not only Levy employees but Heckett employees, iron workers and other employees." This intent also was reflected in statements made by Union official Cisco at a November meeting, in which he suggested that the strike would have been shorter if the Heckett employees had not crossed the picket line. Finally, the fact that the Union brought charges against those employees for crossing the line lends further support to the finding of a secondary objective.

. . . In sum, we believe the ALJ permissibly found that the Union received adequate notice of a validly established reserved gate system, and "chose to ignore it." This conclusion, particularly when taken together with the Union's distribution of leaflets encouraging Heckett employees to honor the picket line, the disciplinary action against the 53 employees who did work, and the statements made by Union representatives, provides more than substantial evidence to support the Board's determination that Local 150's picketing activity was intended to implicate secondary parties and thus was unlawful under section 8(b)(4).

The Union's petition for review is therefore denied, and the Board's cross-application for enforcement of its order is granted.

Case Questions

1. Was the union ever formally notified by LTV about the reserved gate arrangement set up in response to the strike against Levy? Did the court determine that the union was aware of the reserved gate arrangement? Why?
2. What is the relevance of the third *Moore Dry Dock* standard—the requirement that the union picketing be limited to places reasonably close to the situs of the dispute (the operations of the struck employer, Levy)? Where was the situs of Levy's operations in this case?
3. What is the significance of the union's efforts to get Heckett employees to honor the picket line against Levy? What is the significance of the union's efforts to discipline the Heckett employees who crossed the picket line?

Ally Doctrine

Not all union picketing directed against employers other than the primary employer is prohibited. The secondary boycott prohibitions were intended to protect neutral employers from union pressure. If any employer is not neutral—because it is performing the work normally done by the workers of the primary employer, who are now on strike—may the union picket that other employer? That is the issue addressed in the following case.

NLRB v. Business Machine & Office Appliance Mechanics Conference Board, IUE, Local 459 [Royal Typewriter Co.]

228 F.2d 553 (2d Cir. 1955), cert. denied, 351 U.S. 962 (1956)

Lumbard, J.

This case arose out of a labor dispute between the Royal Typewriter Company and the Business Machine and Office Appliance Mechanics Conference Board, Local 459, IUE-CIO, the certified bargaining agent of Royal's typewriter mechanics and other service personnel. The National Labor Relations Board now seeks enforcement of an order directing the Union to cease and desist from certain picketing and to post appropriate notices. . . .

On about March 23, 1954, the Union, being unable to reach agreement with Royal on the terms of a contract, called the Royal service personnel out on strike. The service employees customarily repair typewriters either at Royal's branch offices or at its customers' premises. Royal has several arrangements under which it is obligated to render service to its customers. First, Royal's warranty on each new machine obligates it to provide free inspection and repair for one year. Second, for a fixed periodic fee Royal contracts to service machines not under warranty. Finally, Royal is committed to repairing typewriters rented from it or loaned by it to replace machines undergoing repair. Of course, in addition Royal provides repair service on call by non-contract users.

During the strike Royal differentiated between calls from customers to whom it owed a repair obligation and others. Royal's office personnel were instructed to tell the latter to call some independent repair company listed in the telephone directory. Contract customers, however, were advised to select such an independent from the directory to have the repair made, and to send a receipted invoice to Royal for reimbursement for reasonable repairs within their agreement with Royal. Consequently many of Royal's contract customers had repair services performed by various independent repair companies. In most instances the customer sent Royal the unpaid repair bill and Royal paid the independent company directly. Among the independent companies paid directly by Royal for repairs made for such customers were Typewriter Maintenance and Sales Company and Tytell Typewriter Company. . . .

During May, 1954, the Union picketed four independent typewriter repair companies who had been doing work covered by Royal's contracts pursuant to the arrangement described above. The Board found this picketing unlawful with respect to Typewriter Maintenance and Tytell. Typewriter Maintenance was picketed for about three days and Tytell for several hours on one day. In each instance the picketing, which was peaceful and orderly, took place before entrances used in common by employees, deliverymen and the general public. The signs read substantially as follows (with the appropriate repair company name inserted):

NOTICE TO THE PUBLIC ONLY
EMPLOYEES OF
ROYAL TYPEWRITER COMPANY
ON STRIKE TYTELL TYPEWRITER COMPANY
EMPLOYEES ARE BEING USED AS STRIKEBREAKERS
BUSINESS MACHINE & OFFICE APPLIANCE
MECHANICS UNION, LOCAL 459, IUE-CIO

Both before and after this picketing, which took place in mid-May, Tytell and Typewriter Maintenance did work on Royal accounts and received payment directly from Royal. Royal's records show that Typewriter Maintenance's first voucher was passed for payment by Royal on April 20, 1954, and Tytell's first voucher was passed for payment on May 3, 1954. After these dates each independent serviced various of Royal's customers on numerous occasions and received payment directly from Royal. . . .

On the above facts the Trial Examiner and the Board found that . . . the repair company picketing violated Section 8(b)(4) of the National Labor Relations Act. . . .

We are of the opinion that the Board's finding with respect to the repair company picketing cannot be sustained. The independent repair companies were so allied with Royal that the Union's picketing of their premises was not prohibited by Section 8(b)(4).

We approve the "ally" doctrine which had its origin in a well reasoned opinion by Judge Rifkind in the *Ebasco* case, *Douds v. Architects, Engineers, Chemists & Technicians, Local 231*. Ebasco, a corporation engaged in the business of providing engineering services, had a close business relationship with Project, a firm providing similar services. Ebasco subcontracted some of its work to Project and when it did so Ebasco supervised the work of Project's employees and paid Project for the time spent by Project's employees on Ebasco's work plus a factor for overhead and profit. When Ebasco's employees went on strike, Ebasco transferred a greater percentage of its work to Project, including some jobs that had already been started by Ebasco's employees. When Project refused to heed the Union's requests to stop doing Ebasco's work, the Union picketed Project and induced some of Project's employees to cease work. On these facts Judge Rifkind found that Project was not "doing business" with Ebasco within the meaning of Section 8(b)(4) and that the Union had therefore not committed an unfair labor practice under that Section. He reached this result by looking to the legislative history of the Taft-Hartley Act and to the history of the secondary boycotts which it sought to outlaw. He determined that Project was not a person "wholly unconcerned in the disagreement between an employer and his employees" such as Section 8(b)(4) was designed to protect. . . .

Here there was evidence of only one instance where Royal contacted an independent (Manhattan Typewriter Service, not named in the complaint) to see whether it could handle some of Royal's calls. Apart from that incident there is no evidence that Royal made any arrangement with an independent directly. It is obvious, however, that what the independents did would inevitably tend to break the strike. As Judge Rifkind pointed out in the *Ebasco* case: "The economic effect on Ebasco's employees was precisely that which would flow from Ebasco's hiring strikebreakers to work on its own premises. . . ."

Moreover, there is evidence that the secondary strikes and boycotts sought to be outlawed by Section 8(b)(4) were only those which had been unlawful at common law. And although secondary boycotts were generally unlawful, it has been held that the common law does not proscribe union activity designed to prevent employers from doing the farmed-out work of a struck employer. Thus the picketing of the independent typewriter companies was not the kind of a secondary activity which Section 8(b)(4) of the Taft-Hartley Act was designed to outlaw. Where an employer is attempting to avoid the economic impact of a strike by securing the services of others to do his work, the striking union obviously has a great interest, and we think a proper interest in preventing those services from being rendered. This interest is more fundamental than the interest in bringing pressure on customers of the primary employer. Nor are those who render such services completely uninvolved in the primary strike. By doing the work of the primary employer they secure benefits themselves at the same time that they aid the primary employer. The ally employer may easily extricate himself from the dispute and insulate himself from picketing by refusing to do that work. A case may arise where the ally employer is unable to determine that the work he is doing is "farmed-out." We need not decide whether the picketing of such an employer would be lawful, for that is not the situation here. The existence of the strike, the receipt of checks from Royal, and the picketing itself certainly put the independents on notice that some of the work they were doing might be work farmed-out by Royal. Wherever they worked on new Royal machines they were probably aware that such machines were covered by a Royal warranty. But in any event, before working on a Royal machine they could have inquired of the customer whether it was covered by a Royal contract and refused to work on it if it was. There is no indication that they made any effort to avoid doing Royal's work. The Union was justified in picketing them in order to induce them to make such an effort. We therefore hold that an employer is not within the protection of Section 8(b)(4) when he knowingly does work which would otherwise be done by the striking employees of the primary employer and where this work is paid for by the primary employer pursuant to an arrangement devised and originated by him to enable him to meet his contractual obligations.

Enforcement denied.

Case Questions

1. Against whom was the union on strike? Why did the union picket the independent typewriter repair shops?
2. Was the union's picketing at the independent repair shops primary or secondary? Explain your answer.
3. What is the rationale for the "ally" exception to the secondary picketing prohibitions of Section 8(b)(4)? How does that rationale apply to the facts in this case? Explain.

Publicity: "Consumer" Picketing

The second proviso to Section 8(b)(4) allows the union to use ". . . publicity, other than picketing, for the purpose of truthfully advising the public" that the secondary employer is handling the product of the primary employer. Such publicity is legal unless it has the effect of inducing other employees to refuse to perform their services at the secondary employer's location. This proviso allows the union to distribute handbills addressed to the public, asking for the public to support the union in its strike by refusing to buy the primary product or by refraining from shopping at the secondary employer.

In the case of *NLRB v. Fruit and Vegetable Packers, Local 760 (Tree Fruits)* [377 U.S. 58 (1964)], the Supreme Court held that the publicity proviso did not, by negative implication, prohibit peaceful picketing by a union at a supermarket that sold apples packed by the employer against whom the union was on strike. The union's picketing was directed at consumers and asked only that they refuse to buy the apples; it did not ask them to refrain from shopping at the market. The Supreme Court found that such picketing was not prohibited because it was directed at the primary product rather than the neutral supermarket.

In *Tree Fruits,* the primary product, the apples, was only one of many products sold by the supermarket. May the union engage in consumer picketing when the secondary employer sells only one product—the primary product? In *NLRB v. Retail Store Employees Union, Local 1001, Retail Clerks Int. Association (Safeco)* [447 U.S. 607 (1980)], the union striking against Safeco Title Insurance Co. conducted consumer picketing of local title companies, asking consumers to cancel their Safeco policies. The local title companies sold title insurance, performed escrow services, and conducted title searches; over 90 percent of their gross income was derived from the sale of Safeco title insurance. The Supreme Court held that the consumer picketing was in violation of Section 8(b)(4) because, unlike that in *Tree Fruits,* it was "reasonably calculated to induce customers not to patronize the neutral parties at all. . . . Product picketing that reasonably can be expected to threaten neutral parties with ruin or substantial loss simply does not square with the language or the purpose of Section 8(b)(4)(ii)(B)." The Court also stated that if "secondary picketing were directed against a product representing a major portion of a neutral's business, but significantly less than that represented by a single dominant product. . . . The critical question would be whether, by encouraging customers to reject the struck product, the secondary appeal is reasonably likely to threaten the neutral party with ruin or substantial loss."

The effect of the *Safeco* decision is to restrict consumer picketing (also known as product picketing) to situations in which the primary product accounts for less than a substantial portion of the business of the neutral at whose premises the picketing takes place. Other problems under consumer picketing have involved cases in which the primary product has become mixed with the product of the neutral or secondary employer. In such merged prod-

ETHICAL DILEMMA: CONSUMER AND PUBLICITY PICKETING

You are the human resources manager for FoodMart, a regional grocery retailer. The FoodMart employees are members of the Retail Clerks Union, and FoodMart and the union are engaged in negotiations to renew their collective agreement. The retail grocery business is extremely competitive, and a number of low-cost, low-overhead chains compete directly with FoodMart. The employees of the low-cost grocery chains are not unionized, and their wages are barely above the minimum wage. FoodMart employees' wages average around $7.25 per hour, and FoodMart also offers generous benefit packages, including medical insurance and pensions. As a result, FoodMart's labor costs are much higher than the low-cost chains, and FoodMart has seen its profit margins decline. FoodMart had considered proposing wage and benefit reductions to the union; the union had publicly vowed not to agree to any wage concessions.

To avoid a strike, the CEO suggests that you offer the union a guarantee not to reduce wages and benefits if the union agrees to begin a campaign of consumer and publicity picketing and handbilling in front of the low-cost grocery stores—to inform the public how the low-cost chains treat their employees. What arguments can you make in favor of such a proposal? What arguments can you make against it? Should you make such an offer to the union? Prepare a memo to the CEO outlining the positive and negative aspects of the proposal, and recommending a course of action, with appropriate supporting reasons.

uct cases, the public is unable to separate the primary product from the secondary product; hence, a call to the public to avoid the primary product becomes, in effect, a call to avoid the secondary employer's product altogether. For example, if a union representing striking bakery workers pickets a fast-food restaurant urging customers not to eat the sandwich buns supplied by the struck bakery, the effect of the union's consumer picketing may be to urge consumers to boycott the restaurant totally, *Teamsters Local 327* [170 NLRB 91 (1968), enforced 411 F.2d 147 (6th Cir. 1969)]. In *Kroger Co. v. NLRB* [647 F.2d 634 (6th Cir. 1980)], the union representing striking paper workers picketed grocery stores, asking consumers to refrain from using paper bags to pack their groceries. The picketing was held to violate Section 8(b)(4) because the bags had lost their separate identity and had become "merged" with the products (groceries) of the neutral grocery stores.

The Publicity Proviso

The publicity proviso of Section 8(b)(4) purports to allow publicity, other than picketing, for the purposes of truthfully advising the public that the products of the employer against whom the union is striking are being distributed by another employer. How far does that proviso go in allowing consumer appeals by a union? This question is addressed by the following Supreme Court decision.

EDWARD J. DEBARTOLO CORP. V. FLORIDA GULF COAST BUILDING TRADES COUNCIL

485 U.S. 568 (1988)

White, J.

This case centers around the respondent union's peaceful handbilling of the businesses operating in a shopping mall in Tampa, Florida, owned by petitioner, the Edward J. DeBartolo Corporation (DeBartolo). The union's primary labor dispute was with H. J. High Construction Company (High) over alleged substandard wages and fringe benefits. High was retained by the H. J. Wilson Company (Wilson) to construct a department store in the mall, and neither DeBartolo nor any of the other 85 or so mall tenants had any contractual right to influence the selection of contractors.

The union, however, sought to obtain their influence upon Wilson and High by distributing handbills asking mall customers not to shop at any of the stores in the mall "until the Mall's owner publicly promises that all construction at the Mall will be done using contractors who pay their employees fair wages and fringe benefits."[1] The handbills' message was that "[t]he payment of substandard wages not only diminishes the working person's ability to purchase with earned, rather than borrowed, dollars, but it also undercuts the wage standard of the entire community." The handbills made clear that the union was seeking only a consumer boycott against the other mall tenants, not a secondary strike by their employees. At all four entrances to the mall for about three weeks in December 1979, the union peacefully distributed the handbills without any accompanying picketing or patrolling.

After DeBartolo failed to convince the union to alter the language of the handbills to state that its dispute did not involve DeBartolo or the mall lessees other than Wilson and to limit its distribution to the immediate vicinity of Wilson's construction site, it filed a complaint with the National Labor Relations Board (Board), charging the union with engaging in unfair labor practices under Section 8(b)(4) of the National Labor Relations Act. . . . The Board's General Counsel issued a complaint, but the Board eventually dismissed it, concluding that the handbilling was protected by the publicity proviso of Section 8(b)(4). The Court of Appeals for the Fourth Circuit affirmed the Board, but this Court reversed in *Edward J. DeBartolo Corp. v. NLRB*. There, we concluded that the handbilling did not fall within the proviso's limited scope of exempting "publicity intended to inform the public that the primary employer's product is 'distributed by' the secondary employer" because

---

[1] The handbill read:

PLEASE *DON'T SHOP AT EAST LAKE SQUARE MALL* PLEASE

The FLA. GULF COAST Building TRADES COUNCIL, AFL-CIO is requesting that you do not shop at the stores in the East Lake Square Mall because of The Mall ownership's contribution to substandard wages.

The Wilson's Department Store under construction on these premises is being built by contractors who pay substandard wages and fringe benefits. In the past, the Mall's owners, The Edward J. DeBartolo Corporation, has supported labor and our local economy by insuring that the Mall and its stores be built by contractors who pay fair wages and fringe benefits. Now, however, and for no apparent reason, the Mall owners have taken a giant step backwards by permitting our standards to be torn down. The payment of substandard wages not only diminishes the working person's ability to purchase with earned, rather than borrowed, dollars, but it also undercuts the wage standard of the entire community. Since low construction wages at this time of inflation mean decreased purchasing power, do the owners of East Lake Mall intend to compensate for the decreased purchasing power of workers of the community by encouraging the stores in East Lake Mall to cut their prices and lower their profits? CUT-RATE WAGES ARE NOT FAIR UNLESS MERCHANDISE PRICES ARE ALSO CUT-RATE.

We ask for your support in our protest against substandard wages. Please do not patronize the stores in the East Lake Square Mall until the Mall's owner publicly promises that all construction at the Mall will be done using contractors who pay their employees fair wages and fringe benefits. IF YOU MUST ENTER THE MALL TO DO BUSINESS, please express to the store managers your concern over substandard wages and your support of our efforts.

We are appealing only to the public—the consumer. We are not seeking to induce any person to cease work or to refuse to make deliveries.

DeBartolo and the other tenants, as opposed to Wilson, did not distribute products of High. Since there had not been a determination below whether the union's handbilling fell within the prohibition of Section 8(b)(4), and, if so, whether it was protected by the First Amendment, we remanded the case.

On remand, the Board held that the union's handbilling was proscribed by Section 8 (b)(4)(ii)(B). It stated that under its prior cases "handbilling and other activity urging a consumer boycott constituted coercion." The Board reasoned that "[a]ppealing to the public not to patronize secondary employers is an attempt to inflict economic harm on the secondary employers by causing them to lose business," and "such appeals constitute 'economic retaliation' and are therefore a form of coercion." It viewed the object of the handbilling as attempting "to force the mall tenants to cease doing business with DeBartolo in order to force DeBartolo and/or Wilson's not to do business with High." The Board observed that it need not inquire whether the prohibition of this handbilling raised serious questions under the First Amendment, for "the statute's literal language and the applicable case law require[d]" a finding of a violation. Finally, it reiterated its longstanding position that "as a congressionally created administrative agency, we will presume the constitutionality of the Act we administer." . . .

[T]he Board's construction of the statute, as applied in this case, poses serious questions of the validity of Section 8(b)(4) under the First Amendment. The handbills involved here truthfully revealed the existence of a labor dispute and urged potential customers of the mall to follow a wholly legal course of action, namely, not to patronize the retailers doing business in the mall. The handbilling was peaceful. No picketing or patrolling was involved. On its face, this was expressive activity arguing that substandard wages should be opposed by abstaining from shopping in a mall where such wages were paid. Had the union simply been leafletting the public generally, including those entering every shopping mall in town, pursuant to an annual educational effort against substandard pay, there is little doubt that legislative proscription of such leaflets would pose a substantial issue of validity under the First Amendment. The same may well be true in this case, although here the handbills called attention to a specific situation in the mall allegedly involving the payment of unacceptably low wages by a construction contractor.

That a labor union is the leafletter and that a labor dispute was involved does not foreclose this analysis. We do not suggest that communications by labor unions are never of the commercial speech variety and thereby entitled to a lesser degree of constitutional protection. The handbills involved here, however, do not appear to be typical commercial speech such as advertising the price of a product or arguing its merits, for they pressed the benefits of unionism to the community and the dangers of inadequate wages to the economy and the standard of living of the populace. Of course, commercial speech itself is protected by the First Amendment . . . and however these handbills are to be classified, the Court of Appeals was plainly correct in holding that the Board's construction would require deciding serious constitutional issues. . . .

The case turns on whether handbilling such as involved here must be held to "threaten, coerce, or restrain any person" to cease doing business with another, within the meaning of Section 8(b)(4)(ii)(B). We note first that "induc[ing] or encourag[ing]" employees of the secondary employer to strike is proscribed by 8(b)(4)(i). But more than mere persuasion is necessary to prove a violation of 8(b)(4)(ii): that section requires a showing of threats, coercion, or restraints. Those words, we have said, are "nonspecific, indeed vague," and should be interpreted with "caution" and not given a "broad sweep" . . . and in applying Section 8 (b)(4)(1)(A) they were not to be construed to reach peaceful recognitional picketing. Neither is there any necessity to construe such language to reach the handbills involved in this case. There is no suggestion that the leaflets had any coercive effect on customers of the mall. There was no violence, picketing, or patrolling and only an attempt to persuade customers not to shop in the mall.

The Board nevertheless found that the handbilling "coerced" mall tenants and explained in a footnote that "[a]ppealing to the public not to patronize secondary employers is an attempt to inflict economic harm on the secondary employers by causing them to lose business. As the case law makes clear, such appeals constitute 'economic retaliation' and are therefore a form of coercion." Our decision in *Tree Fruits,* however, makes untenable the notion that any kind of handbilling, picketing, or other appeals to a secondary employer to cease doing business with the employer involved in the labor dispute is "coercion" within the meaning of Section 8 (b)(4)(ii)(B) if it has some economic impact on the neutral. In that case, the union picketed a secondary employer, a retailer, asking the public not to buy a product produced by the primary employer. We held that the impact of this picketing was not coercion within the meaning of Section 8(b)(4) even though, if the appeal succeeded, the retailer would lose revenue.

NLRB v. Retail Store Employees (Safeco), in turn, held that consumer picketing urging a general boycott of a secondary employer aimed at causing him to sever relations with the union's real antagonist was coercive and forbidden by Section 8(b)(4). It is urged that *Safeco* rules this case because the union sought a general boycott of all tenants in the mall. But "picketing is qualitatively 'different from other modes of communication,'" and *Safeco* noted that the picketing there actually threatened the neutral with ruin or substantial loss. As Justice Stevens pointed out in his concurrence in *Safeco,* picketing is "a mixture of conduct and communication" and the conduct element "often provides the most persuasive deterrent to third persons about to enter a business establishment." Handbills containing the same message, he observed, are "much less effective than labor picketing" because they "depend entirely on the persuasive force of the idea."

In *Tree Fruits,* we could not discern with the "requisite clarity" that Congress intended to proscribe all peaceful consumer picketing at secondary sites. There is even less reason to find in the language of Section 8(b)(4)(ii), standing alone, any clear indication that handbilling, without picketing, "coerces" secondary employers. The loss of customers because they read a handbill urging them not to patronize a business, and not because they are intimidated by a line of picketers, is the result of mere persuasion, and the neutral who reacts is doing no more than what its customers honestly want it to do. . . .

It is nevertheless argued that the second proviso to Section 8(b)(4) makes clear that that section, as amended in 1959, was intended to proscribe nonpicketing appeals such as handbilling urging a consumer boycott of a neutral employer. . . . By its terms, the proviso protects nonpicketing communications directed at customers of a distributor of goods produced by an employer with whom the union has a labor dispute. Because handbilling and other consumer appeals not involving such a distributor are not within the proviso, the argument goes, those appeals must be considered coercive within the meaning of Section 8(b)(4)(ii). Otherwise, it is said, the proviso is meaningless, for if handbilling and like communications are never coercive and within the reach of the section, there would have been no need whatsoever for the proviso.

This approach treats the proviso as establishing an exception to a prohibition that would otherwise reach the conduct excepted. But this proviso has a different ring to it. It states that Section 8(b)(4) "shall not be construed" to forbid certain described nonpicketing publicity. That language need not be read as an exception. It may indicate only that without the proviso, the particular nonpicketing communication the proviso protects might have been considered to be coercive, even if other forms of publicity would not be. Section 8(b)(4), with its proviso, may thus be read as not covering nonpicketing publicity, including appeals to customers of a retailer as they approach the store, urging a complete boycott of the retailer because he handles products produced by nonunion shops. . . .

In our view, interpreting Section 8(b)(4) as not reaching the handbilling involved in this case is not foreclosed either by the language of the section or its legislative history. That construction makes unnecessary passing on the serious constitutional questions that would be raised by the Board's understanding of the statute. Accordingly, the judgment of the Court of Appeals is

Affirmed.

Case Questions

1. With whom did the union have a dispute in this case? What union conduct was subject of the unfair labor practice complaint? Against whom was that conduct directed?
2. What does the "publicity proviso" of section 8(b)(4) protect? How does it apply to the facts of this case? Explain your answer.
3. Why does the Court treat handbilling or other appeals to consumers differently from picketing aimed at consumers? Are handbills or other appeals likely to be more or less effective than picketing aimed at consumers? Explain.

Not all union handbilling is protected; in *Warshawsky & Co. v. NLRB* [182 F.3d 948 (D.C. Cir. 1999)], union handbilling directed at employees of neutral subcontractors and intended to induce them to walk off the job was held to be an effort to induce a secondary boycott and a violation of Section 8(b)(4).

The case of *Int. Longshoremen's Association v. NLRB* [56 F.3d 205 (D.C. Cir. 1995)] involved requests by U.S. union officials to Japanese unions asking for support in a dispute with nonunion shipping firms; the Japanese unions responded by stating that they would refuse to unload any cargo that had been loaded by nonunion workers. The U.S. Court of Appeals for the D.C. Circuit held that the Japanese unions were not acting as agents of the U.S. unions, and the U.S. unions' requests for support did not violate Section 8(b)(4).

Section 8(b)(4)(D): Jurisdictional Disputes

Section 8(b)(4)(D) prohibits a union from picketing an employer in order to force that employer to assign work to that union. If the picketing union is not entitled to that work by reason of a certification or NLRB order, such picketing violates Section 8(b)(4)(D). For example, the union representing plasterers and the union representing stonemasons on the construction site of an apartment complex both might demand the right to lay the ceramic tiles in hallways and bathrooms. If either union picketed to force such assignment of the work, it would be a violation of Section 8(b)(4)(D).

When a Section 8(b)(4)(D) complaint is filed with the board, Section 10(k) requires that the board give the parties involved ten days to settle the dispute. If the parties are unable to settle the jurisdictional dispute in ten days, the board must then make an assignment of the work in dispute. Once the board awards the work, the successful union may picket to force the employer to live up to the board order. Section 10(l) requires that the board seek an injunction against the picketing when a complaint alleging a violation of Section 8(b)(4)(D) is filed.

Section 8(e): Hot Cargo Clauses

Hot cargo clauses are provisions in collective-bargaining agreements purporting to permit employees to refuse to handle the product of any employer involved in a labor dispute. Section 8(e), inserted into the NLRA as one of the 1959 Landrum-Griffin amendments, prohibits the negotiation and enforcement of such clauses:

> (e) It shall be an unfair labor practice for any labor organization and any employer to enter into any contract or agreement, express or implied, whereby such employer ceases or refrains or agrees to cease or refrain from handling, using, selling, transporting or otherwise dealing in any of the products of any other employer, or to cease doing business with any other person, and any contract or agreement entered into heretofore or hereafter containing such an agreement shall be to such extent unenforcible and void: Provided, That nothing in this subsection (e) shall apply to an agreement between a labor organization and an employer in the construction industry relating to the contracting or subcontracting of work to be done at the site of the construction, alteration, painting, or repair of a building, structure, or other work: Provided further, That for the purposes of this subsection (e) and section 8(b)(4)(B) the terms "any employer," "any person engaged in commerce or an industry affecting commerce," "any person" when used in relation to the terms "any other producer, processor, or manufacturer," "any employer," or "any other person" shall not include persons in the relation of a jobber, manufacturer, contractor, or

subcontractor working on the goods or premises of the jobber or manufacturer or performing parts of an integrated process of production in the apparel and clothing industry: Provided further, That nothing in this Act shall prohibit the enforcement of any agreement which is within the foregoing exception.

It can be seen that the provisos to Section 8(e) exempt the garment industry and the construction industry from its provisions. The garment industry is completely exempted; the construction industry is exempted to the extent of allowing unions to negotiate hot cargo clauses that relate to work normally done at the work site.

The objective of Section 8(e) is to prohibit language in a collective agreement that purports to authorize conduct that is prohibited by Section 8(b)(4), such as refusing to handle goods produced by a nonunion employer or by an employer who is being struck by a different union. The courts have allowed contract language that authorizes conduct that is primary, such as refusing to cross a primary picket line and refusing to perform the work normally done by the employees of an employer who is the target of a primary strike. One issue that has been problematic under Section 8(e) is whether work preservation clauses outside the construction industry are prohibited by Section 8(e). The courts have consistently held that when unions seek to retain the right to perform work that they have traditionally done or to acquire work that is similar to work they have traditionally done, and such activity to enforce the clauses is directed against the employer with the right of control over the working conditions at issue, such activity is primary. In *NLRB v. International Longshoremen's Association* [473 U.S. 61 (1985)], the Supreme Court considered a union rule penalizing shippers who used prepacked containers to ship cargo that had traditionally been loaded and unloaded by union members at the docks. The Court held that, even though the use of containers had eliminated most of the traditional loading work done by longshoremen, the language that sought to preserve such "unnecessary" work was a legitimate work preservation clause under Sections 8(e) and 8(b)(4). The union's objective through the language was the preservation of work similar in nature to that traditionally performed by the longshoremen, and the employers had the power to control the assignment of such work.

REMEDIES FOR SECONDARY ACTIVITY

As mentioned, the NLRB is required to seek an immediate injunction against the picketing when a complaint alleging a violation of Section 8(b)(4), Section 8(b)(7), or Section 8(e) is filed. The injunction is intended to prevent the activity in question until its legality can be determined. If the board holds the conduct illegal, it will issue a cease-and-desist order against it.

Section 303 of the NLRA also provides that any person suffering harm to business or property by reason of activity that violates Section 8(b)(4) may sue in federal court to recover damages for the injuries sustained and legal fees. Either the primary or secondary employer may sue under Section 303, and they may file a suit regardless of whether an unfair labor practice charge has been filed with the NLRB.

NATIONAL EMERGENCIES

Sections 206 to 210 of the NLRA, which were added by the Taft-Hartley Act of 1947, provide for injunctions forestalling strikes when they threaten the national health or safety. When a strike or threatened strike poses such a threat, the president is authorized to appoint a board of inquiry to report on the issues involved in the dispute. The U.S. attorney general can secure an injunction to forestall the strike for up to eighty days, while the Federal Mediation and Conciliation Service (FMCS) attempts to resolve the dispute. The parties are not bound by the FMCS recommendations, and if no agreement is reached, the NLRB is required to poll the employees to determine if they will accept the employer's last offer. If the last offer is rejected, the injunction is dissolved, and the president may refer the issue to Congress for "appropriate action."

The emergency provisions of the Taft-Hartley Act have been invoked only rarely in recent years. President George W. Bush's action to stop a lockout of longshoremen in West coast ports in October 2002 was the first use of the Taft-Hartley emergency provisions since 1978. The emergency provisions allow the president to delay a strike but do not address the causes of the strike. As a result, the dispute remains despite the invocation of the emergency provisions, and the strike or lockout may resume after the delay period under the injunction expires.

SUMMARY

- When collective bargaining fails to produce an agreement in a labor dispute, either party may resort to pressure tactics to try to force the other side to settle the dispute. Union pressure involves strikes and calls for a boycott, while employers may resort to lockouts. The right to strike is not constitutionally guaranteed, but a strike is protected activity under the NLRA. Picketing, which usually accompanies a strike, is subject to several controls under the NLRA and related legislation.
- The Norris–La Guardia Act restricts the ability of the federal courts to issue injunctions against union conduct in a labor dispute; the term *labor dispute* is defined broadly in the Norris–La Guardia Act and includes strikes that are politically motivated. State courts can regulate violent picketing or picketing in violation of state laws, but when an unfair labor practice complaint has been filed concerning the legality of union picketing on private property, the *Babcock & Wilcox* approach should be used to decide the issue.
- The NLRA prohibits recognitional picketing, but publicity picketing directed to inform the public of a labor dispute is protected. Similarly, secondary picketing—union picketing directed at neutral employers who are not involved in the labor dispute—is an unfair labor practice. Exceptions to the prohibition on secondary picketing include consumer picketing and other publicity activities, such as handbilling; employers who are allies of the struck employer may also be picketed by the union involved in the labor dispute.
- Hot cargo clauses—contract language that would allow unions to engage in secondary activity—are illegal under Section 8(e) of the

NLRA; exceptions to Section 8(e) allow work preservation clauses and exclude the garment industry from the prohibitions of both Section 8(e) and Section 8(b)(4).

- Remedies for illegal secondary activity include injunctions under Section 10(l) and civil suits for damages under Section 303 of the NLRA.

QUESTIONS

1. Why is the right to picket protected by the U.S. Constitution? Is the right to strike also protected by the Constitution?
2. In what situations can the states regulate picketing? Explain your answer.
3. What is recognitional or organization picketing? Under what circumstances is it prohibited by the NLRA?
4. What is primary picketing? What is secondary picketing? What factors determine the legality of picketing against neutral employers?
5. Why is common situs picketing at a construction site treated differently from picketing in a *General Electric*-type situation?
6. What is the ally doctrine? How does it affect the legality of picketing under Section 8(b)(4)?
7. When is consumer picketing prohibited by Section 8(b)(4)?
8. What is a hot cargo clause? Why are hot cargo clauses prohibited by the NLRA?
9. What are the procedures available under the Taft-Hartley Act to attempt to prevent strikes that pose a danger to the national health, safety, or security?

CASE PROBLEMS

1. Plaintiff owned and operated a supermarket in Springfield, Missouri. The defendant union neither represented, nor did it claim to want to organize, the supermarket's clerks. Nevertheless, the union sporadically picketed the supermarket, claiming that the impetus for its picketing was that the supermarket paid substandard wages.

   Initially, the union picketed in the public street, but subsequently, it moved onto the supermarket's sidewalk. After the supermarket filed a trespass complaint with the local police, the pickets moved back to the street but simultaneously filed an unfair labor practice charge with the NLRB. The board issued a complaint, asserting that the supermarket violated Section 8(a)(1) of the NLRA by ordering the pickets off the sidewalk.

   The supermarket's owners initiated a lawsuit, seeking an injunction to keep the pickets off the sidewalk and also to stop other alleged picketing activities. The plaintiffs alleged that the pickets called customers "scab shoppers," took down license numbers of customers' cars, and misstated on their placards that the plaintiff was an Arizona company, coming in from out of state, when in fact it was a Missouri corporation.

   In what kind of picketing was the union engaging? What was the theory on which the NLRB issued its complaint on behalf of the union, and how do you think it will fare before an administrative law judge?

   Does the issuance of that complaint by the board preempt the Missouri state court from enjoining any of the picketers' activities?

All of their activities? Is your answer any different if the Section 8(a)(1) charge is ultimately sustained by the ALJ who hears the case? See *Smitty's Super Markets v. Local 322* [637 S.W.2d 148, 116 L.R.R.M. 3393 (Missouri Ct. Apps. (1982)].

2. Theater Techniques, Inc. (TTI) was a supplier of theatrical props and scenery for Broadway shows. TTI had a subcontract with Nolan Studios to paint scenery and props provided by TTI. Nolan Studios' employees were represented by Local 829, United Scenic Artists, whose collective agreement gave the union jurisdiction over the sculpting and painting of props. When some props from TTI arrived at Nolan already fabricated, the union employees refused to paint them unless Nolan paid a premium rate for the work. Nolan did not inform the union that TTI had contractual control over the disputed work; but Nolan did file a complaint with the NLRB, charging the union with violating Section 8(b)(4)(B) by refusing to handle the props from TTI to force Nolan to stop doing business with TTI.

How should the board decide the unfair labor practice complaint filed by Nolan? Explain your answer. See *United Scenic Artists, Local 829 v. NLRB* [762 F.2d 1027 (D.C. Cir. 1985)].

3. Local 366 of the Brewery, Bottling, Can & Allied Industrial Union called a strike against the Coors bottling plant in Golden, Colorado. Local 366 was affiliated with the AFL-CIO and received nationwide union support for a boycott of Coors beer during the strike.

During the course of this protracted labor dispute, Coors made an agreement with KQED, a broadcasting station in the San Francisco Bay Area, under which the brewer would provide financial support and volunteers for a Coors Day portion of the station's annual fund-raising telethon.

Prior to the telethon, an article appeared in the *San Francisco Bay Guardian,* which stated that Coors "is notorious for anti-union activities during a . . . strike" and had long been "the subject of a labor-backed nationwide boycott." Following the appearance of the article, the coordinator of the Northern California Chapter of the Coors Boycott Committee met with the KQED general manager to inform him of the swelling opposition to Coors Day, allegedly warning him not to stumble into a "shooting war" and that he could not guarantee the safety of the teleauction volunteers. KQED subsequently canceled Coors Day, and Coors sued the coordinator and other union supporters for damages.

Was the boycott group a labor organization under the jurisdiction of the NLRA? If so, did the boycott group violate the NLRA? Did it violate the federal antitrust laws? Did it violate any state laws? If so, would a state court have had jurisdiction of the case? See *Adolph Coors Co. v. Wallace* [570 F. Supp. 202, 115 L.R.R.M. 3100 (N.D. Cal. 1984)].

4. In 1975, Delta Air Lines subcontracted the janitorial work of its offices at the Los Angeles International Airport to the National Cleaning Company. National entered into a collective-bargaining agreement with the Hospital and Service Employees Union, Local 399. In 1976, Delta lawfully terminated its contract with National and made a new contract with Statewide Maintenance Company, a nonunion employer. Consequently, National fired five of the six janitors who had cleaned Delta's offices.

In furtherance of its recognitional dispute with Statewide Maintenance, the union began distributing handbills at Delta's L.A. Airport facilities in front of the downtown Los Angeles office. One or two persons usually distributed the flyers at each facility. The handbilling caused no interruptions in deliveries or refusals by Delta's employees to do their work.

There were four handbills altogether. The first stated, "Please do not fly Delta Airlines. Delta Airlines unfair. Does not provide AFL-CIO conditions of employment. (signed by union)." The other side said, "It takes more than money to fly Delta. It takes nerve. Let's look at the accident record." There followed a list of fifty-five accidents involving Delta between 1963 and 1976, along with the total number of deaths and injuries.

The second handbill, distributed a week later, contained all the information on side two of the first handbill but not the information from side one.

The third handbill, another week later, again consisted of two sides. Side one said:

Please Do Not Fly Delta Airlines. This airline has caused members of Service Employees Union, Local 399, AFL-CIO, at Los Angeles International Airport, to become unemployed. In their place they have contracted with a maintenance company which does not provide Local 399 wages, benefits and standards. We urge all union members to protest Delta's action to the Delta office in your region. If you are concerned about the plight of fellow union members . . . Please Do Not Fly Delta Airlines.

Side two contained the same accident information as the previous two broadsides. Handbill four contained the same accident information as the prior three, with the following prefatory statement:

> As members of the public and in order to protect the wages and conditions of Local 399 members and to publicize our primary dispute with the Statewide Building Maintenance Company, we wish to call to the attention of the consuming public certain information about Delta Airlines from the official records of the Civil Aeronautics Board of the United States Government.

Simultaneous with the handbilling activities, the union published copies of flyers one and three in two union newspapers, along with an advertisement stating singly, "Do Not Fly Delta."

Analyze each of the four handbills. What, if anything, in each constituted an illegal secondary boycott? What, if anything, was protected by the NLRA's publicity proviso? Is the same true with respect to the newspaper ads? See *Service Employees Local 399 v. NLRB* [117 L.R.R.M. 2717, 743 F.2d 1417 (9th Cir. 1984)].

5. Shortly after the Soviet invasion of Afghanistan in 1979, the United States imposed an embargo on exports to the Soviet Union. However, some grain shipments were exempted from the embargo. Nevertheless, the International Longshoremen's Association (ILA), apparently disagreeing with the exemptions, adopted a resolution that its longshoremen would not handle any goods exported to or arriving from the Soviet Union.

Sovfracht Chartering Corporation, a Soviet government maritime agency, chartered a Belgian ship (*The Belgium*) to transport exempt and duly licensed grain from Houston to Russia. The Houston stevedore companies had to hire all longshoremen from ILA hiring halls. When TTT Stevedores, an employer party to an ILA collective-bargaining agreement, sought to load the Soviet-bound grain on board *The Belgium,* it was informed that the ILA local would not provide any of its members to do the work. When informed of this decision, Sovfracht canceled *The Belgium's* stop in Houston.

Was the ILA guilty of a secondary boycott? If so, against whom? What arguments can be made that this action was not illegal activity under the NLRA? See *ILA v. NLRB* [723 F.2d 963, 115 L.R.R.M. 2093 (D.C. Cir. 1983)].

6. The Iron Workers Union had been engaged in organizing the employees of Stokrr's Multi-Ton Corporation. When Stokrr's refused to recognize the union, the union called a strike of the company's employees.

Perkins Trucking Company handled and transported Stokrr's products. Three days into the strike, pickets gathered around a Perkins truck as it attempted to make a pickup at the Stokrr's facility. One of the union pickets jumped on the running board of the Perkins truck and yelled at the driver, "We're going to rape your wife. . . . I'm going to break your legs." The picket then pointed at the driver's face and stated, "Just remember what I look like, because I know who you are. I'm going to get you. . . . [W]e're going to get all your trucks, you run a lot of them." At that point, the police assisted the Perkins truck through the picket line to the loading dock.

Sometime later, eight to twelve strikers arrived at the Perkins terminal at 7 A.M. carrying placards. But they engaged in no picketing of the terminal facility; they stood around, five to ten feet from the terminal gate. They told the assistant shop steward of the union at Perkins that they were "individuals" trying to gain information for their "personal use" and that they wanted to know if Perkins was handling any of Stokrr's freight. They were told that Perkins had not handled any Stokrr's freight for "the last couple of weeks." At about 8 A.M., the strikers departed.

Based on these facts, could it be said that Perkins was an ally of Stokrr's? What provisions of the NLRA, if any, did the union violate? See *Iron Workers, Local 455* [243 NLRB No. 39, 102 L.R.R.M. 1109 (1979)].

7. Caruso was sole proprietor of Linoleum & Carpet City in Spokane, Washington. He also owned a parking lot a quarter of a mile from his business. Periodically, delivery trucks blocked access to the lot.

On October 26, 1973, Caruso found a beer truck and a van blocking the entrance to his lot. Caruso called a tow truck to have the vehicles removed. (He had first called the owner, whose name was on the truck, and asked him to remove it.) The driver of the van settled his share of the tow truck costs, but Contos, the driver of the truck, refused to pay his share. Contos told Caruso he would report him to the Teamsters Union and the union would "break" him.

On November 9, 1973, an article was published in the *Washington Teamster*. The article, titled "Don't Patronize Carpet City in Spokane," was printed once on the front page of the teamster paper and twice more in substantially the same form on page 5. It continued to state that the owner harassed laboring people who used his parking lot. It was signed Teamsters Union, Local 690.

Soon after publication of the first three articles, people began calling Linoleum & Carpet City and stating that they would not shop there. Sales dropped dramatically, and in May 1974, Caruso relocated his business hoping to minimize his losses.

Assess the union's activities in light of the NLRA. Are there any unfair labor practices? Are there any common-law counts that Caruso could pursue against the union for destroying his business? If so, does he face a preemption problem? See *Caruso v. Teamsters Local 690* [120 L.R.R.M. 2233 (Wash. S.C. 1983)].

8. Zellers worked as an elevator installer; he was a member of Local 123 of the Elevator Constructors. Zellers was employed by Eggers Construction Co. and was working at a neutral construction site. The elevator construction crew was directed to use a separate, neutral gate at the work site because another union had set up a picket line at a different gate at the work site. When he saw the other picket line, Zellers refused to enter the work site, even though there was no picket line at the gate he was required to use. Because of his refusal to enter the gate, Zellers was suspended by Eggers. The Elevator Constructors Union filed a grievance protesting the suspension of Zellers. Eggers then filed an unfair labor practice complaint with the NLRB, alleging that the union filing the grievance was in violation of Section 8(b)(4) because it sought to authorize Zellers' refusal to work in order to force the general contractor to get rid of the employer subject to the strike by the other union.

How should the board rule on Eggers' unfair labor practice complaint? Explain your answer. See *NLRB v. Elevator Constructors* [134 L.R.R.M. 2137 (8th Cir. 1990)].

9. The Truck Drivers' Union was engaged in a primary labor dispute with Piggyback Services, Inc., a nonunion employer. The dispute began when the Santa Fe Railroad awarded Piggyback a subcontract to ramp and deramp intermodal freight (freight carried inside trailers and containers on railroad flatcars) at Santa Fe's Richmond, California, rail terminal. That work had been performed by union members for a wholly owned subsidiary of Santa Fe. Piggyback had initially agreed to hire the former union workers, but reneged on that promise in July 1990, and the union began picketing and distributing handbills at Santa Fe's Richmond rail terminal.

In an effort to insulate itself from the union's labor dispute with Piggyback, Santa Fe designated a gate, Gate 1, as the sole entrance to the Richmond facility for employees, customers, visitors, and suppliers of Piggyback. Santa Fe also posted signs at four other entrances to the Richmond facility, designated as Gate 2, Gate 3, Gate 4, and Gate 5, stating that these "neutral" gates were reserved for the exclusive use of Santa Fe's employees, customers, visitors, and suppliers, and that Gate 1 was available only for Piggyback's employees, customers, visitors, and suppliers.

Although Piggyback employees entered only through Gate 1, and the union fully acknowledged that it had no labor dispute with Santa Fe, the union began picketing at the four neutral gates. Handbills distributed by the union at neutral locations urged neutral employees and customers entering the Santa Fe railway yard to either honor the picket line or, alternatively, to cease all work related to Piggyback's day-to-day operations. The union sent letters to the presidents of the seven unions that represented Santa Fe employees; the letters requested that union members employed by Santa Fe not perform work directly related to Piggyback's operations at the Richmond terminal. A similar letter was sent by the union to United Parcel Services (UPS), Santa Fe's primary unionized intermodal trucking customer.

The UPS drivers and other Santa Fe customers honored the picket line by refusing to deliver intermodal freight to the Richmond terminal. In response, Santa Fe established a drop-off site about a mile-and-a-half from Gate 3 for use by UPS and other Santa Fe customers. Although no Piggyback employees were stationed at the UPS drop-off site, the union expanded its activity to that location. The union also picketed at the two railroad spur lines where intermodal freight cars entered the railway yard.

Santa Fe filed an unfair labor practice complaint with the NLRB, alleging that the union picketing violated Section 8(b)(4). How should the NLRB rule on the complaint? Why? Explain your answer. See *NLRB v. General Truck Drivers, Warehousemen, Helpers and Automotive Employees of Contra Costa County, Local No. 315* [20 F.3d 1017 (9th Cir. 1994)].

10. Rainbow, a tour bus company based in Honolulu, provides ground transportation services to various tourist agencies in the Honolulu area. In 1976, Steven Kolt became a part owner and president of the company and adopted its present name.

In 1976, Rainbow was a nonunion business. In the latter part of that year and early the next year, some employees began inquiring into joining a union. Soon thereafter, on the morning of January 29, 1977, the union picketed the Rainbow yard. Approximately thirty to forty pickets were involved. The pickets were somewhat threatening and unruly and temporarily blocked ingress and egress to the Rainbow yard. Rainbow immediately sought to enjoin the picketing in Hawaii state court. On February 2, 1977, the union agreed before the state court judge to reduce the number of pickets to two.

On February 1, 1977, Rainbow commenced the lawsuit that is the subject of this appeal. Rainbow brought two counts. The first alleged violations cognizable under Section 303 of the Labor Management Relations Act.

The second count, a pendent state law claim, alleged the union had engaged in unlawful mass picketing that tortiously interfered with Rainbow's employment contracts and resulted in a loss of business.

On March 2, 1977, the union and two former Rainbow employees filed unfair labor practice charges with the NLRB. They alleged Rainbow had unlawfully interfered with its employees' Section 7 rights by threatening and terminating several of them. Rainbow answered that the union had engaged in activity violative of Sections 8(b)(1)(A) (coercing employees in the exercise of their Section 7 rights); (b)(4) (illegal secondary conduct); and (b)(7) (illegal recognitional picketing when no petition had been timely filed). The NLRB consolidated the complaints, and a hearing was held from July 6 to July 13, 1977.

The ALJ entered his decision on March 29, 1978. The NLRB affirmed the ALJ's findings and adopted his order with minor modifications (241 NLRB. 589, 101 L.R.R.M. 1042, 1979). The NLRB rejected Rainbow's claims and found for the union.

Does the NLRB's decision in favor of the union mean that Rainbow cannot recover damages in this case? Or is there a theory of recovery on which it should be permitted to proceed? See *Rainbow Coaches v. Hawaii Teamsters* [704 F.2d 1443, 113 L.R.R.M. 2383 (9th Cir. 1983)].

INTERNET EXERCISE

Some student groups are calling for a boycott of garments made by low-paid foreign workers employed in "sweatshop" conditions. Not surprisingly, the U.S. union movement supports the efforts of these students. Go to the "Unite! Stop Sweatshops Campaign" website at **http://www.uniteunion.org/sweatshops/index.htm** to get information about the campaign against sweatshop-produced goods. Click on the link to "College Students Against Sweatshops" for more information on the campaign against sweatshop-produced goods. Why would U.S. unions support student efforts to ban sweatshop goods?

INFOTRAC KEYWORDS

http://www.infotrac-college.com

Picketing, boycott

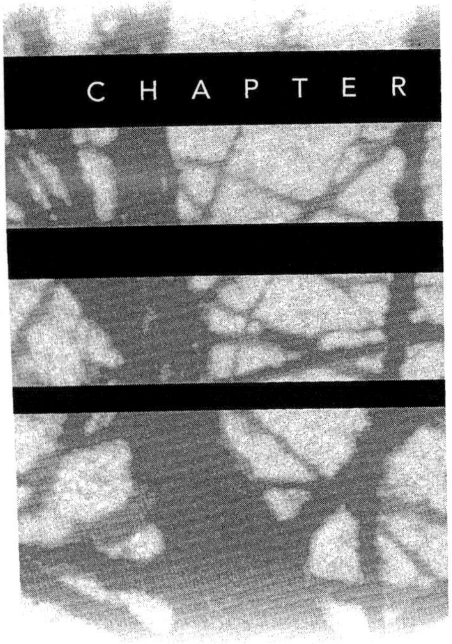

CHAPTER 18

THE ENFORCEMENT AND ADMINISTRATION OF THE COLLECTIVE AGREEMENT

The signing of a collective agreement by a union and an employer may mark the end of the bargaining process; it is also the beginning of a continuing relationship between them. The agreement creates rights for and imposes obligations on both parties. The parties are bound to uphold the terms of the contract for its duration. How can union and management ensure that the "other side" will honor the contract? What means are available to enforce the contract in the event of a breach by either side? How can disputes over the interpretation of the agreement be resolved? This chapter discusses the means available for the enforcement and administration of the collective agreement.

Section 301 of the National Labor Relations Act (NLRA) provides that suits for violations of contracts between an employer and a labor union may be brought in federal and state courts. Therefore, either the union or employer could bring a lawsuit over the other side's failure to live up to the contract. However, lawsuits are a cumbersome means of resolving most contract disputes; they are also expensive and time-consuming. For these reasons, lawsuits are impractical for resolving disputes over how collective agreements should be interpreted or applied.

Either party to the agreement could resort to pressure tactics to try to resolve a contract dispute. The union could go on strike or the employer could lock out the employees to force the other side to live up to the contract. The employer generally is not willing to lock out employees and cease production over minor matters. Nor are union members likely to strike, lose wages, and risk being replaced over insignificant issues.

ARBITRATION

Arbitration
The settlement of disputes by a neutral adjudicator chosen by the parties.

Because of the shortcomings of both lawsuits and pressure tactics as a way to resolve contract disputes, the parties usually agree, as a part of their collective agreement, to establish their own process for resolving disputes peacefully. The peaceful settlement process usually involves **arbitration.** Arbitration is the settlement of disputes by a neutral adjudicator chosen by the parties to the dispute. It provides a means to resolve contractual disputes relatively inexpensively and expeditiously. Arbitration also provides flexibility because the parties are free to tailor the arbitration process to suit their particular situation. The parties generally incorporate arbitration as the final step of the grievance procedure. In return for the agreement by each party to arbitrate their dispute, they give up their right to strike or lock out over such issues.

INTEREST ARBITRATION VERSUS RIGHTS ARBITRATION

In a labor relations setting, arbitration may be used either to settle a dispute over the creation of a new collective agreement or over the interpretation and administration of an existing agreement. When arbitration is used to create a new agreement (or renew an existing one), it is known as *interest arbitration*—the parties seek to protect their economic interests through favorable contract terms. Interest arbitration is common in the public sector, where employees are generally prohibited from striking. Interest arbitration replaces pressure tactics as a means to resolve the negotiating impasse in the public sector. It is much less common in the private sector.

Visit this site for information on interest arbitration in New York: **http://www.perb.state.ny.us/int.asp**

If the dispute involves interpreting an existing agreement rather than creating a new one, the arbitration to resolve it is known as *rights arbitration.* Rights arbitration is the means to define the rights and obligations of each party under the agreement. It is very common in both the public and private sectors. Even though rights arbitration is not required by the NLRA, more than 90 percent of all collective agreements provide for rights arbitration as the means to resolve disputes over the interpretation and/or application of the collective agreement. This chapter is concerned with rights arbitration, and unless otherwise specified, the term *arbitration* refers to rights arbitration.

RIGHTS ARBITRATION AND THE GRIEVANCE PROCESS

Rights arbitration is generally used as the final step in the *grievance process*—a process set up to deal with complaints under the collective agreement. Like rights arbitration, the grievance process is created by the parties to the agreement. It is not required by statute. Because it is voluntarily created by the parties under the collective agreement, the grievance process can be tailored to fit their particular situation or desires.

Grievance
A complaint that one party to a collective agreement is not living up to the obligations of the agreement.

A **grievance** is simply a complaint that either party to the agreement is not living up to the obligations of the agreement. Most grievances are filed by employees complaining about the actions of the employer (or its agents), but management may also file grievances under the agreement.

Grievance procedures vary widely; the parties to an agreement can devise whatever procedure is best suited to their purposes. The following is an example of a four-step grievance procedure, with arbitration as the final step:

ARTICLE XIII: GRIEVANCE PROCEDURE

SECTION 1. Any grievance or dispute between the Company and the Union involving the interpretation or application of any terms of this Agreement shall be adjusted according to the following procedure:

Step One: The employee who believes he has suffered a grievance or been unjustly treated may raise the alleged grievance with his Foreman or Assistant Foreman in an attempt to settle the same. The said employee may be accompanied or represented if he so desires by the Steward. The Foreman shall have two (2) working days to settle the grievance.

Step Two: If the matter is not satisfactorily settled in STEP ONE, it may be taken to the Second Step by the Union's reducing it to writing, on a mutually agreed upon form provided by the Company. Any grievance taken to the Second Step must be signed by a Steward, a Chief Steward, or a Local Union Committee member. Two (2) copies will be delivered to the Supervisor, who will sign and date the grievance upon receipt of it. A meeting will be arranged within four (4) working days following receipt of the form, between the Supervisor, Plant Superintendent, Grievant, Steward, or in his absence, Chief Steward. A written answer shall be given within four (4) working days from the date of the meeting even though an oral decision is given at the meeting. If the answer is not received during the time period, the grievance shall be deemed settled in favor of the grievant or Union.

Step Three: The Steward, or Chief Steward in his absence, may appeal the Second Step decision by completing the "Appeal to Third Step" portion of the grievance form and by delivering the same to the Industrial Relations Department within five (5) working days (excluding Saturday and Sunday) after the decision in the Second Step. The Industrial Relations Department shall arrange a meeting within five (5) working days (excluding Saturday and Sunday) following receipt of the appeal, between the representative designated by the Company, the Shop Grievance Committee, and the International Representative. A written answer shall be given within five (5) working days (excluding Saturday and Sunday) from the date of the meeting even though an oral decision is given at the meeting. Any failure by either party to meet the time limits required shall deem the grievance settled in favor of the other party.

Step Four: Any grievance or dispute involving the interpretation or application of this Agreement, which has not been satisfactorily settled in the foregoing steps, may, at the request of either party, be submitted to an arbitrator or arbitration board selected as hereinafter provided, by written notice delivered to the other party within four (4) calendar weeks subsequent to the decision in Step Three. Any failure, by either party, to meet such time limits shall be deemed a waiver of the grievance. Unless the parties mutually agree upon arbitration by the State Board of Mediation and Arbitration, the matter shall be referred to the American Arbitration Association for arbitration under its rules. The fees and expenses of the arbitrator thus selected shall be divided equally between the parties.

SECTION 2. The arbitration board or the arbitrator is not authorized to add to, modify, or take away from the express terms of this Agreement and shall be limited to the interpretation or application of the provisions of the Agreement of the determination as to whether there is a violation of it. Any decision of the arbitration board or the arbitrator within the scope of the above authority shall be final and binding on both parties.
SECTION 3. Time limits above set forth must be complied with strictly.
SECTION 4. The Company or the Union may institute a grievance at Step Three on any matter concerning general application, and process it through STEP FOUR.

It can be seen that the actual grievance procedure is a series of meetings between union and management representatives. As the grievance remains unresolved and moves through the various steps of the procedure, the rank of the representatives involved increases. Either party may request that a grievance unresolved at Step Three be submitted to arbitration.

THE COURTS AND ARBITRATION

As noted, arbitration as a means to resolve grievances is a voluntary mechanism; the parties to the contract have agreed to use it. But what happens if either party refuses to submit a dispute to arbitration? What remedies are available to the party seeking arbitration? The following case deals with an attempt to use Section 301 of the NLRA to force management to arbitrate a union grievance.

Textile Workers Union of America v. Lincoln Mills of Alabama

353 U.S. 448 (1957)

Douglas, J.

Petitioner-union entered into a collective bargaining agreement in 1953 with respondent-employer. . . . The agreement provided that there would be no strikes or work stoppages and that grievances would be handled pursuant to a specified procedure. The last step in the grievance procedure—a step that could be taken by either party—was arbitration.

This controversy involves several grievances that concern work loads and work assignments. The grievances were processed through the various steps in the grievance procedure and were finally denied by the employer. The union requested arbitration, and the employer refused. Thereupon the union brought this suit in the District Court to compel arbitration.

The District Court concluded that it had jurisdiction and ordered the employer to comply with the grievance arbitration provisions of the collective bargaining agreement. The Court of Appeals reversed by a divided vote.

The starting point of our inquiry is Section 301 of the Labor Management Relations Act of 1947, which provides:

> (a) Suits for violation of contracts between an employer and a labor organization representing employees in an industry affecting commerce as defined in this chapter, or between any such labor organizations, may be brought in any district court of the United States having jurisdiction of the parties, without respect to the amount in controversy or without regard to the citizenship of the parties.

> (b) Any labor organization which represents employees in an industry affecting commerce as defined in this chapter and any employer whose activities affect commerce as defined in this chapter shall be bound by the acts of its agents. Any such labor organization may sue or be sued as an entity and in behalf of the employees whom it represents in the courts of the United States. Any money judgment against a labor organization in a district court of the United States shall be enforceable only against the organization as an entity and against its assets, and shall not be enforceable against any individual member or his assets.

There has been considerable litigation involving Section 301. . . . Courts—the overwhelming number of them—hold that Section 301(a) is more than jurisdictional—that it authorizes federal courts to fashion a body of federal law for the enforcement of these collective bargaining agreements and includes within that federal law specific performance of promises to arbitrate grievances under collective bargaining agreements. That is our construction of Section 301(a), which means that the agreement to arbitrate grievance disputes, contained in this collective bargaining agreement, should be specifically enforced. . . .

Plainly the agreement to arbitrate grievance disputes is the *quid pro quo* for an agreement not to strike. Viewed in this light, the legislation does more than confer jurisdiction in the federal courts over labor organizations. It expresses a federal policy that federal courts should enforce these agreements on behalf of or against labor organizations and that industrial peace can be best obtained only in that way.

It seems, therefore, clear to us that Congress adopted a policy which placed sanctions behind agreements to arbitrate grievance disputes. . . . The question then is, what is the substantive law to be applied in suits under Section 301(a)? We conclude that the substantive law to apply in suits under Section 301(a) is federal law, which the courts must fashion from the policy of our national labor laws. The Labor Management Relations Act expressly furnishes some substantive law. It points out what the parties may or may not do in certain situations. Other problems will lie in the penumbra of express statutory mandates. Some will lack express statutory sanction but will be solved by looking at the policy of the legislation and fashioning a remedy that will effectuate that policy. The range of judicial inventiveness will be determined by the nature of the problem. Federal interpretation of the federal law will govern, not state law. But state law, if compatible with the purpose of Section 301, may be resorted to in order to find the rule that will best effectuate the federal policy. Any state law applied, however, will be absorbed as federal law and will not be an independent source of private rights.

The question remains whether jurisdiction to compel arbitration of grievance disputes is withdrawn by the Norris–La Guardia Act. . . . Section 7 of that Act prescribes stiff procedural requirements for issuing an injunction in a labor dispute. Though a literal reading might bring the dispute within the terms of the Act, we see no justification in policy for restricting Section 301(a) to damage suits, leaving specific performance of a contract to arbitrate grievance disputes to the inapposite procedural requirements of that Act. The congressional policy in favor of the enforcement of agreements to arbitrate grievance disputes being clear, there is no reason to submit them to the requirements of the Norris–La Guardia Act.

The judgment of the Court of Appeals is reversed and the cause is remanded to that court for proceedings in conformity with this opinion.

Reversed.

Case Questions

1. What does Justice Douglas mean when he writes that an agreement to arbitrate is "the *quid pro quo*" for an agreement not to strike?
2. What is the effect of the Norris–La Guardia Act on the ability of the court to order the parties to arbitrate a dispute? Why?
3. Should a court apply state law or federal law when deciding a dispute under Section 301? Why?

As *Lincoln Mills* indicates, if the parties have agreed to arbitration as a means of resolving disputes, the courts will require them to use it. What is voluntary about arbitration, then, is its existence—whether the agreement provides for arbitration. Once the parties have agreed to use arbitration, the courts will enforce that agreement.

What should the role of the court be when it is asked to order that a dispute be arbitrated or when it is asked to enforce an arbitration award? Those issues were addressed by the Supreme Court in three cases that came to be known as the *Steelworkers Trilogy*. In *United Steelworkers of America v. Warrior & Gulf Navigation Co.* [363 U.S. 574 (1960)], the Supreme Court held that when a court is asked to order arbitration under Section 301, an order to arbitrate the grievance should not be denied "unless it may be said with positive assurance that the arbitration clause is not susceptible of an interpretation that covers the asserted dispute. Doubts should be resolved in favor of coverage." In a more recent decision, the Supreme Court again affirmed the holding of *Warrior & Gulf Navigation;* in *AT&T Technologies v. Communications Workers of America* [475 U.S. 643 (1986)], the Court held that it is the role of the courts, not that of the arbitrators, to resolve questions of whether a grievance is subject to arbitration.

The collective agreement's arbitration clause may also affect the right of individual employees to bring employment discrimination suits. In *Wright v. Universal Marine Supply* [525 U.S. 70 (1998)] (see Chapter 5), the U.S. Supreme Court held that, in order to waive individual employee's right to sue over employment discrimination claims, the arbitration clause of a collective agreement must contain a "clear and unmistakable waiver" of the individual employee's rights to sue. *Kennedy v. Superior Printing Co.* [215 F.3d 650 (6th Cir. 2000)] held that an employee who had arbitrated a claim of employment discrimination was not prevented from bringing a court suit over the same discrimination claim because the collective agreement's general nondiscrimination clause was not a "clear and unmistakable waiver."

The limited role of the court ordering arbitration was emphasized in *United Steelworkers v. American Mfg. Co.* [363 U.S. 564 (1960)], the second case in the trilogy. In that case, the Supreme Court held that

> [t]he function of the court . . . is confined to ascertaining whether the party seeking arbitration is making a claim which on its face is governed by the contract. Whether the moving party is right or wrong is a question of contract interpretation for the arbitrator. . . . *The courts, therefore, have no business weighing the merits of the grievance.* [emphasis added]

The duty to arbitrate arises from the collective agreement between the parties, but does the duty to arbitrate continue to exist after the expiration of the collective agreement? In *Litton Financial Printing Div., Litton Business Systems v. NLRB* [501 U.S. 190 (1991)], the Supreme Court held that the duty to arbitrate continues after the expiration of the agreement if the grievance arises "under the agreement"; that is, it involves facts and occurrences that arose prior to expiration, it concerns postexpiration action that infringes a right accrued or vested under the agreement, or it involves disputed contract rights that survive the expiration of the collective agreement.

When one of the parties refuses to comply with the arbitrator's award or decision after the grievance has been arbitrated, the other party may seek to have the award judicially enforced. What is the role of the court that is asked to enforce the arbitration decision? This was the subject of the final case in the trilogy, *United Steelworkers v. Enterprise Wheel & Car Co.* [363 U.S. 593 (1960)]. In that case, the

Supreme Court held that the court is required to enforce the arbitrator's decision unless it is clear to the court that the arbitrator has exceeded the authority given to him or her by the collective agreement. The Court stated that "the question of interpretation of the collective agreement is a question for the arbitrator. It is the arbitrator's construction which was bargained for; and so far as the arbitrator's decision concerns the construction of the contract, the courts have no business overruling him because their interpretation of the contract is different from his." In *Major League Baseball Players Association v. Garvey* [532 U.S. 504 (2001)], the Supreme Court emphasized that even when the court vacates an arbitration award, the court must remand the issue back to arbitration for resolution rather than settling the merits of the dispute according to the court's own judgment.

Under the *Enterprise Wheel & Car* decision, the court should refuse to enforce an arbitration decision that violates the law. How should the court react when an employer claims that an arbitration decision conflicts with the "policy" behind the law?

In *Paperworkers v. Misco, Inc.* [484 U.S. 29 (1987)], the Supreme Court held that a court may refuse to enforce an arbitration award only if the award violates "explicit" public policy as defined by reference to legislation and court decisions rather than "general considerations of supposed public interests." In the following case, an employer argues that an arbitration award reinstating an employee who had failed a drug test should not be enforced because it violates public policy.

Eastern Associated Coal Corporation v. United Mine Workers of America, District 17

531 U.S. 57 (2000)

Justice Breyer delivered the opinion of the Court.

... Eastern Associated Coal Corp., and respondent, United Mine Workers of America, are parties to a collective-bargaining agreement with arbitration provisions. The agreement specifies that, in arbitration, in order to discharge an employee, Eastern must prove it has "just cause." Otherwise the arbitrator will order the employee reinstated. The arbitrator's decision is final.

James Smith worked for Eastern as a member of a road crew, a job that required him to drive heavy truck-like vehicles on public highways. As a truck driver, Smith was subject to Department of Transportation (DOT) regulations requiring random drug testing of workers engaged in "safety-sensitive" tasks.

In March 1996, Smith tested positive for marijuana. Eastern sought to discharge Smith. The union went to arbitration, and the arbitrator concluded that Smith's positive drug test did not amount to "just cause" for discharge. Instead the arbitrator ordered Smith's reinstatement, provided that Smith (1) accept a suspension of 30 days without pay, (2) participate in a substance-abuse program, and (3) undergo drug tests at the discretion of Eastern (or an approved substance-abuse professional) for the next five years.

Between April 1996 and January 1997, Smith passed four random drug tests. But in July 1997 he again tested positive for marijuana. Eastern again sought to discharge Smith. The union again went to arbitration, and the arbitrator again concluded that Smith's use of marijuana did not amount to "just cause" for discharge, in light of two mitigating circumstances. First, Smith had been a good employee for 17 years. And, second, Smith had made a credible and "very personal appeal under oath . . . concerning a personal/family problem which caused this one time lapse in drug usage."

The arbitrator ordered Smith's reinstatement provided that Smith (1) accept a new suspension without pay, this time for slightly more than three months; (2) reimburse Eastern and the union for the costs of both arbitration proceedings; (3) continue to participate in a substance-abuse program; (4) continue to undergo random drug testing; and (5) provide Eastern with a signed, undated letter of resignation, to take effect if Smith again tested positive within the next five years.

Eastern brought suit in federal court seeking to have the arbitrator's award vacated, arguing that the award contravened a public policy against the operation of dangerous machinery by workers who test positive for drugs. The District Court, while recognizing a strong regulation-based public policy against drug use by workers who perform safety-sensitive functions, held that Smith's conditional reinstatement did not violate that policy. And it ordered the award's enforcement.

The Court of Appeals for the Fourth Circuit affirmed on the reasoning of the District Court. [Eastern appealed to the U.S. Supreme Court.] . . .

Eastern claims that considerations of public policy make the arbitration award unenforceable. . . . Eastern does not claim here that the arbitrator acted outside the scope of his contractually delegated authority. Hence we must treat the arbitrator's award as if it represented an agreement between Eastern and the union as to the proper meaning of the contract's words "just cause." . . . We must then decide whether a contractual reinstatement requirement would fall within the legal exception that makes unenforceable "a collective bargaining agreement that is contrary to public policy." The Court has made clear that any such public policy must be "explicit," "well defined," and "dominant." It must be "ascertained 'by reference to the laws and legal precedents and not from general considerations of supposed public interests.'" And, of course, the question to be answered is not whether Smith's drug use itself violates public policy, but whether the agreement to reinstate him does so. To put the question more specifically, does a contractual agreement to reinstate Smith with specified conditions run contrary to an explicit, well-defined, and dominant public policy, as ascertained by reference to positive law and not from general considerations of supposed public interests? . . .

We agree, in principle, that courts' authority to invoke the public policy exception is not limited solely to instances where the arbitration award itself violates positive law. Nevertheless, the public policy exception is narrow and must satisfy the principles set forth in . . . *Misco.* Moreover, in a case like the one before us, where two political branches have created a detailed regulatory regime in a specific field, courts should approach with particular caution pleas to divine further public policy in that area.

Eastern asserts that a public policy against reinstatement of workers who use drugs can be discerned from an examination of that regulatory regime, which consists of the Omnibus Transportation Employee Testing Act of 1991 and DOT's implementing regulations. The Testing Act . . . requires the Secretary of Transportation to promulgate regulations requiring "testing of operators of commercial motor vehicles for the use of a controlled substance." It mandates suspension of those operators who have driven a commercial motor vehicle while under the influence of drugs. And DOT's implementing regulations set forth sanctions applicable to those who test positive for illegal drugs.

In Eastern's view, these provisions embody a strong public policy against drug use by transportation workers in safety-sensitive positions and in favor of random drug testing in order to detect that use. Eastern argues that reinstatement of a driver who has twice failed random drug tests would undermine that policy—to the point where a judge must set aside an employer-union agreement requiring reinstatement.

Eastern's argument, however, loses much of its force when one considers further provisions of the Act that make clear that the Act's remedial aims are complex. The Act says that "rehabilitation is a critical component of any testing program". . . . Neither the Act nor the regulations forbid an employer to reinstate in a safety-sensitive position an employee who fails a random drug test once or twice. The congressional and regulatory directives require only that the above-stated prerequisites to reinstatement be met.

Moreover, when promulgating these regulations, DOT decided not to require employers either to provide rehabilitation or to "hold a job open for a driver" who has tested positive, on the basis that such decisions "should be left to management/driver negotiation." That determination reflects basic background labor law principles, which caution against interference with labor-management agreements about appropriate employee discipline. . . .

We believe that these expressions of positive law embody several relevant policies. As Eastern points out, these policies include Testing Act policies against drug use by employees in safety-sensitive transportation positions and in favor of drug testing. They also include a Testing Act policy favoring rehabilitation of employees who use drugs. And the relevant statutory and regulatory provisions must be read in light of background labor law policy that favors determination of disciplinary questions through arbitration when chosen as a result of labor-management negotiation.

The award before us is not contrary to these several policies, taken together. The award does not condone Smith's conduct or ignore the risk to public safety that drug use by truck drivers may pose. Rather, the award punishes Smith by suspending him for three months, thereby depriving him of nearly $9,000 in lost wages; it requires him to pay the arbitration costs of both sides; it insists upon further substance-abuse treatment and testing; and it makes clear (by requiring Smith to provide a signed letter of resignation) that one more failed test means discharge.

The award violates no specific provision of any law or regulation. It is consistent with DOT rules requiring completion of substance-abuse treatment before returning to work, for it does not preclude Eastern from assigning Smith to a non-safety-sensitive position until Smith completes the prescribed treatment program. It is consistent with the Testing Act's . . . driving license suspension requirements, for those requirements apply only to drivers who, unlike Smith, actually operated vehicles under the influence of drugs. The award is also consistent with the Act's rehabilitative concerns, for it requires substance-abuse treatment and testing before Smith can return to work. . . .

Regarding drug use by persons in safety-sensitive positions, then, Congress has enacted a detailed statute. And Congress has delegated to the Secretary of Transportation authority to issue further detailed regulations on that subject. Upon careful consideration, including public notice and comment, the Secretary has done so. Neither Congress nor the Secretary has seen fit to mandate the discharge of a worker who twice tests positive for drugs. We hesitate to infer a public policy in this area that goes beyond the careful and detailed scheme Congress and the Secretary have created.

We recognize that reasonable people can differ as to whether reinstatement or discharge is the more appropriate remedy here. But both employer and union have agreed to entrust this remedial decision to an arbitrator. We cannot find in the Act, the regulations, or any other law or legal precedent an "explicit," "well defined," "dominant" public policy to which the arbitrator's decision "runs contrary." We conclude that the lower courts correctly rejected Eastern's public policy claim.

The judgment of the Court of Appeals is **affirmed.**

Case Questions

1. Why did the arbitrator order the reinstatement of Smith? What penalties did Smith suffer as a result of testing positive for drug use?
2. What does the employer use to define the public policy it claims requires that Smith be discharged? Does the Court read those materials as defining the same public policy as claimed by the employer?
3. Does the Court enforce the arbitrator's award here? Why?

JUDICIAL ENFORCEMENT OF NO-STRIKE CLAUSES

The decisions in the *Steelworkers Trilogy* emphasized that arbitration was a substitute for industrial strife. The *Lincoln Mills* decision stated that the employer's agreement to arbitrate disputes is the quid pro quo for the union's agreement not to strike over arbitrable disputes.

Many agreements contain no-strike clauses by which the union agrees not to strike over disputes of interpretation of the agreement. In *Teamsters Local 174 v. Lucas Flour* [369 U.S. 95 (1962)], the Supreme Court held that a no-strike clause will be implied by the court, even when the agreement itself is silent on the matter, if the agreement contains an arbitration provision. The implied no-strike clause covers any dispute that is subject to arbitration under the agreement.

If the collective agreement contains an express no-strike clause, or even an implied one under *Lucas Flour*, can a federal court enforce that clause by enjoining a strike in violation of the no-strike clause? What about the anti-injunction provisions of the Norris–La Guardia Act? This issue was presented to the Supreme Court in *Boys Markets, Inc. v. Retail Clerks Union, Local 770* [398 U.S. 235 (1970)]. The Court in *Boys Markets* held that the Norris-La Guardia Act did not prevent a federal court from issuing an injunction to stop a strike over an issue that was subject to the arbitration clause of a collective agreement.

Injunctions under the doctrine of *Boys Markets* may also be issued against employers for breaches of the collective agreement that threaten the arbitration process. In *Oil, Chemical and Atomic Workers International Union, Local 2–286 v. Amoco Oil Co.* [885 F.2d 697 (10th Cir. 1989)], the court affirmed an injunction preventing an employer's unilateral implementation of a drug testing program, pending the outcome of arbitration to determine the employer's right to institute such a program under the collective-bargaining agreement.

The decision in *Boys Markets* allowing federal courts to enjoin strikes in violation of no-strike clauses does not mean that a union may never go on strike during the term of a collective agreement. The *Boys Markets* holding is limited to strikes over issues subject to arbitration under the agreement. In *Jacksonville Bulk Terminals, Inc. v. Int. Longshoremen's Ass'n.* [457 U.S. 702 (1982)], the Supreme Court refused to enjoin a refusal by longshoremen to handle cargo destined for the Soviet Union in protest over the Soviet invasion of Afghanistan. The Court held that the strike was over a political dispute that was not arbitrable under the collective agreement. The policy behind that decision was first set out in the Supreme Court decision of *Buffalo Forge Co. v. United Steelworkers of America* [428 U.S. 397 (1975)], which held that the use of an injunction to stop a strike, as in *Boys Markets,* is appropriate only when the cause of the strike is a dispute that is subject to arbitration under the collective agreement.

Remedies for Breach of No-Strike Clauses

As the preceding cases demonstrate, an employer may enjoin strikes that violate a no-strike clause when the strike is over an arbitrable issue. But even when an injunction will not be issued, an employer may still recover damages for breach of the no-strike clause through a suit under Section 301. In the *Lucas Flour* case, the Supreme Court upheld a damage award for a strike in violation of the implied no-strike clause.

Section 301 Suits. The Supreme Court had held that suits under Section 301 are governed by the appropriate state statutes of limitations, *UAW v. Hoosier Cardinal Corp.* [383 U.S. 696 (1966)]. More recently, in *DelCostello v. Teamsters* [462 U.S. 151 (1983)], the Court held that suits under Section 301 by an individual employee against the employer for breach of the collective agreement and against the union for breach of the duty of fair representation were subject to the six-month limitation period under Section 10(b) of the NLRA.

Section 301, while allowing damage suits for breach of no-strike clauses, places some limitations upon such suits. Section 301(b) specifies that "any money judgment against a labor organization in a district court of the United States shall be enforceable only against the organization as an entity and its assets, and shall not be enforceable against any individual member or his assets." In *Atkinson v. Sinclair Refining Co.* [370 U.S. 238 (1962)], the Supreme Court held that Section 301 does not authorize damage suits against individual union officials when their union is liable for violating a no-strike clause. In *Complete Auto Transit, Inc. v. Reis* [451 U.S. 401 (1981)], the Court held that individual employees are not liable for damages from a wildcat strike not authorized by their union in breach of the collective agreement. If the employer cannot recover damages from the individuals responsible for such a strike, what other steps can the employer take against those individuals?

In *Carbon Fuel Co. v. United Mine Workers* [444 U.S. 212 (1979)], the Supreme Court held that an international union was not liable for damages resulting from a strike by one of its local unions when the international had neither instigated, authorized, supported, nor encouraged the strike. Why would the employer seek damages from the international when the local had gone on strike?

The result of the *Complete Auto Transit* and *Carbon Fuel* cases is to deprive the employer of the right to recover damages from either the union or the individual union members when a strike by the individual union members is not authorized by the union. The remedy of damages is available to the employer only when the union has called or authorized the strike in breach of the collective agreement.

When the employer can pursue arbitration over the union violation of the agreement, the court will stay a suit for damages pending arbitration according to the Supreme Court decision in *Drake Bakeries Inc. v. Bakery Workers Local 50* [370 U.S. 254 (1962)]. The employer's obligation to arbitrate such disputes continues despite the union's breach of its contractual obligations, *Packinghouse Workers Local 721 v. Needham Packing Co.* [376 U.S. 247 (1964)].

Section 301 and Other Remedies. Can a court hear a suit alleging a breach of contract under Section 301 even though the contract is silent about judicial remedies? In *Groves v. Ring Screw Works* [498 U.S. 168 (1990)], the collective agreement provided for arbitration in discharge cases only upon agreement of both parties; it also provided that if a grievance was not resolved through the grievance procedure, the union could go on strike over the issue. Two employees who were discharged by the employer filed suit for wrongful discharge in state court; their union joined the suits as a plaintiff. The employer argued that the union could not file suit because the contract did not require arbitration. The Supreme Court reversed the court of appeals; the Court unanimously held that a contract giving the union the right to strike or the employer the right to lock out does not automatically strip federal courts of the authority to resolve contractual disputes. The union was not precluded from filing suit against the employer to enforce the contract, even though the contract was silent about judicial remedies.

Section 301 Preemption of Other Remedies. In *Allis-Chalmers Corp. v. Leuck* [471 U.S. 202 (1985)], the Supreme Court held that if the resolution of a state law claim depends on the interpretation of a collective agreement, the application of the state law is preempted by federal law; a suit under state law alleging bad-faith handling of a disability benefits claim was preempted by Section 301 because the collective agreement set out provisions for handling disability claims. In *I.B.E.W. v. Hechler* [481 U.S. 851 (1987)], the Supreme Court held that an employee's tort suit against the union for failure to provide a safe place to work was precluded by Section 301 because her claim was "nothing more than a breach of the union's federal duty of fair representation." However, where state law remedies exist independently of any collective agreement and do not require interpretation of the agreement, the state law remedy is not preempted. In *Lingle v. Norge Division of Magic Chef, Inc.* [486 U.S. 399 (1988)], the Supreme Court held that an employee who was discharged for filing a workers' compensation claim could file suit under state law for compensation and punitive damages; her suit was not preempted by Section 301.

California law requires that employers pay discharged employees all wages owed to them immediately at the time of the discharge; the California State commissioner of labor interpreted that law as not applying to employees covered by a collective agreement containing an arbitration clause. In *Livadas v. Bradshaw* [512 U.S. 107 (1994)], the U.S. Supreme Court held that the commissioner's interpretation was preempted by Section 301 because it denied employees benefits for engaging in activity—pursuing arbitration and other remedies under the collective agreement—protected under federal labor law.

THE NLRB AND ARBITRATION

As the preceding cases have demonstrated, the courts favor the policy of voluntary resolution of disputes between labor and management. The courts will therefore refrain from deciding issues that are subject to arbitration, instead deferring to the arbitrator's resolution of such issues. If a grievance under an agreement involves conduct that may also be an unfair labor practice under the NLRA, what is the role of the National Labor Relations Board (NLRB)? Should the board, like the courts, defer to arbitration? Or should the board decide the issue to ensure that the parties' statutory rights are protected? The following case applies to these issues.

United Technologies

268 NLRB No. 83 (NLRB, 1984)

The complaint alleges that the Respondent (United Technologies) violated Section 8(a)(1) by threatening employee Sherfield with disciplinary action if she persisted in processing a grievance to the second step. At the hearing, the Respondent denied that it had violated Section 8(a)(1) as alleged and argued that, in any event, since the dispute was cognizable under the grievance-arbitration provisions of the parties' collective-bargaining agreement, it should be resolved pursuant to those provisions. Accordingly, the Respondent urged the Board to defer the exercise of its jurisdiction in this matter to the grievance-arbitration machinery. The judge, relying on *General American Transportation Corp.*, rejected the Respondent's contention because the conduct complained of constituted an alleged violation of Section 8(a)(1). . . .

On 6 November 1981 the Union filed a third-step grievance alleging that the Respondent, through its general foreman, Peterson, intimidated, coerced, and harassed shop steward Wilson and employee Sherfield at a first-step grievance meeting by threatening disciplinary action against Sherfield if she appealed her grievance to the second step. The remedy the Union sought was that "the Company immediately stop these contract violations and General Foreman Roger Peterson be properly reprimanded and reinstructed for his misuse, abuse, and violation of the contract." The Respondent denied the Union's grievance at the third step, and the Union withdrew it on 27 January 1982 "without prejudice." The next day, the Respondent filed its own grievance alleging that "[n]otwithstanding the union's mistake in its allegations concerning General Foreman Peterson, it has refused to withdraw, with prejudice, its grievance." The Union denied the Respondent's grievance, and the Respondent appealed to the fourth step. Following a fourth-step meeting, the Union again denied the Respondent's grievance and refused the Respondent's request that the matter be submitted to arbitration. Thereafter, the Union filed the charge [with the NLRB]. . . .

The Respondent and the Union were parties to a collective-bargaining agreement which was effective from 24 April 1978 through 24 April 1983. Article VII of the contract established a grievance procedure that includes an oral step, four written steps, and an arbitration provision that calls for final and binding arbitration.

Arbitration as a means of resolving labor disputes has gained widespread acceptance over the years and now occupies a respected and firmly established place in Federal labor policy. The reason for its success is the underlying conviction that the parties to a collective-bargaining agreement are in the best position to resolve, with the help of a neutral third party if necessary, disputes concerning the correct interpretation of their contract. Congressional intent regarding the use of arbitration is abundantly clear. . . .

Similarly, the concept of judicial and administrative deference to the arbitral process and the notion that courts should support, rather than interfere with, this method of dispute resolution have become entrenched in American jurisprudence. Over the years, the Board has played a key role in fostering a climate in which arbitration could flourish.

The Board endowed this sound approach with renewed vigor in the seminal case of *Collyer Insulated Wire,* in which the Board dismissed a complaint alleging unilateral changes in wages and working conditions in violation of Section 8(a)(5) in deference to the parties' grievance-arbitration machinery. The *Collyer* majority articulated several factors favoring deferral: The dispute arose within the confines of a long and productive collective-bargaining relationship; there was no claim of employer animosity to the employees' exercise of protected rights; the parties' contract provided for arbitration in a very broad range of disputes; the arbitration clause clearly encompassed the dispute at issue; the employer had asserted its willingness to utilize arbitration to resolve the dispute; and the dispute was eminently well suited to resolution by arbitration. In these circumstances, deferral to the arbitral process merely gave full effect to the parties' agreement to submit disputes to arbitration. In essence, the *Collyer* majority was holding the parties to their bargain by directing them to avoid substituting the Board's processes for their own mutually agreed-upon method for dispute resolution.

The experience under *Collyer* was extremely positive. . . . In *National Radio* the Board extended the deferral policy to cases involving 8(a)(3) allegations. In that case the complaint alleged, inter alia, the disciplinary suspension and discharge of an active union adherent in violation of Section 8(a)(3) as well as various changes in terms and conditions of employment in violation of Section 8(a)(5). Thus, that case presented a situation where the resolution of the unilateral change issues by an arbitrator would not necessarily have resolved the 8(a)(3) issues raised by the complaint. Nevertheless, the Board decided that deferral to the grievance procedure prior to the issuance of the arbitrator's award was warranted.

Following *National Radio,* the Board routinely dismissed complaints alleging violations of Section 8(a)(3) and (1) in deference to the arbitral forum.

Despite the universal judicial acceptance of the *Collyer* doctrine, however, the Board in *General American Transportation* abruptly changed course and adopted a different standard for arbitral deferral, one that we believe ignores the important policy considerations in favor of deferral. Indeed, by deciding to decline to defer cases alleging violations of Sections 8(a)(1) and (3) and 8(b)(1)(A) and (2), the *General American Transportation* majority essentially emasculated the Board's deferral policy, a policy that had favorably withstood the tests of judicial scrutiny and of practical application. And they did so for reasons that are largely unsupportable. Simply stated, *Collyer* worked well because it was premised on sound legal and pragmatic considerations. Accordingly, we believe it deserves to be resurrected and infused with renewed life. . . .

The facts of the instant case make it eminently well suited for deferral. The dispute centers on a statement a single foreman made to a single employee and a shop steward during the course of a routine first-step grievance meeting allegedly concerning possible adverse consequences that might flow from a decision by the employee to process her grievance to the next step. The statement is alleged to be a threat violative of Section 8(a)(1). It is also, however, clearly cognizable under the broad grievance-arbitration provision of Section VII of the collective-bargaining agreement. Moreover, Respondent has expressed its willingness, indeed its eagerness, to arbitrate the dispute.

So ordered.

Case Questions

1. What was the basis of the union's Section 8(a)(1) charge? Was that question subject to arbitration under the collective agreement?
2. According to the *Collyer Insulated Wire* decision, what factors will the NLRB consider in deciding whether to defer an unfair labor practice complaint to arbitration? How do those factors apply to the present case?
3. Why would the NLRB want to refer a case to arbitration rather than decide the case itself?

When the board has deferred an unfair labor practice charge to arbitration, should the board automatically uphold the arbitrator's decision? This question is addressed in the following case.

Olin Corp.

268 NLRB No. 86 (NLRB, 1984)

In brief, the Union is the exclusive collective-bargaining representative of Respondent's approximately 260 production and maintenance employees. The 1980–83 collective-bargaining agreement contained the following provision:

> Article XIV—Strikes and Lockouts
> During the life of the Agreement, the Company will not conduct a lockout at the Plant and neither the Local Union nor the International Union, nor any officer or representative of either, will cause or permit its members to cause any strike, slowdown or stoppage (total or partial) of work or any interference, directly or indirectly, with the full operation of the plant.

Employee Salvatore B. Spatorico was president of the Union from 1976 until his termination in December 1980. On the morning of 17 December, Respondent suspended two pipefitters for refusing to perform a job that they felt was more appropriately millwright work. A "sick out" ensued during which approximately 43 employees left work that day with medical excuses. Respondent gave formal written reprimands to 39 of the employees who had engaged in the sick out. In a letter dated 29 December, Respondent notified Spatorico that he was discharged based on his entire record and in particular for threatening the sick out, participating in the sick out, and failing to prevent it.

Spatorico's discharge was grieved and arbitrated. After a hearing, the arbitrator found that a sick out had occurred at Respondent's facility on 17 December, that Spatorico "at least partially caused or participated" in it, and that he failed to try to stop it until after it had occurred. The arbitrator concluded that Spatorico's conduct contravened his obligation under article XIV of the collective-bargaining agreement set forth above. The arbitrator also stated, "Union officers implicitly have an affirmative duty not to cause strikes which are in violation of the clause, not to participate in such strikes and to try to stop them when they occur." Accordingly, the arbitrator found that Spatorico had been appropriately discharged.

Noting that the unfair labor practice charges had been referred to arbitration . . . the arbitrator addressed these charges and found "no evidence that the company discharged the grievant for his legitimate Union activities." The arbitrator again stated his conclusion that Spatorico had been discharged for participating in and failing to stop the sick out because Spatorico "is a Union officer but the contract's no strike clause *specifically* prohibits such activity by Union officers." [emphasis added] [The union filed unfair labor practice charges with the NLRB.]

The judge (ALJ) declined to defer to the arbitration award on the grounds that although the arbitrator referred to the unfair labor practice issue he did not consider it "in any serious way." The judge determined that the arbitrator was not competent to decide the unfair labor practice issue because the award was limited to interpretation of the contract. Moreover, he determined that the arbitrator did not explicitly refer to the statutory right and the waiver questions raised by the unfair labor practice charge. On the merits, however, the judge agreed with the arbitrator's conclusion in that he found Spatorico's "participation in the strike was inconsistent with his manifest contractual obligation to attempt to stem the tide of unprotected activity." The judge concluded that article XIV of the collective-bargaining agreement was sufficiently clear and unmistakable to waive, at the least, the sort of conduct in which Spatorico engaged, that, therefore, "Spatorico exposed himself to the greater liability . . ." and that Respondent did not violate Section 8(a)(3) and (1) of the Act by discharging him while merely reprimanding other employees.

We agree with the judge that the complaint should be dismissed. We do so, however, without reaching the merits because we would defer to the arbitrator's award consistent with the standards set forth in *Spielberg Mfg. Co.* In its seminal decision in *Spielberg,* the Board held that it would defer to an arbitration award where the proceedings appear to have been fair and regular, all parties have agreed to be bound, and the decision of the arbitrator is not clearly repugnant to the purposes and policies of the Act. The Board in *Raytheon Co.* further conditioned deferral on the arbitrator's having considered the unfair labor practice issue.

It hardly needs repeating that national policy strongly favors the voluntary arbitration of disputes. The importance of arbitration in the overall scheme of Federal labor law has been stressed in innumerable contexts and forums. . . .

Accordingly, we adopt the following standard for deferral to arbitration awards. We would find that an arbitrator has adequately considered the unfair labor practice if (1) the contractual issue is factually parallel to the unfair labor practice issue, and (2) the arbitrator was presented generally with the facts relevant to resolving the unfair labor practice. In this respect, differences, if any, between the contractual and statutory standards of review should be weighed by the Board as part of its determination under the *Spielberg* standards of whether an award is "clearly repugnant" to the Act. And, with regard to the inquiry into the "clearly repugnant" standard, we would not require an arbitrator's award to be totally consistent with Board precedent. Unless the award is "palpably wrong," i.e. unless the arbitrator's decision is not susceptible to an interpretation consistent with the Act, we will defer.

Finally, we would require that the party seeking to have the Board reject deferral and consider the merits of a given case show that the above standards for deferral have not been met. Thus, the party seeking to have the Board ignore the determination of an arbitrator has the burden of affirmatively demonstrating the defects in the arbitral process or award. . . .

Turning now to the case before us, we find that the arbitral proceeding has met the *Spielberg* standards for deferral, and that the arbitrator adequately considered the unfair labor practice issue.

Case Questions

1. What was the arbitrator's decision on the union's grievance over Spatorico's discharge? Why was the union now seeking to have the NLRB decide its unfair labor practice charges based on that discharge?
2. According to the *Spielberg Mfg. Co.* decision, when will the NLRB accept an arbitration award rather than decide an unfair labor practice complaint? How do those factors apply to the facts in this case?
3. Why should the NLRB defer to an arbitrator's award to settle an unfair labor practice complaint rather than decide the case itself? Do you see any problems with that approach? Explain.

Some courts of appeals have rejected the NLRB's broad deferral policy under *United Technologies* and *Olin*. In *Taylor v. NLRB* [786 F.2d 1516 (11th Cir. 1986)], the court stated that the board's deferral policy inappropriately divests the board of its unfair labor practice jurisdiction under Section 10(b) of the NLRA. The court held that the policy of presuming every arbitration proceeding addresses every possible unfair labor practice issue overlooks situations when the contractual and statutory issues may be factually parallel but involve differing elements of proof or questions of factual relevance. In *Hammondtree v. NLRB* [894 F.2d 438 (D.C. Cir. 1990)], the court held that an employee may not be forced to give up the right to have the board adjudicate an unfair labor practice claim simply because the employer and union have established parallel contractual provisions and procedures for resolving the claim; only where the employee waives unfair labor practice rights or the claim rests on otherwise arbitrable matters may the board defer to arbitration.

CHANGES IN THE STATUS OF EMPLOYERS

SUCCESSOR EMPLOYERS

When a new employer takes over a unionized firm, what is the obligation of the successor employer to recognize the union, to adhere to the collective agreement, and to arbitrate grievances that arose under the collective agreement?

In *John Wiley & Sons, Inc. v. Livingston* [376 U.S. 543 (1964)], the Supreme Court held that the successor employer must arbitrate a grievance arising under the collective agreement where there was a "substantial continuity of identity in the business enterprise" and the employer retained a majority of the employees from the former unionized work force. The union in *Wiley* sought only to force the new employer to arbitrate; it did not seek to force the employer to bargain with it. In *NLRB v. Burns International Security Services, Inc.* [406 U.S. 272 (1972)], the Supreme Court dealt with a case where the union sought to force the new employer to recognize the union and to abide by the collective agreement. The Supreme Court held that the successor employer was not bound by the prior collective agreement but was required to recognize and bargain with the union because it had retained enough employees from the prior, unionized work force to constitute a majority of the new employer's work force.

See **http://www.law.cornell.edu/topics/labor.html** *and choose state statutes to look up state labor laws and Supreme Court decisions.*

What factors should be considered when determining whether a "substantial continuity of identity" of the operation exists, and at what point in the hiring process does the presence of a union's supporters constituting a majority of the work force trigger the duty to bargain with the union? The Supreme Court addressed these issues in the following case.

Fall River Dyeing & Finishing Corp. v. NLRB

482 U.S. 27 (1987)

Blackmun, J.

. . . For over 30 years before 1982, Sterlingwale operated a textile dyeing and finishing plant in Fall River, Massachusetts. Its business consisted basically of two types of dyeing, called, respectively, "converting" and "commission." Under the converting process, which in 1981 accounted for 60 to 70 percent of its business, Sterlingwale bought unfinished fabrics for its own account, dyed and finished them, and then sold them to apparel manufacturers. In commission dyeing, which accounted for the remainder of its business, Sterlingwale dyed and finished fabrics owned by customers according to their specifications. The financing and marketing aspects of converting and commission dyeing are different. Converting requires capital to purchase fabrics and a sales force to promote the finished products. The production process, however, is the same for both converting and commission dyeing.

In the late 1970s the textile-dyeing business, including Sterlingwale's, began to suffer from adverse economic conditions and foreign competition. After 1979, business at Sterlingwale took a serious turn for the worse because of the loss of its export market, and the company reduced the number of its employees. Finally, in February 1982, Sterlingwale laid off all its production employees, primarily because it no longer had the capital to continue the converting business. It retained a skeleton crew of workers and supervisors to ship out the goods remaining on order and to maintain the corporation's building and machinery. In the months following the layoff, Leonard Ansin, Sterlingwale's president, liquidated the inventory of the corporation and, at the same time, looked for a business partner with whom he could "resurrect the business." . . .

For almost as long as Sterlingwale had been in existence, its production and maintenance employees had been represented by the United Textile Workers of America, AFL-CIO, Local 292 (Union).

In late summer 1982, however, Sterlingwale finally went out of business. It made an assignment for the benefit of its creditors [who held] . . . a first mortgage on most of Sterlingwale's real property and . . . a security interest on Sterlingwale's machinery and equipment. . . .

During this same period, a former Sterlingwale employee and officer, Herbert Chace, and Arthur Friedman, president of one of Sterlingwale's major customers, . . . formed petitioner Fall River Dyeing & Finishing Corp. Chace, who had resigned from Sterlingwale in February 1982, had worked there for 27 years, had been vice-president in charge of sales at the time of his departure, and had participated in collective bargaining with the Union during his tenure at Sterlingwale. Chace and Friedman formed petitioner with the intention of engaging strictly in the commission-dyeing business and of taking advantage of the availability of Sterlingwale's assets and workforce. Accordingly, Friedman [acquired] . . . Sterlingwale's plant, real property, and equipment, and [sold] them to petitioner. Petitioner also obtained some of Sterlingwale's remaining inventory at the liquidator's auction. Chace became petitioner's vice-president in charge of operations and Friedman became its president. In September 1982, petitioner began operating out of Sterlingwale's former facilities and began hiring employees. . . . Petitioner's initial hiring goal was to attain one full shift of workers, which meant from 55 to 60 employees. Petitioner planned to "see how business would be" after this initial goal had been met and, if business permitted, to expand to two shifts. The employees who were hired first spent approximately four to six weeks in start-up operations and an additional month in experimental production.

By letter dated October 19, 1982, the Union requested petitioner to recognize it as the bargaining agent for petitioner's employees and to begin collective bargaining. Petitioner refused the request, stating that, in its view, the request had "no legal basis." At that time, 18 of petitioner's 21 employees were former employees of Sterlingwale. By November of that year, petitioner had employees in a complete range of jobs, had its production process in operation, and was handling customer orders; by mid-January 1983, it had attained its initial goal of one shift of workers. Of the 55 workers in this initial shift, a number that represented over half the workers petitioner would eventually hire, 36 were former Sterlingwale employees. Petitioner continued to expand its workforce, and by mid-April 1983 it had reached two full shifts. For the first time, ex-Sterlingwale employees were in the minority but just barely so (52 or 53 out of 107 employees).

Although petitioner engaged exclusively in commission dyeing, the employees experienced the same conditions they had when they were working for Sterlingwale. The production process was unchanged and the employees worked on the same machines, in the same building, with the same job classifications, under virtually the same supervisors. Over half the volume of petitioner's business came from former Sterlingwale customers, . . .

On November 1, 1982, the Union filed an unfair labor practice charge with the Board, alleging that in its refusal to bargain petitioner had violated Section 8(a)(1) and (5) of the National Labor Relations Act. After a hearing, the Administrative Law Judge (ALJ) decided that, on the facts of the case, petitioner was a successor to Sterlingwale. . . . Thus, in the view of the ALJ, petitioner's duty to bargain rose in mid-January because former Sterlingwale employees then were in the majority and because the Union's October demand was still in effect. Petitioner thus committed an unfair labor practice in refusing to bargain. In a brief decision and order, the Board, with one member dissenting, affirmed this decision. The Court of Appeals for the First Circuit, also by a divided vote, enforced the order. . . .

. . . [I]n *NLRB v. Burns International Security Services, Inc.,* this Court first dealt with the issue of a successor employer's obligation to bargain with a union that had represented the employees of its predecessor. . . . These presumptions [of majority support developed in *Burns*] are based not so much on an absolute certainty that the union's majority status will not erode following certification, as on a particular policy decision. The overriding policy of the NLRA is "industrial peace." The presumptions of majority support further this policy by "promot[ing] stability in collective-bargaining relationships, without impairing the free choice of employees." In essence, they enable a union to concentrate on obtaining and fairly administering a collective-bargaining agreement without worrying that, unless it produces immediate results, it will lose majority support and will be decertified. . . . The presumptions also remove any temptation on the part of the employer to avoid good-faith bargaining in the hope that, by delaying, it will undermine the union's support among the employees. . . .

The rationale behind the presumptions is particularly pertinent in the successorship situation and so it is understandable that the Court in *Burns* referred to them. During a transition between employers, a union is in a peculiarly vulnerable position. It has no formal and established bargaining relationship with the new employer, is uncertain about the new employer's plans, and cannot be sure if or when the new employer must bargain with it. While being concerned with the future of its members with the new employer, the union also must protect whatever rights still exist for its members under the collective bargaining agreement with the predecessor employer. Accordingly, during this unsettling transition period, the union needs the presumptions of majority status to which it is entitled to safeguard its members' rights and to develop a relationship with the successor.

The position of the employees also supports the application of the presumptions in the successorship situation. If the employees find themselves in a new enterprise that substantially resembles the old, but without their chosen bargaining representative, they may well feel that their choice of a union is subject to the vagaries of an enterprise's transformation. . . . Without the presumptions of majority support and with the wide variety of corporate transformations possible, an employer could use a successor enterprise as a way of getting rid of a labor contract and of exploiting the employees' hesitant attitude towards the union to eliminate its continuing presence.

In addition to recognizing the traditional presumptions of union majority status, however, the Court in *Burns* was careful to safeguard "the rightful prerogative of owners independently to rearrange their businesses." If the new employer makes a conscious decision to maintain generally the same business and to hire a majority of its employees from the predecessor, then the bargaining obligation of Section 8(a)(5) is activated. This makes sense when one considers that the employer intends to take advantage of the trained workforce of its predecessor. . . .

We now hold that a successor's obligation to bargain is not limited to a situation where the union in question has been recently certified. Where, as here, the union has a rebuttable presumption of majority status, this status continues despite the change in employers. And the new employer has an obligation to bargain with that union so long as the new employer is in fact a successor of the old employer and the majority of its employees were employed by its predecessor.

We turn now to the three rules, as well as to their application to the facts of this case, that the Board has adopted for the successorship situation.

In *Burns* we approved the approach taken by the Board and accepted by courts with respect to determining whether a new company was indeed the successor to the old. This approach, which is primarily factual in nature and is based upon the totality of the circumstances of a given situation, requires that the Board focus on whether the new company has "acquired substantial assets of its predecessor and continued, without interruption or substantial change the predecessor's business operations." Hence, the focus is on whether there is "substantial continuity" between the enterprises. Under this approach, the Board examines a number of factors: whether the business of both employers is essentially the same; whether the employees of the new company are doing the same jobs in the same working conditions under the same supervisors; and whether the new entity has the same production process, produces the same products, and basically has the same body of customers.... In conducting the analysis, the Board keeps in mind the question whether "those employees who have been retained will understandably view their job situations as essentially unaltered." . . .

[W]e find that the Board's determination that there was "substantial continuity" between Sterlingwale and petitioner and that petitioner was Sterlingwale's successor is supported by substantial evidence in the record. Petitioner acquired most of Sterlingwale's real property, its machinery and equipment, and much of its inventory and materials. It introduced no new product line. Of particular significance is the fact that, from the perspective of the employees, their jobs did not change. Although petitioner abandoned converting dyeing in exclusive favor of commission dyeing, this change did not alter the essential nature of the employees' jobs because both types of dyeing involved the same production process. The job classifications of petitioner were the same as those of Sterlingwale; petitioner's employees worked on the same machines under the direction of supervisors most of whom were former supervisors of Sterlingwale. The record, in fact, is clear that petitioner acquired Sterlingwale's assets with the express purpose of taking advantage of its predecessor's workforce. . . .

For the reasons given above, this is a case where the other factors suggest "substantial continuity" between the companies despite the 7-month hiatus. Here, moreover, the extent of the hiatus between the demise of Sterlingwale and the start-up of petitioner is somewhat less than certain. After the February layoff, Sterlingwale retained a skeleton crew of supervisors and employees that continued to ship goods to customers and to maintain the plant. In addition, until the assignment for the benefit of the creditors late in the summer, Ansin was seeking to resurrect the business or to find a buyer for Sterlingwale. The Union was aware of these efforts. Viewed from the employees' perspective, therefore, the hiatus may have been much less than seven months. Although petitioner hired the employees through advertisements, it often relied on recommendations from supervisors, themselves formerly employed by Sterlingwale, and intended the advertisements to reach the former Sterlingwale workforce. Accordingly, we hold that, under settled law, petitioner was a successor to Sterlingwale. We thus must consider if and when petitioner's duty to bargain arose.

In *Burns,* the Court determined that the successor had an obligation to bargain with the union because a majority of its employees had been employed by Wackenhut. The "triggering" fact for the bargaining obligation was this composition of the successor's workforce. The Court, however, did not have to consider the question when the successor's obligation to bargain arose: Wackenhut's contract expired on June 30 and Burns began its services with a majority of former Wackenhut guards on July 1. In other situations, as in the present case, there is a start-up period by the new employer while it gradually builds its operations and hires employees. In these situations, the Board, with the approval of the Courts of Appeals, has adopted the "substantial and representative complement" rule for fixing the moment when the determination as to the composition of the successor's workforce is to be made. If, at this particular moment, a majority of the successor's employees had been employed by its predecessor, then the successor has an obligation to bargain with the union that represented these employees. In deciding when a "substantial and representative complement" exists in a particular employer transition, the Board examines a number of factors. It studies "whether the job classifications designated for the operation were filled or substantially filled and whether the operation was in normal or substantially normal production." In addition, it takes into consideration "the size of the complement on that date and the time expected to elapse before a substantially larger complement would be at work . . . as well as the relative certainty of the employer's expected expansion." . . .

We conclude, . . . that in this situation the successor is in the best position to follow a rule the criteria of which are straightforward. The employer generally will know with tolerable certainty when all its job classifications have been filled or substantially filled, when it has hired a majority of the employees it intends to hire, and when it has begun normal production. Moreover, the "full complement" standard advocated by petitioner is not necessarily easier for a successor to apply than is the "substantial and representative complement." In fact, given the expansionist dreams of many new entrepreneurs, it might well be more difficult for a successor to identify the moment when the "full complement" has been attained, which is when the business will reach the limits of the new employer's initial hopes, than it would be for this same employer to acknowledge the time when its business has begun normal production—the moment identified by the "substantial and representative complement" rule. We therefore hold that the Board's "substantial and representative complement" rule is reasonable in the successorship context. Moreover, its application to the facts of this case is supported by substantial record evidence. The Court of Appeals observed that by mid-January petitioner "had hired employees in virtually all job classifications, had hired at least fifty percent of those it would ultimately employ in the majority of those classifications, and it employed a majority of the employees it would eventually employ when it reached full complement." At that time petitioner had begun normal production. Although petitioner intended to expand to two shifts, and, in fact, reached this goal by mid-April, that expansion was contingent expressly upon the growth of the business. Accordingly, as found by the Board and approved by the Court of Appeals, mid-January was the period when petitioner reached its "substantial and representative complement." Because at that time the majority of petitioner's employees were former Sterlingwale employees, petitioner had an obligation to bargain with the Union then.

We also hold that the Board's "continuing demand" rule is reasonable in the successorship situation. The successor's duty to bargain at the "substantial and representative complement" date is triggered only when the union has made a bargaining demand. Under the "continuing demand" rule, when a union has made a premature demand that has been rejected by the employer, this demand remains in force until the moment when the employer attains the "substantial and representative complement."

Such a rule, particularly when considered along with the "substantial and representative complement" rule, places a minimal burden on the successor and makes sense in light of the union's position. Once the employer has concluded that it has reached the appropriate complement, then, in order to determine whether its duty to bargain will be triggered, it has only to see whether the union already has made a demand for bargaining. Because the union has no established relationship with the successor and because it is unaware of the successor's plans for its operations and hiring, it is likely that, in many cases, a union's bargaining demand will be premature. It makes no sense to require the union repeatedly to renew its bargaining demand in the hope of having it correspond with the "substantial and representative complement" date, when, with little trouble, the employer can regard a previous demand as a continuing one.

The reasonableness of the "continuing demand" rule is demonstrated by the facts of this case. Although the Union had asked Ansin to inform it about his plans for Sterlingwale so that it could become involved in the employer transition, the Union learned about this transition only after it had become a *fait accompli*. Without having any established relationship with petitioner, it therefore is not surprising that the Union's October bargaining demand was premature. The Union, however, made clear after this demand that, in its view, petitioner had a bargaining obligation: the Union filed an unfair labor practice in November. Petitioner responded by denying that it had any duty to bargain. Rather than being a successor confused about when a bargaining obligation might arise, petitioner took an initial position—and stuck with it—that it never would have any bargaining obligation with the Union.

The judgment of the Court of Appeals is affirmed.

It is so ordered.

[Dissent omitted.]

Case Questions

1. What is the NLRB's "substantial and representative complement" rule? How does it apply to the facts in this case? Explain.
2. What factors does the NLRB consider when determining if there is a "substantial continuity" of operation between the former employer and a successor employer? How do those factors apply to the facts here?
3. What is the NLRB's "continuing demand" rule? How does it apply to the facts in this case? Explain.

ETHICAL DILEMMA: TO RETAIN OR NOT TO RETAIN?

Immense Multinational Business (IMB) is planning to purchase the entire plant, assets, and operation of CastCo, a small manufacturing company. The employees at CastCo are represented by the International Molders Union, but IMB's employees are not unionized. IMB plans to maintain most of the operations at CastCo and is considering whether to retain the former CastCo employees as well. What are the benefits of retaining the former CastCo production workers? Are there any arguments against retaining the CastCo workers? Are there any legal restrictions on the decision whether to retain the CastCo workers? How should IMB proceed here?

You, the recently promoted director of human resources for IMB's manufacturing operations, are asked by the CEO to prepare a memo discussing these issues and recommending a course of action. Be sure to support your recommendation.

Following *Fall River Dyeing,* a court held that an employer who assumed operation of a steel mill that had been closed for two years and that had drastically reduced the number of employees and restructured job classifications was not a successor employer because of the lack of a substantial continuity of operation with the former employer, *CitiSteel USA v. NLRB* [53 F.3d 350 (D.C. Cir. 1995)]. However, a two-year hiatus in operations did not preclude the NLRB from holding that the new employer was a successor in *Pennsylvania Transformer Technology, Inc. v. NLRB* [254 F.3d 217 (2001)].

A successor employer can be held liable for the remedy of an unfair labor practice committed by the old employer; in *NLRB v. Winco Petroleum* [668 F.2d 973 (8th Cir. 1982)], a successor was held subject to a bargaining order remedy even though the successor itself was not guilty of a refusal to bargain.

The incumbent union in a successorship situation is entitled to a rebuttable presumption of continuing majority status, but that presumption does not preclude a petition for a representation or decertification election or an otherwise valid challenge to the union's majority status, *MV Transportation* [337 NLRB No. 129 (2002)].

BANKRUPTCY AND THE COLLECTIVE AGREEMENT

The prior cases dealt with the obligations of successor employers. When an employer experiencing financial difficulties seeks protection from creditors under the bankruptcy laws, can the employer also reject the collective agreement?

When a corporation files a petition for the protection of the bankruptcy laws, the financial obligations of the corporation are suspended pending the resolution of the issue by the bankruptcy courts. What happens when a unionized employer files a petition for bankruptcy? Is the employer required to adhere to the terms and conditions of the collective agreement? In the case of *NLRB v. Bildisco & Bildisco* [465 U.S. 513 (1984)], the Supreme Court held that an employer who files for reorganization under Chapter 11 of the Bankruptcy Act does not violate Section 8(a)5 by unilaterally changing the terms of the collective agreement after filing the bankruptcy petition. The Court also held that the bankruptcy court may allow the employer to reject the collective agreement if the court finds that the agreement "burdens the estate" of the employer and if "the equities balance in favor of rejecting the labor contract."

Following the Supreme Court's *Bildisco* decision, Congress amended the Bankruptcy Code to deal with the rejection of a collective agreement. The changes, enacted in Public Law 98-353 (1984), 11 U.S.C. Section 1113, allow the employer petitioning for bankruptcy protection to reject the collective agreement only when the following conditions are met:

1. The employer has made a proposal for contractual modifications, necessary to permit reorganization and treating all interested parties equitably, to the union.
2. The employer must provide the union with such relevant information as is necessary to evaluate the proposal.
3. The employer must offer to "confer in good faith in attempting to reach mutually satisfactory modifications."
4. The bankruptcy court finds that the union has rejected the employer's proposal "without good cause."
5. The court concludes that "the balance of equities clearly favors rejection" of the agreement.

The bankruptcy court is required to hold a hearing on the employer's petition within fourteen days and to issue its determination on the rejection issue within thirty days after the hearing.

The following case involves the operation of Section 1113 when an employer seeks to reject a collective agreement when filing a petition for bankruptcy court protection from creditors.

Hoffman Bros. Packing Co., Inc. United Food and Commercial Workers Union, Local 770 v. Official Unsecured Creditors Committee

173 B.R. 177 (U.S. Bankruptcy Appellate Panel of the 9th Circuit, 1994)

Volinn, Bankruptcy Judge

. . . Hoffman Brothers Packing Co., Inc. (Hoffy), the debtor in possession, is a meat processing plant. Prior to bankruptcy, Hoffy had CBAs (collective bargaining agreements) with four unions representing its employees.

. . . Hoffy filed a Chapter 11 bankruptcy petition on April 19, 1993. Hoffy's stated intention for filing was to prevent its forced liquidation and to effect a "going concern" sale of the business. Over the course of the next month, Hoffy managed to shore up its customer base and inventory supply. It reduced management wages and benefits, effected management layoffs, and arranged new financing with its lender. It also did not make payments on its unions' employee health and welfare benefits as agreed to in the CBAs. These measures, while reducing the company's losses, did not succeed in eliminating the operating deficit and producing a profit sufficient to make Hoffy an attractive marketing prospect.

. . . Hoffy had stopped making payments to each union's health and pension funds prior to the bankruptcy filing date. Hoffy's failure to fund the health insurance threatened to cause Local 770's health insurance coverage to lapse on June 1, 1993. . . . On May 25, 1993, Hoffy met with the unions and asked them to approve its prior breaches, allow Hoffy to continue cuts in their pension benefits, and to change the union's health insurance coverage. The unions did not agree.

Without having come to an agreement with the unions, Hoffy unilaterally switched its workers to a different health plan, Maxicare, on June 1, 1993. The cost savings to the company were significant; however, under the Maxicare plan, the benefits were less than the agreed to options provided in the CBAs.

. . . On July 29, Local 770 filed charges against Hoffy with the NLRB for unfair labor practices. On August 30, 1993, the bankruptcy court heard argument on the motion to reject the CBAs. The court found that Hoffy had complied with the requirements of § 1113 (c) by proposing necessary modifications and providing relevant information to the union, that the union had refused to accept the proposed modifications, that the unions' refusal was without good cause, and that the balance of equities favored rejection. The court authorized Hoffy to reject the CBAs. The order was entered October 1, 1993, and Local 770 timely appealed. . . .

. . . A preliminary question arises as to whether or not a debtor who proposes to sell the business free and clear of a collective bargaining agreement can be said to be bargaining in good faith. To put it otherwise, can a debtor file a Chapter 11 liquidation plan which contemplates sale of all its assets to another party who, effectively, will not be bound by any collective bargaining agreement which may be arrived at with the debtor in possession?

It is probable that Hoffy will command a higher sale price if it is sold as a going concern rather than auctioned off piecemeal and that a going concern Hoffy is more salable without the perceived economic disadvantages of the CBAs. It is arguable that such a procedure, being tantamount to liquidation of the business, may be incompatible with § 1113. It is not as if the debtor has no other alternative. The debtor could file under Chapter 7, and a trustee could operate the business pending sale. But here the debtor chose Chapter 11 and selected a course which by emphasizing economic necessity and the need to disengage without qualification from the CBA in order to get a better sale, seems at odds with § 1113. Under these circumstances, there is some credibility to appellant's contention that the debtor could not and did not deal with the union in good faith. This problem was considered in one of a trilogy of cases in the Second Circuit. *In re Maxwell Newspapers, Inc.*, (1992), the court faced a similar circumstance where the debtor proposed the sale of a newspaper as a going concern. The court found the distinction between reorganization of a debtor and the sale of a going concern asset to a third party to be irrelevant to considerations under § 1113, based on Chapter 11's goal of continuing the enterprise, regardless of the ownership. We agree, and hold that § 1113 does not preclude rejection of CBAs where the purpose or plan of the debtor is to liquidate by a going concern sale of the business.

In order to reject a collective bargaining agreement under § 1113(c), a debtor must demonstrate that:

> (1) the trustee has, prior to the hearing, made a proposal that fulfills the requirements of subsection (b)(1);
>
> (2) the authorized representative of the employees has refused to accept such proposal without good cause; and
>
> (3) the balance of the equities clearly favors rejection of such agreement.
>
> Subsection (b)(1) mandates that a debtor shall:
>
> (A) make a proposal to the authorized representative of the employees covered by such agreement, based on the most complete and reliable information available at the time of such proposal, which provides for those necessary modifications in the employee's benefits and protections that are necessary to permit the reorganization of the debtor and assures that all creditors, the debtor and all of the affected parties are treated fairly and equitably; and
>
> (B) provide . . . the representative of the employees with such relevant information as is necessary to evaluate the proposal.

The debtor must demonstrate that it has made a proposal for "necessary" modifications that are "necessary" for reorganization, and which assures that all creditors are treated "fairly and equitably." The court may authorize rejection only if the union refuses to accept the debtor's proposal "without good cause."

During the course of these proceedings, Hoffy presented to the union an initial list of 12 modifications. By letter dated June 24, 1993, Hoffy outlined its proposals and stated they were "absolutely essential." Significant proposals included reduction of senior wages and an end to the seniority system for layoffs and overtime. Hoffy's letter then stated:

> The modifications outlined below are interdependent; the amendment or exclusion of any one or more of these modifications would force Hoffman to reconsider the whole package and would likely result in the introduction of certain additional modifications which it has not so far proposed.

Local 770 refused to accept Hoffy's 12 proposals. On August 9, Hoffy added six additional proposals. Local 770 responded to Hoffy's 18 proposals by letter on August 12, rejecting 11 of them and stating its reasons for rejecting them. Local 770 also took the position that Hoffy would have to agree to bind its successor to any new CBA and to assume liability in the event the successor refused to be bound. The original CBA did not contain such a clause. The parties did not come to terms, and Hoffy brought a motion for authorization to reject the CBAs pursuant to § 1113 (c).

In all, Hoffy offered 18 proposed modifications, some of which clearly met the § 1113(b) standard of "necessary" modifications "necessary" to the reorganization, i.e. wage rollbacks, elimination of pension funding, and less expensive health insurance. These are straightforward dollar issues. Other proposed modifications are problematic, such as elimination of dues checkoff and seniority, and requiring the union to ratify the debtor's unilateral changes, in essence stipulating to dismissal of its NLRB complaint. These modifications for the most part, while arguably non-economic, were found by the court to be related to the economic benefit of the debtor. This finding is not clearly erroneous.

On the other hand, Local 770 could not tell the court that it made any concessions to Hoffy on its unobjectionable proposals. The union refused to agree to many of the proposed modifications and demanded incorporation of successor liability into any agreement. The parties agree that without such a clause, any new buyer, while not bound by Hoffy's contract with the union, would nevertheless be required to bargain with it pursuant to the LMRA. This, coupled with the fact that the debtor offered in its letter of June 24, 1993 to furnish the name of the purchaser once meaningful negotiations produced one, places the parties more or less in the same position as with the original CBA provision, Article XXVII, relative to change of ownership. Thus, the union's insistence on this added provision created a gratuitous impediment to the debtor's prospects for reorganization.

. . . All things considered, particularly the failing condition of the debtor, and the benefit to all concerned if Hoffy could survive, the court had enough facts before it to justify the conclusion that the equities of the case warranted rejection of the CBA. The court's order authorizing rejection of the CBA therefore is affirmed.

Case Questions

1. What must an employer that files for bankruptcy do to reject a collective agreement?
2. What proposals did Hoffy make? How were those proposals necessary to Hoffy's reorganization? What concessions or proposals did the union make in response to Hoffy's proposals?
3. On what basis did the bankruptcy court decide that the union had rejected the company's proposals without good cause?

In *Wheeling Pittsburgh Steel Corp. v. United Steelworkers* [791 F.2d 1074 (1986)], the Third Circuit Court of Appeals held that it was an error to allow the employer to void the collective agreement where the employer did not give any persuasive rationale for asking the unionized employees to take disproportionate cuts for a five-year period without any provision for improvement if the employer's position improved. In *Teamsters Local 807 v. Carey Trans.* [816 F.2d 82 (1987)], the Second Circuit Court of Appeals upheld rejection of the agreement where unionized employees were expected to take cuts greater than those for nonunion employees because the union wages were 60 percent higher than industry average, whereas the other employees' compensation was barely competitive.

The NLRB has made it clear that filing a petition for bankruptcy protection does not affect the employer's obligation to recognize and bargain with the union, *Airport Bus Service* [273 NLRB 561 (1984)]. In *Willis Elec.* [269 NLRB 1145 (1984)], the NLRB held that an employer unilaterally abrogating an agreement without obtaining bankruptcy court relief is guilty of violating Section 8(a)(5); economic necessity is not a defense for such conduct.

In *NLRB v. Superior Forwarding, Inc.* [762 F.2d 695 (8th Cir. 1985)], the court of appeals held that a bankruptcy court may enjoin the NLRB from proceeding with hearings on unfair labor practice charges that arise from an employer's unilateral modification of a collective agreement, when the unfair labor practice proceedings would threaten the assets of the employer.

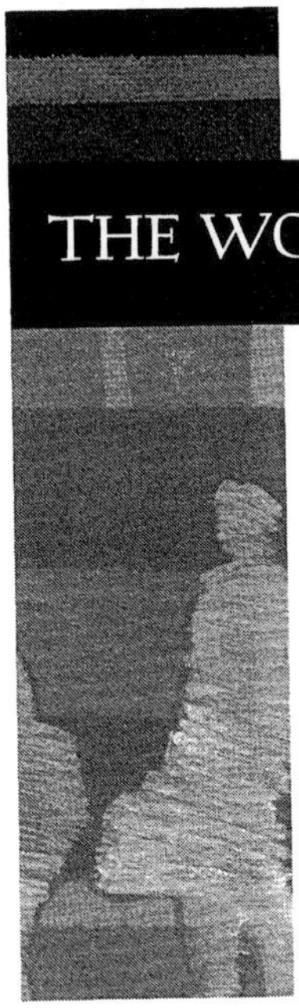

WHEELING-PITTSBURGH STEEL AGREEMENT WITH UNION CLEARS WAY FOR FIRM TO EMERGE FROM BANKRUPTCY

THE WORKING LAW

The United Steelworkers union reached an agreement with Wheeling-Pittsburgh Steel Co. in June 2003; the union members voted to ratify the five-year contract. The contract freezes wages for the first year of the contract and provides for enhanced pensions for hourly employees; it also provides for reorganizing work rules in the company's steel mills. The steel company had filed for Chapter 11 bankruptcy protection in November 2000; that filing was the second time the company had been in bankruptcy proceedings.

The company's agreement with the Steelworkers union was one of the key points of the firm's reorganization plan filed with the bankruptcy court. Reaching an agreement with the union was also a condition for the company to be eligible for a $250 million loan guarantee by the federal Emergency Steel Loan Guaranty Board. The loan will enable the company to continue operations and to upgrade its steel mills. The loan and the agreement with the union were major factors in the company's exit from the protection of the bankruptcy court on August 1, 2003.

Sources: "Labor Pact Clears Way for Wheeling-Pittsburgh Steel's Exit from Bankruptcy," *Pittsburgh Post-Gazette,* July 31, 2003; "Wheeling-Pitt, Union Reach Tentative Deal," *Associated Press,* June 26, 2003; "Wheeling-Pittsburgh Corporation Exits Bankruptcy," *PR Newswire,* August 1, 2003; "Union Pact Leaves Wheeling Set to Exit," *The Daily Deal,* July 31, 2003.

SUMMARY

- Arbitration is the usual method by which the parties to a collective agreement enforce that agreement. The existence of an arbitration clause is voluntary; the NLRA does not require that the parties include an arbitration clause in the agreement. But if the parties do agree to an arbitration clause, it becomes legally enforceable through Section 301 of the NLRA, and arbitration becomes the preferred means of interpreting and enforcing the agreement. When asked to order arbitration, a court should not consider the merits of the grievance but rather only whether the grievance is within the scope of the arbitration clause. When asked to enforce an arbitration award under Section 301, the court should not substitute its judgment for that of the arbitrator but rather only consider whether the arbitrator acted within the scope of his or her authority under the agreement. Courts should refuse to enforce an arbitration award only when the arbitrator exceeded the authority granted under the agreement or when the arbitration award violates "clear and explicit public policy."

- Section 301 also allows a court to enforce a no-strike clause in a collective agreement; despite the Norris–La Guardia Act, a court may grant an injunction to stop a strike that is over an issue subject to arbitration under a collective agreement. Suits under Section 301 may be used to seek damages for violations of the agreement, including the no-strike clause. Remedies under Section 301 may preempt any state law remedies or actions that involve the interpretation or application of the collective agreement.
- The NLRB will defer unfair labor practice complaints to arbitration under the requirements set out in *United Technologies* and will recognize arbitration decisions as resolving unfair labor practice charges when the conditions set out in the *Olin* case are met.
- Successor employers may be required to recognize and bargain with the union that had represented the employees of the former employer when there is a substantial continuity of operation and the employees from the former unionized employer make up a majority of the successor's employees. Section 1113 of the Bankruptcy Code sets out the procedure to be followed by an employer seeking to reject a collective agreement after having filed a petition for bankruptcy protection with the bankruptcy court.

QUESTIONS

1. What is arbitration? Why is arbitration used to resolve contract disputes between unions and employers?
2. What is rights arbitration? What is interest arbitration?
3. When will a court enforce a contractual promise to arbitrate disputes over the interpretation and application of a collective agreement?
4. When should a court refuse to enforce an arbitrator's decision?
5. What remedies are available to an employer against workers striking in violation of a no-strike clause? Against a union striking in violation of a no-strike clause?
6. When will the NLRB defer consideration of an unfair labor practice complaint to arbitration?
7. When is a successor employer obligated to recognize and bargain with the union representing the employees of the former employer?
8. What is the effect of the 1984 amendments to the Bankruptcy Code on the *Bildisco* decision? When can an employer filing under Chapter 11 of the Bankruptcy Code repudiate a collective agreement?

CASE PROBLEMS

1. An employee of the Du Pont Company's plant in East Chicago attacked his supervisor and another employee and destroyed some company equipment all for no apparent reason. He was discharged by the company. He was subsequently arrested and spent thirty days under observation in a hospital psychiatric ward. Two psychiatrists subsequently testified in court that the employee was temporarily insane at the time of the incident, and therefore, he was acquitted of the criminal charges. They also testified that the worker had recovered and was not likely to suffer another mental breakdown.

Following his acquittal, the worker's discharge was challenged by the union on the ground that the employee was not responsible for the assaults due to temporary mental incapacity. Therefore, argued the union, he was not dismissed for "just cause" as called for under the "security of employment" clause in the collective-bargaining agreement.

The company refused to reinstate the employee, and the union moved the grievance to arbitration. The arbitrator ruled in the union's favor and ordered the grievant reinstated to his job. Du Pont filed suit in a federal court in Indiana to overturn the arbitrator's ruling.

If you represented the company in front of the federal judge, what arguments would you make for overturning the arbitrator's award? If you represented the union, what counterarguments would you make in response? How should the judge have ruled? See *E. I. Du Pont De Nemours & Co. v. Grasselli Employees Independent Ass'n. of E. Chicago* [790 F.2d 611 (7th Cir. 1986)].

2. The labor contract between the West Penn Power Company of Arnold, Pennsylvania, and System Local No. 102 of the Utility Workers of America included a provision that employees engaged in the construction or maintenance of power lines would not be required to work outdoors during "inclement weather" and that the responsible supervisor would determine when weather conditions were too severe for outdoor work.

The no-strike clause in the labor agreement required the union and its officers to make a "sincere, active effort to have work resumed at a normal rate" if the employees engaged in a wildcat strike or refused to carry out job assignments.

One day in November, seven employees, including the union's president and vice president, ceased working due to weather conditions, despite their supervisor's repeated orders to keep on working. West Penn subsequently suspended the five rank-and-file employees for five days each, but discharged the two union officers for "their refusal to proceed with a work assignment and to make an active effort as (union officers) to have work resumed by other union employees."

An arbitration panel sustained the union president's discharge, while reducing the vice president's termination to a thirty-day suspension. Both men responded by filing unfair labor practice charges with the NLRB.

What do you think was the basis for the unfair labor practice charges filed by the two union officials? How should the NLRB respond? Should it defer to arbitration in this case? If not, how should it rule on the unfair labor practice charges? What remedy should it impose if it finds the two men were wrongfully discharged? See *West Penn Power Co.* [274 NLRB No. 173 (1985)].

3. Safeway Stores, Inc., discharged a journeyman meat cutter for disobeying an order and threatening a supervisor with physical harm. United Food and Commercial Workers Local 400 filed a grievance on behalf of the employee, and a few days later, representatives of the company and the union met to discuss the grievance.

Unable to reach an informal resolution, the union submitted the grievance to arbitration.

The arbitrator found that the grievant was guilty of disobeying a direct order and that he had compounded his offense by threatening his supervisor with bodily harm. However, the arbitrator refused to sustain the discharge because he also found that the company had not fully disclosed to the union or the grievant all the reasons for the discharge. At the grievance meeting, the company had stated that the reason for the discharge was the incident of insubordination. But during the arbitration hearing, the personnel director testified that his decision to discharge the grievant was based not only on his acts of insubordination but also on his past disciplinary record and a newspaper clipping he had seen concerning the grievant's conviction for assault and battery of his former girlfriend.

The company refused to abide by the arbitrator's decision and sought to have it overturned in the U.S. District Court for the District of Columbia.

If you had been the federal judge sitting in this case, would you have affirmed or overturned the arbitrator's award? See *Safeway Stores, Inc. v. United Food and Commercial Workers Local 400* [621 F.Supp. 1233 (D.D.C. 1985)].

4. *The Cleveland Press* and *The Plain Dealer*, the two daily newspapers in Cleveland, Ohio, were part of a multiemployer bargaining group that had signed a collective-bargaining agreement with the Cleveland Typographical Union, Local 53. The contract stated that each covered employee was entitled to "a regular full-time job . . . for the remainder of his working life."

When the afternoon *Cleveland Press* went out of business, eighty-nine former *Press* employees sued the parent company, E. W. Scripps Company, and *The Plain Dealer* to enforce the lifetime employment guarantee in their collective-bargaining agreement. In addition to their Section 301 action, the plaintiffs also charged that the two defendants had conspired to create a daily newspaper monopoly in the city of Cleveland. The defendants replied, among other defenses, that the plaintiffs had no standing to sue on this second basis.

Should the federal judge enforce the contract guarantee of lifetime jobs? If you say yes, what kind of a remedy should the judge fashion? What evidence do you see to support the plaintiffs' antitrust allegation? If defendants violated the Sherman Act, what impact should this have on their case? See *Province v. Cleveland Press Publishing Co.* [787 F.2d 1047 (6th Cir. 1986)].

5. Nolde Bros. Bakery's collective-bargaining agreement with the Bakery & Confectionery Workers Union, Local 358, provided that any grievance between the parties was subject to binding arbitration. During negotiations over the renewal of the agreement, the union gave notice of its intention to cancel the existing agreement. Negotiations continued for several days past the termination date, and the union threatened to strike. The employer informed the union that it was permanently closing its plant. The employer paid the employees their accrued wages and vacation pay but refused to pay severance pay as called for in the collective agreement. The employer argued that its duty to pay severance pay and its duty to arbitrate the claim for severance pay expired with the collective agreement. The union sued under Section 301 to force the employer to arbitrate the question of whether the employer was required to pay severance pay.

How should the court decide the union's suit? Is the employer required to arbitrate the matter? Explain your answer. See *Nolde Bros. v. Bakery & Confectionery Workers Local 358* [430 U.S. 243 (1977)].

6. The Grissom family owned and operated a motor lodge and restaurant franchised by the Howard Johnson Co.; they employed fifty-three employees, who were represented by the Hotel & Restaurant Employees Union. The Grissoms sold their business to the Howard

Johnson Co. Howard Johnson hired forty-five employees, nine of whom were former employees of the Grissoms. The union requested that Howard Johnson recognize it and meet the obligations of the prior collective agreement, but Howard Johnson refused. The union then sought arbitration of the question of the successor's obligations under the agreement; it filed a suit under Section 301 to compel Howard Johnson to arbitrate.

Is Howard Johnson required to recognize and bargain with the union? Is Howard Johnson required to arbitrate the question of the successor's obligation? Explain your answer. See *Howard Johnson Co. v. Hotel & Restaurant Employees Detroit Local Joint Board* [417 U.S. 249 (1974)].

7. The underlying dispute in this case arose when Waller Brothers, which operates a stone quarry engaged in removing and processing stone and packing the stone in boxes for shipment, purchased an "Instapak" machine, which sprays protective padding around the stone being packed for shipment. Before the purchase of the Instapak, the stone was packed with strips of synthetic material as padding. Employees called "craters" pack the stone for shipment.

The union claims that it was entitled to negotiate a new wage rate for an Instapak machine operator, whereas the company maintains that the operation of the machine is only a function of the crater job classification, which is subject to a previously negotiated wage rate. The company takes the position that both the no-strike clause and the provision for mandatory grievance arbitration contained in the collective-bargaining agreement apply to this dispute. The union for its part relies on the portion of the contract that provides that wage rates are not subject to arbitration and that the union expressly reserves the right to strike in the event of a disagreement on wages.

If the union calls a strike and the company goes into court seeking a *Boys Markets* injunction, should the court grant or deny it? See *Waller Bros. Stone Co. v. District 23* [620 F.2d 132, 104 L.R.R.M. 2168 (6th Cir. 1980)].

8. HMC Management Corp., an apartment rental and management company, discharged two of its employees for substandard work performance. The employees, represented by the Carpenters Union, filed grievances. The employer subsequently decided to rehire one of the employees but not the other one. When the grievance filed by the employee who was not rehired was arbitrated, the arbitrator acknowledged that the employer had sufficient reason to discharge the two employees but held that the employer had acted improperly when it rehired one employee but not the other. The arbitrator ordered that the employer reinstate the other employee. The employer filed suit in federal court to have the arbitration award vacated.

Should the court enforce or vacate the arbitrator's decision? Explain your answer. See *HMC Mgt. Corp. v. Carpenters District Council* [750 F.2d 1302 (5th Cir. 1985)].

9. The appellate court judge who wrote the decision of the three-judge panel in this case began his opinion as follows:

> Coffin, Chief Judge—This tempest has been brewed in a very small teapot. The dispute which precipitated the filing in this court of more than 80 pages of briefs and an extensive appendix began on July 30, 1974, when appellee Anheuser-Busch posted a notice prohibiting employees at its Merrimack, New Hampshire brewery from wearing tank-top shirts on the job. Tank-tops are sleeveless shirts which leave exposed the shoulders, arms and underarms of the wearer. Beginning on July 31, when three employees were sent home after refusing to doff their tank-tops for other shirts, the emotional temperature rose, with over a dozen more employees, including shop stewards, being sent home a few days later. The issue peaked by August 14, when thirteen of the eighteen employees in the Brewery Department wore tank-tops, refused to put on other shirts, and went home. Approximately thirty employees in the Maintenance Department wore tank-

tops on August 15. On August 16 no maintenance employees reported for work and production at the brewery was halted.

The brewery filed a lawsuit in federal district court seeking injunctive relief and damages against the employees' union on the grounds that the collective-bargaining agreement contained a no-strike clause and an arbitration clause.

The union responded that (1) the employees' actions were individual, not concerted, activity; (2) the employees were entitled to wear the tank-tops pending arbitration of the controversy; and (3) the employer should not be permitted to hide behind a *Boys Markets* injunction after management's overreaction had itself precipitated the crisis.

How do you think the court ruled in this dispute? See *Anheuser-Busch v. Teamsters Local 633* [511 F.2d 1097, 88 L.R.R.M. 2785 (1st Cir.), *cert. denied,* 423 U.S. 875, 90 L.R.R.M. 2744 (1975)].

10. Stikes, an employee of Chevron Corp., was discharged for refusing to allow the employer to search her car under a company antidrug policy, adopted in 1984, that required workers to submit to random searches of person and property. Stikes was a member of the bargaining unit represented by the Oil, Chemical and Atomic Workers Union; the collective agreement covering the bargaining unit provided for arbitration of discharge cases. Rather than submit a grievance over her discharge, Stikes filed a suit against Chevron in the state court. The suit charged Chevron with wrongful discharge, intentional infliction of emotional distress, unfair business practice, and violation of rights to privacy under the state constitution. Chevron argued that the suit was preempted by Section 301 because it was a suit to enforce the collective agreement.

Does Stikes have a right to sue under state law over her discharge, or is her suit preempted by Section 301? Explain your answer. See *Stikes v. Chevron USA Inc.* [914 F.2d 1265 (9th Cir. 1990)].

INTERNET EXERCISE

As discussed in this chapter, arbitration is the preferred method of interpreting and enforcing collective agreements. The American Arbitration Association is a nonprofit organization that promotes and regulates arbitration. To find out more about the American Arbitration Association, go to its Web site at **http://www.adr.org** and click the About sidebar link. To get more information about how labor arbitration is conducted, click the Rules link and then scroll down to and click the Labor Arbitration Rules link. For information about handling grievances, go back to the Rules link and then click the Grievance Mediation Procedure link.

The American Arbitration Association also handles nonlabor arbitration, and a growing area is the arbitration of employee-employer disputes, including employment discrimination claims (see Chapter 5). For information on this type of arbitration, go to the Rules/Procedures link, next click the Guides link, and then click the Resolving Employment Disputes—A Practical Guide link.

INFOTRAC KEYWORDS

http://www.infotrac-college.com

interest arbitration, rights arbitration, grievance process, no-strike clause

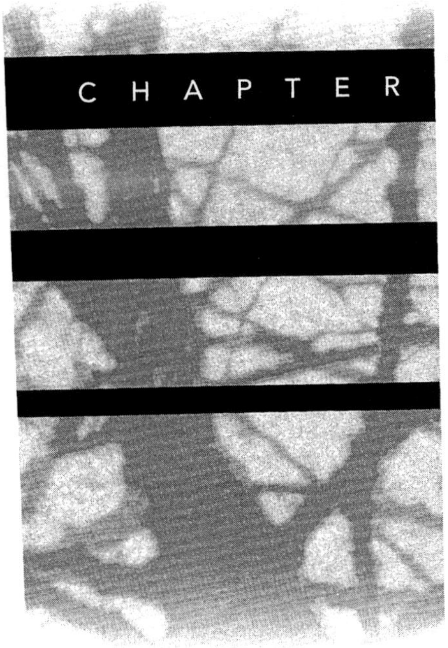

CHAPTER 19

THE RIGHTS OF UNION MEMBERS

Unions, as bargaining agents representing bargaining units of employees, have significant power and control over individual employees. Those employees are precluded from dealing with the employer on matters of wages and working conditions; the employees must go through the union in dealing with the employer. Because employees are dependent on the union, they must be protected from the arbitrary or unreasonable exercise of union power. This chapter explores the legal controls of unions to protect the rights of union members.

PROTECTION OF THE RIGHTS OF UNION MEMBERS

Duty of Fair Representation
Legal duty on a union to represent fairly all members of the bargaining unit.

The legal controls on unions are the result of actions by the courts, the National Labor Relations Board (NLRB), and Congress. The courts and the NLRB have imposed a **duty of fair representation** on the part of the union—an obligation to represent fairly all members of the bargaining unit. Congress has legislated a *union members' "bill of rights"* to guarantee that union internal procedures are fair and has prohibited certain practices by unions that interfere with employees' rights under the National Labor Relations Act (NLRA).

In 1947, the Taft-Hartley Act added a list of union unfair labor practices to the NLRA. Section 7 was amended to give employees the right to refrain from engaging in concerted activity, as well as the right to engage in such activity. Section 8(b)(1)(A) prohibits union activity that interferes with, restrains, or coerces employees in the exercise of their Section 7 rights. Section 8(b)(2) prohibits unions from causing an employer to discriminate against employees in terms and conditions of employ-

ETHICAL DILEMMA: UNION MEMBERSHIP BENEFITS AND COSTS

You are the human resource manager of the Springfield plant of Immense Multinational Business; the plant production employees are represented by a union, and the collective agreement has a union shop clause requiring employees in the bargaining unit to join the union and to maintain their membership in good standing.

You have just hired a new production employee, Waylon Smithers, who asks you if he is required to join the union. He also asks you what benefits he may receive by becoming a union member and what the negative aspects of union membership are. How should you respond to him? Prepare a short memo outlining your response to his questions, supporting your comments with appropriate references.

ment because they are not union members. Section 8(b)(5) protects employees from unreasonable union dues and initiation fees.

The Landrum-Griffin Act of 1959 added the union member's "bill of rights" to the NLRA. Those provisions will be discussed in detail later in this chapter.

THE UNION'S DUTY OF FAIR REPRESENTATION

The duty of fair representation is a judicially created obligation on the part of the union to represent fairly all employees in the bargaining unit. The duty was developed by the courts because of the union's role as exclusive bargaining agent for the bargaining unit. The initial cases dealing with the duty of fair representation arose under the Railway Labor Act; subsequent cases applied the duty to unions under the NLRA as well. In the following case, the Supreme Court developed the concept of the duty of fair representation.

STEELE V. LOUISVILLE & NASHVILLE R.R.

323 U.S. 192 (1944)

Stone, C.J.

The question is whether the Railway Labor Act . . . imposes on a labor organization, acting by authority of the statute as the exclusive bargaining representative of a craft or class of railway employees, the duty to represent all the employees in the craft without discrimination because of their race, and, if so, whether the courts have jurisdiction to protect the minority of the craft or class from the violation of such obligation.

. . . Petitioner, a Negro, is a locomotive fireman in the employ of respondent railroad, suing on his own behalf and that of his fellow employees who, like petitioner, are Negro firemen employed by the Railroad. Respondent Brotherhood, a labor organization, is as provided under Section 2, Fourth of the Railway Labor

Act, the exclusive bargaining representative of the craft of firemen employed by the Railroad and is recognized as such by it and the members of the craft. The majority of the firemen employed by the Railroad are white and are members of the Brotherhood, but a substantial minority are Negroes who, by the constitution and ritual of the Brotherhood, are excluded from its membership. As the membership of the Brotherhood constitutes a majority of all firemen employed on respondent Railroad and as under Section 2, Fourth, the members, because they are the majority, have chosen the Brotherhood to represent the craft, petitioner and other Negro firemen on the road have been required to accept the Brotherhood as their representative for the purposes of the Act.

On March 28, 1940, the Brotherhood, purporting to act as representative of the entire craft of firemen, without informing the Negro firemen or giving them opportunity to be heard, served a notice on respondent Railroad and on twenty other railroads operating principally in the southeastern part of the United States. The notice announced the Brotherhood's desire to amend the existing collective bargaining agreement in such a manner as ultimately to exclude all Negro firemen from the service. By established practice on the several railroads so notified only white firemen can be promoted to serve as engineers, and the notice proposed that only "promotable," i.e., white, men should be employed as firemen or assigned to new runs or jobs or permanent vacancies in established runs or jobs.

On February 18, 1941, the railroads and the Brotherhood, as representative of the craft, entered into a new agreement which provided that not more than 50 percent of the firemen in each class of service in each seniority district of a carrier should be Negroes; that until such percentage should be reached all new runs and all vacancies should be filled by white men; and that the agreement did not sanction the employment of Negroes in any seniority district in which they were not working. . . .

. . . [W]e think that Congress, in enacting the Railway Labor Act and authorizing a labor union, chosen by a majority of a craft, to represent the craft, did not intend to confer plenary power upon the union to sacrifice, for the benefit of its members, rights of the minority of the craft, without imposing on it any duty to protect the minority. Since petitioner and the other Negro members of the craft are not members of the Brotherhood or eligible for membership, the authority to act for them is derived not from their action or consent but wholly from the command of the Act. . . .

Section 2, Second, requiring carriers to bargain with the representative so chosen, operates to exclude any other from representing a craft. The minority members of a craft are thus deprived by the statute of the right, which they would otherwise possess, to choose a representative of their own, and its members cannot bargain individually on behalf of themselves as to matters which are properly the subject of collective bargaining. . . .

The fair interpretation of the statutory language is that the organization chosen to represent a craft is to represent all its members, the majority as well as the minority, and it is to act for and not against those whom it represents. It is a principle of general application that the exercise of a granted power to act in behalf of others involves the assumption toward them of a duty to exercise the power in their interest and behalf, and that such a grant of power will not be deemed to dispense with all duty toward those for whom it is exercised unless so expressed.

We think that the Railway Labor Act imposes upon the statutory representative of a craft at least as exacting a duty to protect equally the interests of the members of the craft as the Constitution imposes upon a legislature to give equal protection to the interests of those for whom it legislates. Congress has seen fit to clothe the bargaining representative with powers comparable to those possessed by a legislative body both to create and restrict the rights of those whom it represents, but it also imposed on the representative a corresponding duty. We hold that the language of the Act to which we have referred, read in the light of the purposes of the Act, expresses the aim of Congress to impose on the bargaining representative of a craft or class of employees the duty to exercise fairly the power conferred upon it in behalf of all those for whom it acts, without hostile discrimination against them.

This does not mean that the statutory representative of a craft is barred from making contracts which may have unfavorable effects on some of the members of the craft represented. Variations in terms of the contract based on differences relevant to the authorized purposes of the contract in conditions to which they are to be applied, such as differences in seniority, the type of work performed, the competence and skill with which it is performed, are within the scope of the bargaining representation of a craft, all of whose members are not identical in their interest or merit. Without attempting to mark the allowable limits of differences in the terms of contracts based on differences of conditions to which they apply, it is enough for present purposes to say that the statutory power to represent a craft and to make contracts as to wages, hours and working conditions does not include the authority to make among members of the craft discriminations not based on such relevant differences. Here the discriminations based on race alone are obviously irrelevant and invidious. Congress plainly did not undertake to authorize the bargaining representative to make such discriminations. . . .

The representative which thus discriminates may be enjoined from so doing, and its members may be enjoined from taking the benefit of such discriminatory action. No more is the Railroad bound by or entitled to take the benefit of a contract which the bargaining representative is prohibited by the statute from making. In both cases the right asserted, which is derived from the duty imposed by the statute on the bargaining representative, is a federal right implied from the statute and the policy which it has adopted. . . .

So long as a labor union assumes to act as the statutory representative of a craft, it cannot rightly refuse to perform the duty, which is inseparable from the power of representation conferred upon it, to represent the entire membership of the craft. While the statute does not deny to such a bargaining labor organization the right to determine eligibility to its membership, it does require the union, in collective bargaining and in making contracts with the carrier, to represent non-union or minority union members of the craft without hostile discrimination, fairly, impartially, and in good faith. Wherever necessary to that end, the union is required to consider requests of non-union members of the craft and expressions of their views with respect to collective bargaining with the employer and to give to them notice of and opportunity for hearing upon its proposed action. . . .

We conclude that the duty which the statute imposes on a union representative of a craft to represent the interests of all its members stands on no different footing and that the statute contemplates resort to the usual judicial remedies of injunction and award of damages when appropriate for breach of that duty.

The judgment is accordingly reversed and remanded. . . .

So ordered.

Case Questions

1. Is Steele a member of the union? Why?
2. To what conduct by the union and the railroad did Steele object?
3. To which employees does the union owe a duty of fair representation? What is the source of the union's duty of fair representation?

The *Steele* case held that the duty of fair representation arose out of the union's exclusive bargaining agent status under Section 2, Ninth, of the Railway Labor Act. In *Syres v. Oil Workers Local 23* [350 U.S. 892 (1955)], the Supreme Court held that the duty of fair representation also extended to unions granted bargaining agent status under Section 9(a) of the NLRA.

Unions, in representing employees, must make decisions that affect different employees in different ways. For example, in negotiating a contract, the union must decide whether to seek increased wages or improved benefits—trade-offs must be made in fashioning contract proposals. Older employees may be more concerned with pensions, whereas younger employees may be more concerned with increased wages. Should the courts monitor the union's negotiation proposals to ensure that all workers are fairly represented? In *Ford Motor Co. v. Huffman* [345 U.S. 330 (1953)], the Supreme Court held that unions should be given broad discretion by the courts in negotiation practices; the courts should ensure only that the union operates "in good faith and honesty of purpose in the exercise of its discretion."

The courts also give unions some leeway in exercising their contractual duties. In *Steelworkers v. Rawson* [495 U.S. 362 (1990)], the Supreme Court held that the allegations that the union had been negligent in its duty under the collective agreement to conduct safety inspections did not amount to a breach of the duty of fair representation because mere negligence, even in the performance of a contractual duty, does not amount to a breach of the duty of fair representation. However, a union's negligent failure to follow hiring hall rules may be a breach of the duty of fair representation, *Jacoby v. NLRB* [233 F.3d 611 (D.C. Cir. 2000)].

Although the courts allow unions broad latitude in negotiations, they may be more concerned with union decisions involving individual employee grievances. In *Vaca v. Sipes* [386 U.S. 171 (1967)], the Supreme Court held that an individual does not have an absolute right to have a grievance taken to arbitration, but the union must make decisions about the merits of a grievance in good faith and in a nonarbitrary manner.

In *Vaca,* the union refused to arbitrate the employee's grievance. If the union decides to arbitrate the grievance but mishandles the employee's claim, does it violate the duty of fair representation? What if the union gives the grievance only perfunctory handling? The following case addresses these questions.

Hines v. Anchor Motor Freight, Inc.

424 U.S. 554 (1976)

White, J.

The issue here is whether a suit against an employer by employees asserting breach of a collective-bargaining contract was properly dismissed where the accompanying complaint against the Union for breach of duty of fair representation has withstood the Union's motion for summary judgment and remains to be tried.

Petitioners, who were formerly employed as truck drivers by respondent Anchor Motor Freight, Inc., were discharged on June 5, 1967. The applicable collective-bargaining contract forbade discharges without just cause. The company charged dishonesty. . . . Anchor's assertion was that petitioners had sought reimbursement for motel expenses in excess of the actual charges sustained by them. At a meeting between the company and the union, Local 377, International Brotherhood of Teamsters, which was also attended by petitioners, Anchor presented motel receipts previously submitted by petitioners which were in excess of the charges shown on the motel's registration cards; a notarized statement of the motel clerk asserting the accuracy of the registration cards; and an affidavit of the motel owner affirming that the registration cards were accurate and that inflated receipts had been furnished petitioners. The Union claimed petitioners were innocent and opposed the discharges. It was then agreed that the matter would be presented to the joint arbitration committee for the area, to which the collective-bargaining contract permitted either party to submit an unresolved grievance. Pending this hearing, petitioners were reinstated. Their suggestion that the motel be investigated was answered by the Union representatives' assurances that "there was nothing to worry about" and that they need not hire their own attorney.

A hearing before the joint area committee was held on July 26, 1967. Anchor presented its case. Both the Union and petitioners were afforded an opportunity to present their case and to be heard. Petitioners denied their dishonesty, but neither they nor the Union presented any other evidence contradicting the documents presented by the company. The committee sustained the discharges. Petitioners then retained an attorney and sought rehearing based on a statement by the motel owner that he had no personal knowledge of the events, but that the discrepancy between the receipts and the registration cards could have been attributable to the motel clerk's recording on the cards less than was actually paid and retaining for himself the difference between the amount receipted and the amount recorded. The committee, after hearing, unanimously denied rehearing "because there was no new evidence presented which would justify reopening this case."

There were later indications that the motel clerk was in fact the culprit; and the present suit was filed in June 1969, against Anchor, the Union and its International. The complaint alleged that the charges of dishonesty made against petitioners by Anchor were false, that there was no just cause for discharge and that the discharges had been in breach of contract. It was also asserted that the falsity of the charges could have been discovered with a minimum of investigation, that the Union had made no effort to ascertain the truth of the charges and that the Union had violated its duty of fair representation by arbitrarily and in bad faith depriving petitioners of their employment and permitting their discharge without sufficient proof.

The Union denied the charges and relied on the decision of the joint area committee. Anchor asserted that petitioners had been properly discharged for just cause. It also defended on the ground that petitioners, diligently and in good faith represented by the Union, had unsuccessfully resorted to the grievance and arbitration machinery provided by the contract and that the adverse decision of the joint arbitration committee was binding upon the Union and petitioners under the contractual provision. . . . Discovery followed, including a deposition of the motel clerk revealing that he had falsified the records and that it was he who had pocketed the difference between the sums shown on the receipts and the registration cards. Motions for summary judgment filed by Anchor and the Unions were granted by the District Court on the ground that the decision of the arbitration committee was final and binding on the employees and "for failure to show facts comprising bad faith, arbitrariness or perfunctoriness on the part of the Unions." Although indicating that the acts of the Union "may not meet professional standards of competency . . . ," the District Court concluded that the facts demonstrated at most bad judgment on the part of the Union, which was insufficient to prove a breach of duty or make out a prima facie case against it. . . .

After reviewing the allegations and the record before it, the Court of Appeals concluded that there were sufficient facts from which bad faith or arbitrary conduct on the part of the local Union could be inferred by the trier of fact and that petitioners should have been afforded an opportunity to prove their charges. To this extent the judgment of the District Court was reversed. The Court of Appeals affirmed the judgment in favor of Anchor and the International. . . .

It is this judgment of the Court of Appeals with respect to Anchor that is now before us. . . .

It is urged that the reversal of the Court of Appeals will undermine not only the finality rule but the entire collective-bargaining process. Employers, it is said, will be far less willing to give up their untrammeled right to discharge without cause and to agree to private settlement procedures. But the burden on employees will remain a substantial one, far too heavy in the opinion of some. To prevail against either the company or the Union, petitioners must show not only that their discharge was contrary to the contract but must also carry the burden of demonstrating breach of duty by the Union. As the District Court indicated, this involves more than demonstrating mere errors in judgment.

Petitioners are not entitled to relitigate their discharge merely because they offer newly discovered evidence that the charges against them were false and that in fact they were fired without cause. The grievance processes cannot be expected to be error-free. The finality provision has sufficient force to surmount occasional instances of mistake. But it is quite another matter to suggest that erroneous arbitration decisions must stand even though the employee's representation by the union has been dishonest, in bad faith or discriminatory; for in that event error and injustice of the grossest sort would multiply. The contractual system would then cease to qualify as an adequate mechanism to secure individual redress for damaging failure of the employer to abide by the contract. Congress has put its blessing on private dispute settlement arrangements provided in collective agreements, but it was anticipated, we are sure, that the contractual machinery would operate within some minimum levels of integrity. In our view, enforcement of the finality provision where the arbitrator has erred is conditioned upon the Union's having satisfied its statutory duty fairly to represent the employee in connection with the arbitration proceedings. . . .

Petitioners, if they prove an erroneous discharge and the Union's breach of duty tainting the decision of the joint committee, are entitled to an appropriate remedy against the employer as well as the Union. It was error to affirm the District Court's final dismissal of petitioners' action against Anchor. To this extent the judgment of the Court of Appeals is reversed.

So ordered.

Case Questions

1. Why were the employees discharged? Were they actually guilty of such misconduct? Explain your answer.
2. What is the basis of the employees' claim that the union had breached its duty of fair representation? What is the effect of the arbitration board decision in this case?
3. What must the employees demonstrate to establish a breach of the duty of fair representation? How would that affect the decision of the arbitration board? Explain.

Union Dues and the Duty of Fair Representation

A union owes a duty of fair representation to all employees in the bargaining unit it represents, whether or not the employees are members of the union. As you recall from Chapter 15, Section 8(a)(3) allows the employer and union to agree on a union security clause (unless there is a state "right-to-work" law that prohibits mandatory union membership or union dues). Union security clauses generally involve either a "union shop" clause, which requires employees to become union members within thirty days of their employment, or an "agency shop" clause, which requires employees to pay union dues and fees. Negotiating a union security clause that incorporates the language of Section 8(a)(3) of the NLRA is not a violation of the union's duty of fair representation, *Marquez v. Screen Actors Guild* [525 U.S. 33 (1998)]. An employer who unilaterally ceases to deduct union dues from employees under a union security clause violates Sections 8(a)(1) and 8(a)(5), *NLRB v. Oklahoma Fixture Co.* [332 F.3d 1284 (10th Cir. 2003)].

Where the collective agreement contains a union shop agreement, a proviso to Section 8(a)(3) states that an employer may not discharge an employee for failing to join the union if union membership is denied for a reason other than failure to pay union dues or fees. In *NLRB v. General Motors Corp.* [373 U.S. 734 (1963)], the Supreme Court held that the effect of that proviso is to reduce an employee's obligation under a union shop clause to "a financial core"—that is, simply to pay union dues and fees. According to the Supreme Court's decision in *Communications Workers of America v. Beck* [487 U.S. 735 (1988)], unions may not use the dues or fees of employees who are not union members to pay for union activities not related to collective bargaining; such employees are entitled to a reduction in dues and fees by the percentage of union expenditures that go for noncollective-bargaining expenses. Employees who are not union members may not be charged for the portion of union dues spent on organizing activities outside the appropriate bargaining unit, *United Food and Commercial Workers Union, Local 1036 v. NLRB* [249 F.3d 1115 (2001)]. In *Chicago Teachers Union, Local No. 1 v. Hudson* [466 U.S. 435 (1986)], the Supreme Court held that the union is required to provide objecting members with information relating to the union expenditures on collective bargaining and political activities and must include an adequate explanation of the basis of dues and fees. The objecting members must also be provided with a reasonable opportunity to challenge, before an impartial decision maker, the amount of the dues or fees; the union must hold in escrow the disputed amounts pending the resolution of the challenges. Unions may require that disputes over the amount of agency fees charged to nonmembers be arbitrated; however, the objecting nonmembers, unless they have specifically agreed to arbitrate their dispute, are not required to exhaust the arbitration process before filing suit in federal court, *Air Line Pilots Association v. Miller* [523 U.S. 866 (1998)].

The following case illustrates how the NLRB applies the *Beck* decision.

International Brotherhood of Teamsters, Local 776, AFL-CIO (Carolina Freight Carriers Corporation)

324 NLRB No. 176 (NLRB 1997)

Michael O. Miller, ALJ

. . . Since before 1994, the Employer had recognized Respondent [union] (and the Teamsters National Freight Industry Negotiating Committee) as the exclusive collective-bargaining representative of its employees in a unit appropriate for collective-bargaining purposes. The collective-bargaining agreement includes a "Union Shop" clause which . . . "[a]ll present employees who are not members of the Local union and all employees who are hired hereafter [to] become and remain members in good standing of the Local Union as a condition of employment on and after the thirty-first (31st) day following the beginning of their employment. . . ."

It further provides that an employee "who has failed to acquire, or thereafter maintain, membership in the Union . . . shall be terminated seventy-two (72) hours after his Employer has received written notice from . . . the Local Union." . . .

Carolina hired Timothy Blosser on May 2, 1994, as a casual dock laborer. As a casual, he had no set or guaranteed hours; his schedule was determined each week. . . .

On May 27, the Union sent Blosser a registered letter outlining what it asserted were his union membership and financial obligations. That letter stated:

> Our Constitution states that after thirty (30) calendar days, you are required to join the Local Union. . . . Your initiation fee is $200.00 plus the first month's dues which is two times your hourly rate, plus one dollar ($1.00) assessment for the death benefit. . . .
>
> According to our records, your first day of employment at Carolina Freight was May 2, 1994. Therefore, per the terms of our agreement with Carolina Freight and as outlined above, you are hereby notified that you must come into the Local Union office and join and/or become a member in good standing in the Local Union on, but not before June 2, 1994.
>
> Upon failure to comply on this date, we shall contact your employer to inform him that you are not eligible to work. If you have any questions regarding Teamsters Local Union No. 776 or are no longer employed by the above-mentioned company, please feel free to call.

The letter omitted any reference to employee rights to opt out of full membership or pay less than the full amount of dues.

On June 1, Blosser responded to the Union's demand . . . he described, as a violation of the duty of fair representation, a union's maintenance and application of a union-security clause requiring membership in good standing without advising the unit employees that their obligation was limited to the payment of uniform initiation fees and dues.

. . . Blosser asserted that nonmembers "do not have to pay a fee equal to union dues," that they "can only be required to pay a fee that equals their share of what the union can prove is its costs of collective bargaining, contract administration, and grievance adjustment with their employer." . . .

The Union replied on June 3, notifying Blosser that "the fees established by our auditor is [sic] 87% of the two times the hourly rate, and $1.00 for the death benefit, plus the $200.00 initiation fee." Accordingly, the dues, he was told, would be $26.10 per month. He had, he was told, seven days to comply before the employer would be informed not to assign him work.

The correspondence continued. Blosser replied, insisting that, "before the union demands fees, an independent accountant's verification of the union's cost of collective bargaining, NOT the union's interpretation" must be provided. Because no such verification had been provided, Blosser asserted that no payment could be demanded and that he would await receipt of that verification. He also asserted that the initiation fee should similarly be reduced by the appropriate percentage, 87 percent according to the Union's calculation. Finally, he requested a copy of the collective bargaining agreement.

On June 20, the Union sent Blosser the "latest auditor's verification of the core fees," those for 1993, noting that the computations of the core fees using the 1994 financial information was [sic] in process. The computation showed the Union's expenses and the portion of those expenses, if any, which were chargeable under *Beck*. It concluded that the expenses chargeable to protesting members amounted to 86.7 percent of the total expenses.

Blosser was also told that copies of the National Master Freight Agreement and the supplement applicable to Carolina are "given to all members when they become members of the Union." A hope was expressed that his dues and initiation fee would be received within 72 hours.

On June 24, the Union sent Blosser a computer-generated letter reiterating his obligation to pay the initiation fee and dues. The sums demanded were the full dues and initiation fee; there was no reference to any adjustments. . . . It also reiterated his obligation to "become a member in good standing" with no reference to his right to choose financial core membership and it threatened to notify his employer that he was ineligible to work if he did not comply within 72 hours.

Blosser wrote back on June 27, asserting that he was entitled to the independent auditor's complete audit or his complete review, as well as his opinion letter, for the Local's expenses as well as those of the Union's District and National levels, where some of the dues money goes. He also threatened to file an additional unfair labor practice charge if he did not get a copy of the collective-bargaining agreement, to which he claimed entitlement as a member of the unit.

On June 29, the Union gave him a copy of the contract. The other information he sought, the Union stated, was "being investigated as to the legality;" he was promised a subsequent response. Blosser never became a member of the [union]; neither did he pay it any fees or dues. He voluntarily left Carolina's employ on June 29.

. . . The union-security clause in Respondent's collective-bargaining agreement requires all employees "to become and remain members in good standing." On May 27, and on June 24, the Union demanded that Blosser "join and/or become a member in good standing in the Local Union." At no time was he told that he had a right to be and remain a nonmember. By failing to so inform him, Respondent breached the duty of fair representation owed to him as a member of the bargaining unit and thereby violated Section 8(b)(1)(A). . . .

As set forth [by the NLRB] in *California Saw & Knife Works* (1995), a union, when it seeks to enforce a union-security clause, is required to inform the employees [who choose not to join the union] of their rights under *Beck*. Thus, they must tell the employees that they are not required to pay the full dues and fees, give those employees information upon which to intelligently decide whether to object, and apprise them of the union's internal procedures for filing objections. Respondent did none of those when it made repeated demands upon Blosser that he join the Union and pay dues. It thus failed in its duty of fair representation, in violation of Section 8(b)(1)(A).

In its various demands that he pay the dues and the initiation fee and join the Union, Respondent gave Blosser only three to seven days in which to decide and act, on pain of the loss of his job if he failed to comply. At the times it did so, Respondent had not yet provided him with the *Beck* notifications to which he was entitled. General Counsel argues that by failing to give Blosser a reasonable time within which to satisfy his dues obligation, Respondent further breached its duty of fair representation.

. . . the complaint further alleges this conduct more generally as unlawful restraint and coercion. I agree. By threatening to cause his termination if he did not join the Union in an unreasonably short time and without the information necessary for him to reasonably decide whether to assume objector status, Respondent has restrained and coerced him in violation of Section 8(b)(1)(A).

Respondent's repeated demands upon Blosser continued to seek payment of the full $200 initiation fee, even after it acknowledged that some portion of the dues were [sic] not chargeable to objectors as representational expenses. . . . The complaint expressly raised the issue of the Union's attempt to collect the full initiation fee from Blosser. Respondent offered no evidence that funds derived from initiation fees were expended differently than those derived from periodic dues and presented no argument on brief that initiation fees should be exempt from the *Beck* apportionment. Accordingly, I find that by seeking to require Blosser, a nonmember objector, to pay the full initiation fee, Respondent breached its duty of fair representation and thereby violated Section 8(b)(1)(A).

In its computation of "core fees," the Union included, as chargeable to objecting employees, its organizing expenses. The complaint alleges that by the inclusion of such expenses the Union has breached its duty of fair representation. . . . It is axiomatic that the organizing of other bargaining units, at least within the same industry and/or geographical area, strengthens a union's hand in bargaining with the employer of objecting employees. Successful organization of the employees of an employer's competitors precludes that employer from arguing, at the bargaining table, that the lesser wages and benefits paid by his union-free competition prevents him from granting wage and benefit increases sought by the union which represents his employees. It also tends to increase the support which his employees will receive should they find it necessary to engage in economic action, such as a strike. Organizing of other employees thus inures "to the benefit of the members of the local union by virtue of their membership in the parent organization."

Moreover, in order to avoid the "free rider" problem . . . it is essential that a union be permitted to charge objecting nonmembers for its expenses in organizing other units. The bargaining unit in which the objector finds him or herself has already been organized. The expense of that organizational effort was borne by the union (and its members in previously organized units) sometime in the past; it can no longer be charged to current employees. Only by permitting a union to pass along the cost of its current organizing efforts to the members of its already organized units can it equitably recoup those expenses.

It may be that some organizing expenses are too remote, in terms of industry or geography, to pose more than a theoretical benefit to the objector's bargaining unit. However . . . I find that organizing expenses are not "necessarily nonchargeable . . . as a matter of law" and recommend dismissal of this allegation.

. . . Having found that the Respondent has engaged in certain unfair labor practices, I find that it must be ordered to cease and desist and to take certain affirmative action designed to effectuate the policies of the Act. . . .

[On review by the NLRB, the Board affirmed the judge's rulings, findings, and conclusions and adopted the recommended Order.]

Case Questions

1. What information does the NLRB require a union to provide to employees who choose not to become members? What information did the union provide to Blosser?
2. Why is the union allowed to include organizing expenses in the expenses chargeable to nonmembers? What is the "free rider" problem?
3. How was the union's conduct coercive? What unfair labor practices did the union commit? Explain.

Shortly after taking office in 2001, President George W. Bush signed Executive Order 13201, which applies to all firms doing business with the federal government. The order requires these firms to post notices in the workplace informing employees subject to a union security agreement that they have the right to refuse to pay the portion of their union dues that is expended for activities unrelated to collective bargaining, contract administration, or grievance adjustment. The secretary of labor is responsible for enforcing the executive order.

COURT RULES SMALL UNIONS NEED NOT PROVIDE AUDITED FINANCIAL STATEMENTS

THE WORKING LAW

In response to a suit by fee-paying nonmembers challenging the deduction of agency fees, the U.S. Court of Appeals for the Ninth Circuit held that small unions need only provide financial statements verified by an outside source rather than having the statements formally audited by a CPA firm. The suit was brought by teachers who were not members of the California Teachers Association, but who were required under the collective agreements to pay agency fees to the union. The suit argued that the various local unions of the Teachers Association, which provided the nonmembers with summary financial information, were not complying with the requirements of the *Chicago Teachers Union Local No. 1 v. Hudson* decision. In addition, the suit argued that the school superintendents of the various school districts were also liable for allowing the deduction of the agency fees without verifying the accuracy of the financial information provided by the union.

The court of appeals reversed the trial court, which held that the unions had to provide audited financial statements and that the school superintendents were liable for failing to verify the union statements. The court of appeals held that small local unions, with less than $50,000 in member dues and agency fees, need not have their financial information audited by a CPA, but only need have the information verified by an outside neutral party. The court of appeals also held that there was no legal basis for holding the school superintendents responsible for the accuracy of the financial information provided by the unions.

Sources: "Independent Verification Required for Local Union's Financial Statements," *National Public Employment Reporter,* November 1, 2002; "Union's 'Fair Share' Notice Needs Independent Audit Verification," *8 Public Employment Law Report No. 2,* April 2003, p. 10; *Harik v. California Teachers Association* [326 F.3d 1042 (9th Cir. 2003)].

Liability for Breach of the Duty of Fair Representation

Most cases involving the duty of fair representation arise from action by the employer; after the employee has been disciplined or discharged, the union's alleged breach of the duty compounds the problem.

How should the damages awarded in such a case be divided between the employer and the union? Which party should bear primary liability? In *Vaca v. Sipes* [386 U.S. 171 (1967)], the Supreme Court also held that an employer cannot escape liability for breach of the collective agreement just because the union has breached its duty of fair representation. Where the employee has established a breach of the collective agreement by the employer and a breach of the duty of fair representation by the union, the employer and the union must share liability. In *Bowen v. U.S. Postal Service* [459 U.S. 212 (1983)], the Supreme Court held that the employer is liable for back pay for the discharge of an employee in breach of the collective agreement, whereas the union breaching the duty of fair representation by refusing to grieve the discharge is responsible for any increase in damages suffered by the employee as a result of the breach of the duty of fair representation. In *Chauffeurs, Teamsters and Helpers, Local No. 391 v. Terry* [494 U.S. 538 (1990)], the Supreme Court held that to recover damages against both the employer and the union, the employee must prove both that the employer's actions violated the collective agreement and that the union's handling of the grievance breached the duty of fair representation.

The NLRB has held that when an employee has established that the union improperly refused to process a grievance or handled it in a perfunctory manner, the board is prepared to resolve doubts about the merits of the grievance in favor of the employee, *Rubber Workers Local 250 (Mack-Wayne Enclosures)* [279 NLRB No. 165, 122 L.R.R.M. 1147 (1986)].

Enforcing the Duty of Fair Representation

In *Miranda Fuel Co.* [140 NLRB 181 (1962)], the NLRB held that a breach of the duty of fair representation by a union was a violation of Section 8(b)(1)(A) of the NLRA. The board reasoned that "Section 7 . . . gives employees the right to be free from unfair or irrelevant or invidious treatment by their exclusive bargaining agent in matters affecting their employment." Although the Court of Appeals for the Second Circuit refused to enforce the board's order in *Miranda* [326 F.2d 172 (1963)], other courts of appeals have affirmed NLRB findings of Section 8(b)(1)(A) violations in subsequent duty of fair representation cases. The NLRB continues to hold that breach of the duty of fair representation by a union is an unfair labor practice.

The NLRB does not have exclusive jurisdiction over claims of the breach of the duty of fair representation; federal courts also may exercise jurisdiction over such claims according to the Supreme Court in *Breininger v. Sheet Metal Workers Local 6* [493 U.S. 67 (1989)]. The cases developing the duty of fair representation that we have seen so far have involved lawsuits filed against both the union and the employer. Such suits are filed under Section 301 of the NLRA and may be filed either in state or federal courts and are subject to federal labor law, not state contract law. In *Steelworkers v. Rawson* [495 U.S. 362 (1990)], the Supreme Court held that a wrongful death suit brought under state law against a union by the heirs of miners killed in an underground fire was preempted by Section 301. According to the Supreme Court in *Chauffeurs, Teamsters and Helpers, Local No. 391 v. Terry* [494 U.S. 558 (1990)], an employee who seeks back pay as a remedy for a union's violation of the duty of fair representation is entitled to a jury trial.

In *DelCostello v. Teamsters* [462 U.S. 151 (1983)], the Supreme Court held that the time limit for bringing a suit under Section 301 alleging a breach of the duty of fair representation is six months; in cases where the employee is required to exhaust internal procedures, the six-month time limit does not begin to run until those procedures have been exhausted, *Frandsen v. BRAC* [782 F.2d 674 (7th Cir. 1986)]. A suit against a union for failing to enforce an arbitration award is an action for breach of the duty of fair representation and is subject to the six-month limitations period, *Carrion v. Enterprise Association, Metal Trades Branch Local Union 638* [227 F.3d 29 (2d Cir. 2000)].

Exhausting Internal Remedies

We have seen that the duty of fair representation may be enforced by either a Section 301 suit or a Section 8(b)(1)(A) unfair labor practice proceeding. Before either action can be initiated, however, the employee alleging breach of the duty of fair representation must attempt to exhaust internal remedies that may be available.

Because most complaints of breaches of the duty of fair representation result from employer actions, such as discharge or discipline, which are then compounded by the union's breach of its duty, the affected employee may have the right to file a grievance under the collective-bargaining agreement to challenge the employer's actions. When contractual remedies—the grievance procedure and arbitration—are available to the employee, he or she must first attempt to use those procedures. This means that the employee must file a grievance and attempt to have it processed through to arbitration before filing a Section 301 suit or a Section 8(b)(1)(A) complaint. The requirement of exhausting contractual remedies flows from the policy of fostering voluntary settlement of disputes. This policy is behind the court's deferral to arbitration (recall the *Steelworkers Trilogy* from Chapter 18) and the NLRB deferral to arbitration (recall the *United Technologies* and the *Olin Corp.* cases from Chapter 18).

The requirement of exhausting contractual remedies is not absolute. In *Glover v. St. Louis–San Francisco Railway* [393 U.S. 324 (1969)], the Supreme Court held that employees need not exhaust contract remedies when the union and employer are cooperating in the violation of employee rights. In such cases, attempts to get the union to file a grievance or to process it through to arbitration would be an exercise in futility.

Aside from contractual remedies, an employee may have available internal union procedures to deal with complaints against the union. Some union constitutions provide for review of complaints of alleged mistreatment of union members by union leaders. For example, if local union officials refuse to submit the employee's grievance to arbitration, the employee may appeal that decision to the membership of the local. An appeal to the international union leadership may also be available. Should an employee be required to exhaust such internal union remedies before filing a suit or unfair practice complaint alleging breach of the duty of fair representation?

In *Clayton v. United Auto Workers* [451 U.S. 679 (1981)], the Supreme Court held that an employee is not required to exhaust internal union remedies when the internal union appeals procedure cannot result in reactivation of the employee's grievance or award the complete relief sought by the employee. In such cases, the employee may file a Section 301 suit or a Section 8(b)(1)(A) complaint without exhausting the internal union remedies. If such remedies could provide the relief sought by the employee, they must be pursued before filing under Section 301 or Section 8(b)(1)(A).

If the alleged breach of the duty of fair representation involves claims of discrimination based on race, sex, religion, or national origin, the affected employees may also have legal remedies under Title VII of the Civil Rights Act of 1964. Just as in *Alexander v. Gardner-Denver* (see Chapter 5), the remedies under Title

VII are separate from any remedies under Section 301 or Section 8(b)(1)(A). The affected employees may then file a complaint with the Equal Employment Opportunity Commission under Title VII as well as filing under Section 301 and/or Section 8(b)(1)(A).

Remedies available under an action for breach of the duty of fair representation depend on whether the employee pursues the claim under Section 301 or Section 8(b)(1)(A). Under Section 301, an action against both the employer and the union can be brought. An employee may recover monetary damages (but not punitive damages) and legal fees and may get an injunction (such as ordering the union to arbitrate the grievance or ordering the employer to reinstate the employee). Under Section 8(b)(1)(A), the NLRB can order the union to (1) pay compensation for lost wages, benefits, and legal fees, (2) arbitrate the grievance, and (3) "cease and desist" from further violations. If the employee's complaint involves action by both the employer and the union, Section 301 would be preferable; if only the union is involved, either Section 301 or Section 8(b)(1)(A) is appropriate.

RIGHTS OF UNION MEMBERS

In addition to being protected by the duty of fair representation, union members have certain rights against the union guaranteed by statute. The union members' "bill of rights" under the Labor Management Reporting and Disclosure Act and Section 8(b)(1) establishes those rights.

See **http://www4.law.cornell.edu/uscode/29/ch11.html** *for the text of the LMRDA.*

UNION DISCIPLINE OF MEMBERS

Section 8(b)(1)(A) prohibits union actions that restrain, coerce, or interfere with employee rights under Section 7. Section 8(b)(1)(A), however, does provide that "This paragraph shall not impair the right of a labor organization to prescribe its own rules with respect to the acquisition or retention of membership therein."

In *NLRB v. Allis-Chalmers Mfg. Co.* [388 U.S. 175 (1967)], the Supreme Court held that a union could impose fines against members who crossed a picket line and worked during an authorized strike. In *NLRB v. Boeing Co.* [412 U.S. 67 (1973)], the Supreme Court held that a union may file suit in a state court to enforce fines imposed against members. However, if union members legally resign from the union before crossing the picket line and return to work during a strike, the union cannot impose fines against them, as held by the Supreme Court in *NLRB v. Textile Workers Granite State Joint Board* [409 U.S. 213 (1972)].

In response to the *Textile Workers Granite State Joint Board* decision, a number of unions adopted rules that limited the right of members to resign from the union during a strike. Such rules violate section 8(b)(1)(A) according to the Supreme Court decision in *Pattern Makers' League of North America v. NLRB* [473 U.S. 95 (1985)].

ACTORS' UNION IMPOSES FINES FOR WORKING DURING STRIKE

THE WORKING LAW

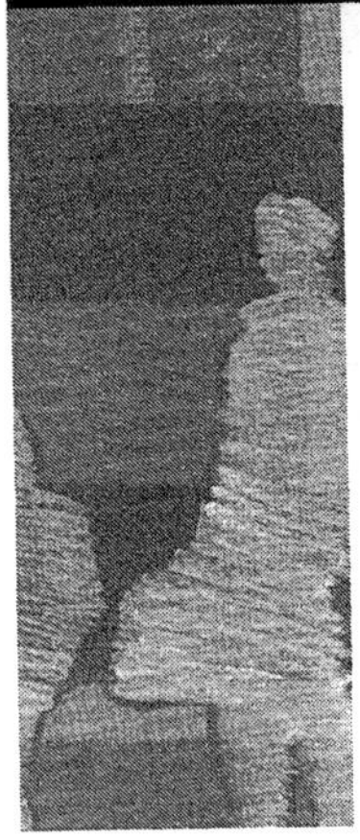

The Screen Actors Guild imposed a fine of $100,000 on actress Elizabeth Hurley for making an Estée Lauder perfume commercial during a six-month strike by commercial actors. The union, which represents the actors and actresses who appear in TV commercials, called the strike over a dispute on residual payments actors receive for each time the commercial is broadcast. Hurley, who appeared before a union trial board to plead her case, complained that she never received notice of the strike. She had already made a "goodwill" donation of $25,000 to the union's strike fund, which was credited against her fine. Professional golfer Tiger Woods, who apologized to the union for making a Buick commercial during the strike, was fined $50,000. Hurley complained that pop singers Britney Spears and 'N Sync were not fined for appearing in a McDonald's commercial during the strike.

Sources: "Hurley Fined $100,000 for Crossing Picket Lines," *Los Angeles Times,* Dec. 19, 2000; "'Scab' Hurley Fined by Her Union for Strike-Breaking," *The Independent* (London), Dec. 18, 2000; "Commercial Spot Costly to Hurley," *The Houston Chronicle,* Dec. 18, 2000.

UNION MEMBERS' BILL OF RIGHTS

The Labor Management Reporting and Disclosure Act (LMRDA) seeks to ensure that union members are guaranteed certain rights when subjected to internal union proceedings. Section 101 of the LMRDA is commonly called the union members' "bill of rights."

Union Disciplinary Procedures

Procedural safeguards against improper disciplinary action are provided by Section 101(a)(5), which states that

> No member of any labor organization may be fined, suspended, expelled, or otherwise disciplined except for nonpayment of dues by such organization or by any officer thereof unless such member has been (A) served with written specific charges; (B) given a reasonable time to prepare his defense; (C) afforded a full and fair hearing.

Section 102 of the LMRDA allows any person whose rights under the act have been violated to bring a civil suit in the federal courts for such relief as may be appropriate. In *Wooddell v. International Brotherhood of Electrical Workers, Local 71* [502 U.S. 93 (1991)], the Supreme Court held that a union member suing under the LMRDA, alleging discrimination against him by the union in job referrals through the union hiring hall, was entitled to a jury trial.

When a union member alleges that his or her rights have been violated by union disciplinary action, what standards should the court apply to determine if the union procedure was reasonable? This question was addressed by the following case.

Boilermakers v. Hardeman

401 U.S. 233 (1971)

Brennan, J.

Respondent was expelled from membership in petitioner union and brought this action under Section 102 [of the LMRDA] in the District Court for the Southern District of Alabama. He alleged that in expelling him the petitioner violated Section 101(a)(5) of the Act. . . .

A jury awarded respondent damages of $152,150. The Court of Appeals for the Fifth Circuit affirmed. We granted certiorari limited to the questions whether the subject matter of the suit was preempted because exclusively within the competence of the National Labor Relations Board and, if not preempted, whether the courts below had applied the proper standard of review to the union proceedings. . . . We reverse.

The case arises out of events in the early part of October 1960. Respondent, George Hardeman, is a boilermaker. He was then a member of petitioner's Local Lodge 112. On October 3, he went to the union hiring hall to see Herman Wise, business manager of the Local Lodge and the official responsible for referring workmen for jobs. Hardeman had talked to a friend of his, an employer who had promised to ask for him by name for a job in the vicinity. He sought assurance from Wise that he would be referred for the job. When Wise refused to make a definite commitment, Hardeman threatened violence if no work was forthcoming in the next few days.

On October 4, Hardeman returned to the hiring hall and waited for a referral. None was forthcoming. The next day, in his words, he "went to the hall . . . and waited from the time the hall opened until we had the trouble. I tried to make up my mind what to do, whether to sue the local or Wise or beat hell of out of Wise, and then I made up my mind." When Wise came out of his office to go to a local job-site, as required by his duties as business manager, Hardeman handed him a copy of a telegram asking for Hardeman by name. As Wise was reading the telegram, Hardeman began punching him in the face.

Hardeman was tried for this conduct on charges of creating dissension and working against the interest and harmony of the Local Lodge, and of threatening and using force to restrain an officer of the Local Lodge from properly discharging the duties of his office. The trial committee found him "guilty as charged," and the Local Lodge sustained the finding and voted his expulsion for an indefinite period. Internal union review of this action, instituted by Hardeman, modified neither the verdict nor the penalty. Five years later, Hardeman brought this suit alleging that petitioner violated Section 101(a)(5) by denying him a full and fair hearing in the union disciplinary proceedings.

We consider first the union's claim that the subject matter of this lawsuit is, in the first instance, with the exclusive competence of the National Labor Relations Board. The union argues that the gravamen of Hardeman's complaint—which did not seek reinstatement, but only damages for wrongful expulsion, consisting of loss of income, loss of pension and insurance rights, mental anguish and punitive damages—is discrimination against him in job referrals; that any such conduct on the part of the union is at the very least arguably an unfair labor practice under Sections 8(b)(1)(A) and 8(b)(2) of the National Labor Relations Act . . . ; and that in such circumstances, "the federal courts must defer to the exclusive competence of the National Labor Relations Board if the danger of . . . interference with national policy is to be averted."

We think the union's argument is misdirected. Hardeman's complaint alleged that his expulsion was unlawful under Section 101(a)(5), and sought compensation for the consequences of the claimed wrongful expulsion. The critical issue presented by Hardeman's complaint was whether the union disciplinary proceedings had denied him a full and fair hearing within the meaning of Section 101(a)(5)(c). Unless he could establish this claim, Hardeman would be out of court. We hold that this claim was not within the exclusive competence of the National Labor Relations Board. . . . Congress explicitly referred claims under Section 101(a)(5) not to the NLRB, but to the federal district courts. This is made explicit in the opening sentence of Section 102. . . .

Two charges were brought against Hardeman in the union disciplinary proceedings. He was charged with violation of Article 13, Section 1, of the Subordinate Lodge Constitution, which forbids attempting to create dissension or working against the interest and harmony of the union, and carries a penalty of expulsion. He was also charged with violations of Article 12, Section 1, of the Subordinate Lodge By-Laws, which forbids the threat or use of force against any officer of the union in order to prevent him from properly discharging the duties of his office; violation may be punished "as warranted by the offense." Hardeman's conviction on both charges was upheld in internal union procedures for review.

The trial judge instructed the jury that "whether or not he [respondent] was rightfully or wrongfully discharged or expelled is a pure question of law for me to determine." He assumed, but did not decide, that the transcript of the union disciplinary hearing contained evidence adequate to support conviction of violating Article 12. He held, however, that there was no evidence at all in the transcript of the union disciplinary proceedings to support the charge of violating Article 13. This holding appears to have been based on the Fifth Circuit's decision in *Boilermakers v. Braswell*. There the Court of Appeals for the Fifth Circuit had reasoned that "penal provisions in union constitutions must be strictly construed," and that as so construed Article 13 was directed only to "threats to the union as an organization and to the effective carrying out of the union's aims," not to merely personal altercations. Since the union tribunals had returned only a general verdict, and since one of the charges was thought to be supported by no evidence whatsoever, the trial judge held that Hardeman had been deprived of the full and fair hearing guaranteed by Section 101(a)(5). The Court of Appeals affirmed, simply citing *Braswell*. . . .

We find nothing in either the language or the legislative history of Section 101(a)(5) that could justify such a substitution of judicial for union authority to interpret the union's regulations in order to determine the scope of offenses warranting discipline of union members. . . .

We think that this is sufficient to indicate that Section 101(a)(5) was not intended to authorize courts to determine the scope of offenses for which a union may discipline its members. And if a union may discipline its members for offenses not proscribed by written rules at all, it is surely a futile exercise for a court to construe the written rules in order to determine whether particular conduct falls within or without their scope.

Of course, Section 101(a)(5)(A) requires that a member subject to discipline be "served with written specific charges." These charges must be, in Senator McClellan's words, "specific enough to inform the accused member of the offense that he has allegedly committed." Where, as here, the union's charges make reference to specific written provisions, Section 101(a)(5)(A) obviously empowers the federal courts to examine those provisions and determine whether the union member had been misled or otherwise prejudiced in the presentation of his defense. But it gives courts no warrant to scrutinize the union regulations in order to determine whether particular conduct may be punished at all.

Respondent does not suggest, and we cannot discern, any possibility of prejudice in the present case. Although the notice of charges with which he was served does not appear as such in the record, the transcript of the union hearing indicates that the notice did not confine itself to a mere statement or citation of the written regulations that Hardeman was said to have violated: the notice appears to have contained a detailed statement of the facts relating to the fight which formed the basis for the disciplinary action. Section 101(a)(5) requires no more.

There remains only the question whether the evidence in the union disciplinary proceeding was sufficient to support the finding of guilt. Section 101(a)(5)(C) of the LMRDA guarantees union members a "full and fair" disciplinary hearing, and the parties and the lower federal courts are in full agreement that this guarantee requires the charging party to provide some evidence at the disciplinary hearing to support the charges made. This is the proper standard of judicial review. We have repeatedly held that conviction on charges unsupported by any evidence is a denial of due process . . . and we feel that Section 101(a)(5)(C) may fairly be said to import a similar requirement into union disciplinary proceedings. . . . [A]ny lesser standard would make useless Section 101(a)(5)(A)'s requirement of written, specific charges. A stricter standard, on the other hand, would be inconsistent with the apparent congressional intent to allow unions to govern their own affairs, and would require courts to judge the credibility of witnesses on the basis of what would be at best, a cold record.

Applying this standard to the present case, we think there is no question that the charges were adequately supported. Respondent was charged with having attacked Wise without warning, and with continuing to beat him for some time. Wise so testified at the disciplinary hearing, and his testimony was fully corroborated by one other witness to the altercation. Even Hardeman, although he claimed he was thereafter held and beaten, admitted having struck the first blow. On such a record there is no question but that the charges were supported by "some evidence."

Reversed.

Case Questions

1. Why did the union expel Hardeman from membership?
2. Does the NLRB have exclusive jurisdiction over complaints alleging that unions failed to provide full and fair procedures for members accused of disciplinary offenses? Explain.
3. What is the court's role under Section 101(a)(5) in interpreting union disciplinary rules? Who is to determine the scope of conduct that warrants discipline?

To have a valid claim under Section 101(a)(5) and Section 102, the union member must have been subjected to discipline by the union. In *Breininger v. Sheet Metal Workers Local 6* [493 U.S. 67 (1989)], the Supreme Court held that Breininger's suit over the union's failure to refer him under a hiring hall agreement because he supported a political rival of the union business manager did not state a claim under the LMRDA. The Court held that the failure to refer him was not "discipline" within the meaning of the act.

Free Speech and Association

Whereas Section 101(a)(5) guarantees union members' procedural rights in union disciplinary proceedings, the other provisions of Section 101(a) provide for other basic rights in participating in union activities. These rights take precedence over any provisions of union constitutions or bylaws that are inconsistent with Section 101 rights. Section 101(b) states that any such inconsistent provisions shall have no effect.

http://www4.law.cornell.edu/uscode/29/481.html *contains the text of Subchapter V on elections.*

Section 101(a)(2) provides for the rights of freedom of speech and assembly for union members. Every union member has the right to meet and assemble with other members and to express any views or opinions, subject to the union's reasonable rules for the conduct of meetings. As long as any item of business is properly before a union meeting, a union member may express his or her views on that item of business. The latitude given to union members to express their opinions at union meetings is very broad. Any restrictions on such expression must be reasonable and required for the orderly conducting of union meetings. Violations of these rights give rise to civil liability. In *Hall v. Cole* [412 U.S. 1 (1973)], a union member was expelled from the union after introducing a series of resolutions alleging undemocratic actions and questionable policies by union officials. The union claimed such resolutions violated a rule against "deliberate and malicious vilification with regard to the execution or duties of any office." The member filed suit under Section 102, alleging violations of his rights guaranteed by Section 101(a)(2). The Supreme Court upheld the trial decision ordering that the member be reinstated in the union and awarding him $5,500 in legal fees.

In *Sheet Metal Workers International Association v. Lynn* [488 U.S. 347 (1989)], an elected business agent of the union filed suit under Section 102 over his removal from office because of statements he made at a union meeting opposing a dues increase sought by the union trustee. The Supreme Court held that his removal from office constituted a violation of the free speech provisions of Section 101(a)(2).

In *United Steelworkers of America v. Sadlowski* [457 U.S. 102 (1982)], the Supreme Court held that a union rule prohibiting contributions from nonmembers in campaigns for union offices did not violate a union member's right of free speech and assembly under Section 101(a)(2), even though it had the effect of making a challenge to incumbent union officers much more difficult.

The courts have recognized some other limits on union members' rights of free speech and assembly. A union member cannot preach "dual unionism"—that is, advocate membership in another union during his union's meeting. Furthermore, the remarks of a union member are subject to libel and slander laws. The right of free assembly does not protect a group of members who engage in a wildcat strike that violates the union's no-strike agreement with the employer.

Right to Participate in Union Affairs

The right of union members to participate in all membership business, such as meetings, discussions, referendums, and elections, is guaranteed by Section 101(a)(1) of the LMRDA. This right to participate is subject to the reasonable rules and regulations of the union's constitution and bylaws. Any provisions that are inconsistent with these rights are of no effect by reason of Section 101(b).

The provisions of the LMRDA allow a union to require that members exhaust internal union remedies before pursuing external action for violation of the rights granted by the LMRDA. Section 101(a)(4) does provide, however, that the internal union proceedings cannot last longer than four months. If the proceedings take longer than four months, the member is not required to pursue them before instituting external proceedings.

Election Procedures

Title IV of the LMRDA requires that union elections be conducted according to certain democratic procedures. Section 401 sets the following requirements:

1. National and international labor organizations must elect their officers at least every five years.
2. Every local union must hold elections at least every three years.
3. Elections shall be by secret ballot or at a convention of delegates chosen by secret ballot.
4. There must be advance notice of the election, freedom of choice among candidates, and publication and one year's preservation of the election results.
5. Dues and assessments cannot be used to support anyone's candidacy.
6. Every candidate has the right to inspect lists of members' names and addresses.
7. Each candidate has the right to have observers at polling places and at the counting of the ballots.

In the case of *International Organization for Masters, Mates & Pilots v. Brown* [498 U.S. 466 (1991)], the Supreme Court held that labor unions must cooperate with all reasonable requests from candidates for union office to distribute campaign literature despite union rules restricting such requests. In that case, the Court decided that a union refusal to provide a membership list to a candidate because of a union rule prohibiting preconvention mailings was in violation of the LMRDA.

The election provisions of the LMRDA also prohibit unduly restrictive eligibility requirements that enable incumbents to become entrenched in office. Such eligibility requirements are the subject of the following case.

Herman v. Local 1011, United Steelworkers of America

207 F.3d 924 (7th Cir. 2000), cert. denied, 531 U.S. 1010 (2000)

Posner, Chief Judge

Section 401(e) of the Labor-Management Reporting and Disclosure Act [LMRDA] makes all union members in good standing eligible to run for office in the union's elections subject to "reasonable qualifications uniformly imposed." The constitution of the steelworkers international union conditions eligibility for local office on the member's having attended at least eight of the local's monthly meetings (or been excused from attendance at them, in which event he must have attended one-third of the meetings from which he was not excused) within the two years preceding the election. Noting that the rule disqualifies 92 percent of the almost 3,000 members of Local 1011 of the steelworkers union, the district judge, at the behest of the Secretary of Labor . . . declared the rule void.

The Act's aim was to make the governance of labor unions democratic. The democratic presumption is that any adult member of the polity, which in this case is a union local, is eligible to run for office. . . .

As an original matter we would think it, not absurd, but still highly questionable, to impose a meeting-attendance requirement on aspirants for union office, at least in the absence of any information, which has not been vouchsafed us, regarding the character of these meetings. All we know is that they are monthly and that the union's constitution requires that all expenditure and other decisions of the union's hierarchy be approved at these meetings; yet despite the formal power that the attendants exercise, only a tiny percentage of the union's membership bothers to attend—on average no more than 3 percent (fewer than 90 persons). We are not told whether an agenda or any other material is distributed to the membership in advance of the meeting to enable members to decide whether to attend and to enable them to participate intelligently if they do attend. We do not know how long the meetings last or what information is disseminated at them orally or in writing to enable the attenders to cast meaningful, informed votes. For all we know the only attenders are a tiny coterie of insiders not eager to share their knowledge with the rest of the union's members. . . .

All we know for sure about this case, so far as bears on the reasonableness of the meeting-attendance requirement, is that the requirement disqualifies the vast majority of the union's members, that it requires members who have not been attending meetings in the past to decide at least eight months before an election that they may want to run for union office (for remember that the meetings are monthly and that a candidate must have attended at least eight within the past two years unless he falls within one of the excuse categories), and that the union itself does not take the requirement very seriously, for it allows members who have attended no meetings to run for office, provided that they fall into one of the excuse categories. The categories are reasonable in themselves—service with the armed forces, illness, being at work during the scheduled time of the meeting, and so forth—and they expand the pool of eligibles from 95 union members to 242, of whom 53 attended not a single meeting. But if the meeting-attendance requirement were regarded as a vital condition of effective officership, equivalent in importance to the LMRDA's requirement that the candidate be a union member in good standing, the fact that a member was without fault in failing to satisfy it would not excuse the failure. . . . So many of the union's members are excused from the meeting-attendance requirement that there could be an election for officers of Local 1011 at which none of the candidates satisfied the requirement.

The requirement is paternalistic. Union members should be capable of deciding for themselves whether a candidate for union office who had not attended eight, or five, or for that matter any meetings within the past two years should by virtue of his poor attendance forfeit the electorate's consideration. The union's rule is antidemocratic in deeming the electors incompetent to decide an issue that is in no wise technical or esoteric—what weight to give to a candidate's failure to have attended a given number of union meetings in the recent past. . . . And since most union members interested in seeking an office in the union are likely to attend meetings just to become known . . . the rule is superfluous.

. . . Under conditions of pervasive apathy, a requirement of attending even a single meeting might disqualify the vast bulk of the membership. That is true here. Only 14 percent of the members attended even one meeting within the last two years. Yet the Department of Labor does not argue that therefore even a one-meeting requirement would be unreasonable.

. . . We think the proper approach, and one that is consistent with the case law . . . is to deem a condition of eligibility that disqualifies the vast bulk of the union's membership from standing for union office presumptively unreasonable. The union must then present convincing reasons, not merely conjectures, why the condition is either not burdensome or though burdensome is supported by compelling need. This approach distinguishes . . . between impact and burden. A requirement that to be eligible to be a candidate a member of the union have attended one meeting of the union in his lifetime would not be burdensome even though it might disqualify a large fraction of the union membership simply because very few members took any interest in the governance of the union. That defense is unavailable here, however. Requiring attendance at eight meetings in two years imposes a burden because it compels the prospective candidate not only to sacrifice what may be scarce free time to sit through eight meetings, but also, if he is disinclined to attend meetings for any reason other than to be able to run for union office, to make up his mind whether to run many months before the election.

The burden is great enough in this case to place the onus of justification on the union. The only justification offered is that the requirement of attending eight meetings in two years encourages union members who might want to run for office, perhaps especially opponents of the incumbents, to attend union meetings (since otherwise they may not be eligible to run), thus bolstering attendance at the meetings and fostering participatory democracy. The slight turnout at the meetings suggests that this goal, though worthy, cannot be achieved by the means adopted; the means are not adapted to the end, suggesting that the real end may be different. So far as appears, the union has given no consideration to alternative inducements to attend meetings that would not involve disqualifying from office more than nine-tenths of its members. . . . Under the rule challenged in this case, a union member who wanted to be sure of qualifying for eligibility to run for office might have to start attending meetings as much as a year in advance of the election, because he might miss one or more meetings for reasons that the union does not recognize as excusing (such as vacation or family leave) and because the union might cancel one or more meetings. And yet a year before the election an issue that might move a union member to incur the time and expense of running for office might not even be on the horizon. . . .

The district court was right to invalidate the meeting-attendance requirement as unreasonable, and the judgment is therefore

AFFIRMED.

Case Questions

1. What does the election rule require of members who want to run for union office? Why would the union impose such a requirement?
2. Why has the secretary of labor (Herman) challenged the election-eligibility rule?
3. What does the court mean by distinguishing "between impact and burden" of the challenged rule? How does the court's approach apply to the rule at issue in this case?

OTHER RESTRICTIONS ON UNIONS

Duties of Union Officers

The provisions of the LMRDA and the Taft-Hartley amendments to the NLRA imposed a number of duties on union officers to eliminate financial corruption and racketeering and to safeguard union funds. All officials handling union money must be bonded, and persons convicted of certain criminal offenses are barred from holding union office for five years.

Unions are also subjected to annual reporting requirements by the LMRDA. The union reports, filed with the secretary of labor, must contain the following information:

1. the name and the title of each officer;
2. the fees and dues required of members;
3. provisions for membership qualification and issuing work permits;
4. the process for electing and removing officers;
5. disciplinary standards for members;
6. details of any union benefit plans;
7. authorization rules for bargaining demands, strikes, and contract ratification.

Any changes in the union constitution, bylaws, or rules must be reported. In addition, detailed financial information must be reported annually; these financial reports must contain information on the following:

1. assets and liabilities at the beginning and end of the fiscal year;
2. union receipts and their sources;
3. salaries paid by the union in excess of $10,000 total;
4. any loans by the union in excess of $250;
5. any other union disbursements.

All reports and information filed with the secretary of labor must also be made available to union members.

Union officials must report any security or financial interest in, or any benefit received from, any employer whose employees are represented by the union and anything of value received from any business dealing connected with the union. The LMRDA imposes on union officers a duty to refrain from dealing with the union as an adverse party in any manner connected with their duties and to refrain from holding or acquiring any personal or pecuniary interest that conflicts with the interests of the union, *Chathas v. Local 134 I.B.E.W.* [233 F.3d 508 (7th Cir. 2000)]. Employers are required to make annual reports of any expenditures or transactions with union representatives and payments to employees or consultants for the purpose of influencing organizational or bargaining activities.

Welfare and Pension Plans

Section 302 of the Taft-Hartley Act, along with the Employee Retirement Income Security Act (ERISA), controls the operation and administration of employee welfare and pension plans. Persons administering such funds must handle them to protect the interests of all employees. Union officials serving as trustees or administrators of such funds may receive only one full-time salary. They must also be careful to keep their roles as trustee and union official separated.

Section 304 of the Taft-Hartley Act, along with the Federal Election Campaign Act of 1976, controls union political contributions and expenditures. Union dues or assessments may not be used to fund political expenditures. However, the union may establish a separate political fund if it is financed by voluntary contributions from union members. Members must be kept informed of the use of such funds and must not be subject to any reprisals in connection with the collection of contributions.

SUMMARY

- The duty of fair representation was developed by the Supreme Court to ensure that unions protected the rights of the employees they represent. The NLRB has determined that a breach of the duty of fair representation is an unfair labor practice in violation of Section 8(b)(1)(A) of the NLRA; Section 301 may also be used to bring a suit for breach of duty of fair representation in the courts. Although unions have some leeway to exercise judgment as to how to represent their members, actions that are discriminatory, arbitrary, or in bad faith are violations of the duty of fair representation.
- Unions owe the duty of fair representation to all employees in the bargaining unit, not just to union members. Employees subject to a union security clause may not be terminated for failing to join the union, as long as membership is denied to them for reasons other than failure to pay union dues or fees. Nonmembers who pay union dues and fees are entitled to a reduction in those dues and fees reflecting union expenditures on matters not related to collective bargaining. Failure to inform such employees of their rights, or to allow them the reductions, is a violation of the duty of fair representation.
- Unions are entitled to make and enforce reasonable rules for internal discipline and maintenance of membership; however, unions cannot enforce such rules against employees who resign from the union. Rules that restrict the right of employees to resign from the union may violate Section 8(b)(1)(A).
- The Labor Management Reporting and Disclosure Act (LMRDA) sets out a "bill of rights" for union members, guaranteeing them certain procedural rights for internal union proceedings. Union officials must comply with the financial and reporting requirements of the LMRDA, and elections for union officers are subject to the requirements of Section 401 of the LMRDA.

QUESTIONS

1. What is meant by the duty of fair representation? What standard of conduct by a union is required by the duty of fair representation? Who is protected by the duty of fair representation?
2. Does an employee in a bargaining unit have the right to have his or her grievance taken to arbitration? When does a union's refusal to arbitrate a grievance breach the duty of fair representation?

3. What remedies are available for a breach of the duty of fair representation? How do the remedies under Section 8(b)(1) differ from those available under Section 301?
4. When can a union enforce its disciplinary rules against employees who resign from the union? When can a union restrict the right of members to resign? Explain your answers.
5. What is the union member's "bill of rights"?
6. What restrictions are placed on union officers by the Taft-Hartley Act and the Labor Management Reporting and Disclosure Act amendments to the NLRA?
7. Can bargaining unit employees who are not union members be required to pay union dues and fees? What information must the union provide to such employees?
8. What requirements does Section 401 of the LMRDA impose on union elections? Who monitors union elections to ensure compliance with Section 401?

CASE PROBLEMS

1. The employee joined the United States Postal Service (USPS) in 1975 as a part-time substitute rural carrier near Spokane, Washington. In 1976, the employee was given a full-time rural route. He obtained this route under a provision in the collective-bargaining agreement giving senior part-timers first priority for new full-time routes.

   City delivery carriers and managers were jealous of the employee for obtaining this route, the court relates. He began to experience harassment from some of his co-workers, and in addition, the route he worked was overburdened. In January 1978, the employee and another man were arrested and charged with stealing equipment from a railroad yard. He pled guilty and received a suspended sentence. The theft was reported in the local press.

   USPS fired the employee, asserting that the conviction meant he no longer was entrusted to safeguard mail or postal funds. He filed a grievance, but the shop steward declined to represent him. The union's steward fulfilled this task instead. When decisions at lower steps were negative, the union considered arbitration. However, the union's general counsel advised against arbitration on the ground that there was little likelihood of success.

   Based on these facts, do you think the union fulfilled its duty of fair representation to the discharged postal worker? See *Johnson v. U.S. Postal Service and National Rural Letter Carriers Association* [756 F.2d 1461 (9th Cir. 1985)].
2. After being on sick leave for half a year because of high blood pressure, Owens attempted to return to work. Owens's family physician had approved his return to work, but Owens's employer's company physician felt that Owens's blood pressure was too high to return, and the employer discharged him. Owens filed a grievance over his discharge, and the union processed the grievance through the grievance procedure. In preparation for taking Owens's grievance to arbitration, the union had Owens examined by another physician; that doctor also believed that Owens should not return to work. In light of their doctor's opinion, the union decided not to take Owens's grievance to arbitration. Owens demanded that his grievance be arbitrated, but the union refused. Owens then sued the union and the employer in state court, alleging breach of the collective agreement and of the duty of fair representation.

   How should the court decide Owens's claims against the union? Against the employer? Explain your answers. See *Vaca v. Sipes* [368 U.S. 171 (1967)].

3. Beginning in 1973, the employer's employees had been represented by Local P-706 of the then Amalgamated Meat Cutters Union. In December 1978, an employee filed a decertification petition in Case 11–RD–284, and the parties entered into a stipulated election agreement. Shortly thereafter, a notice was posted or mailed by the Meat Cutters announcing a meeting on December 30, 1978. Of the 176 unit employees, sixteen attended the meeting and voted 15-1 for what was orally described as a "merger." On January 11, 1979, the NLRB election was held. Local P-706 remained the sole recipient of the 158 valid ballots cast. On May 4, 1979, the board issued its Decision and Certification of Representative to Local P-706, overruling, *inter alia,* the employer's objection, which contended that the Meat Cutters' holding of the merger vote had interfered with the election.

Prior to the board's decision, however, the following events had taken place. Since Local P-706 was an amalgamated local, the merger process was completed on February 17 when the employees of the other employers voted. The employer's employees were expressly excluded from this vote. The February 17 tally was in favor of merger, as of course was the combined tally of the December 30, 1978, and February 17 votes. Pursuant to these votes, sometime in March, Local P-706 surrendered its charter to the Meat Cutters and admittedly became defunct. The board, which was then considering challenges and objections in the decertification proceeding, was not informed of this action.

On July 6, Local 525 filed a petition in Case 11–AC–14 seeking to amend Local P-706's certification to reflect its merger into Local 525. On September 18, the regional director granted the employer's motion to dismiss on the ground that the December 30, 1978, merger vote was procedurally defective because the employees had not been given adequate notice of the union meeting at which the merger vote occurred. Local 525 did not request review of the regional director's decision.

With a view to devising the "quickest way to settle the matter" and thereby remedy the deficiency of the December 30, 1978, vote, Local 525 sent a September 27 letter to all employees of the employer who had either been members of the then defunct Local P-706 or who had since signed membership cards for Local 525. The letter informed the recipients of an October 21 meeting whose sole purpose would be to vote again on the merger issue. This letter indicated that only "Union Members" would be eligible to vote. Of the 176 unit employees, 67 members were sent letters, of which 52 were received. The October 21 vote was 14-0 in favor of merger. Local 525 then petitioned the NLRB to be certified as the employees' collective-bargaining representative.

How should the NLRB have ruled on this petition? See *Fast Food Merchandisers and Food & Commercial Workers, Local 525* [274 NLRB No. 25, 118 L.R.R.M. 1365 (1985)].

4. The plaintiff, Joan Taschner, worked for Thrift-Rack, Inc. in its warehouse for nine years, from 1973 until September 1982. Teamsters Local Union 384 was at all times relevant to this action the exclusive bargaining representative for certain employees, including the plaintiff of Thrift-Rack.

In September 1982, the plaintiff successfully cross-bid for an outside job of driver-salesperson. While working outside as a driver, she developed a severe neurodermatitis condition and allergic reaction, requiring a doctor's supervision and medication. As a result, she was unable to perform her outside job as a driver.

The plaintiff twice requested Thrift-Rack to transfer her to her prior warehouse position, which was still open, or to any other warehouse position. The company, however, rejected her requests on grounds that the plaintiff alleges were not provided for in the collective-bargaining agreement and that were in violation of past practice.

In response to the company's refusal to transfer her, the plaintiff filed a grievance with Local 384. That grievance was denied by the union agent, James Hill, on grounds that no cross-bidding was allowed, that there were two separate seniority lists for union members who were employed by the company, and that an employee must be working in a unit to be allowed to bid for a job in that unit. Plaintiff requested to take her grievance to arbitration, but that request was denied by Hill. Subsequently, the warehouse position was awarded to another employee with less seniority, no experience, and lower qualifications than the plaintiff possessed.

On November 2, 1982, Thrift-Rack again refused the plaintiff's request to transfer to any warehouse position, although there were still warehouse jobs open, some of which may not have been bid upon by warehouse workers. The company refused to give her any work, informing her that there was no work available for her and to go home. Thereafter, the plaintiff called Thrift-Rack every day for about one week. She reported that she was still on medication and could not drive, but that she was available for any other work. She specifically requested transfer to any position in the warehouse. Thrift-Rack continued to refuse to transfer her to any position in the warehouse.

What recourse did the plaintiff have against her union? See *Taschner v. Hill* [589 F. Supp. 127, 118 L.R.R.M. 2044 (E.D. Pa. 1984)].

5. Plaintiff Feist received a Coast Guard license as a third assistant engineer in 1974 and was accepted into the applicant program of the Merchant Engineers' Beneficial Association (MEBA) in 1975. From 1975 on, he served aboard vessels as a licensed third engineer, completed additional schooling, and worked the required number of days to achieve what is known as Group I status. The plaintiff paid all MEBA dues and had satisfied the requirement of a $2,500 initiation fee for membership. The plaintiff claims that in May 1979 he was informed that the District Investigating Committee had voted to deny him membership in the MEBA. Plaintiff's application was denied a second time on September 7, 1979, and again on February 13, 1981. Plaintiff filed suit against the MEBA, alleging that he had satisfied the requirements of membership in the MEBA and had been wrongfully denied membership status and the right to a full hearing, all in violation of the LMRDA.

Acceptance into membership of the MEBA is governed by Article 3 of the National Constitution, Articles 3 and 4 of the District Constitution, and Rules and Regulations No. 3, promulgated by the National Executive Committee. Rules and Regulations No. 3 states, in pertinent part, "The MEBA reserves the absolute right in its own discretion, for any reason whatsoever (a) at any time prior to acceptance into membership to terminate any applicant's status as such, or (b) to reject the application for membership." The plaintiff sued the union, demanding that he be admitted to membership.

How should the federal court have ruled on the plaintiff's demand? See *Feist v. Engineers' Beneficial Ass'n.* [118 L.R.R.M. 2419 (E.D. La. 1983)].

6. The plaintiffs were boilermakers by trade and also union members. When boilermakers were needed on a construction job, an agreement between the parent union and participating building contractors called "Southeastern States Articles of Agreement" provided that the contractor would request the union to provide the workers and would employ those sent by the union if they were qualified. The controversy resulted from an incident in which the plaintiff boilermakers, upon arriving at the work site, found it picketed by a large and belligerent group from another trade, the pipefitters. It was agreed, for purposes of the case, that the pipefitters' acts and presence were illegal. The referred boilermakers made no attempt to pass through the picket line, and this impasse continued unbroken for several days. After the weekend had passed, a replacement group of boilermakers appeared at the work site in a large body, led by the business agent. The newly recruited boilermakers went right through the line, but the pipefitters, along with the plaintiff boilermakers who had respected the picket lines the previous week, continued to hold off, standing apart. Soon thereafter, an official of the contractor came out from the job site and handed termination notices to all in that group, asserting absenteeism as the ground.

The record reflects a fear by the union that it would be in serious trouble if it could not improve its record of complying with its agreements with employers, and this incident of course involved not honoring illegal picket lines and thereby making the boilermakers abettors of illegal conduct by others.

The preceding situation is dealt with in a series of documents that were in evidence. The previously mentioned Articles of Agreement provide as follows:

> 1.4.4. There will be no recognition of any unauthorized or illegal picket line established by any person or organization, and the international and local officers of the Union will immediately upon being informed that such a situation exists, order all employees to cross such picket line.

The Joint Referral Committee Standards entered into by employers and union provide that a registrant is not to be referred for employment from the out-of-work list for ninety days after:

> 4. Involvement in any unauthorized strike, work stoppage, slowdown, or any other activity having the effect of disrupting the job. . . .
> 6. Insistence on recognizing illegal or unauthorized picket lines.

This ninety-day exclusion from referral was often called "benching" in the record of this case.

The employer demanded in writing that the rules be applied to seven men, including the plaintiffs herein, and accordingly, the Union Rules Committee notified all business agents nationwide, effectively blacklisting the offenders. One of the men was obliged to quit a job he had found in Florida. At the time of trial, the three plaintiffs did not yet have work as boilermakers, though the ninety days had long since expired. They were restored to the bottom of the out-of-work list—not to their previous seniority.

Evaluate the discipline handed out to these boilermakers and the manner in which it was meted. Why were they disciplined? Were they accorded due process of law? See *Turner v. Boilermakers Local 455* [755 F.2d 866, 118 L.R.R.M. 3157 (11th Cir. 1985)].

7. On February 23, 1983, Gerald Forrest, a union member, addressed to Carroll Koepplinger, president of the defendant union, a letter setting forth the basis of his objections to the December 1982 election. The local received Forrest's letter and filed it. Forrest did not receive a response from the union, and pursuant to the LMRDA, he thereafter filed a timely complaint with the U.S. Department of Labor. The plaintiff conducted an investigation of the allegations of Forrest's complaint and found probable cause to believe that violations of Title IV had occurred.

At the time of the election, 378 members belonged to the local. They were employed by approximately eighteen employers spread geographically in the states of Illinois and Iowa. Eight separate nomination meetings were held and were generally conducted by Koepplinger. Following the nomination meetings, the Local 518 secretary reviewed the list of the nominees to determine the eligibility of each in accordance with the union requirements. One of those requirements was that no member could be nominated to any office unless the individual had been a member of the local or international union continuously for five years immediately preceding his or her nomination.

As a result of that requirement, four nominees were ruled ineligible to run for office.

The shop stewards distributed the ballots to union members in their shops while the members were working. The instruction sheet did not contain any instructions for shop stewards with respect to the procedure to be followed in issuing ballots. At least two of the shop stewards who distributed ballots were themselves candidates for union office (one of the two was unopposed). After collecting all the voted ballots, the stewards returned the package to the secretary of the local. The voted ballots were stored in an unlocked filing cabinet in the union hall. The secretary took leave of absence from the local from approximately December 23, 1982, to January 3, 1983, during which time Koepplinger had sole responsibility for the conduct of the election.

Koepplinger selected December 30, 10:00 A.M., to tally the ballots. Koepplinger was present at the local union hall during the tally but in a different room from where the tally took place. The candidates were not affirmatively advised of the time and place of the election tally, and no observers were present. It is unclear whether any candidates had actual notice of the counting. The court requested affidavits from the parties on this question. Only the plaintiff filed affidavits. Those affidavits state that the affiants were never advised of the tally by anyone from the local. They do not answer the question of whether actual notice occurred.

The referendum committee that counted the ballots did not count or reconcile the number of unused ballots and the number of voted ballots to account for all of the official printed ballots. After the election, the local maintained all the election records except for the unvoted ballots. Koepplinger threw these away approximately three weeks after the election tally as part of an office clean-up.

According to the election records, there were 328 voted ballots. There were fifteen elected officers of which three were contested races.

Should the court overturn this election? See *Donovan v. Graphic Arts Union* [118 L.R.R.M. 2093 (C.D. Ill. 1984)].

8. Suit was filed as a class action by ten employees of the Kroger Company. These employees claimed that Teamsters International and Teamsters Local 327, which represented their bargaining unit, breached the union's duty to represent all members of the collective-bargaining unit fairly. The employees also charged that Kroger conspired with the union to "reduce" the conditions and benefits of their employment. More specifically, the plaintiffs claimed that Local 327 failed to represent the members of the union fairly in negotiating a collective-bargaining agreement with Kroger, with the result that the union "bargained away substantial benefits relating primarily to seniority." The complaint charged the International Union with failing to furnish a skilled negotiator to aid in the negotiations when requested to do so by the negotiating committee.

The complaint also alleged that the business agent and president of Local 327 conspired with Kroger in formulating an agreement that contained terms and conditions that were contrary to union policies and that diminished the rights of the plaintiffs and the class they sought to represent (all the unit members in two Kroger warehouses in the Nashville, Tennessee, area). The complaint further alleged that Local 327 and its business agent and president fraudulently changed the results of a membership vote on the proposed collective-bargaining agreement to reflect ratification when in fact the proposed agreement had been rejected. Finally, the complaint asserted that the agreement negotiated by Local 327 and Kroger contained a provision that discriminated against female members of the unit by prescribing a lower wage scale for the unit employees in one of the warehouses than for the employees in the other. Virtually all employees in the warehouse with the lower wage rate were women.

Did the union breach its duty of fair representation? See *Storey v. Teamsters Local 327* [759 F.2d 517, 118 L.R.R.M. 3273 (6th Cir. 1985)].

9. In 1983, General Motors Corporation signed a collective-bargaining agreement with the International Brotherhood of Electrical Workers, under the wage provisions of which new employees joining the bargaining unit were to be paid at a different (lower) hourly rate than current members. A so-called two-tier wage scale resulted from the arbitration of a Postal Service dispute that same year. Since then, a number of other unions have accepted two-tier systems as concessions in their collective-bargaining agreements. Labor negotiators commonly refer to such two-tier wage concessions as "selling the unborn."

Can you articulate an argument on behalf of these "unborn" (new employees) that two-tier labor contracts violate the union's duty of fair representation? Do you see an Equal Employment Opportunity implication to such an agreement? See "IRRA Panelists Address Two-Tier Implications for Fair Representation and Equal Opportunity" [No. 1 DLR A–5 (1985)].

INTERNET EXERCISE

Recall from the material on union dues and on the duty of fair representation that unions may require nonmembers who object to the agency fees charged to arbitrate their disputes. The American Arbitration Association, a nonprofit organization that promotes and regulates arbitration, has specific rules for handling union dues disputes. To learn more, go to the American Arbitration Association Web site at **http://www.adr.org** and click the Focus Areas link. Click the Labor link and then click Rules for Impartial Determination of Union Fees.

INFOTRAC KEYWORDS

http://www.infotrac-college.com

rights of union members, union dues, Labor Management Reporting and Disclosure Act

20 CHAPTER

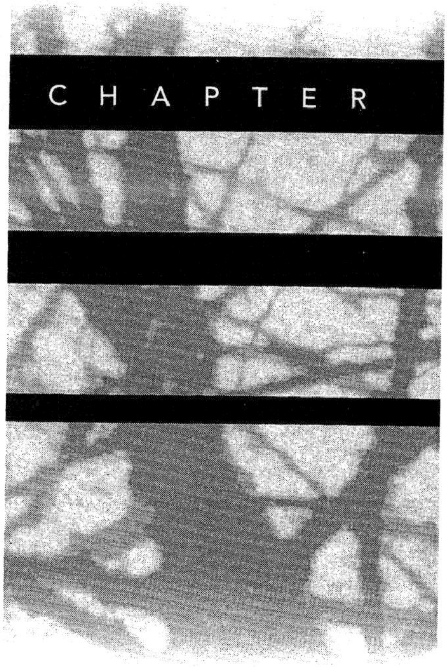

PUBLIC SECTOR LABOR RELATIONS

The rights of public sector employees to organize and bargain collectively are relatively recent legal developments. The National Labor Relations Act (NLRA) excludes employees of the federal, state, and local governments from its coverage. Only in the last few decades have Congress, the executive branch, and the states adopted legal provisions allowing public employees some rights to organize and bargain collectively. This chapter examines the legal provisions that enable public employees to engage in labor relations activities. Labor relations legislation affecting the federal sector is examined in some detail, and certain aspects of state legislation are also considered.

GOVERNMENT AS EMPLOYER

Although many labor relations issues in the public sector are similar to those in the private sector, there are also significant differences. Actions taken by government employers with regard to their employees may raise issues of the constitutional rights of those employees. Both the U.S. Constitution and the various state constitutions regulate and limit government action affecting citizens. Because public sector workers are both citizens and employees, their constitutional rights must be respected by their employers. The public sector employer may therefore be limited in its attempts to discipline or regulate its employees by constitutional provisions. The private sector employer faces no similar constitutional problems.

Another area in which public sector labor relations differs from that of the private sector involves the idea of sovereignty. The government, as government, is sovereign; it cannot vacate or delegate its sovereignty. The government may be obligated by law to perform certain functions and provide certain services, and government officials are given authority to take such actions and make such decisions as are necessary to perform those functions. Collective bargaining involves sharing decision-making power between the employer and the union; the employer and the union jointly determine working conditions, rates of pay, benefits, and so on. For the public sector employer, collective bargaining may involve delegating to the union the authority relating to the employer's statutory obligations. Bargaining may also affect the financial condition of the employer, requiring tax increases or cutbacks in the level of public services provided by the government employer. Because of this concern over sharing or delegating government sovereignty with the union, public sector labor relations statutes may narrowly define "terms and conditions" of employment and limit the matters that are subject to collective bargaining to avoid the government employer abdicating its legal authority. In the federal government, for example, most employees have their wages set by statute; collective bargaining in the federal service is precluded from dealing with any matter that is "provided for by Federal statute." Some state public sector labor relations statutes do not provide for collective bargaining at all but rather for consultation or "meeting and conferring" on working conditions.

See **http://www4.law.cornell.edu/uscode/5/pIIIspFch71.html** *for Title 5 of the U.S. Code.*

A third area in which public sector employment differs from the private sector deals with the right to strike. The right to strike is protected by Section 7 of the NLRA for private sector workers. Public sector workers, in general, do not have the right to strike. The activities of the government employer are usually vital to the public interest; disruptions of these activities because of labor disputes could imperil the welfare of the public. For that reason, the right to strike by public sector workers may be prohibited (as in the federal government and most states) or be limited to certain employees whose refusal to work would not endanger the public safety or welfare (as in several states).

The following case involves a challenge to the prohibitions of strikes by federal employees. The union representing postal clerks argues that such a prohibition violates their members' constitutional rights to strike.

Postal Clerks v. Blount

325 F. Supp. 879 (U.S.D.C., D.C. 1971), aff'd, 404 U.S. 802 (1971)

This action was brought by the United Federation of Postal Clerks (hereafter sometimes referred to as "Clerks"), an unincorporated public employee labor organization which consists primarily of employees of the Post Office Department, and which is the exclusive bargaining representative of approximately 305,000 members of the clerk craft employed by defendant. Defendant Blount is the Postmaster General of the United States. The Clerks seek declaratory and injunctive relief invalidating portions of 5 U.S.C. Section 7311, 18 U.S.C. Section 1918, an affidavit required by 5 U.S.C. Section 3333 to implement the above statutes, and Executive Order

11491. The Government, in response, filed a motion to dismiss or in the alternative for summary judgment, and plaintiff filed its opposition thereto and cross motion for summary judgment. . . .

5 U.S.C. Section 7311(3) prohibits an individual from accepting or holding a position in the federal government or in the District of Columbia if he

> (3) participates in a strike . . . against the Government of the United States or the government of the District of Columbia. . . .

Paragraph C of the appointment affidavit required by 5 U.S.C. Section 3333, which all federal employees are required to execute under oath, states:

> I am not participating in any strike against the Government of the United States or any agency thereof, and I will not so participate while an employee of the Government of the United States or any agency thereof.

18 U.S.C. Section 1918, in making a violation of 5 U.S.C. Section 7311 a crime, provides:

> Whoever violates the provision of Section 7311 of Title 5 that an individual may not accept or hold a position in the Government of the United States or the government of the District of Columbia if he . . .
>
> (3) participates in a strike, or asserts the right to strike, against the Government of the United States or the District of Columbia . . . shall be fined not more than $1,000 or imprisoned not more than one year and a day, or both.

Section 2(e)(2) of Executive Order 11491 exempts from the definition of a labor organization any group which:

> asserts the right to strike against the Government of the United States or any agency thereof, or to assist or participate in such strike, or imposes a duty or obligation to conduct, assist or participate in such a strike.

Section 19(b)(4) of the same Executive Order makes it an unfair labor practice for a labor organization to:

> call or engage in a strike, work stoppage, or slowdown; picket any agency in a labor-management dispute; or condone any such activity by failing to take affirmative action to prevent or stop it; . . .

Plaintiff contends that the right to strike is a fundamental right protected by the Constitution, and that the absolute prohibition of such activity by 5 U.S.C. Section 7311(3), and the other provisions set out above thus constitutes an infringement of the employees' First Amendment rights of association and free speech and operates to deny them equal protection of the law. Plaintiff also argues that the language to "strike" and "participate in a strike" is vague and overbroad and therefore violative of both the First Amendment and the Due Process Clause of the Fifth Amendment. For the purposes of this opinion, we will direct our attention to the attack on the constitutionality of 5 U.S.C. Section 7311(3), the key provision being challenged. . . .

At common law no employee, whether public or private, had a constitutional right to strike in concert with his fellow workers. Indeed, such collective action on the part of employees was often held to be a conspiracy. When the right of private employees to strike finally received full protection, it was by statute, Section 7 of the National Labor Relations Act, which "took this conspiracy weapon away from the employer in employment relations which affect interstate commerce" and guaranteed to employees in the private sector the right to engage in concerted activities for the purpose of collective bargaining. It seems clear that public employees stand on no stronger footing in this regard than private employees and that in the absence of a statute, they too do not possess the right to strike. The Supreme Court has spoken approvingly of such a restriction, and at least one federal district court has invoked the provisions of a predecessor statute, 5 U.S.C. Section 118p-r, to enjoin a strike by government employees. Likewise, scores of state cases have held that state employees do not have a right to engage in concerted work stoppages in the absence of legislative authorization. It is fair to conclude that, irrespective of the reasons given, there is a unanimity of opinion on the part of courts and legislatures that government employees do not have the right to strike.

Congress has consistently treated public employees as being in a different category than private employees. The National Labor Relations Act and the Labor-Management Relations Act of 1947 (Taft-Hartley) both defined "employer" as not including any governmental or political subdivisions, and thereby indirectly withheld the protections of Section 7 from governmental employees. Congress originally enacted the no-strike provision separately from other restrictions on employee activity by attaching riders to appropriations bills which prohibited strikes by government employees. . . .

Given the fact that there is no constitutional right to strike, it is not irrational or arbitrary for the Government to condition employment on a promise not to withhold labor collectively, and to prohibit strikes by those in public employment, whether because of the prerogatives of the sovereign, some sense of higher obligation associated with public service, to assure the continuing functioning of the Government without interruption, to protect public health and safety, or for other reasons. Although plaintiff argues that the provisions in question are unconstitutionally broad in covering all Government employees regardless of the type or importance of the work they do, we hold that it makes no difference whether the jobs performed by certain public employees are regarded as "essential" or "nonessential," or whether similar jobs are performed by workers in private industry who do have the right to strike protected by statute. Nor is it relevant that some positions in private industry are arguably more affected with a public interest than are some positions in the Government service. . . .

Furthermore, it should be pointed out that the fact that public employees may not strike does not interfere with their rights which are fundamental and constitutionally protected. The right to organize collectively and to select representatives for the purposes of engaging in collective bargaining is such a fundamental right. But, as the Supreme Court noted in *Local 232 v. Wisconsin Employment Relations Board,* "The right to strike, because of its more serious impact upon the public interest, is more vulnerable to regulation than the right to organize and select representatives for lawful purposes of collective bargaining which this Court has characterized as a 'fundamental right' and which, as the Court has pointed out, was recognized as such in its decisions long before it was given protection by the National Labor Relations Act."

Executive Order 11491 recognizes the right of federal employees to join labor organizations for the purpose of dealing with grievances, but that Order clearly and expressly defines strikes, work stoppages and slowdowns as unfair labor practices. As discussed above, that Order is the culmination of a longstanding policy. There certainly is no compelling reason to imply the existence of the right to strike from the right to associate and bargain collectively. In the private sphere, the strike is used to equalize bargaining power, but this has universally been held not to be appropriate when its object and purpose can only be to influence the essentially political decisions of Government in the allocation of its resources. Congress has an obligation to ensure that the machinery of the Federal Government continues to function at all times without interference. Prohibition of strikes by its employees is a reasonable implementation of that obligation.

Accordingly, we hold that the provisions of the statute, the appointment affidavit and the Executive Order, as construed above, do not violate any constitutional rights of those employees who are members of plaintiff's union. The Government's motion to dismiss the complaint is granted.

Order to be presented.

Case Questions

1. Do public sector employees have a constitutional right to strike? Is the right to strike protected at common law?
2. Does the right of employees to organize and join unions for purposes of collective bargaining include the right to strike?
3. Are the legislative prohibitions against strikes by federal employees constitutional? What is the rationale behind such prohibitions?

FEDERAL GOVERNMENT LABOR RELATIONS

HISTORICAL BACKGROUND

It is not clear exactly when federal employees began negotiating over the terms of their employment, but informal bargaining began as long ago as 1883. In that year, the Pendleton Act, known as the Civil Service Act, was passed. It granted Congress the sole authority to set wages, hours, and other terms and conditions of federal employment. This act led to informal bargaining and congressional lobbying by federal employees seeking higher wages and better working conditions.

In 1906, President Theodore Roosevelt halted the informal bargaining by issuing an executive order forbidding federal employees or their associations from soliciting increases in pay, either before Congress, its committees, or before the heads of the executive agencies. Employees violating the order faced dismissal.

In the years following the executive order, Congress passed several laws that gave limited organization rights to some federal workers. The Lloyd–La Follette Act of 1912 gave postal workers the right to join unions. In 1920, the federal government negotiated the terms of a contract with the union representing construction workers building the government-sponsored Alaskan Railroad.

It was not until 1962, with the issuing of Executive Order 10988 by President Kennedy, that large numbers of federal employees were given the right to organize. The executive order recognized the right of federal workers to organize and to present their views on terms and conditions of employment to the agencies for which they worked.

Executive Order 10988 was supplemented by Executive Order 11491, which was issued in 1969 by President Nixon. That order placed the entire program of employee-management relations under the supervision and control of the Federal Labor Relations Council.

The Federal Service Labor-Management Relations Law of 1978, which was enacted as part of the Civil Service Reform Act of 1978, was the first comprehensive enactment covering labor relations in the federal government. The Federal Service Labor-Management Relations Act (FSLMRA) took effect in January 1979.

THE FEDERAL SERVICE LABOR-MANAGEMENT RELATIONS ACT

The FSLMRA, which was modeled after the NLRA, established a permanent structure for labor relations in the federal public sector. It created the Federal Labor Relations Authority (FLRA) to administer the act, and it granted federal employees the right to organize and bargain collectively. It also prohibited strikes and other defined unfair practices.

Coverage

The FSLMRA covers federal employees who are employed by a federal agency or who have ceased to work for the agency because of an unfair labor practice. Most federal agencies are covered, but some are specifically exempted. The agencies excluded from FSLMRA coverage are the FBI, the CIA, the National Security Agency, the General Accounting Office, the Tennessee Valley Authority, the FLRA, and the Federal Service Impasses Panel. Furthermore, any agency that the president determines is investigative in nature or has a primary function of intelligence and would thus not be amenable to FSLMRA coverage because of national security may be excluded. The FSLMRA also excludes certain employees from coverage. Noncitizens working outside the United States for federal agencies, supervisory and management employees, and certain foreign service officers are exempted. In addition, the act excludes any federal employee participating in an illegal strike.

The Thurmond Act of 1969 prohibits military personnel from belonging to a union. That act makes it a felony for enlisted personnel to join a union or for military officers or their representatives to recognize or bargain with a union. The Thurmond Act does not apply to civilian employees of the military.

Employees covered by the FSLMRA are granted the right to form, join, or assist any labor organization or to refrain from such activity freely and without reprisal. Employees may act as representatives of a labor organization and present views of the organization to the heads of agencies, the executive branch, and Congress.

Postal Service Employees

The employees of the U.S. Postal Service are not subject to the FSLMRA. The Postal Service Reorganization Act, which created the U.S. Postal Service as an independent agency, provides that postal service employees are subject to the NLRA, with some limitations. The National Labor Relations Board (NLRB) is authorized to determine appropriate bargaining units, hold representation elections, and enforce the unfair labor practice provision of the NLRA for postal service employees. The postal service unions bargain with the U.S. Postal Service over wages, hours, and conditions of employment, but postal service workers are not permitted to strike. Instead, the Postal Service Reorganization Act provides for fact-finding and binding arbitration if an impasse exists after 180 days from the start of bargaining. Supervisory and managerial employees of the Postal Service are not subject to the NLRA provisions.

Administration

The FSLMRA created the Federal Labor Relations Authority (FLRA), which assumed the duties of the Federal Labor Relations Council created by Executive Order 11491. The FLRA is the central authority responsible for the administration of the FSLMRA.

The FLRA is composed of three members who are nominated by the president and confirmed by the Senate. The members serve five-year terms. The FLRA is empowered to determine the appropriateness of units for representation, to supervise or conduct elections to determine if a labor organization has been selected as the exclusive representative by majority of the employees in the appropriate unit, to resolve issues relating to the duty to bargain in good faith, and to resolve complaints of unfair labor practices.

The FLRA has the authority to hold hearings and issue subpoenas. It may order any agency or union to cease and desist from violating the provisions of the FSLMRA, and it can enlist the federal courts in proceedings against unions that strike illegally. The FLRA may take any remedial actions it deems appropriate in carrying out the policies of the act.

Representation Issues

Under the FSLMRA, a union becomes the exclusive representative of an appropriate unit of employees when it has been selected by a majority of votes cast in a representation election. When selected, the union becomes the sole representative of the employees in the unit and is authorized to negotiate the terms and conditions of employment of the employees in the unit. The union must fairly represent all employees in the unit without discrimination or regard to union membership. The FLRA is authorized to settle questions relating to issues of representation, such as the determination of the appropriate unit and the holding of representation elections.

Appropriate Representation Units. The FLRA is empowered to determine the appropriateness of a representation unit of federal employees. The FLRA ensures the employees the fullest possible freedom in exercising their rights under the FSLMRA in determining the unit, and it ensures a clear and identifiable community of interest among the employees in the unit to promote effective dealing with the agency involved. The FLRA may determine the appropriateness of a unit on an agency, plant, installation, functional, or other basis.

Units may not include any management or supervisory employees, confidential employees, employees engaged in personnel work except those in a purely clerical capacity, employees doing investigative work that directly affects national security, employees administering the FSLMRA, or employees primarily engaged in investigation or audit functions relating to the work of individuals whose duties affect the internal security of an agency. Any employees engaged in administering any provision of law relating to labor-management relations may not be represented by a labor organization that is affiliated with an organization representing other individuals under the act. An appropriate unit may include professional and nonprofessional employees only if the professional employees, by majority vote, approve their inclusion.

Representation Elections. The procedures for representation elections under the FSLMRA closely resemble those for elections under the NLRA. The act allows for the holding of consent elections to determine the exclusive representative of a bargaining unit. It also provides that the FLRA may investigate the question of representation, including holding an election, if a petition is filed by any person alleging that 30 percent of the employees in a unit wish to be represented by a union for the purpose of collective bargaining. In addition, when a petition alleging that 30 percent of the members of a bargaining unit no longer wish to be represented by their exclusive representative union, the FLRA will investigate the representation question.

If the FLRA finds reasonable cause to believe that a representation question exists, it will provide, upon reasonable notice, an opportunity for a hearing. If, on the basis of the hearing, the FLRA finds that a question of representation does exist, it will conduct a representation election by secret ballot. An election will not be held if the unit has held a valid election within the preceding twelve months.

When an election is scheduled, a union may intervene and be placed on the ballot if it can show that it is already the unit's exclusive representative or that it has the support of at least 10 percent of the employees in the unit. The election is by secret ballot, with the employees choosing between the union(s) and "no representation." If no choice receives a majority of votes cast, a runoff election is held between the two choices receiving the highest number of votes. The results of the election are certified; if a union receives a majority of votes cast, it becomes the exclusive representative of the employees in the unit.

A union that has obtained exclusive representation status is entitled to be present at any formal discussions between the agency and unit employees concerning grievances, personnel policies and practices, or other conditions of employment. The exclusive representative must also be given the opportunity to be present at any examination of an employee in the unit in connection with an agency investigation that the employee reasonably believes may result in disciplinary action, provided that he or she has requested such representation. (This right is the equivalent of the *Weingarten* rights established by the NLRB for organized employees in the private sector. See Chapter 15.)

Consultation Rights. If the employees of an agency have not designated any union as their exclusive representative on an agencywide basis, a union that represents a substantial number of agency employees may be granted consultation rights. Consultation rights entitle the union to be informed of any substantive change in employment conditions proposed by the agency. The union is to be permitted reasonable time to present its views and recommendations regarding the proposed changes. The agency must consider the union recommendations before taking final action, and it must provide the union with written reasons for taking the final action.

Collective Bargaining

The FSLMRA requires that agencies and exclusive representatives of agency employees meet and negotiate in good faith. Good faith is defined as approaching the negotiations with a sincere resolve to reach a collective-bargaining agreement, meeting at reasonable times and convenient places as frequently as may be necessary, and being represented at negotiations by duly authorized representatives prepared to discuss and negotiate on any condition of employment.

In *National Federation of Federal Employees, Local 1309 v. Dept. of the Interior* [526 U.S. 86 (1999)], the Supreme Court held that the FLRA had the power to determine whether federal employers were required to engage in "midterm" bargaining—bargaining during the term of a collective agreement over subjects that were not included in the agreement. The FLRA, on remand from the Supreme Court, decided that the FSLMRA required employers to engage in midterm bargaining and the refusal to do so was an unfair labor practice under the FSLMRA, *U.S. Dept. of the Interior v. National Federation of Federal Employees, Local 1309* [56 FLRA 45, *reconsideration denied,* 56 FLRA 279 (2000)].

Conditions of Employment. The act defines "conditions of employment" as including personnel policies, practices, and matters—whether established by rule, regulation, or otherwise—that affect working conditions. However, the act excludes the following from being defined as conditions of employment: policies relating to prohibited political activity, matters relating to the classification of any position, and policies or matters that are provided for by federal statute.

Wages. Wages for most federal employees are not subject to collective bargaining because they are determined by statute. Federal "blue-collar" employees are paid under the coordinated Federal Wage System, which provides for pay comparable to pay for similar jobs in the private sector; federal "white-collar" employees are paid under the General Schedule (GS), and increases and changes in GS pay scales are made by presidential order. However, in *Fort Stewart Schools v. Federal Labor Relations Authority* [495 U.S. 641 (1990)], the Supreme Court considered the question of whether schools owned and operated by the U.S. Army were required to negotiate with the union representing school employees over mileage reimbursement, paid leave, and a salary increase. The school declined to negotiate, claiming that the proposals were not subject to bargaining under the FSLMRA. The school claimed that "conditions of employment" under the FSLMRA included any matter insisted upon as a prerequisite to accepting employment but did not include wages. The Supreme Court upheld an order of the FLRA that the school was required to bargain over wages and fringe benefits. Whereas the wages of most federal employees are set by law under the GS of the Civil Service Act, the school employees' wages are exempted from the GS. Wages for the school employees, therefore, were within the conditions of employment over which the school was required to bargain. Section 7106 of the FSLMRA, which provides that "nothing in this chapter shall affect the authority of any management official of any agency to determine the . . . budget . . . of the agency. . . ." did not exempt wages and fringe benefits from the duty to bargain. Agency management seeking to avail themselves of that provision to avoid bargaining over a proposal must demonstrate that the proposal would result in significant and unavoidable increases in costs.

Management Rights. The FSLMRA contains a very strong management-rights clause, which also restricts the scope of collective bargaining. According to that clause, collective bargaining is not to affect the authority of any management official or any agency to determine the mission, budget, organization, number of employees, or the internal security practices of the agency. In addition, management's right to hire, assign, direct, lay off, retain or suspend, reduce in grade or pay, or take disciplinary action against any employee is not subject to negotiation. Decisions to assign work, contract out work, or select candidates to fill positions are not subject to negotiation. The act also precludes bargaining over any actions necessary to carry out the mission of the agency during emergencies.

The duty to bargain extends to matters that are the subject of any rule or regulation as long as the particular rule or regulation is not governmentwide. However, if the agency determines there is a compelling need for such a regulation, it can refuse to bargain over that regulation. The exclusive representative must be given an opportunity to show that no compelling need exists for the regulation. Disputes over the existence of a compelling need are to be resolved by the FLRA.

The agency's duty to bargain includes the obligation to furnish, upon request by the exclusive representative, data and information normally maintained by the agency. Such data must be reasonably available and necessary for full and proper discussion of subjects within the scope of bargaining. Data related to the guidance, training, advice, or counsel of management or supervisors relating to collective bargaining are excluded from the obligation to provide information. The duty to bargain in good faith also includes the duty to execute a written document embodying the terms of agreement, if either party so requests.

Impasse Settlement

The FSLMRA created the Federal Service Impasse Panel, which is authorized to take any actions necessary to resolve an impasse in negotiations. The Federal Mediation and Conciliation Service, created by the Taft-Hartley Act, also assists in the resolution of impasses by providing mediation services for the parties. If the mediation efforts fail to lead to an agreement, either party may request that the Federal Service Impasse Panel consider the dispute. The panel may either recommend procedures for resolving the impasse or assist the parties in any other way it deems appropriate. The formal impasse resolution procedures may include hearings, fact-finding, recommendations for settlement, or directed settlement. The parties may also seek binding arbitration of the impasse with the approval of the panel.

Grievance Arbitration

The FSLMRA provides that all collective agreements under it must contain a grievance procedure; the grievance procedure must provide for binding arbitration as the final step in resolving grievances. If arbitration is invoked, either party may appeal the arbitrator's decision to the FLRA for review within thirty days of the granting of the award. Upon review, the FLRA may overturn the arbitrator's award only if it is contrary to a law, rule, or regulation, or is inconsistent with the standards for review of private sector awards by the federal courts (see Chapter 18). If no appeal is taken from the arbitrator's award within thirty days of the award, the arbitrator's award is final and binding.

When a grievance involves matters that are subject to a statutory review procedure, the employee may choose to pursue the complaint through the statutory procedure or through the negotiated grievance procedure. Examples would be grievances alleging discrimination in violation of Title VII of the Civil Rights Act of 1964; the grievor can elect to pursue the complaint through the grievance process or through the procedure under Title VII. Performance ratings, demotions, and suspensions or removals that are subject to civil service review procedures may be pursued either through the civil service procedures or the grievance procedure.

Unfair Labor Practices

The FSLMRA prohibits unfair labor practices by agencies and unions; the unfair labor practices defined in the act are similar to those defined by Sections 8(a) and 8(b) of the NLRA.

Agency Unfair Practices

Unfair labor practices by agencies under the FSLMRA include interfering with or restraining the exercise of employees' rights under the act, encouraging or discouraging union membership by discrimination in conditions of employment, sponsoring or controlling a union, disciplining or discriminating against an employee for filing a complaint under the act, refusing to negotiate in good faith, and refusing to cooperate in impasse procedures. It is also an unfair labor practice for an agency to enforce any rule or regulation that conflicts with a preexisting collective-bargaining agreement.

Union Unfair Labor Practices

Union unfair labor practices under the FSLMRA include interfering with or restraining the exercise of employees' rights under the act; coercing or fining a member for the purpose of impeding job performance; discriminating against an employee on the basis of race, color, creed, national origin, gender, age, civil service status, political affiliation, marital status, or disability; refusing to negotiate in good faith; and refusing to cooperate in impasse procedures. It is also an unfair labor practice for a union to call or condone a strike, work slowdown, or stoppage or to picket the agency if the picketing interferes with the agency's operations. Informational picketing that does not interfere with agency operations is allowed.

Unfair Labor Practice Procedures

When a complaint alleging unfair labor practices is filed with the FLRA, the General Counsel's Office of the FLRA investigates the complaint and attempts to reach a voluntary settlement. If no settlement is reached and the investigation uncovers evidence that the act has been violated, a complaint is issued. The complaint contains a notice of the charge and sets a date for a hearing before the FLRA. The party against whom the complaint is filed has the opportunity to file an answer to the complaint and to appear at the hearing to contest the charges.

If the FLRA finds, by a preponderance of evidence, that a violation has occurred, it will issue written findings and an appropriate remedial order. FLRA decisions are subject to judicial review by the federal courts of appeals.

Unfair Labor Practice Remedies

The FLRA has broad authority for fashioning remedial orders for unfair labor practices. Remedial orders may include cease-and-desist orders, reinstatement with back pay, renegotiation of the agreement between the parties with retroactive effect, or any other actions deemed necessary to carry out the purposes of the act.

When a union has been found by the FLRA to have intentionally engaged in a strike or work stoppage in violation of the act, the FLRA may revoke the exclusive representation status of the union or take any other disciplinary action deemed appropriate. Employees engaging in illegal strikes are subject to dismissal. The FLRA may also seek injunctions, restraining orders, or contempt citations in the federal courts against striking unions.

The following case involves the review of an FLRA order revoking the exclusive representation status of the air traffic controllers' union because of its involvement in an illegal strike.

Professional Air Traffic Controllers Org. v. FLRA

685 F.2d 547 (D.C. Cir. 1982)

Edwards, J.

Federal employees have long been forbidden from striking against . . . the federal government. . . . The United States Code presently prohibits a person who "participates in a strike . . . against the Government of the United States" from accepting or holding a position in the federal government, and violation of this section is a criminal offense. Newly hired federal employees are required to execute an affidavit attesting that they have not struck and will not strike against the government. In addition, since the inception of formal collective bargaining between federal employee unions and the federal government, unions have been required to disavow the strike as an economic weapon. Since 1969, striking has been expressly designated a union unfair labor practice.

In 1978, Congress enacted the Civil Service Reform Act, Title VII of which provides the first statutory basis for collective bargaining between the federal government and employee unions. . . . Rather, the Act added a new provision applicable to federal employee unions that strike against the government. Under Section 7120(f) of Title VII, Congress provided that the Federal Labor Relations Authority ("FLRA" or "Authority") shall "revoke the exclusive recognition status" of a recognized union, or "take any other appropriate disciplinary action" against any labor organization, where it is found that the union has called, participated in or condoned a strike, work stoppage or slowdown against a federal agency in a labor-management dispute.

In this case we review the first application of Section 7120(f) by the FLRA. After the Professional Air Traffic Controllers Organization ("PATCO") called a nationwide strike of air traffic controllers against the Federal Aviation Administration ("FAA") in the summer of 1981, the Authority revoked PATCO's status as exclusive bargaining representative for the controllers. . . .

The Professional Air Traffic Controllers Organization has been the recognized exclusive bargaining representative for air traffic controllers employed by the Federal Aviation Administration since the early 1970s. Faced with the expiration of an existing collective bargaining agreement, PATCO and the FAA began negotiations for a new contract in early 1981. A tentative agreement was reached in June, but was overwhelmingly rejected by the PATCO rank and file. Following this rejection, negotiations began again in late July. PATCO announced a strike deadline of Monday, August 3, 1981.

Failing to reach a satisfactory accord, PATCO struck the FAA on the morning of August 3. Over seventy percent of the nation's federally employed air traffic controllers walked off the job, significantly reducing the number of private and commercial flights in the United States.

In prompt response to the PATCO job actions, the Government obtained restraining orders against the strike, and then civil and criminal contempt citations when the restraining orders were not heeded. The Government also fired some 11,000 striking air traffic controllers who did not return to work by 11:00 A.M. on August 5, 1981. In addition, on August 3, 1981, the FAA filed an unfair labor practice charge against PATCO with the Federal Labor Relations Authority. On that same day, an FLRA Regional Director issued a complaint on the unfair labor practice charge, alleging strike activity prohibited by 5 U.S.C. Section 7116(b)(7) and seeking revocation of PATCO's certification under the Civil Service Reform Act. . . .

We affirm that FLRA's finding that PATCO "call[ed], or participate[d] in, a strike" in violation of 5 U.S.C. Section 7116(b)(7)(A).

Given our affirmance of the unfair labor practice finding under Section 7116(b)(7)(A), it necessarily follows that the FLRA could conclude that the PATCO National union was aware of the strike and, as a consequence, had a statutory obligation to attempt to stop the strike activity. In addition, we believe that the FLRA was fully justified in taking official notice of proceedings in the District Court for the District of Columbia. During the early morning of August 3, 1981, the District Court issued a restraining order against the PATCO strike. During the evening of that same day, the District Court found both the PATCO National union and its President, Robert Poli, in civil contempt for violation of the restraining order. In these circumstances, PATCO certainly cannot claim lack of knowledge of the strike.

On these bases, and because PATCO offered no evidence to indicate that it even attempted to end the strike, we also affirm the FLRA's unfair labor practice finding under 5 U.S.C. Section 7116(b)(7)(B).

Having determined that the FLRA properly found PATCO in violation of the no-strike provisions of the Civil Service Reform Act, we turn to the . . . question . . . whether the FLRA properly exercised its discretion under the Act to revoke the exclusive recognition status of PATCO. This inquiry requires us to ascertain: (1) what degree of discretion Congress granted to the FLRA when it enacted Section 7120(f); (2) whether the FLRA's exercise of its discretion in this case was proper. . . .

We have concluded that the FLRA has substantial discretion under Section 7120(f) to decide whether or not to revoke the exclusive recognition status of a union found guilty by the FLRA of striking or condoning a strike against the government. A concomitant of this conclusion is that the courts have only a limited role in reviewing the FLRA's exercise of its remedial discretion. . . . As with judicial review of remedial orders of the NLRB, we will uphold the remedial orders of the FLRA "unless it can be shown that the order is a patent attempt to achieve ends other than those which can fairly be said to effectuate the policies of the Act."

We have little trouble deciding that the FLRA did not abuse its discretion in this case. First, the FLRA could take official notice that PATCO has repeatedly violated legal prohibitions against striking and other job actions. In 1970, PATCO called a "sickout" of the air traffic controllers subject to its exclusive representation. "Extensive disruptions in air service resulted as approximately one quarter of the nation's air controllers reported in sick each day between March 24 and April 14. . . ." In 1978, PATCO threatened a nationwide air traffic slowdown. Based on a stipulated record, the union was held in contempt for its actions. In 1980, PATCO controllers engaged in a work slowdown at Chicago's O'Hare Airport. In August 1981, PATCO called the nationwide strike that gives rise to the present action.

Second, all of PATCO's job actions after 1970 occurred while the union was subject to an injunction resulting from its 1970 strike that prohibited such actions. Nor could PATCO have had any doubt about the continued validity of that injunction before it commenced its 1981 strike. After the effective date of the Civil Service Reform Act, PATCO petitioned the District Court for the Eastern District of New York for vacatur of its 1970 injunction on the ground that Title VII of the Act had deprived the District Court of jurisdiction to enjoin federal employee strikes. In June 1981, before the most recent strike began, the District Court reaffirmed the validity of its 1970 injunction and denied PATCO's motion.

Third, after PATCO struck on August 3, 1981, additional restraining orders and injunctions directed only at this strike issued. PATCO openly defied these injunctions as well.

Finally, PATCO's actions before and after August 3, 1981, can only be characterized as defiant. The union threatened its strike, then willfully and intentionally called and participated in it. After the strike commenced, PATCO made no attempt to end it; indeed, PATCO condoned and encouraged it. Even after the striking controllers had been terminated and a majority of the Authority had ordered revocation of its exclusive recognition status, PATCO failed to satisfy Chairman Haughton's request that it end the strike and promise to abide by the no-strike provisions of the Civil Service Reform Act.

In these circumstances the FLRA's decision to revoke PATCO's exclusive recognition status was not an abuse of discretion. The union is a repeat offender that has willfully ignored statutory proscriptions and judicial injunctions. It has shown little or no likelihood of abiding by the legal requirements of labor-management relations in the federal sector. If the extreme remedy that Congress enacted cannot properly be applied to this case, we doubt that it could ever properly be invoked.

Case Questions

1. On what evidence did the Federal Labor Relations Authority (FLRA) determine that the National PATCO union violated its obligation to attempt to stop the strike?
2. Must the FLRA revoke the exclusive recognition status of a union found guilty of striking or condoning a strike against the federal government? Explain.
3. What evidence was the basis of the FLRA decision to revoke PATCO's exclusive representation status? Did the court of appeals agree with that decision? Why?

JUDICIAL REVIEW OF FLRA DECISIONS

As the *PATCO* case illustrates, final orders, other than bargaining unit determinations and arbitration awards, are subject to review in the federal courts of appeals. The party seeking review has ten days from the issuance of the FLRA decision to file a petition for review with the court of appeals for the appropriate circuit. Unless specifically authorized by the appeals court, the filing of a petition for review does not operate to stay the FLRA order.

Upon review, the court may affirm, enforce, modify, or set aside the FLRA order. Findings of fact by the FLRA are deemed conclusive if they are supported by substantial evidence. The order of the court of appeals is subject to discretionary review by the Supreme Court.

THE HATCH ACT

The Hatch Act [5 U.S.C. § 7321 *et seq.*] prohibits certain political activity by federal employees. Federal employees are prevented from taking an active part in the management of political campaigns or from running for office in a partisan political campaign. The act also restricts federal employees from engaging in political activity while on the job. The purpose of the restrictions on the political activities of federal employees is to avoid the appearance of political bias in government actions, to prevent the coercion of federal employees to engage in political action or to support political positions, and to avoid politicizing the federal civil service. The Hatch Act's restrictions on political activity by federal employees were held to be constitutional in *Burrus v. Vegliante* [2003 WL 21648686 (2d Cir. July 14, 2003)]. That case also held that the American Postal Workers Union's use of bulletin boards in nonpublic areas of post offices to display political materials violated the Hatch Act prohibitions against political activities on the job. Most states have legislation similar to the Hatch Act to restrict political activities by state government employees.

UNION SECURITY PROVISIONS

A union that is granted exclusive representation rights under the FSLMRA must accept, as a member, any unit employee who seeks membership. A union may not require union membership as a condition of employment; this means that the collective agreement may not contain a closed shop or union shop provision. For the government employer to require that employees join a union in order to retain their jobs would violate the employees' constitutional rights of association protected by the First Amendment (or Fourteenth Amendment if the employer is a state or local government agency).

Agency shop provisions, which require that an employee pay union dues or fees but do not require union membership, do not raise the same constitutional problems. However, if the employee's dues money is spent by the union on matters other than those relating to collective bargaining or representation issues, the employee is, in effect, forced to contribute to causes and for purposes that he or she may oppose. Does this "forced contribution" violate the employee's constitutional rights?

In *Abood v. Detroit Board of Education* [431 U.S. 209 (1977)], the Supreme Court held that union expenditures for expression of political views, in support of political candidates, or for advancement of ideological causes not related to its duties as bargaining agent can be financed only from dues or assessments paid by employees who do not object to advancing such ideas and who are not coerced into doing so. To do otherwise violates the First Amendment rights of the employees who object to such expenditures. The Court held that employees who object to political expenditures by the union are entitled to a refund of that portion of their dues payments that represents the proportion that union political expenditures bear to the total union expenditures.

In *Chicago Teachers Union, Local No. 1 v. Hudson* [466 U.S. 435 (1986)], the Supreme Court addressed the procedures that the union must make available for employees who object to union expenditures of their dues or fees. The Court held that the union is required to provide objecting members with information relating to the union expenditures on collective bargaining and political activities and must include an adequate explanation of the basis of dues and fees. The members must also be provided a reasonably prompt opportunity to challenge, before an impartial decision maker, the amount of the dues or fees; and the union must hold in escrow the amounts in dispute pending the resolution of the challenges by the members.

The *Abood* and *Chicago Teachers Union* cases hold that individuals who object to a union's political activities are not required to pay that portion of union dues and fees that fund such nonbargaining activities. What standards should a court use to determine which union expenditures are related to its collective-bargaining activities? The Supreme Court considered this question in the case of *Lehnert v. Ferris Faculty Association* [500 U.S. 507 (1991)]. The court set out three criteria for determining which activities can be funded by dues and fees of objecting individuals:

1. The activity must be germane to collective bargaining.
2. It must be justified by the government's interest in promoting labor peace and avoiding "free riders" who benefit from union activities without paying for union services.
3. It must not significantly add to the burdening of free speech inherent in allowing a union shop or agency shop provision.

Using these criteria, the *Lehnert* court held that the teachers' union could not charge objecting individuals for lobbying, electoral activities, or political activities beyond the limited context of contract implementation or negotiation. In addition, the union could not charge for expenses incurred in conducting an illegal work stoppage or for litigation expenses unless the litigation concerned the individual's own bargaining unit. The union could charge objecting individuals for (1) national union programs and publications designed to disseminate information germane to collective bargaining; (2) information services concerning professional development, job opportunities, and miscellaneous matters that benefited all teachers, even though they may not directly concern members of the individual's bargaining unit; (3) participation by local delegates at state or national union meetings at which representation policies and bargaining strategies are developed; and (4) expenses related to preparation for a strike. The court also held that the union could not charge the objecting individuals for public relations efforts designed to enhance the reputation of the teaching profession generally because such efforts were not directly connected to the union's collective-bargaining function.

It should be noted that private sector employees have the same right to object to political expenditures by their unions; in *Communications Workers of America v. Beck* [487 U.S. 735 (1988)], the Supreme Court stated that "We conclude that Section 8(a)(3) . . . authorizes the exaction [from nonmembers or objecting employees] of only those fees and dues necessary to 'performing the duties of an exclusive representative of the employees in dealing with the employer on labor-management issues'" (see Chapter 19).

The FSLMRA provides that union dues may be deducted from an employee's pay only if authorized by the employee. The employer may not charge a service fee for deductions to either the employee or the union. Employee authorizations for dues deduction may not be revoked for a period of one year from their making.

STATE PUBLIC SECTOR LABOR RELATIONS LEGISLATION

In 1954, Wisconsin adopted a public employee labor relations law covering state, county, and municipal employees. Since that first legal provision for state public sector labor relations, approximately forty states have adopted provisions relating to public sector labor relations. The various state laws differ widely in their treatment of issues such as employee coverage, impasse resolution procedures, and restrictions on the scope of bargaining. Because of the diversity of statutes, it is not possible to discuss them in detail; thus, the remaining portion of this chapter discusses certain general features of state public sector labor relations statutes.

COVERAGE OF STATE LAWS

As noted, approximately forty states have provisions for some labor relations activity by state or local employees. Most of those states have adopted statutes that provide for organizing rights and for collective bargaining by public employees. Some states that have no statutes dealing with public sector labor relations allow voluntary collective bargaining by public employees based on court decisions. Other states, while not restricting the rights of public employees to join unions, prohibit collective bargaining by public employees based on statutory prohibitions or court decisions.

Select from the list of states at **http://www.law.cornell.edu/topics/state_statutes3.html#labor**

In states that have public sector labor relations statutes, the pattern of coverage of those statutes varies. Some statutes cover all state and local employees. Others may cover only local or only state employees. Some states have several statutes, with separate statutes covering teachers, police, and firefighters. Some states also allow for the enactment of municipal labor relations legislation.

New York City, for example, has established an Office of Collective Bargaining by passage of a city ordinance.

The courts have generally held that there is no constitutionally protected right to bargain collectively. For that reason, the courts have upheld restrictions or prohibitions on the right to bargain. The right to join unions or to organize, however, has been held to be protected by the constitutional freedom of association under the First and Fourteenth Amendments. Because the right to organize is constitutionally protected, restrictions on that right of public employees have consistently been struck down by the courts.

But while public employees in general may have the right to organize, many states exclude supervisors and managerial or confidential employees from unionizing. Other states may allow those employees to organize but provide for bargaining units separate from other employees. The courts have generally upheld exclusions of managerial, supervisory, and confidential employees from organizing and bargaining.

REPRESENTATION ISSUES

Most of the state statutes authorizing public sector labor relations provide for exclusive bargaining representatives of the employees. The statutes generally create a Public Employee Relations Board (PERB) to administer the act and to determine representation issues and unfair labor practice complaints.

Bargaining Units

Determining appropriate bargaining units is generally the function of the PERB agency created by the particular statute. Some statutes provide for bargaining by all categories of public employees, whereas other statutes may specifically define appropriate units, such as teachers within a particular school district. When the PERB is entrusted with determining the appropriate unit, it generally considers community interest factors such as the nature of work, similarity of working conditions, efficiency of administration, and the desires of the employees. Some statutes require determination based on efficiency of administration. Police and law enforcement officers and firefighters are generally in separate districtwide units (or statewide units for state law enforcement officers). Faculty at public universities may be organized in statewide units or may bargain on an institution unit basis. In general, PERB agencies seek to avoid a proliferation of small units.

Representation Elections

The procedures for holding representation elections for units of public employees generally resemble those under the FSLMRA and the NLRA. The union seeking representation rights petitions the PERB requesting an election. The union must demonstrate some minimum level of employee support within the unit. If the parties fail to reach agreement on the bargaining unit definition, the eligibility of employees to vote, and the date and other details of the election, the PERB settles such issues after holding hearings on them.

The elections are by secret ballot, and the results are certified by the PERB. Either party may file objections to the election with the PERB; the PERB then reviews the challenges and possibly orders a new election when the challenges are upheld.

Bargaining

As noted, a majority of states have provisions requiring, or at least permitting, some form of collective bargaining. Some statutes may use the term "meet and confer" rather than collective bargaining, but in actual operation, the process is not substantially different from collective bargaining.

The scope of bargaining subjects may be restricted to protect the statutory authority of, or to ensure the provision of essential functions by, the public employer. The public employer may also be legally prohibited from agreeing with the union on particular subjects. For example, state law may require a minimum number of evaluations of employees annually, and the employer may not agree to fewer evaluations.

Public sector labor relations statutes generally have broad management-rights clauses. As a result, the subjects of "wages, hours and other terms and conditions" of employment may be defined more narrowly than is the case in the private sector under the NLRA.

The state PERBs generally classify subjects for bargaining as mandatory, permissive, and illegal subjects. Mandatory topics involve the narrowly defined matters relating to wages, hours, and other terms and conditions of employment. Permissive subjects generally are those related to government policy, the employer's function, or matters of management rights. Illegal subjects may include matters to which the employer is precluded by law from agreeing. Some states may prohibit bargaining over certain items that may be classified as permissive in other states.

In *Central State University v. A.A.U.P., Central State Chapter* [526 U.S. 124 (1999)], the U.S. Supreme Court upheld the constitutionality of an Ohio law that required state public universities to set instructional workloads for professors and exempted those workloads from collective bargaining. The following case deals with whether a public employer's attempts to exempt parts of a collective agreement from being subject to arbitration as required by state law violate the duty to bargain in good faith.

City of Bethany v. The Public Employees Relations Board

904 P.2d 604 (Ok. Sup. Ct. 1995)

Kauger, Vice Chief Justice

. . . In March of 1987, the appellee, the International Association of Firefighters, Local 2085 (the Union) and the appellant, the City of Bethany (the City/Bethany), began negotiating for a collective bargaining agreement for the 1987–1988 fiscal year. During the course of negotiations, the City proposed that certain issues would not be subject to arbitration under the new contract. In response to this proposal, the Union, arguing that pursuant to § 51-111, of the [Oklahoma] Fire and Police Arbitration Act (the Act/FPAA), every item of a contract must be arbitrable, declared an impasse on June 10, 1987.

In August of 1987, the Union filed an unfair labor practice charge against the City of Bethany with the Public Employees Relations Board (the PERB/Board). After a hearing, the PERB found that § 51-111 does not allow parties to negotiate for the removal of a class of grievances, issues, or penalties from the arbitration process, that the City had committed an unfair labor practice, and that a cease and desist order should issue. The City was ordered to cease and desist from bargaining in bad faith by proposing and insisting upon illegal bargaining proposals. . . .

On January 15, 1992, the City of Bethany filed a petition for review of the PERB's decision in District Court challenging both the PERB's determination that it committed an unfair labor practice and the constitutionality of § 51-111. The District Court affirmed the PERB, and upheld the constitutionality of § 51-111. The City appealed.

Although 11 O.S.SUPP.1985 § 51-111 permits different grievance administration procedures, it requires that all disputes over any terms contained in the collective bargaining agreement be subject to final and binding grievance arbitration.

Under the Act, union representatives and municipalities are obligated to meet and negotiate in good faith over issues concerning wages, hours, grievances, working conditions and other terms and conditions of employment. These items are mandatory subjects of bargaining and neither party is compelled to agree to a proposal or required to make a concession regarding such items during the negotiation process.

Arbitration is the prime vehicle for resolving a dispute concerning the interpretation of a collective bargaining agreement formed under the FPAA. The legislative proclamation in . . . § 51-111 ensures arbitration's use by requiring an arbitration clause in all collective bargaining agreements entered into under the Act. The statute commands that any controversies over the interpretation or application of collective bargaining agreements are to have an "immediate and speedy resolution by required mediation."

. . . This Court has previously concluded that the statutory language in § 51-111 expresses a clear legislative intent that any disputes arising from the interpretation or application of the binding collective bargaining agreement shall have an immediate and speedy resolution by required arbitration.

. . . [T]he following principles of legislative policy emerge with respect to grievance arbitration:

> (1) The prohibition against strikes by firefighters and police officers is not contained in the constitution. It occurs only in the statute. The Legislature explicitly balanced the requirement that CBAs contain a no-strike provision with the right to grievance arbitration. Invalidating grievance arbitration would destroy this vital, conscious public policy decision.
>
> (2) "Any" dispute over the "interpretation or application of any provision" of the CBA is subject to grievance arbitration. Neither side can bargain to exclude certain contractual provisions from grievance arbitration.
>
> (3) When the parties cannot agree to a grievance arbitration procedure, they may resort to the statutory procedures for selecting impasse arbitrators and use those procedures for selecting a grievance arbitration panel.
>
> (4) Advisory grievance arbitration decisions are not contemplated by the statute. The statute unequivocally mandates "final" grievance arbitration, whatever procedure is used to select the arbitrators.

. . . The duty to bargain in good faith is violated when a party insists upon contract terms which would be illegal if incorporated in the collective bargaining agreement.

Once the grievance arbitration statute, § 51-111, is properly understood, the good faith bargaining duties of the parties with respect to its provisions become clear as well. The parties are free to bargain with respect to the "mechanics" and "procedures" of grievance administration. They may insist on their positions on these issues and press them to impasse. They may also seek to exclude existing "rules, regulations, fiscal procedures, working conditions, etc." from the CBA. With respect to all issues within the scope of bargaining, the parties may strive mightily to negotiate contract language favorable to their interests and to their view of the proper allocation of rights and responsibilities between management and labor in the collective bargaining relationship. What they may not do is create a two-tier grievance system in which some grievances are arbitrable and others are not. This approach, if permitted, would undo the careful balance the Legislature has struck in the statute—grievance arbitration in exchange for no-grievance-strikes pledge from our most important public safety workers. The logic of such a two-tier regime would ultimately lead to the implication that firefighters and police officers could lawfully strike over non-arbitrable grievances. It is inconceivable that the Legislature intended such a result. It is equally unreasonable and unfair that the Legislature intended that firefighters and police officers give up "something for nothing." . . .

A party may not insist at the negotiating table upon terms which would modify statutory requirements for CBAs. We hold that the Firefighters and Policemen's Arbitration Law defines and determines the make-up of a collective bargaining unit and is not a proper subject for negotiation between the City and the bargaining agent for the firefighters.

. . . We also hold that the entities covered by the FPAA violate their duty to bargain in good faith when they assert positions at the collective bargaining table which would, if accepted, require the other side to agree to terms contrary to those mandated by statute. . . . We also recognize as applicable here, and as consistent with the public policy of the State of Oklahoma, the federal labor policy that the goals of labor peace embodied in the collective bargaining statutes cannot be met when one party is asked to agree to terms which are repugnant to the statute's specific language.

. . . The legislative command that public safety workers and their municipal employers submit their contract interpretation disputes to binding arbitration is enforceable and binding on the parties. § 51-111 providing for mandatory grievance arbitration is constitutional. It is an unfair labor practice for a party to insist at the bargaining table that the other party accept proposals to remove certain matters, otherwise a part of the collective bargaining agreement, from the reach of grievance arbitration. To rule otherwise would be to undermine the public policy compromises the Legislature has crafted and, ultimately, would reduce grievance arbitration to a nullity.

The rulings of the PERB and the District Court are **Affirmed.**

Case Questions

1. Why does Oklahoma law require arbitration for contract disputes involving public safety workers?
2. What is the public policy behind legislation requiring public sector arbitration? According to the court, how would an agreement to exempt certain contract provisions from arbitration affect that public policy?
3. How is the duty to bargain in good faith imposed on public sector employers and unions related to the public policy rationale for legislation requiring arbitration of public sector disputes? How does this court decision support that public policy? Explain.

Bargaining and Open-Meeting Laws

Some states have adopted open-meeting, or "sunshine," laws that require meetings of public bodies be open to the public. Such laws could present a problem for collective bargaining by public employers because they may allow members of the general public to take part in the bargaining process. In some states, such as Ohio, collective bargaining is exempted from the open-meeting law. In other states, however, the right of the public to participate in the bargaining is legally protected.

The following case involves the question of whether or not a school board can allow a teacher to comment at a public meeting on matters currently being negotiated with the teachers' union.

City of Madison Joint School District No. 8 v. Wisconsin Employment Relations Commission

429 U.S. 167 (1976)

Burger, C.J.

The question presented on this appeal from the Supreme Court of Wisconsin is whether a State may constitutionally require that an elected board of education prohibit teachers, other than union representatives, to speak at open meetings, at which public participation is permitted, if such speech is addressed to the subject of pending collective-bargaining negotiations.

The Madison Board of Education and Madison Teachers, Inc. (MTI), a labor union, were parties to a collective-bargaining agreement during the calendar year of 1971. In January 1971 negotiations commenced for renewal of the agreement and MTI submitted a number of proposals. One among them called for the inclusion of a so-called "fair share" clause, which would require all teachers, whether members of MTI or not, to pay union dues to defray the costs of collective bargaining. Wisconsin law expressly permits inclusion of "fair share" provisions in municipal employee collective-bargaining agreements. Another proposal presented by the union was a provision for binding arbitration of teacher dismissals. Both of these provisions were resisted by the school board. The negotiations deadlocked in November 1971 with a number of issues still unresolved, among them "fair share" and arbitration.

During the same month, two teachers, Holmquist and Reed, who were members of the bargaining unit, but not members of the union, mailed a letter to all teachers in the district expressing opposition to the "fair share" proposal. Two hundred teachers replied, most commenting favorably on Holmquist and Reed's position. Thereupon a petition was drafted calling for a one-year delay in the implementation of "fair share" while the proposal was more closely analyzed by an impartial committee. The petition was circulated to teachers in the district on December 6, 1971. Holmquist and Reed intended to present the results of their petition effort to the school board and the MTI at the school board's public meeting that same evening.

Because of the stalemate in the negotiations, MTI arranged to have pickets present at the school board meeting. In addition, 300 to 400 teachers attended in support of the union's position. During a portion of the meeting devoted to expression of opinion by the public, the president of MTI took the floor and spoke on the subject of the ongoing negotiations. He concluded his remarks by presenting to the board a petition signed by 1,300–1,400 teachers calling for the expeditious resolution of the negotiations. Holmquist was next given the floor, after John Matthews, the business representative of MTI, unsuccessfully attempted to dissuade him from speaking. Matthews had also spoken to a member of the school board before the meeting and requested that the board refuse to permit Holmquist to speak. Holmquist stated that he represented "an informal committee of 72 teachers in 49 schools" and that he desired to inform the board of education, as he had already informed the union, of the results of an informational survey concerning the "fair share" clause. He then read the petition which had been circulated to the teachers in the district that morning and stated that in the 31 schools from which reports had been received, 53 percent of the teachers had already signed the petition.

Holmquist stated that neither side had adequately addressed the issue of "fair share" and that teachers were confused about the meaning of the proposal. He concluded by saying: "Due to this confusion, we wish to take no stand on the proposal itself, but ask only that all alternatives be presented clearly to all teachers and more importantly to the general public to whom we are all responsible. We ask simply for communication, not confrontation." The sole response from the school board was a question by the president inquiring whether Holmquist intended to present the board with the petition. Holmquist answered that he would. Holmquist's presentation had lasted approximately 2½ minutes.

Later that evening, the board met in executive session and voted a proposal acceding to all of the union's demands with the exception of "fair share." During a negotiating session the following morning, MTI accepted the proposal and a contract was signed on December 14, 1971.

In January 1972, MTI filed a complaint with the Wisconsin Employment Relations Commission (WERC) claiming that the board had committed a prohibited labor practice by permitting Holmquist to speak at the December 6 meeting. MTI claimed that in so doing the board had engaged in negotiations with a member of the bargaining unit other than the exclusive collective-bargaining representative, in violation of Wis. Stat. Sections 111.70(3)(a)(1),(4) (1973). Following a hearing the Commission concluded that the board was guilty of the prohibited labor practice and ordered that it "immediately cease and desist from permitting employees, other than representatives of Madison Teachers Inc., to appear and speak at meetings of the Board of Education, on matters subject to collective bargaining between it and Madison Teachers, Inc." The Commission's action was affirmed by the Circuit Court of Dane County.

The Supreme Court of Wisconsin affirmed. The court recognized that both the Federal and State Constitutions protect freedom of speech and the right to petition the government, but noted that these rights may be abridged in the face of "a clear and present danger that [the speech] will bring about the substantive evils that [the legislature] has a right to prevent." The court held that abridgment of the speech in this case was justified in order "to avoid the dangers attendant upon relative chaos in labor management relations."

The Wisconsin court perceived "clear and present danger" based upon its conclusion that Holmquist's speech before the school board constituted "negotiation" with the board. Permitting such "negotiation," the court reasoned, would undermine the bargaining exclusivity guaranteed the majority union under Wis. Stat. Section 111.70(3)(a)(4) (1973). From that premise it concluded that teachers' First Amendment rights could be limited. Assuming, *arguendo,* that such a "danger" might in some circumstances justify some limitation of First Amendment rights, we are unable to read this record as presenting such danger as would justify curtailing speech.

The Wisconsin Supreme Court's conclusion that Holmquist's terse statement during the public meeting constituted negotiation with the board was based upon its adoption of the lower court's determination that, "[e]ven though Holmquist's statement superficially appears to be merely a 'position statement,' the court deems from the total circumstances that it constituted 'negotiating.'" This cryptic conclusion seems to ignore the ancient wisdom that calling a thing by a name does not make it so. Holmquist did not seek to bargain or offer to enter into any bargain with the board, nor does it appear that he was authorized by any other teachers to enter into any agreement on their behalf. Although his views were not consistent with those of MTI, communicating such views to the employer could not change the fact that MTI alone was authorized to negotiate and to enter into a contract with the board.

Moreover the school board meeting at which Holmquist was permitted to speak was open to the public. He addressed the school board not merely as one of its employees but also as a concerned citizen, seeking to express his views on an important decision of his government. We have held that teachers may not be "compelled to relinquish the First Amendment rights they would otherwise enjoy as citizens to comment on matters of public interest in connection with the operation of the public schools in which they work." . . . Where the State has opened a forum for direct citizen involvement, it is difficult to find justification for excluding teachers who make up the overwhelming proportion of school employees and who are most vitally concerned with the proceedings. It is conceded that any citizen could have presented precisely the same points and provided the board with the same information as did Holmquist.

Regardless of the extent to which true contract negotiations between a public body and its employees may be regulated—an issue we need not consider at this time—the participation in public discussion of public business cannot be confined to one category of interested individuals. To permit one side of a debatable public question to have a monopoly in expressing its views to the government is the antithesis of constitutional guarantees. Whatever its duties as an employer, when the board sits in public meetings to conduct public business and hear the views of citizens, it may not be required to discriminate between speakers on the basis of their employment, or the content of their speech. . . .

The WERC's order is not limited to a determination that a prohibited labor practice had taken place in the past; it also restrains future conduct. By prohibiting the school board from "permitting employees . . . to appear and speak at meetings of the Board of Education" the order constitutes an indirect, but effective, prohibition on persons such as Holmquist from communicating with their government. The order would have a substantial impact upon virtually all communication between teachers and the school board. The order prohibits speech by teachers "on matters subject to collective bargaining." As the dissenting opinion below noted, however, there is virtually no subject concerning the operation of the school system that could not also be characterized as a potential subject of collective bargaining. Teachers not only constitute the overwhelming bulk of employees of the school system, but they are the very core of that system; restraining teachers' expressions to the board on matters involving the operation of the schools would seriously impair the board's ability to govern the district. . . .

The judgment of the Wisconsin Supreme Court is reversed, and the case is remanded to that court for further proceedings not inconsistent with this opinion.

Reversed and remanded.

Case Questions

1. Why did the Wisconsin Supreme Court characterize Holmquist's statement as constituting negotiation? Did the U.S. Supreme Court agree with that characterization? Why?
2. Was Holmquist addressing the school board in his capacity as an employee, as a concerned citizen, or as both? Why is it relevant here? Explain your answer.
3. When can the First Amendment rights of the freedom of speech and the right to petition the government be limited? Were those circumstances applicable to the facts in this case? Explain.

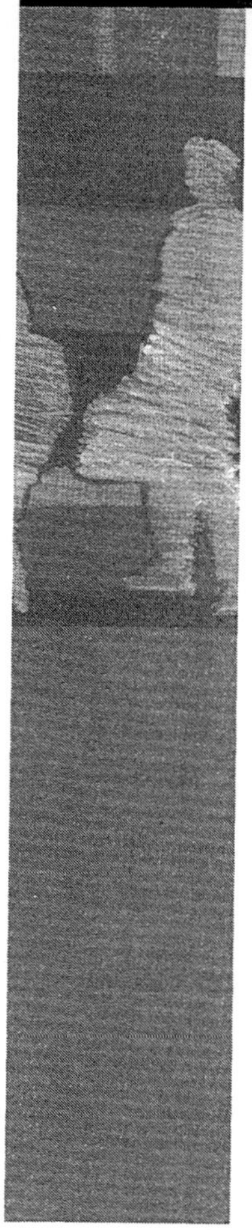

PUBLIC EMPLOYEE'S HORN BLOWING NOT PROTECTED BY FIRST AMENDMENT

THE WORKING LAW

The U.S. Court of Appeals for the First Circuit has held that a police officer's participation in a demonstration that involved blowing a truck's air horn repeatedly to protest the lack of a union contract was not expressive conduct protected by the First Amendment of the U.S. Constitution. Office Paul J. Meaney, of the Woburn, Massachusetts Police Department, drove a truck around city hall as part of a union demonstration to the fact that the city's police and firefighters' unions had been working without a collective-bargaining agreement for the last four years. The demonstration was timed to coincide with the arrival of guests attending the inauguration of Mayor Robert Dever.

After his participation in the demonstration, Meaney was suspended without pay for two weeks by Police Chief Philip Mahoney; the suspension was based on Meaney's "failure to fulfill his professional responsibilities by contributing to a disturbance of the public peace for personal reasons." Meaney appealed the suspension to the mayor; at the hearing on his appeal, Meaney testified that he wanted to "piss off" the mayor and to disrupt the inauguration. The hearing officer concluded that Meaney's actions were based on personal animosity and upheld the suspension. Meaney then appealed to the Massachusetts Civil Service Commission, which overturned the suspension; the Civil Service Commission ruled that the hornblowing was part of Meaney's "lawful, constitutionally protected right as a union member to picket in a peaceful manner."

Meaney then filed a suit against the city, the mayor, and the police chief, seeking damages for the violation of his freedom of speech and for various state tort claims. The trial court dismissed all claims against the city and the state tort claims but entered a judgment against the mayor and police chief, awarding Meaney damages of $7,500 for violation of his freedom of speech under the First Amendment. The police chief and mayor then appealed to the U.S. Court of Appeals for the First Circuit. The court of appeals ruled that Meaney's conduct was motivated by a personal dislike of Dever and a desire to irritate him; the expression of anger toward a supervisor does not relate to a matter of public concern, and therefore is not protected by the First Amendment. The court reversed the trial court verdict awarding damages to Meaney.

Sources: "No Blowing Your Own Horn: Court Rejects Employee's First Amendment Claim," *8 New Hampshire Employment Law Letter,* No. 4 (June 2003); *Meaney v. Dever* [326 F.3d 283 (1st Cir. 2003)].

Impasse Resolution Procedure

Because most state laws restrict or prohibit strikes by public employees, they must provide some alternative means for resolving bargaining impasses. Most statutes provide for a process that includes fact-finding, mediation, and ultimately, interest arbitration.

Mediation is generally the first step in the impasse resolution process; the mediator may be appointed by the PERB at the request of either party. The mediator attempts to offer suggestions and to reduce the number of issues in dispute.

If the mediation is unsuccessful, fact-finding is the second step. Each party presents its case to the fact-finder, who will issue a report defining the issues in dispute and establishing the reasonableness of each side's position. The fact-finder's report may be released to the public in an attempt to bring the pressure of public opinion upon the parties to force a settlement.

If no resolution is reached after mediation and fact-finding, the statutes generally provide for interest arbitration. The arbitration may be either voluntary or compulsory, and it may be binding or nonbinding. Compulsory, binding arbitration is generally found in statutes dealing with employees who provide essential services, such as firefighters and police. Nonbinding arbitration awards may be disregarded by the public employer if it so chooses; binding arbitration awards bind both parties to the arbitrator's settlement of the dispute.

In several states, the arbitration of bargaining disputes has been challenged as being an illegal delegation of the public employer's legal authority to the arbitrator. Most state courts have upheld the legality of arbitration; examples are Maine, Michigan, Minnesota, New York, Pennsylvania, and Washington. In some states, however, courts have held compulsory arbitration to be illegal. Such was the case in Colorado, South Dakota, Texas, and Utah.

Some statutes allow for judicial review of arbitration awards, generally on grounds of whether the award is unreasonable, arbitrary, or capricious.

Strikes by State Workers

Most state public sector labor relations statutes prohibit strikes by public employees. Statutes in other states, such as Hawaii, Michigan, Pennsylvania, and Vermont, allow strikes by employees whose jobs do not immediately affect the public health, safety, and welfare. Still other states' statutes allow for strikes in situations in which the public employer refuses to negotiate or to abide by an arbitration award.

Penalties for illegal strikes vary from state to state. New York's Taylor Law, which prohibits all strikes by public employees, provides for fines and loss of dues check-off provisions for unions involved in illegal strikes. Employees who participate in illegal strikes in New York may face probation, loss of job, and loss of pay. The court may issue injunctions or restraining orders against illegal strikes.

Disciplining public sector employees, even those who have taken part in illegal strikes, may pose constitutional problems for the public sector employer. The employer must ensure that any disciplinary procedure ensures the employees "due process," including adequate notice of and an opportunity to participate in a hearing on the proposed penalty.

ETHICAL DILEMMA: RELIGION IN CITY HALL

You are the director of human resources for the City of Rochester. The city's employees are represented by the Rochester City Employees Association (RCEA). One of the employees at city hall is a devout fundamentalist Christian who frequently asks other employees, particularly non-Christian employees, if they are willing to be "born again" and to pray with her. A number of employees have complained to you, and the union threatens to file a grievance over her behavior.

The state civil service law gives the city the right to impose and enforce reasonable disciplinary rules. The RCEA demands that the city impose a rule prohibiting city employees from engaging in religious conduct on the job and from harassing other employees over matters of religion. You are concerned about the constitutionality of such a rule and of imposing discipline on an employee for religious behavior.

What are the potential constitutional problems raised by the proposed rule? What arguments can you make in favor of the proposed rule? What arguments can you make against it? Prepare a memo discussing these issues for the mayor and city council and recommend whether the city should adopt the rule.

SUMMARY

- Labor relations in the public sector differ from those in the private sector in several ways: (1) government employees are also citizens who have certain rights under the federal and appropriate state constitutions, which may limit disciplinary procedures by government employers; (2) government sovereignty requires that the scope of collective bargaining be restricted; and (3) the right of public employees to strike may be limited or completely prohibited. While legislation in some states permits certain public employees to strike, federal government employees are prohibited from striking. A union that authorizes or conducts a strike against the federal government may have its status as exclusive bargaining representative revoked, and federal employees who go on strike are subject to discharge.
- The Federal Service Labor-Management Relations Act (FSLMRA) regulates federal labor relations; it grants federal employees the right to join or assist unions. Certain federal employees, including members of the armed forces and those involved in intelligence work or national security matters, are excluded from coverage of the FSLMRA. The FSLMRA requires employers and unions to negotiate in good faith, but the act also contains a broad management-rights clause and restricts the scope of collective-bargaining subjects. The Federal Labor Relations Authority (FLRA) administers the FSLMRA; the FLRA determines appropriate representation units, conducts representation elections, and hears complaints of unfair labor practices under the FSLMRA.
- State public sector labor relations legislation varies widely; some states grant certain public employees the right to strike, and most states require that employers negotiate, or "meet and confer," with the unions representing public employees. The scope of collective bargaining

under state public sector legislation is generally restricted by broad management-rights clauses. State public sector labor relations laws are generally administered by a state Public Employee Relations Board (PERB), which conducts representation elections and decides unfair labor practice complaints.

QUESTIONS

1. In what ways does the role of government as employer raise constitutional issues not found in the private sector?
2. Which federal employees are covered by the FSLMRA? Which federal agencies are excluded from the act's coverage?
3. Which statutes govern labor relations of U.S. Postal Service employees?
4. How do union "consultation rights" under the FSLMRA differ from collective bargaining rights under the act?
5. What restrictions are placed on the scope of collective bargaining under the FSLMRA?
6. Which procedures are available for impasse settlement under the FSLMRA?
7. What sanctions are available against unions found to have committed unfair labor practices under the FSLMRA?
8. What legal issues are raised by union security clauses in the public sector? Explain why these issues arise.
9. To what extent may states restrict the right of state public employees to join unions? To what extent may the right of state public sector employees to bargain collectively be restricted?

CASE PROBLEMS

1. In April 1978, public employee Dorothea Yoggerst heard an unconfirmed report that her boss, the director of the Illinois Governor's Office of Management and Human Development, had been discharged. While still at work, she asked a co-worker, "Did you hear the good news?"

   Yoggerst was orally reprimanded by her supervisor. Subsequently, a written memorandum of the reprimand was placed in her personnel file. Two months later, she resigned her job, citing this alleged infringement of her First Amendment right of free speech as her reason for leaving. Yoggerst sued four defendants, including the supervisor who reprimanded her and the personnel director.

   An earlier case heard by the Supreme Court, *Connick v. Myers,* involved the firing of a public employee for distributing to her co-workers a questionnaire that challenged the trustworthiness of her superiors. In that case, the high court enunciated a two-prong test: (1) Did the speech in question address a matter of public concern? (2) How did the employee's right to speak her mind compare to the government's interest in efficient operations? The U.S. Court of Appeals applied this same test in the *Yoggerst* case.

   How do you think the courts ruled in these two cases? See *Yoggerst v. Hedges and McDonough* [739 F.2d 293 (7th Cir. 1984)] and *Connick v. Myers* [461 U.S. 138 (1983)].
2. The Toledo Police Patrolmen's Association is the union representing the employees of the Toledo, Ohio, police department. Several police department employees objected to the

amount of agency fees that they were required to pay because they reflected union political expenditures. The union had charged to objectors an agency fee that was equal to 100 percent of the regular union dues. The union claimed that its collective-bargaining expenditures were $166,020 annually, whereas the dues collected amounted to only $162,138 annually, but the union refused to make its financial records available to the objecting employees. The employees filed suit in federal court, asking the court to order the union to provide financial information and to submit to an audit to verify the procedure used to determine the agency fees.

How should the court rule on the employees' suit? See *Tierney v. City of Toledo* [917 F.2d 927 (6th Cir. 1990)].

3. The federal Department of Health and Human Services (H&HS) decided to institute a total ban on smoking in all of its facilities. The National Treasury Employees Union, which represents the H&HS employees, demanded that the agency bargain with it over the decision. The agency refused, arguing that the decision was not subject to bargaining under the FSLMRA.

How should the Federal Labor Relations Authority rule on the union's claim? See *Dept. of Health and Human Services Family Support Admin. v. Federal Labor Relations Authority* [920 F.2d 45 (D.C. Cir. 1990)].

4. A group of twenty community college faculty instructors in Minnesota refused to join the Minnesota Community College Faculty Association. Under state law, faculty unions were given the exclusive right to engage in discussions with administrators about matters of academic policy. The twenty nonmembers argued that this exclusive representation policy violated principles of free speech and academic freedom enshrined in the First Amendment.

How did the Supreme Court respond? See *Minn. State Bd. for Community Colleges v. Knight* [465 U.S. 271 (1984)].

5. Marjorie Rowland began working at Stebbins High School in Yellow Springs, Ohio, in August 1974. The school principal subsequently asked her to resign when it was learned that she had stated she was bisexual. When she refused, the school suspended her but was forced to rehire her by a preliminary injunction issued by a federal district judge. The administration assigned her to a job with no student contact and, when her contract expired, refused to renew it. Rowland sued.

How do you think the court ruled in this case? See *Rowland v. Mad River Local School District* [730 F.2d 444 (6th Cir. 1984)].

6. On September 22, 1978, all eighteen employees of the public works, fire, and finance departments of the City of Gridley, California, went on strike following the breakdown in negotiations over a new collective-bargaining agreement. The city notified the union that it regarded the strike as illegal and immediately revoked the union's certification as collective-bargaining representative. The city's labor relations officer notified the employees that they would be fired if they did not return to work at their next regular shift. The city council met in emergency session on a Saturday and voted to terminate the employees. On Sunday, the union notified the city that all employees would return to their jobs on Monday. The city refused to reinstate them.

Although the city council had earlier declared that "participation by any employee in a strike . . . is unlawful and shall subject the employee to disciplinary action, up to and including discharge," the union challenged the city's actions on the basis that (1) the discharged employees had been entitled to a hearing, and (2) the sanction of revoking recognition was contrary to the purpose of California's public employee relations laws—that is, to permit the employees to have responsibilities of their own choosing.

The case reached the California Supreme Court. How do you think the court ruled? See

IBEW Local 1245 v. City of Gridley [34 Cal.3d 191 (Supr. Ct. Cal. 1983)].

7. Student Services Inc. was a nonprofit organization that operated a bookstore, bowling alley, vending machines, and other services at Edinboro State College in Pennsylvania. The Retail Clerks Union filed a petition with the Pennsylvania Labor Relations Board seeking a Public Employees Relations Act. After several hearings, an election was held and the union won. The board subsequently certified the union.

The company challenged the board's jurisdiction, stating that it was not a part of the state college and therefore was a private employer covered by the NLRA. The bookstore, bowling alley, and other services were housed rent-free in a building owned by the Commonwealth of Pennsylvania and situated on the college campus. Pennsylvania law defines a "public employer" in pertinent part as "any nonprofit organization or institution and any charitable, religious, scientific, literary, recreational, health, educational or welfare institution receiving grants or appropriations from local, State or Federal governments."

How should the court have ruled on Student Services' status? See *In the Matter of Employees of Student Services, Inc.* [411 A.2d 569 (Pa. Super. 1980)].

8. The Combined Federal Campaign (CFC) is an annual charitable fund-raising drive conducted in the federal workplace during working hours largely through the voluntary efforts of federal employees. Participating organizations confine their fund-raising activities to a thirty-word statement submitted by them for inclusion in the campaign literature.

Volunteer federal employees distribute to their co-workers literature describing the campaign and the participants, along with pledge cards. Designated funds are paid directly to the specified recipient.

The CFC is a relatively recent idea. Prior to 1957, charitable solicitation in the federal workplace occurred on an ad hoc basis. Federal managers received requests from dozens of organizations seeking endorsements and the right to solicit contributions from federal employees at their work sites. In facilities where solicitation was permitted, weekly campaigns were commonplace.

In 1957, President Eisenhower established the forerunner of the CFC to bring order to the solicitation process and to ensure truly voluntary giving by federal employees. The order established an advisory committee and set forth general procedures and standards for a uniform fund-raising program. It permitted no more than three charitable solicitations annually and established a system requiring prior approval by a committee on fund-raising for participation by "voluntary health and welfare" agencies.

A number of organizations joined in challenging these criteria, including the NAACP Legal Defense and Educational Fund, Inc., the Sierra Club Legal Defense Fund, the Puerto Rican Legal Defense and Education Fund, the Federally Employed Women Legal Defense and Education Fund, the Indian Law Resource Center, the Lawyers Committee for Civil Rights under Law, and the Natural Resources Defense Council. Each of the groups attempts to influence public policy through one or more of the following means: political activity, advocacy, lobbying, and litigation on behalf of others.

On what grounds did these organizations challenge the regulations? How do you think the Supreme Court ruled? See *Cornelius v. NAACP Legal Defense and Educational Fund* [473 U.S. 788 (1985)].

9. The Indianapolis city government pressed theft charges against a former employee, Michael McGraw, when his supervisor discovered that he had used the computer to keep customer lists and payment records for his private business—the sale to co-workers and others of Nature-Slim, a liquid diet supplement for people who want to lose weight.

The city decided to press charges for theft after it was unsuccessful in blocking McGraw's application for unemployment compensation benefits. The discharge of McGraw was not related to the alleged misuse of the computer. A jury convicted McGraw on two counts of theft.

The state criminal code defines a thief in the following terms: "A person who knowingly or intentionally exerts unauthorized control over property of another person with intent to deprive the other of any part of its value, or use, commits theft, a class D felony."

Should McGraw's conviction be permitted to stand? Suppose the conviction is overturned. Should he be reinstated? See *Indiana v. McGraw* [480 N.E.2d 552 (Indiana Supr. Ct. 1985)].

10. The legislature of the state of Iowa, concerned about the proliferation of drugs in American society and their alleged availability even inside the nation's prisons, passed a law allowing prison officials to conduct random blood and urinalysis tests on state correction officers. The law allowed testing without any reasonable suspicion that the officers to be tested were in fact users or under the influence of any controlled substance. A total of 1,750 officers filed a class-action suit challenging the law as a search and seizure without a warrant and as a violation of their due process rights.

How should the federal court rule? See *McDonell v. Hunter* [809 F.2d 1302 (8th Cir. 1987)].

INTERNET EXERCISES

1. The Federal Service Labor-Management Relations Act (FSLMRA), 5 U.S.C. Sections 7101–7135 is administered by the Federal Labor Relations Authority (FLRA). The text of the FSLMRA is available online at **http://www.findlaw.com**. Click the link to US Law: Federal, next click the link to U.S. Code, and then enter the legislative citation 5 U.S.C. S. 7101 in the appropriate search boxes. Go to **http://fedbbs.access.gpo.gov/flra01.htm** for the FLRA homepage.

2. State public sector legislation and enforcement agencies are also online. The California Public Employment Relations Board Web site is at **http://www.perb.ca.gov**. Click the Laws & Rules link and then click the link for the Meyers-Milias-Brown Act (MMBA) to get the text of the state public employee law. The New York Public Employee Relations Board Web site is at **http://www.perb.state.ny.us**. Click The Law link to see the text of the Taylor Law, the New York State public employee labor relations legislation.

3. Does your state have public employee relations legislation? You may be able to find out by going to **http://www.findlaw.com** and clicking the States link under the US Laws: Cases & Codes heading. Then click the link for your state.

INFOTRAC KEYWORDS

http://www.infotrac-college.com

public sector labor relations, Federal Service Labor-Management Relations Act, postal service employee, grievance arbitration

APPENDIX A

CIVIL RIGHTS ACT OF 1964

42 U.S.C. § 2000e et seq., as amended by the Civil Rights Act of 1991, P.L. 102-166

Title VII—Nondiscrimination in Employment

Section 701. Definitions

For the purposes of this subchapter—

(a) The term "person" includes one or more individuals, governments, governmental agencies, political subdivisions, labor unions, partnerships, associations, corporations, legal representatives, mutual companies, joint-stock companies, trusts, unincorporated organizations, trustees, trustees in cases under Title 11, or receivers.

(b) The term "employer" means a person engaged in an industry affecting commerce who has fifteen or more employees for each working day in each of twenty or more calendar weeks in the current or preceding calendar year, and any agent of such a person, but such term does not include (1) the United States, a corporation wholly owned by the Government of the United States, an Indian tribe, or any department or agency of the District of Columbia subject by statute to procedures of the competitive service (as defined in section 2102 of Title 5) or (2) a bona fide private membership club (other than a labor organization) which is exempt from taxation under section 501(c) of Title 26, except that during the first year after March 24, 1972, persons having fewer than twenty-five employees (and their agents) shall not be considered employers.

(c) The term "employment agency" means any person regularly undertaking with or without compensation to procure employees for an employer or to procure for employees opportunities to work for an employer and includes an agent of such a person.

(d) The term "labor organization" means a labor organization engaged in an industry affecting commerce, and any agent of such an organization, and includes any organization of any kind, any agency, or employee representation committee, group, association, or plan so engaged in which employees participate and which exists for the purpose, in whole or in part, of dealing with employers concerning grievances, labor disputes, wages, rates of pay, hours, or other terms or conditions of employment, and any conference, general committee, joint or system board, or joint council so engaged which is subordinate to a national or international labor organization.

(e) A labor organization shall be deemed to be engaged in an industry affecting commerce if (1) it maintains or operates a hiring hall or hiring office which procures employees for an employer or procures for employees opportunities to work for an employer; or (2) the number of its members (or, where it is a labor organization composed of other labor organizations or their representatives, if the aggregate number of the members of such other labor organization) is (A) twenty-five or more during the first year after March 24, 1972, or (B) fifteen or more thereafter, and such labor organization—

(1) is the certified representative of employees under the provisions of the National Labor Relations Act, as amended, or the Railway Labor Act, as amended;

(2) although not certified, is a national or international labor organization or a local labor organization recognized or acting as the representative of employees of an employer or employers engaged in an industry affecting commerce; or

(3) has chartered a local labor organization or subsidiary body which is representing or actively seeking to represent employees of employers within the meaning of paragraph (1) or (2); or

(4) has been chartered by a labor organization representing or actively seeking to represent employees within the meaning of paragraph (1) or (2) has the local or subordinate body through which such employees may enjoy membership or become affiliated with such labor organization; or

(5) is a conference, general committee, joint or system board, or joint council subordinate to a national or international labor organization, which includes a labor organization engaged in an industry affecting commerce within the meaning of any of the preceding paragraphs of this subsection.

(f) The term "employee" means an individual employed by an employer, except that the term "employee" shall not include any person elected to public office in any State or political subdivision of any State by the qualified voters thereof, or any person chosen by such officer to be on such officer's personal staff, or an appointee on the policy making level or an immediate adviser with respect to the exercise of the constitutional or legal powers of the office. The exemption set forth in the preceding sentence shall not include employees subject to the civil service laws of a State government, governmental agency or political subdivision.

With respect to employment in a foreign country, such term includes an individual who is a citizen of the United States.

(g) The term "commerce" means trade, traffic, commerce, transportation, transmission, or communication among the several States; or between a State and any place outside thereof; or within the District of Columbia, or a possession of the United States; or between points in the same State but through a point outside thereof.

(h) The term "industry affecting commerce" means any activity, business, or industry in commerce or in which a labor dispute would hinder or obstruct commerce or the free flow of commerce and includes any activity or industry "affecting commerce" within the meaning of the Labor-Management Reporting and Disclosure Act of 1959, and further includes any governmental industry, business, or activity.

(i) The term "State" includes a State of the United States, the District of Columbia, Puerto Rico, the Virgin Islands, American Samoa, Guam, Wake Island, the Canal Zone, and Outer Continental Shelf lands defined in the Outer Continental Shelf Lands Act.

(j) The term "religion" includes all aspects of religious observance and practice, as well as belief, unless an employer demonstrates that he is unable to reasonably accommodate to an employee's or prospective employee's religious observance or practice without undue hardship on the conduct of the employer's business.

(k) The terms "because of sex" or "on the basis of sex" include, but are not limited to, because of or on the basis of pregnancy, childbirth, or related medical conditions; and women affected by pregnancy, childbirth, or related medical conditions shall be treated the same for all employment-related purposes, including receipt of benefits under fringe benefit programs, as other persons not so affected but similar in their ability or inability to work and nothing in section 2000e-2(h) of this title shall be interpreted to permit otherwise. This subsection shall not require an employer to pay for health insurance benefits for abortion, except where the life of the mother would be endangered if the fetus were carried to term, or except where medical complications have arisen from an abortion: Provided, That nothing herein shall preclude an employer from providing abortion benefits or otherwise affect bargaining agreements in regard to abortion.

(l) The term "complaining party" means the Commission, the Attorney General, or a person who may bring an action or proceeding under this title.

(m) The term "demonstrates" means meets the burdens of production and persuasion.

(n) The term "respondent" means an employer, employment agency, labor organization, joint labor-management committee controlling apprenticeship or other training or retraining program, including an on-the-job training program, or Federal entity subject to section 717.

Sec. 702. Subchapter not applicable to employment of aliens outside state and individuals for performance of activities of religious corporations, associations, educational institutions, or societies

(a) This subchapter shall not apply to an employer with respect to the employment of aliens outside any State, or to a religious corporation, association, educational institution, or society with respect to the employment of individuals of a particular religion to perform work connected with the carrying on by such corporation, association, educational institution, or society of its activities.

(b) It shall not be unlawful under section 703 or 704 for an employer (or a corporation controlled by an employer), labor organization, employment agency, or joint management committee controlling apprenticeship or other training or retraining (including on-the-job training programs) to take any action otherwise prohibited by such section, with respect to an employee in a workplace in a foreign country if compliance with such section would cause such employer (or such corporation), such organization, such agency, or such committee to violate the law of the foreign country in which such workplace is located.

(c) (1) If an employer controls a corporation whose place of incorporation is a foreign country, any practice prohibited by section 703 or 704 engaged in by such corporation shall be presumed to be engaged in by such employer.

(2) Sections 703 and 704 shall not apply with respect to the foreign operations of an employer that is a foreign person not controlled by an American employer.

(3) For purposes of this subsection, the determination of whether an employer controls a corporation shall be based on—

(A) the interrelation of operations;

(B) the common management;

(C) the centralized control of labor relations; and

(D) the common ownership or financial control, of the employer and the corporation.

Sec. 703. Unlawful employment practices

(a) It shall be an unlawful employment practice for an employer—

(1) to fail or refuse to hire or to discharge any individual, or otherwise to discriminate against any individual with respect to his compensation, terms, conditions, or privileges of employment, because of such individual's race, color, religion, sex, or national origin; or

(2) to limit, segregate, or classify his employees or applicants for employment in any way which would deprive or tend to deprive any individual of employment opportunities or otherwise adversely affect his status as an employee, because of such individual's race, color, religion, sex, or national origin.

(b) It shall be an unlawful employment practice for an employment agency to fail or refuse to refer for employment, or otherwise to discriminate against, any individual because of his race, color, religion, sex, or national origin, or to classify or refer for employment any individual on the basis of his race, color, religion, sex, or national origin.

(c) It shall be an unlawful employment practice for a labor organization—

(1) to exclude or to expel from its membership, or otherwise to discriminate against, any individual because of his race, color, religion, sex, or national origin;

(2) to limit, segregate, or classify its membership or applicants for membership or to classify or fail or refuse to refer for employment any individual, in any way which would deprive or tend to deprive any individual of employment opportunities, or would limit such employment opportunities or otherwise adversely affect his status as an employee or as an applicant for employment, because of such individual's race, color, religion, sex, or national origin; or

(3) to cause or attempt to cause an employer to discriminate against an individual in violation of this section.

(d) It shall be an unlawful employment practice for any employer, labor organization, or joint labor-management committee controlling apprenticeship or other training or retraining, including on-the-job training programs to discriminate against any individual because of his race, color, religion, sex, or national origin in admission to, or employment in, any program established to provide apprenticeship or other training.

(e) Notwithstanding any other provision of this subchapter, (1) it shall not be an unlawful employment practice for an employer to hire and employ employees, for an employment agency to classify, or refer for employment any individual, for a labor organization to classify its membership or to classify or refer for employment any individual, or for an employer, labor organization, or joint labor-management committee controlling apprenticeship or other training or retraining programs to admit or employ any individual in any such program, on the basis of his religion, sex, or national origin in those certain instances where religion, sex, or national origin is a bona fide occupational qualification reasonably necessary to the normal operation of that particular business or enterprise, and (2) it shall not be an unlawful employment practice for a school, college, university, or other educational institution or institution of learning to hire and employ employees of a particular religion if such school, college, university, or other educational institution or institution of learning is, in whole or in substantial part, owned, supported, controlled, or managed by a particular religion or by a particular religious corporation, association, or society, or if the curriculum of such school, college, university, or other educational institution or institution of learning is directed toward the propagation of a particular religion.

(f) As used in this subchapter, the phrase "unlawful employment practice" shall not be deemed to include any action or measure taken by an employer, labor organization, joint labor-management committee, or employment agency with respect to an individual who is a member of the Communist Party of the United States or of any other organization required to register as a Communist-action or Communist-front organization by final order of the Subversive Activities Control Board pursuant to the Subversive Activities Control Act of 1950.

(g) Notwithstanding any other provision of this title, it shall not be an unlawful employment practice for an employer to fail or refuse to hire and employ an individual for any position, for an employer to discharge an individual from any position, or for an employment agency to fail or refuse to refer any individual for employment in any position, or for a labor organization to fail or refuse to refer any individual for employment in any position, if—

(1) the occupancy of such position, or access to the premises in or upon which any part of the duties of such position is performed or is to be performed, is subject to any requirement imposed in the interest of the national security of the United States under any security program in effect pursuant to or administered under any statute of the United States or any Executive order of the President; and

(2) such individual has not fulfilled or has ceased to fulfill that requirement.

(h) Notwithstanding any other provision of this subchapter, it shall not be an unlawful employment practice for an employer to apply different standards of compensation, or different terms, conditions, or privileges of employment pursuant to a bona fide seniority or merit system, or a system which measures earnings by quantity or quality of production or to employees who work in different locations, provided that such differences are not the result of an intention to discriminate because of race, color, religion, sex, or national origin; nor shall it be an unlawful employment practice for an employer to give and to act upon the results of any professionally developed ability test provided that such test, its administration or action upon the results is not designed, intended or used to discriminate because of race, color, religion, sex or national origin. It shall not be an unlawful employment practice under this subchapter for any employer to differentiate upon the basis of sex in determining the amount of the wages or compensation paid or to be paid to employees of such employer if such differentiation is authorized by the provisions of section 206(d) of Title 29.

(i) Nothing contained in this subchapter shall apply to any business or enterprise on or near an Indian reservation with respect to any publicly announced employment practice of such business or enterprise under which a preferential treatment is given to any individual because he is an Indian living on or near a reservation.

(j) Nothing contained in this subchapter shall be interpreted to require any employer, employment agency, labor organization, or joint labor-management committee subject to this subchapter to grant preferential treatment to any individual or to any group because of the race, color, religion, sex, or national origin of such individual or group on account of an imbalance which may exist with respect to the total number of percentage of persons of any race, color, religion, sex, or national origin employed by any employer, referred or classified for employment by an employment agency or labor organization, admitted to membership or classified by any labor organization, or admitted to, or employed in, any apprenticeship or other training program, in comparison with the total number or percentage of persons of such race, color, religion, sex, or national origin in any community, State, section, or other area, or in the available work force in any community, State, section, or other area.

(k) (1) (A) An unlawful employment practice based on disparate impact is established under this title only if—

(i) a complaining party demonstrates that a respondent uses a particular employment practice that causes a disparate impact on the basis of race, color, religion, sex, or national origin and the respondent fails to demonstrate that the challenged practice is job related for the position in question and consistent with business necessity; or

(ii) the complaining party makes the demonstration described in subparagraph (C) with respect to an alternative employment practice and the respondent refuses to adopt such alternative employment practice.

(B) (i) With respect to demonstrating that a particular employment practice causes a disparate impact as described in subparagraph (A)(i), the complaining party shall demonstrate that each particular challenged employment practice causes a disparate impact, except that if the complaining party can demonstrate to the court that the elements of a respondent's decisionmaking process are not capable of separation for analysis, the decisionmaking process may be analyzed as one employment practice.

(ii) If the respondent demonstrates that a specific employment practice does not cause the disparate impact, the respondent shall not be required to demonstrate that such practice is required by business necessity.

(C) The demonstration referred to by subparagraph (A)(ii) shall be in accordance with the law as it existed on June 4, 1989, with respect to the concept of 'alternative employment practice'.

(2) A demonstration that an employment practice is required by business necessity may not be used as a defense against a claim of intentional discrimination under this title.

(3) Notwithstanding any other provision of this title, a rule barring the employment of an individual who currently and knowingly uses or possesses a controlled substance, as defined in schedules I and II of section 102(6) of the Controlled Substances Act (21 U.S.C. 802(6)), other than the use or possession of a drug taken under the supervision of a licensed health care professional, or any other use or possession authorized by the Controlled Substances Act or any other provision of Federal law, shall be considered an unlawful employment practice under this title only if such rule is adopted or applied with an intent to discriminate because of race, color, religion, sex, or national origin.

(l) It shall be an unlawful employment practice for a respondent, in connection with the selection or referral of applicants or candidates for employment or promotion, to adjust the scores of, use different cutoff scores for, or otherwise alter the results of, employment related tests on the basis of race, color, religion, sex, or national origin.

(m) Except as otherwise provided in this title, an unlawful employment practice is established when the complaining party demonstrates that race, color, religion, sex, or national origin was a motivating factor for any employment practice, even though other factors also motivated the practice.

(n) (1) (A) Notwithstanding any other provision of law, and except as provided in paragraph (2), an employment practice that implements and is within the scope of a litigated or consent judgment or order that resolves a claim of employment discrimination under the Constitution or Federal civil rights laws may not be challenged under the circumstances described in subparagraph (B).

(B) A practice described in subparagraph (A) may not be challenged in a claim under the Constitution or Federal civil rights laws—

(i) by a person who, prior to the entry of the judgment or order described in subparagraph (A), had—

(I) actual notice of the proposed judgment or order sufficient to apprise such person that such judgment or order might adversely affect the interests and legal rights of such person and that an opportunity was available to present objections to such judgment or order by a future date certain; and
(II) a reasonable opportunity to present objections to such judgment or order; or
(ii) by a person whose interests were adequately represented by another person who had previously challenged the judgment or order on the same legal grounds and with a similar factual situation, unless there has been an intervening change in law or fact.

(2) Nothing in this subsection shall be construed to—
(A) alter the standards for intervention under rule 24 of the Federal Rules of Civil Procedure or apply to the rights of parties who have successfully intervened pursuant to such rule in the proceeding in which the parties intervened;
(B) apply to the rights of parties to the action in which a litigated or consent judgment or order was entered, or of members of a class represented or sought to be represented in such action, or of members of a group on whose behalf relief was sought in such action by the Federal Government;
(C) prevent challenges to a litigated or consent judgment or order on the ground that such judgment or order was obtained through collusion or fraud, or is transparently invalid or was entered by a court lacking subject matter jurisdiction; or
(D) authorize or permit the denial to any person of the due process of law required by the Constitution.

(3) Any action not precluded under this subsection that challenges an employment consent judgment or order described in paragraph (1) shall be brought in the court, and if possible before the judge, that entered such judgment or order. Nothing in this subsection shall preclude a transfer of such action pursuant to section 1404 of title 28, United States Code.

Sec. 704. Other unlawful employment practices

(a) It shall be an unlawful employment practice for an employer to discriminate against any of his employees or applicants for employment, for an employment agency, or joint labor-management committee controlling apprenticeship or other training or retraining, including on-the-job training programs, to discriminate against any individual, or for a labor organization to discriminate against any member thereof or applicant for membership, because he has opposed any practice made an unlawful employment practice by this subchapter, or because he has made a charge, testified, assisted, or participated in any manner in an investigation, proceeding, or hearing under this subchapter.

(b) It shall be an unlawful employment practice for an employer, labor organization, employment agency, or joint labor-management committee controlling apprenticeship or other training or retraining, including on-the-job training programs, to print or publish or cause to be printed or published any notice or advertisement relating to employment by such an employer or membership in or any classification or referral for employment by such a labor organization, or relating to any classification or referral for employment by such an employment agency, or relating to admission to, or employment in, any program established to provide apprenticeship or other training by such a joint labor-management committee, indicating any preference, limitation, specification, or discrimination, based on race, color, religion, sex, or national origin, except that such a notice or advertisement may indicate a preference, limitation, specification, or discrimination based on religion, sex, or national origin when religion, sex, or national origin is a bona fide occupational qualification for employment.

Sec. 705. Equal Employment Opportunity Commission

(a) There is hereby created a Commission to be known as the Equal Employment Opportunity Commission, which shall be composed of five members, not more than three of whom shall be members of the same political party. Members of the Commission shall be appointed by the President by and with the advice and consent of the Senate for a term of five years. Any individual chosen to fill a vacancy shall be appointed only for the unexpired term of the member whom he shall succeed, and all members of the Commission shall continue to serve until their successors are appointed and qualified, except that no such member of the Commission shall continue to serve (1) for more than sixty days when the Congress is in session unless a nomination to fill such vacancy shall have been submitted to the Senate, or (2) after the adjournment sine die of the session of the Senate in which such nomination was submitted. The President shall designate one member to serve as Chairman of the Commission, and one member to serve as Vice Chairman. The Chairman shall be responsible on behalf of the Commission for the administrative operations of the Commission, and, except as provided in subsection (b) of this section, shall appoint, in accordance with the provisions of Title 5 governing appointments in the competitive service, such officers, agents, attorneys, administrative law judges, and employees as he deems necessary to assist it in the performance of its functions and to fix their compensation in accordance with the provisions of chapter 51 and subchapter III of chapter 53 of Title 5, relating to classification and General Schedule pay rates: Provided, That assignment, removal, and compensation of administrative law judges shall be in accordance with sections 3105, 3344, 5372, and 7521 of Title 5.

(b) (1) There shall be a General Counsel of the Commission appointed by the President, by and with the advice and consent of the Senate, for a term of four years. The General Counsel shall have responsibility for the conduct of litigation as provided in sections 2000e-5 and 2000e-6 of this title. The General Counsel shall have such other duties as the Commission may prescribe or as may be provided by law and shall concur with the Chairman of the Commission on the appointment and supervision of regional attorneys. The General Counsel of the Commission on the effective date of this Act shall continue in such position and perform the functions specified in this subsection until a successor is appointed and qualifies.

(2) Attorneys appointed under this section may, at the direction of the Commission, appear for and represent the Commission in any case in court, provided that the Attorney General shall conduct all litigation to which the Commission is a party in the Supreme Court pursuant to this subchapter.

(c) A vacancy in the Commission shall not impair the right of the remaining members to exercise all the powers of the Commission and three members thereof shall constitute a quorum.

(d) The Commission shall have an official seal which shall be judicially noticed.

(e) The Commission shall at the close of each fiscal year report to the Congress and to the President concerning the action it has taken, and the moneys it has disbursed. It shall make such further reports on the cause of and means of eliminating discrimination and such recommendations for further legislation as may appear desirable.

(f) The principal office of the Commission shall be in or near the District of Columbia, but it may meet or exercise any or all its powers at any other place. The Commission may establish such regional or State offices as it deems necessary to accomplish the purpose of this subchapter.

(g) The Commission shall have power—

(1) to cooperate with and, with their consent, utilize regional, State, local, and other agencies, both public and private, and individuals;

(2) to pay to witnesses whose depositions are taken or who are summoned before the Commission or any of its agents the same witness and mileage fees as are paid to witnesses in the courts of the United States;

(3) to furnish to persons subject to this subchapter such technical assistance as they may request to further their compliance with this subchapter or an order issued thereunder;

(4) upon the request of (i) any employer, whose employees, or some of them, or (ii) any labor organization, whose members or some of them, refuse or threaten to refuse to cooperate in effectuating the provisions of this subchapter, to assist in such effectuation by conciliation or such other remedial action as is provided by this subchapter;

(5) to make such technical studies as are appropriate to effectuate the purposes and policies of this subchapter and to make the results of such studies available to the public;

(6) to intervene in a civil action brought under section 2000e-5 of this title by an aggrieved party against a respondent other than a government, governmental agency or political subdivision.

(h) (1) The Commission shall, in any of its educational or promotional activities, cooperate with other departments and agencies in the performance of such educational and promotional activities.

(2) In exercising its powers under this title, the Commission shall carry out educational and outreach activities (including dissemination of information in languages other than English) targeted to—

(A) individuals who historically have been victims of employment discrimination and have not been equitably served by the Commission; and

(B) individuals on whose behalf the Commission has authority to enforce any other law prohibiting employment discrimination, concerning rights and obligations under this title or such law, as the case may be.

(i) All offices, agents, attorneys, and employees of the Commission shall be subject to the provisions of section 7324 of Title 5, notwithstanding any exemption contained in such section.

(j) (1) The Commission shall establish a Technical Assistance Training Institute, through which the Commission shall provide technical assistance and training regarding the laws and regulations enforced by the Commission.

(2) An employer or other entity covered under this title shall not be excused from compliance with the requirements of this title because of any failure to receive technical assistance under this subsection.

(3) There are authorized to be appropriated to carry out this subsection such sums as may be necessary for fiscal year 1992.

Sec. 706. Enforcement provision

(a) The Commission is empowered, as hereinafter provided, to prevent any person from engaging in any unlawful employment practice as set forth in section 2000e-2 or 2000e-3 of this title.

(b) Whenever a charge is filed by or on behalf of a person claiming to be aggrieved, or by a member of the Commission, alleging that an employer, employment agency, labor organization, or joint labor-management committee controlling apprenticeship or other training or retraining, including on-the-job training programs, has engaged in an unlawful employment practice, the Commission shall serve a notice of the charge (including the date, place and circumstances of the alleged unlawful employment practice) on such employer, employment agency, labor organization, or joint labor-management committee (hereinafter referred to as the 'respondent') within ten days and shall make an investigation thereof. Charges shall be in writing under oath or affirmation and shall contain such information and be in such form as the Commission requires. Charges shall not be made public by the Commission. If the Commission determines after such investigation that there is not reasonable cause to believe that the charge is true, it shall dismiss the charge and promptly notify the person claiming to be aggrieved and the respondent of its action. In determining whether reasonable cause exists, the Commission shall accord substantial weight to final findings and orders made by State or local authorities in proceedings commenced under state or local law pursuant to the requirements of subsections (c) and (d) of this section. If the Commission determines after such investigation that there is reasonable cause to believe that the charge is true, the Commission shall endeavor to eliminate any such alleged unlawful employment practice by informal methods of conference, conciliation, and persuasion. Nothing said or done during and as a part of such informal endeavors may be made public by the Commission, its officers or employees, or used as evidence in a subsequent proceeding without the written consent of the persons concerned. Any person who makes public information in violation of this subsection shall be fined not more than $1,000 or imprisoned for not more than one year, or both. The Commission shall make its determination on reasonable cause as promptly as possible and, so far as practicable, not later than one hundred and twenty days from the filing of the charge or, where applicable under subsection (c) or (d) of this section, from the date upon which the Commission is authorized to take action with respect to the charge.

(c) In the case of an alleged unlawful employment practice occurring in a State, or political subdivision of a State, which has a State or local law prohibiting the unlawful employment practice alleged and establishing or authorizing a State or local authority to grant or seek relief from such practice or to institute criminal proceedings with respect thereto upon receiving notice thereof, no charge may be filed under subsection (b) of this section by the person aggrieved before the expiration of sixty days after proceedings have been commenced under the State or local law, unless such proceedings have been earlier terminated, provided that such sixty-day period shall be extended to one hundred and twenty days during the first year after the effective date of such State or local law. If any requirement for the commencement of such proceedings is imposed by a State or local authority other than a requirement of the filing of a written and signed statement of the facts upon which the proceeding is based, the proceeding shall be deemed to have been commenced for the purposes of this subsection at the time such statement is sent by registered mail to the appropriate State or local authority.

(d) In the case of any charge filed by a member of the Commission alleging an unlawful employment practice occurring in a State or political subdivision of a State which has a State or local law prohibiting the practice alleged and establishing or authorizing a State or local authority to grant or seek relief from such practice or to institute criminal proceedings with respect thereto upon receiving notice thereof, the Commission shall, before taking any action with respect to such charge, notify the appropriate State or local officials and, upon request, afford them a reasonable time, but not less than sixty days (provided that such sixty-day period shall be extended to one hundred and twenty days during the first year after the effective day of such State or local law), unless a shorter period is requested, to act under such State or local law to remedy the practice alleged.

(e) (1) A charge under this section shall be filed within one hundred and eighty days after the alleged unlawful employment practice occurred and notice of the charge (including the date, place and circumstances of the alleged unlawful employment practice) shall be served upon the person against whom such charge is made within ten days thereafter, except that in a case of an unlawful employment practice with respect to which the person aggrieved has initially instituted proceedings with a State or local agency with authority to grant or seek relief from such practice or to institute criminal proceedings with respect thereto upon receiving notice thereof, such charge shall be filed by or on behalf of the person aggrieved within three hundred days after the alleged unlawful employment practice occurred, or within thirty days after receiving notice that the State or local agency has terminated the proceedings under the State or local law, whichever is earlier, and a copy of such charge shall be filed by the Commission with the State or local agency.

(2) For purposes of this section, an unlawful employment practice occurs, with respect to a seniority system that has been adopted for an intentionally discriminatory purpose in violation of this title (whether or not that discriminatory purpose is apparent on the face of the seniority provision), when the seniority system is adopted, when an individual becomes subject to the seniority system, or when a person aggrieved is injured by the application of the seniority system or provision of the system.

(f) (1) If within thirty days after a charge is filed with the Commission or within thirty days after expiration of any period of reference under subsection (c) or (d) of this section, the Commission has been unable to secure from the respondent a conciliation agreement acceptable to the Commission, the Commission may bring a civil action against any respondent not a government, governmental agency, or political subdivision named in the charge. In the case of a respondent which is a government, governmental agency, or political subdivision, if the Commission has been unable to secure from the respondent a conciliation agreement acceptable to the Commission, the Commission shall take no further action and shall refer the case to the Attorney General who may bring a civil action against such respondent in the appropriate United States district court. The person or persons aggrieved shall have the right to intervene in a civil action brought by the Commission or the Attorney General in a case involving a government, governmental agency, or political subdivision. If a charge filed with the Commission pursuant to subsection (b) of this section is dismissed by the Commission, or if within one hundred and eighty days from the filing of such charge or the expiration of any period of reference under subsection (c) or (d) of this section, whichever is later, the Commission has not filed a civil action under this section or the Attorney General has not filed a civil action in a case involving a government, governmental agency, or political subdivision, or the Commission has not entered into a conciliation agreement to which the person aggrieved is a party, the Commission, or the Attorney General in a case involving a government, governmental agency, or political subdivision, shall so notify the person aggrieved and within ninety days after the giving of such notice a civil action may be brought against the respondent named in the charge (A) by the person claiming to be aggrieved or (B) if such charge was filed by a member of the Commission, by any person whom the charge alleges was aggrieved by the alleged unlawful employment practice. Upon application by the complainant and in such circumstances as the court may deem just, the court may appoint an attorney for such complainant and may authorize the commencement of the action without the payment of fees, costs, or security. Upon timely application, the court may, in its discretion, permit the Commission or the Attorney General in a case involving a government, governmental agency, or political subdivision, to intervene in such civil action upon certification that the case is of general public importance. Upon request, the court may, in its discretion, stay further proceedings for not more than sixty days pending the termination of State or local proceedings described in subsection (c) or (d) of this section or further efforts of the Commission to obtain voluntary compliance.

(2) Whenever a charge is filed with the Commission and the Commission concludes on the basis of a preliminary investigation that prompt judicial action is necessary to carry out the purposes of this Act, the Commission, or the Attorney General in a case involving a government, governmental agency, or political subdivision, may bring an action for appropriate temporary or preliminary relief pending final disposition of such charge. Any temporary restraining order or other order granting preliminary or temporary relief shall be issued in accordance with rule 65 of the Federal Rules of Civil Procedure. It shall be the duty of a court having jurisdiction over proceedings under this section to assign cases for hearing at the earliest practicable date and to cause such cases to be in every way expedited.

(3) Each United States district court and each United States court of a place subject to the jurisdiction of the United States shall have jurisdiction of actions brought under this subchapter. Such an action may be brought in any judicial district in the State in which the unlawful employment practice is alleged to have been committed, in the judicial district in which the employment records relevant to such practice are maintained and administered, or in the judicial district in which the aggrieved person would have worked but for the alleged unlawful employment practice, but if the respondent is not found within any such district, such an action may be brought within the judicial district in which the respondent has his principal office. For purposes of sections 1404 and 1406 of Title 28, the judicial district in which the respondent has his principal office shall in all cases be considered a district in which the action might have been brought.

(4) It shall be the duty of the chief judge of the district (or in his absence, the acting chief judge) in which the case is pending immediately to designate a judge in such district to hear and determine the case. In the event that no judge in the district is available to hear and determine the case, the chief judge of the district, or the acting chief judge, as the case may be, shall certify this fact to the chief judge of the circuit (or in his absence, the acting chief judge) who shall then designate a district or circuit judge of the circuit to hear and determine the case.

(5) It shall be the duty of the judge designated pursuant to this subsection to assign the case

for hearing at the earliest practicable date and to cause the case to be in every way expedited. If such judge has not scheduled the case for trial within one hundred and twenty days after issue has been joined, that judge may appoint a master pursuant to rule 53 of the Federal Rules of Civil Procedure.

(g) (1) If the court finds that the respondent has intentionally engaged in or is intentionally engaging in an unlawful employment practice charged in the complaint, the court may enjoin the respondent from engaging in such unlawful employment practice, and order such affirmative action as may be appropriate, which may include, but is not limited to, reinstatement or hiring of employees, with or without back pay (payable by the employer, employment agency, or labor organization, as the case may be, responsible for the unlawful employment practice), or any other equitable relief as the court deems appropriate. Back pay liability shall not accrue from a date more than two years prior to the filing of a charge with the Commission. Interim earnings or amounts earnable with reasonable diligence by the person or persons discriminated against shall operate to reduce the back pay otherwise allowable.

(2) (A) No order of the court shall require the admission or reinstatement of an individual as a member of a union, or the hiring, reinstatement, or promotion of an individual as an employee, or the payment to him of any back pay, if such individual was refused admission, suspended, or expelled, or was refused employment or advancement or was suspended or discharged for any reason other than discrimination on account of race, color, religion, sex, or national origin or in violation of section 2000e-3 (a) of this title.

(B) On a claim in which an individual proves a violation under section 703(m) and a respondent demonstrates that the respondent would have taken the same action in the absence of the impermissible motivating factor, the court—

(i) may grant declaratory relief, injunctive relief (except as provided in clause (ii)), and attorney's fees and costs demonstrated to be directly attributable only to the pursuit of a claim under section 703(m); and

(ii) shall not award damages or issue an order requiring any admission, reinstatement, hiring, promotion, or payment, described in subparagraph (A).

(h) The provisions of sections 101 to 115 of Title 29 shall not apply with respect to civil actions brought under this section.

(i) In any case in which an employer, employment agency, or labor organization fails to comply with an order of a court issued in a civil action brought under this section, the Commission may commence proceedings to compel compliance with such order.

(j) Any civil action brought under this section and any proceedings brought under subsection (i) of this section shall be subject to appeal as provided in sections 1291 and 1292, Title 28.

(k) In any action or proceeding under this subchapter, the court, in its discretion, may allow the prevailing party, other than the Commission or the United States, a reasonable attorney's fee (including expert fees) as part of the costs, and the Commission and the United States shall be liable for costs the same as a private person.

Sec. 707. Civil actions by Attorney General

(a) Whenever the Attorney General has reasonable cause to believe that any person or group of persons is engaged in a pattern or practice of resistance to the full enjoyment of any of the rights secured by this subchapter, and that the pattern or practice is of such a nature and is intended to deny the full exercise of the rights herein described, the Attorney General may bring a civil action in the appropriate district court of the United States by filing with it a complaint (1) signed by him (or in his absence the Acting Attorney General), (2) setting forth facts pertaining to such pattern or practice, and (3) requesting such relief, including an application for a permanent or temporary injunction, restraining order or other order against the person or persons responsible for such pattern or practice, as he deems necessary to insure the full enjoyment of the rights herein described.

(b) The district courts of the United States shall have and shall exercise jurisdiction of proceedings instituted pursuant to this section, and in any such proceeding the Attorney General may file with the clerk of such court a request that a court of three judges be convened to hear and determine the case. Such request by the Attorney General shall be accompanied by a certificate that, in his opinion, the case is of general public importance. A copy of the certificate and request for a three-judge court shall be immediately furnished by such clerk to the chief judge of the circuit (or in his absence, the presiding circuit judge of the circuit) in which the case is pending. Upon receipt of such request it shall be the duty of the chief judge of the circuit or the presiding circuit judge, as the case may be, to designate immediately three judges in such circuit, of whom at least one shall be a circuit judge and another of whom shall be a district judge of the court in which the proceeding was instituted, to hear and determine such case, and it shall be the duty of the judges so designated to assign the case for hearing at the earliest practicable date, to participate in the hearing and determination thereof, and to cause the case to be in every way expedited. An appeal from the final judgment of such court will lie to the Supreme Court.

In the event the Attorney General fails to file such a request in any such proceeding, it shall be the duty of the chief judge of the district (or in his absence, the acting chief judge) in which the case is pending immediately to designate a judge in such district to hear and determine the case. In the event that no judge in the district is available to hear and determine the case, the chief judge of the district, or the acting chief judge, as the case may be, shall certify this fact to the chief judge of the circuit (or in his absence, the acting chief judge) who shall then designate a district or circuit judge of the circuit to hear and determine the case.

It shall be the duty of the judge designated pursuant to this section to assign the case for hearing at the earliest practicable date and to cause the case to be in every way expedited.

(c) Effective two years after March 24, 1972, the functions of the Attorney General under this section shall be transferred to the Commission, together with such personnel, property, records, and unexpended balances of appropriations, allocations, and other funds employed, used, held, available, or to be made available in connection with such functions unless the President submits, and neither House of Congress vetoes, a reorganization plan pursuant to chapter 9 of Title 5, inconsistent with the provisions of this subsection. The Commission shall carry out such functions in accordance with subsections (d) and (e) of this section.

(d) Upon the transfer of functions provided for in subsection (c) of this section, in all suits commenced pursuant to this section prior to the date of such transfer, proceedings shall continue without abatement, all court orders and decrees shall remain in effect, and the Commission shall be substituted as a party for the United States of America, the Attorney General, or the Acting Attorney General, as appropriate.

(e) Subsequent to March 24, 1972, the Commission shall have authority to investigate and act on a charge of a pattern or practice of discrimination, whether filed by or on behalf of a person claiming to be aggrieved or by a member of the Commission. All such actions shall be conducted in accordance with the procedures set forth in section 2000e-5 of this title.

Sec. 708. Effect on state laws

Nothing in this subchapter shall be deemed to exempt or relieve any person from any liability, duty, penalty, or punishment provided by any present or future law of any State or political subdivision of a State, other than any such law which purports to require or permit the doing of any act which would be an unlawful employment practice under this subchapter.

Sec. 709. Investigations

(a) In connection with any investigation of a charge filed under section 2000e-5 of this title, the Commission or its designated representative shall at all reasonable times have access to, for the purposes of examination, and the right to copy any evidence of any person being investigated or proceeded against that relates to unlawful employment practices covered by this subchapter and is relevant to the charge under investigation.

(b) The Commission may cooperate with State and local agencies charged with the administration of State fair employment practices laws and, with the consent of such agencies, may, for the purpose of carrying out its functions and duties under this subchapter and within the limitation of funds appropriated specifically for such purpose, engage in and contribute to the cost of research and other projects of mutual interest undertaken by such agencies, and utilize the services of such agencies and their employees, and, notwithstanding any other provision of law, pay by advance or reimbursement such agencies and their employees for services rendered to assist the Commission in carrying out this subchapter. In furtherance of such cooperative efforts, the Commission may enter into written agreements with such State or local agencies and such agreements may include provisions under which the Commission shall refrain from processing a charge in any cases or class of cases specified in such agreements or under which the Commission shall relieve any person or class of persons in such State or locality from requirements imposed under this section. The Commission shall rescind any such agreement whenever it determines that the agreement no longer serves the interest of effective enforcement of this subchapter.

(c) Every employer, employment agency, and labor organization subject to this subchapter shall (1) make and keep such records relevant to the determinations of whether unlawful employment practices have been or are being committed, (2) preserve such records for such periods, and (3) make such reports therefrom as the Commission shall prescribe by regulation or order, after public hearing, as reasonable, necessary, or appropriate for the enforcement of this subchapter or the regulations or orders thereunder. The Commission shall, by regulation, require each employer, labor organization, and joint labor-management committee subject to this subchapter which controls an apprenticeship or other training program to maintain such records as are reasonably necessary to carry out the purposes of this subchapter, including, but not limited to, a list of applicants who wish to participate in such program, including the chronological order in which applications were received, and to furnish to the Commission upon request, a detailed description of the manner in which persons are selected to participate in the apprenticeship or other training program. Any employer, employment agency, labor organization, or joint labor-management committee which believes that the application to it of any regulation or order issued under this section would result in undue hardship may apply to the Commission for an exemption from the application of such regulation or order, and, if such application for an exemption is denied, bring a civil action in the United States district court for the district where such records are kept. If the Commission or the court, as the case may be, finds that the application of the regulation or order to the employer, employment agency, or labor organization in question would impose an undue hardship, the Commission or the court, as the case may be, may grant appropriate relief. If any person required to comply with the provisions of this subsection fails or refuses to do so, the United States district court for the district in which such person is found, resides, or transacts business, shall, upon application of the Commission, or the Attorney General in a case involving a government, governmental agency or political subdivision, have jurisdiction to issue to such person an order requiring him to comply.

(d) In prescribing requirements pursuant to subsection (c) of this section, the Commission shall consult with other interested State and Federal agencies and shall endeavor to coordinate its requirements with those adopted by such agencies. The Commission shall furnish upon request and without cost to any State or local agency charged with the administration of a fair employment practice law information obtained pursuant to subsection (c) of this section from any employer, employment agency, labor organization, or joint labor-management committee subject to the jurisdiction of such agency. Such information shall be furnished on condition that it not be made public by the recipient agency prior to the institution of a proceeding under State or local law involving such information. If this condition is violated by a recipient agency, the Commission may decline to honor subsequent requests pursuant to this subsection.

(e) It shall be unlawful for any officer or employee of the Commission to make public in any manner whatever any information obtained by the Commission pursuant to its authority under this section prior to the institution of any proceeding under this subchapter involving such information. Any officer or employee of the Commission who shall make public in any manner whatever any information in violation of this subsection shall be guilty of a misdemeanor and upon conviction thereof, shall be fined not more than $1,000, or imprisoned not more than one year.

Sec. 710. Conduct of hearings and investigations pursuant to section 161 of Title 29

For the purpose of all hearings and investigations conducted by the Commission or its duly authorized agents or agencies, section 161 of Title 29 shall apply.

Sec. 711. Posting of notices; penalties

(a) Every employer, employment agency, and labor organization, as the case may be, shall post and keep posted in conspicuous places upon its premises where notices to employees, applicants for employment, and members are customarily posted a notice to be prepared or approved by the Commission setting forth excerpts from, or summaries of, the pertinent provisions of this subchapter and information pertinent to the filing of a complaint.

(b) A willful violation of this section shall be punishable by a fine of not more than $100 for each separate offense.

Sec. 712. Veterans' special rights or preference

Nothing contained in this subchapter shall be construed to repeal or modify any Federal, State, territorial, or local law creating special rights or preference for veterans.

Sec. 713. Regulations; conformity of regulations with administrative procedure provisions; reliance on interpretations and instructions of commission

(a) The Commission shall have authority from time to time to issue, amend, or rescind suitable procedural regulations to carry out the provisions of this subchapter. Regulations issued under this section shall be in conformity with the standards and limitations of subchapter II of chapter 5 of Title 5.

(b) In any action or proceeding based on any alleged unlawful employment practice, no person shall be subject to any liability or punishment for or on account of (1) the commission by such person of an unlawful employment practice if he pleads and proves that the act or omission complained of was in good faith, in conformity with, and in reliance on any written interpretation or opinion of the Commission, or (2) the failure of such person to publish and file any information required by any provision of this subchapter if he pleads and proves that he failed to publish and file such information in good faith, in conformity with the instructions of the Commission issued under this subchapter regarding the filing of such information. Such a defense, if established, shall be a bar to the action or proceeding, notwithstanding that (A) after such act or omission, such interpretation or opinion is modified or rescinded or is determined by judicial authority to be invalid or of no legal effect, or (B) after publishing or filing the description and annual reports, such publication or filing is determined by judicial authority not to be in conformity with the requirements of this subchapter.

Sec. 714. Application to personnel of commission of sections 111 and 1114 of Title 18; punishment for violation of section 1114 of Title 18

The provisions of sections 111 and 1114, Title 18, shall apply to officers, agents, and employees of the Commission in the performance of their official duties. Notwithstanding the provisions of sections 111 and 1114 of Title 18, whoever in violation of the provisions of section 1114 of such title kills a person while engaged in or on account of the performance of his official functions under this Act shall be punished by imprisonment for any term of years or for life.

Sec. 715. Equal Employment Opportunity Coordinating Council; establishment; composition; duties; report to President and Congress

The Equal Employment Opportunity Commission shall have the responsibility for developing and implementing agreements, policies, and practices designed to maximize effort, promote efficiency, and eliminate conflict, competition, duplication and inconsistency among the operations, functions and jurisdictions of the various departments, agencies and branches of the Federal Government responsible for the implementation and enforcement of equal employment opportunity legislation, orders, and policies. On or before October 1 of each year, the Equal Employment Opportunity Commission shall transmit to the President and to the Congress a report of its activities, together with such recommendations for legislative or administrative changes as it concludes are desirable to further promote the purposes of this section.

Sec. 716. Presidential conferences; acquaintance of leadership with provisions for employment rights and obligations; plans for fair administration; membership

The President shall, as soon as feasible after July 2, 1964, convene one or more conferences for the purpose of enabling the leaders of groups whose members will be affected by this subchapter to become familiar with the rights afforded and obligations imposed by its provisions, and for the purpose of making plans which will result in the fair and effective administration of this subchapter when all of its provisions become effective. The President shall invite the participation in such conference or conferences of (1) the members of the President's Committee on Equal Employment Opportunity, (2) the members of the Commission on Civil Rights, (3) representatives of State and local agencies engaged in furthering equal employment opportunity, (4) representatives of private agencies engaged in furthering equal employment opportunity, and (5) representatives of employers, labor organizations, and employment agencies who will be subject to this subchapter.

Sec. 717. Employment by federal government

(a) All personnel actions affecting employees or applicants for employment (except with regard to aliens employed outside the limits of the United States) in military departments as defined in section 102 of Title 5, in executive agencies as defined in section 105 of Title 5 (including employees and applicants for employment who are paid from nonappropriated funds), in the United States Postal Service and the Postal Rate Commission, in those units of the Government of the District of Columbia having positions in the competitive service, and in those units of the legislative and judicial branches of the Federal Government having positions in the competitive service, and in the Library of Congress shall be made free from any discrimination based on race, color, religion, sex, or national origin.

(b) Except as otherwise provided in this subsection, the Equal Employment Opportunity Commission shall have authority to enforce the provisions of subsection (a) of this section through appropriate remedies, including reinstatement or hiring of employees with or without back pay, as will effectuate the policies of this section, and shall issue such rules, regulations, orders and instructions as it deems necessary and appropriate to carry out its responsibilities under this section. The Equal Employment Opportunity Commission shall—

(1) be responsible for the annual review and approval of a national and regional equal employment opportunity plan which each department and agency and each appropriate unit referred to in subsection (a) of this section shall submit in order to maintain an affirmative program of equal employment opportunity for all such employees and applicants for employment;

(2) be responsible for the review and evaluation of the operation of all agency equal employment opportunity programs, periodically obtaining and publishing (on at least a semiannual basis) progress reports from each such department, agency, or unit; and

(3) consult with and solicit the recommendations of interested individuals, groups, and organizations relating to equal employment opportunity.

The head of each such department, agency, or unit shall comply with such rules, regulations, orders, and instructions which shall include a provision that an employee or applicant for employment shall be notified of any final action taken on any complaint of discrimination filed by him thereunder. The plan submitted by each department, agency, and unit shall include, but not be limited to—

(1) provision for the establishment of training and education programs designed to provide a maximum opportunity for employees to advance so as to perform at their highest potential; and

(2) a description of the qualifications in terms of training and experience relating to equal employment opportunity for the principal and operating officials of each such department, agency, or unit responsible for carrying out the equal employment opportunity program and of the allocation of personnel and resources proposed by such department, agency, or unit to carry out its equal employment opportunity program.

With respect to employment in the Library of Congress, authorities granted in this subsection to the Equal Employment Opportunity Commission shall be exercised by the Librarian of Congress.

(c) Within 90 days of receipt of notice of final action taken by a department, agency, or unit referred to in subsection (a) of this section, or by the Equal Employment Opportunity Commission upon an appeal from a decision or order of such department, agency, or unit on a complaint of discrimination based on race, color, religion, sex or national origin, brought pursuant to subsection (a) of this section, Executive Order 11478 or any succeeding Executive orders, or after one hundred and eighty days from the filing of the initial charge with the department, agency, or unit or with the Equal Employment Opportunity Commission on appeal from a decision or order of such department, agency, or unit until such time as final action may be taken by a department, agency, or unit, an employee or applicant for employment, if aggrieved by the final disposition of his complaint, or by the failure to take final action on his complaint, may file a civil action as provided in section 2000e-5 of this title, in which civil action the head of the department, agency, or unit, as appropriate, shall be the defendant.

(d) The provisions of section 2005e-5 (f) through (k) of this title, as applicable, shall govern civil actions brought hereunder, and the same interest to compensate for delay in payment shall be available as in cases involving nonpublic parties.

(e) Nothing contained in this Act shall relieve any Government agency or official of its or his primary responsibility to assure nondiscrimination in employment as required by the Constitution and statutes or of its or his responsibilities under Executive Order 11478 relating to equal employment opportunity in the Federal Government.

Sec. 718. Procedure for denial, withholding, termination, or suspension of government contract subsequent to acceptance by government of affirmative action plan of employer; time of acceptance of plan

No Government contract, or portion thereof, with any employer, shall be denied, withheld, terminated, or suspended, by any agency or officer of the United States under any equal employment opportunity law or order, where such employer has an affirmative action plan which has previously been accepted by the Government for the same facility within the past twelve months without first according such employer full hearing and adjudication under the provisions of section 554 of Title 5, and the following pertinent sections: Provided, That if such employer has deviated substantially from such previously agreed to affirmative action plan, this section shall not apply: Provided further, That for the purposes of this section an affirmative action plan shall be deemed to have been accepted by the Government at the time the appropriate compliance agency has accepted such plan unless within forty-five days thereafter the Office of Federal Contract Compliance has disapproved such plan.

APPENDIX B

TEXT OF TITLE 42 U.S.C. SECTION 1981

42 U.S.C. Section 1981, as amended by the Civil Rights Act of 1991, P.L. 102–166

Equal Rights under the Law

Section 1981.

(a) All persons within the jurisdiction of the United States shall have the same right in every State and Territory to make and enforce contracts, to sue, be parties, give evidence, and to the full and equal benefit of all laws and proceedings for the security of persons and property as is enjoyed by white citizens, and shall be subject to like punishment, pains, penalties, taxes, licenses, and exactions of every kind, and to no other.

(b) For purposes of this section, the term "make and enforce contracts" includes the making, performance, modification, and termination of contracts, and the enjoyment of all benefits, privileges, terms, and conditions of the contractual relationship.

(c) The rights protected by this section are protected against impairment by nongovernmental discrimination and impairment under color of State law.

Damages in Cases of Intentional Discrimination in Employment

Sec. 1981a.

(a) Right of Recovery—

(1) Civil rights. In an action brought by a complaining party under section 706 or 717 of the Civil Rights Act of 1964 against a respondent who engaged in unlawful intentional discrimination (not an employment practice that is unlawful because of its disparate impact) prohibited under section 703, 704, or 717 of the Act, and provided that the complaining party cannot recover under section 1977 of the Revised Statutes (42 U.S.C. 1981), the complaining party may recover compensatory and punitive damages as allowed in subsection (b), in addition to any relief authorized by section 706(g) of the Civil Rights Act of 1964, from the respondent.

(2) Disability. In an action brought by a complaining party under the powers, remedies, and procedures set forth in section 706 or 717 of the Civil Rights Act of 1964 (as provided in section 107(a) of the Americans with Disabilities Act of 1990 (42 U.S.C. 12117(a)), and section 505(a)(1) of the Rehabilitation Act of 1973 (29 U.S.C. 794a(a)(1)), respectively) against a respondent who engaged in unlawful intentional discrimination (not an employment practice that is unlawful because of its disparate impact) under section 501 of the Rehabilitation Act of 1973 (29 U.S.C. 791) and the regulations implementing section 501, or who violated the requirements of section 501 of the Act or the regulations implementing section 501 concerning the provision of a reasonable accommodation, or section 102 of the Americans with Disabilities Act of 1990 (42 U.S.C. 12112), or committed a violation of section 102(b)(5) of the Act, against an individual, the complaining party may recover compensatory and punitive damages as allowed in subsection (b), in addition to any relief authorized by section 706(g) of the Civil Rights Act of 1964, from the respondent.

(3) Reasonable accommodation and good faith effort. In cases where a discriminatory practice involves the provision of a reasonable accommodation pursuant to section 102(b)(5) of the Americans with Disabilities Act of 1990 or regulations implementing section 501 of the Rehabilitation Act of 1973, damages may not be

awarded under this section where the covered entity demonstrates good faith efforts, in consultation with the person with the disability who has informed the covered entity that accommodation is needed, to identify and make a reasonable accommodation that would provide such individual with an equally effective opportunity and would not cause an undue hardship on the operation of the business.

(b) Compensatory and Punitive Damages—
 (1) Determination of punitive damages. A complaining party may recover punitive damages under this section against a respondent (other than a government, government agency or political subdivision) if the complaining party demonstrates that the respondent engaged in a discriminatory practice or discriminatory practices with malice or with reckless indifference to the federally protected rights of an aggrieved individual.
 (2) Exclusions from compensatory damages. Compensatory damages awarded under this section shall not include backpay, interest on backpay, or any other type of relief authorized under section 706(g) of the Civil Rights Act of 1964.
 (3) Limitations. The sum of the amount of compensatory damages awarded under this section for future pecuniary losses, emotional pain, suffering, inconvenience, mental anguish, loss of enjoyment of life, and other nonpecuniary losses, and the amount of punitive damages awarded under this section, shall not exceed, for each complaining party—
  (A) in the case of a respondent who has more than 14 and fewer than 101 employees in each of 20 or more calendar weeks in the current or preceding calendar year, $50,000;
  (B) in the case of a respondent who has more than 100 and fewer than 201 employees in each of 20 or more calendar weeks in the current or preceding calendar year, $100,000; and
  (C) in the case of a respondent who has more than 200 and fewer than 501 employees in each of 20 or more calendar weeks in the current or preceding calendar year, $200,000; and
  (D) in the case of a respondent who has more than 500 employees in each of 20 or more calendar weeks in the current or preceding calendar year, $300,000.
 (4) Construction. Nothing in this section shall be construed to limit the scope of, or the relief available under, section 1977 of the Revised Statutes (42 U.S.C. 1981).

(c) Jury Trial. If a complaining party seeks compensatory or punitive damages under this section—
 (1) any party may demand a trial by jury; and
 (2) the court shall not inform the jury of the limitations described in subsection (b)(3).

(d) Definitions. As used in this section:
 (1) Complaining party. The term "complaining party" means—
  (A) in the case of a person seeking to bring an action under subsection (a)(1), the Equal Employment Opportunity Commission, the Attorney General, or a person who may bring an action or proceeding under title VII of the Civil Rights Act of 1964 (42 U.S.C. 2000e et seq.); or
  (B) in the case of a person seeking to bring an action under subsection (a)(2), the Equal Employment Opportunity Commission, the Attorney General, a person who may bring an action or proceeding under section 505(a)(1) of the Rehabilitation Act of 1973 (29 U.S.C. 794a(a)(1)), or a person who may bring an action or proceeding under title I of the Americans with Disabilities Act of 1990 (42 U.S.C. 12101 et seq.).
 (2) Discriminatory practice. The term "discriminatory practice" means the discrimination described in paragraph (1), or the discrimination or the violation described in paragraph (2), of subsection (a).

APPENDIX C

EXTRACTS FROM THE AGE DISCRIMINATION IN EMPLOYMENT ACT

29 U.S.C. Section 621 et seq., as amended by P.L. 99–592 (1986); P.L. 101–433 (1990); P.L. 102–166 (1991); and P.L. 104–208 (1996)

Congressional Statement of Findings and Purpose

Section 621.

(a) The Congress hereby finds and declares that—
   (1) in the face of rising productivity and affluence, older workers find themselves disadvantaged in their efforts to retain employment, and especially to regain employment when displaced from jobs;
   (2) the setting of arbitrary age limits regardless of potential for job performance has become a common practice, and certain otherwise desirable practices may work to the disadvantage of older persons;
   (3) the incidence of unemployment, especially long-term unemployment with resultant deterioration of skill, morale, and employer acceptability is, relative to the younger ages, high among older workers; their numbers are great and growing; and their employment problems grave;
   (4) the existence in industries affecting commerce, of arbitrary discrimination in employment because of age, burdens commerce and the free flow of goods in commerce.

(b) It is therefore the purpose of this chapter to promote employment of older persons based on their ability rather than age; to prohibit arbitrary age discrimination in employment; to help employers and workers find ways of meeting problems arising from the impact of age on employment.

Sec. 623. Prohibition of age discrimination

(a) Employer practices
It shall be unlawful for an employer—
   (1) to fail or refuse to hire or to discharge any individual or otherwise discriminate against any individual with respect to his compensation, terms, conditions, or privileges of employment, because of such individual's age;
   (2) to limit, segregate, or classify his employees in any way which would deprive or tend to deprive any individual of employment opportunities or otherwise adversely affect his status as an employee, because of such individual's age; or
   (3) to reduce the wage rate of any employee in order to comply with this chapter.

(b) Employment agency practices
It shall be unlawful for an employment agency to fail or refuse to refer for employment, or otherwise to discriminate against, any individual because of such individual's age, or to classify or refer for employment any individual on the basis of such individual's age.

(c) Labor organization practices
It shall be unlawful for a labor organization—
   (1) to exclude or to expel from its membership, or otherwise to discriminate against, any individual because of his age;
   (2) to limit, segregate, or classify its membership, or to classify or fail or refuse to refer for employment any individual, in any way which would deprive or tend to deprive any individual of employment opportunities or would limit such employment opportunities or otherwise adversely affect his status as an employee or as an applicant for employment, because of such individual's age;
   (3) to cause or attempt to cause an employer to discriminate against an individual in violation of this section.

(d) Opposition to unlawful practices; participation in investigations, proceedings, or litigation

It shall be unlawful for an employer to discriminate against any of his employees or applicants for employment, for an employment agency to discriminate against any individual, or for a labor organization to discriminate against any member thereof or applicant for membership, because such individual, member or applicant for membership has opposed any practice made unlawful by this section, or because such individual, member or applicant for membership has made a charge, testified, assisted, or participated in any manner in an investigation, proceeding, or litigation under this chapter.

(e) Printing or publication of notice or advertisement indicating preference, limitation, etc.
It shall be unlawful for an employer, labor organization, or employment agency to print or publish, or cause to be printed or published, any notice or advertisement relating to employment by such an employer or membership in or any classification or referral for employment by such a labor organization, or relating to any classification or referral for employment by such an employment agency, indicating any preference, limitation, specification, or discrimination, based on age.

(f) Lawful practices; age as occupational qualification; other reasonable factors; laws of foreign workplace; seniority system; employee benefit plans; discharge or discipline for good cause
It shall not be unlawful for an employer, employment agency, or labor organization—
(1) to take any action otherwise prohibited under subsections (a), (b), (c), or (e) of this section where age is a bona fide occupational qualification reasonably necessary to the normal operation of the particular business, or where the differentiation is based on reasonable factors other than age, or where such practices involve an employee in a workplace in a foreign country, and compliance with such subsections would cause such employer, or a corporation controlled by such employer, to violate the laws of the country in which such workplace is located;
(2) to take any action otherwise prohibited under subsection (a), (b), (c), or (e) of this section
(A) to observe the terms of a bona fide seniority system that is not intended to evade the purposes of this chapter, except that no such seniority system shall require or permit the involuntary retirement of any individual specified by section 631(a) of this title because of the age of such individual; or
(B) to observe the terms of a bona fide employee benefit plan—
(i) where, for each benefit or benefit package, the actual amount of payment made or cost incurred on behalf of an older worker is no less than that made or incurred on behalf of a younger worker, as permissible under section 1625.10, title 29, Code of Federal Regulations (as in effect on June 22, 1989); or
(ii) that is a voluntary early retirement incentive plan consistent with the relevant purpose or purposes of this chapter.

Notwithstanding clause (i) or (ii) of subparagraph (B), no such employee benefit plan or voluntary early retirement incentive plan shall excuse the failure to hire any individual, and no such employee benefit plan shall require or permit the involuntary retirement of any individual specified by section 631(a) of this title, because of the age of such individual. An employer, employment agency, or labor organization acting under subparagraph (A), or under clause (i) or (ii) of subparagraph (B), shall have the burden of proving that such actions are lawful in any civil enforcement proceeding brought under this chapter; or
(3) to discharge or otherwise discipline an individual for good cause.

(g) Repealed. [Pub.L. 101–239, Title VI, § 6202(b)(3)(C)(i), Dec. 19, 1989, 103 Stat. 2233]

(h) Practices of foreign corporations controlled by American employers; foreign employers not controlled by American employers; factors determining control
(1) If an employer controls a corporation whose place of incorporation is in a foreign country, any practice by such corporation prohibited under this section shall be presumed to be such practice by such employer.
(2) The prohibitions of this section shall not apply where the employer is a foreign person not controlled by an American employer.
(3) For the purpose of this subsection the determination of whether an employer controls a corporation shall be based upon the—
(A) interrelation of operations,
(B) common management,

(C) centralized control of labor relations, and
(D) common ownership or financial control, of the employer and the corporation.

(i) Employee pension benefit plans; cessation or reduction of benefit accrual or of allocation to employee account; distribution of benefits after attainment of normal retirement age; compliance; highly compensated employees

(1) Except as otherwise provided in this subsection, it shall be unlawful for an employer, an employment agency, a labor organization, or any combination thereof to establish or maintain an employee pension benefit plan which requires or permits

(A) in the case of a defined benefit plan, the cessation of an employee's benefit accrual, or the reduction of the rate of an employee's benefit accrual, because of age, or

(B) in the case of a defined contribution plan, the cessation of allocations to an employee's account, or the reduction of the rate at which amounts are allocated to an employee's account, because of age.

(2) Nothing in this section shall be construed to prohibit an employer, employment agency, or labor organization from observing any provision of an employee pension benefit plan to the extent that such provision imposes (without regard to age) a limitation on the amount of benefits that the plan provides or a limitation on the number of years of service or years of participation which are taken into account for purposes of determining benefit accrual under the plan.

(3) In the case of any employee who, as of the end of any plan year under a defined benefit plan, has attained normal retirement age under such plan—

(A) if distribution of benefits under such plan with respect to such employee has commenced as of the end of such plan year, then any requirement of this subsection for continued accrual of benefits under such plan with respect to such employee during such plan year shall be treated as satisfied to the extent of the actuarial equivalent of in-service distribution of benefits, and

(B) if distribution of benefits under such plan with respect to such employee has not commenced as of the end of such year in accordance with section 1056(a)(3) of this title and section 401(a)(14)(C) of Title 26, and the payment of benefits under such plan with respect to such employee is not suspended during such plan year pursuant to section 1053(a)(3)(B) of this title or section 411(a)(3)(B) of Title 26, then any requirement of this subsection for continued accrual of benefits under such plan with respect to such employee during such plan year shall be treated as satisfied to the extent of any adjustment in the benefit payable under the plan during such plan year attributable to the delay in the distribution of benefits after the attainment of normal retirement age.

The provisions of this paragraph shall apply in accordance with regulations of the Secretary of the Treasury. Such regulations shall provide for the application of the preceding provisions of this paragraph to all employee pension benefit plans subject to this subsection and may provide for the application of such provisions, in the case of any such employee, with respect to any period of time within a plan year.

(4) Compliance with the requirements of this subsection with respect to an employee pension benefit plan shall constitute compliance with the requirements of this section relating to benefit accrual under such plan.

(5) Paragraph (1) shall not apply with respect to any employee who is a highly compensated employee (within the meaning of section 414(q) of Title 26) to the extent provided in regulations prescribed by the Secretary of the Treasury for purposes of precluding discrimination in favor of highly compensated employees within the meaning of subchapter D of chapter 1 of Title 26.

(6) A plan shall not be treated as failing to meet the requirements of paragraph (1) solely because the subsidized portion of any early retirement benefit is disregarded in determining benefit accruals.

(7) Any regulations prescribed by the Secretary of the Treasury pursuant to clause (v) of section 411(b)(1)(H) of Title 26 and subparagraphs

(C) and (D) of section 411(b)(2) of Title 26 shall apply with respect to the requirements of this subsection in the same manner and to the same extent as such regulations apply with respect to the requirements of such sections 411(b)(1)(H) and 411(b)(2) of Title 26.

(8) A plan shall not be treated as failing to meet the requirements of this section solely because such plan provides a normal retirement age described in section 1002(24)(B) of this title and section 411(a)(8)(3) of Title 26.

(9) For purposes of this subsection—

(A) The terms "employee pension benefit plan", "defined benefit plan", "defined contribution plan", and "normal retirement age" have the meanings provided such terms in section 1002 of this title.

(B) The term "compensation" has the meaning provided by section 414(s) of Title 26.

(j) Employment as firefighter or law enforcement officer

It shall not be unlawful for an employer which is a State, a political subdivision of a State, an agency or instrumentality of a State or a political subdivision of a State, or an interstate agency to fail or refuse to hire or to discharge any individual because of such individual's age if such action is taken—

(1) with respect to the employment of an individual as a firefighter or as a law enforcement officer, the employer has complied with section 3(d) (2) of the Age Discrimination in Employment Amendments of 1996 if the individual was discharged after the date described in such section, and the individual has attained—

(A) the age of hiring or retirement, respectively, in effect under applicable State or local law on March 3, 1983; or

(B) (i) if the individual was not hired, the age of hiring in effect on the date of such failure or refusal to hire under applicable State or local law enacted after September 30, 1996; or

(ii) if applicable State or local law was enacted after September 30, 1996, and the individual was discharged, the higher of—

(I) the age of retirement in effect on the date of such discharge under such law; and

(II) age 55; and

(2) pursuant to a bona fide hiring or retirement plan that is not a subterfuge to evade the purposes of this chapter.

(k) Seniority system or employee benefit plan; compliance

A seniority system or employee benefit plan shall comply with this chapter regardless of the date of adoption of such system or plan.

(l) Lawful practices; minimum age as condition of eligibility for retirement benefits; deductions from severance pay; reduction of long-term disability benefits

Notwithstanding clause (i) or (ii) of subsection (f)(2)(B) of this section—

(1) it shall not be a violation of subsection (a), (b), (c), or (e) of this section solely because—

(A) an employee pension benefit plan (as defined in section 1002 (2) of this title) provides for the attainment of a minimum age as a condition of eligibility for normal or early retirement benefits; or

(B) a defined benefit plan (as defined in section 1002(35) of this title) provides for—

(i) payments that constitute the subsidized portion of an early retirement benefit; or

(ii) social security supplements for plan participants that commence before the age and terminate at the age (specified by the plan) when participants are eligible to receive reduced or unreduced old-age insurance benefits under title II of the Social Security Act (42 U.S.C. 401 et seq.), and that do not exceed such old-age insurance benefits.

(2) (A) It shall not be a violation of subsection (a), (b), (c), or (e) of this section solely because following a contingent event unrelated to age—

(i) the value of any retiree health benefits received by an individual eligible for an immediate pension;

(ii) the value of any additional pension benefits that are made available solely as a result of the contingent event unrelated to age and following which the individual is eligible for not less than an immediate and unreduced pension; or

(iii) the values described in both clauses (i) and (ii); are deducted from severance pay made available as a result of the contingent event unrelated to age.

(B) For an individual who receives immediate pension benefits that are actuarially reduced under subparagraph (A)(i), the amount of the deduction available pursuant to subparagraph (A)(i) shall be reduced by the same percentage as the reduction in the pension benefits.

(C) For purposes of this paragraph, severance pay shall include that portion of supplemental unemployment compensation benefits (as described in section 501 (c)(17) of Title 26) that—

(i) constitutes additional benefits of up to 52 weeks;

(ii) has the primary purpose and effect of continuing benefits until an individual becomes eligible for an immediate and unreduced pension; and

(iii) is discontinued once the individual becomes eligible for an immediate and unreduced pension.

(D) For purposes of this paragraph and solely in order to make the deduction authorized under this paragraph, the term "retiree health benefits" means benefits provided pursuant to a group health plan covering retirees, for which (determined as of the contingent event unrelated to age)—

(i) the package of benefits provided by the employer for the retirees who are below age 65 is at least comparable to benefits provided under title XVIII of the Social Security Act (42 U.S.C. 1395 et seq.);

(ii) the package of benefits provided by the employer for the retirees who are age 65 and above is at least comparable to that offered under a plan that provides a benefit package with one-fourth the value of benefits provided under title XVIII of such Act; or

(iii) the package of benefits provided by the employer is as described in clauses (i) and (ii).

(E) (i) If the obligation of the employer to provide retiree health benefits is of limited duration, the value for each individual shall be calculated at a rate of $3,000 per year for benefit years before age 65, and $750 per year for benefit years beginning at age 65 and above.

(ii) If the obligation of the employer to provide retiree health benefits is of unlimited duration, the value for each individual shall be calculated at a rate of $48,000 for individuals below age 65, and $24,000 for individuals age 65 and above.

(iii) The values described in clauses (i) and (ii) shall be calculated based on the age of the individual as of the date of the contingent event unrelated to age. The values are effective on October 16, 1990, and shall be adjusted on an annual basis, with respect to a contingent event that occurs subsequent to the first year after October 16, 1990, based on the medical component of the Consumer Price Index for all-urban consumers published by the Department of Labor.

(iv) If an individual is required to pay a premium for retiree health benefits, the value calculated pursuant to this subparagraph shall be reduced by whatever percentage of the overall premium the individual is required to pay.

(F) If an employer that has implemented a deduction pursuant to subparagraph (A) fails to fulfill the obligation described in subparagraph (E), any aggrieved individual may bring an action for specific performance of the obligation described in subparagraph (E). The relief shall be in addition to any other remedies provided under Federal or State law.

(3) It shall not be a violation of subsection (a), (b), (c), or (e) of this section solely because an employer provides a bona fide employee benefit plan or plans under which long-term disability benefits received by an individual are reduced by any pension benefits (other than those attributable to employee contributions)—
    (A) paid to the individual that the individual voluntarily elects to receive; or
    (B) for which an individual who has attained the later of age 62 or normal retirement age is eligible.

Administration

Sec. 625. The Secretary shall have the power—

(a) to make delegations, to appoint such agents and employees, and to pay for technical assistance on a fee for service basis, as he deems necessary to assist him in the performance of his functions under this chapter;

(b) to cooperate with regional, State, local, and other agencies, and to cooperate with and furnish technical assistance to employers, labor organizations, and employment agencies to aid in effectuating the purposes of this chapter.

Recordkeeping, Investigation, and Enforcement

Sec. 626.

(a) The Commission shall have the power to make investigations and require the keeping of records necessary or appropriate for the administration of this chapter in accordance with the powers and procedures provided in sections 209 and 211 of this title.

(b) The provisions of this chapter shall be enforced in accordance with the powers, remedies, and procedures provided in sections 211(b), 216 (except for subsection (a) thereof), and 217 of this title, and subsection (c) of this section. Any act prohibited under section 623 of this title shall be deemed to be a prohibited act under section 215 of this title. Amounts owing to a person as a result of a violation of this chapter shall be deemed to be unpaid minimum wages or unpaid overtime compensation for purposes of sections 216 and 217 of this title: *Provided,* That liquidated damages shall be payable only in cases of willful violations of this chapter. In any action brought to enforce this chapter the court shall have jurisdiction to grant such legal or equitable relief as may be appropriate to effectuate the purposes of this chapter, including without limitation judgments compelling employment, reinstatement or promotion, or enforcing the liability for amounts deemed to be unpaid minimum wages or unpaid overtime compensation under this section. Before instituting any action under this section, the Commission shall attempt to eliminate the discriminatory practice or practices alleged, and to effect voluntary compliance with the requirements of this chapter through informal methods of conciliation, conference, and persuasion.

(c) (1) Any person aggrieved may bring a civil action in any court of competent jurisdiction for such legal or equitable relief as will effectuate the purposes of this chapter: *Provided,* That the right of any person to bring such action shall terminate upon the commencement of an action by the Commission to enforce the right of such employee under this chapter.
    (2) In an action brought under paragraph (1), a person shall be entitled to a trial by jury of any issue of fact in any such action for recovery of amounts owing as a result of a violation of this chapter, regardless of whether equitable relief is sought by any party in such action.

(d) No civil action may be commenced by an individual under this section until 60 days after a charge alleging unlawful discrimination has been filed with the Commission. Such a charge shall be filed—
    (1) within 180 days after the alleged unlawful practice occurred; or
    (2) in a case to which section 633(b) of this title applies, within 300 days after the alleged unlawful practice occurred, or within 30 days after receipt by the individual of notice of termination of proceeding under State law, whichever is earlier.

    Upon receiving such a charge, the Commission shall promptly notify all persons named in such charge as prospective defendants in the action and shall promptly seek to eliminate any alleged unlawful practice by informal methods of conciliation, conference, and persuasion.

(e) Section 259 of this title shall apply to actions under this chapter. If a charge filed with the Commission under this Act is dismissed or the proceedings of the Commission are otherwise terminated by the Commission, the Commission shall notify the person aggrieved. A civil action may be brought under this section by a person defined in section 11(a) against the respondent named in the charge within 90 days after the date of the receipt of such notice.

(f) (1) An individual may not waive any right or claim under this Act unless the waiver is knowing and voluntary. Except as provided in paragraph (2), a waiver may not be considered knowing and voluntary unless at a minimum—

(A) the waiver is part of an agreement between the individual and written in a manner calculated to be understood by such individual, or by the average individual eligible to participate;

(B) the waiver specifically refers to rights or claims arising under this Act;

(C) the individual does not waive rights or claims that may arise after the date the waiver is executed;

(D) the individual waives rights to claims only in exchange for consideration in addition to anything of value to which the individual already is entitled;

(E) the individual is advised in writing to consult with an attorney prior to executing the agreement;

(F) (i) the individual is given a period of at least 21 days within which to consider the agreement; or

(ii) if a waiver is requested in connection with an exit incentive or other employment termination program offered to a group or class of employees, the individual is given a period of at least 45 days within which to consider the agreement;

(G) the agreement provides that for a period of at least 7 days following the execution of such agreement, the individual may revoke the agreement, and the agreement shall not become effective or enforceable until the revocation period has expired;

(H) if a waiver is requested in connection with an exit incentive or other employment termination program offered to a group or class of employees, the employer (at the commencement of the period specified in subparagraph (F)) informs the individual in writing in a manner calculated to be understood by the average individual eligible to participate, as to—

(i) any class, unit, or group of individuals covered by such program, any eligibility factors for such program, and any time limits applicable to such program; and

(ii) the job titles and ages of all individuals eligible or selected for the program, and the ages of all individuals in the same job classification or organizational unit who are not eligible or selected for the program.

(2) A waiver in settlement of a charge filed with the Equal Employment Opportunity Commission, or an action filed in court by the individual or the individual's representative, alleging age discrimination of a kind prohibited under section 4 or 15 may not be considered knowing and voluntary unless at a minimum—

(A) subparagraphs (A) through (E) of paragraph (1) have been met; and

(B) the individual is given a reasonable period of time within which to consider the settlement agreement.

(3) In any dispute that may arise over whether any of the requirements, conditions, and circumstances set forth in subparagraph (A), (B), (C), (D), (E), (F), (G), or (H) of paragraph (1), or subparagraph (A) or (B) of paragraph (2), have been met, the party asserting the validity of a waiver shall have the burden of proving in a court of competent jurisdiction that a waiver was knowing and voluntary pursuant to paragraph (1) or (2).

(4) No waiver agreement may affect the Commission's rights and responsibilities to enforce this Act. No waiver may be used to justify interfering with the protected right of an employee to file a charge or participate in an investigation or proceeding conducted by the Commission.

Notices to Be Posted

Sec. 627. Every employer, employment agency, and labor organization shall post and keep posted in conspicuous places upon its premises a notice to be prepared or approved by the Commission setting forth information as the Commission deems appropriate to effectuate the purposes of this chapter.

Rules and Regulations; Exemptions

Sec. 628. In accordance with the provisions of subchapter II of chapter 5 of Title 5, the Equal Employment Opportunity Commission may issue such rules and regulations as it may consider necessary or appropriate for carrying out this chapter, and may establish such reasonable exemptions to and from any or all provisions of this chapter as it may find necessary and proper in the public interest.

Criminal Penalties

Sec. 629. Whoever shall forcibly resist, oppose, impede, intimidate or interfere with a duly authorized representative of the Equal Employment Opportunity Commission while it is engaged in the performance of duties under this chapter shall be punished by a fine of not more than $500 or by imprisonment for not more than one year, or by both: *Provided,* however, That no person shall be imprisoned under this section except when there has been a prior conviction hereunder.

Definitions

Sec. 630. For the purposes of this chapter—

(a) The term "person" means one or more individuals, partnerships, associations, labor organizations, corporations, business trusts, legal representatives, or any organized groups of persons.

(b) The term "employer" means a person engaged in an industry affecting commerce who has twenty or more employees for each working day in each of twenty or more calendar weeks in the current or preceding calendar year: *Provided,* That prior to June 30, 1968, employers having fewer than fifty employees shall not be considered employers. The term also means (1) any agent of such a person, and (2) a State or political subdivision of a State and any agency or instrumentality of a State or a political subdivision of a State, and any interstate agency, but such term does not include the United States, or a corporation wholly owned by the Government of the United States.

(c) The term "employment agency" means any person regularly undertaking with or without compensation to procure employees for an employer and includes an agent of such a person; but shall not include an agency of the United States.

(d) The term "labor organization" means a labor organization engaged in an industry affecting commerce, and any agent of such an organization, and includes any organization of any kind, any agency, or employee representation committee, group, association, or plan so engaged in which employees participate and which exists for the purpose, in whole or in part, of dealing with employers concerning grievances, labor disputes, wages, rates of pay, hours, or other terms or conditions of employment, and any conference, general committee, joint or system board, or joint council so engaged which is subordinate to a national or international labor organization.

(e) A labor organization shall be deemed to be engaged in an industry affecting commerce if (1) it maintains or operates a hiring hall or hiring office which procures employees for an employer or procures for employees opportunities to work for an employer, or (2) the number of its members (or, where it is a labor organization composed of other labor organizations or their representatives, if the aggregate number of the members of such other labor organization) is fifty or more prior to July 1, 1968, or twenty-five or more on or after July 1, 1968, and such labor organization—

(1) is the certified representative of employees under the provisions of the National Labor Relations Act, as amended, or the Railway Labor Act, as amended; or

(2) although not certified, is a national or international labor organization or a local labor organization recognized or acting as the representative of employees of an employer or employers engaged in an industry affecting commerce; or

(3) has chartered a local labor organization or subsidiary body which is representing or actively seeking to represent employees of employers within the meaning of paragraph (1) or (2); or

(4) has been chartered by a labor organization representing or actively seeking to represent employees within the meaning of paragraph (1) or (2) as the local or subordinate body through which such employees may enjoy membership or become affiliated with such labor organization; or

(5) is a conference, general committee, joint or system board, or joint council subordinate to a national or international labor organization,

which includes a labor organization engaged in an industry affecting commerce within the meaning of any of the preceding paragraphs and this subsection.

(f) The term "employee" means an individual employed by any employer except that the term "employee" shall not include any person elected to public office in any State or political subdivision of any State by the qualified voters thereof, or any person chosen by such officer to be on such officer's personal staff, or an appointee on the policymaking level or an immediate adviser with respect to the exercise of the constitutional or legal powers of the office. The exemption set forth in the preceding sentence shall not include employees subject to the civil service laws of a State government, governmental agency, or political subdivision.

(g) The term, "commerce" means trade, traffic, commerce, transportation, transmission, or communication among the several States; or between a State and any place outside thereof; or within the District of Columbia, or a possession of the United States; or between points in the same State but through a point outside thereof.

(h) The term "industry affecting commerce" means any activity, business, or industry in commerce or in which a labor dispute would hinder or obstruct commerce or the free flow of commerce and includes any activity or industry "affecting commerce" within the meaning of the Labor-Management Reporting and Disclosure Act of 1959.

(i) The term "State" includes a State of the United States, the District of Columbia, Puerto Rico, the Virgin Islands, American Samoa, Guam, Wake Island, the Canal Zone, and Outer Continental Shelf lands defined in the Outer Continental Shelf Lands Act.

(j) The term "firefighter" means an employee, the duties of whose position are primarily to perform work directly connected with the control and extinguishment of fires or the maintenance and use of firefighting apparatus and equipment, including an employee engaged in this activity who is transferred to a supervisory or administrative position.

(k) The term "law enforcement officer" means an employee, the duties of whose position are primarily the investigation, apprehension, or detention of individuals suspected or convicted of offenses against the criminal laws of a State, including an employee engaged in this activity who is transferred to a supervisory or administrative position. For the purpose of this subsection, "detention" includes the duties of employees assigned to guard individuals incarcerated in any penal institution.

(l) The term "compensation, terms, conditions, or privileges of employment" encompasses all employee benefits, including such benefits provided pursuant to a bona fide employee benefit plan.

Age Limits

Sec. 631.

(a) The prohibitions in this chapter shall be limited to individuals who are at least 40 years of age.

(b) In the case of any personnel action affecting employees or applicants for employment which is subject to the provisions of section 633a of this title, the prohibitions established in section 633a of this title shall be limited to individuals who are at least 40 years of age.

(c) (1) Nothing in this chapter shall be construed to prohibit compulsory retirement of any employee who has attained 65 years of age who, for the 2-year period immediately before retirement, is employed in a bona fide executive or a high policymaking position, if such employee is entitled to an immediate nonforfeitable annual retirement benefit from a pension, profit-sharing, savings, or deferred compensation plan, or any combination of such plans, of the employer of such employee, which equals, in the aggregate, at last $44,000.

(2) In applying the retirement benefit test of paragraph (1) of this subsection, if any such retirement benefit is in a form other than a straight life annuity (with no ancillary benefits), or if employees contribute to any such plan or make rollover contributions, such benefit shall be adjusted in accordance with regulations prescribed by the Secretary, after consultation with the Secretary of the Treasury, so that the benefit is the equivalent of a straight life annuity (with no ancillary benefits) under a plan to which employees do not contribute and under which no rollover contributions are made.

(d) Nothing in this Act shall be construed to prohibit compulsory retirement of any employee who has attained 70 years of age, and who is serving under a contract of unlimited tenure (or similar arrangement providing for unlimited tenure) at an institution of higher education (as defined by section 1141(a) of Title 20).[3]

Annual Report to Congress

Sec. 632. The Equal Employment Opportunity Commission shall submit annually in January a report to the Congress covering its activities for the preceding year and including such information, data, and recommendations for further legislation in connection with the matters covered by this chapter as it may find advisable. Such report shall contain an evaluation and appraisal by the Commission of the effect of the minimum and maximum ages established by this chapter, together with its recommendations to the Congress. In making such evaluation and appraisal, the Commission shall take into consideration any changes which may have occurred in the general age level of the population, the effect of the chapter upon workers not covered by its provisions, and such other factors as it may deem pertinent.

Federal-State Relationship

Sec. 633.

(a) Nothing in this chapter shall affect the jurisdiction of any agency of any State performing like functions with regard to discriminatory employment practices on account of age except that upon commencement of action under this chapter such action shall supersede any State action.

(b) In the case of an alleged unlawful practice occurring in a State which has a law prohibiting discrimination in employment because of age and establishing or authorizing a State authority to grant or seek relief from such discriminatory practice, no suit may be brought under section 626 of this title before the expiration of sixty days after proceedings have been commenced under the State law, unless such proceedings have been earlier terminated: *Provided,* That such sixty-day period shall be extended to one hundred and twenty days during the first year after the effective date of such State law. If any requirement for the commencement of such proceedings is imposed by a State authority other than a requirement of the filing of a written and signed statement of the facts upon which the proceeding is based, the proceeding shall be deemed to have been commenced for the purposes of this subsection at the time such statement is sent by registered mail to the appropriate State authority.

Nondiscrimination on Account of Age in Federal Government Employment

Sec. 633a.

(a) All personnel actions affecting employees or applicants for employment who are at least 40 years of age (except personnel actions with regard to aliens employed outside the limits of the United States) in military departments as defined in section 102 of Title 5, in executive agencies as defined in section 105 of Title 5 (including employees and applicants for employment who are paid from nonappropriated funds), in the United States Postal Service and the Postal Rate Commission, in those units in the government of the District of Columbia having positions in the competitive service, and in those units of the legislative and judicial branches of the Federal Government having positions in the competitive service, and in the Library of Congress shall be made free from any discrimination based on age.

(b) Except as otherwise provided in this subsection, the Equal Employment Opportunity Commission is authorized to enforce the provisions of subsection (a) of this section through appropriate remedies, including reinstatement or hiring of employees with or without backpay, as will effectuate the policies of this section. The Civil Service Commission shall issue such rules, regulations, orders, and instructions as it deems necessary and appropriate to carry out its responsibilities under this section. The Equal Employment Opportunity Commission shall—
   (1) be responsible for the review and evaluation of the operation of all agency programs designed to carry out the policy of this section, periodically obtaining and publishing (on at least a semiannual basis) progress reports from each department, agency, or unit referred to in subsection (a) of this section;
   (2) consult with and solicit the recommendations of interested individuals, groups, and organizations relating to nondiscrimination in employment on account of age; and

[3] This section is repealed December 31, 1993. Pub. L. 99–592, § 6(b), 100 Stat. 3344 (1986).

(3) provide for the acceptance and processing of complaints of discrimination in Federal employment on account of age.

The head of each such department, agency, or unit shall comply with such rules, regulations, orders, and instructions of the Equal Employment Opportunity Commission which shall include a provision that an employee or applicant for employment shall be notified of any final action taken on any complaint of discrimination filed by him thereunder. Reasonable exemptions to the provisions of this section may be established by the Commission but only when the Commission has established a maximum age requirement on the basis of a determination that age is a bona fide occupational qualification necessary to the performance of the duties of the position. With respect to employment in the Library of Congress, authorities granted in this subsection to the Equal Employment Opportunity Commission shall be exercised by the Librarian of Congress.

(c) Any person aggrieved may bring a civil action in any Federal district court of competent jurisdiction for such legal or equitable relief as will effectuate the purposes of this chapter.

(d) When the individual has not filed a complaint concerning age discrimination with the Commission, no civil action may be commenced by any individual under this section until the individual has given the Commission not less than thirty days' notice of an intent to file such action. Such notice shall be filed within one hundred and eighty days after the alleged unlawful practice occurred. Upon receiving a notice of intent to sue, the Commission shall promptly notify all persons named therein as prospective defendants in the action and take any appropriate action to assure the elimination of any unlawful practice.

(e) Nothing contained in this section shall relieve any Government agency or official of the responsibility to assure nondiscrimination on account of age in employment as required under any provision of Federal law.

(f) Any personnel action of any department, agency, or other entity referred to in subsection (a) of this section shall not be subject to, or affected by, any provision of this chapter, other than the provisions of section 631(b) of this title and the provisions of this section.

(g) (1) The Equal Employment Opportunity Commission shall undertake a study relating to the effects of the amendments made to this section by the Age Discrimination in Employment Act Amendments of 1978, and the effects of section 631(b) of this title.

(2) The Equal Employment Opportunity Commission shall transmit a report to the President and to the Congress containing the findings of the Commission resulting from the study of the Commission under paragraph (1) of this subsection. Such report shall be transmitted no later than January 1, 1980.

EXTRACTS FROM THE FAMILY AND MEDICAL LEAVE ACT

APPENDIX D

29 U.S.C. Section 2611 et seq.; P.L. 103–3 (1993)

Section 2611. Definitions

As used in this subchapter:

(1) Commerce

The terms "commerce" and "industry or activity affecting commerce" mean any activity, business, or industry in commerce or in which a labor dispute would hinder or obstruct commerce of the free flow of commerce, and include "commerce" and any "industry affecting commerce", as defined in paragraphs (1) and (3) of section 142 of this title.

(2) Eligible employee

(A) In general

The term "eligible employee" means an employee who has been employed—

(i) for at least 12 months by the employer with respect to whom leave is requested under section 2612 of this title; and

(ii) for at least 1,250 hours of service with such employer during the previous 12-month period.

(B) Exclusions

The term "eligible employee" does not include—

(i) any Federal officer or employee covered under subchapter V of chapter 63 of Title 5; or

(ii) any employee of an employer who is employed at a worksite at which such employer employs less than 50 employees if the total number of employees employed by that employer within 75 miles of that worksite is less than 50.

(C) Determination

For purposes of determining whether an employee meets the hours of service requirement specified in subparagraph (A)(ii), the legal standards established under section 207 of this title shall apply.

(3) Employ; employee; State

The terms "employ", "employee", and "State" have the same meaning given such terms in subsections (c), (e), and (g) of section 203 of this title.

(4) Employer

(A) In general

The term "employer"—

(i) means any person engaged in commerce or in any industry or activity affecting commerce who employs 50 or more employees for each working day during each of 20 or more calendar workweeks in the current or preceding calendar year;

(ii) includes—

(I) any person who acts, directly or indirectly, in the interest of an employer to any of the employees of such employer; and

(II) any successor in interest of an employer; and

(iii) includes any "public agency", as defined in section 203(x) of this title.

(B) Public agency

For purposes of subparagraph (A)(iii), a public agency shall be considered to be a person engaged in commerce or in an industry or activity affecting commerce.

(5) Employment benefits

The term "employment benefits" means all benefits provided or made available to employees by an employer, including group life insurance, health insurance, disability insurance, sick leave, annual leave, educational benefits, and pensions, regardless of whether such benefits are provided by practice or written policy of an employer or through an "employee benefit plan", as defined in section 1002(3) of this title.

(6) Health care provider
The term "health care provider" means—
(A) a doctor of medicine or osteopathy who is authorized to practice medicine or surgery (as appropriate) by the State in which the doctor practices; or
(B) any other person determined by the Secretary to be capable of providing health care services.

(7) Parent
The term "parent" means the biological parent of an employee or an individual who stood in loco parentis to an employee when the employee was a son or daughter.

(8) Person
The term "person" has the same meaning given such term in section 203(a) of this title.

(9) Reduced leave schedule
The term "reduced leave schedule" means a leave schedule that reduces the usual number of hours per workweek, or hours per workday, or an employee.

(10) Secretary
The term "Secretary" means the Secretary of Labor.

(11) Serious health condition
The term "serious health condition" means an illness, injury, impairment, or physical or mental condition that involves—
(A) inpatient care in a hospital, hospice, or residential medical care facility; or
(B) continuing treatment by a health care provider.

(12) Son or daughter
The term "son or daughter" means a biological, adopted, or foster child, a stepchild, a legal ward, or a child of a person standing in loco parentis, who is—
(A) under 18 years of age; or
(B) 18 years of age or older and incapable of self-care because of a mental or physical disability.

(13) Spouse
The term "spouse" means a husband or wife, as the case may be.

Sec. 2612. Leave requirement

(a) In general
(1) Entitlement to leave
Subject to section 2613 of this title, an eligible employee shall be entitled to a total of 12 workweeks of leave during an 12-month period for one or more of the following:
(A) Because of birth of a son or daughter of the employee and in order to care for care for such son or daughter.
(B) Because of the placement of a son or daughter with the employee for adoption or foster care.
(C) In order to care for the spouse, or a son, daughter, or parent, of the employee, if such spouse, son, daughter, or parent has a serious health condition.
(D) Because of a serious health condition that makes the employee unable to perform the functions of the position of such employee.

(2) Expiration of entitlement
The entitlement to leave under subparagraphs (A) and (B) of paragraph (1) for a birth or placement of a son or daughter shall expire at the end of the 12-month period beginning on the date of such birth or placement.

(b) Leave taken intermittently or on reduced leave schedule
(1) In general
Leave under subparagraph (A) or (B) of subsection (a)(1) of this section shall not be taken by an employee intermittently or on a reduced leave schedule unless the employee and the employer of the employee agree otherwise. Subject to paragraph (2), subsection (e)(2) of this section, and section 2613(b)(5) of this title, leave under subparagraph (C) or (D) of subsection (a)(1) of this section may be taken intermittently or on a reduced leave schedule when medically necessary. The taking of leave intermittently or on a reduced leave schedule pursuant to this paragraph shall not result in a reduction in the total amount of leave to which the employee is entitled under subsection (a) or this section beyond the amount of leave actually taken.

(2) Alternative position
If an employee requests intermittent leave, or leave on a reduced leave schedule, under subparagraph (C) or (D) of subsection (a)(1) of this section, that is foreseeable based on planned medical treatment, the employer may

require such employee to transfer temporarily to an available alternative position offered by the employer for which the employee is qualified and that—

(A) has equivalent pay and benefits; and

(B) better accommodates recurring periods of leave than the regular employment position of the employee.

(c) Unpaid leave permitted

Except as provided in subsection (d) of this section, leave granted under subsection (a) of this section may consist of unpaid leave. Where an employee is otherwise exempt under regulations issued by the Secretary pursuant to section 213(a)(1) of this title, the compliance of an employer with this subchapter by providing unpaid leave shall not affect the exempt status of the employee under such section.

(d) Relationship to paid leave

(1) Unpaid leave

If an employer provides paid leave for fewer than 12 workweeks, the additional weeks of leave necessary to attain the 12 workweeks of leave required under this subchapter may be provided without compensation.

(2) Substitution of paid leave

(A) In general

An eligible employee may elect, or an employer may require the employee, to substitute any of the accrued paid vacation leave, personal leave, or family leave of the employee for leave provided under subparagraph (A), (B), or (C) of subsection (a)(1) of this section for any part of the 12-week period of such leave under such subsection.

(B) Serious health condition

An eligible employee may elect, or an employer may require the employee, to substitute any of the accrued paid vacation leave, personal leave, or medical or sick leave of the employee for leave provided under subparagraph (C) or (D) of subsection (a)(1) of this section for any part of the 12-week period of such leave under such subsection, except that nothing in this subchapter shall require an employer to provide paid sick leave or paid medical leave in any situation in which such employer would not normally provide any such paid leave.

(e) Foreseeable leave

(1) Requirement of notice

In any case in which the necessity for leave under subparagraph (A) or (B) of subsection (a)(1) of this section is foreseeable based on an expected birth or placement, the employee shall provide the employer with not less than 30 days' notice, before the date the leave is to begin, of the employee's intention to take leave under such subparagraph, except that if the date of the birth or placement requires leave to begin in less than 30 days, the employee shall provide such notice as is practicable.

(2) Duties of employee

In any case in which the necessity for leave under subparagraph (C) or (D) of subsection (a)(1) of this section is foreseeable based on planned medical treatment, the employee—

(A) shall make a reasonable effort to schedule the treatment so as not to disrupt unduly the operations of the employer, subject to the approval of the health care provider of the employee or the health care provider of the son, daughter, spouse, or parent of the employee, as appropriate; and

(B) shall provide the employer with not less than 30 days' notice, before the date the leave is to begin, of the employee's intention to take leave under such subparagraph, except that if the date of the treatment requires leave to begin in less than 30 days, the employee shall provide such notice as is practicable.

(f) Spouses employed by same employer

In any case in which a husband and wife entitled to leave under subsection (a) of this section are employed by the same employer, the aggregate number of workweeks of leave to which both may be entitled may be limited to 12 workweeks during any 12-month period, if such leave is taken—

(1) under subparagraph (A) or (B) of subsection (a)(1) of this section; or

(2) to care for a sick parent under subparagraph (C) of such subsection.

Sec. 2613. Certification

(a) In general
An employer may require that a request for leave under subparagraph (C) or (D) of section 2612(a)(1) of this title be supported by a certificate issued by the health care provider of the eligible employee or the son, daughter, spouse, parent of the employee, as appropriate. The employee shall provided, in a timely manner, a copy of such certification to the employer.

(b) Sufficient certification
Certification provided under subsection (a) of this section shall be sufficient if it states—
(1) the date on which the serious health condition commenced;
(2) the probable duration of the condition;
(3) the appropriate medical facts within the knowledge of the health care provider regarding the condition;
(4) (A) for purposes of leave under section 2612(a)(1)(C) of this title, a statement that the eligible employee is needed to care for the son, daughter, spouse, or parent and an estimate of the amount of time that such employee is needed to care for the son, daughter, spouse, or parent; and
(B) for purposes of leave under section 2612(a)(1)(D) of this title, a statement that the employee is unable to perform the functions of the position of the employee;
(5) in the case of certification for intermittent leave, or leave on a reduced leave schedule, for planned medical treatment, the dates on which such treatment is expected to be given and the duration of such treatment;
(6) in the case of certification for intermittent leave, or leave on a reduced leave schedule, under section 2612(a)(1)(D) of this title, a statement of the medical necessity for the intermittent leave or leave on a reduced leave schedule, and the expected duration of the intermittent leave or reduced leave schedule; and
(7) in the case of certification for intermittent leave, or leave on a reduced leave schedule, under section 2612(a)(1)(C) of this title, a statement that the employee's intermittent leave or leave on a reduced leave schedule is necessary for the care or the son, daughter, parent, or spouse who has a serious health condition, or will assist in their recovery, and the expected duration and schedule of the intermittent leave or reduced leave schedule.

(c) Second opinion
(1) In general
In any case in which the employer has reason to doubt the validity of the certification provided under subsection (a) of this section for leave under subparagraph (C) or (D) of section 2612(a)(1) of this title, the employer may require, at the expense of the employer, that the eligible employee obtain the opinion of a second health care provider designated or approved by the employer concerning any information certified under subsection (b) of this section for such leave.
(2) Limitation
A health care provider designated or approved under paragraph (1) shall not be employed on a regular basis by the employer.

(d) Resolution of conflicting opinions
(1) In general
In any case in which the second opinion described in subsection (c) of this section differs from the opinion in the original certification provided under subsection (a) of this section, the employer may require, at the expense of the employer, that the employee obtain the opinion of a third health care provider designated or approved jointly by the employer and the employee concerning the information certified under subsection (b) of this section.
(2) Finality
The opinion of the third health care provider concerning the information certified under subsection (b) of this section shall be considered to be final and shall be binding on the employer and the employee.

(e) Subsequent recertification
The employer may require that the eligible employee obtain subsequent recertifications on a reasonable basis.

Sec. 2614. Employment and benefits protection

(a) Restoration to position
(1) In general
Except as provided in subsection (b) of this section, any eligible employee who takes leave under section 2612 of this title for the in-

tended purpose of the leave shall be entitled, on return from such leave—

(A) to be restored by the employer to the position of employment held by the employee when the leave commenced; or

(B) to be restored to an equivalent position with equivalent employment benefits, pay, and other terms and conditions of employment.

(2) Loss of benefits

The taking of leave under section 2612 of this title shall not result in the loss of any employment benefit accrued prior to the date on which the leave commenced.

(3) Limitations

Nothing in this section shall be construed to entitle any restored employee to—

(A) the accrual of any seniority or employment benefits during any period of leave; or

(B) any right, benefit, or position of employment other than any right, benefit, or position to which the employee would have been entitled had the employee not taken the leave.

(4) Certification

As a condition of restoration under paragraph (1) for an employee who has taken leave under section 2612(a)(1)(D) of this title, the employer may have a uniformly applied practice or policy that requires each such employee to receive certification from the health care provider of the employee that the employee is able to resume work, except that nothing in this paragraph shall supersede a valid State or local law or a collective bargaining agreement that governs the return to work of such employees.

(5) Construction

Nothing in this subsection shall be construed to prohibit an employer from requiring an employee on leave under section 2612 of this title to report periodically to the employer on the status and intention of the employee to return to work.

(b) Exemption concerning highly compensated employees

(1) Denial of restoration

An employer may deny restoration under subsection (a) of this section to any eligible employee described in paragraph (2) if—

(A) such denial is necessary to prevent substantial and grievous economic injury to the operations of the employer;

(B) the employer notified the employee of the intent of the employer to deny restoration on such basis at the time the employer determined that such injury would occur; and

(C) in any case in which the leave has commenced, the employee elects not to return to employment after receiving such notice.

(2) Affected employees

An eligible employee described in paragraph (1) is a salaried eligible employee who is among the highest paid 10 percent of the employees employed by the employer within 75 miles of the facility at which the employee is employed.

(c) Maintenance of health benefits

(1) Coverage

Except as provided in paragraph (2), during any period that an eligible employee takes leave under section 2612 of this title, the employer shall maintain coverage under any "group health plan" (as defined in section 5000(b)(1) of Title 26) for the duration of such leave at the level and under the conditions coverage would have been provided if the employee had continued in employment continuously for the duration of such leave.

(2) Failure to return from leave

The employer may recover the premium that the employer paid for maintaining coverage for the employee under such group health plan during any period for unpaid leave under section 2612 of this title if—

(A) the employee fails to return from leave under section 2612 of this title after the period of leave to which the employee is entitled has expired; and

(B) the employee fails to return to work for a reason other than—

(i) the continuation, recurrence, or onset of a serious health condition that entitles the employee to leave under subparagraph (C) or (D) of section 2612 (a)(1) of this title; or

(ii) other circumstances beyond the control of the employee.

(3) Certification
(A) Issuance
An employer may require that a claim that an employee is unable to return to work because of the continuation, recurrence, or onset of the serious health condition described in paragraph (2)(B)(i) be supported by—
(i) a certification issued by the health care provider of the son, daughter, spouse, or parent of the employee, as appropriate, in the case of an employee unable to return to work because of a condition specified in section 2612 (a)(1)(C) of this title, or
(ii) a certification issued by the health care provider of the eligible employee, in the case of an employee unable to return to work because of a condition specified in section 2612(a)(1)(D) of this title.
(B) Copy
The employee shall provide, in a timely manner, a copy of such certification to the employer.
(C) Sufficiency of certification
(i) Leave due to serious health condition of employee
The certification described in subparagraph (A)(ii) shall be sufficient if the certification states that a serious health condition prevented the employee from being able to perform the functions of the position of the employee on the date that the leave of the employee expired.
(ii) Leave due to serious health condition of family member the certification states that the employee is needed to care for the son, daughter, spouse, or parent who has a serious health condition on the date that the leave of the employee expired.

Sec. 2615. Prohibited acts

(a) Interference with rights
(1) Exercise of rights
It shall be unlawful for any employer to interfere with, restrain, or deny the exercise of or the attempt to exercise, any right provided under this subchapter.
(2) Discrimination
It shall be unlawful for any employer to discharge or in any other manner discriminate against any individual for opposing any practice made unlawful by this subchapter.
(b) Interference with proceedings or inquiries
It shall be unlawful for any person to discharge or in any other manner discriminate against any individual because such individual
(1) has filed any charge, or has instituted or caused to be instituted any proceeding, under or related to this subchapter;
(2) has given, or is about to give, any information in connection with any inquiry or proceeding relating to any right provided under this subchapter; or
(3) has testified, or is about to testify, in any inquiry or proceeding relating to any right provided under this subchapter.

• • •

Sec. 2617. Enforcement

(a) Civil action by employees
(1) Liability
Any employer who violates section 2615 of this title shall be liable to any eligible employee affected
(A) for damages equal to—
(i) the amount of—
(I) any wages, salary, employment benefits, or other compensation denied or lost to such employee by reason of the violation; or
(II) in a case in which wages, salary, employment benefits, or other compensation have not been denied or lost to the employee, any actual monetary losses sustained by the employee as a direct result of the violation, such as the cost of providing care, up to a sum equal to 12 weeks of wages or salary for the employee;

(ii) the interest on the amount described in clause (i) calculated at the prevailing rate; and

(iii) an additional amount as liquidated damages equal to the sum of the amount described in clause (i) and the interest described in clause (ii), except that if an employer who has violated section 2615 of this title proves to the satisfaction of the court that the act or omission which violated section 2615 of this title was in good faith and that the employer had reasonable grounds for believing that the act or omission was not a violation of section 2615 of this title, such court may, in the discretion of the court, reduce the amount of the liability to the amount and interest determined under clauses (i) and (ii), respectively; and

(B) for such equitable relief as may be appropriate, including employment, reinstatement, and promotion.

(2) Right of action

An action to recover the damages or equitable relief prescribed in paragraph (1) may be maintained against any employer (including a public agency) in any Federal or State court of competent jurisdiction by any one or more employees for and on behalf of—

(A) the employees; or

(B) the employees and other employees similarly situated.

(3) Fees and costs

The court in such an action shall, in addition to any judgment awarded to the plaintiff, allow a reasonable attorney's fee, reasonable expert witness fees, and other costs of the action to be paid by the defendant.

(4) Limitations

The right provided by paragraph (2) to bring an action by or on behalf of any employee shall terminate—

(A) on the filing of a complaint by the Secretary in an action under subsection (d) of this section in which restraint is sought of any further delay in the payment or the amount described in paragraph (1)(A) to such employee by an employer responsible under paragraph (1) for the payment; or

(B) on the filing of a complaint by the Secretary in an action under subsection (b) of this section in which a recovery is sought of the damages described in paragraph (1)(A) owing to an eligible employee by an employer liable under paragraph (1), unless the action described in subparagraph (A) or (B) is dismissed without prejudice on motion of the Secretary.

(b) Action by Secretary

(1) Administrative action

The Secretary shall receive, investigate, and attempt to resolve complaints of violations of section 2615 of this title in the same manner that the Secretary receives, investigates, and attempts to resolve complaints of violations of sections 206 and 207 of this title.

(2) Civil action

The Secretary may bring an action in any court of competent jurisdiction to recover the damages described in subsection (a)(1)(A) of this section.

(3) Sums recovered

Any sums recovered by the Secretary pursuant to paragraph (2) shall be held in a special deposit account and shall be paid, on order of the Secretary, directly to each employee affected. Any such sums not paid to an employee because of inability to do so within a period of 3 years shall be deposited into the Treasury of the United States as miscellaneous receipts.

(c) Limitation

(1) In general

Except as provided in paragraph (2), an action may be brought under this section not later than 2 years after the date of the last event constituting the alleged violation for which the action is brought.

(2) Willful violation

In the case of such action brought for a willful violation of section 2615 of this title, such action may be brought within 3 years of the date of the last event constituting the alleged violation for which such action is brought.

(3) Commencement

In determining when an action is commenced by the Secretary under this section for the purposes of this subsection, it shall be considered to be commenced on the date when the complaint is filed.

(d) Action for injunction by Secretary
The district courts of the United States shall have jurisdiction, for cause shown, in an action brought by the Secretary
 (1) to restrain violations of section 2615 of this title, including the restraint of any withholding of payment of wages, salary, employment benefits, or other compensation, plus interest, found by the court to be due to eligible employees; or
 (2) to award such other equitable relief as may be appropriate, including employment, reinstatement, and promotion.

(e) Solicitor of Labor
The Solicitor of Labor may appear for and represent the Secretary on any litigation brought under this section.

• • •

Sec. 2619. Notice

(a) In general
Each employer shall post and keep posted, in conspicuous places on the premises of the employer notices, to be prepared or approved by the Secretary, setting forth excerpts from, or summaries of, the pertinent provisions of this subchapter and information pertaining to the filing of a charge.

(b) Penalty
Any employer that willfully violates this section may be assessed a civil money penalty and not to exceed $100 for each separate offense.

Sec. 2651. Effect on other laws

(a) Federal and State antidiscrimination laws
Nothing in this Act or any amendment made by this Act shall be construed to modify or affect any Federal or State law prohibiting discrimination on the basis of race, religion, color, national origin, sex, age, or disability.

(b) State and local laws
Nothing in this Act or any amendment made by this Act shall be construed to supersede any provision of any State or local law that provides greater family or medical leave rights than the rights established under this Act or any amendment made by this Act.

Sec. 2652. Effect on existing employment benefits

(a) More protective
Nothing in this Act or any amendment made by this Act shall be construed to diminish the obligation of an employer to comply with any collective bargaining agreement or any employment benefit program or plan that provides greater family or medical leave rights to employees than the rights established under this Act or any amendment made by this Act.

(b) Less protective
The rights established for employees under this Act or any amendment made by this Act shall not be diminished by any collective bargaining agreement or any employment benefit program or plan.

Sec. 2653. Encouragement of more generous leave policies

Nothing in this Act or any amendment made by this Act shall be construed to discourage employers from adopting or retaining leave policies more generous than any policies that comply with the requirements under this Act or any amendment made by this Act.

EXTRACTS FROM THE AMERICANS WITH DISABILITIES ACT

E APPENDIX

42 U.S.C. §§ 12101-12213

Section 3. (§ 12102) Definitions

As used in this Act:

• • •

(2) DISABILITY.—The term "disability" means, with respect to an individual—
   (A) a physical or mental impairment that substantially limits one or more of the major life activities of such individual;
   (B) a record of such an impairment; or
   (C) being regarded as having such an impairment.

• • •

TITLE I—EMPLOYMENT

Sec. 101. (§ 12111) Definitions

As used in this title:

(1) COMMISSION.—The term "Commission" means the Equal Employment Opportunity Commission established by section 705 of the Civil Rights Act of 1964 (42 U.S.C. 2000e–4).

(2) COVERED ENTITY.—The term "covered entity" means an employer, employment agency, labor organization, or joint labor-management committee.

(3) DIRECT THREAT.—The term "direct threat" means a significant risk to the health or safety of others that cannot be eliminated by reasonable accommodation.

(4) EMPLOYEE.—The term "employee" means an individual employed by an employer. With respect to employment in a foreign country, such term includes an individual who is a citizen of the United States.

(5) EMPLOYER.—
   (A) IN GENERAL.—The term "employer" means a person engaged in an industry affecting commerce who has 15 or more employees for each working day in each of 20 or more calendar weeks in the current or preceding calendar year, and any agent of such person, except that, for two years following the effective date of this title, an employer means a person engaged in an industry affecting commerce who has 25 or more employees for each working day in each of 20 or more calendar weeks in the current or preceding year, and any agent of such person.
   (B) EXCEPTIONS.—The term "employer" does not include—
      (i) the United States, a corporation wholly owned by the government of the United States, or an Indian tribe; or
      (ii) a bona fide private membership club (other than a labor organization) that is exempt from taxation under section 501(c) of the Internal Revenue Code of 1986.

(6) ILLEGAL USE OF DRUGS.—
   (A) IN GENERAL.—The term "illegal use of drugs" means the use of drugs, the possession or distribution of which is unlawful under the Controlled Substances Act (21 U.S.C. 812). Such term does not include the use of a drug taken under supervision by a licensed health care professional, or other uses authorized by the Controlled Substances Act or other provisions of Federal law.
   (B) DRUGS.—The term "drug" means a controlled substance, as defined in schedules I through V of section 202 of the Controlled Substances Act.

(7) PERSON, ETC.—The terms "person", "labor organization", "employment agency", "commerce", and "industry affecting commerce", shall have the same meaning given such terms in section 701 of the Civil Rights Act of 1964 (42 U.S.C. 2000e).

(8) QUALIFIED INDIVIDUAL WITH A DISABILITY.—The term "qualified individual with a disability" means an individual with a disability who, with or without reasonable accommodation, can perform the essential functions of the employment position that such individual holds or desires. For the purposes of this title, consideration shall be given to the employer's judgment as to what functions of a job are essential, and if an employer has prepared a written description before advertising or interviewing applicants for the job, this description shall be considered evidence of the essential functions of the job.

(9) REASONABLE ACCOMMODATION.—The term "reasonable accommodation" may include—
- (A) making existing facilities used by employees readily accessible to and usable by individuals with disabilities; and
- (B) job restructuring, part-time or modified work schedules, reassignment to a vacant position, acquisition or modification of equipment or devices, appropriate adjustment or modifications of examinations, training materials or policies, the provision of qualified readers or interpreters, and other similar accommodations for individuals with disabilities.

(10) UNDUE HARDSHIP.—
- (A) IN GENERAL.—The term "undue hardship" means an action requiring significant difficulty or expense, when considered in light of the factors set forth in subparagraph (B).
- (B) FACTORS TO BE CONSIDERED.—In determining whether an accommodation would impose an undue hardship on a covered entity, factors to be considered include—
  - (i) the nature and cost of the accommodation needed under this Act;
  - (ii) the overall financial resources of the facility or facilities involved in the provision of the reasonable accommodation; the number of persons employed at such facility; the effect on expenses and resources, or the impact otherwise of such accommodation upon the operation of the facility;
  - (iii) the overall financial resources of the covered entity; the overall size of the business of a covered entity with respect to the number of its employees; the number, type, and location of its facilities; and
  - (iv) the type of operation or operations of the covered entity, including the composition, structure, and functions of the workforce of such entity; the geographic separateness, administrative, or fiscal relationship of the facility or facilities in question to the covered entity.

Sec. 102. (§ 12112) Discrimination

(a) GENERAL RULE.—No covered entity shall discriminate against a qualified individual with a disability because of the disability of such individual in regard to job application procedures, the hiring, advancement, or discharge of employees, employee compensation, job training and other terms, conditions, and privileges of employment.

(b) CONSTRUCTION.—As used in subsection (a), the term "discriminate" includes—
- (1) limiting, segregating, or classifying a job applicant or employee in a way that adversely affects the opportunities or status of such applicant or employee because of the disability of such applicant or employee;
- (2) participating in a contractual or other arrangement or relationship that has the effect of subjecting a covered entity's qualified applicant or employee with a disability to the discrimination prohibited by this title (such relationship includes a relationship with an employment or referral agency, labor union, an organization providing fringe benefits to an employee of the covered entity, or an organization providing training and apprenticeship programs);
- (3) utilizing standards, criteria, or methods of administration—
  - (A) that have the effect of discrimination on the basis of disability; or
  - (B) that perpetuate the discrimination of others who are subject to common administrative control;
- (4) excluding or otherwise denying equal jobs or benefits to a qualified individual because of the known disability of an individual with

whom the qualified individual is known to have a relationship or association;

(5) (A) not making reasonable accommodations to the known physical or mental limitations of an otherwise qualified individual with a disability who is an applicant or employee, unless such covered entity can demonstrate that the accommodation would impose an undue hardship on the operation of the business of such covered entity; or

(B) denying employment opportunities to a job applicant or employee who is an otherwise qualified individual with a disability, if such denial is based on the need of such covered entity to make reasonable accommodation to the physical or mental impairments of the employee or applicant;

(6) using qualification standards, employment tests or other selection criteria that screen out or tend to screen out an individual with a disability or a class of individuals with disabilities unless the standard, test or other selection criteria, as used by the covered entity, is shown to be job-related for the position in question and is consistent with business necessity; and

(7) failing to select and administer tests concerning employment in the most effective manner to ensure that, when such test is administered to a job applicant or employee who has a disability that impairs sensory, manual, or speaking skills, such test results accurately reflect the skills, aptitude, or whatever other factor of such applicant or employee that such test purports to measure, rather than reflecting the impaired sensory, manual, or speaking skills of such employee or applicant (except where such skills are the factors that the test purports to measure),

(C) COVERED ENTITIES IN FOREIGN COUNTRIES.—

(1) IN GENERAL.—It shall not be unlawful under this section for a covered entity to take any action that constitutes discrimination under this section with respect to an employee in a workplace in a foreign country if compliance with this section would cause such covered entity to violate the law of the foreign country in which such workplace is located.

(2) CONTROL OF CORPORATION.—

(A) PRESUMPTION.—If an employer controls a corporation whose place of incorporation is a foreign country, any practice that constitutes discrimination under this section and is engaged in by such corporation shall be presumed to be engaged in by such employer.

(B) EXCEPTION.—This section shall not apply with respect to the foreign operations of an employer that is a foreign person not controlled by an American employer.

(C) DETERMINATION.—For purposes of this paragraph, the determination of whether an employer controls a corporation shall be based on—

(i) the interrelation of operations;

(ii) the common management;

(iii) the centralized control of labor relations; and

(iv) the common ownership or financial control of the employer and the corporation.

(d) MEDICAL EXAMINATIONS AND INQUIRIES.—

(1) IN GENERAL.—The prohibition against discrimination as referred to in subsection (a) shall include medical examinations and inquiries.

(2) PREEMPLOYMENT.—

(A) PROHIBITED EXAMINATION OR INQUIRY.—Except as provided in paragraph (3), a covered entity shall not conduct a medical examination or make inquiries of a job applicant as to whether such applicant is an individual with a disability or as to the nature or severity of such disability.

(B) ACCEPTABLE INQUIRY.—A covered entity may make preemployment inquiries into the ability of an applicant to perform job-related functions.

(3) EMPLOYMENT ENTRANCE EXAMINATION.—A covered entity may require a medical examination after an offer of employment has been made to a job applicant and prior to the commencement of the employment duties of such applicant, and may condition an offer of employment on the results of such examination, if—

(A) all entering employees are subjected to such an examination regardless of disability;

(B) information obtained regarding the medical condition or history of the applicant is collected and maintained on separate forms and in separate medical files and is treated as a confidential medical record, except that—

(i) supervisors and managers may be informed regarding necessary restrictions on the work or duties of the employee and necessary accommodations;

(ii) first aid and safety personnel may be informed, when appropriate, if the disability might require emergency treatment; and

(iii) government officials investigating compliance with this Act shall be provided relevant information on request; and

(C) the results of such examination are used only in accordance with this title.

(4) EXAMINATION AND INQUIRY.—

(A) PROHIBITED EXAMINATIONS AND INQUIRIES.—A covered entity shall not require a medical examination and shall not make inquiries of an employee as to whether such employee is an individual with a disability or as to the nature or severity of the disability, unless such examination or inquiry is shown to be job-related and consistent with business necessity.

(B) ACCEPTABLE EXAMINATIONS AND INQUIRIES.—A covered entity may conduct voluntary medical examinations, including voluntary medical histories, which are part of an employee health program available to employees at that work site. A covered entity may make inquiries into the ability of an employee to perform job-related functions.

(C) REQUIREMENT.—Information obtained under subparagraph (B) regarding the medical condition or history of any employee are subject to the requirements of subparagraphs (B) and (C) of paragraph (3).

Sec. 103. (§ 12113) Defenses

(a) IN GENERAL.—It may be a defense to a charge of discrimination under this Act that an alleged application of qualification standards, tests, or selection criteria that screen out or tend to screen out or otherwise deny a job or benefit to an individual with a disability has been shown to be job-related and consistent with business necessity, and such performance cannot be accomplished by reasonable accommodation, as required under this title.

(b) QUALIFICATION STANDARDS.—The term "qualification standards" may include a requirement that an individual shall not pose a direct threat to the health or safety of other individuals in the workplace.

(c) RELIGIOUS ENTITIES.—

(1) IN GENERAL.—This title shall not prohibit a religious corporation, association, educational institution, or society from giving preference in employment to individuals of a particular religion to perform work connected with the carrying on by such corporation, association, educational institution, or society of its activities.

(2) RELIGIOUS TENETS REQUIREMENT.—Under this title, a religious organization may require that all applicants and employees conform to the religious tenets of such organization.

(d) LIST OF INFECTIOUS and COMMUNICABLE DISEASES.—

(1) IN GENERAL.—The Secretary of Health and Human Services, not later than 6 months after the date of enactment of this Act, shall—

(A) review all infectious and communicable diseases which may be transmitted through handling the food supply;

(B) publish a list of infectious and communicable diseases which are transmitted through handling the food supply;

(C) publish the methods by which such diseases are transmitted; and

(D) widely disseminate such information regarding the list of diseases and their modes of transmissibility to the general public.

Such list shall be updated annually.

(2) APPLICATIONS.—In any case in which an individual has an infectious or communicable disease that is transmitted to others through

the handling of food, that is included on the list developed by the Secretary of Health and Human Services under paragraph (1), and which cannot be eliminated by reasonable accommodation, a covered entity may refuse to assign or continue to assign such individual to a job involving food handling.

(3) CONSTRUCTION.—Nothing in this Act shall be construed to preempt, modify, or amend any State, county, or local law, ordinance, or regulation applicable to food handling which is designed to protect the public health from individuals who pose a significant risk to the health or safety of others, which cannot be eliminated by reasonable accommodation, pursuant to the list of infectious or communicable diseases and the modes of transmissibility published by the Secretary of Health and Human Services.

Sec. 104. (§ 12114) Illegal Use of Drugs and Alcohol

(a) QUALIFIED INDIVIDUAL WITH A DISABILITY.—For purposes of this title, the term "qualified individual with a disability" shall not include any employee or applicant who is currently engaging in the illegal use of drugs, when the covered entity acts on the basis of such use.

(b) RULES OF CONSTRUCTION. —Nothing in subsection (a) shall be construed to exclude as a qualified individual with a disability an individual who—

(1) has successfully completed a supervised drug rehabilitation program and is no longer engaging in the illegal use of drugs, or has otherwise been rehabilitated successfully and is no longer engaging in such use;

(2) is participating in a supervised rehabilitation program and is no longer engaging in such use; or

(3) is erroneously regarded as engaging in such use, but is not engaging in such use;

except that it shall not be a violation of this Act for a covered entity to adopt or administer reasonable policies or procedures, including but not limited to drug testing, designed to ensure that an individual described in paragraph (1) or (2) is no longer engaging in the illegal use of drugs.

(c) AUTHORITY OF COVERED ENTITY.—A covered entity—

(1) may prohibit the illegal use of drugs and the use of alcohol in the workplace by all employees;

(2) may require that employees shall not be under the influence of alcohol or be engaging in the illegal use of drugs at the workplace;

(3) may require that employees behave in conformance with the requirements established under the Drug-Free Workplace Act of 1988 (41 U.S.C. 701 et seq.);

(4) may hold an employee who engages in the illegal use of drugs or who is an alcoholic to the same qualification standards for employment or job performance and behavior that such entity holds other employees, even if any unsatisfactory performance or behavior is related to the drug use or alcoholism of such employee; and

(5) may, with respect to Federal regulations regarding alcohol and the illegal use of drugs, require that—

(A) employees comply with the standards established in such regulations of the Department of Defense, if the employees of the covered entity are employed in an industry subject to such regulations, including complying with regulations (if any) that apply to employment in sensitive positions in such an industry, in the case of employees of the covered entity who are employed in such positions (as defined in the regulations of the Department of Defense);

(B) employees comply with the standards established in such regulations of the Nuclear Regulatory Commission, if the employees of the covered entity are employed in an industry subject to such regulations, including complying with regulations (if any) that apply to employment in sensitive positions in such an industry, in the case of employees of the covered entity who are employed in such positions (as defined in the regulations of the Nuclear Regulatory Commission); and

(C) employees comply with the standards established in such regulations of the Department of Transportation, if the employees of the covered entity are employed in a transportation industry subject to such regulations, including complying with such regulations (if any) that apply to employment in sensitive positions in such an industry, in the case of employees of the covered entity who are employed in such positions (as defined in the regulations of the Department of Transportation).

(d) DRUG TESTING.—
  (1) IN GENERAL.—For purposes of this title, a test to determine the illegal use of drugs shall not be considered a medical examination.
  (2) CONSTRUCTION.—Nothing in this title shall be construed to encourage, prohibit, or authorize the conducting of drug testing for the illegal use of drugs by job applicants or employees or making employment decisions based on such test results.

(e) TRANSPORTATION EMPLOYEES.—Nothing in this title shall be construed to encourage, prohibit, restrict, or authorize the otherwise lawful exercise by entities subject to the jurisdiction of the Department of Transportation of authority to—
  (1) test employees of such entities in, and applicants for, positions involving safety-sensitive duties for the illegal use of drugs and for on-duty impairment by alcohol; and
  (2) remove such persons who test positive for illegal use of drugs and on-duty impairment by alcohol pursuant to paragraph (1) from safety-sensitive duties in implementing subsection (c).

Sec. 105. (§ 12115) Posting Notices

Every employer, employment agency, labor organization, or joint labor-management committee covered under this title shall post notices in an accessible format to applicants, employees, and members describing the applicable provisions of this Act, in the manner prescribed by section 711 of the Civil Rights Act of 1964 (42 U.S.C. 2000e–10).

Sec. 106. (§ 12116) Regulations

Not later than 1 year after the date of enactment of this Act, the Commission shall issue regulations in an accessible format to carry out this title in accordance with subchapter II of chapter 5 of title 5, United States Code.

Sec. 107. (§ 12117) Enforcement

(a) POWERS, REMEDIES, AND PROCEDURES.—The powers, remedies, and procedures set forth in sections 705, 706, 707, 709, and 710 of the Civil Rights Act of 1964 (42 U.S.C. 2000e–4, 2000e–5, 2000e–6, 2000e–8, and 2000e–9) shall be the powers, remedies, and procedures this title provides to the Commission, to the Attorney General, or to any person alleging discrimination on the basis of disability in violation of any provision of this Act, or regulations promulgated under section 106, concerning employment.

(b) COORDINATION.—The agencies with enforcement authority for actions which allege employment discrimination under this title and under the Rehabilitation Act of 1973 shall develop procedures to ensure that administrative complaints filed under this title and under the Rehabilitation Act of 1973 are dealt with in a manner that avoids duplication of effort and prevents imposition of inconsistent or conflicting standards for the same requirements under this title and the Rehabilitation Act of 1973. The Commission, the Attorney General, and the Office of Federal Contract Compliance Programs shall establish such coordinating mechanisms (similar to provisions contained in the joint regulations promulgated by the Commission and the Attorney General at part 42 of title 28 and part 1691 of title 29, Code of Federal Regulations, and the Memorandum of Understanding between the Commission and the Office of Federal Contract Compliance Programs dated January 16, 1981 (46 Fed. Reg. 7435, January 23, 1981)) in regulations implementing this title and the Rehabilitation Act of 1973 not later than 18 months after the date of enactment of this Act.

Sec. 108. (§ 12118) Effective Date

This title shall become effective 24 months after the date of enactment.

• • •

SUBCHAPTER IV—MISCELLANEOUS PROVISIONS

Sec. 501. (§ 12201) Construction

(a) IN GENERAL.—Except as otherwise provided in this Act, nothing in this Act shall be construed to apply a lesser standard than the standards applied under title V of the Rehabilitation Act of 1973 (29 U.S.C. 790 et seq.) or the regulations issued by Federal agencies pursuant to such title.

(b) RELATIONSHIP TO OTHER LAWS.—Nothing in this Act shall be construed to invalidate or limit the remedies, rights, and procedures of any Federal law or law of any State or political subdivision of any State or jurisdiction that provides greater or equal protection for the rights of individuals with disabilities than are afforded by this Act. Nothing in this Act shall be construed to preclude the prohibition of, or the imposition of, restrictions on, smoking in places of employment covered by title I, in transportation covered by title II or III or in places of public accommodation covered by title III.

(c) INSURANCE.—Titles I through IV of this Act shall not be construed to prohibit or restrict—
   (1) an insurer, hospital or medical service company, health maintenance organization, or any agent, or entity that administers benefit plans, or similar organizations from underwriting risks, classifying risks, or administering such risks that are based on or not inconsistent with State law; or
   (2) a person or organization covered by this Act from establishing, sponsoring, observing or administering the terms of a bona fide benefit plan that are based on underwriting risks, classifying risks, or administering such risks that are based on or not inconsistent with State law; or
   (3) a person or organization covered by this Act from establishing, sponsoring, observing or administering the terms of a bona fide benefit plan that is not subject to State laws that regulate insurance.

Paragraphs (1), (2), and (3) shall not be used as a subterfuge to evade the purposes of title I and III.

(d) ACCOMMODATIONS AND SERVICES.—Nothing in this Act shall be construed to require an individual with a disability to accept an accommodation, aid, service, opportunity, or benefit which such individual chooses not to accept.

Sec. 502. (§ 12202) State Immunity

A State shall not be immune under the eleventh amendment to the Constitution of the United States from an action in Federal or State court of competent jurisdiction for a violation of this Act. In any action against a State for a violation of the requirements of this Act, remedies (including remedies both at law and in equity) are available for such a violation to the same extent as such remedies are available for such a violation in an action against any public or private entity other than a State.

Sec. 503. (§ 12203) Prohibition Against Retaliation and Coercion

(a) RETALIATION.—No person shall discriminate against any individual because such individual has opposed any act or practice made unlawful by this Act or because such individual made a charge, testified, assisted, or participated in any manner in an investigation, proceeding, or hearing under this Act.

Sec. 511. (§ 12211) Definitions

(a) HOMOSEXUALITY AND BISEXUALITY.—For purposes of the definition of "disability" in section 3(2), homosexuality and bisexuality are not impairments and as such are not disabilities under this Act.

(b) CERTAIN CONDITIONS.—Under this Act, the term "disability" shall not include—
   (1) transvestism, transsexualism, pedophilia, exhibitionism, voyeurism, gender identity disorders not resulting from physical impairments, or other sexual behavior disorders;
   (2) compulsive gambling, kleptomania, or pyromania; or
   (3) psychoactive substance use disorders resulting from current illegal use of drugs.

• • •

APPENDIX F

EXTRACTS FROM THE REHABILITATION ACT

29 U.S.C. §§ 701–796i

Section 706. Definitions

For the purposes of this chapter:

• • •

(7) (A) Except as otherwise provided in subparagraph (B), the term "individual with a disability" means any individual who (i) has a physical or mental impairment which for such individual constitutes or results in a substantial impediment to employment and (ii) can benefit in terms of an employment outcome from vocational rehabilitation services provided pursuant to titles I, II, III, VI, and VIII of this Act.

(B) Subject to subparagraphs (C) and (D), (E) and (F), the term "individual with a disability" means for purposes of sections 2, 14, and 15, and titles IV and V of this Act, any person who (i) has a physical or mental impairment which substantially limits one or more of such person's major life activities, (ii) has a record of such an impairment or (iii) is regarded as having such an impairment.

(C) (i) For purposes of title V, the term "individual with a disability" does not include an individual who is currently engaging in the illegal use of drugs, when a covered entity acts on the basis of such use.

(ii) Nothing in clause (i) shall be construed to exclude as an individual with a disability an individual who—

(I) has successfully completed a supervised drug rehabilitation program and is no longer engaging in the illegal use of drugs, or has otherwise been rehabilitated successfully and is no longer engaging in such use;

(II) is participating in a supervised rehabilitation program and is no longer engaging in such use; or

(III) is erroneously regarded as engaging in such use, but is not engaging in such use;

except that it shall not be a violation of this Act for a covered entity to adopt or administer reasonable policies or procedures, including but not limited to drug testing, designed to ensure that an individual described in subclause (I) or (II) is no longer engaging in the illegal use of drugs.

(iii) Notwithstanding clause (i), for purposes of programs and activities providing health services and services provided under titles I, II, and III, an individual shall not be excluded from the benefits of such programs or activities on the basis of his or her current illegal use of drugs if he or she is otherwise entitled to such services.

(iv) For purposes of programs and activities providing educational services, local educational agencies may take disciplinary action pertaining to the use or possession of illegal drugs or alcohol against any student who is an individual with a disability who currently is engaging in the illegal use of drugs or in the use of alcohol to the same extent that such disciplinary action is taken against students who are not individuals with disabilities. Furthermore, the due process procedures at 34 CFR 104.36 shall not apply to such disciplinary actions.

(v) For purposes of sections 503 and 504 as such sections relate to employment, the term "individual with a disability" does not include any individual who is an alcoholic whose current use of alcohol prevents such individual from performing the duties of the job in question or whose employment, by reason of such current alcohol abuse, would constitute a direct threat to property or the safety of others.

(D) For the purpose of sections 503 and 504, as such sections relate to employment, such term does not include an individual who has a currently contagious disease or infection and who, by reason of such disease or infection, would constitute a direct threat to the health or safety of other individuals or who, by reason of the currently contagious disease or infection, is unable to perform the duties of the job.

Sec. 501. (§ 791) Employment of individuals with disabilities

• • •

(b) **Federal agencies; affirmative action program plans**

Each department, agency, and instrumentality (including the United States Postal Service and the Postal Rate Commission) in the executive branch shall, within one hundred and eighty days after September 26, 1973, submit to the Commission and to the Committee an affirmative action program plan for the hiring, placement and advancement of individuals with disabilities in such department, agency, or instrumentality. Such plan shall include a description of the extent to which and methods whereby the special needs of employees who are individuals with disabilities are being met. Such plan shall be updated annually, and shall be reviewed annually and approved by the Commission, if the Office determines, after consultation with the Committee, that such plan provides sufficient assurances, procedures and commitments to provide adequate hiring, placement, and advancement opportunities for individuals with disabilities.

• • •

Sec. 503. (§ 793) Employment Under Federal Contracts

(a) **Amount of contracts or subcontracts; provision for employment and advancement of qualified individuals with handicaps; regulations**

Any contract in excess of $10,000 entered into by any Federal department or agency for the procurement of personal property and nonpersonal services (including construction) for the United States shall contain a provision requiring that the party contracting with the United States shall take affirmative action to employ and advance in employment qualified individuals with disabilities. The provisions of this section shall apply to any subcontract in excess of $10,000 entered into by a prime contractor in carrying out any contract for the procurement of personal property and nonpersonal services (including construction) for the United States. The President shall implement the provisions of this section by promulgating regulations within ninety days after September 26, 1973.

(b) **Administrative enforcement; complaints; investigations; departmental action**

If any individual with a disability believes any contractor has failed or refused to comply with the provisions of a contract with the United States, relating to employment of individuals with disabilities, such individual may file a complaint with the Department of Labor. The Department shall promptly investigate such complaint and shall take such action thereon as the facts and circumstances warrant, consistent with the terms of such contract and the laws and regulations applicable thereto.

(c) **Waiver by President; national interest special circumstances for waiver of particular agreements**

(1) The requirements of this section may be waived, in whole or in part, by the President with respect to a particular contract or subcontract, in accordance with guidelines set forth in regulations which the President shall prescribe, when the President determines that special circumstances in the national interest

so require and states in writing the reasons for such determination.

• • •

Sec. 504. (§ 794) Nondiscrimination under Federal grants and programs

(a) **Promulgation of rules and regulations**

No otherwise qualified individual with a disability in the United States, as defined in section 706(8) of this title, shall, solely by reason of her or his disability, be excluded from the participation in, be denied the benefits of, or be subjected to discrimination under any program or activity receiving Federal financial assistance or under any program or activity conducted by any Executive agency or by the United States Postal Service. The head of each such agency shall promulgate such regulations as may be necessary to carry out the amendments to this section made by the Rehabilitation, Comprehensive Services, and Developmental Disabilities Act of 1978. Copies of any proposed regulation shall be submitted to appropriate authorizing committees of the Congress and such regulation may take effect no earlier than the thirtieth day after the date on which such regulation is so submitted to such committees.

(b) **"Program or activity" defined**

For the purposes of this section, the term "program or activity" means all of the operations of—

(1) (A) a department, agency, special purpose district, or other instrumentality of a State or of a local government; or

(B) the entity of such State or local government that distributes such assistance and each such department or agency (and each other State or local government entity) to which the assistance is extended, in the case of assistance to a State or local government;

(2) (A) a college, university, or other postsecondary institution or a public system of higher education; or

(B) a local educational agency (as defined in section 2891(12) of Title 20) system of vocational education, or other school system;

(3) (A) an entire corporation, partnership, or other private organization, or an entire sole proprietorship—

(i) if assistance is extended to such corporation, partnership, private organization, or sole proprietorship as a whole; or

(ii) which is principally engaged in the business of providing education, health care, housing, social services, or parks and recreation; or

(B) the entire plant or other comparable, geographically separate facility to which Federal financial assistance is extended, in the case of any other corporation, partnership, private organization sole proprietorship; or

(4) any other entity which is established by two or more of the entities described in paragraph (1), (2), or (3);

any part of which is extended Federal financial assistance.

TEXT OF THE NATIONAL LABOR RELATIONS ACT

APPENDIX G

49 Stat. 449–57 (1935), as amended by 61 Stat. 136–52 (1947), 65 Stat. 601 (1951), 72 Stat. 945 (1958), 73 Stat. 525–42 (1959), 84 Stat. 930 (1970), 88 Stat. 395–97 (1974), 88 Stat. 1972 (1975), 94 Stat. 347 (1980), 94 Stat. 3452 (1980); 29 U.S.C. Section 151 et seq.

Findings and Policies

Section 1. The denial by some employers of the right of employees to organize and the refusal by some employers to accept the procedure of collective bargaining lead to strikes and other forms of industrial strife or unrest, which have the intent or the necessary effect of burdening or obstructing commerce by (a) impairing the efficiency, safety, or operation of the instrumentalities of commerce; (b) occurring in the current of commerce; (c) materially affecting, restraining, or controlling the flow of raw materials or manufactured or processed goods from or into the channels of commerce, or the prices of such materials or goods in commerce; or (d) causing diminution of employment and wages in such volume as substantially to impair or disrupt the market for goods flowing from or into the channels of commerce.

The inequality of bargaining power between employees who do not possess full freedom of association or actual liberty of contract, and employers who are organized in the corporate or other forms of ownership association substantially burdens and affects the flow of commerce, and tends to aggravate recurrent business depressions by depressing wage rates and the purchasing power of wage earners in industry and by preventing the stabilization of competitive wage rates and working conditions within and between industries.

Experience has proved that protection by law of the right of employees to organize and bargain collectively safeguards commerce from injury, impairment, or interruption, and promotes the flow of commerce by removing certain recognized sources of industrial strife and unrest, by encouraging practices fundamental to the friendly adjustment of industrial disputes arising out of differences as to wages, hours, or other working conditions, and by restoring equality of bargaining power between employers and employees.

Experience has further demonstrated that certain practices by some labor organizations, their officers, and members have the intent or the necessary effect of burdening or obstructing commerce by preventing the free flow of goods in such commerce through strikes and other forms of industrial unrest or through concerted activities which impair the interest of the public in the free flow of such commerce. The elimination of such practices is a necessary condition to the assurance of the rights herein guaranteed.

It is hereby declared to be the policy of the United States to eliminate the causes of certain substantial obstructions to the free flow of commerce and to mitigate and eliminate these obstructions when they have occurred by encouraging the practice and procedure of collective bargaining and by protecting the exercise by workers of full freedom of association, self-organization, and designation of representatives of their own choosing, for the purpose of negotiating the terms and conditions of their employment or other mutual aid or protection.

Definitions

Sec. 2. When used in this Act—

(1) The term "person" includes one or more individuals, labor organizations, partnerships, associations, corporations, legal representatives, trustees, trustees in cases under Title II of the United States Code or receivers.

(2) The term "employer" includes any person acting as an agent of an employer, directly or indirectly, but

shall not include the United States or any wholly owned Government corporation, or any Federal Reserve Bank, or any State or political subdivision thereof, or any person subject to the Railway Labor Act, as amended from time to time, or any labor organization (other than when acting as an employer), or anyone acting in the capacity of officer or agent of such labor organization.

(3) The term "employee" shall include any employee, and shall not be limited to the employees of a particular employer, unless the Act explicitly states otherwise, and shall include any individual whose work has ceased as a consequence of, or in connection with, any current labor dispute or because of any unfair labor practice, and who has not obtained any other regular and substantially equivalent employment, but shall not include any individual employed as an agricultural laborer, or in the domestic service of any family or person at his home, or any individual employed by his parent or spouse, or any individual having the status of an independent contractor, or any individual employed as a supervisor, or any individual employed by an employer subject to the Railway Labor Act, as amended from time to time, or by any other person who is not an employer as herein defined.

(4) The term "representatives" includes any individual or labor organization.

(5) The term "labor organization" means any organization of any kind, or any agency or employee representation committee or plan, in which employees participate and which exists for the purpose, in whole or in part, of dealing with employers concerning grievances, labor disputes, wages, rates of pay, hours of employment, or conditions of work.

(6) The term "commerce" means trade, traffic, commerce, transportation, or communication among the several States, or between the District of Columbia or any Territory of the United States and any State or other Territory, or between any foreign country and any State, Territory, or the District of Columbia, or within the District of Columbia or any Territory, or between points in the same State but through any other State or any Territory or the District of Columbia or any foreign country.

(7) The term "affecting commerce" means in commerce, or burdening or obstructing commerce or the free flow of commerce, or having led or tending to lead to a labor dispute burdening or obstructing commerce or the free flow of commerce.

(8) The term "unfair labor practice" means any unfair labor practice listed in section 8.

(9) The term "labor dispute" includes any controversy concerning terms, tenure or conditions of employment, or concerning the association or representation of persons in negotiating, fixing, maintaining, changing, or seeking to arrange terms or conditions of employment, regardless of whether the disputants stand in the proximate relation of employer and employee.

(10) The term "National Labor Relations Board" means the National Labor Relations Board provided for in section 3 of this Act.

(11) The term "supervisor" means any individual having authority, in the interest of the employer, to hire, transfer, suspend, lay off, recall, promote, discharge, assign, reward, or discipline other employees, or responsibly to direct them, or to adjust their grievances, or effectively to recommend such action, if in connection with the foregoing the exercise of such authority is not of a merely routine or clerical nature, but requires the use of independent judgment.

(12) The term "professional employee" means—

(a) any employee engaged in work (i) predominantly intellectual and varied in character as opposed to routine mental, manual, mechanical, or physical work; (ii) involving the consistent exercise of discretion and judgment in its performance; (iii) of such a character that the output produced or the result accomplished cannot be standardized in relation to a given period of time; (iv) requiring knowledge of an advanced type in a field of science or learning customarily acquired by a prolonged course of specialized intellectual instruction and study in an institution of higher learning or a hospital, as distinguished from a general academic education or from an apprenticeship or from training in the performance of routine mental, manual, or physical processes; or

(b) any employee, who (i) has completed the courses of specialized intellectual instruction and study described in clause (iv) or paragraph (a), and (ii) is performing related work under the supervision of a professional person to qualify himself to become a professional employee as defined in paragraph (a).

(13) In determining whether any person is acting as an "agent" of another person so as to make such other

person responsible for his acts, the question of whether the specific acts performed were actually authorized or subsequently ratified shall not be controlling.

(14) The term "health care institution" shall include any hospital, convalescent hospital, health maintenance organization, health clinic, nursing home, extended care facility, or other institution devoted to the care of sick, infirm, or aged person.

National Labor Relations Board

Sec. 3.

(a) The National Labor Relations Board (hereinafter called the "Board") created by this Act prior to its amendment by the Labor Management Relations Act, 1947, is hereby continued as an agency of the United States, except that the Board shall consist of five instead of three members, appointed by the President by and with the advice and consent of the Senate. Of the two additional members so provided for, one shall be appointed for a term of five years and the other for a term of two years. Their successors, and the successors of the other members, shall be appointed for terms of five years each, excepting that any individual chosen to fill a vacancy shall be appointed only for the unexpired term of the member whom he shall succeed. The President shall designate one member to serve as Chairman of the Board. Any member of the Board may be removed by the President, upon notice and hearing, for neglect of duty or malfeasance in office, but for no other cause.

(b) The Board is authorized to delegate to any group of three or more members any or all the powers which it may itself exercise. The Board is also authorized to delegate to its regional directors its power under section 9 to determine the unit appropriate for the purpose of collective bargaining, to investigate and provide for hearings, and determine whether a question of representation exists, and to direct an election or take a secret ballot under subsection (c) or (e) of section 9 and certify the results thereof, except that upon the filing of a request therefor with the Board by any interested person, the Board may review any action of a regional director delegated to him under this paragraph, but such a review shall not, unless specifically ordered by the Board, operate as a stay of any action taken by the regional director. A vacancy in the Board shall not impair the right of the remaining members to exercise all of the powers of the Board, and three members of the Board shall, at all times, constitute a quorum of the Board, except that two members shall constitute a quorum of any group designated pursuant to the first sentence hereof. The Board shall have an official seal which shall be judicially noted.

(c) The Board shall at the close of each fiscal year make a report in writing to Congress and to the President stating in detail the cases it has heard, the decisions it has rendered, and an account of all moneys it has disbursed.

(d) There shall be a General Counsel of the Board who shall be appointed by the President, by and with the advice and consent of the Senate, for a term of four years. The General Counsel of the Board shall exercise general supervision over all attorneys employed by the Board (other than trial examiners and legal assistants to Board members) and over the officers and employees in the regional offices. He shall have final authority, on behalf of the Board, in respect to the investigation of charges and issuance of complaints under section 10, and in respect of the prosecution of such complaints before the Board, and shall have such other duties as the Board may prescribe or as may be provided by law. In case of a vacancy in the office of the General Counsel the President is authorized to designate the officer or employee who shall act as General Counsel during such vacancy, but no person or persons so designated shall so act (1) for more than forty days when the Congress is in session unless a nomination to fill such vacancy shall have been submitted to the Senate, or (2) after the adjournment *sine die* of the session of the Senate in which such nomination was submitted.

Sec. 4.

(a) Each member of the Board and the General Counsel of the Board shall receive a salary of $12,000 a year, shall be eligible for reappointment, and shall not engage in any other business, vocation, or employment. The Board shall appoint an executive secretary, and such attorneys, examiners, and regional directors, and such other employees as it may from time to time find necessary for the proper performance of its duties. The Board may not employ any attorneys for the purpose of reviewing transcripts of hearings or preparing drafts of opinions except that any attorney employed for assignment as a legal assistant to any Board member may for such Board member review such transcripts and prepare such drafts. No trial examiner's report shall be reviewed, either before or after its publication, by any person other than a member of the Board or his legal assistant, and no trial examiner shall advise or consult with the Board with respect to exceptions taken to his findings, rulings, or recommendations. The Board may establish or utilize such regional, local, or other agencies, and utilize such voluntary and uncompensated services, as may from time to time be needed. Attorneys appointed under this section may, at the direction of the Board, appear for and represent the Board in any case in court. Nothing in this Act shall be construed to authorize the Board to appoint individuals for the purpose of conciliation or mediation, or for economic analysis.

(b) All of the expenses of the Board, including all necessary traveling and subsistence expenses outside the District of Columbia incurred by the members or employees of the Board under its orders, shall be allowed and paid on the presentation of itemized vouchers therefor approved by the Board or by any individual it designates for that purpose.

Sec. 5. The principal office of the Board shall be in the District of Columbia, but it may meet and exercise any or all of its powers at any other place. The Board may, by one or more of its members or by such agents or agencies as it may designate, prosecute any inquiry necessary to its functions in any part of the United States. A member who participates in such an inquiry shall not be disqualified from subsequently participating in a decision of the Board in the same case.

Sec. 6. The Board shall have authority from time to time to make, amend, and rescind, in the manner prescribed by the Administrative Procedure Act, such rules and regulations as may be necessary to carry out the provisions of this Act.

Rights of Employees

Sec. 7. Employees shall have the right to self-organization, to form, join, or assist labor organizations, to bargain collectively through representatives of their own choosing, and to engage in other concerted activities for the purpose of collective bargaining or other mutual aid or protection, and shall also have the right to refrain from any or all such activities except to the extent that such right may be affected by an agreement requiring membership in a labor organization as a condition of employment as authorized in section 8(a)(3).

Sec. 8.

(a) It shall be an unfair labor practice for an employer—;

(1) to interfere with, restrain, or coerce employees in the exercise of the rights guaranteed in section 7;

(2) to dominate or interfere with the formation or administration of any labor organization or contribute financial or other support to it: *Provided,* That subject to rules and regulations made and published by the Board pursuant to section 6, an employer shall not be prohibited from permitting employees to confer with him during working hours without loss of time or pay.

(3) by discrimination in regard to hire or tenure of employment or any term or condition of employment to encourage or discourage membership in any labor organization: *Provided,* That nothing in this Act, or in any other statute of the United States, shall preclude an employer from making an agreement with a labor organization (not established, maintained, or assisted by any action defined in section 8(a) of this Act as an unfair labor practice) to require as a condition of employment membership therein on or after the thirtieth day following the beginning of such employment or the effective date of such agreement, whichever is the later, (i) if such labor organization is the representative of the employees as provided in section 9(a), in the appropriate collective-bargaining unit covered by such agreement when made, and (ii) unless following an election held as provided in section 9(3) within one year preceding the effective date of such agreement, the Board shall have certified that at least a majority of the employees eligible to vote in such election have voted to rescind the authority of such labor organization to make such an agreement: *Provided further,* That no employer shall justify any discrimina-

tion against any employee for nonmembership in a labor organization (A) if he has reasonable grounds for believing that such membership was not available to the employee on the same terms and conditions generally applicable to other members, or (B) if he has reasonable grounds for believing that membership was denied or terminated for reasons other than the failure of the employee to tender the periodic dues and the initiation fees uniformly required as a condition of acquiring or retaining membership;

(4) to discharge or otherwise discriminate against an employee because he has filed charges or given testimony under this Act;

(5) to refuse to bargain collectively with the representatives of his employees, subject to the provisions of section 9(a).

(b) It shall be an unfair labor practice for a labor organization or its agents—

(1) to restrain or coerce (A) employees in the exercise of the rights guaranteed in section 7: *Provided,* That this paragraph shall not impair the right of a labor organization to prescribe its own rules with respect to the acquisition or retention of membership therein; or (B) an employer in the selection of his representatives for the purpose of collective bargaining or the adjustment of grievances;

(2) to cause or attempt to cause an employer to discriminate against an employee in violation of subsection (a)(3) or to discriminate against an employee with respect to whom membership in such organization has been denied or terminated on some ground other than his failure to tender the periodic dues and the initiation fees uniformly required as a condition of acquiring or retaining membership;

(3) to refuse to bargain collectively with an employer, provided it is the representative of his employees subject to the provisions of section 9(a);

(4) (i) to engage in, or to induce or encourage any individual employed by any person engaged in commerce or in an industry affecting commerce to engage in, a strike or a refusal in the course of his employment to use, manufacture, process, transport, or otherwise handle or work on any goods, articles, materials, or commodities or to perform any services; or (ii) to threaten, coerce, or restrain any person engaged in commerce or in an industry affecting commerce, where in either case an object thereof is:

(A) forcing or requiring any employer or self-employed person to join any labor or employer organization or to enter into any agreement which is prohibited by section 8(e);

(B) forcing or requiring any person to cease using, selling, handling, transporting, or otherwise dealing in the products of any other producer, processor, or manufacturer, or to cease doing business with any other person, or forcing or requiring any other employer to recognize or bargain with a labor organization as the representative of his employees unless such labor organization has been certified as the representative of such employees under the provisions of section 9: *Provided,* That nothing contained in this clause (B) shall be construed to make unlawful, where not otherwise unlawful, any primary strike or primary picketing;

(C) forcing or requiring any employer to recognize or bargain with a particular labor organization as the representative of his employees if another labor organization has been certified as the representative of such employees under the provisions of section 9;

(D) forcing or requiring any employer to assign particular work to employees in a particular labor organization or in a particular trade, craft, or class rather than to employees in another labor organization or in another trade, craft, or class, unless such employer is failing to conform to an order or certification of the Board determining the bargaining representative for employees performing such work: *Provided,* That nothing contained in this subsection (b) shall be construed to make unlawful a refusal by any person to enter upon the premises of any employer (other than his own employer), if the employees of such employer are engaged in a strike ratified or approved by a representative of such employees whom such employer is required to recognize under this Act: *Provided further*, That for the purposes of this paragraph (4) only, nothing contained in such paragraph shall be construed to prohibit publicity, other than picketing, for the purpose of truthfully advising the public, including consumers and members of a labor organization, that a product or products are produced by an employer with whom the labor organization has a primary dispute and are distributed by another employer, as long as such publicity does not have an effect of inducing any individual employed by any person other than the primary employer in the course of his employment to refuse to pick up, deliver, or transport any goods, or not to perform any services, at the establishment of the employer engaged in such distribution;

(5) to require of employees covered by an agreement authorized under subsection (a)(3) the payment, as a condition precedent to becoming a member of such organization, of a fee in an amount which the Board finds excessive or discriminatory under all the circumstances. In making such a finding, the Board shall consider, among other relevant factors, the practices and customs of labor organizations in the particular industry, and the wages currently paid to the employees affected;

(6) to cause or attempt to cause an employer to pay or deliver or agree to pay or deliver any money or other thing of value, in the nature of an exaction for services which are not performed or not to be performed; and

(7) to picket or cause to be picketed, or threaten to picket or cause to be picketed, any employer where an object thereof is forcing or requiring an employer to recognize or bargain with a labor organization as the representative of his employees, or forcing or requiring the employees of an employer to accept or select such labor organization as their collective bargaining representative, unless such labor organization is currently certified as the representative of such employees:

(A) where the employer has lawfully recognized in accordance with this Act any other labor organization and a question concerning representation may not appropriately be raised under section 9(c) of this Act,

(B) where within the preceding twelve months a valid election under section 9(c) of this Act has been conducted, or

(C) where such picketing has been conducted without a petition under section 9(c) being filed within a reasonable period of time not to exceed thirty days from the commencement of such picketing: *Provided,* That when such a petition has been filed the Board shall forthwith, without regard to the provisions of section 9(c)(1) or the absence of a showing of a substantial interest on the part of the labor organization, direct an election in such unit as the Board finds to be appropriate and shall certify the results thereof: *Provided further,* That nothing in this subparagraph (C) shall be construed to prohibit any picketing or other publicity for the purpose of truthfully advising the public (including consumers) that an employer does not employ members of, or have a contract with, a labor organization, unless an effect of such picketing is to induce any individual employed by any other person in the course of his employment, not to pick up, deliver or transport any goods or not to perform any services.

Nothing in this paragraph (7) shall be construed to permit any act which would otherwise be an unfair labor practice under this section 8(b).

(c) The expressing of any views, argument, or opinion, or the dissemination thereof, whether in written, printed, graphic, or visual form, shall not constitute or be evidence of an unfair labor practice under any of the provisions of this Act, if such expression contains no threat of reprisal or force or promise of benefit.

(d) For the purposes of this section, to bargain collectively is the performance of the mutual obligation of the employer and the representative of the employees to meet at reasonable times and confer in good faith with respect to wages, hours, and other terms and conditions of employment, or the negotiation of an agreement or any question arising thereunder, and the execution of a written contract incorporating any agreement reached if requested by either party, but such obligation does not compel either party to agree to a proposal or require the making of a concession: *Provided,* That where there is in effect a collective-bargaining contract covering employees in an industry affecting commerce, the duty to bargain collectively shall also mean that no party to such contract shall terminate or modify such contract, unless the party desiring such termination or modification—

(1) serves a written notice upon the party to the contract of the proposed termination or modification sixty days prior to the expiration date thereof, or in the event such contract contains no expiration date, sixty days prior to the time it is proposed to make such termination or modification;

(2) offers to meet and confer with the other party for the purpose of negotiating a new contract or a contract containing the proposed modifications;

(3) notifies the Federal Mediation and Conciliation Service within thirty days after such notice of the existence of a dispute, and simultaneously therewith notifies any State or Territorial agency established to mediate and conciliate disputes within the State or Territory where the dispute occurred, provided no agreement has been reached by that time; and

(4) continues in full force and effect, without resorting to strike or lockout, all the terms and conditions of the existing contract for a period of sixty days after such notice is given or until the expiration date of such contract, whichever occurs later.

The duties imposed upon employers, employees, and labor organizations by paragraphs (2), (3), and (4) shall become inapplicable upon an intervening certification of the Board, under which the labor organization or individual, which is a party to the contract, has been superseded as or ceased to be the representative of the employees subject to the provisions of section 9(a), and the duties so imposed shall not be construed as requiring either party to discuss or agree to any modification of the terms and conditions contained in a contract for a fixed period, if such modification is to become effective before such terms and conditions can be reopened under the provisions of the contract. Any employee who engages in a strike within any notice period specified in this subsection, or who engages in any strike with the appropriate period specified in subsection (g) of this section, shall lose his status as an employee of the employer engaged in the particular labor dispute, for the purposes of sections 8, 9, and 10 of this Act, as amended, but such loss of status for such employee shall terminate if and when he is reemployed by such employer. Whenever the collective bargaining involves employees of a health care institution, the provisions of this section 8(d) shall be modified as follows:

(A) The notice of section 8(d)(1) shall be ninety days; the notice of section 8(d)(3) shall be sixty days; and the contract period of section 8(d)(4) shall be ninety days.

(B) Where the bargaining is for an initial agreement following certification or recognition, at least thirty days' notice of the existence of a dispute shall be given by the labor organization to the agencies set forth in section 8(d)(3).

(C) After notice is given to the Federal Mediation and Conciliation Service under either clause (A) or (B) of this sentence, the Service shall promptly communicate with the parties and use its best efforts, by mediation and conciliation, to bring them to agreement. The parties shall participate fully and promptly in such meetings as may be undertaken by the Service for the purpose of aiding in a settlement of the dispute.

(e) it shall be an unfair labor practice for any labor organization and any employer to enter into any contract or agreement, express or implied, whereby such employer ceases or refrains or agrees to cease or refrain from handling, using, selling, transporting or otherwise dealing in any of the products of any other employer, or to cease doing business with any other person, and any contract or agreement entered into heretofore or hereafter containing such an agreement shall be to such extent unenforceable and void: *Provided,* That nothing in this subsection (e) shall apply to an agreement between a labor organization and an employer in the construction industry relating to the contracting or subcontracting of work to be done at the site of the construction, alteration, painting, or repair of a building, structure, or other work: *Provided further,* That for the purposes of this subsection (e) and section 8(b)(4)(B) the terms "any employer," "any person engaged in commerce or in industry affecting commerce," and "any person" when used in relation to the terms "any other producer, processor, or manufacturer," "any other employer," or "any other person" shall not include persons in the relation of a jobber, manufacturer, contractor, or subcontractor working on the goods or premises of the jobber or manufacturer or performing parts of an integrated process of production in the apparel and clothing industry: *Provided further,* That nothing in this Act shall prohibit the enforcement of any agreement which is within the foregoing exception.

(f) It shall not be an unfair labor practice under subsections (a) and (b) of this section for an employer engaged primarily in the building and construction industry to make an agreement covering employees engaged (or who, upon their employment, will be engaged) in the building and construction industry with a labor organization of which building and construction employees are members (not established, maintained, or assisted by any action defined in section 8(a) of this Act as an unfair labor practice) because (1) the majority status of such labor organization has not been established under the provisions of section 9 of this Act prior to the making of such agreement, or (2) such agreement requires as a condition of employment, membership in such labor organization after the seventh day following the beginning of such employment or the effective date of the agreement, whichever is later, or (3) such agreement requires the employer to notify such labor organization of opportunities for employment with such employer, or gives such labor organization an opportunity to refer qualified applicants for such employment, or (4) such agreement specifies minimum training or experience qualifications for employment or provides for priority in opportunities for employment based upon length of service with such employer, in the industry or in the particular geographical area: *Provided,* That nothing in this subsection shall set aside the final proviso to section 8(a)(3) of this Act: *Provided further,* That any agreement which would be invalid, but for clause (1) of this subsection, shall not be a bar to a petition filed pursuant to section 9(c) or 9(e).

(g) A labor organization before engaging in any strike, picketing, or other concerted refusal to work at any health care institution shall, not less than ten days prior to such action, notify the institution in writing and the Federal Mediation and Conciliation Service of that intention, except that in the case of bargaining for an initial agreement following certification or recognition the notice required by this subsection shall not be given the expiration of the period specified in clause (B) of the last sentence of section 8(d) of this Act. The notice shall state the date and time that such action will commence. The notice, once given, may be extended by the written agreement of both parties.

Representatives and Elections

Sec. 9.

(a) Representatives designated or selected for the purposes of collective bargaining by the majority of the employees in a unit appropriate for such purposes, shall be the exclusive representatives of all the employees in such unit for the purposes of collective bargaining in respect to rates of pay, wages, hours or employment, or other conditions of employment: *Provided,* That any individual employee or a group of employees shall have the right at any time to present grievances to their employer and to have such grievances adjusted, without the intervention of the bargaining representative, as long as the adjustment is not inconsistent with the terms of a collective-bargaining contract or agreement then in effect: *Provided further,* That the bargaining representative has been given opportunity to be present at such adjustment.

(b) The Board shall decide in each case whether, in order to assure to employees the fullest freedom in exercising the rights guaranteed by this Act, the unit appropriate for the purposes of collective bargaining shall be the employer unit, craft unit, plant unit, or subdivision thereof: *Provided,* That the Board shall not (1) decide that any unit is appropriate for such purposes if such unit includes both professional employees and employees who are not professional employees unless a majority of such professional employees vote for inclusion in such unit; or (2) decide that any craft unit is inappropriate for such purposes on the ground that a different unit has been established by a prior Board determination, unless a majority of the employees in the proposed craft unit votes against separate representation; or (3) decide that any unit is appropriate for such purposes if it includes, together with other employees, any individual employed as a guard to enforce against employees and other persons rules to protect property of the employer or to protect the safety of persons on the employer's premises; but no labor organization shall be certified as the representative of employees in a bargaining unit of guards if such organization admits to membership, or is affiliated directly or indirectly with an organization which admits to membership, employees other than guards.

(c) (1) Wherever a petition shall have been filed, in accordance with such regulations as may be prescribed by the Board—

(A) by an employee or group of employees or any individual or labor organization acting in their behalf alleging that a substantial number of employees (i) wish to be represented for collective bargaining and that their employer declines to recognize their representative as the representative defined in section 9(a), or (ii) assert that the individual or labor organization, which has been certified or is being recognized by their employer as the bargaining representative, is no longer a representative as defined in section 9(a); or

(B) by an employer, alleging that one or more individuals or labor organizations have presented to him a claim to be recognized as the representative defined in section 9(a):

the Board shall investigate such petition and if it has reasonable cause to believe that a question of representation affecting commerce exists shall provide for an appropriate hearing upon due notice. Such hearing may be conducted by an officer or employee of the regional office, who shall not make any recommendations with respect thereto. If the Board finds upon the record of such hearing that such a question of representation exists, it shall direct an election by secret ballot and shall certify the results thereof.

(2) In determining whether or not a question of representation affecting commerce exists, the same regulations and rules of decision shall apply irrespective of the identity of the person filing the petition or the kind of relief sought and in no case shall the Board deny a labor organization a place on the ballot by reason of an order with respect to such labor organization or its predecessor not issued in conformity with section 10(c).

(3) No election shall be directed in any bargaining unit or any subdivision within which, in the preceding twelve-month period, a valid election shall have been held. Employees engaged in an economic strike who are not entitled to reinstatement shall be eligible to vote under such regulations as the Board shall find are consistent with the purposes and provisions of this Act in any election conducted within twelve months after the commencement of the strike. In any election where none of the choices on the ballot receives a majority, a run-off shall be conducted, the ballot providing for a selection between the two choices receiving the largest and second largest number of valid votes cast in the election.

(4) Nothing in this section shall be construed to prohibit the waiving of hearings by stipulation for the purpose of a consent election in conformity with regulations and rules of decision of the Board.

(5) In determining whether a unit is appropriate for the purposes specified in subsection (b) the extent to which the employees have organized shall not be controlling.

(d) Whenever an order of the Board made pursuant to section 10(c) is based in whole or in part upon facts certified following an investigation pursuant to subsection (c) of this section and there is a petition for the enforcement or review of such order, such certification and the record of such investigation shall be included in the transcript of the entire record required to be filed under section 10(e) or 10(f), and thereupon the decree of the court enforcing, modifying, or setting aside in whole or in part the order of the Board shall be made and entered upon the pleadings, testimony, and proceedings set forth in such transcript.

(e) (1) Upon the filing with the Board, by 30 per centum or more of the employees in a bargaining unit covered by an agreement between their employer and a labor organization made pursuant to section 8(a)(3), of a petition alleging they desire that such authority be rescinded, the Board shall take a secret ballot of the employees in such unit and certify the results thereof to such labor organization and to the employer.

(2) No election shall be conducted pursuant to this subsection in any bargaining unit or any subdivision within which, in the preceding twelve-month period, a valid election shall have been held.

Prevention of Unfair Labor Practices

Sec. 10.

(a) The Board is empowered, as hereinafter provided, to prevent any person from engaging in any unfair labor practice (listed in section 8) affecting commerce. This power shall not be affected by any other means of adjustment or prevention that has been or may be established by agreement, law, or otherwise: *Provided,* That the Board is empowered by agreement with any agency of any State or Territory to cede to such agency jurisdiction over any cases in any industry (other than mining, manufacturing, communications, and transportation except where predominantly local in character) even though such cases may involve labor disputes affecting commerce, unless the provision of the State or Territorial statute applicable to the determination of such cases by such agency is inconsistent with the corresponding provision of this Act or has received a construction inconsistent therewith.

(b) Whenever it is charged that any person has engaged in or is engaging in any such unfair labor practice, the Board, or any agent or agency designated by the Board for such purposes, shall have power to issue and cause to be served upon such person a complaint stating the charges in that respect, and containing a notice of hearing before the Board or a member thereof, or before a designated agent or agency, at a place therein fixed, not less than five days after the serving of said complaint: *Provided,* That no complaint shall issue based upon any unfair labor practice occurring more than six months prior to the filing of the charge with the Board and the service of a copy thereof upon the person against whom such charge is made, unless the person aggrieved thereby was prevented from filing such charge by reason of service in the armed forces, in which event the six-month period shall be computed from the day of his discharge. Any such complaint may be amended by the member, agent, or agency conducting the hearing or the Board in its discretion at any time prior to the issuance of an order based thereon. The person so complained of shall have the right to file an answer to the original or amended complaint and to appear in person or otherwise and give testimony at the place and time fixed in the complaint. In the discretion of the member, agent, or agency conducting the hearing or the Board, any other person may be allowed to intervene in the said proceeding and to present testimony. Any such proceeding shall, so far as practicable, be conducted in accordance with the rules of evidence applicable in the district courts of the United States under the rules of civil procedure for the district courts of the United States, adopted by the Supreme Court of the United States pursuant to the Act of June 19, 1934 (U.S.C., title 28, secs. 723-B, 723-C).

(c) The testimony taken by such member, agent, or agency or the Board shall be reduced to writing and filed with the Board. Thereafter, in its discretion, the Board upon notice may take further testimony or hear argument. If upon the preponderance of the testimony taken the Board shall be of the opinion that any person named in the complaint has engaged in or is engaging in any such unfair labor practice, then the Board shall state its findings of fact and shall issue and cause to be served on such person an order requiring such person to cease and desist from such unfair labor practice, and to take such affirmative action including reinstatement of employees with or without back pay, as will effectuate the policies of this Act: *Provided,* That where an order directs reinstatement of an employee, back pay may be required of the employer or labor organization, as the case may be, responsible for the discrimination suffered by him: *And provided further,* That in determining whether a complaint shall issue alleging a violation of section 8(a)(1) or section 8(a)(2), and in deciding such cases, the same regulations and rules of decision shall apply irrespective of whether or not the labor organization affected is affiliated with a labor organization national or international in scope. Such order may further require such person to make reports from time to time showing the extent to which it has complied with the order. If upon the preponderance of the testimony taken the Board shall not be of the opinion that the person named in the complaint has engaged in or is engaging in any such unfair labor practice, then the Board shall state its findings of fact and shall issue an order dismissing the said complaint. No order of the Board shall require the reinstatement of any individual as an employee who has been suspended or discharged, or the payment to him of any back pay, if such individual was suspended or discharged for cause. In case the evidence is presented before a member of the Board, or before an examiner or examiners thereof, such member, or such examiner or examiners, as the case may be, shall issue and cause to be served on the parties to the proceeding a proposed report, together with a recommended order, which shall be filed with the Board, and if no exceptions are filed within twenty days after service thereof upon such parties, or within such further period as the Board may authorize, such recommended order shall become the order of the Board and become effective as therein prescribed.

(d) Until the record in the case shall have been filed in a court, as hereinafter provided, the Board may at any time, upon reasonable notice and in such manner as it shall deem proper, modify or set aside, in whole or in part, any finding or order made or issued by it.

(e) The Board shall have power to petition any court of appeals of the United States, or if all the courts of appeals to which application may be made are in vacation, any district court of the United States, within any circuit or district, respectively, wherein the unfair labor practice in question occurred or wherein such person resides or transacts business, for the enforcement of such order and for appropriate temporary relief or restraining order, and shall file in the court the record in the proceedings, as provided in section 2112 of title 28, United States Code. Upon the filing of such petition, the court shall cause notice thereof to be served upon such person, and thereupon shall have jurisdiction of the proceeding and of the question determined therein, and shall have power to grant such temporary relief or restraining order as it deems just and proper, and to make and enter a decree enforcing, modifying, and enforcing as so modified, or setting aside in whole or in part the order of the Board. No objection that has not been urged before the Board, its member, agent, or agency, shall be considered by the court, unless the failure or neglect to urge such objection shall be excused because of extraordinary circumstances. The findings of the Board with respect to questions of fact if supported by substantial evidence on the record considered as a whole shall be conclusive. If either party shall apply to the court for leave to adduce additional evidence and shall show to the satisfaction of the court that such additional evidence is material and that there were reasonable grounds for the failure to adduce such evidence in the hearing before the Board, its member, agent, or agency, the court may order such additional evidence to be taken before the Board, its member, agent, or agency, and to be made a part of the record. The Board may modify its findings as to the facts, or make new findings, by reason of additional evidence so taken and filed, and it shall file such modified or new findings, which findings with respect to question of fact if supported by substantial evidence on the record considered as a whole shall be conclusive, and shall file its recommendations, if any, for the modification or setting aside of its original order. Upon the filing of the record with it the jurisdiction of the court shall be exclusive and its judgment and decree shall be final, except that the court shall be subject to review by the appropriate United States court of appeals if application was made to the district court as hereinabove provided, and by the Supreme Court of the United States upon writ of certiorari or certification as provided in section 1254 of title 28.

(f) Any person aggrieved by a final order of the Board granting or denying in whole or in part the relief sought may obtain a review of such order in any circuit court of appeals of the United States in the circuit wherein the unfair labor practice in question was alleged to have been engaged in or wherein such person resides or transacts business, or in the United States Court of Appeals for the District of Columbia, by filing in such court a written petition praying that the order of the Board be modified or set aside. A copy of such petition shall be forthwith transmitted by the clerk of the court to the Board, and thereupon the aggrieved party shall file in the court the record in the proceeding, certified by the Board, as provided in section 2112 of title 28, United States Code. Upon the filing of such petition, the court shall proceed in the same manner as in the case of an application by the Board under subsection (e) of this section, and shall have the same jurisdiction to grant to the Board such temporary relief or restraining order as it deems just and proper, and in like manner to make and enter a decree enforcing, modifying, and enforcing as so modified, or setting aside in whole or in part the order of the Board; the findings of the Board with respect to questions of fact if supported by substantial evidence on the record considered as a whole shall in like manner be conclusive.

(g) The commencement of proceedings under subsection (e) or (f) of this section shall not, unless specifically ordered by the court, operate as a stay of the Board's order.

(h) When granting appropriate temporary relief or a restraining order, or making and entering a decree enforcing, modifying, and enforcing as so modified, or setting aside in whole or in part an order of the Board, as provided in this section, the jurisdiction of courts sitting in equity shall not be limited by the Act entitled "An Act to amend the Judicial Code and to define and limit the jurisdiction of courts sitting in equity, and for other purposes," approved March 23, 1932 (U.S.C., Supp. VII, title 29, secs. 101–115).

(i) Petitions filed under this Act shall be heard expeditiously, and if possible within ten days after they have been docketed.

(j) The Board shall have power, upon issuance of a complaint as provided in subsection (b) charging that any person has engaged in or is engaging in an unfair labor practice, to petition any district court of the United States (including the District Court of the United States for the District of Columbia), within any district wherein the unfair labor practice in question is alleged to have occurred or wherein such person resides or transacts business, for appropriate temporary relief or restraining order. Upon the filing of any such petition the court shall cause notice thereof to be served upon such person, and thereupon shall have jurisdiction to grant to the Board such temporary relief or restraining order as it deems just and proper.

(k) Whenever it is charged that any person has engaged in an unfair labor practice within the meaning of paragraph (4)(D) of section 8(b), the Board is empowered and directed to hear and determine the dispute out of which such unfair labor practice shall have arisen, unless, within ten days after notice that such charge has been filed, the parties to such dispute submit to the Board satisfactory evidence that they have adjusted, or agreed upon methods for the voluntary adjustment of, the dispute. Upon compliance by the parties to the dispute with the decision of the Board or upon such voluntary adjustment of the dispute, such charge shall be dismissed.

(l) Whenever it is charged that any person has engaged in an unfair labor practice within the meaning of paragraph (4) (A), (B), or (C) of section 8(b), or section 8(e) of section 8(b)(7), the preliminary investigation of such charge shall be made forthwith and given priority over all other cases except cases of like character in the office where it is filed or is referred. If, after such investigation, the officer or regional attorney to whom the matter may be referred has reasonable cause to believe such charge is true and that a complaint should issue, he shall, on behalf of the Board, petition any district court of the United States (including the District Court of the United States for the District of Columbia) within any district where the unfair labor practice in question has occurred, is alleged to have occurred, or wherein such person resides or transacts business, for appropriate injunctive relief pending the final adjudication of the Board with respect to such matter. Upon the filing of any such petition the district court shall have jurisdiction to grant such injunctive relief or temporary restraining order as it deems just and proper, not withstanding any other provision of law: *Provided further,* That no temporary restraining order shall be issued without notice unless a petition alleges that substantial and irreparable injury to the charging party will be unavoidable and such temporary restraining order shall be effective no longer than five days and will become void at the expiration of such period: *Provided further,* That such officer or regional attorney shall not apply for any restraining order under section 8(b)(7) if a charge against the employer under section 8(a)(2) has been filed and after the preliminary investigation, he has reasonable cause to believe that such charge is true and that a complaint should issue. Upon filing of any such petition the courts shall cause notice thereof to be served upon any person involved in the charge and such person, including the charging party, shall be given an opportunity to appear by counsel and present any relevant testimony: *Provided further,* That for the purposes of this subsection district courts shall be deemed to have jurisdiction of a labor organization (1) in the district in which such organization maintains its principal office, or (2) in any district in which its duly authorized officers or agents are engaged in promoting or protecting the interests of employee members. The service of legal process upon such officer or agent shall constitute service upon the labor organization and make such organization a party to the suit. In situations where such relief is appropriate the procedure specified herein shall apply to charges with respect to section 8(b)(4)(D).

(m) Whenever it is charged that any person has engaged in an unfair labor practice within the meaning of subsection (a)(3) or (b)(2) of section 8, such charge shall be given priority over all other cases except cases of like character in the office where it is filed or to which it is referred and cases given priority under subsection (l).

Investigatory Powers

Sec. 11. For the purpose of all hearings and investigations, which, in the opinion of the Board, are necessary and proper for the exercise of the powers vested in it by section 9 and section 10—

(1) The Board, or its duly authorized agents or agencies, shall at all reasonable times have access to, for the purpose of examination, and the right to copy any evidence of any person being investigated or proceeded against that relates to any matter under investigation or in question. The Board, or any member thereof, shall upon application of any party to such proceedings, forthwith issue to such party subpoenas requiring the attendance and testimony of witnesses or the production of any evidence in such proceeding or investigation requested in such application. Within five days after the service of a subpoena on any person requiring the production of any evidence in his possession or under his control, such person may petition the Board to revoke, and the Board shall revoke, such subpoena if in its opinion the evidence whose production is required does not relate to any matter under investigation, or any matter in question in such proceedings, or if in its opinion such subpoena does not describe with sufficient particularity the evidence whose production is required. Any member of the Board, or any agent or agency designated by the Board for such purposes, may administer oaths and affirmations, examine witnesses, and receive evidence. Such attendance of witnesses and the production of such evidence may be required from any place in the United States or any Territory or possession thereof, at any designated place of hearing.

(2) In case of contumacy or refusal to obey a subpoena issued to any person, any district court of the United States or the United States courts of any Territory or possession, or the District Court of the United States for the District of Columbia, within the jurisdiction of which the inquiry is carried on or within the jurisdiction of which said person guilty of contumacy or refusal to obey is found or resides or transacts business, upon application by the Board shall have jurisdiction to issue to such person an order requiring such person to appear before the Board, its member, agent, or agency, there to produce evidence if so ordered, or there to give testimony touching the matter under investigation or in question; and any failure to obey such order of the court may be punished by said court as a contempt thereof.

(3) Repealed.

(4) Complaints, orders and other process and papers of the Board, its member, agent, or agency, may be served either personally or by registered or certified mail or by telegraph or by leaving a copy thereof at the principal office or place of business of the person required to be served. The verified return by the individual so serving the same setting forth the manner of such service shall be proof of the same, and the return post office receipt or telegraph receipt therefor when registered or certified and mailed or telegraphed as aforesaid shall be proof of service of the same. Witnesses summoned before the Board, its member, agent, or agency, shall be paid the same fees and mileage that are paid witnesses in the courts of the United States, and witnesses whose depositions are taken and the persons taking the same shall severally be entitled to the same fees as are paid for like services in the courts of the United States.

(5) All process of any court to which application may be made under this Act may be served in the judicial district where the defendant or other person required to be served resides or may be found.

(6) The several departments and agencies of the Government, when directed by the President, shall furnish the Board, upon its request, all records, papers, and information in their possession relating to any matter before the Board.

Sec. 12. Any person who shall willfully resist, prevent, impede, or interfere with any member of the Board or any of its agents or agencies in the performance of duties pursuant to this Act shall be punished by a fine of not more than $5,000 or by imprisonment for not more than one year, or both.

Limitations

Sec. 13. Nothing in this Act, except as specifically provided for herein, shall be construed so as either to interfere with or impede or diminish in any way the right to strike, or to affect the limitations or qualifications on that right.

Sec. 14.

(a) Nothing herein shall prohibit any individual employed as a supervisor from becoming or remaining a member of a labor organization, but no employer subject to this Act shall be compelled to deem individuals defined herein as supervisors as employees for the purpose of any law, either national or local, relating to collective bargaining.

(b) Nothing in this Act shall be construed as authorizing the execution or application of agreements requiring membership in a labor organization as a condition of employment in any State or Territory in which such execution or application is prohibited by State or Territorial law.

(c) (1) The Board, in its discretion, may, by rule of decision or by published rules adopted pursuant to the Administrative Procedure Act, decline to assert jurisdiction over any labor dispute involving any class or category of employers, where, in the opinion of the Board, the effect of such labor dispute on commerce is not sufficiently substantial to warrant the exercise of its jurisdiction: *Provided,* That the Board shall not decline to assert jurisdiction over any labor dispute over which it would assert jurisdiction under the standards prevailing upon August 1, 1959.

(2) Nothing in this Act shall be deemed to prevent or bar any agency or the courts of any State or Territory (including the Commonwealth of Puerto Rico, Guam, and the Virgin Islands), from assuming and asserting jurisdiction over labor disputes over which the Board declines, pursuant to paragraph (1) of this subsection, to assert jurisdiction.

Sec. 15. Wherever the application of the provisions of section 272 of chapter 10 of the Act entitled "An Act to establish a uniform system of bankruptcy throughout the United States," approved July 1, 1898, and Acts amendatory thereof and supplementary thereto (U.S.C., title 11, sec. 672), conflicts with the application of the provisions of this Act, this Act shall prevail: *Provided,* That in any situation where the provisions of this Act cannot be validly enforced, the provisions of such other Acts shall remain in full force and effect.

Sec. 16. If any provision of this Act, or the application of such provision to any person or circumstances, shall be held invalid, the remainder of this Act, or the application of such provision to persons or circumstances other than those as to which it is held invalid, shall not be affected thereby.

Sec. 17. This Act may be cited as the "National Labor Relations Act."

Sec. 18. No petition entertained, no investigation made, no election held, and no certification issued by the National Labor Relations Board, under any of the provisions of section 9 of the National Labor Relations Act, as amended, shall be invalid by reason of the failure of the Congress of Industrial Organizations to have complied with the requirements of section 9(f), (g), or (h) of the aforesaid Act prior to December 22, 1949, or by reason of the failure of the American Federation of Labor to have complied with the provisions of section 9(f), (g), or (h) of the aforesaid Act prior to November 7, 1947: *Provided,* That no liability shall be imposed under any provision of this Act upon any person for failure to honor any election or certificate referred to above, prior to the effective date of this amendment: *Provided, however,* That this proviso shall not have the effect of setting aside or in any way affecting judgments or decrees heretofore entered under section 10(e) or (f) and which have become final.

Individuals with Religious Convictions

Sec. 19. Any employee who is a member of and adheres to established and traditional tenets or teachings of a bona fide religion, body, or sect which has historically held conscientious objections to joining or financially supporting labor organizations shall not be required to join or financially support any labor organization as a condition of employment; except that such employee may be required in a contract between such employees' employer and a labor organization in lieu of periodic dues and initiation fees, to pay sums equal to such dues and initiation fees to a nonreligious nonlabor organization charitable fund exempt from taxation under section 501(c)(3) of title 26 of the Internal Revenue Code, chosen by such employee from a list of at least three such funds, designated in such contract or if the contract fails to designate such funds, then to any such fund chosen by the employee. If such employee who holds conscientious objections pursuant to this section requests the labor organization to use the grievance-arbitration procedure on the employee's behalf, the labor organization is authorized to charge the employee for the reasonable cost of using such procedure.

TEXT OF THE LABOR MANAGEMENT RELATIONS ACT

H APPENDIX

61 Stat. 136–52 (1947), as amended by 73 Stat. 519ff (1959), 83 Stat. 133 (1969), 87 Stat. 314 (1973), 88 Stat. 396–97 (1974); 29 U.S.C. Sections 141–97

AN ACT

To amend the National Labor Relations Act, to provide additional facilities for the mediation of labor disputes affecting commerce, to equalize legal responsibilities of labor organizations and employers, and for other purposes.

Be it enacted by the Senate and House of Representatives of the United States of America in Congress assembled.

Short Title and Declaration of Policy

Section 1.

(a) This Act may be cited as the "Labor Management Relations Act, 1947,"

(b) Industrial strife which interferes with the normal flow of commerce and with the full production of articles and commodities for commerce, can be avoided or substantially minimized if employers, employees, and labor organizations each recognize under law one another's legitimate rights in their relations with each other, and above all recognize under law that neither party has any right in its relations with any other to engage in acts or practices which jeopardize the public health, safety, or interest.

It is the purpose and policy of this Act, in order to promote the full flow of commerce, to prescribe the legitimate rights of both employees and employers in their relations affecting commerce, to provide orderly and peaceful procedures for preventing the interference by either with the legitimate rights of the other, to protect the rights of individual employees in their relations with labor organizations whose activities affect commerce, to define and proscribe practices on the part of labor and management which affect commerce and are inimical to the general welfare, and to protect the rights of the public in connection with labor disputes affecting commerce.

TITLE I

Amendments of National Labor Relations Act

Sec. 101. The National Labor Relations Act is hereby amended to read as follows:

(The text of the National Labor Relations Act as amended appears on Appendix A, supra.)

Effective Date of Certain Changes

Sec. 102. [Omitted.]
Sec. 103. [Omitted.]
Sec. 104. [Omitted.]

TITLE II

Conciliation of Labor Disputes in Industries Affecting Commerce; National Emergencies

Sec. 201. That it is the policy of the United States that—

(a) sound and stable industrial peace and the advancement of the general welfare, health, and safety of the Nation and of the best interest of employers and employees can most satisfactorily be secured by the settlement of issues between employers and employees through the processes of conference and collective bargaining between employers and the representatives of their employees;

(b) the settlement of issues between employers and employees through collective bargaining may be advanced by making available full and adequate governmental facilities for conciliation, mediation, and voluntary arbitration to aid and encourage employers and the representatives of their employees to reach and maintain agreements concerning rates of pay, hours, and working conditions, and to make all reasonable efforts to settle their differences by mutual agreement reached through conferences and collective bargaining or by such methods as may be provided for in any applicable agreement for the settlement of disputes; and

(c) certain controversies which arise between parties to collective-bargaining agreements may be avoided or minimized by making available full and adequate governmental facilities for furnishing assistance to employers and the representatives of their employees in formulating for inclusion within such agreements provision for adequate notice of any proposed changes in the terms of such agreements, for the final adjustment of grievances or questions regarding the application or interpretation of such agreements, and other provisions designed to prevent the subsequent arising of such controversies.

Sec. 202.

(a) There is hereby created an independent agency to be known as the Federal Mediation and Conciliation Service (herein referred to as the "Service," except that for sixty days after the date of the enactment of this Act such term shall refer to the Conciliation Service of the Department of Labor). The Service shall be under the direction of a Federal Mediation and Conciliation Director (hereinafter referred to as the "Director"), who shall be appointed by the President by and with the advice and consent of the Senate. The Director shall receive compensation at the rate of $12,000 per annum. The Director shall not engage in any other business, vocation, or employment.

(b) The Director is authorized, subject to the civil-service laws, to appoint such clerical and other personnel as may be necessary for the execution of the functions of the Service, and shall fix their compensations in accordance with the Classification Act of 1923, as amended, and may, without regard to the provisions of the civil-service laws and the Classification Act of 1923, as amended, appoint and fix the compensation of such conciliators and mediators as may be necessary to carry out the functions of the Service. The Director is authorized to make such expenditures for supplies, facilities, and services as he deems necessary. Such expenditures shall be allowed and paid upon presentation of itemized vouchers therefor approved by the Director or by any employee designated by him for that purpose.

(c) The principal office of the Service shall be in the District of Columbia, but the Director may establish regional offices convenient to localities in which labor controversies are likely to arise. The Director may by order, subject to revocation at any time, delegate any authority and discretion conferred upon him by this Act to any regional director, or other officer or employee of the Service. The Director may establish suitable procedures for cooperation with State and local mediation agencies. The Director shall make an annual report in writing to Congress at the end of the fiscal year.

(d) All mediation and conciliation functions of the Secretary of Labor or the United States Conciliation Service under section 8 of the Act entitled "An Act to create a Department of Labor," approved March 4, 1913 (U.S.C., title 29, sec. 51), and all functions of the United States Conciliation Service under any other law are hereby transferred to the Federal Mediation and Conciliation Service, together with the personnel and records of the United States Conciliation Service. Such transfer shall take effect upon the sixtieth day after the date of enactment of this Act. Such transfer shall not affect any proceedings pending before the United States Conciliation Service or any certification, order, rule, or regulation theretofore made by it or by the Secretary of Labor. The Director and the Service shall not be subject in any way to the jurisdiction or authority of the Secretary of Labor or any official or division of the Department of Labor.

Functions of the Service

Sec. 203.

(a) It shall be the duty of the Service, in order to prevent or minimize interruptions of the free flow of commerce growing out of labor disputes, to assist parties to labor disputes in industries affecting commerce to settle such disputes, through conciliation and mediation.

(b) The Service may proffer its services in any labor dispute in any industry affecting commerce, either upon its own motion or upon the request of one or more of the parties to the dispute, whenever in its judgment such dispute threatens to cause a substantial interruption of commerce. The Director and the Service are directed to avoid attempting to mediate disputes which would have only a minor effect on interstate commerce if State or other conciliation services are available to the parties. Whenever the Service does proffer its services in any dispute, it shall be the duty of the Service promptly to put itself in communication with the parties and to use its best efforts, by mediation and conciliation, to bring them to agreement.

(c) If the Director is not able to bring the parties to agreement by conciliation within a reasonable time, he shall seek to induce the parties voluntarily to seek other means of settling the dispute without resort to strike, lockout, or other coercion, including submission to the employees in the bargaining unit of the employer's last offer of settlement for approval or rejection in a secret ballot. The failure or refusal of either party to agree to any procedure suggested by the Director shall not be deemed a violation of any duty or obligation imposed by this Act.

(d) Final adjustment by a method agreed upon by the parties is hereby declared to be the desirable method for settlement of grievance disputes arising over the application or interpretation of an existing collective-bargaining agreement. The Service is directed to make its conciliation and mediation services available in the settlement of such grievance disputes only as a last resort and in exceptional cases.

(e) The Service is authorized and directed to encourage and support the establishment and operation of joint labor management activities conducted by plant, area, and industrywide committees designed to improve labor management relationships, job security and organizational effectiveness, in accordance with the provisions of section 205A.

Sec. 204.

(a) In order to prevent or minimize interruptions of the free flow of commerce growing out of labor disputes, employers and employees and their representatives, in any industry affecting commerce, shall—

(1) exert every reasonable effort to make and maintain agreements concerning rates of pay, hours, and working conditions, including provision for adequate notice of any proposed change in the terms of such agreements;

(2) whenever a dispute arises over the terms or application of a collective-bargaining agreement and a conference is requested by a party or prospective party thereto, arrange promptly for such a conference to be held and endeavor in such conference to settle such dispute expeditiously; and

(3) in case such dispute is not settled by conference, participate fully and promptly in such meetings as may be undertaken by the Service under this Act for the purpose of aiding a settlement of the dispute.

Sec. 205.

(a) There is hereby created a National Labor-Management Panel which shall be composed of twelve members appointed by the President, six of whom shall be selected from among persons outstanding in the field of management and six of whom shall be selected from among persons outstanding in the field of labor. Each member shall hold office for a term of three years, except that any member appointed to fill a vacancy occurring prior to the expiration of the term for which his predecessor was appointed shall be appointed for the remainder of such term, and the terms of office of the members first taking office shall expire, as designated by the President at the time of appointment, four at the end of the first year, four at the end of the second year, and four at the end of the third year after the date of appointment. Members of the panel, when serving on business of the panel, shall be paid compensation at the rate of $25 per day, and shall also be entitled to receive an allowance for actual and necessary travel and subsistence expenses while so serving away from their places of residence.

(b) It shall be the duty of the panel, at the request of the Director, to advise in the avoidance of industrial controversies and the manner in which mediation and voluntary adjustment shall be administered, particularly with reference to controversies affecting the general welfare of the country.

Sec. 205A.

(a) (1) The Service is authorized and directed to provide assistance in the establishment and operation of plant, area and industrywide labor management committees which—

(A) have been organized jointly by employers and labor organizations representing employees in that plant, area, or industry; and

(B) are established for the purpose of improving labor management relationships, job security, organizational effectiveness, enhancing economic development or involving workers in decisions affecting their jobs including improving communication with respect to subjects of mutual interest and concern.

(2) The Service is authorized and directed to enter into contracts and to make grants, where necessary or appropriate, to fulfill its responsibilities under this section.

(b) (1) No grant may be made, no contract may be entered into and no other assistance may be provided under the provisions of this section to a plant labor management committee unless the employees in that plant are represented by a labor organization and there is in effect at that plant a collective bargaining agreement.

(2) No grant may be made, no contract may be entered into and no other assistance may be provided under the provisions of this section to an area or industrywide labor management committee unless its participants include any labor organizations certified or recognized as the representative of the employees of an employer participating in such committee. Nothing in this clause shall prohibit participation in an area or industrywide committee by an employer whose employees are not represented by a labor organization.

(3) No grant may be made under the provisions of this section to any labor management committee which the Service finds to have as one of its purposes the discouragement of the exercise of rights contained in section 7 of the National Labor Relations Act (29 U.S.C. 157), or the interference with collective bargaining in any plant, or industry.

(c) The Service shall carry out the provisions of this section through an office established for that purpose.

(d) There are authorized to be appropriated to carry out the provisions of this section $10,000,000 for the fiscal year 1979, and such sums as may be necessary thereafter.

(e) Nothing in this section or the amendments made by this section shall affect the terms and conditions of any collective bargaining agreement whether in effect prior to or entered into after the date of enactment of this section.

National Emergencies

Sec. 206. Whenever in the opinion of the President of the United States, a threatened or actual strike or lockout affecting an entire industry or a substantial part thereof engaged in trade, commerce, transportation, transmission, or communication among the several States or with foreign nations, or engaged in the production of goods for commerce, will, if permitted to occur or to continue, imperil the national health or safety, he may appoint a board of inquiry to inquire into the issues involved in the dispute and to make a written report to him within such time as he shall prescribe. Such report shall include a statement of the facts with respect to the dispute, including each party's statement of its position but shall not contain any recommendations. The President shall file a copy of such report with the Service and shall make its contents available to the public.

Sec. 207.

(a) A board of inquiry shall be composed of a chairman and such other members as the President shall determine, and shall have power to sit and act in any place within the United States and to conduct such hearings either in public or in private, as it may deem necessary or proper, to ascertain the facts with respect to the causes and circumstances of the dispute.

(b) Members of a board of inquiry shall receive compensation at the rate of $50 for each day actually spent by them in the work of the board, together with necessary travel and subsistence expenses.

(c) For the purpose of any hearing or inquiry conducted by any board appointed under this title, the provisions of section 9 and 10 (relating to the attendance of witnesses and the production of books, papers, and documents) of the Federal Trade Commission Act of September 16, 1914, as amended (U.S.C. 19, title 15, secs. 49 and 50, as amended), are hereby made applicable to the powers and duties of such board.

Sec. 208.

(a) Upon receiving a report from a board of inquiry the President may direct the Attorney General to petition any district court of the United States having jurisdiction of the parties to enjoin such strike or lock-out or the continuing thereof, and if the court finds that such threatened or actual strike or lockout—
  (i) affects an entire industry or a substantial part thereof engaged in trade, commerce, transportation, transmission, or communication among the several States or with foreign nations, or engaged in the production of goods for commerce, and
  (ii) if permitted to occur or to continue, will imperil the national health or safety, it shall have jurisdiction to enjoin any such strike or lock-out, or the continuing thereof, and to make such other orders as may be appropriate.

(b) In any case, the provisions of the Act of March 23, 1932, entitled "An Act to amend the Judicial Code and to define and limit the jurisdiction of courts sitting in equity, and for other purposes," shall not be applicable.

(c) The order or orders of the court shall be subject to review by the appropriate circuit court of appeals and by the Supreme Court upon writ of certiorari or certification as provided in sections 239 and 240 of the Judicial Code, as amended (U.S.C., title 29, secs. 346 and 347).

Sec. 209.

(a) Whenever a district court has issued an order under section 208 enjoining acts or practices which imperil or threaten to imperil the national health or safety, it shall be the duty of the parties to the labor dispute giving rise to such order to make every effort to adjust and settle their differences, with the assistance of the Service created by this Act. Neither party shall be under any duty to accept, in whole or in part, any proposal of settlement made by the Service.

(b) Upon the issuance of such order, the President shall reconvene the board of inquiry which has previously reported with respect to the dispute. At the end of a sixty-day period (unless the dispute has been settled by that time), the board of inquiry shall report to the President the current position of the parties and the effort which has been made for settlement, and shall include a statement by each party of its position and a statement of the employer's last offer of settlement. The President shall make such report available to the public. The National Labor Relations Board, within the succeeding fifteen days, shall take a secret ballot of the employees of each employer involved in the dispute on the question of whether they wish to accept the final offer of settlement made by their employer as stated by him and shall certify the results thereof to the Attorney General within five days thereafter.

Sec. 210. Upon the certification of the results of such ballot or upon a settlement being reached, whichever happens sooner, the Attorney General shall move the court to discharge the injunction, which motion shall then be granted and the injunction discharged. When such motion is granted, the President shall submit to the Congress a full and comprehensive report of the proceedings, including the findings of the board of inquiry and the ballot taken by the National Labor Relations Board, together with such recommendations as he may see fit to make for consideration and appropriate action.

Compilation of Collective-Bargaining Agreements, Etc.

Sec. 211.

(a) For the guidance and information of interested representatives of employers, employees, and the general public, the Bureau of Labor Statistics of the Department of Labor shall maintain a file of copies of all available collective-bargaining agreements and other available agreements and actions thereunder settling or adjusting labor disputes. Such file shall be open to inspection under appropriate conditions prescribed by the Secretary of Labor, except that no specific information submitted in confidence shall be disclosed.

(b) The Bureau of Labor Statistics in the Department of Labor is authorized to furnish upon request of the Service, or employers, employees, or their representatives, all available data and factual information which may aid in the settlement of any labor dispute, except that no specific information submitted in confidence shall be disclosed.

Exemption of Railway Labor Act

Sec. 212. The provisions of this title shall not be applicable with respect to any matter which is subject to the provisions of the Railway Labor Act, as amended from time to time.

Conciliation of Labor Disputes in the Health Care Industry

Sec. 213.

(a) If, in the opinion of the Director of the Federal Mediation and Conciliation Service a threatened or actual strike or lockout affecting a health care institution will, if permitted to occur or to continue, substantially interrupt the delivery of health care in the locality concerned, the Director may further assist in the resolution of the impasse by establishing within 30 days after the notice to the Federal Mediation and Conciliation Service under clause (A) of the last sentence of section 8(d) (which is required by clause (3) of such section 8(d)), or within 10 days after the notice under clause (B), an impartial Board of Inquiry to investigate the issues involved in the dispute and to make a written report thereon to the parties within fifteen (15) days after the establishment of such a Board. The written report shall contain the findings of fact together with the Board's recommendations for settling the dispute. Each such Board shall be composed of such number of individuals as the Director may deem desirable. No member appointed under this section shall have any interest or involvement in the health care institutions or the employee organizations involved in the dispute.

(b) (1) Members of any board established under this section who are otherwise employed by the Federal Government shall serve without compensation but shall be reimbursed for travel, subsistence, and other necessary expenses incurred by them in carrying out its duties under this section.

(2) Members of any board established under this section who are not subject to paragraph (1) shall receive compensation at a rate prescribed by the Director but not to exceed the daily rate prescribed for GS-18 of the General Schedule under section 5332 of title 5, United States Code, including travel for each day they are engaged in the performance of their duties under this section and shall be entitled to reimbursement for travel, subsistence, and other necessary expenses incurred by them in carrying out their duties under this section.

(c) After the establishment of a board under subsection (a) of this section and for 15 days after any such board has issued its report, no change in the status quo in effect prior to the expiration of the contract in the case of negotiations for a contract renewal, or in effect prior to the time of the impasse in the case of an initial bargaining negotiation, except by agreement, shall be made by the parties to the controversy.

TITLE III

Suits by and against Labor Organizations

Sec. 301.

(a) Suits for violation of contracts between an employer and a labor organization representing employees in an industry affecting commerce as defined in this Act, or between any such labor organizations, may be brought in any district court of the United States having jurisdiction of the parties, without respect to the amount in controversy or without regard to the citizenship of the parties.

(b) Any labor organization which represents employees in an industry affecting commerce as defined in this Act and any employer whose activities affect commerce as defined in this Act shall be bound by the acts of its agents. Any such labor organization may sue or be sued as an entity and in behalf of the employees whom it represents in the courts of the United States. Any money judgment against a labor organization in a district court of the United States shall be enforceable only against the organization as an entity and against its assets, and shall not be enforceable against any individual member or his assets.

(c) For the purposes of actions and proceedings by or against labor organizations in the district courts of the United States, district courts shall be deemed to have jurisdiction of a labor organization (1) in the district in which such organization maintains its principal offices, or (2) in any district in which its duly authorized officers or agents are engaged in representing or acting for employee members.

(d) The service of summons, subpoena, or other legal process of any court of the United States upon an officer or agent of a labor organization, in his capacity as such, shall constitute service upon the labor organization.

(e) For the purpose of this section, in determining whether any person is acting as an "agent" of another person so as to make such other person responsible for his acts, the question of whether the specific acts performed were actually authorized or subsequently ratified shall not be controlling.

Restrictions on Payments to Employee Representatives

Sec. 302.

(a) It shall be unlawful for any employer or association of employers or any person who acts as a labor relations expert, adviser, or consultant to an employer or who acts in the interest of an employer to pay, lend, or deliver, or agree to pay, lend, or deliver, any money or other thing of value—
   (1) to any representative of any of his employees who are employed in an industry affecting commerce; or
   (2) to any labor organization, or any officer or employee thereof, which represents, seeks to represent, or would admit to membership, any of the employees of such employer who are employed in an industry affecting commerce;
   (3) to any employee or group or committee of employees of such employer employed in an industry affecting commerce in excess of their normal compensation for the purpose of causing such employee or group or committee directly or indirectly to influence any other employees in the exercise of the right to organize and bargain collectively through representation of their own choosing; or
   (4) to any officer or employee of a labor organization engaged in an industry affecting commerce with intent to influence him in respect to any of his actions, decisions, or duties as a representative of employees or as such officer or employee of such labor organization.

(b) (1) It shall be unlawful for any person to request, demand, receive, or accept, or agree to receive or accept, any payment, loan, or delivery of any money or other thing of value prohibited by subsection (a).
   (2) It shall be unlawful for any labor organization, or for any person acting as an officer, agent, representative, or employee of such labor organization, to demand or accept from the operator of any motor vehicle (as defined in part II of the Interstate Commerce Act) employed in the transportation of property in commerce, or the employer of any such operator, any money or other thing of value payable to such organization or to an officer, agent, representative or employee thereof as a fee or charge for the unloading, or the connection with the unloading, of the cargo of such vehicle: *Provided,* That nothing in this paragraph shall be construed to make unlawful any payment by an employer to any of his employees as compensation for their services as employees.

(c) The provisions of this section shall not be applicable
   (1) in respect to any money or other thing of value payable by an employer to any of his employees whose established duties include acting openly for such employer in matters of labor relations or personnel administration or to any representative of his employees, or to any officer or employee of a labor organization, who is also an employee or former employee of such employer, as compensation for, or by reason of, his service as an employee of such employer;
   (2) with respect to the payment or delivery of any money or other thing of value in satisfaction of a judgment of any court or a decision or award of an arbitrator or impartial chairman or in compromise, adjustment, settlement, or release of any claim, complaint, grievance or dispute in the absence of fraud or duress;
   (3) with respect to the sale or purchase of an article or commodity at the prevailing market price in the regular course of business;
   (4) with respect to money deducted from the wages of employees in payment of membership dues in a labor organization: *Provided,* That the employer has received from each employee, on whose account such deductions are made, a written assignment which shall not be irrevocable for a period of more than one year, or beyond the termination date of the applicable collective agreement, whichever occurs sooner;
   (5) with respect to money or other thing of value paid to a trust fund established by such representative, for the sole and exclusive benefit

of the employees of such employer, and their families and dependents (or of such employees, families, and dependents jointly with the employees of other employers making similar payments, and their families and dependents): *Provided,* That (A) such payments are held in trust for the purpose of paying, either from principal or income or both, for the benefit of employees, their families and dependents, for medical or hospital care, pensions on retirement or death of employees, compensation for injuries or illness resulting from occupational activity or insurance to provide any of the foregoing, or unemployment benefits or life insurance, disability and sickness insurance, or accident insurance; (B) the detailed basis on which such payments are to be made is specified in a written agreement with the employer, and employees and employers are equally represented in the administration of such fund, together with such neutral persons as the representatives of the employers and the representatives of employees may agree upon and in the event the employer and employee groups deadlock on the administration of such fund and there are no neutral persons empowered to break such deadlock, such agreement provides that the two groups shall agree on an impartial umpire to decide such dispute, or in event of their failure to agree within a reasonable length of time, an impartial umpire to decide such dispute shall, on petition of either group, be appointed by the district court of the United States for the district where the trust fund has its principal office, and shall also contain provisions for an annual audit of the trust fund, a statement of the results of which shall be available for inspection by interested persons at the principal office of the trust fund and at such other places as may be designated in such written agreement; and (C) such payments as are intended to be used for the purpose of providing pensions or annuities for employees are made to a separate trust which provides that the funds held therein cannot be used for any purpose other than paying such pensions or annuities;

(6) with respect to money or other thing of value paid by any employer to a trust fund established by such representative for the purpose of pooled vacation, holiday, severance or similar benefits, or defraying costs of apprenticeship or other training program: *Provided,* That the requirements of clause (B) of the proviso to clause (5) of this subsection shall apply to such trust funds;

(7) with respect to money or other thing of value paid by any employer to a pooled or individual trust fund established by such representative for the purpose of (A) scholarships for the benefit of employees, their families, and dependents for study at educational institutions, or (B) child care centers for preschool and school age dependents of employees: *Provided,* That no labor organization or employer shall be required to bargain on the establishment of any such trust fund, and refusal to do so shall not constitute an unfair labor practice: *Provided further,* That the requirements of clause (B) of the proviso to clause (5) of this subsection shall apply to such trust funds;

(8) with respect to money or any other thing of value paid by any employer to a trust fund established by such representative for the purpose of defraying the costs of legal services for employees, their families, and dependents for counsel or plan of their choice: *Provided,* That the requirements of clause (B) of the proviso to clause (5) of this subsection shall apply to such trust funds: *Provided further,* That no such legal services shall be furnished: (A) to initiate any proceeding directed (i) against any such employer or its officers or agents except in workman's compensation cases, or (ii) against such labor organization, or its parent or subordinate bodies, or their officers or agents, or (iii) against any other employer or labor organization, or their officers or agents, in any matter arising under the National Labor Relations Act, as amended, or this Act; and (B) in any proceeding where a labor organization would be prohibited from defraying the costs of legal services by the provisions of the Labor-Management Reporting and Disclosure Act of 1959; or

(9) with respect to money or other things of value paid by an employer to a plant, area or industrywide labor management committee established for one or more of the purposes set

forth in section 5(b) of the Labor Management Cooperation Act of 1978.

(d) Any person who willfully violates any of the provisions of this section shall, upon conviction thereof, be guilty of a misdemeanor and be subject to a fine of not more than $10,000 or to imprisonment for not more than one year, or both.

(e) The district courts of the United States and the United States courts of the Territories and possessions shall have jurisdiction, for cause shown, and subject to the provisions of section 17 (relating to notice to opposite party) of the Act entitled "An Act to supplement existing laws against unlawful restraints and monopolies, and for other purposes," approved October 15, 1914, as amended (U.S.C., title 28, sec. 381), to restrain violations of this section, without regard to the provisions of sections 6 and 20 of such Act of October 15, 1914, as amended (U.S.C., title 15, sec. 17 and title 29, sec. 52), and the provisions of the Act entitled "An Act to amend the Judicial Code to define and limit the jurisdiction of courts sitting in equity, and for other purposes," approved March 23, 1932 (U.S.C., title 29, secs. 101–115).

(f) This section shall not apply to any contract in force on the date of enactment of this Act, until the expiration of such contract, or until July 1, 1948, whichever first occurs.

(g) Compliance with the restrictions contained in subsection (c)(5)(B) upon contributions to trust funds, otherwise lawful, shall not be applicable to contributions to such trust funds established by collective agreement prior to January 1, 1946, nor shall subsection (c)(5)(A) be construed as prohibiting contributions to such trust funds if prior to January 1, 1947, such funds contained provisions for pooled vacation benefits.

Boycotts and Other Unlawful Combinations

Sec. 303.

(a) It shall be unlawful, for the purpose of this section only, in an industry or activity affecting commerce, for any labor organization to engage in any activity or conduct defined as an unfair labor practice in section 8(b)(4) of the National Labor Relations Act, as amended.

(b) Whoever shall be injured in his business or property by reason of any violation of subsection (a) may sue therefore in any district court of the United States subject to the limitations and provisions of section 301 hereof without respect to the amount in controversy, or in any other court having jurisdiction of the parties, and shall recover the damages by him sustained and the cost of the suit.

Restriction on Political Contributions

Sec. 304. Section 313 of the Federal Corrupt Practices Act, 1925 (U.S.C., 1940 edition, title 2, sec. 251; Supp. V, title 50, App., sec. 1509), as amended, is amended to read as follows:

Sec. 313. It is unlawful for any national bank, or any corporation organized by authority of any law of Congress to make a contribution or expenditure in connection with any election to any political office, or in connection with any primary election or political convention or caucus held to select candidates for any political office, or for any corporation whatever, or any labor organization to make a contribution or expenditure in connection with any election at which Presidential and Vice Presidential electors or a Senator or Representative in, or a Delegate or Resident Commissioner to Congress are to be voted for, or in connection with any primary election or political convention or caucus held to select candidates for any of the foregoing offices, or for any candidate, political committee, or other person to accept or receive any contribution prohibited by this section. Every corporation or labor organization which makes any contribution or expenditure in violation of this section shall be fined not more than $5,000; and every officer or director of any corporation, or officer of any labor organization, who consents to any contribution or expenditure by the corporation or labor organization, as the case may be, in violation of this section shall be fined not more than $1,000 or imprisoned for not more than one year, or both. For the purposes of this section, "labor organization" means any organization of any kind, or any agency or employee representation committee or plan, in which employees participate and which exists for the purpose, in whole or in part, of dealing with employers concerning grievances, labor disputes, wages, rates of pay, hours of employment, or conditions of work.

Strikes by Government Employees

Sec. 305. [Repealed by Ch. 690, 69 Stat. 624, effective August 9, 1955. Sec. 305 made it unlawful for government employees to strike and made strikers subject to immediate discharge, forfeiture of civil-service status, and three-year blacklisting for federal employment.]

TITLE IV

Creation of Joint Committee to Study and Report on Basic Problems Affecting Friendly Labor Relations and Productivity

Sec. 401. There is hereby established a joint congressional committee to be known as the Joint Committee on Labor-Management Relations (hereafter referred to as the committee), and to be composed of seven Members of the Senate Committee on Labor and Public Welfare, to be appointed by the President pro tempore of the Senate, and seven Members of the House of Representatives Committee on Education and Labor, to be appointed by the Speaker of the House of Representatives. A vacancy in membership of the committee, shall not affect the powers of the remaining members to execute the functions of the committee, and shall be filled in the same manner as the original selection. The committee shall select a chairman and a vice chairman from among its members.

Sec. 402. The committee, acting as a whole or by subcommittee shall conduct a thorough study and investigation of the entire field of labor-management relations, including but not limited to—

(1) the means by which permanent friendly cooperation between employers and employees and stability of labor relations may be secured throughout the United States;

(2) the means by which the individual employee may achieve a greater productivity and higher wages, including plans for guaranteed annual wages, incentive profit-sharing and bonus systems;

(3) the internal organization and administration of labor unions, with special attention to the impact on individuals of collective agreements requiring membership in unions as a condition of employment;

(4) the labor relations policies and practices of employers and associations of employers;

(5) the desirability of welfare funds for the benefit of employees and their relation to the social-security system;

(6) the methods and procedures for best carrying out the collective-bargaining processes, with special attention to the effects of industrywide or regional bargaining upon the national economy;

(7) the administration and operation of existing Federal laws relating to labor relations; and

(8) such other problems and subjects in the field of labor-management relations as the committee deems appropriate.

Sec. 403. The committee shall report to the Senate and the House of Representatives not later than March 15, 1948, the results of its study and investigation, together with such recommendations as to necessary legislation and such other recommendations as it may deem advisable, and shall make its final report not later than January 2, 1949.

Sec. 404. The committee shall have the power, without regard to the civil-service laws and the Classification Act of 1923, as amended, to employ and fix the compensation of such officers, experts, and employees as it deems necessary for the performance of its duties, including consultants who shall receive compensation at a rate not to exceed $35 for each day actually spent by them in the work of the committee, together with their necessary travel and subsistence expenses. The committee is further authorized with the consent of the head of the department or agency concerned, to utilize the services, information, facilities, and personnel of all agencies in the executive branch of the Government and may request the governments of the several States, representatives of business, industry, finance, and labor, and such other persons, agencies, organizations, and instrumentalities as it deems appropriate to attend its hearings and to give and present information, advice, and recommendations.

Sec. 405. The committee, or any subcommittee thereof, is authorized to hold such hearings; to sit and act at such times and places during the sessions, recesses, and adjourned periods of the Eightieth Congress; to require by subpoena or otherwise the attendance of such witnesses and the production of such books, papers, and documents; to administer oaths; to take such testimony; to have such printing and binding done; and to make such expenditures within the amount appropriated therefor as it deems advisable. The cost of stenographic services in reporting such hearings shall not be in excess of 25 cents per one hundred words. Subpoenas shall be issued under the signature of the chairman or vice chairman of the committee and shall be served by any person designated by them.

Sec. 406. The members of the committee shall be reimbursed for travel, subsistence, and other necessary expenses incurred by them in the performance of the duties vested in the committee, other than expenses in connection with meetings of the committee held in the District of Columbia during such times as the Congress is in session.

Sec. 407. There is hereby authorized to be appropriated the sum of $150,000, or so much thereof as may be necessary, to carry out the provisions of this title, to be disbursed by the Secretary of the Senate on vouchers signed by the chairman.

TITLE V

Definitions

Sec. 501. When used in this Act—

(1) The term "industry affecting commerce" means any industry or activity in commerce or in which a labor dispute would burden or obstruct commerce or tend to burden or obstruct commerce or the free flow of commerce.

(2) The term "strike" includes any strike or other concerted stoppage of work by employees (including a stoppage by reason of the expiration of a collective-bargaining agreement) and any concerted slow-down or other concerted interruption of operations by employees.

(3) The terms "commerce," "labor disputes," "employer," "employee," "labor organization," "representative," "person," and "supervisor" shall have the same meaning as when used in the National Labor Relations Act as amended by this Act.

Saving Provision

Sec. 502. Nothing in this Act shall be construed to require an individual employee to render labor or service without his consent, nor shall anything in this Act be construed to make the quitting of his labor by an individual employee an illegal act; nor shall any court issue any process to compel the performance by an individual of such labor or service, without his consent; nor shall the quitting of labor by an employee or employees in good faith because of abnormally dangerous conditions for work at the place of employment of such employee or employees be deemed a strike under this Act.

Separability

Sec. 503. If any provision of this Act, or the application of such provision to any person or circumstance, shall be invalid, the remainder of this Act, or the application of such provision to persons or circumstances other than those as to which it is held invalid, shall not be affected thereby.

APPENDIX

TEXT OF THE LABOR-MANAGEMENT REPORTING AND DISCLOSURE ACT OF 1959

73 Stat. 519 (1959), as amended, 79 Stat. 888 (1965), 88 Stat. 852 (1974); 29 U.S.C. Sections 401–531

SHORT TITLE

Section 1. This Act may be cited as the "Labor-Management Reporting and Disclosure Act of 1959."

Declaration of Findings, Purposes, and Policy

Sec. 2.

(a) The Congress finds that, in the public interest, it continues to be the responsibility of the Federal Government to protect employees' rights to organize, choose their own representatives, bargain collectively, and otherwise engage in concerted activities for their mutual aid or protection; that the relations between employers and labor organizations and the millions of workers they represent have a substantial impact on the commerce of the Nation; and that in order to accomplish the objective of a free flow of commerce it is essential that labor organizations, employers, and their officials adhere to the highest standards of responsibility and ethical conduct in administering the affairs of their organizations, particularly as they affect labor-management relations.

(b) The Congress further finds, from recent investigations in the labor and management fields, that there have been a number of instances of breach of trust, corruption, disregard of the rights of individual employees, and other failures to observe high standards of responsibility and ethical conduct which require further and supplementary legislation that will afford necessary protection of the rights and interests of employees and the public generally as they relate to the activities of labor organizations, employers, labor relations consultants, and their officers and representatives.

(c) The Congress, therefore, further finds and declares that the enactment of this Act is necessary to eliminate or prevent improper practices on the part of labor organizations, employers, labor relations consultants, and their officers and representatives which distort and defeat the policies of the Labor Management Relations Act, 1947, as amended, and the Railway Labor Act, as amended, and have the tendency or necessary effect of burdening or obstructing commerce by (1) impairing the efficiency, safety, or operation of the instrumentalities of commerce; (2) occurring in the current of commerce; (3) materially affecting, restraining, or controlling the flow of raw materials or manufactured or processed goods into or from the channels of commerce, or the prices of such materials or goods in commerce; or (4) causing diminution of employment and wages in such volume as substantially to impair or disrupt the market for goods flowing into or from the channels of commerce.

Definitions

Sec. 3. For the purposes of titles I, II, III, IV, V (except section 505), and VI of this Act—

(a) "Commerce" means trade, traffic, commerce, transportation, transmission, or communication among the several States or between any State and any place outside thereof.

(b) "State" includes any State of the United States, the District of Columbia, Puerto Rico, the Virgin Islands, American Samoa, Guam, Wake Island, the Canal Zone, and Outer Continental Shelf lands defined in the Outer Continental Shelf Lands Act (43 U.S.C. §§ 1331–1343).

(c) "Industry affecting commerce" means any activity, business, or industry in commerce or in which a labor dispute would hinder or obstruct commerce or the free flow of commerce and includes any activity or industry "affecting commerce" within the meaning of the Labor Management Relations Act, 1947, as amended, or the Railway Labor Act, as amended.

(d) "Person" includes one or more individuals, labor organizations, partnerships, associations, corporations, legal representatives, mutual companies, joint-stock companies, trusts, unincorporated organizations, trustees, trustees in bankruptcy, or receivers.

(e) "Employer" means any employer or any group or association of employers engaged in an industry affecting commerce (1) which is, with respect to employees engaged in an industry affecting commerce, an employer within the meaning of any law of the United States relating to the employment of any employees or (2) which may deal with any labor organization concerning grievances, labor disputes, wages, rates of pay, hours of employment, or conditions of work, and includes any person acting directly or indirectly as an employer or as an agent of an employer in relation to an employee but does not include the United States or any corporation wholly owned by the Government of the United States or any State or political subdivision thereof.

(f) "Employee" means any individual employed by an employer, and includes any individual whose work has ceased as a consequence of, or in connection with, any current labor dispute or because of any unfair labor practice or because of exclusion or expulsion from a labor organization in any manner or for any reason inconsistent with the requirements of this Act.

(g) "Labor dispute" includes any controversy concerning terms, tenure, or conditions of employment, or concerning the association or representation of persons in negotiating, fixing, maintaining, changing, or seeking to arrange terms or conditions of employment, regardless of whether the disputants stand in the proximate relation of employer and employee.

(h) "Trusteeship" means any receivership, trusteeship, or other method of supervision or control whereby a labor organization suspends the autonomy otherwise available to a subordinate body under its constitution or bylaws.

(i) "Labor organization" means a labor organization engaged in an industry affecting commerce and includes any organization of any kind, any agency, or employee representation committee, group, association, or plan so engaged in which employees participate and which exists for the purpose, in whole or in part, of dealing with employers concerning grievances, labor disputes, wages, rates of pay, hours, or other terms or conditions of employment, and any conference, general committee, joint or system board, or joint council so engaged which is subordinate to a national or international labor organization, other than a State or local central body.

(j) A labor organization shall be deemed to be engaged in an industry affecting commerce if it—

(1) is the certified representative of employees under the provisions of the National Labor Relations Act, as amended, or the Railway Labor Act, as amended; or

(2) although not certified, is a national or international labor organization or a local labor organization recognized or acting as the representative of employees of an employer or employers engaged in an industry affecting commerce; or

(3) has chartered a local labor organization or subsidiary body which is representing or actively seeking to represent employees of employers within the meaning of paragraph (1) or (2), or

(4) has been chartered by a labor organization representing or actively seeking to represent employees within the meaning of paragraph (1) or (2) as the local or subordinate body through which such employees may enjoy membership or become affiliated with such labor organization; or

(5) is a conference, general committee, joint or system board, or joint council, subordinate to a national or international labor organization, which includes a labor organization engaged in an industry affecting commerce within the meaning of any of the preceding paragraphs of this subsection, other than a State or local central body.

(k) "Secret ballot" means the expression by ballot, voting machine, or otherwise, but in no event by proxy, of a choice with respect to any election or vote taken upon any matter, which is cast in such a manner that the person expressing such choice cannot be identified with the choice expressed.

(l) "Trust in which a labor organization is interested" means a trust or other fund or organization (1) which was created or established by a labor organization, or one or more of the trustees or one or more members of the governing body of which is selected or appointed by a labor organization, and (2) a primary purpose of which is to provide benefits for the members of such labor organization or their beneficiaries.

(m) "Labor relations consultant" means any person who, for compensation, advises or represents an employer, employer organization, or labor organization concerning employee organizing, concerted activities, or collective bargaining activities.

(n) "Officer" means any constitutional officer, any person authorized to perform the functions of president, vice president, secretary, treasurer, or other executive functions of a labor organization, and any member of its executive board or similar governing body.

(o) "Member" or "member in good standing", when used in reference to a labor organization, includes any person who has fulfilled the requirements for membership in such organization, and who neither has voluntarily withdrawn from membership nor has been expelled or suspended from membership after appropriate proceedings consistent with lawful provisions of thconstitution and bylaws of such organization.

(p) "Secretary" means the Secretary of Labor.

(q) "Officer, agent, shop steward, or other representative", when used with respect to a labor organization, includes elected officials and key administrative personnel, whether elected or appointed (such as business agents, heads of departments or major units, and organizers who exercise substantial independent authority), but does not include salaried nonsupervisory professional staff, stenographic, and service personnel.

(r) "District court of the United States" means a United States district court and a United States court of any place subject to the jurisdiction of the United States.

TITLE I—BILL OF RIGHTS OF MEMBERS OF LABOR ORGANIZATIONS

Bill of Rights

Sec. 101.

(c) (1) *Equal Rights.*—Every member of a labor organization shall have equal rights and privileges within such organization to nominate candidates, to vote in elections or referendums of the labor organization, to attend membership meetings, and to participate in the deliberations and voting upon the business of such meetings, subject to reasonable rules and regulations in such organization's constitution and bylaws.

(2) *Freedom of Speech and Assembly.*—Every member of any labor organization shall have the right to meet and assemble freely with other members; and to express any views, arguments, or opinions; and to express at meetings of the labor organization his views, upon candidates in an election of the labor organization or upon any business properly before the meeting, subject to the organization's established and reasonable rules pertaining to the conduct of meetings: *Provided,* That nothing herein shall be construed to impair the right of a labor organization to adopt and enforce reasonable rules as to the responsibility of every member toward the organization as an institution and to his refraining from conduct that would interfere with its performance of its legal or contractual obligations.

(3) *Dues, Initiation Fees, and Assessments.*—Except in the case of a federation of national or international labor organizations, the rates of dues and initiation fees payable by members of any labor organization in effect on the date of enactment of this Act shall not be increased, and no general or special assessment shall be levied upon such members, except—

(A) in a case of a local labor organization, (i) by majority vote by secret ballot of the members in good standing voting at a general or special membership meeting, after reasonable notice of the intention to vote upon such question, or (ii) by majority vote of the members in good standing voting in a membership referendum conducted by secret ballot; or

(B) in the case of a labor organization, other than a local labor organization or a federation of national or international labor organizations, (i) by majority vote of the delegates voting at a regular convention, or at a special convention of such labor organization held upon not less than thirty days' written notice to the principal office of each local or constituent labor organization entitled to such notice, or (ii) by majority vote of the members in good standing of such labor organization voting in a membership referendum conducted by secret ballot, or (iii) by majority vote of the members of the executive board or similar governing body of such labor organization, pursuant to express authority contained in the constitution and bylaws of such labor organization: *Provided,* That such action on the part of the executive board or similar governing body shall be effective only until the next regular convention of such labor organization.

(4) *Protection of the Right to Sue.*—No labor organization shall limit the right of any member thereof to institute an action in any court, or in a proceeding before any administrative agency, irrespective of whether or not the labor organization or its officers are named as defendants or respondents in such action or proceeding, or the right of any member of a labor organization to appear as a witness in any judicial, administrative, or legislative proceeding, or to petition any legislature or to communicate with any legislator: *Provided,* That any such member may be required to exhaust reasonable hearing procedures (but not to exceed a four-month lapse of time) within such organization, before instituting legal or administrative proceedings against such organizations or any officer thereof: *And provided further,* That no interested employer or employer association shall directly or indirectly finance, encourage, or participate in, except as a party, any such action, proceeding, appearance, or petition.

(5) *Safeguards Against Improper Disciplinary Action.*—No member of any labor organization may be fined, suspended, expelled, or otherwise disciplined except for nonpayment of dues by such organization or by any officer thereof unless such member has been (A) served with written specific charges; (B) given a reasonable time to prepare his defense; (C) afforded a full and fair hearing.

(b) Any provision of the constitution and bylaws of any labor organization which is inconsistent with the provisions of this section shall be of no force or effect.

Civil Enforcement

Sec. 102. Any person whose rights secured by the provisions of this title have been infringed by any violation of this title may bring a civil action in a district court of the United States for such relief (including injunctions) as may be appropriate. Any such action against a labor organization shall be brought in the district court of the United States for the district where the alleged violation occurred, or where the principal office of such labor organization is located.

Retention of Existing Rights

Sec. 103. Nothing contained in this title shall limit the rights and remedies of any member of a labor organization under any State or Federal law or before any court or other tribunal, or under the constitution and bylaws of any labor organization.

Right to Copies of Collective Bargaining Agreements

Sec. 104. It shall be the duty of the secretary or corresponding principal officer of each labor organization, in the case of a local labor organization, to forward a copy of each collective bargaining agreement made by such labor organization with any employer to any employee who requests such a copy and whose rights as such employee are directly affected by such agreement, and in the case of a labor organization other than a local labor organization, to forward a copy of any such agreement to each constituent unit which has members directly affected by such agreement; and such officer shall maintain at the principal office of the labor organization of which he is an officer copies of any such agreement made or received by such labor organization, which copies shall be available for inspection by any member or by any employee whose rights are affected by such agreement. The provisions of section 210 shall be applicable in the enforcement of this section.

Information as to Act

Sec. 105. Every labor organization shall inform its members concerning the provisions of this Act.

TITLE II—REPORTING BY LABOR ORGANIZATIONS, OFFICERS AND EMPLOYEES OF LABOR ORGANIZATIONS, AND EMPLOYERS

Report of Labor Organizations

Sec. 201.

(a) Every labor organization shall adopt a constitution and bylaws and shall file a copy thereof with the

Secretary, together with a report, signed by its president and secretary or corresponding principal officers, containing the following information—

(1) the name of the labor organization, its mailing address, and any other address at which it maintains its principal office or at which it keeps the records referred to in this title;
(2) the name and title of each of its officers;
(3) the initiation fee or fees required from a new or transferred member and fees for work permits required by the reporting labor organization;
(4) the regular dues or fees or other periodic payments required to remain a member of the reporting labor organization; and
(5) detailed statements, or references to specific provisions of documents filed under this subsection which contain such statements, showing the provision made and procedures followed with respect to each of the following: (A) qualifications for or restrictions on membership, (B) levying of assessments, (C) participation in insurance or other benefit plans, (D) authorization for disbursement of funds of the labor organization, (E) audit of financial transactions of the labor organization, (F) the calling of regular and special meetings, (G) the selection of officers and stewards and of any representatives to other bodies composed of labor organizations' representatives, with a specific statement of the manner in which each officer was elected, appointed, or otherwise selected, (H) discipline or removal of officers or agents for breaches of their trust, (I) imposition of fines, suspensions and expulsions of members, including the grounds for such action and any provision made for notice, hearing, judgment on the evidence, and appeal procedures, (J) authorization for bargaining demands, (K) ratification of contract terms, (L) authorization for strikes, and (M) issuance of work permits. Any change in the information required by this subsection shall be reported to the Secretary at the time the reporting labor organization files with the Secretary the annual financial report required by subsection (b).

(b) Every labor organization shall file annually with the Secretary a financial report signed by its president and treasurer or corresponding principal officers containing the following information in such detail as may be necessary accurately to disclose its financial condition and operations for its preceding fiscal year—

(1) assets and liabilities at the beginning and end of the fiscal year;
(2) receipts of any kind and the sources thereof;
(3) salary, allowances, and other direct or indirect disbursements (including reimbursed expenses) to each officer and also to each employee who, during such fiscal year, received more than $10,000 in the aggregate from such labor organization and any other labor organization affiliated with it or with which it is affiliated, or which is affiliated with the same national or international labor organization;
(4) direct and indirect loans made to any officer, employee, or member, which aggregated more than $250 during the fiscal year, together with a statement of the purpose, security, if any, and arrangements for repayment;
(5) direct and indirect loans to any business enterprise, together with a statement of the purpose, security, if any, and arrangements for repayment; and
(6) other disbursements made by it including the purpose thereof; all in such categories as the Secretary may prescribe.

(c) Every labor organization required to submit a report under this title shall make available the information required to be contained in such report to all of its members, and every such labor organization and its officers shall be under a duty enforceable at the suit of any member of such organization in any State court of competent jurisdiction or in the district court of the United States for the district in which such labor organization maintains its principal office, to permit such member for just cause to examine any books, records, and accounts necessary to verify such report. The court in such action may, in its discretion, in addition to any judgment awarded to the plaintiff or plaintiffs, allow a reasonable attorney's fee to be paid by the defendant, and costs of the action.

Report of Officers and Employees of Labor Organizations

Sec. 202.

(a) Every officer of a labor organization and every employee of a labor organization (other than an employee performing exclusively clerical or custodial services) shall file with the Secretary a signed report listing and describing for his preceding fiscal year—

(1) any stock, bond, security, or other interest, legal or equitable, which he or his spouse or minor child directly or indirectly held in, and any income or any other benefit with monetary value (including reimbursed expenses) which he or his spouse or minor child derived directly or indirectly from, an employer whose employees such labor organization represents or is actively seeking to represent, except payments and other benefits received as a bona fide employee of such employer;

(2) any transaction in which he or his spouse or minor child engaged, directly or indirectly, involving any stock, bond, security, or loan to or from, or other legal or equitable interest in the business of an employer whose employees such labor organization represents or is actively seeking to represent;

(3) any stock, bond, security, or other interest, legal or equitable, which he or his spouse or minor child directly or indirectly held in, and any income or any other benefit with monetary value (including reimbursed expenses) which he or his spouse or minor child directly or indirectly derived from, any business a substantial part of which consists of buying from, selling or leasing to, or otherwise dealing with, the business of an employer whose employees such labor organization represents or is actively seeking to represent;

(4) any stock, bond, security, or other interest, legal or equitable, which he or his spouse or minor child directly or indirectly held in, and any income or any other benefit with monetary value (including reimbursed expenses) which he or his spouse or minor child directly or indirectly derived from, a business any part of which consists of buying from, or selling or leasing directly or indirectly to, or otherwise dealing with such labor organization;

(5) any direct or indirect business transaction or arrangement between him or his spouse or minor child and any employer whose employees his organization represents or is actively seeking to represent, except work performed and payments and benefits received as a bona fide employee of such employer and except purchases and sales of goods or services in the regular course of business at prices generally available to any employee of such employer; and

(6) any payment of money or other thing of value (including reimbursed expenses) which he or his spouse or minor child received directly or indirectly from any employer or any person who acts as a labor relations consultant to an employer, except payments of the kinds referred to in section 302(c) of the Labor Management Relations Act, 1947, as amended.

(b) The provisions of paragraphs (1), (2), (3), (4), and (5) of subsection (a) shall not be construed to require any such officer or employee to report his bona fide investments in securities traded on a securities exchange registered as a national securities exchange under the Securities Exchange Act of 1934, in shares in an investment company registered under the Investment Company Act of 1940, or in securities of a public utility holding company registered under the Public Utility Holding Company Act of 1935, or to report any income derived therefrom.

(c) Nothing contained in this section shall be construed to require any officer or employee of a labor organization to file a report under subsection (a) unless he or his spouse or minor child holds or has held an interest, has received income or any other benefit with monetary value or a loan, or has engaged in a transaction described therein.

Report of Employers

Sec. 203.

(a) Every employer who in any fiscal year made—

(1) any payment or loan, direct or indirect, of money or other thing of value (including reimbursed expenses), or any promise or agreement therefor, to any labor organization or officer, agent, shop steward, or other representative of a labor organization, or employee of any labor organization, except (A) payments or loans made by any national or State bank, credit union, insurance company, savings and loan association or other credit institution and (B) payments of the kind referred to in section 302(c) of the Labor Management Relations Act, 1947, as amended;

(2) any payment (including reimbursed expenses) to any of his employees, or any group or committee of such employees, for the purpose of

causing such employee or group or committee of employees to persuade other employees to exercise or not to exercise, or as to the manner of exercising, the right to organize and bargain collectively through representatives of their own choosing unless such payments were contemporaneously or previously disclosed to such other employees;

(3) any expenditure, during the fiscal year, where an object thereof, directly or indirectly, is to interfere with, restrain, or coerce employees in the exercise of the right to organize and bargain collectively through representatives of their own choosing, or is to obtain information concerning the activities of employees or a labor organization in connection with a labor dispute involving such employer, except for use solely in conjunction with an administrative or arbitral proceeding or a criminal or civil judicial proceeding;

(4) any agreement or arrangement with a labor relations consultant or other independent contractor or organization pursuant to which such person undertakes activities where an object thereof, directly or indirectly, is to persuade employees to exercise or not to exercise, or persuade employees as to the manner of exercising, the right to organize and bargain collectively through representatives of their own choosing, or undertakes to supply such employer with information concerning the activities of employees or a labor organization in connection with a labor dispute involving such employer, except information for use solely in conjunction with an administrative or arbitral proceeding or a criminal or civil judicial proceeding; or

(5) any payment (including reimbursed expenses) pursuant to an agreement or arrangement described in subdivision (4);

shall file with the Secretary a report, in a form prescribed by him, signed by its president and treasurer or corresponding principal officers showing in detail the date and amount of each such payment, loan, promise, agreement, or arrangement and the name, address, and position, if any, in any firm or labor organization of the person to whom it was made and a full explanation of the circumstances of all such payments, including the terms of any agreement or understanding pursuant to which they were made.

(b) Every person who pursuant to any agreement or arrangement with an employer undertakes activities where an object thereof is, directly or indirectly—

(1) to persuade employees to exercise or not to exercise, or persuade employees as to the manner of exercising, the right to organize and bargain collectively through representatives of their own choosing; or

(2) to supply an employer with information concerning the activities of employees or a labor organization in connection with a labor dispute involving such employer, except information for use solely in conjunction with an administrative or arbitral proceeding or a criminal or civil judicial proceeding;

shall file within thirty days after entering into such agreement or arrangement a report with the Secretary, signed by its president and treasurer or corresponding principal officers, containing the name under which such person is engaged in doing business and the address of its principal office, and a detailed statement of the terms and conditions of such agreement or arrangement. Every such person shall file annually, with respect to each fiscal year during which payments were made as a result of such an agreement or arrangement, a report with the Secretary, signed by its president and treasurer or corresponding principal officers, containing a statement (A) of its receipts of any kind from employers on account of labor relations advice or services, designating the sources thereof, and (B) of its disbursements of any kind, in connection with such services and the purposes thereof. In each such case such information shall be set forth in such categories as the Secretary may prescribe.

(c) Nothing in this section shall be construed to require any employer or other person to file a report covering the services of such person by reason of his giving or agreeing to give advice to such employer or representing or agreeing to represent such employer before any court, administrative agency, or tribunal of arbitration or engaging or agreeing to engage in collective bargaining on behalf of such employer with respect to wages, hours, or other terms or conditions of employment or the negotiation of an agreement or any question arising thereunder.

(d) Nothing contained in this section shall be construed to require an employer to file a report under subsection (a) unless he has made an expenditure, payment, loan, agreement, or arrangement of the kind described therein. Nothing contained in this section shall be construed to require any other person to file a report under subsection (b) unless he was a party to an agreement or arrangement of the kind described therein.

(e) Nothing contained in this section shall be construed to require any regular officer, supervisor, or employee of an employer to file a report in connection with services rendered to such employer nor shall any employer be required to file a report covering expenditures made to any regular officer, supervisor, or employee of an employer as compensation for service as a regular officer, supervisor, or employee of such employer.

(f) Nothing contained in this section shall be construed as an amendment to, or modification of the rights protected by, section 8(c) of the National Labor Relations Act, as amended.

(g) The term "interfere with, restrain, or coerce" as used in this section means interference, restraint, and coercion which, if done with respect to the exercise of rights guaranteed in section 7 of the National Labor Relations Act, as amended, would, under section 8(a) of such Act, constitute an unfair labor practice.

Attorney-Client Communications Exempted

Sec. 204. Nothing contained in this Act shall be construed to require an attorney who is a member in good standing of the bar of any State, to include in any report required to be filed pursuant to the provisions of this Act any information which was lawfully communicated to such attorney by any of his clients in the course of a legitimate attorney-client relationship.

Reports Made Public Information

Sec. 205.

(a) The contents of the reports and documents filed with the Secretary pursuant to sections 201, 202, 203, and 211 shall be public information, and the Secretary may publish any information and data which he obtains pursuant to the provisions of this title. The Secretary may use the information and data for statistical and research purposes, and compile and publish such studies, analyses, reports, and surveys based thereon as he may deem appropriate.

(b) The Secretary shall by regulation make reasonable provision for the inspection and examination, on the request of any person, of the information and data contained in any report or other document filed with him pursuant to section 201, 202, 203, or 211.

(c) The Secretary shall by regulation provide for the furnishing by the Department of Labor of copies of reports or other documents filed with the Secretary pursuant to this title, upon payment of a charge based upon the cost of the service. The Secretary shall make available without payment of a charge, or require any person to furnish, to such State agency as is designated by law or by the Governor of the State in which such person has his principal place of business or headquarters, upon request of the Governor of such State, copies of any reports and documents filed by such person with the Secretary pursuant to section 201, 202, 203, or 211, or of information and data contained therein. No person shall be required by reason of any law of any State to furnish to any officer or agency of such State any information included in a report filed by such person with the Secretary pursuant to the provisions of this title, if a copy of such report, or of the portion thereof containing such information, is furnished to such officer or agency. All moneys received in payment of such charges fixed by the Secretary pursuant to this subsection shall be deposited in the general fund of the Treasury.

Retention of Records

Sec. 206. Every person required to file any report under this title shall maintain records on the matters required to be reported which will provide in sufficient detail the necessary basic information and data from which the documents filed with the Secretary may be verified, explained or clarified, and checked for accuracy and completeness, and shall include vouchers, worksheets, receipts, and applicable resolutions, and shall keep such records available for examination for a period of not less than five years after the filing of the documents based on the information which they contain.

Effective Date

Sec. 207.

(a) Each labor organization shall file the initial report required under section 201(a) within ninety days after the date on which it first becomes subject to this Act.

(b) Each person required to file a report under section 201(b), 202, 203(a), or the second sentence of

203(b), or section 211 shall file such report within ninety days after the end of each of its fiscal years; except that where such person is subject to section 201(b), 202, 203(a), the second sentence of 203(b), or section 211, as the case may be, for only a portion of such a fiscal year (because the date of enactment of this Act occurs during such person's fiscal year or such person becomes subject to this Act during its fiscal year) such person may consider that portion as the entire fiscal year in making such report.

Rules and Regulations

Sec. 208. The Secretary shall have authority to issue, amend, and rescind rules and regulations prescribing the form and publication of reports required to be filed under this title and such other reasonable rules and regulations (including rules prescribing reports concerning trusts in which a labor organization is interested) as he may find necessary to prevent the circumvention or evasion of such reporting requirements. In exercising his power under this section the Secretary shall prescribe by general rule simplified reports for labor organizations or employers for whom he finds that by virtue of their size a detailed report would be unduly burdensome, but the Secretary may revoke such provision for simplified forms of any labor organization or employer if he determines, after such investigation as he deems proper and due notice and opportunity for a hearing, that the purposes of this section would be served thereby.

Criminal Provisions

Sec. 209.

(a) Any person who willfully violates this title shall be fined not more than $10,000 or imprisoned for not more than one year, or both.

(b) Any person who makes a false statement or representation of a material fact, knowing it to be false, or who knowingly fails to disclose a material fact, in any document, report, or other information required under the provisions of this title shall be fined not more than $10,000 or imprisoned for not more than one year, or both.

(c) Any person who willfully makes a false entry in or willfully conceals, withholds, or destroys any books, records, reports, or statements required to be kept by any provision of this title shall be fined not more than $10,000 or imprisoned for not more than one year, or both.

(d) Each individual required to sign reports under sections 201 and 203 shall be personally responsible for the filing of such reports and for any statement contained therein which he knows to be false.

Civil Enforcement

Sec. 210. Whenever it shall appear that any person has violated or is about to violate any of the provisions of this title, the Secretary may bring a civil action for such relief (including injunctions) as may be appropriate. Any such action may be brought in the district court of the United States where the violation occurred or, at the option of the parties, in the United States District Court for the District of Columbia.

Surety Company Reports

Sec. 211. Each surety company which issues any bond required by this Act or the Welfare and Pension Plans Disclosure Act shall file annually with the Secretary, with respect to each fiscal year during which any such bond was in force, a report, in such form and detail as he may prescribe by regulation, filed by the president and treasurer or corresponding principal officers of the surety company, describing its bond experience under each such Act, including information as to the premiums received, total claims paid, amounts recovered by way of subrogation, administrative and legal expenses and such related data and information as the Secretary shall determine to be necessary in the public interest and to carry out the policy of the Act. Notwithstanding the foregoing, if the Secretary finds that any such specific information cannot be practicably ascertained or would be uninformative, the Secretary may modify or waive the requirements for such information.

TITLE III—TRUSTEESHIPS

Reports

Sec. 301.

(a) Every labor organization which has or assumes trusteeship over any subordinate labor organization shall file with the Secretary within thirty days after the date of the enactment of this Act or the imposition of any such trusteeship, and semiannually thereafter, a report, signed by its president and treasurer or corresponding principal officers, as well as by the trustees of such subordinate labor organization, containing the following information:

(1) the name and address of the subordinate organization; (2) the date of establishing the trusteeship; (3) a detailed statement of the reason or reasons for establishing or continuing the trusteeship; and (4) the nature and extent of participation by the membership of the subordinate organization in the selection of delegates to represent such organization in regular or special conventions or other policy-determining bodies and in the election of officers of the labor organization which has assumed trusteeship over such subordinate organization. The initial report shall also include a full and complete account of the financial condition of such subordinate organization as of the time trusteeship was assumed over it. During the continuance of a trusteeship the labor organization which has assumed trusteeship over a subordinate labor organization shall file on behalf of the subordinate labor organization the annual financial report required by section 201(b) signed by the president and treasurer or corresponding principal officers of the labor organization which has assumed such trusteeship and the trustees of the subordinate labor organization.

(b) The provisions of sections 201(c), 205, 206, 208, and 210 shall be applicable to reports filed under this title.

(c) Any person who willfully violates this section shall be fined not more than $10,000 or imprisoned for not more than one year, or both.

(d) Any person who makes a false statement or representation of a material fact, knowing it to be false, or who knowingly fails to disclose a material fact, in any report required under the provisions of this section or willfully makes any false entry in or willfully withholds, conceals, or destroys any documents, books, records, reports, or statements upon which such report is based, shall be fined not more than $10,000 or imprisoned for not more than one year, or both.

(e) Each individual required to sign a report under this section shall be personally responsible for the filing of such report and for any statement contained therein which he knows to be false.

Purposes for which a Trusteeship May Be Established

Sec. 302.

Trusteeships shall be established and administered by a labor organization over a subordinate body only in accordance with the constitution and bylaws of the organization which has assumed trusteeship over the subordinate body and for the purpose of correcting corruption or financial malpractice, assuring the performance of collective bargaining agreements or other duties of a bargaining representative, restoring democratic procedures, or otherwise carrying out the legitimate objects of such labor organization.

Unlawful Acts Relating to Labor Organization under Trusteeship

Sec. 303.

(a) During any period when a subordinate body of a labor organization is in trusteeship, it shall be unlawful (1) to count the vote of delegates from such body in any convention or election of officers of the labor organization unless the delegates have been chosen by secret ballot in an election in which all the members in good standing of such subordinate body were eligible to participate, or (2) to transfer to such organization any current receipts or other funds of the subordinate body except the normal per capita tax and assessments payable by subordinate bodies not in trusteeship: *Provided,* That nothing herein contained shall prevent the distribution of the assets of a labor organization in accordance with its constitution and bylaws upon the bona fide dissolution thereof.

(b) Any person who willfully violates this section shall be fined not more than $10,000 or imprisoned for not more than one year, or both.

Enforcement

Sec. 304.

(a) Upon the written complaint of any member or subordinate body of a labor organization alleging that such organization has violated the provisions of this title (except section 301) the Secretary shall investigate the complaint and if the Secretary finds probable cause to believe that such violation has occurred and has not been remedied he shall, without disclosing the identity of the complainant, bring a civil action in any district court of the United States having jurisdiction of the labor organization for such relief (including injunctions) as may be appropriate. Any member or subordinate body of a labor organization affected by any violation of this title (except section 301) may bring a civil action in any district court of the United States having jurisdiction of the labor organization for such relief (including injunctions) as may be appropriate.

(b) For the purpose of actions under this section, district courts of the United States shall be deemed to have jurisdiction of a labor organization (1) in the district in which the principal office of such labor organization is located, or (2) in any district in which its duly authorized officers or agents are engaged in conducting the affairs of the trusteeship.

(c) In any proceeding pursuant to this section a trusteeship established by a labor organization in conformity with the procedural requirements of its constitution and bylaws and authorized or ratified after a fair hearing either before the executive board or before such other body as may be provided in accordance with its constitution or bylaws shall be presumed valid for a period of eighteen months from the date of its establishment and shall not be subject to attack during such period except upon clear and convincing proof that the trusteeship was not established or maintained in good faith for a purpose allowable under section 302. After the expiration of eighteen months the trusteeship shall be presumed invalid in any such proceeding and its discontinuance shall be decreed unless the labor organization shall show by clear and convincing proof that the continuation of the trusteeship is necessary for a purpose allowable under section 302. In the latter event the court may dismiss the complaint or retain jurisdiction of the cause on such conditions and for such period as it deems appropriate.

Report to Congress

Sec. 305. The Secretary shall submit to the Congress at the expiration of three years from the date of enactment of this Act a report upon the operation of this title.

Complaint by Secretary

Sec. 306. The rights and remedies provided by this title shall be in addition to any and all other rights and remedies at law or in equity: *Provided,* That upon the filing of a complaint by the Secretary the jurisdiction of the district court over such trusteeship shall be exclusive and the final judgment shall be res judicata.

TITLE IV—ELECTIONS

Terms of Office; Election Procedures

Sec. 401.

(a) Every national or international labor organization, except a federation of national or international labor organizations, shall elect its officers not less often than once every five years either by secret ballot among the members in good standing or at a convention of delegates chosen by secret ballot.

(b) Every local labor organization shall elect its officers not less often than once every three years by secret ballot among the members in good standing.

(c) Every national or international labor organization, except a federation of national or international labor organizations, and every local labor organization, and its officers, shall be under a duty, enforceable at the suit of any bona fide candidate for office in such labor organization in the district court of the United States in which such labor organization maintains its principal office, to comply with all reasonable requests of any candidate to distribute by mail or otherwise at the candidate's expense campaign literature in aid of such person's candidacy to all members in good standing of such labor organization and to refrain from discrimination in favor of or against any candidate with respect to the use of lists of members, and whenever such labor organizations or its officers authorize the distribution by mail or otherwise to members of campaign literature on behalf of any candidate or of the labor organization itself with reference to such election, similar distribution at the request of any other bona fide candidate shall be made by such labor organization and its officers, with equal treatment as to the expense of such distribution. Every bona fide candidate shall have the right, once within 30 days prior to an election of a labor organization in which he is a candidate, to inspect a list containing the names and last known addresses of all members of the labor organization who are subject to a collective bargaining agreement requiring membership therein as a condition of employment, which list shall be maintained and kept at the principal office of such labor organization by a designated official thereof. Adequate safeguards to insure a fair election shall be provided, including the right of any candidate to have an observer at the polls and at the counting of the ballots.

(d) Officers of intermediate bodies, such as general committees, system boards, joint boards, or joint councils, shall be elected not less often than once every four years by secret ballot among the members in good standing or by labor organization officers representative of such members who have been elected by secret ballot.

(e) In any election required by this section which is to be held by secret ballot a reasonable opportunity shall be given for the nomination of candidates and every member in good standing shall be eligible to be a candidate and to hold office (subject to section 504 and to reasonable qualifications uniformly imposed) and shall have the right to vote for or otherwise support the candidate or candidates of his choice, without being subject to penalty, discipline, or improper interference or reprisal of any kind by such organization or any member thereof. Not less than fifteen days prior to the election notice thereof shall be mailed to each member at his last known home address. Each member in good standing shall be entitled to one vote. No member whose dues have been withheld by his employer for payment to such organization pursuant to his voluntary authorization provided for in a collective bargaining agreement, shall be declared ineligible to vote or be a candidate for office in such organization by reason of alleged delay or default in the payment of dues. The votes cast by members of each local labor organization shall be counted, and the results published, separately. The election officials designated in the constitution and bylaws or the secretary, if no other official is designated, shall preserve for one year the ballots and all other records pertaining to the election. The election shall be conducted in accordance with the constitution and bylaws of such organization insofar as they are not inconsistent with the provisions of this title.

(f) When officers are chosen by a convention of delegates elected by secret ballot, the convention shall be conducted in accordance with the constitution and bylaws of the labor organization insofar as they are not inconsistent with the provisions of this title. The officials designated in the constitution and bylaws or the secretary, if no other is designated, shall preserve for one year the credentials of the delegates and all minutes and other records of the convention pertaining to the election of officers.

(g) No moneys received by any labor organization by way of dues, assessment, or similar levy, and no moneys of an employer shall be contributed or applied to promote the candidacy of any person in an election subject to the provisions of this title. Such moneys of a labor organization may be utilized for notices, factual statements of issues not involving candidates, and other expenses necessary for the holding of an election.

(h) If the Secretary, upon application of any member of a local labor organization, finds after hearing in accordance with the Administrative Procedure Act that the constitution and bylaws of such labor organization do not provide an adequate procedure for the removal of an elected officer guilty of serious misconduct, such officer may be removed, for cause shown and after notice and hearing, by the members in good standing voting in a secret ballot conducted by the officers of such labor organization in accordance with its constitution and bylaws insofar as they are not inconsistent with the provisions of this title.

(i) The Secretary shall promulgate rules and regulations prescribing minimum standards and procedures for determining the adequacy of the removal procedures to which reference is made in subsection (h).

Enforcement

Sec. 402.

(a) A member of a labor organization—
  (1) who has exhausted the remedies available under the constitution and bylaws of such organization and of any parent body or
  (2) who has invoked such available remedies without obtaining a final decision within three calendar months after their invocation,

may file a complaint with the Secretary within one calendar month thereafter alleging the violation of any provision of section 401 (including violation of the constitution and bylaws of the labor organization pertaining to the election and removal of officers). The challenged election shall be presumed valid pending a final decision thereon (as hereinafter provided) and in the interim the affairs of the organization shall be conducted by the officers elected or in such other manner as its constitution and bylaws may provide.

(b) The Secretary shall investigate such complaint and, if he finds probable cause to believe that a violation of this title has occurred and has not been remedied, he shall, within sixty days after the filing of such complaint, bring a civil action against the labor organization as an entity in the district court of the United States in which such labor organization maintains its principal office to set aside the invalid election, if any, and to direct the conduct of an election in hearing and vote upon the removal of officers under the supervision of the Secretary and in accordance with the provisions of this title and such rules and regulations as the Secretary may prescribe. The court shall have power to take such action as it deems proper to preserve the assets of the labor organization.

(c) If, upon a preponderance of the evidence after a trial upon the merits, the court finds—
 (1) that an election has not been held within the time prescribed by section 401, or
 (2) that the violation of section 401 may have affected the outcome of an election

the court shall declare the election, if any, to be void and direct the conduct of a new election under supervision of the Secretary and, so far as lawful and practicable, in conformity with the constitution and bylaws of the labor organization. The Secretary shall promptly certify to the court the names of the persons elected, and the court shall thereupon enter a decree declaring such persons to be the officers of the labor organization. If the proceeding is for the removal of officers pursuant to subsection (h) of section 401, the Secretary shall certify the results of the vote and the court shall enter a decree declaring whether such persons have been removed as officers of the labor organization.

(d) An order directing an election, dismissing a complaint, or designating elected officers of a labor organization shall be appealable in the same manner as the final judgment in a civil action, but an order directing an election shall not be stayed pending appeal.

Application of Other Laws

Sec. 403. No labor organization shall be required by law to conduct elections of officers with greater frequency or in a different form or manner than is required by its own constitution or bylaws, except as otherwise provided by this title. Existing rights and remedies to enforce the constitution and bylaws of a labor organization with respect to elections prior to the conduct thereof shall not be affected by the provisions of this title. The remedy provided by this title for challenging an election already conducted shall be exclusive.

Effective Date

Sec. 404. The provisions of this title shall become applicable—

(1) ninety days after the date of enactment of this Act in the case of a labor organization whose constitution and bylaws can lawfully be modified or amended by action of its constitutional officers or governing body, or

(2) where such modification can only be made by a constitutional convention of the labor organization, not later than the next constitutional convention of such labor organization after the date of enactment of this Act, or one year after such date, whichever is sooner. If no such convention is held within such one-year period, the executive board or similar governing body empowered to act for such labor organization between conventions is empowered to make such interim constitutional changes as are necessary to carry out the provisions of this title.

TITLE V—SAFEGUARDS FOR LABOR ORGANIZATIONS

Fiduciary Responsibility of Officers of Labor Organizations

Sec. 501.

(a) The officers, agents, shop stewards, and other representatives of a labor organization occupy positions of trust in relation to such organization and its members as a group. It is, therefore, the duty of each such person, taking into account the special problems and functions of a labor organization, to hold its money and property solely for the benefit of the organization and its members and to manage, invest, and expend the same in accordance with its constitution and bylaws and any resolutions of the governing bodies adopted thereunder, to refrain from dealing with such organizations as an adverse party or in behalf of an adverse party in any matter connected with his duties and from holding or acquiring any pecuniary or personal interest which conflicts with the interests of such organization, and to account to the organization for any profit received by him in whatever capacity in connection with transactions conducted by him or under his direction on behalf of the organization. A general exculpatory provision in the constitution and bylaws of such a labor organization or a general exculpatory resolution of a governing body purporting to relieve any such person of liability for breach of the duties declared by this section shall be void as against public policy.

(b) When any officer, agent, shop steward, or representative of any labor organization is alleged to have violated the duties declared in subsection (a) and the labor organization or its governing board or officers refuse or fail to sue or recover damages or secure an accounting or other appropriate relief within a reasonable time after being requested to do so by any member of the labor organization, such member may sue such officer, agent, shop steward, or representative in any district court of the United States or in any State court of competent jurisdiction to recover damages or secure an accounting or other appropriate relief for the benefit of the labor organization. No such proceeding shall be brought except upon leave of the court obtained upon verified application and for good cause shown which application may be made ex parte. The trial judge may allot a reasonable part of the recovery in any action under this subsection to pay the fees of counsel prosecuting the suit at the instance of the member of the labor organization and to compensate such member for any expenses necessarily paid or incurred by him in connection with the litigation.

(c) Any person who embezzles, steals, or unlawfully and willfully abstracts or converts to his own use, or the use of another, any of the moneys, funds, securities, property, or other assets of a labor organization of which he is an officer, or by which he is employed, directly or indirectly, shall be fined not more than $10,000 or imprisoned for not more than five years, or both.

Bonding

Sec. 502.

(a) Every officer, agent, shop steward, or other representative or employee of any labor organization (other than a labor organization whose property and annual financial receipts do not exceed $5,000 in value), or of a trust in which a labor organization is interested, who handles funds or other property thereof shall be bonded to provide protection against loss by reason of acts of fraud or dishonesty on his part directly or through connivance with others. The bond of each such person shall be fixed at the beginning of the organization's fiscal year and shall be in an amount not less than 10 per centum of the funds handled by him and his predecessor or predecessors, if any, during the preceding fiscal year, but in no case more than $500,000. If the labor organization or the trust in which a labor organization is interested does not have a preceding fiscal year, the amount of the bond shall be, in the case of a local labor organization, not less than $1,000, and in the case of any other labor organization or of a trust in which a labor organization is interested, not less than $10,000. Such bonds shall be individual or schedule in form, and shall have a corporate surety company as surety thereon. Any person who is not covered by such bonds shall not be permitted to receive, handle, disburse, or otherwise exercise custody or control of the funds or other property of a labor organization or of a trust in which a labor organization is interested. No such bond shall be placed through an agent or broker or with a surety company in which any labor organization or any officer, agent, shop steward, or other representative of a labor organization has any direct or indirect interest. Such surety company shall be a corporate surety which holds a grant of authority from the Secretary of the Treasury under the Act of July 30, 1947 (6 U.S.C. 6–13), as an acceptable surety on Federal bonds: *Provided,* That when in the opinion of the Secretary a labor organization has made other bonding arrangements which would provide the protection required by this section at comparable cost or less, he may exempt such labor organization from placing a bond through a surety company holding such grant of authority.

(b) Any person who willfully violates this section shall be fined not more than $10,000 or imprisoned for not more than one year, or both.

Making of Loans; Payment of Fines

Sec. 503.

(a) No labor organization shall make directly or indirectly any loan or loans to any officer or employee of such organization which results in a total indebtedness on the part of such officer or employee to the labor organization in excess of $2,000.

(b) No labor organization or employer shall directly or indirectly pay the fine of any officer or employee convicted of any willful violation of this Act.

(c) Any person who willfully violates this section shall be fined not more than $5,000 or imprisoned for not more than one year, or both.

Prohibition Against Certain Persons Holding Office

Sec. 504.

(a) No person who is or has been a member of the Communist Party or who has been convicted of, or served any part of a prison term resulting from his conviction of, robbery, bribery, extortion, embezzlement, grand larceny, burglary, arson, violation of narcotics laws, murder, rape, assault with intent to kill, assault which inflicts grievous bodily injury, or a violation of title II or III of this Act, or conspiracy to commit any such crimes, shall serve—

(1) as an officer, director, trustee, member of any executive board or similar governing body, business agent, manager, organizer, or other employee (other than as an employee performing exclusively clerical or custodial duties) of any labor organization, or

(2) as a labor relations consultant to a person engaged in an industry or activity affecting commerce, or as an officer, director, agent, or employee (other than as an employee performing exclusively clerical or custodial duties) of any group or association of employers dealing with any labor organization,

during or for five years after the termination of his membership in the Communist Party, or for five years after such conviction or after the end of such imprisonment, unless prior to the end of such five-year period, in the case of a person so convicted or imprisoned, (A) his citizenship rights, having been revoked as a result of such conviction, have been fully restored, or (B) the Board of Parole of the United States Department of Justice determines that such person's service in any capacity referred to in clause (1) or (2) would not be contrary to the purposes of this Act. Prior to making any such determination the Board shall hold an administrative hearing and shall give notice of such proceeding by certified mail to the State, County, and Federal prosecuting officials in the jurisdiction or jurisdictions in which such person was convicted. The Board's determination in any such proceeding shall be final. No labor organization or officer thereof shall knowingly permit any person to assume or hold any office or paid position in violation of this subsection.

(b) Any person who willfully violates this section shall be fined not more than $10,000 or imprisoned for not more than one year, or both.

(c) For the purposes of this section, any person shall be deemed to have been "convicted" and under the disability of "conviction" from the date of the judgment of the trial court or the date of the final sustaining of such judgment on appeal, whichever is the later event, regardless of whether such conviction occurred before or after the date of enactment of this Act.

TITLE VI—MISCELLANEOUS PROVISIONS

Investigations

Sec. 601.

(a) The Secretary shall have power when he believes it necessary in order to determine whether any person has violated or is about to violate any provision of this Act (except title I or amendments made by this Act to other statutes) to make an investigation and in connection therewith he may enter such places and inspect such records and accounts and question such persons as he may deem necessary to enable him to determine the facts relative thereto. The Secretary may report to interested persons or officials concerning the facts required to be shown in any report required by this Act and concerning the reasons for failure or refusal to file such a report or any other matter which he deems to be appropriate as a result of such an investigation.

(b) For the purpose of any investigation provided for in this Act, the provisions of sections 9 and 10 (relating to the attendance of witnesses and the production of books, papers, and documents) of the Federal Trade Commission Act of September 16, 1914, as amended (15 U.S.C. 49, 50), are hereby made applicable to the jurisdiction, powers, and duties of the Secretary or any officers designated by him.

Extortionate Picketing

Sec. 602.

(a) It shall be unlawful to carry on picketing on or about the premises of any employer for the purpose of, or as part of any conspiracy or in furtherance of any plan or purpose for, the personal profit or enrichment of any individual (except a bona fide increase in wages or other employee benefits) by taking or obtaining any money or other thing of value from such employer against his will or with his consent.

(b) Any person who willfully violates this section shall be fined not more than $10,000 or imprisoned not more than twenty years, or both.

Retention of Rights under Other Federal and State Laws

Sec. 603.

(a) Except as explicitly provided to the contrary, nothing in this Act shall reduce or limit the responsibilities of any labor organization or any officer, agent, shop steward, or other representative of a labor organization, or of any trust in which a labor organization is interested, under any other Federal law or under the laws of any State, and, except as explicitly provided to the contrary, nothing in this Act shall take away any right or bar any remedy to which members of a labor organization are entitled under such other Federal law or law of any State.

(b) Nothing contained in titles I, II, III, IV, V, or VI of this Act shall be construed to supersede or impair or otherwise affect the provisions of the Railway Labor Act, as amended, or any of the obligations, rights, benefits, privileges, or immunities of any carrier, employee, organization, representative, or person subject thereto; nor shall anything contained in said titles (except section 505) of this Act be construed to confer any rights, privileges, immunities, or defenses upon employers, or to impair or otherwise affect the rights of any person under the National Labor Relations Act, as amended.

Effect on State Laws

Sec. 604. Nothing in this Act shall be construed to impair or diminish the authority of any State to enact and enforce general criminal laws with respect to robbery, bribery, extortion, embezzlement, grand larceny, burglary, arson, violation of narcotics laws, murder, rape, assault with intent to kill, or assault which inflicts grievous bodily injury, or conspiracy to commit any of such crimes.

Service of Process

Sec. 605. For the purposes of this Act, service of summons, subpoena, or other legal process of a court of the United States upon an officer or agent of a labor organization in his capacity as such shall constitute service upon the labor organization.

Administrative Procedure Act

Sec. 606. The provisions of the Administrative Procedure Act shall be applicable to the issuance, amendment, or rescission of any rules or regulations, or any adjudication, authorized or required pursuant to the provisions of this Act.

Other Agencies and Departments

Sec. 607. In order to avoid unnecessary expense and duplication of functions among Government agencies, the Secretary may make such arrangements or agreements for cooperation or mutual assistance in the performance of his functions under this Act and the functions of any such agency as he may find to be practicable and consistent with law. The Secretary may utilize the facilities or services of any department, agency, or establishment of the United States or of any State or political subdivision of a State, including the services of any of its employees, with the lawful consent of such department, agency, or establishment; and each department, agency, or establishment of the United States is authorized and directed to cooperate with the Secretary and, to the extent permitted by law, to provide such information and facilities as he may request for his assistance in the performance of his functions under this Act. The Attorney General or his representative shall receive from the Secretary for appropriate action such evidence developed in the performance of his functions under this Act as may be found to warrant consideration for criminal prosecution under the provisions of this Act or other Federal law.

Criminal Contempt

Sec. 608. No person shall be punished for any criminal contempt allegedly committed outside the immediate presence of the court in connection with any civil action prosecuted by the Secretary or any other person in any court of the United States under the provisions of this Act unless the facts constituting such criminal contempt are established by the verdict of the jury in a proceeding in the district court of the United States, which jury shall be chosen and empaneled in the manner prescribed by the law governing trial juries in criminal prosecutions in the district courts of the United States.

Prohibition on Certain Discipline by Labor Organization

Sec. 609. It shall be unlawful for any labor organization, or any officer, agent, shop steward, or other representative of a labor organization, or any employee thereof to fine, suspend, expel, or otherwise discipline any of its members for exercising any right to which he is entitled under the provisions of this Act. The provisions of section 102 shall be applicable in the enforcement of this section.

Deprivation of Rights under Act by Violence

Sec. 610. It shall be unlawful for any person through the use of force or violence, or threat of the use of force or violence, to restrain, coerce, or intimidate, or attempt to restrain, coerce, or intimidate any member of a labor organization for the purpose of interfering with or preventing the exercise of any right to which he is entitled under the provisions of this Act. Any person who willfully violates this section shall be fined not more than $1,000 or imprisoned for not more than one year, or both.

Separability Provisions

Sec. 611. If any provision of this Act, or the application of such provision to any person or circumstances, shall be held invalid, the remainder of this Act or the application of such provision to persons or circumstances other than those as to which it is held invalid, shall not be affected thereby.

GLOSSARY

A

Administrative Law Judges (ALJ). Formerly called Trial Examiners, these judges are independent of both the board and the general counsel.

affirmative action plans. Programs which involve giving preference in hiring or promotion to qualified female or minority employees.

after-acquired evidence. Evidence of the plaintiff employee's misconduct acquired after the plaintiff has filed an EEO charge.

Age Discrimination in Employment Act (ADEA). Federal legislation that prohibits employment discrimination based on age.

agency shop agreement. Agreement requiring employees to pay union dues, but not requiring them to join the union.

ambulatory situs picketing. When the primary employer's business is mobile, picketing by a union following that mobile location.

Americans with Disabilities Act (ADA). A comprehensive piece of civil rights legislation for individuals with disabilities that prohibits discrimination against individuals who are otherwise qualified for employment.

arbitration. The settlement of disputes by a neutral adjudicator chosen by the parties to the dispute.

B

bad faith. Implies malice, evil intent, fraudulent and dishonest speech or behavior.

bargaining unit. Group of employees being represented by a union.

bona fide occupational qualification (BFOQ). An exception to the civil rights laws that allows an employer to hire employees of a specific sex, religion, or national origin when business necessity—the safe and efficient performance of the particular job—requires it.

C

captive-audience speeches. Speeches given by representatives of the employees or mass meeting by the union within twenty-four hours of a representation election.

captive union. (or in-house union) An employer-formed and dominated union usually created because the firm could no longer completely resist worker demands for collective action.

class action suits. An individual plaintiff sues on behalf of a whole class of individuals allegedly suffering the same harm or essentially the same relevant facts.

closed shop. An employer who agrees to hire only those employees who are already union members.

collective bargaining. The performance of the mutual obligation of the employer and the representative of the employees to meet at reasonable times and confer in good faith with respect to wages, hours, and other terms and conditions of employment, or the negotiation of an agreement of any question arising thereunder.

common law. Law developed from court decisions rather than through statutes.

common situs picketing. Picketing of an entire construction site.

comparable worth. A standard of equal pay for jobs of equal value; not the same as equal-pay-for-equal-work.

confidential employees. Those persons whose position involves access to confidential labor relations information.

consent election. Election conducted by the NLRB regional office giving the regional director final authority over any disputes.

construct validity. A method of demonstrating that an employment selection device selects employees based on the traits and characteristics that are required for the job in question.

content validity. A method of demonstrating that an employment selection device reflects the content of the job for which employees are being selected.

contract bar rule. A written labor contract bars an election during the life of the bargaining agreement, subject to the "open season" exception.

contract compliance program. Regulations which provide that all firms having contracts or subcontracts exceeding $10,000 with the federal government must agree to include a no-discrimination clause in the contract.

criminal conspiracy. A crime that may be committed when two or more persons agree to do something unlawful.

criterion-related validity. A method of demonstrating that an employment selection device correlates with the skills and knowledge required for successful job performance.

D

decertification petition. Election petition stating that a current bargaining representative no longer has the support of a majority of the employees in the bargaining unit.

defamation. An intentional, false, and harmful communication. Written defamation is called *libel.* Spoken defamation is called *slander.*

defined-benefit plan. A pension plan that ensures eligible employees and their beneficiaries a specified monthly income for life.

defined-contribution plan. Plan under which an employer makes a fixed-share contribution into a retirement account each year.

dicta. Opinions of a judge or appellate panel of judges which are tangential to the rule, holding, and decision which are at the core of the judicial pronouncement.

disability. Disability means, with respect to an individual, a physical or mental impairment that substantially limits one or more of the major life activities of such individual; a record of such and impairment; or being regarded as having such an impairment.

disparate impact. The discriminatory effect of apparently neutral employment criteria.

disparate treatment. When an employee is treated differently from others due to race, color, religion, sex, or national origin.

duty of fair representation. An NLRB and court imposed obligation on the part of the union to represent fairly all members of the bargaining unit.

E

economic strikes. Strikes over economic issues, such as grievances or a new contract. Unlike unfair labor practice strikers, economic strikers may be permanently replaced by the employer.

emergency standards. These standards are issued when the Secretary of Labor believes that employees are exposed to grave dangers from substances or agents determined to be toxic or physically harmful.

Employee Polygraph Protection Act of 1988. Act that severely restricts the right of an employer to require employees to take lie detector tests.

Employee Retirement Income Security Act (ERISA). An act passed by Congress in 1974 intended to prevent pension fund mismanagement and to protect the interests of employees and their beneficiaries in employee benefit plans.

employment-at-will. Both the employee and the employer are free to unilaterally terminate the relationship at any time and for any legally permissible reason, or even for no reason at all.

Equal Employment Opportunity Commission (EEOC). Federal agency responsible for administration and enforcement of various civil rights legislation.

Equal Pay Act of 1963. Act which requires that men and women performing substantially equal work be paid equally.

Excelsior list. List which contains the names and home addresses of all employees eligible to vote, so that the union can contact them outside their work environment, beyond the boss's observation and control.

exempt employees. Employees whose hours of work and compensation are not stipulated by the FLSA.

express contract. A bargain the terms of which are stated explicitly in writing (or sometimes verbally), as opposed to an implied contract, terms of which must be inferred by the court from the circumstances of the parties' relationship.

F

Fair Labor Standards Act (FLSA). The FLSA provides regulation in four areas: minimum wages, ove time pay provisions, child labor, and equal pay for equal work.

Family and Medical Leave Act (FMLA). This act allows eligible employees to take up to 12 weeks unpaid leave in any 12 months because of the birth, adoption, or foster care of a child, or the need to care for a child, spouse, or parent with a serious health condition, or because the employee's own serious health condition makes the employee unable to perform functions of his or her job.

featherbedding. The practice of getting paid for services not performed and not intended to be performed.

fiduciary. ERISA defines fiduciary as including any person exercising discretionary authority or control respecting the management of the benefit plan, or disposition of plan assets; or who renders, or has authority or responsibility to render, investment advice with respect to any money or property of the plan; or, last, who has *any* discretionary authority or responsibility in the administration of the plan.

forty-eight-hour rule. NLRB's rule stating that an employer who files a petition must submit to the regional office proof of a union's recognition demand within two days of filing the petition.

Four-Fifths Rule. A mathematical formula developed by the EEOC to demonstrate *disparate impact* of a facially-neutral employment practice on selection criterion.

front pay. Monetary damages awarded a plaintiff instead of reinstatement or hiring.

G

good faith. An honest belief, absent malice, in the statement made or the action undertaken. By comparison, bad faith implies malice, evil intent, fraudulent and dishonest speech or behavior.

grievance. A complaint that either party to an agreement is not living up to the obligations of the agreement.

grievance process. A process set up to deal with complaints under the collective bargaining agreement.

H

hiring halls. A job-referral mechanism operated by unions whereby unions refer members to prospective employers.

hostile environment harassment. Harassment which does not involve the conditioning of any job status or benefit on the employee's response to the harassment; rather, the unwelcome harassment has the effect of interfering with the employee's work performance or creating a hostile work environment for the employee.

I

impasse. A deadlock in negotiations.

implied contract. A contractual relationship the terms and conditions of which must be inferred from the contracting parties' behavior toward one another.

independent contractor. A person working as a separate business entity; is not subject to the direction and control of an employer.

in-house union. (or captive union) An employer-formed and dominated union usually created because the firm could no longer completely resist worker demands for collective action.

injunction. A court order to provide remedies prohibiting some action or commanding the righting of some wrongdoing.

integration. The right to offset benefits against those paid by other sources.

intentional infliction of emotional distress. Tortious conduct that is intentional, extreme and outrageous, or at least reckless, and causes severe emotional distress.

interest arbitration. When arbitration is used to create a new agreement or renew an existing one.

interim standards. Interim standards are those that the Secretary of Labor had power to issue for the first two years following the effective date of the OSH Act.

J

just cause. Sometimes called good cause, as distinct from arbitrary behavior and wrongful or illegal motivation for an act.

L

libel. Written defamation.

lockout. An employer's temporary withdrawal of employment to pressure employees to agree to the employer's bargaining proposals.

M

managerial employees. Those persons whose positions involve the formulation or effectuation of management policies.

mandatory bargaining subjects. Those subjects that "vitally affect the terms and conditions of employment" of the employees in the bargaining unit; includes wages, hours, and terms and conditions of employment.

minimum wage. The wage limit, set by the the government; an employer is not allowed to pay an employee less than the wage limit.

Model Employment Termination Act (META). Act which states that "an employer may not terminate the employment of an employee without good cause."

N

National Industrial Recovery Act (NIRA). New Deal legislation that set up a system in which major industries would operate under codes of fair competition. Later ruled unconstitutional.

National Institute of Occupational Safety and Health (NIOSH). An agency created to conduct research and promote the application of the research results to ensure that no worker will suffer diminished health, reduced functional capacity, or decreased life expectancy as a result of his or her work experience.

National Labor Board (NLB). The NLB initially functioned as a mediation board, seeking to persuade the parties to settle their differences peacefully.

National Labor Relations Act (NLRA). The NLRA regulates private sector labor relations by defining basic rights of employees, and prohibiting actions by employers or unions that interfere with or restrict those rights.

National Labor Relations Board (NLRB). The NLRB adjudicates complaints of unfair labor practices under the NLRA, and conducts representation elections.

national origin discrimination. Any discrimination based on the place of origin of an applicant or employee or his or her ancestor(s). and any discrimination based on the physical, cultural or linguistic characteristics of an ethnic group.

Norris–La Guardia Act. Federal legislation that greatly limited the use of labor injunctions by the federal courts.

O

Occupational Safety and Health Act (OSHA). The act requires employers to furnish their employees a workplace that is free from recognized hazards that cause, or are likely to cause, serious injury or death.

Occupational Safety and Health Review Commission (OSHRC). A quasi-judicial agency created to adjudicate contested enforcement actions of OSHA.

overtime pay. Employees covered by FLSA are entitled to overtime pay, at one-and-a-half times their regular pay rate, for hours worked in excess of forty hours per workweek.

P

patrolling. The movement of persons back and forth around the premises of an employer, usually during picketing.

permanent standards. These standards are developed by OSHA and NIOSH and are frequently based on suggestions made by interested parties, such as employers, employees, states and other political subdivisions, and labor unions.

permissive bargaining subjects. Those matters which are not directly related to wages, hours, terms and conditions of employment and that are not prohibited subjects.

picketing. Placing persons outside the premises of an employer to convey information to the public. The information may be conveyed by words, signs, or the distribution of literature.

pressure tactics. Union pressure tactics involve strikes and calls for boycotts, while employers may resort to lockouts.

prima facie case. A case "on the face of it" or "at first sight"; often used to establish that if a certain set of facts are proven, then it is apparent that another fact is established.

Q

quid pro quo. Something for something; giving one valuable thing for another.

quid pro quo harassment. Harassment where the employee's response to the request for sexual favors is considered in granting employment benefits, such as a male supervisor promising a female employee that she will be promoted or receive a favorable performance rating if she sleeps with him.

R

race norming. The practice of using different cutoff scores for different racial, gender, or ethnic groups of applicants, or adjusting test scores or otherwise altering test results of employment-related tests on the basis of race, color, religion, sex, or national origin.

Railway Labor Act. The act allowed railroad employees to designate bargaining representatives of their own choosing, free from employer interference.

Rehabilitation Act of 1973. Act that protects the employment rights of individuals with disabilities; the act's provisions prohibit discrimination against otherwise qualified individuals with disabilities.

rights arbitration. Arbitration of disputes involving the interpretation or application of an existing collective agreement rather than creating a new one.

right-to-work laws. Laws which prohibit union security agreements.

runaway shop. An employer closes in one location and opens in another to avoid unionization.

S

Seniority. Length of service on the job. This measure is frequently used to determine entitlement to employment benefits, promotions, transfers, and job security. Seniority systems usually provide that layoffs of workers be conducted on the basis of inverse seniority-those with the least length of service are laid off before those with greater seniority.

sex-plus discrimination. Discrimination based on gender and another factor—such as an employer who refuses to hire females having pre-school aged children but who does hire males with pre-school aged children.

slander. Spoken defamation.

stare decisis. To abide by and adhere to decided cases.

strike. The organized withholding of labor by workers; the traditional weapon by which workers attempt to pressure employers.

supersedeas. An order to suspend another legal order, rule, or law.

supervisor. A person who, in the interest of the employer, has the authority to direct, hire, fire, discipline, transfer, or suspend other employees, and who uses independent judgment in the exercise of such authority.

T

Title VII of the Civil Rights Act of 1964. Federal legislation that prohibits the refusal or failure to hire, the discharge of any individual, or the discrimination against any individual with respect to compensation, terms, conditions, or privileges of employment because of that individual's race, color, religion, sex, or national origin.

tort. A private or civil wrong or injury, caused by one party to another, either intentionally or negligently.

twenty-four-hour silent period. The NLRB requires that the parties in a representation election refrain from formal campaigning for twenty-four hours prior to the holding of the election.

U

unemployment compensation. Benefits paid to employees out of work through no fault of their own and who are available for suitable work if and when it becomes available.

unfair labor practice strike. A strike by employees in protest of, or precipitated by, employer unfair labor practices.

Uniformed Services Employment and Reemployment Act (USERA). Act that prohibits employers from discriminating against employees because of their service in the military.

Uniform Guidelines on Employee Selection Procedures. A series of regulations adopted by the EEOC and other federal agencies for claims of disparate impact and unfair treatment on the job.

union members' "bill of rights." Federal legislation to guarantee that union internal procedures are fair and to prohibit certain practices by unions that interfere with employees' rights under the NLRA. Contained in the Labor-Management Reporting & Disclosure Act.

union security agreements. An agreement whereby an employer and union agree that employees must either join the union or at least pay union dues in order to remain employees.

union shop agreement. Agreement requiring employees to join the union after a certain period of time.

union shop clause. Clause in an agreement requiring all present and future members of a bargaining unit to become union members after a certain period.

W

Weingarten rights. The right to have a union representative present applies whenever the meeting with management will have the "probable" result of the imposition of discipline, or where such a result is "seriously considered."

whipsaw strikes. Strikes in which the union selectively strikes one firm in the industry.

willful misconduct. The high level of fault that disqualifies an out-of-work worker from unemployment benefits.

workers' compensation. Benefits awarded an employee when injuries are work related.

workweek. A term the FLSA uses to signify seven consecutive days, but the law does not require that the workweek start or end on any particular day of the calendar week.

Y

yellow-dog contracts. Employment contracts requiring employees to agree not to join a union.

LIST OF CASES

INDEX

D

E

G

J

K

N

O

P

U

V

W

Y

Z